A
VICTORIAN ANTHOLOGY
1837–1895

Edited by Edmund Clarence Stedman

Poets' Corner, Westminster Abbey

A

VICTORIAN ANTHOLOGY

1837–1895

SELECTIONS ILLUSTRATING THE EDITOR'S CRITICAL
REVIEW OF BRITISH POETRY IN THE
REIGN OF VICTORIA

EDITED BY

EDMUND CLARENCE STEDMAN

GREENWOOD PRESS, PUBLISHERS
NEW YORK

Originally published in 1895
by Houghton, Mifflin and Company

First Greenwood Reprinting, 1969

Library of Congress Catalogue Card Number 69-14098

SBN 8371-1146-3

To

ELLEN MACKAY HUTCHINSON

INTRODUCTION

WHILE this book is properly termed an Anthology, its scope is limited to the yield of one nation during a single reign. Its compiler's office is not that of one who ranges the whole field of English poetry, from the ballad period to our own time, — thus having eight centuries from which to choose his songs and idyls, each " round and perfect as a star." This has been variously essayed; once, at least, in such a manner as to render it unlikely that any new effort, for years to come, will better the result attained.

On the other hand, the present work relates to the poetry of the English people, and of the English tongue, that knight peerless among languages, at this stage of their manifold development. I am fortunate in being able to make use of such resources for the purpose of gathering, in a single yet inclusive volume, a Victorian garland fairly entitled to its name. The conditions not only permit but require me — while choosing nothing that does not further the general plan — to be somewhat less rigid and eclectic than if examining the full domain of English poesy. That plan is not to offer a collection of absolutely flawless poems, long since become classic and accepted as models ; but in fact to make a truthful exhibit of the course of song during the last sixty years, as shown by the poets of Great Britain in the best of their shorter productions.

Otherwise, and as the title-page implies, this Anthology is designed to supplement my "Victorian Poets," by choice and typical examples of the work discussed in that review. These are given in unmutilated form, except that, with respect to a few extended narrative or dramatic pieces, I do not hesitate to make extracts which are somewhat complete in themselves ; it being difficult otherwise to represent certain names, and yet desirable that they shall be in some wise represented.

At first I thought to follow a strictly chronological method : that is, to give authors succession in the order of their birth-dates ; but had not gone far before it was plain that such an arrangement conveyed no true idea of the poetic movement within the years involved. It was disastrously inconsistent with the course taken in the critical survey now familiar to readers of various editions since its original issue in 1875 and extension in 1887. In that work the leading poets, and the various groups and "schools," are examined for the most part in the order of their coming into vogue. Some of the earlier-born published late in life, or otherwise outlasted their juniors, and thus belong to the later rather than the opening divisions of the period. In the end, I conformed to the plan shown in the ensuing "Table of Contents." This, it will be perceived, is first set off into three divisions of the reign, and secondly into classes of poets, — which in each class, finally, are quoted in order of their seniority. For page-reference, then, the reader will not depend upon the "Contents," but turn to the Indexes of Authors, First Lines, and Titles, at the end of the volume.

It is an arbitrary thing, at the best, to classify poets, like song-birds, into genera and species; nor is this attempted at all in my later division, which aims to present them chronologically. Time itself, however, is a pretty logical curator, and at least decides the associations wherewith we invest the names of singers long gone by. Those so individual as to fall into no obvious alliance are called "distinctive," in the first and middle divisions at large. Song and hymn makers, dramatists, meditative poets, etc., are easily differentiated, and the formation of other groups corresponds with that outlined in "Victorian Poets." Upon the method thus adopted, and with friendly allowance for the personal equation, it seems to me that a conspectus of the last sixty years can be satisfactorily obtained. The shorter pieces named in my critical essays, as having distinction, are usually given here. While representing the poetic leaders most fully, I have not overlooked choice estrays, and I have been regardful of the minor yet significant drifts by which the tendencies of any literary or artistic generation frequently are discerned. In trying to select the best and most characteristic pieces, one sometimes finds, by a paradox, that an author when most characteristic is not always at his best. On the whole, and nearly always with respect to the elder poets whose work has undergone long sifting, poems well known and favored deserve their repute; and preference has not been given, merely for the sake of novelty, to inferior productions. Authors who were closely held to task in the critical volume are represented, in the Anthology, by their work least open to criticism. Finally, I believe that all those discussed in the former book, whether as objects of extended review or as minor contemporaries, are represented here, except a few that have failed to justify their promise or have produced little suited to such a collection. In addition, a showing is made of various poets hopefully come to light since the extension of my survey, in 1887. Others of equal merit, doubtless, are omitted, but with youth on their side they may well await the recognition of future editors.

This Introduction goes beyond the scope of the usual Preface, in order that those who (as students of English poetry) avail themselves of the Anthology, and who have but a limited knowledge of the modern field, may readily understand the general and secondary divisions. To such readers a word concerning the period may be of interest.

In a letter to the editor, Canon Dixon speaks of "the Victorian Period " as " one of the longest in literary history; perhaps the longest." With regard to an individual, or to a reign, length of years is itself an aid to distinction, through its prolongation of a specific tendency or motive. The reign now closing has been one in which a kingdom has become an empire; its power has broadened and its wealth and invention have increased as never before. In science, — and in works of the imagination, despite the realistic stress of journalism, — twenty years of the recent era outvie any fifty between the Protectorate and the beginning of our century. During every temporary lull we fear sterility, but one need not confine his retrospection to the blank from 1700 to 1795 to be assured that an all-round comparison with the past must be in our favor. While, then, it is but a hazardous thing to estimate one's own day, the essays to which the Anthology is a complement would not have been written but for a conviction that the time under review was destined to rank with the foremost times of England's intellectual activity,— to be classed, it well might be, among the few culminating eras of European thought and art, as one to which even the title of "Age" should be applied. We speak of Queen Anne's time; of the Georgian Period, and we have epochs within periods; but we say the Age of Pericles, the Augustan Age, the Elizabethan Age, and it is not beyond conjecture that posterity may award the master epithet to the time of Carlyle and Froude, of Mill and Spencer and Darwin, of Dickens, Thackeray, and their successors, of Tennyson and Browning, — and thus not only for its wonders of power, science, invention, but for an imaginative fertility unequalled since "the spacious days" of the Virgin Queen. The years of her modern successor, whose larger sway betokens such an evolution, have been so prolonged, and so beneficent under the continuous wisdom of her statesmen, that the present reign may find no historic equal in centuries to come. An instinctive recognition of this seems now to prevail. Even the adjective "Victorian" was unfamiliar, if it had been employed at all, when I used it in the title of a magazine essay (the germ of my subsequent volume) published in January, 1873. It is now as well in use as "Elizabethan" or "Georgian," and advisedly, for the cycle bearing the name has so rounded upon itself that an estimate of its characteristic portion can be made *ab extra ;* all the more, because in these latter days "the thoughts of men" are not only "widened," but hastened toward just conclusions, as if in geometrical progression. What, then, my early essays found an ample ground for study, the present compilation seeks to illustrate, and I trust that, although restricted to brief exemplifications, it will somewhat justify this preliminary claim.

In the following pages, then, the period is divided into, first, the early years of the reign; second, the Victorian epoch proper; third, the present time. A survey of the opening division brings out an interesting fact. Of the poets cited as prominent after 1835 and until the death of Wordsworth, scarcely one shows any trace of the artistic and speculative qualities which are essentially Victorian. Well-informed readers may be surprised to find so many antedating the influence of Tennyson, untouched by his captivating and for a long time dominating style. Their work is that of a transition era, holding over into the present reign. It was noted for its songs and sentiment. The feeling of Wordsworth is plain in its meditative verse; yet to this time belong Bulwer, Macaulay, the "Blackwood" and "Bentley" coteries, "Barry Cornwall," and those "strayed Elizabethans," Darley and Beddoes. Milman, Talfourd, Knowles, and others are not quoted, partly on account of their lack of quality, but chiefly because at their best they are late Georgian rather than early Victorian. Praed comes in as the pioneer of our society-verse; Elliott as a bard of "the new day." In fact, the Reform Bill crisis evoked the humanitarian spirit, poetically at its height in the writings of Hood and Mrs. Browning. To include Wordsworth, the Queen's first laureate of her own appointment, farther than by a prelude on "the passing of the elder bards" would be to rob the Georgian Period of the leader of one of its great poetic movements; yet Wordsworth breathes throughout our entire selection, wherever Nature is concerned, or philosophic thought, and not only in the contemplative verse, but in the composite, and never more strenuously than in Palgrave and Arnold, of the middle division, and such a poet as Watson, of the third. Landor, though the comrade of Southey, the foil of Byron, and the delight of Shelley, begins this volume, as he began its predecessor; for Landor with his finish, his classical serenity, and his wonderful retention of the artistic faculty until his death — a score of years after the Accession — belonged to no era more than to our own, — and we may almost say that in poetry he and Swinburne were of the same generation.

Two thirds of our space are naturally required for selections from the typical division. This is seen to begin with the appointment of Tennyson as laureate, since he scarcely had a following until about that date. In him we find, on the reflective side, a sense of Nature akin to Wordsworth's, and on the æsthetic, an artistic perfection foretokened by Keats, — in other words, insight and taste united through his genius had their outcome in the composite idyllic school, supremely representative of the Victorian prime. Tennyson idealized the full advance of nineteenth century speculation, ethical and scientific, in the production of "In Memoriam," and to the end in such a poem as "Vastness." Possibly, also, it was out of his early mediæval romanticism that the next most striking school arose with Rossetti and his fellow Pre-Raphaelites who are grouped as Poets of the Renaissance: their revival including both Greek and Gothic modes and motives, as finally combined in the masterwork of Swinburne. The third and equal force of the epoch is that of Browning, long holding his rugged ground alone, as afterward with half the world to stay him; but, like other men of unique genius, not the founder of a school, — his manner failing in weaker hands. In Arnold's composite verse the reflective prevails over the æsthetic. Besides these chiefs of the quarter-century are various "distinctive" poets, as in the earlier division, each belonging to no general group. Then we have the songsters, for whom all of us confess a kindly feeling; the balladists withal, and the dramatists, — such as they are; also the makers of lighter verse, and other lyrists of a modest station, often yielding something that lends a special grace to an Anthology.

The closing era is of the recent poets of Great Britain, and begins very clearly about twenty years ago. At that date, the direct influences of Tennyson, Browning, Swinburne, and Rossetti began to appear less obviously, or were blended, where apparent, in the verse of a younger generation. The new lyrists had motives of their own, and here and there a new note. There was a lighter touch, a daintiness of wit and *esprit*, a revival of early minstrel "forms," and every token of a blithe and courtly Ecole Intermédiaire: evidence, at least, of emancipation from the stress of the long dominant Victorian chord. The change has become decisive since the "Jubilee Year," to which my supplementary review was extended, and of late we have a distinctly lyrical, though minor song-burst, even if the mother country be not, as in its springtime of pleasant minstrelsy, "a nest of singing-birds." In the later ditties England's hawthorn-edged lanes and meadows come to mind, the skylark carols, and we have verse as pastoral as Mr. Abbey's drawings for Herrick and Goldsmith. This, to my view, if not very great, is more genuine and hopeful than any further iteration of "French Forms," and the same may be occa sionally said for those town-lyrics which strive to express certain garish, wandering phases of the London of to-day. Irish verse, which always has had quality, begins to take on art. But the strongest recent work is found in the ballads of a few men and women, and of these balladists, one born out of Great Britain is first without a seeming effort. As for the drama (considering the whole reign), its significant poetry, beyond a few structures modelled after the antique, and those of Horne, Taylor, and Swinburne, is found mainly in the peculiar and masterful work of Browning; nevertheless, lyrical song indicates a dramatic inspiration, because it is so human, and if the novel did not afford a continuous exercise of the dramatic gift, I would look to see the drama, or verse with pronounced dramatic qualities, attend the rise of the next poetic school. If, on the other hand, there is to ensue a non-imaginative era, a fallow interval, it will be neither strange nor much to be deplored after the productive affluence of the reign now ending with the century.

A selection from the minstrelsy of Great Britain's colonies fills out the scheme of the Anthology. The Australian yield is sufficiently meagre, but I have chosen what seems most local and characteristic. Canada is well in the lists with a group of lyrists whose merit has made their names familiar to readers of our own periodicals, and who feel and healthfully express the sentiment, the atmosphere, of their northern land. I am sure that the space reserved for them in this volume will not seem ill-bestowed. One noteworthy trait of colonial poetry is the frequency with which it takes the ballad form. In a rude way this is seen in the literature of our own colonial period, and along our more recent frontier settlements. By some law akin to that which makes balladry — repeated from mouth to mouth — the natural song of primitive man, of the epic youth of a race or nation, so its form and spirit appear to characterize the verse of a people not primitive, though the colonial pioneers of life and literature in a new land.

To a few exquisite but unnamed quatrains and lyrics by Landor, I have prefixed the felicitous titles given to them by Mr. Aldrich in the little book "Cameos," of which he and I were the editors a score of years ago. From the early minstrels a compiler's selections are not hard to make. The panel already has been struck by time itself, which declares that, even in the case of some uneven roisterer, one or two fortunate catches shall preserve his name. More embarrassment comes from the knowledge that lovers of such poets as Tennyson, who made no imperfect poem, and Browning, who wrote none that was meaningless, are slow to understand why certain pieces, for which an editor, doubtless, shares their own regard, are perforce omitted. To surmise, moreover, which is the one lasting note of a new voice or which of all the younger band is to win renown, this is the labor and the work, seeing that as to finish they are all sensitive enough, except now and then one who invites attention by contempt for it. Nothing is more evident than the good craftsmanship of latter-day English and American verse-makers, — a matter of course, after the object-lessons given by their immediate forbears. All in all, the anthologist must rest his cause upon its good intention. In speaking of those who hunt up and reprint the faulty work of authors, — "the imperfect thing or thought" which in mature years they have tried to suppress, — Palgrave justly says in his "Pro Mortuis," —

> "Nor has the dead worse foe than he
> Who rakes these sweepings of the artist's room,
> And piles them on his tomb."

Conversely, one perhaps earns some right to count himself the artist's friend, whose endeavor is to discover and preserve, from the once cherished treasures of even a humble fellow of the craft, at least "one gem of song, defying age."

Compact Biographical Notes, upon all the poets represented, follow the main text. Where authorities conflict, and usually, also, in the cases of recent authors, effort has been made to secure the desired information at first hand. For this, and for the general result, my hearty thanks are due to the skill and patience of Miss Vernetta E. Coleman, who has prepared the greater portion of the Notes. The faithfulness of the text at large has been enhanced by the coöperation of the Riverside Press, and this is not the first time when I have been grateful to its Corrector and his assistants for really critical attention given to a work passing through their hands.

E. C. S.

New York, *September*, 1895.

NOTE

FOR the text of the selections in this Anthology, transcripts have been made, as far as possible, from the books of the respective authors, many of which volumes are upon the editor's shelves. Much dependence, however, has been placed on the Astor, Mercantile, Columbia College, and Society Libraries, and the Library of the Y. W. C. Association. To the librarians of these institutions the editor's acknowledgments are rendered for courteous assistance. His thanks are due, also, to Mr. R. H. Stoddard, Mr. R. W. Gilder, Prof. Brander Matthews, and Prof. F. D. Sherman, of New York, Mr. Harrison S. Morris, of Philadelphia, Mr. G. H. Ellwanger, of Rochester, and Prof. C. G. D. Roberts, late of Windsor, N. S., for giving him the use of their collections, and to a few other friends for various services. With respect to attractive single poems, and to authors whose original editions could not be obtained, he has found the eight volumes of Mr. Miles's "The Poets and the Poetry of the Century" welcome aids to his research. Use also has been made of Mr. Sharp's "Canterbury Poets" series, Prof. Sladen's "Australian Poets," Mr. Schuyler-Lighthall's "Songs of the Great Dominion," and of several minor collections of Scottish, Irish, and English-dialect verse.

His thanks are rendered to many living British poets, who now, under the amended copyright law, are so closely affiliated with us, for the privilege cheerfully given of taking his own selections from their works. This usufruct has been generously confirmed by the publishers issuing their American editions. The editor desires to express his grateful obligations to Messrs. Macmillan & Co. and Messrs. Longmans, Green & Co., of London and New York; to Messrs. Charles Scribner's Sons, Messrs. Dodd, Mead & Co., Messrs. G. P. Putnam's Sons, and the Frederick A. Stokes Company, of New York; to Messrs. Roberts Brothers and Messrs. Copeland & Day, of Boston; and to Messrs. Stone & Kimball and Messrs. Way & Williams, of Chicago.

TABLE OF CONTENTS

I. EARLY YEARS OF THE REIGN

(TRANSITION PERIOD)

DISTINCTIVE POETS AND DRAMATISTS

POETS OF QUALITY

THE ROISTERERS

MEDITATIVE POETS

ENGLISH SONG WRITERS

SONGS AND BALLADRY OF SCOTLAND

IRISH MINSTRELSY

INCLUDING THE POETS OF YOUNG IRELAND

TABLE OF CONTENTS

"THE OATEN FLUTE"

POETS OF THE NEW DAY

(Humanity — Free Thought — Political, Social, and Artistic Reform)

II. THE VICTORIAN EPOCH

(PERIOD OF TENNYSON, ARNOLD, BROWNING, ROSSETTI, AND SWINBURNE)

COMPOSITE IDYLLIC SCHOOL

BALLADISTS AND LYRISTS

POETS OF THE RENAISSANCE

DRAMATISTS AND PLAYWRIGHTS

ELEGANTIÆ

"THE LAND OF WONDER–WANDER"

III. CLOSE OF THE ERA

(INTERMEDIARY PERIOD)

RECENT POETS OF GREAT BRITAIN

IV. COLONIAL POETS

(INDIA — AUSTRALASIA — DOMINION OF CANADA)

INDIA

See TORU DUTT, RUDYARD KIPLING, *in the preceding division of this Anthology. See also, in the second division,* SIR EDWIN ARNOLD, SIR ALFRED LYALL, *poets of English birth, and sometime resident in India*

AUSTRALASIA

(*See also:* A. DOMETT, R. H. HORNE, W. SHARP, D. B. W. SLADEN)

DOMINION OF CANADA

I

EARLY YEARS OF THE REIGN

(TRANSITION PERIOD)

CLOSE OF SOUTHEY'S LAUREATESHIP: 1837–43
LAUREATESHIP OF WORDSWORTH: 1843–50

Accession of Victoria R., June 20, 1837

THE PASSING OF THE ELDER BARDS

FROM THE "EXTEMPORE EFFUSION UPON THE DEATH OF JAMES HOGG"

THE mighty Minstrel breathes no longer,
Mid mouldering ruins low he lies;
And death upon the braes of Yarrow
Has closed the Shepherd-poet's eyes:

Nor has the rolling year twice measured,
From sign to sign, its steadfast course,
Since every mortal power of Coleridge
Was frozen at its marvellous source;

The 'rapt One, of the godlike forehead,
The heaven-eyed creature sleeps in earth:
And Lamb, the frolic and the gentle,
Has vanished from his lonely hearth.

Like clouds that rake the mountain-summits,
Or waves that own no curbing hand,
How fast has brother followed brother,
From sunshine to the sunless land!

Yet I, whose lids from infant slumber
Were earlier raised, remain to hear
A timid voice, that asks in whispers,
" Who next will drop and disappear? "

WILLIAM WORDSWORTH.

November, 1835.

EARLY YEARS OF THE REIGN

(TRANSITION PERIOD)

DISTINCTIVE POETS AND DRAMATISTS

___

Walter Savage Landor

OVERTURE

FROM "THRASYMEDES AND EUNOË"

WHO will away to Athens with me ? who
Loves choral songs and maidens crown'd
  with flowers,
Unenvious ? mount the pinnace ; hoist the
  sail.
I promise ye, as many as are here,
Ye shall not, while ye tarry with me, taste
From unrins'd barrel the diluted wine
Of a low vineyard or a plant ill prun'd,
But such as anciently the Ægean isles
Pour'd in libation at their solemn feasts :
And the same goblets shall ye grasp,
  emboss'd
With no vile figures of loose languid boors,
But such as gods have liv'd with and have
  led.

THE HAMADRYAD

RHAICOS was born amid the hills where-
  from
Gnidos the light of Caria is discern'd,
And small are the white-crested that play
  near,
And smaller onward are the purple waves.
Thence festal choirs were visible, all crown'd
With rose and myrtle if they were inborn ;
If from Pandion sprang they, on the coast
Where stern Athenè rais'd her citadel,

Then olive was entwin'd with violets
Cluster'd in bosses, regular and large ;
For various men wore various coronals,
But one was their devotion ; 't was to her
Whose laws all follow, her whose smile
  withdraws
The sword from Ares, thunderbolt from
  Zeus,
And whom in his chill caves the mutable
Of mind, Poseidon, the sea-king, reveres,
And whom his brother, stubborn Dis, hath
  pray'd
To turn in pity the averted cheek
Of her he bore away, with promises,
Nay, with loud oath before dread Styx it-
  self,
To give her daily more and sweeter flowers
Than he made drop from her on Enna's dell.
  Rhaicos was looking from his father's
  door
At the long trains that hasten'd to the town
From all the valleys, like bright rivulets
Gurgling with gladness, wave outrunning
  wave,
And thought it hard he might not also go
And offer up one prayer, and press one
  hand,
He knew not whose.   The father call'd him
  in
And said, "Son Rhaicos ! those are idle
  games ;
Long enough I have liv'd to find them so."
And ere he ended, sigh'd ; as old men do
Always, to think how idle such games are.

"I have not yet," thought Rhaicos in his
heart,
And wanted proof.
        "Suppose thou go and help
Echion at the hill, to bark yon oak
And lop its branches off, before we delve
About the trunk and ply the root with axe :
This we may do in winter."
              Rhaicos went ;
For thence he could see farther, and see
more
Of those who hurried to the city-gate.
Echion he found there, with naked arm
Swart-hair'd, strong-sinew'd, and his eyes
intent
Upon the place where first the axe should
fall :
He held it upright. "There are bees about,
Or wasps, or hornets," said the cautious eld,
"Look sharp, O son of Thallinos !" The
youth
Inclin'd his ear, afar, and warily,
And cavern'd in his hand. He heard a buzz
At first, and then the sound grew soft and
clear,
And then divided into what seem'd tune,
And there were words upon it, plaintive
words.
He turn'd, and said, "Echion ! do not strike
That tree : it must be hollow ; for some
god
Speaks from within. Come thyself near."
        Again
Both turn'd toward it : and behold ! there
sat
Upon the moss below, with her two palms
Pressing it, on each side, a maid in form.
Downcast were her long eyelashes, and pale
Her cheek, but never mountain-ash display'd
Berries of color like her lip so pure,
Nor were the anemones about her hair
Soft, smooth, and wavering like the face
beneath.
"What dost thou here ?" Echion, half-
afraid,
Half-angry, cried. She lifted up her eyes,
But nothing spake she. Rhaicos drew one
step
Backward, for fear came likewise over him,
But not such fear : he panted, gasp'd, drew
in
His breath, and would have turn'd it into
words,
But could not into one.
            "O send away

That sad old man !" said she. The old man
went
Without a warning from his master's son,
Glad to escape, for sorely he now fear'd,
And the axe shone behind him in their eyes.
  Hamad. And wouldst thou too shed the
most innocent
Of blood ? No vow demands it ; no god
wills
The oak to bleed.
  Rhaicos. Who art thou ? whence ? why
here ?
And whither wouldst thou go ? Among the
rob'd
In white or saffron, or the hue that most
Resembles dawn or the clear sky, is none
Array'd as thou art. What so beautiful
As that gray robe which clings about thee
close,
Like moss to stones adhering, leaves to
trees,
Yet lets thy bosom rise and fall in turn,
As, touch'd by zephyrs, fall and rise the
boughs
Of graceful platan by the river-side ?
  Hamad. Lovest thou well thy father's
house ?
  Rhaicos.   Indeed
I love it, well I love it, yet would leave
For thine, where'er it be, my father's house,
With all the marks upon the door, that show
My growth at every birthday since the third,
And all the charms, o'erpowering evil eyes,
My mother nail'd for me against my bed,
And the Cydonian bow (which thou shalt
see)
Won in my race last spring from Eutychos.
  Hamad. Bethink thee what it is to leave
a home
Thou never yet hast left, one night, one day.
  Rhaicos. No, 't is not hard to leave it :
't is not hard
To leave, O maiden, that paternal home
If there be one on earth whom we may love
First, last, for ever ; one who says that she
Will love for ever too. To say which word,
Only to say it, surely is enough.
It shows such kindness — if 't were possible
We at the moment think she would indeed.
  Hamad. Who taught thee all this folly at
thy age ?
  Rhaicos. I have seen lovers and have
learn'd to love.
  Hamad. But wilt thou spare the tree ?
  Rhaicos.   My father wants

The bark ; the tree may hold its place awhile.
Hamad. Awhile ? thy father numbers
    then my days ?
Rhaicos. Are there no others where the
    moss beneath
Is quite as tufty ? Who would send thee
    forth
Or ask thee why thou tarriest ? Is thy flock
Anywhere near ?
Hamad.   I have no flock : I kill
Nothing that breathes, that stirs, that feels
    the air,
The sun, the dew. Why should the beauti-
    ful
(And thou art beautiful) disturb the source
Whence springs all beauty ? Hast thou
    never heard
Of Hamadryads ?
Rhaicos.   Heard of them I have :
Tell me some tale about them. May I sit
Beside thy feet ? Art thou not tired ? The
    herbs
Are very soft ; I will not come too nigh ;
Do but sit there, nor tremble so, nor doubt.
Stay, stay an instant : let me first explore
If any acorn of last year be left
Within it ; thy thin robe too ill protects
Thy dainty limbs against the harm one small
Acorn may do. Here 's none. Another day
Trust me ; till then let me sit opposite.
Hamad. I seat me ; be thou seated, and
    content.
Rhaicos. O sight for gods ! ye men be-
    low ! adore
The Aphroditè ! *Is* she there below ?
Or sits she here before me ? as she sate
Before the shepherd on those heights that
    shade
The Hellespont, and brought his kindred
    woe.
Hamad. Reverence the higher Powers ;
    nor deem amiss
Of her who pleads to thee, and would re-
    pay —
Ask not how much — but very much. Rise
    not :
No, Rhaicos, no ! Without the nuptial vow
Love is unholy. Swear to me that none
Of mortal maids shall ever taste thy kiss,
Then take thou mine ; then take it, not
    before.
Rhaicos. Hearken, all gods above ! O
    Aphroditè !
O Herè ! Let my vow be ratified !
But wilt thou come into my father's house?

Hamad. Nay : and of mine I cannot give
    thee part.
Rhaicos. Where is it ?
Hamad.   In this oak.
Rhaicos.   Ay ; now begins
The tale of Hamadryad : tell it through.
Hamad. Pray of thy father never to cut
    down
My tree ; and promise him, as well thou
    mayst,
That every year he shall receive from me
More honey than will buy him nine fat sheep,
More wax than he will burn to all the gods.
Why fallest thou upon thy face ? Some
    thorn
May scratch it, rash young man ! Rise up ;
    for shame !
Rhaicos. For shame I cannot rise. O pity
    me !
I dare not sue for love — but do not hate !
Let me once more behold thee — not once
    more,
But many days : let me love on — unlov'd !
I aim'd too high : on my own head the bolt
Falls back, and pierces to the very brain.
Hamad. Go — rather go, than make me
    say I love.
Rhaicos. If happiness is immortality,
(And whence enjoy it else the gods above ?)
I am immortal too : my vow is heard —
Hark ! on the left — Nay, turn not from me
    now,
I claim my kiss.
Hamad. Do men take first, then claim ?
Do thus the seasons run their course with
    them ?

Her lips were seal'd ; her head sank on
    his breast.
'T is said that laughs were heard within the
    wood :
But who should hear them ? and whose
    laughs ? and why ?

Savory was the smell and long past noon,
Thallinos ! in thy house ; for marjoram,
Basil and mint, and thyme and rosemary,
Were sprinkled on the kid's well roasted
    length,
Awaiting Rhaicos. Home he came at last,
Not hungry, but pretending hunger keen,
With head and eyes just o'er the maple
    plate.
" Thou see'st but badly, coming from the
    sun,

Boy Rhaicos!" said the father. "That
  oak's bark
Must have been tough, with little sap be-
  tween ;
It ought to run ; but it and I are old."
Rhaicos, although each morsel of the bread
Increas'd by chewing, and the meat grew
  cold
And tasteless to his palate, took a draught
Of gold-bright wine, which, thirsty as he
  was,
He thought not of, until his father fill'd
The cup, averring water was amiss,
But wine had been at all times pour'd on kid.
It was religion.
            He thus fortified
Said, not quite boldly, and not quite abash'd,
"Father, that oak is Zeus's own ; that oak
Year after year will bring thee wealth from
  wax
And honey. There is one who fears the
  gods
And the gods love — that one "
                 (He blush'd, nor said
What one)
    "Has promis'd this, and may do more.
Thou hast not many moons to wait until
The bees have done their best ; if then
  there come
Nor wax nor honey, let the tree be hewn."
    "Zeus hath bestow'd on thee a prudent
  mind,"
Said the glad sire : " but look thou often
  there,
And gather all the honey thou canst find
In every crevice, over and above
What has been promis'd ; would they reckon
  that ? "

    Rhaicos went daily; but the nymph as oft,
Invisible. To play at love, she knew,
Stopping its breathings when it breathes
  most soft,
Is sweeter than to play on any pipe.
She play'd on his : she fed upon his sighs ;
They pleas'd her when they gently wav'd
  her hair,
Cooling the pulses of her purple veins,
And when her absence brought them out,
  they pleas'd.
Even among the fondest of them all,
What mortal or immortal maid is more
Content with giving happiness than pain ?
One day he was returning from the wood
Despondently. She pitied him, and said

"Come back !" and twin'd her fingers in
  the hem
Above his shoulder. Then she led his steps
To a cool rill that ran o'er level sand
Through lentisk and through oleander; there
Bath'd she his feet, lifting them on her lap
When bath'd, and drying them in both her
  hands.
He dar'd complain ; for those who most are
  lov'd
Most dare it ; but not harsh was his com-
  plaint.
" O thou inconstant ! " said he, " if stern law
Bind thee, or will, stronger than sternest
  law,
O, let me know henceforward when to hope
The fruit of love that grows for me but
  here."
He spake ; and pluck'd it from its pliant
  stem.
" Impatient Rhaicos ! Why thus intercept
The answer I would give ? There is a bee
Whom I have fed, a bee who knows my
  thoughts
And executes my wishes : I will send
That messenger. If ever thou art false,
Drawn by another, own it not, but drive
My bee away : then shall I know my fate,
And — for thou must be wretched — weep
  at thine.
But often as my heart persuades to lay
Its cares on thine and throb itself to rest,
Expect her with thee, whether it be morn
Or eve, at any time when woods are safe."

  Day after day the Hours beheld them
  blest,
And season after season : years had past,
Blest were they still. He who asserts that
  Love
Ever is sated of sweet things, the same
Sweet things he fretted for in earlier days,
Never, by Zeus ! lov'd he a Hamadryad.

  The nights had now grown longer, and
  perhaps
The Hamadryads find them lone and dull
Among their woods ; one did, alas ! She
  call'd
Her faithful bee : 't was when all bees
  should sleep,
And all did sleep but hers. She was sent
  forth
To bring that light which never wintry blast
Blows out, nor rain nor snow extinguishes,
The light that shines from loving eyes upon

Eyes that love back, till they can see no
more.
Rhaicos was sitting at his father's hearth :
Between them stood the table, not o'er-
spread
With fruits which autumn now profusely
bore,
Nor anise cakes, nor odorous wine ; but
there
The draft-board was expanded ; at which
game
Triumphant sat old Thallinos ; the son
Was puzzled, vex'd, discomfited, distraught.
A buzz was at his ear : up went his hand
And it was heard no longer. The poor bee
Return'd (but not until the morn shone
bright)
And found the Hamadryad with her head
Upon her aching wrist, and show'd one wing
Half-broken off, the other's meshes marr'd,
And there were bruises which no eye could
see
Saving a Hamadryad's.
                        At this sight
Down fell the languid brow, both hands fell
down,
A shriek was carried to the ancient hall
Of Thallinos : he heard it not : his son
Heard it, and ran forthwith into the wood.
No bark was on the tree, no leaf was green,
The trunk was riven through. From that
day forth
Nor word nor whisper sooth'd his ear, nor
sound
Even of insect wing ; but loud laments
The woodmen and the shepherds one long
year
Heard day and night ; for Rhaicos would
not quit
The solitary place, but moan'd and died.

Hence milk and honey wonder not, O guest,
To find set duly on the hollow stone.

THE DEATH OF ARTEMIDORA

" ARTEMIDORA ! Gods invisible,
While thou art lying faint along the couch,
Have tied the sandal to thy veined feet,
And stand beside thee, ready to convey
Thy weary steps where other rivers flow.
Refreshing shades will waft thy weariness
Away, and voices like thine own come nigh,
Soliciting, nor vainly, thy embrace."

Artemidora sigh'd, and would have press'd
The hand now pressing hers, but was too
weak.
Fate's shears were over her dark hair un-
seen
While thus Elpenor spake : he look'd into
Eyes that had given light and life erewhile.
To those above them, those now dim with
tears
And watchfulness. Again he spake of joy,
Eternal. At that word, that sad word, joy,
Faithful and fond her bosom heav'd once
more,
Her head fell back : one sob, one loud deep
sob
Swell'd through the darken'd chamber ;
't was not hers :
With her that old boat incorruptible,
Unwearied, undiverted in its course,
Had plash'd the water up the farther strand.

FROM " MYRTIS "

FRIENDS, whom she look'd at blandly from
her couch
And her white wrist above it, gem-bedew'd,
Were arguing with Pentheusa : she had
heard
Report of Creon's death, whom years before
She listen'd to, well-pleas'd ; and sighs
arose ;
For sighs full often fondle with reproofs
And will be fondled by them. When I
came
After the rest to visit her, she said,
" Myrtis ! how kind ! Who better knows
than thou
The pangs of love ? and my first love was
he ! "
Tell me (if ever, Eros ! are reveal'd
Thy secrets to the earth) have they been
true
To any love who speak about the first ?
What ! shall these holier lights, like twin-
kling stars
In the few hours assign'd them, change
their place,
And, when comes ampler splendor, disap-
pear ?
Idler I am, and pardon, not reply,
Implore from thee, thus question'd ; well
I know
Thou strikest, like Olympian Jove, but
once.

LITTLE AGLAË

TO HER FATHER, ON HER STATUE BEING CALLED LIKE HER

FATHER ! the little girl we see
Is not, I fancy, so like me ;
You never hold her on your knee.

When she came home, the other day,
You kiss'd her ; but I cannot say
She kiss'd you first and ran away.

TO A CYCLAMEN

I COME to visit thee agen,
My little flowerless cyclamen ;
To touch the hand, almost to press,
That cheer'd thee in thy loneliness.
What could thy careful guardian find
Of thee in form, of me in mind,
What is there in us rich or rare,
To make us claim a moment's care ?
Unworthy to be so carest,
We are but withering leaves at best.

DIRCE

STAND close around, ye Stygian set,
With Dirce in one boat convey'd,
Or Charon, seeing, may forget
That he is old, and she a shade.

AN INVOCATION

WE are what suns and winds and waters
make us ;
The mountains are our sponsors, and the
rills
Fashion and win their nursling with their
smiles.
But where the land is dim from tyranny,
There tiny pleasures occupy the place
Of glories and of duties ; as the feet
Of fabled faeries when the sun goes down
Trip o'er the grass where wrestlers strove
by day.
Then Justice, call'd the Eternal One above,
Is more inconstant than the buoyant form
That burst into existence from the froth
Of ever-varying ocean : what is best

Then becomes worst ; what loveliest, most
deform'd.
The heart is hardest in the softest climes,
The passions flourish, the affections die.
O thou vast tablet of these awful truths,
That fillest all the space between the seas,
Spreading from Venice's deserted courts
To the Tarentine and Hydruntine mole,
What lifts thee up ? what shakes thee ? 't is
the breath
Of God. Awake, ye nations ! spring to life !
Let the last work of his right hand appear
Fresh with his image, Man.

FROM "GEBIR"

TAMAR AND THE NYMPH

" 'T WAS evening, though not sunset, and
the tide,
Level with these green meadows, seem'd
yet higher :
'T was pleasant, and I loosen'd from my
neck
The pipe you gave me, and began to play.
O that I ne'er had learn'd the tuneful
art !
It always brings us enemies or love.
Well, I was playing, when above the waves
Some swimmer's head methought I saw
ascend ;
I, sitting still, survey'd it with my pipe
Awkwardly held before my lips half-clos'd.
Gebir ! it was a Nymph ! a Nymph divine !
I cannot wait describing how she came,
How I was sitting, how she first assum'd
The sailor ; of what happen'd there remains
Enough to say, and too much to forget.
The sweet deceiver stepp'd upon this bank
Before I was aware ; for with surprise
Moments fly rapid as with love itself.
Stooping to tune afresh the hoarsen'd reed,
I heard a rustling, and where that arose
My glance first lighted on her nimble feet.
Her feet resembled those long shells ex-
plor'd
By him who to befriend his steed's dim sight
Would blow the pungent powder in the eye.
Her eyes too ! O immortal gods ! her eyes
Resembled — what could they resemble ?
what
Ever resemble those ? Even her attire
Was not of wonted woof nor vulgar art :

Her mantle show'd the yellow samphire-pod,
Her girdle the dove-color'd wave serene.
'Shepherd,' said she, 'and will you wrestle now
And with the sailor's hardier race engage ? '
I was rejoiced to hear it, and contriv'd
How to keep up contention : could I fail
By pressing not too strongly, yet to press ?
' Whether a shepherd, as indeed you seem,
Or whether of the hardier race you boast,
I am not daunted ; no ; I will engage.'
' But first,' said she, ' what wager will you lay ? '
' A sheep,' I answered : 'add whate'er you will.'
' I cannot,' she replied, 'make that return :
Our hided vessels in their pitchy round
Seldom, unless from rapine, hold a sheep.
But I have sinuous shells of pearly hue
Within, and they that lustre have imbib'd
In the sun's palace-porch, where when un-yok'd
His chariot-wheel stands midway in the wave :
Shake one and it awakens, then apply
Its polish'd lips to your attentive ear,
And it remembers its august abodes,
And murmurs as the ocean murmurs there.
And I have others given me by the nymphs,
Of sweeter sound than any pipe you have :
But we, by Neptune ! for no pipe contend ;
This time a sheep I win, a pipe the next.'
Now came she forward eager to engage,
But first her dress, her bosom then survey'd
And heav'd it, doubting if she could deceive.
Her bosom seem'd, inclos'd in haze like heaven,
To baffle touch, and rose forth undefin'd ;
Above her knee she drew the robe succinct,
Above her breast, and just below her arms.
' This will preserve my breath when tightly bound,
If struggle and equal strength should so constrain.'
Thus, pulling hard to fasten it, she spake,
And, rushing at me, clos'd : I thrill'd throughout
And seem'd to lessen and shrink up with cold.
Again with violent impulse gush'd my blood,
And hearing nought external, thus absorb'd,
I heard it, rushing through each turbid vein,
Shake my unsteady swimming sight in air.
Yet with unyielding though uncertain arms

I clung around her neck ; the vest beneath
Rustled against our slippery limbs entwin'd :
Often mine springing with eluded force
Started aside and trembled till replaced :
And when I most succeeded, as I thought,
My bosom and my throat felt so compress'd
That life was almost quivering on my lips.
Yet nothing was there painful : these are signs
Of secret arts and not of human might ;
What arts I cannot tell ; I only know
My eyes grew dizzy and my strength decay'd ;
I was indeed o'ercome — with what regret,
And more, with what confusion, when I reach'd
The fold, and yielding up the sheep, she cried,
' This pays a shepherd to a conquering maid.'
She smil'd, and more of pleasure than disdain
Was in her dimpled chin and liberal lip,
And eyes that languish'd, lengthening, just like love.
She went away ; I on the wicker gate
Leant, and could follow with my eyes alone
The sheep she carried easy as a cloak ;
But when I heard its bleating, as I did,
And saw, she hastening on, its hinder feet
Struggle, and from her snowy shoulder slip,
One shoulder its poor efforts had unveil'd,
Then all my passions mingling fell in tears ;
Restless then ran I to the highest ground
To watch her ; she was gone ; gone down the tide ;
And the long moonbeam on the hard wet sand
Lay like a jasper column half uprear'd."

TO YOUTH

WHERE art thou gone, light-ankled Youth ?
  With wing at either shoulder,
And smile that never left thy mouth
  Until the Hours grew colder :

Then somewhat seem'd to whisper near
  That thou and I must part ;
I doubted it ; I felt no fear,
  No weight upon the heart.

If aught befell it, Love was by
    And roll'd it off again ;
So, if there ever was a sigh,
    'T was not a sigh of pain.

I may not call thee back ; but thou
    Returnest when the hand
Of gentle Sleep waves o'er my brow
    His poppy-crested wand ;

Then smiling eyes bend over mine,
    Then lips once press'd invite ;
But sleep hath given a silent sign,
    And both, alas ! take flight.

TO AGE

WELCOME, old friend ! These many years
    Have we liv'd door by door :
The Fates have laid aside their shears
    Perhaps for some few more.

I was indocile at an age
    When better boys were taught,
But thou at length hast made me sage,
    If I am sage in aught.

Little I know from other men,
    Too little they from me,
But thou hast pointed well the pen
    That writes these lines to thee.

Thanks for expelling Fear and Hope,
    One vile, the other vain ;
One's scourge, the other's telescope,
    I shall not see again :

Rather what lies before my feet
    My notice shall engage.
He who hath brav'd Youth's dizzy heat
    Dreads not the frost of Age.

ROSE AYLMER

AH what avails the sceptred race,
    Ah what the form divine !
What every virtue, every grace !
    Rose Aylmer, all were thine.
Rose Aylmer, whom these wakeful eyes
    May weep, but never see,
A night of memories and of sighs
    I consecrate to thee.

ROSE AYLMER'S HAIR, GIVEN BY HER SISTER

BEAUTIFUL spoils ! borne off from van-
    quish'd death !
Upon my heart's high altar shall ye lie,
Mov'd but by only one adorer's breath,
    Retaining youth, rewarding constancy.

CHILD OF A DAY

CHILD of a day, thou knowest not
    The tears that overflow thine urn,
The gushing eyes that read thy lot,
    Nor, if thou knewest, couldst return.
And why the wish ! the pure and blest
    Watch like thy mother o'er thy sleep.
O peaceful night ! O envied rest !
    Thou wilt not ever see her weep.

FIESOLAN IDYL

HERE, where precipitate Spring with one
    light bound
Into hot Summer's lusty arms expires,
And where go forth at morn, at eve, at
    night,
Soft airs that want the lute to play with 'em,
And softer sighs that know not what they
    want,
Aside a wall, beneath an orange-tree,
Whose tallest flowers could tell the lowlier
    ones
Of sights in Fiesole right up above,
While I was gazing a few paces off
At what they seem'd to show me with their
    nods,
Their frequent whispers and their pointing
    shoots,
A gentle maid came down the garden-steps
And gather'd the pure treasure in her lap.
I heard the branches rustle, and stepp'd
    forth
To drive the ox away, or mule, or goat,
Such I believ'd it must be. How could I
Let beast o'erpower them ? when hath wind
    or rain
Borne hard upon weak plant that wanted
    me,
And I (however they might bluster round)

Walk'd off ? 'T were most ungrateful : for
sweet scents
Are the swift vehicles of still sweeter
thoughts,
And nurse and pillow the dull memory
That would let drop without them her best
stores.
They bring me tales of youth and tones of
love,
And 'tis and ever was my wish and way
To let all flowers live freely, and all die
(Whene'er their Genius bids their souls
depart)
Among their kindred in their native place.
I never pluck the rose ; the violet's head
Hath shaken with my breath upon its bank
And not reproach'd me ; the ever-sacred
cup
Of the pure lily hath between my hands
Felt safe, unsoil'd, nor lost one grain of gold.
I saw the light that made the glossy leaves
More glossy ; the fair arm, the fairer cheek
Warm'd by the eye intent on its pursuit ;
I saw the foot that, although half-erect
From its gray slipper, could not lift her up
To what she wanted : I held down a branch
And gather'd her some blossoms ; since
their hour
Was come, and bees had wounded them,
and flies
Of harder wing were working their way
through
And scattering them in fragments under
foot.
So crisp were some, they rattled unevolv'd,
Others, ere broken off, fell into shells, ,
Unbending, brittle, lucid, white like snow,
And like snow not seen through, by eye or
sun :
Yet every one her gown receiv'd from me
Was fairer than the first. I thought not so,
But so she prais'd them to reward my care.
I said, " You find the largest."
" This indeed,"
Cried she, " is large and sweet." She held
one forth,
Whether for me to look at or to take
She knew not, nor did I ; but taking it
Would best have solv'd (and this she felt)
her doubt.
I dar'd not touch it ; for it seem'd a part
Of her own self ; fresh, full, the most
mature
Of blossoms, yet a blossom ; with a touch
To fall, and yet unfallen. She drew back

The boon she tender'd, and then, finding not
The ribbon at her waist to fix it in,
Dropp'd it, as loth to drop it, on the rest.

FAREWELL TO ITALY

I LEAVE thee, beauteous Italy ! no more
From the high terraces, at even-tide,
To look supine into thy depths of sky,
Thy golden moon between the cliff and me,
Or thy dark spires of fretted cypresses
Bordering the channel of the milky way.
Fiesole and Valdarno must be dreams
Hereafter, and my own lost Affrico
Murmur to me but in the poet's song.
I did believe (what have I not believ'd?),
Weary with age, but unoppress'd by pain,
To close in thy soft clime my quiet day
And rest my bones in the mimosa's shade.
Hope ! Hope ! few ever cherish'd thee so
little ;
Few are the heads thou hast so rarely rais'd;
But thou didst promise this, and all was
well.
For we are fond of thinking where to lie
When every pulse hath ceas'd, when the
lone heart
Can lift no aspiration — reasoning
As if the sight were unimpair'd by death,
Were unobstructed by the coffin-lid,
And the sun cheer'd corruption ! Over all
The smiles of Nature shed a potent charm,
And light us to our chamber at the grave.

THE MAID'S LAMENT

ELIZABETHAN

I LOV'D him not ; and yet now he is gone
I feel I am alone.
I check'd him while he spoke ; yet could
he speak,
Alas ! I would not check.
For reasons not to love him once I sought,
And wearied all my thought
To vex myself and him : I now would give
My love, could he but live
Who lately liv'd for me, and when he found
'T was vain, in holy ground
He hid his face amid the shades of death.
I waste for him my breath

Who wasted his for me ; but mine returns,
And this lone bosom burns
With stifling heat, heaving it up in sleep
And waking me to weep
Tears that had melted his soft heart : for
years
Wept he as bitter tears.
Merciful God! such was his latest prayer,
These may she never share!
Quieter is his breath, his breast more cold,
Than daisies in the mould,
Where children spell, athwart the church-
yard gate,
His name and life's brief date.
Pray for him, gentle souls, whoe'er you be,
And oh ! pray too for me !

MARGARET

MOTHER, I cannot mind my wheel ;
My fingers ache, my lips are dry ;
Oh, if you felt the pain I feel !
But oh, who ever felt as I !
No longer could I doubt him true,
All other men may use deceit ;
He always said my eyes were blue,
And often swore my lips were sweet.

ON MUSIC

MANY love music but for music's sake ;
Many because her touches can awake
Thoughts that repose within the breast half
dead,
And rise to follow where she loves to lead.
What various feelings come from days
gone by !
What tears from far-off sources dim the
eye !
Few, when light fingers with sweet voices
play,
And melodies swell, pause, and melt
away,
Mind how at every touch, at every tone,
A spark of life hath glisten'd and hath gone.

PLAYS

ALAS, how soon the hours are over
Counted us out to play the lover !
And how much narrower is the stage
Allotted us to play the sage !

But when we play the fool, how wide
The theatre expands ! beside,
How long the audience sits before us !
How many prompters ! what a chorus !

THERE FALLS WITH EVERY WEDDING CHIME

THERE falls with every wedding chime
A feather from the wing of Time.
You pick it up, and say " How fair
To look upon its colors are ! "
Another drops day after day
Unheeded ; not one word you say.
When bright and dusky are blown past,
Upon the hearse there nods the last.

SHAKESPEARE AND MILTON

THE tongue of England, that which myriads
Have spoken and will speak, were paralyz'd
Hereafter, but two mighty men stand
forth
Above the flight of ages, two alone ;
One crying out,
All nations spoke through me.
The other :
True ; and through this trumpet burst
God's word ; the fall of Angels, and the
doom
First of immortal, then of mortal, Man.
Glory! be glory! not to me, to God.

MACAULAY

THE dreamy rhymer's measur'd snore
Falls heavy on our ears no more ;
And by long strides are left behind
The dear delights of woman-kind,
Who win their battles like their loves,
In satin waistcoats and kid gloves,
And have achiev'd the crowning work
When they have truss'd and skewer'd a
Turk.
Another comes with stouter tread,
And stalks among the statelier dead.
He rushes on, and hails by turns
High-crested Scott, broad-breasted Burns,
And shows the British youth, who ne'er
Will lag behind, what Romans were,
When all the Tuscans and their Lars
Shouted, and shook the towers of Mars.

ROBERT BROWNING

THERE is delight in singing, though none
    hear
Beside the singer ; and there is delight
In praising, though the praiser sit alone
And see the prais'd far off him, far above.
Shakspeare is not our poet, but the world's,
Therefore on him no speech ! and brief for
    thee,
Browning ! Since Chaucer was alive and
    hale,
No man hath walk'd along our roads with
    step
So active, so inquiring eye, or tongue
So varied in discourse. But warmer climes
Give brighter plumage, stronger wing : the
    breeze
Of Alpine heights thou playest with, borne
    on
Beyond Sorrento and Amalfi, where
The Siren waits thee, singing song for song.

ON THE DEATH OF M. D'OSSOLI AND HIS WIFE MARGARET FULLER

OVER his millions Death has lawful power,
But over thee, brave D'Ossoli ! none, none.
After a longer struggle, in a fight
Worthy of Italy, to youth restor'd,
Thou, far from home, art sunk beneath the
    surge
Of the Atlantic ; on its shore ; in reach
Of help ; in trust of refuge ; sunk with
    all
Precious on earth to thee . . . a child, a
    wife !
Proud as thou wert of her, America
Is prouder, showing to her sons how high
Swells woman's courage in a virtuous
    breast.
She would not leave behind her those she
    lov'd :
Such solitary safety might become
Others ; not her ; not her who stood beside
The pallet of the wounded, when the worst
Of France and Perfidy assail'd the walls
Of unsuspicious Rome. Rest, glorious soul,
Renown'd for strength of genius, Margaret !
Rest with the twain too dear ! My words
    are few,
And shortly none will hear my failing voice,

But the same language with more full ap-
    peal
Shall hail thee. Many are the sons of song
Whom thou hast heard upon thy native
    plains
Worthy to sing of thee : the hour is come ;
Take we our seats and let the dirge begin.

TO IANTHE

YOU smil'd, you spoke, and I believ'd,
By every word and smile deceiv'd.
Another man would hope no more ;
Nor hope I what I hop'd before :
But let not this last wish be vain ;
Deceive, deceive me once again !

IANTHE'S TROUBLES

YOUR pleasures spring like daisies in the
    grass,
    Cut down and up again as blithe as
        ever ;
From you, Ianthe, little troubles pass
    Like little ripples in a sunny river.

THE APPEAL

REMAIN, ah not in youth alone,
    Though youth, where you are, long will
        stay,
But when my summer days are gone,
    And my autumnal haste away.
    " Can I be always by your side ? "
    No ; but the hours you can, you must,
Nor rise at Death's approaching stride,
    Nor go when dust is gone to dust.

THE TEST

I HELD her hand, the pledge of bliss,
    Her hand that trembled and withdrew ;
She bent her head before my kiss . . .
    My heart was sure that hers was true.
Now I have told her I must part,
    She shakes my hand, she bids adieu,
Nor shuns the kiss. Alas, my heart !
    Hers never was the heart for you.

IN AFTER TIME

No, my own love of other years !
  No, it must never be.
Much rests with you that yet endears,
  Alas ! but what with me ?
Could those bright years o'er me revolve
  So gay, o'er you so fair,
The pearl of life we would dissolve
  And each the cup might share.
You show that truth can ne'er decay,
  Whatever fate befalls ;
I, that the myrtle and the bay
  Shoot fresh on ruin'd walls.

A PROPHECY

PROUD word you never spoke, but you will
    speak
  Four not exempt from pride some future
    day.
Resting on one white hand a warm wet
    cheek,
  Over my open volume you will say,
"This man loved *me!*" then rise and
    trip away.

COWSLIPS

WITH rosy hand a little girl press'd down
A boss of fresh-cull'd cowslips in a rill :
Often as they sprang up again, a frown
Show'd she dislik'd resistance to her will :
But when they droop'd their heads and
    shone much less,
She shook them to and fro, and threw them
    by,
And tripp'd away. "Ye loathe the heavi-
    ness
Ye love to cause, my little girls !" thought I,
"And what has shone for you, by you must
    die !"

WRINKLES

WHEN Helen first saw wrinkles in her face
('T was when some fifty long had settled
    there
And intermarried and branch'd off awide)
She threw herself upon her couch and wept :
On this side hung her head, and over that

Listlessly she let fall the faithless brass
That made the men as faithless.
                    But when you
Found them, or fancied them, and would
    not hear
That they were only vestiges of smiles,
Or the impression of some amorous hair
Astray from cloister'd curls and roseate
    band,
Which had been lying there all night per-
    haps
Upon a skin so soft, " No, no," you said,
"Sure, they are coming, yes, are come, are
    here :
Well, and what matters it, while thou art
    too !"

ADVICE

To write as your sweet mother does
  Is all you wish to do.
Play, sing, and smile for others, Rose !
  Let others write for you.

Or mount again your Dartmoor grey,
  And I will walk beside,
Until we reach that quiet bay
  Which only hears the tide.

Then wave at me your pencil, then
  At distance bid me stand,
Before the cavern'd cliff, again
  The creature of your hand.

And bid me then go past the nook
  To sketch me less in size ;
There are but few content to look
  So little in your eyes.

Delight us with the gifts you have,
  And wish for none beyond :
To some be gay, to some be grave,
  To one (blest youth !) be fond.

Pleasures there are how close to Pain,
  And better unpossest !
Let poetry's too throbbing vein
  Lie quiet in your breast.

HOW TO READ ME

To turn my volumes o'er nor find
  (Sweet unsuspicious friend !)
Some vestige of an erring mind
  To chide or discommend,

Believe that all were lov'd like you
With love from blame exempt,
Believe that all my griefs were true
And all my joys but dreamt.

TIME TO BE WISE

YES ; I write verses now and then,
But blunt and flaccid is my pen,
No longer talk'd of by young men
    As rather clever ;
In the last quarter are my eyes,
You see it by their form and size ;
Is it not time then to be wise ?
    Or now or never.

Fairest that ever sprang from Eve !
While Time allows the short reprieve,
Just look at me ! would you believe
    'T was once a lover ?
I cannot clear the five-bar gate ;
But, trying first its timber's state,
Climb stiffly up, take breath, and wait
    To trundle over.

Through gallopade I cannot swing
The entangling blooms of Beauty's spring :
I cannot say the tender thing,
    Be 't true or false,
And am beginning to opine
Those girls are only half divine
Whose waists yon wicked boys entwine
    In giddy waltz.

I fear that arm above that shoulder ;
I wish them wiser, graver, older,
Sedater, and no harm if colder,
    And panting less.
Ah ! people were not half so wild
In former days, when, starchly mild,
Upon her high-heel'd Essex smil'd
    The brave Queen Bess.

THE ONE WHITE HAIR

    THE wisest of the wise
    Listen to pretty lies
        And love to hear them told ;
    Doubt not that Solomon
    Listen'd to many a one, —
Some in his youth, and more when he grew
        old.

I never was among
The choir of Wisdom's song,
    But pretty lies lov'd I
As much as any king,
When youth was on the wing,
And (must it then be told ?) when youth
        had quite gone by.

Alas ! and I have not
The pleasant hour forgot
    When one pert lady said,
"O Walter ! I am quite
Bewilder'd with affright !
I see (sit quiet now) a white hair on your
        head ! "

Another more benign
Snipp'd it away from mine,
    And in her own dark hair
Pretended it was found . . .
She leap'd, and twirl'd it round . . .
Fair as she was, she never was so fair !

ON HIMSELF

I STROVE with none, for none was worth my
    strife ;
    Nature I lov'd, and next to Nature, Art ;
I warm'd both hands before the fire of
    life ;
    It sinks, and I am ready to depart.

ON LUCRETIA BORGIA'S HAIR

BORGIA, thou once wert almost too august
And high for adoration ; now thou 'rt
    dust ;
All that remains of thee these plaits un-
    fold,
Calm hair meandering in pellucid gold.

PERSISTENCE

MY hopes retire ; my wishes as before
Struggle to find their resting-place in
    vain :
The ebbing sea thus beats against the
    shore ;
The shore repels it ; it returns again.

MAN

In his own image the Creator made,
  His own pure sunbeam quicken'd thee, O
    man !
Thou breathing dial ! since thy day began
  The present hour was ever mark'd with
    shade !

TO SLEEP

Come, Sleep ! but mind ye ! if you come
    without
The little girl that struck me at the rout,
By Jove ! I would not give you half-a-crown
For all your poppy-heads and all your down.

ON LIVING TOO LONG

Is it not better at an early hour
  In its calm cell to rest the weary head,
While birds are singing and while blooms
    the bower,
  Than sit the fire out and go starv'd to bed?

A THOUGHT

Blythe bell, that calls to bridal halls,
  Tolls deep a darker day ;
The very shower that feeds the flower
  Weeps also its decay.

HEARTSEASE

There is a flower I wish to wear,
  But not until first worn by you —
Heartsease — of all earth's flowers most
    rare ;
Bring it ; and bring enough for two.

VERSES WHY BURNT

How many verses have I thrown
Into the fire because the one
Peculiar word, the wanted most,
Was irrecoverably lost !

DEATH UNDREADED

Death stands above me, whispering low
  I know not what into my ear :
Of his strange language all I know
  Is, there is not a word of fear.

MEMORY

The Mother of the Muses, we are taught,
Is Memory : she has left me ; they remain,
And shake my shoulder, urging me to sing
About the summer days, my loves of old.
Alas ! alas ! is all I can reply.
Memory has left with me that name alone,
Harmonious name, which other bards may
    sing,
But her bright image in my darkest hour
Comes back, in vain comes back, call'd or
    uncall'd.
Forgotten are the names of visitors
Ready to press my hand but yesterday ;
Forgotten are the names of earlier friends
Whose genial converse and glad counte-
    nance
Are fresh as ever to mine ear and eye ;
To these, when I have written and besought
Remembrance of me, the word *Dear* alone
Hangs on the upper verge, and waits in
    vain.
A blessing wert thou, O oblivion,
If thy stream carried only weeds away,
But vernal and autumnal flowers alike
It hurries down to wither on the strand.

FOR AN EPITAPH AT FIESOLE

Lo ! where the four mimosas blend their
    shade
In calm repose at last is Landor laid ;
For ere he slept he saw them planted
    here
By her his soul had ever held most dear,
And he had liv'd enough when he had
    dried her tear.

George Darley

THE FLOWER OF BEAUTY

Sweet in her green dell the flower of
　beauty slumbers,
　Lull'd by the faint breezes sighing
　　through her hair ;
Sleeps she, and hears not the melancholy
　numbers
Breath'd to my sad lute amid the lonely
　air.

Down from the high cliffs the rivulet is
　teeming,
　To wind round the willow-banks that lure
　　him from above ;
O that, in tears from my rocky prison
　streaming,
　I, too, could glide to the bower of my love !

Ah, where the woodbines with sleepy arms
　have wound her,
　Opes she her eyelids at the dream of my
　　lay,
Listening, like the dove, while the fountains
　echo round her,
　To her lost mate's call in the forests far
　away.

Come, then, my bird ! for the peace thou
　ever bearest,
　Still Heaven's messenger of comfort to
　　me ;
Come ! this fond bosom, my faithfullest,
　my fairest,
　Bleeds with its death-wound — but deeper
　yet for thee.

SUMMER WINDS

Up the dale and down the bourne,
　O'er the meadow swift we fly ;
Now we sing, and now we mourn,
　Now we whistle, now we sigh.

By the grassy-fringed river
　Through the murmuring reeds we sweep,
Mid the lily-leaves we quiver,
　To their very hearts we creep.

Now the maiden rose is blushing
　At the frolic things we say,

While aside her cheek we 're rushing,
　Like some truant bees at play.

Through the blooming groves we rustle,
　Kissing every bud we pass, —
As we did it in the bustle,
　Scarcely knowing how it was.

Down the glen, across the mountain,
　O'er the yellow heath we roam,
Whirling round about the fountain
　Till its little breakers foam.

Bending down the weeping willows,
　While our vesper hymn we sigh ;
Then unto our rosy pillows
　On our weary wings we hie.

There of idlenesses dreaming,
　Scarce from waking we refrain,
Moments long as ages deeming
　Till we 're at our play again.

SONGS FROM "SYLVIA; OR, THE MAY QUEEN"

I

CHORUS OF SPIRITS

Gently ! — gently ! — down ! — down !
　From the starry courts on high,
Gently step adown, down
　The ladder of the sky.

Sunbeam steps are strong enough
　For such airy feet :
Spirits, blow your trumpets rough,
　So as they be sweet !

Breathe them loud, the Queen descending
　Yet a lowly welcome breathe,
Like so many flowerets bending
　Zephyr's breezy foot beneath.

II

MORNING-SONG

Awake thee, my Lady-love !
　Wake thee, and rise !
The sun through the bower peeps
　Into thine eyes !

Behold how the early lark
　Springs from the corn !
Hark, hark how the flower-bird
　Winds her wee horn !

The swallow's glad shriek is heard
　All through the air ;
The stock-dove is murmuring
　Loud as she dare.

Apollo's wing'd bugleman
　Cannot contain,
But peals his loud trumpet-call
　Once and again.

Then wake thee, my Lady-love !
　Bird of my bower !
The sweetest and sleepiest
　Bird at this hour !

III

NEPHON'S SONG

LADY and gentlemen fays, come buy !
No pedlar has such a rich packet as I.

Who wants a gown
　Of purple fold,
Embroider'd down
　The seams with gold ?
　　See here ! — a Tulip richly laced
　　To please a royal fairy's taste !

Who wants a cap
　Of crimson grand ?
By great good hap
　I 've one on hand :
　　Look, sir ! — a Cock's-comb, flowering
　　　red,
　　'T is just the thing, sir, for your head !

Who wants a frock
　Of vestal hue ?
Or snowy smock ? —
　Fair maid, do you ?
　　O me ! — a Ladysmock so white !
　　Your bosom's self is not more bright.

Who wants to sport
　A slender limb ?
I 've every sort
　Of hose for him :
　　Both scarlet, striped, and yellow ones :
　　This Woodbine makes such pantaloons !

Who wants — (hush ! hush !)
　A box of paint ?
'T will give a blush
　Yet leave no taint :
　　This rose with natural rouge is fill'd,
　　From its own dewy leaves distill'd.

Then lady and gentlemen fays, come
　buy !
You never will meet such a merchant
　as I !

IV

ROMANZO TO SYLVIA

I 'VE taught thee Love's sweet lesson
　　o'er,
A task that is not learn'd with tears :
　Was Sylvia e'er so blest before
In her wild, solitary years ?
　　Then what does he deserve, the
　　　Youth,
　　Who made her con so dear a truth !

Till now in silent vales to roam,
Singing vain songs to heedless flowers,
　Or watch the dashing billows foam,
Amid thy lonely myrtle bowers,
　　To weave light crowns of various
　　　hue, —
　　Were all the joys thy bosom knew.

The wild bird, though most musical,
Could not to thy sweet plaint reply ;
　The streamlet and the waterfall
Could only weep when thou didst sigh !
　　Thou couldst not change one dulcet
　　　word
　　Either with billow, or with bird.

For leaves and flowers, but these alone,
Winds have a soft discoursing way ;
　Heav'n's starry talk is all its own, —
It dies in thunder far away.
　　E'en when thou wouldst the Moon
　　　beguile
　　To speak, — she only deigns to smile !

Now, birds and winds, be churlish still,
Ye waters keep your sullen roar,
　Stars be as distant as ye will, —
Sylvia need court ye now no more :
　　In Love there is society
　　She never yet could find with ye !

Bryan Waller Procter

("BARRY CORNWALL")

THE SEA

THE sea ! the sea ! the open sea !
The blue, the fresh, the ever free !
Without a mark, without a bound,
It runneth the earth's wide regions round ;
It plays with the clouds ; it mocks the skies ;
Or like a cradled creature lies.

I 'm on the sea ! I 'm on the sea !
I am where I would ever be ;
With the blue above, and the blue below,
And silence wheresoe'er I go ;
If a storm should come and awake the deep,
What matter ? *I* shall ride and sleep.

I love, O, how I love to ride
On the fierce, foaming, bursting tide,
When every mad wave drowns the moon
Or whistles aloft his tempest tune,
And tells how goeth the world below,
And why the sou'west blasts do blow.

I never was on the dull, tame shore,
But I lov'd the great sea more and more,
And backwards flew to her billowy breast,
Like a bird that seeketh its mother's nest ;
And a mother she was, and is, to me ;
For I was born on the open sea !

The waves were white, and red the morn,
In the noisy hour when I was born ;
And the whale it whistled, the porpoise
    roll'd,
And the dolphins bared their backs of gold ;
And never was heard such an outcry wild
As welcom'd to life the ocean-child !

I 've liv'd since then, in calm and strife,
Full fifty summers, a sailor's life,
With wealth to spend and a power to range,
But never have sought nor sighed for
    change ;
And Death, whenever he comes to me,
Shall come on the wild, unbounded sea !

THE HUNTER'S SONG

RISE ! Sleep no more ! 'T is a noble morn :
The dews hang thick on the fringed thorn,

And the frost shrinks back, like a beaten
    hound,
Under the steaming, steaming ground.
Behold, where the billowy clouds flow by,
And leave us alone in the clear gray sky !
Our horses are ready and steady. — So, ho !
I 'm gone, like a dart from the Tartar's bow.
    Hark, hark ! — Who calleth the maiden
        Morn
    From her sleep in the woods and the
        stubble corn ?
        The horn, — the horn !
    The merry, sweet ring of the hunter's horn.

Now, thorough the copse, where the fox is
    found,
And over the stream, at a mighty bound,
And over the high lands, and over the low,
O'er furrows, o'er meadows, the hunters go !
Away ! — as a hawk flies full at its prey,
So flieth the hunter, away, — away !
From the burst at the cover till set of sun,
When the red fox dies, and — the day is
    done !
    Hark, hark ! — What sound on the wind
        is borne ?
    'T is the conquering voice of the hunter's
        horn.
        The horn, — the horn !
    The merry, bold voice of the hunter's horn.

Sound ! Sound the horn ! To the hunter
    good
What 's the gulley deep or the roaring flood ?
Right over he bounds, as the wild stag
    bounds,
At the heels of his swift, sure, silent hounds.
O, what delight can a mortal lack,
When he once is firm on his horse's back,
With his stirrups short, and his snaffle
    strong,
And the blast of the horn for his morning
    song ?
    Hark, hark ! — Now, home ! and dream
        till morn
    Of the bold, sweet sound of the hunter's
        horn !
        The horn, — the horn !
    O, the sound of all sounds is the hunter's
        horn !

THE POET'S SONG TO HIS WIFE

How many summers, love,
  Have I been thine ?
How many days, thou dove,
  Hast thou been mine ?
Time, like the winged wind
  When 't bends the flowers,
Hath left no mark behind,
  To count the hours.

Some weight of thought, though loth,
  On thee he leaves ;
Some lines of care round both
  Perhaps he weaves ;
Some fears, — a soft regret
  For joys scarce known ;
Sweet looks we half forget ; —
  All else is flown !

Ah ! — With what thankless heart
  I mourn and sing !
Look, where our children start,
  Like sudden Spring !
With tongues all sweet and low,
  Like a pleasant rhyme,
They tell how much I owe
  To thee and Time !

THE STORMY PETREL

A THOUSAND miles from land are we,
Tossing about on the roaring sea ;
From billow to bounding billow cast,
Like fleecy snow on the stormy blast :
The sails are scatter'd abroad, like weeds,
The strong masts shake like quivering
  reeds,
The mighty cables, and iron chains,
The hull, which all earthly strength disdains,
They strain and they crack, and hearts like
  stone
Their natural hard, proud strength disown.

Up and down ! Up and down !
From the base of the wave to the billow's
  crown,
And midst the flashing and feathery foam
The Stormy Petrel finds a home, —
A home, if such a place may be,
For her who lives on the wide, wide sea,
On the craggy ice, in the frozen air,
And only seeketh her rocky lair

To warm her young, and to teach them
  spring
At once o'er the waves on their stormy
  wing.

O'er the Deep ! O'er the Deep !
Where the whale, and the shark, and the
  sword-fish sleep,
Outflying the blast and the driving rain,
The Petrel telleth her tale — in vain ;
For the mariner curseth the warning bird
Who bringeth him news of the storms un-
  heard !
Ah ! thus does the prophet, of good or ill,
Meet hate from the creatures he serveth
  still :
Yet he ne'er falters : — So, Petrel ! spring
Once more o'er the waves on thy stormy
  wing !

PEACE ! WHAT DO TEARS AVAIL ?

PEACE ! what do tears avail ?
She lies all dumb and pale,
  And from her eye
The spirit of lovely life is fading,
  And she must die !
Why looks the lover wroth ? the friend up-
  braiding ?
  Reply, reply !

Hath she not dwelt too long
'Midst pain, and grief, and wrong ?
  Then, why not die ?
Why suffer again her doom of sorrow,
  And hopeless lie ?
Why nurse the trembling dream until to-
  morrow ?
  Reply, reply !

Death ! Take her to thine arms,
In all her stainless charms,
  And with her fly
To heavenly haunts, where, clad in bright-
  ness,
  The Angels lie.
Wilt bear her there, O Death ! in all her
  whiteness ?
  Reply, reply !

LIFE

WE are born ; we laugh ; we weep ;
  We love ; we droop ; we die !

Ah ! wherefore do we laugh or weep ?
  Why do we live, or die ?
Who knows that secret deep ?
  Alas, not I !

Why doth the violet spring
  Unseen by human eye ?
Why do the radiant seasons bring
  Sweet thoughts that quickly fly ?
Why do our fond hearts cling
  To things that die ?

We toil, — through pain and wrong ;
  We fight, — and fly ;
We love ; we lose ; and then, ere long,
  Stone-dead we lie.
O life ! is *all* thy song
  " Endure and — die " ?

THE BLOOD HORSE

GAMARRA is a dainty steed,
Strong, black, and of a noble breed,
Full of fire, and full of bone,
With all his line of fathers known ;
Fine his nose, his nostrils thin,
But blown abroad by the pride within !
His mane is like a river flowing,
And his eyes like embers glowing
In the darkness of the night,
And his pace as swift as light.

Look, — how 'round his straining throat
Grace and shifting beauty float !
Sinewy strength is on his reins,
And the red blood gallops through his veins ;
Richer, redder, never ran
Through the boasting heart of man.
He can trace his lineage higher
Than the Bourbon dare aspire, —
Douglas, Guzman, or the Guelph,
Or O'Brien's blood itself !

He, who hath no peer, was born
Here, upon a red March morn :
But his famous fathers dead
Were Arabs all, and Arab bred,
And the last of that great line
Trod like one of a race divine !
And yet, — he was but friend to one
Who fed him at the set of sun,
By some lone fountain fringed with green :
With him, a roving Bedouin,
He liv'd, — (none else would he obey
Through all the hot Arabian day,) —

And died untam'd upon the sands
Where Balkh amidst the desert stands !

SIT DOWN, SAD SOUL

SIT down, sad soul, and count
  The moments flying :
Come, — tell the sweet amount
  That 's lost by sighing !
How many smiles ? — a score ?
Then laugh, and count no more ;
  For day is dying.

Lie down, sad soul, and sleep,
  And no more measure
The flight of Time, nor weep
  The loss of leisure ;
But here, by this lone stream,
Lie down with us, and dream
  Of starry treasure.

We dream : do thou the same :
  We love — for ever ;
We laugh ; yet few we shame,
  The gentle, never.
Stay, then, till Sorrow dies ;
Then — hope and happy skies
  Are thine for ever !

GOLDEN-TRESSED ADELAIDE

SING, I pray, a little song,
  Mother dear !
Neither sad nor very long :
It is for a little maid,
Golden-tressed Adelaide !
Therefore let it suit a merry, merry ear,
  Mother dear !

Let it be a merry strain,
  Mother dear !
Shunning e'en the thought of pain :
For our gentle child will weep,
If the theme be dark and deep ;
And we will not draw a single, single tear,
  Mother dear !

Childhood should be all divine,
  Mother dear !
And like an endless summer shine ;
Gay as Edward's shouts and cries,
Bright as Agnes' azure eyes :
Therefore, bid thy song be merry : — dost
    thou hear,
  Mother dear ?

A POET'S THOUGHT

TELL me, what is a poet's thought?
  Is it on the sudden born?
Is it from the starlight caught?
Is it by the tempest taught,
  Or by whispering morn?

Was it cradled in the brain?
  Chain'd awhile, or nurs'd in night?
Was it wrought with toil and pain?
Did it bloom and fade again,
  Ere it burst to light?

No more question of its birth:
  Rather love its better part!
'T is a thing of sky and earth,
Gathering all its golden worth
  From the Poet's heart.

A PETITION TO TIME

TOUCH us gently, Time!
  Let us glide adown thy stream
Gently, — as we sometimes glide
  Through a quiet dream.
Humble voyagers are We,
Husband, wife, and children three —
(One is lost, — an angel, fled
To the azure overhead.)

Touch us gently, Time!
  We 've not proud nor soaring wings:
Our ambition, our content,
  Lies in simple things.
Humble voyagers are We,
O'er Life's dim, unsounded sea,
Seeking only some calm clime ; —
Touch us gently, gentle Time!

Charles Jeremiah Wells

FROM "JOSEPH AND HIS BRETHREN"

RACHEL

RACHEL, the beautiful (as she was call'd),
Despis'd our mother Leah, for that she
Was tender-ey'd, lean-favor'd, and did lack
The pulpy ripeness swelling the white skin
To sleek proportions beautiful and round,
With wrinkled joints so fruitful to the eye.
All this is fair : and yet we know it true
That 'neath a pomane breast and snowy side
A heart of guile and falsehood may be hid,
As well as where the soil is deeper tinct.
So here with this same Rachel was it found :
The dim blue-laced veins on either brow,
Neath the transparent skin meandering,
That with the silver-leaved lily vied ;
Her full dark eye, whose brightness glisten'd through
The sable lashes soft as camel-hair ;
Her slanting head curv'd like the maiden moon
And hung with hair luxuriant as a vine
And blacker than a storm ; her rounded ear
Turn'd like a shell upon some golden shore ;
Her whispering foot that carried all her weight,

Nor left its little pressure on the sand ;
Her lips as drowsy poppies, soft and red,
Gathering a dew from her escaping breath ;
Her voice melodious, mellow, deep, and clear,
Lingering like sweet music in the ear ;
Her neck o'ersoften'd like to unsunn'd curd ;
Her tapering fingers rounded to a point ;
The silken softness of her veined hand ;
Her dimpled knuckles answering to her chin ;
And teeth like honeycombs o' the wilderness :
All these did tend to a bad proof in her.
For armed thus in beauty she did steal
The eye of Jacob to her proper self,
Engross'd his time, and kept him by her side,
Casting on Leah indifference and neglect ;
Whereat great Heaven took our mother's part
And struck young Rachel with a barrenness,
While she bore children : thus the matter went ;
Till Rachel, feeling guilty of her fault,
Turn'd to some penitence, which Heaven heard ;
And then she bore this Joseph, who must, and does,

Inherit towards the children all the pride
And scorn his mother had towards our
    mother :
Wherefore he suffers in our just rebuke.

PHRAXANOR TO JOSEPH

Phrax. Oh ! ignorant boy, it is the secret
    hour,
The sun of love doth shine most goodly
    fair.
Contemptible darkness never yet did dull
The splendor of love's palpitating light.
At love's slight curtains, that are made of
    sighs,
Though e'er so dark, silence is seen to stand
Like to a flower closed in the night ;
Or, like a lovely image drooping down
With its fair head aslant and finger rais'd,
And mutely on its shoulder slumbering.
Pulses do sound quick music in Love's ear,
And blended fragrance in his startled breath
Doth hang the hair with drops of magic dew.
All outward thoughts, all common circum-
    stance,
Are buried in the dimple of his smile :
And the great city like a vision sails
From out the closing doors of the hush'd
    mind.
His heart strikes audibly against his ribs
As a dove's wing doth freak upon a cage,
Forcing the blood athro' the cramped veins
Faster than dolphins do o'ershoot the tide
Cours'd by the yawning shark. Therefore
    I say
Night-blooming Cereus, and the star-flower
    sweet,
The honeysuckle, and the eglantine,
And the ring'd vinous tree that yields red
    wine,
Together with all intertwining flowers,
Are plants most fit to ramble o'er each
    other,
And form the bower of all-precious Love,
Shrouding the sun with fragrant bloom and
    leaves
From jealous interception of Love's gaze.
This is Love's cabin in the light of day,
But oh ! compare it not with the black
    night;
Delay thou sun, and give me instant night —
Its soft, mysterious, and secret hours ;
The whitest clouds are pillows to bright
    stars,
Ah ! therefore shroud thine eyes.

THE PATRIARCHAL HOME

Joseph. Still I am patient, tho' you 're
    merciless.
Yet to speak out my mind, I do avouch
There is no city feast, nor city show,
The encampment of the king and soldiery,
Rejoicings, revelries, and victories,
Can equal the remembrance of my home
In visible imagination.
Even as he was I see my father now,
His grave and graceful head's benignity
Musing beyond the confines of this world,
His world within with all its mysteries.
What pompless majesty was in his mien,
An image of integrity creates,
Pattern of nature, in perfection.
Lo ! in the morning when we issued forth,
The patriarch surrounded by his sons,
Girt round with looks of sweet obedience,
Each struggling who should honor him the
    most ;
While from the wrinkles deep of many
    years,
Enfurrow'd smiles, like violets in snow,
Touch'd us with heat and melancholy cold,
Mingling our joy with sorrow for his age :
There were my brothers, habited in skins ;
Ten goodly men, myself, and a sweet youth
Too young to mix in anything but joy ;
And in his hands each led a milk-white
    steer,
Hung o'er with roses, garlanded with flow-
    ers,
Laden with fragrant panniers of green
    boughs
Of bays and myrtle interleav'd with herbs,
Wherein was stor'd our country wine and
    fruit,
And bread with honey sweeten'd, and dried
    figs,
And pressed curds, and choicest rarities,
Stores of the cheerless season of the year ;
While at our sides the women of our tribe,
With pitchers on their heads, fill'd to the
    brim
With wine, and honey, and with smoking
    milk,
Made proud the black-ey'd heifers with the
    swell
Of the sweet anthem sung in plenty's praise.
Thus would we journey to the wilderness,
And fixing on some peak that did o'erlook
The spacious plains that lay display'd be-
    neath,

Where we could see our cattle, like to specks
In the warm meads, browsing the juicy
    grass,
There pitch our tent, and feast, and revel
    out, —
The minutes flying faster than our feet
That vaulted nimbly to the pipe and voice,
Making fatigue more sweet by appetite.
There stood the graceful Reuben by my
    sire,
Piping a ditty, ardent as the sun,
And, like him, stealing renovation
Into the darkest corner of the soul,
And filling it with light. There, women
    group'd,
My sisters and their maids, with ears sub-
    dued,
With bosoms panting from the eager dance,
Against each other lean'd ; as I have seen
A graceful tuft of lilies of the vale
Oppress'd with rain, upon each other bend,
While freshness has stol'n o'er them. Some
    way off
My brothers pitch'd the bar, or plough'd for
    fame,
Each two with their two heifers harness'd
    fast
Unto the shaft, and labor'd till the sweat
Had crept about them like a sudden thaw.
Anon they tied an eagle to a tree,
And strove at archery ; or with a bear
Struggled for strength of limb. These
    were no slaves —
No villain's sons to rifle passengers.
The sports being done, the winners claim'd
    the spoil :
Or hide, or feather, or renowned bow,
Or spotted cow, or fleet and pamper'd horse.
And then my father bless'd us, and we sang
Our sweet way home again. Oft I have
    ach'd
In memory of these so precious hours,
And wept upon those keys that were my
    pride,
And soak'd my pillow thro' the heavy night.
Alas ! God willing, I'll be patient yet.

THE TRIUMPH OF JOSEPH

In the royal path
Came maidens rob'd in white, enchain'd in
    flowers,
Sweeping the ground with incense-scented
    palms :
Then came the sweetest voices of the land,

And cried, ' Bow ye the knee !' — and then
    aloud
Clarions and trumpets broke forth in the air:
After a multitude of men-at-arms,
Of priests, of officers, and horsed chiefs,
Came the benignant Pharaoh, whose great
    pride
Was buried in his smile. I did but glimpse
His car, for 't was of burnish'd gold. No
    eye
Save that of eagles could confront the blaze
That seem'd to burn the air, unless it fell
Either on sapphire or carbuncle huge
That riveted the weight. This car was
    drawn
By twelve jet horses, being four abreast,
And pied in their own foam. Within the
    car
Sat Pharaoh, whose bare head was girt
    around
By a crown of iron ; and his sable hair,
Like strakey as a mane, fell where it would,
And somewhat hid his glossy sun-brent neck
And carcanet of precious sardonyx.
His jewell'd armlets, weighty as a sword,
Clasp'd his brown naked arms — a crimson
    robe,
Deep edged with silver, and with golden
    thread,
Upon a bear-skin kirtle deeply blush'd,
Whose broad resplendent braid and shield-
    like clasps
Were boss'd with diamonds large, by rubies
    fir'd,
Like beauty's eye in rage, or roses white
Lit by the glowing red. Beside him lay
A bunch of poppied corn ; and at his feet
A tamed lion as his footstool crouch'd.
Cas'd o'er in burnish'd plates I, hors'd, did
    bear
A snow-white eagle on a silver shaft,
From whence great Pharaoh's royal banner
    stream'd,
An emblem of his might and dignity ;
And as the minstrelsy burst clanging forth,
With shouts that broke like thunder from
    the host,
The royal bird with kindred pride of power
Flew up the measure of his silken cord,
And arch'd his cloud-like wings as he would
    mount,
And babble of this glory to the sun.
Then follow'd Joseph in a silver car,
Drawn by eight horses, white as evening
    clouds :

His feet were resting upon Pharaoh's sword;
And on his head a crown of drooping corn
Mock'd that of Ceres in high holiday.
His robes were simple, but were full of
    grace,
And (out of love and truth I speak him
    thus)

I never did behold a man less proud,
More dignified or grateful to admire.
His honors nothing teas'd him from him-
    self;
And he but fill'd his fortunes like a man
Who did intend to honor them as much
As they could honor him.

Sir Henry Taylor

FROM "PHILIP VAN ARTE-VELDE"

JOHN OF LAUNOY

I NEVER look'd that he should live so long.
He was a man of that unsleeping spirit,
He seem'd to live by miracle : his food
Was glory, which was poison to his mind
And peril to his body.   He was one
Of many thousand such that die betimes,
Whose story is a fragment, known to few.
Then comes the man who has the luck to live,
And he 's a prodigy.   Compute the chances,
And deem there 's ne'er a one in dangerous
    times
Who wins the race of glory, but than him
A thousand men more gloriously endow'd
Have fallen upon the course ; a thousand
    others
Have had their fortunes founder'd by a
    chance,
Whilst lighter barks push'd past them ; to
    whom add
A smaller tally, of the singular few
Who, gifted with predominating powers,
Bear yet a temperate will and keep the
    peace.
The world knows nothing of its greatest
    men.

REVOLUTIONS

There was a time, so ancient records tell,
There were communities, scarce known by
    name
In these degenerate days, but once far-
    fam'd,
Where liberty and justice, hand in hand,
Order'd the common weal ; where great
    men grew

Up to their natural eminence, and none,
Saving the wise, just, eloquent, were great ;
Where power was of God's gift, to whom
    he gave
Supremacy of merit, the sole means
And broad highway to power, that ever
    then
Was meritoriously administer'd,
Whilst all its instruments from first to last,
The tools of state for service high or low,
Were chosen for their aptness to those ends
Which virtue meditates.   To shake the
    ground
Deep-founded whereupon this structure
    stood,
Was verily a crime ; a treason it was,
Conspiracies to hatch against this state
And its free innocence.   But now, I ask,
Where is there on God's earth that polity
Which it is not, by consequence converse,
A treason against nature to uphold ?
Whom may we now call free ? whom great?
    whom wise ?
Whom innocent ? the free are only they
Whom power makes free to execute all ills
Their hearts imagine ; they alone are great
Whose passions nurse them from their cra-
    dles up
In luxury and lewdness, — whom to see
Is to despise, whose aspects put to scorn
Their station's eminence ; the wise, they
    only
Who wait obscurely till the bolts of heaven
Shall break upon the land, and give them
    light
Whereby to walk ; the innocent, — alas !
Poor innocency lies where four roads meet,
A stone upon her head, a stake driven
    through her,
For who is innocent that cares to live ?
The hand of power doth press the very life
Of innocency out !   What then remains

But in the cause of nature to stand forth,
And turn this frame of things the right side
    up ?
For this the hour is come, the sword is
    drawn,
And tell your masters vainly they resist.

SONG

Down lay in a nook my lady's brach,
    And said — my feet are sore,
I cannot follow with the pack
    A hunting of the boar.

And though the horn sounds never so clear
    With the hounds in loud uproar,
Yet I must stop and lie down here,
    Because my feet are sore.

The huntsman when he heard the same,
    What answer did he give ?
The dog that 's lame is much to blame,
    He is not fit to live.

SONG

Quoth tongue of neither maid nor wife
    To heart of neither wife nor maid,
Lead we not here a jolly life
    Betwixt the shine and shade ?

Quoth heart of neither maid nor wife
    To tongue of neither wife nor maid,
Thou wag'st, but I am worn with strife,
    And feel like flowers that fade.

PHILIP VAN ARTEVELDE

        Dire rebel though he was,
Yet with a noble nature and great gifts
Was he endow'd, — courage, discretion,
    wit,
An equal temper, and an ample soul,
Rock-bound and fortified against assaults
Of transitory passion, but below
Built on a surging subterranean fire
That stirr'd and lifted him to high attempts.
So prompt and capable, and yet so calm,
He nothing lack'd in sovereignty but the
    right,
Nothing in soldiership except good fortune.
Wherefore with honor lay him in his grave,
And thereby shall increase of honor come
Unto their arms who vanquish'd one so wise,
So valiant, so renown'd.

FROM "EDWIN THE FAIR"

THE WIND IN THE PINES

The tale was this :
The wind, when first he rose and went
    abroad
Through the waste region, felt himself at
    fault,
Wanting a voice ; and suddenly to earth
Descended with a wafture and a swoop,
Where, wandering volatile from kind to
    kind,
He woo'd the several trees to give him one.
First he besought the ash ; the voice she lent
Fitfully with a free and lashing change
Flung here and there its sad uncertainties :
The aspen next ; a flutter'd frivolous twit-
    ter
Was her sole tribute : from the willow came,
So long as dainty summer dress'd her out,
A whispering sweetness, but her winter note
Was hissing, dry, and reedy : lastly the pine
Did he solicit, and from her he drew
A voice so constant, soft, and lowly deep,
That there he rested, welcoming in her
A mild memorial of the ocean-cave
Where he was born.

A CHARACTERIZATION

His life was private ; safely led, aloof
From the loud world, — which yet he under-
    stood
Largely and wisely, as no worldling could.
For he, by privilege of his nature proof
Against false glitter, from beneath the roof
Of privacy, as from a cave, survey'd
With steadfast eye its flickering light and
    shade,
And gently judged for evil and for good.
But whilst he mix'd not for his own behoof
In public strife, his spirit glow'd with zeal,
Not shorn of action, for the public weal, —
For truth and justice as its warp and woof,
For freedom as its signature and seal.
His life, thus sacred from the world, dis-
    charged
From vain ambition and inordinate care,
In virtue exercis'd, by reverence rare
Lifted, and by humility enlarged,
Became a temple and a place of prayer.
In latter years he walk'd not singly there ;

For one was with him, ready at all hours
His griefs, his joys, his inmost thoughts to
share,
Who buoyantly his burthens help'd to bear,
And deck'd his altars daily with fresh flow-
ers.
Lines on the Hon. Edward Ernest Villiers.

ARETINA'S SONG

I'M a bird that's free
Of the land and sea,
I wander whither I will ;
But oft on the wing,
I falter and sing,
Oh, fluttering heart, be still,
Be still,
Oh, fluttering heart, be still !

I'm wild as the wind,
But soft and kind,
And wander whither I may ;
The eyebright sighs,
And says with its eyes,
Thou wandering wind, oh stay,
Oh stay,
Thou wandering wind, oh stay !
A Sicilian Summer.

THE HERO

WHAT makes a hero ? — not success, not
fame,
Inebriate merchants, and the loud acclaim

Of glutted Avarice, — caps toss'd up in
air,
Or pen of journalist with flourish fair ;
Bells peal'd, stars, ribbons, and a titular
name —
These, though his rightful tribute, he can
spare ;
His rightful tribute, not his end or aim,
Or true reward ; for never yet did these
Refresh the soul, or set the heart at
ease.
What makes a hero ? — An heroic mind,
Express'd in action, in endurance prov'd.
And if there be preëminence of right,
Deriv'd through pain well suffer'd, to the
height
Of rank heroic, 't is to bear unmov'd,
Not toil, not risk, not rage of sea or
wind,
Not the brute fury of barbarians blind,
But worse — ingratitude and poisonous
darts,
Launch'd by the country he had serv'd
and lov'd :
This, with a free, unclouded spirit pure,
This, in the strength of silence to endure,
A dignity to noble deeds imparts
Beyond the gauds and trappings of re-
nown ;
This is the hero's complement and crown ;
This miss'd, one struggle had been want-
ing still,
One glorious triumph of the heroic will,
One self-approval in his heart of hearts.

Lord Macaulay

(THOMAS BABINGTON MACAULAY)

THE BATTLE OF NASEBY

BY OBADIAH - BIND - THEIR - KINGS - IN -
CHAINS-AND-THEIR-NOBLES-WITH-
LINKS-OF-IRON, SERGEANT IN
IRETON'S REGIMENT

OH ! wherefore come ye forth in triumph
from the north,
With your hands, and your feet, and your
raiment all red ?

And wherefore doth your rout send forth a
joyous shout ?
And whence be the grapes of the wine-press
that ye tread ?

Oh ! evil was the root, and bitter was the
fruit,
And crimson was the juice of the vintage
that we trod ;
For we trampled on the throng of the
haughty and the strong,
Who sate in the high places and slew the
saints of God.

It was about the noon of a glorious day of
June,
That we saw their banners dance and their
cuirasses shine,
And the man of blood was there, with his
long essenced hair,
And Astley, and Sir Marmaduke, and Ru-
pert of the Rhine.

Like a servant of the Lord, with his bible
and his sword,
The general rode along us to form us for
the fight ;
When a murmuring sound broke out, and
swell'd into a shout
Among the godless horsemen upon the
tyrant's right.

And hark ! like the roar of the billows on
the shore,
The cry of battle rises along their charging
line :
For God ! for the cause ! for the Church !
for the laws !
For Charles, king of England, and Rupert
of the Rhine !

The furious German comes, with his clari-
ons and his drums,
His bravoes of Alsatia and pages of White-
hall ;
They are bursting on our flanks ! Grasp
your pikes ! Close your ranks !
For Rupert never comes, but to conquer, or
to fall.

They are here — they rush on — we are
broken — we are gone —
Our left is borne before them like stubble
on the blast.
O Lord, put forth thy might ! O Lord,
defend the right !
Stand back to back, in God's name ! and
fight it to the last !

Stout Skippon hath a wound — the centre
hath given ground.
Hark ! hark ! what means the trampling
of horsemen on our rear ?
Whose banner do I see, boys ? 'T is he !
thank God ! 't is he, boys !
Bear up another minute ! Brave Oliver is
here !

Their heads all stooping low, their points
all in a row :

Like a whirlwind on the trees, like a deluge
on the dikes,
Our cuirassiers have burst on the ranks of
the Accurst,
And at a shock have scatter'd the forest of
his pikes.

Fast, fast, the gallants ride, in some safe
nook to hide
Their coward heads, predestin'd to rot on
Temple Bar ;
And he — he turns ! he flies ! shame on
those cruel eyes
That bore to look on torture, and dare not
look on war !

Ho, comrades ! scour the plain ; and ere ye
strip the slain,
First give another stab to make your search
secure ;
Then shake from sleeves and pockets their
broad-pieces and lockets,
The tokens of the wanton, the plunder of the
poor.

Fools ! your doublets shone with gold, and
your hearts were gay and bold,
When you kiss'd your lily hands to your
lemans to-day ;
And to-morrow shall the fox from her
chambers in the rocks
Lead forth her tawny cubs to howl about
the prey.

Where be your tongues, that late mock'd
at heaven and hell and fate ?
And the fingers that once were so busy with
your blades ?
Your perfum'd satin clothes, your catches
and your oaths ?
Your stage-plays and your sonnets, your
diamonds and your spades ?

Down, down, for ever down with the mitre
and the crown,
With the Belial of the court, and the Mam-
mon of the Pope !
There is woe in Oxford halls, there is wail
in Durham's stalls ;
The Jesuit smites his bosom, the bishop
rends his cope.

And she of the seven hills shall mourn her
children's ills,
And tremble when she thinks on the edge
of England's sword ;

And the kings of earth in fear shall shudder
 when they hear
What the hand of God hath wrought for the
 Houses and the Word !

EPITAPH ON A JACOBITE

To my true king I offer'd free from stain
Courage and faith : vain faith, and courage
 vain.
For him, I threw lands, honors, wealth,
 away,
And one dear hope, that was more priz'd
 than they.
For him I languish'd in a foreign clime,
Gray-hair'd with sorrow in my manhood's
 prime ;
Heard on Lavernia Scargill's whispering
 trees,
And pin'd by Arno for my lovelier Tees ;
Beheld each night my home in fever'd sleep,
Each morning started from the dream to
 weep ;
Till God, who saw me tried too sorely, gave
The resting place I ask'd, an early grave.
Oh thou, whom chance leads to this nameless
 stone
From that proud country which was once
 mine own,
By those white cliffs I never more must see,
By that dear language which I spake like
 thee,
Forget all feuds, and shed one English tear
O'er English dust. A broken heart lies here.

IVRY

Now glory to the Lord of hosts, from whom
 all glories are !
And glory to our sovereign liege, King
 Henry of Navarre !
Now let there be the merry sound of music
 and of dance,
Through thy corn-fields green, and sunny
 vines, O pleasant land of France !
And thou, Rochelle, our own Rochelle,
 proud city of the waters,
Again let rapture light the eyes of all thy
 mourning daughters.
As thou wert constant in our ills, be joyous
 in our joy ;
For cold and stiff and still are they who
 wrought thy walls annoy.

Hurrah ! hurrah ! a single field hath turn'd
 the chance of war !
Hurrah ! hurrah ! for Ivry, and Henry of
 Navarre.

Oh ! how our hearts were beating, when, at
 the dawn of day,
We saw the army of the League drawn out
 in long array ;
With all its priest-led citizens, and all its
 rebel peers,
And Appenzel's stout infantry, and Eg-
 mont's Flemish spears.
There rode the brood of false Lorraine, the
 curses of our land ;
And dark Mayenne was in the midst, a
 truncheon in his hand ;
And, as we look'd on them, we thought of
 Seine's empurpled flood,
And good Coligni's hoary hair all dabbled
 with his blood ;
And we cried unto the living God, who rules
 the fate of war,
To fight for His own holy name, and Henry
 of Navarre.

The king is come to marshal us, in all his
 armor drest ;
And he has bound a snow-white plume upon
 his gallant crest.
He look'd upon his people, and a tear was
 in his eye ;
He look'd upon the traitors, and his glance
 was stern and high.
Right graciously he smil'd on us, as roll'd
 from wing to wing,
Down all our line, a deafening shout : God
 save our lord the king !
"And if my standard-bearer fall, as fall full
 well he may,
For never I saw promise yet of such a
 bloody fray,
Press where ye see my white plume shine
 amidst the ranks of war,
And be your oriflamme to-day the helmet
 of Navarre. "

Hurrah ! the foes are moving.   Hark to
 the mingled din,
Of fife, and steed, and trump, and drum,
 and roaring culverin.
The fiery duke is pricking fast across Saint
 André's plain,
With all the hireling chivalry of Guelders
 and Almayne.

Now by the lips of those ye love, fair gentle-
men of France,
Charge for the golden lilies — upon them
with the lance !
A thousand spurs are striking deep, a thou-
sand spears in rest,
A thousand knights are pressing close be-
hind the snow-white crest ;
And in they burst, and on they rush'd,
while, like a guiding star,
Amidst the thickest carnage blaz'd the hel-
met of Navarre.

Now, God be prais'd, the day is ours : Ma-
yenne hath turn'd his rein ;
D'Aumale hath cried for quarter ; the
Flemish count is slain.
Their ranks are breaking like thin clouds
before a Biscay gale ;
The field is heap'd with bleeding steeds,
and flags, and cloven mail.
And then we thought on vengeance, and,
all along our van,
Remember Saint Bartholomew ! was pass'd
from man to man.
But out spake gentle Henry — " No French-
man is my foe :
Down, down with every foreigner, but let
your brethren go : "
Oh ! was there ever such a knight, in friend-
ship or in war,
As our sovereign lord, King Henry, the sol-
dier of Navarre ?

Right well fought all the Frenchmen who
fought for France to-day ;
And many a lordly banner God gave them
for a prey.

But we of the religion have borne us best
in fight ;
And the good lord of Rosny hath ta'en the
cornet white —
Our own true Maximilian the cornet white
hath ta'en,
The cornet white with crosses black, the flag
of false Lorraine.
Up with it high ; unfurl it wide ; — that all
the host may know
How God hath humbled the proud house
which wrought His Church such
woe.
Then on the ground, while trumpets sound
their loudest point of war,
Fling the red shreds, a footcloth meet for
Henry of Navarre.

Ho ! maidens of Vienna ; ho ! matrons of
Lucerne —
Weep, weep, and rend your hair for those
who never shall return.
Ho ! Philip, send, for charity, thy Mexican
pistoles,
That Antwerp monks may sing a mass for
thy poor spearmen's souls.
Ho ! gallant nobles of the League, look that
your arms be bright ;
Ho ! burghers of St. Genevieve, keep watch
and ward to-night ;
For our God hath crush'd the tyrant, our
God hath rais'd the slave,
And mock'd the counsel of the wise, and
the valor of the brave.
Then glory to His holy name, from whom
all glories are ;
And glory to our sovereign lord, King Henry
of Navarre !

Richard Hengist Horne

FROM " ORION : AN EPIC POEM "

MEETING OF ORION AND ARTEMIS

Afar the hunt in vales below has sped,
But now behind the wooded mount ascends,
Threading its upward mazes of rough
boughs,
Moss'd trunks and thickets, still invisible,
Although its jocund music fills the air

With cries and laughing echoes, mellow'd
all
By intervening woods and the deep hills.

The scene in front two sloping mountain-
sides
Display'd ; in shadow one, and one in light
The loftiest on its summit now sustain'd
The sun-beams, raying like a mighty wheel
Half seen, which left the front-ward sur-
face dark

In its full breadth of shade ; the coming sun
Hidden as yet behind : the other mount,
Slanting oppos'd, swept with an eastward
    face,
Catching the golden light. Now, while the
    peal
Of the ascending chase told that the rout
Still midway rent the thickets, suddenly
Along the broad and sunny slope appear'd
The shadow of a stag that fled across,
Follow'd by a Giant's shadow with a spear !

"Hunter of Shadows, thou thyself a
    Shade,"
Be comforted in this, — that substance holds
No higher attributes ; one sovereign law
Alike develops both, and each shall hunt
Its proper object, each in turn commanding
The primal impulse, till gaunt Time become
A Shadow cast on Space — to fluctuate,
Waiting the breath of the Creative Power
To give new types for substance yet un-
    known :
So from faint nebulæ bright worlds are born;
So worlds return to vapor. Dreams design
Most solid lasting things, and from the eye
That searches life, death evermore retreats.

Substance unseen, pure mythos, or mi-
    rage,
The shadowy chase has vanish'd ; round the
    swell
Of the near mountain sweeps a bounding
    stag ;
Round whirls a god-like Giant close behind ;
O'er a fallen trunk the stag with slippery
    hoofs
Stumbles — his sleek knees lightly touch
    the grass —
Upward he springs — but in his forward
    leap,
The Giant's hand hath caught him fast be-
    neath
One shoulder tuft, and, lifted high in air,
Sustains ! Now Phoibos' chariot rising
    bursts
Over the summits with a circling blaze,
Gilding those frantic antlers, and the head
Of that so glorious Giant in his youth,
Who, as he turns, the form succinct beholds
Of Artemis, — her bow, with points drawn
    back,
A golden hue on her white rounded breast
Reflecting, while the arrow's ample barb
Gleams o'er her hand, and at his heart is
    aim'd.

The Giant lower'd his arm — away the
    stag
Breast forward plunged into a thicket near;
The Goddess paus'd, and dropp'd her ar-
    row's point —
Rais'd it again — and then again relax'd
Her tension, and while slow the shaft came
    gliding
Over the centre of the bow, beside
Her hand, and gently droop'd, so did the
    knee
Of that heroic shape do reverence
Before the Goddess. Their clear eyes had
    ceas'd
To flash, and gaz'd with earnest softening
    light.

DISTRAUGHT FOR MEROPÉ.

O Meropé !
And where art thou, while idly thus I rave ?
Runs there no hope — no fever through thy
    veins,
Like that which leaps and courses round
    my heart ?
Shall I resign thee, passion-perfect maid,
Who in mortality's most finish'd work
Rank'st highest — and lov'st me, even as I
    love ?
Rather possess thee with a tenfold stress
Of love ungovernable, being denied !
'Gainst fraud what should I cast down in
    reply ?
What but a sword, since force must do me
    right,
And strength was given unto me with my
    birth,
In mine own hand, and by ascendancy
Over my giant brethren. Two remain,
Whom prayers to dark Hephaistos and my
    sire
Poseidon, shall awaken into life ;
And we will tear up gates, and scatter
    towers,
Until I bear off Meropé. Sing on !
Sing on, great tempest ! in the darkness
    sing !
Thy madness is a music that brings calm
Into my central soul ; and from its waves
That now with joy begin to heave and gush,
The burning Image of all life's desire,
Like an absorbing fire-breath'd phantom-
    god,
Rises and floats ! — here touching on the
    foam,
There hovering over it ; ascending swift

Starward, then swooping down the hemi-
sphere
Upon the lengthening javelins of the blast.
Why paus'd I in the palace-groves to dream
Of bliss, with all its substance in my reach ?
Why not at once, with thee enfolded, whirl
Deep down the abyss of ecstasy, to melt
All brain and being where no reason is,
Or else the source of reason ?   But the roar
Of Time's great wings, which ne'er had
driven me
By dread events, nor broken-down old age,
Back on myself, the close experience
Of false mankind, with whispers cold and
dry
As snake-songs midst stone hollows, thus
has taught me,
The giant hunter, laugh'd at by the world,
Not to forget the substance in the dream
Which breeds it.   Both must melt and
merge in one.
Now shall I overcome thee, body and soul,
And like a new-made element brood o'er
thee
With all devouring murmurs !   Come, my
love !
Come, life's blood-tempest ! — come, thou
blinding storm,
And clasp the rigid pine — this mortal
frame
Wrap with thy whirlwinds, rend and wrestle
down,
And let my being solve its destiny,
Defying, seeking, thine extremest power;
Famish'd and thirsty for the absorbing
doom
Of that immortal death which leads to life,
And gives a glimpse of Heaven's parental
scheme.

IN FOREST DEPTHS

Within the isle, far from the walks of
men,
Where jocund chase was never heard, nor
hoof
Of Satyr broke the moss, nor any bird
Sang, save at times the nightingale — but
only
In his prolong'd and swelling tones, nor e'er
With wild joy and hoarse laughing melody,
Closing the ecstasy, as is his wont, —
A forest, separate and far withdrawn
From all the rest, there grew.   Old as the
earth,

Of cedar was it, lofty in its glooms
When the sun hung o'erhead, and, in its
darkness,
Like Night when giving birth to Time's
first pulse.
Silence had ever dwelt there ; but of late
Came faint sounds, with a cadence droning
low,
From the far depths, as of a cataract
Whose echoes midst incumbent foliage died.
From one high mountain gush'd a flowing
stream,
Which through the forest pass'd, and found
a fall
Within, none knew where, then roll'd
tow'rds the sea.

There, underneath the boughs, mark
where the gleam
Of sunrise through the roofing's chasm is
thrown
Upon a grassy plot below, whereon
The shadow of a stag stoops to the stream
Swift rolling tow'rds the cataract, and
drinks deeply.
Throughout the day unceasingly it drinks,
While ever and anon the nightingale,
Not waiting for the evening, swells his
hymn —
His one sustain'd and heaven-aspiring
tone —
And when the sun hath vanish'd utterly,
Arm over arm the cedars spread their shade,
With arching wrist and long extended
hands,
And graveward fingers lengthening in the
moon,
Above that shadowy stag whose antlers still
Hang o'er the stream.   Now came a rich-
ton'd voice
Out of the forest depths, and sang this lay,
With deep speech intervall'd and tender
pause.

" If we have lost the world what gain is
ours !
Hast thou not built a palace of more grace
Than marble towers ?   These trunks are
pillars rare,
Whose roof embowers with far more gran-
deur. Say,
Hast thou not found a bliss with Meropé,
As full of rapture as existence new ?
'T is thus with me.   I know that thou art
bless'd.

Our inmost powers, fresh wing'd, shall soar
  and dream
In realms of Elysian gleam, whose air —
  light — flowers,
Will ever be, though vague, most fair, most
  sweet,
Better than memory. — Look yonder, love !
What solemn image through the trunks is
  straying ?
And now he doth not move, yet never turns
On us his visage of rapt vacancy !
It is Oblivion. In his hand — though nought
Knows he of this — a dusky purple flower
Droops over its tall stem. Again, ah see !
He wanders into mist, and now is lost.
Within his brain what lovely realms of
  death
Are pictur'd, and what knowledge through
  the doors
Of his forgetfulness of all the earth
A path may gain ? Then turn thee, love,
  to me :
Was I not worth thy winning, and thy toil,
O earth-born son of Ocean ? Melt to rain."

EOS

Level with the summit of that eastern
  mount,
By slow approach, and like a promontory
Which seems to glide and meet a coming
  ship,
The pale-gold platform of the morning came
Towards the gliding mount. Against a sky
Of delicate purple, snow-bright courts and
  halls,
Touch'd with light silvery green, gleaming
  across,
Fronted by pillars vast, cloud-capitall'd,
With shafts of changeful pearl, all rear'd
  upon
An isle of clear aerial gold, came floating ;
And in the centre, clad in fleecy white,
With lucid lilies in her golden hair,
Eos, sweet Goddess of the Morning, stood.

From the bright peak of that surrounded
  mount,
One step sufficed to gain the tremulous floor
Whereon the palace of the Morning shone,
Scarcely a bow-shot distant ; but that step,
Orion's humbled and still mortal feet
Dared not adventure. In the Goddess' face
Imploringly he gaz'd. " Advance ! " she
  said,

In tones more sweet than when some hea-
  venly bird,
Hid in a rosy cloud, its morning hymn
Warbles unseen, wet with delicious dews,
And to earth's flowers, all looking up in
  prayer,
Tells of the coming bliss. " Believe — ad-
  vance !
Or, as the spheres move onward with their
  song
That calls me to awaken other lands,
That moment will escape which ne'er re-
  turns."
Forward Orion stepp'd : the platform
  bright
Shook like the reflex of a star in water
Mov'd by the breeze, throughout its whole
  expanse ;
And even the palace glisten'd fitfully,
As with electric shiver it sent forth
Odors of flowers divine and all fresh life.
Still stood he where he stepp'd, nor to
  return
Attempted. To essay one pace beyond
He felt no power — yet onward he advanced
Safe to the Goddess, who, with hand out-
  stretch'd,
Into the palace led him. Grace and
  strength,
With sense of happy change to finer earth,
Freshness of nature, and belief in good,
Came flowing o'er his soul, and he was
  bless'd.

'T is always morning somewhere in the
  world,
And Eos rises, circling constantly
The varied regions of mankind. No pause
Of renovation and of freshening rays
She knows, but evermore her love breathes
  forth
On field and forest, as on human hope,
Health, beauty, power, thought, action, and
  advance.
All this Orion witness'd, and rejoiced.

AKINETOS

'T was eve, and Time, his vigorous course
  pursuing,
Met Akinetos walking by the sea.
At sight of him the Father of the Hours
Paus'd on the sand, — which shrank, grew
  moist, and trembled
At that unwonted pressure of the God.

And thus with look and accent stern, he
   spake :

"Thou art the mortal who, with hand un-
   mov'd,
Eatest the fruit of others' toil; whose heart
Is but a vital engine that conveys
Blood, to no purpose, up and down thy frame;
Whose forehead is a large stone sepulchre
Of knowledge ! and whose life but turns to
   waste
My measur'd hours, and earth's material
   mass !"

   .   .   .   .
   Whereto the Great Unmov'd no answer
   made,—
And Time continued, sterner than before :
"O not-to-be-approv'd ! thou Apathy,
Who gazest downward on that empty
   shell,—
Is it for thee, who bear'st the common lot
Of man, and art his brother in the fields,
From birth to funeral pyre ; is it for thee,
Who didst derive from thy long-living sire
More knowledge than endows far better
   sons,
Thy lamp to burn within, and turn aside
Thy face from all humanity, or behold it
Without emotion, like some sea-shell'd
   thing
Staring around from a green hollow'd rock,
Not aiding, loving, caring—hoping aught—
Forgetting Nature, and by her forgot ?"

   Whereto, with mildness, Akinetos said,
"Hast thou consider'd of Eternity ?"
"Profoundly have I done so, in my youth,"
Chronos replied, and bow'd his furrow'd
   head ;
"Most, when my tender feet from Chaos
   trod
Stumbling,—and, doubtful of my eyes, my
   hands
The dazzling air explor'd. But, since that
   date,
So many ages have I told ; so many,
Fleet after fleet on newly opening seas,
Descry before me, that of late my thoughts
Have rather dwelt on all around my path,
With anxious care. Well were it thus with
   thee."

   Then Akinetos calmly spake once more,
With eyes still bent upon the tide-ribb'd
   sands :

"And dost thou of To-morrow also think ?"
Whereat, as one dismay'd by sudden
   thought
Of many crowding things that call him
   thence,
Time, with bent brows, went hurrying on
   his way.

   Slow tow'rds his cave the Great Unmov'd
   repair'd,
And, with his back against the rock, sat
   down
Outside, half smiling in the pleasant air ;
And in the lonely silence of the place
He thus, at length, discours'd unto himself:

"Orion, ever active and at work,
Honest and skilful, not to be surpass'd,
Drew misery on himself and those he lov'd ;
Wrought his companions' death,—and now
   hath found,
At Artemis' hand, his own. So fares it ever
With the world's builder. He, from wall
   to beam,
From pillar to roof, from shade to corporal
   form,
From the first vague Thought to the Temple
   vast,
A ceaseless contest with the crowd endures,
For whom he labors. Why then should
   we move ?
Our wisdom cannot change whate'er 's de-
   creed,
Nor e'en the acts or thoughts of brainless
   men :
Why then be mov'd ? Best reason is most
   vain.
He who will do and suffer, must — and
   end.
Hence, death is not an evil, since it leads
To somewhat permanent, beyond the noise
Man maketh on the tabor of his will,
Until the small round burst, and pale he
   falls.
His ear is stuff'd with the grave's earth,
   yet feels
The inaudible whispers of Eternity,
While Time runs shouting to Oblivion
In the upper fields ! I would not swell
   that cry."

   Thus Akinetos sat from day to day,
Absorb'd in indolent sublimity,
Reviewing thoughts and knowledge o'er
   and o'er ;

And now he spake, now sang unto himself,
Now sank to brooding silence. From above,
While passing, Time the rock touch'd ! —
    and it ooz'd
Petrific drops — gently at first — and slow.
Reclining lonely in his fix'd repose,
The Great Unmov'd unconsciously became
Attach'd to that he press'd,— and gradu-
    ally —
While his thoughts drifted to no shore — a
    part
O' the rock. There clung the dead excres-
    cence, till
Strong hands, descended from Orion,
    made
Large roads, built markets, granaries, and
    steep walls,—
Squaring down rocks for use, and common
    good.

GENIUS

FAR out at sea — the sun was high,
    While veer'd the wind, and flapp'd the
        sail —
We saw a snow-white butterfly
    Dancing before the fitful gale,
            Far out at sea !

The little wanderer, who had lost
    His way, of danger nothing knew;
Settled awhile upon the mast,
    Then flutter'd o'er the waters blue,
            Far out at sea.

Above, there gleam'd the boundless sky ;
    Beneath, the boundless ocean sheen ;
Between them danced the butterfly,
    The spirit-life of this vast scene,
            Far out at sea.

The tiny soul then soar'd away,
    Seeking the clouds on fragile wings,
Lur'd by the brighter, purer ray
    Which hope's ecstatic morning brings,
            Far out at sea.

Away he sped with shimmering glee !
    Scarce seen — now lost — yet onward
        borne !
Night comes ! — with wind and rain — and
        he
No more will dance before the Morn,
            Far out at sea.

He dies unlike his mates, I ween ;
    Perhaps not sooner, or worse cross'd ;
And he hath felt, thought, known, and seen
    A larger life and hope — though lost
            Far out at sea !

PELTERS OF PYRAMIDS

A SHOAL of idlers, from a merchant craft
Anchor'd off Alexandria, went ashore,
And mounting asses in their headlong glee,
Round Pompey's Pillar rode with hoots and
    taunts,
As men oft say, " What art thou more than
    we ? "
Next in a boat they floated up the Nile,
Singing and drinking, swearing senseless
    oaths,
Shouting, and laughing most derisively
At all majestic scenes. A bank they reach'd,
And clambering up, play'd gambols among
    tombs ;
And in portentous ruins (through whose
    depths,
The mighty twilight of departed Gods,
Both sun and moon glanced furtive, as in
    awe)
They hid, and whoop'd, and spat on sacred
    things.

At length, beneath the blazing sun they
    lounged
Near a great Pyramid. Awhile they stood
With stupid stare, until resentment grew,
In the recoil of meanness from the vast ;
And gathering stones, they with coarse
    oaths and jibes
(As they would say, " What art thou more
    than we ? ")
Pelted the Pyramid ! But soon these men,
Hot and exhausted, sat them down to
    drink —
Wrangled, smok'd, spat, and laugh'd, and
    drowsily
Curs'd the bald Pyramid, and fell asleep.

Night came : — a little sand went drift-
    ing by —   .
And morn again was in the soft blue hea-
    vens.
The broad slopes of the shining Pyramid
Look'd down in their austere simplicity
Upon the glistening silence of the sands
Whereon no trace of mortal dust was seen.

SOLITUDE AND THE LILY

THE LILY

I BEND above the moving stream,
And see myself in my own dream,—
Heaven passing, while I do not pass.
Something divine pertains to me,
Or I to it ; — reality
Escapes me on this liquid glass.

SOLITUDE

The changeful clouds that float or poise on
    high,
Emblem earth's night and day of history :
Renew'd for ever, evermore to die.
Thy life-dream is thy fleeting loveliness ;
But mine is concentrated consciousness,
A life apart from pleasure or distress.
    The grandeur of the Whole
    Absorbs my soul,
While my caves sigh o'er human littleness.

THE LILY

Ah, Solitude,
Of marble Silence fit abode !
I do prefer my fading face,
My loss of loveliness and grace,
    With cloud-dreams ever in my view ;
Also the hope that other eyes
May share my rapture in the skies,
And, if illusion, feel it true.

THE SLAVE

A SEA-PIECE, OFF JAMAICA

BEFORE us in the sultry dawn arose
    Indigo-tinted mountains ; and ere noon
We near'd an isle that lay like a fes-
    toon,
And shar'd the ocean's glittering repose.

We saw plantations spotted with white huts;
    Estates midst orange groves and towering
    trees ;

Rich yellow lawns embrown'd by soft
    degrees ;
Plots of intense gold freak'd with shadynuts.

A dead hot silence tranced sea, land, and
    sky :
And now a long canoe came gliding forth,
    Wherein there sat an old man fierce and
    swarth,
Tiger-faced, black-fang'd, and with jaun-
    diced eye.

Pure white, with pale blue chequer'd, and
    red fold
    Of head-cloth 'neath straw brim, this
    Master wore ;
    While in the sun-glare stood with high-
    rais'd oar
A naked Image all of burnish'd gold.

Golden his bones — high-valued in the mart,
    His minted muscles, and his glossy skin ;
    Golden his life of action — but within
The slave is human in a bleeding heart.

THE PLOUGH

A LANDSCAPE IN BERKSHIRE

ABOVE yon sombre swell of land
    Thou seest the dawn's grave orange hue,
With one pale streak like yellow sand,
    And over that a vein of blue.

The air is cold above the woods ;
    All silent is the earth and sky,
Except with his own lonely moods
    The blackbird holds a colloquy.

Over the broad hill creeps a beam,
    Like hope that gilds a good man's brow,
And now ascends the nostril-stream
    Of stalwart horses come to plough.

Ye rigid Ploughmen, bear in mind
    Your labor is for future hours !
Advance — spare not — nor look behind :
    Plough deep and straight with all your
    powers.

Thomas Lovell Beddoes

FROM "TORRISMOND"

IN A GARDEN BY MOONLIGHT

Veronica. Come then, a song ; a winding
  gentle song,
To lead me into sleep. Let it be low
As zephyr, telling secrets to his rose,
For I would hear the murmuring of my
  thoughts ;
And more of voice than of that other
  music
That grows around the strings of quivering
  lutes ;
But most of thought ; for with my mind I
  listen,
And when the leaves of sound are shed upon
  it,
If there 's no seed remembrance grows not
  there.
So life, so death ; a song, and then a
  dream !
Begin before another dewdrop fall
From the soft hold of these disturbed
  flowers,
For sleep is filling up my senses fast,
And from these words I sink.

SONG

How many times do I love thee, dear ?
  Tell me how many thoughts there be
    In the atmosphere
    Of a new-fall'n year,
Whose white and sable hours appear
  The latest flake of Eternity :
So many times do I love thee, dear.

How many times do I love again ?
  Tell me how many beads there are
    In a silver chain
    Of evening rain,
Unravell'd from the tumbling main,
  And threading the eye of a yellow star :
So many times do I love again.

Elvira. She sees no longer : leave her
  then alone,
Encompass'd by this round and moony
  night.
A rose-leaf for thy lips, and then good-
  night :
So life, so death ; a song, and then a
  dream !

DREAM-PEDLARY

IF there were dreams to sell,
  What would you buy ?
Some cost a passing bell ;
  Some a light sigh,
That shakes from Life's fresh crown
Only a rose-leaf down.
If there were dreams to sell,
Merry and sad to tell,
And the crier rung the bell,
  What would you buy ?

A cottage lone and still,
  With bowers nigh,
Shadowy, my woes to still,
  Until I die.
Such pearl from Life's fresh crown
Fain would I shake me down.
Were dreams to have at will,
This would best heal my ill,
  This would I buy.

But there were dreams to sell
  Ill didst thou buy ;
Life is a dream, they tell,
  Waking, to die.
Dreaming a dream to prize,
Is wishing ghosts to rise ;
And, if I had the spell
To call the buried well,
  Which one would I ?

If there are ghosts to raise,
  What shall I call
Out of hell's murky haze,
  Heaven's blue pall ?
Raise my lov'd long-lost boy
To lead me to his joy.
There are no ghosts to raise ;
Out of death lead no ways ;
  Vain is the call.

Know'st thou not ghosts to sue ?
  No love thou hast.
Else lie, as I will do,
  And breathe thy last.
So out of Life's fresh crown
Fall like a rose-leaf down.
Thus are the ghosts to woo ;
Thus are all dreams made true,
  Ever to last !

BALLAD OF HUMAN LIFE

WHEN we were girl and boy together,
  We toss'd about the flowers
  And wreath'd the blushing hours
Into a posy green and sweet.
  I sought the youngest, best,
  And never was at rest
Till I had laid them at thy fairy feet.
But the days of childhood they were fleet,
  And the blooming sweet-briar-breath'd
    weather,
  When we were boy and girl together.

Then we were lad and lass together,
  And sought the kiss of night
  Before we felt aright,
Sitting and singing soft and sweet.
  The dearest thought of heart
  With thee 't was joy to part,
And the greater half was thine, as meet.
Still my eyelid 's dewy, my veins they beat
  At the starry summer-evening weather,
  When we were lad and lass together.

And we are man and wife together,
  Although thy breast, once bold
  With song, be clos'd and cold
Beneath flowers' roots and birds' light feet.
  Yet sit I by thy tomb,
  And dissipate the gloom
With songs of loving faith and sorrow sweet.
And fate and darkling grave kind dreams
    do cheat,
  That, while fair life, young hope, despair
    and death are,
  We 're boy and girl, and lass and lad, and
    man and wife together.

SONGS FROM "DEATH'S JEST-BOOK"

I

TO SEA, TO SEA !

To sea, to sea ! The calm is o'er ;
  The wanton water leaps in sport,
And rattles down the pebbly shore ;
  The dolphin wheels, the sea-cows snort,
A.id unseen Mermaids' pearly song
Comes bubbling up, the weeds among.
  Fling broad the sail, dip deep the oar :
  To sea, to sea ! the calm is o'er.

To sea, to sea ! our wide-wing'd bark
  Shall billowy cleave its sunny way,
And with its shadow, fleet and dark,
  Break the cav'd Tritons' azure day,
Like mighty eagle soaring light
O'er antelopes on Alpine height.
  The anchor heaves, the ship swings free,
  The sails swell full. To sea, to sea !

II

DIRGE

IF thou wilt ease thine heart
Of love and all its smart,
  Then sleep, dear, sleep ;
And not a sorrow
  Hang any tear on your eye-lashes ;
    Lie still and deep,
Sad soul, until the sea-wave washes
  The rim o' the sun to-morrow,
    In eastern sky.

But wilt thou cure thine heart
Of love and all its smart,
  Then die, dear, die ;
'T is deeper, sweeter,
  Than on a rose bank to lie dreaming
    With folded eye ;
  And then alone, amid the beaming
  Of love's stars, thou 'lt meet her
    In eastern sky.

III

ATHULF'S DEATH SONG

A CYPRESS-BOUGH, and a rose-wreath sweet,
A wedding-robe, and a winding-sheet,
  A bridal-bed and a bier.
  Thine be the kisses, maid,
  And smiling Love's alarms ;
And thou, pale youth, be laid
  In the grave's cold arms.
  Each in his own charms,
  Death and Hymen both are here ;
    So up with scythe and torch,
    And to the old church porch,
  While all the bells ring clear :
  And rosy, rosy the bed shall bloom,
  And earthy, earthy heap up the tomb.

Now tremble dimples on your cheek,
Sweet be your lips to taste and speak,
  For he who kisses is near :

By her the bridegod fair,
　In youthful power and force ;
By him the grizard bare,
　Pale knight on a pale horse,
To woo him to a corpse.
　Death and Hymen both are here ;
So up with scythe and torch,
　And to the old church porch,
While all the bells ring clear :
And rosy, rosy the bed shall bloom,
And earthy, earthy heap up the tomb.

IV

SECOND DIRGE

WE do lie beneath the grass
In the moonlight, in the shade
Of the yew-tree. They that pass
Hear us not. We are afraid
They would envy our delight,
In our graves by glow-worm night.
Come follow us, and smile as we ;
We sail to the rock in the ancient
　　waves,
Where the snow falls by thousands into the
　　sea,
And the drown'd and the shipwreck'd
　　have happy graves.

SONGS FROM "THE BRIDES' TRAGEDY"

I

HESPERUS SINGS

POOR old pilgrim Misery,
　Beneath the silent moon he sate,
A-listening to the screech owl's cry
　And the cold wind's goblin prate ;
Beside him lay his staff of yew
　With wither'd willow twin'd,
His scant gray hair all wet with dew,
　His cheeks with grief ybrin'd ;
And his cry it was ever, alack !
Alack, and woe is me !

Anon a wanton imp astray
　His piteous moaning hears,
And from his bosom steals away
　His rosary of tears :
With his plunder fled that urchin elf,
　And hid it in your eyes ;
Then tell me back the stolen pelf,
　Give up the lawless prize ;
Or your cry shall be ever, alack !
Alack, and woe is me !

II

LOVE GOES A-HAWKING

A HO ! A ho !
Love's horn doth blow,
　And he will out a-hawking go.
His shafts are light as beauty's sighs,
And bright as midnight's brightest eyes
　And round his starry way
The swan-wing'd horses of the skies,
With summer's music in their manes,
　Curve their fair necks to zephyr's reins,
And urge their graceful play.

A ho ! A ho !
Love's horn doth blow,
　And he will out a-hawking go.
The sparrows flutter round his wrist,
The feathery thieves that Venus kist
　And taught their morning song,
The linnets seek the airy list,
And swallows too, small pets of Spring,
Beat back the gale with swifter wing,
　And dart and wheel along.

A ho ! A ho !
Love's horn doth blow,
　And he will out a-hawking go.
Now woe to every gnat that skips
To filch the fruit of ladies' lips,
　His felon blood is shed ;
And woe to flies, whose airy ships
On beauty cast their anchoring bite,
And bandit wasp, that naughty wight,
　Whose sting is slaughter-red.

Robert Stephen Hawker

THE SONG OF THE WESTERN MEN

A GOOD sword and a trusty hand !
A merry heart and true !
King James's men shall understand
What Cornish lads can do.

And have they fix'd the where and when ?
And shall Trelawny die ?
Here's twenty thousand Cornish men
Will know the reason why !

Out spake their captain brave and bold,
A merry wight was he :
" If London Tower were Michael's hold,
We 'll set Trelawny free !

" We 'll cross the Tamar, land to land,
The Severn is no stay,
With ' one and all, ' and hand in hand,
And who shall bid us nay ?

" And when we come to London Wall,
A pleasant sight to view,
Come forth ! come forth, ye cowards all,
Here's men as good as you !

" Trelawny he 's in keep and hold,
Trelawny he may die ;
But here's twenty thousand Cornish bold,
Will know the reason why ! "

MAWGAN OF MELHUACH

'T WAS a fierce night when old Mawgan
died,
Men shudder'd to hear the rolling tide :
The wreckers fled fast from the awful shore,
They had heard strange voices amid the
roar.

"Out with the boat there," some one cried,—
" Will he never come ? we shall lose the tide :
His berth is trim and his cabin stor'd,
He 's a weary long time coming on board."

The old man struggled upon the bed :
He knew the words that the voices said ;
Wildly he shriek'd as his eyes grew dim,
" He was dead ! he was dead ! when I bur-
ied him."

Hark yet again to the devilish roar,
" He was nimbler once with a ship on shore ;
Come ! come ! old man, 't is a vain delay,
We must make the offing by break of day."

Hard was the struggle, but at the last,
With a stormy pang old Mawgan past,
And away, away, beneath their sight,
Gleam'd the red sail at pitch of night.

FEATHERSTONE'S DOOM

TWIST thou and twine ! in light and gloom
A spell is on thine hand ;
The wind shall be thy changeful loom,
Thy web the shifting sand.

Twine from this hour, in ceaseless toil,
On Blackrock's sullen shore ;
Till cordage of the sand shall coil
Where crested surges roar.

'T is for that hour, when, from the wave,
Near voices wildly cried ;
When thy stern hand no succor gave,
The cable at thy side.

Twist thou and twine ! in light and gloom
The spell is on thine hand ;
The wind shall be thy changeful loom,
Thy web the shifting sand.

"PATER VESTER PASCIT ILLA"

OUR bark is on the waters : wide around
The wandering wave ; above, the lonely sky.
Hush ! a young sea-bird floats, and that
quick cry
Shrieks to the levell'd weapon's echoing
sound,
Grasps its lank wing, and on, with reckless
bound !
Yet, creature of the surf, a sheltering breast
To-night shall haunt in vain thy far-off nest,
A call unanswer'd search the rocky ground.
Lord of leviathan ! when Ocean heard
Thy gathering voice, and sought his native
breeze ;
When whales first plunged with life, and
the proud deep
Felt unborn tempests heave in troubled
sleep ;

Thou didst provide, e'en for this nameless
    bird,
Home, and a natural love, amid the surging
    seas.

THE SILENT TOWER OF BOTTREAU

TINTADGEL bells ring o'er the tide,
The boy leans on his vessel side ;
He hears that sound, and dreams of home
Soothe the wild orphan of the foam.
    "Come to thy God in time !"
    Thus saith their pealing chime :
    Youth, manhood, old age past,
    "Come to thy God at last."

But why are Bottreau's echoes still ?
Her tower stands proudly on the hill ;
Yet the strange chough that home hath
    found,
The lamb lies sleeping on the ground.
    "Come to thy God in time !"
    Should be her answering chime :
    "Come to thy God at last !"
    Should echo on the blast.

The ship rode down with courses free,
The daughter of a distant sea :
Her sheet was loose, her anchor stor'd,
The merry Bottreau bells on board.
    "Come to thy God in time !"
    Rung out Tintadgel chime ;
    Youth, manhood, old age past,
    "Come to thy God at last !"

The pilot heard his native bells
Hang on the breeze in fitful swells ;
"Thank God," with reverent brow he cried,
"We make the shore with evening's tide."
    "Come to thy God in time !"
    It was his marriage chime :
    Youth, manhood, old age past,
    His bell must ring at last.

"Thank God, thou whining knave, on land,
But thank, at sea, the steersman's hand,"
The captain's voice above the gale :
"Thank the good ship and ready sail."
    "Come to thy God in time !"
    Sad grew the boding chime :

"Come to thy God at last !"
    Boom'd heavy on the blast.

Uprose that sea ! as if it heard
The mighty Master's signal-word :
What thrills the captain's whitening lip ?
The death-groans of his sinking ship.
    "Come to thy God in time !"
    Swung deep the funeral chime :
    Grace, mercy, kindness past,
    "Come to thy God at last !"

Long did the rescued pilot tell —
When gray hairs o'er his forehead fell,
While those around would hear and weep —
That fearful judgment of the deep.
    "Come to thy God in time !"
    He read his native chime :
    Youth, manhood, old age past,
    His bell rung out at last.

Still when the storm of Bottreau's waves
Is wakening in his weedy caves,
Those bells, that sullen surges hide,
Peal their deep notes beneath the tide :
    "Come to thy God in time !"
    Thus saith the ocean chime :
    Storm, billow, whirlwind past,
    "Come to thy God at last !"

TO ALFRED TENNYSON

THEY told me in their shadowy phrase,
    Caught from a tale gone by,
That Arthur, King of Cornish praise,
    Died not, and would not die.

Dreams had they, that in fairy bowers
    Their living warrior lies,
Or wears a garland of the flowers
    That grow in Paradise.

I read the rune with deeper ken,
    And thus the myth I trace : —
A bard should rise, mid future men,
    The mightiest of his race.

He would great Arthur's deeds rehearse
    On gray Dundagel's shore ;
And so the King in laurell'd verse
    Shall live, and die no more !

Edward, Lord Lytton

(EDWARD LYTTON BULWER)

THE CARDINAL'S SOLILOQUY

FROM "RICHELIEU; OR, THE CONSPI-
RACY"

Rich. [*reading*]. "In silence, and at night,
the Conscience feels
That life should soar to nobler ends than
Power."
So sayest thou, sage and sober moralist!
But wert thou tried? Sublime Philosophy,
Thou art the Patriarch's ladder, reaching
heaven,
And bright with beckoning angels — but,
alas!
We see thee, like the Patriarch, but in
dreams,
By the first step, dull-slumbering on the
earth.
I am not happy! — with the Titan's lust
I woo'd a goddess, and I clasp a cloud.
When I am dust, my name shall, like a star,
Shine through wan space, a glory, and a
prophet
Whereby pale seers shall from their aëry
towers
Con all the ominous signs, benign or evil,
That make the potent astrologue of kings.
But shall the Future judge me by the ends
That I have wrought, or by the dubious
means
Through which the stream of my renown
hath run
Into the many-voiced unfathom'd Time?
Foul in its bed lie weeds, and heaps of slime,
And with its waves — when sparkling in
the sun,
Ofttimes the secret rivulets that swell
Its might of waters — blend the hues of
blood.
Yet are my sins not those of Circumstance,
That all-pervading atmosphere, wherein
Our spirits, like the unsteady lizard, take
The tints that color, and the food that nur-
tures?
O! ye, whose hour-glass shifts its tran-
quil sands
In the unvex'd silence of a student's cell;
Ye, whose untempted hearts have never
toss'd

Upon the dark and stormy tides where life
Gives battle to the elements, — and man
Wrestles with man for some slight plank,
whose weight
Will bear but one, while round the desper-
ate wretch
The hungry billows roar, and the fierce Fate,
Like some huge monster, dim-seen through
the surf,
Waits him who drops; — ye safe and for-
mal men,
Who write the deeds, and with unfeverish
hand
Weigh in nice scales the motives of the
Great,
Ye cannot know what ye have never tried!
History preserves only the fleshless bones
Of what we are, and by the mocking skull
The would-be wise pretend to guess the
features.
Without the roundness and the glow of life
How hideous is the skeleton! Without
The colorings and humanities that clothe
Our errors, the anatomists of schools
Can make our memory hideous.
                    I have wrought
Great uses out of evil tools, and they
In the time to come may bask beneath the
light
Which I have stolen from the angry gods,
And warn their sons against the glorious
theft,
Forgetful of the darkness which it broke.
I have shed blood, but I have had no foes
Save those the State had; if my wrath was
deadly,
'T is that I felt my country in my veins,
And smote her sons as Brutus smote his
own.
And yet I am not happy: blanch'd and
sear'd
Before my time; breathing an air of hate,
And seeing daggers in the eyes of men,
And wasting powers that shake the thrones
of earth
In contest with the insects; bearding kings
And brav'd by lackies; murder at my bed;
And lone amidst the multitudinous web,
With the dread Three, that are the Fates
who hold

The woof and shears — the Monk, the Spy,
the Headsman.
And this is power? Alas! I am not happy.
[*After a pause.*
And yet the Nile is fretted by the weeds
Its rising roots not up ; but never yet
Did one least barrier by a ripple vex
My onward tide, unswept in sport away.
Am I so ruthless then that I do hate
Them who hate me? Tush, tush! I do not
hate ;
Nay, I forgive. The Statesman writes the
doom,
But the Priest sends the blessing. I for-
give them,
But I destroy ; forgiveness is mine own,
Destruction is the State's! For private life,
Scripture the guide — for public, Machiavel.
Would fortune serve me if the Heaven were
wroth?
For chance makes half my greatness. I
was born
Beneath the aspect of a bright-eyed star,
And my triumphant adamant of soul
Is but the fix'd persuasion of success.
Ah! — here! — that spasm! — again! —
How Life and Death
Do wrestle for me momently! And yet
The King looks pale. I shall outlive the
King!
And then, thou insolent Austrian — who
didst gibe
At the ungainly, gaunt, and daring lover,
Sleeking thy looks to silken Buckingham,
Thou shalt — no matter! I have outliv'd
love.
O beautiful, all golden, gentle youth!
Making thy palace in the careless front
And hopeful eye of man, ere yet the soul
Hath lost the memories which (so Plato
dream'd)
Breath'd glory from the earlier star it
dwelt in —
Oh, for one gale from thine exulting morn-
ing,
Stirring amidst the roses, where of old
Love shook the dew-drops from his glan-
cing hair !
Could I recall the past, or had not set
The prodigal treasures of the bankrupt soul

In one slight bark upon the shoreless sea ;
The yoked steer, after his day of toil,
Forgets the goad, and rests : to me alike
Or day or night — Ambition has no rest !
Shall I resign? who can resign himself?
For custom is ourself ; as drink and food
Become our bone and flesh, the aliments
Nurturing our nobler part, the mind,
thoughts, dreams,
Passions, and aims, in the revolving cycle
Of the great alchemy, at length are made
Our mind itself ; and yet the sweets of
leisure,
An honor'd home far from these base in-
trigues,
An eyrie on the heaven-kiss'd heights of
wisdom. —
[*Taking up the book.*
Speak to me, moralist ! — I 'll heed thy
counsel.

WHEN STARS ARE IN THE QUIET SKIES

WHEN stars are in the quiet skies,
　Then most I pine for thee ;
Bend on me then thy tender eyes,
　As stars look on the sea !
For thoughts, like waves that glide by night,
　Are stillest when they shine ;
Mine earthly love lies hush'd in light
　Beneath the heaven of thine.

There is an hour when angels keep
　Familiar watch o'er men,
When coarser souls are wrapp'd in sleep —
　Sweet spirit, meet me then !
There is an hour when holy dreams
　Through slumber fairest glide ;
And in that mystic hour it seems
　Thou shouldst be by my side.

My thoughts of thee too sacred are
　For daylight's common beam :
I can but know thee as my star,
　My angel and my dream ;
When stars are in the quiet skies,
　Then most I pine for thee ;
Bend on me then thy tender eyes,
　As stars look on the sea !

NOTE. Another lyric by Lord Lytton will be found in the BIOGRAPHICAL NOTES.

William Edmondstoune Aytoun

THE EXECUTION OF MONTROSE

Come hither, Evan Cameron !
  Come, stand beside my knee :
I hear the river roaring down
  Towards the wintry sea.
There 's shouting on the mountain-side,
  There 's war within the blast ;
Old faces look upon me,
  Old forms go trooping past :
I hear the pibroch wailing
  Amidst the din of fight,
And my dim spirit wakes again
  Upon the verge of night.

'T was I that led the Highland host
  Through wild Lochaber's snows,
What time the plaided clans came down
  To battle with Montrose.
I 've told thee how the Southrons fell
  Beneath the broad claymore,
And how we smote the Campbell clan
  By Inverlochy's shore.
I 've told thee how we swept Dundee,
  And tam'd the Lindsays' pride ;
But never have I told thee yet
  How the great Marquis died.

A traitor sold him to his foes ;
  O deed of deathless shame !
I charge thee, boy, if e'er thou meet
  With one of Assynt's name —
Be it upon the mountain's side,
  Or yet within the glen,
Stand he in martial gear alone,
  Or back'd by armed men —
Face him, as thou wouldst face the man
  Who wrong'd thy sire's renown ;
Remember of what blood thou art,
  And strike the caitiff down !

They brought him to the Watergate,
  Hard bound with hempen span,
As though they held a lion there,
  And not a fenceless man.
They set him high upon a cart,
  The hangman rode below,
They drew his hands behind his back
  And bar'd his noble brow.
Then, as a hound is slipp'd from leash,
  They cheer'd the common throng,

And blew the note with yell and shout
  And bade him pass along.

It would have made a brave man's heart
  Grow sad and sick that day,
To watch the keen malignant eyes
  Bent down on that array.
There stood the Whig west-country lords,
  In balcony and bow ;
There sat their gaunt and wither'd dames,
  And their daughters all a-row.
And every open window
  Was full as full might be
With black-rob'd Covenanting carles,
  That goodly sport to see !

But when he came, though pale and wan,
  He look'd so great and high,
So noble was his manly front,
  So calm his steadfast eye,
The rabble rout forbore to shout,
  And each man held his breath,
For well they knew the hero's soul
  Was face to face with death.
And then a mournful shudder
  Through all the people crept,
And some that came to scoff at him
  Now turn'd aside and wept.

But onwards — always onwards,
  In silence and in gloom,
The dreary pageant labor'd,
  Till it reach'd the house of doom.
Then first a woman's voice was heard
  In jeer and laughter loud,
And an angry cry and a hiss arose
  From the heart of the tossing crowd :
Then as the Graeme look'd upwards,
  He saw the ugly smile
Of him who sold his king for gold,
  The master-fiend Argyle !

The Marquis gaz'd a moment,
  And nothing did he say,
But the cheek of Argyle grew ghastly pale
  And he turn'd his eyes away.
The painted harlot by his side,
  She shook through every limb,
For a roar like thunder swept the street,
  And hands were clench'd at him ;
And a Saxon soldier cried aloud,
  " Back, coward, from thy place !

For seven long years thou hast not dar'd
  To look him in the face."

Had I been there with sword in hand,
  And fifty Camerons by,
That day through high Dunedin's streets
  Had peal'd the slogan-cry.
Not all their troops of trampling horse,
  Nor might of mailed men,
Not all the rebels in the south
  Had borne us backwards then !
Once more his foot on Highland heath
  Had trod as free as air,
Or I, and all who bore my name,
  Been laid around him there !

It might not be. They placed him next
  Within the solemn hall,
Where once the Scottish kings were
    thron'd
  Amidst their nobles all.
But there was dust of vulgar feet
  On that polluted floor,
And perjur'd traitors fill'd the place
  Where good men sate before.
With savage glee came Warristoun
  To read the murderous doom ;
And then uprose the great Montrose
  In the middle of the room.

" Now, by my faith as belted knight,
  And by the name I bear,
And by the bright Saint Andrew's cross
  That waves above us there,
Yea, by a greater, mightier oath —
  And oh, that such should be !
By that dark stream of royal blood
  That lies 'twixt you and me,
I have not sought in battle-field
  A wreath of such renown,
Nor dar'd I hope on my dying day
  To win the martyr's crown !

" There is a chamber far away
  Where sleep the good and brave,
But a better place ye have nam'd for
    me
  Than by my father's grave.
For truth and right, 'gainst treason's
    might,
  This hand hath always striven,
And ye raise it up for a witness still
  In the eye of earth and heaven.
Then nail my head on yonder tower,
  Give every town a limb,

And God who made shall gather them :
  I go from you to Him ! "

The morning dawn'd full darkly,
  The rain came flashing down,
And the jagged streak of the levin-bolt
  Lit up the gloomy town :
The thunder crash'd across the heaven,
  The fatal hour was come ;
Yet aye broke in with muffled beat
  The 'larum of the drum.
There was madness on the earth below
  And anger in the sky,
And young and old, and rich and poor,
  Came forth to see him die.

Ah, God ! that ghastly gibbet !
  How dismal 't is to see
The great tall spectral skeleton,
  The ladder and the tree !
Hark ! hark ! it is the clash of arms —
  The bells begin to toll —
" He is coming ! he is coming !
  God's mercy on his soul ! "
One last long peal of thunder :
  The clouds are clear'd away,
And the glorious sun once more looks
    down
  Amidst the dazzling day.

" He is coming ! he is coming ! "
  Like a bridegroom from his room,
Came the hero from his prison
  To the scaffold and the doom.
There was glory on his forehead,
  There was lustre in his eye,
And he never walk'd to battle
  More proudly than to die :
There was color in his visage,
  Though the cheeks of all were wan,
And they marvell'd as they saw him pass,
  That great and goodly man !

He mounted up the scaffold,
  And he turn'd him to the crowd ;
But they dar'd not trust the people,
  So he might not speak aloud.
But he look'd upon the heavens,
  And they were clear and blue,
And in the liquid ether
  The eye of God shone through;
Yet a black and murky battlement
  Lay resting on the hill,
As though the thunder slept within —
  All else was calm and still.

The grim Geneva ministers
  With anxious scowl drew near,
As you have seen the ravens flock
  Around the dying deer.
He would not deign them word nor sign,
  But alone he bent the knee,
And veil'd his face for Christ's dear
    grace
  Beneath the gallows-tree.
Then radiant and serene he rose,
  And cast his cloak away :
For he had ta'en his latest look
  Of earth and sun and day.

A beam of light fell o'er him,
  Like a glory round the shriven,
And he climb'd the lofty ladder
  As it were the path to heaven.
Then came a flash from out the cloud,
  And a stunning thunder-roll ;
And no man dar'd to look aloft,
  For fear was on every soul.
There was another heavy sound,
  A hush and then a groan ;
And darkness swept across the sky —
  The work of death was done !

MASSACRE OF THE MACPHER-SON

FHAIRSHON swore a feud
  Against the clan M'Tavish —
March'd into their land
  To murder and to rafish ;
For he did resolve
  To extirpate the vipers,
With four-and-twenty men,
  And five-and-thirty pipers.

But when he had gone
  Half-way down Strath-Canaan,
Of his fighting tail
  Just three were remainin'.
They were all he had
  To back him in ta battle :
All the rest had gone
  Off to drive ta cattle.

"Fery coot !" cried Fhairshon —
  So my clan disgraced is ;

Lads, we 'll need to fight
  Pefore we touch ta peasties.
Here 's Mhic-Mac-Methusaleh
  Coming wi' his fassals —
Gillies seventy-three,
  And sixty Dhuinéwassels ! "

"Coot tay to you, sir !
  Are you not ta Fhairshon ?
Was you coming here
  To visit any person ?
You are a plackguard, sir ?
  It is now six hundred
Coot long years, and more,
  Since my glen was plunder'd. "

"Fat is tat you say ?
  Dar you cock your peaver ?
I will teach you, sir,
  Fat is coot pehavior !
You shall not exist
  For another day more ;
I will shot you, sir,
  Or stap you with my claymore ! "

"I am fery glad
  To learn what you mention,
Since I can prevent
  Any such intention."
So Mhic-Mac-Methusaleh
  Gave some warlike howls,
Trew his skhian-dhu,
  An' stuck it in his powels.

In this fery way
  Tied ta faliant Fhairshon,
Who was always thought
  A superior person.
Fhairshon had a son,
  Who married Noah's daughter,
And nearly spoil'd ta flood
  By trinking up ta water —

Which he would have done,
  I at least believe it,
Had ta mixture peen
  Only half Glenlivet.
This is all my tale :
  Sirs, I hope 't is new t' ye !
Here 's your fery good healths,
  And tamn ta whusky tuty !

POETS OF QUALITY

Thomas Love Peacock

THE MEN OF GOTHAM

SEAMEN three ! what men be ye ?
Gotham's three Wise Men we be.
Whither in your bowl so free ?
To rake the moon from out the sea.
The bowl goes trim ; the moon doth
    shine ;
  And our ballast is old wine :
  And your ballast is old wine.

Who art thou, so fast adrift ?
I am he they call Old Care.
Here on board we will thee lift.
No : I may not enter there.
Wherefore so ? 'T is Jove's decree —
  In a bowl Care may not be :
  In a bowl Care may not be.

Fear ye not the waves that roll ?
No : in charmed bowl we swim.
What the charm that floats the bowl ?
Water may not pass the brim.
The bowl goes trim ; the moon doth
    shine ;
  And our ballast is old wine :
  And your ballast is old wine.

THE WAR-SONG OF DINAS VAWR

THE mountain sheep are sweeter,
But the valley sheep are fatter ;
We therefore deem'd it meeter
To carry off the latter.
We made an expedition ;
We met an host and quell'd it ;
We forced a strong position
And kill'd the men who held it.

On Dyfed's richest valley,
Where herds of kine were browsing,
We made a mighty sally,
To furnish our carousing.
Fierce warriors rush'd to meet us ;
We met them, and o'erthrew them :
They struggled hard to beat us,
But we conquer'd them, and slew them.

As we drove our prize at leisure,
 The king march'd forth to catch us ;
His rage surpass'd all measure,
But his people could not match us.
He fled to his hall-pillars ;
And, ere our force we led off,
Some sack'd his house and cellars,
While others cut his head off.

We there, in strife bewildering,
Spilt blood enough to swim in :
We orphan'd many children
And widow'd many women.
The eagles and the ravens
We glutted with our foemen :
The heroes and the cravens,
The spearmen and the bowmen.

We brought away from battle,
And much their land bemoan'd them,
Two thousand head of cattle
And the head of him who own'd them :
Ednyfed, King of Dyfed,
His head was borne before us ;
His wine and beasts supplied our feasts,
And his overthrow, our chorus.

MARGARET LOVE PEACOCK

THREE YEARS OLD

LONG night succeeds thy little day :
 O, blighted blossom ! can it be
That this gray stone and grassy clay
 Have clos'd our anxious care of thee ?

The half-form'd speech of artless thought,
 That spoke a mind beyond thy years,
The song, the dance by Nature taught,
 The sunny smiles, the transient tears,

The symmetry of face and form,
 The eye with light and life replete,
The little heart so fondly warm,
 The voice so musically sweet, —

These, lost to hope, in memory yet
 Around the hearts that lov'd thee cling,
Shadowing with long and vain regret
 The too fair promise of thy Spring.

Winthrop Mackworth Praed

THE VICAR

SOME years ago, ere time and taste
  Had turn'd our parish topsy-turvy,
When Darnel Park was Darnel Waste,
  And roads as little known as scurvy,
The man who lost his way between
  St. Mary's Hill and Sandy Thicket
Was always shown across the green,
  And guided to the parson's wicket.

Back flew the bolt of lissom lath ;
  Fair Margaret, in her tidy kirtle,
Led the lorn traveller up the path
  Through clean-clipp'd rows of box and
    myrtle ;
And Don and Sancho, Tramp and Tray,
  Upon the parlor steps collected,
Wagg'd all their tails, and seem'd to say,
  "Our master knows you ; you 're ex-
    pected."

Up rose the reverend Doctor Brown,
  Up rose the doctor's " winsome marrow ; "
The lady laid her knitting down,
  Her husband clasp'd his ponderous Bar-
    row.
Whate'er the stranger's caste or creed,
  Pundit or papist, saint or sinner,
He found a stable for his steed,
  And welcome for himself, and dinner.

If, when he reach'd his journey's end,
  And warm'd himself in court or college,
He had not gain'd an honest friend,
  And twenty curious scraps of knowledge ;
If he departed as he came,
  With no new light on love or liquor,—
Good sooth, the traveller was to blame,
  And not the vicarage, nor the vicar.

His talk was like a stream which runs
  With rapid change from rocks to roses ;
It slipp'd from politics to puns ;
  It pass'd from Mahomet to Moses ;
Beginning with the laws which keep
  The planets in their radiant courses,
And ending with some precept deep
  For dressing eels or shoeing horses.

He was a shrewd and sound divine,
  Of loud dissent the mortal terror ;

And when, by dint of page and line,
  He 'stablish'd truth or startled error,
The Baptist found him far too deep,
  The Deist sigh'd with saving sorrow,
And the lean Levite went to sleep
  And dream'd of tasting pork to-morrow.

His sermon never said or show'd
  That earth is foul, that heaven is gracious,
Without refreshment on the road
  From Jerome, or from Athanasius ;
And sure a righteous zeal inspir'd
  The hand and head that penn'd and
    plann'd them,
For all who understood admir'd,
  And some who did not understand them.

He wrote too, in a quiet way,
  Small treatises, and smaller verses,
And sage remarks on chalk and clay,
  And hints to noble lords and nurses ;
True histories of last year's ghost ;
  Lines to a ringlet or a turban ;
And trifles to the Morning Post,
  And nothings for Sylvanus Urban.

He did not think all mischief fair,
  Although he had a knack of joking ;
He did not make himself a bear,
  Although he had a taste for smoking ;
And when religious sects ran mad,
  He held, in spite of all his learning,
That if a man's belief is bad,
  It will not be improv'd by burning.

And he was kind, and lov'd to sit
  In the low hut or garnish'd cottage,
And praise the farmer's homely wit,
  And share the widow's homelier pottage.
At his approach complaint grew mild,
  And when his hand unbarr'd the shutter
The clammy lips of fever smil'd
  The welcome which they could not utter.

He always had a tale for me
  Of Julius Cæsar or of Venus ;
From him I learn'd the rule of three,
  Cat's-cradle, leap-frog, and Quæ genus.
I used to singe his powder'd wig,
  To steal the staff he put such trust in,
And make the puppy dance a jig
  When he began to quote Augustine.

Alack, the change ! In vain I look
For haunts in which my boyhood trifled ;
The level lawn, the trickling brook,
The trees I climb'd, the beds I rifled.
The church is larger than before,
You reach it by a carriage entry :
It holds three hundred people more,
And pews are fitted for the gentry.

Sit in the vicar's seat : you 'll hear
The doctrine of a gentle Johnian,
Whose hand is white, whose voice is
    clear,
Whose tone is very Ciceronian.
Where is the old man laid ?   Look
   down,
And construe on the slab before you :
" Hic jacet Gulielmus Brown,
Vir nullâ non donandus lauro."

THE NEWLY–WEDDED

Now the rite is duly done,
Now the word is spoken,

And the spell has made us one
  Which may ne'er be broken ;
Rest we, dearest, in our home,
  Roam we o'er the heather :
We shall rest, and we shall roam,
  Shall we not ? together.

From this hour the summer rose
  Sweeter breathes to charm us ;
From this hour the winter snows
  Lighter fall to harm us :
Fair or foul — on land or sea —
  Come the wind or weather,
Best and worst, whate'er they be,
  We shall share together.

Death, who friend from friend can part,
  Brother rend from brother,
Shall but link us, heart and heart,
  Closer to each other :
We will call his anger play,
  Deem his dart a feather,
When we meet him on our way
  Hand in hand together.

Charles Hartley Langhorne

THEOCRITUS

THEOCRITUS ! Theocritus ! ah, thou hadst
  pleasant dreams
Of the crystal spring Burinna, and the
  Haleus' murmuring streams ;
Of Physcus, and Neaethus, and fair Are-
  thusa's fount,
Of Lacinion's beetling crag, and Latymnus'
  woody mount ;
Of the fretted rocks and antres hoar that
  overhang the sea,
And the sapphire sky and thymy plains of
  thy own sweet Sicily ;
And of the nymphs of Sicily, that dwelt in
  oak and pine —
Theocritus ! Theocritus ! what pleasant
  dreams were thine !

And of the merry rustics who tend the goats
  and sheep,
And the maids who trip to milk the cows
  at morning's dewy peep,
Of Clearista with her locks of brightest
  sunny hair,

And the saucy girl Eunica, and sweet Chloe
  kind and fair ;
And of those highly favor'd ones, Endymion
  and Adonis,
Loved by Selena the divine, and the beau-
  teous Dionis ;
Of the silky-hair'd caprella, and the gentle
  lowing kine —
Theocritus ! Theocritus ! what pleasant
  dreams were thine !

Of the spring time, and the summer, and
  the zephyr's balmy breeze ;
Of the dainty flowers, and waving elms,
  and the yellow humming bees ;
Of the rustling poplar and the oak, the tam-
  arisk and the beech,
The dog-rose and anemone, — thou hadst
  a dream of each !
Of the galingale and hyacinth, and the lily's
  snowy hue,
The couch-grass, and green maiden-hair,
  and celandine pale blue,
The gold-bedropt cassidony, the fern, and
  sweet woodbine —

Theocritus ! Theocritus ! what pleasant
dreams were thine !

Of the merry harvest-home, all beneath the
good green tree,
The poppies and the spikes of corn, the
shouting and the glee
Of the lads so blithe and healthy, and the
girls so gay and neat,
And the dance they lead around the tree
with ever twinkling feet ;
And the bushy piles of lentisk to rest the
aching brow,
And reach and pluck the damson down from
the overladen bough,
And munch the roasted bean at ease, and
quaff the Ptelean wine —
Theocritus ! Theocritus ! what pleasant
dreams were thine !

And higher dreams were thine to dream —
of Heracles the brave,
And Polydeukes good at need, and Castor
strong to save ;
Of Dionysius and the woe he wrought the
Theban king ;

And of Zeus the mighty centre of Olympus'
glittering ring ;
Of Tiresias, the blind old man, the fam'd
Aonian seer ;
Of Hecatè, and Cthonian Dis, whom all
mankind revere ;
And of Daphnis lying down to die beneath
the leafy vine —
Theocritus ! Theocritus ! what pleasant
dreams were thine !

But mostly sweet and soft thy dreams —
of Cypris' loving kiss,
Of the dark-haired maids of Corinth, and
the feasts of Sybaris ;
Of alabaster vases of Assyrian perfume,
Of ebony, and gold, and pomp, and softly-
curtain'd room ;
Of Faunus piping in the woods to the Sa-
tyrs' noisy rout,
And the saucy Panisks mocking him with
many a jeer and flout ;
And of the tender-footed Hours, and
Pieria's tuneful Nine —
Theocritus ! Theocritus ! what pleasant
dreams were thine !

THE ROISTERERS

Richard Harris Barham

("THOMAS INGOLDSBY")

THE JACKDAW OF RHEIMS

The Jackdaw sat on the Cardinal's chair !
Bishop and abbot and prior were there ;
Many a monk, and many a friar,
Many a knight, and many a squire,
With a great many more of lesser degree, —
In sooth, a goodly company ;
And they serv'd the Lord Primate on
bended knee.
Never, I ween,
Was a prouder seen,
Read of in books, or dreamt of in dreams,
Than the Cardinal Lord Archbishop of
Rheims !

In and out
Through the motley rout,
That little Jackdaw kept hopping about ;

Here and there
Like a dog in a fair,
Over comfits and cates,
And dishes and plates,
Cowl and cope, and rochet and pall,
Mitre and crosier ! he hopp'd upon all !
With a saucy air,
He perch'd on the chair
Where, in state, the great Lord Cardinal sat,
In the great Lord Cardinal's great red hat ;
And he peer'd in the face
Of his Lordship's Grace,
With a satisfied look, as if he would say,
"We two are the greatest folks here to-
day ! "
And the priests, with awe,
As such freaks they saw,
Said, "The Devil must be in that little
Jackdaw ! "

The feast was over, the board was clear'd,
The flawns and the custards had all disap-
          pear'd,
And six little Singing-boys, — dear little
          souls !
In nice clean faces, and nice white stoles,
          Came in order due,
          Two by two,
Marching that grand refectory through.
A nice little boy held a golden ewer,
Emboss'd and fill'd with water, as pure
As any that flows between Rheims and
          Namur,
Which a nice little boy stood ready to catch
In a fine golden hand-basin made to match.
Two nice little boys, rather more grown,
Carried   lavender-water   and   eau-de-Co-
          logne ;
And a nice little boy had a nice cake of soap,
Worthy of washing the hands of the Pope.
          One little boy more
          A napkin bore,
Of   the   best   white   diaper,   fringed   with
          pink,
And a Cardinal's hat mark'd in " permanent
          ink."

The great Lord Cardinal turns at the sight
Of these nice little boys dress'd all in white :
          From his finger he draws
          His costly turquoise ;
And, not thinking at all about little Jack-
          daws,
          Deposits it straight
          By the side of his plate,
While the nice little boys on his Eminence
          wait ;
Till, when nobody 's dreaming of any such
          thing,
That little Jackdaw hops off with the ring !
     .   .   .   .
          There 's a cry and a shout,
          And a deuce of a rout,
And nobody seems to know what they 're
          about,
But the monks have their pockets all turn'd
          inside out ;
          The friars are kneeling,
          And hunting, and feeling
The carpet, the floor, and the walls, and the
          ceiling.
          The Cardinal drew
          Off each plum-color'd shoe,
And left his red stockings expos'd to the
          view :

          He peeps, and he feels
          In the toes and the heels ;
They turn up the dishes, — they turn up
          the plates, —
They take up the poker and poke out the
          grates,
          — They turn up the rugs,
          They examine the mugs :
          But no ! — no such thing ;
          They can't find THE RING !
And the Abbot declar'd that, " when no-
          body twigg'd it,
Some rascal or other had popp'd in and
          prigg'd it ! "

The Cardinal rose with a dignified look,
He call'd for his candle, his bell, and his
          book :
          In holy anger, and pious grief,
          He solemnly curs'd that rascally thief !
He curs'd him at board, he curs'd him
          in bed,
From the sole of his foot to the crown of
          his head !
He curs'd him in sleeping, that every
          night
He should dream of the devil, and wake
          in a fright ;
He curs'd him in eating, he curs'd him
          in drinking,
He curs'd him in coughing, in sneezing,
          in winking ;
He curs'd him in sitting, in standing, in
          lying ;
He curs'd him in walking, in riding, in
          flying ;
He curs'd him in living, he curs'd him
          in dying !
Never was heard such a terrible curse !
          But what gave rise
          To no little surprise,
Nobody seem'd one penny the worse !

          The day was gone,
          The night came on,
The monks and the friars they search'd till
          dawn ;
          When the sacristan saw,
          On crumpled claw,
Come limping a poor little lame Jack-
          daw.
          No longer gay,
          As on yesterday;
His feathers all seem'd to be turn'd the
          wrong way;

His pinions droop'd — he could hardly stand,
His head was as bald as the palm of your hand ;
His eye so dim,
So wasted each limb,
That, heedless of grammar, they all cried,
" THAT 'S HIM !
That 's the scamp that has done this scandalous thing !
That 's the thief that has got my Lord Cardinal's Ring ! "
The poor little Jackdaw,
When the monks he saw,
Feebly gave vent to the ghost of a caw ;
And turn'd his bald head, as much as to say,
" Pray, be so good as to walk this way ! "
Slower and slower
He limp'd on before,
Till they came to the back of the belfry-door,
Where the first thing they saw,
Midst the sticks and the straw,
Was the RING, in the nest of that little Jackdaw.

Then the great Lord Cardinal call'd for his book,
And off that terrible curse he took ;
The mute expression
Serv'd in lieu of confession,
And, being thus coupled with full restitution,
The Jackdaw got plenary absolution !
— When those words were heard,
That poor little bird
Was so changed in a moment, 't was really absurd.
He grew sleek and fat ;
In addition to that,
A fresh crop of feathers came thick as a mat.
His tail waggled more
Even than before ;
But no longer it wagg'd with an impudent air,
No longer he perch'd on the Cardinal's chair.
He hopp'd now about
With a gait devout ;
At matins, at vespers, he never was out ;
And, so far from any more pilfering deeds,
He always seem'd telling the Confessor's beads.

If any one lied, or if any one swore,
Or slumber'd in pray'r-time and happen'd to snore,
That good Jackdaw
Would give a great " Caw ! "
As much as to say, " Don't do so any more ! "
While many remark'd, as his manners they saw,
That they " never had known such a pious Jackdaw ! "
He long liv'd the pride
Of that country side,
And at last in the odor of sanctity died ;
When, as words were too faint
His merits to paint,
The Conclave determin'd to make him a Saint ;
And on newly-made Saints and Popes, as you know,
It 's the custom, at Rome, new names to bestow,
So they canoniz'd him by the name of Jem Crow !

MR. BARNEY MAGUIRE'S ACCOUNT OF THE CORONATION

Och ! the Coronation ! what celebration
For emulation can with it compare ?
When to Westminster the Royal Spinster,
And the Duke of Leinster, all in order did repair !
'T was there you 'd see the New Polishemen
Make a scrimmage at half after four,
And the Lords and Ladies, and the Miss O'Gradys,
All standing round before the Abbey door.

Their pillows scorning, that self-same morning
Themselves adorning, all by the candle-light,
With roses and lilies, and daffy-down-dillies
And gould and jewels, and rich di'monds bright.
And then approaches five hundred coaches,
With Gineral Dullbeak. — Och ! 't was mighty fine
To see how asy bould Corporal Casey,
With his sword drawn, prancing made them kape the line.

Then the Guns' alarums, and the King of
    Arums,
All in his Garters and his Clarence shoes,
Opening the massy doors to the bould Am-
    bassydors,
The Prince of Potboys, and great hay-
    then Jews :
'T would have made you crazy to see Ester-
    hazy
All jool's from his jasey to his di'mond
    boots,
With Alderman Harmer, and that swate
    charmer
The famale heiress, Miss Anjā-ly Coutts.

And Wellington, walking with his swoord
    drawn, talking
To Hill and Hardinge, haroes of great
    fame :
And Sir De Lacy, and the Duke Dalmasey
    (They call'd him Sowlt afore he changed
    his name),
Themselves presading Lord Melbourne,
    lading
The Queen, the darling, to her royal chair,
And that fine ould fellow, the Duke of Pell-
    Mello,
The Queen of Portingal's Chargy-de-fair.

Then the noble Prussians, likewise the
    Russians,
In fine laced jackets with their goulden
    cuffs,
And the Bavarians, and the proud Hunga-
    rians,
And Everythingarians all in furs and
    muffs.
Then Misther Spaker, with Misther Pays
    the Quaker,
All in the gallery you might persave ;
But Lord Brougham was missing, and gone
    a-fishing,
Ounly crass Lord Essex would not give
    him lave.

There was Baron Alten himself exalting,
    And Prince Von Schwartzenburg, and
    many more ;
Och ! I 'd be bother'd and entirely smoth-
    er'd
To tell the half of 'em was to the fore ;
With the swate Peeresses, in their crowns
    and dresses,
And Aldermanesses, and the Boord of
    Works ;

But Mehemet Ali said, quite gintaly,
    " I 'd be proud to see the likes among the
    Turks ! "

Then the Queen, Heaven bless her ! och !
    they did dress her
In her purple garaments and her goulden
    Crown ;
Like Venus, or Hebe, or the Queen of
    Sheby,
With eight young ladies houlding up her
    gown.
Sure 't was grand to see her, also for to he-ar
    The big drums bating, and the trumpets
    blow,
And Sir George Smart ! Oh ! he play'd a
    Consarto,
With his four and twenty fiddlers all on
    a row.

Then the Lord Archbishop held a goulden
    dish up,
For to resave her bounty and great
    wealth,
Saying, " Plase your glory, great Queen
    Vic-tory,
Ye 'll give the Clargy lave to drink your
    health ! "
Then his Riverence, retrating, discoors'd
    the mating :
" Boys ! Here 's your Queen ! deny it if
    you can ;
And if any bould traitor, or infarior cray-
    thur
Sneezes at that, I 'd like to see the man ! "

Then the Nobles kneeling to the Pow'rs
    appealing,
" Heaven send your Majesty a glorious
    reign ! "
And Sir Claudius Hunter he did confront
    her,
All in his scarlet gown and goulden
    chain.
The great Lord May'r, too, sat in his chair
    too,
But mighty sarious, looking fit to cry,
For the Earl of Surrey, all in his hurry,
Throwing the thirteens, hit him in his
    eye.

Then there was preaching, and good store
    of speeching,
With Dukes and Marquises on bended
    knee ;

And they did splash her with real Macas-
　shur,
And the Queen said, "Ah ! then thank ye
　all for me ! "
Then the trumpets braying, and the organ
　playing,
And the sweet trombones, with their sil-
　ver tones ;
But Lord Rolle was rolling ; — 't was
　mighty consoling
To think his Lordship did not break his
　bones !

Then the crames and custard, and the beef
　and mustard,
All on the tombstones like a poultherer's
　shop ;
With lobsters and white-bait, and other
　swate-meats,
And wine and nagus, and Imparial Pop !

There was cakes and apples in all the
　Chapels,
With fine polonies, and rich mellow
　pears, —
Och ! the Count Von Strogonoff, sure he
　got prog enough,
The sly ould Divil, undernathe the stairs.

Then the cannons thunder'd, and the people
　wonder'd,
Crying, "God save Victoria, our Royal
　Queen ! " —
Och ! if myself should live to be a hun-
　dred,
Sure it 's the proudest day that I 'll have
　seen ! —
And now, I 've ended, what I pretended,
This narration splendid in swate poe-thry,
Ye dear bewitcher, just hand the pitcher,
Faith, it 's myself that 's getting dhry.

William Maginn

THE IRISHMAN AND THE LADY

THERE was a lady liv'd at Leith,
　A lady very stylish, man ;
And yet, in spite of all her teeth,
　She fell in love with an Irishman —
　　A nasty, ugly Irishman,
　　A wild, tremendous Irishman,
　A tearing, swearing, thumping, bumping,
　　ranting, roaring Irishman.

His face was no ways beautiful,
　For with small-pox 't was scarr'd across;
And the shoulders of the ugly dog
　Were almost double a yard across.
　　Oh, the lump of an Irishman,
　　The whiskey-devouring Irishman,
　The great he-rogue with his wonderful
　　brogue — the fighting, rioting Irish-
　　man.

One of his eyes was bottle-green,
　And the other eye was out, my dear ;
And the calves of his wicked-looking legs
　Were more than two feet about, my dear.
　　Oh, the great big Irishman,
　　The rattling, battling Irishman —
　The stamping, ramping, swaggering, stag-
　　gering, leathering swash of an Irish-
　　man.

He took so much of Lundy-foot
　That he used to snort and snuffle — O !
And in shape and size the fellow's neck
　Was as bad as the neck of a buffalo.
　　Oh, the horrible Irishman,
　　The thundering, blundering Irishman—
　The slashing, dashing, smashing, lashing,
　　thrashing, hashing Irishman.

His name was a terrible name, indeed,
　Being Timothy Thady Mulligan ;
And whenever he emptied his tumbler of
　punch
　He 'd not rest till he fill'd it full
　　again.
　　The boozing, bruising Irishman,
　　The 'toxicated Irishman —
　The whiskey, frisky, rummy, gummy,
　　brandy, no dandy Irishman.

This was the lad the lady lov'd,
　Like all the girls of quality ;
And he broke the skulls of the men of
　Leith,
　Just by the way of jollity.
　　Oh, the leathering Irishman,
　　The barbarous, savage Irishman —
　The hearts of the maids, and the gentle-
　　men's heads, were bother'd I 'm sure
　　by this Irishman.

THE SOLDIER-BOY

I GIVE my soldier-boy a blade,
  In fair Damascus fashion'd well ;
Who first the glittering falchion sway'd,
  Who first beneath its fury fell,
I know not ; but I hope to know
  That for no mean or hireling trade,
To guard no feeling base or low,
  I give my soldier-boy a blade.

Cool, calm, and clear, the lucid flood
  In which its tempering work was done :
As calm, as clear, as cool of mood,
  Be thou whene'er it sees the sun.

For country's claim, at honor's call,
  For outraged friend, insulted maid,
At mercy's voice to bid it fall,
  I give my soldier-boy a blade.

The eye which mark'd its peerless edge,
  The hand that weigh'd its balanced poise,
Anvil and pincers, forge and wedge,
  Are gone with all their flame and noise —
And still the gleaming sword remains ;
  So, when in dust I low am laid,
Remember by these heart-felt strains,
  I gave my soldier-boy a blade.

Francis Mahony

("FATHER PROUT")

THE SHANDON BELLS

Sabbata pango ;
Fvnera plango ;
Solemnia clango.
INSCRIPTION ON AN OLD BELL.

WITH deep affection
And recollection
I often think of
  Those Shandon bells,
Whose sounds so wild would,
In the days of childhood,
Fling round my cradle
  Their magic spells.
On this I ponder
Where'er I wander,
And thus grow fonder,
  Sweet Cork, of thee,
With thy bells of Shandon,
That sound so grand on
The pleasant waters
  Of the river Lee.

I've heard bells chiming
Full many a clime in,
Tolling sublime in
  Cathedral shrine,
While at a glibe rate
Brass tongues would vibrate —
But all their music
  Spoke naught like thine ;
For memory, dwelling
On each proud swelling
Of the belfry, knelling
  Its bold notes free,
Made the bells of Shandon
Sound far more grand on

The pleasant waters
  Of the river Lee.

I've heard bells tolling
Old Adrian's Mole in,
Their thunder rolling
  From the Vatican,
And cymbals glorious
Swinging uproarious
In the gorgeous turrets
  Of Notre Dame ;
But thy sounds were sweeter
Than the dome of Peter
Flings o'er the Tiber,
  Pealing solemnly :
Oh ! the bells of Shandon
Sound far more grand on
The pleasant waters
  Of the river Lee.

There's a bell in Moscow ;
While on tower and kiosk oh !
In Saint Sophia
  The Turkman gets,
And loud in air
Calls men to prayer,
From the tapering summit
  Of tall minarets.
Such empty phantom
I freely grant them ;
But there's an anthem
  More dear to me :
'T is the bells of Shandon,
That sound so grand on
The pleasant waters
  Of the river Lee.

MEDITATIVE POETS

William Sidney Walker

DEATH'S ALCHEMY

THEY say that thou wert lovely on thy bier,
More lovely than in life ; that when the
   thrall
Of earth was loos'd, it seem'd as though a
   pall
Of years were lifted, and thou didst appear
Such as of old amidst thy home's calm
   sphere
Thou sat'st, a kindly Presence felt by all

In joy or grief, from morn to evening-
   fall,
The peaceful Genius of that mansion dear.
Was it the craft of all-persuading Love
That wrought this marvel ? or is Death in-
   deed
A mighty master, gifted from above
With alchemy benign, to wounded hearts
Minist'ring thus, by quaint and subtle arts,
Strange comfort, whereon after-thought
   may feed ?

Hartley Coleridge

TO THE NAUTILUS

WHERE Ausonian summers glowing
Warm the deep to life and joyance,
And gentle zephyrs, nimbly blowing,
Wanton with the waves that flowing
By many a land of ancient glory,
And many an isle renown'd in story,
Leap along with gladsome buoyance,
    There, Marinere,
      Dost thou appear
In faery pinnace gaily flashing,
Through the white foam proudly dash-
   ing,
The joyous playmate of the buxom breeze,
The fearless fondling of the mighty seas.

Thou the light sail boldly spreadest,
O'er the furrow'd waters gliding,
Thou nor wreck nor foeman dreadest,
Thou nor helm nor compass needest,
While the sun is bright above thee,
While the bounding surges love thee :
In their deepening bosoms hiding
    Thou canst not fear,
    Small Marinere,
For though the tides with restless motion
Bear thee to the desert ocean,
Far as the ocean stretches to the sky,
'T is all thine own, 't is all thy empery.

Lame is art, and her endeavor
Follows nature's course but slowly,
Guessing, toiling, seeking ever,
Still improving, perfect never ;
Little Nautilus, thou showest
Deeper wisdom than thou knowest,
Lore, which man should study lowly :
    Bold faith and cheer,
    Small Marinere,
Are thine within thy pearly dwelling :
Thine, a law of life compelling,
Obedience, perfect, simple, glad and free,
To the great will that animates the sea.

THE BIRTH OF SPEECH

WHAT was't awaken'd first the untried
   ear
Of that sole man who was all human kind ?
Was it the gladsome welcome of the wind,
Stirring the leaves that never yet were sere ?
The four mellifluous streams which flow'd so
   near,
Their lulling murmurs all in one combin'd ?
The note of bird unnam'd ? The startled
   hind
Bursting the brake — in wonder, not in fear,
Of her new lord ? Or did the holy ground
Send forth mysterious melody to greet
The gracious pressure of immaculate feet ?

Did viewless seraphs rustle all around,
Making sweet music out of air as sweet,
Or his own voice awake him with its sound ?

WHITHER ?

WHITHER is gone the wisdom and the power
That ancient sages scatter'd with the notes
Of thought-suggesting lyres ?   The music
   floats
In the void air ; e'en at this breathing hour,
In every cell and every blooming bower
The sweetness of old lays is hovering still :
But the strong soul, the self-constraining
   will,
The rugged root that bare the winsome
   flower
Is weak and wither'd.   Were we like the
   Fays
That sweetly nestle in the foxglove bells,
Or lurk and murmur in the rose-lipp'd shells
Which Neptune to the earth for quit-rent
   pays,
Then might our pretty modern Philomels
Sustain our spirits with their roundelays.

TO SHAKESPEARE

THE soul of man is larger than the sky,
Deeper than ocean or the abysmal dark
Of the unfathom'd centre.   Like that Ark
Which in its sacred hold uplifted high,
O'er the drown'd hills, the human family,
And stock reserv'd of every living kind,
So, in the compass of the single mind,
The seeds and pregnant forms in essence lie,
That make all worlds.   Great Poet, 't was
   thy art
To know thyself, and in thyself to be
Whate'er love, hate, ambition, destiny,
Or the firm, fatal purpose of the heart,
Can make of Man.   Yet thou wert still the
   same,
Serene of thought, unhurt by thy own flame.

IDEALITY

THE vale of Tempe had in vain been fair,
Green Ida never deem'd the nurse of Jove ;
Each fabled stream, beneath its covert
   grove,
Had idly murmur'd to the idle air ;

The shaggy wolf had kept his horrid lair
In Delphi's cell, and old Trophonius'
   cave,
And the wild wailing of the Ionian wave
Had never blended with the sweet de-
   spair
Of Sappho's death-song : if the sight in-
   spir'd
Saw only what the visual organs show,
If heaven-born phantasy no more requir'd
Than what within the sphere of sense may
   grow.
The beauty to perceive of earthly things,
The mounting soul must heavenward prune
   her wings.

SONG

SHE is not fair to outward view
   As many maidens be,
Her loveliness I never knew
   Until she smil'd on me ;
Oh! then I saw her eye was bright,
A well of love, a spring of light.

But now her looks are coy and cold,
   To mine they ne'er reply,
And yet I cease not to behold
   The love-light in her eye :
Her very frowns are fairer far
Than smiles of other maidens are.

PRAYER

BE not afraid to pray — to pray is right.
Pray, if thou canst, with hope; but ever
   pray,
Though hope be weak, or sick with long
   delay ;
Pray in the darkness, if there be no light.
Far is the time, remote from human sight,
When war and discord on the earth shall
   cease ;
Yet every prayer for universal peace
Avails the blessed time to expedite.
Whate'er is good to wish, ask that of
   Heaven,
Though it be what thou canst not hope to
   see :
Pray to be perfect, though material leaven
Forbid the spirit so on earth to be;
But if for any wish thou darest not pray,
Then pray to God to cast that wish away.

"MULTUM DILEXIT"

SHE sat and wept beside His feet; the weight
Of sin oppress'd her heart; for all the blame,
And the poor malice of the worldly shame,
To her was past, extinct, and out of date :
Only the sin remain'd, — the leprous state;
She would be melted by the heat of love,
By fires far fiercer than are blown to prove
And purge the silver ore adulterate.

She sat and wept, and with her untress'd
  hair
Still wip'd the feet she was so bless'd to
  touch ;
And He wip'd off the soiling of despair
From her sweet soul, because she lov'd so
  much.
I am a sinner, full of doubts and fears :
Make me a humble thing of love and
  tears.

Anna Jameson

TAKE ME, MOTHER EARTH

TAKE me, Mother Earth, to thy cold breast,
And fold me there in everlasting rest !
    The long day is o'er,
    I 'm weary, I would sleep ;
    But deep, deep,
    Never to waken more.

I have had joy and sorrow, I have prov'd
What life could give, have lov'd, and been
    belov'd ;

    I am sick, and heart-sore,
    And weary; let me sleep ;
    But deep, deep,
    Never to waken more.

To thy dark chamber, Mother Earth, I
    come,
Prepare thy dreamless bed in my last home:
    Shut down the marble door,
    And leave me ! Let me sleep ;
    But deep, deep,
    Never to waken more !

Chauncy Hare Townshend

THY JOY IN SORROW

GIVE me thy joy in sorrow, gracious Lord,
And sorrow's self shall like to joy appear !
Although the world should waver in its
    sphere
I tremble not if Thou thy peace afford ;
But, Thou withdrawn, I am but as a chord
That vibrates to the pulse of hope and fear :
Nor rest I more than harps which to the
    air

Must answer when we place their tuneful
    board
Against the blast, which thrill unmeaning
    woe
Even in their sweetness. So no earthly wing
E'er sweeps me but to sadden.   Oh, place
    Thou
My heart beyond the world's sad vibrat-
    ing —
And where but in Thyself ?   Oh, circle me,
That I may feel no touches save of Thee.

John Henry Newman

THE SIGN OF THE CROSS

WHENE'ER across this sinful flesh of
    mine
I draw the Holy Sign,

All good thoughts stir within me, and re-
    new
Their slumbering strength divine ;
Till there springs up a courage high and true
To suffer and to do.

And who shall say, but hateful spirits
  around,
For their brief hour unbound,
Shudder to see, and wail their overthrow ?
While on far heathen ground
Some lonely Saint hails the fresh odor,
  though
Its source he cannot know.

ENGLAND

TYRE of the West, and glorying in the name
More than in Faith's pure fame !
O trust not crafty fort nor rock renown'd
Earn'd upon hostile ground ;
Wielding Trade's master-keys, at thy proud
  will
To lock or loose its waters, England ! trust
  not still.

Dread thine own power ! Since haughty
  Babel's prime,
High towers have been man's crime.
Since her hoar age, when the huge moat
  lay bare,.
Strongholds have been man's snare.
Thy nest is in the crags; ah, refuge frail !
Mad counsel in its hour, or traitors, will
  prevail.

He who scann'd Sodom for His righteous
  men
Still spares thee for thy ten ;
But, should vain tongues the Bride of
  Heaven defy,
He will not pass thee by ;
For, as earth's kings welcome their spotless
  guest,
So gives He them by turn, to suffer or be
  blest.

REVERSES

WHEN mirth is full and free,
Some sudden gloom shall be ;
When haughty power mounts high,
The Watcher's axe is nigh.
All growth has bound ; when greatest found,
  It hastes to die.

When the rich town, that long
Has lain its huts among,
Uprears its pageants vast,
And vaunts — it shall not last !
Bright tints that shine are but a sign
  Of summer past.

And when thine eye surveys,
With fond adoring gaze,
And yearning heart, thy friend,
Love to its grave doth tend.
All gifts below, save Truth, but grow
  Towards an end.

THE PILLAR OF THE CLOUD

LEAD, Kindly Light, amid the encircling
  gloom,
Lead Thou me on !
The night is dark, and I am far from
  home —
Lead Thou me on !
Keep Thou my feet ; I do not ask to see
The distant scene, — one step enough for
  me.

I was not ever thus, nor pray'd that Thou
  Shouldst lead me on.
I lov'd to choose and see my path ; but
  now
Lead Thou me on !
I lov'd the garish day, and, spite of
  fears,
Pride rul'd my will : remember not past
  years.

So long Thy power hath bless'd me, sure it
  still
Will lead me on,
O'er moor and fen, o'er crag and torrent,
  till
The night is gone ;
And with the morn those angel faces
  smile
Which I have lov'd long since, and lost
  awhile.

THE ELEMENTS

(A TRAGIC CHORUS)

MAN is permitted much
To scan and learn
In Nature's frame ;
Till he well-nigh can tame
Brute mischiefs, and can touch
Invisible things, and turn
All warring ills to purposes of good.
Thus, as a god below,
He can control,
And harmonize, what seems amiss to flow
As sever'd from the whole
And dimly understood.

But o'er the elements
　　One Hand alone,
　　One Hand has sway.
What influence day by day
In straiter belt prevents
The impious Ocean, thrown
Alternate o'er the ever-sounding shore ?
　　Or who has eye to trace
　　How the Plague came ?
Forerun the doublings of the Tempest's
　　race ?
　　Or the Air's weight and flame
　　On a set scale explore ?

Thus God has will'd
That man, when fully skill'd,
Still gropes in twilight dim;
Encompass'd all his hours
　　By fearfullest powers
Inflexible to him.
That so he may discern
　　His feebleness,
And e'en for earth's success
To Him in wisdom turn,
Who holds for us the keys of either
　　home,
Earth and the world to come.

Sara Coleridge

FROM "PHANTASMION"

ONE FACE ALONE

ONE face alone, one face alone,
　　These eyes require ;
But, when that long'd-for sight is shown,
　　What fatal fire
Shoots through my veins a keen and liquid
　　flame,
That melts each fibre of my wasting frame!

One voice alone, one voice alone,
　　I pine to hear ;
But, when its meek mellifluous tone
　　Usurps mine ear,
Those slavish chains about my soul are
　　wound,
Which ne'er, till death itself, can be un-
　　bound.

One gentle hand, one gentle hand,
　　I fain would hold ;
But, when it seems at my command,
　　My own grows cold ;

Then low to earth I bend in sickly swoon,
Like lilies drooping 'mid the blaze of
　　noon.

HE CAME UNLOOK'D FOR

HE came unlook'd for, undesir'd,
A sunrise in the northern sky,
More than the brightest dawn admir'd,
To shine and then forever fly.

His love, conferr'd without a claim,
Perchance was like the fitful blaze,
Which lives to light a steadier flame,
And, while that strengthens, fast decays.

Glad fawn along the forest springing,
Gay birds that breeze-like stir the leaves,
Why hither haste, no message bringing,
To solace one that deeply grieves ?

Thou star that dost the skies adorn,
So brightly heralding the day,
Bring one more welcome than the morn,
Or still in night's dark prison stay.

Charles Whitehead

AS YONDER LAMP

As yonder lamp in my vacated room
With arduous flame disputes the darksome
　　night,
And can, with its involuntary light,

But lifeless things that near it stand, illume;
Yet all the while it doth itself consume ;
And, ere the sun begin its heavenly height
With courier beams that meet the shep-
　　herd's sight,
There, whence its life arose, shall be its
　　tomb : —

So wastes my life away. Perforce confin'd
To common things, a limit to its sphere,
It shines on worthless trifles undesign'd,

With fainter ray each hour imprison'd here.
Alas! to know that the consuming mind
Shall leave its lamp cold, ere the sun appear!

John Sterling

SHAKESPEARE

How little fades from earth when sink to
    rest
The hours and cares that mov'd a great
    man's breast!
Though naught of all we saw the grave may
    spare,
His life pervades the world's impregnate air;
Though Shakespeare's dust beneath our
    footsteps lies,
His spirit breathes amid his•native skies ;
With meaning won from him forever glows
Each air that England feels, and star it
    knows ;
His whisper'd words from many a mother's
    voice
Can make her sleeping child in dreams re-
    joice,
And gleams from spheres he first conjoin'd
    to earth
Are blent with rays of each new morning's
    birth.
Amid the sights and tales of common things,
Leaf, flower, and bird, and wars, and deaths
    of kings,
Of shore, and sea, and nature's daily round,
Of life that tills, and tombs that load the
    ground,
His visions mingle, swell, command, pace
    by,
And haunt with living presence heart and
    eye ;
And tones from him by other bosoms caught
Awaken flush and stir of mounting thought,
And the long sigh, and deep impassion'd
    thrill,
Rouse custom's trance, and spur the falter-
    ing will.
Above the goodly land more his than ours
He sits supreme enthron'd in skyey towers,
And sees the heroic brood of his creation
Teach larger life to his ennobled nation.
O shaping brain! O flashing fancy's hues !
O boundless heart kept fresh by pity's
    dews !

O wit humane and blithe ! O sense sublime
For each dim oracle of mantled Time !
Transcendent Form of Man ! in whom we
    read
Mankind's whole tale of Impulse, Thought,
    and Deed ;
Amid the expanse of years beholding thee,
We know how vast our world of life may be ;
Wherein, perchance, with aims as pure as
    thine,
Small tasks and strengths may be no less
    divine.

LOUIS XV

THE King with all his kingly train
Had left his Pompadour behind,
And forth he rode in Senart's wood
The royal beasts of chase to find.
That day by chance the Monarch mused,
And turning suddenly away,
He struck alone into a path
That far from crowds and courtiers lay.

He saw the pale green shadows play
Upon the brown untrodden earth ;
He saw the birds around him flit
As if he were of peasant birth ;
He saw the trees that know no king
But him who bears a woodland axe ;
He thought not, but he look'd about
Like one who skill in thinking lacks.

Then close to him a footstep fell,
And glad of human sound was he,
For truth to say he found himself
A weight from which he fain would flee.
But that which he would ne'er have guess'd
Before him now most plainly came ;
The man upon his weary back
A coffin bore of rudest frame.

"Why, who art thou ? " exclaim'd the
    King,
" And what is that I see thee bear ? "
" I am a laborer in the wood,
And 't is a coffin for Pierre.

Close by the royal hunting-lodge
You may have often seen him toil ;
But he will never work again,
And I for him must dig the soil."

The laborer ne'er had seen the King,
And this he thought was but a man,
Who made at first a moment's pause,
And then anew his talk began :
" I think I do remember now, —
He had a dark and glancing eye,
And I have seen his slender arm
With wondrous blows the pick-axe ply.

" Pray tell me, friend, what accident
Can thus have kill'd our good Pierre ? "
" Oh! nothing more than usual, Sir,
He died of living upon air.
'T was hunger kill'd the poor good man,
Who long on empty hopes relied ;
He could not pay gabell and tax,
And feed his children, so he died."

The man stopp'd short, and then went
        on, —
" It is, you know, a common thing ;
Our children's bread is eaten up
By Courtiers, Mistresses, and King."
The King look'd hard upon the man,
And afterwards the coffin eyed,
Then spurr'd to ask of Pompadour,
How came it that the peasants died.

TO A CHILD

DEAR child ! whom sleep can hardly tame,
As live and beautiful as flame,
Thou glancest round my graver hours
As if thy crown of wild-wood flowers
Were not by mortal forehead worn,
But on the summer breeze were borne,
Or on a mountain streamlet's waves
Came glistening down from dreamy caves.

With bright round cheek, amid whose glow
Delight and wonder come and go,
And eyes whose inward meanings play,
Congenial with the light of day,
And brow so calm, a home for Thought
Before he knows his dwelling wrought ;
Though wise indeed thou seemest not,
Thou brightenest well the wise man's lot.

That shout proclaims the undoubting mind,
That laughter leaves no ache behind ;
And in thy look and dance of glee,
Unforced, unthought of, simply free,
How weak the schoolman's formal art
Thy soul and body's bliss to part !
I hail thee Childhood's very Lord,
In gaze and glance, in voice and word.

In spite of all foreboding fear,
A thing thou art of present cheer ;
And thus to be belov'd and known
As is a rushy fountain's tone,
As is the forest's leafy shade,
Or blackbird's hidden serenade :
Thou art a flash that lights the whole ;
A gush from Nature's vernal soul.

And yet, dear Child ! within thee lives
A power that deeper feeling gives,
That makes thee more than light or air,
Than all things sweet and all things fair ;
And sweet and fair as aught may be,
Diviner life belongs to thee,
For 'mid thine aimless joys began
The perfect Heart and Will of Man.

Thus what thou art foreshows to me
How greater far thou soon shalt be ;
And while amid thy garlands blow
The winds that warbling come and go,
Ever within not loud but clear
Prophetic murmur fills the ear,
And says that every human birth
Anew discloses God to earth.

Jane Welsh Carlyle

TO A SWALLOW BUILDING
UNDER OUR EAVES

THOU too hast travell'd, little fluttering
        thing —

Hast seen the world, and now thy weary wing
        Thou too must rest.
But much, my little bird, couldst thou but
        tell,
I'd give to know why here thou lik'st so well
        To build thy nest.

For thou hast pass'd fair places in thy flight;
A world lay all beneath thee where to light;
   And, strange thy taste,
Of all the varied scenes that met thine eye,
Of all the spots for building 'neath the sky,
   To choose this waste.

Did fortune try thee ? was thy little purse
Perchance run low, and thou, afraid of
   worse,
   Felt here secure ?
Ah, no ! thou need'st not gold, thou happy
   one !
Thou know'st it not. Of all God's crea-
   tures, man
   Alone is poor.

What was it, then ? some mystic turn of
   thought
Caught under German eaves, and hither
   brought,
   Marring thine eye
For the world's loveliness, till thou art
   grown
A sober thing that dost but mope and moan,
   Not knowing why ?

Nay, if thy mind be sound, I need not
   ask,
Since here I see thee working at thy task
   With wing and beak.
A well-laid scheme doth that small head
   contain,
At which thou work'st, brave bird, with
   might and main,
   Nor more need'st seek.

In truth, I rather take it thou hast got
By instinct wise much sense about thy lot,
   And hast small care
Whether an Eden or a desert be
Thy home, so thou remainst alive, and
   free
   To skim the air.

God speed thee, pretty bird ; may thy small
   nest
With little ones all in good time be blest.
   I love thee much ;
For well thou managest that life of thine,
While I ! Oh, ask not what I do with
   mine !
   Would I were such !

Richard Chenevix Trench

AFTER THE BATTLE

WE crown'd the hard-won heights at
   length,
   Baptiz'd in flame and fire ;
We saw the foeman's sullen strength,
   That grimly made retire —

Saw close at hand, then saw more far
   Beneath the battle-smoke
The ridges of his shatter'd war,
   That broke and ever broke.

But one, an English household's pride,
   Dear many ways to me,
Who climb'd that death-path by my side,
   I sought, but could not see.

Last seen, what time our foremost rank
   That iron tempest tore ;
He touch'd, he scal'd the rampart bank —
   Seen then, and seen no more.

One friend to aid, I measur'd back
   With him that pathway dread ;
No fear to wander from our track —
   Its waymarks English dead.

Light thicken'd : but our search was
   crown'd,
   As we too well divin'd ;
And after briefest quest we found
   What we most fear'd to find.

His bosom with one death-shot riven,
   The warrior-boy lay low ;
His face was turn'd unto the heaven,
   His feet unto the foe.

As he had fallen upon the plain,
   Inviolate he lay ;
No ruffian spoiler's hand profane
   Had touch'd that noble clay.

And precious things he still retain'd,
   Which, by one distant hearth,

Lov'd tokens of the lov'd, had gain'd
A worth beyond all worth.

I treasur'd these for them who yet
Knew not their mighty wo ;
I softly seal'd his eyes, and set
One kiss upon his brow.

A decent grave we scoop'd him, where
Less thickly lay the dead,
And decently compos'd him there
Within that narrow bed.

O theme for manhood's bitter tears :
The beauty and the bloom
Of less than twenty summer years
Shut in that darksome tomb !

Of soldier-sire the soldier-son ;
Life's honor'd .eventide
One lives to close in England, one
In maiden battle died :

And they, that should have been the
mourn'd,
The mourners' parts obtain :
Such thoughts were ours, as we return'd
To earth its earth again.

Brief words we read of faith and prayer
Beside that hasty grave;
Then turn'd away, and left him there,
The gentle and the brave :

I calling back with thankful heart,
With thoughts to peace allied,
Hours when we two had knelt apart
Upon the lone hillside ;

And, comforted, I prais'd the grace
Which him had led to be
An early seeker of that Face
Which he should early see.

SONNET

ALL beautiful things bring sadness, nor
alone
Music, whereof that wisest poet spake ;
Because in us keen longings they awake
After the good for which we pine and groan,
From which exil'd we make continual
moan,
Till once again we may our spirits slake
At those clear streams, which man did first
forsake,
When he would dig for fountains of his
own.
All beauty makes us sad, yet not in vain :
For who would be ungracious to refuse,
Or not to use, this sadness without pain,
Whether it flows upon us from the hues
Of sunset, from the time of stars and
dews,
From the clear sky, or waters pure of
stain ?

Thomas Miller

THE OLD BARON

HIGH on a leaf-carv'd ancient oaken chair
The Norman Baron sat within his hall,
Wearied with a long chase by wold and
mere ;
His hunting spear was rear'd against the
wall ;
Upon the hearth-stone a large wood-fire
blaz'd,
Crackled, or smok'd, or hiss'd, as the green
boughs were rais'd.

Above an arch'd and iron-studded door,
The grim escutcheon's rude devices stood ;

On each side rear'd a black and gristly
boar,
With hearts and daggers grav'd on grounds
of blood,
And deep-dyed gules o'er which plum'd hel-
mets frown;
Beneath this motto ran, — "Beware ! I
trample down."

And high around were suits of armor placed,
And shields triangular, with the wild-boar's
head ;
Arrows, and bows, and swords the rafters
graced,
And red-deer's antlers their wide branches
spread ;

A rough wolf's hide was nail'd upon the wall,
Its white teeth clench'd as when it in the
    dell did fall.

An angel-lamp from the carv'd ceiling
    hung ;
Its outstretch'd wings the blazing oil con-
    tain'd,
While its long figure in the wide hall
    swung,
Blackening the roof to which its arms were
    chain'd ;
The iron hair fell backward like a veil,
And through the gusty door it sent a weary
    wail.

The heavy arras flutter'd in the wind
That through the grated windows sweeping
    came,
And in its foldings glitter'd hart and hind,
While hawk, and horse, and hound, and kir-
    tled dame,

Moved on the curtain'd waves, then sank in
    shade,
Just as the fitful wind along the arras
    played.

On the oak table, filled with blood-red wine,
A silver cup of quaint engraving stood,
On which a thin-limb'd stag of old design,
Chas'd by six long-ear'd dogs, made for a
    wood ;
Sounding a horn a huntsman stood in view,
Whose swollen cheeks uprais'd the silver as
    he blew.

At the old Baron's feet a wolf-dog lay,
Watching his features with unflinching eye;
An aged minstrel, whose long locks were
    gray,
On an old harp his wither'd hands did try ;
A crimson banner's rustling folds hung low,
And threw a rosy light upon his wrinkled
    brow.

John, Lord Hanmer

THE PINE WOODS

WE stand upon the moorish mountain side,
From age to age, a solemn company ;
There are no voices in our paths, but we
Hear the great whirlwinds roaring loud and
    wide ;
And like the sea-waves have our boughs
    replied,
From the beginning, to their stormy glee ;
The thunder rolls above us, and some tree

Smites with his bolt, yet doth the race
    abide,
Answering all times ; but joyous, when the
    sun
Glints on the peaks that clouds no longer
    bear,
And the young shoots to flourish have be-
    gun,
And the quick seeds through the blue
    odorous air
From the expanding cones fall one by one ;
And silence as in temples dwelleth there.

Lord Houghton

(RICHARD MONCKTON MILNES)

AN ENVOY TO AN AMERICAN
LADY

BEYOND the vague Atlantic deep,
Far as the farthest prairies sweep,
Where forest-glooms the nerve appal,
Where burns the radiant Western fall,

One duty lies on old and young, —
With filial piety to guard,
As on its greenest native sward,
The glory of the English tongue.
That ample speech ! That subtle speech !
Apt for the need of all and each :
Strong to endure, yet prompt to bend
Wherever human feelings tend.

Preserve its force — expand its powers ;
And through the maze of civic life,
In Letters, Commerce, even in Strife,
Forget not it is yours and ours.

THE BROOK-SIDE

I WANDER'D by the brook-side,
I wander'd by the mill ;
I could not hear the brook flow,
The noisy wheel was still ;
There was no burr of grasshopper,
No chirp of any bird,
But the beating of my own heart
Was all the sound I heard.

I sat beneath the elm-tree ;
I watch'd the long, long shade,
And, as it grew still longer,
I did not feel afraid ;
For I listen'd for a footfall,

I listen'd for a word,
But the beating of my own heart
Was all the sound I heard.

He came not, — no, he came not —
The night came on alone,
The little stars sat, one by one,
Each on his golden throne ;
The evening wind pass'd by my cheek,
The leaves above were stirr'd,
But the beating of my own heart
Was all the sound I heard.

Fast silent tears were flowing,
When something stood behind ;
A hand was on my shoulder,
I knew its touch was kind :
It drew me nearer — nearer,
We did not speak one word,
For the beating of our own hearts
Was all the sound we heard.

Frances Anne Kemble

THE BLACK WALL-FLOWER

I FOUND a flower in a desolate plot,
Where no man wrought, — by a deserted
    cot,
Where no man dwelt ; a strange, dark-
    color'd gem,
Black heavy buds on a pale leafless stem.
I pluck'd it, wondering, and with it hied
To my brave May, and showing it I cried :
"Look, what a dismal flower ! did ever
    bloom,
Born of our earth and air, wear such a
    gloom ?
It looks as it should grow out of a tomb :
Is it not mournful ? " " No," replied the
    child ;
And, gazing on it thoughtfully, she smil'd.
She knows each word of that great book of
    God,
Spread out between the blue sky and the
    sod :
" There are no mournful flowers — they are
    all glad ;
This is a solemn one, but not a sad."

Lo ! with the dawn the black buds open'd
    slowly.
Within each cup a color deep and holy,
As sacrificial blood, glow'd rich and red,
And through the velvet tissue mantling
    spread ;
While in the midst of this dark crimson
    heat
A precious golden heart did throb and
    beat ;
Through ruby leaves the morning light did
    shine,
Each mournful bud had grown a flow'r di-
    vine ;
And bitter sweet to senses and to soul,
A breathing came from them, that fill'd the
    whole
Of the surrounding tranced and sunny
    air
With its strange fragrance, like a silent
    prayer.
Then cried I, "From the earth's whole
    wreath I 'll borrow
No flower but thee ! thou exquisite type of
    sorrow ! "

FAITH

BETTER trust all and be deceiv'd,
And weep that trust, and that deceiv-
ing,
Than doubt one heart that, if believ'd,
Had blessed one's life with true believing.

Oh, in this mocking world, too fast
The doubting fiend o'ertakes our youth !
Better be cheated to the last
Than lose the blessèd hope of truth.

Henry Alford

LADY MARY

THOU wert fair, Lady Mary,
As the lily in the sun :
And fairer yet thou mightest be,
Thy youth was but begun :
Thine eye was soft and glancing,
Of the deep bright blue ;
And on the heart thy gentle words
Fell lighter than the dew.

They found thee, Lady Mary,
With thy palms upon thy breast,
Even as thou hadst been praying,
At thine hour of rest :
The cold pale moon was shining
On thy cold pale cheek ;
And the morn of the Nativity
Had just begun to break.

They carv'd thee, Lady Mary,
All of pure white stone,
With thy palms upon thy breast,
In the chancel all alone :
And I saw thee when the winter moon
Shone on thy marble cheek,
When the morn of the Nativity
Had just begun to break.

But thou kneelest, Lady Mary,
With thy palms upon thy breast,
Among the perfect spirits,
In the land of rest :

Thou art even as they took thee
At thine hour of prayer,
Save the glory that is on thee
From the sun that shineth there.

We shall see thee, Lady Mary,
On that shore unknown,
A pure and happy angel
In the presence of the throne ;
We shall see thee when the light divine
Plays freshly on thy cheek,
And the resurrection morning
Hath just begun to break.

COLONOS

COLONOS ! can it be that thou hast still
Thy laurel and thine olives and thy vine ?
Do thy close-feather'd nightingales yet trill
Their warbles of thick-sobbing song divine ?
Does the gold sheen of the crocus o'er thee
    shine
And dew-fed clusters of the daffodil,
And round thy flowery knots Cephisus
    twine,
Aye oozing up with many a bubbling rill ?
Oh, might I stand beside thy leafy knoll,
In sight of the far-off city-towers, and see
The faithful-hearted pure Antigone
Toward the dread precinct, leading sad and
    slow
That awful temple of a kingly soul,
Lifted to heaven by unexampled woe !

John Mitford

THE ROMAN LEGIONS

OH, aged Time ! how far, and long,
Travell'd have thy pinions strong,
Since the masters of the world

Here their eagle-wings unfurl'd.
Onward as the legions pass'd,
Was heard the Roman trumpet's blast,
And see the mountain portals old
Now their opening gates unfold.

Slow moves the Consul's car between
Bright glittering helms and axes keen ;
O'er moonlit rocks, and ramparts bare,
High the Pretorian banners glare.
Afar is heard the torrent's moan,
The winds through rifted caverns groan ;
The vulture's huge primeval nest,
Wild toss'd the pine its shatter'd crest ;
Darker the blackening forest frown'd :
Strange murmurs shook the trembling
　　ground.
In the old warrior's midnight dream
Gigantic shadows seem'd to gleam, —
The Caudine forks, and Cannæ's field
Again their threatening cohorts yield.
Seated on the Thunderer's throne,
He saw the shapes of gods unknown,
Saw in Olympus' golden hall
The volleyed lightning harmless fall,
The great and Capitolian lord
Dim sink, 'mid nameless forms abhorr'd.
Shook the Tarpeian cliff ; around
The trembling Augur felt the sound ;
Saw, God of Light ! in deathly shade,
Thy rich, resplendent tresses fade,

And from the empty car of day
The ethereal coursers bound away.

Then frequent rose the signal shrill,
Oft heard on Alba's echoing hill,
Or down the Apulian mountains borne,
The mingled swell of trump and horn ;
The stern centurion frown'd to hear
Unearthly voices murmuring near ;
Back to his still and Sabine home
Fond thoughts and favorite visions roam.
Sweet Vesta ! o'er the woods again
He views thy small and silent fane ;
He sees the whitening torrents leap
And flash round Tibur's mountain-steep ;
Sees Persian ensigns wide unroll'd,
Barbaric kings in chains of gold ;
O'er the long Appian's crowded street,
Sees trophied arms and eagles meet,
Through the tall arch their triumph pour,
Till rose the trumpet's louder roar ;
From a thousand voices nigh
Burst on his ear the banner-cry,
And o'er the concave rocks, the sound
" AVRELIVS," smote with stern rebound.

Arthur Henry Hallam

WRITTEN IN EDINBURGH

EVEN thus, methinks, a city rear'd should
　　be,
Yea, an imperial city, that might hold
Five times an hundred noble towns in fee,
And either with their might of Babel old,
Or the rich Roman pomp of empery
Might stand compare, highest in arts en-
　　roll'd,

Highest in arms ; brave tenement for the
　　free,
Who never crouch to thrones, or sin for gold.
Thus should her towers be rais'd — with
　　vicinage ⸳
Of clear bold hills, that curve her very
　　streets,
As if to vindicate, 'mid choicest seats
Of art, abiding Nature's majesty ;
And the broad sea beyond, in calm or rage
Chainless alike, and teaching Liberty.

Aubrey Thomas De Vere

AN EPICUREAN'S EPITAPH

WHEN from my lips the last faint sigh is
　　blown
By Death, dark waver of Lethean plumes,
O ! press not then with monumental
　　stone

This forehead smooth, nor weigh me down
　　with glooms
From green bowers, gray with dew,
　　Of Rosemary and Rue.
Choose for my bed some bath of sculptur'd
　　marble
Wreath'd with gay nymphs ; and lay me
　　— not alone —

Where sunbeams fall, flowers wave, and
  light birds warble,
To those who lov'd me murmuring in soft
  tone,
" Here lies our friend, from pain secure and
  cold ;
And spreads his limbs in peace under the
  sun-warm'd mould ! "

FLOWERS I WOULD BRING

FLOWERS I would bring if flowers could
  make thee fairer,
And music, if the Muse were dear to thee ;
(For loving these would make thee love the
  bearer)
But sweetest songs forget their melody,
And loveliest flowers would but conceal the
  wearer : —
A rose I mark'd, and might have pluck'd ;
  but she
Blush'd as she bent, imploring me to spare
  her,
Nor spoil her beauty by such rivalry.
Alas ! and with what gifts shall I pursue
  thee,
What offerings bring, what treasures lay
  before thee ;
When earth with all her floral train doth
  woo thee,
And all old poets and old songs adore thee ;
And love to thee is naught ; from passionate
  mood
Secur'd by joy's complacent plenitude !

HUMAN LIFE

SAD is our youth, for it is ever going,
Crumbling away beneath our very feet ;
Sad is our life, for onward it is flowing,
In current unperceiv'd because so fleet ;
Sad are our hopes for they were sweet in
  sowing,
But tares, self-sown, have overtopp'd the
  wheat ;
Sad are our joys, for they were sweet in
  blowing ;
And still, O still, their dying breath is
  sweet :
And sweet is youth, although it hath bereft
  us
Of that which made our childhood sweeter
  still ;

And sweet our life's decline, for it hath left
  us
A nearer Good to cure an older Ill :
And sweet are all things, when we learn to
  prize them
Not for their sake, but His who grants them
  or denies them.

SORROW

COUNT each affliction, whether light or
  grave,
God's messenger sent down to thee ; do
  thou
With courtesy receive him ; rise and bow ;
And, ere his shadow pass thy threshold,
  crave
Permission first his heavenly feet to lave ;
Then lay before him all thou hast. Allow
No cloud of passion to usurp thy brow,
Or mar thy hospitality ; no wave
Of mortal tumult to obliterate
The soul's marmoreal calmness. Grief
  should be
Like joy, majestic, equable, sedate,
Confirming, cleansing, raising, making free ;
Strong to consume small troubles ; to com-
  mend
Great thoughts, grave thoughts, thoughts
  lasting to the end.

LOVE'S SPITE

You take a town you cannot keep ;
  And, forced in turn to fly,
O'er ruins you have made shall leap
  Your deadliest enemy !
Her love is yours — and be it so —
But can you keep it ? No, no, no !

Upon her brow we gaz'd with awe,
  And lov'd, and wish'd to love, in vain
But when the snow begins to thaw
  We shun with scorn the miry plain.
Women with grace may yield : but she
Appear'd some Virgin Deity.

Bright was her soul as Dian's crest
  Whitening on Vesta's fane its sheen :
Cold look'd she as the waveless breast
  Of some stone Dian at thirteen.
Men lov'd : but hope they deem'd to be
A sweet Impossibility !

THE QUEEN'S VESPERS

HALF kneeling yet, and half reclining,
  She held her harp against her knees :
Aloft the ruddy roofs were shining,
  And sunset touch'd the trees.
From the gold border gleam'd like snow
Her foot : a crown enrich'd her brow :
Dark gems confin'd that crimson vest
Close-moulded on her neck and breast.

In silence lay the cloistral court
  And shadows of the convent towers :
Well order'd now in stately sort
  Those royal halls and bowers.
The choral chaunt had just swept by ;
Bright arms lay quivering yet on high :
Thereon the warriors gaz'd, and then
Glanced lightly at the Queen again.

While from her lip the wild hymn floated,
  Such grace in those uplifted eyes
And sweet, half absent looks, they noted
  That, surely, through the skies
A Spirit, they deem'd, flew forward ever
Above that song's perpetual river,
And, smiling from its joyous track,
Upon her heavenly face look'd back.

CARDINAL MANNING

I LEARN'D his greatness first at Lavington :
The moon had early sought her bed of
  brine,
But we discours'd till now each starry sign
Had sunk : our theme was one and one
  alone :
"Two minds supreme," he said, "our earth
  has known ;
One sang in science ; one serv'd God in
  song ;

Aquinas — Dante." Slowly in me grew
  strong
A thought, "These two great minds in him
  are one ;
'Lord, what shall this man do ? ' " Later
  at Rome
Beside the dust of Peter and of Paul
Eight hundred mitred sires of Christendom
In Council sat. I mark'd him 'mid them
  all ;
I thought of that long night in years gone by
And cried, " At last my question meets re-
  ply."

SONG

SEEK not the tree of silkiest bark
  And balmiest bud,
To carve her name while yet 't is dark
  Upon the wood !
The world is full of noble tasks
  And wreaths hard won :
Each work demands strong hearts, strong
  hands,
  Till day is done.

Sing not that violet-veined skin,
  That cheek's pale roses,
The lily of that form wherein
  Her soul reposes !
Forth to the fight, true man ! true knight !
  The clash of arms
Shall more prevail than whisper'd tale,
  To win her charms.

The warrior for the True, the Right,
  Fights in Love's name ;
The love that lures thee from that fight
  Lures thee to shame !
That love which lifts the heart, yet leaves
  The spirit free, —
That love, or none, is fit for one
  Man-shap'd like thee.

Thomas Burbidge

TO IMPERIA

THOU art not, and thou never canst be mine ;
The die of fate for me is thrown,
And thou art made
No more to me than some resplendent shade

Flung on the canvas by old art divine ;
Or vision of shap'd stone ;
Or the far glory of some starry sign
Which hath a beauty unapproachable
To aught but sight, — a throne
High in the heavens and out of reach ;
Therefore with this low speech

I bid thee now a long and last farewell
Ere I depart, in busy crowds to dwell,
Yet be alone.

All pleasures of this pleasant Earth be
    thine !
Yea, let her servants fondly press
Unto thy feet,
Bearing all sights most fair, all scents most
    sweet :
Spring, playing with her wreath of budded
    vine ;
Summer, with stately tress
Prink'd with green wheat-ears and the
    white corn-bine ;
And Autumn, crown'd from the yellow
    forest-tree ;
— And Winter, in his dress
Begemm'd with icicles, from snow dead-
    white
Shooting their wondrous light ;
These be thine ever. But I ask of thee
One blessing only to beseech for me, —
Forgetfulness.

IF I DESIRE

IF I desire with pleasant songs
    To throw a merry hour away,
Comes Love unto me, and my wrongs
    In careful tale he doth display,
And asks me how I stand for singing
While I my helpless hands am wringing.

And then another time if I
    A noon in shady bower would pass,
Comes he with stealthy gestures sly
    And flinging down upon the grass,
Quoth he to me : My master dear,
Think of this noontide such a year !

And if elsewhere I lay my head
    On pillow with intent to sleep,
Lies Love beside me on the bed,
    And gives me ancient words to keep ;
Says he : These looks, these tokens number,
May be, they 'll help you to a slumber.

So every time when I would yield
    An hour to quiet, comes he still ;
And hunts up every sign conceal'd
    And every outward sign of ill ;
And gives me his sad face's pleasures
For merriment's or sleep's or leisure's.

MOTHER'S LOVE

HE sang so wildly, did the Boy,
    That you could never tell
If 't was a madman's voice you heard,
    Or if the spirit of a bird
Within his heart did dwell :
A bird that dallies with his voice
    Among the matted branches ;
Or on the free blue air his note
To pierce, and fall, and rise, and float,
    With bolder utterance launches.
None ever was so sweet as he,
    The boy that wildly sang to me ;
Though toilsome was the way and long,
He led me not to lose the song.

But when again we stood below
    The unhidden sky, his feet
Grew slacker, and his note more slow,
    But more than doubly sweet.
He led me then a little way
    Athwart the barren moor,
And then he stayed and bade me stay
    Beside a cottage door ;
I could have stayed of mine own will,
    In truth, my eye and heart to fill
With the sweet sight which I saw there,
At the dwelling of the cottager.

A little in the doorway sitting,
    The mother plied her busy knitting,
And her cheek so softly smil'd,
You might be sure, although her gaze
    Was on the meshes of the lace,
Yet her thoughts were with her child.
But when the boy had heard her voice,
    As o'er her work she did rejoice,
His became silent altogether,
And slily creeping by the wall,
    He seiz'd a single plume, let fall
By some wild bird of longest feather ;
And all a-tremble with his freak,
He touch'd her lightly on the cheek.

Oh, what a loveliness her eyes
    Gather in that one moment's space,
While peeping round the post she spies
    Her darling's laughing face !
Oh, mother's love is glorifying,
    On the cheek like sunset lying ;
In the eyes a moisten'd light,
Softer than the moon at night !

EVENTIDE

COMES something down with eventide
  Beside the sunset's golden bars,
Beside the floating scents, beside
  The twinkling shadows of the stars.

Upon the river's rippling face,
  Flash after flash the white
Broke up in many a shallow place ;
  The rest was soft and bright.

By chance my eye fell on the stream ;
  How many a marvellous power,
Sleeps in us, — sleeps, and doth not
    dream !
This knew I in that hour.

For then my heart, so full of strife,
  No more was in me stirr'd ;
My life was in the river's life,
  And I nor saw nor heard.

I and the river, we were one :
  The shade beneath the bank,
I felt it cool ; the setting sun
  Into my spirit sank.

A rushing thing in power serene
  I was ; the mystery
I felt of having ever been
  And being still to be.

Was it a moment or an hour ?
  I knew not ; but I mourn'd
When from that realm of awful power
  I to these fields return'd.

William Henry Whitworth

TIME AND DEATH

I SAW old Time, destroyer of mankind ;
Calm, stern, and cold he sate, and often
  shook
And turn'd his glass, nor ever car'd to look
How many of life's sands were still behind.
And there was Death, his page, aghast to
  find
How tremblingly, like aspens o'er a brook,
His blunted dart fell harmless ; so he took

His master's scythe, and idly smote the
  wind.
Smite on, thou gloomy one, with powerless
  aim !
For Sin, thy mother, at her dying breath
Wither'd that arm, and left thee but a name.
Hope clos'd the grave, when He of Naza-
  reth,
Who led captivity His captive, came
And vanquish'd the great conquerors, Time
  and Death.

ENGLISH SONG WRITERS

(*See also :* B. W. PROCTER.)

John Kenyon

CHAMPAGNE ROSÉ

LILY on liquid roses floating —
  So floats yon foam o'er pink champagne :
Fain would I join such pleasant boating,
  And prove that ruby main,
  And float away on wine !

Those seas are dangerous, graybeards
  swear,
  Whose sea-beach is the goblet's brim ;
And true it is they drown old care —
  But what care we for him,
  So we but float on wine !

And true it is they cross in pain,
  Who sober cross the Stygian ferry ;
But only make our Styx champagne,
  And we shall cross right merry,
    Floating away in wine !

Old Charon's self shall make him mellow,
  Then gaily row his boat from shore ;
While we, and every jovial fellow,
  Hear, unconcern'd, the oar
    That dips itself in wine !

William Howitt

THE DEPARTURE OF THE SWALLOW

AND is the swallow gone ?
  Who beheld it ?
    Which way sail'd it ?
  Farewell bade it none ?

No mortal saw it go :
  But who doth hear
  Its summer cheer
As it flitteth to and fro ?

So the freed spirit flies !
  From its surrounding clay
  It steals away
Like the swallow from the skies.

Whither ? wherefore doth it go ?
  'T is all unknown :
  We feel alone
That a void is left below.

Thomas Haynes Bayly

SHE WORE A WREATH OF ROSES

SHE wore a wreath of roses
  The night that first we met ;
Her lovely face was smiling
  Beneath her curls of jet.
Her footstep had the lightness,
  Her voice the joyous tone, —
The tokens of a youthful heart,
  Where sorrow is unknown.
I saw her but a moment,
  Yet methinks I see her now,
With the wreath of summer flowers
  Upon her snowy brow.

A wreath of orange-blossoms,
  When next we met, she wore ;
The expression of her features
  Was more thoughtful than before ;
And standing by her side was one
  Who strove, and not in vain,
To soothe her, leaving that dear home
  She ne'er might view again.
I saw her but a moment,
  Yet methinks I see her now,

With the wreath of orange-blossoms
  Upon her snowy brow.

And once again I see that brow ;
  No bridal-wreath is there,
The widow's sombre cap conceals
  Her once luxuriant hair.
She weeps in silent solitude,
  And there is no one near
To press her hand within his own,
  And wipe away the tear.
I see her broken-hearted ;
  Yet methinks I see her now,
In the pride of youth and beauty,
  With a garland on her brow.

OH ! WHERE DO FAIRIES HIDE THEIR HEADS ?

OH ! where do fairies hide their heads
  When snow lies on the hills,
When frost has spoil'd their mossy beds,
  And crystalliz'd their rills ?
Beneath the moon they cannot trip
  In circles o'er the plain ;
And draughts of dew they cannot sip
  Till green leaves come again.

Perhaps, in small, blue diving-bells,
  They plunge beneath the waves,
Inhabiting the wreathed shells
  That lie in coral caves ;
Perhaps, in red Vesuvius,
  Carousals they maintain ;
And cheer their little spirits thus,
  Till green leaves come again.

When they return there will be mirth,
  And music in the air,
And fairy wings upon the earth,
  And mischief everywhere.
The maids, to keep the elves aloof,
  Will bar the doors in vain ;
No key-hole will be fairy-proof,
  When green leaves come again.

Mary Howitt

THE SEA FOWLER

THE baron hath the landward park, the
    fisher hath the sea ;
But the rocky haunts of the sea-fowl be-
    long alone to me.

The baron hunts the running deer, the
    fisher nets the brine ;
But every bird that builds a nest on ocean-
    cliffs is mine.

Come on then, Jock and Alick, let's to the
    sea-rocks bold :
I was train'd to take the sea-fowl ere I was
    five years old.

The wild sea roars, and lashes the granite
    crags below,
And round the misty islets the loud, strong
    tempests blow.

And let them blow ! Roar wind and wave,
    they shall not me dismay ;
I've faced the eagle in her nest and snatch'd
    her young away.

The eagle shall not build her nest, proud
    bird although she be,
Nor yet the strong-wing'd cormorant, with-
    out the leave of me.

The eider-duck has laid her eggs, the tern
    doth hatch her young,
And the merry gull screams o'er her brood ;
    but all to me belong.

Away, then, in the daylight, and back again
    ere eve ;
The eagle could not rear her young, unless
    I gave her leave.

The baron hath the landward park, the
    fisher hath the sea ;
But the rocky haunts of the sea-fowl be-
    long alone to me.

CORNFIELDS

WHEN on the breath of autumn breeze,
  From pastures dry and brown,
Goes floating like an idle thought
  The fair white thistle-down,
Oh then what joy to walk at will
Upon the golden harvest hill !

What joy in dreamy ease to lie
  Amid a field new shorn,
And see all round on sun-lit slopes
  The pil'd-up stacks of corn ;
And send the fancy wandering o'er
All pleasant harvest-fields of yore.

I feel the day — I see the field,
  The quivering of the leaves,
And good old Jacob and his house
  Binding the yellow sheaves ;
And at this very hour I seem
To be with Joseph in his dream.

I see the fields of Bethlehem
  And reapers many a one,
Bending unto their sickles' stroke,
  And Boaz looking on ;
And Ruth, the Moabite so fair,
Among the gleaners stooping there.

Again I see a little child,
  His mother's sole delight,
God's living gift of love unto
  The kind good Shunammite ;
To mortal pangs I see him yield,
And the lad bear him from the field.

The sun-bath'd quiet of the hills,
  The fields of Galilee,
That eighteen hundred years ago
  Were full of corn, I see ;
And the dear Saviour takes his way
'Mid ripe ears on the Sabbath day.

Oh, golden fields of bending corn,
  How beautiful they seem !
The reaper-folk, the pil'd-up sheaves,
  To me are like a dream.
The sunshine and the very air
Seem of old time, and take me there.

Thomas Kibble Hervey

I THINK ON THEE

I THINK on thee in the night,
  When all beside is still,
And the moon comes out, with her pale, sad
    light,
  To sit on the lonely hill ;
When the stars are all like dreams,
  And the breezes all like sighs,
And there comes a voice from the far-off
    streams
  Like thy spirit's low replies.

I think on thee by day,
  'Mid the cold and busy crowd,
When the laughter of the young and gay
  Is far too glad and loud.
I hear thy soft, sad tone,
  And thy young, sweet smile I see :
My heart — my heart were all alone,
  But for its dreams of thee !

Of thee who wert so dear, —
  And yet I do not weep,
For thine eyes were stain'd by many a tear
  Before they went to sleep ;
And, if I haunt the past,
  Yet may I not repine
That thou hast won thy rest, at last,
  And all the grief is mine.

I think upon thy gain,
  Whate'er to me it cost,
And fancy dwells with less of pain
  On all that I have lost, —
Hope, like the cuckoo's oft-told tale,
  Alas, it wears her wing !

And love that, like the nightingale,
  Sings only in the spring.

Thou art my spirit's all,
  Just as thou wert in youth,
Still from thy grave no shadows fall
  Upon my lonely truth ;
A taper yet above thy tomb,
  Since lost its sweeter rays,
And what is memory, through the gloom,
  Was hope, in brighter days.

I am pining for the home
  Where sorrow sinks to sleep,
Where the weary and the weepers come,
  And they cease to toil and weep.
Why walk about with smiles
  That each should be a tear,
Vain as the summer's glowing spoils
  Flung o'er an early bier ?

Oh, like those fairy things,
  Those insects of the East,
That have their beauty in their wings,
  And shroud it while at rest ;
That fold their colors of the sky
  When earthward they alight,
And flash their splendors on the eye,
  Only to take their flight ; —

I never knew how dear thou wert,
  Till thou wert borne away !
I have it yet about my heart,
  The beauty of that day !
As if the robe thou wert to wear,.
  Beyond the stars, were given
That I might learn to know it there,
  And seek thee out, in heaven !

Charles Swain

TRIPPING DOWN THE FIELD-PATH

TRIPPING down the field-path,
 Early in the morn,
There I met my own love
 'Midst the golden corn ;
Autumn winds were blowing,
 As in frolic chase,
All her silken ringlets
 Backward from her face;
Little time for speaking
 Had she, for the wind,
Bonnet, scarf, or ribbon,
 Ever swept behind.

Still some sweet improvement
 In her beauty shone ;
Every graceful movement
 Won me, — one by one !
As the breath of Venus
 Seemed the breeze of morn,
Blowing thus between us,
 'Midst the golden corn.
Little time for wooing
 Had we, for the wind
Still kept on undoing
 What we sought to bind.

Oh ! that autumn morning
 In my heart it beams,
Love's last look adorning
 With its dream of dreams :
Still, like waters flowing
 In the ocean shell,
Sounds of breezes blowing
 In my spirit dwell ;
Still I see the field-path ; —
 Would that I could see
Her whose graceful beauty
 Lost is now to me !

TAKE THE WORLD AS IT IS

TAKE the world as it is ! — there are good
 and bad in it,
And good and bad will be from now to
 the end ;
And they, who expect to make saints in a
 minute,
Are in danger of marring more hearts
 than they 'll mend.

If ye wish to be happy ne'er seek for the
 faults,
 Or you 're sure to find something or
 other amiss ;
'Mid much that debases, and much that
 exalts,
 The world 's not a bad one if left as it is.

Take the world as it is ! — if the surface be
 shining,
 Ne'er rake up the sediment hidden be-
 low !
There 's wisdom in this, but there 's none
 in repining
 O'er things which can rarely be mended,
 we know.
There 's beauty around us, which let us
 enjoy ;
 And chide not, unless it may be with a
 kiss ;
Though Earth 's not the Heaven we thought
 when a boy,
 There 's something to live for, if ta'en as
 it is.

Take the world as it is ! — with its smiles
 and its sorrow,
 Its love and its friendship, — its false-
 hood and truth,
Its schemes that depend on the breath of
 to-morrow,
 Its hopes which pass by like the dreams
 of our youth :
Yet, oh ! whilst the light of affection may
 shine,
 The heart in itself hath a fountain of
 bliss ;
In the worst there 's some spark of a nature
 divine,
 And the wisest and best take the world
 as it is.

LIFE

LIFE 's not our own, — 't is but a loan
 To be repaid ;
Soon the dark Comer 's at the door,
The debt is due : the dream is o'er, —
 Life 's but a shade.

Thus all decline that bloom or shine,
 Both star and flower ;

'T is but a little odor shed,
A light gone out, a spirit fled,
A funeral hour.

Then let us show a tranquil brow
Whate'er befalls ;
That we upon life's latest brink
May look on Death's dark face, — and
think
An angel calls.

THE ROSE THOU GAV'ST

THE rose thou gav'st at parting —
Hast thou forgot the hour ?
The moon was on the river,
The dew upon the flower :
Thy voice was full of tenderness,
But, ah ! thy voice misleads ;
The rose is like thy promises,
Its thorn is like thy deeds.

The winter cometh bleakly,
And dark the time must be ;
Bnt I can deem it summer
To what thou 'st prov'd to me.
The snow that meets the sunlight
Soon hastens from the scene ;
But melting snow is lasting,
To what thy faith hath been.

'T WAS JUST BEFORE THE HAY WAS MOWN

'T WAS just before the hay was mown,
The season had been wet and cold,
When my good dame began to groan,
And speak of days and years of old :
Ye were a young man then, and gay,
And raven black your handsome hair ;
Ah ! Time steals many a grace away,
And leaves us many a grief to bear.

Tush ! tush ! said I, we 've had our time,
And if 't were here again 't would go ;
The youngest cannot keep their prime,
The darkest head some gray must show.
We 've been together forty years,
And though it seem but like a day,
We 've much less cause, dear dame, for
tears,
Than many who have trod life's way.

Goodman, said she, ye 're always right,
And 't is a pride to hear your tongue ;
And though your fine old head be white,
'T is dear to me as when 't were young.
So give your hand, — 't was never shown
But in affection unto me ;
And I shall be beneath the stone,
And lifeless, when I love not thee.

Eliza Cook

THE QUIET EYE

THE orb I like is not the one
That dazzles with its lightning gleam ;
That dares to look upon the sun,
As though it challenged brighter beam.
That orb may sparkle, flash, and roll ;
Its fire may blaze, its shaft may fly ;
But not for me : I prize the soul
That slumbers in a quiet eye.

There 's something in its placid shade
That tells of calm, unworldly thought ;
Hope may be crown'd, or joy delay'd —
No dimness steals, no ray is caught.
Its pensive language seems to say,
" I know that I must close and die ; "
And death itself, come when it may,
Can hardly change the quiet eye.

There 's meaning in its steady glance,
Of gentle blame or praising love,
That makes me tremble to advance
A word, that meaning might re-
prove.
The haughty threat, the fiery look,
My spirit proudly can defy,
But never yet could meet and brook
The upbraiding of a quiet eye.

There 's firmness in its even light,
That augurs of a breast sincere :
And, oh ! take watch how ye excite
That firmness till it yield a tear.
Some bosoms give an easy sigh,
Some drops of grief will freely
start,
But that which sears the quiet eye
Hath its deep fountain in the heart.

THE SEA-CHILD

HE crawls to the cliff and plays on a brink
Where every eye but his own would shrink ;
No music he hears but the billow's noise,
And shells and weeds are his only toys.
No lullaby can the mother find
To sing him to rest like the moaning wind ;
And the louder it wails and the fiercer it
    sweeps,
The deeper he breathes and the sounder he
    sleeps.

And now his wandering feet can reach
The rugged tracks of the desolate beach ;
Creeping about like a Triton imp,
To find the haunts of the crab and shrimp.
He clings, with none to guide or help,
To the furthest ridge of slippery kelp ;
And his bold heart glows while he stands
    and mocks
The seamew's cry on the jutting rocks.

Few years have wan'd — and now he stands
Bareheaded on the shelving sands.
A boat is moor'd, but his young hands
    cope
Right well with the twisted cable rope ;
He frees the craft, she kisses the tide ;
The boy has climb'd her beaten side :
She drifts — she floats — he shouts with
    glee ;
His soul hath claim'd its right on the sea.

'T is vain to tell him the howling breath
Rides over the waters with wreck and
    death :
He 'll say there 's more of fear and pain
On the plague-ridden earth than the storm-
    lash'd main.
'T would be as wise to spend thy power
In trying to lure the bee from the flower,
The lark from the sky, or the worm from
    the grave,
As in weaning the Sea-Child from the wave.

William Cox Bennett

BABY MAY

CHEEKS as soft as July peaches,
Lips whose dewy scarlet teaches
Poppies paleness — round large eyes
Ever great with new surprise,
Minutes fill'd with shadeless gladness,
Minutes just as brimm'd with sadness,
Happy smiles and wailing cries,
Crows and laughs and tearful eyes,
Lights and shadows swifter born
Than on wind-swept Autumn corn,
Ever some new tiny notion
Making every limb all motion —
Catching up of legs and arms,
Throwings back and small alarms,
Clutching fingers — straightening jerks,
Twining feet whose each toe works,
Kickings up and straining risings,
Mother's ever new surprisings,
Hands all wants and looks all wonder
At all things the heavens under,
Tiny scorns of smil'd reprovings
That have more of love than lovings,

Mischiefs done with such a winning
Archness, that we prize such sinning,
Breakings dire of plates and glasses,
Graspings small at all that passes,
Pullings off of all that 's able
To be caught from tray or table ;
Silences — small meditations,
Deep as thoughts of cares for nations,
Breaking into wisest speeches
In a tongue that nothing teaches,
All the thoughts of whose possessing
Must be wooed to light by guessing ;
Slumbers — such sweet angel-seemings,
That we 'd ever have such dreamings,
Till from sleep we see thee breaking,
And we 'd always have thee waking ;
Wealth for which we know no measure,
Pleasure high above all pleasure,
Gladness brimming over gladness,
Joy in care — delight in sadness,
Loveliness beyond completeness,
Sweetness distancing all sweetness,
Beauty all that beauty may be —
That 's May Bennett, that 's my baby.

BE MINE, AND I WILL GIVE THY NAME

BE mine, and I will give thy name
 To Memory's care,
So well, that it shall breathe, with fame,
 Immortal air,
That time and change and death shall
  be
Scorn'd by the life I give to thee.

I will not, like the sculptor, trust
 Thy shape to stone ;
That, years shall crumble into dust,
 Its form unknown ;
No — the white statue's life shall be
Short, to the life I 'll give to thee.

Not to the canvas worms may fret
 Thy charms I 'll give ;
Soon shall the world those charms for-
  get,
 If there they live ;
The life that colors lend shall be
Poor to the life I 'll give to thee.

For thou shalt live, defying time
 And mocking death,
In music on — O life sublime ! —
 A nation's breath ;
Love, in a people's songs, shall be
The eternal life I 'll give to thee.

A CHRISTMAS SONG

BLOW, wind, blow,
Sing through yard and shroud ;
Pipe it shrilly and loud,
 Aloft as well as below ;
Sing in my sailor's ear
The song I sing to you,
" Come home, my sailor true,
For Christmas that comes so near. "

Go, wind, go,
Hurry his home-bound sail,
Through gusts that are edged with hail,
 Through winter, and sleet, and snow ;
Song, in my sailor's ear,
Your shrilling and moans shall be,
For he knows they sing him to me
And Christmas that comes so near.

SONGS AND BALLADRY OF SCOTLAND

(*See also:* AYTOUN, J. W. CARLYLE, MACAULAY, NICOLL, SCOTT)

Alexander Laing

MY AIN WIFE

I WADNA gi'e my ain wife
 For ony wife I see ;
I wadna gi'e my ain wife
 For ony wife I see ;
A bonnier yet I 've never seen,
 A better canna be —
I wadna gi'e my ain wife
 For ony wife I see !

O couthie is my ingle-cheek,
 An' cheerie is my Jean ;

I never see her angry look,
 Nor hear her word on ane.
She 's gude wi' a' the neebours roun'
 An' aye gude wi' me —
I wadna gi'e my ain wife
 For ony wife I see.

An' O her looks sae kindlie,
 They melt my heart outright,
When o'er the baby at her breast
 She hangs wi' fond delight ;
She looks intill its bonnie face,
 An' syne looks to me —
I wadna gi'e my ain wife
 For ony wife I see.

Thomas Carlyle

THE SOWER'S SONG

Now hands to seed-sheet, boys !
　We step and we cast; old Time 's on wing;
And would ye partake of Harvest's joys,
　The corn must be sown in spring.
　　Fall gently and still, good corn,
　　　Lie warm in thy earthy bed;
　　And stand so yellow some morn,
　　　For beast and man must be fed.

Old earth is a pleasure to see
　In sunshiny cloak of red and green;
The furrow lies fresh, this year will be
　As years that are past have been.
　　Fall gently and still, good corn,
　　　Lie warm in thy earthy bed;
　　And stand so yellow some morn,
　　　For beast and man must be fed.

Old earth, receive this corn,
　The son of six thousand golden sires;
All these on thy kindly breast were born;
　One more thy poor child requires.
　　Fall gently and still, good corn,
　　　Lie warm in thy earthy bed;
　　And stand so yellow some morn,
　　　For beast and man must be fed.

Now steady and sure again,
　And measure of stroke and step we keep;
Thus up and down we cast our grain;
　Sow well and you gladly reap.
　　Fall gently and still, good corn,
　　　Lie warm in thy earthy bed;
　　And stand so yellow some morn,
　　　For beast and man must be fed.

ADIEU

Let time and chance combine, combine,
　Let time and chance combine;
The fairest love from heaven above,
　That love of yours was mine,
　　My dear,
　That love of yours was mine.

The past is fled and gone, and gone,
　The past is fled and gone;
If naught but pain to me remain,
　I 'll fare in memory on,
　　My dear,
　I 'll fare in memory on.

The saddest tears must fall, must fall,
　The saddest tears must fall;
In weal or woe, in this world below,
　I love you ever and all,
　　My dear,
　I love you ever and all.

A long road full of pain, of pain,
　A long road full of pain;
One soul, one heart, sworn ne'er to
　　part, —
　We ne'er can meet again,
　　My dear,
　We ne'er can meet again.

Hard fate will not allow, allow,
　Hard fate will not allow;
We blessed were as the angels are,
　Adieu forever now,
　　My dear,
　Adieu forever now.

Robert Gilfillan

'T IS SAIR TO DREAM

'T is sair to dream o' them we like,
　That waking we sall never see;
Yet, oh ! how kindly was the smile
　My laddie in my sleep gave me !
I thought we sat beside the burn
　That wimples down the flowery glen,

Where, in our early days o' love,
　We met that ne'er sall meet again !

The simmer sun sank 'neath the wave,
　And gladden'd, wi' his parting ray,
The woodland wild and valley green,
　Fast fading into gloamin' grey.
He talk'd of days o' future joy,
　And yet my heart was haflins sair.

For when his eye it beam'd on me,
A withering death-like glance was there !

I thought him dead, and then I thought
That life was young and love was free,
For o'er our heads the mavis sang,
And hameward hied the janty bee !
We pledged our love and plighted troth,
But cauld, cauld was the kiss he gave,
When starting from my dream, I found
His troth was plighted to the grave !

I canna weep, for hope is fled,
And nought would do but silent mourn,
Were 't no for dreams that should na come,
To whisper back my love's return ;
'T is sair to dream o' them we like,
That waking we sall never see;
Yet, oh ! how kindly was the smile
My laddie in my sleep gave me !

THE EXILE'S SONG

OH ! why left I my hame ?
Why did I cross the deep ?
Oh ! why left I the land
Where my forefathers sleep ?
I sigh for Scotia's shore,
And I gaze across the sea,

But I canna get a blink
O' my ain countrie.

The palm-tree waveth high,
And fair the myrtle springs;
And, to the Indian maid,
The bulbul sweetly sings.
But I dinna see the broom
Wi' its tassels on the lee,
Nor hear the lintie's sang
O' my ain countrie.

Oh ! here no Sabbath bell
Awakes the Sabbath morn,
Nor song of reapers heard
Amang the yellow corn :
For the tyrant's voice is here,
And the wail of slaverie;
But the sun of freedom shines
In my ain countrie.

There 's a hope for every woe,
And a balm for every pain,
But the first joys o' our heart
Come never back again.
There 's a track upon the deep,
And a path across the sea;
But the weary ne'er return
To their ain countrie.

David Macbeth Moir

CASA'S DIRGE

VAINLY for us the sunbeams shine,
Dimm'd is our joyous hearth;
O Casa, dearer dust than thine
Ne'er mix'd with mother earth !
Thou wert the corner-stone of love,
The keystone of our fate;
Thou art not ! Heaven scowls dark above,
And earth is desolate.

Ocean may rave with billows curl'd,
And moons may wax and wane,
And fresh flowers blossom; but this world
Shall claim not thee again.
Clos'd are the eyes which bade rejoice
Our hearts till love ran o'er;
Thy smile is vanish'd, and thy voice
Silent for evermore.

Yes ; thou art gone — our hearth's de-
light,
Our boy so fond and dear;
No more thy smiles to glad our sight,
No more thy songs to cheer;
No more thy presence, like the sun,
To fill our home with joy:
Like lightning hath thy race been run,
As bright as swift, fair boy.

Now winter with its snow departs,
The green leaves clothe the tree;
But summer smiles not on the hearts
That bleed and break for thee:
The young May weaves her flowery
crown.
Her boughs in beauty wave;
They only shake their blossoms down
Upon thy silent grave.

Dear to our souls is every spot
  Where thy small feet have trod;
There odors, breath'd from Eden, float,
  And sainted is the sod;
The wild bee with its buglet fine,
  The blackbird singing free,
Melt both thy mother's heart and mine:
  They speak to us of thee !

Only in dreams thou comest now
  From Heaven's immortal shore,
A glory round that infant brow,
  Which Death's pale signet bore:
'T was thy fond looks, 't was thy fond lips,
  That lent our joys their tone;
And life is shaded with eclipse,
  Since thou from earth art gone.

Thine were the fond, endearing ways,
  That tenderest feeling prove;
A thousand wiles to win our praise,
  To claim and keep our love;
Fondness for us thrill'd all thy veins;
  And, Casa, can it be
That nought of all the past remains
  Except vain tears for thee ?

Idly we watch thy form to trace
  In children on the street;
Vainly, in each familiar place,
  We list thy pattering feet;
Then, sudden, o'er these fancies crush'd,
  Despair's black pinions wave;
We know that sound for ever hush'd:
  We look upon thy grave.

O heavenly child of mortal birth !
  Our thoughts of thee arise,
Not as a denizen of earth,
  But inmate of the skies:
To feel that life renew'd is thine
  A soothing balm imparts;
We quaff from out Faith's cup divine,
  And Sabbath fills our hearts.

Thou leanest where the fadeless wands
  Of amaranth bend o'er;
Thy white wings brush the golden sands
  Of Heaven's refulgent shore.
Thy home is where the psalm and song
  Of angels choir abroad,
And blessed spirits, all day long,
  Bask round the throne of God.

There chance and change are not; the soul
  Quaffs bliss as from a sea,
And years, through endless ages, roll,
  From sin and sorrow free:
There gush for aye fresh founts of joy,
  New raptures to impart;
Oh ! dare we call thee still *our* boy,
  Who now a seraph art ?

A little while — a little while —
  Ah ! long it cannot be !
And thou again on us wilt smile,
  Where angels smile on thee.
How selfish is the worldly heart:
  How sinful to deplore !
Oh ! that we were where now thou art,
  Not lost, but gone before.

William Thom

THE MITHERLESS BAIRN

WHEN a' ither bairnies are hush'd to their
    hame,
By aunty, or cousin, or frecky grand-dame,
Wha stands last an' lanely, an' sairly for-
    fairn ?
'T is the puir dowie laddie — the mitherless
    bairn !

The mitherless bairnie creeps to his lane
    bed;
Nane covers his cauld back, or haps his bare
    head;

His wee hackit heelies are hard as the airn,
An' lithless the lair o' the mitherless bairn.

Aneath his cauld brow, siccan dreams hover
    there,
O' hands that wont kindly to kaim his dark
    hair !
But mornin' brings clutches, a' reckless an'
    stern,
That lo'e na the locks o' the mitherless bairn.

The sister, wha sang o'er his saftly rock'd
    bed,
Now rests in the mools whare their mammie
    is laid;

While the father toils sair his wee bannock
  to earn,
An' kens na the wrangs o' his mitherless
  bairn.

Her spirit that pass'd in yon hour of his
  birth
Still watches his lone lorn wand'rings on
  earth,
Recording in heaven the blessings they
  earn

Wha couthilie deal wi' the mitherless
  bairn !

Oh ! speak him na harshly — he trembles
  the while,
He bends to your biddin', and blesses your
  smile:
In the dark hour o' anguish, the heartless
  shall learn
That God deals the blow for the mitherless
  bairn !

Thomas Aird

THE SWALLOW

THE swallow, bonny birdie, comes sharp
  twittering o'er the sea,
And gladly is her carol heard for the sunny
  days to be;
She shares not with us wintry glooms, but
  yet, no faithless thing,
She hunts the summer o'er the earth with
  wearied little wing.

The lambs like snow all nibbling go upon
  the ferny hills;
Light winds are in the leafy woods, and
  birds, and bubbling rills;
Then welcome, little swallow, by our morn-
  ing lattice heard,
Because thou com'st when Nature bids
  bright days be thy reward !

Thine be sweet mornings with the bee
  that's out for honey-dew;

And glowing be the noontide for the grass-
  hopper and you;
And mellow shine, o'er day's decline, the
  sun to light thee home:
What can molest thy airy nest ? sleep till
  the day-spring come !

The river blue that rushes through the val-
  ley hears thee sing,
And murmurs much beneath the touch of
  thy light-dipping wing.
The thunder-cloud, over us bowed, in
  deeper gloom is seen,
When quick reliev'd it glances to thy
  bosom's silvery sheen.

The silent Power, that brought thee back
  with leading-strings of love
To haunts where first the summer sun fell
  on thee from above,
Shall bind thee more to come aye to the
  music of our leaves,
For here thy young, where thou hast sprung,
  shall glad thee in our eaves.

James Ballantine

MUCKLE-MOU'D MEG

*Oh, wha hae ye brought us hame now, my
  brave lord,
Strappit flaught ower his braid saddle-
  bow ?

Some bauld Border reiver to feast at our
  board,
An' herry our pantry, I trow.
He's buirdly an' stalwart in lith an' in limb;
  Gin ye were his master in war
The field was a saft eneugh litter for him,
  Ye needna hae brought him sae far.

Then saddle an' munt again, harness an'
    dunt again,
An' when ye gae hunt again, strike higher
    game."

"Hoot, whisht ye, my dame, for he comes
    o' gude kin,
An' boasts o' a lang pedigree ;
This night he maun share o' our gude cheer
    within,
At morning's grey dawn he maun dee.
He 's gallant Wat Scott, heir o' proud
    Harden Ha',
Wha ettled our lands clear to sweep ;
But now he is snug in auld Elibank's paw,
An' shall swing frae our donjon-keep.
Tho' saddle an' munt again, harness an'
    dunt again,
I 'll ne'er when I hunt again strike higher
    game."

"Is this young Wat Scott ? an' wad ye rax
    his craig,
When our daughter is fey for a man ?
Gae, gaur the loun marry our muckle-
    mou'd Meg,
Or we 'll ne'er get the jaud aff our han' ! "
"Od ! hear our gudewife, she wad fain save
    your life ;
Wat Scott, will ye marry or hang ? "
But Meg's muckle mou set young Wat's
    heart agrue,
Wha swore to the woodie he 'd gang.
Ne'er saddle nor munt again, harness nor
    dunt again,

Wat ne'er shall hunt again, ne'er see his
    hame.

Syne muckle-mou'd Meg press'd in close to
    his side,
An' blinkit fu' sleely and kind,
But aye as Wat glower'd at his braw prof-
    fer'd bride,
He shook like a leaf in the wind.
"A bride or a gallows, a rope or a wife ! "
The morning dawn'd sunny and clear —
Wat boldly strode forward to part wi' his
    life,
Till he saw Meggy shedding a tear ;
Then saddle an' munt again, harness an'
    dunt again,
Fain wad Wat hunt again, fain wad be hame.

Meg's tear touch'd his bosom, the gibbet
    frown'd high,
An' slowly Wat strode to his doom ;
He gae a glance round wi' a tear in his
    eye,
Meg shone like a star through the gloom.
She rush'd to his arms, they were wed on
    the spot,
An' lo'ed ither muckle and lang ;
Nae bauld border laird had a wife like Wat
    Scott ;
'T was better to marry than hang.
So saddle an' munt again, harness an' dunt
    again,
Elibank hunt again, Wat 's snug at hame.

(*Compare* R. BROWNING, *p. 364.*)

John Stuart Blackie

MY BATH

(*Scene* — Kinnaird Burn, near Pitlochrie.)

COME here, good people great and small,
    that wander far abroad,
To drink of drumly German wells, and
    make a weary road
To Baden and to Wiesbaden, and how they
    all are nam'd,
To Carlsbad and to Kissingen, for healing
    virtue fam'd ;
Come stay at home, and keep your feet from
    dusty travel free,

And I will show you what rare bath a good
    God gave to me ;
'T is hid among the Highland hills beneath
    the purple brae,
With cooling freshness free to all, nor doc=
    tor's fee to pay.

No craft of mason made it here, nor carpen-
    ter, I wot ;
Nor tinkering fool with hammering tool to
    shape the charmed spot ;
But down the rocky-breasted glen the foamy
    torrent falls
Into the amber caldron deep, fenced round
    with granite walls.

Nor gilded beam, nor pictur'd dome, nor
    curtain, roofs it in,
But the blue sky rests, and white clouds
    float, above the bubbling linn,
Where God's own hand hath scoop'd it out
    in Nature's Titan hall,
And from her cloud-fed fountains drew its
    waters free to all.

Oh come and see my Highland bath, and
    prove its freshening flood,
And spare to taint your skin with swathes
    of drumly German mud :
Come plunge with me into the wave like
    liquid topaz fair,
And to the waters give your back that
    spout down bravely there ;
Then float upon the swirling flood, and, like
    a glancing trout,
Plash about, and dash about, and make a
    lively rout,
And to the gracious sun display the glory
    of your skin,
As you dash about and splash about in the
    foamy-bubbling linn.

Oh come and prove my bonnie bath ; in
    sooth 't is furnish'd well
With trees, and shrubs, and spreading ferns,
    all in the rocky dell,
And roses hanging from the cliff in grace
    of white and red,
And little tiny birches nodding lightly over-
    head,
And spiry larch with purple cones, and tips
    of virgin green,
And leafy shade of hazel copse with sunny
    glints between :
Oh might the Roman wight be here who
    praised Bandusia's well,
He 'd find a bath to Nymphs more dear in
    my sweet Highland dell.

Some folks will pile proud palaces, and
    some will wander far
To scan the blinding of a sun, or the blink-
    ing of a star ;
Some sweat through Afric's burning sands ;
    and some will vex their soul
To find heaven knows what frosty prize be-
    neath the Arctic pole.
God bless them all ; and may they find what
    thing delights them well
In east or west, or north or south, — but I
    at home will dwell

Where fragrant ferns their fronds uncurl,
    and healthful breezes play,
And clear brown waters grandly swirl be-
    neath the purple brae.

Oh come and prove my Highland bath, the
    burn, and all the glen,
Hard-toiling wights in dingy nooks, and
    scribes with inky pen,
Strange thoughtful men with curious quests
    that vex your fretful brains,
And scheming sons of trade who fear to
    count your slippery gains ;
Come wander up the burn with me, and
    thread the winding glen,
And breathe the healthful power that flows
    down from the breezy Ben,
And plunge you in the deep brown pool ;
    and from beneath the spray
You'll come forth like a flower that blooms
    'neath freshening showers in May !

THE EMIGRANT LASSIE

As I came wandering down Glen Spean,
    Where the braes are green and grassy,
With my light step I overtook
    A weary-footed lassie.

She had one bundle on her back,
    Another in her hand,
And she walk'd as one who was full loath
    To travel from the land.

Quoth I, " My bonnie lass ! " — for she
    Had hair of flowing gold,
And dark brown eyes, and dainty limbs,
    Right pleasant to behold —

" My bonnie lass, what aileth thee,
    On this bright summer day,
To travel sad and shoeless thus
    Upon the stony way ?

" I 'm fresh and strong, and stoutly shod,
    And thou art burden'd so ;
March lightly now, and let me bear
    The bundles as we go."

" No, no ! " she said, " that may not be ;
    What 's mine is mine to bear ;
Of good or ill, as God may will,
    I take my portion'd share."

" But you have two, and I have none ;
    One burden give to me ;
I 'll take that bundle from thy back
    That heavier seems to be."

" No, no ! " she said ; " *this*, if you will,
    That holds — no hand but mine
May bear its weight from dear Glen Spean
    'Cross the Atlantic brine ! "

" Well, well ! but tell me what may be
    Within that precious load,
Which thou dost bear with such fine care
    Along the dusty road ?

" Belike it is some present rare
    From friend in parting hour ;
Perhaps, as prudent maidens wont,
    Thou tak'st with thee thy dower."

She droop'd her head, and with her hand
    She gave a mournful wave :
" Oh, do not jest, dear sir ! — it is
    Turf from my mother's grave ! "

I spoke no word : we sat and wept
    By the road-side together ;
No purer dew on that bright day
    Was dropp'd upon the heather.

THE WORKING MAN'S SONG

I AM no gentleman, not I !
    No bowing, scraping thing !
I bear my head more free and high
    Than titled count or king.
I am no gentleman, not I !
    No, no, no !
And only to one Lord on high
    My head I bow.

I am no gentleman, not I !
    No vain and varnish'd thing !

And from my heart, without a die,
    My honest thoughts I fling.
I am no gentleman, not I !
    No, no, no !
Our stout John Knox was none — and why
    Should I be so ?

I am no gentleman, not I !
    No mincing, modish thing,
In gay saloon a butterfly,
    Some wax-doll Miss to wing.
I am no gentleman, not I !
    No, no, no !
No moth, to sport in fashion's eye,
    A Bond Street beau.

I am no gentleman, not I !
    No bully, braggart thing,
With jockeys on the course to vie,
    With bull-dogs in the ring.
I am no gentleman, not I !
    No, no, no !
The working man might sooner die
    Than sink so low.

I am no gentleman, not I !
    No star-bedizen'd thing !
My fathers filch'd no dignity,
    By fawning to a king.
I am no gentleman, not I !
    No, no, no !
And to the wage of honesty
    My rank I owe.

I am no gentleman, not I !
    No bowing, scraping thing !
I bear my head more free and high
    Than titled count or king.
I am no gentleman, not I !
    No, no, no !
And thank the blessed God on high,
    Who made me so !

William Miller

WILLIE WINKIE

WEE Willie Winkie rins through the town,
Up stairs and doon stairs, in his nicht-gown,
Tirlin' at the window, cryin' at the lock,
" Are the weans in their bed ? — for it 's
    now ten o'clock."

Hey, Willie Winkie ! are ye comin' ben ?
The cat 's singin' gay thrums to the sleepin'
    hen,
The doug 's spelder'd on the floor, and disna
    gie a cheep ;
But here 's a waukrife laddie, that winna
    fa' asleep.

Ony thing but sleep, ye rogue ! — glow'rin'
  like the moon,
Rattlin' in an airn jug wi' an airn spoon,
Rumblin', tumblin' roun' about, crawin' like
  a cock,
Skirlin' like a kenna-what —wauknin' sleep-
  in' folk !

Hey, Willie Winkie ! the wean 's in a
  creel !
Waumblin' aff a bodie's knee like a vera
  eel,
Ruggin' at the cat's lug, and ravellin' a'
  her thrums :
Hey, Willie Winkie !—See, there he comes !

Charles Mackay

TELL ME, YE WINGED WINDS

TELL me, ye winged winds,
  That round my pathway roar,
Do ye not know some spot
  Where mortals weep no more ?
Some lone and pleasant dell,
  Some valley in the west,
Where, free from toil and pain,
  The weary soul may rest ?
The loud wind dwindled to a whisper low,
And sigh'd for pity as it answer'd, " No."

Tell me, thou mighty deep,
  Whose billows round me play,
Knowst thou some favor'd spot,
  Some island far away,
Where weary man may find
  The bliss for which he sighs,
Where sorrow never lives,
  And friendship never dies ?
The loud waves, rolling in perpetual flow,
Stopp'd for a while, and sigh'd to answer,
  " No."

And thou, serenest moon,
  That, with such lovely face,
Dost look upon the earth
  Asleep in night's embrace ;
Tell me, in all thy round
  Hast thou not seen some spot
Where miserable man
  May find a happier lot ?
Behind a cloud the moon withdrew in woe,
And a voice, sweet but sad, responded,
  " No."

Tell me, my secret soul,
  Oh ! tell me, Hope and Faith,
Is there no resting-place
  From sorrow, sin, and death ?

Is there no happy spot
  Where mortals may be blest,
Where grief may find a balm,
  And weariness a rest ?
Faith, Hope, and Love, best boons to mortals
  given,
Wav'd their bright wings, and whisper'd,
  " Yes, in heaven."

EARL NORMAN AND JOHN TRUMAN

THROUGH great Earl Norman's acres wide,
  A prosperous and a good land,
'T will take you fifty miles to ride
  O'er grass, and corn, and woodland.
His age is sixty-nine, or near,
  And I 'm scarce twenty-two, man,
And have but fifty pounds a year, —
  Poor John Truman !
But would I change ? I' faith ! not I,
  Oh no ! not I, says Truman !

Earl Norman dwells in halls of state,
  The grandest in the county ;
Has forty cousins at his gate,
  To feed upon his bounty.
But then he 's deaf — the doctors' care,
  While I in whispers woo, man,
And find my physic in the air, —
  Stout John Truman !
D 'ye think I 'd change for thrice his gold ?
  Oh no ! not I, says Truman !

Earl Norman boasts a gartered knee,
  A proof of royal graces ;
I wear, by Nelly wrought for me,
  A silken pair of braces.
He sports a star upon his breast,
  And I a violet blue, man, —

The gift of her who loves me best,
Proud John Truman !
I'd be myself, and not the Earl,
Oh, that would I, says Truman.

WHAT MIGHT BE DONE

WHAT might be done if men were wise —
What glorious deeds, my suffering
brother,
Would they unite
In love and right,
And cease their scorn of one another ?

Oppression's heart might be imbued
With kindling drops of loving-kindness,
And knowledge pour,
From shore to shore,
Light on the eyes of mental blindness.

All slavery, warfare, lies, and wrongs,
All vice and crime, might die together ;
And wine and corn,
To each man born,
Be free as warmth in summer weather.

The meanest wretch that ever trod,
The deepest sunk in guilt and sorrow,
Might stand erect
In self-respect,
And share the teeming world to-morrow.

What might be done ? This might be
done,
And more than this, my suffering
brother —
More than the tongue
E'er said or sung,
If men were wise and lov'd each other.

IRISH MINSTRELSY

INCLUDING THE POETS OF YOUNG IRELAND

(*See also :* DE VERE, MAGINN, MAHONY, SIMMONS)

Samuel Lover

RORY O'MORE; OR, GOOD OMENS

YOUNG Rory O'More courted Kathleen
Bawn,
He was bold as a hawk, — she as soft as
the dawn ;
He wish'd in his heart pretty Kathleen to
please,
And he thought the best way to do that
was to tease.
" Now, Rory, be aisy," sweet Kathleen
would cry
(Reproof on her lip, but a smile in her
eye),
" With your tricks I don't know, in troth,
what I'm about,
Faith you've teas'd till I've put on my
cloak inside out."
" Oh ! jewel," says Rory, " that same is the
way

You've thrated my heart for this many a
day ;
And 't is plaz'd that I am, and why not to
be sure ?
For 't is all for good luck," says bold Rory
O'More.

" Indeed, then," says Kathleen, " don't think
of the like,
For I half gave a promise to soothering
Mike ;
The ground that I walk on he loves, I'll be
bound."
" Faith," says Rory, " I'd rather love you
than the ground."
" Now, Rory, I'll cry if you don't let me go ;
Sure I drame ev'ry night that I'm hating
you so ! "
" Oh," says Rory, " that same I'm de-
lighted to hear,
For drames always go by conthrairies, my
dear ;

Oh! jewel, keep draming that same till
you die,
And bright morning will give dirty night
the black lie !
And 't is plaz'd that I am, and why not, to
be sure ?
Since 't is all for good luck," says bold
Rory O'More.

" Arrah, Kathleen, my darlint, you 've
teas'd me enough,
Sure I 've thrash'd for your sake Dinny
Grimes and Jim Duff ;
And I 've made myself, drinking your
health, quite a baste,
So I think, after that, I may talk to the
praste."
Then Rory, the rogue, stole his arm round
her neck,
So soft and so white, without freckle or
speck,
And he look'd in her eyes that were beam-
ing with light,
And he kiss'd her sweet lips ; — don't you
think he was right ?
" Now Rory, leave off, sir ; you 'll hug me
no more,
That 's eight times to-day you have kiss'd
me before."
" Then here goes another," says he, " to
make sure,
For there 's luck in odd numbers," says
Rory O'More.

WIDOW MACHREE

WIDOW Machree, it 's no wonder you frown,
Och hone ! Widow Machree.
Faith, it ruins your looks, that same dirty
black gown,
Och hone ! Widow Machree.
How alter'd your air,
With that close cap you wear —
'T is destroying your hair
Which should be flowing free ;
Be no longer a churl
Of its black silken curl,
Och hone ! Widow Machree !

Widow Machree, now the summer is come,
Och hone ! Widow Machree,

When everything smiles, should a beauty
look glum ?
Och hone ! Widow Machree.
See the birds go in pairs,
And the rabbits and hares —
Why even the bears
Now in couples agree ;
And the mute little fish,
Though they can't spake, they wish,
Och hone ! Widow Machree.

Widow Machree, and when winter comes
in,
Och hone ! Widow Machree,
To be poking the fire all alone is a sin,
Och hone ! Widow Machree.
Sure the shovel and tongs
To each other belongs,
And the kettle sings songs
Full of family glee ;
While alone with your cup,
Like a hermit, you sup,
Och hone ! Widow Machree.

And how do you know, with the comforts
I 've towld,
Och hone ! Widow Machree,
But you 're keeping some poor fellow out in
the cowld ?
Och hone ! Widow Machree.
With such sins on your head
Sure your peace would be fled,
Could you sleep in your bed
Without thinking to see
Some ghost or some sprite,
That would wake you each night,
Crying, " Och hone ! Widow Ma-
chree " ?

Then take my advice, darling Widow Ma-
chree,
Och hone ! Widow Machree.
And with my advice, faith I wish you 'd
take me,
Och hone ! Widow Machree.
You 'd have me to desire
Then to sit by the fire,
And sure Hope is no liar
In whispering to me,
That the ghosts would depart,
When you 'd me near your heart,
Och hone ! Widow Machree.

John Banim

SOGGARTH AROON

AM I the slave they say,
  Soggarth aroon ? [1]
Since you did show the way,
  Soggarth aroon,
Their slave no more to be,
While they would work with me
Old Ireland's slavery,
  Soggarth aroon.

Why not her poorest man,
  Soggarth aroon,
Try and do all he can,
  Soggarth aroon,
Her commands to fulfil
Of his own heart and will,
Side by side with you still,
  Soggarth aroon ?

Loyal and brave to you,
  Soggarth aroon,
Yet be not slave to you,
  Soggarth aroon,
Nor, out of fear to you,
Stand up so near to you —
Och ! out of fear to *you*,
  Soggarth aroon !

Who, in the winter's night,
  Soggarth aroon,
When the cold blast did bite,
  Soggarth aroon,

Came to my cabin-door,
And on my earthen-floor
Knelt by me, sick and poor,
  Soggarth aroon ?

Who, on the marriage day,
  Soggarth aroon,
Made the poor cabin gay,
  Soggarth aroon,
And did both laugh and sing,
Making our hearts to ring
At the poor christening,
  Soggarth aroon ?

Who, as friend only met,
  Soggarth aroon,
Never did flout me yet,
  Soggarth aroon ;
And when my hearth was dim,
Gave, while his eye did brim,
What I should give to him,
  Soggarth aroon ?

Och ! you, and only you,
  Soggarth aroon !
And for this I was true to you,
  Soggarth aroon !
Our love they 'll never shake,
When for ould Ireland's sake
We a true part did take,
  Soggarth aroon !

Gerald Griffin

A PLACE IN THY MEMORY

A PLACE in thy memory, Dearest !
  Is all that I claim :
To pause and look back when thou hearest
  The sound of my name.
Another may woo thee, nearer ;
  Another may win and wear;
I care not though he be dearer,
  If I am remember'd there.

Remember me, not as a lover
  Whose hope was cross'd,
Whose bosom can never recover
  The light it hath lost !
As the young bride remembers the mother
  She loves, though she never may see,
As a sister remembers a brother,
  O Dearest, remember me !

Could I be thy true lover, Dearest !
  Couldst thou smile on me,

[1] *Ságart arún* — Priest, dear.

I would be the fondest and dearest
That ever lov'd thee :
But a cloud on my pathway is glooming
That never must burst upon thine ;
And heaven, that made thee all blooming,
Ne'er made thee to wither on mine.

Remember me then ! O remember
My calm light love,
Though bleak as the blasts of November
My life may prove !
That life will, though lonely, be sweet
If its brightest enjoyment should be
A smile and kind word when we meet
And a place in thy memory.

NOCTURNE

Sleep that like the couched dove
Broods o'er the weary eye,
Dreams that with soft heavings move
The heart of memory,
Labor's guerdon, golden rest, —
Wrap thee in its downy vest, —
Fall like comfort on thy brain
And sing the hush song to thy pain !

Far from thee be startling fears,
And dreams the guilty dream ;
No banshee scare thy drowsy ears
With her ill-omen'd scream ;
But tones of fairy minstrelsy
Float like the ghosts of sound o'er thee,
Soft as the chapel's distant bell,
And lull thee to a sweet farewell.

Ye for whom the ashy hearth
The fearful housewife clears,
Ye whose tiny sounds of mirth
The nighted carman hears,
Ye whose pygmy hammers make
The wonderers of the cottage wake,
Noiseless be your airy flight,
Silent as the still moonlight.

Silent go, and harmless come,
Fairies of the stream :
Ye, who love the winter gloom
Or the gay moonbeam,
Hither bring your drowsy store
Gather'd from the bright lusmore ;
Shake o'er temples, soft and deep,
The comfort of the poor man, sleep.

James Clarence Mangan

DARK ROSALEEN

O my Dark Rosaleen,
Do not sigh, do not weep !
The priests are on the ocean green,
They march along the deep.
There 's wine from the royal Pope,
Upon the ocean green ;
And Spanish ale shall give you hope,
My Dark Rosaleen !
My own Rosaleen !
Shall glad your heart, shall give you
hope,
Shall give you health, and help, and
hope,
My Dark Rosaleen !

Over hills, and through dales,
Have I roam'd for your sake ;
All yesterday I sail'd with sails
On river and on lake.

The Erne, at its highest flood,
I dash'd across unseen,
For there was lightning in my blood,
My Dark Rosaleen !
My own Rosaleen !
O ! there was lightning in my blood,
Red lightning lighten'd through my blood,
My Dark Rosaleen !

All day long, in unrest,
To and fro, do I move,
The very soul within my breast
Is wasted for you, love !
The heart in my bosom faints
To think of you, my queen,
My life of life, my saint of saints,
My own Rosaleen !
To hear your sweet and sad complaints,
My life, my love, my saint of saints,
My Dark Rosaleen !

Woe and pain, pain and woe,
　Are my lot, night and noon,
To see your bright face clouded so,
　Like to the mournful moon.
But yet will I rear your throne
　Again in golden sheen ;
'T is you shall reign, shall reign alone,
　My Dark Rosaleen !
　My own Rosaleen !
'T is you shall have the golden throne,
'T is you shall reign, and reign alone,
　My Dark Rosaleen !

Over dews, over sands,
　Will I fly for your weal :
Your holy, delicate white hands
　Shall girdle me with steel.
At home in your emerald bowers,
　From morning's dawn till e'en,
You 'll pray for me, my flower of flowers,
　My Dark Rosaleen !
　My fond Rosaleen !
You 'll think of me through daylight's
　　hours,
My virgin flower, my flower of flowers,
　My Dark Rosaleen !

I could scale the blue air,
　I could plough the high hills,
O, I could kneel all night in prayer,
　To heal your many ills !
And one beamy smile from you
　Would float like light between
My toils and me, my own, my true,
　My Dark Rosaleen !
　My fond Rosaleen !
Would give me life and soul anew,
A second life, a soul anew,
　My Dark Rosaleen !

O ! the Erne shall run red
　With redundance of blood,
The earth shall rock beneath our tread,
　And flames warp hill and wood,
And gun-peal and slogan cry
　Wake many a glen serene,
Ere you shall fade, ere you shall die,
　My Dark Rosaleen !
　My own Rosaleen !
The Judgment Hour must first be nigh,
Ere you can fade, ere you can die,
　My Dark Rosaleen !

SOUL AND COUNTRY

ARISE, my slumbering soul ! arise,
And learn what yet remains for thee
　　To dree or do !
The signs are flaming in the skies ;
A struggling world would yet be free,
　　And live anew.
The earthquake hath not yet been born
That soon shall rock the lands around,
　　Beneath their base ;
Immortal Freedom's thunder horn
As yet yields but a doleful sound
　　To Europe's race.

Look round, my soul ! and see, and say
If those about thee understand
　　Their mission here :
The will to smite, the power to slay,
Abound in every heart and hand
　　Afar, anear ;
But, God ! must yet the conqueror's sword
Pierce mind, as heart, in this proud year ?
　　O, dream it not !
It sounds a false, blaspheming word,
Begot and born of moral fear,
　　And ill-begot.

To leave the world a name is nought :
To leave a name for glorious deeds
　　And works of love,
A name to waken lightning thought
And fire the soul of him who reads,
　　This tells above.
Napoleon sinks to-day before
The ungilded shrine, the single soul
　　Of Washington :
Truth's name alone shall man adore
Long as the waves of Time shall roll
　　Henceforward on.

My countrymen ! my words are weak :
My health is gone, my soul is dark,
　　My heart is chill ;
Yet would I fain and fondly seek
To see you borne in freedom's bark
　　O'er ocean still.
Beseech your God ! and bide your hour !
He cannot, will not long be dumb :
　　Even now his tread
Is heard o'er earth with coming power ;
And coming, trust me, it will come, —
　　Else were He dead.

Helen Selina, Lady Dufferin

LAMENT OF THE IRISH EMIGRANT

I 'M sittin' on the stile, Mary,
  Where we sat side by side
On a bright May mornin' long ago,
  When first you were my bride.
The corn was springin' fresh and green,
  And the lark sang loud and high,
And the red was on your lip, Mary,
  And the love-light in your eye.

The place is little changed, Mary,
  The day is bright as then,
The lark's loud song is in my ear,
  And the corn is green again ;
But I miss the soft clasp of your hand,
  And your breath, warm on my cheek :
And I still keep list'nin' for the words
  You never more will speak.

'T is but a step down yonder lane,
  And the little church stands near —
The church where we were wed, Mary ;
  I see the spire from here.
But the graveyard lies between, Mary,
  And my step might break your rest —
For I 've laid you, darling, down to sleep,
  With your baby on your breast.

I 'm very lonely now, Mary,
  For the poor make no new friends ;
But, oh ! they love the better still
  The few our Father sends.
And you were all I had, Mary,
  My blessin' and my pride :
There 's nothing left to care for now,
  Since my poor Mary died.

Yours was the good, brave heart, Mary,
  That still kept hoping on,
When the trust in God had left my soul,
  And my arm's young strength was
    gone ;
There was comfort ever on your lip,
  And the kind look on your brow —
I bless you, Mary, for that same,
  Though you cannot hear me now.

I thank you for the patient smile
  When your heart was fit to break,
When the hunger pain was gnawin' there,
  And you hid it for my sake ;
I bless you for the pleasant word,
  When your heart was sad and sore —
Oh ! I 'm thankful you are gone, Mary,
  Where grief can't reach you more !

I 'm biddin' you a long farewell,
  My Mary — kind and true !
But I 'll not forget you, darling,
  In the land I 'm goin' to :
They say there 's bread and work for
    all,
  And the sun shines always there,
But I 'll not forget old Ireland,
  Were it fifty times as fair !

And often in those grand old woods
  I 'll sit, and shut my eyes,
And my heart will travel back again
  To the place where Mary lies ;
And I 'll think I see the little stile
  Where we sat side by side,
And the springin' corn, and the bright May
    morn,
  When first you were my bride.

Caroline Elizabeth Sarah Norton
(LADY STIRLING—MAXWELL)

WE HAVE BEEN FRIENDS TOGETHER

WE have been friends together,
  In sunshine and in shade ;
Since first beneath the chestnut-trees
  In infancy we played.

But coldness dwells within thy heart,
  A cloud is on thy brow ;
We have been friends together —
  Shall a light word part us now ?

We have been gay together ;
  We have laugh'd at little jests ;

For the fount of hope was gushing
  Warm and joyous in our breasts.
But laughter now hath fled thy lip,
  And sullen glooms thy brow ;
We have been gay together —
  Shall a light word part us now ?

We have been sad together,
  We have wept, with bitter tears,
O'er the grass-grown graves, where slumber'd
  The hopes of early years.
The voices which are silent there
  Would bid thee clear thy brow ;
We have been sad together —
  Oh ! what shall part us now ?

THE KING OF DENMARK'S RIDE

WORD was brought to the Danish king
  (Hurry !)
That the love of his heart lay suffering,
And pin'd for the comfort his voice would
    bring ;
  (Oh ! ride as though you were flying !)
Better he loves each golden curl
On the brow of that Scandinavian girl
Than his rich crown jewels of ruby and
    pearl ;
  And his rose of the isles is dying !

Thirty nobles saddled with speed,
  (Hurry !)
Each one mounting a gallant steed
Which he kept for battle and days of need ;
  (Oh ! ride as though you were flying !)
Spurs were struck in the foaming flank ;
Worn-out chargers stagger'd and sank ;
Bridles were slacken'd, and girths were
    burst ;
But ride as they would, the king rode first,
  For his rose of the isles lay dying !

His nobles are beaten, one by one ;
  (Hurry !)
They have fainted, and falter'd, and homeward gone ;
His little fair page now follows alone,
  For strength and for courage trying.
The king look'd back at that faithful child ;
Wan was the face that answering smil'd ;
They passed the drawbridge with clattering
    din,
Then he dropp'd ; and only the king rode in
  Where his rose of the isles lay dying !

The king blew a blast on his bugle horn ;
  (Silence !)
No answer came ; but faint and forlorn
An echo return'd on the cold gray morn,
  Like the breath of a spirit sighing.
The castle portal stood grimly wide ;
None welcom'd the king from that weary
    ride ;
For dead, in the light of the dawning day,
The pale sweet form of the welcomer lay,
  Who had yearn'd for his voice while
    dying !

The panting steed, with a drooping crest,
  Stood weary.
The king return'd from her chamber of rest,
The thick sobs choking in his breast ;
  And, that dumb companion eyeing,
The tears gush'd forth which he strove to
    check ;
He bowed his head on his charger's neck :
" O steed — that every nerve didst strain,
Dear steed, our ride hath been in vain
  To the halls where my love lay dying ! "

LOVE NOT

LOVE not, love not ! ye hapless sons of clay !
Hope's gayest wreaths are made of earthly
    flowers —
Things that are made to fade and fall away
Ere they have blossom'd for a few short
    hours.
    Love not !

Love not ! the thing ye love may change :
The rosy lip may cease to smile on you,
The kindly-beaming eye grow cold and
    strange,
The heart still warmly beat, yet not be true.
    Love not !

Love not ! the thing you love may die,
May perish from the gay and gladsome
    earth ;
The silent stars, the blue and smiling sky,
Beam o'er its grave, as once upon its birth.
    Love not !

Love not ! oh warning vainly said
In present hours as in the years gone by ;
Love flings a halo round the dear ones'
    head,
Faultless, immortal, till they change or die
    Love not !

John Francis Waller

KITTY NEIL

" Ah, sweet Kitty Neil, rise up from that
    wheel,
  Your neat little foot will be weary from
    spinning ;
Come trip down with me to the sycamore-
    tree,
  Half the parish is there, and the dance
    is beginning.
The sun is gone down, but the full harvest-
    moon
  Shines sweetly and cool on the dew-
    whiten'd valley,
While all the air rings with the soft, loving
    things
  Each little bird sings in the green
    shaded alley."

With a blush and a smile Kitty rose up the
    while,
  Her eye in the glass, as she bound her
    hair, glancing ;
'T is hard to refuse when a young lover
    sues,
  So she could n't but choose to — go
    off to the dancing.
And now on the green the glad groups are
    seen,
  Each gay-hearted lad with the lass of
    his choosing ;
And Pat, without fail, leads out sweet
    Kitty Neil, —
  Somehow, when he ask'd, she ne'er
    thought of refusing.

Now, Felix Magee puts his pipes to his
    knee,
  And with flourish so free sets each
    couple in motion ;
With a cheer and a bound, the lads patter
    the ground,
  The maids move around just like swans
    on the ocean :
Cheeks bright as the rose — feet light as
    the doe's,
  Now coyly retiring, now boldly ad-
    vancing —

Search the world all round, from the sky
    to the ground,
  No such sight can be found as an
    Irish lass dancing !

Sweet Kate ! who could view your bright
    eyes of deep blue,
  Beaming humidly through their dark
    lashes so mildly,
Your fair-turned arm, heaving breast,
    rounded form,
  Nor feel his heart warm, and his pulses
    throb wildly;
Young Pat feels his heart, as he gazes, de-
    part,
  Subdued by the smart of such painful
    yet sweet love ;
The sight leaves his eye, as he cries with a
    sigh,
  " *Dance light, for my heart it lies under
    your feet, love !* "

A SPINNING–WHEEL SONG

Mellow the moonlight to shine is begin-
    ning ;
Close by the window young Eileen is spin-
    ning ;
Bent o'er the fire, her blind grandmother,
    sitting,
Is croaning, and moaning, and drowsily
    knitting :
" Eileen, achora, I hear some one tapping."
" 'T is the ivy, dear mother, against the
    glass flapping."
" Eileen, I surely hear somebody sighing."
" 'T is the sound, mother dear, of the sum-
    mer wind dying."
Merrily, cheerily, noisily whirring,
Swings the wheel, spins the reel, while the
    foot 's stirring ;
Sprightly, and lightly, and airily ringing,
Thrills the sweet voice of the young maiden
    singing.

" What 's that noise that I hear at the win-
    dow, I wonder ? "
" 'T is the little birds chirping the holly-
    bush under."

" What makes you be shoving and moving
　　your stool on,
And singing all wrong that old song of
　　' The Coolun ? ' "
There 's a form at the casement — the form
　　of her true-love —
And he whispers, with face bent, " I 'm
　　waiting for you, love ;
Get up on the stool, through the lattice
　　step lightly,
We 'll rove in the grove while the moon 's
　　shining brightly."
Merrily, cheerily, noisily whirring,
Swings the wheel, spins the reel, while the
　　foot 's stirring ;
Sprightly, and lightly, and airily ring-
　　ing,
Thrills the sweet voice of the young maiden
　　singing.

The maid shakes her head, on her lip lays
　　her fingers,

Steals up from her seat — longs to go, and
　　yet lingers ;
A frighten'd glance turns to her drowsy
　　grandmother,
Puts one foot on the stool, spins the wheel
　　with the other.
Lazily, easily, swings now the wheel
　　round ;
Slowly and slowly is heard now the reel's
　　sound ;
Noiseless and light to the lattice above
　　her
The maid steps — then leaps to the arms
　　of her lover.
Slower — and slower — and slower the
　　wheel swings ;
Lower — and lower — and lower the reel
　　rings ;
Ere the reel and the wheel stopp'd their
　　ringing and moving,
Through the grove the young lovers by
　　moonlight are roving.

Sir Samuel Ferguson

THE FAIRY THORN

AN ULSTER BALLAD

" Get up, our Anna dear, from the weary
　　spinning wheel ;
For your father 's on the hill, and your
　　mother is asleep ;
Come up above the crags, and we 'll dance
　　a highland reel
Around the fairy thorn on the steep."

At Anna Grace's door 't was thus the maid-
　　ens cried,
Three merry maidens fair in kirtles of the
　　green ;
And Anna laid the sock and the weary wheel
　　aside,
The fairest of the four, I ween.

They 're glancing through the glimmer of
　　the quiet eve,
Away in milky wavings of neck and ankle
　　bare ;
The heavy-sliding stream in its sleepy song
　　they leave,
And the crags in the ghostly air ;

And linking hand in hand, and singing as
　　they go,
The maids along the hill-side have ta'en
　　their fearless way,
Till they come to where the rowan trees in
　　lovely beauty grow
Beside the Fairy Hawthorn gray.

The hawthorn stands between the ashes tall
　　and slim,
Like matron with her twin grand-daugh-
　　ters at her knee ;
The rowan berries cluster o'er her low head
　　gray and dim
In ruddy kisses sweet to see.

The merry maidens four have ranged them
　　in a row,
Between each lovely couple a stately
　　rowan stem,
And away in mazes wavy like skimming
　　birds they go, —
Oh, never caroll'd bird like them !

But solemn is the silence of the silvery
　　haze
That drinks away their voices in echoless
　　repose,

And dreamily the evening has still'd the
    haunted braes,
And dreamier the gloaming grows.

And sinking one by one, like lark-notes from
    the sky
    When the falcon's shadow saileth across
        the open shaw,
Are hush'd the maidens' voices, as cowering
    down they lie
    In the flutter of their sudden awe.

For, from the air above and the grassy
    ground beneath,
    And from the mountain-ashes and the old
        white thorn between,
A power of faint enchantment doth through
    their beings breathe,
    And they sink down together on the
        green.

They sink together silent, and, stealing side
    by side,
    They fling their lovely arms o'er their
        drooping necks so fair,
Then vainly strive again their naked arms
    to hide,
    For their shrinking necks again are bare.

Thus clasp'd and prostrate all, with their
    heads together bow'd,
    Soft o'er their bosoms beating — the only
        human sound —
They hear the silky footsteps of the silent
    fairy crowd,
    Like a river in the air, gliding round.

Nor scream can any raise, nor prayer can
    any say,

But wild, wild, the terror of the speechless
    three,
    For they feel fair Anna Grace drawn silently
        away,
By whom they dare not look to see.

They feel their tresses twine with her part-
    ing locks of gold,
    And the curls elastic falling, as her head
        withdraws ;
They feel her sliding arms from their
    tranced arms unfold,
    But they dare not look to see the
        cause :

For heavy on their senses the faint enchant-
    ment lies
    Through all that night of anguish and
        perilous amaze ;
And neither fear nor wonder can ope their
    quivering eyes,
    Or their limbs from the cold ground
        raise,

Till out of night the earth has roll'd her
    dewy side,
    With every haunted mountain and
        streamy vale below ;
When, as the mist dissolves in the yellow
    morning-tide,
    The maidens' trance dissolveth so.

Then fly the ghastly three as swiftly as they
    may,
    And tell their tale of sorrow to anxious
        friends in vain :
They pin'd away and died within the year
    and day,
    And ne'er was Anna Grace seen again.

Thomas Osborne Davis

THE SACK OF BALTIMORE[1]

THE summer sun is falling soft on Carbery's
    hundred isles,
The summer sun is gleaming still through
    Gabriel's rough defiles ;
Old Innisherkin's crumbled fane looks like
    a moulting bird,
And in a calm and sleepy swell the ocean
    tide is heard :

The hookers lie upon the beach; the children
    cease their play ;
The gossips leave the little inn ; the house-
    holds kneel to pray ;
And full of love, and peace, and rest, its
    daily labor o'er,
Upon that cosy creek there lay the town of
    Baltimore.

A deeper rest, a starry trance, has come with
    midnight there ;

[1] His last poem.

No sound, except that throbbing wave, in
earth, or sea, or air !
The massive capes and ruin'd towers seem
conscious of the calm ;
The fibrous sod and stunted trees are breath-
ing heavy balm.
So still the night, these two long barques
round Dunashad that glide
Must trust their oars, methinks not few,
against the ebbing tide.
Oh, some sweet mission of true love must
urge them to the shore !
They bring some lover to his bride who sighs
in Baltimore.

All, all asleep within each roof along that
rocky street,
And these must be the lover's friends, with
gently gliding feet —
A stifled gasp, a dreamy noise ! " The roof
is in a flame ! "
From out their beds and to their doors rush
maid and sire and dame,
And meet upon the threshold stone the
gleaming sabre's fall,
And o'er each black and bearded face the
white or crimson shawl.
The yell of " Allah ! " breaks above the
prayer, and shriek, and roar :
O blessed God ! the Algerine is lord of Bal-
timore !

Then flung the youth his naked hand against
the shearing sword ;
Then sprung the mother on the brand with
which her son was gor'd ;
Then sunk the grandsire on the floor, his
grand-babes clutching wild ;
Then fled the maiden moaning faint, and
nestled with the child:
But see ! yon pirate strangled lies, and
crush'd with splashing heel,
While o'er him in an Irish hand there sweeps
his Syrian steel
Though virtue sink, and courage fail, and
misers yield their store,
There's one hearth well avenged in the sack
of Baltimore.

Midsummer morn in woodland nigh the
birds begin to sing,
They see not now the milking maids, — de-
serted is the spring ;
Midsummer day this gallant rides from dis-
tant Bandon's town,

These hookers cross'd from stormy Skull,
that skiff from Affadown ;
They only found the smoking walls with
neighbors' blood besprent,
And on the strewed and trampled beach
awhile they wildly went,
Then dash'd to sea, and pass'd Cape Clear,
and saw, five leagues before,
The pirate-galley vanishing that ravaged
Baltimore.

Oh, some must tug the galley's oar, and
some must tend the steed ;
This boy will bear a Scheik's chibouk, and
that a Bey's jerreed.
Oh, some are for the arsenals by beauteous
Dardanelles ;
And some are in the caravan to Mecca's
sandy dells.
The maid that Bandon gallant sought is
chosen for the Dey :
She's safe — she's dead — she stabb'd him
in the midst of his Serai !
And when to die a death of fire that noble
maid they bore,
She only smiled, O'Driscoll's child ; she
thought of Baltimore.

'Tis two long years since sunk the town
beneath that bloody band,
And all around its trampled hearths a larger
concourse stand,
Where high upon a gallows-tree a yelling
wretch is seen :
'T is Hackett of Dungarvan—he who steer'd
the Algerine !
He fell amid a sullen shout with scarce a
passing prayer,
For he had slain the kith and kin of many
a hundred there.
Some mutter'd of MacMurchadh, who
brought the Norman o'er ;
Some curs'd him with Iscariot, that day in
Baltimore.

THE BOATMAN OF KINSALE

His kiss is sweet, his word is kind,
His love is rich to me ;
I could not in a palace find
A truer heart than he.
The eagle shelters not his nest
From hurricane and hail
More bravely than he guards my breast —
The Boatman of Kinsale.

The wind that round the Fastnet sweeps
  Is not a whit more pure,
The goat that down Cnoc Sheehy leaps
  Has not a foot more sure.
No firmer hand nor freer eye
  E'er faced an autumn gale,
De Courcy's heart is not so high —
  The Boatman of Kinsale.

The brawling squires may heed him not,
  The dainty stranger sneer,
But who will dare to hurt our cot
  When Myles O'Hea is here ?
The scarlet soldiers pass along :
  They'd like, but fear to rail :
His blood is hot, his blow is strong —
  The Boatman of Kinsale.

His hooker 's in the Scilly van,
  When seines are in the foam,
But money never made the man,
  Nor wealth a happy home.
So, bless'd with love and liberty,
  While he can trim a sail,
He'll trust in God, and cling to me —
  The Boatman of Kinsale.

THE WELCOME

COME in the evening, or come in the morning ;
Come when you 're look'd for, or come without warning :
Kisses and welcome you 'll find here before you,
And the oftener you come here the more
  I 'll adore you !
Light is my heart since the day we were
  plighted ;
Red is my cheek that they told me was
  blighted ;
The green of the trees looks far greener than
  ever,
And the linnets are singing, " True lovers
  don't sever ! "

I 'll pull you sweet flowers, to wear if you
  choose them, —

Or, after you 've kiss'd them, they 'll lie on
  my bosom ;
I 'll fetch from the mountain its breeze to
  inspire you ;
I 'll fetch from my fancy a tale that won't
  tire you.
Oh ! your step 's like the rain to the summer-
  vex'd farmer,
Or sabre and shield to a knight without
  armor ;
I 'll sing you sweet songs till the stars rise
  above me,
Then, wandering, I 'll wish you in silence
  to love me.

We 'll look through the trees at the cliff
  and the eyrie ;
We 'll tread round the rath on the track
  of the fairy ;
We 'll look on the stars, and we 'll list to
  the river,
Till you ask of your darling what gift you
  . can give her :
Oh ! she 'll whisper you — " Love, as unchangeably beaming,
And trust, when in secret, most tunefully
  streaming ;
Till the starlight of heaven above us shall
  quiver,
As our souls flow in one down eternity's
  river."

So come in the evening, or come in the morning ;
Come when you 're looked for, or come without warning :
Kisses and welcome you 'll find here before you,
And the oftener you come here the more
  I 'll adore you !
Light is my heart since the day we were
  plighted ;
Red is my cheek that they told me was
  blighted ;
The green of the trees looks far greener
  than ever,
And the linnets are singing, " True lovers
  don't sever ! "

Sir Charles Gavan Duffy

THE IRISH RAPPAREES

RIGH Shemus[1] he has gone to France, and
    left his crown behind ;
Ill luck be theirs, both day and night, put
    running in his mind !
Lord Lucan followed after with his
    Slashers brave and true,
And now the doleful keen is raised —
    " What will poor Ireland do ?
What must poor Ireland do ?
Our luck," they say, " has gone to France
    — what can poor Ireland do ? "

O, never fear for Ireland, for she has sol-
    diers still,
For Rory's boys are in the wood, and Re-
    my's on the hill !
And never had poor Ireland more loyal
    hearts than these —
May God be kind and good to them, the
    faithful Rapparees !
The fearless Rapparees !
The jewel were you, Rory, with your Irish
    Rapparees !

O, black 's your heart, Clan Oliver, and
    colder than the clay !
O, high 's your head, Clan Sassenach, since
    Sarsfield 's gone away !
It 's little love you bear to us for sake of
    long ago ;
But hold your hand, for Ireland still can
    strike a deadly blow —
Can strike a mortal blow :
Och, duar-na-Críosd ! 't is she that still
    could strike a deadly blow !

The Master's bawn, the Master's seat, a
    surly bodagh fills ;
The Master's son, an outlawed man, is
    riding on the hills.
But God be prais'd that round him throng,
    as thick as summer bees,
The swords that guarded Limerick wall —
    his loyal Rapparees !
His loving Rapparees !
Who dare say no to Rory Oge, with all his
    Rapparees ?

Black Billy Grimes of Latnamard, he rack'd
    us long and sore —
God rest the faithful hearts he broke ! —
    we 'll never see them more ;
But I 'll go bail he 'll break no more, while
    Truagh has gallows-trees ;
For why ? — he met, one lonesome night,
    the fearless Rapparees !
The angry Rapparees !
They never sin no more, my boys, who
    cross the Rapparees !

Now, Sassenach and Cromweller, take
    heed of what I say,
Keep down your black and angry looks
    that scorn us night and day :
For there 's a just and wrathful Judge that
    every action sees,
And He 'll make strong, to right our wrong,
    the faithful Rapparees !
The fearless Rapparees !
The men that rode at Sarsfield's side, the
    roving Rapparees !

Denis Florence MacCarthy

BLESS THE DEAR OLD VER-
DANT LAND

BLESS the dear old verdant land !
    Brother, wert thou born of it ?
As thy shadow life doth stand
Twining round its rosy band,
Did an Irish mother's hand
    Guide thee in the morn of it ?

Did a father's first command
    Teach thee love or scorn of it ?

Thou who tread'st its fertile breast,
    Dost thou feel a glow for it ?
Thou of all its charms possest,
Living on its first and best,
Art thou but a thankless guest
    Or a traitor foe for it ?

[1] King James II.

If thou lovest, where 's the test ?
　Wilt thou strike a blow for it ?

Has the past no goading sting
　That can make thee rouse for it ?
Does thy land's reviving spring,
　Full of buds and blossoming,
Fail to make thy cold heart cling,
　Breathing lover's vows for it ?
With the circling ocean's ring
　Thou wert made a spouse for it.

Hast thou kept as thou shouldst keep
　Thy affections warm for it,
Letting no cold feeling creep
Like an ice-breath o'er the deep,
Freezing to a stony sleep
　Hopes the heart would form for it,
Glories that like rainbows peep
　Through the darkening storm for it ?

Son of this down-trodden land,
　Aid us in the fight for it.
We seek to make it great and grand,
Its shipless bays, its naked strand,
By canvas-swelling breezes fanned :
　Oh, what a glorious sight for it,
The past expiring like a brand
　In morning's rosy light for it !

Think, this dear old land is thine,
　And thou a traitor slave of it :
Think how the Switzer leads his kine,
When pale the evening star doth shine ;

His song has home in every line,
　Freedom in every stave of it ;
Think how the German loves his Rhine
　And worships every wave of it !

Our own dear land is bright as theirs,
　But oh ! our hearts are cold for it ;
Awake ! we are not slaves, but heirs.
Our fatherland requires our cares,
Our speech with men, with God our prayers;
　Spurn blood-stain'd Judas gold for it :
Let us do all that honor dares —
　Be earnest, faithful, bold for it !

THE IRISH WOLF-HOUND

FROM "THE FORAY OF CON O'DONNELL "

As fly the shadows o'er the grass,
　He flies with step as light and sure,
He hunts the wolf through Tostan pass,
　And starts the deer by Lisanoure.
The music of the Sabbath bells,
　O Con ! has not a sweeter sound
Than when along the valley swells
　The cry of John Mac Donnell's hound.

His stature tall, his body long,
　His back like night, his breast like snow,
His fore-leg pillar-like and strong,
　His hind-leg like a bended bow ;
Rough curling hair, head long and thin,
　His ear a leaf so small and round ;
Not Bran, the favorite dog of Fin,
　Could rival John Mac Donnell's hound.

Bartholomew Dowling

THE REVEL

(EAST INDIA)

WE meet 'neath the sounding rafter,
　And the walls around are bare ;
As they shout back our peals of laughter
　It seems that the dead are there.
Then stand to your glasses, steady !
　We drink in our comrades' eyes :
One cup to the dead already —
　Hurrah for the next that dies !

Not here are the goblets glowing,
　Not here is the vintage sweet ;

'T is cold, as our hearts are growing,
　And dark as the doom we meet.
But stand to your glasses, steady !
　And soon shall our pulses rise :
A cup to the dead already —
　Hurrah for the next that dies !

There 's many a hand that 's shaking,
　And many a cheek that 's sunk ;
But soon, though our hearts are breaking,
　They 'll burn with the wine we 've drunk.
Then stand to your glasses, steady !
　'T is here the revival lies :
Quaff a cup to the dead already —
　Hurrah for the next that dies !

Time was when we laugh'd at others ;
　We thought we were wiser then ;
Ha ! ha ! let them think of their mothers,
　Who hope to see them again.
No ! stand to your glasses, steady !
　The thoughtless is here the wise :
One cup to the dead already —
　Hurrah for the next that dies !

Not a sigh for the lot that darkles,
　Not a tear for the friends that sink ;
We 'll fall, 'midst the wine-cup's sparkles,
　As mute as the wine we drink.
Come stand to your glasses, steady !
　'T is this that the respite buys :
A cup to the dead already —
　Hurrah for the next that dies !

There 's a mist on the glass congealing,
　'T is the hurricane's sultry breath ;
And thus does the warmth of feeling
　Turn ice in the grasp of Death.

But stand to your glasses, steady !
　For a moment the vapor flies :
Quaff a cup to the dead already —
　Hurrah for the next that dies !

Who dreads to the dust returning ?
　Who shrinks from the sable shore,
Where the high and haughty yearning
　Of the soul can sting no more ?
No, stand to your glasses, steady !
　The world is a world of lies :
A cup to the dead already —
　And hurrah for the next that dies !

Cut off from the land that bore us,
　Betray'd by the land we find,
When the brightest have gone before us,
　And the dullest are most behind —
Stand, stand to your glasses, steady !
　'T is all we have left to prize :
One cup to the dead already —
　Hurrah for the next that dies !

John Kells Ingram

THE MEMORY OF THE DEAD

Who fears to speak of Ninety-Eight ?
　Who blushes at the name ?
When cowards mock the patriot's fate,
　Who hangs his head for shame ?
He 's all a knave or half a slave
　Who slights his country thus ;
But a true man, like you, man,
　Will fill your glass with us.

We drink the memory of the brave,
　The faithful and the few :
Some lie far off beyond the wave,
　Some sleep in Ireland, too ;
All, all are gone — but still lives on
　The fame of those who died :
All true men, like you, men,
　Remember them with pride.

Some on the shores of distant lands
　Their weary hearts have laid,
And by the stranger's heedless hands
　Their lonely graves were made ;
But, though their clay be far away
　Beyond the Atlantic foam,
In true men, like you, men,
　Their spirit 's still at home.

The dust of some is Irish earth ;
　Among their own they rest ;
And the same land that gave them birth
　Has caught them to her breast ;
And we will pray that from their clay
　Full many a race may start
Of true men, like you, men,
　To act as brave a part.

They rose in dark and evil days
　To right their native land ;
They kindled here a living blaze
　That nothing shall withstand.
Alas, that Might can vanquish Right !
　They fell, and pass'd away ;
But true men, like you, men,
　Are plenty here to-day.

Then here 's their memory — may it be
　For us a guiding light,
To cheer our strife for liberty,
　And teach us to unite !
Through good and ill, be Ireland's still,
　Though sad as theirs your fate ;
And true men be you, men,
　Like those of Ninety-Eight.

Thomas D'Arcy McGee

THE CELTIC CROSS

THROUGH storm and fire and gloom, I see
    it stand,
    Firm, broad, and tall,
The Celtic Cross that marks our Father-
    land,
    Amid them all !
Druids and Danes and Saxons vainly rage
    Around its base ;
It standeth shock on shock, and age on age,
    Star of our scatter'd race.

O Holy Cross ! dear symbol of the dread
    Death of our Lord,
Around thee long have slept our martyr
    dead
    Sward over sward.
An hundred bishops I myself can count
    Among the slain :
Chiefs, captains, rank and file, a shining
    mount
    Of God's ripe grain.

The monarch's mace, the Puritan's clay-
    more,
    Smote thee not down ;
On headland steep, on mountain summit
    hoar,
    In mart and town,
In Glendalough, in Ara, in Tyrone,
    We find thee still,
Thy open arms still stretching to thine own,
    O'er town and lough and hill.

And would they tear thee out of Irish soil,
    The guilty fools !
How time must mock their antiquated toil
    And broken tools !
Cranmer and Cromwell from thy grasp re-
    tir'd,
    Baffled and thrown ;
William and Anne to sap thy site con-
    spir'd, —
    The rest is known.

Holy Saint Patrick, father of our faith,
    Belov'd of God !
Shield thy dear Church from the impend-
    ing scaith,
    Or, if the rod

Must scourge it yet again, inspire and raise
    To emprise high
Men like the heroic race of other days,
    Who joyed to die.

Fear ! wherefore should the Celtic people
    fear
    Their Church's fate ?
The day is not — the day was never near —
    Could desolate
The Destin'd Island, all whose seedy clay
    Is holy ground :
Its cross shall stand till that predestin'd
    day
When Erin's self is drown'd.

THE IRISH WIFE

I WOULD not give my Irish wife
    For all the dames of the Saxon land ;
I would not give my Irish wife
    For the Queen of France's hand ;
For she to me is dearer
    Than castles strong, or lands, or life :
An outlaw — so I 'm near her
    To love till death my Irish wife.

O what would be this home of mine,
    A ruin'd, hermit-haunted place,
But for the light that nightly shines
    Upon its walls from Kathleen's face !
What comfort in a mine of gold,
    What pleasure in a royal life,
If the heart within lay dead and cold,
    If I could not wed my Irish wife ?

I knew the law forbade the banns ;
    I knew my king abhorr'd her race ;
Who never bent before their clans
    Must bow before their ladies' grace.
Take all my forfeited domain,
    I cannot wage with kinsmen strife :
Take knightly gear and noble name,
    And I will keep my Irish wife.

My Irish wife has clear blue eyes,
    My heaven by day, my stars by night ;
And twin-like truth and fondness lie
    Within her swelling bosom white
My Irish wife has golden hair,
    Apollo's harp had once such strings,

Apollo's self might pause to hear
　Her bird-like carol when she sings.

I would not give my Irish wife
　For all the dames of the Saxon land ;
I would not give my Irish wife
　For the Queen of France's hand ;
For she to me is dearer
　Than castles strong, or lands, or life :
In death I would be near her,
　And rise beside my Irish wife.

THE EXILE'S DEVOTION

IF I forswear the art divine
　That glorifies the dead,
What comfort then can I call mine,
　What solace seek instead ?
For from my birth our country's fame
　Was life to me, and love ;
And for each loyal Irish name
　Some garland still I wove.

I 'd rather be the bird that sings
　Above the martyr's grave,
Than fold in fortune's cage my wings
　And feel my soul a slave ;
I 'd rather turn one simple verse
　True to the Gaelic ear

Than sapphic odes I might rehearse
　With senates listening near.

Oh, native land ! dost ever mark,
　When the world's din is drown'd
Betwixt the daylight and the dark,
　A wandering solemn sound
That on the western wind is borne
　Across thy dewy breast ?
It is the voice of those who mourn
　For thee, in the far West.

For them and theirs I oft essay
　Thy ancient art of song,
And often sadly turn away,
　Deeming my rashness wrong ;
For well I ween, a loving will
　Is all the art I own :
Ah me ! could love suffice for skill,
　What triumphs I had known !

My native land ! my native land !
　Live in my memory still !
Break on my brain, ye surges grand !
　Stand up, mist-cover'd hill !
Still on the mirror of the mind
　The scenes I love, I see :
Would I could fly on the western wind,
　My native land, to thee !

Jane Francesca Speranza, Lady Wilde

(" SPERANZA ")

THE VOICE OF THE POOR

WAS sorrow ever like unto our sorrow ?
　O God above !
Will our night never change into a mor-
　row
Of joy and love ?
A deadly gloom is on us — waking — sleep-
　ing —
Like the darkness at noon-tide
That fell upon the pallid Mother, weep-
　ing
By the Crucified.

Before us die our brothers of starvation :
　Around are cries of famine and de-
　spair :

Where is hope for us, or comfort, or salva-
　tion ?
　Where, oh, where ?
If the angels ever hearken, downward bend-
　ing,
They are weeping, we are sure,
At the litanies of human groans ascend=
　ing
From the crush'd hearts of the poor.

When the human rests in love upon the
　human,
　All grief is light ;
But who bends one kind glance to illumine
　Our life-long night ?
The air around is ringing with their laugh-
　ter ;
God has only made the rich to smile :

But we, in our rags and want and woe, we
    follow after,
Weeping the while.

And the laughter seems but utter'd to de-
    ride us :
    When, oh ! when,
Will fall the frozen barriers that divide
    us
From other men ?
Will ignorance for ever thus enslave
    us !
Will misery for ever lay us low ?
All are eager with their insults, but to
    save us
None, none, we know.

We never knew a childhood's mirth and
    gladness,
Nor the proud heart of youth free and
    brave ;
Oh ! a death-like dream of wretchedness
    and sadness
Is our life's weary journey to the
    grave.
Day by day we lower sink and lower,
    Till the god-like soul within

Falls crush'd, beneath the fearful demon
    power
Of poverty and sin.

So we toil on — on, with fever burning
    In heart and brain ;
So we toil on — on, through bitter scorning,
    Want, woe and pain :
We dare not raise our eyes to the blue
    heaven
Or the toil must cease ;
We dare not breathe the fresh air God has
    given,
One hour in peace.

We must toil, though the light of life is
    burning,
    Oh, how dim !
We must toil on our sick bed, feebly turn-
    ing
    Our eyes to Him
Who alone can hear the pale lip faintly
    saying
With scarce mov'd breath,
And the paler hands, uplifted, and the pray-
    ing, —
    "Lord, grant us *Death !*"

Mary Eva Kelly

TIPPERARY

WERE you ever in sweet Tipperary, where
    the fields are so sunny and green,
And the heath-brown Slieve-bloom and the
    Galtees look down with so proud a
    mien ?
'T is there you would see more beauty than
    is on all Irish ground —
God bless you, my sweet Tipperary ! for
    where could your match be found ?

They say that your hand is fearful, that
    darkness is in your eye ;
But I 'll not let them dare to talk so black
    and bitter a lie.
O, no ! *macushla storin*, bright, bright, and
    warm are you,
With hearts as bold as the men of old, to
    yourself and your country true.

And when there is gloom upon you, bid
    them think who brought it there —

Sure a frown or a word of hatred was not
    made for your face so fair ;
You 've a hand for the grasp of friendship
    — another to make them quake,
And they 're welcome to whichsoever it
    pleases them to take.

Shall our homes, like the huts of Connaught,
    be crumbled before our eyes ?
Shall we fly, like a flock of wild geese, from
    all that we love and prize ?
No ! by those that were here before us, no
    churl shall our tyrant be,
Our land it is theirs by plunder — but, by
    Brigid, ourselves are free !

No ! we do not forget the greatness did
    once to sweet *Eiré* belong ;
No treason or craven spirit was ever our
    race among ;
And no frown or word of hatred we give —
    but to pay them back ;
In evil we only follow our enemies' dark-
    some track.

O, come for awhile among us and give us
the friendly hand !
And you 'll see that old Tipperary is a lov-
ing and gladsome land ;

From Upper to Lower Ormonde, bright
welcomes and smiles will spring :
On the plains of Tipperary the stranger is
like a king.

Ellen Mary Patrick Downing

WERE I BUT HIS OWN WIFE

WERE I but his own wife, to guard and to
guide him,
'T is little of sorrow should fall on my
dear ;
I 'd chant my low love-verses, stealing be-
side him,
So faint and so tender his heart would
but hear ;
I 'd pull the wild blossoms from valley and
highland,
And there at his feet I would lay them
all down ;
I 'd sing him the songs of our poor stricken
island,
Till his heart was on fire with a love like
my own.

There 's a rose by his dwelling, — I 'd tend
the lone treasure,
That he might have flowers when the
summer would come ;
There 's a harp in his hall, — I would wake
its sweet measure,
For he must have music to brighten his
home.

Were I but his own wife, to guide and to
guard him,
'T is little of sorrow should fall on my
dear ;
For every kind glance my whole life would
award him,
In sickness I 'd soothe and in sadness I 'd
cheer.

My heart is a fount welling upward for-
ever !
When I think of my true-love, by night
or by day,
That heart keeps its faith like a fast-flow-
ing river
Which gushes forever and sings on its
way.
I have thoughts full of peace for his soul to
repose in,
Were I but his own wife, to win and to
woo ;
O sweet, if the night of misfortune were
closing,
To rise like the morning star, darling,
for you !

"THE OATEN FLUTE"

William Barnes

(DORSET)

WOONE SMILE MWORE

O ! MEÄRY, when the zun went down,
Woone night in spring, w' viry rim,
Behind the nap wi' woody crown,
An' left your smilèn feäce so dim ;

Your little sister there, inside,
Wi' bellows on her little knee,
Did blow the vire, a-glearèn wide
Drough window-peänes, that I could
zee, —
As you did stan' wi' me, avore
The house, a-peärten,—woone smile mwore.

The chatt'rèn birds, a-risèn high,
An' zinkèn low, did swiftly vlee
Vrom shrinkèn moss, a-growèn dry,
Upon the leänèn apple tree.
An' there the dog, a-whippèn wide
His heäiry taïl, an' comèn near,
Did fondly lay ageän your zide
His coal-black nose an' russet ear :
To win what I 'd a-won avore,
Vrom your gaÿ feäce, his woone smile
    mwore.

An' while your mother bustled sprack,
A-gettèn supper out in hall,
An' cast her sheäde, a-whiv'rèn black
Avore the vire, upon the wall ;
Your brother come, wi' easy peäce,
In drough the slammèn geäte, along
The path, wi' healthy-bloomèn feäce,
A-whis'lèn shrill his last new zong :
An' when he come avore the door,
He met vrom you his woone smile mwore.

Now you that wer the daughter there,
Be mother on a husband's vloor,
An' mid ye meet wi' less o' ceäre
Than what your heärty mother bore ;
An' if abroad I have to rue
The bitter tongue, or wrongvul deed,
Mid I come hwome to sheäre wi' you
What 's needvul free o' pinchèn need :
An' vind that you ha' still in store
    My evenèn meal, an' woone smile
    mwore.

BLACKMWORE MAIDENS

The primrwose in the sheäde do blow,
The cowslip in the zun,
The thyme upon the down do grow,
The clote where streams do run ;
An' where do pretty maidens grow
An' blow, but where the tow'r
Do rise among the bricken tuns,
In Blackmwore by the Stour.

If you could zee their comely gaït,
An' pretty feäces' smiles,
A-trippèn on so light o' waïght,
An' steppèn off the stiles ;
A-gwaïn to church, as bells do swing
An' ring 'ithin the tow'r,
You 'd own the pretty maïdens' pleäce
Is Blackmwore by the Stour.

If you vrom Wimborne took your road,
To Stower or Paladore,
An' all the farmers' housen show'd
Their daughters at the door ;
You 'd cry to bachelors at hwome —
" Here, come : 'ithin an hour
You 'll vind ten maïdens to your mind,
In Blackmwore by the Stour."

An' if you look'd 'ithin their door,
To zee em in their pleäce,
A-doèn housework up avore
Their smilèn mother's feäce ;
You 'd cry — " Why, if a man would wive
An' thrive, 'ithout a dow'r,
Then let en look en out a wife
In Blackmwore by the Stour."

As I upon my road did pass
A school-house back in Maÿ,
There out upon the beäten grass
Wer maïdens at their plaÿ ;
An' as the pretty souls did tweil
An' smile, I cried, " The flow'r
O' beauty, then, is still in bud
In Blackmwore by the Stour."

THE HEÄRE

(1) There be the greyhounds ! lo'k ! an'
    there 's the heäre !
(2) What houn's, the squier's, Thomas ?
    where, then, where ?
(1) Why, out in Ash Hill, near the barn,
    behind
Thik tree. (3) The pollard ? (1) Pol-
    lard ! no ! b 'ye blind ?
(2) There, I do zee em over-right thik
    cow.
(3) The red woone ? (1) No, a mile be-
    yand her now.
(3) Oh ! there 's the heäre, a-meäkèn for
    the drong.
(2) My goodness ! How the dogs do
    zweep along,
A-pokèn out their pweinted noses' tips.
(3) He can't allow hizzelf much time vor
    slips !
(1) They 'll hab en, after all, I 'll bet a
    crown.
(2) Done vor a crown. They woon't !
    He 's gwaïn to groun'.
(3) He is ! (1) He idden ! (3) Ah ! 't is
    well his tooes
Ha' got noo corns, inside o' hobnail shoes.

(1) He's geäme a-runnèn too. Why, he
do mwore
Than eärn his life. (3) His life wer his
avore.
(1) There, now the dogs wull turn en.
(2) No! He's right.
(1) He idden! (2) Ees he is! (3)
He's out o' zight.
(1) Aye, aye. His mettle wull be well a-
tried
Agwaïn down Verny Hill, o' t' other zide.
They'll have en there. (3) O no! a vew
good hops
Wull teäke en on to Knapton Lower Copse.
(2) An' that's a meesh that he've a-took
avore.
(3) Ees, that's his hwome. (1) He'll
never reach his door.
(2) He wull. (1) He woon't. (3) Now,
hark, d'ye heär em now?
(2) O! here's a bwoy a-come athirt the
brow
O' Knapton Hill. We'll ax en. (1) Here,
my bwoy!
Canst tell us where's the heäre? (4)
He's got awoy.
(2) Ees, got awoy, in coo'se, I never zeed
A heäre a-scotèn on wi' half his speed.
(1) Why, there, the dogs be wold, an' half
a-done.
They can't catch anything wi' lags to run.
(2) Vrom vu'st to last they had but little
chance
O' catchèn o''n. (3) They had a perty
dance.
(1) No, catch en, no! I little thought
they would;
He know'd his road too well to Knapton
Wood.
(3) No! no! I wish the squier would let
me feäre
On rabbits till his hounds do catch thik
heäre.

THE CASTLE RUINS

A HAPPY day at Whitsuntide,
As soon's the zun begun to vall,
We all stroll'd up the steep hill-zide
To Meldon, gret an' small;
Out where the Castle wall stood high
A-mwoldrèn to the zunny sky.

An' there wi' Jenny took a stroll
Her youngest sister, Poll, so gaÿ,
Bezide John Hind, ah! merry soul,
An' mid her wedlock faÿ;
An' at our zides did plaÿ an' run
My little maïd an' smaller son.

Above the beäten mwold upsprung
The driven doust, a-spreadèn light,
An' on the new-leav'd thorn, a-hung,
Wer wool a-quiv'rèn white;
An' corn, a-sheenèn bright, did bow,
On slopèn Meldon's zunny brow.

There, down the roofless wall did glow
The zun upon the grassy vloor,
An' weakly-wandrèn winds did blow,
Unhinder'd by a door;
An' smokeless now avore the zun
Did stan' the ivy-girded tun.

My bwoy did watch the daws' bright
wings
A-flappèn vrom their ivy bow'rs;
My wife did watch my maïd's light
springs,
Out here an' there vor flow'rs;
And John did zee noo tow'rs, the pleäce
Vor him had only Polly's feäce.

An' there, of all that pried about
The walls, I overlook'd em best,
An' what o' that? Why, I meäde out
Noo mwore than all the rest:
That there wer woonce the nest of zome
That wer a-gone avore we come.

When woonce above the tun the smoke
Did wreathy blue among the trees,
An' down below, the livèn vo'k
Did tweil as brisk as bees;
Or zit wi' weary knees, the while
The sky wer lightless to their tweil.

Edwin Waugh

(LANCASHIRE)

THE DULE'S I' THIS BONNET O' MINE

THE dule's i' this bonnet o' mine ;
　My ribbins 'll never be reet ;
Here, Mally, aw 'm like to be fine,
　For Jamie 'll be comin' to-neet ;
He met me i' th' lone t' other day, —
　Aw 're gooin' for wayter to th' well, —
An' he begg'd that aw 'd wed him i'
　May ; —
　　Bi th' mass, iv he 'll let me, aw will !

When he took my two honds into his,
　Good Lord, heaw they trembled between ;
An' aw durstn't look up in his face,
　Becose on him seein' my e'en ;
My cheek went as red as a rose ; —
　There 's never a mortal can tell
Heaw happy aw felt ; for, thea knows,
　One could n't ha' ax'd him theirsel'.

But th' tale wur at th' end o' my tung, —
　To let it eawt would n't be reet, —
For aw thought to seem forrud wur wrung,
　So aw towd him aw 'd tell him to-neet ;
But Mally, thae knows very weel, —
　Though it is n't a thing one should own, —
Iv aw 'd th' pikein' o' th' world to mysel',
　Aw 'd oather ha' Jamie or noan.

Neaw, Mally, aw 've towd tho my mind ;
　What would to do iv 't wur thee ?
" Aw 'd tak him just while he 're inclin'd,
　An' a farrantly bargain he 'd be ;
For Jamie 's as gradely a lad
　As ever stepp'd eawt into th' sun ; —
So, jump at thy chance, an' get wed,
　An' may th' best o' th' job when it 's
　　done ! "

Eh, dear, but it 's time to be gwon, —
　Aw should n't like Jamie to wait ;
Aw connut for shame be too soon,
　An' aw would n't for th' world be too
　　late ;
Aw 'm o' ov a tremble to th' heel, —
　Dost think 'at my bonnet 'll do ? —
" Be off, lass, — thae looks very weel ;
　He wants noan o' th' bonnet, thae foo ! "

TH' SWEETHEART GATE

OH, there 's mony a gate eawt ov eawr
　　teawn-end,
　But nobbut one for me ;
It winds by a rindlin' wayter side,
　An' o'er a posied lea,
It wanders into a shady dell ;
　An' when aw 've done for th' day,
Aw never can sattle this heart o' mine,
　Beawt walkin' deawn that way.

It 's noather garden, nor posied lea,
　Nor wayter rindlin' clear ;
But deawn i' th vale there 's a rosy nook,
　An' my true love lives theer.
It 's olez summer where th' heart 's content,
　Tho' wintry winds may blow ;
An' there 's never a gate 'at 's so kind to th'
　　fuut,
　As th' gate one likes to go.

When aw set off o' sweetheartin,' aw 've
　A theawsan' things to say ;
But th' very first glent o' yon chimbley-top
　It drives 'em o' away ;
An' when aw meet wi' my bonny lass,
　It sets my heart a-jee ; —
Oh, there 's summut i' th' leet o' yon two
　　blue e'en
　That plays the dule wi' me !

When th' layrock 's finished his wark aboon,
　An' laid his music by,
He flutters deawn to his mate, an' stops
　Till dayleet stirs i' th' sky.
Though Matty sends me away at dark,
　Aw know that hoo 's reet full well ; —
An' it 's heaw aw love a true-hearted lass,
　No mortal tung can tell !

Aw wish that Candlemas day were past,
　When wakin' time comes on ;
An' aw wish that Kesmass time were here,
　An' Matty an' me were one.
Aw wish this wanderin' wark were o'er —
　This maunderin' to an' fro ;
That aw could go whoam to my own true
　　love,
　An' stop at neet an' o'.

OWD PINDER

OWD Pinder were a rackless foo,
  An' spent his days i' spreein';
At th' end ov every drinkin'-do,
  He 're sure to crack o' deein';
" Go, sell my rags, an' sell my shoon;
  Aw 's never live to trail 'em;
My ballis-pipes are eawt o' tune,
  An' th' wynt begins to fail 'em!

" Eawr Matty 's very fresh an' yung;
  'T would ony mon bewilder;
Hoo 'll wed again afore it 's lung,
  For th' lass is fond o' childer;
My bit o' brass 'll fly, — yo 'n see, —
  When th' coffin-lid has screen'd me;
It gwos again my pluck to dee,
  An' lev her wick beheend me.

" Come, Matty, come, an' cool my yed,
  Aw 'm finish'd, to my thinkin';"
Hoo happ'd him nicely up, an' said, —
  " Thae 's brought it on wi' drinkin'!"

" Nay, nay," said he, "my fuddle 's
    done;
  We 're partin' t' one fro' t' other;
So, promise me that when a 'm gwon,
  Thea 'll never wed another!"

" Th' owd tale," said hoo, an' laft her
    stoo,
  " It 's rayley past believin';
Thee think o' th' world thea 'rt goin' to,
  An' leave this world to th' livin';
What use to me can deead folk be?
  Thae 's kilt thisel' wi spreein';
An' iv that 's o' thae wants wi' me,
  Get forrud wi' thi deein'!"

He scrat his yed, he rubb'd his e'e,
  An' then he donn'd his breeches;
" Eawr Matty gets as fause," said he,
  " As one o' Pendle witches;
Iv ever aw 'm to muster wit,
  It mun be now or never;
Aw think aw 'll try to live a bit;
  It would n't do to lev her!"

Samuel Laycock

(LANCASHIRE)

WELCOME, BONNY BRID!

THA 'rt welcome, little bonny brid,
But should n't ha' come just when tha
    did;
    Toimes are bad.
We 're short o' pobbies for eawr Joe,
But that, of course, tha did n't know,
    Did ta, lad?

Aw 've often yeard mi feyther tell,
'At when aw coom i' th' world misel
    Trade wur slack;
An' neaw it 's hard wark pooin' throo —
But aw munno fear thee; iv aw do
    Tha 'll go back.

Cheer up! these toimes 'ull awter soon;
Aw 'm beawn to beigh another spoon —
    One for thee;
An' as tha 's sich a pratty face,
Aw 'll let thee have eawr Charley's place
    On mi knee.

God bless thee, love, aw 'm fain tha 'rt come,
Just try an' mak thisel awhoam:
    What ar 't co'd?
Tha 'rt loike thi mother to a tee,
But tha 's thi feyther's nose, aw see,
    Well, aw 'm blow'd!

Come, come, tha need n't look so shy,
Aw am no' blackin' thee, not I;
    Settle deawn,
An' tak this haup'ney for thisel',
There 's lots o' sugar-sticks to sell
    Deawn i' th' teawn.

Aw know when furst aw coom to th' leet
Aw 're fond o' owt 'at tasted sweet;
    Tha 'll be th' same.
But come, tha 's never towd thi dad
What he 's to co thi yet, mi lad —
    What 's thi name?

Hush! hush! tha munno cry this way,
But get this sope o' cinder tay
    While it 's warm;

Mi mother us'd to give it me,
When aw wur sich a lad as thee,
In her arm.

Hush a babby, hush a bee —
Oh, what a temper ! dear a-me,
Heaw tha skroikes !
Here 's a bit o' sugar, sithee ;
Howd thi noise, an' then aw 'll gie thee
Owt tha loikes.

We 'n nobbut getten coarsish fare,
But eawt o' this tha 'st ha' thi share,
Never fear.
Aw hope tha 'll never want a meel,
But allus fill thi bally weel
While tha 'rt here.

Thi feyther 's noan bin wed so long,
An' yet tha sees he 's middlin' throng
Wi' yo' o :
Besides thi little brother, Ted,
We 'n one up-steers, asleep i' bed
Wi' eawr Joe.

But though we 'n childer two or three,
We 'll mak' a bit o' reawm for thee —
Bless thee, lad !
Tha 'rt th' prattiest brid we han i' th'
nest ;
Come, hutch up closer to mi breast —
Aw 'm thi dad.

POETS OF THE NEW DAY

(HUMANITY — FREE THOUGHT — POLITICAL, SOCIAL, AND ARTISTIC, REFORM)

Ebenezer Elliott

ELEGY ON WILLIAM COBBETT

O BEAR him where the rain can fall,
And where the winds can blow ;
And let the sun weep o'er his pall
As to the grave ye go !

And in some little lone churchyard,
Beside the growing corn,
Lay gentle Nature's stern prose bard,
Her mightiest peasant-born.

Yes ! let the wild-flower wed his grave,
That bees may murmur near,
When o'er his last home bend the brave,
And say — "A man lies here !"

For Britons honor Cobbett's name,
Though rashly oft he spoke ;
And none can scorn, and few will blame,
The low-laid heart of oak.

See, o'er his prostrate branches, see !
E'en factious hate consents
To reverence, in the fallen tree,
His British lineaments.

Though gnarl'd the storm-toss'd boughs
that brav'd
The thunder's gather'd scowl,
Not always through his darkness rav'd
The storm-winds of the soul.

O, no ! in hours of golden calm
Morn met his forehead bold ;
And breezy evening sang her psalm
Beneath his dew-dropp'd gold.

The wren its crest of fibred fire
With his rich bronze compar'd,
While many a youngling's songful sire
His acorn'd twiglets shar'd.

The lark, above, sweet tribute paid,
Where clouds with light were riven ;
And true love sought his bluebell'd shade,
"To bless the hour of heaven."

E'en when his stormy voice was loud,
And guilt quak'd at the sound,
Beneath the frown that shook the proud
The poor a shelter found.

Dead oak ! thou livest. Thy smitten hands,
　The thunder of thy brow,
Speak with strange tongues in many lands,
　And tyrants hear thee, now !

Beneath the shadow of thy name,
　Inspir'd by thy renown,
Shall future patriots rise to fame,
　And many a sun go down.

A POET'S EPITAPH

Stop, mortal ! Here thy brother lies —
　The poet of the poor.
His books were rivers, woods, and skies,
　The meadow and the moor ;
His teachers were the torn heart's wail,
　The tyrant and the slave,
The street, the factory, the jail,
　The palace — and the grave.
Sin met thy brother everywhere !
　And is thy brother blam'd ?
From passion, danger, doubt, and care,
　He no exemption claim'd.
The meanest thing, earth's feeblest worm,
　He fear'd to scorn or hate ;
But, honoring in a peasant's form
　The equal of the great,
He bless'd the steward, whose wealth makes
　The poor man's little, more ;
Yet loath'd the haughty wretch that takes
　From plunder'd labor's store.

A hand to do, a head to plan,
　A heart to feel and dare —
Tell man's worst foes, here lies the man
　Who drew them as they are.

THE BUILDERS

Spring, summer, autumn, winter,
　Come duly, as of old ;
Winds blow, suns set, and morning saith,
　" Ye hills, put on your gold."

The song of Homer liveth,
　Dead Solon is not dead ;
Thy splendid name, Pythagoras,
　O'er realms of suns is spread.

But Babylon and Memphis
　Are letters traced in dust :
Read them, earth's tyrants ! ponder well
　The might in which ye trust !

They rose, while all the depths of guilt
　Their vain creators sounded ;
They fell, because on fraud and force
　Their corner-stones were founded.

Truth, mercy, knowledge, justice,
　Are powers that ever stand ;
They build their temples in the soul,
　And work with God's right hand.

William Johnson Fox

THE BARONS BOLD

The Barons bold on Runnymede
　By union won their charter ;
True men were they, prepar'd to bleed,
　But not their rights to barter :
And they swore that England's laws
　Were above a tyrant's word ;
And they prov'd that freedom's cause
　Was above a tyrant's sword :
　　Then honor we
　　The memory
Of those Barons brave united ;
　　And like their band,
　　Join hand to hand :
Our wrongs shall soon be righted.

The Commons brave, in Charles's time,
　By union made the Crown fall,
And show'd the world how royal crime
　Should lead to royal downfall :
And they swore that rights and laws
　Were above a monarch's word ;
And they raised the nation's cause
　Above the monarch's sword :
　　Then honor we
　　The memory
Of those Commons brave, united ;
　　And like their band,
　　Join hand to hand :
Our wrongs shall soon be righted.

The People firm, from Court and Peers,
　By union won Reform, sirs,

And, union safe, the nation steers
   Through sunshine and through storm,
      sirs :
And we swear that equal laws
   Shall prevail o'er lordlings' words,
And can prove that freedom's cause
   Is too strong for hireling swords :
      Then honor we
        The victory
Of the people brave, united ;
      Let all our bands
        Join hearts and hands :
Our wrongs shall all be righted.

LIFE IS LOVE

The fair varieties of earth,
   The heavens serene and blue above,
The rippling smile of mighty seas —
   What is the charm of all, but love ?

By love they minister to thought,
   Love makes them breathe the poet's
      song ;
When their Creator best is prais'd,
   'T is love inspires the adoring throng.

Knowledge, and power, and will supreme,
   Are but celestial tyranny,
Till they are consecrate by love,
   The essence of divinity.

For love is strength, and faith, and hope ;
   It crowns with bliss our mortal state ;
And, glancing far beyond the grave,
   Foresees a life of endless date.

That life is love ; and all of life
   Time or eternity can prove ;
Both men and angels, worms and gods,
   Exist in universal love.

Thomas Hood

THE DREAM OF EUGENE ARAM

'T was in the prime of summer time,
   An evening calm and cool,
And four-and-twenty happy boys
   Came bounding out of school :
There were some that ran and some that
   leap'd,
   Like troutlets in a pool.

Away they sped with gamesome minds,
   And souls untouch'd by sin ;
To a level mead they came, and there
   They drave the wickets in :
Pleasantly shone the setting sun
   Over the town of Lynn.

Like sportive deer they cours'd about,
   And shouted as they ran,
Turning to mirth all things of earth,
   As only boyhood can ;
But the Usher sat remote from all,
   A melancholy man !

His hat was off, his vest apart,
   To catch heaven's blessed breeze ;
For a burning thought was in his brow,
   And his bosom ill at ease :
So he lean'd his head on his hands, and read
   The book between his knees.

Leaf after leaf, he turn'd it o'er,
   Nor ever glanced aside,
For the peace of his soul he read that
   book
   In the golden eventide :
Much study had made him very lean,
   And pale, and leaden-eyed.

At last he shut the ponderous tome,
   With a fast and fervent grasp
He strain'd the dusky covers close,
   And fix'd the brazen hasp :
" Oh, God ! could I so close my mind,
   And clasp it with a clasp ! "

Then leaping on his feet upright,
   Some moody turns he took, —
Now up the mead, then down the mead,
   And past a shady nook, —
And, lo ! he saw a little boy
   That por'd upon a book.

" My gentle lad, what is 't you read —
   Romance or fairy fable ?
Or is it some historic page,
   Of kings and crowns unstable ? "
The young boy gave an upward glance, —
   " It is ' The Death of Abel.' "

The Usher took six hasty strides,
 As smit with sudden pain,
Six hasty strides beyond the place,
 Then slowly back again ;
And down he sat beside the lad,
 And talk'd with him of Cain ;

And, long since then, of bloody men,
 Whose deeds tradition saves ;
Of lonely folk cut off unseen,
 And hid in sudden graves ;
Of horrid stabs, in groves forlorn,
 And murders done in caves ;

And how the sprites of injur'd men
 Shriek upward from the sod ;
Aye, how the ghostly hand will point
 To show the burial clod ;
And unknown facts of guilty acts
 Are seen in dreams from God !

He told how murderers walk the earth
 Beneath the curse of Cain,
With crimson clouds before their eyes,
 And flames about their brain :
For blood has left upon their souls
 Its everlasting stain.

" And well," quoth he, " I know, for truth,
 Their pangs must be extreme, —
Woe, woe, unutterable woe, —
 Who spill life's sacred stream !
For why ? Methought, last night, I wrought
 A murder, in a dream !

" One that had never done me wrong,
 A feeble man and old :
I led him to a lonely field ;
 The moon shone clear and cold :
Now here, said I, this man shall die,
 And I will have his gold !

" Two sudden blows with a ragged stick,
 And one with a heavy stone,
One hurried gash with a hasty knife, —
 And then the deed was done ;
There was nothing lying at my foot
 But lifeless flesh and bone !

" Nothing but lifeless flesh and bone,
 That could not do me ill ;
And yet I fear'd him all the more,
 For lying there so still :
There was a manhood in his look,
 That murder could not kill.

" And, lo ! the universal air
 Seem'd lit with ghastly flame ;
Ten thousand thousand dreadful eyes
 Were looking down in blame :
I took the dead man by his hand,
 And call'd upon his name !

" Oh, God ! it made me quake to see
 Such sense within the slain !
But when I touch'd the lifeless clay,
 The blood gush'd out amain !
For every clot, a burning spot
 Was scorching in my brain !

" My head was like an ardent coal,
 My heart as solid ice ;
My wretched, wretched soul, I knew,
 Was at the Devil's price ;
A dozen times I groan'd : the dead
 Had never groan'd but twice.

" And now, from forth the frowning sky,
 From the Heaven's topmost height,
I heard a voice — the awful voice
 Of the blood-avenging sprite :
' Thou guilty man ! take up thy dead
 And hide it from my sight !'

" I took the dreary body up,
 And cast it in a stream,
A sluggish water, black as ink,
 The depth was so extreme : —
My gentle Boy, remember this
 Is nothing but a dream !

" Down went the corse with hollow plunge
 And vanish'd in the pool ;
Anon I cleans'd my bloody hands,
 And wash'd my forehead cool,
And sat among the urchins young,
 That evening in the school.

" Oh, Heaven ! to think of their white souls,
 And mine so black and grim !
I could not share in childish prayer
 Nor join in Evening Hymn :
Like a Devil of the Pit I seem'd,
 'Mid holy Cherubim !

" And peace went with them, one and all,
 And each calm pillow spread ;
But Guilt was my grim Chamberlain
 That lighted me to bed,
And drew my midnight curtains round,
 With fingers bloody red !

"All night I lay in agony,
  In anguish dark and deep,
My fever'd eyes I dar'd not close,
  But star'd aghast at Sleep :
For Sin had render'd unto her
  The keys of hell to keep.

"All night I lay in agony,
  From weary chime to chime,
With one besetting horrid hint,
  That rack'd me all the time ;
A mighty yearning like the first
  Fierce impulse unto crime ;

"One stern tyrannic thought, that made
  All other thoughts its slave :
Stronger and stronger every pulse
  Did that temptation crave,
Still urging me to go and see
  The Dead Man in his grave !

"Heavily I rose up, as soon
  As light was in the sky,
And sought the black accursed pool
  With a wild misgiving eye :
And I saw the Dead in the river bed,
  For the faithless stream was dry.

"Merrily rose the lark, and shook
  The dew-drop from its wing ;
But I never mark'd its morning flight,
  I never heard it sing,
For I was stooping once again
  Under the horrid thing.

"With breathless speed, like a soul in chase,
  I took him up and ran ;
There was no time to dig a grave
  Before the day began :
In a lonesome wood, with heaps of leaves,
  I hid the murder'd man.

"And all that day I read in school,
  But my thought was other where ;
As soon as the mid-day task was done,
  In secret I was there :
And a mighty wind had swept the leaves,
  And still the corse was bare !

"Then down I cast me on my face,
  And first began to weep,
For I knew my secret then was one
  That earth refus'd to keep :
Or land or sea, though he should be
  Ten thousand fathoms deep.

"So wills the fierce avenging Sprite,
  Till blood for blood atones !
Aye, though he 's buried in a cave,
  And trodden down with stones,
And years have rotted off his flesh, —
  The world shall see his bones.

"Oh, God ! that horrid, horrid dream
  Besets me now awake !
Again — again, with dizzy brain,
  The human life I take ;
And my red right hand grows raging
    hot,
  Like Cranmer's at the stake.

"And still no peace for the restless clay
  Will wave or mould allow ;
The horrid thing pursues my soul, —
  It stands before me now !"
The fearful Boy look'd up, and saw
  Huge drops upon his brow.

That very night, while gentle sleep
  The urchin eyelids kiss'd,
Two stern-faced men set out from Lynn,
  Through the cold and heavy mist ;
And Eugene Aram walk'd between,
  With gyves upon his wrist.

FLOWERS

I WILL not have the mad Clytie,
Whose head is turn'd by the sun ;
The tulip is a courtly quean,
Whom, therefore I will shun ;
The cowslip is a country wench,
The violet is a nun ;
But I will woo the dainty rose,
The queen of every one.

The pea is but a wanton witch,
In too much haste to wed,
And clasps her rings on every hand ;
The wolfsbane I should dread ;
Nor will I dreary rosemarye,
That always mourns the dead ;
But I will woo the dainty rose,
With her cheeks of tender red.

The lily is all in white, like a saint,
And so is no mate for me,
And the daisy's cheek is tipp'd with a
  blush,
She is of such low degree ;

Jasmine is sweet, and has many loves,
And the broom's betroth'd to the bee ;
But I will plight with the dainty rose,
For fairest of all is she.

FAIR INES

O SAW ye not fair Ines ?
She 's gone into the West,
To dazzle when the sun is down,
And rob the world of rest :
She took our daylight with her,
The smiles that we love best,
With morning blushes on her cheek,
And pearls upon her breast.

O turn again, fair Ines,
Before the fall of night,
For fear the Moon should shine alone,
And stars unrivall'd bright ;
And blessed will the lover be
That walks beneath their light,
And breathes the love against thy cheek
I dare not even write.

Would I had been, fair Ines,
That gallant cavalier
Who rode so gayly by thy side,
And whisper'd thee so near !
Were there no bonny dames at home,
Or no true lovers here,
That he should cross the seas to win
The dearest of the dear ?

I saw thee, lovely Ines,
Descend along the shore,
With bands of noble gentlemen,
And banners wav'd before ;
And gentle youth and maidens gay,
And snowy plumes they wore ; —
It would have been a beauteous dream, —
If it had been no more !

Alas, alas, fair Ines,
She went away with song,
With Music waiting on her steps,
And shoutings of the throng ;
But some were sad, and felt no mirth,
But only Music's wrong,
In sounds that sang Farewell, Farewell,
To her you 've lov'd so long.

Farewcll, farewell, fair Ines !
That vessel never bore

So fair a lady on its deck,
Nor danced so light before :
Alas for pleasure on the sea,
And sorrow on the shore !
The smile that bless'd one lover's heart
Has broken many more !

THE DEATH-BED

WE watch'd her breathing thro' the night,
  Her breathing soft and low,
As in her breast the wave of life
  Kept heaving to and fro.

So silently we seem'd to speak,
  So slowly mov'd about,
As we had lent her half our powers
  To eke her living out.

Our very hopes belied our fears,
  Our fears our hopes belied —
We thought her dying when she slept,
  And sleeping when she died.

For when the morn came dim and sad,
  And chill with early showers,
Her quiet eyelids clos'd — she had
  Another morn than ours.

BALLAD

IT was not in the winter
Our loving lot was cast ;
It was the time of roses,
We pluck'd them as we pass'd.

That churlish season never frown'd
On early lovers yet :
Oh, no — the world was newly crown'd
With flowers when first we met !

'T was twilight, and I bade you go,
But still you held me fast ;
It was the time of roses,
We pluck'd them as we pass'd.

What else could peer thy glowing cheek,
That tears began to stud ?
And when I ask'd the like of Love,
You snatch'd a damask bud ;

And op'd it to the dainty core,
Still glowing to the last.
It was the time of roses,
We pluck'd them as we pass'd.

LEAR

A POOR old king with sorrow for my crown,
Thron'd upon straw, and mantled with the
　　wind —
For pity, my own tears have made me blind
That I might never see my children's frown ;
And maybe madness like a friend has
　　thrown
A folded fillet over my dark mind,
So that unkindly speech may sound for
　　kind, —
Albeit I know not. — I am childish grown,
And have not gold to purchase wit withal,
I that have once maintain'd most royal
　　state,
A very bankrupt now that may not call
My child, my child — all-beggar'd save in
　　tears,
Wherewith I daily weep an old man's
　　fate,
Foolish — and blind — and overcome with
　　years !

BALLAD

SPRING it is cheery,
　　Winter is dreary,
Green leaves hang, but the brown must fly ;
　　When he 's forsaken,
　　Wither'd and shaken,
What can an old man do but die ?

　　Love will not clip him,
　　Maids will not lip him,
Maud and Marian pass him by ;
　　Youth it is sunny,
　　Age has no honey,
What can an old man do but die ?

　　June it was jolly,
　　O for its folly !
A dancing leg and a laughing eye ;
　　Youth may be silly,
　　Wisdom is chilly,
What can an old man do but die ?

　　Friends they are scanty,
　　Beggars are plenty,
If he has followers, I know why ;
　　Gold 's in his clutches,
　　(Buying him crutches !)
What can an old man do but die ?

FROM " MISS KILMANSEGG AND HER PRECIOUS LEG "

HER DEATH

'T IS a stern and startling thing to think
How often mortality stands on the brink
　　Of its grave without any misgiving :
And yet in this slippery world of strife,
In the stir of human bustle so rife,
There are daily sounds to tell us that Life
　　Is dying, and Death is living !

Ay, Beauty the Girl, and Love the Boy,
Bright as they are with hope and joy,
　　How their souls would sadden instanter,
To remember that one of those wedding
　　bells,
Which ring so merrily through the dells,
　　Is the same that knells
　　Our last farewells,
　　Only broken into a canter !

But breath and blood set doom at nought :
How little the wretched Countess thought,
　　When at night she unloos'd her sandal,
That the Fates had woven her burial cloth,
And that Death, in the shape of a Death's
　　Head Moth,
　　Was fluttering round her candle !

As she look'd at her clock of or-molu,
For the hours she had gone so wearily
　　through
　　At the end of a day of trial,
How little she saw in her pride of prime
The dart of Death in the Hand of Time —
　　That hand which mov'd on the dial !

As she went with her taper up the stair,
How little her swollen eye was aware
　　That the Shadow which follow'd was
　　　double !
Or when she clos'd her chamber door,
It was shutting out, and for evermore,
　　The world — and its worldly trouble.

Little she dreamt, as she laid aside
Her jewels, after one glance of pride,
　　They were solemn bequests to Vanity ;
Or when her robes she began to doff
That she stood so near to the putting off
　　Of the flesh that clothes humanity.

And when she quench'd the taper's light,
How little she thought, as the smoke took
    flight,
That her day was done — and merged in a
    night
    Of dreams and durations uncertain,
      Or, along with her own,
      That a Hand of Bone
Was closing mortality's curtain !

But life is sweet, and mortality blind,
And youth is hopeful, and Fate is kind
    In concealing the day of sorrow ;
And enough is the present tense of toil,
For this world is to all a stiffish soil,
And the mind flies back with a glad recoil
    From the debts not due till to-morrow.

Wherefore else does the spirit fly
And bids its daily cares good-bye,
    Along with its daily clothing ?
Just as the felon condemn'd to die,
    With a very natural loathing,
Leaving the Sheriff to dream of ropes,
From his gloomy cell in a vision elopes
To caper on sunny greens and slopes,
    Instead of the dance upon nothing.

Thus, even thus, the Countess slept,
While Death still nearer and nearer crept,
    Like the Thane who smote the sleeping ;
But her mind was busy with early joys,
Her golden treasures and golden toys,
      That flash'd a bright
      And golden light
Under lids still red with weeping.

The golden doll that she used to hug !
Her coral of gold, and the golden mug !
    Her godfather's golden presents !
The golden service she had at her meals,
The golden watch, and chain, and seals,
Her golden scissors, and thread, and reels,
    And her golden fishes and pheasants!

The golden guineas in silken purse,
And the Golden Legends she heard from
    her nurse,
    Of the Mayor in his gilded carriage,
And London streets that were pav'd with
    gold,
And the Golden Eggs that were laid of old,
      With each golden thing
      To the golden ring
At her own auriferous Marriage !

And still the golden light of the sun
Through her golden dream appear'd to run,
Though the night that roar'd without was
    one
    To terrify seamen or gypsies,
While the moon, as if in malicious mirth,
Kept peeping down at the ruffled earth,
As though she enjoy'd the tempest's birth,
    In revenge of her old eclipses.

But vainly, vainly, the thunder fell,
For the soul of the Sleeper was under a spell
    That time had lately embitter'd :
The Count, as once at her foot he knelt —
That foot which now he wanted to melt !
But — hush ! — 't was a stir at her pillow
    she felt,
    And some object before her glitter'd.

'T was the Golden Leg ! — she knew its
    gleam !
And up she started, and tried to scream, —
    But, ev'n in the moment she started,
Down came the limb with a frightful smash,
And, lost in the universal flash
That her eyeballs made at so mortal a crash,
    The Spark, call'd Vital, departed !
  .   .   .   .

Gold, still gold ! hard, yellow, and cold,
For gold she had liv'd, and she died for
    gold,
    By a golden weapon — not oaken ;
In the morning they found her all alone —
Stiff, and bloody, and cold as stone —
But her Leg, the Golden Leg, was gone,
    And the " Golden Bowl was broken ! "

Gold — still gold ! it haunted her yet :
At the Golden Lion the Inquest met —
    Its foreman a carver and gilder,
And the Jury debated from twelve till three
What the Verdict ought to be,
And they brought it in as Felo-de-Se,
    " Because her own Leg had kill'd her !"

HER MORAL

Gold ! Gold ! Gold ! Gold !
Bright and yellow, hard and cold,
Molten, graven, hammer'd, and roll'd ;
Heavy to get, and light to hold ;
Hoarded, barter'd, bought, and sold,
Stolen, borrow'd, squander'd, doled :
Spurn'd by the young, but hugg'd by the old
To the very verge of the churchyard mould ;

Price of many a crime untold ;
Gold ! Gold ! Gold ! Gold !
Good or bad a thousand-fold !
  How widely its agencies vary :
To save — to ruin — to curse — to bless —
As even its minted coins express,
Now stamp'd with the image of Good Queen
    Bess,
And now of a bloody Mary.

RUTH

SHE stood breast high amid the corn,
Clasp'd by the golden light of morn,
Like the sweetheart of the sun,
Who many a glowing kiss had won.

On her cheek an autumn flush,
Deeply ripen'd ; — such a blush
In the midst of brown was born,
Like red poppies grown with corn.

Round her eyes her tresses fell,
Which were blackest none could tell,
But long lashes veil'd a light
That had else been all too bright.

And her hat, with shady brim,
Made her tressy forehead dim ;
Thus she stood amid the stooks,
Praising God with sweetest looks :

Sure, I said, heav'n did not mean
Where I reap thou shouldst but glean,
Lay thy sheaf adown and come,
Share my harvest and my home.

THE WATER LADY

ALAS, the moon should ever beam
To show what man should never see !
I saw a maiden on a stream,
And fair was she !

I stayed awhile, to see her throw
Her tresses back, that all beset
The fair horizon of her brow
With clouds of jet.

I stayed a little while to view
Her cheek, that wore in place of red
The bloom of water, tender blue,
Daintily spread.

I stayed to watch, a little space,
Her parted lips if she would sing ;
The waters clos'd above her face
With many a ring.

And still I stayed a little more :
Alas, she never comes again !
I throw my flowers from the shore,
And watch in vain.

I know my life will fade away,
I know that I must vainly pine,
For I am made of mortal clay,
But she 's divine !

ODE

AUTUMN

I

I SAW old Autumn in the misty morn
Stand shadowless, like silence, listening
To silence, for no lonely bird would sing
Into his hollow ear from woods forlorn,
Nor lowly hedge nor solitary thorn ; —
Shaking his languid locks all dewy bright
With tangled gossamer that fell by night,
    Pearling his coronet of golden corn.

II

Where are the songs of Summer ? — With
    the sun,
Oping the dusky eyelids of the south,
Till shade and silence waken up as one,
And Morning sings with a warm odorous
    mouth.
Where are the merry birds ? — Away, away,
On panting wings through the inclement
    skies,
    Lest owls should prey
    Undazzled at noon-day,
And tear with horny beak their lustrous
    eyes.

III

Where are the blooms of Summer ? — In
    the west,
Blushing their last to the last sunny hours,
When the mild Eve by sudden Night is
    prest
Like tearful Proserpine, snatch'd from her
    flow'rs
    To a most gloomy breast.

Where is the pride of Summer, — the green
    prime, —
The many, many leaves all twinkling ? —
    Three
On the moss'd elm ; three on the naked
    lime
Trembling, — and one upon the old oak
    tree !
Where is the Dryad's immortality ? —
Gone into mournful cypress and dark yew,
Or wearing the long gloomy Winter through
In the smooth holly's green eternity.

IV

The squirrel gloats on his accomplish'd
    hoard,
The ants have brimm'd their garners with
    ripe grain,
    And honey bees have stor'd
The sweets of Summer in their luscious
    cells ;
The swallows all have wing'd across the
    main ;
But here the Autumn melancholy dwells,
    And sighs her tearful spells
Amongst the sunless shadows of the plain.
    Alone, alone,
    Upon a mossy stone,
She sits and reckons up the dead and
    gone
With the last leaves for a love-rosary,
Whilst all the wither'd world looks drearily,
Like a dim picture of the drowned past
In the hush'd mind's mysterious far away,
Doubtful what ghostly thing will steal the
    last
Into that distance, gray upon the gray.

V

O go and sit with her, and be o'ershaded
Under the languid downfall of her hair :
She wears a coronal of flowers faded
Upon her forehead, and a face of care ; —
There is enough of wither'd everywhere
To make her bower, — and enough of
    gloom ;   *
There is enough of sadness to invite,
If only for the rose that died, — whose
    doom
Is Beauty's, — she that with the living bloom
Of conscious cheeks most beautifies the
    light ; —
There is enough of sorrowing, and quite

Enough of bitter fruits the earth doth
    bear, —
Enough of chilly droppings for her
    bowl ;
Enough of fear and shadowy despair,
To frame her cloudy prison for the
    soul !

THE SONG OF THE SHIRT

With fingers weary and worn,
    With eyelids heavy and red,
A woman sat in unwomanly rags,
    Plying her needle and thread —
        Stitch ! stitch ! stitch !
In poverty, hunger, and dirt,
    And still with a voice of dolorous pitch
She sang the " Song of the Shirt ! "

" Work ! work ! work !
    While the cock is crowing aloof !
And work — work — work,
    Till the stars shine through the roof !
It 's Oh ! to be a slave
    Along with the barbarous Turk,
Where woman has never a soul to save,
    If this is Christian work !

" Work — work — work
    Till the brain begins to swim ;
Work — work — work
    Till the eyes are heavy and dim.
Seam, and gusset, and band,
    Band, and gusset, and seam,
Till over the buttons I fall asleep,
    And sew them on in a dream !

" Oh, Men, with Sisters dear !
    Oh, Men, with Mothers and Wives !
It is not linen you 're wearing out,
    But human creatures' lives !
        Stitch — stitch — stitch,
    In poverty, hunger, and dirt,
Sewing at once, with a double thread,
    A Shroud as well as a Shirt.

" But why do I talk of Death ?
    That Phantom of grisly bone,
I hardly fear his terrible shape,
    It seems so like my own —
It seems so like my own,
    Because of the fasts I keep ;
Oh, God ! that bread should be so dear,
    And flesh and blood so cheap !

" Work — work — work !
  My labor never flags ;
And what are its wages ?   A bed of straw,
  A crust of bread — and rags.
That shatter'd roof — and this naked floor —
  A table — a broken chair —
And a wall so blank, my shadow I thank
  For sometimes falling there.

" Work — work — work !
From weary chime to chime,
  Work — work — work —
As prisoners work for crime !
    Band, and gusset, and seam,
    Seam, and gusset, and band,
Till the heart is sick, and the brain be-
      numb'd,
    As well as the weary hand.

" Work — work — work,
In the dull December light,
  And work — work — work,
When the weather is warm and bright,
    While underneath the eaves
    The brooding swallows cling
As if to show me their sunny backs
    And twit me with the spring.

" Oh ! but to breathe the breath
Of the cowslip and primrose sweet,
  With the sky above my head,
And the grass beneath my feet,
    For only one short hour
    To feel as I used to feel,
Before I knew the woes of want
    And the walk that costs a meal,

" Oh, but for one short hour !
  A respite however brief !
No blessed leisure for Love or Hope,
  But only time for Grief !
    A little weeping would ease my heart,
    But in their briny bed
My tears must stop, for every drop
    Hinders needle and thread ! "

With fingers weary and worn,
  With eyelids heavy and red,
A woman sat in unwomanly rags,
    Plying her needle and thread —
      Stitch ! stitch ! stitch !
    In poverty, hunger, and dirt,
And still with a voice of dolorous pitch,
  Would that its tone could reach the Rich !
    She sang this " Song of the Shirt ! "

THE LAY OF THE LABORER

A SPADE ! a rake ! a hoe !
  A pickaxe, or a bill !
A hook to reap, or a scythe to mow,
  A flail, or what ye will,
And here 's a ready hand
  To ply the needful tool,
And skill'd enough, by lessons rough,
  In Labor's rugged school.

To hedge, or dig the ditch,
  To lop or fell the tree,
To lay the swarth on the sultry field,
  Or plough the stubborn lea ;
The harvest stack to bind,
  The wheaten rick to thatch,
And never fear in my pouch to find
  The tinder or the match.

To a flaming barn or farm
  My fancies never roam ;
The fire I yearn to kindle and burn
  Is on the hearth of Home ;
Where children huddle and crouch
  Through dark long winter days,
Where starving children huddle and crouch,
  To see the cheerful rays
A-glowing on the haggard cheek,
  And not in the haggard's blaze !

To Him who sends a drought
  To parch the fields forlorn,
The rain to flood the meadows with mud,
  The blight to blast the corn,
To Him I leave to guide
  The bolt in its crooked path,
To strike the miser's rick, and show
  The skies blood-red with wrath.

A spade ! a rake ! a hoe !
  A pickaxe, or a bill !
A hook to reap, or a scythe to mow,
  A flail, or what ye will ;
The corn to thrash, or the hedge to plash,
  The market-team to drive,
Or mend the fence by the cover side,
  And leave the game alive.

Ay, only give me work,
  And then you need not fear
That I shall snare his worship's hare,
  Or kill his grace's deer ;
Break into his lordship's house,
  To steal the plate so rich ;

Or leave the yeoman that had a purse
    To welter in a ditch.

Wherever Nature needs,
    Wherever Labor calls,
No job I'll shirk of the hardest work,
    To shun the workhouse walls ;
Where savage laws begrudge
    The pauper babe its breath,
And doom a wife to a widow's life,
    Before her partner's death.

My only claim is this,
    With labor stiff and stark,
By lawful turn my living to earn
    Between the light and dark ;
My daily bread, and nightly bed,
    My bacon and drop of beer —
But all from the hand that holds the land,
    And none from the overseer !

No parish money, or loaf,
    No pauper badges for me,
A son of the soil, by right of toil
    Entitled to my fee.
No alms I ask, give me my task :
    Here are the arm, the leg,
The strength, the sinews of a Man,
    To work, and not to beg.

Still one of Adam's heirs,
    Though doom'd by chance of birth
To dress so mean, and to eat the lean
    Instead of the fat of the earth ;
To make such humble meals
    As honest labor can,
A bone and a crust, with a grace to God,
    And little thanks to man !

A spade ! a rake ! a hoe !
    A pickaxe, or a bill !
A hook to reap, or a scythe to mow,
    A flail, or what ye will ;
Whatever the tool to ply,
    Here is a willing drudge,
With muscle and limb, and woe to him
    Who does their pay begrudge !

Who every weekly score
    Docks labor's little mite,
Bestows on the poor at the temple-door,
    But robb'd them over night.
The very shilling he hop'd to save,
    As health and morals fail,
Shall visit me in the New Bastile,
    The Spital or the Gaol !

THE BRIDGE OF SIGHS

ONE more unfortunate,
    Weary of breath,
    Rashly importunate,
Gone to her death !

Take her up tenderly,
    Lift her with care ;
    Fashioned so slenderly,
Young, and so fair !

Look at her garments
Clinging like cerements ;
Whilst the wave constantly
Drips from her clothing ;
Take her up instantly,
Loving, not loathing.

Touch her not scornfully ;
Think of her mournfully,
Gently and humanly ;
Not of the stains of her,
All that remains of her
Now is pure womanly.

Make no deep scrutiny
Into her mutiny
Rash and undutiful :
Past all dishonor,
Death has left on her
Only the beautiful.

Still, for all slips of hers,
One of Eve's family —
Wipe those poor lips of hers
Oozing so clammily.

Loop up her tresses
Escaped from the comb,
Her fair auburn tresses ;
Whilst wonderment guesses
Where was her home ?

Who was her father ?
Who was her mother ?
Had she a sister ?
Had she a brother ?
Or was there a dearer one
Still, and a nearer one
Yet, than all other ?

Alas ! for the rarity
Of Christian charity
Under the sun !
Oh ! it was pitiful !

Near a whole city full,
Home she had none.

Sisterly, brotherly,
Fatherly, motherly
Feelings had changed :
Love, by harsh evidence,
Thrown from its eminence ;
Even God's providence
Seeming estranged.

Where the lamps quiver
So far in the river,
With many a light
From window and casement,
From garret to basement,
She stood with amazement,
Houseless by night.

The bleak wind of March
Made her tremble and shiver,
But not the dark arch,
Or the black flowing river ;
Mad from life's history,
Glad to death's mystery,
Swift to be hurl'd —
Any where, any where
Out of the world !

In she plunged boldly,
No matter how coldly
The rough river ran, —
Over the brink of it,
Picture it — think of it,
Dissolute Man !
Lave in it, drink of it,
Then, if you can !

Take her up tenderly,
Lift her with care ;
Fashion'd so slenderly,
Young, and so fair !

Ere her limbs frigidly
Stiffen too rigidly,

Decently, kindly,
Smooth and compose them ;
And her eyes, close them,
Staring so blindly !

Dreadfully staring
Thro' muddy impurity,
As when with the daring
Last look of despairing
Fix'd on futurity.

Perishing gloomily,
Spurr'd by contumely,
Cold inhumanity,
Burning insanity,
Into her rest,
Cross her hands humbly,
As if praying dumbly,
Over her breast.

Owning her weakness,
Her evil behavior,
And leaving, with meekness,
Her sins to her Saviour !

STANZAS

FAREWELL, Life ! my senses swim,
And the world is growing dim ;
Thronging shadows cloud the light,
Like the advent of the night ;
Colder, colder, colder still,
Upward steals a vapor chill ;
Strong the earthy odor grows —
I smell the mould above the rose !

Welcome, Life ! the Spirit strives !
Strength returns and hope revives ;
Cloudy fears and shapes forlorn
Fly like shadows at the morn ;
O'er the earth there comes a bloom ;
Sunny light for sullen gloom,
Warm perfume for vapor cold —
I smell the rose above the mould !

Bartholomew Simmons

STANZAS TO THE MEMORY OF THOMAS HOOD

TAKE back into thy bosom, earth,
This joyous, May-eyed morrow,

The gentlest child that ever mirth
Gave to be rear'd by sorrow !
'T is hard — while rays half green, half
gold,
Through vernal bowers are burning,

And streams their diamond-mirrors hold
  To summer's face returning —
To say we 're thankful that his sleep
  Shall never more be lighter,
In whose sweet-tongued companionship
  Stream, bower, and beam grew brighter !

But all the more intensely true
  His soul gave out each feature
Of elemental love — each hue
  And grace of golden nature ;
The deeper still beneath it all
  Lurk'd the keen jags of anguish ;
The more the laurels clasp'd his brow
  Their poison made it languish.
Seem'd it that like the nightingale
  Of his own mournful singing,
The tenderer would his song prevail
  While most the thorn was stinging.

So never to the desert-worn
  Did fount bring freshness deeper,
Than that his placid rest this morn
  Has brought the shrouded sleeper.
That rest may lap his weary head
  Where charnels choke the city,
Or where, mid woodlands, by his bed
  The wren shall wake its ditty ;
But near or far, while evening's star
  Is dear to hearts regretting,
Around that spot admiring thought
  Shall hover, unforgetting.

And if this sentient, seething world
  Is, after all, ideal,
Or in the immaterial furl'd
  Alone resides the real,
Freed one ! there 's a wail for thee this
    hour
  Through thy lov'd elves' dominions ;
Hush'd is each tiny trumpet-flower,
  And droopeth Ariel's pinions ;
Even Puck, dejected, leaves his swing,
  To plan, with fond endeavor,
What pretty buds and dews shall keep
  Thy pillow bright for ever.

And higher, if less happy, tribes,
  The race of early childhood,

Shall miss thy whims of frolic wit,
  That in the summer wild-wood,
Or by the Christmas hearth, were hail'd,
  And hoarded as a treasure
Of undecaying merriment
  And ever-changing pleasure.
Things from thy lavish humor flung
  Profuse as scents, are flying
This kindling morn, when blooms are born
  As fast as blooms are dying.

Sublimer art owned thy control :
  The minstrel's mightiest magic,
With sadness to subdue the soul,
  Or thrill it with the tragic.
Now listening Aram's fearful dream,
  We see beneath the willow
That dreadful thing, or watch him steal,
  Guilt-lighted, to his pillow.
Now with thee roaming ancient groves,
  We watch the woodman felling
The funeral elm, while through its boughs
  The ghostly wind comes knelling.

Dear worshipper of Dian's face
  In solitary places,
Shalt thou no more steal, as of yore,
  To meet her white embraces ?
Is there no purple in the rose
  Henceforward to thy senses ?
For thee have dawn and daylight's close
  Lost their sweet influences ?
No ! — by the mental night untam'd
  Thou took'st to death's dark portal,
The joy of the wide universe
  Is now to thee immortal !

How fierce contrasts the city's roar
  With thy new-conquer'd quiet ! —
This stunning hell of wheels that pour
  With princes to their riot !
Loud clash the crowds — the busy clouds
  With thunder-noise are shaken,
While pale, and mute, and cold, afar
  Thou liest, men-forsaken.
Hot life reeks on, nor recks that one —
  The playful, human-hearted —
Who lent its clay less earthiness,
  Is just from earth departed.

Harriet Martineau

ON, ON, FOREVER

BENEATH this starry arch
  Nought resteth or is still ;
But all things hold their march,
  As if by one great will :
Moves one, move all : hark to the foot-fall !
  On, on, forever !

Yon sheaves were once but seed ;
  Will ripens into deed ;
As cave-drops swell the streams,
Day-thoughts feed nightly dreams ;
And sorrow tracketh wrong,
As echo follows song :
  On, on, forever !

By night, like stars on high,
  The Hours reveal their train ;
They whisper and go by :
  I never watch in vain.
Moves one, move all : hark to the foot-
    fall !
  On, on, forever !

They pass the cradle-head,
And there a promise shed ;
They pass the moist new grave,
And bid rank verdure wave ;
They bear through every clime
The harvests of all time.
  On, on, forever !

Laman Blanchard

NELL GWYNNE'S LOOKING-GLASS

GLASS antique, 'twixt thee and Nell
Draw we here a parallel.
She, like thee, was forced to bear
All reflections, foul or fair.
  Thou art deep and bright within,
  Depths as bright belong'd to Gwynne ;
  Thou art very frail as well,
  Frail as flesh is, — so was Nell.

Thou, her glass, art silver-lin'd,
She too, had a silver mind :
Thine is fresh till this far day,
Hers till death ne'er wore away :
  Thou dost to thy surface win
  Wandering glances, so did Gwynne ;
  Eyes on thee long love to dwell,
  So men's eyes would do on Nell.

Life-like forms in thee are sought,
Such the forms the actress wrought ;
Truth unfailing rests in you,
Nell, whate'er she was, was true.
  Clear as virtue, dull as sin,
  Thou art oft, as oft was Gwynne ;
  Breathe on thee, and drops will swell :
  Bright tears dimm'd the eyes of Nell.

Thine 's a frame to charm the sight,
Fram'd was she to give delight,
Waxen forms here truly show
Charles above and Nell below ;
  But between them, chin with chin,
  Stuart stands as low as Gwynne, —
  Paired, yet parted, — meant to tell
  Charles was opposite to Nell.

Round the glass wherein her face
Smil'd so oft, her "arms" we trace ;
Thou, her mirror, hast the pair,
Lion here, and leopard there.
  She had part in these, — akin
  To the lion-heart was Gwynne ;
  And the leopard's beauty fell
  With its spots to bounding Nell.

Oft inspected, ne'er seen through,
Thou art firm, if brittle too ;
So her will, on good intent,
Might be broken, never bent.
  What the glass was, when therein
  Beam'd the face of glad Nell Gwynne,
  Was that face by beauty's spell
  To the honest soul of Nell.

HIDDEN JOYS

PLEASURES lie thickest where no pleasures
    seem :
There 's not a leaf that falls upon the ground
But holds some joy, of silence, or of sound,
Some sprite begotten of a summer dream.
The very meanest things are made supreme
With innate ecstacy. No grain of sand
But moves a bright and million-peopled
    land,
And hath its Edens and its Eves, I deem.

For Love, though blind himself, a curious
    eye
Hath lent me, to behold the hearts of
    things,
And touch'd mine ear with power. Thus,
    far or nigh,
Minute or mighty, fix'd or free with
    wings,
Delight from many a nameless covert
    sly
Peeps sparkling, and in tones familiar
    sings.

Thomas Wade

THE NET-BRAIDERS

WITHIN a low-thatch'd hut, built in a lane
    Whose narrow pathway tendeth toward
       the ocean,
A solitude which, save of some rude swain
    Or fisherman, doth scarce know human
       motion —
Or of some silent poet, to the main
    Straying, to offer infinite devotion
To God, in the free universe — there dwelt
Two women old, to whom small store was
    dealt

Of the world's misnam'd good : mother
    and child,
    Both aged and mateless. These two life
       sustain'd
By braiding fishing-nets ; and so beguil'd
    Time and their cares, and little e'er com-
       plain'd
Of Fate or Providence : resign'd and mild,
    Whilst day by day, for years, their hour-
       glass rain'd
Its trickling sand, to track the wing of time,
They toil'd in peace ; and much there was
    sublime

In their obscure contentment : of mankind
    They little knew, or reck'd ; but for their
       being
They bless'd their Maker, with a simple
    mind ;
    And in the constant gaze of his all-
       seeing
Eye, to his poorest creatures never blind,
    Deeming they dwelt, they bore their
       sorrows fleeing,

Glad still to live, but not afraid to die,
In calm expectance of Eternity.

And since I first did greet those braiders
    poor,
    If ever I behold fair women's cheeks
Sin-pale in stately mansions, where the
    door
    Is shut to all but pride, my cleft heart
       seeks
For refuge in my thoughts, which then ex-
    plore
       That pathway lone near which the wild
       sea breaks,
And to Imagination's humble eyes
That hut, with all its want, is Paradise !

BIRTH AND DEATH

METHINKS the soul within the body held
Is as a little babe within the womb,
Which flutters in its antenatal tomb,
But stirs and heaves the prison where 't is
    cell'd,
And struggles in strange darkness, undis-
    pell'd
By all its strivings towards the breath and
    bloom
Of that aurorean being soon to come —
Strivings of feebleness, by nothing quell'd :
And even as birth to the enfranchis'd
    child,
Which shows to its sweet senses all the
    vast
Of beauty visible and audible,
Is death unto the spirit undefil'd ;
Setting it free of limit, and the past,
And all that in its prison-house befell.

Thomas Cooper

CHARTIST SONG

THE time shall come when wrong shall end,
When peasant to peer no more shall bend;
When the lordly Few shall lose their sway,
And the Many no more their frown obey.
  Toil, brothers, toil, till the work is
      done,
  Till the struggle is o'er, and the Charter
      won!

The time shall come when the artisan.
Shall homage no more the titled man;
When the moiling men who delve the mine
By Mammon's decree no more shall pine.
  Toil, brothers, toil, till the work is done,
  Till the struggle is o'er, and the Charter
      won.

The time shall come when the weavers'
      band
Shall hunger no more in their fatherland;
When the factory-child can sleep till day,
And smile while it dreams of sport and
      play.

Toil, brothers, toil, till the work is done,
Till the struggle is o'er, and the Charter
won.

The time shall come when Man shall hold
His brother more dear than sordid gold;
When the negro's stain his freeborn mind
Shall sever no more from human-kind.
  Toil, brothers, toil, till the world is free,
  Till Justice and Love hold jubilee.

The time shall come when kingly crown
And mitre for toys of the past are shown;
When the fierce and false alike shall fall,
And mercy and truth encircle all.
  Toil, brothers, toil, till the world is free,
  Till Mercy and Truth hold jubilee!

The time shall come when earth shall be
A garden of joy, from sea to sea,
When the slaughterous sword is drawn no
      more,
And goodness exults from shore to shore.
  Toil, brothers, toil, till the world is free,
  Till goodness shall hold high jubilee!

Sarah Flower Adams

HYMN

HE sendeth sun, he sendeth shower,
Alike they 're needful for the flower:
And joys and tears alike are sent
To give the soul fit nourishment.
As comes to me or cloud or sun,
Father! thy will, not mine, be done!

Can loving children e'er reprove
With murmurs whom they trust and love?
Creator! I would ever be
A trusting, loving child to thee:
As comes to me or cloud or sun,
Father! thy will, not mine, be done!

Oh, ne'er will I at life repine:
Enough that thou hast made it mine.
When falls the shadow cold of death
I yet will sing, with parting breath,
As comes to me or shade or sun,
Father! thy will, not mine, be done!

LOVE

O LOVE! thou makest all things even
      In earth or heaven;
Finding thy way through prison-bars
      Up to the stars;
Or, true to the Almighty plan,
That out of dust created man,
Thou lookest in a grave, — to see
      Thine immortality!

NEARER TO THEE

NEARER, my God, to thee,
      Nearer to thee!
E'en though it be a cross
      That raiseth me;
Still all my song shall be,
Nearer, my God, to thee,
      Nearer to thee!

Though like the wanderer,
　The sun gone down,
Darkness be over me,
　My rest a stone ;
Yet in my dreams I 'd be
Nearer, my God, to thee,
　Nearer to thee !

There let the way appear
　Steps unto heaven ;
All that thou send'st to me
　In mercy given ;
Angels to beckon me
Nearer, my God, to thee,
　Nearer to thee !

Then, with my waking thoughts
　Bright with thy praise,
Out of my stony griefs
　Bethel I 'll raise ;
So by my woes to be
Nearer, my God, to thee,
　Nearer to thee !

Or if on joyful wing
　Cleaving the sky,
Sun, moon, and stars forgot,
　Upward I fly,
Still all my song shall be,
Nearer, my God, to thee,
　Nearer to thee !

Elizabeth Barrett Browning

THE CRY OF THE CHILDREN

Do ye hear the children weeping, O my
　　brothers,
　　Ere the sorrow comes with years ?
They are leaning their young heads against
　. their mothers,
　　And *that* cannot stop their tears.
The young lambs are bleating in the mead-
　ε　ows,
　The young birds are chirping in the nest,
The young fawns are playing with the
　　shadows,
　The young flowers are blowing toward
　　the west :
But the young, young children, O my
　　brothers,
　　They are weeping bitterly !
They are weeping in the playtime of the
　　others,
　　In the country of the free.

Do you question the young children in the
　　sorrow
　　Why their tears are falling so ?
The old man may weep for his to-morrow
　　Which is lost in Long Ago ;
The old tree is leafless in the forest,
　The old year is ending in the frost,
The old wound, if stricken, is the sorest,
　The old hope is hardest to be lost :
But the young, young children, O my
　　brothers,
　Do you ask them why they stand

Weeping sore before the bosoms of their
　　mothers,
　　In our happy Fatherland ?

They look up with their pale and sunken
　　faces,
　　And their looks are sad to see,
For the man's hoary anguish draws and
　　presses
　　Down the cheeks of infancy ;
" Your old earth," they say, " is very dreary,
　Our young feet," they say, " are very
　　weak ;
Few paces have we taken, yet are weary —
　Our grave-rest is very far to seek :
Ask the aged why they weep, and not the
　　children,
　　For the outside earth is cold,
And we young ones stand without, in our
　　bewildering,
　　And the graves are for the old."

" True," say the children, " it may happen
　　That we die before our time :
Little Alice died last year, her grave is
　　shapen
　　Like a snowball, in the rime.
We looked into the pit prepared to take
　　her :
　Was no room for any work in the close
　　clay !
From the sleep wherein she lieth none will
　　wake her,
　Crying, 'Get up, little Alice ! it is day.'

If you listen by that grave, in sun and
    shower,
  With your ear down, little Alice never
    cries :
Could we see her face, be sure we should
    not know her,
  For the smile has time for growing in her
    eyes :
And merry go her moments, lull'd and
    still'd in
  The shroud by the kirk-chime.
It is good when it happens," say the chil-
    dren,
  " That we die before our time."

Alas, alas, the children ! they are seeking
  Death in life, as best to have :
They are binding up their hearts away from
    breaking,
  With a cerement from the grave.
Go out, children, from the mine and from
    the city,
  Sing out, children, as the little thrushes
    do ;
Pluck your handfuls of the meadow-cow-
    slips pretty,
  Laugh aloud, to feel your fingers let
    them through !
But they answer, " Are your cowslips of
    the meadows
  Like our weeds anear the mine ?
Leave us quiet in the dark of the coal-
    shadows,
  From your pleasures fair and fine !

" For oh," say the children, " we are weary,
  And we cannot run or leap ;
If we car'd for any meadows, it were merely
  To drop down in them and sleep.
Our knees tremble sorely in the stooping,
  We fall upon our faces, trying to go ;
And, underneath our heavy eyelids droop-
    ing,
  The reddest flower would look as pale as
    snow.
For, all day, we drag our burden tiring
  Through the coal-dark, underground,
Or, all day, we drive the wheels of iron
  In the factories, round and round.

" For all day, the wheels are droning, turn-
    ing ;
  Their wind comes in our faces,
Till our hearts turn, our heads with pulses
    burning,
  And the walls turn in their places :

Turns the sky in the high window blank and
    reeling,
  Turns the long light that drops adown the
    wall,
Turn the black flies that crawl along the
    ceiling,
  All are turning, all the day, and we with
    all.
And all day, the iron wheels are droning,
  And sometimes we could pray,
' O ye wheels,' (breaking out in a mad
    moaning)
  'Stop ! be silent for to-day ! ' "

Ay, be silent ! Let them hear each other
    breathing
  For a moment, mouth to mouth !
Let them touch each other's hands, in a
    fresh wreathing
  Of their tender human youth !
Let them feel that this cold metallic motion
  Is not all the life God fashions or reveals :
Let them prove their living souls against
    the notion
  That they live in you, or under you, O
    wheels !
Still, all day, the iron wheels go onward,
  Grinding life down from its mark ;
And the children's souls, which God is call-
    ing sunward,
  Spin on blindly in the dark.

Now tell the poor young children, O my
    brothers,
  To look up to Him and pray ;
So the blessed One who blesseth all the
    others,
  Will bless them another day.
They answer, " Who is God that He should
    hear us,
  While the rushing of the iron wheels is
    stirr'd ?
When we sob aloud, the human creatures
    near us
  Pass by, hearing not, or answer not a
    word.
And we hear not (for the wheels in their
    resounding)
  Strangers speaking at the door :
Is it likely God, with angels singing round
    Him,
  Hears our weeping any more ?

" Two words, indeed, of praying we re-
    member,
  And at midnight's hour of harm,

'Our Father,' looking upward in the cham-
ber,
   We say softly for a charm.
We know no other words except ' Our
Father,'
   And we think that, in some pause of
     angels' song,
God may pluck them with the silence sweet
     to gather,
   And hold both within His right hand
     which is strong.
'Our Father !' If He heard us, He would
     surely
   (For they call Him good and mild)
Answer, smiling down the steep world very
     purely,
   'Come and rest with me, my child.'

" But, no !" say the children, weeping
     faster,
   " He is speechless as a stone :
And they tell us, of His image is the master
   Who commands us to work on.
Go to !" say the children, — " up in heaven,
   Dark, wheel-like, turning clouds are all
     we find.
Do not mock us ; grief has made us unbe-
     lieving :
   We look up for God, but tears have made
     us blind."
Do you hear the children weeping and dis-
     proving,
   O my brothers, what ye preach ?
For God's possible is taught by His world's
     loving,
   And the children doubt of each.

And well may the children weep before you!
   They are weary ere they run ;
They have never seen the sunshine, nor the
     glory
   Which is brighter than the sun.
They know the grief of man, without its
     wisdom ;
   They sink in man's despair, without its
     calm ;
Are slaves, without the liberty in Christdom,
   Are martyrs, by the pang without the
     palm :
Are worn as if with age, yet unretrievingly
     The harvest of its memories cannot
     reap, —
Are orphans of the earthly love and heav-
     enly.
   Let them weep ! let them weep !

They look up with their pale and sunken
     faces,
   And their look is dread to see,
For they mind you of their angels in high
     places,
   With eyes turned on Deity.
" How long," they say, " how long, O cruel
     nation,
   Will you stand, to move the world, on a
     child's heart, —
Stifle down with a mailed heel its palpita-
     tion,
   And tread onward tc your throne amid
     the mart ?
Our blood splashes upward, O gold-heaper,
   And your purple shows your path !
But the child's sob in the silence curses
     deeper
   Than the strong man in his wrath."

MY HEART AND I

ENOUGH ! we 're tired, my heart and I.
   We sit beside the headstone thus,
   And wish that name were carv'd for us.
The moss reprints more tenderly
   The hard types of the mason's knife,
   As Heaven's sweet life renews earth's life
With which we 're tired, my heart and I.

You see we 're tired, my heart and I.
   We dealt with books, we trusted men,
   And in our own blood drench'd the pen,
As if such colors could not fly.
   We walk'd too straight for fortune's end,
   We lov'd too true to keep a friend ;
At last we 're tired, my heart and I.

How tired we feel, my heart and I !
   We seem of no use in the world ;
   Our fancies hang gray and uncurl'd
About men's eyes indifferently ;
   Our voice which thrill'd you so, will let
   You sleep ; our tears are only wet :
What do we here, my heart and I ?

So tired, so tired, my heart and I !
   It was not thus in that old time
   When Ralph sat with me 'neath the lime
To watch the sunset from the sky.
   " Dear love, you 're looking tired," he
     said :
   I, smiling at him, shook my head.
'T is now we 're tired, my heart and I.

So tired, so tired, my heart and I !
  Though now none takes me on his arm
  To fold me close and kiss me warm
Till each quick breath end in a sigh
  Of happy languor. Now, alone,
  We lean upon this graveyard stone,
Uncheer'd, unkiss'd, my heart and I.

Tired out we are, my heart and I.
  Suppose the world brought diadems
  To tempt us, crusted with loose gems
Of powers and pleasures ? Let it try.
  We scarcely care to look at even
  A pretty child, or God's blue heaven,
We feel so tired, my heart and I.

Yet who complains ? My heart and I ?
  In this abundant earth no doubt
  Is little room for things worn out :
Disdain them, break them, throw them by !
  And if before the days grew rough
  We *once* were lov'd, us'd, — well enough,
I think, we 've far'd, my heart and I.

SONNETS FROM THE PORTU-
GUESE

I

I THOUGHT once how Theocritus had sung
Of the sweet years, the dear and wish'd-
    for years,
Who each one in a gracious hand appears
To bear a gift for mortals, old or young :
And, as I mus'd it in his antique tongue,
I saw, in gradual vision through my tears,
The sweet, sad years, the melancholy years,
Those of my own life, who by turns had flung
A shadow across me. Straightway I was
    'ware,
So weeping, how a mystic Shape did move
Behind me, and drew me backward by the
    hair ;
And a voice said in mastery, while I
    strove, —
" Guess now who holds thee ! " — " Death,"
    I said. But, there,
The silver answer rang — " Not Death, but
    Love."

IV

THOU hast thy calling to some palace-floor,
Most gracious singer of high poems ! where
The dancers will break footing, from the care
Of watching up thy pregnant lips for more.

And dost thou lift this house's latch too poor
For hand of thine ? and canst thou think
    and bear
To let thy music drop here unaware
In folds of golden fulness at my door ?
Look up and see the casement broken in,
The bats and owlets builders in the roof !
My cricket chirps against thy mandolin.
Hush, call no echo up in further proof
Of desolation ! there 's a voice within
That weeps . . . as thou must sing . . .
    alone, aloof.

V

I LIFT my heavy heart up solemnly,
As once Electra her sepulchral urn,
And, looking in thine eyes, I overturn
The ashes at thy feet. Behold and see
What a great heap of grief lay hid in me,
And how the red wild sparkles dimly burn
Through the ashen grayness. If thy foot
    in scorn
Could tread them out to darkness utterly,
It might be well perhaps. But if instead
Thou wait beside me for the wind to blow
The gray dust up, . . . those laurels on
    thine head,
O my Beloved, will not shield thee so,
That none of all the fires shall scorch and
    shred
The hair beneath. Stand further off then !
    go !

VI

Go from me. Yet I feel that I shall stand
Henceforward in thy shadow. Nevermore
Alone upon the threshold of my door
Of individual life, I shall command
The uses of my soul, nor lift my hand
Serenely in the sunshine as before,
Without the sense of that which I fore-
    bore —
Thy touch upon the palm. The widest
    land
Doom takes to part us, leaves thy heart in
    mine
With pulses that beat double. What I do
And what I dream include thee, as the
    wine
Must taste of its own grapes. And when I
    sue
God for myself, He hears that name of
    thine,
And sees within my eyes the tears of two.

IX

Can it be right to give what I can give ?
To let thee sit beneath the fall of tears
As salt as mine, and hear the sighing years
Re-sighing on my lips renunciative
Through those infrequent smiles which fail
    to live
For all thy adjurations ?   O my fears,
That this can scarce be right !   We are not
    peers
So to be lovers ; and I own, and grieve,
That givers of such gifts as mine are, must
Be counted with the ungenerous.   Out, alas !
I will not soil thy purple with my dust,
Nor breathe my poison on thy Venice-glass,
Nor give thee any love — which were unjust.
Beloved, I only love thee ! let it pass.

XVIII

I never gave a lock of hair away
To a man, Dearest, except this to thee,
Which now upon my fingers thoughtfully
I ring out to the full brown length and
    say
"Take it."   My day of youth went yester-
    day ;
My hair no longer bounds to my foot's glee,
Nor plant I it from rose or myrtle-tree,
As girls do, any more : it only may
Now shade on two pale cheeks the mark of
    tears,
Taught drooping from the head that hangs
    aside
Through sorrow's trick.   I thought the
    funeral-shears
Would take this first, but Love is justi-
    fied, —
Take it thou, — finding pure, from all those
    years,
The kiss my mother left here when she died.

XX

Beloved, my Beloved, when I think
That thou wast in the world a year ago,
What time I sat alone here in the snow
And saw no footprint, heard the silence
    sink
No moment at thy voice, but, link by link,
Went counting all my chains as if that so
They never could fall off at any blow
Struck by thy possible hand, — why, thus I
    drink

Of life's great cup of wonder !   Wonderful,
Never to feel thee thrill the day or night
With personal act or speech, — nor ever
    cull
Some prescience of thee with the blossoms
    white
Thou sawest growing !   Atheists are as
    dull,
Who cannot guess God's presence out of
    sight.

XXII

When our two souls stand up erect and
    strong,
Face to face, silent, drawing nigh and
    nigher,
Until the lengthening wings break into fire
At either curved point, — what bitter wrong
Can the earth do to us, that we should not
    long
Be here contented ?   Think !   In mounting
    higher,
The angels would press on us and aspire
To drop some golden orb of perfect song
Into our deep, dear silence.   Let us stay
Rather on earth, Beloved, — where the unfit
Contrarious moods of men recoil away
And isolate pure spirits, and permit
A place to stand and love in for a day,
With darkness and the death-hour rounding
    it.

XXIII

Is it indeed so ?   If I lay here dead,
Wouldst thou miss any life in losing mine ?
And would the sun for thee more coldly
    shine
Because of grave-damps falling round my
    head ?
I marvelled, my Beloved, when I read
Thy thought so in the letter.   I am thine —
But . . . *so* much to thee ?   Can I pour
    thy wine
While my hands tremble ?   Then my soul,
    instead
Of dreams of death, resumes life's lower
    range.
Then, love me, Love ! look on me — breathe
    on me !
As brighter ladies do not count it strange,
For love, to give up acres and degree,
I yield the grave for thy sake, and ex-
    change
My near sweet view of heaven, for earth
    with thee !

XXVI

I LIV'D with visions for my company
Instead of men and women, years ago,
And found them gentle mates, nor thought
    to know
A sweeter music than they play'd to me.
But soon their trailing purple was not free
Of this world's dust, their lutes did silent
    grow,
And I myself grew faint and blind below
Their vanishing eyes. Then THOU didst
    come — to be,
Beloved, what they seem'd. Their shining
    fronts,
Their songs, their splendors, (better, yet
    the same,
As river-water hallow'd into fonts)
Met in thee, and from out thee overcame
My soul with satisfaction of all wants :
Because God's gift puts man's best dreams
    to shame.

XXXV

IF I leave all for thee, wilt thou exchange
And be all to me ? Shall I never miss
Home-talk and blessing and the commcn
    kiss
That comes to each in turn, nor count it
    strange,
When I look up, to drop on a new range
Of walls and floors, another home than this ?
Nay, wilt thou fill that place by me which
    is
Fill'd by dead eyes too tender to know
    change
That 's hardest ? If to conquer love, has
    tried,
To conquer grief, tries more, as all things
    prove,
For grief indeed is love and grief beside.
Alas, I have griev'd so I am hard to love.
Yet love me — wilt thou ? Open thine
    heart wide,
And fold within the wet wings of thy dove.

XXXVIII

FIRST time he kiss'd me, he but only kiss'd
The fingers of this hand wherewith I write ;
And ever since, it grew more clean and
    white,
Slow to world-greetings, quick with its
    "Oh, list,"

When the angels speak. A ring of ame-
    thyst
I could not wear here, plainer to my sight,
Than that first kiss. The second pass'd in
    height
The first, and sought the forehead, and half
    miss'd,
Half falling on the hair. O beyond meed !
That was the chrism of love, which love's
    own crown,
With sanctifying sweetness, did precede.
The third upon my lips was folded down
In perfect, purple state ; since when, in-
    deed,
I have been proud and said, "My love, my
    own."

XXXIX

BECAUSE thou hast the power and own'st
    the grace
To look through and behind this mask of
    me,
(Against which, years have beat thus
    blanchingly
With their rains,) and behold my soul's
    true face,
The dim and weary witness of life's race, —
Because thou hast the faith and love to see,
Through that same soul's distracting
    lethargy,
The patient angel waiting for a place
In the new Heavens, — because nor sin
    nor woe,
Nor God's infliction, nor death's neighbor-
    hood,
Nor all which others viewing, turn to go,
Nor all which makes me tired of all, self-
    view'd, —
Nothing repels thee, . . . Dearest, teach
    me so
To pour out gratitude, as thou dost, good !

XLI

I THANK all who have lov'd me ir their
    hearts,
With thanks and love from mine. Deep
    thanks to all
Who paus'd a little near the prison-wall
To hear my music in its louder parts
Ere they went onward, each one to the
    mart's
Or temple's occupation, beyond call.
But thou, who, in my voice's sink and fall
When the sob took it, thy divinest Art's

Own instrument didst drop down at thy
　　foot
To hearken what I said between my
　　tears, . . .
Instruct me how to thank thee! Oh, to
　　shoot
My soul's full meaning into future years,
That *they* should lend it utterance, and
　　salute
Love that endures, from Life that disap-
　　pears!

XLIII

How do I love thee? Let me count the
　　ways.
I love thee to the depth and breadth and
　　height
My soul can reach, when feeling out of
　　sight
For the ends of Being and ideal Grace.
I love thee to the level of every day's
Most quiet need, by sun and candlelight.
I love thee freely, as men strive for Right;
I love thee purely, as they turn from Praise.
I love thee with the passion put to use
In my old griefs, and with my childhood's
　　faith.
I love thee with a love I seem'd to lose
With my lost saints, — I love thee with the
　　breath,
Smiles, tears, of all my life! — and, if God
　　choose,
I shall but love thee better after death.

A MUSICAL INSTRUMENT

What was he doing, the great god Pan,
　　Down in the reeds by the river?
Spreading ruin and scattering ban,
Splashing and paddling with hoofs of a goat,
And breaking the golden lilies afloat
　　With the dragon-fly on the river.

He tore out a reed, the great god Pan,
　　From the deep cool bed of the river:
The limpid water turbidly ran,
And the broken lilies a-dying lay,
And the dragon-fly had fled away,
　　Ere he brought it out of the river.

High on the shore sat the great god Pan,
　　While turbidly flow'd the river;
And hack'd and hew'd as a great god
　　can,

With his hard bleak steel at the patient reed,
Till there was not a sign of a leaf indeed
　　To prove it fresh from the river.

He cut it short, did the great god Pan,
　　(How tall it stood in the river!)
Then drew the pith, like the heart of a man,
Steadily from the outside ring,
And notch'd the poor dry empty thing
　　In holes, as he sat by the river.

"This is the way," laugh'd the great god
　　Pan,
　　(Laugh'd while he sat by the river,)
"The only way, since gods began
To make sweet music, they could succeed."
Then, dropping his mouth to a hole in the
　　reed,
　　He blew in power by the river.

Sweet, sweet, sweet, O Pan!
　　Piercing sweet by the river!
Blinding sweet, O great god Pan!
The sun on the hill forgot to die,
And the lilies reviv'd, and the dragon-fly
　　Came back to dream on the river.

Yet half a beast is the great god Pan,
　　To laugh as he sits by the river,
Making a poet out of a man:
The true gods sigh for the cost and pain, —
For the reed which grows nevermore again
　　As a reed with the reeds in the river.

FROM "CASA GUIDI WINDOWS"

JULIET OF NATIONS

I heard last night a little child go singing
　　'Neath Casa Guidi windows, by the
　　church,
O bella libertà, O bella! — stringing
　　The same words still on notes he went in
　　search
So high for, you concluded the upspringing
　　Of such a nimble bird to sky from perch
Must leave the whole bush in a tremble
　　green,
　　And that the heart of Italy must beat,
While such a voice had leave to rise serene
　　'Twixt church and palace of a Florence
　　street:
A little child, too, who not long had been
　　By mother's finger steadied on his feet,
And still *O bella libertà* he sang.

Then I thought, musing, of the innumer-
ous
Sweet songs which still for Italy out-
rang
From older singers' lips who sang not thus
Exultingly and purely, yet, with pang
Fast sheath'd in music, touch'd the heart
of us
So finely that the pity scarcely pain'd.
I thought how Filicaja led on others,
Bewailers for their Italy enchain'd,
And how they call'd her childless among
mothers,
Widow of empires, ay, and scarce re-
frain'd
Cursing her beauty to her face, as brothers
Might a sham'd sister's, — " Had she
been less fair
She were less wretched ; " — how, evoking
so
From congregated wrong and heap'd de-
spair
Of men and women writhing under blow,
Harrow'd and hideous in a filthy lair,
Some personating Image wherein woe
Was wrapp'd in beauty from offending
much,
They call'd it Cybele, or Niobe,
Or laid it corpse-like on a bier for
such,
Where all the world might drop for Italy
Those cadenced tears which burn not
where they touch, —
" Juliet of nations, canst thou die as we ?
And was the violet that crown'd thy
head
So over-large, though new buds made it
rough,
It slipp'd down and across thine eyelids
dead,
O sweet, fair Juliet ? " Of such songs
enough,
Too many of such complaints ! behold,
instead,
Void at Verona, Juliet's marble trough :
As void as that is, are all images
Men set between themselves and actual
wrong,
To catch the weight of pity, meet the
stress
Of conscience, — since 't is easier to gaze
long
On mournful masks and sad effigies
Than on real, live, weak creatures crush'd
by strong.

SURSUM CORDA

The sun strikes, through the windows, up
the floor ;
Stand out in it, my own young Florentine,
Not two years old, and let me see thee
more !
It grows along thy amber curls, to shine
Brighter than elsewhere. Now, look
straight before,
And fix thy brave blue English eyes on
mine,
And from my soul, which fronts the fu-
ture so,
With unabash'd and unabated gaze,
Teach me to hope for, what the angels
know
When they smile clear as thou dost. Down
God's ways
With just alighted feet, between the
snow
And snowdrops, where a little lamb may
graze,
Thou hast no fear, my lamb, about the
road,
Albeit in our vain-glory we assume
That, less than we have, thou hast learnt
of God.
Stand out, my blue-eyed prophet ! — thou,
to whom
The earliest world-day light that ever
flow'd,
Through Casa Guidi windows chanced to
come !
Now shake the glittering nimbus of thy
hair,
And be God's witness that the elemental
New springs of life are gushing every-
where
To cleanse the water-courses, and prevent all
Concrete obstructions which infest the
air !
That earth 's alive, and gentle or ungentle
Motions within her, signify but
growth ! —
The ground swells greenest o'er the labor-
ing moles.
Howe'er the uneasy world is vex'd and
wroth,
Young children, lifted high on parent souls,
Look round them with a smile upon the
mouth,
And take for music every bell that tolls ;
(Who said we should be better if like
these ?)

But *we* sit murmuring for the future though
   Posterity is smiling on our knees,
Convicting us of folly. Let us go —
   We will trust God. The blank interstices
Men take for ruins, He will build into
   With pillar'd marbles rare, or knit across
With generous arches, till the fane 's com-
     plete.
This world has no perdition, if some loss.

Such cheer I gather from thy smiling, Sweet!
   The self-same cherub-faces which emboss
The Vail, lean inward to the Mercy-seat.

A COURT LADY

HER hair was tawny with gold, her eyes
   with purple were dark,
Her cheeks' pale opal burnt with a red and
   restless spark.

Never was lady of Milan nobler in name
   and in race ;
Never was lady of Italy fairer to see in the
   face.

Never was lady on earth more true as
   woman and wife,
Larger in judgment and instinct, prouder
   in manners and life.

She stood in the early morning, and said
   to her maidens, " Bring
That silken robe made ready to wear at
   the court of the king.

" Bring me the clasps of diamond, lucid,
   clear of the mote,
Clasp me the large at the waist, and clasp
   me the small at the throat.

" Diamonds to fasten the hair, and dia-
   monds to fasten the sleeves,
Laces to drop from their rays, like a powder
   of snow from the eaves."

Gorgeous she enter'd the sunlight which
   gather'd her up in a flame,
While, straight in her open carriage, she to
   the hospital came.

In she went at the door, and gazing from
   end to end,
" Many and low are the pallets, but each
   is the place of a friend."

Up she pass'd through the wards, and
   stood at a young man's bed :
Bloody the band on his brow, and livid the
   droop of his head.

" Art thou a Lombard, my brother ?
   Happy art thou," she cried,
And smiled like Italy on him : he dream'd
   in her face and died.

Pale with his passing soul, she went on still
   to a second :
He was a grave hard man, whose years by
   dungeons were reckon'd.

Wounds in his body were sore, wounds in
   his life were sorer.
" Art thou a Romagnole ? " Her eyes
   drove lightnings before her.

" Austrian and priest had join'd to double
   and tighten the cord
Able to bind thee, O strong one, — free by
   the stroke of a sword.

" Now be grave for the rest of us, using
   the life overcast
To ripen our wine of the present, (too new,)
   in glooms of the past."

Down she stepp'd to a pallet where lay a
   face like a girl's,
Young, and pathetic with dying, — a deep
   black hole in the curls.

" Art thou from Tuscany, brother ? and
   seest thou, dreaming in pain,
Thy mother stand in the piazza, searching
   the List of the slain ? "

Kind as a mother herself, she touch'd his
   cheeks with her hands :
" Blessed is she who has borne thee, al-
   though she should weep as she
   stands."

On she pass'd to a Frenchman, his arm
   carried off by a ball :
Kneeling, . . . " O more than my brother !
   how shall I thank thee for all ?

" Each of the heroes around us has fought
   for his land and line,
But *thou* hast fought for a stranger, in hate
   of a wrong not thine.

"Happy are all free peoples, too strong to
    be dispossess'd :
But blessed are those among nations, who
    dare to be strong for the rest ! "

Ever she pass'd on her way, and came to a
    couch where pin'd
One with a face from Venetia, white with a
    hope out of mind.

Long she stood and gaz'd, and twice she
    ,tried at the name,
But two great crystal tears were all that
    falter'd and came.

Only a tear for Venice ? — she turn'd as in
    passion and loss,
And stoop'd to his forehead and kiss'd it,
    as if she were kissing the cross.

Faint with that strain of heart she mov'd
    on then to another,
Stern and strong in his death. " And dost
    thou suffer, my brother ? "

Holding his hands in hers : — " Out of the
    Piedmont lion
Cometh the sweetness of freedom ! sweet-
    est to live or to die on."

Holding his cold rough hands, — " Well,
    oh, well have ye done
In noble, noble Piedmont, who would not
    be noble alone."

Back he fell while she spoke. She rose to
    her feet with a spring, —
" That was a Piedmontese ! and this is the
    Court of the King."

MOTHER AND POET

TURIN, AFTER NEWS FROM GAETA, 1861

DEAD ! One of them shot by the sea in
    the east,
    And one of them shot in the west by the
    sea.
Dead ! both my boys ! When you sit at
    the feast
    And are wanting a great song for Italy
    free,
    Let none look at me !

Yet I was a poetess only last year,
    And good at my art, for a woman, men
    said ;
But this woman, this, who is agoniz'd here,
    — The east sea and west sea rhyme on
    in her head
    For ever instead.

What art can a woman be good at ? Oh,
    vain !
    What art is she good at, but hurting her
    breast
With the milk-teeth of babes, and a smile
    at the pain ?
    Ah boys, how you hurt ! you were strong
    as you press'd,
    And I proud, by that test.

What art 's for a woman ? To hold on her
    knees
    Both darlings ; to feel all their arms
    round her throat,
Cling, strangle a little, to sew by degrees
    And 'broider the long-clothes and neat
    little coat ;
    To dream and to doat.

To teach them . . . It stings there ! I
    made them indeed
    Speak plain the word country. I taught
    them, no doubt,
That a country 's a thing men should die
    for at need.
    I prated of liberty, rights, and about
    The tyrant cast out.

And when their eyes flash'd . . . O my
    beautiful eyes ! . . .
    I exulted ; nay, let them go forth at the
    wheels
Of the guns, and denied not. But then
    the surprise
    When one sits quite alone ! Then one
    weeps, then one kneels !
    God, how the house feels !

At first, happy news came, in gay letters
    moil'd
    With my kisses, — of camp-life and
    glory, and how
They both lov'd me ; and, soon coming
    home to be spoil'd,
    In return would fan off every fly from
    my brow
    With their green laurel-bough.

Then was triumph at Turin : " Ancona
     was free ! "
And someone came out of the cheers in
     the street,
With a face pale as stone, to say something
     to me.
  My Guido was dead ! I fell down at his
     feet,
  While they cheer'd in the street.

I bore it ; friends sooth'd me ; my grief
     look'd sublime
  As the ransom of Italy. One boy re-
     main'd
To be leant on and walk'd with, recalling
     the time
  When the first grew immortal, while
     both of us strain'd
  To the height he had gain'd.

And letters still came, shorter, sadder, more
     strong,
  Writ now but in one hand, " I was not to
     faint, —
One lov'd me for two — would be with me
     ere long :
  And *Viva l' Italia !* — *he* died for, our
     saint,
  Who forbids our complaint."

My Nanni would add, "he was safe, and
     aware
  Of a presence that turn'd off the balls, —
     was impress'd
It was Guido himself, who knew what I
     could bear,
  And how 't was impossible, quite dispos-
     sess'd,
  To live on for the rest."

On which, without pause, up the telegraph-
     line,
  Swept smoothly the next news from
     Gaeta : — *Shot.*
Tell his mother. Ah, ah, " his," " their "
     mother, — not " mine,"
  No voice says " *My* mother " again to
     me. What !
  You think Guido forgot ?

Are souls straight so happy that, dizzy with
     Heaven,
  They drop earth's affections, conceive
     not of woe ?

I think not. Themselves were too lately
     forgiven
  Through THAT Love and Sorrow which
     reconcil'd so
  The Above and Below.

O Christ of the five wounds, who look'dst
     through the dark
  To the face of Thy mother ! consider, I
     pray,
How we common mothers stand desolate,
     mark,
  Whose sons, not being Christs, die with
     eyes turn'd away,
  And no last word to say !

Both boys dead ? but that 's out of nature.
     We all
  Have been patriots, yet each house must
     always keep one.
'T were imbecile, hewing out roads to a wall ;
  And, when Italy 's made, for what end is
     it done
  If we have not a son ?

Ah, ah, ah ! when Gaeta 's taken, what
     then ?
  When the fair wicked queen sits no more
     at her sport
Of the fire-balls of death crashing souls out
     of men ?
  When the guns of Cavalli with final re-
     tort
  Have cut the game short ?

When Venice and Rome keep their new
     jubilee,
  When your flag takes all heaven for its
     white, green, and red,
When *you* have your country from moun-
     tain to sea,
  When King Victor has Italy's crown on
     his head,
  (And *I* have my Dead) —

What then ? Do not mock me. Ah, ring
     your bells low,
  And burn your lights faintly ! *My*
     country is *there,*
Above the star prick'd by the last peak of
     snow :
  My Italy 's THERE, with my brave civic
     Pair,
  To disfranchise despair !

Forgive me. Some women bear children
    in strength,
  And bite back the cry of their pain in
    self-scorn ;
But the birth-pangs of nations will wring
    us at length
  Into wail such as this — and we sit on
    forlorn
    When the man-child is born.

Dead ! One of them shot by the sea in the
    east,
  And one of them shot in the west by the
    sea,
Both ! both my boys ! If in keeping the feast
  You want a great song for your Italy free,
    Let none look at *me*.

[This was Laura Savio, of Turin, a poet and patriot,
whose sons were killed at Ancona and Gaeta.]

FROM "AURORA LEIGH"

MOTHERLESS

I WRITE. My mother was a Florentine,
Whose rare blue eyes were shut from see-
    ing me
When scarcely I was four years old ; my
    life,
A poor spark snatch'd up from a failing
    lamp
Which went out therefore. She was weak
    and frail ;
She could not bear the joy of giving life —
The mother's rapture slew her. If her kiss
Had left a longer weight upon my lips,
It might have steadied the uneasy breath,
And reconcil'd and fraterniz'd my soul
With the new order. As it was, indeed,
I felt a mother-want about the world,
And still went seeking, like a bleating lamb
Left out at night, in shutting up the fold, —
As restless as a nest-deserted bird
Grown chill through something being away,
    though what
It knows not. I, Aurora Leigh, was born
To make my father sadder, and myself
Not overjoyous, truly. Women know
The way to rear up children (to be just,)
They know a simple, merry, tender knack
Of tying sashes, fitting baby-shoes,
And stringing pretty words that make no
    sense,
And kissing full sense into empty words ;

Which things are corals to cut life upon,
Although such trifles : children learn by
    such,
Love's holy earnest in a pretty play,
And get not over-early solemniz'd, —
But seeing, as in a rose-bush, Love 's Divine,
Which burns and hurts not, — not a single
    bloom, —
Become aware and unafraid of Love.
Such good do mothers. Fathers love as
    well
— Mine did, I know, — but still with
    heavier brains,
And wills more consciously responsible,
And not as wisely, since less foolishly ;
So mothers have God's license to be miss'd.

BOOKS

Or else I sat on in my chamber green,
And liv'd my life, and thought my thoughts,
    and pray'd
My prayers without the vicar ; read my
    books,
Without considering whether they were fit
To do me good. Mark, there. We get no
    good
By being ungenerous, even to a book,
And calculating profits . . . so much help
By so much reading. It is rather when
We gloriously forget ourselves, and plunge
Soul-forward, headlong, into a book's pro-
    found,
Impassion'd for its beauty and salt of
    truth —
'T is then we get the right good from a
    book.

THE POETS

I had found the secret of a garret-room
Pil'd high with cases in my father's name ;
Pil'd high, pack'd large, — where, creeping
    in and out
Among the giant fossils of my past,
Like some small nimble mouse between the
    ribs
Of a mastodon, I nibbled here and there
At this or that box, pulling through the gap,
In heats of terror, haste, victorious joy,
The first book first. And how I felt it
    beat
Under my pillow, in the morning's dark,
An hour before the sun would let me read !
My books !

At last, because the time was ripe,
I chanced upon the poets.
                    As the earth
Plunges in fury, when the internal fires
Have reach'd and prick'd her heart, and,
            throwing flat
The marts and temples, the triumphal
            gates
And towers of observation, clears herself
To elemental freedom — thus, my soul,
At poetry's divine first finger touch,
Let go conventions and sprang up surpris'd,
Convicted of the great eternities
Before two worlds.
                    What's this, Aurora Leigh,
You write so of the poets, and not laugh?
Those virtuous liars, dreamers after dark,
Exaggerators of the sun and moon,
And soothsayers in a tea-cup?
                    I write so
Of the only truth-tellers, now left to God, —
The only speakers of essential truth,
Oppos'd to relative, comparative,
And temporal truths ; the only holders by
His sun-skirts, through conventional gray
            glooms ;
The only teachers who instruct mankind,
From just a shadow on a charnel wall,
To find man's veritable stature out,
Erect, sublime, — the measure of a man,
And that 's the measure of an angel, says
The apostle.

THE FERMENT OF NEW WINE

And so, like most young poets, in a flush
Of individual life, I pour'd myself
Along the veins of others, and achiev'd
Mere lifeless imitations of live verse,
And made the living answer for the dead,
Profaning nature. " Touch not, do not taste,
Nor handle," — we're too legal, who write
            young :
We beat the phorminx till we hurt our
            thumbs,
As if still ignorant of counterpoint ;
We call the Muse . . . "O Muse, benignant
            Muse ! " —
As if we had seen her purple-braided head
With the eyes in it start between the
            boughs
As often as a stag's. What make-believe,
With so much earnest ! what effete results,
From virile efforts ! what cold wire-drawn
            odes,

From such white heats ! bucolics, where
            the cows
Would scare the writer if they splash'd the
            mud
In lashing off the flies, — didactics, driven
Against the heels of what the master said ;
And counterfeiting epics, shrill with trumps
A babe might blow between two straining
            cheeks
Of bubbled rose, to make his mother laugh ;
And elegiac griefs, and songs of love,
Like cast-off nosegays pick'd up on the
            road,
The worse for being warm : all these things,
            writ
On happy mornings, with a morning heart,
That leaps for love, is active for resolve,
Weak for art only.   Oft, the ancient forms
Will thrill, indeed, in carrying the young
            blood.
The wine-skins, now and then, a little
            warp'd,
Will crack even, as the new wine gurgles
            in.
Spare the old bottles ! — spill not the new
            wine.

By Keats's soul, the man who never stepp'd
In gradual progress like another man,
But, turning grandly on his central self,
Enspher'd himself in twenty perfect years
And died, not young, — (the life of a long
            life,
Distill'd to a mere drop, falling like a tear
Upon the world's cold cheek to make it
            burn
For ever ;) by that strong excepted soul,
I count it strange, and hard to understand,
That nearly all young poets should write
            old ;
That Pope was sexagenarian at sixteen,
And beardless Byron academical,
And so with others.   It may be, perhaps,
Such have not settled long and deep enough
In trance, to attain to clairvoyance, — and
            still
The memory mixes with the vision, spoils,
And works it turbid.
                    Or perhaps, again
In order to discover the Muse-Sphinx,
The melancholy desert must sweep round,
Behind you, as before. —
                    For me, I wrote
False poems, like the rest, and thought
            them true,

Because myself was true in writing them.
I, peradventure, have writ true ones since
With less complacence.

ENGLAND

Whoever lives true life, will love true love.
I learn'd to love that England. Very oft,
Before the day was born, or otherwise
Through secret windings of the afternoons,
I threw my hunters off and plunged myself
Among the deep hills, as a hunted stag
Will take the waters, shivering with the
    fear
And passion of the course. And when, at
    last
Escap'd, — so many a green slope built on
    slope
Betwixt me and the enemy's house behind,
I dar'd to rest, or wander, — like a rest
Made sweeter for the step upon the grass, —
And view the ground's most gentle dimple-
    ment,
(As if God's finger touch'd but did not press
In making England !) such an up and down
Of verdure, — nothing too much up or down,
A ripple of land ; such little hills, the sky
Can stoop to tenderly and the wheatfields
    climb ;
Such nooks of valleys, lin'd with orchises,
Fed full of noises by invisible streams ;
And open pastures, where you scarcely tell
White daisies from white dew, — at inter-
    vals
The mythic oaks and elm-trees standing out
Self-pois'd upon their prodigy of shade, —
I thought my father's land was worthy too
Of being my Shakespeare's. . . .
. . . Breaking into voluble ecstacy,
I flatter'd all the beauteous country round,
As poets use . . . the skies, the clouds, the
    fields,
The happy violets hiding from the roads
The primroses run down to, carrying
    gold, —
The tangled hedgerows, where the cows
    push out
Impatient horns and tolerant churning
    mouths
'Twixt dripping ash-boughs, — hedgerows
    all alive
With birds and gnats and large white but-
    terflies
Which look as if the May-flower had sought
    life

And palpitated forth upon the wind,—
Hills, vales, woods, netted in a silver mist,
Farms, granges, doubled up among the hills,
And cattle grazing in the water'd vales,
And cottage-chimneys smoking from the
    woods,
And cottage-gardens smelling everywhere,
Confus'd with smell of orchards. " See," I
    said,
" And see ! is God not with us on the earth ?
And shall we put Him down by aught we
    do ?
Who says there 's nothing for the poor and
    vile
Save poverty and wickedness ? behold ! "
And ankle-deep in English grass I leap'd,
And clapp'd my hands, and call'd all very
    fair.

" BY SOLITARY FIRES "

                O my God, my God,
O supreme Artist, who as sole return
For all the cosmic wonder of Thy work,
Demandest of us just a word . . . a name,
" My Father ! " — thou hast knowledge,
    only thou,
How dreary 't is for women to sit still
On winter nights by solitary fires,
And hear the nations praising them far off,
Too far ! ay, praising our quick sense of
    love,
Our very heart of passionate womanhood,
Which could not beat so in the verse with-
    out
Being present also in the unkiss'd lips,
And eyes undried because there 's none to
    ask
The reason they grew moist.
                To sit alone,
And think, for comfort, how, that very
    night,
Affianced lovers, leaning face to face
With sweet half-listenings for each other's
    breath,
Are reading haply from some page of ours,
To pause with a thrill, as if their cheeks
    had touch'd,
When such a stanza, level to their mood,
Seems floating their own thoughts out —
    " So I feel
For thee," — " And I, for thee : this poet
    knows
What everlasting love is ! " — how, that
    night

A father issuing from the misty roads
Upon the luminous round of lamp and
  hearth
And happy children, having caught up first
The youngest there until it shrunk and
  shriek'd
To feel the cold chin prick its dimple
  through
With winter from the hills, may throw i'
  the lap
Of the eldest (who has learn'd to drop her
  lids
To hide some sweetness newer than last
  year's)
Our book and cry, . . . " Ah you, you care
  for rhymes ;
So here be rhymes to pore on under trees,
When April comes to let you ! I 've been
  told
They are not idle as so many are,
But set hearts beating pure as well as
  fast :
It 's yours, the book ; I 'll write your name
  in it, —
That so you may not lose, however lost
In poet's lore and charming reverie,
The thought of how your father thought of
  you
In riding from the town."
                    To have our books
Apprais'd by love, associated with love,
While *we* sit loveless ! is it hard, you think ?
At least 't is mournful. Fame, indeed, 't was
  said,
Means simply love. It was a man said that.
And then there 's love and love : the love
  of all
(To risk, in turn, a woman's paradox,)
Is but a small thing to the love of one.
You bid a hungry child be satisfied
With a heritage of many corn-fields : nay,
He says he 's hungry, — he would rather
  have
That little barley-cake you keep from him
While reckoning up his harvests. So with
  us.

ROMNEY AND AURORA

But oh, the night ! oh, bitter-sweet ! oh,
  sweet !
O dark, O moon and stars, O ecstasy
Of darkness ! O great mystery of love, —
In which absorb'd, loss, anguish, treason's
  self

Enlarges rapture, — as a pebble dropp'd
In some full wine-cup, over-brims the wine !
While we two sate together, lean'd that
  night
So close, my very garments crept and
  thrill'd
With strange electric life ; and both my
  cheeks
Grew red, then pale, with touches from my
  hair
In which his breath was ; while the golden
  moon
Was hung before our faces as the badge
Of some sublime inherited despair,
Since ever to be seen by only one, —
A voice said, low and rapid as a sigh,
Yet breaking, I felt conscious, from a
  smile, —
" Thank God, who made me blind, to make
  me see !
Shine on, Aurora, dearest light of souls,
Which rul'st for evermore both day and
  night !
I am happy."
                    I flung closer to his breast,
As sword that, after battle, flings to
  sheathe ;
And, in that hurtle of united souls,
The mystic motions, which in common moods
Are shut beyond our sense, broke in on us,
And, as we sate, we felt the old earth spin,
And all the starry turbulence of worlds
Swing round us in their audient circles, till
If that same golden moon were overhead
Or if beneath our feet, we did not know.

THE SLEEP

Of all the thoughts of God that are
Borne inward into souls afar,
Along the Psalmist's music deep,
Now tell me if that any is
For gift or grace surpassing this —
" He giveth His beloved, sleep " ?

What would we give to our beloved ?
The hero's heart to be unmoved,
The poet's star-tun'd harp to sweep,
The patriot's voice to teach and rouse,
The monarch's crown to light the brows ? —
He giveth His beloved, sleep.

What do we give to our beloved ?
A little faith all undisproved,

A little dust to overweep,
And bitter memories to make
The whole earth blasted for our sake :
He giveth His beloved, sleep.

"Sleep soft, beloved ! " we sometimes say
Who have no tune to charm away
Sad dreams that through the eyelids creep:
But never doleful dream again
Shall break the happy slumber when
He giveth His beloved, sleep.

O earth, so full of dreary noises !
O men, with wailing in your voices !
O delved gold, the wailers heap !
O strife, O curse, that o'er it fall !
God strikes a silence through you all,
And giveth His beloved, sleep.

His dews drop mutely on the hill,
His cloud above it saileth still,
Though on its slope men sow and reap :
More softly than the dew is shed,

Or cloud is floated overhead,
He giveth His beloved, sleep.

Ay, men may wonder while they scan
A living, thinking, feeling man
Confirm'd in such a rest to keep ;
But angels say, and through the word
I think their happy smile is *heard* —
"He giveth His beloved, sleep."

For me, my heart that erst did go
Most like a tired child at a show,
That sees through tears the mummers leap,
Would now its wearied vision close,
Would childlike on His love repose
Who giveth His beloved, sleep.

And friends, dear friends, when it shall be
That this low breath is gone from me,
And round my bier ye come to weep,
Let One, most loving of you all,
Say, "Not a tear must o'er her fall !
He giveth His beloved, sleep."

Alfred Domett

A GLEE FOR WINTER

HENCE, rude Winter ! crabbed old fel-
low,
Never merry, never mellow !
Well-a-day ! in rain and snow
What will keep one's heart aglow ?
Groups of kinsmen, old and young,
Oldest they old friends among ;
Groups of friends, so old and true
That they seem our kinsmen too ;
These all merry all together
Charm away chill Winter weather.

What will kill this dull old fellow ?
Ale that's bright, and wine that's mel-
low !
Dear old songs for ever new ;
Some true love, and laughter too ;
Pleasant wit, and harmless fun,
And a dance when day is done.
Music, friends so true and tried,
Whisper'd love by warm fireside,
Mirth at all times all together,
Make sweet May of Winter weather.

A CHRISTMAS HYMN

(OLD STYLE: 1837)

IT was the calm and silent night !
    Seven hundred years and fifty-three
Had Rome been growing up to might,
    And now was Queen of land and sea.
No sound was heard of clashing wars ;
    Peace brooded o'er the hush'd domain ;
Apollo, Pallas, Jove and Mars,
    Held undisturb'd their ancient reign,
        In the solemn midnight
            Centuries ago.

'T was in the calm and silent night !
    The senator of haughty Rome
Impatient urged his chariot's flight,
    From lordly revel rolling home.
Triumphal arches gleaming swell
    His breast with thoughts of boundless
        sway ;
What reck'd the Roman what befell
    A paltry province far away,
        In the solemn midnight
            Centuries ago !

Within that province far away
 Went plodding home a weary boor :
A streak of light before him lay,
 Fall'n through a half-shut stable door
Across his path. He pass'd — for nought
 Told what was going on within ;
How keen the stars ! his only thought ;
 The air how calm and cold and thin,
  In the solemn midnight
   Centuries ago !

O strange indifference ! — low and high
 Drows'd over common joys and cares :
The earth was still — but knew not why ;
 The world was listening — unawares.
How calm a moment may precede
 One that shall thrill the world for
  ever !
To that still moment none would heed,
 Man's doom was link'd, no more to
  sever,
  In the solemn midnight
   Centuries ago.

It *is* the calm and solemn night !
 A thousand bells ring out, and throw
Their joyous peals abroad, and smite
 The darkness, charm'd and holy now.
The night that erst no name had worn,
 To it a happy name is given ;
For in that stable lay new-born
 The peaceful Prince of Earth and Hea-
  ven,
  In the solemn midnight
   Centuries ago.

FROM "A CHRISTMAS HYMN"

(NEW STYLE : 1875)

To murder one so young !
 To still that wonder-teeming tongue
Ere half the fulness of its mellow'd glory
 Had flash'd in mild sheet-lightnings forth!
Who knows, had that majestic Life grown
  hoary,
 Long vers'd in all man's weakness, woes
  and worth,
What beams had pierced the clouds that
  veil this voyage of care !
 Not Zeus, nor Baal's throne,
 Nor Osiris alone,
But Doubt, or worse assurance of Despair,
Or Superstition's brood that blends the tiger
 with the hare.

Who knows but we had caught
 Some hint from pure impassion'd
  Thought,
How Matter's links and Spirit's, that still
  fly us,
 Can break and still leave Spirit free ;
How Will can act o'ermaster'd by no bias ;
 Why Good omnipotent lets Evil be ;
What balm heals beauteous Nature's uni-
  versal flaw ;
 And how, below, above,
 It is Love, and only Love
Bids keen Sensation glut Destruction's
 maw —
Love rolls this groaning Sea of Life on
 pitiless rocks of Law !

William Bell Scott

GLENKINDIE

ABOUT Glenkindie and his man
A false ballant hath long been writ ;
Some bootless loon had written it,
 Upon a bootless plan :
But I have found the true at last,
And here it is, — so hold it fast !
'T was made by a kind damosel
Who lov'd him and his man right well.

Glenkindie, best of harpers, came
 Unbidden to our town ;
And he was sad, and sad to see,
 For love had worn him down.

It was love, as all men know,
 The love that brought him down,
The hopeless love for the King's daugh-
  ter,
 The dove that heir'd a crown.

Now he wore not that collar of gold,
 His dress was forest green ;
His wondrous fair and rich mantel
 Had lost its silvery sheen.

But still by his side walk'd Rafe, his boy,
 In goodly cramoisie :
Of all the boys that ever I saw
 The goodliest boy was he.

O Rafe the page ! O Rafe the page !
 Ye stole the heart frae me :
O Rafe the page ! O Rafe the page !
 I wonder where ye be :
We ne'er may see Glenkindie more,
 But may we never see thee ?

Glenkindie came within the hall ;
 We set him on the dais,
And gave him bread, and gave him wine,
 The best in all the place.

We set for him the guests' high chair,
 And spread the naperie :
Our Dame herself would serve for him,
 And I for Rafe, perdie !

But down he sat on a low low stool,
 And thrust his long legs out,
And lean'd his back to the high chair,
 And turn'd his harp about.

He turn'd it round, he strok'd the strings,
 He touch'd each tirling-pin,
He put his mouth to the sounding-board
 And breath'd his breath therein.

And Rafe sat over against his face,
 And look'd at him wistfullie :
I almost grat ere he began,
 They were so sad to see.

The very first stroke he strack that day,
 We all came crowding near ;
And the second stroke he strack that day,
 We all were smit with fear.

The third stroke that he strack that day,
 Full fain we were to cry ;
The fourth stroke that he strack that day,
 We thought that we would die.

No tongue can tell how sweet it was,
 How far, and yet how near :
We saw the saints in Paradise,
 And bairnies on their bier.

And our sweet Dame saw her good
 lord —
 She told me privilie :
She saw him as she saw him last,
 On his ship upon the sea.

Anon he laid his little harp by,
 He shut his wondrous eyes ;

We stood a long time like dumb things,
 Stood in a dumb surprise.

Then all at once we left that trance,
 And shouted where we stood ;
We clasp'd each other's hands and vow'd
 We would be wise and good.

Soon he rose up and Rafe rose too,
 He drank wine and broke bread ;
He clasp'd hands with our trembling Dame,
 But never a word he said ;
They went, — Alack and lack-a-day !
 They went the way they came.

I follow'd them all down the floor,
 And O but I had drouth
To touch his cheek, to touch his hand,
 To kiss Rafe's velvet mouth !

But I knew such was not for me.
 They went straight from the door ;
We saw them fade within the mist,
 And never saw them more.

YOUTH AND AGE

OUR night repast was ended : quietness
Return'd again : the boys were in their
 books ;
The old man slept, and by him slept his dog :
My thoughts were in the dream-land of to-
 morrow :
A knock is heard ; anon the maid brings
 in
A black-seal'd letter that some over-work'd
Late messenger leaves. Each one looks
 round and scans,
But lifts it not, and I at last am told
To read it. " Died here at his house this
 day " —
Some well-known name not needful here
 to print,
Follows at length. Soon all return again
To their first stillness, but the old man
 coughs,
And cries, " Ah, he was always like the
 grave,
And still he was but young ! " while those
 who stand
On life's green threshold smile within them-
 selves,
Thinking how very old he was to them,
And what long years, what memorable
 deeds,

Are theirs in prospect ! Little care have
    they
What old man dies, what child is born, in-
    deed ;
Their day is coming, and their sun shall
    shine !

PYGMALION

" MISTRESS of gods and men ! I have been
    thine
From boy to man, and many a myrtle rod
Have I made grow upon thy sacred sod,
Nor ever have I pass'd thy white shafts nine
Without some votive offering for the shrine,
Carv'd beryl or chas'd bloodstone ; — aid
    me now,
And I will live to fashion for thy brow
Heart-breaking priceless things : oh, make
    her mine."

Venus inclin'd her ear, and through the
    Stone
Forthwith slid warmth like spring through
    sapling-stems,
And lo, the eyelid stirr'd, beneath had
    grown
The tremulous light of life, and all the hems
Of her zon'd peplos shook. Upon his breast
She sank, by two dread gifts at once op-
    press'd.

MY MOTHER

THERE was a gather'd stillness in the room:
Only the breathing of the great sea rose
From far off, aiding that profound repose,
With regular pulse and pause within the
    gloom
Of twilight, as if some impending doom
Was now approaching ; — I sat moveless
    there,
Watching with tears and thoughts that were
    like prayer,
Till the hour struck, — the thread dropp'd
    from the loom ;
And the Bark pass'd in which freed souls
    are borne.
The dear still'd face lay there ; that sound
    forlorn
Continued ; I rose not, but long sat by :
And now my heart oft hears that sad sea-
    shore,
When she is in the far-off land, and I
Wait the dark sail returning yet once more.

THE NORNS WATERING
YGGDRASILL

(FOR A PICTURE)

WITHIN the unchanging twilight
    Of the high land of the gods,
Between the murmuring fountain
    And the Ash-tree, tree of trees,
The Norns, the terrible maidens,
    For evermore come and go.

Yggdrasill the populous Ash-tree,
    Whose leaves embroider heaven,
Fills all the gray air with music —
    To Gods and to men sweet sounds,
But speech to the fine-ear'd maidens
    Who evermore come and go.

That way to their doomstead thrones
    The Aesir ride each day,
And every one bends to the saddle
    As they pass beneath the shade ;
Even Odin, the strong All-father,
Bends to the beautiful maidens
    Who cease not to come and go.

The tempest crosses the high boughs,
    The great snakes heave below,
The wolf, the boar, and antler'd harts
    Delve at the life-giving roots,
But all of them fear the wise maidens,
The wise-hearted water-bearers
    Who evermore come and go.

And men far away, in the night-hours
    To the north-wind listening, hear ;
They hear the howl of the were-wolf,
    And know he hath felt the sting
Of the eyes of the potent maidens
    Who sleeplessly come and go.

They hear on the wings of the north-wind
    A sound as of three that sing ;
And the skald, in the blae mist wandering
    High on the midland fell,
Heard the very words of the o'ersong
    Of the Norns who come and go.

But alas for the ears of mortals
    Chance-hearing that fate-laden song !
The bones of the skald lie there still :
    For the speech of the leaves of the Tree
Is the song of the three Queen-maidens
    Who evermore come and go.

TO THE DEAD

(A PARAPHRASE)

GONE art thou ? gone, and is the light of
    day
Still shining, is my hair not touch'd with
    gray ?
But evening draweth nigh, I pass the door,
And see thee walking on the dim-lit shore.

Gone, art thou ? gone, and weary on the
    brink
Of Lethe waiting there.   O do not drink,

Drink not, forget not, wait a little while,
I shall be with thee ; we again may smile.

HERO-WORSHIP

How would the centuries long asunder
Look on their sires with angry wonder,
Could some strong necromantic power
Revive them for one spectral hour !
Bondsmen of the past are we, —
Predestin'd bondsmen : could we see
The dead now deified, again
Peering among environing men,
        We might be free.

William James Linton

EVICTION[1]

LONG years their cabin stood
    Out on the moor ;
More than one sorrow-brood
    Pass'd through their door ;
Ruin them over-cast,
Worse than one wintry blast ;
Famine's plague follow'd fast :
    God help the poor !

There on that heap of fern,
    Gasping for breath,
Lieth the wretched kérn,
    Waiting for death :
Famine had brought him low ;
Fever had caught him so, —
O thou sharp-grinding woe,
    Outwear thy sheath !

Dying, or living here —
    Which is the worse ?
Misery's heavy tear,
    Back to thy source !
Who dares to lift her head
Up from the scarcely dead ?
Who pulls the crazy shed
    Down on the corse ?

What though some rent was due,
    Hast thou no grace ?
So may God pardon you,
    Shame of your race !

What though that home may be
Wretched and foul to see,
What if God harry thee
    Forth from His face ?

Widow'd and orphan'd ones,
    Flung from your rest !
Where will you lay your bones ?
    Bad was your best.
Out on the dreary road,
Where shall be their abode ?
One of them sleeps with God :
    Where are the rest ?

PATIENCE[1]

BE patient, O be patient !   Put your ear
    against the earth ;
Listen there how noiselessly the germ o' the
    seed has birth ;
How noiselessly and gently it upheaves its
    little way
Till it parts the scarcely-broken ground,
    and the blade stands up in the day.

Be patient, O be patient ! the germs of
    mighty thought
Must have their silent undergrowth, must
    underground be wrought ;
But, as sure as ever there 's a Power that
    makes the grass appear,
Our land shall be green with Liberty, the
    blade-time shall be here.

[1] From his early Poems of Freedom.

Be patient, O be patient ! go and watch the
    wheat-ears grow,
So imperceptibly that ye can mark nor
    change nor throe :
Day after day, day after day till the ear is
    fully grown ;
And then again day after day, till the
    ripen'd field is brown.

Be patient, O be patient ! though yet our
    hopes are green,
The harvest-field of Freedom shall be
    crown'd with the sunny sheen.
Be ripening, be ripening ! mature your
    silent way
Till the whole broad land is tongued with
    fire on Freedom's harvest day.

OUR CAUSE[1]

So, Freedom, thy great quarrel may we
    serve,
With truest zeal that, sensitive of blame,
Ever thy holy banner would preserve
As pure as woman's love or knightly fame.

And though detraction's flood we proudly
    breast,
Or, weakening, sink in that unfathom'd sea,
Ever we 'll keep aloft our banner, lest
Even the black spray soil its purity.

My life be branded and my name be flung
To infamy ; — beloved, I will wear
Thy beauty on my shield, till even the
    tongue
Of falsehood echo truth, and own thee fair.

HEART AND WILL[1]

Our England's heart is sound as oak ;
    Our English will is firm ;
And through our actions Freedom spoke
    In history's proudest term :
When Blake was lord from shore to shore,
    And Cromwell rul'd the land,
And Milton's words were shields of power
    To stay the oppressor's hand.

Our England's heart is yet as sound,
    As firm our English will ;
And tyrants, be they cowl'd or crown'd,
    Shall find us fearless still.
And though our Vane be in his tomb,
    Though Hampden's blood is cold,

Their spirits live to lead our doom
    As in the days of old.

Our England's heart is stout as oak ;
    Our English will as brave
As when indignant Freedom spoke
    From Eliot's prison grave.
And closing yet again with Wrong,
    A world in arms shall see
Our England foremost of the strong
    And first among the free.

FROM "A THRENODY: IN MEMORY OF ALBERT DARASZ"

O blessed Dead ! beyond all earthly pains
    Beyond the calculation of low needs ;
    Thy growth no longer chok'd by earthly
      weeds ;
Thy spirit clear'd from care's corrosive
    chains.
    O blessed Dead ! O blessed Life-in-death
    Transcending all life's poor decease of
      breath !

Thou walkest not upon some desolate moor
    In the storm-wildering midnight, when
      thine own,
    Thy trusted friend, hath lagg'd and left
      thee lone.
He knows not poverty who, being poor,
    Hath still one friend. But he who fain
      had kept
    The comrade whom his zeal hath over
      stept.

Thou sufferest not the friendly cavilling
    Impugning motive ; nor that worse than
      spear
    Of foeman, — biting doubt of one most
      dear
Laid in thy deepest heart, a barbed sting
    Never to be withdrawn. For we were
      friends :
    Alas ! and neither to the other bends.

Thou hast escap'd continual falling off
    Of old companions ; and that aching voice
    Of the proud heart which has been over
      buoy'd
With friendship's idle breath ; and now the
      scoff
    Of failure even as idly passeth by
    Thy poor remains : — *Thou* soaring
      through the sky.

[1] From his early Poems of Freedom.

Knowing no more that malady of hope —
  The sickness of deferral, thou canst
  look
Thorough the heavens and, healthily pa-
  tient, brook
Delay, — defeat. For in thy vision's scope
  Most distant cometh. We might see it
  too,
But dizzying faintness overveils our
  view.

And when disaster flings us in the dust,
  Or when we wearily drop on the highway-
  side,
  Or when in prison'd, exil'd depths the
  pride
Of suffering bows its head, as oft it must,
  We cannot, looking on thy wasted corse,
  Perceive the future. Lend us of thy
  force !

LOVE AND YOUTH

Two winged genii in the air
I greeted as they pass'd me by :
The one a bow and quiver bare,
  The other shouted joyously.
Both I besought to stay their speed,
But never Love nor Youth had heed
  Of my wild cry.

As swift and careless as the wind,
Youth fled, nor ever once look'd back ;
A moment Love was left behind,
  But follow'd soon his fellow's track.
Yet loitering at my heart he bent
His bow, then smil'd with changed intent :
  The string was slack.

TOO LATE

YES ! thou art fair, and I had lov'd
If we in earlier hours had met ;
But ere tow'rd me thy beauty mov'd
The sun of Love's brief day had set.

Though I may watch thy opening bloom,
And its rich promise gladly see,
'T will not procrastinate my doom :
The ripen'd fruit is not for me.

Yet, had I shar'd thy course of years,
And young as Hope beheld thy charms,
The love that only now endears
Perchance had given thee to my arms.

Vain, vain regret ! Another day
Will kiss the buds of younger flowers,
But ne'er will evening turn away
From love untimelier than ours.

WEEP NOT! SIGH NOT!

WEEP not ! tears must vainly fall,
  Though they fall like rain :
Sorrow's flood shall not recall
  Love 's dear life again.
    Vain thy tears,
    Vain thy sobs ;
    As vain heart-throbs
      Of lonely years
  Since thou Love hast slain.

Sigh not ! As a passed wind
Is but sought in vain,
Sighs nor groans may not unbind
  Death's unbroken chain.
    Sighs and tears
    Nought avail,
    Nor cheeks grown pale
      In lonely years.
  Love comes not again.

SPRING AND AUTUMN

"THOU wilt forget me." "Love has no
  such word."
The soft Spring wind is whispering to the
  trees.
Among lime-blossoms have the hovering
  bees
    Those whispers heard ?

" Or thou wilt change." "Love changeth
  not," he said.
The purple heather cloys the air with
  scent
Of honey. O'er the moors her lover went,
    Nor turn'd his head.

LOVE'S BLINDNESS

THEY call her fair. I do not know :
  I never thought to look.
Who heeds the binder's costliest show
  When he may read the book ?

What need a list of parts to me
  When I possess the whole ?
Who only watch her eyes to see
  The color of her soul.

I may not praise her mouth, her chin,
　Her feet, her hands, her arms :
My love lacks leisure to begin
　The schedule of her charms.

To praise is only to compare :
　And therefore Love is blind.
I lov'd before I was aware
　Her beauty was of kind.

THE SILENCED SINGER

THE nest is built, the song hath ceas'd :
The minstrel joineth in the feast,
So singeth not.　The poet's verse,
Crippled by Hymen's household curse,
Follows no more its hungry quest.
Well if Love's feathers line the nest.

Yet blame not that beside the fire
Love hangeth up his unstrung lyre !
How sing of hope when Hope hath fled,
Joy whispering lip to lip instead ?

Or how repeat the tuneful moan
When the Obdùrate 's all my own ?

Love, like the lark, while soaring sings :
Wouldst have him spread again his wings ?
What careth he for higher skies
Who on the heart of harvest lies,
And finds both sun and firmament
Clos'd in the round of his content ?

EPICUREAN

IN Childhood's unsuspicious hours
The fairies crown'd my head with flowers.

Youth came : I lay at Beauty's feet ;
She smil'd and said my song was sweet.

Then Age, and, Love no longer mine,
My brows I shaded with the vine.

With flowers and love and wine and song,
O Death ! life hath not been too long.

Robert Nicoll

WE 'LL A' GO PU' THE HEATHER

WE 'LL a' go pu the heather,
　Our byres are a' to theek :
Unless the peat-stack get a hap,
　We 'll a' be smoor'd wi' reek.
Wi' rantin' sang awa' we 'll gang,
　While summer skies are blue,
To fend against the winter cauld
　The heather we will pu'.

I like to pu' the heather,
　We 're aye sae mirthfu' where
The sunshine creeps atour the crags,
　Like ravell'd golden hair.
Where on the hill-tap we can stand
　Wi' joyfu' heart I trow,
And mark ilk grassy bank and holm,
　As we the heather pu'.

I like to pu' the heather,
　Where harmless lambkins run,
Or lay them down beside the burn
　Like gowans in the sun ;
Where ilka foot can tread upon
　The heath-flower wet wi' dew,
When comes the starnie ower the hill,
　While we the heather pu'.

I like to pu' the heather,
　For ane can gang awa',
But no before a glint o' love
　On some ane's e'e doth fa'.
Sweet words we dare to whisper there,
　" My hinny and my doo,"
Till maistly we wi' joy could greet
　As we the heather pu'.

We 'll a' go pu' the heather,
　For at yon mountain fit
There stands a broom bush by a burn,
　Where twa young folk can sit :
He meets me there at morning's rise,
　My beautiful and true.
My father said the word — the morn
　The heather we will pu'.

BONNIE BESSIE LEE

BONNIE Bessie Lee had a face fu' o'
　smiles,
And mirth round her ripe lip was aye
　dancing slee ;
And light was the footfa', and winsome the
　wiles,
O' the flower o' the parochin — our ain
　Bessie Lee.

Wi' the bairns she would rin, and the school
    laddies paik,
And o'er the broomy braes like a fairy
    would flee,
Till auld hearts grew young again wi' love
    for her sake :
There was life in the blithe blink o'
    Bonnie Bessie Lee.

She grat wi' the waefu', and laugh'd wi'
    the glad,
And light as the wind 'mang the dancers
    was she ;
And a tongue that could jeer, too, the little
    limmer had,
Whilk keepit aye her ain side for Bonnie
    Bessie Lee.

And she whiles had a sweetheart, and some-
    times had twa —
A limmer o' a lassie ! — but, atween you
    and me,
Her warm wee bit heartie she ne'er threw
    awa',
Though mony a ane had sought it frae
    Bonnie Bessie Lee.

But ten years had gane since I gaz'd on
    her last,
For ten years had parted my auld hame
    and me ;
And I said to mysel', as her mither's door
    I past,
" Will I ever get anither kiss frae Bon-
    nie Bessie Lee ? "

But Time changes a' thing — the ill-natur'd
    loon !
Were it ever sae rightly he 'll no let it
    be ;
But I rubbit at my een, and I thought I
    would swoon,
How the carle had come roun' about our
    ain Bessie Lee !

The wee laughing lassie was a gudewife
    grown auld,
Twa weans at her apron and ane on her
    knee ;
She was douce, too, and wiselike — and
    wisdom 's sae cauld :
I would rather ha'e the ither ane than
    this Bessie Lee !

THE HERO

My hero is na deck'd wi' gowd,
    He has nae glittering state ;
Renown upon a field o' blood
    In war he hasna met.
He has nae siller in his pouch,
    Nae menials at his ca' ;
The proud o' earth frae him would turn,
    And bid him stand awa'.

His coat is hame-spun hodden-gray,
    His shoon are clouted sair,
His garments, maist unhero-like,
    Are a' the waur o' wear :
His limbs are strong — his shoulders broad,
    His hands were made to plough ;
He 's rough without, but sound within ;
    His heart is bauldly true.

He toils at e'en, he toils at morn,
    His wark is never through ;
A coming life o' weary toil
    Is ever in his view.
But on he trudges, keeping aye
    A stout heart to the brae,
And proud to be an honest man
    Until his dying day.

His hame a hame o' happiness
    And kindly love may be ;
And monie a nameless dwelling-place
    Like his we still may see.
His happy altar-hearth so bright
    Is ever bleezing there ;
And cheerfu' faces round it set
    Are an unending prayer.

The poor man in his humble hame,
    Like God, who dwells aboon,
Makes happy hearts around him there,
    Sae joyfu' late and soon.
His toil is sair, his toil is lang ;
    But weary nights and days,
Hame — happiness akin to his —
    A hunder-fauld repays.

Go, mock at conquerors and kings !
    What happiness give they ?
Go, tell the painted butterflies
    To kneel them down and pray !
Go, stand erect in manhood's pride,
    Be what a man should be,
Then come, and to my hero bend
    Upon the grass your knee !

Wathen Marks Wilks Call

THE PEOPLE'S PETITION

O LORDS ! O rulers of the nation !
O softly cloth'd ! O richly fed !
O men of wealth and noble station !
Give us our daily bread.

For you we are content to toil,
For you our blood like rain is shed ;
Then, lords and rulers of the soil,
Give us our daily bread.

Your silken robes, with endless care,
Still weave we ; still uncloth'd, unfed,
We make the raiment that ye wear :
Give us our daily bread.

In the red forge-light do we stand,
We early leave — late seek our bed,
Tempering the steel for your right hand :
Give us our daily bread.

We sow your fields, ye reap the fruit ;
We live in misery and in dread ;
Hear but our prayer, and we are mute :
Give us our daily bread.

Throughout old England's pleasant fields
There is no spot where we may tread,
No house to us sweet shelter yields :
Give us our daily bread.

Fathers are we ; we see our sons,
We see our fair young daughters, dead ;
Then hear us, O ye mighty ones !
Give us our daily bread.

'T is vain — with cold, unfeeling eye
Ye gaze on us, uncloth'd, unfed ;
'T is vain — ye will not hear our cry,
Nor give us daily bread.

We turn from you, our lords by birth,
To him who is our Lord above ;
We all are made of the same earth,
Are children of one love.

Then, Father of this world of wonders,
Judge of the living and the dead,
Lord of the lightnings and the thunders,
Give us our daily bread !

SUMMER DAYS

IN summer, when the days were long,
We walk'd, two friends, in field and
　　wood ;
Our heart was light, our step was strong,
And life lay round us, fair as good,
In summer, when the days were long.

We stray'd from morn till evening came,
We gather'd flowers, and wove us crowns ;
We walk'd mid poppies red as flame,
Or sat upon the yellow downs,
And always wish'd our life the same.

In summer, when the days were long,
We leap'd the hedgerow, cross'd the brook ;
And still her voice flow'd forth in song,
Or else she read some graceful book,
In summer, when the days were long.

And then we sat beneath the trees,
With shadows lessening in the noon ;
And in the sunlight and the breeze
We revell'd, many a glorious June,
While larks were singing o'er the leas.

In summer, when the days were long,
We pluck'd wild strawberries, ripe and
　　red,
Or feasted, with no grace but song,
On golden nectar, snow-white bread,
In summer, when the days were long.

We lov'd, and yet we knew it not,
For loving seem'd like breathing then ;
We found a heaven in every spot ;
Saw angels, too, in all good men,
And dream'd of gods in grove and grot.

In summer, when the days are long,
Alone I wander, muse alone ;
I see her not, but that old song
Under the fragrant wind is blown,
In summer, when the days are long.

Alone I wander in the wood,
But one fair spirit hears my sighs ;
And half I see the crimson hood,
The radiant hair, the calm glad eyes,
That charm'd me in life's summer mood.

In summer, when the days are long,
I love her as I lov'd of old ;
My heart is light, my step is strong,

For love brings back those hours of gold,
In summer, when the days are long.

Charles Weldon

THE POEM OF THE UNIVERSE

The Poem of the Universe
　Nor rhythm has nor rhyme ;
Some God recites the wondrous song
　A stanza at a time.

Great deeds is he foredoom'd to do,
　With Freedom's flag unfurl'd,
Who hears the echo of that song
　As it goes down the world.

Great words he is compell'd to speak
　Who understands the song ;
He rises up like fifty men,
　Fifty good men and strong.

A stanza for each century :
　Now heed it, all who can !
Who hears it, he, and only he,
　Is the elected man.

Emily Brontë

SONG

The linnet in the rocky dells,
　The moor-lark in the air,
The bee among the heather bells
　That hide my lady fair.

The wild deer browse above her breast ;
　The wild birds raise their brood ;
And they, her smiles of love caress'd,
　Have left her solitude.

I ween that, when the grave's dark wall
　Did first her form retain,
They thought their hearts could ne'er recall
　The light of joy again.

They thought the tide of grief would flow
　Uncheck'd through future years ;
But where is all their anguish now,
　And where are all their tears ?

Well, let them fight for honor's breath,
　Or pleasure's shade pursue :
The dweller in the land of death
　Is changed and careless too.

And, if their eyes should watch and weep
　Till sorrow's source were dry,
She would not, in her tranquil sleep,
　Return a single sigh.

Blow, west-wind, by the lonely mound,
　And murmur, summer streams !
There is no need of other sound
　To soothe my lady's dreams.

THE OLD STOIC

Riches I hold in light esteem,
　And Love I laugh to scorn ;
And lust of fame was but a dream
　That vanish'd with the morn ;

And if I pray, the only prayer
　That moves my lips for me
Is, " Leave the heart that now I bear,
　And give me liberty ! "

Yes, as my swift days near their goal,
　'T is all that I implore :
In life and death a chainless soul,
　With courage to endure.

WARNING AND REPLY

In the earth—the earth—thou shalt be laid
　A gray stone standing over thee ;
Black mould beneath thee spread,
　And black mould to cover thee.

" Well — there is rest there,
　So fast come thy prophecy ﹐

The time when my sunny hair
  Shall with grass roots entwined be."

But cold — cold is that resting-place,
  Shut out from joy and liberty,
And all who lov'd thy living face
  Will shrink from it shudderingly.

" Not so. Here the world is chill,
  And sworn friends fall from me ;
But there — they will own me still,
  And prize my memory."

Farewell, then, all that love,
  All that deep sympathy :
Sleep on : Heaven laughs above,
  Earth never misses thee.

Turf-sod and tombstone drear
  Part human company ;
One heart breaks only — here,
  But that heart was worthy thee !

STANZAS

OFTEN rebuk'd, yet always back returning
  To those first feelings that were born with
    me,
And leaving busy chase of wealth and
    learning
  For idle dreams of things which cannot
    be ;

To-day, I will seek not the shadowy region ;
  Its unsustaining vastness waxes drear ;
And visions rising, legion after legion,
  Bring the unreal world too strangely near.

I 'll walk, but not in old heroic traces,
  And not in paths of high morality,
And not among the half-distinguish'd faces,
  The clouded forms of long-past history.

I 'll walk where my own nature would be
    leading :
  It vexes me to choose another guide :
Where the gray flocks in ferny glens are
    feeding ;
  Where the wild wind blows on the moun-
    tain side.

What have those lonely mountains worth
    revealing ?
  More glory and more grief than I can
    tell :
The earth that wakes one human heart to
    feeling
  Can centre both the worlds of Heaven
    and Hell.

HER LAST LINES

No coward soul is mine,
No trembler in the world's storm-troubled
    sphere :
  I see Heaven's glories shine,
And faith shines equal, arming me from
    fear.

O God within my breast,
Almighty, ever-present Deity !
  Life — that in me has rest,
As I — undying Life — have power in thee !

Vain are the thousand creeds
That move men's hearts : unutterably vain ;
  Worthless as wither'd weeds,
Or idlest froth amid the boundless main,

To waken doubt in one
Holding so fast by thine infinity ;
  So surely anchor'd on
The steadfast rock of immortality.

With wide-embracing love
Thy spirit animates eternal years,
  Pervades and broods above,
Changes, sustains, dissolves, creates, and
    rears.

Though earth and man were gone,
And suns and universes ceas'd to be,
  And Thou were left alone,
Every existence would exist in Thee.

There is not room for Death,
Nor atom that his might could render
    void :
  Thou — Thou art Being and Breath,
And what Thou art may never be de-
    stroy'd.

Mary Ann Evans (Lewes) Cross

("GEORGE ELIOT")

"O MAY I JOIN THE CHOIR INVISIBLE"

Longum illud,tempus, quum non ero, magis me movet, quam hoc exiguum. — Cicero, ad Att., xii. 18.

O MAY I join the choir invisible
Of those immortal dead who live again
In minds made better by their presence : live
In pulses stirr'd to generosity,
In deeds of daring rectitude, in scorn
For miserable aims that end with self,
In thoughts sublime that pierce the night like stars,
And with their mild persistence urge man's search
To vaster issues.
      So to live is heaven :
To make undying music in the world,
Breathing as beauteous order that controls
With growing sway the growing life of man.
So we inherit that sweet purity
For which we struggled, fail'd, and agoniz'd
With widening retrospect that bred despair.
Rebellious flesh that would not be subdued,
A vicious parent shaming still its child,
Poor anxious penitence, is quick dissolv'd ;
Its discords, quench'd by meeting harmonies,
Die in the large and charitable air.
And all our rarer, better, truer self,
That sobb'd religiously in yearning song,
That watch'd to ease the burthen of the world,
Laboriously tracing what must be,
And what may yet be better, — saw within
A worthier image for the sanctuary,
And shap'd it forth before the multitude,
Divinely human, raising worship so
To higher reverence more mix'd with love, —
That better self shall live till human Time
Shall fold its eyelids, and the human sky
Be gather'd like a scroll within the tomb
Unread forever.
      This is life to come,
Which martyr'd men have made more glorious

For us who strive to follow. May I reach
That purest heaven, be to other souls
The cup of strength in some great agony,
Enkindle generous ardor, feed pure love,
Beget the smiles that have no cruelty,
Be the sweet presence of a good diffus'd,
And in diffusion ever more intense !
So shall I join the choir invisible
Whose music is the gladness of the world.

SONGS FROM "THE SPANISH GYPSY"

THE DARK

SHOULD I long that dark were fair ?
Say, O song,
Lacks my love aught, that I should long ?

Dark the night, with breath all flow'rs,
And tender broken voice that fills
With ravishment the listening hours :
Whisperings, wooings,
Liquid ripples and soft ring-dove cooings
In low-ton'd rhythm that love's aching stills.
Dark the night,
Yet is she bright,
For in her dark she brings the mystic star,
Trembling yet strong, as is the voice of love,
From some unknown afar.
O radiant Dark ! O darkly-fostered ray !
Thou hast a joy too deep for shallow Day.

SONG OF THE ZÍNCALI

ALL things journey : sun and moon,
Morning, noon, and afternoon,
   Night and all her stars :
'Twixt the east and western bars
   Round they journey,
     Come and go.
   We go with them !
For to roam and ever roam
Is the Zíncali's loved home.

Earth is good, the hillside breaks
By the ashen roots and makes
   Hungry nostrils glad ;
Then we run till we are mad,
   Like the horses,

And we cry,
None shall catch us !
Swift winds wing us — we are free —
Drink the air — we Zíncali !

Falls the snow : the pine-branch split,
Call the fire out, see it flit,
　Through the dry leaves run,
Spread and glow, and make a sun
　In the dark tent :
　　O warm dark !
　　Warm as conies !

Strong fire loves us, we are warm !
Who the Zíncali shall harm ?

Onward journey : fires are spent ;
Sunward, sunward ! lift the tent,
　Run before the rain,
Through the pass, along the plain.
　Hurry, hurry,
　　Lift us, wind !
Like the horses.
For to roam and ever roam
Is the Zíncali's loved home.

Ernest Charles Jones

EARTH'S BURDENS

WHY groaning so, thou solid earth,
　Though sprightly summer cheers ?
Or is thine old heart dead to mirth ?
　Or art thou bow'd by years ?

" Nor am I cold to summer's prime,
　Nor knows my heart decay ;
Nor am I bow'd by countless time,
　Thou atom of a day !

" I lov'd to list when tree and tide
　Their gentle music made,
And lightly on my sunny side
　To feel the plough and spade.

" I lov'd to hold my liquid way
　Through floods of living light ;
To kiss the sun's bright hand by day,
　And count the stars by night.

" I lov'd to hear the children's glee,
　Around the cottage door,
And peasant's song right merrily
　The glebe come ringing o'er.

" But man upon my back has roll'd
　Such heavy loads of stone,
I scarce can grow the harvest gold :
　'Tis therefore that I groan.

" And when the evening dew sinks mild
　Upon my quiet breast,
I feel the tear of the houseless child
　Break burning on my rest.

" Oh ! where are all the hallow'd sweets,
　The harmless joys I gave ?
The pavement of your sordid streets
　Are stones on Virtue's grave.

" And thick and fast as autumn leaves
　My children drop away,
A gathering of unripen'd sheaves
　By premature decay.

" Gaunt misery holds the cottage door,
　And olden honor's flown,
And slaves are slavish more and more :
　'Tis therefore that I groan."

John Ruskin

THE WRECK

ITS masts of might, its sails so free,
Had borne the scatheless keel
Through many a day of darken'd sea,

And many a storm of steel ;
When all the winds were calm, it met
(With home-returning prore)
　With the lull
　Of the waves
On a low lee shore.

The crest of the conqueror
On many a brow was bright ;
The dew of many an exile's eye
Had dimm'd the dancing sight ;
And for love and for victory
One welcome was in store,
    In the lull
      Of the waves
    On a low lee shore

The voices of the night are mute
Beneath the moon's eclipse ;
The silence of the fitful flute
Is on the dying lips.
The silence of my lonely heart
Is kept forevermore
    In the lull
      Of the waves
    On a low lee shore.

TRUST THOU THY LOVE

TRUST thou thy Love : if she be proud, is
    she not sweet ?
Trust thou thy Love : if she be mute, is
    she not pure ?
Lay thou thy soul full in her hands, low at
    her feet ; —
Fail, Sun and Breath ! — yet, for thy
    peace, *she* shall endure.

Ebenezer Jones

SONG OF THE KINGS OF GOLD

OURS all are marble halls,
Amid untrodden groves
Where music ever calls,
Where faintest perfume roves ;
And thousands toiling moan,
That gorgeous robes may fold
The haughty forms alone
Of us — the Kings of Gold.
    (*Chorus.*)
  We cannot count our slaves,
  Nothing bounds our sway,
  Our will destroys and saves,
  We let, we create, we slay.
    Ha ! ha ! who are Gods ?

Purple, and crimson, and blue,
Jewels, and silks, and pearl,
All splendors of form and hue,
Our charm'd existence furl ;
When dared shadow dim
The glow in our winecups roll'd ?
When droop'd the banquet-hymn
Rais'd for the Kings of Gold ?
    (*Chorus.*)

The earth, the earth, is ours !
Its corn, its fruits, its wine,
Its sun, its rain, its flowers,
Ours, all, all ! — cannot shine
One sunlight ray, but where
Our mighty titles hold ;
Wherever life is, there
Possess the Kings of Gold.
    (*Chorus.*)

And all on earth that lives,
Woman, and man, and child,
Us trembling homage gives ;
Aye trampled, sport-defil'd,
None dareth raise one frown,
Or slightest questioning hold ;
Our scorn but strikes them down
To adore the Kings of Gold.
    (*Chorus.*)

.   .   .   .

In a glorious sea of hate,
Eternal rocks we stand ;
Our joy is our lonely state,
And our trust, our own right hand ;
We frown, and nations shrink ;
They curse, but our swords are old ;
And the wine of their rage deep drink
The dauntless Kings of Gold.
    (*Chorus.*)
  We cannot count our slaves,
  Nothing bounds our sway,
  Our will destroys and saves,
  We let, we create, we slay.
    Ha ! ha ! who are Gods ?

THE FACE

THESE dreary hours of hopeless gloom
Are all of life I fain would know ;
I would but feel my life consume,
While bring they back mine ancient woe ;
For, midst the clouds of grief and shame
That crowd around, one face I see ;
It is the face I dare not name,
The face none ever name to me.

I saw it first when in the dance
Borne, like a falcon, down the hall,
He stay'd to cure some rude mischance
My girlish deeds had caused to fall ;
He smil'd, he danced with me, he made
A thousand ways to soothe my pain ;
And sleeplessly all night I pray'd
That I might see that smile again.

I saw it next, a thousand times ;
And every time its kind smile near'd ;
Oh ! twice ten thousand glorious chimes
My heart rang out, when he appear'd ;

What was I then, that others' thought
Could alter so my thought of him;
That I could be by others taught
His image from my heart to dim !

I saw it last, when black and white
Shadows went struggling o'er it wild ;
When he regain'd my long-lost sight,
And I with cold obeisance smil'd ; —
I did not see it fade from life ;
My letters o'er his heart they found ;
They told me in death's last hard strife
His dying hands around them wound.

Although my scorn that face did maim,
Even when its love would not depart ;
Although my laughter smote its shame
And drave it swording through his heart ;
Although its death-gloom grasps my brain
With crushing unrefus'd despair ;
That I may dream that face again
God still must find alone my prayer.

THE RHAPSODISTS

Philip James Bailey

FROM "FESTUS"

YOUTH, LOVE, AND DEATH

Lucifer. And we might trust these youths
    and maidens fair,
The world was made for nothing but love,
    love.
Now I think it was made most to be burn'd.
    Festus. The night is glooming on us.
    It is the hour
When lovers will speak lowly, for the sake
Of being nigh each other ; and when love
Shoots up the eye, like morning on the east,
Making amends for the long northern night
They pass'd, ere either knew the other
    lov'd ;
The hour of hearts ! Say gray-beards what
    they please,
The heart of age is like an emptied wine-
    cup ;

Its life lies in a heel-tap : how can age
    judge ?
'T were a waste of time to ask how they
    wasted theirs ;
But while the blood is bright, breath sweet,
    skin smooth,
And limbs all made to minister delight ;
Ere yet we have shed our locks, like trees
    their leaves,
And we stand staring bare into the air ;
He is a fool who is not for love and beauty
It is I, the young, to the young speak. I
    am of them,
And always shall be. What are years to
    me ?
You traitor years, that fang the hands ye
    have lick'd,
Vicelike ; henceforth your venom-sacs are
    gone.
I have conquer'd. Ye shall perish : yea,
    shall fall

Like birdlets beaten by some resistless
  storm
'Gainst a dead wall, dead. I pity ye, that
  such
Mean things should have rais'd in man or
  hope or fear ;
Those Titans of the heart that fight at
  heaven,
And sleep, by fits, on fire, whose slightest
  stir 's
An earthquake. I am bound and bless'd
  to youth.
None but the brave and beautiful can love.
Oh give me to the young, the fair, the
  free,
The brave, who would breast a rushing,
  burning world
Which came between him and his heart's
  delight.
Mad must I be, and what 's the world ?
  Like mad
For itself. And I to myself am all things,
  too.
If my heart thunder'd would the world
  rock ? Well,
Then let the mad world fight its shadow
  down.
Soon there may be nor sun nor world nor
  shadow.
But thou, my blood, my bright red running
  soul,
Rejoice thou like a river in thy rapids.
Rejoice, thou wilt never pale with age, nor
  thin ;
But in thy full dark beauty, vein by vein
Serpent-wise, me encircling, shalt to the end
Throb, bubble, sparkle, laugh, and leap
  along.
Make merry, heart, while the holidays shall
  last.
Better than daily dwine, break sharp with
  life ;
Like a stag, sunstruck, top thy bounds and
  die.
Heart, I could tear thee out, thou fool, thou
  fool,
And strip thee into shreds upon the wind.
What have I done that thou shouldst maze
  me thus ?
  Lucifer. Let us away ; we have had
    enough of hearts.
  Festus. Oh for the young heart like a
    fountain playing,
Flinging its bright fresh feelings up to the
  skies

It loves and strives to reach ; strives, loves
  in vain.
It is of earth, and never meant for heaven,
Let us love both and die. The sphinx-like
  heart
Loathes life the moment that life's riddle
  is read.
The knot of our existence solv'd, all things
Loose-ended lie, and useless. Life is had,
And lo ! we sigh, and say, can this be all ?
It is not what we thought ; it is very well,
But we want something more. There is
  but death.
And when we have said and seen, done, had,
  enjoy'd
And suffer'd, maybe, all we have wish'd or
  fear'd,
From fame to ruin, and from love to loath--
  ing,
There can come but one more change --
  try it — death.
Oh ! it is great to feel that nought of earth,
Hope, love, nor dread, nor care for what 's
  to come,
Can check the royal lavishment of life ;
But, like a streamer strown upon the wind,
We fling our souls to fate and to the future.
For to die young is youth's divinest gift ;
To pass from one world fresh into another,
Ere change hath lost the charm of soft
  regret,
And feel the immortal impulse from within
Which makes the coming life cry alway,
  on !
And follow it while strong, is heaven's last
  mercy.
There is a fire-fly in the south, but shines
When on the wing. So is 't with mind.
  When once
We rest, we darken. On ! saith God to the
  soul,
As unto the earth for ever. On it goes,
A rejoicing native of the infinite,
As is a bird, of air ; an orb, of heaven.

THE POET

Festus. Thanks, thanks ! With the
  Muse is always love and light,
And self-sworn loyalty to truth. For know,
Poets are all who love, who feel, great
  truths,
And tell them : and the truth of truths is
  love.
There was a time — oh, I remember well !

When, like a sea-shell with its sea-born
   strain,
My soul aye rang with music of the lyre,
And my heart shed its lore as leaves their
   dew —
A honey dew, and throve on what it shed.
All things I lov'd ; but song I lov'd in
   chief.
Imagination is the air of mind,
Judgment its earth and memory its main,
Passion its fire.   I was at home in heaven.
Swiftlike, I liv'd above ; once touching
   earth,
The meanest thing might master me : long
   wings
But baffled.   Still and still I harp'd on
   song.
Oh ! to create within the mind is bliss,
And shaping forth the lofty thought, or
   lovely,
We seek not, need not heaven : and when
   the thought,
Cloudy and shapeless, first forms on the
   mind,
Slow darkening into some gigantic make,
How the heart shakes with pride and fear,
   as heaven
Quakes under its own thunder ; or as
   might,
Of old, the mortal mother of a god,
When first she saw him lessening up the
   skies.
And I began the toil divine of verse,
Which, like a burning bush, doth guest a
   god.
But this was only wing-flapping — not
   flight ;
The pawing of the courser ere he win ;
Till by degrees, from wrestling with my
   soul,
I gather'd strength to keep the fleet
   thoughts fast,
And made them bless me.   Yes, there was
   a time
When tomes of ancient song held eye and
   heart ;
Were the sole lore I reck'd of : the great
   bards
Of Greece, of Rome, and mine own master
   land,
And they who in the holy book are death-
   less ;
Men who have vulgariz'd sublimity,
And bought up truth for the nations ; held
   it whole ;

Men who have forged gods — utter'd —
   made them pass :
Sons of the sons of God, who in olden days
Did leave their passionless heaven for earth
   and woman,
Brought an immortal to a mortal breast,
And, rainbowlike the sweet earth clasping,
   left
A bright precipitate of soul, which lives
Ever, and through the lines of sullen men,
The dumb array of ages, speaks for all ;
Flashing by fits, like fire from an enemy's
   front ;
Whose thoughts, like bars of sunshine in
   shut rooms,
Mid gloom, all glory, win the world to
   light ;
Who make their very follies like their
   souls,
And like the young moon with a ragged
   edge,
Still in their imperfection beautiful ;
Whose weaknesses are lovely as their
   strengths,
Like the white nebulous matter between
   stars,
Which, if not light, at least is likest light ;
Men whom we build our love round like an
   arch
Of triumph, as they pass us on their way
To glory, and to immortality ;
Men whose great thoughts possess us like
   a passion,
Through every limb and the whole heart ;
   whose words
Haunt us, as eagles haunt the mountain
   air ;
Whose thoughts command all coming times
   and minds,
As from a tower, a warden — fix them-
   selves
Deep in the heart as meteor stones in earth,
Dropp'd from some higher sphere : the
   words of gods,
And fragments of the undeem'd tongues of
   heaven ;
Men who walk up to fame as to a friend,
Or their own house, which from the wrong-
   ful heir
They have wrested, from the world's hard
   hand and gripe ;
Men who, like death, all bone but all un-
   arm'd,
Have ta'en the giant world by the throat,
   and thrown him,

And made him swear to maintain their
name and fame
At peril of his life ; who shed great thoughts
As easily as an oak looseneth its golden
leaves
In a kindly largesse to the soil it grew on ;
Whose names are ever on the world's broad
tongue,
Like sound upon the falling of a force ;
Whose words, if wing'd, are with angels'
wings ;
Who play upon the heart as on a harp,
And make our eyes bright as we speak of
them ;
Whose hearts have a look southwards, and
are open
To the whole noon of nature ; these I have
wak'd,
And wept o'er, night by night ; oft ponder-
ing thus :
Homer is gone : and where is Jove ? and
where
The rival cities seven ? His song outlives
Time, tower, and god — all that then was,
save heaven.

HELEN'S SONG

The rose is weeping for her love,
The nightingale ;
And he is flying fast above,
To her he will not fail.
Already golden eve appears ;
He wings his way along ;
Ah ! look, he comes to kiss her tears,
And soothe her with his song.

The moon in pearly light may steep
The still blue air ;
The rose hath ceas'd to droop and weep,
For lo ! her love is there ;
He sings to her, and o'er the trees
She hears his sweet notes swim ;
The world may weary ; she but sees
Her love, and hears but him.

LUCIFER AND ELISSA

Elissa.   Nigh one year ago,
I watch'd that large bright star, much
where 't is now :
Time hath not touch'd its everlasting light-
ning,
Nor dimm'd the glorious glances of its eye ;
Nor passion clouded it, nor any star

Eclips'd ; it is the leader still of heaven.
And I who lov'd it then can love it now ;
But am not what I was, in one degree.
Calm star ! who was it nam'd thee Lucifer,
From him who drew the third of heaven
down with him ?
Oh ! it was but the tradition of thy beauty !
For if the sun hath one part, and the moon
one,
Thou hast the third part of the host of
heaven —
Which is its power — which power is but
its beauty !
Lucifer. It was no tradition, lady, but
of truth !
Elissa. I thought we parted last to
meet no more.
Lucifer. It was so, lady ; but it is not so.
Elissa. Am I to leave, or thou, then ?
Lucifer.   Neither, yet.
Elissa. And who art thou that I should
fear and serve ?
Lucifer. I am the morning and the
evening star,
The star thou lovedst ; thy lover too ; as
once
I told thee incredulous ; star and spirit I
am ;
A power, an ill which doth outbalance being.
Behold life's tyrant evil, peer of good,
The great infortune of the universe.
Am I not more than mortal in my form ?
Millions of years have circled round my
brow,
Like worlds upon their centres, — still I
live,
And age but presses with a halo's weight.
This single arm hath dash'd the light of
heaven ;
This one hand dragg'd the angels from
their thrones : —
Am I not worthy to have lov'd thee, lady ?
Thou mortal model of all heavenliness !
Yet all these spoils have I abandon'd,
cower'd
My powers, my course becalm'd, and
stoop'd from the high
Destruction of the skies for thee, and him
Who loving thee is with thee lost, both lost.
Thou hast but serv'd the purpose of the
fiend ;
Art but the gilded vessel of selfish sin
Whose poison hath drunken made a soul to
death :
Thou, useless now. I come to bid thee die.

Elissa. Wicked, impure, tormentor of the world,
I knew thee not. Yet doubt not thou it was
Who darkenedst for a moment with base aim
God to evade, and shun in this world, man,
Love's heart ; with selfish end alone redeeming
Me from the evil, the death-fright. Take, nathless,
One human soul's forgiveness, such the sum
Of thanks I feel for heaven's great grace that thou
From the overflowings of love's cup mayst quench
Thy breast's broad burning desert, and fertilize
Aught may be in it, that boasts one root of good.
    Lucifer. It is doubtless sad to feel one day our last.
    Elissa. I knew, forewarn'd, I was dying. God is good.
The heavens grow darker as they purer grow,
And both, as we approach them ; so near death
The soul grows darker and diviner hourly.
Could I love less, I should be happier now.
But always 't is to that mad extreme, death
Alone appears the fitting end to bliss
Like that my spirit presseth for.
    Lucifer.   Thy death
Gentle shall be as e'er hath been thy life.
I 'll hurt thee not, for once upon this breast,
Fell, like a snowflake on a fever'd lip,
Thy love. Thy soul shall, dreamlike, pass from thee.
One instant, and thou wakest in heaven for aye.
    Elissa. Lost, say'st thou in one breath, and sav'd in heaven.

.   .   .   .

I ever thought thee to be more than mortal,
And since thus mighty, grant me — and thou mayst
This one, this only boon, as friend to friend —
Bring him I love, one moment ere I die ;
Life, love, all his. . . .
    Lucifer.   Cease !
As a wind-flaw, darting from some rifted cloud,
Seizes upon a water-patch mid main,
And into white wrath worries it, so my mind
This petty controversy distracts. He comes,
I say, but never shalt thou view him, living.
    Elissa. But I will, will see him, and while I am alive.
I hear him. He is come.
    Lucifer.   The ends of things
Are urgent. Still, to this mortuary deed
Reluctant, fix I death's black seal. He 's here !
    Elissa. I hear him ; he is come ; it is he ; it is he !
    Lucifer. Die graciously, as ever thou hast liv'd.
Die, thou shalt never look upon him again.
    Elissa. My love ! haste, Festus ! I am dying.
    Lucifer.   Dead !
As ocean racing fast and fierce to reach
Some headland, ere the moon with maddening ray
Forestall him, and rebellious tides excite
To vain strife, nor of the innocent skiff that thwarts
His path, aught heeds, but with dispiteous foam
Wrecks deathful, I, made hasty by time's end
Impending, thus fill up fate's tragic form.
A word could kill her. See, she hath gone to heaven.

Dora Greenwell

A SONG OF FAREWELL

The Spring will come again, dear friends,
The swallow o'er the sea ;
The bud will hang upon the bough,
The blossom on the tree ;

And many a pleasant sound will rise to greet her on her way,
The voice of bird, and leaf, and stream, and warm winds in their play ;
Ah ! sweet the airs that round her breathe ! and bountiful is she.

She bringeth all the things that fresh, and
    sweet, and hopeful be ;
She scatters promise on the earth with
    open hand and free,
But not for me, my friends,
    But not for me !

Summer will come again, dear friends,
Low murmurs of the bee
Will rise through the long sunny day
Above the flowery lea ;
And deep the dreamy woods will own the
    slumbrous spell she weaves,
And send a greeting, mix'd with sighs,
    through all their quivering leaves.
Oh, precious are her glowing gifts ! and
    plenteous is she,
She bringeth all the lovely things that
    bright and fragrant be,
She scatters fulness on the Earth with lav-
    ish hand and free,
But not for me, my friends,
    But not for me !

Autumn will come again, dear friends,
His spirit-touch shall be
With gold upon the harvest-field,
With crimson on the tree ;

He passeth o'er the silent woods, they
    wither at his breath,
Slow fading in a still decay, a change that
    is not Death.
Oh ! rich and liberal, and wise, and provi-
    dent is he !
He taketh to his garner-house the things
    that ripen'd be,
He gathereth his store from Earth, and
    silently —
    And he will gather me, my friends,
    He will gather me !

TO CHRISTINA ROSSETTI

Thou hast fill'd me a golden cup
With a drink divine that glows,
With the bloom that is flowing up
From the heart of the folded rose.
The grapes in their amber glow,
And the strength of the blood-red wine,
All mingle and change and flow
In this golden cup of thine,
With the scent of the curling vine,
With the balm of the rose's breath, —
For the voice of love is thine,
And thine is the Song of Death !

George Macdonald

LIGHT

Thou art the joy of age :
Thy sun is dear when long the shadow
    falls.
Forth to its friendliness the old man crawls,
And, like the bird hung out in his poor
    cage
To gather song from radiance, in his chair
Sits by the door ; and sitteth there
His soul within him, like a child that lies
Half dreaming, with half-open eyes,
At close of a long afternoon in summer —
High ruins round him, ancient ruins, where
The raven is almost the only comer ;
Half dreams, half broods, in wonderment
At thy celestial descent,
Through rifted loops alighting on the gold
That waves its bloom in many an airy rent :
So dreams the old man's soul, that is not
    old,
But sleepy 'mid the ruins that enfold.

What soul-like changes, evanescent
    moods,
Upon the face of the still passive earth,
Its hills, and fields, and woods,
Thou with thy seasons and thy hours art
    ever calling forth !
Even like a lord of music bent
Over his instrument,
Who gives to tears and smiles an equal
    birth !
When clear as holiness the morning ray
Casts the rock's dewy darkness at its
    feet,
Mottling with shadows all the mountain
    gray ;
When, at the hour of sovereign noon,
Infinite silent cataracts sheet
Shadowless through the air of thunder-
    breeding June ;
And when a yellower glory slanting passes
'Twixt longer shadows o'er the meadow
    grasses ;

When now the moon lifts up her shining
   shield,
High on the peak of a cloud-hill reveal'd ;
Now crescent, low, wandering sun-dazed
   away,
Unconscious of her own star-mingled ray,
Her still face seeming more to think than
   see,
Makes the pale world lie dreaming dreams
   of thee !
No mood of mind, no melody of soul,
But lies within thy silent soft control.

Of operative single power,
And simple unity the one emblem,
Yet all the colors that our passionate eyes
   devour,
In rainbow, moonbow, or in opal gem,
Are the melodious descant of divided thee.
Lo thee in yellow sands ! lo thee
In the blue air and sea !
In the green corn, with scarlet poppies lit,
Thy half souls parted, patient thou dost sit.
Lo thee in speechless glories of the west !
Lo thee in dewdrop's tiny breast !
Thee on the vast white cloud that floats
   away,
Bearing upon its skirt a brown moon-ray !
Regent of color, thou dost fling
Thy overflowing skill on everything !
The thousand hues and shades upon the
   flowers
Are all the pastime of thy leisure hours ;
And all the jewelled ores in mines that hid-
   den be
Are dead till touch'd by thee.

WORLD AND SOUL

This infant world has taken long to make !
Nor hast Thou done the making of it yet,
But wilt be working on when death has set
A new mound in some church-yard for my
   sake.
On flow the centuries without a break ;
Uprise the mountains, ages without let ;
The lichens suck the rock's breast — food
   they get :
Years more than past, the young earth yet
   will take.
But in the dumbness of the rolling time,
No veil of silence shall encompass me :
Thou wilt not once forget and let me be ;
Rather wouldst Thou some old chaotic prime
Invade, and, with a tenderness sublime,
Unfold a world, that I, thy child, might see.

BABY

Where did you come from, baby dear ?
Out of the everywhere into the here.

Where did you get those eyes so blue ?
Out of the sky as I came through.

What makes the light in them sparkle and
   spin ?
Some of the starry spikes left in.

Where did you get that little tear ?
I found it waiting when I got here.

What makes your forehead so smooth and
   high ?
A soft hand strok'd it as I went by.

What makes your cheek like a warm white
   rose ?
I saw something better than any one
   knows.

Whence that three-corner'd smile of bliss ?
Three angels gave me at once a kiss.

Where did you get this pearly ear ?
God spoke, and it came out to hear.

Where did you get those arms and hands ?
Love made itself into bonds and bands.

Feet, whence did you come, you darling
   things ?
From the same box as the cherubs' wings.

How did they all just come to be you ?
God thought about me, and so I grew.

But how did you come to us, you dear ?
God thought about you, and so I am
   here.

SONG

I dream'd that I woke from a dream,
And the house was full of light ;
At the window two angel Sorrows
Held back the curtains of night.

The door was wide, and the house
Was full of the morning wind ;
At the door two armed warders
Stood silent, with faces blind.

I ran to the open door,
For the wind of the world was sweet ;
The warders with crossing weapons
Turn'd back my issuing feet.

I ran to the shining windows —
There the winged Sorrows stood ;

Silent they held the curtains,
And the light fell through in a flood.

I clomb to the highest window —
Ah ! there, with shadow'd brow,
Stood one lonely radiant Sorrow,
And that, my love, was thou.

Gerald Massey

• THE DESERTER FROM THE CAUSE

HE is gone : better so. We should know
　　who stand under
　Our banner : let none but the trusty
　　remain !
For there's stern work at hand, and the
　　time comes shall sunder
　The shell from the pearl, and the chaff
　　from the grain.
And the heart that through danger and
　　death will be dutiful,
　Soul that with Cranmer in fire would
　　shake hands,
With a life like a palace-home built for
　　the beautiful,
　Freedom of all her beloved demands.

He is gone from us ! Yet shall we march
　　on victorious,
　Hearts burning like beacons — eyes fix'd
　　on the goal !
And if we fall fighting, we fall like the
　　glorious,
　With face to the stars, and all heaven
　　in the soul.
And aye for the brave stir of battle we 'll
　　barter
　The sword of life sheath'd in the peace
　　of the grave ;
And better the fieriest fate of the martyr,
　Than live like the coward, and die like
　　the slave !

CHRISTIE'S PORTRAIT

YOUR tiny picture makes me yearn ;
　We are so far apart !
My darling, I can only turn
　And kiss you in my heart.
A thousand tender thoughts a-wing
　Swarm in a summer clime,

And hover round it murmuring
　Like bees at honey-time.

Upon a little girl I look
　Whose pureness makes me sad ;
I read as in a holy book,
　I grow in secret glad.
It seems my darling comes to me
　With something I have lost
Over life's toss'd and troubled sea,
　On some celestial coast.

I think of her when spirit-bow'd ;
　A glory fills the place !
Like sudden light on swords, the proud
　Smile flashes in my face :
And others see, in passing by,
　But cannot understand
The vision shining in mine eye,
　My strength of heart and hand.

That grave content and touching grace
　Bring tears into mine eyes ;
She makes my heart a holy place
　Where hymns and incense rise.
Such calm her gentle spirit brings
　As, smiling overhead,
White-statued saints with peaceful wings
　Shadow the sleeping dead.

Our Christie is no rosy Grace
　With beauty all may see,
But I have never felt a face
　Grow half so dear to me.
No curling hair about her brows,
　Like many merry girls ;
Well, straighter to my heart it goes,
　And round it curls and curls.

Meek as the wood anemone glints
　To see if heaven be blue,
Is my pale flower with her sweet tints
　Of heaven shining through.

She will be poor and never fret,
  Sleep sound and lowly lie ;
Will live her quiet life, and let
  The great world-storm go by.

Dear love !, God keep her in his grasp,
  Meek maiden, or brave wife,
Till his good angels softly clasp
  Her closed book of life !
And this fair picture of the sun,
  With birthday blessings given,
Shall fade before a glorious one
  Taken of her in heaven.

HIS BANNER OVER ME

SURROUNDED by unnumber'd foes,
Against my soul the battle goes !

Yet though I weary, sore distrest,
I know that I shall reach my rest :
  I lift my tearful eyes above, —
  His banner over me is love.

Its sword my spirit will not yield,
Though flesh may faint upon the field ;
He waves before my fading sight
The branch of palm, — the crown of light ;
  I lift my brightening eyes above, —
  His banner over me is love.

My cloud of battle-dust may dim,
His veil of splendor curtain him !
And in the midnight of my fear
I may not feel him standing near ;
  But, as I lift mine eyes above,
  His banner over me is love.

Alexander Smith

FROM "A LIFE-DRAMA"

FORERUNNERS

Walter. I have a strain of a departed
  bard ;
One who was born too late into this world.
A mighty day was past, and he saw nought
But ebbing sunset and the rising stars, —
Still o'er him rose those melancholy stars !
Unknown his childhood, save that he was
  born
'Mong woodland waters full of silver
  breaks ;
. . . .
I was to him but Labrador to Ind ;
His pearls were plentier than my pebble-
  stones.
He was the sun, I was that squab — the
  earth,
And bask'd me in his light until he drew
Flowers from my barren sides. Oh ! he
  was rich,
And I rejoiced upon his shore of pearls,
A weak enamor'd sea. Once he did say,
"My Friend ! a Poet must ere long arise,
And with a regal song sun-crown this age,
As a saint's head is with a halo crown'd ; —
One, who shall hallow Poetry to God
And to its own high use, for Poetry is
The grandest chariot wherein king-thoughts
  ride ; —

One, who shall fervent grasp the sword of
  song,
As a stern swordsman grasps his keenest
  blade,
To find the quickest passage to the heart.
A mighty Poet, whom this age shall choose
To be its spokesman to all coming times.
In the ripe full-blown season of his soul,
He shall go forward in his spirit's strength,
And grapple with the questions of all time,
And wring from them their meanings. As
  King Saul
Call'd up the buried prophet from his
  grave
To speak his doom, so shall this Poet-king
Call up the dead Past from its awful grave
To tell him of our future. As the air
Doth sphere the world, so shall his heart
  of love —
Loving mankind, not peoples. As the lake
Reflects the flower, tree, rock, and bending
  heaven,
Shall he reflect our great humanity ;
And as the young Spring breathes with liv-
  ing breath
On a dead branch, till it sprouts fragrantly
Green leaves and sunny flowers, shall he
  breathe life
Through every theme he touch, making all
  Beauty
And Poetry for ever like the stars."
His words set me on fire ; I cried aloud,

"Gods! what a portion to forerun this
    Soul!"
He grasp'd my hand, — I look'd upon his
    face, —
A thought struck all the blood into his
    cheeks,
Like a strong buffet. His great flashing
    eyes
Burn'd on mine own. He said, "A grim
    old king,
Whose blood leap'd madly when the trum-
    pets bray'd
To joyous battle 'mid a storm of steeds,
Won a rich kingdom on a battle-day;
But in the sunset he was ebbing fast,
Ring'd by his weeping lords. His left
    hand held
His white steed, to the belly splash'd with
    blood,
That seem'd to mourn him with its droop-
    ing head;
His right, his broken brand; and in his
    ear
His old victorious banners flap the winds.
He called his faithful herald to his side, —
'Go! tell the dead I come!' With a proud
    smile,
The warrior with a stab let out his soul,
Which fled and shriek'd through all the
    other world,
'Ye dead! My master comes!' And
    there was pause
Till the great shade should enter. Like
    that herald,
Walter, I'd rush across this waiting world
And cry, ' *He* comes!'" Lady, wilt hear
    the song? [*Sings.*

A MINOR POET

He sat one winter 'neath a linden tree
In my bare orchard; "See, my friend,"
    he said,
"The stars among the branches hang like
    fruit,
So, hopes were thick within me. When
    I'm gone
The world will like a valuator sit
Upon my soul, and say, 'I was a cloud
That caught its glory from a sunken sun,
And gradual burn'd into its native gray.'"
On an October eve, 't was his last wish
To see again the mists and golden woods;
Upon his death-bed he was lifted up,
The slumb'rous sun within the lazy west

With their last gladness fill'd his dying
    eyes.
No sooner was he hence than critic-worms
Were swarming on the body of his fame,
And thus they judged the dead: "This
    Poet was
An April tree whose vermeil-loaded boughs
Promis'd to Autumn apples juiced and red,
But never came to fruit." "He is to us
But a rich odor, — a faint music-swell."
"Poet he was not in the larger sense;
He could write pearls, but he could never
    write
A Poem round and perfect as a star."
"Politic, i' faith. His most judicious act
Was dying when he did; the next five years
Had finger'd all the fine dust from his
    wings,
And left him poor as we. He died — 't was
    shrewd!
And came with all his youth and unblown
    hopes
On the world's heart, and touch'd it into
    tears."

SEA-MARGE

The lark is singing in the blinding sky,
Hedges are white with May. The bride-
    groom sea
Is toying with the shore, his wedded bride,
And, in the fulness of his marriage joy,
He decorates her tawny brow with shells,
Retires a space, to see how fair she looks,
Then proud, runs up to kiss her. All is
    fair —
All glad, from grass to sun! Yet more I
    love
Than this, the shrinking day that some-
    times comes
In Winter's front, so fair 'mong its dark
    peers,
It seems a straggler from the files of June,
Which in its wanderings had lost its wits,
And half its beauty; and, when it return'd,
Finding its old companions gone away,
It join'd November's troop, then marching
    past;
And so the frail thing comes, and greets
    the world
With a thin crazy smile, then bursts in
    tears,
And all the while it holds within its hand
A few half-wither'd flowers. I love and
    pity it!

BEAUTY

BEAUTY still walketh on the earth and air,
Our present sunsets are as rich in gold
As ere the Iliad's music was out-roll'd ;
The roses of the Spring are ever fair,
'Mong branches green still ring-doves coo
　　and pair,
And the deep sea still foams its music old.
So, if we are at all divinely soul'd,
This beauty will unloose our bonds of care.
'T is pleasant, when blue skies are o'er us
　　bending
Within old starry-gated Poesy,
To meet a soul set to no worldly tune,
Like thine, sweet Friend ! Oh, dearer this
　　to me
Than are the dewy trees, the sun, the moon,
Or noble music with a golden ending.

TO ——

THE broken moon lay in the autumn sky,
　　And I lay at thy feet ;
You bent above me ; in the silence I
　　Could hear my wild heart beat.

I spoke ; my soul was full of trembling fears
　　At what my words would bring :
You rais'd your face, your eyes were full
　　of tears,
　　As the sweet eyes of Spring.

You kiss'd me then, I worshipp'd at thy
　　feet
　　Upon the shadowy sod.
Oh, fool, I lov'd thee ! lov'd thee, lovely
　　cheat !
　　Better than Fame or God.

My soul leap'd up beneath thy timid kiss ;
　　What then to me were groans,
Or pain, or death ?　Earth was a round of
　　bliss,
　　I seem'd to walk on thrones.

And you were with me 'mong the rushing
　　wheels,
　　'Mid Trade's tumultuous jars ;
And where to awe-struck wilds the Night
　　reveals
　　Her hollow gulfs of stars.

Before your window, as before a shrine,
　　I 've knelt 'mong dew-soak'd flowers,
While distant music-bells, with voices fine,
　　Measur'd the midnight hours.

There came a fearful moment : I was pale,
　　You wept, and never spoke,
But clung around me as the woodbine frail
　　Clings, pleading, round an oak.

Upon my wrong I steadied up my soul,
　　And flung thee from myself ;
I spurn'd thy love as 't were a rich man's
　　dole, ——
　　It was my only wealth.

I spurn'd thee ! I, who lov'd thee, could
　　have died,
　　That hop'd to call thee " wife,"
And bear thee, gently-smiling at my side,
　　Through all the shocks of life !

Too late, thy fatal beauty and thy tears,
　　Thy vows, thy passionate breath ;
I 'll meet thee not in Life, nor in the spheres
　　Made visible by Death.

EARLY HYMNODY

(*See also :* S. F. ADAMS, ALFORD, E. B. BROWNING, H. COLERIDGE, DE VERE, FOX,
MARTINEAU, NEWMAN)

James Montgomery

AT HOME IN HEAVEN

" FOREVER with the Lord ! "
　　Amen, so let it be ;
Life from the dead is in that word,
　　'T is immortality.

Here in the body pent,
　　Absent from him I roam,
Yet nightly pitch my moving tent
　　A day's march nearer home.

My Father's house on high,
Home of my soul, how near
At times, to faith's foreseeing eye,
Thy golden gates appear !

Ah ! then my spirit faints
To reach the land I love,
The bright inheritance of saints,
Jerusalem above.

Yet clouds will intervene,
And all my prospect flies ;
Like Noah's dove, I flit between
Rough seas and stormy skies.

Anon the clouds dispart,
The winds and waters cease,

While sweetly o'er my gladden'd heart
Expands the bow of peace.

Beneath its glowing arch,
Along the hallow'd ground,
I see cherubic armies march,
A camp of fire around.

I hear at morn and even,
At noon and midnight hour,
The choral harmonies of heaven
Earth's Babel-tongues o'erpower.

Then, then I feel that he,
Remember'd or forgot,
The Lord, is never far from me,
Though I perceive him not.

Charlotte Elliott

JUST AS I AM

Just as I am, without one plea
But that thy blood was shed for me,
And that thou bid'st me come to thee,
O Lamb of God, I come !

Just as I am, and waiting not
To rid my soul of one dark blot,
To thee, whose blood can cleanse each spot,
O Lamb of God, I come !

Just as I am, though toss'd about,
With many a conflict, many a doubt,
Fightings and fears within, without,
O Lamb of God, I come !

Just as I am, poor, wretched, blind ;
Sight, riches, healing of the mind,
Yea, all I need, in thee to find,
O Lamb of God, I come !

Just as I am, thou wilt receive,
Wilt welcome, pardon, cleanse, relieve ;
Because thy promise I believe,
O Lamb of God, I come !

Just as I am — thy love unknown
Has broken every barrier down ;
Now to be thine, yea, thine alone,
O Lamb of God, I come !

Just as I am, of that free love,
The breadth, length, depth, and height to
prove,
Here for a season, then above,
O Lamb of God, I come !

LET ME BE WITH THEE

Let me be with thee where thou art,
My Saviour, my eternal rest !
Then only will this longing heart
Be fully and forever blest.

Let me be with thee where thou art,
Thy unveil'd glory to behold ;
Then only will this wandering heart
Cease to be treacherous, faithless, cold.

Let me be with thee where thou art,
Where spotless saints thy name adore ;
Then only will this sinful heart
Be evil and defil'd no more.

Let me be with thee where thou art,
Where none can die, where none re-
move ;
There neither death nor life will part
Me from thy presence and thy love !

James Edmeston

PRAYER TO THE TRINITY

LEAD us, heavenly Father, lead us
O'er the world's tempestuous sea ;
Guard us, guide us, keep us, feed us,
For we have no help but thee ;
    Yet possessing
    Every blessing,
If our God our Father be.

Saviour, breathe forgiveness o'er us ;
All our weakness thou dost know ;

Thou didst tread this earth before us,
Thou didst feel its keenest woe ;
    Lone and dreary,
    Faint and weary,
Through the desert thou didst go.

Spirit of our God, descending,
  Fill our hearts with heavenly joy ,
Love with every passion blending,
  Pleasure that can never cloy :
    Thus provided,
    Pardon'd, guided,
Nothing can our peace destroy.

Henry Hart Milman

HYMN FOR THE SIXTEENTH SUNDAY AFTER TRINITY

WHEN our heads are bow'd with woe,
When our bitter tears o'erflow,
When we mourn the lost, the dear :
Gracious Son of Mary, hear !

Thou our throbbing flesh hast worn,
Thou our mortal griefs hast borne,
Thou hast shed the human tear :
Gracious Son of Mary, hear !

When the sullen death-bell tolls
For our own departed souls—
When our final doom is near,
Gracious Son of Mary, hear !

Thou hast bow'd the dying head,
Thou the blood of life hast shed,
Thou hast fill'd a mortal bier ·
Gracious Son of Mary, hear !

When the heart is sad within
With the thought of all its sin,
When the spirit shrinks with fear,
Gracious Son of Mary, hear !

Thou the shame, the grief hast known ;
Though the sins were not Thine own,
Thou hast deign'd their load to bear :
Gracious Son of Mary, hear !

BURIAL HYMN

BROTHER, thou art gone before us,
  And thy saintly soul is flown
Where tears are wip'd from every eye,
  And sorrow is unknown.
From the burden of the flesh,
  And from care and sin releas'd,
Where the wicked cease from troubling,
  And the weary are at rest.

The toilsome way thou 'st travell'd o'er,
  And hast borne the heavy load ;
But Christ hath taught thy wandering feet
  To reach his bless'd abode ;
Thou 'rt sleeping now, like Lazarus,
  On his Father's faithful breast,
Where the wicked cease from troubling,
  And the weary are at rest.

Sin can never taint thee now,
  Nor can doubt thy faith assail ;
Nor thy meek trust in Jesus Christ
  And the Holy Spirit fail;
And there thou 'rt sure to meet the good,
  Whom on earth thou lovest best,
Where the wicked cease from troubling,
  And the weary are at rest.

" Earth to earth," and " dust to dust,"
  Thus the solemn priest hath said ;
So we lay the turf above thee now,
  And seal thy narrow bed ;

But thy spirit, brother, soars away
　Among the faithful blest,
Where the wicked cease from troubling,
　And the weary are at rest.

And when the Lord shall summon us
　Whom thou now hast left behind,
May we, untainted by the world,
　As sure a welcome find ;
May each, like thee, depart in peace,
　To be a glorious, happy guest,
Where the wicked cease from troubling,
　And the weary are at rest.

RIDE ON IN MAJESTY

RIDE on ! ride on in majesty !
In lowly pomp ride on to die ;

O Christ, thy triumphs now begin
O'er captive death and conquer'd sin !

Ride on ! ride on in majesty !
The winged armies of the sky
Look down with sad and wondering eyes
To see the approaching sacrifice.

Ride on ! ride on in majesty !
The last and fiercest strife is nigh ;
The Father on his sapphire throne
Expects his own anointed Son.

Ride on ! ride on in majesty !
In lowly pomp ride on to die ;
Bow thy meek head to mortal pain,
Then take, O God, thy power, and reign !

John Keble

WHO RUNS MAY READ

THERE is a book, who runs may read,
　Which heavenly truth imparts,
And all the lore its scholars need,
　Pure eyes and Christian hearts.

The works of God above, below,
　Within us and around,
Are pages in that book, to show
　How God himself is found.

The glorious sky, embracing all,
　Is like the Maker's love,
Wherewith encompass'd, great and small
　In peace and order move.

The moon above, the Church below,
　A wondrous race they run,
But all their radiance, all their glow,
　Each borrows of its sun.

The Saviour lends the light and heat
　That crowns his holy hill ;
The saints, like stars, around his seat,
　Perform their courses still.

The saints above are stars in heaven —
　What are the saints on earth ?
Like trees they stand whom God has given,
　Our Eden's happy birth.

Faith is their fix'd unswerving root,
　Hope their unfading flower,
Fair deeds of charity their fruit,
　The glory of their bower.

The dew of heaven is like thy grace.
　It steals in silence down ;
But where it lights, the favor'd place
　By richest fruits is known.

One Name, above all glorious names,
　With its ten thousand tongues
The everlasting sea proclaims,
　Echoing angelic songs.

The raging fire, the roaring wind,
　Thy boundless power display :
But in the gentler breeze we find
　Thy spirit's viewless way.

Two worlds are ours : 't is only sin
　Forbids us to descry
The mystic heaven and earth within,
　Plain as the sea and sky.

Thou, who hast given me eyes to see
　And love this sight so fair,
Give me a heart to find out thee,
　And read thee everywhere.

SEED TIME HYMN

LORD, in thy name thy servants plead,
　And thou hast sworn to hear ;
Thine is the harvest, thine the seed,
　The fresh and fading year :

Our hope, when autumn winds blew wild,
　We trusted, Lord, with thee ;
And still, now spring has on us smil'd,
　We wait on thy decree.

The former and the latter rain,
　The summer sun and air,
The green ear, and the golden grain,
　All thine, are ours by prayer.

Thine too by right, and ours by grace,
　The wondrous growth unseen,
The hopes that soothe, the fears that brace,
　The love that shines serene.

So grant the precious things brought forth
　By sun and moon below,
That thee in thy new heaven and earth
　We never may forego.

HOLY MATRIMONY

THE voice that breath'd o'er Eden,
　That earliest wedding-day,
The primal marriage blessing,
　It hath not pass'd away.

Still in the pure espousal
　Of Christian man and maid,
The holy Three are with us,
　The threefold grace is said.

For dower of blessed children,
　For love and faith's sweet sake,
For high mysterious union,
　Which nought on earth may break.

Be present, awful Father,
　To give away this bride,
As Eve thou gav'st to Adam
　Out of his own pierced side :

Be present, Son of Mary,
　To join their loving hands,
As thou didst bind two natures
　In thine eternal bands :

Be present, Holiest Spirit,
　To bless them as they kneel,
As thou for Christ, the Bridegroom,
　The heavenly Spouse dost seal.

Oh, spread thy pure wing o'er them,
　Let no ill power find place,
When onward to thine altar
　The hallow'd path they trace,

To cast their crowns before thee
　In perfect sacrifice,
Till to the home of gladness
　With Christ's own Bride they rise. AMEN.

Sir John Bowring

FROM THE RECESSES

FROM the recesses of a lowly spirit
My humble prayer ascends : O Father !
　hear it.
Upsoaring on the wings of fear and meek-
　ness,
　　Forgive its weakness.

I know, I feel, how mean and how un-
　worthy
The trembling sacrifice I pour before thee ;
What can I offer in thy presence holy,
　　But sin and folly ?

For in thy sight, who every bosom viewest,
Cold are our warmest vows and vain our
　truest ;
Thoughts of a hurrying hour ; our lips re-
　peat them,
　　Our hearts forget them.

We see thy hand — it leads us, it supports
　us ;
We hear thy voice — it counsels and it
　courts us ;
And then we turn away — and still thy
　kindness
　　Pardons our blindness.

And still thy rain descends, thy sun is glowing,
Fruits ripen round, flowers are beneath us blowing,
And, as if man were some deserving creature,
　Joys cover nature.

Oh how long-suffering, Lord! but thou delightest
To win with love the wandering ; thou invitest
By smiles of mercy, not by frowns or terrors,
　Man from his errors.

Who can resist thy gentle call, appealing
To every generous thought and grateful feeling ?
That voice paternal whispering, watching ever,
　My bosom ? — never.

Father and Saviour! plant within that bosom
These seeds of holiness ; and bid them blossom
In fragrance and in beauty bright and vernal,
　And spring eternal.

Then place them in those everlasting gardens
Where angels walk, and seraphs are the wardens ;

Where every flower that creeps through death's dark portal
　Becomes immortal.

WHAT OF THE NIGHT?

WATCHMAN, tell us of the night,
　What its signs of promise are !
Traveller, o'er yon mountain's height
　See that glory-beaming star !
Watchman, doth its beauteous ray
　Aught of hope or joy foretell ?
Traveller, yes ! it brings the day,
　Promis'd day of Israel.

Watchman, tell us of the night :
　Higher yet that star ascends !
Traveller, blessedness and light,
　Peace and truth, its course portends.
Watchman, will its beams alone
　Gild the spot that gave them birth ?
Traveller, ages are its own,
　And it bursts o'er all the earth !

Watchman, tell us of the night,
　For the morning seems to dawn.
Traveller, darkness takes its flight,
　Doubt and terror are withdrawn.
Watchman, let thy wand'rings cease ;
　Hie thee to thy quiet home.
Traveller, lo ! the Prince of Peace,
　Lo ! the Son of God is come.

Henry Francis Lyte

ABIDE WITH ME

ABIDE with me ! Fast falls the eventide ;
The darkness deepens : Lord, with me abide !
When other helpers fail, and comforts flee,
Help of the helpless, O abide with me !

Swift to its close ebbs out life's little day ;
Earth's joys grow dim ; its glories pass away :
Change and decay in all around I see ;
O thou, who changest not, abide with me !

Not a brief glance I beg, a passing word,
But as thou dwell'st with thy disciples, Lord,

Familiar, condescending, patient, free, —
Come, not to sojourn, but abide, with me !

Come not in terrors, as the King of kings ;
But kind and good, with healing in thy wings :
Tears for all woes, a heart for every plea ;
Come, Friend of sinners, and thus bide with me !

Thou on my head in early youth didst smile,
And, though rebellious and perverse meanwhile,
Thou hast not left me, oft as I left thee :
On to the close, O Lord, abide with me !

I need thy presence every passing hour.
What but thy grace can foil the Tempter's
  power ?
Who like thyself my guide and stay can
  be ?
Through cloud and sunshine, O abide with
  me !

I fear no foe with thee at hand to bless :
Ills have no weight, and tears no bitterness.
Where is death's sting, where, grave, thy
  victory ?
I triumph still, if thou abide with me.

Hold thou thy cross before my closing eyes ;
Shine through the gloom, and point me to
  the skies :
Heaven's morning breaks, and earth's vain
  shadows flee :
In life and death, O Lord, abide with me !

"LO, WE HAVE LEFT ALL"

JESUS, I my cross have taken,
  All to leave, and follow thee ;
Destitute, despis'd, forsaken,
  Thou, from hence, my all shalt be.
Perish every fond ambition,
  All I 've sought and hop'd and known,
Yet how rich is my condition,
  God and heaven are still my own !

Let the world despise and leave me,
  They have left my Saviour, too ;
Human hearts and looks deceive me ;
  Thou art not, like man, untrue ;
And, while thou shalt smile upon me,
  God of wisdom, love, and might,
Foes may hate and friends may shun me :
  Show thy face, and all is bright.

Go, then, earthly fame and treasure !
  Come, disaster, scorn, and pain !
In thy service pain is pleasure ;
  With thy favor loss is gain.
I have call'd thee Abba, Father ;
  I have stay'd my heart on thee :
Storms may howl, and clouds may gather,
  All must work for good to me.

Man may trouble and distress me,
  'T will but drive me to thy breast ;

Life with trials hard may press me,
  Heaven will bring me sweeter rest.
Oh, 't is not in grief to harm me,
  While thy love is left to me !
Oh, 't were not in joy to charm me,
  Were that joy unmix'd with thee !

Take, my soul, thy full salvation,
  Rise o'er sin and fear and care ;
Joy to find in every station
  Something still to do or bear.
Think what Spirit dwells within thee ;
  What a Father's smile is thine ;
What a Saviour died to win thee :
  Child of heaven, shouldst thou repine ?

Haste then on from grace to glory,
  Arm'd by faith, and wing'd by prayer ;
Heaven's eternal day 's before thee,
  God's own hand shall guide thee there.
Soon shall close thy earthly mission,
  Swift shall pass thy pilgrim days,
Hope soon change to glad fruition,
  Faith to sight, and prayer to praise !

THE SECRET PLACE

THERE is a safe and secret place
  Beneath the wings divine,
Reserv'd for all the heirs of grace :
  Oh, be that refuge mine !

The least and feeblest there may bide
  Uninjur'd and unaw'd ;
While thousands fall on every side,
  He rests secure in God.

The angels watch him on his way,
  And aid with friendly arm ;
And Satan, roaring for his prey,
  May hate, but cannot harm.

He feeds in pastures large and fair
  Of love and truth divine ;
O child of God, O glory's heir,
  How rich a lot is thine !

A hand almighty to defend,
  An ear for every call,
An honor'd life, a peaceful end,
  And heaven to crown it all !

Samuel Wilberforce

JUST FOR TO-DAY

Lord, for to-morrow and its needs
 I do not pray ;
Keep me from any stain of sin
 Just for to-day :
Let me both diligently work
 And duly pray ;
Let me be kind in word and deed
 Just for to-day,
Let me be slow to do my will —
 Prompt to obey :

Help me to sacrifice myself
 Just for to-day.
Let me no wrong or idle word
 Unthinking say —
Set thou thy seal upon my lips,
 Just for to-day.
So for to-morrow and its needs
 I do not pray,
But keep me, guide me, hold me, Lord,
 Just for to-day.

Christopher Wordsworth

GIVING TO GOD

O Lord of heaven, and earth, and sea !
To thee all praise and glory be ;
How shall we show our love to thee,
 Who givest all — who givest all ?

The golden sunshine, vernal air,
Sweet flowers and fruit thy love declare ;
When harvests ripen, thou art there,
 Who givest all — who givest all.

For peaceful homes and healthful days,
For all the blessings earth displays,
We owe thee thankfulness and praise,
 Who givest all — who givest all.

For souls redeem'd, for sins forgiven,
For means of grace and hopes of heaven,
What can to thee, O Lord ! be given,
 Who givest all — who givest all ?

We lose what on ourselves we spend,
We have, as treasures without end,
Whatever, Lord, to thee we lend,
 Who givest all — who givest all.

Whatever, Lord, we lend to thee,
Repaid a thousand-fold will be ;
Then gladly will we give to thee,
 Who givest all — who givest all.

Horatius Bonar

LOST BUT FOUND

I was a wandering sheep,
 I did not love the fold ;
I did not love my Shepherd's voice,
 I would not be controll'd.
I was a wayward child,
 I did not love my home,
I did not love my Father's voice,
 I lov'd afar to roam.

The Shepherd sought his sheep ;
 The Father sought his child ;
They follow'd me o'er vale and hill,
 O'er deserts waste and wild.

They found me nigh to death,
 Famish'd, and faint, and lone ;
They bound me with the bands of love ;
 They sav'd the wandering one.

They spoke in tender love,
 They rais'd my drooping head ;
They gently clos'd my bleeding wounds,
 My fainting soul they fed.
They wash'd my filth away,
 They made me clean and fair ;
They brought me to my home in peace,
 The long-sought wanderer.

Jesus my Shepherd is,
　'T was he that lov'd my soul ;
'T was he that wash'd me in his blood,
　'T was he that made me whole ;
　'T was he that sought the lost,
　That found the wandering sheep ;
'T was he that brought me to the fold,
　'T is he that still doth keep.

I was a wandering sheep,
　I would not be controll'd ;
But now I love my Shepherd's voice,
　I love, I love the fold.
I was a wayward child,
　I once preferr'd to roam ;
But now I love my Father's voice,
　I love, I love his home.

THE VOICE FROM GALILEE

I HEARD the voice of Jesus say,
　Come unto me and rest ;
Lay down, thou weary one, lay down
　Thy head upon my breast.
I came to Jesus as I was,
　Weary, and worn, and sad,
I found in him a resting-place,
　And he has made me glad.

I heard the voice of Jesus say,
　Behold, I freely give
The living water, — thirsty one,
　Stoop down, and drink, and live.
I came to Jesus and I drank
　Of that life-giving stream ;
My thirst was quench'd, my soul reviv'd,
　And now I live in him.

I heard the voice of Jesus say,
　I am this dark world's light,
Look unto me, thy morn shall rise
　And all thy day be bright.
I look'd to Jesus, and I found
　In him my Star, my Sun ;
And in that light of life I' ll walk
　Till travelling days are done.

THY WAY, NOT MINE

THY way, not mine, O Lord,
　However dark it be !
Lead me by thine own hand,
　Choose out the path for me.

Smooth let it be, or rough,
　It will be still the best ;
Winding or straight, it matters not
　Right onward to thy rest.

I dare not choose my lot ;
　I would not, if I might ;
Choose thou for me, my God ;
　So shall I walk aright.

The kingdom that I seek
　Is thine ; so let the way
That leads to it be thine,
　Else I must surely stray.

Take thou my cup, and it
　With joy or sorrow fill,
As best to thee may seem ;
　Choose thou my good and ill ;

Choose thou for me my friends,
　My sickness or my health ;
Choose thou my cares for me,
　My poverty or wealth.

Not mine, not mine the choice,
　In things or great or small ;
Be thou my guide, my strength,
　My wisdom, and my all.

ABIDE WITH US

'T IS evening now !
O Saviour, wilt not thou
Enter my home and heart,
Nor ever hence depart,
Even when the morning breaks,
And earth again awakes ?
Thou wilt abide with me,
And I with thee.

The world is old !
Its air grows dull and cold ;
Upon its aged face
The wrinkles come apace ;
Its western sky is wan,
Its youth and joy are gone.
O Master, be our light,
When o'er us falls the night.

Evil is round !
Iniquities abound ;
Our cottage will be lone
When the great Sun is gone ;

O Saviour, come and bless,
Come share our loneliness ;
We need a comforter ;
Take up thy dwelling here.

THE MASTER'S TOUCH

In the still air the music lies unheard ;
In the rough marble beauty hides un-
    seen ;
To wake the music and the beauty needs
The master's touch, the sculptor's chisel
    keen.

Great Master, touch us with thy skilful
    hand,
Let not the music that is in us die ;
Great Sculptor, hew and polish us ; nor
    let,
Hidden and lost, thy form within us lie.

Spare not the stroke ; do with us as thou
    wilt ;
Let there be nought unfinish'd, broken,
    marr'd ;
Complete thy purpose, that we may become
Thy perfect image, O our God and Lord.

A LITTLE WHILE

BEYOND the smiling and the weeping
    I shall be soon ;
Beyond the waking and the sleeping,
Beyond the sowing and the reaping,
    I shall be soon.

Love, rest, and home !
Sweet hope !
Lord, tarry not, but come.

Beyond the blooming and the fading
    I shall be soon ;
Beyond the shining and the shading,
Beyond the hoping and the dreading,
    I shall be soon.

Beyond the rising and the setting
    I shall be soon ;
Beyond the calming and the fretting,
Beyond remembering and forgetting,
    I shall be soon.

Beyond the gathering and the strowing
    I shall be soon ;
Beyond the ebbing and the flowing,
Beyond the coming and the going,
    I shall be soon.

Beyond the parting and the meeting
    I shall be soon ;
Beyond the farewell and the greeting,
Beyond this pulse's fever beating,
    I shall be soon.

Beyond the frost chain and the fever
    I shall be soon ;
Beyond the rock waste and the river,
Beyond the ever and the never,
    I shall be soon.
Love, rest, and home !
Sweet hope !
Lord, tarry not, but come.

John Samuel Bewley Monsell

LITANY

WHEN my feet have wander'd
    From the narrow way
Out into the desert,
    Gone like sheep astray ;
Soil'd and sore with travel
Through the ways of men,
All too weak to bear me
Back to Thee again :
Hear me, O my Father !
From Thy mercy-seat,
Save me by the passion
Of the bleeding feet !

When my hands, unholy
    Through some sinful deed
Wrought in me, have freshly
    Made my Saviour's bleed :
And I cannot lift up
Mine to Thee in prayer,
Tied and bound, and holden
Back by my despair :
Then, my Father ! loose them,
Break for me their bands,
Save me by the passion
Of the bleeding hands !

When my thoughts, unruly,
  Dare to doubt of Thee,
And thy ways to question
  Deem is to be free :
Till, through cloud and darkness,
Wholly gone astray,
They find no returning
To the narrow way :
Then, my God ! mine only
Trust and truth art Thou ;
Save me by the passion
Of the bleeding brow !

When my heart, forgetful
  Of the love that yet,
Though by man forgotten,
  Never can forget ;
All its best affections
Spent on things below,
In its sad despondings
Knows not where to go :
Then, my God ! mine only
Hope and help Thou art ;
Save me by the passion
Of the bleeding heart !

Frederick William Faber

THE WILL OF GOD

I worship thee, sweet will of God !
  And all thy ways adore ;
And every day I live, I seem
  To love thee more and more.

Thou wert the end, the blessed rule
  Of our Saviour's toils and tears ;
Thou wert the passion of his heart
  Those three and thirty years.

And he hath breath'd into my soul
  A special love of thee,
A love to lose my will in his,
  And by that loss be free.

I love to see thee bring to nought
  The plans of wily men ;
When simple hearts outwit the wise,
  Oh, thou art loveliest then.

The headstrong world it presses hard
  Upon the church full oft,
And then how easily thou turn'st
  The hard ways into soft.

I love to kiss each print where thou
  Hast set thine unseen feet ;
I cannot fear thee, blessed will !
  Thine empire is so sweet.

When obstacles and trials seem
  Like prison walls to be,
I do the little I can do,
  And leave the rest to thee.

I know not what it is to doubt,
  My heart is ever gay ;
I run no risk, for, come what will,
  Thou always hast thy way.

I have no cares, O blessed will !
  For all my cares are thine :
I live in triumph, Lord ! for thou
  Hast made thy triumphs mine.

And when it seems no chance or change
  From grief can set me free,
Hope finds its strength in helplessness,
  And gayly waits on thee.

Man's weakness, waiting upon God,
  Its end can never miss,
For men on earth no work can do
  More angel-like than this.

Ride on, ride on, triumphantly,
  Thou glorious will, ride on !
Faith's pilgrim sons behind thee take
  The road that thou hast gone.

He always wins who sides with God,
  To him no chance is lost ;
God's will is sweetest to him, when
  It triumphs at his cost.

Ill that he blesses is our good,
  And unbless'd good is ill ;
And all is right that seems most wrong,
  If it be his sweet will.

PARADISE

O Paradise, O Paradise,
  Who doth not crave for rest,
Who would not seek the happy land
  Where they that lov'd are blest ?
    Where loyal hearts and true
    Stand ever in the light,
  All rapture through and through,
    In God's most holy sight.

O Paradise, O Paradise,
  The world is growing old ;
Who would not be at rest and free
  Where love is never cold ?

O Paradise, O Paradise,
  Wherefore doth death delay ?
Bright death, that is the welcome dawn
  Of our eternal day.

O Paradise, O Paradise,
  'T is weary waiting here ;
I long to be where Jesus is,
  To feel, to see him near.

O Paradise, O Paradise,
  I want to sin no more,
I want to be as pure on earth
  As on thy spotless shore.

O Paradise, O Paradise,
  I greatly long to see
The special place my dearest Lord
  Is destining for me.

O Paradise, O Paradise,
  I feel 't will not be long ;
Patience ! I almost think I hear
  Faint fragments of thy song ;
    Where loyal hearts and true
    Stand ever in the light,
  All rapture through and through,
    In God's most holy sight.

THE RIGHT MUST WIN

Oh, it is hard to work for God,
  To rise and take his part
Upon this battle-field of earth,
  And not sometimes lose heart !

He hides himself so wondrously,
  As though there were no God ;
He is least seen when all the powers
  Of ill are most abroad.

Or he deserts us at the hour
  The fight is all but lost ;
And seems to leave us to ourselves
  Just when we need him most.

Ill masters good ; good seems to change
  To ill with greatest ease ;
And, worst of all, the good with good
  Is at cross-purposes.

Ah ! God is other than we think ;
  His ways are far above,
Far beyond reason's height, and reach'd
  Only by childlike love.

Workman of God ! Oh, lose not heart,
  But learn what God is like ;
And in the darkest battle-field
  Thou shalt know where to strike.

Thrice bless'd is he to whom is given
  The instinct that can tell
That God is on the field when he
  Is most invisible.

Bless'd, too, is he who can divine
  Where real right doth lie,
And dares to take the side that seems
  Wrong to man's blindfold eye.

For right is right, since God is God ;
  And right the day must win ;
To doubt would be disloyalty,
  To falter would be sin.

Arthur Penrhyn Stanley

TEACH US TO DIE

WHERE shall we learn to die ?
Go, gaze with steadfast eye
On dark Gethsemane
Or darker Calvary,
Where through each lingering hour
The Lord of grace and power,
Most lowly and most high,
Has taught the Christian how to die.

When in the olive shade
His long last prayer he pray'd,
When on the cross to heaven
His parting spirit was given,
He show'd that to fulfil
The Father's gracious will,
Not asking how or why,
Alone prepares the soul to die.

No word of anxious strife,
No anxious cry for life ;
By scoff and torture torn,
He speaks not scorn for scorn ;
Calmly forgiving those
Who deem themselves his foes,
In silent majesty
He points the way at peace to die.

Delighting to the last
In memories of the past ;
Glad at the parting meal
In lowly tasks to kneel ;

Still yearning to the end
For mother and for friend ;
His great humility
Loves in such acts of love to die.

Beyond his depth of woes
A wider thought arose,
Along his path of gloom,
Thought for his country's doom ;
Athwart all pain and grief,
Thought for the contrite thief :
The far-stretch'd sympathy
Lives on when all beside shall die.

Bereft, but not alone,
The world is still his own ;
The realm of deathless truth
Still breathes immortal youth ;
Sure, though in shuddering dread,
That all is finished,
With purpose fix'd and high
The friend of all mankind must die.

Oh, by those weary hours
Of slowly-ebbing powers ;
By those deep lessons heard
In each expiring word ;
By that unfailing love
Lifting the soul above,
When our last end is nigh,
So teach us, Lord, with thee to die.

Christopher Newman Hall

MY TIMES ARE IN THY HAND

My times are in thy hand !
  I know not what a day
Or e'en an hour may bring to me,
But I am safe while trusting thee,
  Though all things fade away.
    All weakness, I
    On him rely
Who fix'd the earth and spread the starry
  sky.

My times are in thy hand !
  Pale poverty or wealth,
Corroding care or calm repose,
Spring's balmy breath or winter's snows,
  Sickness or buoyant health, —
    Whate'er betide,
    If God provide,
'T is for the best ; I wish no lot beside.

My times are in thy hand !
  Should friendship pure illume

And strew my path with fairest flowers,
Or should I spend life's dreary hours
  In solitude's dark gloom,
    Thou art a friend,
    Till time shall end
Unchangeably the same ; in thee all beau-
    ties blend.

My times are in thy hand !
  Many or few, my days
I leave with thee, — this only pray,
That by thy grace, I, every day
    Devoting to thy praise,
    May ready be
    To welcome thee
Whene'er thou com'st to set my spirit free.

My times are in thy hand !
  Howe'er those times may end,
Sudden or slow my soul's release,
Midst anguish, frenzy, or in peace,
  I 'm safe with Christ my friend.

    If he is nigh,
    Howe'er I die,
'T will be the dawn of heavenly ecstasy.

My times are in thy hand !
  To thee I can intrust
My slumbering clay, till thy command
Bids all the dead before thee stand,
    Awaking from the dust.
    Beholding thee,
    What bliss 't will be
With all thy saints to spend eternity !

To spend eternity
  In heaven's unclouded light !
From sorrow, sin, and frailty free,
Beholding and resembling thee, —
    O too transporting sight !
    Prospect too fair
    For flesh to bear !
Haste ! haste ! my Lord, and soon trans-
    port me there !

Anne Brontë

A PRAYER

My God (oh, let me call thee mine,
  Weak, wretched sinner though I be),
My trembling soul would fain be thine ;
  My feeble faith still clings to thee.

Not only for the past I grieve,
  The future fills me with dismay ;
Unless Thou hasten to relieve,
  Thy suppliant is a castaway.

I cannot say my faith is strong,
  I dare not hope my love is great ;
But strength and love to thee belong ;
  Oh, do not leave me desolate !

I know I owe my all to thee ;
  Oh, take the heart I cannot give !
Do Thou my strength — my Saviour be,
  And make me to thy glory live.

William John Blew

O LORD, THY WING OUTSPREAD

O Lord, thy wing outspread,
  And us thy flock infold ;
Thy broad wing spread, that covered
  Thy mercy-seat of old :
And o'er our nightly roof,
  And round our daily path,
Keep watch and ward, and hold aloof
  The devil and his wrath.

For thou dost fence our head,
  And shield — yea, thou alone —
The peasant on his pallet-bed,
  The prince upon his throne.
Make then our heart thine ark,
  Whereon thy Mystic Dove
May brood, and lighten it, when dark,
  With beams of peace and love ;

That dearer far to thee
   Than gold or cedar-shrine
The bodies of thy saints may be,
   The souls by thee made thine :

So nevermore be stirr'd
   That voice within our heart,
The fearful word that once was heard, —
   " Up, let us hence depart ! "

Cecil Frances Alexander

THERE IS A GREEN HILL

THERE is a green hill far away,
   Without a city wall,
Where the dear Lord was crucified,
   Who died to save us all.

We may not know, we cannot tell
   What pains he had to bear,
But we believe it was for us
   He hung and suffer'd there.

He died that we might be forgiven,
   He died to make us good,

That we might go at last to heaven,
   Sav'd by his precious blood.

There was no other good enough
   To pay the price of sin ;
He only could unlock the gate
   Of heaven, and let us in.

O dearly, dearly has he lov'd,
   And we must love him too,
And trust in his redeeming blood,
   And try his works to do.

Elizabeth Cecilia Clephane

THE LOST SHEEP

("THE NINETY AND NINE")

THERE were ninety and nine that safely lay
   In the shelter of the fold ;
But one was out on the hills away,
   Far off from the gates of gold,
Away on the mountains wild and bare,
Away from the tender Shepherd's care.

" Lord, thou hast here thy ninety and nine :
   Are they not enough for thee ? "
But the Shepherd made answer : " 'T is of
   mine
Has wander'd away from me ;
And although the road be rough and steep
I go to the desert to find my sheep."

But none of the ransom'd ever knew
   How deep were the waters cross'd,
Nor how dark was the night that the Lord
   pass'd through
Ere he found his sheep that was lost.

Out in the desert he heard its cry —
Sick and helpless, and ready to die.

" Lord, whence are those blood-drops all
   the way,
   That mark out the mountain track ? "
" They were shed for one who had gone
   astray
   Ere the Shepherd could bring him back."
" Lord, whence are thy hands so rent and
   torn ? "
" They are pierced to-night by many a
   thorn."

But all through the mountains, thunder-
   riven,
   And up from the rocky steep,
There rose a cry to the gate of heaven,
   " Rejoice ! I have found my sheep ! "
And the angels echoed around the throne,
   " Rejoice, for the Lord brings back his
   own ! "

Sabine Baring-Gould

CHILD'S EVENING HYMN

Now the day is over,
  Night is drawing nigh,
Shadows of the evening
  Steal across the sky.

Now the darkness gathers,
  Stars begin to peep,
Birds and beasts and flowers
  Soon will be asleep.

Jesu, give the weary
  Calm and sweet repose ;
With thy tenderest blessing
  May our eyelids close.

Grant to little children
  Visions bright of thee ;
Guard the sailors tossing
  On the deep blue sea.

Comfort every sufferer
  Watching late in pain ;
Those who plan some evil
  From their sin restrain.

Through the long night-watches
  May thine angels spread
Their white wings above me,
  Watching round my bed.

When the morning wakens,
  Then may I arise
Pure and fresh and sinless
  In thy holy eyes.

Glory to the Father,
  Glory to the Son,
And to thee, bless'd Spirit,
  Whilst all ages run.   AMEN.

Frances Ridley Havergal

I GAVE MY LIFE FOR THEE

I GAVE my life for thee,
  My precious blood I shed
That thou mightst ransom'd be,
  And quicken'd from the dead.
I gave my life for thee ;
What hast thou given for me ?

I spent long years for thee
  In weariness and woe,
That an eternity
  Of joy thou mightest know.
I spent long years for thee ;
Hast thou spent one for me ?

My Father's home of light,
  My rainbow-circled throne,
I left, for earthly night,
  For wanderings sad and lone.
I left it all for thee ;
Hast thou left aught for me ?

I suffer'd much for thee,
  More than thy tongue may tell
Of bitterest agony,
  To rescue thee from hell.
I suffer'd much for thee ;
What canst thou bear for me ?

And I have brought to thee,
  Down from my home above,
Salvation full and free,
  My pardon and my love.
Great gifts I brought to thee ;
What hast thou brought to me ?

Oh, let thy life be given,
  Thy years for him be spent,
World-fetters all be riven,
  And joy with suffering blent ;
I gave myself for thee :
Give thou thyself to me ?

II

THE VICTORIAN EPOCH

(PERIOD OF TENNYSON, ARNOLD, BROWNING, ROSSETTI, AND SWINBURNE)

DEATH OF WILLIAM WORDSWORTH: APRIL 23, 1850
ALFRED TENNYSON APPOINTED LAUREATE: NOVEMBER 21, 1850

PRELUDE

ENGLAND! since Shakespeare died no loftier day
  For thee than lights herewith a century's goal, —
  Nor statelier exit of heroic soul
Conjoined with soul heroic, — nor a lay
Excelling theirs who made renowned thy sway
  Even as they heard the billows which outroll
  Thine ancient sea, and left their joy and dole
In song, and on the strand their mantles gray.
Star-rayed with fame thine Abbey windows loom
  Above his dust whom the Venetian barge
  Bore to the main; who passed the two-fold marge
To slumber in thy keeping, — yet make room
  For the great Laurifer, whose chanting large
And sweet shall last until our tongue's far doom.

E. C. S.

THE VICTORIAN EPOCH

(PERIOD OF TENNYSON, ARNOLD, BROWNING, ROSSETTI, AND SWINBURNE)

COMPOSITE IDYLLIC SCHOOL

Frederick Tennyson

THIRTY-FIRST OF MAY

Awake ! — the crimson dawn is glowing,
  And blissful breath of Morn
From golden seas is earthward flowing
  Thro' mountain-peaks forlorn ;
'Twixt the tall roses, and the jasmines near,
  That darkly hover in the twilight air,
I see the glory streaming, and I hear
  The sweet wind whispering like a messenger.

'Tis time to sing ! — the Spirits of Spring
  Go softly by mine ear,
And out of Fairyland they bring
  Glad tidings to me here ;
'Tis time to sing ! now is the pride of
    Youth
  Pluming the woods, and the first rose appears,
And Summer from the chambers of the
    South
  Is coming up to wipe away all tears.

They bring glad tidings from afar
  Of Her that cometh after
To fill the earth, to light the air,
  With music and with laughter ;
Ev'n now she leaneth forward, as she stands,
  And her fire-wing'd horses, shod with
    gold,
Stream, like a sunrise, from before her
    hands,
  And thro' the Eastern gates her wheels
    are roll'd.

'Tis time to sing — the woodlands ring
  New carols day by day ;
The wild birds of the islands sing
  Whence they have flown away ;
'Tis time to sing : the nightingale is
    come,
  And 'mid the laurels chants he all night
    long,
And bids the leaves be still, the winds be
    dumb,
  And like the starlight flashes forth his
    song.

Immortal Beauty from above,
  Like sunlight breath'd on cloud,
Touches the weary soul with love,
  And hath unwound the shroud
Of buried Nature till she looks again
  Fresh in infantine smiles and childish
    tears,
And o'er the rugged hearts of aged men
  Sheds the pure dew of Youth's delicious
    years.

The heart of the awaken'd Earth
  Breathes odorous ecstasy ;
Let ours beat time unto her mirth,
  And hymn her jubilee !
The glory of the Universal Soul
  Ascends from mountain-tops, and lowly
    flowers,
The mighty pulses throbbing through the
    Whole
  Call unto us for answering life in ours.

Arise ! young Queen of forests green,
  A path was strewn for thee
With hyacinth, and gold bells atween,
  And red anemone ;
Arise ! young Queen of beauty and delight,
  Lift up in this fair land thine happy eyes ;
The valleys yearn, and gardens for thy
    sight,
  But chief this heart that prays for thee
    with sighs.

How oft into the opening blue
  I look'd up wistfully,
In hope to see thee wafted thro'
  Bright rifts of stormy sky ;
Many gray morns, sad nights, and weary
    days,
  Without thy golden smile my heart was
    dying ;
Oh ! in the valleys let me see thy face,
  And thy loose locks adown the wood-
    walks flying.

Come, with thy flowers, and silver showers,
  Thy rainbows, and thy light ;
Fold in thy robe the naked Hours,
  And fill them with thy might ;
Though less I seek thee for the loveliness
  Thou laughest from thee over land and
    sea,
Than for the hues wherein gay Fancies dress
  My drooping spirit at the sight of thee.

Come, with thy voice of thousand joys,
  Thy leaves, and fluttering wings ;
Come with thy breezes, and the noise
  Of rivulets and of springs ;
Though less I seek thee for thine harmo-
    nies
  Of winds and waters, and thy songs
    divine,
Than for that Angel that within me lies,
  And makes glad music echoing unto
    thine.

O Gardens blossoming anew !
  O Rivers, and fresh Rills !
O Mountains in your mantles blue !
  O dales of daffodils !
What ye can do no mortal spirit can,
  Ye have a strength within we cannot
    borrow,
Blessed are ye beyond the heart of Man,
  Your Joy, your Love, your Life beyond
    all Sorrow !

THE BLACKBIRD

How sweet the harmonies of afternoon !
  The Blackbird sings along the sunny
    breeze
His ancient song of leaves, and summer
    boon ;
  Rich breath of hayfields streams thro'
    whispering trees ;
And birds of morning trim their bustling
    wings,
And listen fondly — while the Blackbird
    sings.

How soft the lovelight of the West re-
    poses
  On this green valley's cheery solitude,
On the trim cottage with its screen of
    roses,
  On the gray belfry with its ivy hood,
And murmuring mill-race, and the wheel
    that flings
Its bubbling freshness — while the Black-
    bird sings.

The very dial on the village church
  Seems as 't were dreaming in a dozy
    rest ;
The scribbled benches underneath the porch
  Bask in the kindly welcome of the West ;
But the broad casements of the old Three
    Kings
Blaze like a furnace — while the Blackbird
    sings.

And there beneath the immemorial elm
  Three rosy revellers round a table sit,
And thro' gray clouds give laws unto the
    realm,
  Curse good and great, but worship their
    own wit,
And roar of fights, and fairs, and junket-
    ings,
Corn, colts, and curs — the while the Black-
    bird sings.

Before her home, in her accustom'd seat,
  The tidy Grandam spins beneath the
    shade
Of the old honeysuckle, at her feet
  The dreaming pug, and purring tabby
    laid ;
To her low chair a little maiden clings,
And spells in silence — while the Blackbird
    sings.

Sometimes the shadow of a lazy cloud
  Breathes o'er the hamlet with its gardens
    green,
While the far fields with sunlight overflow'd
  Like golden shores of Fairyland are seen ;
Again, the sunshine on the shadow springs,
And fires the thicket where the Blackbird
    sings.

The woods, the lawn, the peaked Manor-
    house,
  With its peach-cover'd walls, and rookery
    loud,
The trim, quaint garden alleys, screen'd
    with boughs,
  The lion-headed gates, so grim and proud,
The mossy fountain with its murmurings,
Lie in warm sunshine — while the Blackbird
    sings.

The ring of silver voices, and the sheen
  Of festal garments — and my Lady
    streams
With her gay court across the garden green ;
  Some laugh, and dance, some whisper
    their love-dreams ;
And one calls for a little page ; he strings
Her lute beside her — while the Blackbird
    sings.

A little while — and lo ! the charm is heard,
  A youth, whose life has been all Summer,
    steals
Forth from the noisy guests around the
    board,
  Creeps by her softly ; at her footstool
    kneels ;
And, when she pauses, murmurs tender
    things
Into her fond ear — while the Blackbird
    sings.

The smoke-wreaths from the chimneys curl
    up higher,
  And dizzy things of eve begin to float
Upon the light ; the breeze begins to tire ;
  Half way to sunset with a drowsy note
The ancient clock from out the valley
    swings ;
The Grandam nods — and still the Black-
    bird sings.

Far shouts and laughter from the farmstead
    peal,
  Where the great stack is piling in the sun ;

Thro' narrow gates o'erladen wagons reel,
  And barking curs into the tumult run ;
While the inconstant wind bears off, and
    brings
The merry tempest — and the Blackbird
    sings.

On the high wold the last look of the sun
  Burns, like a beacon, over dale and stream;
The shouts have ceased, the laughter and
    the fun ;
  The Grandam sleeps, and peaceful be her
    dream ;
Only a hammer on an anvil rings ;
The day is dying — still the Blackbird sings.

Now the good Vicar passes from his gate
  Serene, with long white hair ; and in his
    eye
Burns the clear spirit that hath conquer'd
    Fate,
  And felt the wings of immortality ;
His heart is throng'd with great imaginings,
And tender mercies — while the Blackbird
    sings.

Down by the brook he bends his steps, and
    thro'
  A lowly wicket ; and at last he stands
Awful beside the bed of one who grew
  From boyhood with him — who with
    lifted hands
And eyes, seems listening to far welcomings,
And sweeter music than the Blackbird sings.

Two golden stars, like tokens from the
    Blest,
  Strike on his dim orbs from the setting
    sun ;
His sinking hands seem pointing to the
    West ;
  He smiles as though he said — "Thy will
    be done : "
His eyes, they see not those illuminings;
His ears, they hear not what the Blackbird
    sings.

FROM "NIOBE"

I TOO remember, in the after years,
The long-hair'd Niobe, when she was old,
Sitting alone, without the city gates,
Upon the ground ; alone she sat, and
    mourn'd.
Her watchers, mindful of her royal state,

Her widowhood, and sorrows, follow'd her
Far off, when she went forth, to be alone
In lonely places ; and at set of sun
They won her back by some fond phantasy,
By telling her some tale of the gone days
Of her dear lost ones, promising to show her
Some faded garland, or some broken toy,
Dusty and dim, which they had found, or
    feign'd
To have found, some plaything of their
    infant hours.
Within the echoes of a ruin'd court
She sat and mourn'd, with her lamenting
    voice,
Melodious in sorrow, like the sound
Of funeral hymns ; for in her youth she sang
Along the myrtle valleys in the spring,
Plucking the fresh pinks and the hyacinths,
With her fair troop of girls, who answer'd
    her
Silverly sweet, so that the lovely tribe
Were Nature's matchless treble to the last
Delicious pipe, pure, warbling, dewy clear.
In summer and in winter, that lorn voice
Went up, like the struck spirit of this world,
Making the starry roof of heaven tremble
With her lament, and agony, and all
The crowned Gods in their high tabernacles
Sigh unawares, and think upon their deeds.
Her guardians let her wander at her will,
For all could weep for her ; had she not
    been
The first and fairest of that sunny land,
And bless'd with all things ; doubly crown'd
    with power
And beauty, doubly now discrown'd and
    fallen ?
Oh ! none would harm her, only she herself ;
And chiefly then when they would hold her
    back,
And sue her to take comfort in her home,
Or in the bridal chambers of her youth,
Or in the old gardens, once her joy and
    pride,
Or the rose-bowers along the river-shore
She lov'd of old, now silent and forsaken.
For then she fled away, as though in fear,
As if she saw the spectres of her hours
Of joyaunce pass before her in the shapes
Of her belov'd ones. But most she chose
Waste places, where the moss and lichen
    crawl'd,
And the wild ivy flutter'd, and the rains
Wept thro' the roofless ruins, and all
    seem'd

To mourn in symbols, and to answer to her,
Showing her outward that she was within.
The unregarding multitude pass'd on,
Because her woe was a familiar sight.
But some there were that shut their ears
    and fled,
And they were childless ; the rose-lipp'd
    and young
Felt that imperial voice and desolate
Strike cold into their hearts ; children at
    play
Were smit with sudden silence, with their
    toys
Clutch'd in their hands, forgetful of the
    game.
Aged she was, yet beautiful in age.
Her beauty, thro' the cloud of years and
    grief,
Shone as a wintry sun ; she never smil'd,
Save when a darkness pass'd across the sun,
And blotted out from her entranced eyes
Disastrous shapes that rode upon his disk,
Tyrannous visions, armed presences ;
And then she sigh'd and lifted up her head,
And shed a few warm tears.   But when he
    rose,
And her sad eyes unclos'd before his beams,
She started up with terrors in her look,
That wither'd up all pity in affright,
And ran about, like one with Furies torn,
And rent her hair, and madly threaten'd
    Heaven,
And call'd for retribution on the Gods,
Crying, "O save me from Him, He is
    there ;
Oh, let me wear my little span of life.
I see Him in the centre of the sun ;
His face is black with wrath ! thou angry
    God,
I am a worthless thing, a childless mother,
Widow'd and wasted, old and comfortless,
But still I am alive ; wouldst thou take
    all ?
Thou who hast snatch'd my hopes and my
    delights,
Thou who hast kill'd my children, wouldst
    thou take
The little remnant of my days of sorrow,
Which the sharp winds of the first winter
    days,
Or the first night of frost, may give unto
    thee ?
For never shall I seek again that home
Where they are not ; cold, cold shall be the
    hearth

Where they were gather'd, cold as is my
   heart !
Oh ! if my living lot be bitterness,
'T is sweeter than to think, that, if I go
Down to the dust, then I shall think no more
Of them I lov'd and lost, the thoughts of
   whom
Are all my being, and shall speak no more,
In answer to their voices in my heart,
As though it were mine ear, rewording all
Their innocent delights, and fleeting pains,
Their infant fondnesses, their little wants,
And simple words. Oh ! while I am, I
   dream
Of those who are not ; thus my anguish
   grows
My solace, as the salt surf of the seas

Clothes the sharp crags with beauty." Then
   her mood
Would veer to madness, like a windy
   change
That brings up thunder, and she rais'd her
   voice,
Crying, "And yet they are not, they who
   were,
And never more shall be ! accursed
   dreams ! "
And, suddenly becoming motionless,
The bright hue from her cheeks and fore-
   head pass'd,
And, full of awful resignation, fixing
Her large undazzled orbs upon the sun,
She shriek'd, "Strike, God, thou canst not
   harm me more ! "

Charles Tennyson Turner

THE LION'S SKELETON

How long, O lion, hast thou fleshless lain ?
What rapt thy fierce and thirsty eyes
   away ?
First came the vulture : worms, heat, wind,
   and rain
Ensued, and ardors of the tropic day.
I know not — if they spar'd it thee — how
   long
The canker sate within thy monstrous
   mane,
Till it fell piecemeal, and bestrew'd the
   plain,
Or, shredded by the storming sands, was
   flung
Again to earth ; but now thine ample front,
Whereon the great frowns gather'd, is laid
   bare ;
The thunders of thy throat, which erst
   were wont
To scare the desert, are no longer there ;
Thy claws remain, but worms, wind, rain,
   and heat
Have sifted out the substance of thy feet.

THE VACANT CAGE

Our little bird in his full day of health
With his gold-coated beauty made us glad,
And when disease approach'd with cruel
   stealth,
A sadder interest our smiles forbad.

How oft we watch'd him, when the night
   hours came,
His poor head buried near his bursting
   heart,
Which beat within a puff'd and troubled
   frame ;
But he has gone at last, and play'd his part :
The seed-glass, slighted by his sickening
   taste,
The little moulted feathers, saffron-tipp'd,
The fountain, where his fever'd bill was
   dipp'd,
The perches, which his failing feet embraced,
All these remain — not even his bath re-
   mov'd —
But where 's the spray and flutter that we
   lov'd ?

THE LACHRYMATORY

From out the grave of one whose budding
   years
Were cropp'd by death, when Rome was in
   her prime,
I brought the phial of his kinsman's tears,
There placed, as was the wont of ancient
   time ;
Round me, that night, in meads of aspho-
   del,
The souls of the early dead did come and
   go,
Drawn by that flask of grief, as by a spell,
That long-imprison'd shower of human woe

As round Ulysses, for the draught of blood,
The heroes throng'd, those spirits flock'd
    to me,
Where, lonely, with that charm of tears, I
    stood ;
Two, most of all, my dreaming eyes did see ;
The young Marcellus, young, but great and
    good,
And Tully's daughter, mourn'd so tenderly.

THE BUOY-BELL

How like the leper, with his own sad cry
Enforcing his own solitude, it tolls !
That lonely bell set in the rushing shoals,
To warn us from the place of jeopardy ?
O friend of man ! sore-vex'd by ocean's
    power,
The changing tides wash o'er thee day by
    day ;
Thy trembling mouth is fill'd with bitter
    spray,
Yet still thou ringest on from hour to hour ;
High is thy mission, though thy lot is
    wild —
To be in danger's realm a guardian sound ;
In seamen's dreams a pleasant part to bear,
And earn their blessing as the year goes
    round,
And strike the key-note of each grateful
    prayer,
Breath'd in their distant homes by wife or
    child !

THE FOREST GLADE

As one dark morn I trod a forest glade,
A sunbeam enter'd at the further end,
And ran to meet me thro' the yielding
    shade —
As one, who in the distance sees a friend,
And, smiling, hurries to him ; but mine
    eyes,
Bewilder'd by the change from dark to
    bright,
Receiv'd the greeting with a quick sur-
    prise
At first, and then with tears of pure de-
    light ;
For sad my thoughts had been — the tem-
    pest's wrath
Had gloom'd the night, and made the
    morrow gray ;

That heavenly guidance humble sorrow
    hath,
Had turn'd my feet into that forest-way,
Just when His morning light came down
    the path,
Among the lonely woods at early day.

THE LATTICE AT SUNRISE

As on my bed at dawn I mus'd and pray'd,
I saw my lattice prank'd upon the wall,
The flaunting leaves and flitting birds
    withal —
A sunny phantom interlaced with shade ;
" Thanks be to heaven," in happy mood I
    said,
" What sweeter aid my matins could befall
Than the fair glory from the East hath
    made ?
What holy sleights hath God, the Lord of
    all,
To bid us feel and see ! we are not free
To say we see not, for the glory comes
Nightly and daily, like the flowing sea ;
His lustre pierceth through the midnight
    glooms
And, at prime hour, behold ! He follows
    me
With golden shadows to my secret rooms."

THE ROOKERY

METHOUGHT, as I beheld the rookery pass
Homeward at dusk upon the rising wind,
How every heart in that close-flying mass
Was well befriended by the Almighty
    mind :
He marks each sable wing that soars or
    drops,
He sees them forth at morning to their
    fare,
He sets them floating on His evening air,
He sends them home to rest on the tree-
    tops :
And when through umber'd leaves the
    night-winds pour,
With lusty impulse rocking all the grove,
The stress is measur'd by an eye of love,
No root is burst, though all the branches
    roar ;
And, in the morning, cheerly as before,
The dark clan talks, the social instincts
    move.

ORION

How oft I 've watch'd thee from the gar-
den croft,
In silence, when the busy day was done,
Shining with wondrous brilliancy aloft,
And flickering like a casement 'gainst the
sun !
I 've seen thee soar from out some snowy
cloud,
Which held the frozen breath of land and
sea,
Yet broke and sever'd as the wind grew
loud —
But earth-bound winds could not dismem-
ber thee,
Nor shake thy frame of jewels ; I have
guess'd
At thy strange shape and function, haply
felt
The charm of that old myth about thy belt
And sword ; but, most, my spirit was pos-
sess'd
By His great Presence, Who is never far
From his light-bearers, whether man or star.

TO THE GOSSAMER-LIGHT

QUICK gleam, that ridest on the gossa-
mer !
How oft I see thee, with thy wavering lance,
Tilt at the midges in their evening dance,
A gentle joust set on by summer air !
How oft I watch thee from my garden-
chair !
And, failing that, I search the lawns and
bowers,
To find thee floating o'er the fruits and
flowers,
And doing thy sweet work in silence there.
Thou art the poet's darling, ever sought
In the fair garden or the breezy mead ;
The wind dismounts thee not ; thy buoyant
thread
Is as the sonnet, poising one bright thought,
That moves but does not vanish : borne
along
Like light, — a golden drift through all
the song !

LETTY'S GLOBE

WHEN Letty had scarce pass'd her third
glad year,
And her young, artless words began to
flow,
One day we gave the child a color'd
sphere
Of the wide earth, that she might mark and
know,
By tint and outline, all its sea and land.
She patted all the world ; old empires
peep'd
Between her baby fingers ; her soft hand
Was welcome at all frontiers. How she
leap'd,
And laugh'd and prattled in her world-
wide bliss ;
But when we turn'd her sweet unlearned
eye
On our own isle, she rais'd a joyous cry,
"Oh ! yes, I see it, Letty's home is there ! "
And, while she hid all England with a
kiss,
Bright over Europe fell her golden hair !

HER FIRST-BORN

IT was her first sweet child, her heart's de-
light :
And, though we all foresaw his early doom,
We kept the fearful secret out of sight ;
We saw the canker, but she kiss'd the
bloom.
And yet it might not be : we could not
brook
To vex her happy heart with vague alarms,
To blanch with fear her fond intrepid
look,
Or send a thrill through those encircling
arms.
She smil'd upon him, waking or at rest :
She could not dream her little child would
die :
She toss'd him fondly with an upward
eye :
She seem'd as buoyant as a summer spray,
That dances with a blossom on its breast,
Nor knows how soon it will be borne away.

Alfred, Lord Tennyson

THE DESERTED HOUSE

LIFE and Thought have gone away
   Side by side,
   Leaving door and windows wide :
Careless tenants they !

   All within is dark as night :
   In the windows is no light ;
   And no murmur at the door,
   So frequent on its hinge before.

Close the door, the shutters close,
   Or thro' the windows we shall see
   The nakedness and vacancy
Of the dark deserted house.

Come away : no more of mirth
   Is here or merry-making sound.
The house was builded of the earth,
   And shall fall again to ground.

Come away : for Life and Thought
   Here no longer dwell ;
   But in a city glorious —
A great and distant city — have bought
   A mansion incorruptible.
Would they could have stay'd with us !

THE LOTOS-EATERS

"COURAGE ! " he said, and pointed toward
   the land,
" This mounting wave will roll us shoreward
   soon."
In the afternoon they came unto a land
In which it seemed always afternoon.
All round the coast the languid air did
   swoon,
Breathing like one that hath a weary dream.
Full-faced above the valley stood the moon ;
And like a downward smoke, the slender
   stream
Along the cliff to fall and pause and fall
   did seem.

A land of streams ! some, like a downward
   smoke,
Slow-dropping veils of thinnest lawn, did go;
And some thro' wavering lights and shadows
   broke,
Rolling a slumbrous sheet of foam below.

They saw the gleaming river seaward flow
From the inner land : far off, three moun-
   tain-tops,
Three silent pinnacles of aged snow,
Stood sunset-flush'd : and, dew'd with show-
   ery drops,
Up-clomb the shadowy pine above the woven
   copse.

The charmed sunset linger'd low adown
In the red West : thro' mountain clefts the
   dale
Was seen far inland, and the yellow down
Border'd with palm, and many a winding
   vale
And meadow, set with slender galingale ;
A land where all things always seem'd the
   same !
And round about the keel with faces pale,
Dark faces pale against that rosy flame,
The mild - eyed melancholy Lotos - eaters
   came.

Branches they bore of that enchanted stem,
Laden with flower and fruit, whereof they
   gave
To each, but whoso did receive of them,
And taste, to him the gushing of the wave
Far far away did seem to mourn and rave
On alien shores ; and if his fellow spake,
His voice was thin, as voices from the grave ;
And deep-asleep he seem'd, yet all awake,
And music in his ears his beating heart did
   make.

They sat them down upon the yellow sand,
Between the sun and moon upon the shore ;
And sweet it was to dream of Fatherland,
Of child, and wife, and slave ; but evermore
Most weary seem'd the sea, weary the oar,
Weary the wandering fields of barren foam.
Then some one said, " We will return no
   more ; "
And all at once they sang, " Our island home
Is far beyond the wave ; we will no longer
   roam."

CHORIC SONG

I

THERE is sweet music here that softer falls
Than petals from blown roses on the grass,
Or night-dews on still waters between walls

Of shadowy granite, in a gleaming pass ;
Music that gentlier on the spirit lies,
Than tir'd eyelids upon tir'd eyes ;
Music that brings sweet sleep down from
    the blissful skies.
Here are cool mosses deep,
And thro' the moss the ivies creep,
And in the stream the long-leav'd flowers
    weep,
And from the craggy ledge the poppy hangs
    in sleep.

II

Why are we weigh'd upon with heaviness,
And utterly consum'd with sharp distress,
While all things else have rest from weari-
    ness ?
All things have rest : why should we toil
    alone,
We only toil, who are the first of things,
And make perpetual moan,
Still from one sorrow to another thrown :
Nor never fold our wings,
And cease from wanderings,
Nor steep our brows in slumber's holy balm ;
Nor harken what the inner spirit sings,
" There is no joy but calm ! "
Why should we only toil, the roof and crown
    of things ?

III

Lo ! in the middle of the wood,
The folded leaf is wooed from out the bud
With winds upon the branch, and there
Grows green and broad, and takes no care,
Sun-steep'd at noon, and in the moon
Nightly dew-fed ; and turning yellow
Falls, and floats adown the air.
Lo ! sweeten'd with the summer light,
The full-juiced apple, waxing over-mellow,
Drops in a silent autumn night.
All its allotted length of days,
The flower ripens in its place,
Ripens and fades, and falls, and hath no toil,
Fast-rooted in the fruitful soil.

IV

Hateful is the dark-blue sky,
Vaulted o'er the dark-blue sea.
Death is the end of life ; ah, why
Should life all labor be ?
Let us alone. Time driveth onward fast,
And in a little while our lips are dumb.
Let us alone. What is it that will last ?
All things are taken from us, and become

Portions and parcels of the dreadful Past.
Let us alone. What pleasure can we have
To war with evil ? Is there any peace
In ever climbing up the climbing wave ?
All things have rest, and ripen toward the
    grave
In silence ; ripen, fall, and cease :
Give us long rest or death, dark death, or
    dreamful ease.

V

How sweet it were, hearing the downward
    stream,
With half-shut eyes ever to seem
Falling asleep in a half-dream !
To dream and dream, like yonder amber
    light,
Which will not leave the myrrh-bush on the
    height ;
To hear each other's whisper'd speech ;
Eating the Lotos day by day,
To watch the crisping ripples on the beach,
And tender curving lines of creamy spray ;
To lend our hearts and spirits wholly
To the influence of mild-minded melan-
    choly ;
To muse and brood and live again in mem-
    ory,
With those old faces of our infancy
Heap'd over with a mound of grass,
Two handfuls of white dust, shut in an urn
    of brass !

VI

Dear is the memory of our wedded lives,
And dear the last embraces of our wives
And their warm tears : but all hath suffer'd
    change :
For surely now our household hearths are
    cold :
Our sons inherit us : our looks are strange :
And we should come like ghosts to trouble
    joy.
Or else the island princes over-bold
Have eat our substance, and the minstrel
    sings
Before them of the ten years' war in Troy,
And our great deeds, as half-forgotten
    things.
Is there confusion in the little isle ?
Let what is broken so remain.
The Gods are hard to reconcile :
'T is hard to settle order once again.
There *is* confusion worse than death,

Trouble on trouble, pain on pain,
Long labor unto aged breath,
Sore task to hearts worn out by many wars
And eyes grown dim with gazing on the
  pilot-stars.

VII

But propp'd on beds of amaranth and moly,
How sweet (while warm airs lull us, blow-
  ing lowly)
With half-dropp'd eyelid still,
Beneath a heaven dark and holy,
To watch the long bright river drawing
  slowly
His waters from the purple hill —
To hear the dewy echoes calling
From cave to cave thro' the thick-twin'd
  vine —
To watch the emerald-color'd water falling
Thro' many a wov'n acanthus-wreath di-
  vine!
Only to hear and see the far-off sparkling
  brine,
Only to hear were sweet, stretch'd out be-
  neath the pine.

VIII

The Lotos blooms below the barren peak :
The Lotos blows by every winding creek :
All day the wind breathes low with mel-
  lower tone :
Thro' every hollow cave and alley lone
Round and round the spicy downs the yel-
  low Lotos-dust is blown.
We have had enough of action, and of mo-
  tion we,
Roll'd to starboard, roll'd to larboard, when
  the surge was seething free,
Where the wallowing monster spouted his
  foam-fountains in the sea.
Let us swear an oath, and keep it with an
  equal mind,
In the hollow Lotos-land to live and lie
  reclin'd
On the hills like Gods together, careless of
  mankind.
For they lie beside their nectar, and the
  bolts are hurl'd
Far below them in the valleys, and the
  clouds are lightly curl'd
Round their golden houses, girdled with the
  gleaming world :
Where they smile in secret, looking over
  wasted lands,

Blight and famine, plague and earthquake,
  roaring deeps and fiery sands,
Clanging fights, and flaming towns, and
  sinking ships, and praying hands.
But they smile, they find a music centred
  in a doleful song
Steaming up, a lamentation and an ancient
  tale of wrong,
Like a tale of little meaning tho' the words
  are strong ;
Chanted from an ill-us'd race of men that
  cleave the soil,
Sow the seed, and reap the harvest with
  enduring toil,
Storing yearly little dues of wheat, and
  wine and oil ;
Till they perish and they suffer — some,
  't is whisper'd — down in hell
Suffer endless anguish, others in Elysian
  valleys dwell,
Resting weary limbs at last on beds of
  asphodel.
Surely, surely, slumber is more sweet than
  toil, the shore
Than labor in the deep mid-ocean, wind
  and wave and oar ;
Oh rest ye, brother mariners, we will not
  wander more.

ULYSSES

It little profits that an idle king,
By this still hearth, among these barren
  crags,
Match'd with an aged wife, I mete and dole
Unequal laws unto a savage race,
That hoard, and sleep, and feed, and know
  not me.
I cannot rest from travel : I will drink
Life to the lees : all times I have enjoy'd
Greatly, have suffer'd greatly, both with
  those
That lov'd me, and alone ; on shore, and
  when
Thro' scudding drifts the rainy Hyades
Vex'd the dim sea.   I am become a name ;
For always roaming with a hungry heart
Much have I seen and known : cities of men
And manners, climates, councils, govern-
  ments,
Myself not least, but honor'd of them all ;
And drunk delight of battle with my peers,
Far on the ringing plains of windy Troy.
I am a part of all that I have met ;
Yet all experience is an arch wherethro'

Gleams that untravell'd world, whose mar-
gin fades
For ever and for ever when I move.
How dull it is to pause, to make an end,
To rust unburnish'd, not to shine in use !
As tho' to breathe were life.   Life pil'd on
life
Were all too little, and of one to me
Little remains : but every hour is sav'd
From that eternal silence, something more,
A bringer of new things ; and vile it were
For some three suns to store and hoard
myself,
And this gray spirit yearning in desire
To follow knowledge like a sinking star,
Beyond the utmost bound of human thought.
This is my son, mine own Telemachus,
To whom I leave the sceptre and the isle —
Well-lov'd of me, discerning to fulfil
This labor, by slow prudence to make mild
A rugged people, and thro' soft degrees
Subdue them to the useful and the good.
Most blameless is he, centred in the sphere
Of common duties, decent not to fail
In offices of tenderness, and pay
Meet adoration to my household gods,
When I am gone.   He works his work, I
mine.
There lies the port ; the vessel puffs her
sail :
There gloom the dark broad seas.   My
mariners,
Souls that have toil'd, and wrought, and
thought with me —
That ever with a frolic welcome took
The thunder and the sunshine, and oppos'd
Free hearts, free foreheads — you and I are
old ;
Old age hath yet his honor and his toil ;
Death closes all ; but something ere the end,
Some work of noble note, may yet be done,
Not unbecoming men that strove with Gods.
The lights begin to twinkle from the rocks :
The long day wanes : the slow moon climbs :
the deep
Moans round with many voices.   Come, my
friends,
'T is not too late to seek a newer world.
Push off, and sitting well in order smite
The sounding furrows ; for my purpose holds
To sail beyond the sunset, and the baths
Of all the western stars, until I die.
It may be that the gulfs will wash us down :
It may be we shall touch the Happy Isles,
And see the great Achilles, whom we knew.

Tho' much is taken, much abides ; and tho'
We are not now that strength which in old
days
Mov'd earth and heaven, that which we
are, we are :
One equal temper of heroic hearts,
Made weak by time and fate, but strong in
will
To strive, to seek, to find, and not to yield.

SIR GALAHAD

My good blade carves the casques of men,
My tough lance thrusteth sure,
My strength is as the strength of ten,
Because my heart is pure.
The shattering trumpet shrilleth high,
The hard brands shiver on the steel,
The splinter'd spear-shafts crack and fly,
The horse and rider reel :
They reel, they roll in clanging lists,
And when the tide of combat stands,
Perfume and flowers fall in showers,
That lightly rain from ladies' hands.

How sweet are looks that ladies bend
On whom their favors fall !
For them I battle till the end,
To save from shame and thrall :
But all my heart is drawn above,
My knees are bow'd in crypt and shrine :
I never felt the kiss of love,
Nor maiden's hand in mine.
More bounteous aspects on me beam,
Me mightier transports move and thrill ;
So keep I fair thro' faith and prayer
A virgin heart in work and will.

When down the stormy crescent goes,
A light before me swims,
Between dark stems the forest glows,
I hear a noise of hymns :
Then by some secret shrine I ride ;
I hear a voice, but none are there ;
The stalls are void, the doors are wide,
The tapers burning fair.
Fair gleams the snowy altar-cloth,
The silver vessels sparkle clean,
The shrill bell rings, the censer swings,
And solemn chaunts resound between.

Sometimes on lonely mountain-meres
I find a magic bark ;
I leap on board : no helmsman steers :
I float till all is dark.

A gentle sound, an awful light !
Three angels bear the holy Grail :
With folded feet, in stoles of white,
On sleeping wings they sail.
Ah, blessed vision ! blood of God !
My spirit beats her mortal bars,
As down dark tides the glory slides,
And star-like mingles with the stars.

When on my goodly charger borne
Thro' dreaming towns I go,
The cock crows ere the Christmas morn,
The streets are dumb with snow.
The tempest crackles on the leads,
And, ringing, springs from brand and
mail ;
But o'er the dark a glory spreads,
And gilds the driving hail.
I leave the plain, I climb the height ;
No branchy thicket shelter yields ;
But blessed forms in whistling storms
Fly o'er waste fens and windy fields.

A maiden knight — to me is given
Such hope, I know not fear ;
I yearn to breathe the airs of heaven
That often meet me here.
I muse on joy that will not cease,
Pure spaces cloth'd in living beams,
Pure lilies of eternal peace,
Whose odors haunt my dreams ;
And, stricken by an angel's hand,
This mortal armor that I wear,
This weight and size, this heart and eyes,
Are touch'd, are turn'd to finest air.

The clouds are broken in the sky,
And thro' the mountain-walls
A rolling organ-harmony
Swells up, and shakes and falls.
Then move the trees, the copses nod,
Wings flutter, voices hover clear :
" O just and faithful knight of God !
Ride on ! the prize is near."
So pass I hostel, hall, and grange ;
By bridge and ford, by park and pale,
All-arm'd I ride, whate'er betide,
Until I find the holy Grail.

SIR LAUNCELOT AND QUEEN GUINEVERE

LIKE souls that balance joy and pain,
With tears and smiles from heaven again

The maiden Spring upon the plain
Came in a sun-lit fall of rain.
In crystal vapor everywhere
Blue isles of heaven laugh'd between,
And far, in forest-deeps unseen,
The topmost elm-tree gather'd green
From draughts of balmy air.

Sometimes the linnet pip'd his song :
Sometimes the throstle whistled strong
Sometimes the sparhawk, wheel'd along,
Hush'd all the groves from fear of wrong ;
By grassy capes with fuller sound
In curves the yellowing river ran,
And drooping chestnut-buds began
To spread into the perfect fan,
Above the teeming ground.

Then, in the boyhood of the year,
Sir Launcelot and Queen Guinevere
Rode thro' the coverts of the deer,
With blissful treble ringing clear.
She seem'd a part of joyous Spring ;
A gown of grass-green silk she wore,
Buckled with golden clasps before ;
A light-green tuft of plumes she bore
Clos'd in a golden ring.

Now on some twisted ivy-net,
Now by some tinkling rivulet,
In mosses mix'd with violet
Her cream-white mule his pastern set :
And fleeter now she skimm'd the plains
Than she whose elfin prancer springs
By night to eery warblings,
When all the glimmering moorland rings
With jingling bridle-reins.

As fast she fled thro' sun and shade,
The happy winds upon her play'd,
Blowing the ringlet from the braid :
She look'd so lovely, as she sway'd
The rein with dainty finger-tips,
A man had given all other bliss,
And all his worldly worth for this,
To waste his whole heart in one kiss
Upon her perfect lips.

BREAK, BREAK, BREAK

BREAK, break, break,
On thy cold gray stones, O Sea !
And I would that my tongue could utter
The thoughts that arise in me.

O well for the fisherman's boy,
That he shouts with his sister at play !
O well for the sailor lad,
That he sings in his boat on the bay !

And the stately ships go on
To their haven under the hill ;
But O for the touch of a vanish'd hand,
And the sound of a voice that is still !

Break, break, break,
At the foot of thy crags, O Sea !
But the tender grace of a day that is dead
Will never come back to me.

SONGS FROM "THE PRINCESS"

AS THRO' THE LAND

As thro' the land at eve we went,
And pluck'd the ripen'd ears,
We fell out, my wife and I,
Oh, we fell out I know not why,
And kiss'd again with tears.
And blessings on the falling out
That all the more endears,
When we fall out with those we love
And kiss again with tears !
For when we came where lies the child
We lost in other years,
There above the little grave,
Oh, there above the little grave,
We kiss'd again with tears.

SWEET AND LOW

SWEET and low, sweet and low,
Wind of the western sea,
Low, low, breathe and blow,
Wind of the western sea !
Over the rolling waters go,
Come from the dying moon, and blow,
Blow him again to me ;
While my little one, while my pretty one,
sleeps.

Sleep and rest, sleep and rest,
Father will come to thee soon ;
Rest, rest, on mother's breast,
Father will come to thee soon ;
Father will come to his babe in the nest;
Silver sails all out of the west
Under the silver moon :
Sleep, my little one, sleep, my pretty one,
sleep.

BUGLE SONG

THE splendor falls on castle walls
And snowy summits old in story :
The long light shakes across the lakes,
And the wild cataract leaps in glory.
Blow, bugle, blow, set the wild echoes flying,
Blow, bugle ; answer, echoes, dying, dying
dying.

O hark, O hear ! how thin and clear,
And thinner, clearer, farther going !
O sweet and far from cliff and scar
The horns of Elfland faintly blowing !
Blow, let us hear the purple glens replying :
Blow, bugle ; answer, echoes, dying, dying,
dying.

O love, they die in yon rich sky,
They faint on hill or field or river :
Our echoes roll from soul to soul,
And grow for ever and for ever.
Blow, bugle, blow, set the wild echoes flying.
And answer, echoes, answer, dying, dying,
dying.

TEARS, IDLE TEARS

TEARS, idle tears, I know not what they
mean,
Tears from the depth of some divine despair
Rise in the heart, and gather to the eyes,
In looking on the happy Autumn-fields,
And thinking of the days that are no more.

Fresh as the first beam glittering on a sail,
That brings our friends up from the under-
world,
Sad as the last which reddens over one
That sinks with all we love below the verge ;
So sad, so fresh, the days that are no more.

Ah, sad and strange as in dark summer
dawns
The earliest pipe of half-awaken'd birds
To dying ears, when unto dying eyes
The casement slowly grows a glimmering
square ;
So sad, so strange, the days that are no more.

Dear as remember'd kisses after death,
And sweet as those by hopeless fancy feign'd
On lips that are for others ; deep as love,
Deep as first love, and wild with all regret ;
O Death in Life, the days that are no more.

THY VOICE IS HEARD

THY voice is heard thro' rolling drums
  That beat to battle where he stands ;
Thy face across his fancy comes,
  And gives the battle to his hands :
A moment, while the trumpets blow,
  He sees his brood about thy knee ;
The next, like fire he meets the foe,
  And strikes him dead for thine and thee.

ASK ME NO MORE

ASK me no more : the moon may draw the
      sea ;
  The cloud may stoop from heaven and
      take the shape
With fold to fold, of mountain or of cape ;
But O too fond, when have I answer'd thee ?
      Ask me no more.

Ask me no more : what answer should I
      give ?
  I love not hollow cheek or faded eye :
Yet, O my friend, I will not have thee
      die !
Ask me no more, lest I should bid thee live ;
      Ask me no more.

Ask me no more : thy fate and mine are
      seal'd :
  I strove against the stream and all in
      vain :
Let the great river take me to the main :
No more, dear love, for at a touch I yield ;
      Ask me no more.

ODE ON THE DEATH OF THE DUKE OF WELLINGTON

I

BURY the Great Duke
  With an empire's lamentation,
Let us bury the Great Duke
  To the noise of the mourning of a mighty
      nation,
Mourning when their leaders fall,
Warriors carry the warrior's pall,
And sorrow darkens hamlet and hall.

II

Where shall we lay the man whom we de-
      plore ?
Here, in streaming London's central roar.

Let the sound of those he wrought for,
And the feet of those he fought for,
Echo round his bones for evermore.

III

Lead out the pageant : sad and slow,
As fits an universal woe,
Let the long long procession go,
And let the sorrowing crowd about it grow,
And let the mournful martial music blow ;
The last great Englishman is low.

IV

Mourn, for to us he seems the last,
Remembering all his greatness in the Past.
No more in soldier fashion will he greet
With lifted hand the gazer in the street.
O friends, our chief state-oracle is mute :
Mourn for the man of long-enduring blood,
The statesman-warrior, moderate, resolute,
Whole in himself, a common good.
Mourn for the man of amplest influence,
Yet clearest of ambitious crime,
Our greatest yet with least pretence,
Great in council and great in war,
Foremost captain of his time,
Rich in saving common-sense,
And, as the greatest only are,
In his simplicity sublime.
O good gray head which all men knew,
O voice from which their omens all men
      drew,
O iron nerve to true occasion true,
O fall'n at length that tower of strength
Which stood four-square to all the winds
      that blew !
Such was he whom we deplore.
The long self-sacrifice of life is o'er.
The great World-victor's victor will be seen
      no more.

V

All is over and done :
Render thanks to the Giver,
England, for thy son.
Let the bell be toll'd.
Render thanks to the Giver,
And render him to the mould.
Under the cross of gold
That shines over city and river,
There he shall rest for ever
Among the wise and the bold.
Let the bell be toll'd :

And a reverent people behold
The towering car, the sable steeds :
Bright let it be with its blazon'd deeds,
Dark in its funeral fold.
Let the bell be toll'd :
And a deeper knell in the heart be knoll'd ;
And the sound of the sorrowing anthem
    roll'd
Thro' the dome of the golden cross ;
And the volleying cannon thunder his loss ;
He knew their voices of old.
For many a time in many a clime
His captain's-ear has heard them boom
Bellowing victory, bellowing doom :
When he with those deep voices wrought,
Guarding realms and kings from shame ;
With those deep voices our dead captain
    taught
The tyrant, and asserts his claim
In that dread sound to the great name,
Which he has worn so pure of blame,
In praise and in dispraise the same,
A man of well-attemper'd frame.
O civic muse, to such a name,
To such a name for ages long,
To such a name,
Preserve a broad approach of fame,
And ever-echoing avenues of song.

VI

Who is he that cometh, like an honor'd
    guest,
With banner and with music, with soldier
    and with priest,
With a nation weeping, and breaking on my
    rest ?
Mighty Seaman, this is he
Was great by land as thou by sea.
Thine island loves thee well, thou famous
    man,
The greatest sailor since our world began.
Now, to the roll of muffled drums,
To thee the greatest soldier comes ;
For this is he
Was great by land as thou by sea ;
His foes were thine ; he kept us free ;
O give him welcome, this is he
Worthy of our gorgeous rites,
And worthy to be laid by thee ;
For this is England's greatest son,
He that gain'd a hundred fights,
Nor ever lost an English gun ;
This is he that far away
Against the myriads of Assaye

Clash'd with his fiery few and won ;
And underneath another sun,
Warring on a later day,
Round affrighted Lisbon drew
The treble works, the vast designs
Of his labor'd rampart lines,
Where he greatly stood at bay,
Whence he issued forth anew,
And ever great and greater grew,
Beating from the wasted vines
Back to France her banded swarms,
Back to France with countless blows,
Till o'er the hills her eagles flew
Beyond the Pyrenean pines,
Follow'd up in valley and glen
With blare of bugle, clamor of men,
Roll of cannon and clash of arms,
And England pouring on her foes.
Such a war had such a close.
Again their ravening eagle rose
In anger, wheel'd on Europe-shadowing
    wings,
And barking for the thrones of kings ;
Till one that sought but Duty's iron crown
On that loud sabbath shook the spoiler
    down ;
A day of onsets of despair !
Dash'd on every rocky square
Their surging charges foam'd themselves
    away ;
Last, the Prussian trumpet blew ;
Thro' the long-tormented air
Heaven flash'd a sudden jubilant ray,
And down we swept and charged and over-
    threw.
So great a soldier taught us there,
What long-enduring hearts could do
In that world-earthquake, Waterloo !
Mighty Seaman, tender and true,
And pure as he from taint of craven guile,
O saviour of the silver-coasted isle,
O shaker of the Baltic and the Nile,
If aught of things that here befall
Touch a spirit among things divine,
If love of country move thee there at all,
Be glad, because his bones are laid by thine !
And thro' the centuries let a people's voice
In full acclaim,
A people's voice,
The proof and echo of all human fame,
A people's voice, when they rejoice
At civic revel and pomp and game,
Attest their great commander's claim
With honor, honor, honor, honor to him,
Eternal honor to his name.

VII

A people's voice ! we are a people yet.
Tho' all men else their nobler dreams for-
    get,
Confus'd by brainless mobs and lawless
    Powers ;
Thank Him who isl'd us here, and roughly
    set
His Briton in blown seas and storming
    showers,
We have a voice, with which to pay the
    debt
Of boundless love and reverence and regret
To those great men who fought, and kept
    it ours.
And keep it ours, O God, from brute con-
    trol ;
O Statesmen, guard us, guard the eye, the
    soul
Of Europe, keep our noble England whole,
And save the one true seed of freedom sown
Betwixt a people and their ancient throne,
That sober freedom out of which there
    springs
Our loyal passion for our temperate kings ;
For, saving that, ye help to save mankind
Till public wrong be crumbled into dust,
And drill the raw world for the march of
    mind,
Till crowds at length be sane and crowns
    be just.
But wink no more in slothful overtrust.
Remember him who led your hosts ;
He bade you guard the sacred coasts.
Your cannons moulder on the seaward wall ;
His voice is silent in your council-hall
For ever ; and whatever tempests lour
For ever silent ; even if they broke
In thunder, silent ; yet remember all
He spoke among you, and the Man who
    spoke ;
Who never sold the truth to serve the hour,
Nor palter'd with Eternal God for power ;
Who let the turbid streams of rumor flow
Thro' either babbling world of high and low ;
Whose life was work, whose language rife
With rugged maxims hewn from life ;
Who never spoke against a foe ;
Whose eighty winters freeze with one re-
    buke
All great self - seekers trampling on the
    right :
Truth - teller was our England's Alfred
    nam'd ;

Truth-lover was our English Duke ;
Whatever record leap to light
He never shall be sham'd.

VIII

Lo, the leader in these glorious wars
Now to glorious burial slowly borne,
Follow'd by the brave of other lands,
He, on whom from both her open hands
Lavish Honor shower'd all her stars,
And affluent Fortune emptied all her horn.
Yea, let all good things await
Him who cares not to be great,
But as he saves or serves the state.
Not once or twice in our rough island-story,
The path of duty was the way to glory :
He that walks it, only thirsting
For the right, and learns to deaden
Love of self, before his journey closes,
He shall find the stubborn thistle bursting
Into glossy purples, which outredden
All voluptuous garden-roses.
Not once or twice in our fair island-story,
The path of duty was the way to glory :
He, that ever following her commands,
On with toil of heart and knees and hands,
Thro' the long gorge to the far light has
    won
His path upward, and prevail'd,
Shall find the toppling crags of Duty scal'd
Are close upon the shining table-lands
To which our God Himself is moon and
    sun.
Such was he : his work is done.
But while the races of mankind endure,
Let his great example stand
Colossal, seen of every land,
And keep the soldier firm, the statesman
    pure :
Till in all lands and thro' all human story
The path of duty be the way to glory :
And let the land whose hearths he sav'd
    from shame
For many and many an age proclaim
At civic revel and pomp and game,
And when the long-illumin'd cities flame,
Their ever-loyal iron leader's fame,
With honor, honor, honor, honor to him,
Eternal honor to his name.

IX

Peace, his triumph will be sung
By some yet unmoulded tongue

Far on in summers that we shall not see :
Peace, it is a day of pain
For one about whose patriarchal knee
Late the little children clung :
O peace, it is a day of pain
For one, upon whose hand and heart and
   brain
Once the weight and fate of Europe hung.
Ours the pain, be his the gain !
More than is of man's degree
Must be with us, watching here
At this, our great solemnity.
Whom we see not we revere ;
We revere, and we refrain
From talk of battles loud and vain,
And brawling memories all too free
For such a wise humility
As befits a solemn fane :
We revere, and while we hear
The tides of Music's golden sea
Setting toward eternity,
Uplifted high in heart and hope are we,
Until we doubt not that for one so true
There must be other nobler work to do
Than when he fought at Waterloo,
And victor he must ever be.
For tho' the Giant Ages heave the hill
And break the shore, and evermore
Make and break, and work their will ;
Tho' world on world in myriad myriads
   roll
Round us, each with different powers,
And other forms of life than ours,
What know we greater than the soul ?
On God and Godlike men we build our
   trust.
Hush, the Dead March wails in the people's
   ears :
The dark crowd moves, and there are sobs
   and tears :
The black earth yawns : the mortal disap-
   pears ;
Ashes to ashes, dust to dust ;
He is gone who seem'd so great.—
Gone ; but nothing can bereave him
Of the force he made his own
Being here, and we believe him
Something far advanced in State,
And that he wears a truer crown
Than any wreath that man can weave him.
Speak no more of his renown,
Lay your earthly fancies down,
And in the vast cathedral leave him,
God accept him, Christ receive him.

THE CHARGE OF THE LIGHT BRIGADE

HALF a league, half a league,
   Half a league onward,
All in the valley of Death
   Rode the six hundred.
" Forward, the Light Brigade !
Charge for the guns ! " he said :
Into the valley of Death
   Rode the six hundred.

" Forward, the Light Brigade ! "
Was there a man dismay'd ?
Not tho' the soldier knew
   Some one had blunder'd :
Theirs not to make reply,
Theirs not to reason why,
Theirs but to do and die :
Into the valley of Death
   Rode the six hundred.

Cannon to right of them,
Cannon to left of them,
Cannon in front of them
   Volley'd and thunder'd ;
Storm'd at with shot and shell,
Boldly they rode and well,
Into the jaws of Death,
Into the mouth of Hell
   Rode the six hundred.

Flash'd all their sabres bare,
Flash'd as they turn'd in air
Sabring the gunners there,
Charging an army, while
   All the world wonder'd :
Plunged in the battery-smoke
Right thro' the line they broke ;
Cossack and Russian
Reel'd from the sabre-stroke
   Shatter'd and sunder'd.
Then they rode back, but not
   Not the six hundred.

Cannon to right of them,
Cannon to left of them,
Cannon behind them
   Volley'd and thunder'd ;
Storm'd at with shot and shell,
While horse and hero fell,
They that had fought so well
Came thro' the jaws of Death,
Back from the mouth of Hell,

All that was left of them,
Left of six hundred.

When can their glory fade ?
O the wild charge they made !
All the world wonder'd.
Honor the charge they made !
Honor the Light Brigade,
Noble six hundred !

NORTHERN FARMER

OLD STYLE

WHEER 'asta beän saw long and meä liggin'
 'ere aloän ?
Noorse ? thourt nowt o' a noorse : whoy,
 Doctor's abeän an' agoän :
Says that I moänt 'a naw moor aäle : but
 I beänt a fool :
Git ma my aäle, fur I beänt a-gawin' to
 breäk my rule.

Doctors, they knaws nowt, fur a says what 's
 nawways true :
Naw soort o' koind o' use to saäy the things
 that a do.
I 've 'ed my point o' aäle ivry noight sin' I
 beän 'ere.
An' I 've 'ed my quart ivry market-noight
 for foorty year.

Parson 's a beän loikewoise, an' a sittin' 'ere
 o' my bed.
" The amoighty 's a taäkin o' you[1] to 'issén,
 my friend," a said,
An' a towd ma my sins, an 's toithe were
 due, an' I gied it in hond :
I done my duty boy 'um, as I 'a done boy
 the lond.

Larn'd a ma' beä. I reckons I 'annot sa
 mooch to larn.
But a cast oop, thot a did, 'bout Bessy Mar-
 ris's barne.
Thaw a knaws I hallus voäted wi' Squoire
 an' choorch an' staäte,
An' i' the woost o' toimes I wur niver agin
 the raäte.

An' I hallus coom'd to 's chooch afoor moy
 Sally wur deäd,
An' 'eärd 'um a bummin' awaäy loike a
 buzzard-clock[2] ower my 'eäd,

[1] ou as in hour.   [2] Cockchafer.   [3] Bittern.

An' I niver knaw'd whot a meän'd but I
 thowt a 'ad summut to saäy,
An' I thowt a said whot a owt to 'a said
 an' I coom'd away.

Bessy Marris's barne ! tha knaws she laäid
 it to meä.
Mowt a beän, mayhap, for she wur a bad
 un, sheä.
'Siver, I kep 'um, I kep 'um, my lass, tha
 mun understond ;
I done moy duty boy 'um as I 'a done boy
 the lond.

But Parson a cooms an' a goäs, an' a says
 it eäsy an' freeä,
" The almoighty 's a taäkin o' you to 'issén,
 my friend," says 'eä.
I weänt saäy men be loiars, thaw summun
 said it in 'aäste :
But 'e reäds wonn sarmin a weeäk, an' I 'a
 stubb'd Thurnaby waäste.

D' ya moind the waäste, my lass ? naw, naw,
 tha was not born then ;
Theer wur a boggle in it, I often 'eärd 'um
 mysen ;
Moäst loike a butter-bump,[3] fur I 'eärd 'um
 about an' about,
But I stubb'd 'um oop wi' the lot, an' raäv'd
 an' rembled 'um out.

Keäper's it wur ; fo' they fun 'um theer
 a-laäid of 'is faäce
Down i' the woild enemies[4] afoor I coom'd
 to the plaäce.
Noäks or Thimbleby — toäner[5] 'ed shot 'um
 as deäd as a naäil.
Noäks wur 'ang'd for it oop at 'soize — but
 git ma my aäle.

Dubbut looök at the waäste : theer warn't
 not feeäd for a cow ;
Nowt at all but bracken an' fuzz, an' looök
 at it now —
Warnt worth nowt a haäcre, an' now theer 's
 lots o' feeäd,
Fourscoor[1] yows upon it an' some on it
 down i' seeäd.[6]

Nobbut a bit on it 's left, an' I meän'd to 'a
 stubb'd it at fall,
Done it ta-year I meän'd, an' runn'd plow
 thruff it an' all,

[4] Anemones.   [5] One or other.   [6] Clover.

f godamoighty an' parson 'ud nobbut let
    ma aloän,
Ieä, wi' haäte hoonderd haäcre o' Squoire's,
    an' lond o' my oän.

)o godamoighty knaw what a 's doin'
    a-taäkin' o' meä ?
beänt wonn as saws 'ere a beän an' yon-
    der a peä ;
.n' Squoire 'ull be sa mad an' all — a' dear
    a' dear !
.nd I 'a managed for Squoire coom Michael-
    mas thutty year.

. mowt 'a taäen owd Joänes, as 'ant not a
    'aäpoth o' sense,
'r a mowt 'a taäen young Robins — a niver
    mended a fence :
ut godamoighty a moost taäke meä an'
    taäke ma now
Vi' aäf the cows to cauve an' Thurnaby
    hoälms to plow !

ooök 'ow quoloty smoiles when they seeäs
    ma a passin' boy,
ays to thessén, naw doubt, " what a man a
    beä sewer-loy ! "
ur they knaws what I beän to Squoire sin
    fust a coom'd to the 'All ;
done moy duty by Squoire an' I done moy
    duty boy hall.

quoire 's i' Lunnon, an' summun I reckons
    'ull 'a to wroite,
or whoä 's to howd the lond ater meä thot
    muddles ma quoit ;
.rtin-sewer I beä, thot a weänt niver give
    it to Joänes,
aw, nor a moänt to Robins — a niver rem-
    bles the stoäns.

.t summun 'ull come ater meä mayhap
    wi' 'is kittle o' steäm
uzzin' an' maäzin' the blessed feälds wi'
    the Divil's oän teäm.
.n' I mun doy I mun doy, thaw loife they
    says is sweet,
ut sin' I mun doy I mun doy, for I
    couldn abeär to see it.

'hat atta stannin' theer fur, an' doesn bring
    ma the aäle ?
octor 's a' toättler, lass, an a 's hallus i' the
    owd taäle ;

I weänt breäk rules fur Doctor, a knaws
    naw moor nor a floy ;
Git ma my aäle I tell tha, an' if I mun doy
    I mun doy.

THE DAISY

WRITTEN AT EDINBURGH

O LOVE, what hours were thine and mine,
  In lands of palm and southern pine ;
    In lands of palm, of orange-blossom,
Of olive, aloe, and maize and vine.

What Roman strength Turbia show'd
  In ruin, by the mountain road ;
    How like a gem, beneath, the city
Of little Monaco, basking, glow'd.

How richly down the rocky dell
  The torrent vineyard streaming fell
    To meet the sun and sunny waters,
That only heav'd with a summer swell.

What slender campanili grew
  By bays, the peacock's neck in hue ;
    Where, here and there, on sandy beaches
A milky-bell'd amaryllis blew.

How young Columbus seem'd to rove,
  Yet present in his natal grove,
    Now watching high on mountain cornice,
And steering, now, from a purple cove,

Now pacing mute by ocean's rim ;
  Till, in a narrow street and dim,
    I stay'd the wheels at Cogoletto,
And drank, and loyally drank to him.

Nor knew we well what pleas'd us most,
Not the clipp'd palm of which they boast ;
    But distant color, happy hamlet,
A moulder'd citadel on the coast,

Or tower, or high hill-convent, seen
A light amid its olives green ;
    Or olive-hoary cape in ocean ;
Or rosy blossom in hot ravine,

Where oleanders flush'd the bed
Of silent torrents, gravel-spread ;
    And, crossing, oft we saw the glisten
Of ice, far up on a mountain head.

We lov'd that hall tho' white and cold,
Those niched shapes of noble mould,
  A princely people's awful princes,
The grave, severe Genovese of old.

At Florence too what golden hours,
In those long galleries, were ours ;
  What drives about the fresh Cascinè,
Or walks in Boboli's ducal bowers.

In bright vignettes, and each complete,
Of tower or duomo, sunny-sweet,
  Or palace, how the city glitter'd,
Thro' cypress avenues, at our feet.

But when we cross'd the Lombard plain
Remember what a plague of rain ;
  Of rain at Reggio, rain at Parma ;
At Lodi, rain, Piacenza, rain.

And stern and sad (so rare the smiles
Of sunlight) look'd the Lombard piles ;
  Porch-pillars on the lion resting,
And sombre, old, colonnaded aisles.

O Milan, O the chanting quires,
The giant windows' blazon'd fires,
  The height, the space, the gloom, the
    glory !
A mount of marble, a hundred spires !

I climb'd the roofs at break of day ;
Sun-smitten Alps before me lay.
  I stood among the silent statues,
And statued pinnacles, mute as they.

How faintly-flush'd, how phantom-fair,
Was Monte Rosa, hanging there
  A thousand shadowy-pencill'd valleys
And snowy dells in a golden air.

Remember how we came at last
To Como ; shower and storm and blast
  Had blown the lake beyond his limit,
And all was flooded ; and how we past

From Como, when the light was gray,
And in my head, for half the day,
  The rich Virgilian rustic measure
Of Lari Maxume, all the way,

Like ballad-burthen music, kept,
As on The Lariano crept
  To that fair port below the castle
Of Queen Theodolind, where we slept ;

Or hardly slept, but watch'd awake
A cypress in the moonlight shake,
  The moonlight touching o'er a terrace
One tall Agave above the lake.

What more ? we took our last adieu,
And up the snowy Splugen drew,
  But ere we reach'd the highest summit
I pluck'd a daisy, I gave it you.

It told of England then to me,
And now it tells of Italy.
  O love, we two shall go no longer
To lands of summer across the sea ;

So dear a life your arms enfold
Whose crying is a cry for gold :
  Yet here to-night in this dark city,
When ill and weary, alone and cold,

I found, tho' crush'd to hard and dry,
This nursling of another sky
  Still in the little book you lent me,
And where you tenderly laid it by :

And I forgot the clouded Forth,
The gloom that saddens Heaven and Earth,
  The bitter east, the misty summer
And gray metropolis of the North.

Perchance, to lull the throbs of pain,
Perchance, to charm a vacant brain,
  Perchance, to dream you still beside me,
My fancy fled to the South again.

THE FLOWER

Once in a golden hour
  I cast to earth a seed.
Up there came a flower,
  The people said, a weed.

To and fro they went
  Thro' my garden-bower,
And muttering discontent
  Curs'd me and my flower.

Then it grew so tall
  It wore a crown of light,
But thieves from o'er the wall
  Stole the seed by night.

Sow'd it far and wide
  By every town and tower,

Till all the people cried,
  " Splendid is the flower."

Read my little fable :
  He that runs may read.
Most can raise the flowers now,
  For all have got the seed.

And some are pretty enough,
  And some are poor indeed ;
And now again the people
  Call it but a weed.

COME INTO THE GARDEN, MAUD

OME into the garden, Maud,
  For the black bat, night, has flown,
ome into the garden, Maud,
  I am here at the gate alone ;
nd the woodbine spices are wafted abroad,
  And the musk of the rose is blown.

r a breeze of morning moves,
  And the planet of Love is on high,
eginning to faint in the light that she loves
  On a bed of daffodil sky,
 faint in the light of the sun she loves,
  To faint in his light, and to die.

l night have the roses heard
  The flute, violin, bassoon ;
ll night has the casement jessamine stirr'd
  To the dancers dancing in tune ;
ll silence fell with the waking bird,
  And a hush with the setting moon.

said to the lily, " There is but one
  With whom she has heart to be gay.
hen will the dancers leave her alone ?
  She is weary of dance and play."
w half to the setting moon are gone,
  And half to the rising day ;
w on the sand and loud on the stone
  The last wheel echoes away.

aid to the rose, " The brief night goes
  In babble and revel and wine.
young lord-lover, what sighs are those,
  For one that will never be thine ?
t mine, but mine," so I sware to the rose,
  " For ever and ever, mine."

And the soul of the rose went into my
    blood,
  As the music clash'd in the hall :
And long by the garden lake I stood,
  For I heard your rivulet fall
From the lake to the meadow and on to
    the wood,
  Our wood, that is dearer than all ;

From the meadow your walks have left so
    sweet
  That whenever a March-wind sighs
He sets the jewel-print of your feet
  In violets blue as your eyes,
To the woody hollows in which we meet
  And the valleys of Paradise.

The slender acacia would not shake
  One long milk-bloom on the tree ;
The white lake-blossom fell into the lake
  As the pimpernel doz'd on the lea ;
But the rose was awake all night for your
    sake,
  Knowing your promise to me ;
The lilies and roses were all awake,
  They sigh'd for the dawn and thee.

Queen rose of the rosebud garden of girls,
  Come hither, the dances are done,
In gloss of satin and glimmer of pearls,
  Queen lily and rose in one ;
Shine out, little head, sunning over with
    curls,
  To the flowers, and be their sun.

There has fallen a splendid tear
  From the passion-flower at the gate.
She is coming, my dove, my dear;
  She is coming, my life, my fate ;
The red rose cries, " She is near, she is
    near ; "
  And the white rose weeps, " She is late ; "
The larkspur listens, " I hear, I hear ; "
  And the lily whispers, " I wait."

She is coming, my own, my sweet ;
  Were it ever so airy a tread,
My heart would hear her and beat,
  Were it earth in an earthy bed ;
My dust would hear her and beat,
  Had I lain for a century dead ;
Would start and tremble under her feet,
  And blossom in purple and red.

THE SHELL

FROM "MAUD"

SEE what a lovely shell,
Small and pure as a pearl,
Lying close to my foot,
Frail, but a work divine,
Made so fairily well
With delicate spire and whorl,
How exquisitely minute,
A miracle of design !

What is it ? a learned man
Could give it a clumsy name.
Let him name it who can,
The beauty would be the same.

The tiny cell is forlorn,
Void of the little living will
That made it stir on the shore.
Did he stand at the diamond door
Of his house in a rainbow frill ?
Did he push, when he was uncurl'd,
A golden foot or a fairy horn
Thro' his dim water-world ?

Slight, to be crush'd with a tap
Of my finger-nail on the sand,
Small, but a work divine,
Frail, but of force to withstand,
Year upon year, the shock
Of cataract seas that snap
The three-decker's oaken spine
Athwart the ledges of rock,
Here on the Breton strand !

THE PASSING OF ARTHUR

FROM "IDYLLS OF THE KING"

THEN saw they how there hove a dusky
 barge,
Dark as a funeral scarf from stem to stern,
Beneath them ; and descending they were
 ware
That all the decks were dense with stately
 forms,
Black-stol'd, black-hooded, like a dream —
 by these
Three Queens with crowns of gold : and
 from them rose
A cry that shiver'd to the tingling stars,
And, as it were one voice, an agony
Of lamentation, like a wind that shrills
All night in a waste land, where no one
 comes,
Or hath come, since the making of the
 world.

Then murmur'd Arthur, "Place me in the
 barge."
So to the barge they came. There those
 three Queens
Put forth their hands, and took the King
 and wept.
But she, that rose the tallest of them all
And fairest, laid his head upon her lap,
And loos'd the shatter'd casque, and chaf'
 'his hands,
And call'd him by his name, complaining
 loud,
And dropping bitter tears against a brow
Strip'd with dark blood : for all his face
 was white
And colorless, and like the wither'd moon
Smote by the fresh beam of the springing
 east ;
And all his greaves and cuisses dash'd with
 drops
Of onset ; and the light and lustrous
 curls —
That made his forehead like a rising sun
High from the daïs-throne — were parch'
 with dust ;
Or, clotted into points and hanging loose,
Mix'd with the knightly growth that fringe
 his lips.
So like a shatter'd column lay the King ;
Not like that Arthur who, with lance in
 rest,
From spur to plume a star of tournament,
Shot thro' the lists at Camelot, and charge
Before the eyes of ladies and of kings.

Then loudly cried the bold Sir Bedivere
" Ah ! my Lord Arthur, whither shall I go
Where shall I hide my forehead and my
 eyes ?
For now I see the true old times are dead
When every morning brought a noble
 chance,
And every chance brought out a noble
 knight.
Such times have been not since the light
 that led
The holy Elders with the gift of myrrh.
But now the whole Round Table is dissolv
Which was an image of the mighty world

nd I, the last, go forth companionless,
nd the days darken round me, and the
    years,
mong new men, strange faces, other
    minds."

And slowly answer'd Arthur from the
    barge :
The old order changeth, yielding place to
    new,
nd God fulfils himself in many ways,
est one good custom should corrupt the
    world.
omfort thyself : what comfort is in me ?
have liv'd my life, and that which I have
    done
ay He within himself make pure ! but
    thou,
' thou shouldst never see my face again,
ray for my soul. More things are
    wrought by prayer
han this world dreams of. Wherefore,
    let thy voice
ise like a fountain for me night and day.
or what are men better than sheep or goats
hat nourish a blind life within the brain,
', knowing God, they lift not hands of
    prayer
oth for themselves and those who call
    them friend ?
or so the whole round earth is every way
ound by gold chains about the feet of God.
ut now farewell. I am going a long way
Vith these thou seëst — if indeed I go
'or all my mind is clouded with a
    doubt) —
o the island-valley of Avilion ;
There falls not hail, or rain, or any snow,
or ever wind blows loudly ; but it lies
eep-meadow'd, happy, fair with orchard
    lawns
nd bowery hollows crown'd with summer
    sea,
There I will heal me of my grievous
    wound."

So said he, and the barge with oar and sail
lov'd from the brink, like some full-
    breasted swan
hat, fluting a wild carol ere her death,
uffles her pure cold plume, and takes
    the flood
'ith swarthy webs. Long stood Sir
    Bedivere
evolving many memories, till the hull

Look'd one black dot against the verge of
    dawn,
And on the mere the wailing died away.

RIZPAH

WAILING, wailing, wailing, the wind over
    land and sea —
And Willy's voice in the wind, " O mother,
    come out to me."
Why should he call me to-night, when he
    knows that I cannot go ?
For the downs are as bright as day, and the
    full moon stares at the snow.

We should be seen, my dear ; they would
    spy us out of the town.
The loud black nights for us, and the storm
    rushing over the down,
When I cannot see my own hand, but am
    led by the creak of the chain,
And grovel and grope for my son till I find
    myself drench'd with the rain.

Anything fallen again ? nay — what was
    there left to fall ?
I have taken them home, I have number'd
    the bones, I have hidden them all.
What am I saying ? and what are *you* ?
    do you come as a spy ?
Falls ? what falls ? who knows ? As the
    tree falls so must it lie.

Who let her in ? how long has she been ?
    you — what have you heard ?
Why did you sit so quiet ? you never have
    spoken a word.
O — to pray with me — yes — a lady —
    none of their spies —
But the night has crept into my heart, and
    begun to darken my eyes.

Ah — you, that have liv'd so soft, what
    should *you* know of the night,
The blast and the burning shame and the
    bitter frost and the fright ?
I have done it, while you were asleep —
    you were only made for the day.
I have gather'd my baby together — and
    now you may go your way.

Nay — for it 's kind of you, Madam, to sit
    by an old dying wife.
But say nothing hard of my boy, I have
    only an hour of life.

I kiss'd my boy in the prison, before he
    went out to die.
"They dar'd me to do it," he said, and he
    never has told me a lie.
I whipp'd him for robbing an orchard once
    when he was but a child —
"The farmer dar'd me to do it," he said ;
    he was always so wild —
And idle — and could n't be idle — my
    Willy — he never could rest.
The King should have made him a sol-
    dier; he would have been one of his
    best.

But he liv'd with a lot of wild mates, and
    they never would let him be good ;
They swore that he dare not rob the mail,
    and he swore that he would ;
And he took no life, but he took one purse,
    and when all was done
He flung it among his fellows — I 'll none
    of it, said my son.

I came into court to the Judge and the
    lawyers. I told them my tale,
God's own truth — but they kill'd him,
    they kill'd him for robbing the mail.
They hang'd him in chains for a show —
    he had always borne a good name —
To be hang'd for a thief — and then put
    away — is n't that enough shame ?
Dust to dust — low down — let us hide !
    but they set him so high
That all the ships of the world could stare
    at him, passing by.
God 'ill pardon the hell-black raven and
    horrible fowls of the air,
But not the black heart of the lawyer who
    kill'd him and hang'd him there.

And the jailer forced me away. I had bid
    him my last goodbye ;
They had fasten'd the door of his cell,
    " O mother ! " I heard him cry.
I could n't get back tho' I tried, he had
    something further to say,
And now I never shall know it. The
    jailer forced me away.

Then since I could n't but hear that cry of
    my boy that was dead,
They seiz'd me and shut me up : they
    fasten'd me down on my bed.
" Mother, O mother ! " — he call'd in the
    dark to me year after year —

They beat me for that, they beat me —
    you know that I could n't but hea
And then at the last they found I ha
    grown so stupid and still
They let me abroad again — but th
    creatures had work'd their will.

Flesh of my flesh was gone, but bone of m
    bone was left —
I stole them all from the lawyers — an
    you, will you call it a theft ? —
My baby, the bones that had suck'd m
    the bones that had laugh'd ar
    had cried —
Theirs ? O no ! they are mine — n
    theirs — they had mov'd in my sid

Do you think I was scar'd by the bones
    I kiss'd 'em, I buried 'em all —
I can't dig deep, I am old — in the nig
    by the churchyard wall.
My Willy 'ill rise up whole when th
    trumpet of judgment 'ill sound,
But I charge you never to say that I la
    him in holy ground.

They would scratch him up — they wou
    hang him again on the cursed tree.
Sin ? O yes — we are sinners, I know –
    let all that be,
And read me a Bible verse of the Lord
    good will toward men—
" Full of compassion and mercy, the Lord
    — let me hear it again ;
" Full of compassion and mercy — lon
    suffering." Yes, O yes !
For the lawyer is born but to murder — th
    Saviour lives but to bless.
He 'll never put on the black cap except f
    the worst of the worst,
And the first may be last — I have heard
    in church — and the last may be firs
Suffering — O long-suffering — yes, as th
    Lord must know,
Year after year in the mist and the win
    and the shower and the snow.

Heard, have you ? what ? they have tol
    you he never repented his sin.
How do they know it ? are *they* his mother
    are *you* of his kin ?
Heard ! have you ever heard, when th
    storm on the downs began,
The wind that 'ill wail like a child and th
    sea that 'ill moan like a man ?

lection, Election and Reprobation — it 's
   all very well.
But I go to-night to my boy, and I shall
   not find him in Hell.
For I car'd so much for my boy that the
   Lord has look'd into my care,
And He means me, I 'm sure, to be happy
   with Willy, I know not where.

And if *he* be lost — but to save *my* soul,
   that is all your desire :
Do you think that I care for *my* soul if my
   boy be gone to the fire ?
I have been with God in the dark — go, go,
   you may leave me alone —
You never have borne a child — you are
   just as hard as a stone.

Madam, I beg your pardon ! I think that
   you mean to be kind,
But I cannot hear what you say for my
   Willy's voice in the wind —
The snow and the sky so bright — he us'd
   but to call in the dark,
And he calls to me now from the church
   and not from the gibbet — for hark !
Nay — you can hear it yourself — it is
   coming — shaking the walls —
Willy — the moon 's in a cloud — Good-
   night. I am going. He calls.

FLOWER IN THE CRANNIED WALL

FLOWER in the crannied wall,
I pluck you out of the crannies,
I hold you here, root and all, in my hand,
Little flower — but *if* I could understand
What you are, root and all, and all in all,
I should know what God and man is.

SONG IN "THE FORESTERS"*

THERE is no land like England
   Where'er the light of day be ;
There are no hearts like English hearts,
   Such hearts of oak as they be.
There is no land like England
   Where'er the light of day be ;
There are no men like Englishmen,
   So tall and bold as they be.

And these will strike for England
   And man and maid be free

To foil and spoil the tyrant
   Beneath the greenwood tree.

There is no land like England
   Where'er the light of day be ;
There are no wives like English wives,
   So fair and chaste as they be.
There is no land like England
   Where'er the light of day be ;
There are no maids like the English maids,
   So beautiful as they be.

And these shall wed with freemen,
   And all their sons be free,
To sing the songs of England
   Beneath the greenwood tree.

VASTNESS

MANY a hearth upon our dark globe sighs
   after many a vanish'd face,
Many a planet by many a sun may roll with
   the dust of a vanish'd race.

Raving politics, never at rest — as this poor
   earth's pale history runs, —
What is it all but a trouble of ants in the
   gleam of a million million of suns ?

Lies upon this side, lies upon that side,
   truthless violence mourn'd by the
   Wise,
Thousands of voices drowning his own in a
   popular torrent of lies upon lies ;

Stately purposes, valor in battle, glorious
   annals of army and fleet,
Death for the right cause, death for the
   wrong cause, trumpets of victory,
   groans of defeat ;

Innocence seeth'd in her mother's milk,
   and Charity setting the martyr
   aflame ;
Thraldom who walks with the banner of
   Freedom, and recks not to ruin a
   realm in her name ;

Faith at her zenith, or all but lost in the
   gloom of doubts that darken the
   schools ;
Craft with a bunch of all-heal in her hand,
   follow'd up by her vassal legion of
   fools ;

Trade flying over a thousand seas with her
  spice and her vintage, her silk and
  her corn ;
Desolate offing, sailorless harbors, famish-
  ing populace, wharves forlorn ;

Star of the morning, Hope in the sunrise ;
  gloom of the evening, Life at a close ;
Pleasure who flaunts on her wide downway
  with her flying robe and her poison'd
  rose ;

Pain, that has crawl'd from the corpse of
  Pleasure, a worm which writhes all
  day, and at night
Stirs up again in the heart of the sleeper,
  and stings him back to the curse of
  the light ;

Wealth with his wines and his wedded
  harlots ; honest Poverty, bare to the
  bone ;
Opulent Avarice, lean as Poverty ; Flattery
  gilding the rift in a throne ;

Fame blowing out from her golden trum-
  pet a jubilant challenge to Time and
  to Fate ;
Slander, her shadow, sowing the nettle on
  all the laurell'd graves of the Great ;

Love for the maiden, crown'd with mar-
  riage, no regrets for aught that has
  been,
Household happiness, gracious children,
  debtless competence, golden mean ;

National hatreds of whole generations, and
  pigmy spites of the village spire ;
Vows that will last to the last death-ruckle,
  and vows that are snapp'd in a mo-
  ment of fire ;

He that has liv'd for the lust of a minute,
  and died in the doing it, flesh with-
  out mind ;
He that has nail'd all flesh to the Cross, till
  Self died out in the love of his kind ;

Spring and Summer and Autumn and
  Winter, and all these old revolutions
  of earth ;
All new-old revolutions of Empire —
  change of the tide — what is all of it
  worth ?

What the philosophies, all the sciences
  poesy, varying voices of prayer ?
All that is noblest, all that is basest, a
  that is filthy with all that is fair ?

What is it all, if we all of us end but i
  being our own corpse-coffins at last
Swallow'd in Vastness, lost in Silence
  drown'd in the deeps of a meaning
  less Past ?

What but a murmur of gnats in the gloom
  or a moment's anger of bees in thei
  hive ? —
. . . . . .
Peace, let it be ! for I loved him, and lov
  him for ever : the dead are not dea
  but alive.

THE SILENT VOICES *

WHEN the dumb Hour, cloth'd in black,
Brings the Dreams about my bed,
Call me not so often back,
Silent Voices of the dead,
Toward the lowland ways behind me,
And the sunlight that is gone !
Call me rather, silent Voices,
Forward to the starry track
Glimmering up the heights beyond me
On, and always on !

CROSSING THE BAR

SUNSET and evening star,
  And one clear call for me !
And may there be no moaning of the bar,
  When I put out to sea,

But such a tide as moving seems asleep,
  Too full for sound and foam,
When that which drew from out the bound
  less deep
  Turns again home.

Twilight and evening bell,
  And after that the dark !
And may there be no sadness of farewell,
  When I embark ;

For tho' from out our bourne of Time an
  Place
  The flood may bear me far,
I hope to see my Pilot face to face
  When I have cross'd the bar.

Earl of Beaconsfield

(BENJAMIN D'ISRAELI)

WELLINGTON

Not only that thy puissant arm could bind
The tyrant of a world; and, conquering Fate,
Enfranchise Europe, do I deem thee great ;
But that in all thy actions I do find
Exact propriety : no gusts of mind
Fitful and wild, but that continuous state
Of order'd impulse mariners await
In some benignant and enriching wind, —

The breath ordain'd of Nature. Thy calm
    mien
Recalls old Rome, as much as thy high
    deed ;
Duty thine only idol, and serene
When all are troubled ; in the utmost need
Prescient ; thy country's servant ever seen,
Yet sovereign of thyself, whate'er may
    speed.

Thomas Westwood

O WIND OF THE MOUNTAIN!

O Wind of the Mountain, Wind of the
    Mountain, hear !
I have a prayer to whisper in thine ear :—
Hush, pine-tree, hush ! Be silent, syca-
    more !
Cease thy wild waving, ash-tree, old and
    hoar !
Flow softly, stream ! My voice is faint
    with fear —
O Wind of the Mountain, Wind of the
    Mountain, hear !

In the dull city, by the lowland shore,
Pale grows the cheek, so rosy-fresh of yore.
Woe for the child — the fair blithe-hearted
    child —
Once thy glad playmate on the breezy
    wild !
Hush, pine-tree, hush ! — my voice is faint
    with fear —
O Wind of the Mountain, Wind of the
    Mountain, hear !

Pale grows the cheek, and dim the sunny
    eyes,
And the voice falters, and the laughter dies.
Woe for the child ! She pines, on that sad
    shore,
For the free hills and happy skies of yore.
Hush, river, hush ! — my voice is faint with
    fear —
O Wind of the Mountain, Wind of the
    Mountain, hear !

O Wind of the Mountain, thou art swift
    and strong —
Follow, for love's sake, though the way be
    long.
Follow, oh ! follow, over down and dale,
To the far city in the lowland vale.
Hush, pine-tree, hush ! — my voice is faint
    with fear —
O Wind of the Mountain, Wind of the
    Mountain, hear !

Kiss the dear lips, and bid the laughters
    rise ;
Flush the wan cheek, and brighten the dim
    eyes ;
Sing songs of home, and soon, from grief
    and pain,
Win back thy playmate, blessed Wind,
    again !
Win back my darling — while away my
    fear —
O Wind of the Mountain, Wind of the
    Mountain, hear !

IN THE GOLDEN MORNING OF
THE WORLD

In the golden morning of the world,
When creation's freshness was unfurl'd,
Had earth truer, fonder hearts than now ?
One, at least, in this our day, I know,
(Whisper soft, *ah! benedicite!*)
Faithful-fond as any heart could be
In the golden morning of the world.

And were faces, in that orient time,
Flush'd, in sooth, with more resplendent prime,
More consummate loveliness than now?
Nay, one maiden face, at least, I know
(Whisper soft, *ah! benedicite!*)
Just as fair as any face could be
In the golden morning of the world.

But dark shadows reign, and storms are rife,
In the once serene clear heaven of life.
Oh! sweet angel, at the shining gate,
By God's mercy, keep one earthly fate,
One dear life — *ah! benedicite!*
Happy, calm, as any such could be
In the golden morning of the world!

Arthur Hugh Clough

IN A LECTURE-ROOM

AWAY, haunt thou not me,
Thou vain Philosophy!
Little hast thou bestead,
Save to perplex the head,
And leave the spirit dead.
Unto thy broken cisterns wherefore go,
While from the secret treasure-depths below,
Fed by the skyey shower,
And clouds that sink and rest on hill-tops high,
Wisdom at once, and Power,
Are welling, bubbling forth, unseen, incessantly?
Why labor at the dull mechanic oar,
When the fresh breeze is blowing,
And the strong current flowing,
Right onward to the Eternal Shore?

A PROTEST

LIGHT words they were, and lightly, falsely said;
She heard them, and she started, — and she rose,
As in the act to speak; the sudden thought
And unconsider'd impulse led her on.
In act to speak she rose, but with the sense
Of all the eyes of that mix'd company
Now suddenly turn'd upon her, some with age
Harden'd and dull'd, some cold and critical;
Some in whom vapors of their own conceit,
As moist malarious mists the heavenly stars,
Still blotted out their good, the best at best

By frivolous laugh and prate conventional
All too untun'd for all she thought to say, —
With such a thought the mantling blood to her cheek
Flush'd up, and o'er-flush'd itself, blank night her soul
Made dark, and in her all her purpose swoon'd.
She stood as if for sinking. Yet anon,
With recollections clear, august, sublime,
Of God's great truth, and right immutable,
Which, as obedient vassals, to her mind
Came summon'd of her will, in self-negation
Quelling her troublous earthly consciousness,
She queen'd it o'er her weakness. At the spell
Back roll'd the ruddy tide, and leaves her cheek
Paler than erst, and yet not ebbs so far
But that one pulse of one indignant thought
Might hurry it hither in flood. So as she stood
She spoke. God in her spoke, and made her heard.

QUA CURSUM VENTUS

As ships, becalm'd at eve, that lay
With canvas drooping, side by side,
Two towers of sail at dawn of day
Are scarce long leagues apart descried;

When fell the night, upsprung the breeze,
And all the darkling hours they plied,
Nor dreamt but each the self-same seas
By each was cleaving, side by side:

E'en so — but why the tale reveal
Of those whom, year by year unchanged,
Brief absence join'd anew to feel,
Astounded, soul from soul estranged ?

At dead of night their sails were fill'd,
And onward each rejoicing steer'd :
Ah, neither blame, for neither will'd,
Or wist, what first with dawn appear'd !

To veer, how vain ! On, onward strain,
Brave barks ! In light, in darkness too,
Through winds and tides one compass
    guides, —
To that, and your own selves, be true.

But O blithe breeze, and O great seas,
Though ne'er, that earliest parting past,
On your wide plain they join again,
Together lead them home at last !

One port, methought, alike they sought,
One purpose hold where'er they fare, —
O bounding breeze, O rushing seas,
At last, at last, unite them there !

FROM "THE BOTHIE OF TOBER-NA-VUOLICH"

THE BATHERS

THERE is a stream, I name not its name,
    lest inquisitive tourist
Hunt it, and make it a lion, and get it at
    last into guide-books,
Springing far off from a loch unexplor'd
    in the folds of great mountains,
Falling two miles through rowan and
    stunted alder, enveloped
Then for four more in a forest of pine,
    where broad and ample
Spreads, to convey it, the glen with heath-
    ery slopes on both sides :
Broad and fair the stream, with occasional
    falls and narrows ;
But, where the glen of its course ap-
    proaches the vale of the river,
Met and block'd by a huge interposing
    mass of granite,
Scarce by a channel deep-cut, raging up,
    and raging onward,
Forces its flood through a passage so nar-
    row a lady would step it.

There, across the great rocky wharves, a
    wooden bridge goes,
Carrying a path to the forest ; below,
    three hundred yards, say,
Lower in level some twenty-five feet,
    through flats of shingle,
Stepping-stones and a cart-track cross in
    the open valley.
But in the interval here the boiling,
    pent-up water
Frees itself by a final descent, attaining a
    basin,
Ten feet wide and eighteen long, with
    whiteness and fury
Occupied partly, but mostly pellucid, pure,
    a mirror ;
Beautiful there for the color deriv'd from
    green rocks under ;
Beautiful, most of all, where beads of
    foam up-rising
Mingle their clouds of white with the deli-
    cate hue of the stillness.
Cliff over cliff for its sides, with rowan and
    pendant birch boughs,
Here it lies, unthought of above at the
    bridge and pathway,
Still more enclosed from below by wood
    and rocky projection.
You are shut in, left alone with yourself
    and perfection of water,
Hid on all sides, left alone with yourself
    and the goddess of bathing.
Here, the pride of the plunger, you stride
    the fall and clear it ;
Here, the delight of the bather, you roll in
    beaded sparklings,
Here into pure green depth drop down
    from lofty ledges.
Hither, a month agone, they had come,
    and discover'd it ; hither
(Long a design, but long unaccountably left
    unaccomplish'd),
Leaving the well-known bridge and path-
    way above to the forest,
Turning below from the track of the carts
    over stone and shingle,
Piercing a wood, and skirting a narrow and
    natural causeway
Under the rocky wall that hedges the bed
    of the streamlet,
Rounded a craggy point, and saw on a sud-
    den before them
Slabs of rock, and a tiny beach, and perfec-
    tion of water,

Picture-like beauty, seclusion sublime, and
　　the goddess of bathing.
There they bath'd, of course, and Arthur,
　　the glory of headers,
Leap'd from the ledges with Hope, he
　　twenty feet, he thirty ;
There, overbold, great Hobbes from a ten-
　　foot height descended,
Prone, as a quadruped, prone with hands
　　and feet protending ;
There in the sparkling champagne, ecstatic,
　　they shriek'd and shouted.
" Hobbes's gutter " the Piper entitles
　　the spot, profanely,
Hope " the Glory " would have, after
　　Arthur, the glory of headers :
But, for before they departed, in shy and
　　fugitive reflex
Here in the eddies and there did the splen-
　　dor of Jupiter glimmer ;
Adam adjudged it the name of Hesperus,
　　star of the evening.
Hither, to Hesperus, now, the star of the
　　evening above them,
Come in their lonelier walk the pupils
　　twain and Tutor ;
Turn'd from the track of the carts, and
　　passing the stone and shingle,
Piercing the wood, and skirting the stream
　　by the natural causeway,
Rounded the craggy point, and now at their
　　ease look'd up ; and
Lo, on the rocky ledge, regardant, the
　　Glory of headers,
Lo, on the beach, expecting the plunge, not
　　cigarless, the Piper. —
And they look'd, and wonder'd, incredu-
　　lous, looking yet once more.
Yes, it was he, on the ledge, bare-limb'd,
　　an Apollo, down-gazing,
Eying one moment the beauty, the life, ere
　　he flung himself in it,
Eying through eddying green waters the
　　green-tinting floor underneath them,
Eying the bead on the surface, the bead,
　　like a cloud, rising to it,
Drinking in, deep in his soul, the beautiful
　　hue and the clearness,
Arthur, the shapely, the brave, the unboast-
　　ing, the glory of headers ;
Yes, and with fragrant weed, by his knap-
　　sack, spectator and critic,
Seated on slab by the margin, the Piper,
　　the Cloud-compeller.

PESCHIERA

What voice did on my spirit fall,
Peschiera, when thy bridge I crost ?
" 'T is better to have fought and lost,
Than never to have fought at all."

The tricolor — a trampled rag —
Lies dirt and dust ; the lines I track
By sentries' boxes, yellow, black,
Lead up to no Italian flag.

I see the Croat soldier stand
Upon the grass of your redoubts ;
The eagle with his black wing flouts
The breadth and beauty of your land.

Yet not in vain, although in vain,
O men of Brescia ! on the day
Of loss past hope, I heard you say
Your welcome to the noble pain.

You said : " Since so it is, good-bye,
Sweet life, high hope ; but whatsoe'er
May be, or must, no tongue shall dare
To tell, ' The Lombard fear'd to die !' "

You said (there shall be answer fit) :
" And if our children must obey,
They must ; but, thinking on this day,
'T will less debase them to submit."

You said (O not in vain you said) :
" Haste, brothers, haste, while yet we
　　may ;
The hours ebb fast of this one day,
While blood may yet be nobly shed."

Ah ! not for idle hatred, not
For honor, fame, nor self-applause,
But for the glory of the cause,
You did what will not be forgot.

And though the stranger stand, 't is true,
By force and fortune's right he stands :
By fortune, which is in God's hands,
And strength, which yet shall spring in
　　you.

This voice did on my spirit fall,
Peschiera, when thy bridge I crost :
" 'T is better to have fought and lost,
Than never to have fought at all."

FROM "AMOURS DE VOYAGE"

JUXTAPOSITION

JUXTAPOSITION, in fine ; and what is juxta-
position ?
Look you, we travel along in the railway-
carriage or steamer,
And, *pour passer le temps*, till the tedious
journey be ended,
Lay aside paper or book, to talk with the
girl that is next one ;
And, *pour passer le temps*, with the terminus
all but in prospect,
Talk of eternal ties and marriages made in
heaven.
Ah, did we really accept with a perfect
heart the illusion !
Ah, did we really believe that the Pre-
sent indeed is the Only !
Or through all transmutation, all shock
and convulsion of passion,
Feel we could carry undimmed, unextin-
guished, the light of our knowledge !
But for his funeral train which the bride-
groom sees in the distance,
Would he so joyfully, think you, fall in
with the marriage-procession ?
But for that final discharge, would he dare
to enlist in that service ?
But for that certain release, ever sign to
that perilous contract ?
But for that exit secure, ever bend to that
treacherous doorway ? —
Ah, but the bride, meantime, — do you
think she sees it as he does ?
But for the steady fore-sense of a freer
and larger existence,
Think you that man could consent to be
circumscribed here into action ?
But for assurance within of a limitless ocean
divine, o'er
Whose great tranquil depths unconscious
the wind-toss'd surface
Breaks into ripples of trouble that come
and change and endure not, —
But that in this, of a truth, we have our
being, and know it,
Think you we men could submit to live and
move as we do here ?
Ah, but the women, — God bless them ! —
they don't think at all about it.
Yet we must eat and drink, as you say.
And as limited beings

Scarcely can hope to attain upon earth to
an Actual Abstract,
Leaving to God contemplation, to His hands
knowledge confiding,
Sure that in us if it perish, in Him it abid-
eth and dies not,
Let us in His sight accomplish our petty
particular doings, —
Yes, and contented sit down to the victual
that He has provided.
Allah is great, no doubt, and Juxtaposition
his prophet.
Ah, but the women, alas ! they don't look
at it in that way.
Juxtaposition is great ; — but, my friend,
I fear me, the maiden
Hardly would thank or acknowledge the
lover that sought to obtain her,
Not as the thing he would wish, but the
thing he must even put up with, —
Hardly would tender her hand to the wooer
that candidly told her
That she is but for a space, an *ad-interim*
solace and pleasure, —
That in the end she shall yield to a perfect
and absolute something,
Which I then for myself shall behold, and
not another, —
Which, amid fondest endearments, mean-
time I forget not, forsake not.
Ah, ye feminine souls, so loving and so ex-
acting,
Since we cannot escape, must we even sub-
mit to deceive you ?
Since, so cruel is truth, sincerity shocks
and revolts you,
Will you have us your slaves to lie to you,
flatter and — leave you ?

ITE DOMUM SATURÆ, VENIT HESPERUS

THE skies have sunk, and hid the upper
snow,
(Home, Rose, and home, Provence and La
Palie !)
The rainy clouds are filling fast below,
And wet will be the path, and wet shall we.
Home, Rose, and home, Provence and La
Palie !

Ah dear ! and where is he, a year agone,
Who stepp'd beside and cheer'd us on and
on ?

My sweetheart wanders far away from me
In foreign land or on a foreign sea.
Home, Rose, and home, Provence and La
    Palie !

The lightning zigzags shoot across the sky,
(Home, Rose, and home, Provence and La
    Palie !)
And through the vale the rains go sweep-
    ing by ;
Ah me ! and when in shelter shall we be ?
(Home, Rose, and home, Provence and La
    Palie !)

Cold, dreary cold, the stormy winds feel
    they
O'er foreign lands and foreign seas that
    stray.
(Home, Rose, and home, Provence and La
    Palie !)
And doth he e'er, I wonder, bring to mind
The pleasant huts and herds he left be-
    hind ?

And doth he sometimes in his slumbering
    see
The feeding kine, and doth he think of
    me,
My sweetheart wandering wheresoe'er it
    be ?
Home, Rose, and home, Provence and La
    Palie !

The thunder bellows far from snow to
    snow,
(Home, Rose, and home, Provence and La
    Palie !)
And loud and louder roars the flood be-
    low.
Heigh-ho ! but soon in shelter shall we be :
Home, Rose, and home, Provence and La
    Palie !

Or shall he find before his term be sped
Some comelier maid that he shall wish to
    wed ?
(Home, Rose, and home, Provence and La
    Palie !)
For weary is work, and weary day by day
To have your comfort miles on miles away.
(Home, Rose, and home, Provence and La
    Palie !)

Or may it be that I shall find my mate,
And he, returning, see himself too late ?

For work we must, and what we see, we see,
And God he knows, and what must be,
    must be,
When sweethearts wander far away from
    me.
Home, Rose, and home, Provence and La
    Palie !

The sky behind is brightening up anew,
(Home, Rose, and home, Provence and La
    Palie !)
The rain is ending, and our journey too;
Heigh-ho ! aha ! for here at home are
    we : —
In, Rose, and in, Provence and La Palie !

AH ! YET CONSIDER IT AGAIN

OLD things need not be therefore true,
O brother men, nor yet the new ;
Ah ! still awhile the old thought retain,
And yet consider it again !

The souls of now two thousand years
Have laid up here their toils and fears,
And all the earnings of their pain, —
Ah, yet consider it again !

We ! what do we see ? each a space
Of some few yards before his face ;
Does that the whole wide plan explain ?
Ah, yet consider it again !

Alas ! the great world goes its way,
And takes its truth from each new day ;
They do not quit, nor can retain,
Far less consider it again.

WHERE LIES THE LAND

WHERE lies the land to which the ship
    would go ?
Far, far ahead, is all her seamen know.
And where the land she travels from ?
    Away,
Far, far behind, is all that they can say.

On sunny noons upon the deck's smooth
    face,
Link'd arm in arm, how pleasant here to
    pace !
Or o'er the stern reclining, watch below
The foaming wake far widening as we go.

On stormy nights, when wild northwesters
    rave,
How proud a thing to fight with wind and
    wave !
The dripping sailor on the reeling mast
Exults to bear, and scorns to wish it past.

Where lies the land to which the ship would
    go ?
Far, far ahead, is all her seamen know.
And where the land she travels from ?
    Away,
Far, far behind, is all that they can say.

John Campbell Shairp

CAILLEACH BEIN-Y-VREICH [1]

WEIRD wife of Bein-y-Vreich ! horo ! horo !
    Aloft in the mist she dwells ;
Vreich horo ! Vreich horo ! Vreich horo !
    All alone by the lofty wells.

Weird, weird wife ! with the long gray
    locks,
    She follows her fleet-foot stags,
Noisily moving through splinter'd rocks,
    And crashing the grisly crags.

Tall wife, with the long gray hose ! in
    haste
    The rough stony beach she walks ;
But dulse or seaweed she will not taste,
    Nor yet the green kail stalks.

And I will not let my herds of deer,
    My bonny red deer go down ;
I will not let them down to the shore,
    To feed on the sea-shells brown.

Oh, better they love in the corrie's recess,
    Or on mountain top to dwell,
And feed by my side on the green, green
    cress,
    That grows by the lofty well.

Broad Bein-y-Vreich is grisly and drear,
    But wherever my feet have been
The well-springs start for my darling deer,
    And the grass grows tender and green.

And there high up on the calm nights clear,
    Beside the lofty spring,
They come to my call, and I milk them
    there,
    And a weird wild song I sing.

But when hunter men round my dun deer
    prowl,
    I will not let them nigh ;
Through the rended cloud I cast one scowl,
    They faint on the heath and die.

And when the north wind o'er the desert
    bare
    Drives loud, to the corries below
I drive my herds down, and bield them
    there
    From the drifts of the blinding snow.

Then I mount the blast, and we ride full
    fast,
    And laugh as we stride the storm,
I, and the witch of the Cruachan Ben,
    And the scowling-eyed Seul-Gorm.

Menella Bute Smedley

THE LITTLE FAIR SOUL

A LITTLE fair soul that knew no sin
    Look'd over the edge of Paradise,
And saw one striving to come in,
    With fear and tumult in his eyes.

"Oh, brother, is it you ?" he cried ;
    "Your face is like a breath from
    home ;
Why do you stay so long outside ?
    I am athirst for you to come ı

---

[1] A beanshith or fairy seen by hunters.

"Tell me first how our mother fares,
  And has she wept too much for me?"
"White are her cheeks and white her hairs,
  But not from gentle tears for thee."

"Tell me, where are our sisters gone?"
  "Alas, I left them weary and wan."
"And tell me is the baby grown?"
  "Alas! he is almost a man.

"Cannot you break the gathering days,
  And let the light of death come through,
Ere his feet stumble in the maze
  Cross'd safely by so few, so few?

"For like a crowd upon the sea
  That darkens till you find no shore,
So was that face of life to me,
  Until I sank for evermore;

"And like an army in the snow
  My days went by, a treacherous train,
Each smiling as he struck his blow,
  Until I lay among them slain."

"Oh, brother, there was a path so clear!"
  "There might be, but I never sought."
"Oh, brother, there was a sword so near!"
  "There might be, but I never fought."

"Yet sweep this needless gloom aside,
  For you are come to the gate at last!"

Then in despair that soul replied,
  "The gate is fast, the gate is fast!"

"I cannot move this mighty weight,
  I cannot find this golden key;
But hosts of heaven around us wait,
  And none has ever said 'No' to me.

"Sweet Saint, put by thy palm and scroll,
  And come and undo the door for me!"
"Rest thee still, thou little fair soul,
  It is not mine to keep the key."

"Kind Angel, strike these doors apart!
  The air without is dark and cold."
"Rest thee still, thou little pure heart,
  Not for my word will they unfold."

Up all the shining heights he pray'd
  For that poor Shadow in the cold!
Still came the word, "Not ours to aid;
  We cannot make the doors unfold."

But that poor Shadow, still outside,
  Wrung all the sacred air with pain;
And all the souls went up and cried
  Where never cry was heard in vain.

No eye beheld the pitying Face,
  The answer none might understand,
But dimly through the silent space
  Was seen the stretching of a Hand.

Robert Leighton

THE DRIED-UP FOUNTAIN

OUTSIDE the village, by the public road,
  I know a dried-up fountain, overgrown
With herbs, the haunt of legendary toad,
  And grass, by Nature sown.

I know not where its trickling life was still'd;
  No living ears its babbling tongue has
    caught;
But often, as I pass, I see it fill'd
  And running o'er with thought.

I see it as it was in days of old,
  The blue-ey'd maiden stooping o'er its
    brim,
And smoothing in its glass her locks of gold,
  Lest she should meet with *him*.

She knows that he is near, yet I can see
  Her sweet confusion when she hears him
    come.
No tryst had they, though every evening he
  Carries her pitchers home.

The ancient beggar limps along the road
  At thirsty noon, and rests him by its
    brink;
The dusty pedlar lays aside his load,
  And pauses there to drink.

And there the village children come to
    play,
  When busy parents work in shop and
    field.
The swallows, too, find there the loamy clay
  When 'neath the eaves they build.

When cows at eve come crooning home,
the boy
Leaves them to drink, while his mechanic
skill
Within the brook sets up, with inward joy,
His tiny water-mill.

And when the night is hush'd in summer
sleep,
And rest has come to laborer and team,

I hear the runnel through the long grass
creep,
As 't were a whispering dream.

Alas ! 't is all a dream. Lover and lass,
Children and wanderers, are in their
graves ;
And where the fountain flow'd a greener
grass —
Its *In Memoriam* — waves.

Matthew Arnold

WRITTEN IN EMERSON'S ESSAYS

" O MONSTROUS, dead, unprofitable world,
That thou canst hear, and hearing, hold thy
way !
A voice oracular hath peal'd to-day,
To-day a hero's banner is unfurl'd ;
Hast thou no lip for welcome ? " — So I
said.
Man after man, the world smil'd and
pass'd by ;
A smile of wistful incredulity
As though one spake of life unto the
dead —
Scornful, and strange, and sorrowful, and
full
Of bitter knowledge. Yet the will is
free ;
Strong is the soul, and wise, and beauti-
ful ;
The seeds of god-like power are in us still ;
Gods are we, bards, saints, heroes, if we
will ! —
Dumb judges, answer, truth or mockery ?

THE WORLD AND THE QUIETIST

" WHY, when the world's great mind
Hath finally inclin'd,
Why," you say, Critias, "be debating still ?
Why, with these mournful rhymes
Learn'd in more languid climes,
Blame our activity
Who, with such passionate will,
Are what we mean to be ? "

Critias, long since, I know
(For Fate decreed it so),

Long since the world hath set its heart to
live ;
Long since, with credulous zeal
It turns life's mighty wheel,
Still doth for laborers send
Who still their labor give,
And still expects an end.

Yet, as the wheel flies round,
With no ungrateful sound
Do adverse voices fall on the world's ear.
Deafen'd by his own stir
The rugged laborer
Caught not till then a sense
So glowing and so near
Of his omnipotence.

So, when the feast grew loud
In Susa's palace proud,
A white-rob'd slave stole to the Great
King's side.
He spake — the Great King heard ;
Felt the slow-rolling word
Swell his attentive soul ;
Breath'd deeply as it died,
And drain'd his mighty bowl.

FROM "SOHRAB AND RUSTUM"

THE COMBAT

HE ceas'd, but while he spake, Rustum
had risen,
And stood erect, trembling with rage ; his
club
He left to lie, but had regain'd his spear,
Whose fiery point now in his mail'd right
hand

Blaz'd bright and baleful, like that autumn-
  star,
The baleful sign of fevers ; dust had soil'd
His stately crest, and dimm'd his glitter-
  ing arms.
His breast heav'd, his lips foam'd, and
  twice his voice
Was chok'd with rage ; at last these words
  broke way : —
  "Girl ! nimble with thy feet, not with
  thy hands !
Curl'd minion, dancer, coiner of sweet
  words !
Fight, let me hear thy hateful voice no
  more !
Thou art not in Afrasiab's gardens now
With Tartar girls, with whom thou art
  wont to dance ;
But on the Oxus-sands, and in the dance
Of battle, and with me, who make no play
Of war ; I fight it out, and hand to hand.
Speak not to me of truce, and pledge, and
  wine !
Remember all thy valor ; try thy feints
And cunning ! all the pity I had is gone ;
Because thou hast sham'd me before both
  the hosts
With thy light skipping tricks, and thy
  girl's wiles."
  He spoke, and Sohrab kindled at his
  taunts,
And he too drew his sword ; at once they
  rush'd
Together, as two eagles on one prey
Come rushing down together from the
  clouds,
One from the east, one from the west ;
  their shields
Dash'd with a clang together, and a din
Rose, such as that the sinewy woodcutters
Make often in the forest's heart at morn,
Of hewing axes, crashing trees — such blows
Rustum and Sohrab on each other hail'd.
And you would say that sun and stars took
  part
In that unnatural conflict ; for a cloud
Grew suddenly in Heaven, and dark'd the
  sun
Over the fighters' heads ; and a wind rose
Under their feet, and moaning swept the
  plain,
And in a sandy whirlwind wrapp'd the
  pair.
In gloom they twain were wrapp'd, and
  they alone ;

For both the on-looking hosts on either
  hand
Stood in broad daylight, and the sky was
  pure,
And the sun sparkled on the Oxus stream.
But in the gloom they fought, with blood-
  shot eyes
And laboring breath ; first Rustum struck
  the shield
Which Sohrab held stiff out ; the steel-
  spik'd spear
Rent the tough plates, but fail'd to reach
  the skin,
And Rustum pluck'd it back with angry
  groan.
Then Sohrab with his sword smote Rus-
  tum's helm,
Nor clove its steel quite through ; but all
  the crest
He shore away, and that proud horsehair
  plume,
Never till now defil'd, sank to the dust ;
And Rustum bow'd his head ; but then
  the gloom
Grew blacker, thunder rumbled in the air,
And lightnings rent the cloud ; and Ruksh,
  the horse,
Who stood at hand, utter'd a dreadful
  cry ; —
No horse's cry was that, most like the roar
Of some pain'd desert-lion, who all day
Has trail'd the hunter's javelin in his side,
And comes at night to die upon the
  sand —
The two hosts heard that cry, and quak'd
  for fear,
And Oxus curdled as it cross'd his stream.
But Sohrab heard, and quail'd not, but
  rush'd on,
And struck again ; and again Rustum
  bow'd
His head ; but this time all the blade, like
  glass,
Sprang in a thousand shivers on the helm,
And in the hand the hilt remain'd alone.
Then Rustum rais'd his head ; his dread-
  ful eyes
Glar'd, and he shook on high his menacing
  spear,
And shouted :   *Rustum !* — Sohrab heard
  that shout,
And shrank amaz'd : back he recoil'd one
  step,
And scann'd with blinking eyes the ad-
  vancing form ;

And then he stood bewilder'd, and he dropp'd
His covering shield, and the spear pierced his side.
He reel'd, and staggering back, sank to the ground ;
And then the gloom dispers'd, and the wind fell,
And the bright sun broke forth, and melted all
The cloud ; and the two armies saw the pair ; —
Saw Rustum standing, safe upon his feet,
And Sohrab, wounded, on the bloody sand.

OXUS

But the majestic river floated on,
Out of the mist and hum of that low land,
Into the frosty starlight, and there mov'd,
Rejoicing, through the hush'd Chorasmian waste,
Under the solitary moon ; — he flow'd
Right for the polar star, past Orgunjè,
Brimming, and bright, and large ; then sands begin
To hem his watery march, and dam his streams,
And split his currents ; that for many a league
The shorn and parcell'd Oxus strains along
Through beds of sand and matted rushy isles —
Oxus, forgetting the bright speed he had
In his high mountain-cradle in Pamere,
A foil'd circuitous wanderer — till at last
The long'd-for dash of waves is heard, and wide
His luminous home of waters opens, bright
And tranquil, from whose floor the new-bath'd stars
Emerge, and shine upon the Aral Sea.

FROM "BALDER DEAD"

THE INCREMATION

But now the sun had pass'd the height of Heaven,
And soon had all that day been spent in wail ;
But then the Father of the ages said : —
" Ye Gods, there well may be too much of wail !
Bring now the gather'd wood to Balder's ship ;

Heap on the deck the logs, and build the pyre."
But when the Gods and Heroes heard, they brought
The wood to Balder's ship, and built a pile,
Full the deck's breadth, and lofty; then the corpse
Of Balder on the highest top they laid,
With Nanna on his right, and on his left
Hoder, his brother, whom his own hand slew.
And they set jars of wine and oil to lean
Against the bodies, and stuck torches near,
Splinters of pine-wood, soak'd with turpentine ;
And brought his arms and gold, and all his stuff,
And slew the dogs who at his table fed,
And his horse, Balder's horse, whom most he lov'd,
And threw them on the pyre, and Odin threw
A last choice gift thereon, his golden ring.
The mast they fix'd, and hoisted up the sails,
Then they put fire to the wood ; and Thor
Set his stout shoulder hard against the stern
To push the ship through the thick sand ; — sparks flew
From the deep trench she plough'd, so strong a God
Furrow'd it ; and the water gurgled in.
And the ship floated on the waves, and rock'd.
But in the hills a strong east-wind arose,
And came down moaning to the sea ; first squalls
Ran black o'er the sea's face, then steady rush'd
The breeze, and fill'd the sails, and blew the fire ;
And wreath'd in smoke the ship stood out to sea.
Soon with a roaring rose the mighty fire,
And the pile crackled ; and between the logs
Sharp quivering tongues of flame shot out, and leap'd,
Curling and darting, higher, until they lick'd
The summit of the pile, the dead, the mast,
And ate the shrivelling sails ; but still the ship

Drove on, ablaze above her hull with fire.
And the Gods stood upon the beach, and
gaz'd.
And while they gaz'd, the sun went lurid
down
Into the smoke-wrapp'd seas, and night
came on.
Then the wind fell, with night, and there
was calm ;
But through the dark they watch'd the
burning ship
Still carried o'er the distant waters on,
Farther and farther, like an eye of fire.
And long, in the far dark, blaz'd Balder's
pile ;
But fainter, as the stars rose high, it
flar'd ;
The bodies were consum'd, ash chok'd the
pile.
And as, in a decaying winter-fire,
A charr'd log, falling, makes a shower of
sparks —
So with a shower of sparks the pile fell in,
Reddening the sea around ; and all was
dark.
  But the Gods went by starlight up the
shore
To Asgard, and sate down in Odin's hall
At table, and the funeral-feast began.
All night they ate the boar Serimner's
flesh,
And from their horns, with silver rimm'd,
drank mead,
Silent, and waited for the sacred morn.

THE FORSAKEN MERMAN

COME, dear children, let us away ;
Down and away below !
Now my brothers call from the bay,
Now the great winds shoreward blow,
Now the salt tides seaward flow ;
Now the wild white horses play,
Champ and chafe and toss in the spray.
Children dear, let us away !
This way, this way !

Call her once before you go —
Call once yet !
In a voice that she will know :
" Margaret ! Margaret ! "
Children's voices should be dear
(Call once more) to a mother's ear ;
Children's voices, wild with pain —
Surely she will come again !

Call her once and come away ;
This way, this way !
" Mother dear, we cannot stay !
The wild white horses foam and fret."
Margaret ! Margaret !

Come, dear children, come away down ;
Call no more !
One last look at the white-wall'd town,
And the little gray church on the windy
shore ;
Then come down !
She will not come though you call all day ;
Come away, come away !

Children dear, was it yesterday
We heard the sweet bells over the bay ?
In the caverns where we lay,
Through the surf and through the swell,
The far-off sound of a silver bell ?
Sand-strewn caverns, cool and deep,
Where the winds are all asleep ;
Where the spent lights quiver and gleam,
Where the salt weed sways in the stream,
Where the sea-beasts, ranged all round,
Feed in the ooze of their pasture-ground ;
Where the sea-snakes coil and twine,
Dry their mail and bask in the brine ;
Where great whales come sailing by,
Sail and sail, with unshut eye,
Round the world for ever and aye ?
When did music come this way ?
Children dear, was it yesterday ?

Children dear, was it yesterday
(Call yet once) that she went away ?
Once she sate with you and me,
On a red gold throne in the heart of the sea,
And the youngest sate on her knee.
She comb'd its bright hair, and she tended
it well,
When down swung the sound of a far-off
bell.
She sigh'd, she look'd up through the clear
green sea ;
She said : " I must go, for my kinsfolk
pray
In the little gray church on the shore to-
day.
'T will be Easter-time in the world — ah
me !
And I lose my poor soul, Merman ! here
with thee."
I said : " Go up, dear heart, through the
waves ;

Say thy prayer, and come back to the kind
    sea-caves ! "
She smil'd, she went up through the surf
    in the bay.

Children dear, was it yesterday ?
Children dear, were we long alone ?
" The sea grows stormy, the little ones
    moan ;"
Long prayers," I said, " in the world they
    say ;
Come ! " I said ; and we rose through the
    surf in the bay.
We went up the beach, by the sandy down
Where the sea-stocks bloom, to the white-
    wall'd town ;
Through the narrow pav'd streets, where
    all was still,
To the little gray church on the windy
    hill.
From the church came a murmur of folk
    at their prayers,
But we stood without in the cold blowing
    airs.
We climb'd on the graves, on the stones
    worn with rains,
And we gaz'd up the aisle through the
    small leaded panes.
She sate by the pillar ; we saw her clear :
" Margaret, hist ! come quick, we are here !
Dear heart," I said, " we are long alone ;
The sea grows stormy, the little ones moan."
But, ah, she gave me never a look,
For her eyes were seal'd to the holy book !
Loud prays the priest : shut stands the door.
Come away, children, call no more!
Come away, come down, call no more !

Down, down, down !
Down to the depths of the sea !
She sits at her wheel in the humming town,
Singing most joyfully.
Hark what she sings : " O joy, O joy,
For the humming street, and the child with
    its toy !
For the priest, and the bell, and the holy
    well ;
For the wheel where I spun,
And the blessed light of the sun ! "
And so she sings her fill,
Singing most joyfully,
Till the spindle drops from her hand,
And the whizzing wheel stands still.
She steals to the window, and looks at the
    sand,

And over the sand at the sea ;
And her eyes are set in a stare ;
And anon there breaks a sigh,
And anon there drops a tear,
From a sorrow-clouded eye,
And a heart sorrow-laden,
A long, long sigh;
For the cold strange eyes of a little Mer-
    maiden
And the gleam of her golden hair.

Come away, away, children ;
Come, children, come down !
The hoarse wind blows colder ;
Lights shine in the town.
She will start from her slumber
When gusts shake the door ;
She will hear the winds howling,
Will hear the waves roar.
We shall see, while above us
The waves roar and whirl,
A ceiling of amber,
A pavement of pearl.
Singing : " Here came a mortal,
But faithless was she !
And alone dwell for ever
The kings of the sea."

But, children, at midnight,
When soft the winds blow,
When clear falls the moonlight,
When spring-tides are low ;
When sweet airs come seaward
From heaths starr'd with broom,
And high rocks throw mildly
On the blanch'd sands a gloom ;
Up the still, glistening beaches,
Up the creeks we will hie,
Over banks of bright seaweed
The ebb-tide leaves dry.
We will gaze, from the sand-hills,
At the white, sleeping town ;
At the church on the hill-side —
And then come back down.
Singing : " There dwells a lov'd one,
But cruel is she !
She left lonely for ever
The kings of the sea."

PHILOMELA

Hark ! ah, the nightingale —
The tawny-throated !
Hark, from that moonlit cedar what a
    burst !

What triumph ! hark ! — what pain !
O wanderer from a Grecian shore,
Still, after many years, in distant lands,
Still nourishing in thy bewilder'd brain
That wild, unquench'd, deep-sunken, old-
 world pain —
Say, will it never heal ?
And can this fragrant lawn
With its cool trees, and night,
And the sweet, tranquil Thames,
And moonshine, and the dew,
To thy rack'd heart and brain
Afford no balm ?

Dost thou to-night behold,
Here, through the moonlight on this English
 grass,
The unfriendly palace in the Thracian
 wild ?
Dost thou again peruse
With hot cheeks and sear'd eyes
The too clear web, and thy dumb sister's
 shame ?
Dost thou once more assay
Thy flight, and feel come over thee,
Poor fugitive, the feathery change
Once more, and once more seem to make
 resound
With love and hate, triumph and agony,
Lone Daulis, and the high Cephissian vale ?
Listen, Eugenia —
How thick the bursts come crowding
 through the leaves !
Again — thou hearest ?
Eternal passion !
Eternal pain !

DOVER BEACH

The sea is calm to-night.
The tide is full, the moon lies fair
Upon the straits ; — on the French coast the
 light
Gleams and is gone ; the cliffs of England
 stand,
Glimmering and vast, out in the tranquil
 bay.
Come to the window, sweet is the night-
 air !
Only, from the long line of spray
Where the sea meets the moon-blanch'd
 sand,
Listen ! you hear the grating roar
Of pebbles which the waves draw back, and
 fling,

At their return, up the high strand,
Begin, and cease, and then again begin,
With tremulous cadence slow, and bring
The eternal note of sadness in.

Sophocles long ago
Heard it on the Ægæan, and it brought
Into his mind the turbid ebb and flow
Of human misery ; we
Find also in the sound a thought,
Hearing it by this distant northern sea.

The sea of faith
Was once, too, at the full, and round earth's
 shore
Lay like the folds of a bright girdle furl'd.
But now I only hear
Its melancholy, long, withdrawing roar,
Retreating, to the breath
Of the night-winds, down the vast edges
 drear
And naked shingles of the world.

Ah, love, let us be true
To one another ! for the world, which
 seems
To lie before us like a land of dreams,
So various, so beautiful, so new,
Hath really neither joy, nor love, nor light,
Nor certitude, nor peace, nor help for pain ;
And we are here as on a darkling plain
Swept with confus'd alarms of struggle and
 flight,
Where ignorant armies clash by night.

FROM "EMPEDOCLES ON ETNA"

And you, ye stars,
Who slowly begin to marshal,
As of old, in the fields of heaven,
Your distant, melancholy lines !
Have you, too, surviv'd yourselves ?
Are you, too, what I fear to become ?
You, too, once liv'd ;
You too mov'd joyfully,
Among august companions,
In an older world, peopled by Gods,
In a mightier order,
The radiant, rejoicing, intelligent Sons of
 Heaven.
But now, ye kindle
Your lonely, cold-shining lights,
Unwilling lingerers
In the heavenly wilderness,

For a younger, ignoble world ;
And renew, by necessity,
Night after night your courses,
In echoing, unnear'd silence,
Above a race you know not —
Uncaring and undelighted,
Without friend and without home ;
Weary like us, though not
Weary with our weariness.

No, no, ye stars ! there is no death with
    you,
No languor, no decay ! languor and death,
They are with me, not you ! ye are alive —
Ye, and the pure dark ether where ye ride
Brilliant above me ! And thou, fiery world,
That sapp'st the vitals of this terrible
    mount
Upon whose charr'd and quaking crust I
    stand —
Thou, too, brimmest with life ! — the sea of
    cloud,
That heaves its white and billowy vapors up
To moat this isle of ashes from the world,
Lives ; and that other fainter sea, far down,
O'er whose lit floor a road of moonbeams
    leads
To Etna's Liparëan sister-fires
And the long dusky line of Italy —
That mild and luminous floor of waters
    lives,
With held-in joy swelling its heart ; I only,
Whose spring of hope is dried, whose spirit
    has fail'd,
I, who have not, like these, in solitude
Maintain'd courage and force, and in myself
Nurs'd an immortal vigor — I alone
Am dead to life and joy, therefore I read
In all things my own deadness.

THE BURIED LIFE

Light flows our war of mocking words,
    and yet,
Behold, with tears mine eyes are wet !
I feel a nameless sadness o'er me roll.
Yes, yes, we know that we can jest,
We know, we know that we can smile !
But there 's a something in this breast,
To which thy light words bring no rest,
And thy gay smiles no anodyne ;
Give me thy hand, and hush awhile,
And turn those limpid eyes on mine,
And let me read there, love ! thy inmost
    soul.

Alas ! is even love too weak
To unlock the heart, and let it speak ?
Are even lovers powerless to reveal
To one another what indeed they feel ?
I knew the mass of men conceal'd
Their thoughts, for fear that if reveal'd
They would by other men be met
With blank indifference, or with blame
    reprov'd ;
I knew they liv'd and mov'd
Trick'd in disguises, alien to the rest
Of men, and alien to themselves — and yet
The same heart beats in every human
    breast !

But we, my love ! — doth a like spell be-
    numb
Our hearts, our voices ? — must we too be
    dumb ?

Ah ! well for us, if even we,
Even for a moment, can get free
Our heart, and have our lips unchain'd ;
For that which seals them hath been deep-
    ordain'd !

Fate, which foresaw
How frivolous a baby man would be —
By what distractions he would be possess'd,
How he would pour himself in every strife,
And well-nigh change his own identity —
That it might keep from his capricious play
His genuine self, and force him to obey
Even in his own despite his being's law,
Bade through the deep recesses of our
    breast
The unregarded river of our life
Pursue with indiscernible flow its way ;
And that we should not see
The buried stream, and seem to be
Eddying at large in blind uncertainty,
Though driving on with it eternally.

But often, in the world's most crowded
    streets,
But often, in the din of strife,
There rises an unspeakable desire
After the knowledge of our buried life ;
A thirst to spend our fire and restless force
In tracking out our true, original course ;
A longing to inquire
Into the mystery of this heart which beats
So wild, so deep in us — to know
Whence our lives come and where they
    go.

And many a man in his own breast then
delves,
But deep enough, alas ! none ever mines.
And we have been on many thousand lines,
And we have shown, on each, spirit and
power ;
But hardly have we, for one little hour,
Been on our own line, have we been our-
selves —
Hardly had skill to utter one of all
The nameless feelings that course through
our breast,
But they course on for ever unexpress'd.
And long we try in vain to speak and act
Our hidden self, and what we say and do
Is eloquent, is well —but 't is not true !
And then we will no more be rack'd
With inward striving, and demand
Of all the thousand nothings of the hour
Their stupefying power ;
Ah yes, and they benumb us at our call !
Yet still, from time to time, vague and
forlorn,
From the soul's subterranean depth upborne
As from an infinitely distant land,
Come airs, and floating echoes, and convey
A melancholy into all our day.

Only — but this is rare —
When a beloved hand is laid in ours,
When, jaded with the rush and glare
Of the interminable hours,
Our eyes can in another's eyes read clear,
When our world-deafen'd ear
Is by the tones of a lov'd voice caress'd —
A bolt is shot back somewhere in our
breast,
And a lost pulse of feeling stirs again.
The eye sinks inward, and the heart lies
plain,
And what we mean, we say, and what we
would, we know.
A man becomes aware of his life's flow,
And hears its winding murmur, and he sees
The meadows where it glides, the sun, the
breeze.

And there arrives a lull in the hot race
Wherein he doth for ever chase
The flying and elusive shadow, rest.
An air of coolness plays upon his face,
And an unwonted calm pervades his breast.
And then he thinks he knows
The hills where his life rose,
And the sea where it goes.

MEMORIAL VERSES

APRIL, 1850

GOETHE in Weimar sleeps, and Greece,
Long since, saw Byron's struggle cease.
But one such death remain'd to come ;
The last poetic voice is dumb —
We stand to-day by Wordsworth's tomb.

When Byron's eyes were shut in death,
We bow'd our head and held our breath.
He taught us little ; but our soul
Had *felt* him like the thunder's roll.
With shivering heart the strife we saw
Of passion with eternal law ;
And yet with reverential awe
We watch'd the fount of fiery life
Which serv'd for that Titanic strife.

When Goethe's death was told, we said :
Sunk, then, is Europe's sagest head.
Physician of the iron age,
Goethe has done his pilgrimage.
He took the suffering human race,
He read each wound, each weakness clear :
And struck his finger on the place,
And said : *Thou ailest here, and here !*
He look'd on Europe's dying hour
Of fitful dream and feverish power ;
His eye plunged down the weltering strife,
The turmoil of expiring life —
He said : *The end is everywhere,
Art still has truth, take refuge there !*
And he was happy, if to know
Causes of things, and far below
His feet to see the lurid flow
Of terror, and insane distress,
And headlong fate, be happiness.

And Wordsworth ! — Ah, pale ghosts, re-
joice !
For never has such soothing voice
Been to your shadowy world convey'd,
Since erst, at morn, some wandering shade
Heard the clear song of Orpheus come
Through Hades, and the mournful gloom.
Wordsworth has gone from us — and ye,
Ah, may ye feel his voice as we !
He too upon a wintery clime
Had fallen —on this iron time
Of doubts, disputes, distractions, fears.
He found us when the age had bound
Our souls in its benumbing round ;
He spoke, and loos'd our hearts in tears.

He laid us as we lay at birth
On the cool flowery lap of earth,
Smiles broke from us, and we had ease ;
The hills were round us, and the breeze
Went o'er the sun-lit fields again ;
Our foreheads felt the wind and rain.
Our youth return'd ; for there was shed
On spirits that had long been dead,
Spirits dried up and closely furl'd,
The freshness of the early world.

Ah ! since dark days still bring to light
Man's prudence and man's fiery might,
Time may restore us in his course
Goethe's sage mind and Byron's force ;
But where will Europe's latter hour
Again find Wordsworth's healing power ?
Others will teach us how to dare,
And against fear our breast to steel ;
Others will strengthen us to bear —
But who, ah ! who, will make us feel ?
The cloud of mortal destiny,
Others will front it fearlessly —
But who, like him, will put it by ?
Keep fresh the grass upon his grave,
O Rotha, with thy living wave !
Sing him thy best ! for few or none
Hears thy voice right, now he is gone.

GEIST'S GRAVE

FOUR years ! — and didst thou stay above
The ground, which hides thee now, but four ?
And all that life, and all that love,
Were crowded, Geist ! into no more ?

Only four years those winning ways,
Which make me for thy presence yearn,
Call'd us to pet thee or to praise,
Dear little friend ! at every turn ?

That loving heart, that patient soul,
Had they indeed no longer span,
To run their course, and reach their goal,
And read their homily to man ?

That liquid, melancholy eye,
From whose pathetic, soul-fed springs
Seem'd urging the Virgilian cry,[1]
The sense of tears in mortal things —

That steadfast, mournful strain, consol'd
By spirits gloriously gay,
And temper of heroic mould —
What, was four years their whole short day ?

Yes, only four ! — and not the course
Of all the centuries yet to come,
And not the infinite resource
Of Nature, with her countless sum

Of figures, with her fulness vast
Of new creation evermore,
Can ever quite repeat the past,
Or just thy little self restore.

Stern law of every mortal lot !
Which man, proud man, finds hard to
      bear,
And builds himself I know not what
Of second life I know not where.

But thou, when struck thine hour to go,
On us, who stood despondent by,
A meek last glance of love didst throw,
And humbly lay thee down to die.

Yet would we keep thee in our heart —
Would fix our favorite on the scene,
Nor let thee utterly depart
And be as if thou ne'er hadst been.

And so there rise these lines of verse
On lips that rarely form them now ;
While to each other we rehearse :
Such ways, such arts, such looks hadst thou !

We stroke thy broad brown paws again,
We bid thee to thy vacant chair,
We greet thee by the window-pane,
We hear thy scuffle on the stair.

We see the flaps of thy large ears
Quick rais'd to ask which way we go ;
Crossing the frozen lake, appears
Thy small black figure on the snow !

Nor to us only art thou dear
Who mourn thee in thine English home :
Thou hast thine absent master's tear,
Dropp'd by the far Australian foam.

Thy memory lasts both here and there,
And thou shalt live as long as we.
And after that — thou dost not care !
In us was all the world to thee.

Yet, fondly zealous for thy fame,
Even to a date beyond our own
We strive to carry down thy name,
By mounded turf, and graven stone.

[1] Sunt lacrimæ rerum !

We lay thee, close within our reach,
Here, where the grass is smooth and warm,
Between the holly and the beech,
Where oft we watch'd thy couchant form,

Asleep, yet lending half an ear
To travellers on the Portsmouth road ; —
There build we thee, O guardian dear,
Mark'd with a stone, thy last abode !

Then some, who through this garden pass,
When we too, like thyself, are clay,
Shall see thy grave upon the grass,
And stop before the stone, and say :

People who lived here long ago
Did by this stone, it seems, intend
To name for future times to know
The dachs-hound, Geist, their little friend.

Charles Kent

POPE AT TWICKENHAM

BEYOND a hundred years and more,
A garden lattice like a door
   Stands open in the sun,
Admitting fitful winds that set
Astir the fragrant mignonette
   In waves of speckled dun :

Sweet waves, above whose odorous flow
Red roses bud, red roses blow,
   In beds that gem the lawn —
Enamell'd rings and stars of flowers,
By summer beams and vernal showers
   From earth nutritious drawn.

Within the broad bay-window, there,
Lo ! huddled in his easy-chair,
   One hand upon his knee,
A hand so thin, so wan, so frail,
It tells of pains and griefs a tale,
   A small bent form I see.

The day is fair, the hour is noon,
From neighboring thicket thrills the boon
   The nuthatch yields in song :
All drench'd with recent rains, the leaves
Are dripping — drip the sheltering eaves,
   The dropping notes among.

And twinkling diamonds in the grass
Show where the flitting zephyrs pass,
   That shake the green blades dry ;
And golden radiance fills the air
And gilds the floating gossamer
   That glints and trembles by.

Yet, blind to each familiar grace,
Strange anguish on his pallid face,
   And eyes of dreamful hue,

That lonely man sits brooding there,
Still huddled in his easy-chair,
   With memories life will rue.

Where bay might crown that honor'd
   head,
A homely crumpled nightcap spread
   Half veils the careworn brows ;
In morning-gown of rare brocade
His puny shrunken shape array'd
   His sorrowing soul avows :

Avows in every dropping line
Dejection words not thus define
   So eloquent of woe ;
Yet never to those mournful eyes,
The heart's full-brimming fountains, rise
   Sweet tears to overflow.

No token here of studied grief,
But plainest signs that win belief,
   A simple scene and true.
Beside the mourner's chair display'd,
The matin meal's slight comforts laid
   Trimly the board bestrew.

'Mid silvery sheen of burnish'd plate,
The chill'd and tarnish'd chocolate
   On snow-white damask stands ;
Untouch'd the trivial lures remain
In dainty pink-tinged porcelain,
   Still ranged by usual hands.

A drowsy bee above the cream
Hums loitering in the sunny gleam
   That tips each rim with gold ;
A checker'd maze of light and gloom
Floats in the quaintly-litter'd room
   With varying charms untold.

Why sits that silent watcher there,
Still brooding with that face of care,
  That gaze of tearless pain ?
What bonds of woe his spirit bind,
What treasure lost can leave behind
  Such stings within his brain ?

He dreams of one who lies above,
He never more in life can love —
  That mother newly dead ;

He waits the artist-friend whose skill
Shall catch the angel-beauty still
  Upon her features spread.

A reverent sorrow fills the air,
And makes a throne of grief the chair
  Where filial genius mourns :
Death proving still, at direst need,
Life's sceptre-wand — a broken reed,
  Love's wreath — a crown of thorns.

William Caldwell Roscoe

TO LA SANSCŒUR

I know not how to call you light,
Since I myself was lighter ;
Nor can you blame my changing plight
Who were the first inviter.

I know not which began to range
Since we were never constant ;
And each when each began to change
Was found a weak remonstrant.

But this I know, the God of Love
Doth shake his hand against us,
And scorning says we ne'er did prove
True passion — but pretences.

THE MASTER-CHORD

Like a musician that with flying finger
Startles the voice of some new instrument,
And, though he know that in one string are
    blent
All its extremes of sound, yet still doth lin-
    ger
Among the lighter threads, fearing to start
The deep soul of that one melodious wire,
Lest it, unanswering, dash his high desire,

And spoil the hopes of his expectant heart ;
Thus, with my mistress oft conversing, I
Stir every lighter theme with careless voice,
Gathering sweet music and celestial joys
From the harmonious soul o'er which I fly ;
Yet o'er the one deep master-chord I hover,
And dare not stoop, fearing to tell — I love
    her.

EARTH

Sad is my lot ; among the shining spheres
Wheeling, I weave incessant day and night,
And ever, in my never-ending flight,
Add woes to woes, and count up tears on
    tears.
Young wives' and new-born infants' hapless
    biers
Lie on my breast, a melancholy sight ;
Fresh griefs abhor my fresh returning light ;
Pain and remorse and want fill up my years.
My happier children's farther-piercing eyes
Into the blessed solvent future climb,
And knit the threads of joy and hope and
    warning ;
But I, the ancient mother, am not wise,
And, shut within the blind obscure of time,
Roll on from morn to night, and on from
    night to morning.

William Johnson Cory

MIMNERMUS IN CHURCH

You promise heavens free from strife,
  Pure truth, and perfect change of will ;
But sweet, sweet is this human life,
  So sweet, I fain would breathe it
    still ;

Your chilly stars I can forego,
This warm kind world is all I know.

You say there is no substance here,
  One great reality above :
Back from that void I shrink in fear,
  And child-like hide myself in love.

Show me what angels feel.   Till then,
I cling, a mere weak man, to men.

You bid me lift my mean desires
    From faltering lips and fitful veins
To sexless souls, ideal quires,
    Unwearied voices, wordless strains :
My mind with fonder welcome owns
One dear dead friend's remember'd tones.

Forsooth the present we must give
    To that which cannot pass away ;
All beauteous things for which we live
By laws of time and space decay.
But oh, the very reason why
I clasp them, is because they die.

HERACLEITUS[1]

THEY told me, Heracleitus, they told me
    you were dead,
They brought me bitter news to hear and
    bitter tears to shed.
I wept, as I remember'd how often you
    and I
Had tir'd the sun with talking and sent him
    down the sky.

And now that thou art lying, my dear old
    Carian guest,
A handful of gray ashes, long, long ago at
    rest,

Still are thy pleasant voices, thy nightin-
    gales, awake ;
For Death, he taketh all away, but them
    he cannot take.

A POOR FRENCH SAILOR'S SCOTTISH SWEETHEART

I CANNOT forget my Joe,
    I bid him be mine in sleep ;
But battle and woe have changed him so
    There's nothing to do but weep.

My mother rebukes me yet,
    And I never was meek before ;
His jacket is wet, his lip cold set,
    He'll trouble our home no more.

Oh, breaker of reeds that bend !
    Oh, quencher of tow that smokes !
I'd rather descend to my sailor friend
    Than prosper with lofty folks.

I'm lying beside the gowan,
    My Joe in the English bay ;
I'm Annie Rowan, his Annie Rowan,
    He called me his Bien-Aimée.

I'll hearken to all you quote,
    Though I'd rather be deaf and free ;
The little he wrote in the sinking boat
    Is Bible and charm for me.

Author Unfound

EPITAPH OF DIONYSIA

HERE doth Dionysia lie :
She whose little wanton foot,
Tripping (ah, too carelessly !),
Touch'd this tomb, and fell into't.

Trip no more shall she, nor fall.
And her trippings were so few !
Summers only eight in all
Had the sweet child wander'd through.

But, already, life's few suns
Love's strong seeds had ripen'd warm.
All her ways were winning ones ;
All her cunning was to charm.

And the fancy, in the flower,
While the flesh was in the bud,
Childhood's dawning sex did dower
With warm gusts of womanhood.

Oh what joys by hope begun,
Oh what kisses kiss'd by thought,
What love-deeds by fancy done,
Death to endless dust hath wrought !

Had the fates been kind as thou,
Who, till now, was never cold,
Once Love's aptest scholar, now
Thou hadst been his teacher bold ;

[1] After Callimachus.

But, if buried seeds upthrow
Fruits and flowers ; if flower and fruit
By their nature fitly show
What the seeds are, whence they shoot,

Dionysia, o'er this tomb,
Where thy buried beauties be,
From their dust shall spring and bloom
Loves and graces like to thee.

Coventry Patmore

FROM "THE ANGEL IN THE HOUSE"

THE DEAN'S CONSENT

THE Ladies rose. I held the door,
  And sigh'd, as her departing grace
Assur'd me that she always wore
  A heart as happy as her face ;
And, jealous of the winds that blew,
  I dreaded, o'er the tasteless wine,
What fortune momently might do
  To hurt the hope that she 'd be mine.

Towards my mark the Dean's talk set :
  He praised my "Notes on Abury,"
Read when the Association met
  At Sarum ; he was pleas'd to see
I had not stopp'd, as some men had,
  At Wrangler and Prize Poet ; last,
He hop'd the business was not bad
  I came about : then the wine pass'd.

A full glass prefaced my reply :
  I lov'd his daughter, Honor ; I told
My estate and prospects ; might I try
  To win her ? At my words so bold
My sick heart sank. Then he : He gave
  His glad consent, if I could get
Her love. A dear, good Girl ! she 'd have
  Only three thousand pounds as yet ;
More by and by. Yes, his good will
  Should go with me ; he would not stir ;

He and my father in old time still
  Wish'd I should one day marry her ;
But God so seldom lets us take
  Our chosen pathway, when it lies
In steps that either mar or make
  Or alter others' destinies,
That, though his blessing and his pray'r
  Had help'd, should help, my suit, yet he
Left all to me, his passive share
  Consent and opportunity.

My chance, he hop'd, was good : I 'd won
  Some name already ; friends and place
Appear'd within my reach, but none
  Her mind and manners would not grace.
Girls love to see the men in whom
  They invest their vanities admir'd ;
Besides, where goodness is, there room
  For good to work will be desir'd.
'T was so with one now pass'd away ;
  And what she was at twenty-two,
Honor was now ; and he might say
  Mine was a choice I could not rue.

He ceas'd, and gave his hand. He had
  won
  (And all my heart was in my word)
From me the affection of a son,
  Whichever fortune Heaven conferr'd !
Well, well, would I take more wine ? Then
  go
To her ; she makes tea on the lawn
  These fine warm afternoons. And so
  We went whither my soul was drawn ;
And her light-hearted ignorance
  Of interest in our discourse
Fill'd me with love, and seem'd to enhance
  Her beauty with pathetic force,
As, through the flowery mazes sweet,
  Fronting the wind that flutter'd blithe,
And lov'd her shape, and kiss'd her feet,
  Shown to their insteps proud and lithe,
She approach'd, all mildness and young
  trust,
  And ever her chaste and noble air
Gave to love's feast its choicest gust,
  A vague, faint augury of despair.

HONORIA'S SURRENDER

From little signs, like little stars,
  Whose faint impression on the sense
The very looking straight at mars,
  Or only seen by confluence ;
From instinct of a mutual thought,
  Whence sanctity of manners flow'd ;

From chance unconscious, and from what
　Concealment, overconscious, show'd ;
Her hand's less weight upon my arm,
　Her lovelier mien ; that match'd with
　　this ;
I found, and felt with strange alarm,
　I stood committed to my bliss.

I grew assur'd, before I ask'd,
　That she 'd be mine without reserve,
And in her unclaim'd graces bask'd,
　At leisure, till the time should serve,
With just enough of dread to thrill
　The hope, and make it trebly dear ;
Thus loth to speak the word to kill
　Either the hope or happy fear.

Till once, through lanes returning late,
　Her laughing sisters lagg'd behind ;
And, ere we reach'd her father's gate,
　We paus'd with one presentient mind ;
And, in the dim and perfum'd mist,
　Their coming stay'd, who, friends to me,
And very women, lov'd to assist
　Love's timid opportunity.

Twice rose, twice died my trembling word ;
　The faint and frail Cathedral chimes
Spake time in music, and we heard
　The chafers rustling in the limes.
Her dress, that touch'd me where I stood,
　The warmth of her confided arm,
Her bosom's gentle neighborhood,
　Her pleasure in her power to charm ;
Her look, her love, her form, her touch,
　The least seem'd most by blissful turn,
Blissful but that it pleas'd too much,
　And taught the wayward soul to yearn.
It was as if a harp with wires
　Was travers'd by the breath I drew ;
And, oh, sweet meeting of desires,
　She, answering, own'd that she lov'd too.

Honoria was to be my bride !
　The hopeless heights of hope were scal'd ;
The summit won, I paus'd and sigh'd,
　As if success itself had fail'd.
It seem'd as if my lips approach'd
　To touch at Tantalus' reward,
And rashly on Eden life encroach'd,
　Half-blinded by the flaming sword.
The whole world's wealthiest and its best,
　So fiercely sought, appear'd, when found,
Poor in its need to be possess'd,
　Poor from its very want of bound.

My queen was crouching at my side,
　By love unsceptred and brought low,
Her awful garb of maiden pride
　All melted into tears like snow ;
The mistress of my reverent thought,
　Whose praise was all I ask'd of fame,
In my close-watch'd approval sought
　Protection as from danger and blame ;
Her soul, which late I lov'd to invest
　With pity for my poor desert,
Buried its face within my breast,
　Like a pet fawn by hunters hurt.

THE MARRIED LOVER

Why, having won her, do I woo ?
　Because her spirit's vestal grace
Provokes me always to pursue,
　But, spirit-like, eludes embrace ;
Because her womanhood is such
　That, as on court-days subjects kiss
The Queen's hand, yet so near a touch
　Affirms no mean familiarness,
Nay, rather marks more fair the height
　Which can with safety so neglect
To dread, as lower ladies might,
　That grace could meet with disrespect,
Thus she with happy favor feeds
　Allegiance from a love so high
That thence no false conceit proceeds
　Of difference bridged, or state put by ;
Because, although in act and word
　As lowly as a wife can be,
Her manners, when they call me lord,
　Remind me 't is by courtesy ;
Not with her least consent of will,
　Which would my proud affection hurt,
But by the noble style that still
　Imputes an unattain'd desert ;
Because her gay and lofty brows,
　When all is won which hope can ask,
Reflect a light of hopeless snows
　That bright in virgin ether bask ;
Because, though free of the outer court
　I am, this Temple keeps its shrine
Sacred to Heaven ; because, in short,
　She 's not and never can be mine.

Feasts satiate ; stars distress with height ;
　Friendship means well, but misses reach,
And wearies in its best delight
　Vex'd with the vanities of speech ;
Too long regarded, roses even
　Afflict the mind with fond unrest ;
And to converse direct with Heaven
　Is oft a labor in the breast ;

Whate'er the up-looking soul admires,
Whate'er the senses' banquet be,
Fatigues at last with vain desires,
Or sickens by satiety ;
But truly my delight was more
In her to whom I 'm bound for aye
Yesterday than the day before,
And more to-day than yesterday.

THE GIRL OF ALL PERIODS

" AND even our women," lastly grumbles
Ben,
" Leaving their nature, dress and talk like
men ! "
A damsel, as our train stops at Five Ashes,
Down to the station in a dog-cart dashes.
A footman buys her ticket, " Third class,
parly ; "
And, in huge-button'd coat and " Cham-
pagne Charley "
And such scant manhood else as use allows
her,
Her two shy knees bound in a single trouser,
With, 'twixt her shapely lips, a violet
Perch'd as a proxy for a cigarette,
She takes her window in our smoking car-
riage,
And scans us, calmly scorning men and
marriage.
Ben frowns in silence ; older, I know bet-
ter
Than to read ladies 'havior in the letter.
This aping man is crafty Love's devising
To make the woman's difference more sur-
prising ;
And, as for feeling wroth at such rebelling,
Who 'd scold the child for now and then
repelling
Lures with " I won't ! " or for a moment's
straying
In its sure growth towards more full obey-
ing ?
" Yes, she had read the ' Legend of the
Ages,'
And George Sand too, skipping the wicked
pages."
And, whilst we talk'd, her protest firm and
perky
Against mankind, I thought, grew lax and
jerky ;
And, at a compliment, her mouth's com-
pressure
Nipp'd in its birth a little laugh of pleas-
ure ;

And smiles, forbidden her lips, as weakness
horrid,
Broke, in grave lights, from eyes and chin
and forehead ; .
And, as I push'd kind 'vantage 'gainst the
scorner,
The two shy knees press'd shyer to the cor-
ner ;
And Ben began to talk with her, the rather
Because he found out that he knew her
father,
Sir Francis Applegarth, of Fenny Compton,
And danced once with her sister Maude at
Brompton ;
And then he star'd until he quite confus'd
her,
More pleas'd with her than I, who but ex-
cus'd her ;
And, when she got out, he, with sheepish
glances,
Said he 'd stop too, and call on old Sir
Francis.

FROM "THE UNKNOWN EROS"

THE TOYS

MY little son, who look'd from thought-
ful eyes
And mov'd and spoke in quiet grown-up
wise,
Having my law the seventh time disobey'd,
I struck him, and dismiss'd
With hard words and unkiss'd,
His Mother, who was patient, being dead.
Then, fearing lest his grief should hinder
sleep,
I visited his bed,
But found him slumbering deep,
With darken'd eyelids, and their lashes yet
From his late sobbing wet.
And I, with moan,
Kissing away his tears, left others of my
own ;
For, on a table drawn beside his head,
He had put, within his reach,
A box of counters and a red-vein'd stone,
A piece of glass abraded by the beach,
And six or seven shells,
A bottle with bluebells
And two French copper coins, ranged there
with careful art,
To comfort his sad heart.
So when that night I pray'd
To God, I wept, and said :

Ah, when at last we lie with tranced breath,
Not vexing Thee in death,
And Thou rememberest of what toys
We made our joys,.
How weakly understood
Thy great commanded good,
Then, fatherly not less
Than I whom Thou hast moulded from the
    clay,
Thou 'lt leave Thy wrath, and say,
" I will be sorry for their childishness."

THE TWO DESERTS

Not greatly mov'd with awe am I
To learn that we may spy
Five thousand firmaments beyond our own.
The best that 's known
Of the heavenly bodies does them credit
    small.
View'd close, the Moon's fair ball
Is of ill objects worst,
A corpse in Night's highway, naked, fire-
    scarr'd, accurst ;
And now they tell
That the Sun is plainly seen to boil and
    burst
Too horribly for hell.
So, judging from these two,
As we must do,
The Universe, outside our living Earth,
Was all conceiv'd in the Creator's mirth,
Forecasting at the time Man's spirit deep,
To make dirt cheap.
Put by the Telescope !
Better without it man may see,
Stretch'd awful in the hush'd midnight,
The ghost of his eternity.

Give me the nobler glass that swells to the
    eye
The things which near us lie,
Till Science rapturously hails,
In the minutest water-drop,
A torment of innumerable tails.
These at the least do live.
But rather give
A mind not much to pry
Beyond our royal-fair estate
Betwixt these deserts blank of small and
    great.
Wonder and beauty our own courtiers are,
Pressing to catch our gaze,
And out of obvious ways
Ne'er wandering far.

REGINA CŒLI

SAY, did his sisters wonder what could
    Joseph see
In a mild, silent little Maid like thee ?
And was it awful, in that narrow house,
With God for Babe and Spouse ?
Nay, like thy simple, female sort, each one
Apt to find Him in Husband and in Son,
Nothing to theé came strange in this.
Thy wonder was but wondrous bliss :
Wondrous, for, though
True Virgin lives not but does know,
(Howbeit none ever yet confess'd,)
That God lies really in her breast,
Of thine He made His special nest !
And so
All mothers worship little feet,
And kiss the very ground they 've trod ;
But, ah, thy little Baby sweet
Who was indeed thy God !

Walter C. Smith

DAUGHTERS OF PHILISTIA

FROM " OLRIG GRANGE "

LADY ANNE DEWHURST on a crimson couch
Lay, with a rug of sable o'er her knees,
In a bright boudoir in Belgravia ;
Most perfectly array'd in shapely robe
Of sumptuous satin, lit up here and there
With scarlet touches, and with costly lace,
Nice-finger'd maidens knotted in Brabant ;

And all around her spread magnificence
Of bronzes, Sèvres vases, marquetrie,
Rare buhl, and bric-à-brac of every kind,
From Rome and Paris and the centuries
Of far-off beauty. All of goodly color,
Or graceful form that could delight the
    eye,
In orderly disorder lay around,
And flowers with perfume scented the
    warm air.

Stately and large and beautiful was she
Spite of her sixty summers, with an eye
Train'd to soft languors, that could also
    flash,
Keen as a sword and sharp — a black
    bright eye,
Deep sunk beneath an arch of jet. She had
A weary look, and yet the weariness
Seem'd not so native as the worldliness
Which blended with it. Weary and
    worldly, she
Had quite resign'd herself to misery
In this sad vale of tears, but fully meant
To nurse her sorrow in a sumptuous fashion,
And make it an expensive luxury ;
For nothing she esteem'd that nothing cost.

Beside her, on a table round, inlaid
With precious stones by Roman art de-
    sign'd,
Lay phials, scent, a novel and a Bible,
A pill box, and a wine glass, and a book
On the Apocalypse ; for she was much
Addicted unto physic and religion,
And her physician had prescrib'd for her
Jellies and wines and cheerful Literature.
The Book on the Apocalypse was writ
By her chosen pastor, and she took the
    novel
With the dry sherry, and the pills pre-
    scrib'd.
A gorgeous, pious, comfortable life
Of misery she lived ; and all the sins
Of all her house, and all the nation's sins,
And all shortcomings of the Church and
    State,
And all the sins of all the world beside,
Bore as her special cross, confessing them
Vicariously day by day, and then
She comforted her heart, which needed it,
With bric-à-brac and jelly and old wine.

Beside the fire, her elbow on the mantel,
And forehead resting on her finger-tips,
Shading a face where sometimes loom'd a
    frown,
And sometimes flash'd a gleam of bitter
    scorn,
Her daughter stood ; no more a graceful
    girl,
But in the glory of her womanhood,
Stately and haughty. One who might have
    been
A noble woman in a nobler world,
But now was only woman of her world ;

With just enough of better thought to
    know
It was not noble, and despise it all,
And most herself for making it her all.
A woman, complex, intricate, involv'd ;
Wrestling with self, yet still by self sub-
    dued ;
Scorning herself for being what she was,
And yet unable to be that she would ;
Uneasy with the sense of possible good
Never attain'd, nor sought, except in fits
Ending in failures ; conscious, too, of power
Which found no purpose to direct its force,
And so came back upon herself, and grew
An inward fret. The caged bird some-
    times dash'd
Against the wires, and sometimes sat and
    pin'd,
But mainly peck'd her sugar, and eyed her
    glass,
And trill'd her graver thoughts away in
    song.

Mother and daughter — yet a childless
    mother,
And motherless her daughter ; for the
    world
Had gash'd a chasm between, impassable,
And they had nought in common, neither
    love,
Nor hate, nor anything except a name.
Yet both were of the world ; and she not
    least
Whose world was the religious one, and
    stretch'd
A kind of isthmus 'tween the Devil and
    God,
A slimy, oozy mud, where mandrakes grew,
Ghastly, with intertwisted roots, and things
Amphibious haunted, and the leathern bat
Flicker'd about its twilight evermore.

THE SELF-EXILED

THERE came a soul to the gate of Heaven
    ' Gliding slow —
A soul that was ransom'd and forgiven,
    And white as snow :
And the angels all were silent.

A mystic light beam'd from the face
    Of the radiant maid,
But there also lay on its tender grace
    A mystic shade :
And the angels all were silent.

As sunlit clouds by a zephyr borne
    Seem not to stir,
So to the golden gates of morn
    They carried her :
And the angels all were silent.

" Now open the gate, and let her in,
    And fling it wide,
For she has been cleans'd from stain of
    sin,"
    St. Peter cried :
And the angels all were silent.

" Though I am cleans'd from stain of sin,"
    She answer'd low,
" I came not hither to enter in,
    Nor may I go : "
And the angels all were silent.

" I come," she said, " to the pearly door,
    To see the Throne
Where sits the Lamb on the Sapphire Floor,
    With God alone : "
And the angels all were silent.

" I come to hear the new song they sing
    To Him that died,
And note where the healing waters spring
    From His pierced side : "
And the angels all were silent.

" But I may not enter there," she said,
    " For I must go
Across the gulf where the guilty dead
    Lie in their woe : "
And the angels all were silent.

" If I enter heaven I may not pass
    To where they be,
Though the wail of their bitter pain, alas !
    Tormenteth me : "
And the angels all were silent.

" If I enter heaven I may not speak
    My soul's desire
For them that are lying distraught and
    weak
    In flaming fire : "
And the angels all were silent.

" I had a brother, and also another
    Whom I lov'd well ;
What if, in anguish, they curse each other
    In the depths of hell ? "
And the angels all were silent.

" How could I touch the golden harps,
    When all my praise
Would be so wrought with grief-full warps
    Of their sad days ? "
And the angels all were silent.

" How love the lov'd who are sorrowing,
    And yet be glad ?
How sing the songs ye are fain to sing,
    While I am sad ? "
And the angels all were silent.

" Oh, clear as glass is the golden street
    Of the city fair,
And the tree of life it maketh sweet
    The lightsome air : "
And the angels all were silent.

" And the white-rob'd saints with their
    crowns and palms
    Are good to see,
And oh, so grand are the sounding psalms
    But not for me : "
And the angels all were silent.

" I come where there is no night," she said,
    " To go away,
And help, if I yet may help, the dead
    That have no day."
And the angels all were silent.

St. Peter he turned the keys about,
    And answer'd grim :
" Can you love the Lord, and abide with-
    out,
    Afar from Him ? "
And the angels all were silent.

" Can you love the Lord who died for you,
    And leave the place
Where His glory is all disclos'd to view,
    And tender grace ? "
And the angels all were silent.

" They go not out who come in here ;
    It were not meet :
Nothing they lack, for He is here,
    And bliss complete."
And the angels all were silent.

" Should I be nearer Christ," she said,
    " By pitying less
The sinful living or woeful dead
    In their helplessness ? "
And the angels all were silent.

" Should I be liker Christ were I
    To love no more
The lov'd, who in their anguish lie
    Outside the door ? "
And the angels all were silent.

" Did He not hang on the curs'd tree,
    And bear its shame,
And clasp to His heart, for love of me,
    My guilt and blame ? "
And the angels all were silent.

" Should I be liker, nearer Him,
    Forgetting this,
Singing all day with the Seraphim,
    In selfish bliss ? "
And the angels all were silent.

The Lord Himself stood by the gate,
    And heard her speak

Those tender words compassionate,
    Gentle and meek :
And the angels all were silent.

Now, pity is the touch of God
    In human hearts,
And from that way He ever trod
    He ne'er departs :
And the angels all were silent.

And He said, " Now will I go with you,
    Dear child of love,
I am weary of all this glory, too,
    In heaven above : "
And the angels all were silent.

" We will go seek and save the lost,
    If they will hear,
They who are worst but need me most,
    And all are dear : "
And the angels were not silent.

Francis Turner Palgrave

THE ANCIENT AND MODERN MUSES

THE monument outlasting bronze
    Was promis'd well by bards of old ;
The lucid outline of their lay
    Its sweet precision keeps for aye,
    Fix'd in the ductile language-gold.

But we who work with smaller skill,
    And less refin'd material mould, —
His close conglomerate English speech,
    Bequest of many tribes, that each
    Brought here and wrought at from of
        old,

Residuum rough, eked out by rhyme,
    Barbarian ornament uncouth, —
Our hope is less to last through Art
    Than deeper searching of the heart,
    Than broader range of utter'd truth.

One keen-cut group, one deed or aim
    Athenian Sophocles could show,
And rest content ; but Shakespeare's
       stage
Must hold the glass to every age, —
    A thousand forms and passions glow

Upon the world-wide canvas. So
    With larger scope our art we play ;
And if the crown be harder won,
Diviner rays around it run,
    With strains of fuller harmony.

PRO MORTUIS

WHAT should a man desire to leave ?
    A flawless work ; a noble life :
Some music harmoniz'd from strife,
Some finish'd thing, ere the slack hands at
       eve
    Drop, should be his to leave.

One gem of song, defying age ;
    A hard-won fight ; a well-work'd farm;
    A law no guile can twist to harm ;
Some tale, as our lost Thackeray's bright,
       or sage
    As the just Hallam's page.

Or, in life's homeliest, meanest spot,
    With temperate step from year to year
    To move within his little sphere,
Leaving a pure name to be known, or not, —
    This is a true man's lot.

He dies : he leaves the deed or name,
  A gift forever to his land,
  In trust to Friendship's prudent hand,
Round 'gainst all adverse shocks to guard
    his fame,
    Or to the world proclaim.

But the imperfect thing or thought, —
  The crudities and yeast of youth,
  The dubious doubt, the twilight truth,
The work that for the passing day was
    wrought,
    The schemes that came to nought,

The sketch half-way 'twixt verse and
    prose
  That mocks the finish'd picture true,
  The quarry whence the statue grew,
The scaffolding 'neath which the palace rose,
    The vague abortive throes

And fever-fits of joy or gloom : —
  In kind oblivion let them be !
  Nor has the dead worse foe than he
Who rakes these sweepings of the artist's
    room,
    And piles them on his tomb.

Ah, 't is but little that the best,
  Frail children of a fleeting hour,
  Can leave of perfect fruit or flower !
Ah, let all else be graciously supprest
    When man lies down to rest !

WILLIAM WORDSWORTH

1845

GENTLE and grave, in simple dress,
And features by keen mountain air
Moulded to solemn ruggedness,
The man we came to see sat there :
Not apt for speech, nor quickly stirr'd
Unless when heart to heart replied;
A bearing equally remov'd
From vain display or sullen pride.

The sinewy frame yet spoke of one
Known to the hillsides : on his head
Some five-and-seventy winters gone
Their crown of perfect white had shed: —
As snow-tipp'd summits toward the sun
In calm of lonely radiance press,
Touch'd by the broadening light of death
With a serener pensiveness.

O crown of venerable age !
O brighter crown of well-spent years !
The bard, the patriot, and the sage,
The heart that never bow'd to fears !
That was an age of soaring souls ;
Yet none with a more liberal scope
Survey'd the sphere of human things ;
None with such manliness of hope.

Others, perchance, as keenly felt,
As musically sang as he ;
To Nature as devoutly knelt,
Or toil'd to serve humanity :
But none with those ethereal notes,
That star-like sweep of self-control ;
The insight into worlds unseen,
The lucid sanity of soul.

The fever of our fretful life,
The autumn poison of the air,
The soul with its own self at strife,
He saw and felt, but could not share :
With eye made clear by pureness, pierce
The life of Man and Nature through ;
And read the heart of common things,
Till new seem'd old, and old was new.

To his own self not always just,
Bound in the bonds that all men share, —
Confess the failings as we must,
The lion's mark is always there !
Nor any song so pure, so great
Since his, who closed the sightless eyes
Our Homer of the war in Heaven,
To wake in his own Paradise.

O blaring trumpets of the world !
O glories, in their budding sere !
O flaunting roll of Fame unfurl'd !
Here was the king — the hero here !
It was a strength and joy for life
In that great presence once to be ;
That on the boy he gently smil'd,
That those white hands were laid on m

A LITTLE CHILD'S HYMN

FOR NIGHT AND MORNING

THOU that once, on mother's knee,
Wast a little one like me,
When I wake or go to bed
Lay thy hands about my head :
Let me feel thee very near,
Jesus Christ, our Saviour dear.

Be beside me in the light,
Close by me through all the night ;
Make me gentle, kind, and true,
Do what mother bids me do ;
Help and cheer me when I fret,
And forgive when I forget.

Once wast thou in cradle laid,
Baby bright in manger-shade,
With the oxen and the cows,
And the lambs outside the house :
Now thou art above the sky :
Canst thou hear a baby cry ?

Thou art nearer when we pray,
Since thou art so far away ;
Thou my little hymn wilt hear,
Jesus Christ, our Saviour dear,
Thou that once, on mother's knee,
Wast a little one like me.

A DANISH BARROW

ON THE EAST DEVON COAST

LIE still, old Dane, below thy heap !
A sturdy-back and sturdy-limb,
Whoe'er he was, I warrant him
Upon whose mound the single sheep
Browses and tinkles in the sun,
Within the narrow vale alone.

Lie still, old Dane ! This restful scene
Suits well thy centuries of sleep :
The soft brown roots above thee creep,

The lotus flaunts his ruddy sheen,
And, — vain memento of the spot, —
The turquoise-eyed forget-me-not.

Lie still ! Thy mother-land herself
Would know thee not again : no more
The Raven from the northern shore
Hails the bold crew to push for pelf,
Through fire and blood and slaughter'd
kings
'Neath the black terror of his wings.

And thou, — thy very name is lost !
The peasant only knows that here
Bold Alfred scoop'd thy flinty bier,
And pray'd a foeman's prayer, and tost
His auburn head, and said, "One more
Of England's foes guards England's
shore,"

And turn'd and pass'd to other feats,
And left thee in thine iron robe,
To circle with the circling globe,
While Time's corrosive dewdrop eats
The giant warrior to a crust
Of earth in earth, and rust in rust.

So lie : and let the children play
And sit like flowers upon thy grave
And crown with flowers, — that hardly
have
A briefer blooming-tide than they ; —
By hurrying years urged on to rest,
As thou, within the Mother's breast.

Thomas Henry Huxley

TENNYSON

(WESTMINSTER ABBEY: OCTOBER 12, 1892)

GIB DIESEN TODTEN MIR HERAUS ! [1]

(The Minster speaks)

BRING me my dead !
To me that have grown,
Stone laid upon stone,
As the stormy brood
Of English blood
Has wax'd and spread
And fill'd the world,
With sails unfurl'd ;

With men that may not lie ;
With thoughts that cannot die.

Bring me my dead !
Into the storied hall,
Where I have garner'd all
My harvest without weed ;
My chosen fruits of goodly seed ,
And lay him gently down among
The men of state, the men of song :
The men that would not suffer wrong :
The thought-worn chieftains of the mind :
Head-servants of the human kind.

[1] Don Carlos.

Bring me my dead !
The autumn sun shall shed
Its beams athwart the bier's
Heap'd blooms : a many tears
Shall flow ; his words, in cadence sweet and
    strong,
Shall voice the full hearts of the silent
    throng.
Bring me my dead !

And oh ! sad wedded mourner, seeking sti
For vanish'd hand clasp : drinking in th
    fill
Of holy grief ; forgive, that pious theft
Robs thee of all, save memories, left :
Not thine to kneel beside the grassy moun
While dies the western glow ; and all aroun
Is silence ; and the shadows closer creep
And whisper softly : All must fall asleep.

Arthur Joseph Munby

DORIS: A PASTORAL

I SAT with Doris, the shepherd-maiden ;
    Her crook was laden with wreathed
    flowers :
I sat and woo'd her, through sunlight
    wheeling
    And shadows stealing, for hours and
    hours.

And she, my Doris, whose lap encloses
    Wild summer-roses of sweet perfume,
The while I sued her, kept hush'd and
    hearken'd,
    Till shades had darken'd from gloss to
    gloom.

She touch'd my shoulder with fearful finger;
    She said, " We linger, we must not stay :
My flock 's in danger, my sheep will wan-
    der ;
    Behold them yonder, how far they
    stray ! "

I answer'd bolder, " Nay, let me hear you,
    And still be near you, and still adore !
No wolf nor stranger will touch one year-
    ling :
    Ah ! stay, my darling, a moment more ! "

She whisper'd, sighing, " There will be
    sorrow
Beyond to-morrow, if I lose to-day ;
My fold unguarded, my flock unfolded,
    I shall be scolded and sent away."

Said I, denying, " If they do miss you,
    They ought to kiss you when you get
    home ;

And well rewarded by friend and neighbo
    Should be the labor from which yo
    come."

" They might remember," she answer'
    meekly,
    " That lambs are weakly, and sheep ar
    wild ;
But if they love me, it 's none so fervent :
    I am a servant, and not a child."

Then each hot ember glow'd within me,
    And love did win me to swift reply :
" Ah ! do but prove me ; and none sha
    bind you,
    Nor fray nor find you, until I die."

She blush'd and started, and stood awai
    ing,
    As if debating in dreams divine ;
But I did brave them ; I told her plainly
    She doubted vainly, she must be mine.

So we, twin-hearted, from all the valley
    Did rouse and rally her nibbling ewes ;
And homeward drave them, we two togethe
    Through blooming heather and gleamin
    dews.

That simple duty fresh grace did lend he
    My Doris tender, my Doris true ;
That I, her warder, did always bless her,
    And often press her to take her due.

And now in beauty she fills my dwelling,
    With·love excelling, and undefil'd ;
And love doth guard her, both fast an
    fervent,
    No more a servant, nor yet a child.

FROM "DOROTHY: A COUNTRY STORY"

DOROTHY

DOROTHY goes with her pails to the ancient
    well in the courtyard
Daily at gray of morn, daily ere twilight
    at eve ;
Often and often again she winds at the
    mighty old windlass,
Still with her strong red arms landing
    the bucket aright :
Then, her beechen yoke press'd down on
    her broad square shoulders,
Stately, erect, like a queen, she with her
    burden returns :
She with her burden returns to the fields
    that she loves, to the cattle
Lowing beside the troughs, welcoming
    her and her pails.
Dorothy — who is she ?   She is only a ser-
    vant-of-all-work ;
Servant at White Rose Farm, under the
    cliff in the vale :
Under the sandstone cliff, where martins
    build in the springtime,
Hard by the green level meads, hard by
    the streams of the Yore.
Oh, what a notable lass is our Dolly, the
    pride of the dairy !
Stalwart and tall as a man, strong as a
    heifer to work :
Built for beauty, indeed, but certainly built
    for labor —
Witness her muscular arm, witness the
    grip of her hand !

.   .   .   .

Weakly her mistress was, and weakly the
    two little daughters ;
But by her master's side Dorothy wrought
    like a son :
Wrought out of doors on the farm, and
    labor'd in dairy and kitchen,
Doing the work of two ; help and sup-
    port of them all.
Rough were her broad brown hands, and
    within, ah me ! they were horny ;
Rough were her thick ruddy arms,
    shapely and round as they were ;
Rough too her glowing cheeks ; and her
    sunburnt face and forehead
Browner than cairngorm seem'd, set in
    her amber-bright hair.

Yet 't was a handsome face ; the beautiful
    regular features
Labor could never spoil, ignorance could
    not degrade :
And in her clear blue eyes bright gleams
    of intelligence linger'd ;
And on her warm red mouth, Love might
    have 'lighted and lain.
Never an unkind word nor a rude unseemly
    expression
Came from that soft red mouth ; nor in
    those sunny blue eyes
Lived there a look that belied the frankness
    of innocent girlhood —
Fearless, because it·is pure ; gracious,
    and gentle, and calm.
Have you not seen such a face, among rural
    hardworking maidens
Born but of peasant stock, free from our
    Dorothy's shame ?
Just such faces as hers — a countenance
    open and artless,
Where no knowledge appears, culture,
    nor vision of grace ;
Yet which an open-air life and simple and
    strenuous labor
Fills with a charm of its own — precious,
    and warm from the heart ?
Hers was full of that charm ; and besides,
    was something ennobled,
Something adorn'd, by thoughts due to a
    gentle descent :
So that a man should say, if he saw her
    afield at the milking,
Or with her sickle at work reaping the
    barley or beans,
" There is a strapping wench — a lusty lass
    of a thousand,
" Able to fend for herself, fit for the
    work of a man ! "
But if he came more near, and she lifted
    her face to behold him,
" Ah," he would cry, " what a change !
    Surely a *lady* is here ! "
Yes — if a lady be one who is gracious and
    quiet in all things,
Thinking no evil at all, helpful wherever
    she can ;
Then too at White Rose Farm, by the
    martins' cliff in the valley,
There was a lady ; and she was but the
    servant of all.
True, when she spoke, her speech was the
    homely speech of the country ;

Rough with quaint antique words, pic-
turesque sayings of old :
And, for the things that she said, they were
nothing but household phrases —
News of the poultry and kine, tidings of
village and home ;
But there was something withal in her
musical voice and her manner
Gave to such workaday talk touches of
higher degree.
So too, abroad and alone, when she saw the
sun rise o'er the meadows,
Or amid golden clouds saw him descend-
ing at eve ;
Though no poetic thought, no keen and
rapturous insight,
Troubled her childlike soul, yet she could
wonder and gaze ;
Yet she could welcome the morn for its
beauty as well as its brightness
And, in the evening glow, think — not of
supper alone.

COUNTRY KISSES

Curious, the ways of these folk of humble
and hardy condition :
Kisses, amongst ourselves, bless me, how
much they imply !
Ere you can come to a kiss, you must
scale the whole gamut of court-
ship —
Introduction first ; pretty attentions and
words ;
Tentative looks ; and at length, perhaps the
touch of a finger ;
Then the confession ; and *then* (if she al-
low it) the kiss.
So that a kiss comes last — 't is the crown
and seal of the whole thing ;
Passion avow'd by you, fondly accepted
by her.
But in our Dorothy's class, a kiss only
marks the beginning :
Comes me a light-hearted swain, think-
ing of nothing at all ;
Flings his fustian sleeve round the ample
waist of the maiden ;
Kisses her cheek, and she — laughingly
thrusts him away.
Why, 't is a matter of course ; every good-
looking damsel expects it ;
'T is but the homage, she feels, paid to her
beauty by men :

So that, at Kiss-in-the-Ring — an innoce:
game and a good one —
Strangers in plenty may kiss : nay, sh
pursues, in her turn.

DOROTHY'S ROOM

'T was but a poor little room : a farn
servant's loft in a garret ;
One small window and door ; never
chimney at all ;
One little stool by the bed, and a remna:
of cast-away carpet ;
But on the floor, by the wall, carefull
dusted and bright,
Stood the green-painted box, our Dorothy
closet and wardrobe,
Holding her treasures, her all — all tha
she own'd in the world !
Linen and hosen were there, coarse line:
and home-knitted hosen ;
Handkerchiefs bought at the fair, aproı
and smocks not a few ;
Kirtles for warmth when afield, and frock
for winter and summer,
Blue-spotted, lilac, gray ; cotton an
woolen and serge ;
All her simple attire, save the clothes sh
felt most like herself in —
Rough, coarse workaday clothes, fit fc
a laborer's wear.
There was her Sunday array — the boot:
and the shawl, and the bonnet,
Solemnly folded apart, not to be lightl
assumed ;
There was her jewelry, too : 't was a brooc
(she had worn it this evening)
Made of cairngorm stone — really to
splendid for her !
Which on a Martlemas Day Mr. Rober
had bought for a fairing :
Little she thought, just then, how sh
would value it now !
As for her sewing gear, her housewife, he
big brass thimble,
Knitting and suchlike work, such as he:
fingers could do,
That was away downstairs, in a dresser
drawer in the kitchen,
Ready for use of a night, when she wa
tidied and clean.
Item, up there in the chest were her books
"The Dairyman's Daughter ;"
Ballads ; "The Olney Hymns ;" Bibl
and Prayer-book, of course :

That was her library ; these were the limits
    of Dorothy's reading ;
Wholesome, but scanty indeed : was it
    then all that she knew ?
Nay, for like other good girls, she had
    profited much by her schooling
Under the mighty three — Nature, and
    Labor, and Life :
Mightier they than books ; if books could
    have only come after,
Thoughts of instructed minds filtering
    down into hers.
That was impossible now ; what she had
    been, she was, and she would be ;
Only a farm-serving lass — only a peas-
    ant, I fear !

Well — on that green-lidded box, her name
    was painted in yellow ;
Dorothy Crump were the words. Crump ?
    What a horrible name !
Yes, but they gave it to her, because (like
    the box) 't was her mother's ;
Ready to hand — though of course *she*
    had no joy in the name :
She had no kin — and indeed, she never
    had needed a surname ;
Never had used one at all, never had
    made one her own :
" Dolly " she was to herself, and to every
    one else she was " Dolly " ;
Nothing but " Dolly " ; and so, that was
    enough for a name.
Thus then, her great, green box, her one
    undoubted possession,
Stood where it was ; like her, " never
    went nowhere " at all ;
Waited, perhaps, as of old, some beautiful
    Florentine bride-chest,
Till, in the fulness of time, He, the Be-
    loved, appears.—
Was there naught else in her room ? nothing
    handy for washing or dressing ?
Yes ; on a plain deal stand, basin, and
    ewer, and dish :
All of them empty, unused ; for the sink
    was the place of her toilet ;
Save on a Sunday — and then, she too
    could dress at her ease ;
Then, by the little sidewall of the diamonded
    dormer-window
She at a sixpenny glass brush'd out her
    bonny bright hair.
Ah, what a poor little room ! Would *you*
    like to sleep in it, ladies ?

Innocence sleeps there unharm'd ; Honor,
    and Beauty, and Peace —
Love, too, has come ; and with these, even
    dungeons were easily cheerful ;
But, for our Dorothy's room, it is no
    dungeon at all.
No ! through the latticed panes of the
    diamonded dormer-window
Dorothy looks on a world free and fa-
    miliar and fair :
Looks on the fair farm-yard, where the
    poultry and cattle she lives with
Bellow and cackle and low — music de-
    lightful to her ;
Looks on the fragrant fields, with cloud-
    shadows flying above them,
Singing of birds in the air, woodlands
    and waters around.
She in those fragrant meads has wrought,
    every year of her girlhood ;
Over those purple lands she, too, has
    follow'd the plough ;
And, like a heifer afield, or a lamb that is
    yean'd in the meadows,
She, to herself and to us, seems like a
    part of it all.

BEAUTY AT THE PLOUGH

Thus then, one beautiful day, in the sweet,
    cool air of October,
High up on Breakheart Field, under the
    skirts of the wood,
Dolly was ploughing : she wore (why did
    I not sooner describe it ?)
Just such a dress as they all — all the
    farm-servants around ;
Only, it seem'd to be hers by a right divine
    and a fitness —
Color and pattern and shape suited so
    aptly to her.
First, on her well-set head a lilac hood-
    bonnet of cotton,
Framing her amberbright hair, shading
    her neck from the sun ;
Then, on her shoulders a shawl ; a coarse
    red kerchief of woolen,
Matching the glow of her cheeks, lighting
    her berry-brown skin ;
Then came a blue cotton frock — dark blue,
    and spotted with yellow —
Sleev'd to the elbows alone, leaving her
    bonny arms bare ;
So that those ruddy brown arms, with the
    dim, dull blue for a background

Seem'd not so rough as they were —
  softer in color and grain.
All round her ample waist her frock was
  gather'd and kilted,
Showing her kirtle, that hung down to
  the calf of the leg :
Lancashire linsey it was, with bands of
  various color
Striped on a blue-gray ground : sober,
  and modest, and warm ;
Showing her stout firm legs, made stouter
  by home-knitted stockings ;
Ending in strong laced boots, such as a
  ploughman should wear :
Big solid ironshod boots, that added an
  inch to her stature ;
Studded with nails underneath, shoed
  like a horse, at the heels.
After a day at plough, all clotted with
  earth from the furrows,
  Oh, how unlike were her boots, Rosa
  Matilda, to yours !

FLOS FLORUM

ONE only rose our village maiden wore ;
Upon her breast she wore it, in that part
Where many a throbbing pulse doth heave
  and start
At the mere thought of Love and his sweet
  lore.
No polish'd gems hath she, no moulded ore,
Nor any other masterpiece of art :
She hath but Nature's ●masterpiece, her
  heart ;
And that show'd ruddy as the rose she bore
Because that he, who sought for steadfast-
  ness
Vainly in other maids, had found it bare
Under the eyelids of this maiden fair,
Under the folds of her most simple dress.
She let him find it ; for she lov'd him, too,
As he lov'd her : and all this tale is true.

SWEET NATURE'S VOICE

FROM "SUSAN: A POEM OF DEGREES "

HER Master gave the signal, with a look :
Then, timidly as if afraid, she took
In her rough hands the Laureate's dainty
  book,
And straight began. But when she did
  begin,
Her own mute sense of poesy within

Broke forth to hail the poet, and to greet
His graceful fancies and the accents swee
In which they are express'd. Oh, lately
  lost,
Long loved, long honor'd, and whose Cap
  tain's post
No living bard is competent to fill —
How strange, to the deep heart that now i
  still,
And to the vanish'd hand, and to the ear
Whose soft melodious measures are so dea
To us who cannot rival them — how strange
If thou, the lord of such a various range,
Hadst heard this new voice telling Arden'
  tale !
For this was no prim maiden, scant an
  pale,
Full of weak sentiment, and thin delight
In pretty rhymes, who mars the resonan
  might
Of noble verse with arts rhetorical
And simulated frenzy : not at all !
This was a peasant woman ; large an
  strong,
Redhanded, ignorant, unused to song —
Accustom'd rather to the rudest prose.
And yet, there lived within her rustic clothe
A heart as true as Arden's ; and a brain,
Keener than his, that counts it false and vai
To seem aught else than simply what she is
How singular, her faculty of bliss !
Bliss in her servile work ; bliss deep an
  full
In things beyond the vision of the dull,
Whate'er their rank : things beautiful a
  these
Sonorous lines and solemn harmonies
Suiting the tale they tell of ; bliss in love —
Ah, chiefly that ! which lifts her soul abov
Its common life, and gives to labors coars
Such fervor of imaginative force
As makes a passion of her basest toil.
  Surely this servant-dress was but a foil
To her more lofty being ! As she read,
Her accent was as pure, and all she said
As full of interest and of varied grace
As were the changeful moods, that o'er he
  face
Pass'd, like swift clouds across a windy sky
At each sad stage of Enoch's history.
Such ease, such pathos, such abandonmen
To what she utter'd, moulded as she went
Her soft sweet voice, and with such self
  control
Did she, interpreting the poet's soul,

Bridle her own, that when the tale was done
I look'd at her, amaz'd : she seem'd iike one
Who from some sphere of music had come
    down,
And donn'd the white cap and the cotton
    gown

As if to show how much of skill and art
May dwell unthought of, in the humblest
    heart.
Yet there was no great mystery to tell :
She felt it deeply, so she read it well.

Isa Craig Knox

THE WOODRUFFE

THOU art the flower of grief to me,
    'T is in thy flavor !
Thou keepest the scent of memory,
    A sickly savor.
In the moonlight, under the orchard tree,
Thou wert pluck'd and given to me,
    For a love favor.

In the moonlight, under the orchard tree,
    Ah, cruel flower !
Then wert pluck'd and given to me,
    While a fruitless shower
Of blossoms rain'd on the ground where grew
The woodruffe bed all wet with dew,
    In the witching hour.

Under the orchard tree that night
    Thy scent was sweetness,
And thou, with thy small star clusters bright
    Of pure completeness,
Shedding a pearly lustre bright,
Seem'd, as I gaz'd in the meek moonlight,
    A gift of meetness.

"It keeps the scent for years," said he,
    (And thou hast kept it) ;
"And when you scent it, think of me."
    (He could not mean thus bitterly.)
    Ah ! I had swept it
Into the dust where dead things rot,
Had I then believ'd his love was not
    What I have wept it.

Between the leaves of this holy book,
    O flower undying !
A worthless and wither'd weed in look,
    I keep thee lying.
The bloom of my life with thee was pluck'd,
And a close-press'd grief its sap hath suck'd,
    Its strength updrying.

Thy circles of leaves, like pointed spears,
    My heart pierce often ;
They enter, it inly bleeds, no tears
    The hid wounds soften ;
Yet one will I ask to bury thee
In the soft white folds of my shroud with
    me,
    Ere they close my coffin.

Sir Edwin Arnold

FROM " THE LIGHT OF ASIA "

NIRVÂNA

THE Books say well, my Brothers ! each
    man's life
The outcome of his former living is ;
The bygone wrongs bring forth sorrows and
    woes,
The bygone right breeds bliss.

That which ye sow ye reap. See yonder
    fields !
The sesamum was sesamum, the corn

Was corn. The Silence and the Darkness
    knew !
So is a man's fate born.

He cometh, reaper of the things he sow'd,
Sesamum, corn, so much cast in past
    birth ;
And so much weed and poison-stuff, which
    mar
Him and the aching earth.

If he shall labor rightly, rooting these,
And planting wholesome seedlings where
    they grew,

Fruitful and fair and clean the ground
   shall be,
And rich the harvest due.

If he who liveth, learning whence woe
   springs,
Endureth patiently, striving to pay
His utmost debt for ancient evils done
   In Love and Truth alway ;

If making none to lack, he thoroughly purge
   The lie and lust of self forth from his
     blood ;
Suffering all meekly, rendering for offence
   Nothing but grace and good ;

If he shall day by day dwell merciful,
   Holy and just and kind and true ; and
     rend
Desire from where it clings with bleeding
     roots,
   Till love of life have end :

He — dying — leaveth as the sum of him
   A life-count clos'd, whose ills are dead
     and quit,
Whose good is quick and mighty, far and
     near,
   So that fruits follow it.

No need hath such to live as ye name life ;
   That which began in him when he began
Is finish'd : he hath wrought the purpose
     through
   Of what did make him Man.

Never shall yearnings torture him, nor sins
   Stain him, nor ache of earthly joys and
     woes
Invade his safe eternal peace ; nor deaths
   And lives recur. He goes

Unto NIRVÂNA. He is one with Life
   Yet lives not. He is blest, ceasing to be.
OM, MANI PADME, OM ! the Dewdrop slips
   Into the shining sea !

THE CALIPH'S DRAUGHT

UPON a day in Ramadan —
   When sunset brought an end of fast,
And in his station every man
   Prepar'd to share the glad repast —
Sate Mohtasim in royal state,
   The pillaw smok'd upon the gold ;

The fairest slave of those that wait
   Mohtasim's jewell'd cup did hold.

Of crystal carven was the cup,
   With turquoise set along the brim,
A lid of amber clos'd it up ;
   'T was a great king that gave it him.
The slave pour'd sherbet to the brink,
   Stirr'd in wild honey and pomegranate,
With snow and rose - leaves cool'd the
     drink,
   And bore it where the Caliph sate.

The Caliph's mouth was dry as bone,
   He swept his beard aside to quaff :
The news-reader beneath the throne
   Went droning on with *ghain* and *kaf.*
The Caliph drew a mighty breath,
   Just then the reader read a word —
And Mohtasim, as grim as death,
   Set down the cup and snatch'd his sword.

" *Ann' amratan shureefatee !* "
   "Speak clear !" cries angry Mohtasim ;
" *Fe lasr ind' ilj min ulji,*"—
   Trembling the newsman read to him
How in Ammoria, far from home,
   An Arab girl of noble race
Was captive to a lord of Roum ;
   And how he smote her on the face,

And how she cried, for life afraid,
   " Ya, Mohtasim ! help, O my king !"
And how the Kafir mock'd the maid,
   And laugh'd, and spake a bitter thing,
"Call louder, fool ! Mohtasim's ears
   Are long as Barak's — if he heed —
Your prophet's ass ; and when he hears,
   He'll come upon a spotted steed !"

The Caliph's face was stern and red,
   He snapp'd the lid upon the cup ;
" Keep this same sherbet, slave," he said,
   " Till such time as I drink it up.
Wallah ! the stream my drink shall be,
   My hallow'd palm my only bowl,
Till I have set that lady free,
   And seen that Roumi dog's head roll."

At dawn the drums of war were beat,
   Proclaiming, " Thus saith Mohtasim,
' Let all my valiant horsemen meet,
   And every soldier bring with him
A spotted steed.' " So rode they forth,
   A sight of marvel and of fear ;

Pied horses prancing fiercely north,
  Three lakhs — the cup borne in the rear !

When to Ammoria he did win,
  He smote and drove the dogs of Roum,
And rode his spotted stallion in,
  Crying, " *Labbayki !* I am come ! "
Then downward from her prison-place
  Joyful the Arab lady crept ;
She held her hair before her face,
  She kiss'd his feet, she laugh'd and wept.

She pointed where that lord was laid :
  They drew him forth, he whin'd for grace :
Then with fierce eyes Mohtasim said —
  " She whom thou smotest on the face
Had scorn, because she call'd her king :
  Lo ! he is come ! and dost thou think
To live, who didst this bitter thing
  While Mohtasim at peace did drink ? "

Flash'd the fierce sword — roll'd the lord's
    head ;
  The wicked blood smok'd in the sand.
" Now bring my cup ! " the Caliph said.
  Lightly he took it in his hand, —
As down his throat the sweet drink ran
  Mohtasim in his saddle laugh'd,
And cried, " *Taiba asshrab alan !*
  By God ! delicious is this draught ! "

AFTER DEATH IN ARABIA

HE who died at Azan sends
This to comfort all his friends :

Faithful friends ! It lies, I know,
Pale and white and cold as snow ;
And ye say, " Abdallah 's dead ! "
Weeping at the feet and head.
I can see your falling tears,
I can hear your sighs and prayers ;
Yet I smile and whisper this, —
" *I* am not the thing you kiss ;
Cease your tears, and let it lie ;
It *was* mine, it is not I."

Sweet friends ! What the women lave
For its last bed of the grave,
Is a tent which I am quitting,
Is a garment no more fitting,
Is a cage from which, at last,
Like a hawk my soul hath pass'd.
Love the inmate, not the room, —
The wearer, not the garb, — the plume

Of the falcon, not the bars
Which kept him from these splendid stars.

Loving friends ! Be wise, and dry
Straightway every weeping eye, —
What ye lift upon the bier
Is not worth a wistful tear.
'T is an empty sea-shell, — one
Out of which the pearl is gone ;
The shell is broken, it lies there ;
The pearl, the all, the soul, is here.
'T is an earthen jar, whose lid
Allah seal'd, the while it hid
That treasure of his treasury,
A mind that lov'd him ; let it lie !
Let the shard be earth's once more,
Since the gold shines in his store !

Allah glorious ! Allah good !
Now thy world is understood ;
Now the long, long wonder ends ;
Yet ye weep, my erring friends,
While the man whom ye call dead,
In unspoken bliss, instead,
Lives and loves you ; lost, 't is true,
By such light as shines for you ;
But in light ye cannot see
Of unfulfill'd felicity, —
In enlarging paradise,
Lives a life that never dies.

Farewell, friends ! Yet not farewell ;
Where I am, ye, too, shall dwell.
I am gone before your face,
A moment's time, a little space.
When ye come where I have stepp'd
Ye will wonder why ye wept ;
Ye will know, by wise love taught,
That here is all, and there is naught.
Weep awhile, if ye are fain, —
Sunshine still must follow rain ;
Only not at death, — for death,
Now I know, is that first breath
Which our souls draw when we enter
Life, which is of all life centre.

Be ye certain all seems love,
View'd from Allah's throne above ;
Be ye stout of heart, and come
Bravely onward to your home !
La Allah illa Allah ! yea !
Thou love divine ! Thou love alway !

He that died at Azan gave
This to those who made his grave.

RAGLAN

AH ! not because our Soldier died before
   his field was won ;
Ah ! not because life would not last till
   life's long task were done.
Wreathe one less leaf, grieve with less
   grief, — of all our hosts that led
Not last in work and worth approv'd, —
   Lord Raglan lieth dead.

His nobleness he had of none, War's Master
   taught him war,
And prouder praise that Master gave than
   meaner lips can mar ;
Gone to his grave, his duty done ; if farther
   any seek,
He left his life to answer them, — a soldier's,
   — let it speak !

'T was his to sway a blunted sword, — to
   fight a fated field,
While idle tongues talk'd victory, to strug-
   gle not to yield ;
Light task for placeman's ready pen to plan
   a field for fight,
Hard work and hot with steel and shot to
   win that field aright.

Tears have been shed for the brave dead ;
   mourn him who mourn'd for all !
Praise hath been given for strife well striven;
   praise him who strove o'er all,
Nor count that conquest little, though no
   banner flaunt it far,
That under him our English hearts beat
   Pain and Plague and War.

And if he held those English hearts too
   good to pave the path
To idle victories, shall we grudge what
   noble palm he hath ?
Like ancient Chief he fought a-front, and
   mid his soldiers seen,
His work was aye as stern as theirs ; oh !
   make his grave as green.

They know him well, — the Dead who died
   that Russian wrong should cease,
Where Fortune doth not measure men, —
   their souls and his have peace ;
Ay ! as well spent in sad sick tent as they
   in bloody strife,
For English Homes our English Chief gave
   what he had, — his life.

FROM "WITH SA'DI IN THE GARDEN"

MAHMUD AND AYAZ: A PARAPHRASE ON SA'DI

THEY mock'd the Sovereign of Ghaznîn :
   one saith,
" Ayaz hath no great beauty, by my faith !
   A Rose that 's neither rosy-red nor fra-
   grant,
The Bulbul's love for such astonisheth ! "

This went to Mahmud's ears ; ill-pleas'd he
   sate,
Bow'd on himself, reflecting ; then to that
   Replied : " My love is for his kindly
   nature,
Not for his stature, nor his face, nor state ! "

And I did hear how, in a rocky dell,
Bursting a chest of gems a camel fell ;
   King Mahmud wav'd his sleeve, permit-
   ting plunder,
But spurr'd his own steed onward, as they
   tell.

His horsemen parted from their Lord amain,
Eager for pearls, and corals, and such gain :
   Of all those neck-exalting courtiers
None except Ayaz near him did remain.

The King look'd back — " How many hast
   thou won,
Curl'd comfort of my heart ? "   He an-
   swer'd " None !
   I gallop'd up the pass in rear of thee ;
I quit thee for no pearls beneath the sun ! "

Oh, if to God thou hast propinquity,
For no wealth heedless of His service be !
   If Lovers true of God shall ask from God
Aught except God, that 's infidelity.

If thine eyes fix on any gift of Friend,
Thy gain, not his, is thy desire's end :
   If thy mouth gape in avarice, Heaven's
   message
Unto Heart's ear by that road shall not wend.

SONG WITHOUT A SOUND

THE Bulbul wail'd, " Oh, Rose ! all night I
   sing,
And Thou, Beloved ! utterest not one
   thing."

"Dear Bird!" she answer'd, "scent and
  blossoming
Are music of my Song without a sound."

The Cypress to the Tulip spake: "What
  bliss
Seest thou in sunshine, dancing still like
  this?"
"My cup," the Tulip said, "the wind's lips
  kiss;
  Dancing I hear the Song without a
  sound."

The gray Owl hooted to the Dove at morn,
"Why art thou happy on thy jungle-
  thorn?"
"Hearest thou not," she cooed, "o'er
  Earth's face borne
This music of the Song without a sound?"

"Ah, Darweesh!" moan'd a King,
  "Vainly I pray
For Allah's comfort, kneeling day by day."
"Sultan!" quoth he, "be meek, and hear
  alway
The music of His Mercy without sound."

"Poet!" a Queen sigh'd, "why alone to
  thee
Come visions of that world we cannot see —
Not great nor rich?" "I borrow min-
  strelsy,"
  Smiling he said, "from Songs without a
  sound."

Shirin-i-man! dear Lover! true and sweet,
Ask no more if I love, nor kiss my feet;
But hear, with cheek against my bosom's
  beat,
The music of the Song without a sound!

THE MUSMEE

The Musmee has brown velvet eyes
  Curtain'd with satin, sleepily;
You wonder if those lids would rise
  The newest, strangest sight to see;
But when she chatters, laughs, or plays
Kôto, biwa, or samisen,

No jewel gleams with brighter rays
  Than flash from those dark lashes then.

The Musmee has a small brown face,
  "Musk-melon seed" its perfect shape:
Jetty arch'd eyebrows; nose to grace
  The rosy mouth beneath; a nape,
And neck, and chin, and smooth, soft cheeks
  Carv'd out of sun-burn'd ivory,
With teeth, which, when she smiles or
  speaks,
  Pearl merchants might come leagues to
  see!

The Musmee's hair could teach the night
  How to grow dark, the raven's wing
How to seem ebon! Grand the sight
  When, in rich masses, towering,
She builds each high black-marble coil,
  And binds the gold and scarlet in;
And thrusts, triumphant, through the toil
  The Kanzâshi, her jewell'd pin.

The Musmee has wee, faultless feet,
  With snow-white *tabi* trimly deck'd,
Which patter down the city street
  In short steps, slow and circumspect;
A velvet string between her toes
  Holds to its place th' unwilling shoe:
Pretty and pigeon-like she goes,
  And on her head a hood of blue.

The Musmee wears a wondrous dress —
  Kimono, obi, imoji —
A rose-bush in Spring loveliness
  Is not more color-glad to see!
Her girdle holds her silver pipe,
  And heavy swing her long silk sleeves
With cakes, love-letters, *mikan* ripe,
  Small change, musk-bag, and writing-
  leaves.

The Musmee's heart is slow to grief,
  And quick to pleasure, dance, and song;
The Musmee's pocket-handkerchief
  A square of paper! All day long
Gentle, and sweet, and debonair
  Is, rich or poor, this Asian lass:
Heaven have her in its tender care,
  O medetó gozarimas! [1]

---

[1] Japanese for "May it be well with thee!"

Stopford Augustus Brooke

VERSAILLES

(1784)

In Carnival we were, and supp'd that night
In a long room that overlook'd the Square,
When that strange matter happ'd of which
    you ask.
We rang all pleasure's carillon that week ;
Feasts and rich shows, and hunting in the
    woods,
Light love that liv'd on change, deep drink-
    ing, mirth
As mad as Nero's on the Palatine ;
The women were as wild as we, and, like
The King's, our money flew about in
    showers.
They said, " The people starv'd " ; it could
    not be ;
We spent a million on the Carnival.
And now for fifty years gone by I have
    heard
" The people starve " — Why then do the
    useless beasts
Gender so fast ? Less mouths, more bread !
    For me,
I do not care whether they live or die, —
Canaille the dunghill breeds, — but Drum-
    mond car'd,
The young Scotch musketeer whose waking
    dream
You wish to hear from me, who only live
Of all our joyous company. I am old,
My life burns like the thinnest flame, but
    then
It was a glorious fire, and on that night
I led the feast, and roof and table rang
With revelry : till at the height of noise
A sudden silence fell, and while we smil'd,
Waiting for whom should break it, the
    great clock
Struck three in the still air — and a hush'd
    sound
Like coming wind pass'd by, and in its
    breath
I thought I heard, far off, a wail and roar
As if a city perish'd at one stroke ;
The rest heard not, but Drummond starting
    up
And muttering — " Death, Death and his
    troops are nigh," —
Strode to the window. Half asleep he
    seem'd,

Pale as that madman Damiens on the day
He met the torture — and across the bar
He lean'd, and saw the white square in the
    moon.
Men mock'd, and let him be — they knew
    his mood ;
One of his Highland trances, so they said ;
But I kept watch — the grim gray North
    in him,
Midst of our Gallic lightness, pleas'd me
    well.
I watch'd and mark'd above his head the
    moon,
That shone like pearl amid the western
    heaven,
Suddenly swallow'd up by a vast cloud,
With edges like red lightning, but the rest
Of the sky and stars was clear, and the
    rushing noise
Now louder swell'd, like cataracts of rain.
And then I saw how Drummond toss'd his
    arms
High o'er his head, and, crying " Horror,
    horror,"
Fell like a stabb'd man prone upon the
    floor.
We laid him on a couch and cried, " Speak
    — speak,
What is it, what have you seen ? "
                    " I have seen Death," he said,
" And Doom," — and truly with his matted
    hair,
And eyes which as he rose upon his hands
Seem'd 'neath their cavern'd arches coals of
    fire,
He look'd like a gaunt, shaggy mountain
    wolf
Caught in a pit, and mad with rage and
    fear.
" You heard," he said, " that sighing rush
    of wind
And then the awful cry, far off, as if
The world had groan'd and died — I heard,
    and trance
Fell on my brain, and in the trance I saw
The square below me in the moonlight fill
With nobles, dames, and maidens, pages, all
The mighty names of France, and midst
    them walk'd
The King and Queen, not ours, but those
    that come
Hereafter, and I heard soft speech of love

And laughter please the night — when
 momently
The moon went out, and from the darkness
 stream'd
A hissing flood of rain that where it fell
Changed into blood, and 'twixt the court-
 yard stones
Blood well'd as water from a mountain
 moss ;
And the gay crowd, unwitting, walk'd in
 it :
Bubbling it rose past ankle, knee, and waist,
From waist to throat ; and still they walk'd
 as if
They knew it not, until a fierce wind lash'd
The crimson sea, and beat it into waves,
And when its waves smote on their faces,
 then
They knew and shriek'd, but all in vain ;
 the blood,
Storming upon them, whelm'd and drown'd
 them all ;
At which a blinding lightning like a knife
Gash'd the cloud's breast, and dooming
 thunder peal'd.
I woke, and crying 'Horror' knew no
 more.
I've seen the fates of France ; the day of
 God
And vengeance is at hand ; take heed —
 repent —
Leave me to rest."
 We laugh'd to hear him preach,
And left him on the couch, where like a
 man
Drunken he slept, but when he rose, his
 hue
Was changed, a cloud was on his eyes, his
 mouth
Was stern. He sang, he ruffled, lov'd no
 more,
Provok'd no man, and went about like one
Who — can you think it ? — thought there
 was a God
Who, midst his court, car'd how his people
 liv'd.
We all were doom'd, he said, and France
 was doom'd,
He would not stay ! And so gave up his
 sword,
And went to Scotland, where in some grim
 tower
He lov'd and married — fool ! — a name-
 less girl,
And made the peasants happy, I am told ;

But we liv'd out our life, and met no
 doom ;
And now I am old, and Louis, my good
 friend
The Well-belov'd, is dead long since, and
 soon
My time will come ! — The people starve,
 they say,
And curse. I know they curse and hate us !
 Well,
We will ride down and slay the mutinous
 dogs ;
Why, yesterday my horses in the crowd
Threw down a mother and a child, and
 splash'd
A hideous dwarf, who shook his fist and
 curs'd ;
I laugh'd, but as he curs'd with skill, I
 ask'd
The ruffian's name — " Marat," they said,
 " a leech,
Who physics horses and the common herd,
Brute healing brute — the people's friend,
 and yet
He takes our wages — writes us down, but
 keeps
A place in d'Artois' stable !" These are
 the scum
That Drummond fear'd — Artois shall flog
 the man.

THE JUNGFRAU'S CRY

I, VIRGIN of the Snows, have liv'd
 Uncounted years apart ;
Mated with Sunlight, Stars and Heaven,
 But I am cold at heart.

High mates ! Ye teach me purity,
 And lonely thought and truth ;
But I have never liv'd, and yet
 I have eternal youth.

Blow, tropic winds, and warm rains, fall,
 And melt my snowy crest ;
Let soft woods clothe my shoulders fair,
 Deep grass lie on my breast.

And let me feed a thousand herds,
 And hear the tinkling bells,
Till the brown châlets cluster close
 In all my stream-fed dells.

So may I hear the sweep of scythes,
 And beating of the flails,

My maidens singing as they spin,
    And the voice of nightingales.

And little children in their joy,
    And, where my violets hide,
Soft interchange of lovers' vows,
    Sweet hymns at eventide.

Alas! cold Sunlight, Stars and Heaven,
    My high companions, call.
The ice-clad life is pure and stern :
    I am weary of it all.

SONGS FROM "RIQUET OF THE TUFT"

QUEEN'S SONG

YOUNG Sir Guyon proudly said,
" Love shall never be my fate."
" None can say so but the dead,"
Shriek'd the witch wife at his gate.

" Go and dare my shadow'd dell,
Love will quell your happy mood."
Guyon, laughing his farewell,
Rode into the faery wood.

There he met a maiden wild,
By a tree she stood alone ;
When she look'd at him and smil'd,
At a breath his heart was gone.

In her arms she twin'd him fast,
And, like wax within the flame,
Melted memory of the past,
Soul and body, name and fame.

Late at night the steed came back,
" Where's our good knight ? " cried his
    men ;
Far and near they sought his track,
But Guyon no one saw again.

PRINCE RIQUET'S SONG

O LONG ago, when Faery-land
Arose new born, King Oberon
Walk'd pensive on the yellow strand,
And wearied, for he liv'd alone.

" Why have I none, he said, to love ? "
When soft a wind began to fleet
Across the moonlit sea, and drove
A lonely shallop to his feet.

Of pearl, and rubies red, and gold,
That shell was made, and in it lay
Titania fast asleep, and roll'd
In roses, and in flowers of May.

He wak'd her with a loving kiss,
Her arms around him softly clung ;
And none can ever tell the bliss
These had when Faery-land was young.

John Nichol

MARE MEDITERRANEUM

A LINE of light ! it is the inland sea,
    The least in compass and the first in
        fame ;
The gleaming of its waves recalls to me
    Full many an ancient name.

As through my dreamland float the days of
        old,
    The forms and features of their heroes
        shine :
I see Phœnician sailors bearing gold
    From the Tartessian mine.

Seeking new worlds, storm-toss'd Ulysses
        ploughs
    Remoter surges of the winding main ;

And Grecian captains come to pay their
        vows,
    Or gather up the slain.

I see the temples of the Violet Crown
    Burn upward in the hour of glorious
        flight ;
And mariners of uneclips'd renown,
    Who won the great sea fight.

I hear the dashing of a thousand oars,
    The angry waters take a deeper dye ;
A thousand echoes vibrate from the shores
    With Athens' battle-cry.

Again the Carthaginian rovers sweep,
    With sword and commerce, on from shore
        to shore ;

In visionary storms the breakers leap
　　Round Syrtes, as of yore.

Victory, sitting on the Seven Hills,
　　Had gain'd the world when she had mas-
　　　　ter'd thee ;
Thy bosom with the Roman war - note
　　thrills,
　　Wave of the inland sea.

Then, singing as they sail in shining ships,
　　I see the monarch minstrels of Romance,
And hear their praises murmur'd through
　　the lips
　　Of the fair dames of France.

Across the deep another music swells,
　　On Adrian bays a later splendor smiles ;
Power hails the marble city where she
　　dwells
　　Queen of a hundred isles.

Westward the galleys of the Crescent roam,
　　And meet the Pisan ; challenge on the
　　　　breeze,
Till the long Dorian palace lords the foam
　　With stalwart Genoese.

But the light fades ; the vision wears
　　away ;
　　I see the mist above the dreary wave.
Blow, winds of Freedom, give another day
　　Of glory to the brave !

H. W. L.

THE roar of Niagara dies away,
　　The fever heats of war and traffic fade,
While the soft twilight melts the glare of
　　day
　　In this new Helicon, the Muses' glade.

The roof that shelter'd Washington's
　　retreat,
　　Thy home of homes, America, I find
In this memorial mansion, where we greet
　　The full-ton'd lyrist, with the gentle
　　mind.

Here have thy chosen spirits met and
　　flower'd,
　　Season on season, 'neath magnetic spells
Of him who, in his refuge, rose-embower'd,
　　Remote from touch of envious passion
　　dwells.

Here Concord's sage and Harvard's wit
　　contend :
　　The wise, the true, the learned of the land,
Grave thoughts, gay fantasies together
　　blend
　　In subtle converse, 'neath his fostering
　　hand.

With other forms than those of mortal
　　guest
　　The house is haunted ; visions of the
　　morn,
Voices of night that soothe the soul to rest,
　　Attend the shapes, by aery wand reborn ;

Serene companions of a vanish'd age,
　　Noiseless they tread the once familiar
　　floors ,
Or, later offspring of the poet's page,
　　They throng the threshold, crowd the
　　corridors.

"Sweet Preciosa" beside the listening stair
　　Flutters expectant while Victorian sings ;
Evangeline, with cloistral eyes of prayer,
　　Folds her white hands, in shade of angels'
　　wings.

Conquistadors of Castile pace the hall ;
　　Or red-skinn'd warriors pass the challenge
　　round ;
Or Minnehaha's laughter, as the fall
　　Of woodland waters, makes a silver
　　sound.

Thor rolls the thunders of his fiery vaunt,
　　The answering battle burns in Olaf's
　　eyes ;
Or love-crown'd Elsie lures us with the
　　chaunt
　　That lull'd the waves, 'neath star-hung
　　Genoan skies.

Here grim-faced captains of colonial days
　　Salute the builders of old German rhyme ;
And choral troops of children hymn the
　　praise
　　Of their own master minstrel of all time.

Fair shrine of pure creations ! linger long
　　His bright example, may his fame
　　increase :
Discord nor distance ever dim his song,
　　Whose ways are pleasantness, whose
　　paths are peace.

Nor Hawthorne's manse, with ancient moss
bespread,
Nor Irving's hollow, is with rest so rife

As this calm haven, where the leaves are
shed
Round Indian summers of a golden life.

Francis, Earl of Rosslyn

BEDTIME

'T is bedtime ; say your hymn, and bid
"Good-night ;
God bless Mamma, Papa, and dear ones
all."
Your half-shut eyes beneath your eyelids
fall,
Another minute, you will shut them quite.
Yes, I will carry you, put out the light,
And tuck you up, although you are so
tall !
What will you give me, sleepy one, and
call
My wages, if I settle you all right ?
I laid her golden curls upon my arm,
I drew her little feet within my hand,
Her rosy palms were joined in trustful bliss,
Her heart next mine beat gently, soft and
warm
She nestled to me, and, by Love's command,
Paid me my precious wages — " Baby's
Kiss."

MEMORY

I STILL keep open Memory's chamber : still
Drink from the fount of Youth's perennial
stream.
It may be in old age an idle dream
Of those dear children ; but beyond my will
They come again, and dead affections thrill
My pulseless heart, for now once more they
seem
To be alive, and wayward fancies teem
In my fond brain, and all my senses fill.
Come, Alice, leave your books ; 't is I who
call ;
Bind up your hair, and teasing — did you
say
Kissing — that kitten ?   Evey, come with
me ;
Mary, grave darling, take my hand : yes,
all !
I have three hands to-day !   A Holiday.
A Holiday, Papa ?   Woe 's me ! 't is Mem-
ory !

Sir Lewis Morris

AT LAST

LET me at last be laid
On that hillside I know which scans the vale,
Beneath the thick yews' shade,
For shelter when the rains and winds pre-
vail.
It cannot be the eye
Is blinded when we die,
So that we know no more at all
The dawns increase, the evenings fall ;
Shut up within a mouldering chest of wood
Asleep, and careless of our children's good.

Shall I not feel the spring,
The yearly resurrection of the earth,
Stir thro' each sleeping thing
With the fair throbbings and alarms of
birth,

Calling at its own hour
On folded leaf and flower,
Calling the lamb, the lark, the bee,
Calling the crocus and anemone,
Calling new lustre to the maiden's eye,
And to the youth love and ambition high ?

Shall I no more admire
The winding river kiss the daisied plain ?
Nor see the dawn's cold fire
Steal downward from the rosy hills again ?
Nor watch the frowning cloud,
Sublime with mutterings loud,
Burst on the vale, nor eves of gold,
Nor crescent moons, nor starlights cold,
Nor the red casements glimmer on the
hill
At Yule-tides, when the frozen leas are
still ?

Or should my children's tread
Through Sabbath twilights, when the hymns
    are done,
Come softly overhead,
Shall no sweet quickening through my
    bosom run,
Till all my soul exale
Into the primrose pale,
And every flower which springs above
Breathes a new perfume from my love ;
And I shall throb, and stir, and thrill be-
    neath
With a pure passion stronger far than
    death ?

Sweet thought ! fair, gracious dream,
Too fair and fleeting for our clearer view !
How should our reason deem
That those dear souls, who sleep beneath
    the blue
In rayless caverns dim,
'Mid ocean monsters grim,
Or whitening on the trackless sand,
Or with strange corpses on each hand
In battle-trench or city graveyard lie,
Break not their prison-bonds till time shall
    die ?

Nay, 't is not so indeed :
With the last fluttering of the falling breath
The clay-cold form doth breed
A viewless essence, far too fine for death ;
And, ere one voice can mourn,
On upward pinions borne,
They are hidden, they are hidden, in some
    thin air,
Far from corruption, far from care,
Where through a veil they view their
    former scene,
Only a little touch'd by what has been.

Touch'd but a little ; and yet,
Conscious of every change that doth befall,
By constant change beset,
The creatures of this tiny whirling ball,
Fill'd with a higher being,
Dower'd with a clearer seeing,
Risen to a vaster scheme of life,
To wider joys and nobler strife,
Viewing our little human hopes and fears
As we our children's fleeting smiles and
    tears.

Then, whether with fire they burn
This dwelling-house of mine when I am fled,

And in a marble urn
My ashes rest by my beloved dead,
Or in the sweet cold earth
I pass from death to birth,
And pay kind Nature's life-long debt
In heart's-ease and in violet —
In charnel-yard or hidden ocean wave,
Where'er I lie, I shall not scorn my grave.

SONG

Love took my life and thrill'd it
    Through all its strings,
Play'd round my mind and fill'd it
    With sound of wings,
But to my heart he never came
To touch it with his golden flame.

Therefore it is that singing
    I do rejoice,
Nor heed the slow years bringing
    A harsher voice,
Because the songs which he has sung
Still leave the untouch'd singer young.

But whom in fuller fashion
    The Master sways,
For him, swift wing'd with passion,
    Fleet the brief days.
Betimes the enforced accents come,
And leave him ever after dumb.

ON A THRUSH SINGING IN AUTUMN

Sweet singer of the Spring, when the new
    world
Was fill'd with song and bloom, and the
    fresh year
Tripp'd, like a lamb playful and void of
    fear,
Through daisied grass and young leaves
    scarce unfurl'd,
Where is thy liquid voice
That all day would rejoice ?
Where now thy sweet and homely call,
Which from gray dawn to evening's chill-
    ing fall
Would echo from thin copse and tassell'd
    brake,
For homely duty tun'd and love's sweet
    sake ?

The spring-tide pass'd, high summer soon
    should come.
The woods grew thick, the meads a deeper
    hue ;
The pipy summer growths swell'd, lush and
    tall ;
The sharp scythes swept at daybreak
    through the dew.
Thou didst not heed at all,
Thy prodigal voice grew dumb ;
No more with song mightst thou beguile,
She sitting on her speckled eggs the while,
Thy mate's long vigil as the slow days went,
Solacing her with lays of measureless con-
    tent.

Nay, nay, thy voice was Duty's, nor would
    dare
Sing were Love fled, though still the world
    were fair ;
The summer wax'd and wan'd, the nights
    grew cold,
The sheep were thick within the wattled fold,
The woods began to moan,
Dumb wert thou and alone ;
Yet now, when leaves are sere, thy ancient
    note
Comes low and halting from thy doubtful
    throat.

Oh, lonely loveless voice, what dost thou
    here
In the deep silence of the fading year ?

Thus do I read answer of thy song :
  " I sang when winds blew chilly all day
    long ;
I sang because hope came and joy was near,
I sang a little while, I made good cheer ;
In summer's cloudless day
My music died away ;
But now the hope and glory of the year
Are dead and gone, a little while I sing
Songs of regret for days no longer here,
And touch'd with presage of the far-off
    Spring."

Is this the meaning of thy note, fair bird ?
Or do we read into thy simple brain
Echoes of thoughts which human hearts
    have stirr'd,
High-soaring joy and melancholy pain ?
Nay, nay, that lingering note
Belated from thy throat —
" Regret," is what it sings, " regret, regret !
The dear days pass, but are not wholly
    gone.
In praise of those I let my song go on ;
'T is sweeter to remember than forget."

Philip Gilbert Hamerton

THE SANYASSI

" I HAVE subdued at last the will to live,
  Expelling nature from my weary heart ;
And now my life, so calm, contemplative,
  No longer selfish, freely may depart.
The vital flame is burning less and less ;
And memory fuses to forgetfulness.

" Sometimes I gaze on vacancy so long
  That all my brain grows vacant, and I
    feel
That wondrous influence which doth make
  me strong
  In resolution and unworldly zeal,
Until, abstracted from all time and sense,
I sink into eternal indolence.

" And now I feel my inward life grow still,
  A being by itself, which fondly clings
To consciousness which I can never kill,

Yet is abstracted from all outward
    things,
And slumbers often, and is overgrown ;
The sense of self increases when alone.

" I have subdued the will, but gain'd the
    power
  To dwell among the denizens of earth ;
I spread my spirit over tree and flower,
  And human hearts, and things of meaner
    birth ;
And thinking thus to give my soul away,
I found it grew more conscious every day.

" The simple crowds who hourly pass me by,
  I think have lately grown afraid of me ;
There is some virtue in this sunken eye,
  For sometimes in my dreams I faintly
    see
The workings of the spirit in the brain,
And living floods that gush in every vein.

" Now, as I am weary of this vain endeavor
  To lift my spirit to eternal sleep ;
I seek the marble stairs, the sacred river,
  The liquid graves below, where, calm and
    deep,
Beneath where that bright, silent water
    flows,
Stretch wide the regions of divine repose."

With thoughts like these the Indian suicide
  Dragg'd forth his stiffen'd limbs from
    his old lair ;
He had no garment on his shrivell'd hide,
  He shunn'd the grove, and sought the
    solar glare,
He never look'd aside, and his dead march
Had for its goal a gate of one proud arch.

It rose in sculptur'd splendor on the view
  From the surrounding foliage of dark
    green,
Whose masses of broad shadow did subdue
  Its prominent light. The blue sky shone
    between.
A crowd was on the river's sacred marge,
And on the Ganges many a gaudy barge.

Down to that river he descended now ;
  And as he press'd the last steps of the stair,
A glance of pleasure from beneath his brow
  Fell on two jars of porous earthenware.
He seiz'd them with his feeble hands, and
    tied
One of them to his girdle on each side,

And floated slowly from the crowded Ghaut;
  And since no friendly hand was stretch'd
    to save,
Found in those quiet waters what he
    sought —
A long rest and an honorable grave.

His faith was righteous, and his ending
  blest ;
And now his soul enjoys eternal rest.

THE WILD HUNTSMEN

" WILD huntsmen ? " — 'T was a flight of
  swans,
But so invisibly they flew,
That in his mind the pallid hind
  Could hear a bugle horn.
Faintly sounds the airy note,
And the deepest bay from the staghound's
  throat
Like the yelp of a cur on the air doth float ;
  And hardly heard is the wild halloo
  On the straggling night-breeze borne !

They fly on the blast of the forest
  That whistles round the wither'd tree,
But where they go we may not know,
  Nor see them as they fly.
With hound and horn they ride away
In the dreary twilight cold and gray,
That hovers near the dying day;
  And the peasant hears but cannot see
  Those huntsmen pass him by.

Hark ! 't is the goblin of the wood,
  Rushing down the dark hill-side ;
With steeds that neigh and hounds that
    bay,
  All viewless sweeps the throng.
And heavily where the fallow-deer feeds
Clatter the hoofs of their hunting steeds,
Like the mountain gale on the valley's
    meads ;
  Till far away the spectres ride,
  In distant lands along.

Roden Noel

THE SECRET OF THE NIGHT-INGALE

THE ground I walk'd on felt like air,
Air buoyant with the year's young mirth ;
Far, filmy, undulating fair,
The down lay, a long wave of earth ;
And a still green foam of woods rose high
Over the hill-line into the sky.

In meadowy pasture browse the kine,
Thin wheat-blades color a brown plough-
  line ;
Fresh rapture of the year's young joy
Was in the unfolded luminous leaf,
And birds that shower as they toy
Melodious rain that knows not grief,
A song-maze where my heart in bliss
Lay folded, like a chrysalis.

They allur'd my feet far into the wood,
Down a winding glade with leaflets wall'd,
With an odorous dewy dark imbued ;
Rose, and maple, and hazel call'd
Me into the shadowy solitude ;
Wild blue germander eyes enthrall'd
Made me free of the balmy bowers,
Where a wonderful garden-party of flow-
　　ers,
Laughing sisterhood under the trees,
Dancing merrily, play'd with the bees ;
Anemone, starwort, bands in white,
Like girls for a first communion dight,
And pale yellow primrose ere her flight,
Usher'd me onward wondering
To a scene more fair than the court of a
　　king.
Ah ! they were very fair themselves,
Sweet maids of honor, woodland elves !
Frail flowers that arrive with the cuckoo,
Pale lilac, hyacinth purple of hue,
And the little pink geranium,
All smil'd and nodded to see me come ;
All gave me welcome ; " No noise," they
　　said,
" For we will show you the bridal bed,
Where Philomel, our queen, was wed ;
Hush ! move with a tender, reverent foot,
Like a shy light over bole and root ; "
And they blew in the delicate air for flute.

Into the heart of the verdure stole
My feet, and a music enwound my soul ;
Zephyr flew over a cool bare brow —
I am near, very near to the secret now !
For the rose-covers, all alive with song,
Flash with it, plain now low and long ;
Sprinkle a holy water of notes ;
On clear air melody leans and floats ;
The blithe-wing'd minstrel merrily moves,
Dim bushes burn with mystical loves !

Lo ! I arrive ! immers'd in green,
Where the wood divides, though barely
　　seen,
A nest in one of the blue leaf-rifts !
There over the border a bird uplifts
Her downy head, bill'd, luminous-ey'd ;
Behold the chosen one, the bride !
And the singer, he singeth by her side.
Leap, heart ! be aflame with them ! loud,
　　not dumb,
Give a voice to their epithalamium !
Whose raptures wax not pale nor dim
Beside the fires of seraphim.

These are glorious, glowing stairs,
In gradual ascent to theirs ;
With human loves acclaim and hail
The holy lore of the nightingale !

SEA SLUMBER–SONG

Sea-birds are asleep,
The world forgets to weep,
Sea murmurs her soft slumber-song
On the shadowy sand
Of this elfin land ;
" I, the Mother mild,
Hush thee, O my child,
Forget the voices wild !
Isles in elfin light
Dream, the rocks and caves,
Lull'd by whispering waves,
Veil their marbles bright,
Foam glimmers faintly white
Upon the shelly sand
Of this elfin land ;
Sea-sound, like violins,
To slumber woos and wins,
I murmur my soft slumber-song,
Leave woes, and wails, and sins,
Ocean's shadowy might
Breathes good-night,
　　Good-night ! "

DYING

They are waiting on the shore
For the bark to take them home ;
They will toil and grieve no more ;
The hour for release hath come.

All their long life lies behind,
Like a dimly blending dream ;
There is nothing left to bind
To the realms that only seem.

They are waiting for the boat,
There is nothing left to do ;
What was near them grows remote,
Happy silence falls like dew ;
Now the shadowy bark is come,
And the weary may go home.

By still water they would rest,
In the shadow of the tree ;
After battle sleep is best,
After noise tranquillity.

THE MERRY–GO–ROUND

THE merry-go-round, the merry-go-round,
  the merry-go-round at Fowey !
They whirl around, they gallop around, man,
  woman, and girl, and boy ;
They circle on wooden horses, white, black,
  brown, and bay,
To a loud monotonous tune that hath a
  trumpet bray.
All is dark where the circus stands on the
  narrow quay,
Save for its own yellow lamps, that illumine
  it brilliantly :
Painted purple and red, it pours a broad
  strong glow
Over an old-world house, with a pillar'd
  place below ;
For the floor of the building rests on bandy
  columns small,
And the bulging pile may, tottering, sud-
  denly bury all.
But there upon wooden benches, hunch'd
  in the summer night,
Sit wrinkled sires of the village arow, whose
  hair is white ;
They sit like the mummies of men, with a
  glare upon them cast
From a rushing flame of the living, like
  their own mad past ;
They are watching the merry-make, and
  their face is very grave ;
Over all are the silent stars ! beyond, the
  cold gray wave.
And while I gaze on the galloping horses
  circling round,
The men caracoling up and down to a weird,
  monotonous sound,
I pass into a bewilderment, and marvel why
  they go ;
It seems the earth revolving, with our vain
  to and fro !
For the young may be glad and eager, but
  some ride listlessly,
And the old look on with a weary, dull,
  and lifeless eye ;
I know that in an hour the fair will all be
  gone,
Stars shining over a dreary void, the Deep
  have sound alone.
I gaze with orb suffus'd at human things
  that fly,
And I am lost in the wonder of our dim
  destiny. . . .

The merry-go-round, the merry-go-round,
  the merry-go-round at Fowey !
They whirl around, they gallop around, man,
  woman, and girl, and boy.

LAMENT

I AM lying in the tomb, love,
  Lying in the tomb,
Tho' I move within the gloom, love,
  Breathe within the gloom !
Men deem life not fled, dear,
  Deem my life not fled,
Tho' I with thee am dead, dear,
  I with thee am dead,
    O my little child !

What is the gray world, darling,
  What is the gray world,
Where the worm lies curl'd, darling,
  The deathworm lies curl'd ?
They tell me of the spring, dear !
  Do I want the spring ?
Will she waft upon her wing, dear,
  The joy-pulse of her wing,
  Thy songs, thy blossoming,
    O my little child !

For the hallowing of thy smile, love,
  The rainbow of thy smile,
Gleaming for a while, love,
  Gleaming to beguile,
Replunged me in the cold, dear,
  Leaves me in the cold.
And I feel so very old, dear,
  Very, very old !

Would they put me out of pain, dear,
  Out of all my pain,
Since I may not live again, dear,
  Never live again !

I am lying in the grave, love,
  In thy little grave,
Yet I hear the wind rave, love,
  And the wild wave !
I would lie asleep, darling,
  With thee lie asleep,
Unhearing the world weep, darling,
  Little children weep !
    O my little child !

THE TOY CROSS

MY little boy at Christmas-tide
Made me a toy cross ;
Two sticks he did, in boyish pride,
With brazen nail emboss.

Ah me ! how soon, on either side
His dying bed's true cross,
She and I were crucified,
Bemoaning our life-loss !

But He, whose arms in death spread wide
Upon the holy tree,
Were clasp'd about him when he died —
Clasp'd for eternity !

"THAT THEY ALL MAY BE ONE"

WHENE'ER there comes a little child,
My darling comes with him ;
Whene'er I hear a birdie wild
Who sings his merry whim,

Mine sings with him :
If a low strain of music sails
Among melodious hills and dales,
When a white lamb or kitten leaps,
Or star, or vernal flower peeps,
When rainbow dews are pulsing joy,
Or sunny waves, or leaflets toy,
Then he who sleeps
Softly wakes within my heart ;
With a kiss from him I start ;
He lays his head upon my breast,
Tho' I may not see my guest,
Dear bosom-guest !
In all that 's pure and fair and good,
I feel the spring-time of thy blood,
Hear thy whisper'd accents flow
To lighten woe,
Feel them blend,
Although I fail to comprehend.
And if one woundeth with harsh word,
Or deed, a child, or beast, or bird,
It seems to strike weak Innocence
Through him, who hath for his defence
Thunder of the All-loving Sire,
And mine, to whom He gave the fire.

Sir Alfred Lyall

MEDITATIONS OF A HINDU PRINCE

ALL the world over, I wonder, in lands
that I never have trod,
Are the people eternally seeking for the
signs and steps of a God ?
Westward across the ocean, and North-
ward across the snow,
Do they all stand gazing, as ever, and what
do the wisest know ?

Here, in this mystical India, the deities
hover and swarm
Like the wild bees heard in the tree-tops,
or the gusts of a gathering storm ;
In the air men hear their voices, their feet
on the rocks are seen,
Yet we all say, " Whence is the message,
and what may the wonders mean ? "

A million shrines stand open, and ever the
censer swings,
As they bow to a mystic symbol, or the
figures of ancient kings ;

And the incense rises ever, and rises the
endless cry
Of those who are heavy laden, and of cow-
ards loth to die.

For the Destiny drives us together, like
deer in a pass of the hills ;
Above is the sky, and around us the sound
of the shot that kills ;
Push'd by a power we see not, and struck
by a hand unknown,
We pray to the trees for shelter, and press
our lips to a stone.

The trees wave a shadowy answer, and the
rock frowns hollow and grim,
And the form and the nod of the demon
are caught in the twilight dim ;
And we look to the sunlight falling afar on
the mountain crest, —
Is there never a path runs upward to a
refuge there and a rest ?

The path, ah ! who has shown it, and which
   is the faithful guide ?
The haven, ah ! who has known it ? for
   steep is the mountain side,
Forever the shot strikes surely, and ever
   the wasted breath
Of the praying multitude rises, whose an-
   swer is only death.

Here are the tombs of my kinsfolk, the
   fruit of an ancient name,
Chiefs who were slain on the war-field, and
   women who died in flame ;
They are gods, these kings of the foretime,
   they are spirits who guard our race :
Ever I watch and worship ; they sit with a
   marble face.

And the myriad idols around me, and the
   legion of muttering priests,
The revels and rites unholy, the dark un-
   speakable feasts !
What have they wrung from the Silence ?
   Hath even a whisper come
Of the secret, Whence and Whither ?
   Alas ! for the gods are dumb.

Shall I list to the word of the English, who
   come from the uttermost sea ?
"The Secret, hath it been told you, and
   what is your message to me ? "

It is nought but the wide-world story how
   the earth and the heavens began,
How the gods are glad and angry, and a
   Deity once was man.

I had thought, " Perchance in the cities
   where the rulers of India dwell,
Whose orders flash from the far land, who
   girdle the earth with a spell,
They have fathom'd the depths we float on,
   or measur'd the unknown main — "
Sadly they turn from the venture, and say
   that the quest is vain.

Is life, then, a dream and delusion, and
   where shall the dreamer awake ?
Is the world seen like shadows on water, and
   what if the mirror break ?
Shall it pass as a camp that is struck, as a
   tent that is gathered and gone
From the sands that were lamp-lit at eve,
   and at morning are level and lone ?

Is there nought in the heaven above, whence
   the hail and the levin are hurl'd,
But the wind that is swept around us by the
   rush of the rolling world ?
The wind that shall scatter my ashes, and
   bear me to silence and sleep
With the dirge, and the sounds of lamenting,
   and voices of women who weep.

Alfred Austin

AT HIS GRAVE

HUGHENDEN, MAY, 1881

LEAVE me a little while alone,
Here at his grave that still is strown
   With crumbling flower and wreath ;
The laughing rivulet leaps and falls,
The thrush exults, the cuckoo calls,
   And he lies hush'd beneath.

With myrtle cross and crown of rose,
And every lowlier flower that blows,
   His new-made couch is dress'd ;
Primrose and cowslip, hyacinth wild,
Gather'd by monarch, peasant, child,
   A nation's grief attest.

I stood not with the mournful crowd
That hither came when round his shroud
   Pious farewells were said.

In the fam'd city that he sav'd,
By minaret crown'd, by billow lav'd,
   I heard that he was dead.

Now o'er his tomb at last I bend,
No greeting get, no greeting tend,
   Who never came before
Unto his presence, but I took,
From word or gesture, tone or look,
   Some wisdom from his door.

And must I now unanswer'd wait,
And, though a suppliant at the gate,
   No sound my ears rejoice ?
Listen ! Yes, even as I stand,
I feel the pressure of his hand,
   The comfort of his voice.

How poor were Fame, did grief confess
That death can make a great life less,
    Or end the help it gave !
Our wreaths may fade, our flowers may
        wane,
But his well-ripen'd deeds remain,
    Untouch'd, above his grave.

Let this, too, soothe our widow'd minds ;
Silenced are the opprobrious winds
    Whene'er the sun goes down ;
And free henceforth from noonday noise,
He at a tranquil height enjoys
    The starlight of renown.

Thus hence we something more may take
Than sterile grief, than formless ache,
    Or vainly utter'd vow ;
Death hath bestow'd what life withheld
And he round whom detraction swell'd
    Hath peace with honor now.

The open jeer, the covert taunt,
The falsehood coin'd in factious haunt,
    These loving gifts reprove.
They never were but thwarted sound
Of ebbing waves that bluster round
    A rock that will not move.

And now the idle roar rolls off,
Hush'd is the gibe and sham'd the scoff,
    Repress'd the envious gird ;
Since death, the looking-glass of life,
Clear'd of the misty breath of strife,
    Reflects his face unblurr'd.

From callow youth to mellow age,
Men turn the leaf and scan the page,
    And note, with smart of loss,
How wit to wisdom did mature,
How duty burn'd ambition pure,
    And purged away the dross.

Youth is self-love ; our manhood lends
Its heart to pleasure, mistress, friends,
    So that when age steals nigh,
How few find any worthier aim
Than to protract a flickering flame,
    Whose oil hath long run dry !

But he, unwitting youth once flown,
With England's greatness link'd his own,
    And, steadfast to that part,
Held praise and blame but fitful sound,
And in the love of country found
    Full solace for his heart.

Now in an English grave he lies :
With flowers that tell of English skies
    And mind of English air,
A grateful sovereign decks his bed,
And hither long with pilgrim tread
    Will English feet repair.

Yet not beside his grave alone
We seek the glance, the touch, the tone;
    His home is nigh, — but there,
See from the hearth his figure fled,
The pen unrais'd, the page unread,
    Untenanted the chair !

Vainly the beechen boughs have made
A fresh green canopy of shade,
    Vainly the peacocks stray ;
While Carlo, with despondent gait,
Wonders how long affairs of State
    Will keep his lord away.

Here most we miss the guide, the friend ;
Back to the churchyard let me wend,
    And, by the posied mound,
Lingering where late stood worthier feet,
Wish that some voice, more strong, more
        sweet,
    A loftier dirge would sound.

At least I bring not tardy flowers :
Votive to him life's budding powers,
    Such as they were, I gave —
He not rejecting, so I may
Perhaps these poor faint spices lay,
    Unchidden, on his grave !

SONGS FROM "PRINCE LU-
CIFER"

GRAVE-DIGGER'S SONG

THE crab, the bullace, and the sloe,
    They burgeon in the Spring ;
And, when the west wind melts the snow,
    The redstarts build and sing.
But Death's at work in rind and root,
    And loves the green buds best ;
And when the pairing music 's mute,
    He spares the empty nest,
        Death ! Death !
    Death is master of lord and clown.
    Close the coffin, and hammer it down.

When nuts are brown and sere without,
    And white and plump within,
And juicy gourds are pass'd about,
    And trickle down the chin ;

When comes the reaper with his scythe,
  And reaps and nothing leaves,
Oh, then it is that Death is blithe,
  And sups among the sheaves.
        Death ! Death !
  Lower the coffin and slip the cord :
  Death is master of clown and lord.

When logs about the house are stack'd,
  And next year's hose is knit,
And tales are told and jokes are crack'd,
  And faggots blaze and spit ;
Death sits down in the ingle-nook,
  Sits down and doth not speak :
But he puts his arm round the maid that 's
      warm,
  And she tingles in the cheek.
        Death ! Death !
  Death is master of lord and clown ;
  Shovel the clay in, tread it down.

MOTHER-SONG

WHITE little hands !
  Pink little feet !
Dimpled all over,
  Sweet, sweet, sweet !
What dost thou wail for ?
  The unknown ? the unseen ?
The ills that are coming,
  The joys that have been ?

Cling to me closer,
  Closer and closer,
Till the pain that is purer
  Hath banish'd the grosser.
Drain, drain at the stream, love,
  Thy hunger is freeing,
That was born in a dream, love,
  Along with thy being !

Little fingers that feel
  For their home on my breast,
Little lips that appeal
  For their nurture, their rest !
Why, why dost thou weep, dear ?
  Nay, stifle thy cries,
Till the dew of thy sleep, dear,
  Lies soft on thine eyes.

AGATHA

SHE wanders in the April woods,
  That glisten with the fallen shower ;
She leans her face against the buds,
  She stops, she stoops, she plucks a flower.

She feels the ferment of the hour :
She broodeth when the ringdove broods ;
  The sun and flying clouds have power
Upon her cheek and changing moods.
  She cannot think she is alone,
  As o'er her senses warmly steal
Floods of unrest she fears to own,
  And almost dreads to feel.

Among the summer woodlands wide
  Anew she roams, no more alone ;
The joy she fear'd is at her side,
  Spring's blushing secret now is known.
The primrose and its mates have flown,
  The thrush's ringing note hath died ;
  But glancing eye and glowing tone
Fall on her from her god, her guide.
  She knows not, asks not, what the goal,
    She only feels she moves towards
        bliss,
  And yields her pure unquestioning soul
    To touch and fondling kiss.

And still she haunts those woodland ways,
  Though all fond fancy finds there now
To mind of spring or summer days,
  Are sodden trunk and songless bough.
  The past sits widow'd on her brow,
Homeward she wends with wintry gaze,
  To walls that house a hollow vow,
To hearth where love hath ceas'd to blaze :
  Watches the clammy twilight wane,
    With grief too fix'd for woe or tear ;
  And, with her forehead 'gainst the pane,
    Envies the dying year.

THE HAYMAKERS' SONG

HERE 's to him that grows it,
        Drink, lads, drink !
That lays it in and mows it,
        Clink, jugs, clink !
To him that mows and makes it,
That scatters it and shakes it,
That turns, and teds, and rakes it,
        Clink, jugs, clink !

Now here 's to him that stacks it,
        Drink, lads, drink !
That thrashes and that tacks it,
        Clink, jugs, clink !
That cuts it out for eating,
When March-dropp'd lambs are bleating,
And the slate-blue clouds are sleeting,
        Drink, lads, drink !

And here's to thane and yeoman,
Drink, lads, drink !
To horseman and to bowman,
Clink, jugs, clink !

To lofty and to low man,
Who bears a grudge to no man,
But flinches from no foeman,
Drink, lads, drink !

Thomas Ashe

MARIAN

PASSING feet pause, as they pass,
By this little slab of slate.
People, if they go this way,
By the linchen'd wicket gate,
At each other look and say,
"Pity, pity ! sad it was ! "
Here have fallen as many tears
As the months in her short years.

Seven and ten brief sunny springs ;
Scarce so many winter snows :
Here the little speedwell keeps
Watch beside the pale dog-rose ;
On this hillock, while she sleeps
Underneath, the red-breast sings.
Wedded on an April day !
In the Autumn laid away !

PHANTOMS

MY days are full of pleasant memories
Of all those women sweet,
Whom I have known ! How tenderly their
eyes
Flash thro' the days — too fleet ! —
Which long ago went by with sun and rain,
Flowers, or the winter snow ;
And still thro' memory's palace-halls are
fain
In rustling robes to go !
Or wed, or widow'd, or with milkless breasts,
Around those women stand,
Like mists that linger on the mountain
crests
Rear'd in a phantom land ;
And love is in their mien and in their look,
And from their lips a stream
Of tender words flows, smooth as any brook,
And softer than a dream :
And, one by one, holding my hands, they say
Things of the years agone ;
And each head will a little turn away,
And each one still sigh on ;

Because they think such meagre joy we
had ;
For love was little bold,
And youth had store, and chances to be
glad,
And squander'd so his gold.
Blue eyes, and gray, and blacker than the
sloe,
And dusk and golden hair,
And lips that broke in kisses long ago,
Like sun-kiss'd flowers, are there ;
And warm fire-side, and sunny orchard wall,
And river-brink and bower,
And wood and hill, and morning and day-
fall,
And every place and hour !
And each on each a white unclouded brow
Still as a sister bends,
As they would say, "love makes us kindred
now,
Who sometime were his friends."

BY THE SALPÉTRIÈRE

I SAW a poor old woman on the bench
That you may find by the Salpétrière.
The yellow leaves were falling, and the
wind
Gave hint of bitter days to come ere long.
And yet the sun was bright : and as I knew
A little sun, with the Parisiennes,
Means light of heart, I could not but de-
mand
"Why, now, so near to weeping, citizen ?"
She look'd up at me with vague surprise,
And said, "You see I'm old ; I'm very
old :
I'm eighty years and nine ; and people say
This winter will be hard. And we have
here,
We poor old women in this hospital,
A mortal dread of one strange bitter thing.
We would be buried in a coffin, we ;
For each her own. It is not much you
crave,

Who 've striven ninety years, and come to this,
And we would have the priest to say a prayer
To the good God for us, within the church,
Before we go the way that go we must.
And sou by sou we save : — a coffin costs, —
You hear, Sir ? — sixteen francs ; and if we go
To church en route, 't is six francs for the priest.
There 's some of us have sav'd it all, and smile,
With the receipt sew'd up, lest they should lose
This passport to the grave of honest folk.
But one may die before ; and then there is
One coffin for us all, and we are borne
To our last place, and slipp'd within the grave,
And back they take the coffin for the next.
And if you 've sixteen francs, and not the six,
No church, but just a sprinkle with the brush,
And half a prayer, and you must take your chance.
Good God ! and I shall die : I know I shall :
I feel it here ! and I have ten francs just :
No more ! " My tears fell like a shower of rain.
I said, " Old woman, here 's the other twelve ; "
And fled, with great strides, like a man possess'd.

A VISION OF CHILDREN

I DREAM'D I saw a little brook
  Run rippling down the Strand ;
With cherry-trees and apple-trees
  Abloom on either hand :

The sparrows gather'd from the Squares,
  Upon the branches green ;
The pigeons flock'd from Palace-Yard,
  Afresh their wings to preen ;
And children down St. Martin's Lane,
  And out of Westminster,
Came trooping, many a thousand strong,
  With a bewilder'd air.
They hugg'd each other round the neck
  And titter'd for delight,
To see the yellow daffodils,
  And see the daisies white ;
They roll'd upon the grassy slopes,
  And drank the water clear,
While 'busses the Embankment took,
  Asham'd to pass anear ;
And sandwich-men stood still aghast,
  And costermongers smil'd ;
And the policeman on his beat
  Pass'd, weeping like a child.

POETA NASCITUR

THE flame-wing'd seraph spake a word
  To one of Galilee : —
" Be not afraid : know, of the Lord
  Is that is born of thee."

And by the poet's bliss and woe
  Learn we the will of Heaven :
He is God's instrument ; and so
  Swords in his heart are seven.

He is God's oracle and slave,
  As once the priestesses ;
His griefs in keeping we should have,
  To heal, or make them less.

Theodore Watts

ODE TO MOTHER CAREY'S CHICKEN

(ON SEEING A STORM-PETREL IN A CAGE ON A COTTAGE WALL AND RELEASING IT)

GAZE not at me, my poor unhappy bird ;
  That sorrow is more than human in thine eye ;
Too deep already is my spirit stirr'd
  To see thee here, child of the sea and sky,

Coop'd in a cage with food thou canst not eat,
Thy "snow-flake" soil'd, and soil'd those conquering feet
That walk'd the billows, while thy "sweet-sweet-sweet"
  Proclaim'd the tempest nigh.

Bird whom I welcom'd while the sailors curs'd,
  Friend whom I bless'd wherever keels may roam,

Prince of my childish dreams, whom mer-
    maids nurs'd
  In purple of billows — silver of ocean-
    foam,
Abash'd I stand before the mighty grief
That quells all other : Sorrow's king and
    chief :
To ride the wind and hold the sea in fief,
    Then find a cage for home !

From out thy jail thou seest yon heath and
    woods,
  But canst thou hear the birds or smell
    the flowers ?
Ah, no ! those rain-drops twinkling on the
    buds
Bring only visions of the salt sea-showers.
" The sea ! " the linnets pipe from hedge
    and heath ;
" The sea ! " the honeysuckles whisper and
    breathe ;
And tumbling waves, where those wild-roses
    wreathe,
    Murmur from inland bowers.

These winds so soft to others, — how they
    burn !
  The mavis sings with gurgle and ripple
    and plash,
To thee yon swallow seems a wheeling tern.
And when the rain recalls the briny lash
Old Ocean's kiss thou lovest, — when thy
    sight
Is mock'd with Ocean's horses — manes of
    white,
The long and shadowy flanks, the shoulders
    bright —
    Bright as the lightning's flash, —

When all these scents of heather and brier
    and whin,
  All kindly breaths of land-shrub, flower,
    and vine,
Recall the sea-scents, till thy feather'd skin
Tingles in answer to a dream of brine, —
When thou, remembering there thy royal
    birth,
Dost see between the bars a world of dearth,
Is there a grief — a grief on all the earth —
    So heavy and dark as thine ?

But I can buy thy freedom — I (thank
    God !),
  Who lov'd thee more than albatross or
    gull,

Lov'd thee when on the waves thy footstep
    trod,
  Dream'd of thee when, becalm'd, we lay
    a-hull —
'T is I thy friend who once, a child of six,
To find where Mother Carey fed her chicks
Climb'd up the stranded punt, and with
    two sticks
    Tried all in vain to scull, —

Thy friend who ow'd a Paradise of Storm, —
  The little dreamer of the cliffs and coves
Who knew thy mother, saw her shadowy
    form
  Behind the cloudy bastions where she
    moves,
And heard her call : " Come ! for the wel-
    kin thickens,
And tempests mutter and the lightning
    quickens ! "
Then, starting from his dream, would find
    the chickens
    Were only blue rock-doves, —

Thy friend who ow'd another Paradise
  Of calmer air, a floating isle of fruit,
Where sang the Nereids on a breeze of spice
  While Triton, from afar, would sound
    salute :
There wast thou winging, though the skies
    were calm,
For marvellous strains, as of the morning's
    shalm,
Were struck by ripples round that isle of
    palm
    Whose shores were " Carey's lute.'

And now to see thee here, my king, my king,
  Far-glittering memories mirror'd in those
    eyes,
As if there shone within each iris-ring
  An orbed world — ocean and hills and
    skies ! —
Those black wings ruffled whose triumphant
    sweep
Conquer'd in sport ! — yea, up the glimmer-
    ing steep
Of highest billow, down the deepest deep,
    Sported with victories !

To see thee here ! — a coil of wilted weeds
  Beneath those feet that danced on dia-
    mond spray,
Rider of sportive Ocean's reinless steeds —
Winner in Mother Carey's sabbath-fray

When, stung by magic of the witch's chant,
They rise, each foamy-crested combatant —
They rise and fall and leap and foam and
    gallop and pant
Till albatross, sea-swallow, and cormorant
    Would flee like doves away !

And shalt thou ride no more where thou
    hast ridden,
    And feast no more in hyaline halls and
    caves,
Master of Mother Carey's secrets hidden,
    Master most equal of the wind and waves,
Who never, save in stress of angriest blast,
Ask'd ship for shelter, — never, till at last
The foam-flakes, hurl'd against the sloping
    mast,
    Slash'd thee like whirling glaives !

Right home to fields no seamew ever kenn'd,
    Where scarce the great sea-wanderer
    fares with thee,
I come to take thee — nay, 't is I, thy
    friend —
Ah, tremble not — I come to set thee free ;
I come to tear this cage from off this wall,
And take thee hence to that fierce festival
Where billows march and winds are musical,
    Hymning the Victor-Sea !

.   .   .   .

Yea, lift thine eyes, my own can bear them
    now :
    Thou 'rt free ! thou 'rt free. Ah, surely
    a bird can smile !
Dost know me, Petrel ? Dost remember how
    I fed thee in the wake for many a mile,
Whilst thou wouldst pat the waves, then,
    rising, take
The morsel up and wheel about the wake ?
Thou 'rt free, thou 'rt free, but for thine
    own dear sake
    I keep thee caged awhile.

Away to sea ! no matter where the coast :
    The road that turns to home turns never
    wrong :
Where waves run high my bird will not be
    lost :
    His home I know : 't is where the winds
    are strong, —
Where, on her throne of billows, rolling
    hoary
And green and blue and splash'd with
    sunny glory,

Far, far from shore — from farthest prom-
    ontory —
The mighty Mother sings the triumphs of
    her story,
    Sings to my bird the song !

THE SONNET'S VOICE

(A METRICAL LESSON BY THE SEASHORE)

Yon silvery billows breaking on the beach
Fall back in foam beneath the star-shine
    clear,
The while my rhymes are murmuring in
    your ear
A restless lore like that the billows teach ;
For on these sonnet-waves my soul would
    reach
From its own depths, and rest within you,
    dear,
As, through the billowy voices yearning here,
Great nature strives to find a human speech.
A sonnet is a wave of melody :
From heaving waters of the impassion'd
    soul
A billow of tidal music one and whole
Flows in the "octave ;" then returning free,
Its ebbing surges in the "sestet" roll
Back to the deeps of Life's tumultuous sea.

COLERIDGE

I see thee pine like her in golden story
Who, in her prison, woke and saw, one day,
The gates thrown open — saw the sunbeams
    play,
With only a web 'tween her and summer's
    glory ;
Who, when that web — so frail, so transi-
    tory
It broke before her breath — had fallen
    away,
Saw other webs and others rise for aye
Which kept her prison'd till her hair was
    hoary.
Those songs half-sung that yet were all-
    divine —
That woke Romance, the queen, to reign
    afresh —
Had been but preludes from that lyre of
    thine,
Could thy rare spirit's wings have pierced
    the mesh
Spun by the wizard who compels the flesh,
But lets the poet see how heav'n can shine.

THE BREATH OF AVON

TO THE PILGRIMS OF GREATER BRITAIN
ON SHAKESPEARE'S BIRTHDAY

I

WHATE'ER of woe the Dark may hide in
    womb
For England, mother of kings of battle and
    song —
Be it rapine, racial hates, mysterious wrong,
Blizzard of Chance, or fiery dart of Doom —
Let breath of Avon, rich of meadow-bloom,
Bind her to that great daughter sever'd
    long —
To near and far-off children young and
    strong —
With fetters woven of Avon's flower per-
    fume.
Welcome, ye English-speaking pilgrims, ye
Whose hands around the world are join'd
    by him,
Who make his speech the language of the
    sea,
Till winds of Ocean waft from rim to rim
The breath of Avon: let this great day
    be
A Feast of Race no power shall ever dim.

II

From where the steeds of Earth's twin
    oceans toss
Their manes along Columbia's chariot-
    way —
From where Australia's long blue billows
    play —
From where the morn, quenching the
    Southern Cross,
Startling the frigate-bird and albatross
Asleep in air, breaks over Table Bay —
Come hither, Pilgrims, where these rushes
    sway
'Tween grassy banks of Avon soft as moss !
For, if ye found the breath of Ocean sweet,
Sweeter is Avon's earthy, flowery smell,
Distill'd from roots that feel the coming
    spell
Of May, who bids all flowers that lov'd him
    meet
In meadows that, remembering Shake-
    speare's feet,
Hold still a dream of music where they
    fell.

THE FIRST KISS

IF only in dreams may man be fully blest,
Is heav'n a dream ? Is she I clasp'd
    dream ?
Or stood she here even now where dew
    drops gleam
And miles of furze shine golden down the
    West ?
I seem to clasp her still — still on my breast
Her bosom beats, — I see the blue eye
    beam : —
I think she kiss'd these lips, for now they
    seem
Scarce mine : so hallow'd of the lips they
    press'd !
Yon thicket's breath — can that be eglan-
    tine ?
Those birds — can they be morning's chori-
    ters ?
Can this be earth ? Can these be banks of
    furze ?
Like burning bushes fir'd of God they shine
I seem to know them, though this body of
    mine
Pass'd into spirit at the touch of hers !

TOAST TO OMAR KHAYYÁM

AN EAST ANGLIAN ECHO-CHORUS

Chorus

IN this red wine, where Memory's eyes
    seem glowing
  Of days when wines were bright by
    Ouse and Cam,
And Norfolk's foaming nectar glittered
    showing
What beard of gold John Barleycorn was
    growing,
We drink to thee whose lore is Nature
    knowing,
      Omar Khayyám !

I

Star-gazer who canst read, when night is
    strowing
  Her scriptured orbs on Time's frail ori-
    flamme,
  Nature's proud blazon : " Who shall
    bless or damn ?
Life, Death, and Doom are all of my
    bestowing ! "

Chorus
Omar Khayyám !

II

[m]aster whose stream of balm and music,
    flowing
Through Persian gardens, widened till
    it swam —
A fragrant tide no bank of Time shall
    dam —
[th]rough Suffolk meads where gorse and
    may were blowing,

Chorus
Omar Khayyám !

III

[w]ho blent thy song with sound of cattle
    lowing,
And caw of rooks that perch on ewe
    and ram,
And hymn of lark, and bleat of orphan
    lamb,
[an]d swish of scythe in Bredfield's dewy
    mowing ?

Chorus
Omar Khayyám !

IV

'T was Fitz, " Old Fitz," whose knowledge,
    farther going
Than lore of Omar, " Wisdom's starry
    Cham,"
Made richer still thine opulent epigram :
Sowed seed from seed of thine immortal
    sowing.

Chorus
Omar Khayyám !

In this red wine, where Memory's eyes
    seem glowing
Of days when wines were bright by
    Ouse and Cam,
And Norfolk's foaming nectar glittered,
    showing
What beard of gold John Barleycorn was
    growing,
We drink to thee whose lore is Nature's
    knowing,
    Omar Khayyám !

David Gray

THE DEAR OLD TOILING ONE

OH, many a leaf will fall to-night,
As she wanders through the wood !
And many an angry gust will break
The dreary solitude.
I wonder if she 's past the bridge,
Where Luggie moans beneath,
While rain-drops clash in planted lines
On rivulet and heath.
Disease hath laid his palsied palm
Upon my aching brow ;
The headlong blood of twenty-one
Is thin and sluggish now.
'T is nearly ten ! A fearful night,
Without a single star
To light the shadow on her soul
With sparkle from afar :
The moon is canopied with clouds,
And her burden it is sore ;
What would wee Jackie do, if he
Should never see her more ?
Ay, light the lamp, and hang it up
At the window fair and free ;

'T will be a beacon on the hill
To let your mother see.
And trim it well, my little Ann,
For the night is wet and cold,
And you know the weary, winding way
Across the miry wold.
All drench'd will be her simple gown,
And the wet will reach her skin :
I wish that I could wander down,
And the red quarry win,
To take the burden from her back,
And place it upon mine ;
With words of cheerful condolence,
Not utter'd to repine.
You have a kindly mother, dears,
As ever bore a child,
And Heaven knows I love her well
In passion undefil'd.
Ah me ! I never thought that she
Would brave a night like this,
While I sat weaving by the fire
A web of fantasies.
How the winds beat this home of ours
With arrow-falls of rain ;

This lonely home upon the hill
They beat with might and main.
And 'mid the tempest one lone heart
Anticipates the glow,
Whence, all her weary journey done,
Shall happy welcome flow.
'T is after ten ! O, were she here,
Young man although I be,
I could fall down upon her neck,
And weep right gushingly !
I have not lov'd her half enough,
The dear old toiling one,
The silent watcher by my bed,
In shadow or in sun.

I DIE, BEING YOUNG

"Whom the gods love die young." The
    thought is old,
And yet it sooth'd the sweet Athenian mind.
I take it with all pleasure, overbold
Perhaps, yet to its virtue much inclin'd
By an inherent love for what is fair.
This is the utter poetry of woe,
That the bright-flashing gods should cure
    despair
By love, and make youth precious here below.

I die, being young ; and, dying, could be
    come
A pagan, with the tender Grecian trust.
Let death, the fell anatomy, benumb
The hand that writes, and fill my mouth
    with dust :
Chant no funereal theme, but, with
    choral
Hymn, O ye mourners, hail immortal youth
    auroral.

MY EPITAPH

Below lies one whose name was traced in
    sand.
He died, not knowing what it was to
    live :
Died, while the first sweet consciousness of
    manhood
To maiden thought electrified his soul,
Faint heatings in the calyx of the rose.
Bewilder'd reader, pass without a sigh,
In a proud sorrow ! There is life with
    God
In other kingdom of a sweeter air.
In Eden every flower is blown : Amen.

John Addington Symonds

AN EPISODE

Vasari tells that Luca Signorelli,
The morning star of Michael Angelo,
Had but one son, a youth of seventeen sum-
    mers,
Who died. That day the master at his
    easel
Wielded the liberal brush wherewith he
    painted
At Orvieto, on the Duomo's walls,
Stern forms of Death and Heaven and Hell
    and Judgment.
Then came they to him, and cried : "Thy
    son is dead,
Slain in a duel ; but the bloom of life
Yet lingers round red lips and downy
    cheek."
Luca spoke not, but listen'd. Next they
    bore
His dead son to the silent painting-room,
And left on tiptoe son and sire alone.

Still Luca spoke and groan'd not ; but he
    rais'd
The wonderful dead youth, and smooth'd
    his hair,
Wash'd his red wounds, and laid him on the
    bed,
Naked and beautiful, where rosy curtains
Shed a soft glimmer of uncertain splen-
    dor
Life-like upon the marble limbs below.
Then Luca seiz'd his palette : hour by
    hour
Silence was in the room ; none durst ap-
    proach :
Morn wore to noon, and noon to eve, when
    shyly
A little maid peep'd in, and saw the painter
Painting his dead son with unerring hand-
    stroke,
Firm and dry-ey'd before the lordly can-
    vas.

LUX EST UMBRA DEI

ᴀʏ, Death, thou art a shadow ! Even as
          light
ꜱ but the shadow of invisible God,
ₐnd of that shade the shadow is thin Night,
ʹeiling the earth whereon our feet have
          trod ;
ꜱo art Thou but the shadow of this life,
ᴛself the pale and unsubstantial shade
ᴼf living God, fulfill'd by love and strife
ʹhroughout the universe Himself hath
          made :
ₐnd as frail Night, following the flight of
          earth,
ᴼbscures the world we breathe in, for a
          while,
ꜱo Thou, the reflex of our mortal birth,
ʹeilest the life wherein we weep and
          smile :
ᴮut when both earth and life are whirl'd
          away,
ᵂhat shade can shroud us from God's
          deathless day ?

THE NIGHTINGALE

ᴡᴇɴᴛ a roaming through the woods alone,
ₐnd heard the nightingale that made her
          moan.

ᴴard task it were to tell how dewy-still
    Were flowers and ferns and foliage in
          the rays
ᴼf Hesper, white amid the daffodil
    Of twilight fleck'd with faintest chryso-
          prase ;
    And all the while, embower'd in leafy
          bays,
ʹhe bird prolong'd her sharp soul-thrilling
          tone.

went a roaming through the woods alone,
ₐnd heard the nightingale that made her
          moan.

ᴮut as I stood and listened, on the air
    Arose another voice more clear and keen,
ᵀhat startled silence with a sweet despair,
    And still'd the bird beneath her leafy
          screen :
    The star of Love, those lattice-boughs
          between,
ᵍrew large and lean'd to listen from his
          zone.

I went a roaming through the woods alone,
And heard the nightingale that made her
          moan.

The voice, methought, was neither man's
          nor boy's,
    Nor bird's nor woman's, but all these in
          one :
In Paradise perchance such perfect noise
    Resounds from angel choirs in unison,
    Chanting with cherubim their antiphon
To Christ and Mary on the sapphire throne.

I went a roaming through the woods alone,
And heard the nightingale that made her
          moan.

Then down the forest aisles there came a
          boy,
    Unearthly pale, with passion in his eyes ;
Who sang a song whereof the sound was joy,
    But all the burden was of love that dies
    And death that lives — a song of sobs
          and sighs,
A wild swan's note of Death and Love in
          one.

I went a roaming through the woods alone,
And heard the nightingale that made her
          moan.

Love burn'd within his luminous eyes, and
          Death
    Had made his fluting voice so keen and
          high,
The wild wood trembled as he pass'd be-
          neath,
    With throbbing throat singing, Love-led,
          to die :
    Then all was hush'd, till in the thicket
          nigh
The bird resum'd her sharp soul-thrilling
          tone.

I went a roaming through the woods alone,
And heard the nightingale that made her
          moan.

But in my heart and in my brain the cry,
    The wail, the dirge, the dirge of Death
          and Love,
Still throbs and throbs, flute-like, and will
          not die,
    Piercing and clear the night-bird's tune
          above, —

The aching, anguish'd, wild-swan's note,
  whereof
The sweet sad flower of song was over-
  blown.

I went a roaming through the woods alone,
And heard the nightingale that made her
  moan.

THE FALL OF A SOUL

I SAT unsphering Plato ere I slept :
Then through my dream the choir of gods
  was borne,
Swift as the wind and splendid as the morn,
Fronting the night of stars ; behind them
  swept
Tempestuous darkness o'er a drear descent,
Wherein I saw a crowd of charioteers
Urging their giddy steeds with cries and
  cheers,
To join the choir that aye before them
  went :
But one there was who fell, with broken car
And horses swooning down the gulf of
  gloom ;
Heavenward his eyes, though prescient of
  their doom,
Reflected glory like a falling star,
While with wild hair blown back and list-
  less hands
Ruining he sank toward undiscover'd lands.

FAREWELL

IT is buried and done with,
  The love that we knew :
Those cobwebs we spun with
  Are beaded with dew.

I lov'd thee ; I leave thee :
  To love thee was pain :
I dare not believe thee,
  To love thee again.

Like spectres unshriven
  Are the years that I lost;
To thee they were given
  Without count of cost.

I cannot revive them
  By penance or prayer :
Hell's tempest must drive them
  Through turbulent air.

Farewell, and forget me ;
  For I too am free
From the shame that beset me,
  The sorrow of thee.

IL FIOR DEGLI EROICI FUROR

(SAXIFRAGA PYRAMIDALIS)

I BLOOM but once, and then I perish;
  This plume of snow
No sun or soft south wind will cherish —
  'T is drooping now.

Black streams beneath me foam and thun-
  der ;
  Their icy breath,
There where the rocks are rent asunder,
  Wooes me with death.

Still like a fair imperial streamer
  I float and flaunt;
I am no light luxurious dreamer,
  Whom dangers daunt.

For me no delicate life-lover
  Will dare to bow ;
My pyramid of bloom shall cover
  No craven's brow.

But should some youth on whom the splen-
  dor
  Of hope is high,
Who loves with love superb and tender
  What cannot die,

Pass by this dark and awful dwelling,
  He shall not shrink
From slippery rock or sick waves swell-
  ing
  To the black brink;

But stoop and pluck the song I utter
  Of death and joy :
Yea, my free plume of snow shall flutter
  To greet the boy.

VENICE

VENICE, thou Siren of sea-cities, wrought
By mirage, built on water, stair o'er stair,
Of sunbeams and cloud-shadows, phantom
  fair,
With naught of earth to mar thy sea-born
  thought !

hou floating film upon the wonder-fraught
cean of dreams ! Thou hast no dream so
rare
s are thy sons and daughters, they who
wear
oam-flakes of charm from thine enchant-
ment caught !
dark brown eyes ! O tangles of dark hair !
heaven-blue eyes, blonde tresses where
the breeze
lays over sun-burn'd cheeks in sea-blown
air !
irm limbs of moulded bronze ! frank
debonair
miles of deep-bosom'd women ! Loves
that seize
Ian's soul, and waft her on storm-melo-
dies !

THYSELF

IVE me thyself ! It were as well to cry :
ive me the splendor of this night of June !
ive me yon star upon the swart lagoon
rembling in unapproach'd serenity !
ur gondola, that four swift oarsmen ply,
hoots from the darkening Lido's sandy
dune,
plits with her steel the mirrors of the
moon,
hivers the star-beams that before us fly.
ive me thyself ! This prayer is even a
knell,
Varning me back to mine own impotence.
elf gives not self ; and souls sequester'd
dwell
n the dark fortalice of thought and sense,
Vhere, though life's prisoners call from
cell to cell,
ach pines alone and may not issue thence.

THE SONNET

I

HE Sonnet is a fruit which long hath slept
nd ripen'd on life's sun-warm'd orchard-
wall ;
gem which, hardening in the mystical
line. of man's heart, to quenchless flame
hath leapt ;
medal of pure gold art's nympholept
tamps with love's lips and brows imperial ;
branch from memory's briar, whereon
the fall
f thought-eternalizing tears hath wept :

A star that shoots athwart star-steadfast
heaven ;
A fluttering aigrette of toss'd passion's
brine ;
A leaf from youth's immortal missal torn ;
A bark across dark seas of anguish driven ;
A feather dropp'd from breast-wings aqui-
line ;
A silvery dream shunning red lips of morn

II

There is no mood, no heart-throb fugitive,
No spark from man's imperishable mind,
No moment of man's will, that may not
find
Form in the Sonnet ; and thenceforward
live
A potent elf, by art's imperative
Magic to crystal spheres of song confin'd :
As in the moonstone's orb pent spirits
wind
'Mid dungeon depths day-beams they take
and give.
Spare thou no pains ; carve thought's pure
diamond
With fourteen facets, scattering fire and
light : —
Uncut, what jewel burns but darkly bright ?
And Prospero vainly waves his runic wand,
If spurning art's inexorable law
In Ariel's prison-sphere he leave one flaw.

III

The Sonnet is a world, where feelings caught
In webs of phantasy, combine and fuse
Their kindred elements 'neath mystic dews
Shed from the ether round man's dwelling
wrought ;
Distilling heart's content, star-fragrance
fraught
With influences from the breathing fires
Of heaven in everlasting endless gyres
Enfolding and encircling orbs of thought.
Our Sonnet's world hath two fix'd hemi-
spheres :
This, where the sun with fierce strength
masculine
Pours his keen rays and bids the noonday
shine ;
That, where the moon and the stars, con-
cordant powers,
Shed milder rays, and daylight disappears
In low melodious music of still hours.

Alexander Hay Japp

A MUSIC LESSON

FINGERS on the holes, Johnny,
  Fairly in a raw :
Lift this and then that,
  And blaw, blaw, blaw !
That 's hoo to play, Johnny,
  On the pipes sae shrill :
Never was the piper yet
  But needit a' his skill.

And lang and sair he tried it, tae,
  Afore he wan the knack
O' making bag and pipe gie
  His verra yearnin's back.
The echo tae his heart-strings
  Frae sic a thing to come ;
Oh, is it no a wonder —
  Like a voice frae out the dumb ?

Tak' tentie, noo, my Johnny lad,
  Ye maunna hurry thro',
Tak' time and try it ower again —
  Sic a blast ye blew !
It 's no alane by blawing strang,
  But eke by blawing true,
That ye can mak' the music
  To thrill folk thro' and thro'.

The waik folk and the learnin',
  'T is them that mak's the din ;
But for the finish'd pipers
  They count it as a sin :
And maybe it 's the verra same
  A' the warld thro',
The learners are the verra ones
  That mak' the most ado !

Ye ken the Southrons taunt us —
  I sayna they 're unfair —
Aboot oor squallin' music,
  And their taunts hae hurt me sair ;
But if they 'd heard a piper true
  At nicht come ower the hill,
Playin' up a pibroch
  Upon the wind sae still :

Risin' noo, and fallin' noo,
  And floatin' on the air,
The sounds come saftly on ye
  Amaist ere ye 're aware,

And wind themsels aboot the heart,
  That hasna yet forgot
The witchery o' love and joy
  Within some lanely spot :

I 'm sure they wadna taunt us sae,
  Nor say the bagpipe 's wild,
Nor speak o' screachin' noises
  Enuch to deave a child :
They would say the bagpipe only
  Is the voice of hill and glen ;
And would listen to it sorrowing,
  Within the haunts of men.

Fingers on the holes, Johnny,
  Fairly in a raw :
Lift this and then that,
  And blaw, blaw, blaw !
That 's hoo to play, Johnny,
  On the pipes sae shrill :
Never was the piper yet
  But needit a' his skill.

LANDOR

LIKE crown'd athlete that in a race has run,
And points his finger at those left behind,
And follows on his way as now inclin'd,
With song and laughter in the glowing sun,
And joys at that which he hath joyous done,
And, like a child, will wanton with the
  wind,
And pluck the flowers his radiant brows to
  bind —
Re-crown himself as conscious he hath won ;
And still regardless of his fellow-men
He follows on his road intent and fain
To please himself, and caring not to gain
The world's applause which he might seek
  in vain :
A soldier, yet would, careless, sport and
  play
And leave the reckoning for a distant day.

SHELLEY

THE odor of a rose : light of a star :
The essence of a flame blown on by wind,
That lights and warms all near it, bland
  and kind,
But aye consumes itself, as though at war

With what supports and feeds it ; — from
   afar
It draws its life, but evermore inclin'd
To leap into the flame that makes men
   blind
Who seek the secret of all things that are.
Such wert thou, Shelley, bound for airiest
   goal :
Interpreter of quintessential things :
Who mounted ever up on eagle-wings
Of phantasy : had aim'd at heaven and
   stole
Promethean fire for men to be as gods,
And dwell in free, aerial abodes.

MEMORIES

My love he went to Burdon Fair, .
And of all the gifts that he saw there
Was none could his great love declare ;

So he brought me marjoram smelling rare —
Its sweetness filled all the air.
   Oh, the days I dote on yet,
   Marjoram, pansies, mignonette !

My love he sail'd across the sea,
And all to make a home for me.
Oh, sweet his last kiss on the lea,
The pansies pluck'd beneath the tree,
When he said, " My love, I 'll send for
   thee ! "
   Oh, the days I dote on yet,
   Marjoram, pansies, mignonette !

His mother sought for me anon ;
So long my name she would not own.
Ah, gladly would she now atone,
For we together make our moan !
She brought the mignonette I 've sown.
   Oh, the days I dote on yet,
   Marjoram, pansies, mignonette !

Cosmo Monkhouse

SONG

Who calls me bold because I won my love,
   And did not pine,
And waste my life with secret pain, but
   strove
   To make him mine ?

Us'd no arts ; 't was Nature's self that
   taught
   My eye to speak,
And bid the burning blush to paint unsought
   My flashing cheek ;

That made my voice to tremble when I bid
   My love " Goodby,"
So weak that every other sound was hid,
   Except a sigh.

Oh, was it wrong to use the truth I knew,
   That hearts are mov'd,
And spring warm-struck with life and love
   anew,
   By being lov'd ?

One night there came a tear, that, big and
   loth,
   Stole 'neath my brow.

'T was thus I won my heart's own heart,
   and both
   Are happy now.

A DEAD MARCH

Play me a march, low-ton'd and slow —
   a march for a silent tread,
Fit for the wandering feet of one who
   dreams of the silent dead,
Lonely, between the bones below and the
   souls that are overhead.

Here for a while they smil'd and sang,
   alive in the interspace,
Here with the grass beneath the foot, and
   the stars above the face,
Now are their feet beneath the grass, and
   whither has flown their grace ?

Who shall assure us whence they come, or
   tell us the way they go ?
Verily, life with them was joy, and, now
   they have left us, woe,
Once they were not, and now they are not,
   and this is the sum we know.

Orderly range the seasons due, and orderly
    roll the stars.
How shall we deem the soldier brave who
    frets of his wounds and scars ?
Are we as senseless brutes that we should
    dash at the well-seen bars ?

No, we are here, with feet unfix'd, but ever
    as if with lead
Drawn from the orbs which shine above to
    the orb on which we tread,
Down to the dust from which we came and
    with which we shall mingle dead.

No, we are here to wait, and work, and
    strain our banish'd eyes,
Weary and sick of soil and toil, and hungry
    and fain for skies
Far from the reach of wingless men, and
    not to be scal'd with cries.

No, we are here to bend our necks to the
    yoke of tyrant Time,
Welcoming all the gifts he gives us — glo-
    ries of youth and prime,
Patiently watching them all depart as our
    heads grow white as rime.

Why do we mourn the days that go — for
    the same sun shines each day,
Ever a spring her primrose hath, and ever
    a May her may ;
Sweet as the rose that died last year is the
    rose that is born to-day.

Do we not too return, we men, as ever the
    round earth whirls ?
Never a head is dimm'd with gray but an-
    other is sunn'd with curls ;
She was a girl and he was a boy, but yet
    there are boys and girls.

Ah, but alas for the smile of smiles that
    never but one face wore ;
Ah, for the voice that has flown away like
    a bird to an unseen shore ;
Ah, for the face — the flower of flowers —
    that blossoms on earth no more.

THE SPECTRUM

How many colors here do we see set,
Like rings upon God's finger ? Some say
    three,

Some four, some six, some seven. All agree
To left of red, to right of violet,
Waits darkness deep as night and black a
    jet.
And so we know what Noah saw we see,
Nor less nor more — of God's emblazonry
A shred — a sign of glory known not yet.
If red can glide to yellow, green to blue,
What joys may yet await our wider eyes
When we rewake upon a wider shore !
What deep pulsations, exquisite and new !
What keener, swifter raptures may surprise
Men born to see the rainbow and no more

THE SECRET

She passes in her beauty bright
    Amongst the mean, amongst the gay,
And all are brighter for the sight,
    And bless her as she goes her way.

And now a gleam of pity pours,
    And now a spark of spirit flies,
Uncounted, from the unlock'd stores
    Of her rich lips and precious eyes.

And all men look, and all men smile,
    But no man looks on her as I :
They mark her for a little while,
    But I will watch her till I die.

And if I wonder now and then
    Why this so strange a thing should be—
That she be seen by wiser men
    And only duly lov'd by me :

I only wait a little longer,
    And watch her radiance in the room
'Here making light a little stronger,
    And there obliterating gloom,

(Like one who, in a tangled way,
    Watches the broken sun fall through,
Turning to gold the faded spray,
    And making diamonds of dew).

Until at last, as my heart burns,
    She gathers all her scatter'd light,
And undivided radiance turns
    Upon me like a sea of light.

And then I know they see in part
    That which God lets me worship whole
He gives them glances of her heart,
    But me, the sunshine of her soul.

Robert Buchanan

THE BALLAD OF JUDAS IS-CARIOT

'T was the body of Judas Iscariot
Lay in the Field of Blood ;
'T was the soul of Judas Iscariot
Beside the body stood.

Black was the earth by night,
And black was the sky ;
Black, black were the broken clouds,
Tho' the red Moon went by.

'T was the body of Judas Iscariot
Strangled and dead lay there ;
'T was the soul of Judas Iscariot
Look'd on it in despair.

The breath of the World came and went
Like a sick man's in rest ;
Drop by drop on the World's eyes
The dews fell cool and blest.

Then the soul of Judas Iscariot
Did make a gentle moan —
" I will bury underneath the ground
My flesh and blood and bone.

" I will bury deep beneath the soil,
Lest mortals look thereon,
And when the wolf and raven come
The body will be gone !

" The stones of the field are sharp as steel,
And hard and bold, God wot ;
And I must bear my body hence
Until I find a spot ! "

'T was the soul of Judas Iscariot
So grim, and gaunt, and gray,
Rais'd the body of Judas Iscariot,
And carried it away.

And as he bare it from the field
Its touch was cold as ice,
And the ivory teeth within the jaw
Rattled aloud, like dice.

As the soul of Judas Iscariot
Carried its load with pain,
The Eye of Heaven, like a lanthorn's eye,
Open'd and shut again.

Half he walk'd, and half he seem'd
Lifted on the cold wind ;
He did not turn, for chilly hands
Were pushing from behind.

The first place that he came unto
It was the open wold,
And underneath were prickly whins,
And a wind that blew so cold.

The next place that he came unto
It was a stagnant pool,
And when he threw the body in
It floated light as wool.

He drew the body on his back,
And it was dripping chill,
And the next place that he came unto
Was a Cross upon a hill.

A Cross upon the windy hill,
And a Cross on either side,
Three skeletons that swing thereon,
Who had been crucified.

And on the middle cross-bar sat
A white Dove slumbering ;
Dim it sat in the dim light,
With its head beneath its wing.

And underneath the middle Cross
A grave yawn'd wide and vast,
But the soul of Judas Iscariot
Shiver'd, and glided past.

The fourth place that he came unto
It was the Brig of Dread,
And the great torrents rushing down
Were deep, and swift, and red.

He dar'd not fling the body in
For fear of faces dim,
And arms were wav'd in the wild water
To thrust it back to him.

'T was the soul of Judas Iscariot
Turn'd from the Brig of Dread,
And the dreadful foam of the wild water
Had splash'd the body red.

For days and nights he wander'd on
Upon an open plain,

And the days went by like blinding mist,
And the nights like rushing rain.

For days and nights he wander'd on,
All thro' the Wood of Woe ;
And the nights went by like moaning wind,
And the days like drifting snow.

'T was the soul of Judas Iscariot
Came with a weary face —
Alone, alone, and all alone,
Alone in a lonely place !

He wander'd east, he wander'd west,
And heard no human sound ;
For months and years, in grief and tears,
He wander'd round and round.

For months and years, in grief and tears,
He walk'd the silent night ;
Then the soul of Judas Iscariot
Perceiv'd a far-off light.

A far-off light across the waste,
As dim as dim might be,
That came and went like a lighthouse
    gleam
On a black night at sea.

'T was the soul of Judas Iscariot
Crawl'd to the distant gleam ;
And the rain came down, and the rain was
    blown
Against him with a scream.

For days and nights he wander'd on,
Push'd on by hands behind ;
And the days went by like black, black
    rain,
And the nights like rushing wind.

'T was the soul of Judas Iscariot,
Strange, and sad, and tall,
Stood all alone at dead of night
Before a lighted hall.

And the wold was white with snow,
And his foot-marks black and damp,
And the ghost of the silver Moon arose,
Holding her yellow lamp.

And the icicles were on the eaves,
And the walls were deep with white,
And the shadows of the guests within
Pass'd on the window light.

The shadows of the wedding guests
Did strangely come and go,
And the body of Judas Iscariot
Lay stretch'd along the snow.

The body of Judas Iscariot
Lay stretch'd along the snow ;
'T was the soul of Judas Iscariot
Ran swiftly to and fro.

To and fro, and up and down,
He ran so swiftly there,
As round and round the frozen Pole
Glideth the lean white bear.

'T was the Bridegroom sat at the table
    head,
And the lights burn'd bright and clear —
"Oh, who is that," the Bridegroom said,
"Whose weary feet I hear ? "

'T was one look'd from the lighted hall,
And answer'd soft and slow,
"It is a wolf runs up and down
With a black track in the snow. "

The Bridegroom in his robe of white
Sat at the table-head —
"Oh, who is that who moans without ? "
The blessed Bridegroom said.

'T was one look'd from the lighted hall,
And answer'd fierce and low,
"'T is the soul of Judas Iscariot
Gliding to and fro."

'T was the soul of Judas Iscariot
Did hush itself and stand,
And saw the Bridegroom at the door
With a light in his hand.

The Bridegroom stood in the open door,
And he was clad in white,
And far within the Lord's Supper
Was spread so long and bright.

The Bridegroom shaded his eyes an
    look'd,
And his face was bright to see —
"What dost thou here at the Lord's Sup
    per
With thy body's sins ? " said he.

'T was the soul of Judas Iscariot
Stood black, and sad, and bare —

"I have wander'd many nights and days ;
  There is no light elsewhere. "

'Twas the wedding guests cried out within,
  And their eyes were fierce and bright —
" Scourge the soul of Judas Iscariot
  Away into the night ! "

The Bridegroom stood in the open door,
  And he wav'd hands still and slow,
And the third time that he wav'd his hands
  The air was thick with snow.

And of every flake of falling snow,
  Before it touch'd the ground,
There came a dove, and a thousand doves
  Made sweet sound.

'Twas the body of Judas Iscariot
  Floated away full fleet,
And the wings of the doves that bare it off
  Were like its winding-sheet.

'Twas the Bridegroom stood at the open
    door,
  And beckon'd, smiling sweet ;
'Twas the soul of Judas Iscariot
  Stole in, and fell at his feet.

" The Holy Supper is spread within,
  And the many candles shine,
And I have waited long for thee
  Before I pour'd the wine ! "

The supper wine is pour'd at last,
  The lights burn bright and fair,
Iscariot washes the Bridegroom's feet,
  And dries them with his hair.

SPRING SONG IN THE CITY

WHO remains in London,
  In the streets with me,
Now that Spring is blowing
  Warm winds from the sea ;
Now that trees grow green and tall,
  Now the sun shines mellow,
And with moist primroses all
  English lanes are yellow ?

Little barefoot maiden,
  Selling violets blue,
Hast thou ever pictur'd
  Where the sweetlings grew ?

Oh, the warm wild woodland ways,
  Deep in dewy grasses,
Where the wind-blown shadow strays,
  Scented as it passes !

Pedlar breathing deeply,
  Toiling into town,
With the dusty highway
  You are dusky brown ;
Hast thou seen by daisied leas,
  And by rivers flowing,
Lilac-ringlets which the breeze
  Loosens lightly blowing ?

Out of yonder wagon
  Pleasant hay-scents float,
He who drives it carries
  A daisy in his coat :
Oh, the English meadows, fair
  Far beyond all praises !
Freckled orchids everywhere
  Mid the snow of daisies !

Now in busy silence
  Broods the nightingale,
Choosing his love's dwelling
  In a dimpled dale ;
Round the leafy bower they raise
  Rose-trees wild are springing ;
Underneath, thro' the green haze,
  Bounds the brooklet singing.

And his love is silent
  As a bird can be,
For the red buds only
  Fill the red rose-tree ;
Just as buds and blossoms blow
  He 'll begin his tune,
When all is green and roses glow
  Underneath the moon.

Nowhere in the valleys
  Will the wind be still,
Everything is waving,
  Wagging at his will :
Blows the milkmaid's kirtle clean,
  With her hand press'd on it ;
Lightly o'er the hedge so green
  Blows the ploughboy's bonnet.

Oh, to be a-roaming
  In an English dell !
Every nook is wealthy,
  All the world looks well,

Tinted soft the Heavens glow,
  Over Earth and Ocean,
Waters flow, breezes blow,
  All is light and motion !

THE WAKE OF TIM O'HARA

(SEVEN DIALS)

To the Wake of O'Hara
  Came company ;
All St. Patrick's Alley
  Was there to see,
With the friends and kinsmen
  Of the family.
On the long deal table lay Tim in white,
And at his pillow the burning light.
Pale as himself, with the tears on her
    cheek,
The mother receiv'd us, too full to speak ;
But she heap'd the fire, and on the board
Set the black bottle with never a word,
While the company gather'd, one and all,
Men and women, big and small :
Not one in the Alley but felt a call
  To the Wake of Tim O'Hara.

At the face of O'Hara,
  All white with sleep,
Not one of the women
  But took a peep,
And the wives new-wedded
  Began to weep.
The mothers gather'd round about,
And prais'd the linen and laying out, —
For white as snow was his winding-sheet,
And all was peaceful, and clean, and sweet ;
And the old wives, praising the blessed
    dead,
Were thronging around the old press-bed,
Where O'Hara's widow, tatter'd and torn,
Held to her bosom the babe new-born,
And star'd all around her, with eyes for-
    lorn,
  At the Wake of Tim O'Hara.

For the heart of O'Hara
  Was good as gold,
And the life of O'Hara
  Was bright and bold,
And his smile was precious
  To young and old !
Gay as a guinea, wet or dry,
With a smiling mouth, and a twinkling
    eye !

Had ever an answer for chaff and fun ;
Would fight like a lion, with any one !
Not a neighbor of any trade
But knew some joke that the boy had
    made ;
Not a neighbor, dull or bright,
But minded *something* — frolic or fight,
And whisper'd it round the fire that night,
  At the Wake of Tim O'Hara.

  " To God be glory
    In death and life,
  He 's taken O'Hara
    From trouble and strife ! "
  Said one-eyed Biddy,
    The apple-wife.
" God bless old Ireland ! " said Mistress
    Hart,
Mother to Mike of the donkey-cart ;
" God bless old Ireland till all be done,
She never made wake for a better son ! "
And all join'd chorus, and each one said
Something kind of the boy that was dead ;
And the bottle went round from lip to lip,
And the weeping widow, for fellowship,
Took the glass of old Biddy and had a sip,
  At the Wake of Tim O'Hara.

  Then we drank to O'Hara
    With drams to the brim,
  While the face of O'Hara
    Look'd on so grim,
  In the corpse-light shining
    Yellow and dim.
The cup of liquor went round again,
And the talk grew louder at every drain ;
Louder the tongue of the women grew !
The lips of the boys were loosening too !
The widow her weary eyelids clos'd,
And, soothed by the drop o' drink, she
    doz'd ;
The mother brighten'd and laugh'd to hear
Of O'Hara's fight with the grenadier,
And the hearts of all took better cheer,
  At the Wake of Tim O'Hara.

  Tho' the face of O'Hara
    Look'd on so wan,
  In the chimney-corner
    The row began—
  Lame Tony was in it,
    The oyster-man ;
For a dirty low thief from the North
    came near,
And whistled " Boyne Water " in his ear,

And Tony, with never a word of grace,
Flung out his fist in the blackguard's face ;
And the girls and women scream'd out for
    fright,
And the men that were drunkest began to
    fight :
Over the tables and chairs they threw, —
The corpse-light tumbled, — the trouble
    grew, —
The new-born join'd in the hullabaloo, —
    At the Wake of Tim O'Hara.

    " Be still ! be silent !
      Ye do a sin !
    Shame be his portion
      Who dares begin ! "
'T was Father O'Connor
    Just enter'd in !
All look'd down, and the row was done,
And sham'd and sorry was every one ;
But the Priest just smil'd quite easy and
    free —
" Would ye wake the poor boy from his
    sleep ? " said he :
And he said a prayer, with a shining face,
Till a kind of brightness fill'd the place ;
The women lit up the dim corpse-light,
The men were quieter at the sight,
And the peace of the Lord fell on all that
    night
    At the Wake of Tim O'Hara.

TWO SONS

    I HAVE two sons, wife —
      Two, and yet the same ;
    One his wild way runs, wife,
      Bringing us to shame.
The one is bearded, sunburnt, grim, and
    fights across the sea,
The other is a little child who sits upon
    your knee.

    One is fierce and cold, wife,
      As the wayward deep ;
    Him no arms could hold, wife,
      Him no breast could keep.
He has tried our hearts for many a year,
    not broken them ; for he
Is still the sinless little one that sits upon
    your knee.

    One may fall in fight, wife —
      Is he not our son ?
    Pray with all your might, wife,
      For the wayward one ;

Pray for the dark, rough soldier, who fights
    across the sea,
Because you love the little shade who smiles
    upon your knee.

    One across the foam, wife,
      As I speak may fall ;
    But this one at home, wife,
      Cannot die at all.
They both are only one ; and how thankful
    should we be,
We cannot lose the darling son who sits
    upon your knee !

ON A YOUNG POETESS'S GRAVE

UNDER her gentle seeing,
    In her delicate little hand,
They placed the Book of Being,
    To read and understand.

The Book was mighty and olden,
    Yea, worn and eaten with age ;
Though the letters look'd great and golden,
    She could not read a page.

The letters flutter'd before her,
    And all look'd sweetly wild :
Death saw her, and bent o'er her,
    As she pouted her lips and smil'd.

And weary a little with tracing
    The Book, she look'd aside,
And lightly smiling, and placing
    A Flower in its leaves, she died.

She died, but her sweetness fled not,
    As fly the things of power, —
For the Book wherein she read not
    Is the sweeter for the Flower.

THE SUMMER POOL

THERE is a singing in the summer air,
The blue and brown moths flutter o'er the
    grass,
The stubble bird is creaking in the wheat,
And perch'd upon the honeysuckle-hedge
Pipes the green linnet. Oh, the golden
    world !
The stir of life on every blade of grass,
The motion and the joy on every bough,
The glad feast everywhere, for things that
    love
The sunshine, and for things that love the
    shade !

Aimlessly wandering with weary feet,
Watching the wool-white clouds that wan-
    der by,
I come upon a lonely place of shade, —
A still green Pool, where with soft sound
    and stir
The shadows of o'erhanging branches sleep,
Save where they leave one dreamy space of
    blue,
O'er whose soft stillness ever and anon
The feathery cirrus blows.   Here un-
    aware
I pause, and leaning on my staff I add
A shadow to the shadows ; and behold !
Dim dreams steal down upon me, with a
    hum
Of little wings, a murmuring of boughs,
The dusky stir and motion dwelling here,
Within this small green world.   O'ershad-
    ow'd
By dusky greenery, tho' all around
The sunshine throbs on fields of wheat
    and bean,
Downward I gaze into the dreamy blue,
And pass into a waking sleep, wherein
The green boughs rustle, feathery wreaths
    of cloud
Pass softly, piloted by golden airs :
The air is still, — no birds sing any
    more, —
And helpless as a tiny flying thing,
I am alone in all the world with God.

The wind dies — not a leaf stirs — on the
    Pool
The fly scarce moves ; earth seems to hold
    her breath
Until her heart stops, listening silently
For the far footsteps of the coming rain !

While thus I pause, it seems that I have
    gain'd
New eyes to see ; my brain grows sensitive
To trivial things that, at another hour,
Had pass'd unheeded.   Suddenly the air
Shivers, the shadows in whose midst I
    stand
Tremble and blacken — the blue eye o' the
    Pool
Is clos'd and clouded ; with a sudden gleam
Oiling its wings, a swallow darteth past,
And weedling flowers beneath my feet
    thrust up
Their leaves, to feel the fragrant shower.
    Oh, hark !

The thirsty leaves are troubled into sighs,
And up above me, on the glistening boughs,
Patters the summer rain !

                    Into a nook,
Screen'd by thick foliage of oak and beech,
I creep for shelter ; and the summer shower
Murmurs around me.   Oh, the drowsy
    sounds !
The pattering rain, the numerous sigh of
    leaves,
The deep, warm breathing of the scented
    air,
Sink sweet into my soul — until at last
Comes the soft ceasing of the gentle fall,
And lo ! the eye of blue within the Pool
Opens again, while with a silvern gleam
Dew-diamonds twinkle moistly on the
    leaves,
Or, shaken downward by the summer wind,
Fall melting on the Pool in rings of light !

WE ARE CHILDREN

CHILDREN indeed are we — children that
    wait
Within a wondrous dwelling, while on high
Stretch the sad vapors and the voiceless
    sky ;
The house is fair, yet all is desolate
Because our Father comes not ; clouds of
    fate
Sadden above us — shivering we espy
The passing rain, the cloud before the gate,
And cry to one another, " He is nigh ! "
At early morning, with a shining Face,
He left us innocent and lily-crown'd ;
And now this late — night cometh on
    apace —
We hold each other's hands and look
    around,
Frighted at our own shades !   Heaven send
    us grace !
When He returns, all will be sleeping
    sound.

WHEN WE ARE ALL ASLEEP

WHEN He returns, and finds the world so
    drear,
All sleeping, young and old, unfair and
    fair,
Will he stoop down and whisper in each
    ear,
" Awaken ! " or for pity's sake forbear,

Saying, "How shall I meet their frozen
   stare
Of wonder, and their eyes so full of fear?
How shall I comfort them in their despair,
If they cry out, 'Too late! let us sleep
   here'?"
Perchance He will not wake us up, but
   when
He sees us look so happy in our rest,
Will murmur, "Poor dead women and dead
   men!
Dire was their doom, and weary was their
   quest.
Wherefore awake them into life again?
Let them sleep on untroubled — it is best."

THE DREAM OF THE WORLD
WITHOUT DEATH

FROM "THE BOOK OF ORM"

Now, sitting by her side, worn out with
   weeping,
Behold, I fell to sleep, and had a vision,
Wherein I heard a wondrous Voice inton-
   ing:

Crying aloud, "The Master on His throne
Openeth now the seventh seal of wonder,
And beckoneth back the angel men name
   Death.

"And at His feet the mighty Angel kneel-
   eth,
Breathing not; and the Lord doth look
   upon him,
Saying, 'Thy wanderings on earth are
   ended.'

"And lo! the mighty Shadow sitteth idle
Even at the silver gates of heaven,
Drowsily looking in on quiet waters,
And puts his silence among men no longer."

.   .   .   .

The world was very quiet. Men in traffic
Cast looks over their shoulders; pallid sea-
   men
Shiver'd to walk upon the decks alone;

And women barr'd their doors with bars of
   iron,
In the silence of the night; and at the sun-
   rise
Trembled behind the husbandmen afield.

I could not see a kirkyard near or far;
I thirsted for a green grave, and my vision
Was weary for the white gleam of a tomb-
   stone.

But harkening dumbly, ever and anon
I heard a cry out of a human dwelling,
And felt the cold wind of a lost one's going.

One struck a brother fiercely, and he fell,
And faded in a darkness; and that other
Tore his hair, and was afraid, and could
   not perish.

One struck his aged mother on the mouth,
And she vanish'd with a gray grief from
   his hearth-stone.
One melted from her bairn, and on the
   ground

With sweet unconscious eyes the bairn lay
   smiling.
And many made a weeping among moun-
   tains,
And hid themselves in caverns, and were
   drunken.

I heard a voice from out the beauteous earth,
Whose side roll'd up from winter into
   summer,
Crying, "I am grievous for my children."

I heard a voice from out the hoary ocean,
Crying, "Burial in the breast of me were
   better,
Yea, burial in the salt flags and green
   crystals."

I heard a voice from out the hollow ether,
Saying, "The thing ye curs'd hath been
   abolish'd —
Corruption and decay, and dissolution!"

And the world shriek'd, and the summer-
   time was bitter,
And men and women fear'd the air behind
   them;
And for lack of its green graves the world
   was hateful.

.   .   .   .

Now at the bottom of a snowy mountain
I came upon a woman thin with sorrow,
Whose voice was like the crying of a sea-
   gull:

Saying, " O Angel of the Lord, come hither,
And bring me him I seek for on thy bosom,
That I may close his eyelids and embrace
    him.

" I curse thee that I cannot look upon him !
I curse thee that I know not he is sleep-
    ing !
Yet know that he has vanish'd upon God !

" I laid my little girl upon a wood-bier,
And very sweet she seem'd, and near unto
    me ;
And slipping flowers into her shroud was
    comfort.

" I put my silver mother in the darkness,
And kiss'd her, and was solaced by her
    kisses,
And set a stone, to mark the place, above
    her.

" And green, green were their sleeping-
    places,
So green that it was pleasant to remem-
    ber
That I and my tall man would sleep beside
    them.

" The closing of dead eyelids is not dread-
    ful,
For comfort comes upon us when we close
    them,
And tears fall, and our sorrow grows famil-
    iar ;

" And we can sit above them where they
    slumber,
And spin a dreamy pain into a sweetness,
And know indeed that we are very near
    them.

" But to reach out empty arms is surely
    dreadful,
And to feel the hollow empty world is
    awful,
And bitter grows the silence and the dis-
    tance.

" There is no space for grieving or for weep-
    ing ;
No touch, no cold, no agony to strive with,
And nothing but a horror and a blankness ! "

   *   .   .   .   .

Now behold I saw a woman in a mud-hut
Raking the white spent embers with her
    fingers,
And fouling her bright hair witl the white
    ashes.

Her mouth was very bitter with the ashes ;
Her eyes with dust were blinded ; and her
    sorrow
Sobb'd in the throat of her like gurgling
    water.

And all around the voiceless hills were
    hoary,
But red lights scorch'd their edges ; and
    above her
There was a soundless trouble of the vapors.

" Whither, and O whither," said the woman,
" O Spirit of the Lord, hast thou convey'd
    them,
My little ones, my little son and daughter ?

" For, lo ! we wander'd forth at early morn-
    ing,
And winds were blowing round us, and
    their mouths
Blew rose-buds to the rose-buds, and their
    eyes

" Look'd violets at the violets, and their
    hair
Made sunshine in the sunshine, and their
    passing
Left a pleasure in the dewy leaves behind
    them ;

" And suddenly my little son look'd upward
And his eyes were dried like dew-drops ;
    and his going
Was like a blow of fire upon my face ;

" And my little son was gone. My little
    daughter
Look'd round me for him, clinging to my
    vesture ;
But the Lord had drawn him from me, and
    I knew it

" By the sign He gives the stricken, that
    the lost one
Lingers nowhere on the earth, on the hill
    or valley,
Neither underneath the grasses nor the
    tree-roots.

And my shriek was like the splitting of an ice-reef,
And I sank among my hair, and all my palm
Was moist and warm where the little hand had fill'd it.

Then I fled and sought him wildly, hither and thither —
Though I knew that he was stricken from me wholly
By the token that the Spirit gives the stricken.

" I sought him in the sunlight and the starlight,
I sought him in great forests, and in waters
Where I saw my own pale image looking at me.

"And I forgot my little bright-hair'd daughter,
Though her voice was like a wild-bird's far behind me,
Till the voice ceas'd, and the universe was silent.

" And stilly, in the starlight, came I backward
To the forest where I miss'd him ; and no voices
Brake the stillness as I stoop'd down in the starlight,

"And saw two little shoes filled up with dew,
And no mark of little footsteps any far-ther,
And knew my little daughter had gone also."

.   .   .   .

But beasts died ; yea, the cattle in the yoke,
The milk-cow in the meadow, and the sheep,
And the dog upon the doorstep : and men envied.

And birds died ; yea, the eagle at the sun-gate,
The swan upon the waters, and the farm-fowl,
And the swallows on the housetops : and men envied.

And reptiles ; yea, the toad upon the road-side,
The slimy, speckled snake among the grass,
The lizard on the ruin : and men envied.

The dog in lonely places cried not over
The body of his master ; but it miss'd him,
And whin'd into the air, and died, and rot-ted.

The traveller's horse lay swollen in the pathway,
And the blue fly fed upon it ; but no trav-eller
Was there ; nay, not his footprint on the ground.

The cat mew'd in the midnight, and the blind
Gave a rustle, and the lamp burnt blue and faint,
And the father's bed was empty in the morning.

The mother fell to sleep beside the cra-dle,
Rocking it, while she slumber'd, with her foot,
And waken'd, — and the cradle there was empty.

I saw a two-years' child, and he was play-ing ;
And he found a dead white bird upon the doorway,
And laugh'd, and ran to show it to his mother.

The mother moan'd, and clutch'd him, and was bitter,
And flung the dead white bird across the threshold ;
And another white bird flitted round and round it,

And utter'd a sharp cry, and twitter'd and twitter'd,
And lit beside its dead mate, and grew busy,
Strewing it over with green leaves and yel-low.

.   .   .   .

So far, so far to seek for were the limits
Of affliction; and men's terror grew a
    homeless
Terror, yea, and a fatal sense of blankness.

There was no little token of distraction,
There was no visible presence of bereave-
    ment,
Such as the mourner easeth out his heart
    on.

There was no comfort in the slow farewell,
No gentle shutting of beloved eyes,
Nor beautiful broodings over sleeping fea-
    tures.

There were no kisses on familiar faces,
No weaving of white grave-clothes, no
    last pondering
Over the still wax cheeks and folded fin-
    gers.

There was no putting tokens under pillows,
There was no dreadful beauty slowly fading,
Fading like moonlight softly into darkness.

There were no churchyard paths to walk
    on, thinking
How near the well-beloved ones are lying.
There were no sweet green graves to sit
    and muse on,

Till grief should grow a summer medita-
    tion,
The shadow of the passing of an angel,
And sleeping should seem easy, and not
    cruel.

Nothing but wondrous parting and a
    blankness.

.   .   .   .

But I woke, and, lo! the burthen was up-
    lifted,
And I pray'd within the chamber where
    she slumber'd,
And my tears flow'd fast and free, but
    were not bitter.

I eas'd my heart three days by watching
    near her,
And made her pillow sweet with scent and
    flowers,
And could bear at last to put her in the
    darkness.

And I heard the kirk-bells ringing very
    slowly,
And the priests were in their vestments,
    and the earth
Dripp'd awful on the hard wood, yet I bore
    it.

And I cried, " O unseen Sender of Corrup-
    tion,
I bless Thee for the wonder of Thy mercy,
Which softeneth the mystery and the part-
    ing :

" I bless thee for the change and for the
    comfort,
The bloomless face, shut eyes, and waxen
    fingers, —
For Sleeping, and for Silence, and Corrup-
    tion."

THE FAËRY FOSTER-MOTHER

Bright Eyes, Light Eyes! Daughter of a
    Fay !
I had not been a wedded wife a twelve-
    month and a day,
I had not nurs'd my little one a month
    upon my knee,
When down among the blue-bell banks
    rose elfins three times three,
They gripp'd me by the raven hair, I could
    not cry for fear,
They put a hempen rope around my waist
    and dragg'd me here,
They made me sit and give thee suck as
    mortal mothers can,
Bright Eyes, Light Eyes ! strange and
    weak and wan !

Dim Face, Grim Face! lie ye there so
    still ?
Thy red, red lips are at my breast, and thou
    may'st suck thy fill ;
But know ye, tho' I hold thee firm, and
    rock thee to and fro,
'T is not to soothe thee into sleep, but just
    to still my woe ?
And know ye, when I lean so calm against
    the wall of stone,
'T is when I shut my eyes and try to think
    thou art mine own ?
And know ye, tho' my milk be here, my
    heart is far away,
Dim Face, Grim Face ! Daughter of a
    Fay !

Gold Hair, Cold Hair ! Daughter to a King !
Wrapp'd in bands of snow-white silk with
jewels glittering,
Tiny slippers of the gold upon thy feet so
thin,
Silver cradle velvet-lin'd for thee to slum-
ber in,
Pygmy pages, crimson-hair'd, to serve thee
on their knees,
To fan thy face with ferns and bring thee
honey bags of bees, —
I was but a peasant lass, my babe had but
the milk,
Gold Hair, Cold Hair ! raimented in silk !

Pale Thing, Frail Thing ! dumb and weak
and thin,
Altho' thou ne'er dost utter sigh thou 'rt
shadow'd with a sin ;
Thy minnie scorns to suckle thee, thy min-
nie is an elf,
Upon a bed of rose's-leaves she lies and
fans herself ;
And though my heart is aching so for one
afar from me,
I often look into thy face and drop a tear
for thee,
And I am but a peasant born, a lowly cot-
ter's wife,
Pale Thing, Frail Thing ! sucking at my life !

Weak Thing, Meek Thing ! take no blame
from me,
Altho' my babe may moan for lack of what
I give to thee ;
For though thou art a faëry child, and
though thou art my woe,
To feel thee sucking at my breast is all
the bliss I know ;
It soothes me, tho' afar away I hear my
daughter call,
My heart were broken if I felt no little
lips at all !
If I had none to tend at all, to be its nurse
and slave,
Weak Thing, Meek Thing ! I should
shriek and rave !

Bright Eyes, Light Eyes ! lying on my knee !
If soon I be not taken back unto mine
own countree,
To feel my own babe's little lips, as I am
feeling thine,
To smooth the golden threads of hair, to
see the blue eyes shine, —

I 'll lean my head against the wall and
close my weary eyes,
And think my own babe draws the milk
with balmy pants and sighs,
And smile and bless my little one and
sweetly pass away,
Bright Eyes, Light Eyes ! Daughter of a
Fay !

THE CHURCHYARD

How slowly creeps the hand of Time
On the old clock's green-mantled face !
Yea, slowly as those ivies climb,
The hours roll round with patient pace ;
The drowsy rooks caw on the tower,
The tame doves hover round and round ;
Below, the slow grass hour by hour
Makes green God's sleeping-ground.

All moves, but nothing here is swift ;
The grass grows deep, the green boughs
shoot ;
From east to west the shadows drift ;
The earth feels heavenward underfoot ;
The slow stream through the bridge doth
stray
With water-lilies on its marge,
And slowly, pil'd with scented hay,
Creeps by the silent barge.

All stirs, but nothing here is loud :
The cushat broods, the cuckoo cries ;
Faint, far up, under a white cloud,
The lark trills soft to earth and skies ;
And underneath the green graves rest ;
And through the place, with slow foot-
falls,
With snowy cambric on his breast,
The old gray Vicar crawls.

And close at hand, to see him come,
Clustering at the playground gate,
The urchins of the schoolhouse, dumb
And bashful, hang the head and wait ;
The little maidens curtsey deep,
The boys their forelocks touch mean-
while,
The Vicar sees them, half asleep,
And smiles a sleepy smile.

Slow as the hand on the clock's face,
Slow as the white cloud in the sky,
He cometh now with tottering pace
To the old vicarage hard by ·

Smother'd it stands in ivy leaves,
  Laurels and yews make dark the ground ;
The swifts that build beneath the eaves
  Wheel in still circles round.

And from the portal, green and dark,
  He glances at the church-clock old —

Gray soul ! why seek his eyes to mark
  The creeping of that finger cold ?
He cannot see, but still as stone
  He pauses, listening for the chime,
And hears from that green tower intone
  The eternal voice of Time.

Emily Pfeiffer

A SONG OF WINTER

BARB'D blossom of the guarded gorse,
  I love thee where I see thee shine :
Thou sweetener of our common-ways,
And brightener of our wintry days.

Flower of the gorse, the rose is dead,
  Thou art undying, O be mine !
Be mine with all thy thorns, and prest
Close on a heart that asks not rest.

I pluck thee and thy stigma set
  Upon my breast and on my brow ;
Blow, buds, and plenish so my wreath
That none may know the wounds beneath.

O crown of thorn that seem'st of gold,
  No festal coronal art thou ;
Thy honey'd blossoms are but hives
That guard the growth of winged lives.

I saw thee in the time of flowers
  As sunshine spill'd upon the land,
Or burning bushes all ablaze
With sacred fire ; but went my ways ;

I went my ways, and as I went
  Pluck'd kindlier blooms on either hand ;
Now of those blooms so passing sweet
None lives to stay my passing feet.

And still thy lamp upon the hill
  Feeds on the autumn's dying sigh,
And from thy midst comes murmuring
A music sweeter than in spring.

Barb'd blossoms of the guarded gorse,
  Be mine to wear until I die,
And mine the wounds of love which still
Bear witness to his human will.

TO A MOTH THAT DRINKETH OF THE RIPE OCTOBER

I

A MOTH belated, sun and zephyr-kist,
Trembling about a pale arbutus bell,
Probing to wildering depths its honey'd
    cell, —
A noonday thief, a downy sensualist !
Not vainly, sprite, thou drawest careless
    breath,
Strikest ambrosia from the cool-cupp'd
    flowers,
And flutterest through the soft, uncounted
    hours,
To drop at last in unawaited death ;
'T is something to be glad ! and those fine
    thrills,
Which move thee, to my lip have drawn
    the smile
Wherewith we look on joy.   Drink ! drown
    thine ills,
If ill have any part in thee ; erewhile
May the pent force — thy bounded life, set
    free,
Fill larger sphere with equal ecstasy.

II

With what fine organs art thou dower'd,
    frail elf !
Thy harp is pitch'd too high for dull annoy,
Thy life a love-feast, and a silent joy,
As mute and rapt as Passion's silent self.
I turn from thee, and see the swallow
    sweep
Like a wing'd will, and the keen-scented
    hound
That snuffs with rapture at the tainted
    ground, —
All things that freely course, that swim or
    leap, —

Then, hearing glad-voiced creatures men
        call dumb,
I feel my heart, oft sinking 'neath the
        weight
Of Nature's sorrow, lighten at the sum
Of Nature's joy; its half-unfolded fate
Breathes hope — for all but those beneath
        the ban
Of the inquisitor and tyrant, man.

TO THE HERALD HONEYSUCKLE

DEEP Honeysuckle ! in the silent eve
When wild-rose cups are clos'd, and when
        each bird
Is sleeping by its mate, then all unheard
The dew's soft kiss thy wakeful lips receive.

'T is then the sighs that throng them seem
        to weave
A spell whereby the drowsy night is stirr'd
To fervid meanings, which no fullest
        word
Of speech or song so sweetly could achieve.
Herald of bliss ! whose fragrant trumpet
        blew
Love's title to our hearts ere love was
        known,
'T was well thy flourish told a tale so
        true,
Well that Love's dazzling presence was
        foreshown ;
Had his descent on us been as the dew
On thee, our rarer sense he had o'er-
        thrown.

Frederic William Henry Myers

.FROM "SAINT PAUL"

Lo, as some bard on isles of the Aegean
    Lovely and eager when the earth was
        young,
Burning to hurl his heart into a paean,
    Praise of the hero from whose loins he
        sprung ; —

He, I suppose, with such a care to carry,
    Wander'd disconsolate and waited long,
Smiting his breast, wherein the notes would
        tarry,
    Chiding the slumber of the seed of song :

Then in the sudden glory of a minute
    Airy and excellent the proem came,
Rending his bosom, for a god was in it,
    Waking the seed, for it had burst in flame.

So even I athirst for his inspiring,
    I who have talk'd with Him forget again,
Yes, many days with sobs and with desiring
    Offer to God a patience and a pain ;

Then through the mid complaint of my
        confession,
Then through the pang and passion of
        my prayer,
Leaps with a start the shock of his posses-
        sion,
    Thrills me and touches, and the Lord is
        there.

Lo, if some pen should write upon your
        rafter
    MENE and MENE in the folds of flame,
Think you could any memories thereafter
    Wholly retrace the couplet as it came ?

Lo, if some strange intelligible thunder
    Sang to the earth the secret of a star,
Scarce could ye catch, for terror and for
        wonder,
    Shreds of the story that was peal'd so
        far.

Scarcely I catch the words of his reveal-
        ing,
Hardly I hear Him, dimly understand,
Only the Power that is within me pealing
    Lives on my lips and beckons to my hand.

Whoso has felt the Spirit of the Highest
    Cannot confound nor doubt Him nor
        deny :
Yea, with one voice, O world, though thou
        deniest,
    Stand thou on that side, for on this am I.

Rather the earth shall doubt when her
        retrieving
    Pours in the rain and rushes from the
        sod,
Rather than he for whom the great con-
        ceiving
    Stirs in his soul to quicken into God.

Ay, though thou then shouldst strike him
    from his glory
Blind and tormented, madden'd and
    alone,
Even on the cross would he maintain his
    story,
Yes, and in hell would whisper, I have
    known.

A SONG

THE pouring music, soft and strong,
    Some God within her soul has lit,
Her face is rosy with the song
    And her gray eyes are sweet with it.

A woman so with singing fir'd,
    Has earth a lovelier sight than this?
Oh, he that look'd had soon desir'd
    Those lips to fasten with a kiss.

But let not him that race begin
    Who seeks not toward its utmost goal;
Give me an hour for drinking in
    Her fragrant and her early soul.

To happier hearts I leave the rest,
    Who less and more than I shall know,
For me, world-weary, it is best
    To listen for an hour and go:

To lift her hand, and press, and part,
    And think upon her long and long,
And bear for ever in my heart
    The tender traces of a song.

ON A GRAVE AT GRINDEL-WALD

HERE let us leave him; for his shroud the
    snow,
For funeral-lamps he has the planets
    seven,
For a great sign the icy stair shall go
    Between the heights to heaven.

One moment stood he as the angels
    stand,
    High in the stainless eminence of air;
The next, he was not, to his fatherland
    Translated unaware.

A LAST APPEAL

O SOMEWHERE, somewhere, God un-
    known,
    Exist and be!
I am dying; I am all alone;
    I must have thee!

God! God! my sense, my soul, my all,
    Dies in the cry:—
Saw'st thou the faint star flame and fall?
    Ah! it was I.

IMMORTALITY

So when the old delight is born anew,
    And God re-animates the early bliss,
Seems it not all as one first trembling kiss
    Ere soul knew soul with whom she has to
        do?
O nights how desolate, O days how few,
    O death in life, if life be this, be this!
O weigh'd alone as one shall win or miss
    The faint eternity which shines therethro'!
Lo, all that age is as a speck of sand
Lost on the long beach where the tides are
    free,
And no man metes it in his hollow hand
Nor cares to ponder it, how small it be;
    At ebb it lies forgotten on the land
And at full tide forgotten in the sea.

A LETTER FROM NEWPORT

φαίη κ' ἀθανάτους καὶ ἀγήρως ἔμμεναι αἰεὶ
ὃς τότ' ἐπαντιάσει ὅτ' Ἰάονες ἄθροοι εἶεν.

THE crimson leafage fires the lawn,
    The pil'd hydrangeas blazing glow;
How blue the vault of breezy dawn
    Illumes the Atlantic's crested snow!
'Twixt sea and sands how fair to ride
    Through whispering airs a starlit way,
And watch those flashing towers divide
    Heaven's darkness from the darkling
        bay!

Ah, friend, how vain their pedant's part,
    Their hurrying toils how idly spent,
How have they wrong'd the gentler heart
    Which thrills the awakening continent,
Who have not learnt on this bright shore
    What sweetness issues from the strong,
Where flowerless forest, cataract-roar,
    Have found a blossom and a song!

Ah, what imperial force of fate
   Links our one race in high emprize !
Nor aught henceforth can separate
   Those glories mingling as they rise ;
For one in heart, as one in speech,
   At last have Child and Mother grown, —
Fair Figures ! honoring each in each
   A beauty kindred with her own.

Through English eyes more calmly soft
   Looks from gray deeps the appealing
     charm ;
Reddens on English cheeks more oft
   The rose of innocent alarm ; —
Our old-world heart more gravely feels,
   Has learnt more force, more self-con-
     trol ;
For us through sterner music peals
   The full accord of soul and soul.

But ah, the life, the smile untaught,
   The floating presence feathery-fair !
The eyes and aspect that have caught
   The brilliance of Columbian air !
No oriole through the forest flits
   More sheeny-plum'd, more gay and free ;
On no nymph's marble forehead sits
   Proudlier a glad virginity.

So once the Egyptian, gravely bold,
   Wander'd the Ionian folk among.
Heard from their high Letôon roll'd
   That song the Delian maidens sung ;
Danced in his eyes the dazzling gold,
   For with his voice the tears had sprung,—
" They die not, these ! they wax not old,
   They are ever-living, ever-young ! "

Spread then, great land ! thine arms afar,
   Thy golden harvest westward roll ;
Banner with banner, star with star,
   Ally the tropics and the pole ; —
There glows no gem than these more bright
   From ice to fire, from sea to sea ;
Blossoms no fairer flower to light
   Through all thine endless empery.

And thou come hither, friend ! thou too
   Their kingdom enter as a boy ;
Fed with their glorious youth renew
   Thy dimm'd prerogative of joy : —
Come with small question, little thought,
   Through thy worn veins what pulse
     shall flow,
With what regrets, what fancies fraught,
   Shall silver-footed summer go : —

If round one fairest face shall meet
   Those many dreams of many fair,
And wandering homage seek the feet
   Of one sweet queen, and linger there ;
Or if strange winds betwixt be driven,
   Unvoyageable oceans foam,
Nor this new earth, this airy heaven,
   For thy sad heart can find a home.

I SAW, I SAW THE LOVELY CHILD

I saw, I saw the lovely child,
   I watch'd her by the way,
I learnt her gestures sweet and wild,
   Her loving eyes and gay.

Her name ? — I heard not, nay, nor care :
   Enough it was for me
To find her innocently fair
   And delicately free.

Oh, cease and go ere dreams be done,
   Nor trace the angel's birth,
Nor find the Paradisal one
   A blossom of the earth !

Thus is it with our subtlest joys, —
   How quick the soul's alarm !
How lightly deed or word destroys
   That evanescent charm !

It comes unbidden, comes unbought,
   Unfetter'd flees away ;
His swiftest and his sweetest thought
   Can never poet say.

Edward Dowden

RENUNCIANTS

Seems not our breathing light ?
   Sound not our voices free ?
Bid to Life's festal bright
   No gladder guests there be.

Ah stranger, lay aside
   Cold prudence ! I divine
The secret yon would hide,
   And you conjecture mine.

You too have temperate eyes,
　Have put your heart to school,
Are prov'd. I recognize
　A brother of the rule.

I knew it by your lip,
　A something when you smil'd,
Which meant " close scholarship,
　A master of the guild."

Well, and how good is life ;
　Good to be born, have breath,
The calms good, and the strife,
　Good life, and perfect death.

Come, for the dancers wheel,
　Join we the pleasant din, —
Comrade, it serves to feel
　The sackcloth next the skin.

LEONARDO'S "MONNA LISA"

MAKE thyself known, Sibyl, or let despair
Of knowing thee be absolute : I wait
Hour-long and waste a soul. What word of fate
Hides 'twixt the lips which smile and still forbear ?
Secret perfection ! Mystery too fair !
Tangle the sense no more, lest I should hate
The delicate tyranny, the inviolate
Poise of thy folded hands, the fallen hair.

Nay, nay,— I wrong thee with rough words; still be
Serene, victorious, inaccessible ;
Still smile but speak not ; lightest irony
Lurk ever 'neath thy eyelids' shadow ; still
O'ertop our knowledge ; Sphinx of Italy,
Allure us and reject us at thy will !

TWO INFINITIES

A LONELY way, and as I went my eyes
Could not unfasten from the Spring's sweet things,
Lush-sprouted grass, and all that climbs and clings
In loose, deep hedges, where the primrose lies
In her own fairness, buried blooms surprise
The plunderer bee and stop his murmurings,
And the glad flutter of a finch's wings
Outstartle small blue-speckled butterflies.
Blissfully did one speedwell plot beguile
My whole heart long ; I lov'd each separate flower,
Kneeling. I look'd up suddenly —Dear God !
There stretch'd the shining plain for many a mile,
The mountains rose with what invincible power !
And how the sky was fathomless and broad !

Margaret Veley

FIRST OR LAST ?

A WIFE TO HER HUSBAND

My life ebbs from me — I must die.
Must die — it has a ghostly sound,
A far-off thunder drawing nigh,
An echo as from underground.
Yes, I must die who fain would live ;
You cannot give me life — alas !
Dear Love of mine, you can but give
One latest kiss before I pass.

Dear, we have had our summer bliss,
Kisses on cheek, and lip, and brow,
But soul to soul, as now we kiss,
I think we never kiss'd till now.

Give both your hands, and let the earth
Roll onward — let what will befall.
This is an hour of wondrous birth,
And can it be the end of all ?

Ah, your sad face ! I know you think
(Clasp me, O love, your faith is mine,
Only my weakness made me shrink)
That I am standing on the brink
Of night where never dawn will shine,
Of slumber whence I shall not wake,
Of darkness where no life will grope ;
I know your hopeless creed, and take
My part therein for your dear sake, —
We stand asunder if I hope.

And yet I dream'd of a fair land
Where you and I were met at last,
And face to face, and hand in hand,
Smil'd at the sorrow overpast.
The eastern sky was touch'd with fire,
In the dim woodlands cooed the dove,
Earth waited, tense with strong desire,
For day — your coming, O my love !
The breeze awoke to breathe your name,
And through the leafy maze I came
With feet that could not turn aside,
With eyes that would not be denied —
My lips, my heart a rosy flame,
Because you kiss'd me ere I died.
Death could but part us for a while ;
Beyond the boundary of years
We met again — oh, do not smile
That tender smile, more sad than tears !

Forget my vision sweet and vain,
Your faith is mine — your faith is best ;
Let others count the joys they gain,
I am a thousand times more blest.
They can but give a scanty dole
Out of a life made safe in heaven,
While I am sovereign o'er the whole,
I can give all — and all is given !
Faith such as ours defies the grave,
Nor needs a dream of bliss above —
Shall not this moment make me brave ?
O aloe-flower of perfect love !

What though the end of all be come,
The latest hour, the latest breath,
This is life's triumph, and its sum,
The aloe-flower of love and death !

And yet your kisses wake a life
That throbs in anguish through my **heart,**
Leads up to wage despairing strife,
And shudders, loathing to depart.
Can such desire be born in vain,
Crush'd by inevitable doom ?
While you let live can Love be slain ?
Can Love lie dead within my tomb ?
And when you die — that hopeless day
When darkness comes and utmost need,
And I am dead and cold, you say,
Will Death have power to hold his
    prey ?
Shall I not know ? Shall I not heed ?
When your last sun, with waning light,
Below the sad horizon dips,
Shall I not rush from out the night
To die once more upon your lips ?

Ah, the black moment comes !   Draw
    nigh,
Stoop down, O Love, and hold me fast.
O empty earth !   O empty sky !
There is no answer, though I die
Breathing my soul out in the cry,
Is it the first kiss — or the last ?

Lady Currie

("VIOLET FANE")

A MAY SONG

A LITTLE while my love and I,
  Before the mowing of the hay,
Twin'd daisy-chains and cowslip-balls,
And caroll'd glees and madrigals,
  Before the hay, beneath the may,
My love (who lov'd me then) and I.

For long years now my love and I
  Tread sever'd paths to varied ends ;
We sometimes meet, and sometimes say
The trivial things of every day,
  And meet as comrades, meet as friends,
My love (who lov'd me once) and I.

But never more my love and I
  Will wander forth, as once, together,
Or sing the songs we us'd to sing
  In spring-time, in the cloudless weather ;
Some chord is mute that us'd to ring,
  Some word forgot we us'd to say
  Amongst the may, before the hay,
My love (who loves me not) and I

A FOREBODING

I DO not dread an alter'd heart,
  Or that long line of land or sea
Should separate my love from me,
I dread that drifting slow apart —
  All unresisted, unrestrain'd —
  Which comes to some when they have
    gain'd
  The dear endeavor of their soul.

As two light skiffs that sail'd together,
Through days and nights of tranquil
    weather,
  Adown some inland stream, might be
Drifted asunder, each from each ;
When, floating with the tide, they reach
    The hop'd-for end, the promis'd goal,
  The sudden glory of the sea.

IN GREEN OLD GARDENS

IN green old gardens, hidden away
  From sight of revel and sound of strife,
    Where the bird may sing out his soul
      ere he dies,
Nor fears for the night, so he lives his day ;
Where the high red walls, which are grow-
      ing gray
    With their lichen and moss embroi-
      deries,
  Seem sadly and sternly to shut out Life,
Because it is often as sad as they ;

Where even the bee has time to glide
  (Gathering gayly his honey'd store)
    Right to the heart of the old-world
      flowers, —
China-asters and purple stocks,
Dahlias and tall red hollyhocks,
    Laburnums raining their golden show-
      ers,
  Columbines prim of the folded core,
And lupins, and larkspurs, and "London
      pride";

Where the heron is waiting amongst the
      reeds,
    Grown tame in the silence that reigns
      around,
    Broken only, now and then,
  By shy woodpecker or noisy jay,
By the far-off watch-dog's muffled bay;
    But where never the purposeless laugh-
      ter of men,
  Or the seething city's murmurous sound
Will float up under the river-weeds.

Here may I live what life I please,
  Married and buried out of sight, —
    Married to pleasure, and buried to
      pain, —
Hidden away amongst scenes like these,
Under the fans of the chestnut trees ;
    Living my child-life over again,

With the further hope of a fuller delight,
Blithe as the birds and wise as the bees.

In green old gardens hidden away
  From sight of revel and sound of
      strife, —
    Here have I leisure to breathe and
      move,
And to do my work in a nobler way ;
To sing my songs, and to say my say ;
    To dream my dreams, and to love my
      love ;
  To hold my faith, and to live my life,
Making the most of its shadowy day.

AFTERWARDS

I KNOW that these poor rags of woman-
      hood, —
    This oaten pipe, whereon the wild winds
      play'd
    Making sad music, — tatter'd and out-
      fray'd,
Cast off, play'd out, — can hold no more of
      good,
    Of love, or song, or sense of sun and
      shade.

What homely neighbors elbow me (hard by
    'Neath the black yews) I know I shall
      not know,
    Nor take account of changing winds
      that blow,
Shifting the golden arrow, set on high
    On the gray spire, nor mark who come
      and go.

Yet would I lie in some familiar place,
    Nor share my rest with uncongenial
      dead, —
    Somewhere, maybe, where friendly feet
      will tread, —
As if from out some little chink of space
    Mine eyes might see them tripping over-
      head.

And though too sweet to deck a sepulchre
    Seem twinkling daisy-buds, and meadow
      grass ;
    And so, would more than serve me, lest
      they pass
Who fain would know what woman rested
      there,
    What her demeanor, or her story was,—

For these I would that on a sculptur'd
      stone
(Fenced round with ironwork to keep se-
      cure)

Should sleep a form with folded palms
      demure,
In aspect like the dreamer that was gone,
   With these words carv'd, "*I hop'd, but was
      not sure.*"

Samuel Waddington

THE INN OF CARE

AT Nebra, by the Unstrut, —
So travellers declare, —
There stands an ancient tavern,
It is the "Inn of Care."
To all the world 't is open ;
It sets a goodly fare ;
And every soul is welcome
That deigns to sojourn there.

The landlord with his helpers,
(He is a stalwart host),
To please his guest still labors
With " bouilli " and with " roast ; "
And ho ! he laughs so roundly,
He laughs, and loves to boast
That he who bears the beaker
May live to share the " toast."

Lucus a non lucendo —
Thus named might seem the inn,
So careless is its laughter,
So loud its merry din ;
Yet ere to doubt its title
You do, in sooth, begin,
Go, watch the pallid faces
Approach and pass within.

To Nebra, by the Unstrut,
May all the world repair,
And meet a hearty welcome,
And share a goodly fare ;
The world ! ' t is worn and weary —
'T is tir'd of gilt and glare ;
The inn ! 't is nam'd full wisely,
It is the " Inn of Care."

SOUL AND BODY

WHERE wert thou, Soul, ere yet my body
      born
Became thy dwelling-place ?   Didst thou
      on earth,
Or in the clouds, await this body's birth ?
Or by what chance upon that winter's morn
Didst thou this body find, a babe forlorn ?
Didst thou in sorrow enter, or in mirth ?
Or for a jest, perchance, to try its worth
Thou tookest flesh, ne'er from it to be torn ?
Nay, Soul, I will not mock thee ; well I
      know
Thou wert not on the earth, nor in the sky ;
For with my body's growth thou too didst
      grow ;
But with that body's death wilt thou too die ?
I know not, and thou canst not tell me, so
In doubt we 'll go together, — thou and I.

Ernest Myers

GORDON

I

ON through the Libyan sand
Rolls ever, mile on mile,
League on long league, cleaving the rain-
      less land,
Fed by no friendly wave, the immemorial
      Nile.

II

Down through the cloudless air,
Undimm'd, from heaven's sheer height,
Bend their inscrutable gaze, austere and
      bare,
In long-proceeding pomp, the stars of Lib-
      yan night.

III

Beneath the stars, beside the unpausiug
       flood,
Earth trembles at the wandering lion's roar ;
Trembles again, when in blind thirst of
       blood
Sweep the wild tribes along the startled
       shore.

IV

They sweep and surge and struggle, and
       are gone :
The mournful desert silence reigns again,
The immemorial River rolleth on,
The order'd stars gaze blank upon the
       plain.

V

O awful Presence of the lonely Nile,
O awful Presence of the starry sky,
Lo, in this little while
Unto the mind's true-seeing inward eye
There hath arisen there
Another haunting Presence as sublime,
As great, as sternly fair ;
Yea, rather fairer far
Than stream, or sky, or star,
To live while star shall burn or river roll,
Unmarr'd by marring Time,
The crown of Being, a heroic soul.

VI

Beyond the weltering tides of worldly
       change
He saw the invisible things,
The eternal Forms of Beauty and of Right ;
Wherewith well pleas'd his spirit wont to
       range,
Rapt with divine delight,
Richer than empires, royaler than kings.

VII

Lover of children, lord of fiery fight,
Saviour of empires, servant of the poor,
Not in the sordid scales of earth, unsure,
Deprav'd, adulterate,
He measur'd small and great,
But by some righteous balance wrought in
       heaven,
To his pure hand by Powers empyreal given ;
Therewith, by men unmov'd, as God he
       judged aright.

VIII

As on the broad sweet-water'd river tost
Falls some poor grain of salt,
And melts to naught, nor leaves embitter‑
       ing trace ;
As in the o'er-arching vault
With unrepell'd assault
A cloudy climbing vapor, lightly lost,
Vanisheth utterly in the starry space ;
So from our thought, when his enthron'd
       estate
We inly contemplate,
All wrangling phantoms fade, and leave us
       face to face.

IX

Dwell in us, sacred spirit, as in thee
Dwelt the eternal Love, the eternal Life,
Nor dwelt in only thee ; not thee alone
We honor reverently,
But in thee all who in some succoring
       strife,
By day or dark, world-witness'd or un‑
       known,
Crush'd by the crowd, or in late harvest
       hail'd,
Warring thy war have triumph'd, or have
       fail'd.

X

Nay, but not only there
Broods thy great Presence, o'er the Libyan
       plain.
It haunts a kindlier clime, a dearer air,
The liberal air of England, thy lov'd home.
Thou through her sunlit clouds and flying
       rain
Breathe, and all winds that sweep her island
       shore —
Rough fields of riven foam,
Where in stern watch her guardian break‑
       ers roar.
Ay, thron'd with all her mighty memories,
Wherefrom her nobler sons their nurture
       draw,
With all of good or great
For aye incorporate
That rears her race to faith and generous
       shame,
To high-aspiring awe,
To hate implacable of thick-thronging lies,
To scorn of gold and gauds and clamorous
       fame ;

With all we guard most dear and most
    divine,
All records rank'd with thine,
Here be thy home, brave soul, thy undecay-
    ing shrine.

ETSI OMNES, EGO NON

HERE where under earth his head
Finds a last and lonely bed,
Let him speak upon the stone :
Etsi omnes, ego non.

Here he shall not know the eyes
Bent upon their sordid prize
Earthward ever, nor the beat
Of the hurrying faithless feet.

None to make him perfect cheer
Join'd him on his journey drear ;
Some too soon, who fell away ;
Some too late, who mourn to-day.

Yet while comrades one by one
Made denial and were gone,
Not the less he labor'd on :
Etsi omnes, ego non.

Surely his were heart and mind
Meet for converse with his kind,
Light of genial fancy free,
Grace of sweetest sympathy.

But his soul had other scope,
Holden of a larger hope,

Larger hope and larger love.
Meat to eat men knew not of :

Knew not, know not — yet shall sound
From this place of holy ground
Even this legend thereupon,
Etsi omnes, ego non.

"THE SEA-MAIDS' MUSIC"

ONE moment the boy, as he wander'd by
    night
Where the far-spreading foam in the moon-
    beam was white,
One moment he caught on the breath of
    the breeze
The voice of the sisters that sing in the seas.

One moment, no more : though the boy
    linger'd long,
No more might he hear of the mermaidens'
    song,
But the pine-woods behind him moan'd
    low from the land,
And the ripple gush'd soft at his feet on
    the sand.

Yet or ever they ceas'd, the strange sound
    of their joy
Had lighted a light in the breast of the
    boy :
And the seeds of a wonder, a splendor to be
Had been breath'd through his soul from
    the songs of the sea.

George Francis Savage-Armstrong

AUTUMN MEMORIES

WHEN russet beech-leaves drift in air,
    And withering bracken gilds the ling,
And red haws brighten hedgerows bare,
    And only plaintive robins sing ;
When autumn whirlwinds curl the sea,
    And mountain-tops are cold with haze,
Then saddest thoughts revisit me, —
    I sit and dream of the olden days.

When chestnut-leaves lie yellow on ground,
    And brown nuts break the prickled husk,
And nests on naked boughs are found,
    And swallows shrill no more at dusk,

And folks are glad in house to be,
    And up the flue the faggots blaze,
Then climb my little boys my knee
    To hear me tell of the olden days.

THE MYSTERY

YEAR after year
    The leaf and the shoot ;
The babe and the nestling,
    The worm at the root ;
The bride at the altar,
    The corpse on the bier —
The Earth and its story,
    Year after year.

Whither are tending,
　And whence do they rise,
The cycles of changes,
　The worlds in their skies,
The seasons that roll'd
　Ere I flash'd from the gloom,
And will roll on as now
　When I'm dust in the tomb?

ONE IN THE INFINITE

ROLL on, and with thy rolling crust
　That round thy poles thou twirlest,
Roll with thee, Earth, this grain of dust,
　As through the Vast thou whirlest;
On, on through zones of dark and light
　Still waft me, blind and reeling,
Around the sun, and with his flight
　In wilder orbits wheeling.

Speed on through deeps without a shore,
　This Atom with thee bearing,
Thyself a grain of dust — no more —
　'Mid fume of systems flaring.
Ah, what am I to thirst for power,
　Or pore on Nature's pages, —
Whirl'd onward, living for an hour,
　And dead through endless ages?

MY GUIDE

SHE leads me on through storm and calm,
　My glorious Angel girt with light;
By dazzling isles of tropic balm,
　By coasts of ice in northern night.
Now far amid the mountain shades
　Her footprints gleam like golden fire,
And now adown the leafy glades
　I chase the music of her lyre.

And now amid the tangled pines
　That darkly robe the gorgeous steep
She beckons where in woven lines
　The sunbeams through the darkness
　　creep,
And shows in glimpses far below
　The champaign stretching leagues away,

Fair cities veil'd in summer's glow
　Or sparkling in the cloudless ray.

At times on seas with tempest loud,
　The pilot of my bark, she stands,
And, through the rifts of driving cloud,
　To tranquil bays of bounteous lands,
The grassy creek, the bowery shore,
　The fringe of many a charmed realm,
She steers me safe by magic lore,
　Her white arm leaning on the helm.

When, sick at heart and worn, mine eyes
　I bend to earth in long despair,
She lifts her finger to the skies,
　The violet deeps of lucid air,
The myriad myriad orbs that roll
　In endless throngs in living space,
And all the vision of her soul
　Is mirror'd in her radiant face.

"THE FATHER"

IF it were only a dream,
　Were it not good to cherish,
Seeing to lose its beam
　Is in despair to perish —
Maker and Father and Friend,
　Yearning in pity to guide me,
Leading me on to the end,
　Ever in love beside me,
Never in storm or gloom
　Deaf to a cry of sorrow,
Kindling beyond the tomb
　Light of an endless morrow?

Yea, if 't were only a dream,
　Better it were to clasp it,
Brood on it until it seem
　Real as the lives that grasp it.
Helpless, feeble, and lost,
　Groping in Wisdom's traces,
Whirl'd like a leaf, and tost
　Out in the awful spaces, —
Oh, how the heart betray'd
　Bounds, into life upleaping,
Trusting that He who made
　Watch over all is keeping!

James Chapman Woods

THE SOUL STITHY

My soul, asleep between its body-throes,
Mid leagues of darkness watch'd a furnace
glare,
And breastless arms that wrought labori-
ous there, —
Power without plan, wherefrom no purpose
grows, —
Welding white metal on a forge with blows,
Whence stream'd the singing sparks like
flaming hair,
Which whirling gusts ever abroad would
bear :
And still the stithy hammers fell and rose.
And then I knew those sparks were souls
of men,
And watch'd them driven like starlets down
the wind.
A myriad died and left no trace to tell ;
An hour like will-o'-the-wisps some lit the
fen ;
Now one would leave a trail of fire behind :
And still the stithy-hammers rose and fell.

THE WORLD'S DEATH-NIGHT

I THINK a stormless night-time shall ensue
Unto the world, yearning for hours of
calm :
Not these the end, — nor sudden-closing
palm
Of a God's hand beneath the skies we
knew,
Nor fall from a fierce heaven of fiery dew
In place of the sweet dewfall, the world's
balm,
Nor swell of elemental triumph-psalm
Round the long-buffeted bulk, rent through
and through.
But in the even of its endless night,
With shoreless floods of moonlight on its
breast,
And baths of healing mist about its scars,
An instant sums its circling years of flight,
And the tir'd earth hangs crystall'd into
rest,
Girdled with gracious watchings of the
stars.

BALLADISTS AND LYRISTS

Louisa Macartney Crawford

KATHLEEN MAVOURNEEN

Kathleen Mavourneen ! the gray dawn
is breaking,
The horn of the hunter is heard on the hill;
The lark from her light wing the bright
dew is shaking, —
Kathleen Mavourneen ! what, slumber-
ing still ?
Oh, hast thou forgotten how soon we must
sever ?
Oh ! hast thou forgotten this day we must
part ?
It may be for years, and it may be forever !
Oh, why art thou silent, thou voice of
my heart ?
Oh ! why art thou silent, Kathleen Mavour-
neen ?

Kathleen Mavourneen, awake from thy
slumbers !
The blue mountains glow in the sun's
golden light ;
Ah, where is the spell that once hung on
my numbers ?
Arise in thy beauty, thou star of my
night !
Mavourneen, Mavourneen, my sad tears
are falling,
To think that from Erin and thee I
must part !
It may be for years, and it may be for-
ever !
Then why art thou silent, thou voice of
my heart ?
Then why art thou silent, Kathleen Ma-
vourneen ?

Sir Francis Hastings Doyle

THE OLD CAVALIER

" For our martyr'd Charles I pawn'd my
     plate,
     For his son I spent my all,
That a churl might dine, and drink my wine,
     And preach in my father's hall :
That father died on Marston Moor,
     My son on Worcester plain ;
But the king he turn'd his back on me
     When he got his own again.

" The other day, there came, God wot !
     A solemn, pompous ass,
Who begged to know if I did not go
     To the sacrifice of Mass :
I told him fairly to his face,
     That in the field of fight
I had shouted loud for Church and King,
     When he would have run outright.

" He talk'd of the Man of Babylon
     With his rosaries and copes,
As if a Roundhead was n't worse
     Than half a hundred Popes.
I don't know what the people mean,
     With their horror and affright ;
All Papists that I ever knew
     Fought stoutly for the right.

" I now am poor and lonely,
     This cloak is worn and old,
But yet it warms my loyal heart,
     Through sleet, and rain, and cold,
When I call to mind the Cavaliers,
     Bold Rupert at their head,
Bursting through blood and fire, with cries
     That might have wak'd the dead.

" Then spur and sword was the battle word,
     And we made their helmets ring,
Howling like madmen, all the while,
     For God and for the King.
And though they snuffled psalms, to give
     The Rebel-dogs their due,
When the roaring shot pour'd close and hot
     They were stalwart men and true.

" On the fatal field of Naseby,
     Where Rupert lost the day
By hanging on the flying crowd
     Like a lion on his prey,

I stood and fought it out, until,
     In spite of plate and steel,
The blood that left my veins that day
     Flow'd up above my heel.

" And certainly, it made those quail
     Who never quail'd before,
To look upon the awful front
     Which Cromwell's horsemen wore.
I felt that every hope was gone,
     When I saw their squadrons form,
And gather for the final charge
     Like the coming of the storm.

" Oh ! where was Rupert in that hour
     Of danger, toil, and strife ?
It would have been to all brave men
     Worth a hundred years of life
To have seen that black and gloomy force
     As it poured down in line,
Met midway by the Royal horse
     And Rupert of the Rhine.

" All this is over now, and I
     Must travel to the tomb,
Though the king I serv'd has got his own
     In poverty and gloom.
Well, well, I serv'd him for himself,
     So I must not now complain,
But I often wish that I had died
     With my son on Worcester plain."

THE PRIVATE OF THE BUFFS

Last night, among his fellow roughs,
     He jested, quaff'd, and swore :
A drunken private of the Buffs,
     Who never look'd before.
To-day, beneath the foeman's frown,
     He stands in Elgin's place,
Ambassador from Britain's crown,
     And type of all her race.

Poor, reckless, rude, low-born, untaught,
     Bewilder'd, and alone,
A heart, with English instinct fraught,
     He yet can call his own.
Ay, tear his body limb from limb,
     Bring cord, or axe, or flame ·
He only knows, that not through him
     Shall England come to shame.

ar Kentish hop-fields round him seem'd,
Like dreams, to come and go ;
right leagues of cherry-blossom gleam'd,
One sheet of living snow ;
he smoke, above his father's door,
In gray soft eddyings hung :
ust he then watch it rise no more,
Doom'd by himself, so young ?

es, honor calls ! — with strength like steel
He put the vision by.
et dusky Indians whine and kneel;
An English lad must die.

And thus, with eyes that would not shrink,
With knee to man unbent,
Unfaltering on its dreadful brink,
To his red grave he went.

Vain, mightiest fleets, of iron fram'd ;
Vain, those all-shattering guns ;
Unless proud England keep, untam'd,
The strong heart of her sons.

So, let his name through Europe ring —
A man of mean estate,
Who died, as firm as Sparta's king,
Because his soul was great.

William Makepeace Thackeray

AT THE CHURCH GATE

ALTHOUGH I enter not,
Yet round about the spot
    Ofttimes I hover;
And near the sacred gate,
With longing eyes I wait,
    Expectant of her.

The minster bell tolls out
Above the city's rout,
    And noise and humming ;
They 've hush'd the minster bell :
The organ 'gins to swell ;
    She 's coming, she 's coming !

My lady comes at last,
Timid and stepping fast
    And hastening thither,
With modest eyes downcast ;
She comes — she 's here, she 's past !
    May heaven go with her !

Kneel undisturb'd, fair saint !
Pour out your praise or plaint
    Meekly and duly ;
I will not enter there,
To sully your pure prayer
    With thoughts unruly.

But suffer me to pace
Round the forbidden place,
    Lingering a minute,
Like outcast spirits, who wait,
And see, through heaven's gate,
    Angels within it.

THE BALLAD OF BOUILLABAISSE

A STREET there is in Paris famous,
    For which no rhyme our language yields,
Rue Neuve des petits Champs its name
        is —
The New Street of the Little Fields ;
And there 's an inn, not rich and splen-
        did,
    But still in comfortable case —
The which in youth I oft attended,
    To eat a bowl of Bouillabaisse.

This Bouillabaisse a noble dish is —
    A sort of soup, or broth, or brew,
Or hotchpotch of all sorts of fishes,
    That Greenwich never could outdo ;
Green herbs, red peppers, mussels, saffern,
    Soles, onions, garlic, roach, and dace ;
All these you eat at Terré's tavern,
    In that one dish of Bouillabaisse.

Indeed, a rich and savory stew 't is ;
    And true philosophers, methinks,
Who love all sorts of natural beauties,
    Should love good victuals and good
        drinks.
And Cordelier or Benedictine
    Might gladly, sure, his lot embrace,
Nor find a fast-day too afflicting,
    Which served him up a Bouillabaisse.

I wonder if the house still there is ?
    Yes, here the lamp is as before ;
The smiling, red-cheeked écaillère is
    Still opening oysters at the door.

Is Terré still alive and able ?
  I recollect his droll grimace ;
He 'd come and smile before your table,
  And hop'd you lik'd your Bouillabaisse.

We enter ; nothing 's changed or older.
  "How 's Monsieur Terré, waiter, pray ? "
The waiter stares and shrugs his shoulder ;—
  "Monsieur is dead this many a day."
"It is the lot of saint and sinner.
  So honest Terré 's run his race ! "
"What will Monsieur require for dinner ? "
  "Say, do you still cook Bouillabaisse ? "

"Oh, oui, Monsieur, " 's the waiter's an-
        swer ;
  "Quel vin Monsieur désire-t-il ? "
"Tell me a good one." "That I can, sir ;
  The Chambertin with yellow seal."
"So Terré 's gone, " I say and sink in
  My old accustom'd corner-place ;
"He 's done with feasting and with drink-
        ing,
  With Burgundy and Bouillabaisse."

My old accustom'd corner here is —
  The table still is in the nook ;
Ah ! vanish'd many a busy year is,
  This well-known chair since last I took.
When first I saw ye, *Cari luoghi*,
  I 'd scarce a beard upon my face,
And now a grizzled, grim old fogy,
  I sit and wait for Bouillabaisse.

Where are you, old companions trusty
  Of early days, here met to dine ?
Come, waiter ! quick, a flagon crusty —
  I 'll pledge them in the good old wine.
The kind old voices and old faces
  My memory can quick retrace ;
Around the board they take their places,
  And share the wine and Bouillabaisse.

There 's Jack has made a wondrous mar-
        riage ;
  There 's laughing Tom is laughing yet ;
There 's brave Augustus drives his carriage ;
  There 's poor old Fred in the Gazette ;
On James's head the grass is growing :
  Good Lord ! the world has wagg'd apace
Since here we set the Claret flowing,
  And drank, and ate the Bouillabaisse.

Ah me ! how quick the days are flitting !
  I mind me of a time that 's gone,

When here I 'd sit, as now I 'm sitting,
  In this same place — but not alone.
A fair young form was nestled near me,
  A dear, dear face look'd fondly up,
And sweetly spoke and smil'd to cheer me
  — There 's no one now to share my cup.

.   .   .   .

I drink it as the Fates ordain it.
  Come, fill it, and have done with rhymes
Fill up the lonely glass, and drain it
  In memory of dear old times.
Welcome the wine, whate'er the seal is ;
  And sit you down and say your grace
With thankful heart, whate'er the meal is
  —Here comes the smoking Bouillabaisse

THE AGE OF WISDOM

Ho ! pretty page, with the dimpled chin,
  That never has known the barber's shear,
All your wish is woman to win ;
This is the way that boys begin :
  Wait till you come to forty year.

Curly gold locks cover foolish brains ;
  Billing and cooing is all your cheer —
Sighing, and singing of midnight strains,
Under Bonnybell's window panes :
  Wait till you come to forty year.

Forty times over let Michaelmas pass ;
  Grizzling hair the brain doth clear ;
Then you know a boy is an ass,
Then you know the worth of a lass,
  Once you have come to forty year.

Pledge me round ; I bid ye declare,
  All good fellows whose beards are gray,
Did not the fairest of the fair
Common grow and wearisome ere
  Ever a month was pass'd away ?

The reddest lips that ever have kiss'd,
  The brightest eyes that ever have shone,
May pray and whisper and we not list,
Or look away and never be miss'd,
  Ere yet ever a month is gone.

Gillian 's dead ! God rest her bier —
  How I loved her twenty years syne !
Marian 's married ; but I sit here,
Alone and merry at forty year,
  Dipping my nose in the Gascon wine.

SORROWS OF WERTHER

WERTHER had a love for Charlotte
Such as words could never utter ;
Would you know how first he met her ?
She was cutting bread and butter.

Charlotte was a married lady,
And a moral man was Werther,
And for all the wealth of Indies
Would do nothing for to hurt her.

So he sigh'd and pin'd and ogled,
And his passion boil'd and bubbled,
Till he blew his silly brains out,
And no more was by it troubled.

Charlotte, having seen his body
Borne before her on a shutter,
Like a well-conducted person,
Went on cutting bread and butter.

THE PEN AND THE ALBUM

I AM Miss Catherine's book" (the Album speaks) ;
I 've lain among your tomes these many weeks ;
'm tir'd of your old coats and yellow cheeks.

Quick, Pen ! and write a line with a good grace ;
ome ! draw me off a funny little face ;
nd, prithee, send me back to Chesham Place."

PEN

am my master's faithful old Gold Pen ;
've serv'd him three long years, and drawn since then
housands of funny women and droll men.

Album ! could I tell you all his ways
nd thoughts, since I am his, these thousand days,
ord, how your pretty pages I 'd amaze !

ALBUM

Is ways ? his thoughts ? Just whisper me a few ;
ell me a curious anecdote or two,
nd write 'em quickly off, good Mordan, do !

PEN

Since he my faithful service did engage
To follow him through his queer pilgrimage,
I 've drawn and written many a line and page.

Caricatures I scribbled have, and rhymes,
And dinner cards, and picture pantomimes,
And merry little children's books at times.

I 've writ the foolish fancy of his brain ;
The aimless jest that, striking, hath caus'd pain ;
The idle word that he 'd wish back again.

I v'e help'd him to pen many a line for bread ;
To joke, with sorrow aching in his head ;
And make your laughter when his own heart bled.

I 've spoke with men of all degree and sort —
Peers of the land, and ladies of the Court ;
O, but I 've chonicled a deal of sport.

Feasts that were ate a thousand days ago,
Biddings to wine that long hath ceas'd to flow,
Gay meetings with good fellows long laid low ;

Summons to bridal, banquet, burial, ball,
Tradesman's polite reminders of his small
Account due Christmas last — I 've answer'd all.

Poor Diddler's tenth petition for a half
Guinea ; Miss Bunyan's for an autograph ;
So I refuse, accept, lament, or laugh,

Condole, congratulate, invite, praise, scoff,
Day after day still dipping in my trough,
And scribbling pages after pages off.

Day after day the labor 's to be done,
And sure as comes the postman and the sun,
The indefatigable ink must run.

.   .   .   .

Go back, my pretty little gilded tome,
To a fair mistress and a pleasant home,
Where soft hearts greet us whensoe'er we come.

Dear, friendly eyes, with constant kindness
    lit,
However rude my verse, or poor my wit,
Or sad or gay my mood, you welcome it.

Kind lady ! till my last of lines is penn'd,
My master's love, grief, laughter, at an end,
Whene'er I write your name, may I write
    friend !

Not all are so that were so in past years ;
Voices, familiar once, no more he hears ;
Names, often writ, are blotted out in tears.

So be it : — joys will end and tears will
    dry —
Album ! my master bids me wish good-
    by ;
He 'll send you to your mistress presently.

And thus with thankful heart he closes
    you ;
Blessing the happy hour when a friend he
    knew
So gentle, and so generous, and so true.

Nor pass the words as idle phrases by;
Stranger ! I never writ a flattery,
Nor sign'd the page that register'd a lie.

THE MAHOGANY TREE

CHRISTMAS is here ;
Winds whistle shrill,
Icy and chill,
Little care we ;
Little we fear
Weather without,
Shelter'd about
The Mahogany Tree.

Once on the boughs
Birds of rare plume
Sang, in its bloom ;
Night birds are we ;
Here we carouse,
Singing, like them,
Perch'd round the stem
Of the jolly old tree.

Here let us sport,
Boys, as we sit —
Laughter and wit
Flashing so free.

Life is but short —
When we are gone,
Let them sing on,
Round the old tree.

Evenings we knew,
Happy as this ;
Faces we miss,
Pleasant to see.
Kind hearts and true,
Gentle and just,
Peace to your dust !
We sing round the tree.

Care, like a dun,
Lurks at the gate :
Let the dog wait ;
Happy we 'll be !
Drink every one ;
Pile up the coals,
Fill the red bowls,
Round the old tree.

Drain we the cup. —
Friend, art afraid ?
Spirits are laid
In the Red Sea.
Mantle it up ;
Empty it yet ;
Let us forget,
Round the old tree.

Sorrows, begone !
Life and its ills,
Duns and their bills,
Bid we to flee.
Come with the dawn,
Blue-devil sprite,
Leave us to-night,
Round the old tree.

THE END OF THE PLAY

THE play is done — the curtain drops,
    Slow falling to the prompter's bell ;
A moment yet the actor stops,
    And looks around, to say farewell.
It is an irksome word and task ;
    And, when he 's laugh'd and said his say,
He shows, as he removes the mask,
    A face that 's anything but gay.

One word, ere yet the evening ends :
    Let 's close it with a parting rhyme,

And pledge a hand to all young friends,
  As fits the merry Christmas time ;
In life's wide scene you, too, have parts,
  That fate ere long shall bid you play ;
Good-night ! — with honest gentle hearts
  A kindly greeting go alway !

Good-night ! — I 'd say the griefs, the joys,
  Just hinted in this mimic page,
The triumphs and defeats of boys,
  Are but repeated in our age ;
I 'd say your woes were not less keen,
  Your hopes more vain, than those of
    men,
Your pangs or pleasures of fifteen
  At forty-five played o'er again.

I 'd say we suffer and we strive
  Not less nor more as men than boys,
With grizzled beards at forty-five,
  As erst at twelve in corduroys,
And if, in time of sacred youth,
  We learn'd at home to love and pray,
Pray heaven that early love and truth
  May never wholly pass away.

And in the world, as in the school,
  I 'd say how fate may change and shift,
The prize be sometimes with the fool,
  The race not always to the swift ;
The strong may yield, the good may fall,
  The great man be a vulgar clown,
The knave be lifted over all,
  The kind cast pitilessly down.

Who knows the inscrutable design ?
  Blessed be He who took and gave !
Why should your mother, Charles, not
    mine,
  Be weeping at her darling's grave ?
We bow to heaven that will'd it so,
  That darkly rules the fate of all,
That sends the respite or the blow,
  That 's free to give or to recall.

This crowns his feast with wine and wit —
  Who brought him to that mirth and state ?
His betters, see, below him sit,
  Or hunger hopeless at the gate.
Who bade the mud from Dives' wheel
  To spurn the rags of Lazarus ?
Come, brother, in that dust we 'll kneel,
  Confessing heaven that rul'd it thus.

So each shall mourn, in life's advance,
  Dear hopes, dear friends, untimely kill'd,
Shall grieve for many a forfeit chance,
  And longing passion unfulfill'd.
Amen ! — whatever fate be sent,
  Pray God the heart may kindly glow,
Although the head with cares be bent,
  And whiten'd with the winter snow.

Come wealth or want, come good or ill,
  Let young and old accept their part,
And bow before the awful will,
  And bear it with an honest heart.
Who misses or who wins the prize —
  Go, lose or conquer as you can ;
But if you fail, or if you rise,
  Be each, pray God, a gentleman.

A gentleman, or old or young !
  (Bear kindly with my humble lays ;)
The sacred chorus first was sung
  Upon the first of Christmas days ;
The shepherds heard it overhead —
  The joyful angels rais'd it then :
Glory to heaven on high, it said,
  And peace on earth to gentle men !

My song, save this, is little worth ;
  I lay the weary pen aside,
And wish you health, and love, and mirth,
  As fits the solemn Christmas-tide.
As fits the holy Christmas birth,
  Be this, good friends, our carol still :
Be peace on earth, be peace on earth,
  To men of gentle will.

Charles Dickens

THE IVY GREEN

Oh, a dainty plant is the Ivy green,
  That creepeth o'er ruins old !
Of right choice food are his meals I ween,
  In his cell so lone and cold.
The wall must be crumbled, the stone de-
    cayed,

To pleasure his dainty whim ;
And the mouldering dust that years have
    made
  Is a merry meal for him.
    Creeping where no life is seen,
    A rare old plant is the Ivy green.

Fast he stealeth on, though he wears no
    wings,
And a staunch old heart has he.
How closely he twineth, how tight he clings
    To his friend the huge Oak Tree !
And slily he traileth along the ground,
    And his leaves he gently waves,
As he joyously hugs and crawleth round
    The rich mould of dead men's graves.
        Creeping where grim death has been,
        A rare old plant is the Ivy green.

Whole ages have fled and their works de
    cayed,
And nations have scattered been ;
But the stout old Ivy shall never fade,
    From its hale and hearty green.
The brave old plant, in its lonely days,
    Shall fatten upon the past :
For the stateliest building man can raise
    Is the Ivy's food at last.
        Creeping on, where time has been,
        A rare old plant is the Ivy green.

Charles Kingsley

FROM " THE SAINT'S TRAGEDY "

SONG

OH ! that we two were Maying
Down the stream of the soft spring breeze ;
Like children with violets playing
In the shade of the whispering trees.

Oh ! that we two sat dreaming
On the sward of some sheep - trimm'd
    down,
Watching the white mist steaming
Over river and mead and town.

Oh ! that we two lay sleeping
In our nest in the churchyard sod,
With our limbs at rest on the quiet earth's
    breast,
And our souls at home with God.

CRUSADER CHORUS

(Men at Arms pass singing)

THE tomb of God before us,
Our fatherland behind,
Our ships shall leap o'er billows steep,
Before a charmed wind.

Above our van great angels
Shall fight along the sky ;
While martyrs pure and crowned saints
To God for rescue cry.

The red-cross knights and yeomen
Throughout the holy town,
In faith and might, on left and right,
Shall tread the paynim down.

Till on the Mount Moriah
The Pope of Rome shall stand ;
The Kaiser and the King of France
Shall guard him on each hand.

There shall he rule all nations,
With crosier and with sword ;
And pour on all the heathen
The wrath of Christ the Lord.

.   .   .   .

(Young Knights pass)

The rich East blooms fragrant before us ;
All Fairy-land beckons us forth ;
We must follow the crane in her flight o'er
    the main,
From the posts and the moors of the North

Our sires in the youth of the nations
Swept westward through plunder and blood
But a holier quest calls us back to the
    East,
We fight for the kingdom of God.

Then shrink not, and sigh not, fair ladies,
The red cross which flames on each arm
    and each shield,
Through philter and spell, and the black
    charms of hell,
Shall shelter our true love in camp and in
    field.

(Old Monk looking after them)

Jerusalem, Jerusalem !
The burying-place of God !
Why gay and bold, in steel and gold,
O'er the paths where Christ hath trod ?

THE SANDS OF DEE

" O MARY, go and call the cattle home,
  And call the cattle home,
  And call the cattle home
Across the sands of Dee ! "
The western wind was wild and dank wi'
      foam,
  And all alone went she.

The western tide crept up along the sand,
  And o'er and o'er the sand,
  And round and round the sand,
  As far as eye could see.
The rolling mist came down and hid the
      land —
  And never home came she.

" Oh ! is it weed, or fish, or floating hair —
  A tress o' golden hair,
  A drowned maiden's hair
  Above the nets at sea ?
Was never salmon yet that shone so fair
  Among the stakes on Dee."

They row'd her in across the rolling foam,
  The cruel crawling foam,
  The cruel hungry foam,
  To her grave beside the sea :
But still the boatmen hear her call the
      cattle home
  Across the sands of Dee !

THE THREE FISHERS

THREE fishers went sailing out into the
      West,
  Out into the West as the sun went down ;
Each thought on the woman who lov'd
      him the best ;
And the children stood watching them
      out of the town ;
For men must work, and women must weep,
And there's little to earn, and many to
      keep,
  Though the harbor bar be moaning.

Three wives sat up in the light-house tower,
And they trimm'd the lamps as the sun
      went down;
They look'd at the squall, and they look'd
      at the shower,
  And the night rack came rolling up
      ragged and brown !

But men must work, and women must weep,
Though storms be sudden, and waters deep,
  And the harbor bar be moaning.

Three corpses lay out on the shining sands
  In the morning gleam as the tide went
      down,
And the women are weeping and wringing
      their hands
  For those who will never come back to
      the town ;
For men must work, and women must
      weep,
And the sooner it's over, the sooner to
      sleep —
  And good-by to the bar and its moan-
      ing.

A MYTH

A FLOATING, a floating
Across the sleeping sea,
All night I heard a singing bird
Upon the topmast tree.

" Oh, came you from the isles of Greece
Or from the banks of Seine ;
Or off some tree in forests free,
Which fringe the western main ? "

" I came not off the old world
Nor yet from off the new —
But I am one of the birds of God
Which sing the whole night through. "

" Oh, sing and wake the dawning —
Oh, whistle for the wind ;
The night is long, the current strong,
My boat it lags behind. "

" The current sweeps the old world,
The current sweeps the new ;
The wind will blow, the dawn will glow,
Ere thou hast sail'd them through. "

THE DEAD CHURCH

WILD, wild wind, wilt thou never cease thy
      sighing ?
Dark, dark night, wilt thou never wear
      away ?
Cold, cold church, in thy death sleep lying,
Thy Lent is past, thy Passion here, but not
      thine Easterday.

Peace, faint heart, though the night be
    dark and sighing ;
Rest, fair corpse, where thy Lord himself
    hath lain.
Weep, dear Lord, where thy bride is lying ;
Thy tears shall wake her frozen limbs to
    life and health again.

ANDROMEDA AND THE SEA-NYMPHS

FROM "ANDROMEDA"

Aw'D by her own rash words she was
    still : and her eyes to the seaward
Look'd for an answer of wrath : far off, in
    the heart of the darkness,
Bright white mists rose slowly ; beneath
    them the wandering ocean
Glimmer'd and glow'd to the deepest
    abyss ; and the knees of the maiden
Trembled and sank in her fear, as afar, like
    a dawn in the midnight,
Rose from their seaweed chamber the choir
    of the mystical sea-maids.
Onward toward her they came, and her
    heart beat loud at their coming,
Watching the bliss of the gods, as waken'd
    the cliffs with their laughter.
Onward they came in their joy, and before
    them the roll of the surges
Sank, as the breeze sank dead, into smooth
    green foam-fleck'd marble,
Aw'd ; and the crags of the cliff, and the
    pines of the mountain were silent.
    Onward they came in their joy, and
    around them the lamps of the sea-nymphs,
Myriad fiery globes, swam panting and
    heaving ; and rainbows,
Crimson and azure and emerald, were
    broken in star-showers, lighting
Far through the wine-dark depths of the
    crystal, the gardens of Nereus,
Coral and sea-fan and tangle, the blooms
    and the palms of the ocean.
    Onward they came in their joy, more
    white than the foam which they scatter'd,
Laughing and singing, and tossing and twining, while eager, the Tritons
Blinded with kisses their eyes, unreprov'd,
    and above them in worship
Hover'd the terns, and the seagulls swept
    past them on silvery pinions

Echoing softly their laughter ; around then
    the wantoning dolphins
Sigh'd as they plunged, full of love ; an
    the great sea-horses which bore then
Curv'd up their crests in their pride to th
    delicate arms of the maiden,
Pawing the spray into gems, till the fiery
    rainfall, unharming,
Sparkled and gleam'd on the limbs of th
    nymphs, and the coils of the mermen
    Onward they went in their joy, bath'c
    round with the fiery coolness,
Needing nor sun nor moon, self-lighted
    immortal : but others,
Pitiful, floated in silence apart ; in thei
    bosoms the sea-boys,
Slain by the wrath of the seas, swept dowr
    by the anger of Nereus ;
Hapless, whom never again on strand or on
    quay shall their mothers
Welcome with garlands and vows to th
    temple, but wearily pining
Gaze over island and bay for the sails o
    the sunken ; they heedless
Sleep in soft bosoms forever, and dream o
    the surge and the sea-maids.
    Onward they pass'd in their joy ; on thei
    brows neither sorrow nor anger ;
Self-sufficing, as gods, never heeding the
    woe of the maiden.

THE LAST BUCCANEER

OH, England is a pleasant place for them
    that 's rich and high ;
But England is a cruel place for such poor
    folks as I ;
And such a port for mariners I ne'er shall
    see again,
As the pleasant Isle of Avès, beside the
    Spanish main.

There were forty craft in Avès that were
    both swift and stout,
All furnish'd well with small arms and
    cannons round about ;
And a thousand men in Avès made laws so
    fair and free
To choose their valiant captains and obey
    them loyally.

Thence we sail'd against the Spaniard with
    his hoards of plate and gold,
Which he wrung by cruel tortures from the
    Indian folk of old ;

Likewise the merchant captains, with hearts
as hard as stone,
Which flog men and keel-haul them and
starve them to the bone.

Oh, the palms grew high in Avès and fruits
that shone like gold,
And the colibris and parrots they were
gorgeous to behold ;
And the negro maids to Avès from bondage
fast did flee,
To welcome gallant sailors a sweeping in
from sea.

Oh, sweet it was in Avès to hear the land-
ward breeze
A-swing with good tobacco in a net between
the trees,
With a negro lass to fan you while you list-
en'd to the roar
Of the breakers on the reef outside that
never touched the shore.

But Scripture saith, an ending to all fine
things must be,
So the King's ships sail'd on Avès and
quite put down were we.
All day we fought like bulldogs, but they
burst the booms at night ;
And I fled in a piragua sore wounded from
the fight.

Nine days I floated starving, and a negro
lass beside,
Till for all I tried to cheer her, the poor
young thing she died ;
But as I lay a gasping a Bristol sail came by,
And brought me home to England here to
beg until I die.

And now I'm old and going I'm sure I
can't tell where ;
One comfort is, this world's so hard I can't
be worse off there :
If I might but be a sea-dove I'd fly across
the main,
To the pleasant Isle of Aves, to look at it
once again.

LORRAINE

'Are you ready for your steeple-chase,
Lorraine, Lorraine, Lorrèe ?
   Barum, Barum, Barum, Barum,
   Barum, Barum, Baree.

You 're booked to ride your capping race
to-day at Coulterlee,
You 're booked to ride Vindictive, for all the
world to see,
To keep him straight, and keep him first,
and win the run for me. "
   Barum, Barum, Barum, Barum,
   Barum, Barum, Baree.

She clasp'd her new-born baby, poor Lor-
raine, Lorraine, Lorrèe,
   Barum, Barum, Barum, Barum,
   Barum, Barum, Baree.
" I cannot ride Vindictive, as any man
might see,
And I will not ride Vindictive, with this
baby on my knee ;
He 's kill'd a boy, he 's kill'd a man, and
why must he kill me ? "

" Unless you ride Vindictive, Lorraine,
Lorraine, Lorrèe,
Unless you ride Vindictive to-day at Coul-
terlee,
And land him safe across the brook, and
win the blank for me,
It 's you may keep your baby, for you 'll get
no keep from me. "

" That husbands could be cruel," said Lor-
raine, Lorraine, Lorrèe,
" That husbands could be cruel, I have
known for seasons three ;
But oh, to ride Vindictive while a baby cries
for me,
And be kill'd across a fence at last for all
the world to see ! "

She master'd young Vindictive — O, the
gallant lass was she !
And kept him straight and won the race as
near as near could be ;
But he kill'd her at the brook against a
pollard willow tree ;
Oh ! he kill'd her at the brook, the brute
for all the world to see,
And no one but the baby cried for poor
Lorraine, Lorrèe.

A FAREWELL

My fairest child, I have no song to give you ;
  No lark could pipe to skies so dull and gray:
Yet, ere we part, one lesson I can leave you
  For every day.

Be good, sweet maid, and let who will be
  clever ;
Do noble things, not dream them, all day
  long :

And so make life, death, and that vast for
  ever
    One grand, sweet song.

Adelaide Anne Procter

A WOMAN'S QUESTION

BEFORE I trust my fate to thee,
  Or place my hand in thine,
Before I let thy future give
  Color and form to mine,
Before I peril all for thee, question thy soul
  to-night for me.

I break all slighter bonds, nor feel
  A shadow of regret :
Is there one link within the Past
  That holds thy spirit yet ?
Or is thy faith as clear and free as that
  which I can pledge to thee ?

Does there within thy dimmest dreams
  A possible future shine,
Wherein thy life could henceforth breathe,
  Untouch'd, unshar'd by mine ?
If so, at any pain or cost, O, tell me before
  all is lost.

Look deeper still. If thou canst feel,
  Within thy inmost soul,
That thou hast kept a portion back,
  While I have stak'd the whole ;
Let no false pity spare the blow, but in true
  mercy tell me so.

Is there within thy heart a need
  That mine cannot fulfil ?
One chord that any other hand
  Could better wake or still ?
Speak now — lest at some future day my
  whole life wither and decay.

Lives there within thy nature hid
  The demon-spirit Change,
Shedding a passing glory still
  On all things new and strange ?
It may not be thy fault alone — but shield
  my heart against thy own.

Couldst thou withdraw thy hand one day
  And answer to my claim,

That Fate, and that to-day's mistake —
  Not thou — had been to blame ?
Some soothe their conscience thus ; but thou
  wilt surely warn and save me now.

Nay, answer *not*, — I dare not hear,
  The words would come too late ;
Yet I would spare thee all remorse,
  So, comfort thee, my fate —
Whatever on my heart may fall — remem-
  ber, I would risk it all !

A DOUBTING HEART

WHERE are the swallows fled ?
  Frozen and dead,
Perchance, upon some bleak and stormy
  shore.
  O doubting heart !
  Far over purple seas
  They wait, in sunny ease,
  The balmy southern breeze,
To bring them to their northern homes once
  more.

Why must the flowers die ?
  Prison'd they lie
In the cold tomb, heedless of tears or rain.
  O doubting heart !
  They only sleep below
  The soft white ermine snow,
  While winter winds shall blow,
To breathe and smile upon you soon
  again.

The sun has hid its rays
  These many days ;
Will dreary hours never leave the earth ?
  O doubting heart !
  The stormy clouds on high
  Veil the same sunny sky,
  That soon (for spring is nigh)
Shall wake the summer into golden mirth.

Fair hope is dead, and light
  Is quench'd in night.

What sound can break the silence of de-
    spair ?
O doubting heart !
Thy sky is overcast,
Yet stars shall rise at last,
Brighter for darkness past,
And angels' silver voices stir the air.

THE REQUITAL

LOUD roared the tempest,
    Fast fell the sleet ;
A little Child Angel
    Passed down the street,
With trailing pinions
    And weary feet.

The moon was hidden ;
    No stars were bright ;
So she could not shelter
    In heaven that night,
For the Angels' ladders
    Are rays of light.

She beat her wings
    At each window-pane,
And pleaded for shelter,
    But all in vain ; —
" Listen," they said,
    " To the pelting rain ! "

She sobb'd, as the laughter
    And mirth grew higher,
" Give me rest and shelter
    Beside your fire,
And I will give you
    Your heart's desire."

The dreamer sat watching
    His embers gleam,
While his heart was floating
    Down hope's bright stream ;
. . . So he wove her wailing
    Into his dream.

The worker toil'd on,
    For his time was brief ;
The mourner was nursing
    Her own pale grief ;
They heard not the promise
    That brought relief.

But fiercer the tempest
    Rose than before,

When the Angel paus'd
    At a humble door,
And ask'd for shelter
    And help once more.

A weary woman,
    Pale, worn, and thin,
With the brand upon her
    Of want and sin,
Heard the Child Angel
    And took her in :

Took her in gently,
    And did her best
To dry her pinions ;
    And made her rest
With tender pity
    Upon her breast.

When the eastern morning
    Grew bright and red,
Up the first sunbeam
    The Angel fled ;
Having kiss'd the woman
    And left her — dead.

PER PACEM AD LUCEM

I DO not ask, O Lord, that life may be
    A pleasant road ;
I do not ask that Thou wouldst take from
    me
    Aught of its load ;

I do not ask that flowers should always
    spring
    Beneath my feet ;
I know too well the poison and the sting
    Of things too sweet.

For one thing only, Lord, dear Lord, I plead,
    Lead me aright —
Though strength should falter, and though
    heart should bleed —
    Through Peace to Light.

I do not ask, O Lord, that thou shouldst
    shed
    Full radiance here ;
Give but a ray of peace, that I may tread
    Without a fear.

I do not ask my cross to understand,
    My way to see ;

Better in darkness just to feel Thy hand
  And follow Thee.

Joy is like restless day; but peace divine
  Like quiet night :

Lead me, O Lord, — till perfect Day shall
  shine,
Through Peace to Light.

Dinah Maria Mulock Craik

PHILIP, MY KING

Look at me with thy large brown eyes,
    Philip, my king!
Round whom the enshadowing purple lies
Of babyhood's royal dignities.
Lay on my neck thy tiny hand
  With love's invisible sceptre laden ;
I am thine Esther to command
  Till thou shalt find a queen-handmaiden,
    Philip, my king.

Oh the day when thou goest a-wooing,
    Philip, my king !
When some beautiful lips 'gin suing,
And some gentle heart's bars undoing
Thou dost enter, love-crown'd, and there
  Sittest love-glorified.   Rule kindly,
Tenderly, over thy kingdom fair,
  For we that love, ah ! we love so blindly,
    Philip, my king.

Up from thy sweet mouth, — up to thy
    brow,
    Philip, my king !
The spirit that here lies sleeping now
May rise like a giant and make men
    bow
As to one heaven-chosen among his peers.
  My Saul, than thy brethren taller and
    fairer,
Let me behold thee in future years !
  Yet thy head needeth a circlet rarer,
    Philip, my king.

— A wreath not of gold, but palm.   One
    day,
    Philip, my king !
Thou too must tread, as we trod, a way
Thorny and cruel and cold and gray :

Rebels within thee, and foes without,
  Will snatch at thy crown.   But march
    on, glorious,
Martyr, yet monarch ! till angels shout,
  As thou sit'st at the feet of God victo-
    rious,
    " Philip, the king ! "

TOO LATE

" DOWGLAS, DOWGLAS, TENDIR AND TREU "

Could ye come back to me, Douglas,
    Douglas,
  In the old likeness that I knew,
I would be so faithful, so loving, Douglas,
  Douglas, Douglas, tender and true.

Never a scornful word should grieve ye,
  I 'd smile on ye sweet as the angels do :
Sweet as your smile on me shone ever,
  Douglas, Douglas, tender and true.

Oh, to call back the days that are not !
  My eyes were blinded, your words were
    few :
Do you know the truth now, up in heaven,
  Douglas, Douglas, tender and true ?

I never was worthy of you, Douglas ;
  Not half worthy the like of you :
Now all men beside seem to me   like
    shadows —
  I love you, Douglas, tender and true.

Stretch out your hand to me, Douglas,
    Douglas,
  Drop forgiveness from heaven like dew ;
As I lay my heart on your dead heart,
    Douglas,
  Douglas, Douglas, tender and true !

Earl of Southesk

(SIR JAMES CARNEGIE)

THE FLITCH OF DUNMOW

Come Micky and Molly and dainty Dolly,
  Come Betty and blithesome Bill ;
Ye gossips and neighbors, away with your
    labors !
  Come to the top of the hill.
For there are Jenny and jovial Joe ;
Jolly and jolly, jolly they go,
  Jogging over the hill.

By apple and berry, 't is twelve months
    merry
  Since Jenny and Joe were wed !
And never a bother or quarrelsome pother
  To trouble the board or bed.
So Joe and Jenny are off to Dunmow :
Happy and happy, happy they go,
  Young and rosy and red.

Oh, Jenny 's as pretty as doves in a ditty ;
  And Jenny, her eyes are black ;
And Joey 's a fellow as merry and mellow
  As ever shoulder'd a sack.
So quick, good people, and come to the
    show !
Merry and merry, merry they go,
  Bumping on Dobbin's back.

They 've prank'd up old Dobbin with ribands
    and bobbin,
  And tether'd his tail in a string !
The fat flitch of bacon is not to be taken
  By many that wear the ring !
Good luck, good luck, to Jenny and Joe !
Jolly and jolly, jolly they go.
  Hark ! how merry they sing.

" O merry, merry, merry are we,
Happy as birds that sing in a tree !

All of the neighbors are merry to-day,
Merry are we and merry are they.
O merry are we ! for love, you see,
Fetters a heart and sets it free.

" O happy, happy, happy is life
For Joe (that 's me) and Jenny my wife !
All of the neighbors are happy, and say —
' Never were folk so happy as they ! '
O happy are we ! for love, you see,
Fetters a heart and sets it free.

" O jolly, jolly, jolly we go,
I and my Jenny, and she and her Joe.
All of the neighbors are jolly, and sing —
' She is a queen, and he is a king ! '
O jolly are we ! for love, you see,
Fetters a heart and sets it free."

NOVEMBER'S CADENCE

The bees about the Linden-tree,
When blithely summer blooms were spring-
    ing,
Would hum a heartsome melody,
The simple baby-soul of singing ;
And thus my spirit sang to me
When youth its wanton way was wing-
    ing :
  " Be glad, be sad—thou hast the choice —
  But mingle music with thy voice. "

The linnets on the Linden-tree,
Among the leaves in autumn dying,
Are making gentle melody,
A mild, mysterious, mournful sighing ;
And thus my spirit sings to me
While years are flying, flying, flying :
  " Be sad, be sad, thou hast no choice,
  But mourn with music in thy voice. "

Mortimer Collins

A GREEK IDYL

He sat the quiet stream beside,
His white feet laving in the tide,

And watch'd the pleasant waters glide
  Beneath the skies of summer.
She singing came from mound to mound,
Her footfall on the thymy ground

Unheard ; his tranquil haunt she found —
 That beautiful new comer.

He said — "My own Glycerium !
The pulses of the woods are dumb,
How well I knew that thou wouldst come,
 Beneath the branches gliding."
The dreamer fancied he had heard
Her footstep, whensoever stirr'd
The summer wind or languid bird
 Amid the boughs abiding.

She dipp'd her fingers in the brook,
And gaz'd awhile with happy look
Upon the windings of a book
 Of Cyprian hymnings tender.
The ripples to the ocean raced —
The flying minutes pass'd in haste :
His arm was round the maiden's waist,
 That waist so very slender.

O cruel Time ! O tyrant Time !
Whose winter all the streams of rhyme,
The flowing waves of love sublime,
 In bitter passage freezes.
I only see the scambling goat,
The lotos on the waters float,
While an old shepherd with an oat
 Pipes to the autumn breezes.

KATE TEMPLE'S SONG

ONLY a touch, and nothing more :
Ah ! but never so touch'd before !
Touch of lip, was it ? Touch of hand ?
Either is easy to understand.
Earth may be smitten with fire or frost —
Never the touch of true love lost.

Only a word, was it ? Scarce a word !
Musical whisper, softly heard,
Syllabled nothing — just a breath —
'T will outlast life, and 't will laugh at
 death.
Love with so little can do so much —
Only a word, sweet ! Only a touch !

THE IVORY GATE

Sunt geminae Somni portae : quarum altera fertur
Cornea ; qua veris facilis datur exitus umbris :
Altera candenti perfecta nitens elephanto ;
Sed falsa ad coelum mittunt insomnia Manes.
 VERGIL.

WHEN, lov'd by poet and painter,
 The sunrise fills the sky,
When night's gold urns grow fainter,
 And in depths of amber die —
When the morn-breeze stirs the curtain,
 Bearing an odorous freight —
Then visions strange, uncertain,
 Pour thick through the Ivory Gate.

Then the oars of Ithaca dip so
 Silently into the sea
That they wake not sad Calypso,
 And the Hero wanders free :
He breasts the ocean-furrows,
 At war with the words of Fate,
And the blue tide's low susurrus
 Comes up to the Ivory Gate.

Or, clad in the hide of leopard,
 'Mid Ida's freshest dews,
Paris, the Teucrian shepherd,
 His sweet Oenone wooes :
On the thought of her coming bridal
 Unutter'd joy doth wait,
While the tune of the false one's idyl
 Rings soft through the Ivory Gate.

Or down from green Helvellyn
 The roar of streams I hear,
And the lazy sail is swelling
 To the winds of Windermere :
That girl with the rustic bodice
 'Mid the ferry's laughing freight
Is as fair as any goddess
 Who sweeps through the Ivory Gate.

Ah, the vision of dawn is leisure —
 But the truth of day is toil ;
And we pass from dreams of pleasure
 To the world's unstay'd turmoil.
Perchance, beyond the river
 Which guards the realms of Fate,
Our spirits may dwell forever
 'Mong dreams of the Ivory Gate.

William Allingham

THE FAIRIES

A CHILD'S SONG

Up the airy mountain,
  Down the rushy glen,
We dare n't go a-hunting
  For fear of little men ;
Wee folk, good folk,
  Trooping all together ;
Green jacket, red cap,
  And white owl's feather !

Down along the rocky shore
  Some make their home, —
They live on crispy pancakes
  Of yellow tide-foam ;
Some in the reeds
  Of the black mountain-lake,
With frogs for their watch-dogs,
  All night awake.

High on the hill-top
  The old King sits ;
He is now so old and gray
  He 's nigh lost his wits.
With a bridge of white mist
  Columbkill he crosses,
On his stately journeys
  From Slieveleague to Rosses ;
Or going up with music
  On cold starry nights,
To sup with the Queen
  Of the gay Northern Lights.

They stole little Bridget
  For seven years long ;
When she came down again
  Her friends were all gone.
They took her lightly back,
  Between the night and morrow,
They thought that she was fast asleep,
  But she was dead with sorrow.
They have kept her ever since
  Deep within the lakes,
On a bed of flag-leaves,
  Watching till she wakes.

By the craggy hill-side,
  Through the mosses bare,
They have planted thorn-trees
  For pleasure here and there.

Is any man so daring
  As dig one up in spite,
He shall find the thornies set
  In his bed at night.

Up the airy mountain,
  Down the rushy glen,
We dare n't go a-hunting
  For fear of little men ;
Wee folk, good folk,
  Trooping all together ;
Green jacket, red cap,
  And white owl's feather !

LOVELY MARY DONNELLY

Oh, lovely Mary Donnelly, it 's you I love
    the best !
If fifty girls were round you I 'd hardly see
    the rest.
Be what it may the time of day, the place
    be where it will,
Sweet looks of Mary Donnelly, they bloom
    before me still.

Her eyes like mountain water that 's flow-
    ing on a rock,
How clear they are, how dark they are ! and
    they give me many a shock.
Red rowans warm in sunshine and wetted
    with a show'r,
Could ne'er express the charming lip that
    has me in its pow'r.

Her nose is straight and handsome, her
    eyebrows lifted up,
Her chin is very neat and pert, and smooth
    like a china cup,
Her hair 's the brag of Ireland, so weighty
    and so fine ;
It 's rolling down upon her neck, and
    gather'd in a twine.

The dance o' last Whit-Monday night ex-
    ceeded all before ;
No pretty girl for miles about was missing
    from the floor ;
But Mary kept the belt of love, and O but
    she was gay !
She danced a jig, she sung a song, that took
    my heart away.

When she stood up for dancing, her steps
    were so complete,
The music nearly kill'd itself to listen to
    her feet ;
The fiddler moan'd his blindness, he heard
    her so much prais'd,
But bless'd himself he was n't deaf when
    once her voice she rais'd.

And evermore I 'm whistling or lilting what
    you sung,
Your smile is always in my heart, your
    name beside my tongue ;
But you 've as many sweethearts as you 'd
    count on both your hands,
And for myself there 's not a thumb or
    little finger stands.

Oh, you 're the flower o' womankind in
    country or in town ;
The higher I exalt you, the lower I 'm cast
    down.
If some great lord should come this way,
    and see your beauty bright,
And you to be his lady, I 'd own it was but
    right.

O might we live together in a lofty palace
    hall,
Where joyful music rises, and where scar-
    let curtains fall !
O might we live together in a cottage mean
    and small,
With sods of grass the only roof, and mud
    the only wall !

O lovely Mary Donnelly, your beauty 's my
    distress :
It 's far too beauteous to be mine, but I 'll
    never wish it less.
The proudest place would fit your face, and
    I am poor and low ;
But blessings be about you, dear, wherever
    you may go !

THE SAILOR

A ROMAIC BALLAD

THOU that hast a daughter
    For one to woo and wed,
Give her to a husband
    With snow upon his head ;
Oh, give her to an old man,
    Though little joy it be,

Before the best young sailor
    That sails upon the sea !

How luckless is the sailor
    When sick and like to die ;
He sees no tender mother,
    No sweetheart standing by.
Only the captain speaks to him, —
    Stand up, stand up, young man,
And steer the ship to haven,
    As none beside thee can.

Thou say'st to me, " Stand up, stand up ;"
    I say to thee, take hold,
Lift me a little from the deck,
    My hands and feet are cold.
And let my head, I pray thee,
    With handkerchiefs be bound ;
There, take my love's gold handkerchief,
    And tie it tightly round.

Now bring the chart, the doleful chart ;
    See, where these mountains meet —
The clouds are thick around their head,
    The mists around their feet ;
Cast anchor here ; 't is deep and safe
    Within the rocky cleft ;
The little anchor on the right,
    The great one on the left.

And now to thee, O captain,
    Most earnestly I pray,
That they may never bury me
    In church or cloister gray ;
But on the windy sea-beach,
    At the ending of the land,
All on the surfy sea-beach,
    Deep down into the sand.

For there will come the sailors,
    Their voices I shall hear,
And at casting of the anchor
    The yo-ho loud and clear ;
And at hauling of the anchor
    The yo-ho and the cheer, —
Farewell, my love, for to thy bay
    I nevermore may steer!

A DREAM

I HEARD the dogs howl in the moonlight
    night ;
I went to the window to see the sight ;
All the Dead that ever I knew
Going one by one and two by two.

On they pass'd, and on they pass'd ;
Townsfellows all, from first to last ;
Born in the moonlight of the lane,
Quench'd in the heavy shadow again.

Schoolmates, marching as when we play'd
At soldiers once —but now more staid ;
Those were the strangest sight to me
Who were drown'd, I knew, in the awful
    sea.

Straight and handsome folk ; bent and
    weak, too ;
Some that I lov'd, and gasp'd to speak
    to ;
Some but a day in their churchyard bed ;
Some that I had not known were dead.

A long, long crowd —where each seem'd
    lonely,
Yet of them all there was one, one only,
Raised a head or look'd my way :
She linger'd a moment, — she might not
    stay.

How long since I saw that fair pale face !
Ah ! Mother dear ! might I only place
My head on thy breast, a moment to
    rest,
While thy hand on my tearful cheek were
    prest !

On, on, a moving bridge they made
Across the moon-stream, from shade to
    shade,
Young and old, women and men ;
Many long-forgot, but remember'd then.

And first there came a bitter laughter ;
A sound of tears the moment after ;
And then a music so lofty and gay,
That every morning, day by day,
I strive to recall it if I may.

HALF-WAKING

I THOUGHT it was the little bed
    I slept in long ago ;
A straight white curtain at the head,
    And two smooth knobs below.

I thought I saw the nursery fire,
    And in a chair well-known
My mother sat, and did not tire
    With reading all alone.

If I should make the slightest sound
    To show that I'm awake,
She'd rise, and lap the blankets round,
    My pillow softly shake ;

Kiss me, and turn my face to see
    The shadows on the wall,
And then sing "Rousseau's Dream" to me,
    Till fast asleep I fall.

But this is not my little bed ;
    That time is far away :
With strangers now I live instead,
    From dreary day to day.

DAY AND NIGHT SONGS

THESE little Songs,
Found here and there,
Floating in air
By forest and lea,
Or hill-side heather,
In houses and throngs,
Or down by the sea—
Have come together,
How, I can't tell :
But I know full well
No witty goose-wing
On an inkstand begot 'em ;
Remember each place
And moment of grace,
In summer or spring,
Winter or autumn,
By sun, moon, stars,
Or a coal in the bars,
In market or church,
Graveyard or dance,
When they came without search,
Were found as by chance.
A word, a line,
You may say are mine ;
But the best in the songs,
Whatever it be,
To you, and to me,
And to no one belongs.

George Walter Thornbury

THE THREE SCARS

THIS I got on the day that Goring
Fought through York, like a wild beast
    roaring —
The roofs were black, and the streets were
    full,
The doors built up with packs of wool ;
But our pikes made way through a storm
    of shot,
Barrel to barrel till locks grew hot ;
Frere fell dead, and Lucas was gone,
But the drum still beat and the flag went on.

This I caught from a swinging sabre,
All I had from a long night's labor ;
When Chester flam'd, and the streets were
    red,
In splashing shower fell the molten lead,
The fire sprang up, and the old roof split,
The fire-ball burst in the middle of it ;
With a clash and a clang the troopers they
    ran,
For the siege was over ere well began.

This I got from a pistol butt
(Lucky my head 's not a hazel nut);
The horse they raced, and scudded and
    swore ;
There were Leicestershire gentlemen, sev-
    enty score ;
Up came the "Lobsters," cover'd with
    steel —
Down we went with a stagger and reel ;
Smash at the flag, I tore it to rag,
And carried it off in my foraging bag.

MELTING OF THE EARL'S PLATE

HERE 's the gold cup all bossy with satyrs
    and saints,
And my race-bowl (now, women, no whin-
    ing and plaints !)
From the paltriest spoon to the costliest
    thing,
We 'll melt it all down for the use of the
    king.

Here 's the chalice stamp'd over with sigil
    and cross, —
Some day we 'll make up to the chapel the
    loss.

Now bring me my father's great emerald
    ring,
For I 'll melt down the gold for the good
    of the king.

And bring me the casket my mother has got,
And the jewels that fall to my Barbara's
    lot ;
Then dry up your eyes and do nothing but
    sing,
For we 're helping to coin the gold for the
    king.

This dross we 'll transmute into weapons of
    steel,
Temper'd blades for the hand, sharpest
    spurs for the heel ;
And when Charles, with a shout, into Lon-
    don we bring,
We 'll be glad to remember this deed for
    the king.

Bring the hawk's silver bells and the nurs-
    ery spoon,
The crucible 's ready — we 're nothing too
    soon ;
For I hear the horse neigh that shall carry
    the thing
That 'll bring up a smile in the eyes of the
    king.

There go my old spurs, and the old silver
    jug, —
'T was just for a moment a pang and a tug ;
But now I am ready to dance and to sing,
To think I 've thrown gold in the chest of
    my king.

The earrings lose shape, and the coronet
    too,
I feel my eyes dim with a sort of a dew.
Hurrah for the posset dish ! — Everything
Shall run into bars for the use of the king.

That spoon is a sword, and this thimble a
    pike ;
It 's but a week's garret in London be-
    like —
Then a dash at Whitehall, and the city
    shall ring
With the shouts of the multitude bringing
    the king.

THE THREE TROOPERS

DURING THE PROTECTORATE

INTO the Devil tavern
  Three booted troopers strode,
From spur to feather spotted and splash'd
  With the mud of a winter road.
In each of their cups they dropp'd a crust,
  And star'd at the guests with a frown ;
Then drew their swords, and roar'd for a
    toast,
  " God send this Crum-well-down ! "

A blue smoke rose from their pistol locks,
  Their sword blades were still wet ;
There were long red smears on their jer-
    kins of buff,
  As the table they overset.
Then into their cups they stirr'd the crusts,
  And curs'd old London town ;
Then wav'd their swords, and drank with
    a stamp,
  " God send this Crum-well-down ! "

The 'prentice dropp'd his can of beer,
  The host turn'd pale as a clout ;
The ruby nose of the toping squire
  Grew white at the wild men's shout.
Then into their cups they flung the crusts,
  And show'd their teeth with a frown ;
They flash'd their swords as they gave the
    toast,
  " God send this Crum-well-down ! "

The gambler dropp'd his dog's-ear'd cards,
  The waiting-women scream'd,
As the light of the fire, like stains of
    blood,
  On the wild men's sabres gleam'd.
Then into their cups they splash'd the
    crusts,
  And curs'd the fool of a town,
And leap'd on the table, and roar'd a toast,
  " God send this Crum-well-down ! "

Till on a sudden fire-bells rang,
  And the troopers sprang to horse ;
The eldest mutter'd between his teeth,
  Hot curses — deep and coarse.
In their stirrup cups they flung the crusts,
  And cried as they spurr'd through town,
With their keen swords drawn and their
    pistols cock'd,
  " God send this Crum-well-down ! "

Away they dash'd through Temple Bar,
  Their red cloaks flowing free,
Their scabbards clash'd, each back-piece
    shone —
  None lik'd to touch the three.
The silver cups that held the crusts
  They flung to the startled town,
Shouting again, with a blaze of swords,
  " God send this Crum-well-down ! "

THE WHITE ROSE OVER THE WATER

EDINBURGH, 1744

THE old men sat with hats pull'd down,
  Their claret cups before them :
Broad shadows hid their sullen eyes,
  The tavern lamps shone o'er them,
As a brimming bowl, with crystal fill'd,
  Came borne by the landlord's daughter,
Who wore in her bosom the fair white rose,
  That grew best over the water.

Then all leap'd up, and join'd their hands
  With hearty clasp and greeting,
The brimming cups, outstretch'd by all,
  Over the wide bowl meeting.
" A health," they cried, " to the witching eyes
  Of Kate, the landlord's daughter !
But don't forget the white, white rose
  That grows best over the water."

Each others' cups they touch'd all round,
  The last red drop outpouring ;
Then with a cry that warm'd the blood,
  One heart-born chorus roaring —
" Let the glass go round, to pretty Kate,
  The landlord's black-eyed daughter ;
But never forget the white, white rose
  That grows best over the water."

Then hats flew up and swords sprang out,
  And lusty rang the chorus —
" Never," they cried, " while Scots are Scots,
  And the broad Frith 's before us."
A ruby ring the glasses shine
  As they toast the landlord's daughter,
Because she wore the white, white rose
  That grew best over the water.

A poet cried, " Our thistle 's brave,
  With all its stings and prickles ;
The shamrock with its holy leaf
  Is spar'd by Irish sickles.

But bumpers round, for what are these
  To Kate, the landlord's daughter,
Who wears at her bosom the rose as white,
  That grows best over the water ? "

They dash'd the glasses at the wall,
  No lip might touch them after ;
The toast had sanctified the cups
  That smash'd against the rafter ;
Then chairs thrown back, they up again
  To toast the landlord's daughter,
But never forgot the white, white rose
  That grew best over the water.

THE JACOBITE ON TOWER HILL

HE tripp'd up the steps with a bow and a
    smile,
Offering snuff to the chaplain the while,
A rose at his button-hole that afternoon —
'Twas the tenth of the month, and the month
    it was June.

Then shrugging his shoulders he look'd at
    the man
With the mask and the axe, and a murmur-
    ing ran
Through the crowd, who, below, were all
    pushing to see
The gaoler kneel down, and receiving his fee.

He look'd at the mob, as they roar'd, with
    a stare,
And took snuff again with a cynical air.
" I 'm happy to give but a moment's delight
To the flower of my country agog for a
    sight."

Then he look'd at the block, and with
    scented cravat
Dusted room for his neck, gaily doffing
    his hat,
Kiss'd his hand to a lady, bent low to the
    crowd,
Then smiling, turn'd round to the heads-
    man and bow'd.

" God save King James ! " he cried bravely
    and shrill,
And the cry reach'd the houses at foot of
    the hill,
" My friend, with the axe, à votre service,"
    he said ;
And ran his white thumb 'long the edge of
    the blade.

When the multitude hiss'd he stood firm as
    a rock ;
Then kneeling, laid down his gay head on
    the block ;
He kiss'd a white rose, — in a moment
    't was red
With the life of the bravest of any that
    bled.

THE DEATH OF MARLBOROUGH

THE sun shines on the chamber wall,
  The sun shines through the tree,
Now, though unshaken by the wind,
  The leaves fall ceaselessly ;
The bells from Woodstock's steeple
  Shake Blenheim's fading bough.
" This day you won Malplaquet," —
  " Aye, something then, but now ! "

They lead the old man to a chair,
  Wandering, pale and weak ;
His thin lips move — so faint the sound
  You scarce can hear him speak.
They lift a picture from the wall,
  Bold eyes and swelling brow ;
" The day you won Malplaquet,"—
  " Aye, something then, but now ! "

They reach him down a rusty sword,
  In faded velvet sheath :
The old man drops the heavy blade,
  And mutters 'tween his teeth ;
There 's sorrow in his fading eye,
  And pain upon his brow ;
" With this you won Malplaquet," —
  " Aye, something then, but now ! "

Another year, a stream of lights
  Flows down the avenue ;
A mile of mourners, sable clad,
  Walk weeping two by two ;
The steward looks into the grave
  With sad and downcast brow :
" This day he won Malplaquet, —
  Aye, something then, but now ! "

THE OLD GRENADIER'S STORY

TOLD ON A BENCH OUTSIDE THE INVALIDES

'T WAS the day beside the Pyramids,
  It seems but an hour ago,
That Kleber's Foot stood firm in squares,
  Returning blow for blow.

The Mamelukes were tossing
  Their standards to the sky,
When I heard a child's voice say, "My men,
  Teach me the way to die!"

'T was a little drummer, with his side
  Torn terribly with shot;
But still he feebly beat his drum,
  As though the wound were not.
And when the Mameluke's wild horse
  Burst with a scream and cry,
He said, "O men of the Forty-third,
  Teach me the way to die!"

"My mother has got other sons,
  With stouter hearts than mine,
But none more ready blood for France
  To pour out free as wine.
Yet still life 's sweet," the brave lad moan'd,
  "Fair are this earth and sky;
Then, comrades of the Forty-third,
  Teach me the way to die!"

I saw Salenche, of the granite heart,
  Wiping his burning eyes —
It was by far more pitiful
  Than mere loud sobs and cries.
One bit his cartridge till his lip
  Grew black as winter sky,
But still the boy moan'd, "Forty-third,
  Teach me the way to die!"

O never saw I sight like that!
  The sergeant flung down flag,
Even the fifer bound his brow
  With a wet and bloody rag,
Then look'd at locks and fix'd their steel,
  But never made reply,
Until he sobb'd out once again,
  "Teach me the way to die!"

Then, with a shout that flew to God,
  They strode into the fray;

I saw their red plumes join and wave,
  But slowly melt away.
The last who went — a wounded man —
  Bade the poor boy good-bye,
And said, "We men of the Forty-third
  Teach you the way to die!"

I never saw so sad a look
  As the poor youngster cast,
When the hot smoke of cannon
  In cloud and whirlwind pass'd.
Earth shook, and Heaven answer'd;
  I watch'd his eagle eye,
As he faintly moan'd, "The Forty-third
  Teach me the way to die!"

Then, with a musket for a crutch,
  He limp'd unto the fight;
I, with a bullet in my hip,
  Had neither strength nor might.
But, proudly beating on his drum,
  A fever in his eye,
I heard him moan "The Forty-third
  Taught me the way to die!"

They found him on the morrow,
  Stretch'd on a heap of dead;
His hand was in the grenadier's
  Who at his bidding bled.
They hung a medal round his neck,
  And clos'd his dauntless eye;
On the stone they cut, "*The Forty-third
  Taught him the way to die!*"

'T is forty years from then till now —
  The grave gapes at my feet —
Yet when I think of such a boy
  I feel my old heart beat.
And from my sleep I sometimes wake,
  Hearing a feeble cry,
And a voice that says, "Now, Forty-third,
  Teach me the way to die!"

John Veitch

THE LAIRD OF SCHELYNLAW

SCHELYNLAW TOWER is fair on the brae,
  Its muirs are green and wide,
And Schelynlaw's ewes are the brawest ewes
  In a' the country-side.

The birk grows there and the rowan red,
  And the burnie brattles down,
And there are nae sic knowes as Schelynlaw's,
  With the heather and bent sae brown.

But wife, three bairns are a' frae him gane,
  Twa sons in a deidly raid ;
And but yestreen his bonnie lass Jean
  In Traquair kirkyard was laid.

A lane auld man in his ain auld keep, —
  What ane could wish him ill ?
Not e'en Traquair wi' his black fause heart
  And his loons that range the hill.

Out in the morn to the muirland dun
  Rode ane frae Schelynlaw's gate,
Into the mist of the hill he rode,
  His errand might not wait.

The opening arms of the grey hill haur
  Folded the rider dim ;
Oh, cloud of the muir ! 't is a gruesome deed
  Ye hide in your misty rim.

Up he made for the Black Syke Rig,
  And round by the Fingland Glen,
But he turn'd and turn'd him aye in the
    mist ;
  Its glower was as faces of men !

And oft a voice sounded low in his ear,
  " The sun is no' gaun to daw —
For that straik o' blude and that clot o'
    blude,
  On the breist o' auld Schelynlaw ! "

'T was late o' nicht — to the House of
    Traquair
A horseman came jaded and rude,
None asked him whence or why he came,
  Nor whose on his hands was the blude.

" But hae ye the Bond ? " said hard
    Traquair.
  " The Bond i' faith I hae ;
The deid sign nae mair, the lands are thine,
  But foul was the stroke I gae :

" I 've ridden wi' you ower moss and fell,
  In moonlight and in mirk,
And monie a stalwart man I 've hewn, —
  So shrive me, Haly Kirk !

" Lewinshope Tam and Wulrus Will
  I slew, and Jock o' the Ha' ;
But there 's my richt hand to burn in flame,
  Could I bring back auld Schelynlaw ! "

Schelynlaw's lands were ne'er bought or
    sold,
  Yet they fell to the house of Traquair ;
But Jock o' Grieston that rode that morn
  Was ne'er seen to ride ony mair.

High in state rose the noble Earl,
  Well did he please the King ;
He could tell any lie to the States or the
    Kirk,
  His warrant the signet-ring.

Many a year has come and gone,
  His pride and his power are away,
A graceless son has the old lord's lands,
  And the father's hairs are grey.

The Court is back to Edinburgh town,
  Lairds and braw leddies ride there ;
A dole some give to a bow'd-down man,
  In pity, — 't is auld Traquair !

Jean Ingelow

THE HIGH TIDE ON THE COAST OF LINCOLNSHIRE

(1571)

The old mayòr climb'd the belfry tower,
  The ringers ran by two, by three ;
" Pull, if ye never pull'd before ;
  Good ringers, pull your best," quoth he.
" Play uppe, play uppe, O Boston bells !
Ply all your changes, all your swells,
  Play uppe, ' The Brides of Enderby.' "

Men say it was a stolen tyde —
  The Lord that sent it, He knows all ;
But in myne ears doth still abide
  The message that the bells let fall :
And there was nought of strange, beside
The flight of mews and peewits pied
  By millions crouch'd on the old sea wall.

I sat and spun within the doore,
  My thread brake off, I rais'd myne eyes;
The level sun, like ruddy ore,
  Lay sinking in the barren skies ;

And dark against day's golden death
She moved where Lindis wandereth,
My sonne's faire wife, Elizabeth.

"Cusha! Cusha! Cusha!" calling,
Ere the early dews were falling,
Farre away I heard her song,
"Cusha! Cusha!" all along;
Where the reedy Lindis floweth,
    Floweth, floweth,
From the meads where melick groweth
Faintly came her milking song —

"Cusha! Cusha! Cusha!" calling,
"For the dews will soone be falling;
Leave your meadow grasses mellow,
    Mellow, mellow;
Quit your cowslips, cowslips yellow;
Come uppe, Whitefoot, come uppe, Light-
    foot;
Quit the stalks of parsley hollow,
    Hollow, hollow;
Come uppe, Jetty, rise and follow,
From the clovers lift your head;
Come uppe, Whitefoot, come uppe, Light-
    foot,
Come uppe, Jetty, rise and follow,
Jetty, to the milking shed."

If it be long, ay, long ago,
    When I beginne to think howe long,
Againe I hear the Lindis flow,
    Swift as an arrowe, sharpe and strong;
And all the aire, it seemeth mee,
Bin full of floating bells (sayth shee),
That ring the tune of Enderby.

Alle fresh the level pasture lay,
    And not a shadowe mote be seene,
Save where full fyve good miles away
    The steeple tower'd from out the greene;
And lo! the great bell farre and wide
Was heard in all the country side
That Saturday at eventide.

The swanherds where their sedges are
    Mov'd on in sunset's golden breath,
The shepherde lads I heard afarre,
    And my sonne's wife, Elizabeth;
Till floating o'er the grassy sea
Came downe that kyndly message free,
The "Brides of Mavis Enderby."

Then some look'd uppe into the sky,
    And all along where Lindis flows

To where the goodly vessels lie,
    And where the lordly steeple shows.
They sayde, "And why should this thing
    be?
What danger lowers by land or sea?
They ring the tune of Enderby!

"For evil news from Mablethorpe,
    Of pyrate galleys warping down;
For shippes ashore beyond the scorpe,
    They have not spar'd to wake the towne:
But while the west bin red to see,
And storms be none, and pyrates flee,
Why ring 'The Brides of Enderby'?"

I look'd without, and lo! my sonne
    Came riding downe with might and main:
He rais'd a shout as he drew on,
    Till all the welkin rang again,
"Elizabeth! Elizabeth!"
(A sweeter woman ne'er drew breath
Than my sonne's wife, Elizabeth.)

"The olde sea wall (he cried) is downe,
    The rising tide comes on apace,
And boats adrift in yonder towne
    Go sailing uppe the market-place."
He shook as one that looks on death:
"God save you, mother!" straight he saith;
"Where is my wife, Elizabeth?"

"Good sonne, where Lindis winds her way,
    With her two bairns I marked her long;
And ere yon bells beganne to play
    Afar I heard her milking song."
He looked across the grassy lea,
To right, to left, "Ho, Enderby!"
They rang "The Brides of Enderby!"

With that he cried and beat his breast;
    For, lo! along the river's bed
A mighty eygre rear'd his crest,
    And uppe the Lindis raging sped.
It swept with thunderous noises loud;
Shap'd like a curling snow-white cloud,
Or like a demon in a shroud.

And rearing Lindis backward press'd
    Shook all her trembling bankes amaine;
Then madly at the eygre's breast
    Flung uppe her weltering walls again.
Then bankes came downe with ruin and
    rout —
Then beaten foam flew round about —
Then all the mighty floods were out.

So farre, so fast the eygre drave,
  The heart had hardly time to beat
Before a shallow seething wave
  Sobb'd in the grasses at oure feet :
The feet had hardly time to flee
Before it brake against the knee,
And all the world was in the sea.

Upon the roofe we sate that night,
  The noise of bells went sweeping by ;
I mark'd the lofty beacon light
  Stream from the church tower, red and
    high —
A lurid mark and dread to see ;
And awsome bells they were to mee,
That in the dark rang " Enderby."

They rang the sailor lads to guide
  From roofe to roofe who fearless row'd ;
And I — my sonne was at my side,
And yet the ruddy beacon glow'd :
And yet he moan'd beneath his breath,
" O come in life, or come in 'death !
O lost ! my love, Elizabeth."

And didst thou visit him no more ?
  Thou didst, thou didst, my daughter
    deare ;
The waters laid thee at his doore,
  Ere yet the early dawn was clear.
Thy pretty bairns in fast embrace,
The lifted sun shone on thy face,
Downe drifted to thy dwelling-place.

That flow strew'd wrecks about the grass,
  That ebbe swept out the flocks to
    sea ;
A fatal ebbe and flow, alas !
  To manye more than myne and mee ;
But each will mourn his own (she saith) ;
And sweeter woman ne'er drew breath
Than my sonne's wife, Elizabeth.

I shall never hear her more
By the reedy Lindis shore,
" Cusha ! Cusha ! Cusha ! " calling,
Ere the early dews be falling ;
I shall never hear her song,
" Cusha ! Cusha ! " all along
Where the sunny Lindis floweth,
  Goeth, floweth ;
From the meads where melick groweth,
  When the water winding down,
  Onward floweth to the town.

I shall never see her more
Where the reeds and rushes quiver,
  Shiver, quiver ;
Stand beside the sobbing river,
Sobbing, throbbing, in its falling
To the sandy lonesome shore ;
I shall never hear her calling,
" Leave your meadow grasses mellow,
    Mellow, mellow ;
Quit your cowslips, cowslips yellow ;
Come uppe, Whitefoot, come uppe, Light-
    foot ;
Quit your pipes of parsley hollow,
    Hollow, hollow ;
Come uppe, Lightfoot, rise and follow ;
    Lightfoot, Whitefoot,
From your clovers lift the head ;
Come uppe, Jetty, follow, follow,
Jetty, to the milking shed."

SAILING BEYOND SEAS

METHOUGHT the stars were blinking
    bright,
  And the old brig's sails unfurl'd ;
I said, " I will sail to my love this night
  At the other side of the world."
I stepp'd aboard, — we sail'd so fast, —
  The sun shot up from the bourn ;
But a dove that perch'd upon the mast
  Did mourn, and mourn, and mourn.
    O fair dove ! O fond dove !
    And dove with the white breast,
    Let me alone, the dream is my own,
    And my heart is full of rest.

My true love fares on this great hill,
  Feeding his sheep for aye ;
I look'd in his hut, but all was still,
  My love was gone away.
I went to gaze in the forest creek,
  And the dove mourn'd on apace ;
No flame did flash, nor fair blue reek
  Rose up to show me his place.
    O last love ! O first love !
    My love with the true heart,
    To think I have come to this your
      home,
    And yet — we are apart !

My love ! He stood at my right hand,
  His eyes were grave and sweet.
Methought he said, " In this far land,
  O, is it thus we meet ?

Ah, maid most dear, I am not here ;
  I have no place, — no part, —
No dwelling more by sea or shore,
  But only in thy heart."
    O fair dove ! O fond dove !
    Till night rose over the bourn,
    The dove on the mast, as we sail'd fast,
    Did mourn, and mourn, and mourn.

THE LONG WHITE SEAM

As I came round the harbor buoy,
  The lights began to gleam,
No wave the land-lock'd water stirr'd,
  The crags were white as cream ;
And I mark'd my love by candle-light
  Sewing her long white seam.
    It 's aye sewing ashore, my dear,
    Watch and steer at sea,
    It 's reef and furl, and haul the line,
    Set sail and think of thee.

I climb'd to reach her cottage door ;
  O sweetly my love sings !
Like a shaft of light her voice breaks forth,
  My soul to meet it springs
As the shining water leap'd of old,
  When stirr'd by angel wings.
    Aye longing to list anew,
    Awake and in my dream,
    But never a song she sang like this,
    Sewing her long white seam.

Fair fall the lights, the harbor lights,
  That brought me in to thee,
And peace drop down on that low roof
  For the sight that I did see,
And the voice, my dear, that rang so
  clear
All for the love of me.
    For O, for O, with brows bent low
    By the candle's flickering gleam,
    Her wedding gown it was she wrought,
    Sewing the long white seam.

Robert Dwyer Joyce

CROSSING THE BLACKWATER
A. D. 1603

We stood so steady,
  All under fire,
We stood so steady,
Our long spears ready
  To vent our ire :
To dash on the Saxon,
Our mortal foe,
And lay him low
  In the bloody mire.

'T was by Blackwater,
  When snows were white,
'T was by Blackwater,
Our foes for the slaughter
  Stood full in sight ;
But we were ready
With our long spears,
And we had no fears
  But we 'd win the fight.

Their bullets came whistling
  Upon our rank,
Their bullets came whistling,

Their spears were bristling
  On th' other bank :
Yet we stood steady,
And each good blade,
Ere the morn did fade,
  At their life-blood drank.

" Hurrah ! for Freedom ! "
  Came from our van,
" Hurrah ! for Freedom !
Our swords — we 'll feed 'em
  As best we can —
With vengeance we 'll feed 'em ! "
Then down we crash'd,
Through the wild ford dash'd,
  And the fray began.

Horses to horses,
  And man to man :
O'er dying horses,
And blood and corses,
  O'Sullivan,
Our general, thunder'd,
And we were not slack
To slay at his back
  Till the fight began.

O, how we scatter'd
   The foemen then, —
Slaughter'd and scatter'd,
And chas'd and shatter'd,
   By shore and glen !
To the wall of Moyallo
Few fled that day :
Will they bar our way
   When we come again ?

Our dead freres we buried,
   They were but few,
Our dead freres we buried
Where the dark waves hurried,
   And flash'd and flew :
O sweet be their slumber
Who thus have died
In the battle's tide,
   Inisfail, for you !

Ellen O'Leary

TO GOD AND IRELAND TRUE

I SIT beside my darling's grave,
   Who in the prison died,
And though my tears fall thick and fast
   I think of him with pride :
Ay, softly fall my tears like dew,
For one to God and Ireland true.

"I love my God o'er all," he said,
   "And then I love my land,
And next I love my Lily sweet,
   Who pledged me her white hand :
To each — to all — I'm ever true,
To God, to Ireland, and to you."

No tender nurse his hard bed smooth'd
   Or softly rais'd his head ;
He fell asleep and woke in heaven
   Ere I knew he was dead ;
Yet why should I my darling rue ?
He was to God and Ireland true.

Oh, 'tis a glorious memory !
   I'm prouder than a queen,
To sit beside my hero's grave
   And think on what has been ;
And, O my darling, I am true
To God — to Ireland — and to you !

Hamilton Aïdé

REMEMBER OR FORGET

I SAT beside the streamlet,
   I watch'd the water flow,
As we together watch'd it
   One little year ago :
The soft rain patter'd on the leaves,
   The April grass was wet.
Ah ! folly to remember ;
   'T is wiser to forget.

The nightingales made vocal
   June's palace pav'd with gold ;
I watch'd the rose you gave me
   Its warm red heart unfold ;
But breath of rose and bird's song
   Were fraught with wild regret.
'T is madness to remember ;
   'T were wisdom to forget.

I stood among the gold corn,
   Alas ! no more, I knew,

To gather gleaner's measure
   Of the love that fell from you.
For me, no gracious harvest —
   Would God we ne'er had met !
'T is hard, Love, to remember, but
   'T is harder to forget.

The streamlet now is frozen,
   The nightingales are fled,
The cornfields are deserted,
   And every rose is dead.
I sit beside my lonely fire,
   And pray for wisdom yet :
For calmness to remember,
   Or courage to forget.

THE DANUBE RIVER

Do you recall that night in June,
   Upon the Danube river ?
We listen'd to a Ländler tune,
   We watch'd the moonbeams quiver.

I oft since then have watch'd the moon,
But never, love, oh ! never,
Can I forget that night in June,
Adown the Danube river.

Our boat kept measure with its oar,
The music rose in snatches,
From peasants dancing on the shore
With boisterous songs and catches.
I know not why that Ländler rang
Through all my soul — but never
Can I forget the songs they sang
Adown the Danube river.

WHEN WE ARE PARTED

When we are parted let me lie
In some far corner of thy heart,
Silent, and from the world apart,
Like a forgotten melody :
Forgotten of the world beside,
Cherish'd by one, and one alone,
For some lov'd memory of its own ;
So let me in thy heart abide
When we are parted.

When we are parted, keep for me
The sacred stillness of the night ;
That hour, sweet Love, is mine by right ;
Let others claim the day of thee !
The cold world sleeping at our feet,
My spirit shall discourse with thine ; —
When stars upon thy pillow shine,
At thy heart's door I stand and beat,
Though we are parted.

THE FORSAKEN

She sat beside the mountain springs,
Her feet were on the water's brink,
And oft she wept when she beheld
The birds that lighted there to drink ;
She wept : but as they spread their wings,
Her sweet voice follow'd them on high :
" He will return — I know him well ;
He would not leave me here to die."

And there she sat, as months roll'd on,
Unmindful of the changing year ;
She heeded not the sun, or snow,
All seasons were alike to her.
She look'd upon the frozen stream,
She listen'd to the night bird's cry :
" He will return — I know him well ;
He would not leave me here to die."

And still she sits beside the springs,
And combs the gold drips of her hair ;
Red berries for a bridal crown
At early morn she places there.
At every shadow on the grass
She starts, and murmurs with a sigh,
" He will return — I know him well ;
He would not leave me here to die. "

Joseph Skipsey

MOTHER WEPT

Mother wept, and father sigh'd ;
With delight a-glow
Cried the lad, " To-morrow," cried,
" To the pit I go."

Up and down the place he sped,
Greeted old and young,
Far and wide the tidings spread,
Clapp'd his hands and sung.

Came his cronies, some to gaze
Rapt in wonder ; some
Free with counsel ; some with praise ;
Some with envy dumb.

" May he," many a gossip cried,
" Be from peril kept ; "
Father hid his face and sighed,
Mother turned and wept.

THE DEWDROP

Ah, be not vain. In yon flower-bell,
As rare a pearl, did I appear,
As ever grew in ocean shell,
To dangle at a Helen's ear.

So was I till a cruel blast
Arose and swept me to the ground,
When, in the jewel of the past,
Earth but a drop of water found.

THE BUTTERFLY

THE butterfly from flower to flower
The urchin chas'd ; and, when at last
He caught it in my lady's bower,
He cried, " Ha, ha ! " and held it fast.

Awhile he laugh'd, but soon he wept,
When looking at the prize he 'd caught
He found he had to ruin swept
The very glory he had sought.

Richard Garnett

THE ISLAND OF SHADOWS

YES, Cara mine, I know that I shall stand
Upon the seashore soon,
And watch the waves that die upon the
strand,
And the immortal moon.

One mew will hover 'mid the drowsy
damp
That clogs the breezes there,
One star suspend her solitary lamp,
High in the viewless air.

My straining eyes will mark a distant
oar,
Grazing the supple sea,
And a light pinnace speeding to the shore,
And in it thou wilt be.

The empty veins with life no more are
warm,
The eyes no longer shine,
The pale star gazes through the pallid form,
What matter ? thou art mine.

The Love which, while it walk'd the earth,
could meet
No place to lay its head,
Now reigns unchallenged in the winding-
sheet,
Nor fears its kindred dead.

For Love dwells with the dead, though
more sedate,
Chasten'd, and mild it seems ;
While Avarice, Envy, Jealousy, and Hate,
With them are only dreams.

I step into the boat, our steady prore
Furrows the still moonlight ;
The sea is merry with our plashing oar,
With our quick rudder white.

No word has pass'd thy lips, but yet I know
Well where our course will be ;
We leave the worn-out world — is it not
so ? —
The uncorrupted sea

To cross, and gain some isle in whose sweet
shade
Even Slavery is free ;
And careless Care on smoothest rose-leaves
laid
Becomes Tranquillity.

Far, far the haunts where, rob'd in gory
weeds,
Grim War his court doth hold,
And mumbling Superstition counts his
beads,
And Avarice his gold.

But Love and Death, the comrades and the
twins,
Uninterrupted reign ;
Where is it that one ends and one be-
gins ?
And are they one or twain ?

And all is like thy soul, pensive and fair,
Veil'd in a shadowy dress,
And strewn with gems more rich were they
more rare,
And steep'd in balminess.

No drossy shape of earthliness appears
On the phantastic coast,
No grosser sound strikes the attuned ears
Than footfall of a ghost.

Seclusion, quiet, silence, slumber, dreams,
No murmur of a breath ;
The same still image on the same still
streams,
Of Love caressing Death.

So let us hasten, Love! Our steady
    prore
Furrows the still moonlight ;
The sea is merry with our plashing oar,
    With our quick rudder white.

THE FAIR CIRCASSIAN

FORTY Viziers saw I go
Up to the Seraglio,
Burning, each and every man,
For the fair Circassian.

Ere the morn had disappear'd,
Every Vizier wore a beard ;
Ere the afternoon was born,
Every Vizier came back shorn.

" Let the man that woos to win
Woo with an unhairy chin ; "
Thus she said, and as she bid
Each devoted Vizier did.

From the beards a cord she made,
Loop'd it to the balustrade,
Glided down and went away
To her own Circassia.

When the Sultan heard, wax'd he
Somewhat wroth, and presently
In the noose themselves did lend
Every Vizier did suspend.

Sages all, this rhyme who read,
Guard your beards with prudent heed,
And beware the wily plans
Of the fair Circassians.

THE BALLAD OF THE BOAT

THE stream was smooth as glass, we said :
    " Arise and let 's away ; "
The Siren sang beside the boat that in the
    rushes lay ;
And spread the sail, and strong the oar, we
    gaily took our way.
When shall the sandy bar be cross'd ?
    When shall we find the bay ?

The broadening flood swells slowly out o'er
    cattle-dotted plains,
The stream is strong and turbulent, and
    dark with heavy rains,

The laborer looks up to see our shallop
    speed away.
When shall the sandy bar be cross'd ?
    When shall we find the bay ?

Now are the clouds like fiery shrouds ; the
    sun, superbly large,
Slow as an oak to woodman's stroke sinks
    flaming at their marge.
The waves are bright with mirror'd light
    as jacinths on our way.
When shall the sandy bar be cross'd ?
    When shall we find the bay ?

The moon is high up in the sky, and now
    no more we see
The spreading river's either bank, and
    surging distantly
There booms a sullen thunder as of break-
    ers far away.
Now shall the sandy bar be cross'd, now
    shall we find the bay !

The seagull shrieks high overhead, and
    dimly to our sight
The moonlit crests of foaming waves gleam
    towering through the night.
We 'll steal upon the mermaid soon, and
    start her from her lay,
When once the sandy bar is cross'd, and
    we are in the bay.

What rises white and awful as a shroud-
    enfolded ghost ?
What roar of rampant tumult bursts in
    clangor on the coast ?
Pull back ! pull back ! The raging flood
    sweeps every oar away.
O stream, is this thy bar of sand ? O boat,
    is this the bay ?

THE LYRICAL POEM

PASSION the fathomless spring, and words
    the precipitate waters,
Rhythm the bank that binds these to their
    musical bed.

THE DIDACTIC POEM

SOULLESS, colorless strain, thy words are
    the words of wisdom.
Is not a mule a mule, bear he a burden of
    gold ?

ON AN URN

BOTH thou and I alike, my Bacchic urn,
From clay are sprung, and must to clay re-
    turn ;
But happier fate this day is mine and thine,
For I am full of life, and thou of wine ;
Our powers for mutual aid united be,
Keep thou me blithe, and flowing I 'll keep
    thee.

AGE

I WILL not rail, or grieve when torpid eld
Frosts the slow-journeying blood, for I shall
    see
The lovelier leaves hang yellow on the
    tree,
The nimbler brooks in icy fetters held.
Methinks the aged eye, that first beheld
The fitful ravage of December wild,
Then knew himself indeed dear Nature's
    child,
Seeing the common doom, that all com-
    pell'd.
No kindred we to her beloved broods,
If, dying these, we drew a selfish breath ;
But one path travel all her multitudes,
And none dispute the solemn Voice that
    saith :

"Sun, to thy setting ; to your autumn,
    woods ;
Stream, to thy sea ; and man, unto thy
    death ! "

TO AMERICA

AFTER READING SOME UNGENEROUS
CRITICISMS

WHAT though thy Muse the singer's art
    essay
With lip now over-loud, now over-low ?
'T is but the augury that makes her so
Of the high things she hath in charge to
    say.
How shall the giantess of gold and clay,
Girt with two oceans, crown'd with Arctic
    snow,
Sandall'd with shining seas of Mexico,
Be par'd to trim proportion in a day ?
Thou art too great ! Thy million-billow'd
    surge
Of life bewilders speech, as shoreless sea
Confounds the ranging eye from verge to
    verge
With mazy strife or smooth immensity.
Not soon or easily shall thence emerge
A Homer or a Shakespeare worthy thee.

John Todhunter

THE BANSHEE

GREEN, in the wizard arms
Of the foam-bearded Atlantic,
An isle of old enchantment,
A melancholy isle,
Enchanted and dreaming lies :
And there, by Shannon's flowing,
In the moonlight, spectre-thin,
The spectre Erin sits.

An aged desolation,
She sits by old Shannon's flowing,
A mother of many children,
Of children exil'd and dead,
In her home, with bent head, homeless,
Clasping her knees she sits,
Keening, keening !

And at her keene the fairy-grass
Trembles on dun and barrow ;

Around the foot of her ancient crosses
The grave-grass shakes and the nettle
    swings ;
In haunted glens the meadow-sweet
Flings to the night wind
Her mystic mournful perfume ;
The sad spearmint by holy wells
Breathes melancholy balm.
Sometimes she lifts her head,
With blue eyes tearless,
And gazes athwart the reck of night
Upon things long past,
Upon things to come.

And sometimes, when the moon
Brings tempest upon the deep,
And rous'd Atlantic thunders from his
    caverns in the west,
The wolfhound at her feet
Springs up with a mighty bay,

And chords of mystery sound from the
  wild harp at her side,
Strung from the heart of poets ;
And she flies on the wings of tempest
Around her shuddering isle,
With gray hair streaming :
A meteor of evil omen,
The spectre of hope forlorn,
Keening, keening !

She keenes, and the strings of her wild
  harp shiver
On the gusts of night :
O'er the four waters she keenes — over
  Moyle she keenes,
O'er the sea of Milith, and the Strait of
  Strongbow,
And the Ocean of Columbus.

And the Fianna hear, and the ghost of her
  cloudy hovering heroes ;

And the Swan, Fianoula, wails o'er the
  waters of Inisfail,
Chanting her song of destiny,
The rune of the weaving Fates.
And the nations hear in the void and quak-
  ing time of night,
Sad unto dawning, dirges,
Solemn dirges,
And snatches of bardic song ;
Their souls quake in the void and quaking
  time of night,
And they dream of the weird of kings,
And tyrannies moulting, sick
In the dreadful wind of change.

Wail no more, lonely one, mother of exiles,
  wail no more,
Banshee of the world — no more !
Thy sorrows are the world's, thou art no
  more alone ;
Thy wrongs, the world's.

R. St. John Tyrwhitt

THE GLORY OF MOTION

Three twangs of the horn, and they're all
  out of cover !
Must brave you, old bull-finch, that's
  right in the way !
A rush, and a bound, and a crash, and I'm
  over !
They're silent and racing and for'ard
  away ;
Fly, Charley, my darling ! Away and we
  follow ;
There's no earth or cover for mile upon
  mile ;
We're wing'd with the flight of the stork
  and the swallow ;
The heart of the eagle is ours for a
  while.

The pasture-land knows not of rough
  plough or harrow !
The hoofs echo hollow and soft on the
  sward ;
The soul of the horses goes into our
  marrow ;
My saddle's a kingdom, and I am its
  lord :

And rolling and flowing beneath us like
  ocean,
Gray waves of the high ridge and furrow
  glide on,
And small flying fences in musical motion,
  Before us, beneath us, behind us, are
  gone.

O puissant of bone and of sinew availing,
  On thee how I've long'd for the brooks
  and the showers !
O white-breasted camel, the meek and un-
  failing,
  To speed through the glare of the long
  desert hours !
And, bright little barbs, ye make worthy
  pretences
  To go with the going of Solomon's sires ;
But you stride not the stride, and you fly
  not the fences !
  And all the wide Hejaz is naught to the
  shires.

O gay gondolier ! from thy night-flitting
  shallop
I have heard the soft pulses of oar and
  guitar ;

But sweeter the rhythmical rush of the
   gallop,
The fire in the saddle, the flight of the
   star.
Old mare, my beloved, no stouter or
   faster
Hath ever strode under a man at his
   need ;
Be glad in the hand and embrace of thy
   master,
And pant to the passionate music of
   speed.

Can there e'er be a thought to an elderly
   person
So keen, so inspiring, so hard to forget,
So fully adapted to break into burgeon
As this — that the steel is n't out of him
   yet ;
That flying speed tickles one's brain with a
   feather ;
That one's horse can restore one the
   years that are gone ;
That, spite of gray winter and weariful
   weather,
The blood and the pace carry on, carry on?

Clement Scott

RUS IN URBE

POETS are singing the whole world over
Of May in melody, joys for June ;
Dusting their feet in the careless clover,
   And filling their hearts with the black-
     bird's tune.
The " brown bright nightingale " strikes
   with pity
The sensitive heart of a count or clown ;
But where is the song for our leafy city,
   And where the rhymes for our lovely
     town ?

"O for the Thames, and its rippling
   reaches,
   Where almond rushes, and breezes
     sport !
Take me a walk under Burnham Beeches ;
   Give me a dinner at Hampton Court ! "
Poets, be still, though your hearts I harden ;
   We 've flowers by day and have scents at
     dark,
The limes are in leaf in the cockney garden,
   And lilacs blossom in Regent's Park.

" Come for a blow," says a reckless fellow,
   Burn'd red and brown by passionate
     sun ;
" Come to the downs, where the gorse is
   yellow ;
The season of kisses has just begun !
Come to the fields where bluebells shiver,
   Hear cuckoo's carol, or plaint of dove ;
Come for a row on the silent river ;
   Come to the meadows and learn to
     love ! "

Yes, I will come when this wealth is
   over
Of soften'd color and perfect tone —
The lilac 's better than fields of clover ;
   I 'll come when blossoming May has
     flown.
When dust and dirt of a trampled city
   Have dragg'd the yellow laburnum
     down,
I 'll take my holiday — more 's the pity —
   And turn my back upon London town.

Margaret ! am I so wrong to love it,
   This misty town that your face shines
     through ?
A crown of blossom is wav'd above it ;
   But heart and life of the whirl — 't is
     you !
Margaret ! pearl ! I have sought and
   found you ;
   And, though the paths of the wind are
     free,
I 'll follow the ways of the world around
   you,
   And build my nest on the nearest tree !

LILIAN ADELAIDE NEILSON

WHAT shall my gift be to the dead one
   lying
   Wrapp'd in the mantle of her mother
     earth ?
No tear, no voice, no prayer, or any sigh-
   ing,
   Gives back her face made beautiful by
     birth.

Honor was due to one whose soul was
tender,
  Whose nature quicken'd at the touch of
  art ;
Now that the struggle 's over, God will send
  her
  Mercy and peace to soothe her troubled
  heart.

Tears will be shed ; for who dare raise the
  finger
  Of scorn when all is buried in the grave ?
Some pity near her memory will linger :
  Upon life's stormy sea she toss'd — a
  wave !

Life's weary hill she bravely fell in breast-
  ing,
  Her work was done ; "Oh, take me
  home," she sighs ;

Whisper it low, she sleeps not, "she is
  resting," —
  So fell the curtain, and she clos'd her eyes.

The flowers she lov'd will deck the cross
  that shows us
  Where all remains of what was once so
  fair.
Yes ! she is dead, but still, perhaps, she
  knows us
  Who say "Implora pace !" for our
  prayer.

They gave love's playthings, who were
  wont to win her,
  As Juliet coax'd to happiness her nurse ;
But I, who knew the goodness that was in
  her,
  Place humbly on her grave — this leaf of
  verse !

Sarah Williams

OMAR AND THE PERSIAN

THE victor stood beside the spoil, and by
  the grinning dead :
"The land is ours, the foe is ours, now
  rest, my men, " he said.
But while he spoke there came a band of
  foot-sore, panting men :
"The latest prisoner, my lord, we took
  him in the glen,
And left behind dead hostages that we
  would come again."

The victor spoke : "Thou, Persian dog !
  hast cost more lives than thine.
That was thy will, and thou shouldst die
  full thrice, if I had mine.
Dost know thy fate, thy just reward ?"
  The Persian bent his head,
"I know both sides of victory, and only
  grieve," he said,
"Because there will be none to fight
  'gainst thee when I am dead.

No Persian faints at sight of Death, — we
  know his face too well, —
He waits for us on mountain side, in town,
  or shelter'd dell ;

But I crave a cup of wine, thy first and
  latest boon,
For I have gone three days athirst, and
  fear lest I may swoon,
Or even wrong mine enemy, by dying now,
  too soon."

The cup was brought ; but ere he drank
  the Persian shudder'd white.
Omar replied, "What fearest thou ? The
  wine is clear and bright ;
We are no poisoners, not we, nor traitors
  to a guest,
No dart behind, nor dart within, shall
  pierce thy gallant breast ;
Till thou hast drain'd the draught, O foe,
  thou dost in safety rest."

The Persian smil'd, with parched lips, upon
  the foemen round,
Then pour'd the precious liquid out, un-
  tasted, on the ground.
" Till that is drunk, I live," said he, " and
  while I live, I fight ;
So, see you to your victory, for 't is undone
  this night ;
Omar the worthy, battle fair is but thy
  god-like right."

Upsprang a wrathful army then, — Omar
  restrain'd them all,
Upon no battle-field had rung more clear
  his martial call,
The dead men's hair beside his feet as by a
  breeze was stirr'd,

The farthest henchman in the camp the
  noble mandate heard :
" Hold ! if there be a sacred thing, it is
  the warrior's word."

Sir Walter Besant

TO DAPHNE

LIKE apple-blossom, white and red ;
  Like hues of dawn, which fly too
    soon ;
Like bloom of peach, so softly spread ;
  Like thorn of May and rose of June —
Oh, sweet ! oh, fair ! beyond compare,
    Are Daphne's cheeks,
Are Daphne's blushing cheeks, I swear.

That pretty rose, which comes and goes
  Like April sunshine in the sky,

I can command it when I choose —
  See how it rises if I cry.
Oh, sweet ! oh, fair ! beyond compare,
    Are Daphne's cheeks,
Are Daphne's blushing cheeks, I swear.

Ah ! when it lies round lips and eyes,
  And fades away, again to spring,
No lover, sure, could ask for more
  Than still to cry, and still to sing:
Oh, sweet ! oh, fair ! beyond compare,
    Are Daphne's cheeks,
Are Daphne's blushing cheeks, I swear.

Lady Lindsay

SONNET

(SUGGESTED BY MR. WATTS'S PICTURE OF LOVE
AND DEATH)

YEA, Love is strong as life ; he casts out
    fear,
And wrath, and hate, and all our envious
    foes ;
He stands upon the threshold, quick to close
The gate of happiness ere should appear
Death's dreaded presence — ay, but Death
    draws near,
And large and gray the towering outline
    grows,
Whose face is veil'd and hid ; and yet Love
    knows
Full well, too well, alas ! that Death is
    here.
Death tramples on the roses ; Death comes
    in,
Though Love, with outstretch'd arms and
    wings outspread,

Would bar the way — poor Love, whose
    wings begin
To droop, half-torn as are the roses dead
Already at his feet — but Death must win,
And Love grows faint beneath that ponder-
    ous tread !

MY HEART IS A LUTE

ALAS, that my heart is a lute,
  Whereon you have learn'd to play !
For a many years it was mute,
  Until one summer's day
You took it, and touch'd it, and made it
    thrill,
And it thrills and throbs, and quivers still !

I had known you, dear, so long !
  Yet my heart did not tell me why
It should burst one morn into song,
  And wake to new life with a cry,

Like a babe that sees the light of the sun,
And for whom this great world has just
  begun.

Your lute is enshrin'd, cas'd in,
Kept close with love's magic key,

So no hand but yours can win
And wake it to minstrelsy ;
Yet leave it not silent too long, nor
  alone,
Lest the strings should break, and the
  music be done.

VARIOUS DISTINCTIVE POETS

Thomas Gordon Hake

OLD SOULS

THE world, not hush'd, lay as in trance ;
  It saw the future in its van,
And drew its riches in advance
  To meet the greedy wants of man ;
Till length of days, untimely sped,
Left its account unaudited.

The sun, untir'd, still rose and set, —
  Swerv'd not an instant from its beat ;
It had not lost a moment yet,
  Nor used in vain its light and heat ;
But, as in trance, from when it rose
To when it sank, man crav'd repose.

A holy light that shone of yore
  He saw, despis'd, and left behind :
His heart was rotting to the core
  Lock'd in the slumbers of the mind :
Not beat of drum, nor sound of fife,
Could rouse it to a sense of life.

A cry was heard, inton'd and slow,
  Of one who had no wares to vend :
His words were gentle, dull, and low,
  And he call'd out, " Old souls to
    mend ! "
He peddled on from door to door,
And look'd not up to rich or poor.

His step kept on as if in pace
  With some old timepiece in his head,
Nor ever did its way retrace ;
  Nor right nor left turn'd he his tread,
But utter'd still his tinker's cry
To din the ears of passers-by.

So well they knew the olden note
  Few heeded what the tinker spake,
Though here and there an ear it smote
  And seem'd a sudden hold to take ;
But they had not the time to stay,
And it would do some other day.

Still on his way the tinker wends,
  Though jobs be far between and few ;
But here and there a soul he mends
  And makes it look as good as new.
Once set to work, once fairly hir'd,
His dull old hammer seems inspir'd.

Over the task his features glow ;
  He knocks away the rusty flakes ;
A spark flies off at every blow ;
  At every rap new life awakes.
The soul once cleans'd of outward sins,
His subtle handicraft begins.

Like iron unanneal'd and crude,
  The soul is plunged into the blast ;
To temper it, however rude,
  'T is next in holy water cast ;
Then on the anvil it receives
The nimblest stroke the tinker gives.

The tinker's task is at an end :
  Stamp'd was the cross by that last blow
Again his cry, " Old souls to mend ! "
  Is heard in accents dull and low.
He pauses not to seek his pay, —
That too will do another day.

One stops and says, " This soul of mine
  Has been a tidy piece of ware,

But rust and rot in it combine,
  And now corruption lays it bare.
Give it a look : there was a day
When it the morning hymn could say."

The tinker looks into his eye,
  And there detects besetting sin,
The decent old-establish'd lie,
  That creeps through all the chinks
    within.
Lank are its tendrils, thick its shoots,
And like a worm's nest coil the roots.

Like flowers that deadly berries bear,
  His seed, if tended from the pod,
Had grown in beauty with the year,
  Like deodara drawn to God ;
Now, like a dank and curly brake,
It fosters venom for the snake.

The tinker takes the weed in tow,
  And roots it out with tooth and nail ;
His labor patient to bestow,
  Lest like the herd of men he fail.
How best to extirpate the weed
Has grown with him into a creed.

His tack is steady, slow, and sure :
  He plucks it out, despite the howl,
With gentle hand and look demure,
  As cunning maiden draws a fowl.
He knows the job he is about,
And pulls till all the lie is out.

" Now steadfastly regard the man
  Who wrought your cure of rust and
    rot !
You saw him ere the work began :
  Is he the same, or is he not ?
You saw the tinker ; now behold
The Envoy of a God of old."

This said, he on the forehead stamps
  The downward stroke and one across,
Then straight upon his way he tramps ;
  His time for profit, not for loss ;
His task no sooner at an end
Than out he cries, " Old souls to mend !"

As night comes on he enters doors,
  He crosses halls, he goes upstairs,
He reaches first and second floors,
  Still busied on his own affairs.
None stop him or a question ask ;
None heed the workman at his task.

Despite his cry, " Old souls to mend ! "
  Which into dull expression breaks,
Not mov'd are they, nor ear they lend
  To him who from old habit speaks ;
Yet does the deep and one-ton'd cry
Send thrills along eternity.

He gads where out-door wretches walk,
  Where outcasts under arches creep ;
Among them holds his simple talk.
  He lets them hear him in their sleep.
They who his name have still denied,
He lets them see him crucified.

On royal steps he takes a stand
  To light the beauties to the ball ;
He holds a lantern in his hand,
  And lets this simple saying fall.
They deem him but some sorry wit
Serving the Holy Spirit's writ.

They know not souls can rust and rot,
  And deem him, while he says his say,
The tipsy watchman who forgot
  To call out, " Carriage stops the way ! "
They know not what it can portend,
This mocking cry, " Old souls to mend ! "

While standing on the palace stone,
  He is in workhouse, brothel, jail ;
He is to play and ball-room gone,
  To hear again the beauties rail ;
With tender pity to behold
The dead alive in pearls and gold.

In meaning deep, in whispers low
  As bubble bursting on the air,
He lets the solemn warning flow
  Through jewell'd ears of creatures fair,
Who, while they dance, their paces blend
With his mild words, " Old souls to mend ! "

And when to church their sins they take,
  And bring them back to lunch again,
And fun of empty sermons make,
  He whispers softly in their train ;
And sits with them if two or more
Think of a promise made of yore.

Of those who stay behind to sup,
  And in remembrance eat the bread,
He leads the conscience to the cup,
  His hands across the table spread.
When contrite hearts before him bend,
Glad are his words, " Old souls to mend ! "

The little ones before the font
   He clasps within his arms to bless ;
For Childhood's pure and guileless front
   Smiles back his own sweet gentleness.
"Of such," he says, "my kingdom is,
For they betray not with a kiss."

He goes to hear the vicars preach :
   They do not always know his face,
Him they pretend the way to teach,
   And, as one absent, ask his grace.
Not then his words, "Old souls to mend !"
Their spirits pierce or bosoms rend.

He goes to see the priests revere
   His image as he lay in death :
They do not know that he is there ;
   They do not feel his living breath,
Though to his secret they pretend
With incense sweet, old souls to mend.

He goes to hear the grand debate
   That makes his own religion law ;
But him the members, as he sate
   Below the gangway, never saw.
They us'd his name to serve their end,
And others left old souls to mend.

Before the church-exchange he stands,
   Where those who buy and sell him, meet:
He sees his livings changing hands,
   And shakes the dust from off his feet.
Maybe his weary head he bows,
While from his side fresh ichor flows.

From mitred peers he turns his face.
   Where priests convok'd in session plot,
He would remind them of his grace
   But for his now too humble lot ;
So his dull cry on ears devout
He murmurs sadly from without.

He goes where judge the law defends,
   And takes the life he can't bestow,
And soul of sinner recommends
   To grace above, but not below ;
Reserving for a fresh surprise
Whom it shall meet in Paradise.

He goes to meeting, where the saint
   Exempts himself from deadly ire,
But in a strain admir'd and quaint
   Consigns all others to the fire,
While of the damn'd he mocks the howl,
And on the tinker drops his scowl.

Go here, go there, they cite his word,
   While he himself is nigh forgot.
He hears them use the name of Lord,
   He present though they know him not.
Though he be there, they vision lack,
And talk of him behind his back.

Such is the Church and such the State.
   Both set him up and put him down, —
Below the houses of debate,
   Above the jewels of the crown.
But when "Old souls to mend !" he says,
They send him off about his ways.

He is the humble, lowly one,
   In coat of rusty velveteen,
Who to his daily work has gone ;
   In sleeves of lawn not ever seen.
No mitre on his forehead sticks :
His crown is thorny, and it pricks.

On it the dews of mercy shine ;
   From heaven at dawn of day they fell ;
And it he wears by right divine,
   Like earthly kings, if truth they tell ;
And up to heaven the few to send,
He still cries out, "Old souls to mend !"

THE SIBYL

A MAID who mindful of her playful time
   Steps to her summer, bearing childhood
      on
To woman's beauty, heedless of her prime :
   The early day but not the pastime gone :
She is the Sibyl, uttering a doom
Out of her spotless bloom.

She is the Sibyl; seek not, then, her voice ; —
   A laugh, a song, a sorrow, but thy share,
With woes at hand for many who rejoice
   That she shall utter ; that shall many
      hear ;
That warn all hearts who seek of her their
      fates,
Her love but one awaits.

She is the Sibyl ; days that distant lie
   Bend to the promise that her word shall
      give ;
Already has she eyes that prophesy,
   For of her beauty shall all beauty live :
Unknown to her, in her slow opening bloom,
She turns the leaves of doom.

Edward FitzGerald

FROM HIS PARAPHRASE OF THE RUBÁIYÁT OF OMAR KHAYYÁM

OVERTURE

WAKE! For the Sun who scatter'd into
flight
The stars before him from the field of
night,
   Drives night along with them from
Heav'n, and strikes
The Sultán's turret with a shaft of light.

Before the phantom of false morning died,
Methought a Voice within the tavern cried,
   " When all the temple is prepar'd
within,
Why nods the drowsy worshipper outside ? "

And, as the Cock crew, those who stood
before
The tavern shouted — " Open then the
door !
   You know how little while we have to
stay,
And, once departed, may return no more."

PARADISE ENOW

With me along the strip of herbage strown
That just divides the desert from the sown,
   Where name of slave and sultán is for-
got —
And peace to Máhmúd on his golden
throne !

A book of verses underneath the bough,
A jug of wine, a loaf of bread — and Thou
   Beside me singing in the wilderness —
Oh, wilderness were Paradise enow !

Some for the glories of this world ; and
some
Sigh for the Prophet's Paradise to come ;
   Ah, take the cash, and let the credit go,
Nor heed the rumble of a distant drum !

Look to the blowing Rose about us — " Lo,
Laughing," she says, " into the world I
blow,
   At once the silken tassel of my purse
Tear, and its treasure on the garden throw."

And those who husbanded the golden grain,
And those who flung it to the winds like
rain,
   Alike to no such aureate earth are turn'd
As, buried once, men want dug up again.

The worldly hope men set their hearts
upon
Turns ashes — or it prospers ; and anon,
   Like snow upon the desert's dusty face,
Lighting a little hour or two — was gone.

Think, in this batter'd caravanserai
Whose portals are alternate Night and
Day,
   How Sultán after Sultán with his pomp
Abode his destin'd hour, and went his
way.

They say the lion and the lizard keep
The courts where Jamshyd gloried and
drank deep :
   And Bahrám, that great hunter — the
wild ass
Stamps o'er his head, but cannot break his
sleep.

I sometimes think that never blows so red
The rose as where some buried Cæsar bled ;
   That every hyacinth the garden wears
Dropp'd in her lap from some once lovely
head.

And this reviving herb whose tender green
Fledges the river-lip on which we lean —
   Ah, lean upon it lightly ! for who knows
From what once lovely lip it springs un-
seen !

Ah, my Beloved, fill the cup that clears
To-day of past regrets and future fears :
   To-morrow ! — Why to-morrow I may be
Myself with Yesterday's sev'n thousand
years.

For some we lov'd, the loveliest and the
best
That from his vintage rolling Time has
prest,
   Have drunk their cup a round or two be-
fore,
And one by one crept silently to rest.

And we, that now make merry in the room
They left, and Summer dresses in new
bloom,
 Ourselves must we beneath the couch of
  earth
Descend — ourselves to make a couch —
 for whom ?

Ah, make the most of what we yet may
 spend,
Before we too into the dust descend;
 Dust into dust, and under dust, to lie,
Sans wine, sans song, sans singer, and —
 sans end !

THE MASTER-KNOT

Up from Earth's centre through the
 Seventh Gate
I rose, and on the throne of Saturn sate,
 And many a knot unravell'd by the road ;
But not the master-knot of human fate.

There was the door to which I found no key ;
There was the veil through which I could
 not see ;
 Some little talk awhile of Me and Thee
There was — and then no more of Thee
 and Me.

Earth could not answer ; nor the seas that
 mourn
In flowing purple, of their Lord forlorn ;
 Nor rolling Heaven, with all his signs
  reveal'd
And hidden by the sleeve of night and morn.

Then of the Thee in Me who works behind
The veil, I lifted up my hands to find
 A lamp amid the darkness ; and I heard,
As from Without — " *The Me within Thee*
 blind ! "

Then to the lip of this poor earthen urn
I lean'd, the secret of my life to learn :
 And lip to lip it murmur'd — " While
  you live,
Drink ! — for, once dead, you never shall
 return."

I think the Vessel, that with fugitive
Articulation answer'd, once did live,
 And drink ; and ah ! the passive lip I
  kiss'd,
How many kisses might it take — and give !

For I remember stopping by the way
To watch a Potter thumping his wet Clay :
 And with its all-obliterated tongue
It murmur'd — " Gently, brother, gently,
 pray ! "

Listen — a moment listen ! — Of the same
Poor earth from which that human whisper
 came
 The luckless mould in which mankind
  was cast
They did compose, and call'd him by the
 name.

And not a drop that from our cups we
 throw
For earth to drink of, but may steal below
 To quench the fire of anguish in some
  eye
There hidden — far beneath, and long ago.

THE PHANTOM CARAVAN

And if the wine you drink, the lip you
 press,
End in what all begins and ends in — Yes ;
 Think then you are To-day what Yester-
  day
You were — To-morrow you shall not be
 less.

So when the Angel of the darker drink
At last shall find you by the river-brink,
 And, offering his cup, invite your Soul
Forth to your lips to quaff — you shall not
 shrink.

Why, if the Soul can fling the dust aside,
And naked on the air of Heaven ride,
 Wer 't not a shame — wer 't not a shame
 for him
In this clay carcase crippled to abide ?

'T is but a tent where takes his one-day's
 rest
A Sultán to the realm of Death addrest ;
 The Sultán rises, and the dark Ferrásh
Strikes, and prepares it for another guest.

And fear not lest existence closing your
Account, and mine, should know the like
 no more ;
 The Eternal Sáki from that bowl has
  pour'd
Millions of bubbles like us, and will pour.

When you and I behind the veil are past,
Oh but the long long while the world shall
last,
  Which of our coming and departure heeds
As the Sev'n Seas should heed a pebble-
cast.

A moment's halt — a momentary taste
Of Being from the well amid the waste —
  And lo ! — the phantom caravan has
reach'd
The Nothing it set out from — Oh, make
haste !

THE MOVING FINGER WRITES

I sent my Soul through the invisible,
Some letter of that after-life to spell :
  And by and by my Soul return'd to me,
And answer'd "I myself am Heav'n and
Hell."

Heav'n but the vision of fulfill'd desire,
And Hell the shadow of a soul on fire,
  Cast on the darkness into which our-
selves,
So late emerged from, shall so soon expire.

We are no other than a moving row
Of magic shadow-shapes that come and go
  Round with this sun-illumin'd lantern
held
In midnight by the Master of the Show;

Impotent pieces of the game He plays
Upon this checker-board of nights and
days ;
  Hither and thither moves, and checks,
and slays,
And one by one back in the closet lays.

The ball no question makes of ayes and noes
But right or left as strikes the Player goes ;
  And He that toss'd you down into the
field,
He knows about it all — HE knows — HE
knows !

The Moving Finger writes ; and, having
writ,
Moves on : nor all your piety nor wit
  Shall lure it back to cancel half a line,
Nor all your tears wash out a word of it.

And that inverted bowl they call the Sky,
Whereunder crawling coop'd we live and
die,
  Lift not your hands to *It* for help — for
It
As impotently rolls as you or I.

AND YET — AND YET !

Yet ah, that Spring should vanish with the
rose !
That Youth's sweet-scented manuscript
should close !
  The nightingale that in the branches
sang,
Ah whence, and whither flown again, who
knows !

Would but the desert of the fountain yield
One glimpse — if dimly, yet indeed, re-
veal'd,
  To which the fainting traveller might
spring,
As springs the trampled herbage of the
field !

Would but some winged Angel ere too late
Arrest the yet unfolded roll of fate,
  And make the stern Recorder otherwise
Enregister, or quite obliterate !

Ah Love ! could you and I with Him con-
spire
To grasp this sorry scheme of things entire,
  Would not we shatter it to bits— and
then
Re-mould it nearer to the heart's desire !

. . . .

Yon rising moon that looks for us again —
How oft hereafter will she wax and wane ;
How oft hereafter rising look for us
Through this same garden — and for *one*
in vain !

And when like her, oh Sáki, you shall pass
Among the guests star-scatter'd on the
grass,
  And in your blissful errand reach the
spot
Where I made one — turn down an empty
glass !

Robert Browning

SONG FROM "PARACELSUS"

OVER the sea our galleys went,
With cleaving prows in order brave,
To a speeding wind and a bounding wave —
    A gallant armament:
Each bark built out of a forest-tree,
    Left leafy and rough as first it grew,
And nail'd all over the gaping sides,
Within and without, with black-bull hides,
Seeth'd in fat and suppled in flame,
To bear the playful billow's game ;
So each good ship was rude to see,
Rude and bare to the outward view,
    But each upbore a stately tent ;
Where cedar-pales in scented row
Kept out the flakes of the dancing brine :
And an awning droop'd the mast below,
In fold on fold of the purple fine,
That neither noontide, nor star-shine,
Nor moonlight cold which maketh mad,
    Might pierce the regal tenement.
When the sun dawn'd, oh, gay and glad
We set the sail and plied the oar ;
But when the night-wind blew like breath,
For joy of one day's voyage more,
We sang together on the wide sea,
Like men at peace on a peaceful shore ;
Each sail was loos'd to the wind so free,
Each helm made sure by the twilight star,
And in a sleep as calm as death,
We, the strangers from afar,
    Lay stretch'd along, each weary crew
In a circle round its wondrous tent,
Whence gleam'd soft light and curl'd rich
    scent,
    And, with light and perfume, music too :
So the stars wheel'd round, and the darkness
    past,
And at morn we started beside the mast,
And still each ship was sailing fast !

One morn, the land appear'd ! — a speck
Dim trembling betwixt sea and sky —
Avoid it, cried our pilot, check
    The shout, restrain the longing eye !
But the heaving sea was black behind
For many a night and many a day,
And land, though but a rock, drew nigh ;
So we broke the cedar pales away,
Let the purple awning flap in the wind,
    And a statue bright was on every deck !

We shouted, every man of us,
And steer'd right into the harbor thus,
With pomp and pæan glorious.

An hundred shapes of lucid stone !
    All day we built a shrine for each —
A shrine of rock for every one —
Nor paus'd we till in the westering sun
    We sate together on the beach
To sing, because our task was done ;
When lo ! what shouts and merry songs !
What laughter all the distance stirs !
What raft comes loaded with its throngs
Of gentle islanders ?
" The isles are just at hand," they cried ;
    " Like cloudlets faint at even sleeping,
Our temple-gates are open'd wide,
    Our olive-groves thick shade are keep-
        ing
For the lucid shapes you bring " — they
        cried.
Oh, then we awoke with sudden start
From our deep dream ; we knew, too late,
How bare the rock, how desolate,
To which we had flung our precious freight :
    Yet we call'd out — " Depart !
Our gifts, once given, must here abide :
    Our work is done ; we have no heart
To mar our work, though vain " — we cried.

CAVALIER TUNES

I

MARCHING ALONG

KENTISH Sir Byng stood for his King,
Bidding the crop-headed Parliament swing :
And, pressing a troop unable to stoop
And see the rogues flourish and honest folk
    droop,
Marching along, fifty-score strong,
Great-hearted gentlemen, singing this song.

God for King Charles ! Pym and such carles
To the Devil that prompts 'em their trea-
    sonous parles !
Cavaliers, up ! Lips from the cup,
Hands from the pasty, nor bite take nor sup
Till you 're —
        (Chorus)
    Marching along, fifty-score strong,
    Great-hearted gentlemen, singing this song.

Hampden to hell, and his obsequies' knell
Serve Hazelrig, Fiennes, and young Harry
   as well !
England, good cheer ! Rupert is near !
Kentish and loyalists, keep we not here,
      (*Chorus*)
  Marching along, fifty-score strong,
  Great-hearted gentlemen, singing this song ?

Then, God for King Charles ! Pym and
  his snarls
To the Devil that pricks on such pestilent
  carles !
Hold by the right, you double your might ;
So, onward to Nottingham, fresh for the
  fight,
      (*Chorus*)
  March we along, fifty-score strong,
  Great-hearted gentlemen, singing this song !

II

GIVE A ROUSE

KING CHARLES, and who 'll do him right
  now ?
King Charles, and who 's ripe for fight
  now ?
Give a rouse : here 's, in hell's despite
  now,
King Charles !

Who gave me the goods that went since ?
Who rais'd me the house that sank once ?
Who help'd me to gold I spent since ?
Who found me in wine you drank once ?
      (*Chorus*)
  King Charles, and who 'll do him right
    now ?
  King Charles, and who 's ripe for fight
    now ?
  Give a rouse : here 's, in hell's despite now,
  King Charles !

To whom us'd my boy George quaff else,
By the old fool's side that begot him ?
For whom did he cheer and laugh else,
While Noll's damn'd troopers shot him ?
      (*Chorus*)
  King Charles, and who 'll do him right
    now ?
  King Charles, and who 's ripe for fight
    now ?
  Give a rouse : here 's, in hell's despite now,
  King Charles !

III

BOOT AND SADDLE

BOOT, saddle, to horse, and away !
Rescue my castle before the hot day
Brightens to blue from its silvery gray,
      (*Chorus*)
  Boot, saddle, to horse, and away !

Ride past the suburbs, asleep as you 'd
  say ;
Many 's the friend there, will listen and
  pray
" God's luck to gallants that strike up the
  lay —
      (*Chorus*)
  Boot, saddle, to horse, and away ! "

Forty miles off, like a roebuck at bay,
Flouts Castle Brancepeth the Roundheads'
  array :
Who laughs, " Good fellows ere this, by
  my fay,
      (*Chorus*)
  Boot, saddle, to horse, and away ! "

Who ? My wife Gertrude ; that, honest
  and gay,
Laughs when you talk of surrendering,
  " Nay !
I 've better counsellors ; what counsel they ?
      (*Chorus*)
  ' *Boot, saddle, to horse, and away ! ' "*

MY LAST DUCHESS

FERRARA

THAT 's my last Duchess painted on the
  wall,
Looking as if she were alive. I call
That piece a wonder, now : Frà Pandolf's
  hands
Work'd busily a day, and there she stands.
Will 't please you sit and look at her ?
  said
" Frà Pandolf " by design : for never read
Strangers like you that pictur'd counte
  nance,
The depth and passion of its earnest glance
But to myself they turn'd (since none put
  by
The curtain I have drawn for you, but I)

And seem'd as they would ask me, if they
   durst,
How such a glance came there ; so, not the
   first
Are you to turn and ask thus. Sir, 't was
   not
Her husband's presence only, call'd that
   spot
Of joy into the Duchess' cheek : perhaps
Frà Pandolf chanced to say " Her mantle
   laps
Over my lady's wrist too much," or
   " Paint
Must never hope to reproduce the faint
Half-flush that dies along her throat : " such
   stuff
Was courtesy, she thought, and cause
   enough
For calling up that spot of joy. She had
A heart — how shall I say ? — too soon
   made glad,
Too easily impress'd ; she lik'd whate'er
She look'd on, and her looks went every-
   where.
Sir, 't was all one ! My favor at her breast,
The dropping of the daylight in the West,
The bough of cherries some officious fool
Broke in the orchard for her, the white mule
She rode with round the terrace — all and
   each
Would draw from her alike the approving
   speech,
Or blush, at least. She thank'd men, —
   good ! but thank'd
Somehow — I know not how — as if she
   rank'd
My gift of a nine-hundred-years-old name
With anybody's gift. Who 'd stoop to blame
This sort of trifling ? Even had you skill
In speech — (which I have not) — to make
   your will
Quite clear to such an one, and say, " Just
   this
Or that in you disgusts me ; here you miss,
Or there exceed the mark " — and if she
   let
Herself be lesson'd so, nor plainly set
Her wits to yours, forsooth, and made ex-
   cuse,
— E'en then would be some stooping ; and
   I choose
Never to stoop. Oh sir, she smil'd, no
   doubt,
Whene'er I pass'd her ; but who pass'd
   without

Much the same smile ? This grew ; I gave
   commands ;
Then all smiles stopp'd together. There
   she stands
As if alive. Will 't please you rise ? We 'll
   meet
The company below, then. I repeat,
The Count your master's known munifi-
   cence
Is ample warrant that no just pretence
Of mine for dowry will be disallow'd ;
Though his fair daughter's self, as I avow'd
At starting, is my object. Nay, we 'll go
Together down, sir. Notice Neptune,
   though,
Taming a sea-horse, thought a rarity,
Which Claus of Innsbruck cast in bronze
   for me ?

INCIDENT OF THE FRENCH CAMP

You know, we French storm'd Ratisbon :
   A mile or so away
On a little mound, Napoleon
   Stood on our storming-day ;
With neck out-thrust, you fancy how,
   Legs wide, arms lock'd behind,
As if to balance the prone brow
   Oppressive with its mind.

Just as perhaps he mus'd " My plans
   That soar, to earth may fall,
Let once my army leader Lannes
   Waver at yonder wall, " —
Out 'twixt the battery smokes there flew
   A rider, bound on bound
Full-galloping ; nor bridle drew
   Until he reach'd the mound.

Then off there flung in smiling joy,
   And held himself erect
By just his horse's mane, a boy :
   You hardly could suspect —
(So tight he kept his lips compress'd,
   Scarce any blood came through)
You look'd twice ere you saw his breast
   Was all but shot in two.

" Well," cried he, " Emperor, by God's
   grace
We 've got you Ratisbon !
The Marshal 's in the market-place,
   And you 'll be there anon

To see your flag-bird flap his vans
  Where I, to heart's desire,
Perch'd him !" The chief's eye flash'd ;
    his plans
  Soar'd up again like fire.

The chief's eye flash'd ; but presently
  Soften'd itself, as sheathes
A film the mother-eagle's eye
  When her bruis'd eaglet breathes.
"You 're wounded !" "Nay," the soldier's
    pride
  Touch'd to the quick, he said :
"I 'm kill'd, Sire !" And his chief beside,
  Smiling the boy fell dead.

IN A GONDOLA

He sings

I send my heart up to thee, all my heart
  In this my singing.
For the stars help me, and the sea bears
    part ;
  The very night is clinging
Closer to Venice' streets to leave one space
Above me, whence thy face
May light my joyous heart to thee its
  dwelling-place.

She speaks

Say after me, and try to say
My very words, as if each word
Came from you of your own accord,
In your own voice, in your own way :
"This woman's heart and soul and brain
Are mine as much as this gold chain
She bids me wear ; which" (say again)
"I choose to make by cherishing
A precious thing, or choose to fling
Over the boat-side, ring by ring."
And yet once more say . . . no word
    more !
Since words are only words. Give o'er !

Unless you call me, all the same,
Familiarly by my pet name,
Which if the Three should hear you call,
And me reply to, would proclaim
At once our secret to them all.
Ask of me, too, command me, blame —
Do, break down the partition-wall
'Twixt us, the daylight world beholds
Curtain'd in dusk and splendid folds !

What 's left but — all of me to take ?
I am the Three's : prevent them, slake
Your thirst ! 'T is said, the Arab sage,
In practising with gems, can loose
Their subtle spirit in his cruce
And leave but ashes : so, sweet mage,
Leave them my ashes when thy use
Sucks out my soul, thy heritage !

He sings

Past we glide, and past, and past !
  What 's that poor Agnese doing
Where they make the shutters fast ?
  Gray Zanobi 's just a-wooing
To his couch the purchas'd bride :
  Past we glide !

Past we glide, and past, and past !
  Why 's the Pucci Palace flaring
Like a beacon to the blast ?
  Guests by hundreds, not one caring
If the dear host's neck were wried :
  Past we glide !

She sings

The moth's kiss, first !
Kiss me as if you made believe
You were not sure, this eve,
How my face, your flower, had purs'd
Its petals up ; so, here and there
You brush it, till I grow aware
Who wants me, and wide ope I burst.

The bee's kiss, now !
Kiss me as if you enter'd gay
My heart at some noonday, —
A bud that dares not disallow
The claim, so, all is render'd up,
And passively its shatter'd cup
Over your head to sleep I bow.

He sings

What are we two ?
I am a Jew,
And carry thee, farther than friends can
    pursue,
To a feast of our tribe;
Where they need thee to bribe
The devil that blasts them unless he imbibe
Thy . . . Scatter the vision for ever ! And
    now,
As of old, I am I, thou art thou !

Say again, what we are ?
The sprite of a star,
I lure thee above where the destinies bar
My plumes their full play
Till a ruddier ray
Than my pale one announce there is wither-
    ing away
Some . . . Scatter the vision for ever !
    And now,
As of old, I am I, thou art thou !

He muses

Oh, which were best, to roam or rest ?
The land's lap or the water's breast ?
To sleep on yellow millet-sheaves,
Or swim in lucid shallows, just
Eluding water-lily leaves,
An inch from Death's black fingers, thrust
To lock you, whom release he must ;
Which life were best on Summer eves ?

He speaks, musing

Lie back : could thought of mine improve
    you ?
From this shoulder let there spring
A wing ; from this, another wing ;
Wings, not legs and feet, shall move
    you !
Snow-white must they spring, to blend
With your flesh, but I intend
They shall deepen to the end,
Broader, into burning gold,
Till both wings crescent-wise enfold
Your perfect self, from 'neath your feet
To o'er your head, where, lo, they meet
As if a million sword-blades hurl'd
Defiance from you to the world !
Rescue me thou, the only real !
And scare away this mad ideal
That came, nor motions to depart !
Thanks ! Now, stay ever as thou art !

Still he muses

What if the Three should catch at last
Thy serenader ? While there 's cast
Paul's cloak about my head, and fast
Gian pinions me, Himself has past
His stylet through my back ; I reel ;
And . . . is it thou I feel ?

They trail me, these three godless knaves,
Past every church that saints and saves,

Nor stop till, where the cold sea raves
By Lido's wet accursed graves,
They scoop mine, roll me to its brink,
And . . . on thy breast I sink !

She replies, musing

Dip your arm o'er the boat side, elbow-
    deep,
As I do : thus : were death so unlike sleep,
Caught this way ? Death 's to fear from
    flame or steel,
Or poison doubtless ; but from water —
    feel !

Go find the bottom ! Would you stay me ?
    There !
Now pluck a great blade of that ribbon-
    grass
To plait in where the foolish jewel was,
I flung away : since you have prais'd my
    hair,
'T is proper to be choice in what I wear.

He speaks

Row home ? must we row home ? Too surely
Know I where its front 's demurely
Over the Guidecca pil'd ;
Window just with window mating,
Door on door exactly waiting,
All 's the set face of a child :
But behind it, where 's a trace
Of the staidness and reserve,
And formal lines without a curve,
In the same child's playing-face ?
No two windows look one way
O'er the small sea-water thread
Below them. Ah, the autumn day
I, passing, saw you overhead !
First, out a cloud of curtain blew,
Then a sweet cry, and last came you —
To catch your lory that must needs
Escape just then, of all times then,
To peck a tall plant's fleecy seeds
And make me happiest of men.
I scarce could breathe to see you reach
So far back o'er the balcony,
To catch him ere he climb'd too high
Above you in the Smyrna peach,
That quick the round smooth cord of gold,
This coil'd hair on your head, unroil'd,
Fell down you like a gorgeous snake
The Roman girls were wont, of old,
When Rome there was, for coolness' sake

To let lie curling o'er their bosoms.
Dear lory, may his beak retain
Ever its delicate rose stain,
As if the wounded lotus-blossoms
Had mark'd their thief to know again.
Stay longer yet, for others' sake
Than mine! What should your chamber
     do?
— With all its rarities that ache
In silence while day lasts, but wake
At night-time and their life renew,
Suspended just to pleasure you
Who brought against their will together
These objects, and, while day lasts, weave
Around them such a magic tether
That dumb they look : your harp, believe,
With all the sensitive tight strings
Which dare not speak, now to itself
Breathes slumberously, as if some elf
Went in and out the chords, — his wings
Make murmur, wheresoe'er they graze,
As an angel may, between the maze
Of midnight palace-pillars, on
And on, to sow God's plagues, have gone
Through guilty glorious Babylon.
And while such murmurs flow, the nymph
Bends o'er the harp-top from her shell
As the dry limpet for the lymph
Come with a tune he knows so well.
And how your statues' hearts must swell!
And how your pictures must descend
To see each other, friend with friend!
Oh, could you take them by surprise,
You 'd find Schidone's eager Duke
Doing the quaintest courtesies
To that prim saint by Haste-thee-Luke!
And, deeper into her rock den,
Bold Castelfranco's Magdalen
You 'd find retreated from the ken
Of that rob'd counsel-keeping Ser —
As if the Tizian thinks of her,
And is not, rather, gravely bent
On seeing for himself what toys
Are these his progeny invent,
What litter now the board employs
Whereon he sign'd a document
That got him murder'd! Each enjoys
Its night so well, you cannot break
The sport up : so, indeed must make
More stay with me, for others' sake.

She speaks

To-morrow, if a harp-string, say,
Is used to tie the jasmine back

That overfloods my room with sweets,
Contrive your Zorzi somehow meets
My Zanze! If the ribbon 's black,
The Three are watching : keep away!

Your gondola — let Zorzi wreathe
A mesh of water-weeds about
Its prow, as if he unaware
Had struck some quay or bridge-foot
     stair!
That I may throw a paper out
As you and he go underneath.

There 's Zanze's vigilant taper; safe are
     we.
Only one minute more to-night with me?
Resume your past self of a month ago!
Be you the bashful gallant, I will be
The lady with the colder breast than snow.
Now bow you, as becomes, nor touch my
     hand
More than I touch yours when I step to
     land.
Just say, " All thanks, Siora ! " —
                              Heart to heart
And lips to lips ! Yet once more, ere we
     part,
Clasp me and make me thine, as mine thou
     art!

He is surprised, and stabbed

It was ordain'd to be so, sweet ! — and best
Comes now, beneath thine eyes, upon thy
     breast.
Still kiss me ! Care not for the cowards !
     Care
Only to put aside thy beauteous hair
My blood will hurt ! The Three, I do not
     scorn
To death, because they never liv'd : but I
Have liv'd indeed, and so — (yet one more
     kiss) — can die !

SONG FROM "PIPPA PASSES"

THE year 's at the spring,
And day 's at the morn ;
Morning 's at seven ;
The hill-side 's dew-pearl'd ;
The lark 's on the wing ;
The snail 's on the thorn :
God 's in His heaven —
All 's right with the world.

"HOW THEY BROUGHT THE GOOD NEWS FROM GHENT TO AIX"

[16—]

I SPRANG to the stirrup, and Joris, and he ;
I gallop'd, Dirck gallop'd, we gallop'd all
   three ;
"Good speed ! " cried the watch, as the
   gate-bolts undrew ;
"Speed ! " echoed the wall to us galloping
   through ;
Behind shut the postern, the lights sank to
   rest,
And into the midnight we gallop'd abreast.

Not a word to each other ; we kept the
   great pace
Neck by neck, stride by stride, never
   changing our place ;
I turn'd in my saddle and made its girths
   tight,
Then shorten'd each stirrup, and set the
   pique right,
Rebuckled the cheek-strap, chain'd slacker
   the bit,
Nor gallop'd less steadily Roland a whit.

'T was moonset at starting ; but while we
   drew near
Lokeren, the cocks crew and twilight
   dawn'd clear ;
At Boom, a great yellow star came out to
   see ;
At Düffeld, 't was morning as plain as could
   be ;
And from Mechelm church-steeple we heard
   the half chime,
So, Joris broke silence with, "Yet there is
   time ! "

At Aershot, up leap'd of a sudden the sun,
And against him the cattle stood black
   every one,
To stare thro' the mist at us galloping past,
And I saw my stout galloper Roland at
   last,
With resolute shoulders, each butting away
The haze, as some bluff river headland its
   spray :

And his low head and crest, just one sharp
   ear bent back
For my voice, and the other prick'd out
   on his track ;

And one eye's black intelligence, — ever
   that glance
O'er its white edge at me, his own master,
   askance !
And the thick heavy spume-flakes which
   aye and anon
His fierce lips shook upwards in galloping
   on.

By Hasselt, Dirck groan'd ; and cried
   Joris " Stay spur !
Your Roos gallop'd bravely, the fault 's
   not in her,
We 'll remember at Aix " — for one heard
   the quick wheeze
Of her chest, saw the stretch'd neck and
   staggering knees,
And sunk tail, and horrible heave of the
   flank,
As down on her haunches she shudder'd
   and sank.

So, we were left galloping, Joris and I,
Past Looz and past Tongres, no cloud in
   the sky ;
The broad sun above laugh'd a pitiless
   laugh,
'Neath our feet broke the brittle bright
   stubble like chaff ;
Till over by Dalhem a dome-spire sprang
   white,
And "Gallop," gasped Joris, "for Aix is in
   sight !

"How they 'll greet us ! " — and all in a
   moment his roan
Roll'd neck and croup over, lay dead as a
   stone ;
And there was my Roland to bear the
   whole weight
Of the news which alone could save Aix
   from her fate,
With his nostrils like pits full of blood to
   the brim,
And with circles of red for his eye-sockets'
   rim.

Then I cast loose my buffcoat, each holster
   let fall,
Shook off both my jack-boots, let go belt
   and all,
Stood up in the stirrup, lean'd, patted his
   ear,
Call'd my Roland his pet name, my horse
   without peer ;

Clapp'd my hands, laugh'd and sang, any
noise, bad or good,
Till at length into Aix Roland gallop'd
and stood.

And all I remember is, friends flocking
round
As I sat with his head 'twixt my knees on
the ground ;
And no voice but was praising this Roland
of mine,
As I pour'd down his throat our last
measure of wine,
Which (the burgesses voted by common
consent)
Was no more than his due who brought
good news from Ghent.

THE LOST LEADER

Just for a handful of silver he left us,
Just for a ribbon to stick in his coat —
Found the one gift of which fortune bereft
us,
Lost all the others she lets us devote ;
They, with the gold to give, dol'd him out
silver,
So much was theirs who so little allow'd ;
How all our copper had gone for his ser-
vice !
Rags — were they purple, his heart had
been proud !
We that had lov'd him so, follow'd him,
honor'd him,
Liv'd in his mild and magnificent eye,
Learn'd his great language, caught his
clear accents,
Made him our pattern to live and to
die !
Shakespeare was of us, Milton was for us,
Burns, Shelley, were with us, — they
watch from their graves !
He alone breaks from the van and the free-
men,
He alone sinks to the rear and the slaves !

We shall march prospering, — not thro'
his presence ;
Songs may inspirit us, — not from his
lyre ;
Deeds will be done, — while he boasts his
quiescence,
Still bidding crouch whom the rest bade
aspire.

Blot out his name, then, record one lost
soul more,
One task more declin'd, one more foot-
path untrod,
One more devil's-triumph and sorrow for
angels,
One wrong more to man, one more insult
to God !
Life's night begins : let him never come
back to us !
There would be doubt, hesitation, and
pain,
Forced praise on our part — the glimmer of
twilight,
Never glad confident morning again !
Best fight on well, for we taught him —
strike gallantly,
Menace our heart ere we master his own ;
Then let him receive the new knowledge
and wait us,
Pardon'd in heaven, the first by the
throne !

YOUTH AND ART

It once might have been, once only :
We lodged in a street together,
You, a sparrow on the housetop lonely,
I, a lone she-bird of his feather.

Your trade was with sticks and clay,
You thumb'd, thrust, patted and polish'd,
Then laugh'd, " They will see, some day,
Smith made, and Gibson demolish'd."

My business was song, song, song ;
I chirp'd, cheep'd, trill'd and twitter'd,
" Kate Brown 's on the boards ere long,
And Grisi's existence embitter'd ! "

I earn'd no more by a warble
Than you by a sketch in plaster ;
You wanted a piece of marble,
I needed a music-master.

We studied hard in our styles,
Chipp'd each at a crust like Hindoos,
For air, look'd out on the tiles,
For fun, watch'd each other's windows.

You lounged, like a boy of the South,
Cap and blouse — nay, a bit of beard too ;
Or you got it, rubbing your mouth
With fingers the clay adher'd to.

And I — soon managed to find
Weak points in the flower-fence facing,
Was forced to put up a blind
And be safe in my corset-lacing.

No harm ! It was not my fault
If you never turn'd your eye's tail up
As I shook upon E *in alt,*
Or ran the chromatic scale up :

For spring bade the sparrows pair,
And the boys and girls gave guesses,
And stalls in our street look'd rare
With bulrush and watercresses.

Why did not you pinch a flower
In a pellet of clay and fling it ?
Why did not I put a power
Of thanks in a look, or sing it ?

I did look, sharp as a lynx,
(And yet the memory rankles)
When models arriv'd, some minx
Tripp'd up stairs, she and her ankles.

But I think I gave you as good !
" That foreign fellow, — who can know
How she pays, in a playful mood,
For his tuning her that piano ? "

Could you say so, and never say,
" Suppose we join hands and fortunes,
And I fetch her from over the way,
Her, piano, and long tunes and short
tunes ? "

No, no : you would not be rash,
Nor I rasher and something over ;
You 've to settle yet Gibson's hash,
And Grisi yet lives in clover.

But you meet the Prince at the Board,
I 'm queen myself at *bals-parés,*
I 've married a rich old lord,
And you 're dubb'd knight and an R. A.

Each life 's unfulfill'd, you see ;
It hangs still, patchy and scrappy :
We have not sigh'd deep, laugh'd free,
Starv'd, feasted, despair'd, — been happy;

And nobody calls you a dunce,
And people suppose me clever ;
This could but have happen'd once,
And we miss'd it, lost it forever.

HOME THOUGHTS FROM ABROAD

I

OH, to be in England now that April 's
there
And whoever wakes in England sees, some
morning, unaware,
That the lowest boughs and the brushwood
sheaf
Round the elm-tree bole are in tiny leaf,
While the chaffinch sings on the orchard
bough
In England — now !

II

And after April, when May follows
And the white-throat builds, and all the
swallows !
Hark, where my blossom'd pear-tree in
the hedge
Leans to the field and scatters on the clover
Blossoms and dewdrops — at the bent
spray's edge —
That 's the wise thrush : he sings each song
twice over
Lest you should think he never could re-
capture
The first fine careless rapture !
And, though the fields look rough with
hoary dew,
All will be gay when noontide wakes anew
The buttercups, the little children's dower,
Far brighter than this gaudy melon-flower !

A FACE

IF one could have that little head of
hers !
Painted upon a background of pale gold,
Such as the Tuscan's early art prefers !
No shade encroaching on the matchless
mould
Of those two lips, which should be opening
soft
In the pure profile ; not as when she
laughs,
For that spoils all : but rather as if aloft
Yon hyacinth, she loves so, lean'd its
staff's
Burthen of honey-color'd buds to kiss
And capture 'twixt the lips apart for this.

Then her lithe neck, three fingers might
surround,
How it should waver, on the pale gold
ground,
Up to the fruit-shap'd, perfect chin it
lifts !
I know, Correggio loves to mass, in rifts
Of heaven, his angel faces, orb on orb
Breaking its outline, burning shades ab-
sorb ;
But these are only mass'd there, I should
think,
Waiting to see some wonder momently
Grow out, stand full, fade slow against the
sky .
(That's the pale ground you'd see this
sweet face by),
All heaven, meanwhile, condens'd into one
eye
Which fears to lose the wonder, should it
wink.

"DE GUSTIBUS—"

I

YOUR ghost will walk, you lover of trees,
(If our loves remain)
In an English lane,
By a cornfield-side a-flutter with poppies.
Hark, those two in the hazel coppice —
A boy and a girl, if the good fates please,
Making love, say, —
The happier they !
Draw yourself up from the light of the
moon,
And let them pass, as they will too soon,
With the beanflower's boon,
And the blackbird's tune,
And May, and June !

II

What I love best in all the world
Is a castle, precipice-encurl'd,
In a gash of the wind-griev'd Apennine.
Or look for me, old fellow of mine,
(If I get my head from out the mouth
O' the grave, and loose my spirit's bands,
And come again to the land of lands) —
In a sea-side house to the farther South,
Where the bak'd cicala dies of drouth,
And one sharp tree — 't is a cypress —
stands,

By the many hundred years red-rusted,
Rough iron-spik'd, ripe fruit-o'ercrusted,
My sentinel to guard the sands
To the water's edge. For, what expands
Before the house, but the great opaque
Blue breadth of sea without a break ?
While, in the house, for ever crumbles
Some fragment of the frescoed walls,
From blisters where a scorpion sprawls.
A girl bare-footed brings, and tumbles
Down on the pavement, green-flesh melons,
And says there's news to-day — the king
Was shot at, touch'd in the liver-wing,
Goes with his Bourbon arm in a sling :
— She hopes they have not caught the felons.
Italy, my Italy !
Queen Mary's saying serves for me —
(When fortune's malice
Lost her Calais)
Open my heart and you will see
Grav'd inside of it, "Italy."
Such lovers old are I and she :
So it always was, so shall ever be.

THE BISHOP ORDERS HIS TOMB AT SAINT PRAXED'S CHURCH

ROME, 15—

VANITY, saith the preacher, vanity !
Draw round my bed : is Anselm keeping
back ?
Nephews — sons mine . . . ah God, I know
not ! Well —
She, men would have to be your mother
once,
Old Gandolf envied me, so fair she was !
What's done is done, and she is dead be-
side,
Dead long ago, and I am Bishop since,
And as she died so must we die ourselves,
And thence ye may perceive the world's a
dream.
Life, how and what is it ? As here I lie
In this state-chamber, dying by degrees,
Hours and long hours in the dead night, I
ask,
"Do I live, am I dead ?" Peace, peace
seems all.
Saint Praxed's ever was the church for
peace ;
And so, about this tomb of mine. I fought
With tooth and nail to save my niche, ye
know :

— Old Gandolf cozen'd me, despite my
care;
Shrewd was that snatch from out the
corner South
He graced his carrion with, God curse the
same !
Yet still my niche is not so cramp'd but
thence
One sees the pulpit on the epistle-side,
And somewhat of the choir, those silent
seats,
And up into the aëry dome where live
The angels, and a sunbeam's sure to lurk :
And I shall fill my slab of basalt there,
And 'neath my tabernacle take my rest,
With those nine columns round me, two and
two,
The odd one at my feet where Anselm
stands :
Peach-blossom marble all, the rare, the
ripe
As fresh-pour'd red wine of a mighty pulse,
— Old Gandolf with his paltry onion-stone.
Put me where I may look at him ! True
peach,
Rosy and flawless : how I earn'd the prize !
Draw close : that conflagration of my
church
— What then ? So much was sav'd if
aught were miss'd !
My sons, ye would not be my death ? Go
dig
The white-grape vineyard where the oil-
press stood,
Drop water gently till the surface sink,
And if ye find . . . Ah God, I know not,
I ! . . .
Bedded in store of rotten figleaves soft,
And corded up in a tight olive-frail,
Some lump, ah God, of *lapis lazuli*,
Big as a Jew's head cut off at the nape,
Blue as a vein o'er the Madonna's breast . .
Sons, all have I bequeathed you, villas, all,
That brave Frascati villa with its bath,
So, let the blue lump poise between my
knees,
Like God the Father's globe on both his
hands
Ye worship in the Jesu Church so gay,
For Gandolf shall not choose but see and
burst !
Swift as a weaver's shuttle fleet our years :
Man goeth to the grave, and where is he ?
Did I say, basalt for my slab, sons?
Black —

'T was ever antique-black I meant ! How
else
Shall ye contrast my frieze to come be-
neath ?
The bas-relief in bronze ye promis'd me,
Those Pans and Nymphs ye wot of, and
perchance
Some tripod, thyrsus, with a vase or so,
The Saviour at his sermon on the mount,
Saint Praxed in a glory, and one Pan
Ready to twitch the Nymph's last garment
off,
And Moses with the tables . . . but I know
Ye mark me not ! What do they whisper
thee,
Child of my bowels, Anselm ? Ah, ye hope
To revel down my villas while I gasp
Brick'd o'er with beggar's mouldy traver-
tine
Which Gandolf from his tomb-top chuckles
at !
Nay, boys, ye love me — all of jasper, then !
'T is jasper ye stand pledged to, lest I
grieve
My bath must needs be left behind, alas !
One block, pure green as a pistachio-nut,
There's plenty jasper somewhere in the
world —
And have I not Saint Praxed's ear to pray
Horses for ye, and brown Greek manu-
scripts,
And mistresses with great smooth marbly
limbs ?
— That's if ye carve my epitaph aright,
Choice Latin, pick'd phrase, Tully's every
word,
No gaudy ware like Gandolf's second line —
Tully, my masters ? Ulpian serves his
need !
And then how shall I lie through centuries,
And hear the blessed mutter of the mass,
And see God made and eaten all day long,
And feel the steady candle-flame, and taste
Good strong thick stupefying incense·
smoke !
For as I lie here, hours of the dead night,
Dying in state and by such slow degrees,
I fold my arms as if they clasp'd a crook,
And stretch my feet forth straight as stone
can point,
And let the bedclothes, for a mortcloth,
drop
Into great laps and folds of sculptor's work :
And as yon tapers dwindle, and strange
thoughts

Grow, with a certain humming in my ears,
About the life before I liv'd this life,
And this life too, popes, cardinals and
  priests,
Saint Praxed at his sermon on the mount,
Your tall pale mother with her talking eyes,
And new-found agate urns as fresh as day,
And marble's language, Latin pure, dis-
  creet,
— Aha, ELUCESCEBAT quoth our friend ?
No Tully, said I, Ulpian at the best !
Evil and brief hath been my pilgrimage.
All *lapis*, all, sons ! Else I give the Pope
My villas ! Will ye ever eat my heart ?
Ever your eyes were as a lizard's quick,
They glitter like your mother's for my
  soul,
Or ye would heighten my impoverish'd
  frieze,
Piece out its starv'd design, and fill my
  vase
With grapes, and add a vizor and a Term,
And to the tripod ye would tie a lynx
That in his struggle throws the thyrsus
  down,
To comfort me on my entablature
Wherein I am to lie till I must ask,
" Do I live, am I dead ? " There, leave me,
  there !
For ye have stabb'd me with ingratitude
To death : ye wish it — God, ye wish it !
  Stone —
Gritstone, a-crumble ! Clammy squares
  which sweat
As if the corpse they keep were oozing
  through —
And no more *lapis* to delight the world !
Well, go ! I bless ye. Fewer tapers
  there,
But in a row : and, going, turn your backs
— Ay, like departing altar-ministrants,
And leave me in my church, the church for
  peace
That I may watch at leisure if he leers —
Old Gandolf — at me, from his onion-stone,
As still he envied me, so fair she was !

MEETING AT NIGHT

THE gray sea and the long black land ;
And the yellow half-moon large and
  low :
And the startled little waves that leap
In fiery ringlets from their sleep,

As I gain the cove with pushing prow,
And quench its speed i' the slushy sand.

Then a mile of warm sea-scented beach ;
Three fields to cross till a farm appears ;
A tap at the pane, the quick sharp scratch
And blue spurt of a lighted match,
And a voice less loud, through joys and
  fears,
Than the two hearts beating each to each !

PARTING AT MORNING

ROUND the cape of a sudden came the sea,
And the sun look'd over the mountain's rim :
And straight was a path of gold for him,
And the need of a world of men for me.

EVELYN HOPE

BEAUTIFUL Evelyn Hope is dead !
  Sit and watch by her side an hour.
That is her book-shelf, this her bed ;
  She pluck'd that piece of geranium-
    flower,
Beginning to die too, in the glass ;
  Little has yet been changed, I think :
The shutters are shut, no light may pass
  Save two long rays thro' the hinge's chink.

Sixteen years old when she died !
  Perhaps she had scarcely heard my name ;
It was not her time to love ; beside,
  Her life had many a hope and aim,
Duties enough and little cares,
  And now was quiet, now astir,
Till God's hand beckon'd unawares, —
  And the sweet white brow is all of her.

Is it too late then, Evelyn Hope ?
  What, your soul was pure and true,
The good stars met in your horoscope,
  Made you of spirit, fire and dew —
And, just because I was thrice as old
  And our paths in the world diverged so
    wide,
Each was nought to each, must I be told ?
  We were fellow mortals, nought beside ?

No, indeed ! for God above
  Is great to grant, as mighty to make,
And creates the love to reward the love :
  I claim you still, for my own love's sake !

Delay'd it may be for more lives yet,
Through worlds I shall traverse, not a
few :
Much is to learn, much to forget
Ere the time be come for taking you.

But the time will come, at last it will,
When, Evelyn Hope, what meant (I
shall say)
In the lower earth, in the years long still,
That body and soul so pure and gay ?
Why your hair was amber, I shall divine,
And your mouth of your own geranium's
red —
And what you would do with me, in fine,
In the new life come in the old one's
stead.

I have liv'd (I shall say) so much since
then,
Given up myself so many times,
Gain'd me the gains of various men,
Ransack'd the ages, spoil'd the climes ;
Yet one thing, one, in my soul's full scope,
Either I miss'd or itself miss'd me :
And I want and find you, Evelyn Hope !
What is the issue ? let us see !

I lov'd you, Evelyn, all the while !
My heart seem'd full as it could hold ;
There was place and to spare for the frank
young smile,
And the red young mouth, and the hair's
young gold.
So hush, — I will give you this leaf to
keep :
See, I shut it inside the sweet cold
hand !
There, that is our secret : go to sleep !
You will wake, and remember, and
understand.

"CHILDE ROLAND TO THE DARK TOWER CAME" [1]

My first thought was, he lied in every
word,
That hoary cripple, with malicious eye
Askance to watch the working of his lie
On mine, and mouth scarce able to afford
Suppression of the glee, that purs'd and
scor'd
Its edge, at one more victim gain'd
thereby.

What else should he be set for, with his
staff ?
What, save to waylay with his lies, en-
snare
All travellers who might find him posted
there,
And ask the road ? I guess'd what skull-
like laugh
Would break, what crutch 'gin write my
epitaph
For pastime in the dusty thoroughfare,

If at his counsel I should turn aside
Into that ominous tract which, all agree,
Hides the Dark Tower. Yet acquiescingly
I did turn as he pointed : neither pride
Nor hope rekindling at the end descried,
So much as gladness that some end
might be.

For, what with my whole world-wide
wandering,
What with my search drawn out thro'
years, my hope
Dwindled into a ghost not fit to cope
With that obstreperous joy success would
bring, —
I hardly tried now to rebuke the spring
My heart made, finding failure in its
scope.

As when a sick man very near to death
Seems dead indeed, and feels begin and
end
The tears and takes the farewell of each
friend,
And hears one bid the other go, draw breath
Freelier outside, ("since all is o'er," he
saith,
"And the blow fallen no grieving can
amend ;")

While some discuss if near the other graves
Be room enough for this, and when a day
Suits best for carrying the corpse away,
With care about the banners, scarves and
staves,
And still the man hears all, and only craves
He may not shame such tender love and
stay.

Thus, I had so long suffer'd, in this quest,
Heard failure prophesied so oft, been writ
So many times among "The Band" — to
wit,

[1] See Edgar's song in "Lear."

The knights who to the Dark Tower's
   search address'd
Their steps — that just to fail as they,
   seem'd best.
   And all the doubt was now — should I
   be fit ?

So, quiet as despair, I turn'd from him,
   That hateful cripple, out of his highway
Into the path he pointed. All the day
Had been a dreary one at best, and dim
Was settling to its close, yet shot one grim
Red leer to see the plain catch its estray.

For mark ! no sooner was I fairly found
   Pledged to the plain, after a pace or two,
   Than, pausing to throw backward a last
   view
O'er the safe road, 't was gone ; gray plain
   all round :
Nothing but plain to the horizon's bound.
I might go on ; nought else remain'd to do.

So, on I went. I think I never saw
   Such starv'd ignoble nature ; nothing
   throve :
   For flowers — as well expect a cedar
   grove !
But cockle, spurge, according to their law
Might propagate their kind, with none to
   awe,
   You 'd think ; a burr had been a treasure
   trove.

No ! penury, inertness and grimace,
   In some strange sort, were the land's
   portion. " See
Or shut your eyes," said Nature peevishly,
" It nothing skills : I cannot help my case :
'T is the Last Judgment's fire must cure this
   place,
   Calcine its clods and set my prisoners
   free."

If there push'd any ragged thistle-stalk
   Above its mates, the head was chopp'd ;
   the bents
   Were jealous else. What made those
   holes and rents
In the dock's harsh swarth leaves, bruis'd
   as to baulk
All hope of greenness ? 'T is a brute must
   walk
   Pashing their life out, with a brute's in-
   tents.

As for the grass, it grew as scant as hair
   In leprosy ; thin dry blades prick'd the
   mud
   Which underneath look'd kneaded up
   with blood.
One stiff blind horse, his every bone
   a-stare,
Stood stupefied, however he came there :
   Thrust out past · service from the devil's
   stud !

Alive ? he might be dead for aught I
   know,
   With that red, gaunt and collop'd neck
   a-strain,
   And shut eyes underneath the rusty
   mane ;
Seldom went such grotesqueness with such
   woe ;
I never saw a brute I hated so ;
   He must be wicked to deserve such pain.

I shut my eyes and turn'd them on my
   heart.
   As a man calls for wine before he fights,
   I ask'd one draught of earlier, happier
   sights,
Ere fitly I could hope to play my part.
Think first, fight afterwards — the soldier's
   art :
   One taste of the old time sets all to
   rights.

Not it ! I fancied Cuthbert's reddening
   face
   Beneath its garniture of curly gold,
   Dear fellow, till I almost felt him fold
An arm in mine to fix me to the place,
That way he us'd. Alas, one night's dis-
   grace !
   Out went my heart's new fire and left it
   cold.

Giles then, the soul of honor — there he
   stands
   Frank as ten years ago when knighted
   first.
   What honest man should dare (he said)
   he durst.
Good — but the scene shifts — faugh !
   what hangman hands
Pin to his breast a parchment ? His own
   bands
   Read it. Poor traitor, spit upon and
   curst !

Better this present than a past like that ;
　Back therefore to my darkening path
　　again !
No sound, no sight as far as eye could
　. strain.
Will the night send a howlet or a bat ?
I asked : when something on the dismal flat
　Came to arrest my thoughts and change
　　their train.

A sudden little river cross'd my path
　As unexpected as a serpent comes.
No sluggish tide congenial to the glooms ;
This, as it froth'd by, might have been a
　　bath
For the fiend's glowing hoof — to see the
　　wrath
　Of its black eddy bespate with flakes and
　　spumes.

So petty yet so spiteful ! All along,
　Low scrubby alders kneel'd down over
　　it ;
Drench'd willows flung them headlong
　　in a fit
Of mute despair, a suicidal throng :
The river which had done them all the
　　wrong,
　Whate'er that was, roll'd by, deterr'd
　　no whit.

Which, while I forded, — good saints, how
　I fear'd
To set my foot upon a dead man's cheek,
　Each step, or feel the spear I thrust to
　　seek
For hollows, tangled in his hair or beard !
— It may have been a water-rat I spear'd,
　But, ugh ! it sounded like a baby's shriek.

Glad was I when I reach'd the other bank.
　Now for a better country. Vain pre-
　　sage !
Who were the strugglers, what war did
　　they wage
Whose savage trample thus could pad the
　　dank
Soil to a plash ? Toads in a poison'd tank,
　Or wild cats in a red-hot iron cage —

The fight must so have seem'd in that fell
　　cirque.
　What penn'd them there, with all the
　　plain to choose ?
No foot-print leading to that horrid mews,

None out of it. Mad brewage set to work
　Their brains, no doubt, like galley-slaves
　　the Turk
Pits for his pastime, Christians against
　　Jews.

And more than that — a furlong on — why,
　　there !
　What bad use was that engine for, that
　　wheel,
　Or brake, not wheel — that harrow fit to
　　reel
Men's bodies out like silk ? with all the
　　air
Of Tophet's tool, on earth left unaware,
　Or brought to sharpen its rusty teeth of
　　steel.

Then came a bit of stubb'd ground, once a
　　wood,
　Next a marsh, it would seem, and now
　　mere earth
Desperate and done with ; (so a fool finds
　　mirth,
Makes a thing and then mars it, till his
　　mood
Changes and off he goes !) within a rood —
　Bog, clay, and rubble, sand and stark
　　black dearth.

Now blotches rankling, color'd gay and grim,
　Now patches where some leanness of the
　　soil's
Broke into moss or substances like boils ;
Then came some palsied oak, a cleft in him
Like a distorted mouth that splits its rim
Gaping at death, and dies while it recoils.

And just as far as ever from the end,
　Nought in the distance but the evening,
　　nought
To point my footstep further ! At the
　　thought,
A great black bird, Apollyon's bosom-
　　friend,
Sail'd past, nor beat his wide wing dragon-
　　penn'd
　That brush'd my cap — perchance the
　　guide I sought.

For, looking up, aware I somehow grew,
　Spite of the dusk, the plain had given
　　place
　All round to mountains — with such
　　name to grace

Mere ugly heights and heaps now stolen in
   view.
How thus they had surpris'd me, — solve
   it, you !
   How to get from them was no clearer
      case.

Yet half I seem'd to recognize some trick
   Of mischief happen'd to me, God knows
      when —
   In a bad dream perhaps. Here ended,
      then,
Progress this way. When, in the very nick
Of giving up, one time more, came a click
   As when a trap shuts — you 're inside the
      den.

Burningly it came on me all at once,
   This was the place ! those two hills on
      the right,
   Couch'd like two bulls lock'd horn in
      horn in fight,
While, to the left, a tall scalp'd mountain
   . . . Dunce,
Dotard, a-dozing at the very nonce,
   After a life spent training for the sight !

What in the midst lay but the Tower itself ?
   The round squat turret, blind as the
      fool's heart,
   Built of brown stone, without a counter-
      part
In the whole world. The tempest's mock-
   ing elf
Points to the shipman thus the unseen shelf
He strikes on, only when the timbers start.

Not see ? because of night perhaps ? —
   why, day
   Came back again for that ! before it left,
   The dying sunset kindled through a cleft :
The hills, like giants at a hunting, lay,
Chin upon hand, to see the game at bay, —
   " Now stab and end the creature — to
      the heft ! "

Not hear ? when noise was everywhere ! it
   toll'd
   Increasing like a bell. Names in my ears
   Of all the lost adventurers my peers, —
How such a one was strong, and such was
   bold,
And such was fortunate, yet each of old
   Lost, lost ! one moment knell'd the woe
      of years.

There they stood, ranged along the hill-
   sides, met
To view the last of me, a living frame
For one more picture ! in a sheet of flame
I saw them and I knew them all. And yet
Dauntless the slug-horn to my lips I set,
   And blew " *Childe Roland to the Dark*
      Tower came."

RESPECTABILITY

DEAR, had the world in its caprice
   Deign'd to proclaim " I know you both,
   Have recogniz'd your plighted troth,
Am sponsor for you : live in peace ! "
How many precious months and years
   Of youth had pass'd, that speed so fast,
   Before we found it out at last,
The world, and what it fears ?

How much of priceless life were spent
   With men that every virtue decks,
   And women models of their sex,
Society's true ornament, —
Ere we dar'd wander, nights like this,
   Thro' wind and rain, and watch the Seine,
   And feel the Boulevart break again
To warmth and light and bliss ?

I know ! the world proscribes not love ;
   Allows my fingers to caress
   Your lips' contour and downiness,
Provided it supply a glove.
The world's good word ! — the Institute !
   Guizot receives Montalembert !
   Eh ? Down the court three lampions
      flare :
Put forward your best foot !

MEMORABILIA

AH, did you once see Shelley plain,
   And did he stop and speak to you,
And did you speak to him again ?
   How strange it seems, and new !

But you were living before that,
   And also you are living after ;
And the memory I started at —
   My starting moves your laughter !

I cross'd a moor, with a name of its own
   And a certain use in the world, no doubt,
Yet a hand's-breadth of it shines alone
   'Mid the blank miles round about :

For there I picked up on the heather
  And there I put inside my breast
A moulted feather, an eagle-feather !
  Well, I forget the rest.

ONE WAY OF LOVE

ALL June I bound the rose in sheaves.
Now, rose by rose, I strip the leaves
And strow them where Pauline may pass.
She will not turn aside ? Alas !
Let them lie. Suppose they die ?
The chance was they might take her eye.

How many a month I strove to suit
These stubborn fingers to the lute !
To-day I venture all I know.
She will not hear my music ? So !
Break the string ; fold music's wing :
Suppose Pauline had bade me sing !

My whole life long I learn'd to love.
This hour my utmost art I prove
And speak my passion — heaven or hell ?
She will not give me heaven ? 'T is well !
Lose who may — I still can say,
Those who win heaven, bless'd are they !

ONE WORD MORE

THERE they are, my fifty men and women
Naming me the fifty poems finish'd !
Take them, Love, the book and me to-
  gether.
Where the heart lies, let the brain lie also.

Rafael made a century of sonnets,
Made and wrote them in a certain volume
Dinted with the silver-pointed pencil
Else he only us'd to draw Madonnas :
These, the world might view — but One,
  the volume.   •
Who that one, you ask ? Your heart in-
  structs you.
Did she live and love it all her lifetime ?
Did she drop, his lady of the sonnets,
Die, and let it drop beside her pillow
Where it lay in place of Rafael's glory,
Rafael's cheek so duteous and so loving —
Cheek, the world was wont to hail a
  painter's,
Rafael's cheek, her love had turn'd a
  poet's ?

You and I would rather read that volume,
(Taken to his beating bosom by it)
Lean and list the bosom-beats of Rafael,
Would we not ? than wonder at Madon-
  nas —
Her, San Sisto names, and Her, Foligno,
Her, that visits Florence in a vision,
Her, that 's left with lilies in the Louvre —
Seen by us and all the world in circle.

You and I will never read that volume.
Guido Reni like his own eye's apple
Guarded long the treasure book and lov'd it.
Guido Reni dying, all Bologna
Cried, and the world with it, " Ours — the
  treasure ! "
Suddenly, as rare things will, it vanish'd.

Dante once prepar'd to paint an angel :
Whom to please ? You whisper " Bea-
  trice."
While he mus'd and traced it and retraced
  it,
(Peradventure with a pen corroded
Still by drops of that hot ink he dipp'd
  for,
When, his left-hand i' the hair o' the
  wicked,
Back he held the brow and prick'd its
  stigma,
Bit into the live man's flesh for parchment,
Loos'd him, laugh'd to see the writing
  rankle,
Let the wretch go festering thro' Flor-
  ence) —
Dante, who lov'd well because he hated,
Hated wickedness that hinders loving,
Dante standing, studying his angel, —
In there broke the folk of his Inferno.
Says he — " Certain people of impor-
  tance "
(Such he gave his daily, dreadful line to)
Enter'd and would seize, forsooth, the poet.
Says the poet — " Then I stopp'd my paint-
  ing."
You and I would rather see that angel,
Painted by the tenderness of Dante,
Would we not ? — than read a fresh In-
  ferno.

You and I will never see that picture.
While he mus'd on love and Beatrice,
While he soften'd o'er his outlin'd angel,
In they broke, those " people of impor-
  tance : "

We and Bice bear the loss forever.
What of Rafael's sonnets, Dante's picture ?

This : no artist lives and loves that longs
    not
Once, and only once, and for One only,
(Ah, the prize !) to find his love a language
Fit and fair and simple and sufficient —
Using nature that 's an art to others,
Not, this one time, art that 's turn'd his
    nature.
Ay, of all the artists living, loving,
None but would forego his proper dowry, —
Does he paint ? he fain would write a
    poem, —
Does he write ? he fain would paint a pic-
    ture,
Put to proof art alien to the artist's,
Once, and only once, and for One only,
So to be the man and leave the artist,
Save the man's joy, miss the artist's sorrow.

Wherefore ? Heaven's gift takes earth's
    abatement !
He who smites the rock and spreads the
    water
Bidding drink and live a crowd beneath
    him,
Even he, the minute makes immortal,
Proves, perchance, his mortal in the minute,
Desecrates, belike, the deed in doing,
While he smites, how can he but remem-
    ber,
So he smote before, in such a peril,
When they stood and mock'd — " Shall
    smiting help us ? "
When they drank and sneer'd — " A stroke
    is easy ! "
When they wip'd their mouths and went
    their journey,
Throwing him for thanks — " But drought
    was pleasant. "

Thus old memories mar the actual tri-
    umph ;
Thus the doing savors of disrelish ;
Thus achievement lacks a gracious some-
    what ;
O'er-importun'd brows becloud the man-
    date,
Carelessness or consciousness, the gesture.
For he bears an ancient wrong about him,
Sees and knows again those phalanx'd faces,
Hears, yet one time more, the 'custom'd
    prelude —

" How shouldst thou, of all men, smite,
    and save us ? "
Guesses what is like to prove the sequel —
" Egypt's flesh-pots —nay, the drought was
    better."

Oh, the crowd must have emphatic war-
    rant !
Theirs, the Sinai-forehead's cloven bril-
    liance,
Right-arm's rod-sweep, tongue's imperial
    fiat.
Never dares the man put off the prophet.

Did he love one face from out the thou
    sands,
(Were she Jethro's daughter, white and
    wifely,
Were she but the Æthiopian bondslave,)
He would envy yon dumb patient camel,
Keeping a reserve of scanty water
Meant to save his own life in the desert ;
Ready in the desert to deliver
(Kneeling down to let his breast be open'd)
Hoard and life together for his mistress.

I shall never, in the years remaining,
Paint you pictures, no, nor carve you
    statues,
Make you music that should all-express me ;
So it seems : I stand on my attainment.
This of verse alone, one life allows me :
Verse and nothing else have I to give you
Other heights in other lives, God willing —
All the gifts from all the heights, your own,
    Love !

Yet a semblance of resource avails us —
Shade so finely touch'd, love's sense must
    seize it.
Take these lines, look lovingly and nearly,
Lines I write the first time and the last
    time.
He who works in fresco, steals a hair-brush
Curbs the liberal hand, subservient proudly,
Cramps his spirit, crowds its all in little,
Makes a strange art of an art familiar,
Fills his lady's missal-marge with flowerets
He who blows thro' bronze, may breathe
    thro' silver,
Fitly serenade a slumbrous princess.
He who writes, may write for once, as I do

Love, you saw me gather men and women,
Live or dead or fashion'd by my fancy,

Enter each and all, and use their service,
Speak from every mouth, — the speech, a
    poem.
Hardly shall I tell my joys and sorrows,
Hopes and fears, belief and disbelieving :
I am mine and yours — the rest be all
    men's,
Karshook, Cleon, Norbert and the fifty.
Let me speak this once in my true person,
Not as Lippo, Roland or Andrea,
Though the fruit of speech be just this
    sentence —
Pray you, look on these my men and wo-
    men,
'Take and keep my fifty poems finish'd ;
Where my heart lies, let my brain lie
    also !
Poor the speech ; be how I speak, for all
    things.

Not but that you know me ! Lo, the
    moon's self !
Here in London, yonder late in Florence,
Still we find her face, the thrice trans-
    figur'd.
Curving on a sky imbrued with color,
Drifted over Fiesole by twilight,
Came she, our new crescent of a hair's-
    breadth.
Full she flar'd it, lamping Samminiato,
Rounder 'twixt the cypresses, and rounder,
Perfect till the nightingales applauded.
Now, a piece of her old self, impoverish'd,
Hard to greet, she traverses the house-
    roofs,
Hurries with unhandsome thrift of silver,
Goes dispiritedly, — glad to finish.
What, there 's nothing in the moon note-
    worthy ?
Nay — for if that moon could love a
    mortal,
Use, to charm him (so to fit a fancy)
All her magic ('t is the old sweet mythos)
She would turn a new side to her mortal,
Side unseen of herdsman, huntsman, steers-
    man —
Blank to Zoroaster on his terrace,
Blind to Galileo on his turret,
Dumb to Homer, dumb to Keats — him,
    even !
Think, the wonder of the moonstruck mor-
    tal —
When she turns round, comes again in
    heaven,
Opens out anew for worse or better ?

Proves she like some portent of an ice-
    berg
Swimming full upon the ship it founders,
Hungry with huge teeth of splinter'd crys-
    tals ?
Proves she as the pav'd-work of a sapphire
Seen by Moses when he climb'd the moun-
    tain ?
Moses, Aaron, Nadab and Abihu
Climb'd and saw the very God, the High-
    est,
Stand upon the pav'd-work of a sapphire.
Like the bodied heaven in his clearness
Shone the stone, the sapphire of that pav'd-
    work,
When they ate and drank and saw God
    also !

What were seen ? None knows, none ever
    shall know.
Only this is sure — the sight were other,
Not the moon's same side, born late in
    Florence,
Dying now impoverish'd here in London.
God be thank'd, the meanest of his crea-
    tures
Boasts two soul-sides, one to face the world
    with,
One to show a woman when he loves
    her.

This I say of me, but think of you, Love !
This to you — yourself my moon of poets !
Ah, but that 's the world's side — there 's
    the wonder —
Thus they see you, praise you, think they
    know you.
There in turn I stand with them and praise
    you,
Out of my own self, I dare to phrase it.
But the best is when I glide from out
    them,
Cross a step or two of dubious twilight,
Come out on the other side, the novel
Silent silver lights and darks undream'd
    of,
Where I hush and bless myself with si-
    lence.

Oh, their Rafael of the dear Madonnas,
Oh, their Dante of the dread Inferno,
Wrote one song — and in my brain I sing
    it,
Drew one angel — borne, see, on my
    bosom.

ABT VOGLER

(AFTER HE HAS BEEN EXTEMPORIZING UPON
THE MUSICAL INSTRUMENT OF HIS INVEN-
TION)

WOULD that the structure brave, the mani-
    fold music I build,
Bidding my organ obey, calling its keys
    to their work,
Claiming each slave of the sound, at a
    touch, as when Solomon will'd
Armies of angels that soar, legions of
    demons that lurk,
Man, brute, reptile, fly, — alien of end and
    of aim,
Adverse, each from the other heaven-
    high, hell-deep remov'd, —
Should rush into sight at once as he nam'd
    the ineffable Name,
And pile him a palace straight, to pleas-
    ure the princess he lov'd !

Would it might tarry like his, the beauti-
    ful building of mine,
This which my keys in a crowd press'd
    and importun'd to raise !
Ah, one and all, how they help'd, would
    dispart now and now combine,
Zealous to hasten the work, heighten
    their master his praise !
And one would bury his brow with a blind
    plunge down to hell,
Burrow awhile and build, broad on the
    roots of things,
Then up again swim into sight, having
    bas'd me my palace well,
Founded it, fearless of flame, flat on the
    nether springs.

And another would mount and march, like
    the excellent minion he was,
Ay, another and yet another, one crowd
    but with many a crest,
Raising my rampir'd walls of gold as trans-
    parent as glass,
Eager to do and die, yield each his place
    to the rest :
For higher still and higher (as a runner tips
    with fire,
When a great illumination surprises a
    festal night —
Outlining round and round Rome's dome
    from space to spire)
Up, the pinnacled glory reach'd, and
    the pride of my soul was in sight.

In sight ? Not half ! for it seem'd it was
    certain, to match man's birth,
Nature in turn conceiv'd, obeying an
    impulse as I ;
And the emulous heaven yearn'd down,
    made effort to reach the earth,
As the earth had done her best, in my
    passion, to scale the sky :
Novel splendors burst forth, grew familiar
    and dwelt with mine,
Not a point nor peak but found, but fix'd
    its wandering star ;
Meteor-moons, balls of blaze : and they did
    not pale nor pine,
For earth had attain'd to heaven, there
    was no more near nor far.

Nay more ; for there wanted not who walk'd
    in the glare and glow,
Presences plain in the place ; or, fresh
    from the Protoplast,
Furnish'd for ages to come, when a kindlier
    wind should blow,
Lur'd now to begin and live, in a house
    to their liking at last ;
Or else the wonderful Dead who have
    pass'd through the body and gone,
But were back once more to breathe in
    an old world worth their new :
What never had been, was now ; what was
    as it shall be anon ;
And what is, — shall I say, match'd
    both ? for I was made perfect too.

All through my keys that gave their sounds
    to a wish of my soul,
All through my soul that prais'd as its
    wish flow'd visibly forth,
All through music and me ! For think, had
    I painted the whole,
Why, there it had stood, to see, nor
    the process so wonder-worth.
Had I written the same, made verse —
    still, effect proceeds from cause,
Ye know why the forms are fair, ye hear
    how the tale is told ;
It is all triumphant art, but art in obedience
    to laws,
Painter and poet are proud, in the artist-
    list enroll'd : —

But here is the finger of God, a flash of the
    will that can,
Existent behind all laws : that made
    them, and, lo, they are !

And I know not if, save in this, such gift
  be allow'd to man,
That out of three sounds he frame, not a
  fourth sound, but a star.
Consider it well : each tone of our scale in
  itself is nought ;
It is everywhere in the world — loud,
  soft, and all is said :
Give it to me to use ! I mix it with two in
  my thought,
And, there ! Ye have heard and seen :
  consider and bow the head !

Well, it is gone at last, the palace of music
  I rear'd ;
Gone ! and the good tears start, the
  praises that come too slow ;
For one is assur'd at first, one scarce can
  say that he fear'd,
That he even gave it a thought, the gone
  thing was to go.
Never to be again ! But many more of the
  kind
As good, nay, better perchance : is this
  your comfort to me ?
To me, who must be sav'd because I cling
  with my mind
To the same, same self, same love, same
  God : ay, what was, shall be.

Therefore to whom turn I but to Thee, the
  ineffable Name ?
Builder and maker, thou, of houses not
  made with hands !
What, have fear of change from thee who
  art ever the same ?
Doubt that thy power can fill the heart
  that thy power expands ?
There shall never be one lost good ! What
  was, shall live as before ;
The evil is null, is nought, is silence im-
  plying sound ;
What was good, shall be good, with, for
  evil, so much good more ;
On the earth the broken arcs ; in the
  heaven, a perfect round.

All we have will'd or hop'd or dream'd of
  good, shall exist ;
Not its semblance, but itself ; no beauty,
  nor good, nor power
Whose voice has gone forth, but each sur-
  vives for the melodist,
When eternity affirms the conception of
  an hour.

The high that prov'd too high, the heroic for
  earth too hard,
The passion that left the ground to lose
  itself in the sky,
Are music sent up to God by the lover and
  the bard ;
Enough that he heard it once : we shall
  hear it by and by.

And what is our failure here but a tri-
  umph's evidence
For the fulness of the days ? Have we
  wither'd or agoniz'd ?
Why else was the pause prolong'd but that
  singing might issue thence ?
Why rush'd the discords in, but that
  harmony should be priz'd ?
Sorrow is hard to bear, and doubt is slow to
  clear,
Each sufferer says his say, his scheme of
  the weal and woe :
But God has a few of us whom he whispers
  in the ear ;
The rest may reason and welcome ; 't is
  we musicians know.

Well, it is earth with me ; silence resumes
  her reign :
I will be patient and proud, and soberly
  acquiesce.
Give me the keys. I feel for the common
  chord again,
Sliding by semitones, till I sink to the
  minor, — yes,
And I blunt it into a ninth, and I stand on
  alien ground,
Surveying awhile the heights I roll'd from
  into the deep :
Which, hark, I have dar'd and done, for
  my resting-place is found,
The C Major of this life : so, now I will
  try to sleep.

PROSPICE

FEAR death ? — to feel the fog in my throat,
  The mist in my face,
When the snows begin, and the blasts denote
  I am nearing the place,
The power of the night, the press of the
  storm,
  The post of the foe ;
Where he stands, the Arch Fear in a
  visible form,
  Yet the strong man must go :

For the journey is done and the summit
attain'd,
And the barriers fall,
Though a battle's to fight ere the guerdon
be gain'd,
The reward of it all.
I was ever a fighter, so — one fight
more,
The best and the last!
I would hate that death bandaged my eyes,
and forbore,
And bade me creep past.
No! let me taste the whole of it, fare like
my peers
The heroes of old,
Bear the brunt, in a minute pay glad life's
arrears
Of pain, darkness and cold.
For sudden the worst turns the best to the
brave,
The black minute's at end,
And the elements' rage, the fiend-voices
that rave,
Shall dwindle, shall blend,
Shall change, shall become first a peace out
of pain.
Then a light, then thy breast,
O thou soul of my soul! I shall clasp thee
again,
And with God be the rest!

MISCONCEPTIONS

THIS is a spray the bird clung to,
Making it blossom with pleasure,
Ere the high tree-top she sprung to,
Fit for her nest and her treasure:
Oh, what a hope beyond measure
Was the poor spray's, which the flying feet
hung to, —
So to be singled out, built in, and sung
to!

This is a heart the queen leant on,
Thrill'd in a minute erratic,
Ere the true bosom she bent on,
Meet for love's regal dalmatic.
Oh, what a fancy ecstatic
Was the poor heart's, ere the wanderer
went on, —
Love to be sav'd for it, proffer'd to, spent
on!

EPITAPH

INSCRIBED ON A ROCK ABOVE THE GRAVE OF
LEVI LINCOLN THAXTER, APRIL, 1885.

THOU whom these eyes saw never, say
friends true,
Who say my soul, help'd onward by my
song,
Though all unwittingly, has help'd thee
too?
I gave but of the little that I knew:
How were the gift requited, while along
Life's path I pace, couldst thou make
weakness strong,
Help me with knowledge — for Life's old.
Death's new!

MUCKLE-MOUTH MEG [1]

FROWN'D the Laird on the Lord: "So, red-
handed I catch thee?
Death-doom'd by our Law of the Border!
We 've a gallows outside and a chiel to dis-
patch thee:
Who trespasses — hangs: all 's in order."

He met frown with smile, did the young
English gallant:
Then the Laird's dame: "Nay, Husband,
I beg!
He 's comely: be merciful! Grace for the
callant
— If he marries our Muckle-mouth
Meg!"

"No mile-wide-mouth'd monster of yours
do I marry:
Grant rather the gallows!" laugh'd he.
"Foul fare kith and kin of you — why do
you tarry?"
"To tame your fierce temper!" quoth
she.

"Shove him quick in the Hole, shut him
fast for a week:
Cold, darkness, and hunger work won-
ders:
Who lion-like roars now, mouse-fashion
will squeak,
And 'it rains' soon succeed to 'it thun-
ders.'"

---

[1] Compare J. Ballantine, p. 83.

A week did he bide in the cold and dark
— Not hunger : for duly at morning
In flitted a lass, and a voice like a lark
Chirp'd, "Muckle-mouth Meg still ye 're
scorning ?

" Go hang, but here 's parritch to hearten
ye first ! "
" Did Meg's muckle-mouth boast within
some
Such music as yours, mine should match it
or burst :
No frog-jaws ! So tell folk, my Win-
some ! "

Soon week came to end, and, from Hole's
door set wide,
Out he march'd, and there waited the
lassie :
" Yon gallows, or Muckle-mouth Meg for
a bride !
Consider ! Sky 's blue and turf 's grassy:

" Life 's sweet ; shall I say ye wed Muckle-
mouth Meg ? "
" Not I," quoth the stout heart : " too
eerie
The mouth that can swallow a bubblyjock's
egg :
Shall I let it munch mine ? Never,
dearie ! "

" Not Muckle-mouth Meg ? Wow, the
obstinate man !
Perhaps he would rather wed me ! "
" Ay, would he — with just for a dowry
your can ! "
" I 'm Muckle-mouth Meg," chirp'd she.

" Then so — so — so — so — " as he kiss'd
her apace —
" Will I widen thee out till thou turnest

From Margaret Minnikin-mou', by God's
grace,
To Muckle-mouth Meg in good earnest ! "

EPILOGUE

AT the midnight in the silence of the sleep-
time,
When you set your fancies free,
Will they pass to where — by death, fools
think, imprison'd —
Low he lies who once so lov'd you, whom
you lov'd so,
• — Pity me ?

Oh to love so, be so lov'd, yet so mis-
taken !
What had I on earth to do
With the slothful, with the mawkish, the
unmanly ?
Like the aimless, helpless, hopeless did I
drivel
— Being — who ?

One who never turn'd his back but march'd
breast forward,
Never doubted clouds would break,
Never dream'd, though right were worsted,
wrong would triumph,
Held we fall to rise, are baffled to fight
better,
Sleep to wake.

No, at noonday in the bustle of man's
work-time
Greet the unseen with a cheer !
Bid him forward, breast and back as either
should be,
" Strive and thrive ! " cry " Speed, — fight
on, fare ever
There as here ! "

Sydney Dobell

HOW 'S MY BOY?

" Ho, Sailor of the sea !
How 's my boy — my boy ? "
" What 's your boy 's name, good wife,
And in what good ship sail'd he ? "

" My boy John —
He that went to sea —
What care I for the ship, sailor ?
My boy 's my boy to me.

"You come back from sea,
And not know my John ?
I might as well have ask'd some landsman
Yonder down in the town.
There 's not an ass in all the parish
But he knows my John.

"How 's my boy — my boy ?
And unless you let me know
I 'll swear you are no sailor,
Blue jacket or no,
Brass buttons or no, sailor,
Anchor and crown or no !
Sure his ship was the ' Jolly Briton ' " —
"Speak low, woman, speak low !"
"And why should I speak low, sailor,
About my own boy John ?
If I was loud as I am proud
I 'd sing him over the town !
Why should I speak low, sailor ?"
"That good ship went down."

"How 's my boy — my boy ?
What care I for the ship, sailor ?
I was never aboard her.
Be she afloat or be she aground,
Sinking or swimming, I 'll be bound,
Her owners can afford her !
I say, how 's my John ?"
"Every man on board went down,
Every man aboard her."
"How 's my boy — my boy ?
What care I for the men, sailor ?
I 'm not their mother —
How 's my boy — my boy ?
Tell me of him and no other !
How 's my boy — my boy ?"

A NUPTIAL EVE

Oh, happy, happy maid,
In the year of war and death
She wears no sorrow !
By her face so young and fair,
By the happy wreath
That rules her happy hair,
She might be a bride to-morrow !
She sits and sings within her moonlit bower,
Her moonlit bower in rosy June,
Yet ah, her bridal breath,
Like fragrance from some sweet night-
   blowing flower,
Moves from her moving lips in many a
   mournful tune !

She sings no song of love's despair,
She sings no lover lowly laid,
No fond peculiar grief
Has ever touched or bud or leaf
Of her unblighted spring.
She sings because she needs must sing ;
She sings the sorrow of the air
Whereof her voice is made.
That night in Britain howsoe'er
On any chords the fingers stray'd
They gave the notes of care.
A dim sad legend old
Long since in some pale shade
Of some far twilight told,
She knows not when or where,
She sings, with trembling hand on trembling
   lute-strings laid : —

The murmur of the mourning ghost
  That keeps the shadowy kine
"Oh, Keith of Ravelston,
  The sorrows of thy line !"

Ravelston, Ravelston,
  The merry path that leads
Down the golden morning hill,
  And thro' the silver meads ;

Ravelston, Ravelston,
  The stile beneath the tree,
The maid that kept her mother's kine,
  The song that sang she !

She sang her song, she kept her kine,
  She sat beneath the thorn
When Andrew Keith of Ravelston
  Rode thro' the Monday morn ;

His henchmen sing, his hawk-bells ring,
  His belted jewels shine !
Oh, Keith of Ravelston,
  The sorrows of thy line !

Year after year, where Andrew came,
  Comes evening down the glade,
And still there sits a moonshine ghost
  Where sat the sunshine maid.

Her misty hair is faint and fair,
  She keeps the shadowy kine ;
Oh, Keith of Ravelston,
  The sorrows of thy line !

I lay my hand upon the stile,
  The stile is lone and cold,

The burnie that goes babbling by
  Says nought that can be told.

Yet, stranger ! here, from year to year,
  She keeps her shadowy kine ;
Oh, Keith of Ravelston,
  The sorrows of thy line !

Step out three steps, where Andrew stood —
  Why blanch thy cheeks for fear ?
The ancient stile is not alone,
  'T is not the burn I hear !

She makes her immemorial moan,
  She keeps her shadowy kine ;
Oh, Keith of Ravelston,
  The sorrows of thy line !

TOMMY'S DEAD

You may give over plough, boys,
You may take the gear to the stead,
All the sweat o' your brow, boys,
Will never get beer and bread.
The seed 's waste, I know, boys,
There 's not a blade will grow, boys,
'T is cropp'd out, I trow, boys,
  And Tommy 's dead.

Send the colt to fair, boys,
He 's going blind, as I said,
My old eyes can't bear, boys,
To see him in the shed ;
The cow 's dry and spare, boys,
She 's neither here nor there, boys,
I doubt she 's badly bred ;

Stop the mill to-morn, boys,
There 'll be no more corn, boys,
Neither white nor red ;
There 's no sign of grass, boys,
You may sell the goat and the ass, boys,
The land 's not what it was, boys,
And the beasts must be fed :
You may turn Peg away, boys,
You may pay off old Ned,
We 've had a dull day, boys,
  And Tommy 's dead.

Move my chair on the floor, boys,
Let me turn my head :
She 's standing there in the door, boys,
Your sister Winifred !
Take her away from me, boys,

Your sister Winifred !
Move me round in my place, boys,
  Let me turn my head,
Take her away from me, boys,
As she lay on her death-bed,
The bones of her thin face, boys,
As she lay on her death-bed !
I don't know how it be, boys,
  When all 's done and said,
But I see her looking at me, boys,
Wherever I turn my head ;
Out of the big oak-tree, boys,
  Out of the garden-bed,
And the lily as pale as she, boys,
And the rose that used to be red.

There 's something not right, boys,
But I think it 's not in my head,
I 've kept my precious sight, boys —
  The Lord be hallowed !
Outside and in
The ground is cold to my tread,
The hills are wizen and thin,
The sky is shrivell'd and shred,
The hedges down by the loan
I can count them bone by bone,
The leaves are open and spread,
But I see the teeth of the land,
And hands like a dead man's hand,
And the eyes of a dead man's head.
There 's nothing but cinders and sand,
The rat and the mouse have fed,
And the summer 's empty and cold ;
Over valley and wold
Wherever I turn my head
There 's a mildew and a mould,
The sun 's going out overhead,
  And I 'm very old,
  And Tommy 's dead.

What am I staying for, boys ?
You 're all born and bred,
'T is fifty years and more, boys,
Since wife and I were wed,
And she 's gone before, boys,
  And Tommy 's dead.

She was always sweet, boys,
Upon his curly head,
She knew she 'd never see 't, boys,
And she stole off to bed ;
I 've been sitting up alone, boys,
For he 'd come home, he said,
But it 's time I was gone, boys,
For Tommy 's dead.

Put the shutters up, boys,
Bring out the beer and bread,
Make haste and sup, boys,
For my eyes are heavy as lead ;
There 's something wrong i' the cup, boys,
There 's something ill wi' the bread,
I don't care to sup, boys,
And Tommy 's dead.

I 'm not right, I doubt, boys,
I 've such a sleepy head,
I shall never more be stout, boys,
You may carry me to bed.
What are you about, boys ?
The prayers are all said,
The fire 's rak'd out, boys,
And Tommy 's dead.

The stairs are too steep, boys,
You may carry me to the head,
The night 's dark and deep, boys,
Your mother 's long in bed,
'Tis time to go to sleep, boys,
And Tommy 's dead.

I 'm not us'd to kiss, boys,
You may shake my hand instead.
All things go amiss, boys,
You may lay me where she is, boys,
And I 'll rest my old head :
'Tis a poor world, this, boys,
And Tommy 's dead.

HOME IN WAR-TIME

SHE turn'd the fair page with her fairer
    hand —
More fair and frail than it was wont to be —
O'er each remember'd thing he lov'd to see
She linger'd, and as with a fairy's wand
Enchanted it to order. Oft she fann'd
New motes into the sun ; and as a bee
Sings thro' a brake of bells, so murmur'd
    she,
And so her patient love did understand
The reliquary room. Upon the sill
She fed his favorite bird. " Ah, Robin,
    sing !
He loves thee." Then she touches a sweet
    string
Of soft recall, and towards the Eastern hill
Smiles all her soul — for him who cannot
    hear
The raven croaking at his carrion ear.

AMERICA

NOR force nor fraud shall sunder us ! O ye
Who north or south, on east or western land,
Native to noble sounds, say truth for truth,
Freedom for freedom, love for love, and God
For God ; O ye who in eternal youth
Speak with a living and creative flood
This universal English, and do stand
Its breathing book ; live worthy of that
    grand
Heroic utterance — parted, yet a whole,
Far yet unsever'd, — children brave and free
Of the great Mother-tongue, and ye shall be
Lords of an empire wide as Shakespeare's
    soul,
Sublime as Milton's immemorial theme,
And rich as Chaucer's speech, and fair as
    Spenser's dream.

EPIGRAM ON THE DEATH OF EDWARD FORBES

NATURE, a jealous mistress, laid him low.
He woo'd and won her ; and, by love made
    bold,
She show'd him more than mortal man
    should know,
Then slew him lest her secret should be told.

SEA BALLAD

FROM " BALDER "

" How many ? " said our good Captain.
" Twenty sail and more."
We were homeward bound,
Scudding in a gale with our jib towards
    the Nore.
Right athwart our tack,
The foe came thick and black,
Like Hell-birds and foul weather — you
    might count them by the score.

The Betsy Jane did slack
To see the game in view.
They knew the Union-Jack,
And the tyrant's flag we knew !
Our Captain shouted " Clear the decks !"
    and the Bo'sun's whistle blew.

Then our gallant Captain,
With his hand he seiz'd the wheel,

And pointed with his stump to the mid-
dle of the foe.
" Hurrah, lads, in we go ! "
(You should hear the British cheer,
Fore and aft.)

" There are twenty sail," sang he,
" But little Betsy Jane bobs to nothing on
the sea ! "
(You should hear the British cheer,
Fore and aft.)

" See yon ugly craft
With the pennon at her main !
Hurrah, my merry boys,
There goes the Betsy Jane ! "
(You should hear the British cheer,
Fore and aft.)

The foe, he beats to quarters, and the
Russian bugles sound ;
And the little Betsy Jane she leaps upon
the sea.
" Port and starboard! " cried our Captain;
" Pay it in, my hearts ! " sang he.

" We 're old England's sons,
And we 'll fight for her to-day ! "
(You should hear the British cheer.
Fore and aft.)
" Fire away ! "
In she runs,
And her guns
Thunder round.

DANTE, SHAKESPEARE, MILTON

FROM "BALDER"

Doctor. Ah ! thou, too,
ad Alighieri, like a waning moon
etting in storm behind a grove of bays !
Balder. Yes, the great Florentine, who
wove his web
nd thrust it into hell, and drew it forth
mmortal, having burn'd all that could burn,
nd leaving only what shall still be found
ntouch'd, nor with the smell of fire upon it,
nder the final ashes of this world.
Doctor. Shakespeare and Milton !
Balder. Switzerland and home.
ne'er see Milton, but I see the Alps,
s once, sole standing on a peak supreme,
o the extremest verge summit and gulf

I saw, height after depth, Alp beyond Alp,
O'er which the rising and the sinking soul
Sails into distance, heaving as a ship
O'er a great sea that sets to strands unseen.
And as the mounting and descending bark,
Borne on exulting by the under deep,
Gains of the wild wave something not the
wave,
Catches a joy of going, and a will
Resistless, and upon the last lee foam
Leaps into air beyond it, so the soul
Upon the Alpine ocean mountain-toss'd,
Incessant carried up to heaven, and plunged
To darkness, and still wet with drops of
death
Held into light eternal, and again
Cast down, to be again uplift in vast
And infinite succession, cannot stay
The mad momentum, but in frenzied sight
Of horizontal clouds and mists and skies
And the untried Inane, springs on the surge
Of things, and passing matter by a force
Material, thro' vacuity careers,
Rising and falling.
Doctor. And my Shakespeare ! Call
Milton your Alps, and which is *he* among
The tops of Andes ? Keep your Paradise,
And Eves, and Adams, but give me the
Earth
That Shakespeare drew, and make it grave
and gay
With Shakespeare's men and women; let
me laugh
Or weep with them, and you — a wager, —
aye,
A wager by my faith — either his muse
Was the recording angel, or that hand
Cherubic, which fills up the Book of Life,
Caught what the last relaxing gripe let
fall
By a death-bed at Stratford, and hence-
forth
Holds Shakespeare's pen. Now strain your
sinews, poet,
And top your Pelion, — Milton Switzerland,
And English Shakespeare —
Balder. This dear English land !
This happy England, loud with brooks and
birds,
Shining with harvests, cool with dewy trees,
And bloom'd from hill to dell ; but whose
best flowers
Are daughters, and Ophelia still more fair
Than any rose she weaves ; whose noblest
floods

The pulsing torrent of a nation's heart;
Whose forests stronger than her native oaks
Are living men ; and whose unfathom'd
   lakes
Forever calm the unforgotten dead
In quiet graveyards willow'd seemly round,
O'er which To-day bends sad, and sees his
   face.
Whose rocks are rights, consolidate of old
Thro' unremember'd years, around whose
   base
The ever-surging peoples roll and roar
Perpetual, as around her cliffs the seas
That only wash them whiter ; and whose
   mountains,
Souls that from this mere footing of the
   earth
Lift their great virtues thro' all clouds of
   Fate
Up to the very heavens, and make them rise
To keep the gods above us !

ON THE DEATH OF MRS. BROWNING

WHICH of the Angels sang so well in
   Heaven
That the approving Archon of the quire
Cried, "Come up hither ! " and he, going
   higher,
Carried a note out of the choral seven ;
Whereat that cherub to whom choice is
   given
Among the singers that on earth aspire
Beckon'd thee from us, and thou, and thy
   lyre
Sudden ascended out of sight ? Yet even
In Heaven thou weepest ! Well, true wife,
   to weep !
Thy voice doth so betray that sweet offence
That no new call should more exalt thee
   hence
But for thy harp. Ah, lend it, and such grace
Shall still advance thy neighbor that thou
   keep
Thy seat, and at thy side a vacant place !

FRAGMENT OF A SLEEP-SONG

SISTER Simplicitie,
Sing, sing a song to me,
Sing me to sleep.

Some legend low and long,
Slow as the summer song
Of the dull Deep.

Some legend long and low,
Whose equal ebb and flow
To and fro creep
On the dim marge of gray
'Tween the soul's night and day,
Washing " awake " away
Into " asleep."

Some legend low and long,
Never so weak or strong
As to let go
While it can hold this heart
Withouten sigh or smart,
Or as to hold this heart
When it sighs " No."

Some long low swaying song,
As the sway'd shadow long
Sways to and fro
Where, thro' the crowing cocks,
And by the swinging clocks,
Some weary mother rocks
Some weary woe.

Sing up and down to me
Like a dream-boat at sea,
So, and still so,
Float through the " then " and " when,"
Rising from when to then,
Sinking from then to when
While the waves go.

Low and high, high and low,
Now and then, then and now,
Now, now ;
And when the now is then, and when the
   then is now,
And when the low is high, and when the
   high is low,
Low, low ;
Let me float, let the boat
Go, go ;
Let me glide, let me slide
Slow, slow ;
Gliding boat, sliding boat,
Slow, slow ;
Glide away, slide away
So, so.

George Meredith

FROM "MODERN LOVE"

"ALL OTHER JOYS"

ALL other joys of life he strove to warm,
And magnify, and catch them to his lip ;
But they had suffer'd shipwreck with the
ship,
And gaz'd upon him sallow from the storm.
Or if Delusion came, 't was but to show
The coming minute mock the one that went.
Cold as a mountain in its star-pitch'd tent
Stood high Philosophy, less friend than foe ;
Whom self-caged Passion, from its prison-
bars,
Is always watching with a wondering hate.
Not till the fire is dying in the grate,
Look we for any kinship with the stars.
Oh, wisdom never comes when it is gold,
And the great price we pay for it full worth !
We have it only when we are half earth :
Little avails that coinage to the old !

HIDING THE SKELETON

AT dinner she is hostess, I am host.
Went the feast ever cheerfuller ?   She
keeps
The topic over intellectual deeps
In buoyancy afloat.   They see no ghost.
With sparkling surface-eyes we ply the
ball :
It is in truth a most contagious game ;
HIDING THE SKELETON shall be its name.
Such play as this the devils might appall !
But here 's the greater wonder ; in that
we,
Enamor'd of our acting and our wits,
Admire each other like true hypocrites.
Warm-lighted glances, Love's Ephemeræ,
Shoot gayly o'er the dishes and the wine.
We waken envy of our happy lot.
Last, sweet, and golden, shows our mar-
riage-knot.
Dear guests, you now have seen Love's
corpse-light shine !

THE COIN OF PITY

THEY say that Pity in Love's service dwells,
. porter at the rosy temple's gate.
I miss'd him going : but it is my fate
To come upon him now beside his wells ;

Whereby I know that I Love's temple leave,
And that the purple doors have clos'd behind.
Poor soul ! if in those early days unkind
Thy power to sting had been but power to
grieve,
We now might with an equal spirit meet,
And not be match'd like innocence and vice
She for the Temple's worship has paid price,
And takes the coin of Pity as a cheat.
She sees thro' simulation to the bone :
What 's best in her impels her to the worst.
Never, she cries, shall Pity soothe Love's
thirst,
Or foul hypocrisy for truth atone !

ONE TWILIGHT HOUR

WE saw the swallows gathering in the sky,
And in the osier-isle we heard their noise.
We had not to look back on summer joys,
Or forward to a summer of bright dye ;
But in the largeness of the evening earth
Our spirits grew as we went side by side.
The hour became her husband, and my bride.
Love that had robb'd us so, thus bless'd our
dearth !
The pilgrims of the year wax'd very loud
In multitudinous chatterings, as the flood
Full brown came from the west, and like
pale blood
Expanded to the upper crimson cloud.
Love, that had robb'd us of immortal things,
This little moment mercifully gave,
And still I see across the twilight wave
The swan sail with her young beneath her
wings.

JUGGLING JERRY

PITCH here the tent, while the old horse
grazes :
By the old hedge-side we 'll halt a stage.
It 's nigh my last above the daisies :
My next leaf 'll be man's blank page.
Yes, my old girl ! and it 's no use crying :
Juggler, constable, king, must bow.
One that outjuggles all 's been spying
Long to have me, and he has me now.

We 've travell'd times to this old common :
Often we 've hung our pots in the gorse.
We 've had a stirring life, old woman !
You, and I, and the old gray horse.

Races, and fairs, and royal occasions,
  Found us coming to their call :
Now they 'll miss us at our stations :
  There 's a Juggler outjuggles all !

Up goes the lark, as if all were jolly !
  Over the duck-pond the willow shakes.
Easy to think that grieving 's folly,
  When the hand 's firm as driven stakes !
Ay ! when we 're strong, and braced, and
    manful,
  Life 's a sweet fiddle ; but we 're a batch
Born to become the Great Juggler's han'-
    ful :
  Balls he shies up, and is safe to catch.

Here 's where the lads of the village cricket ;
  I was a lad not wide from here ;
Couldn't I whip off the bale from the
    wicket ?
  Like an old world those days appear !
Donkey, sheep, geese, and thatch'd ale-
    house — I know them !
They are old friends of my halts, and
    seem,
Somehow, as if kind thanks I owe them :
  Juggling don't hinder the heart's esteem.

Juggling 's no sin, for we must have victual ;
  Nature allows us to bait for the fool.
Holding one's own makes us juggle no lit-
    tle ;
  But, to increase it, hard juggling 's the
    rule.
You that are sneering at my profession,
  Have n't you juggled a vast amount ?
There 's the Prime Minister, in one Ses-
    sion,
  Juggles more games than my sins 'll
    count.

I 've murder'd insects with mock thunder :
  Conscience, for that, in men don't quail.
I 've made bread from the bump of wonder :
  That 's my business, and there 's my tale.
Fashion and rank all prais'd the professor ;
  Ay ! and I 've had my smile from the
    Queen :
Bravo, Jerry ! she meant : God bless her !
  Ain't this a sermon on that scene ?

I 've studied men from my topsy-turvy
  Close, and, I reckon, rather true.
Some are fine fellows : some, right scurvy :
  Most, a dash between the two.

But it 's a woman, old girl, that makes me
  Think more kindly of the race ;
And it 's a woman, old girl, that shakes me
  When the Great Juggler I must face.

We two were married, due and legal :
  Honest we 've liv'd since we 've been one.
Lord ! I could then jump like an eagle :
  You danced bright as a bit o' the sun.
Birds in a May-bush we were ! right
    merry !
  All night we kiss'd — we juggled all day.
Joy was the heart of Juggling Jerry !
  Now from his old girl he 's juggled away.

It 's past parsons to console us :
  No, nor no doctor fetch for me :
I can die without my bolus ;
  Two of a trade, lass, never agree !
Parson and Doctor ! — don't they love
    rarely,
  Fighting the devil in other men's fields !
Stand up yourself and match him fairly ;
  Then see how the rascal yields !

I, lass, have liv'd no gypsy, flaunting
  Finery while his poor helpmate grubs ;
Coin I 've stor'd, and you won't be wanting :
  You shan't beg from the troughs and tubs.
Nobly you 've stuck to me, though in his
    kitchen
  Many a Marquis would hail you Cook !
Palaces you could have rul'd and grown rich
    in,
  But your old Jerry you never forsook.

Hand up the chirper ! ripe ale winks in it ;
  Let 's have comfort and be at peace.
Once a stout draught made me light as a
    linnet.
  Cheer up ! the Lord must have his lease
May be — for none see in that black hol-
    low —
  It 's just a place where we 're held in
    pawn,
And, when the Great Juggler makes us to
    swallow,
  It 's just the sword-trick — I ain't quite
    gone !

Yonder came smells of the gorse, so nutty,
  Gold-like and warm ; it 's the prime of
    May.
Better than mortar, brick, and putty,
  Is God's house on a blowing day.

Lean me more up the mound ; now I feel
   it :
All   the   old   heath-smells !   Ain't it
   strange ?
There 's the world laughing, as if to conceal
   it,
But He 's by us, juggling the change.

I mind it well, by the sea-beach lying,
   Once — it 's long gone — when two gulls
   we beheld,
Which, as the moon got up, were flying
   Down a big wave that spark'd and
   swell'd.
Crack ! went a gun : one fell : the second
   Wheel'd round him twice, and was off
   for new luck :
There   in   the   dark   her white wing
   beckon'd : —
Drop me a kiss — I 'm the bird dead-
   struck !

THE LARK ASCENDING

HE rises and begins to round,
He drops the silver chain of sound
Of many links without a break,
In chirrup, whistle, slur and shake,
All intervolv'd and spreading wide,
Like water-dimples down a tide
Where ripple ripple overcurls
And eddy into eddy whirls ;
A press of hurried notes that run
So fleet they scarce are more than one,
Yet changingly the trills repeat
And linger ringing while they fleet,
Sweet to the quick o' the ear, and dear
To her beyond the handmaid ear,
Who sits beside our inner springs,
Too often dry for this he brings,
Which seems the very jet of earth
At sight of sun, her music's mirth,
As up he wings the spiral stair,
A song of light, and pierces air
With fountain ardor, fountain play,
To reach the shining tops of day,
And drink in everything discern'd
An ecstasy to music turn'd,
Impell'd by what his happy bill
Disperses ; drinking, showering still,
Unthinking save that he may give
His voice the outlet, there to live
Renew'd in endless notes of glee,
So thirsty of his voice is he,

For all to hear and all to know
That he is joy, awake, aglow,
The tumult of the heart to hear
Through pureness filter'd crystal-clear,
And know the pleasure sprinkled bright
By simple singing of delight,
Shrill, irreflective, unrestrain'd,
Rapt, ringing, on the jet sustain'd
Without a break, without a fall,
Sweet-silvery, sheer lyrical,
Perennial, quavering up the chord
Like myriad dews of sunny sward
That trembling into fulness shine,
And sparkle dropping argentine ;
Such wooing as the ear receives
From zephyr caught in choric leaves
Of aspens when their chattering net
Is flush'd to white with shivers wet ;
And such the water-spirit's chime
On mountain heights in morning's prime,
Too freshly sweet to seem excess,
Too animate to need a stress ;•
But wider over many heads
The starry voice ascending spreads,
Awakening, as it waxes thin,
The best in us to him akin ;
And every face to watch him rais'd,
Puts on the light of children prais'd,
So rich our human pleasure ripes
When sweetness on sincereness pipes,
Though nought be promis'd from the seas,
But only a soft-ruffling breeze
Sweep glittering on a still content,
Serenity in ravishment.

For singing till his heaven fills,
'T is love of earth that he instils,
And ever winging up and up,
Our valley is his golden cup,
And he the wine which overflows
To lift us with him as he goes :
The woods and brooks, the sheep and kine
He is, the hills, the human line,
The meadows green, the fallows brown,
The dreams of labor in the town ;
He sings the sap, the quicken'd veins ;
The wedding song of sun and rains
He is, the dance of children, thanks
Of sowers, shout of primrose-banks,
And eye of violets while they breathe ;
All these the circling song will wreathe,
And you shall hear the herb and tree,
The better heart of men shall see,
Shall feel celestially, as long
As you crave nothing save the song.

Was never voice of ours could say
Our inmost in the sweetest way,
Like yonder voice aloft, and link
All hearers in the song they drink :
Our wisdom speaks from failing blood,
Our passion is too full in flood,
We want the key of his wild note
Of truthful in a tuneful throat,
The song seraphically free
Of taint of personality,
So pure that it salutes the suns
The voice of one for millions,
In whom the millions rejoice
For giving their one spirit voice.

Yet men have we, whom we revere,
Now names, and men still housing here,
Whose lives, by many a battle-dint
Defaced, and grinding wheels on flint,
Yield substance, though they sing not,
    sweet
For song our highest heaven to greet :
Whom heavenly singing gives us new,
Enspheres them brilliant in our blue,
From firmest base to farthest leap,
Because their love of Earth is deep,
And they are warriors in accord
With life to serve and pass reward,
So touching purest and so heard
In the brain's reflex of yon bird ;
Wherefore their soul in me, or mine,
Through self-forgetfulness divine,
In them, that song aloft maintains,
To fill the sky and thrill the plains
With showerings drawn from human stores,
As he to silence nearer soars,
Extends the world at wings and dome,
More spacious making more our home,
Till lost on his aërial rings
In light, and then the fancy sings.

LUCIFER IN STARLIGHT

On a starr'd night Prince Lucifer uprose.
Tir'd of his dark dominion swung the
    fiend
Above the rolling ball in cloud part screen'd,
Where sinners hugg'd their spectre of re-
    pose.
Poor prey to his hot fit of pride were those.
And now upon his Western wing he lean'd,
Now his huge bulk o'er Africa careen'd,
Now the black planet shadow'd Arctic
    snows.

Soaring through wider zones that prick'd
    his scars
With memory of the old revolt from Awe,
He reach'd a middle height, and at the
    stars,
Which are the brain of heaven, he look'd,
    and sank.
Around the ancient track march'd, rank on
    rank,
The army of unalterable law.

THE SPIRIT OF SHAKESPEARE

I

Thy greatest knew thee, Mother Earth ;
    unsour'd
He knew thy sons. He prob'd from hell to
    hell
Of human passions, but of love deflower'd
His wisdom was not, for he knew thee well.
Thence came the honey'd corner at his lips,
The conquering smile wherein his spirit
    sails
Calm as the God who the white sea-wave
    whips,
Yet full of speech and intershifting tales,
Close mirrors of us : thence had he the
    laugh
We feel is thine ; broad as ten thousand
    beeves
At pasture ! thence thy songs, that winnow
    chaff
From grain, bid sick Philosophy's last
    leaves
Whirl, if they have no response — they en-
    forced
To fatten Earth when from her soul di-
    vorced.

II

How smiles he at a generation rank'd
In gloomy noddings over life ! They pass.
Not he to feed upon a breast unthank'd,
Or eye a beauteous face in a crack'd glass.
But he can spy that little twist of brain
Which mov'd some weighty leader of the
    blind,
Unwitting 't was the goad of personal pain,
To view in curs'd eclipse our Mother's mind,
And show us of some rigid harridan
The wretched bondmen till the end of time
O liv'd the Master now to paint us Man,
That little twist of brain would ring a chime

Of whence it came and what it caus'd, to
    start
Thunders of laughter, clearing air and
    heart.

THE TWO MASKS

MELPOMENE among her livid people,
Ere stroke of lyre, upon Thaleia looks,
Warn'd by old contests that one museful
    ripple,
Along those lips of rose with tendril hooks,
Forbodes disturbance in the springs of pa-
    thos,
Perchance may change of masks midway
    demand,

Albeit the man rise mountainous as Athos,
The woman wild as Cape Leucadia stand.

For this the Comic Muse exacts of crea-
    tures
Appealing to the fount of tears : that they
Strive never to outleap our human fea-
    tures,
And do Right Reason's ordinance obey,
In peril of the hum to laughter nighest.
But prove they under stress of action's
    fire
Nobleness, to that test of Reason high-
    est,
She bows : she waves them for the loftier
    lyre.

Sebastian Evans

A DIRGE FOR SUMMER

SUMMER dieth : — o'er his bier
Chant a requiem low and clear !
Chant it for his dying flowers,
Chant it for his flying hours.
Let them wither all together
Now the world is past the prime
Of the golden olden-time.

Let them die, and dying Summer
Yield his kingdom to the comer
From the islands of the West :
He is weary, let him rest !
And let mellow Autumn's yellow
Fall upon the leafy prime
Of the golden olden-time.

Go, ye days, your deeds are done !
Be yon clouds about the sun
Your imperial winding-sheet ;
Let the night winds as they fleet
Tell the story of the glory
Of the free great-hearted prime
Of the golden olden-time.

WHAT THE TRUMPETER SAID

AT a pot-house bar as I chanced to pass
I saw three men by the flare of the gas :
Soldiers two, with their red-coats gay,
And the third from Chelsea, a pensioner
    gray,

With three smart hussies as bold as they.
Drunk and swearing and swaggering all,
With their foul songs scaring the quiet
    Mall,
While the clash of glasses and clink of
    spurs
Kept time to the roystering quiristers,
And the old man sat and stamp'd with his
    stump :
When I heard a trumpeter trumpet a
    trump : —
    " To the wars ! — To the wars !
        March, march !
    Quit your petty little tittle-tattle,
    Quit the bottle for the battle,
        And march !
    To the wars, to the wars !
    March, march with a tramp !
        To the wars !
Up, you toper at your tipple, bottle after
    bottle at the tap !
Quit your pretty dirty Betty ! Clap her
    garter in your cap,
        And march !
    To the trench and the sap !
    To the little victual of the camp !
    To the little liquor of the camp !
    To the breach and the storm !
    To the roaring and the glory of the
        wars !
    To the rattle and the battle and the
        scars ! "
Trumpeter, trumpet it out !

Christina Georgina Rossetti

THE UNSEEN WORLD

AT HOME

WHEN I was dead, my spirit turn'd
To seek the much-frequented house :
I pass'd the door, and saw my friends
Feasting beneath green orange-boughs ;
From hand to hand they push'd the wine,
They suck'd the pulp of plum and peach ;
They sang, they jested, and they laugh'd,
For each was lov'd of each.

I listen'd to their honest chat :
Said one : " To-morrow we shall be
Plod plod along the featureless sands,
And coasting miles and miles of sea."
Said one : " Before the turn of tide
We will achieve the eyrie-seat."
Said one : " To-morrow shall be like
To-day, but much more sweet."

" To-morrow," said they, strong with hope,
And dwelt upon the pleasant way :
" To-morrow," cried they, one and all,
While no one spoke of yesterday.
Their life stood full at blessed noon ;
I, only I, had pass'd away :
" To-morrow and to-day," they cried ;
I was of yesterday.

I shiver'd comfortless, but cast
No chill across the table-cloth ;
I, all forgotten, shiver'd, sad
To stay, and yet to part how loth :
I pass'd from the familiar room,
I who from love had pass'd away,
Like the remembrance of a guest
That tarrieth but a day.

REMEMBER

REMEMBER me when I am gone away,
Gone far away into the silent land ;
When you can no more hold me by the
hand,
Nor I half turn to go yet turning stay.
Remember me when no more, day by day,
You tell me of our future that you plann'd :
Only remember me ; you understand
It will be late to counsel then or pray.

Yet if you should forget me for a while
And afterwards remember, do not grieve :
For if the darkness and corruption leave
A vestige of the thoughts that once I
had,
Better by far you should forget and smile
Than that you should remember and be
sad.

AFTER DEATH

THE curtains were half drawn, the floor
. was swept
And strewn with rushes, rosemary and may
Lay thick upon the bed on which I lay,
Where through the lattice ivy-shadows
crept.
He lean'd above me, thinking that I slept
And could not hear him ; but I heard him
say :
" Poor child, poor child : " and as he turn'd
away
Came a deep silence, and I knew he wept.
He did not touch the shroud, or raise the
fold
That hid my face, or take my hand in
his,
Or ruffle the smooth pillows for my head :
He did not love me living ; but once dead
He pitied me ; and very sweet it is
To know he still is warm though I am cold.

WIFE TO HUSBAND

PARDON the faults in me,
For the love of years ago :
Good-by.
I must drift across the sea,
I must sink into the snow,
I must die.

You can bask in this sun,
You can drink wine, and eat :
Good-by.
I must gird myself and run,
Though with unready feet :
I must die.

Blank sea to sail upon,
Cold bed to sleep in :
Good-by.

While you clasp, I must be gone
For all your weeping :
I must die.

A kiss for one friend,
And a word for two, —
Good-by : —
A lock that you must send,
A kindness you must do :
I must die.

Not a word for you,
Not a lock or kiss,
Good-by.
We, one, must part in two ;
Verily death is this :
I must die.

UP-HILL

Does the road wind up-hill all the way ?
Yes, to the very end.
Will the day's journey take the whole long
day ?
From morn to night, my friend.

But is there for the night a resting-place ?
A roof for when the slow dark hours be-
gin.
May not the darkness hide it from my
face ?
You cannot miss that inn.

Shall I meet other wayfarers at night ?
Those who have gone before.
Then must I knock, or call when just in
sight ?
They will not keep you standing at that
door.

Shall I find comfort, travel-sore and weak ?
Of labor you shall find the sum.
Will there be beds for me and all who
seek ?
Yea, beds for all who come.

"IT IS FINISHED"

Dear Lord, let me recount to Thee
Some of the great things thou hast done
For me, even me
Thy little one.

It was not I that car'd for Thee, —
But Thou didst set Thy heart upon
Me, even me
Thy little one.

And therefore was it sweet to Thee
To leave Thy Majesty and Throne,
And grow like me
A Little One,

A swaddled Baby on the knee
Of a dear Mother of Thine own,
Quite weak like me
Thy little one.

Thou didst assume my misery,
And reap the harvest I had sown,
Comforting me
Thy little one.

Jerusalem and Galilee, —
Thy love embraced not those alone,
But also me
Thy little one.

Thy unblemish'd Body on the Tree
Was bar'd and broken to atone
For me, for me
Thy little one.

Thou lovedst me upon the Tree, —
Still me, hid by the ponderous stone,
Me always, — me
Thy little one.

And love of me arose with Thee
When death and hell lay overthrown :
Thou lovedst me
Thy little one.

And love of me went up with Thee
To sit upon Thy Father's Throne :
Thou lovest me
Thy little one :

Lord, as Thou me, so would I Thee
Love in pure love's communion,
For Thou lov'st me
Thy little one :

Which love of me brings back with Thee
To Judgment when the Trump is blown,
Still loving me
Thy little one.

FROM "MONNA INNOMINATA"

ABNEGATION

If there be any one can take my place
And make you happy whom I grieve to
 grieve,
Think not that I can grudge it, but be-
 lieve
I do commend you to that nobler grace,
That readier wit than mine, that sweeter
 face ;
Yea, since your riches make me rich, con-
 ceive
I too am crown'd, while bridal crowns I
 weave,
And thread the bridal dance with jocund
 pace.
For if I did not love you, it might be
That I should grudge you some one dear
 delight ;
But since the heart is yours that was mine
 own,
Your pleasure is my pleasure, right my
 right,
Your honorable freedom makes me free,
And you companion'd I am not alone.

TRUST

If I could trust mine own self with your
 fate,
Shall I not rather trust it in God's
 hand ?
Without whose will one lily doth not
 stand,
Nor sparrow fall at his appointed date ;
Who numbereth the innumerable sand,
Who weighs the wind and water with a
 weight,
To whom the world is neither small nor
 great,
Whose knowledge foreknew every plan we
 plann'd.
Searching my heart for all that touches
 you,
I find there only love and love's good-
 will
Helpless to help and impotent to do,
Of understanding dull, of sight most dim ;
And therefore I commend you back to
 Him
Whose love your love's capacity can fill.

FLUTTERED WINGS

The splendor of the kindling day,
 The splendor of the setting sun,
These move my soul to wend its way,
 And have done
With all we grasp and toil amongst and
 say.

The paling roses of a cloud,
 The fading bow that arches space,
These woo my fancy toward my shroud ;
 Toward the place
Of faces veil'd, and heads discrown'd and
 bow'd.

The nation of the awful stars,
 The wandering star whose blaze is
 brief,
These make me beat against the bars
 Of my grief ;
My tedious grief, twin to the life it mars.

O fretted heart toss'd to and fro,
 So fain to flee, so fain to rest !
All glories that are high or low,
 East or west,
Grow dim to thee who art so fain to go.

PASSING AND GLASSING

All things that pass
 Are woman's looking-glass ;
They show her how her bloom must fade,
And she herself be laid
With wither'd roses in the shade ;
 With wither'd roses and the fallen peach,
 Unlovely, out of reach
 Of summer joy that was.

All things that pass
 Are woman's tiring-glass ;
The faded lavender is sweet,
Sweet the dead violet
Cull'd and laid by and car'd for yet ;
 The dried-up violets and dried lavender
 Still sweet, may comfort her,
 Nor need she cry Alas !

All things that pass
 Are wisdom's looking-glass ;
Being full of hope and fear, and still
Brimful of good or ill,
According to our work and will ;

For there is nothing new beneath the sun ;
Our doings have been done,
And that which shall be was.

THE THREAD OF LIFE

THE irresponsive silence of the land,
The irresponsive sounding of the sea,
Speak both one message of one sense to
    me : —
Aloof, aloof, we stand aloof, so stand
Thou too aloof, bound with the flawless
    band
Of inner solitude ; we bind not thee ;
But who from thy self-chain shall set thee
    free ?
What heart shall touch thy heart ? what
    hand thy hand ? —
And I am sometimes proud and sometimes
    meek,
And sometimes I remember days of old
When fellowship seem'd not so far to seek
And all the world and I seem'd much less
    cold,
And at the rainbow's foot lay surely gold,
And hope felt strong and life itself not
    weak.

FROM " LATER LIFE "

VI

WE lack, yet cannot fix upon the lack :
Not this, nor that ; yet somewhat, cer-
    tainly.
We see the things we do not yearn to see
Around us : and what see we glancing back ?
Lost hopes that leave our hearts upon the
    rack,
Hopes that were never ours yet seem'd to
    be,
For which we steer'd on life's salt stormy
    sea
Braving the sunstroke and the frozen pack.
If thus to look behind is all in vain,
And all in vain to look to left or right,
Why face we not our future once again,
Launching with hardier hearts across the
    main,
Straining dim eyes to catch the invisible
    sight,
And strong to bear ourselves in patient
    pain ?

IX

STAR Sirius and the Pole Star dwell afar
Beyond the drawings each of other's
    strength :
One blazes through the brief bright sum-
    mer's length
Lavishing life-heat from a flaming car ;
While one unchangeable upon a throne
Broods o'er the frozen heart of earth
    alone,
Content to reign the bright particular star
Of some who wander or of some who
    groan.
They own no drawings each of other's
    strength,
Nor vibrate in a visible sympathy,
Nor veer along their courses each toward
    each :
Yet are their orbits pitch'd in harmony
Of one dear heaven, across whose depth
    and length
Mayhap they talk together without speech.

AN ECHO FROM WILLOWWOOD

" OH YE, ALL YE THAT WALK IN WILLOW-
                    WOOD "

Two gaz'd into a pool, he gaz'd and she,
Not hand in hand, yet heart in heart, I
    think,
Pale and reluctant on the water's brink,
As on the brink of parting which must be.
Each eyed the other's aspect, she and he,
Each felt one hungering heart leap up and
    sink,
Each tasted bitterness which both must
    drink,
There on the brink of life's dividing sea.
Lilies upon the surface, deep below
Two wistful faces craving each for each,
Resolute and reluctant without speech : —
A sudden ripple made the faces flow
One moment join'd, to vanish out of reach :
So these hearts join'd, and ah ! were parted
    so.

TWIST ME A CROWN

TWIST me a crown of wind-flowers ;
    That I may fly away
To hear the singers at their song,
    And players at their play.

Put on your crown of wind-flowers :
But whither would you go ?
Beyond the surging of the sea
And the storms that blow.

Alas ! your crown of wind-flowers
Can never make you fly :
I twist them in a crown to-day,
And to-night they die.

GOOD-BY

" GOOD-BY in fear, good-by in sorrow,
Good-by, and all in vain,
Never to meet again, my dear — "
" Never to part again."
" Good-by to-day, good-by to-morrow,
Good-by till earth shall wane,
Never to meet again, my dear — "
" Never to part again."

Robert, Earl of Lytton

("OWEN MEREDITH")

INDIAN LOVE-SONG

MY body sleeps : my heart awakes.
My lips to breathe thy name are mov'd
In slumber's ear : then slumber breaks ;
And I am drawn to thee, belov'd.
Thou drawest me, thou drawest me,
Through sleep, through night. I hear
the rills,
And hear the leopard in the hills,
And down the dark I feel to thee.

The vineyards and the villages
Were silent in the vales, the rocks ;
I follow'd past the myrrhy trees,
And by the footsteps of the flocks.
Wild honey, dropp'd from stone to stone,
Where bees have been, my path suggests.
The winds are in the eagles' nests.
The moon is hid. I walk alone.

Thou drawest me, thou drawest me
Across the glimmering wildernesses,
And drawest me, my love, to thee,
With dove's eyes hidden in thy tresses.
The world is many : my love is one ;
I find no likeness for my love.
The cinnamons grow in the grove ;
The Golden Tree grows all alone.

O who hath seen her wondrous hair,
Or seen my dove's eyes in the woods ?
Or found her voice upon the air,
Her steps along the solitudes ?
Or where is beauty like to hers ?
She draweth me, she draweth me.
I sought her by the incense-tree,
And in the aloes, and in the firs.

Where art thou, O my heart's delight,
With dove's eyes hidden in thy locks ?
My hair is wet with dews of night.
My feet are torn upon the rocks.
The cedarn scents, the spices, fail
About me. Strange and stranger seems
The path. There comes a sound of
streams
Above the darkness on the vale.

No trees drop gums ; but poison flowers
From rifts and clefts all round me fall ;
The perfumes of thy midnight bowers,
The fragrance of thy chambers, all
Is drawing me, is drawing me.
Thy baths prepare ; anoint thine hair ;
Open the window : meet me there :
I come to thee, to thee, to thee !

Thy lattices are dark, my own.
Thy doors are still. My love, look out.
Arise, my dove with tender tone.
The camphor-clusters all about
Are whitening. Dawn breaks silently.
And all my spirit with the dawn
Expands ; and, slowly, slowly drawn,
Through mist and darkness moves toward
thee.

AUX ITALIENS

AT Paris it was, at the Opera there ; —
And she look'd like a queen in a book,
that night,
With the wreath of pearl in her raven
hair,
And the brooch on her breast, so bright.

Of all the operas that Verdi wrote,
  The best, to my taste, is the Trovatore ;
And Mario can soothe with a tenor note
  The souls in Purgatory.

The moon on the tower slept soft as snow :
  And who was not thrill'd in the strangest
    way,
As we heard him sing, while the gas burn'd
    low,
  " Non ti scordar di me " ?

The Emperor there, in his box of state,
  Look'd grave, as if he had just then seen
The red flag wave from the city-gate
  Where his eagles in bronze had been.

The Empress, too, had a tear in her eye.
  You 'd have said that her fancy had gone
    back again,
For one moment, under the old blue sky,
  To the old glad life in Spain.

Well ! there in our front-row box we sat,
  Together, my bride-betroth'd and I ;
My gaze was fix'd on my opera-hat,
  And hers on the stage hard by.

And both were silent, and both were sad.
  Like a queen she lean'd on her full white
    arm,
With that regal, indolent air she had ;
  So confident of her charm !

I have not a doubt she was thinking then
  Of her former lord, good soul that he was !
Who died the richest and roundest of men,
  The Marquis of Carabas.

I hope that, to get to the kingdom of heaven,
  Through a needle's eye he had not to pass.
I wish him well, for the jointure given
  To my lady of Carabas.

Meanwhile, I was thinking of my first love,
  As I had not been thinking of aught for
    years,
Till over my eyes there began to move
  Something that felt like tears.

I thought of the dress that she wore last time,
  When we stood, 'neath the cypress-trees,
    together,
In that lost land, in that soft clime,
  In the crimson evening weather ;

Of that muslin dress (for the eve was
    hot),
  And her warm white neck in its golden
    chain,
And her full, soft hair, just tied in a knot,
  And falling loose again ;

And the jasmine-flower in her fair young
    breast,
  (O the faint, sweet smell of that jasmine-
    flower !)
And the one bird singing alone to his nest,
  And the one star over the tower.

I thought of our little quarrels and strife,
  And the letter that brought me back my
    ring.
And it all seem'd then, in the waste of
    life,
  Such a very little thing !

For I thought of her grave below the hill,
  Which the sentinel cypress-tree stands
    over ;
And I thought . . . " were she only living
    still,
  How I could forgive her, and love her ! "

And I swear, as I thought of her thus, in
    that hour,
  And of how, after all, old things were
    best,
That I smelt the smell of that jasmine-
    flower
  Which she used to wear in her breast.

It smelt so faint, and it smelt so sweet,
  It made me creep, and it made me cold !
Like the scent that steals from the crum-
    bling sheet
  Where a mummy is half unroll'd.

And I turn'd, and look'd. She was sitting
    there
  In a dim box, over the stage ; and dress'd
In that muslin dress with that full soft
    hair,
  And that jasmine in her breast !

I was here ; and she was there ;
  And the glittering horseshoe curv'd be-
    tween : —
From my bride-betroth'd, with her raven
    hair,
  And her sumptuous scornful mien,

To my early love, with her eyes downcast,
  And over her primrose face the shade
(In short from the Future back to the Past),
  There was but a step to be made.

To my early love from my future bride
  One moment I look'd. Then I stole to
    the door,
I travers'd the passage ; and down at her
    side
  I was sitting, a moment more.

My thinking of her, or the music's strain,
  Or something which never will be ex-
    prest,
Had brought her back from the grave
    again,
  With the jasmine in her breast.

She is not dead, and she is not wed !
  But she loves me now, and she lov'd me
    then !
And the very first word that her sweet lips
    said,
  My heart grew youthful again.

The Marchioness there, of Carabas,
  She is wealthy, and young, and handsome
    still,
And but for her . . . well, we 'll let that
    pass,
  She may marry whomever she will.

But I will marry my own first love,
  With her primrose face : for old things
    are best,
And the flower in her bosom, I prize it
    above
  The brooch in my lady's breast.

The world is fill'd with folly and sin,
  And Love must cling where it can, I
    say :
For Beauty is easy enough to win ;
  But one is n't lov'd every day.

And I think, in the lives of most women
    and men,
  There 's a moment when all would go
    smooth and even,
If only the dead could find out when
  To come back, and be forgiven.

But O the smell of that jasmine-flower !
  And O that music ! and O the way

That voice rang out from the donjon
    tower,
  Non ti scordar di me,
  Non ti scordar di me!

THE CHESS-BOARD

My little love, do you remember,
  Ere we were grown so sadly wise,
Those evenings in the bleak December,
Curtain'd warm from the snowy weather,
When you and I play'd chess together,
  Checkmated by each other's eyes ?
Ah, still I see your soft white hand
Hovering warm o'er Queen and Knight !
  Brave Pawns in valiant battle stand ;
The double Castles guard the wings ;
The Bishop, bent on distant things,
Moves, sidling through the fight.
  Our fingers touch ; our glances meet,
  And falter ; falls your golden hair
Against my cheek ; your bosom sweet
Is heaving. Down the field, your Queen
Rides slow her soldiery all between,
  And checks me unaware.
  Ah me ! the little battle 's done,
Dispers'd is all its chivalry ;
Full many a move, since then, have we
'Mid Life's perplexing checkers made,
And many a game with Fortune play'd, —
  What is it we have won ?
This, this at least — if this alone ; —
That never, never, never more,
As in those old still nights of yore
  (Ere we were grown so sadly wise),
Can you and I shut out the skies,
Shut out the world, and wintry weather,
And, eyes exchanging warmth with eyes,
Play chess, as then we play'd, together !

TEMPORA ACTA

FROM " BABYLONIA "

O, FOR the times which were (if any
  Time be heroic) heroic indeed !
    When the men were few,
    And the deeds to do
Were mighty, and many,
    And each man in his hand held a noble
      deed.
Now the deeds are few,
  And the men are many,
    And each man has, at most, but a noble
      need.

THE DINNER HOUR

FROM "LUCILE"

O HOUR of all hours, the most blest upon
    earth,
Blest hour of our dinners !
        The land of his birth;
The face of his first love ; the bills that he
    owes ;
The twaddle of friends, and venom of foes;
The sermon he heard when to church he
    last went ;
The money he borrow'd, the money he
    spent ;
All of these things a man, I believe, may
    forget,
And not be the worse for forgetting; but yet
Never, never, oh, never ! earth's luckiest
    sinner
Hath unpunish'd forgotten the hour of his
    dinner !
Indigestion, that conscience of every bad
    stomach,
Shall relentlessly gnaw and pursue him with
    some ache
Or some pain ; and trouble, remorseless,
    his best ease,
As the Furies once troubled the sleep of
    Orestes.

We may live without poetry, music, and art ;
We may live without conscience, and live
    without heart ;
We may live without friends ; we may live
    without books ;
But civilized man cannot live without cooks.
He may live without books, — what is
    knowledge but grieving ?
He may live without hope, — what is hope
    but deceiving ?
He may live without love, — what is pas-
    sion but pining ?
But where is the man that can live without
    dining ?

THE LEGEND OF THE DEAD
LAMBS

DEATH, though already in the world, as
    yet
Had only tried his timorous tooth to whet
On grass and leaves. But he began to grow
Greedier, greater, and resolv'd to know

The taste of stronger food than such light
    fare.
To feed on human flesh he did not dare,
Till many a meaner meal had slowly given
The young destroyer strength to vanquish
    even
His restless rival in destruction, Man.
Meanwhile, on lesser victims he began
To test his power ; and in a cold spring
    night
Two weanling lambs first perish'd from his
    bite.
The bleatings of their dam at break of day
Drew to the spot where her dead lamb-
    kins lay
The other beasts. They, understanding not,
In wistful silence round that fatal spot
Stood eyeing the dead lambs with looks
    forlorn.

Adam, who was upon the march that morn,
Missing his bodyguard, turn'd back to see
What they were doing ; and there also he
Saw the two frozen lambkins lying dead,
But understood not. At the last he said,
" Since the lambs cannot move, methinks
    't were best
That I should carry them."

                        So on his breast
He laid their little bodies, and again
Set forward, follow'd o'er the frosty plain
By his bewilder'd flocks. And in dismay
They held their peace. That was a silent
    day.
At night he laid the dead lambs on the
    grass.
That night still colder than the other was,
And when the morning broke there were
    two more
Dead lambs to carry. Adam took the four,
And in his arms he bore them, no great way,
Till eventide. That was a sorrowful day.

But, ere the next, two other lambkins died.
Frost-bitten in the dark. Then Adam tried
To carry them, all six. But the poor sheep
Said, " Nay, we thank thee, Adam. Let
    them sleep !
Thou canst not carry them. 'T is all in vain.
We fear our lambkins will not wake again.
And, if they wake, they could not walk —
    for see,
Their little legs are stiffen'd. Let them
    be ! "

So Adam left the lambs.   And all the
  herd
Follow'd him sorrowing, and not a word
Was spoken.   Never until then had they
Their own forsaken.   That was the worst
  day.

Eve said to Adam, as they went along,
" Adam, last night the cold was bitter
  strong.
Warm fleeces to keep out the freezing wind
Have those six lambkins thou hast left
  behind ;
But they will never need them any more.
Go, fetch them here ! and I will make, be-
  fore
This day be done, stout garments for us
  both,
Lest we, too, wake no more."   Said Adam,
  loth
To do her bidding, " Why dost thou sup-
  pose
Our lambs will nevermore have need of
  those
Warm fleeces ?   They are sleeping."   But
  Eve said,
" They are not sleeping, Adam.   They are
  dead."
" Dead ?   What is that ? "   " I know not.
  But I know
That they no more can feel the north wind
  blow,
Nor the sun burn.   They cannot hear the
  bleat
Of their own mothers, cannot suffer heat
Or cold, or thirst or hunger, weariness
Or want, again."   " How dost thou know
  all this ? "
Ask'd Adam.   And Eve whisper'd in his
  ear,
" The Serpent told me."   " Is the Serpent
  here ?
If here he be, why hath he," Adam cried,
" No good gift brought me ? "   Adam's
  wife replied,
" The best of gifts, if rightly understood,
He brings thee, and that gift is counsel
  good.

The Serpent is a prudent beast ; and right !
For we were miserably cold last night,
And may to-night be colder ; and hard by
Those dead lambs in their woolly fleeces
  lie,
Yet need them not as we do.   They are dead.
Go fetch them hither ! "

                  Adam shook his head,
But went.
    Next morning, to the beasts' surprise,
Adam and Eve appear'd before their eyes
In woollen fleeces warmly garmented.
And all the beasts to one another said,
" How wonderful is Man, who can make
  wool
As good as sheep's wool, and more beauti-
  ful ! "

Only the Fox, who sniff'd and grinn'd, had
  guess'd
Man's unacknowledged theft : and to the
  rest
He sneer'd, " How wonderful is Woman's
  whim !
See, Adam's wife hath made a sheep of
  him ! "

THE UTMOST

SOME clerks aver that as the tree doth
  fall
Even forever so that tree shall lie,
And that Death's act doth make perpetual
The last state of the souls of men that die.
If this be so, — if this, indeed, were sure,
Then not a moment longer would I live ;
Who, being now as I would fain endure,
If man's last state doth his last hour sur-
  vive,
Should be among the blessed souls ? I fear
Life's many changes, not Death's change-
  lessness.
So perfect is this moment's passing cheer,
I needs must tremble lest it pass to less.
Thus but in fickle love of life I live,
Lest fickle life me of my love deprive.

James Thomson

MELENCOLIA

FROM "THE CITY OF DREADFUL NIGHT"

ANEAR the centre of that northern crest
  Stands out a level upland bleak and
    bare,
From which the city east and south and
    west
  Sinks gently in long waves ; and throned
    there
An Image sits, stupendous, superhuman,
The bronze colossus of a winged Woman,
  Upon a graded granite base foursquare.

Low-seated she leans forward massively,
  With cheek on clench'd left hand, the
    forearm's might
Erect, its elbow on her rounded knee ;
  Across a clasp'd book in her lap the right
Upholds a pair of compasses ; she gazes
With full set eyes, but wandering in thick
    mazes
  Of sombre thought beholds no outward
    sight.

Words cannot picture her ; but all men
    know
  That solemn sketch the pure sad artist
    wrought
Three centuries and three score years ago,
  With fantasies of his peculiar thought :
The instruments of carpentry and science
Scatter'd about her feet, in strange alliance
  With the keen wolf-hound sleeping un-
    distraught ;

Scales, hour-glass, bell, and magic-square
    above ;
  The grave and solid infant perch'd be-
    side,
With open winglets that might bear a dove,
  Intent upon its tablets, heavy-eyed ;
Her folded wings as of a mighty eagle
But all too impotent to lift the regal
  Robustness of her earth-born strength
    and pride ;

And with those wings, and that light
    wreath which seems
  To mock her grand head and the knotted
    frown

Of forehead charged with baleful thoughts
    and dreams,
  The household bunch of keys, the house-
    wife's gown
Voluminous, indented, and yet rigid
As if a shell of burnish'd metal frigid,
  The feet thick-shod to tread all weak-
    ness down ;

The comet hanging o'er the waste dark seas,
  The massy rainbow curv'd in front of it
Beyond the village with the masts and
    trees ;
  The snaky imp, dog-headed, from the
    Pit,
Bearing upon its batlike leathern pinions
Her name unfolded in the sun's dominions,
  The " MELENCOLIA " that transcends
    all wit.

Thus has the artist copied her, and thus
  Surrounded to expound her form sublime,
Her fate heroic and calamitous ;
  Fronting the dreadful mysteries of Time,
Unvanquish'd in defeat and desolation,
Undaunted in the hopeless conflagration
  Of the day setting on her baffled prime.

Baffled and beaten back she works on still,
  Weary and sick of soul she works the
    more,
Sustain'd by her indomitable will :
  The hands shall fashion and the brain
    shall pore,
And all her sorrow shall be turn'd to
    labor,
Till Death the friend-foe piercing with his
    sabre
  That mighty heart of hearts ends bitter
    war.

But as if blacker night could dawn on
    night,
  With tenfold gloom on moonless night
    unstarr'd,
A sense more tragic than defeat and blight,
  More desperate than strife with hope
    debarr'd,
More fatal than the adamantine Never
Encompassing her passionate endeavor,
  Dawns glooming in her tenebrous
    regard :

The sense that every struggle brings de-
 feat
Because Fate holds no prize to crown
 success ;
That all the oracles are dumb or cheat
Because they have no secret to ex-
 press ;
That none can pierce the vast black veil
 uncertain
Because there is no light beyond the cur-
 tain ;
That all is vanity and nothingness.

Titanic from her high throne in the north,
 That City's sombre Patroness and Queen,
In bronze sublimity she gazes forth
 Over her Capital of teen and threne,
Over the river with its isles and bridges,
The marsh and moorland, to the stern rock-
 ridges,
 Confronting them with a coeval mien.

The moving moon and stars from east to
 west
 Circle before her in the sea of air ;
Shadows and gleams glide round her sol-
 emn rest.
 Her subjects often gaze up to her there :
The strong to drink new strength of iron
 endurance,
The weak new terrors ; all, renew'd assur-
 ance
 And confirmation of the old despair.

LIFE'S HEBE

In the early morning-shine
Of a certain day divine,
I beheld a Maiden stand
With a pitcher in her hand ;
Whence she pour'd into a cup,
Until it was half fill'd up,
Nectar that was golden light
In the cup of crystal bright.

And the first who took the cup
With pure water fill'd it up ;
As he drank then, it was more
Ruddy golden than before :
And he leap'd and danced and sang
As to Bacchic cymbals' clang.

But the next who took the cup
With the red wine fill'd it up ;

What he drank then was in hue
Of a heavy sombre blue :
First he reel'd and then he crept,
Then lay faint but never slept.

And the next who took the cup
With the white milk fill'd it up ;
What he drank at first seem'd blood,
Then turn'd thick and brown as mud :
And he mov'd away as slow
As a weary ox may go.

But the next who took the cup
With sweet honey fill'd it up ;
Nathless that which he did drink
Was thin fluid black as ink :
As he went he stumbled soon,
And lay still in deathlike swoon.

She the while without a word
Unto all the cup preferr'd ;
Blandly smil'd and sweetly laugh'd
As each mingled his own draught.

And the next who took the cup
To the sunshine held it up,
Gave it back and did not taste ;
It was empty when replaced :
First he bow'd a reverent bow,
Then he kiss'd her on the brow.

But the next who took the cup
Without mixture drank it up ;
When she took it back from him
It was full unto the brim :
He with a right bold embrace
Kiss'd her sweet lips face to face.

Then she sang with blithest cheer :
Who has thirst, come here, come here !
Nectar that is golden light
In the cup of crystal bright,
Nectar that is sunny fire
Warm as warmest heart's desire :
Pitcher never lacketh more,
Arm is never tir'd to pour :
Honey, water, milk, or wine
Mingle with the draught divine,
Drink it pure, or drink it not ;
Each is free to choose his lot ;
Am I old ? or am I cold ?
Only two have kiss'd me bold !

She was young and fair and gay
As that young and glorious day.

FROM "HE HEARD HER SING"

AND thus all-expectant abiding I waited not
   long, for soon
A boat came gliding and gliding out in the
   light of the moon,
Gliding with muffled oars, slowly, a thin
   dark line,
Round from the shadowing shores into the
   silver shine
Of the clear moon westering now, and
   still drew on and on,
While the water before its prow breaking
   and glistering shone,
Slowly in silence strange ; and the rower
   row'd till it lay
Afloat within easy range deep in the curve
   of the bay ;
And besides the rower were two : a Wo-
   man, who sat in the stern,
And Her by her fame I knew, one of those
   fames that burn,
Startling and kindling the world, one whose
   likeness we everywhere see ;
And a man reclining half-curl'd with an in-
   dolent grace at her knee,
The Signor, lord of her choice ; and he
   lightly touch'd a guitar ; —
A guitar for that glorious voice ! Illumine
   the sun with a star !
She sat superb and erect, stately, all-happy,
   serene,
Her right hand toying uncheck'd with the
   hair of that page of a Queen ;
With her head and her throat and her bust
   like the bust and the throat and the
   head
Of Her who has long been dust, of her who
   shall never be dead,
Preserv'd by the potent art made trebly
   potent by love,
While the transient ages depart from under
   the heavens above, —
Preserv'd in the color and line on the can-
   vas fulgently flung
By Him the Artist divine who triumph'd
   and vanish'd so young :
Surely there rarely hath been a lot more to
   be envied in life
Than thy lot, O Fornarina, whom Raphael's
   heart took to wife.

There was silence yet for a time save the
   tinkling capricious and quaint,
Then She lifted her voice sublime, no
   longer tender and faint,

Pathetic and tremulous, no ! but firm as a
   column it rose,
Rising solemn and slow with a full rich
   swell to the close,
Firm as a marble column soaring with
   noble pride
In a triumph of rapture solemn to some
   Hero deified ;
In a rapture of exultation made calm by its
   stress intense,
In a triumph of consecration and a jubila-
   tion immense.
And the Voice flow'd on and on, and ever
   it swell'd as it pour'd,
Till the stars that throbb'd as they shone
   seem'd throbbing with it in ac-
   cord ;
Till the moon herself in my dream, still
   Empress of all the night,
Was only that voice supreme translated into
   pure light :
And I lost all sense of the earth though I
   still had sense of the sea ;
And I saw the stupendous girth of a tree
   like the Norse World-Tree ;
And its branches fill'd all the sky, and the
   deep sea water'd its root,
And the clouds were its leaves on high and
   the stars were its silver fruit ;
Yet the stars were the notes of the singing
   and the moon was the voice of the
   song,
Through the vault of the firmament ring-
   ing and swelling resistlessly strong ;
And the whole vast night was a shell for
   that music of manifold might,
And was strain'd by the stress of the swell
   of the music yet vaster than night.
And I saw as a crystal fountain whose shaft
   was a column of light
More high than the loftiest mountain ascend
   the abyss of the night ;
And its spray fill'd all the sky, and the
   clouds were the clouds of its spray,
Which glitter'd in star-points on high and
   fill'd with pure silver the bay ;
And ever in rising and falling it sang as it
   rose and it fell,
And the heavens with their pure azure
   walling all puls'd with the pulse of
   its swell,
For the stars were the notes of the singing
   and the moon was the voice of the
   song
Through the vault of the firmament ringing
   and swelling ineffably strong ;

And the whole vast night was a shell for
that music of manifold might,
And was strain'd by the stress of the
swell of the music yet vaster than
night :
And the fountain in swelling and soaring
and filling beneath and above,
Grew flush'd with red fire in outpour-
ing, transmuting great power into
love,
Great power with a greater love flush-
ing, immense and intense and su-
preme,
As if all the World's heart-blood outgush-
ing ensanguin'd the trance of my
dream ;

And the waves of its blood seem'd to dash
on the shore of the sky to the cope
With the stress of the fire of a passion and
yearning of limitless scope,
Vast fire of a passion and yearning, keen
torture of rapture intense,
A most unendurable burning consuming the
soul with the sense : —
" Love, love only, forever love with its
torture of bliss ;
All the world's glories can never equal two
souls in one kiss :
Love, and ever love wholly ; love in all
time and all space ;
Life is consummate then solely in the death
of a burning embrace. "

Harriet Eleanor Hamilton King

PALERMO

FROM " THE DISCIPLES "

Whosoe'er
Had look'd upon the glory of that day
In Sicily beneath the summer sun,
Would not have dream'd that Death was
reigning there
In shape so terrible ; — for all the road
Was like an avenue of Paradise,
Life, and full flame of loveliness of life.
The red geraniums blaz'd in banks breast-
high,
And from the open doors in the white walls
Scents of magnolia and of heliotrope
Came to the street ; filmy aurora-flowers
Open'd and died in the hour, and fell away
In many-color'd showers upon the ground ;
Nebulous masses of the pale blue stars
Made light upon the darkness of the green,
Through openings in the thickets over-
arch'd ;
Where roses, white and yellow and full-
rose,
Weigh'd down their branches, till the
ground was swept
By roses, and strewn with them, as the air
Shook the thick clusters, and the Indian
reeds
Bow'd to its passing with their feathery
heads ;
And trumpet-blossoms push'd out great
white horns

From the green sheath, till all the green
was hid
By the white spread of giant-blowing wings.
In the cool shadow heaps of tuberose
Lay by the fountains in the market-place,
Among the purple fruit. The jalousies
Of the tall houses shut against the sun
Were wreath'd with trails of velvet-glossy
bells ;
And here and there one had not been un-
clos'd
Yesterday, and the vivid shoots had run
Over it in a night, and seal'd it fast
With tendril, and bright leaf, and drops of
flower.
And in and out the balconies thin stems
Went twisting, and the chains of passion-
flowers,
Bud, blossom, and phantasmal orb of fruit
Alternate, swung, and lengthen'd every
hour.
And fine-leav'd greenery crept from bower
to bower
With thick white star-flakes scatter'd ; and
the bloom
Of orient lilies, and the rainbow-blue
Of iris shot up stately from the grass ;
And through the wavering shadows crim-
son sparks
Pois'd upon brittle stalks, glanced up and
down ;
And shining darkness of the cypress clos'd
The deep withdrawing glades of evergreen,
Lit up far off with oleander pyres.

Out of the rocky dust of the wayside
The lamps of the aloes burn'd themselves
    aloft,
Immortal ; and the prickly cactus-knots
In the hot sunshine overleant the walls,
The lizards darting in and out of them ;
But in the shadier side the maidenhair
Sprung thick from every crevice. Passing
    these,
He issued on to the Piazza, where
The wonder of the world, the Fountain
    streams
From height to height of marble, dashing
    down
White waves forever over whitest limbs,
That shine in multitudes amid the spray
And sound of silver waters without end,
Rolling and rising and showering sud-
    denly.
There standing where the fig-trees made
    a shade
Close in the angle, he beheld the streets
Stretch fourways to the beautiful great
    gates ;
With all their burnish'd domes and carven
    stones
In wavering color'd lines of light and
    shade.
And downwards, from the greatest of the
    gates,
Porta Felice, swept the orange-groves ;
And avenues of coral-trees led down
In all their hanging splendors to the
    shore ;
And out beyond them, sleeping in the light,
The islands, and the azure of the sea.
And upwards, through a labyrinth of
    spires,
And turrets, and steep alabaster walls,
The city rose, and broke itself away
Amidst the forests of the hills, and reach'd
The heights of Monreale, crown'd with all
Its pinnacles and all its jewell'd fronts
Shining to seaward ; — but the tolling bells
Out of the gilded minarets smote the
    ear : —
Until at last, through miles of shadowy air,
The blue and violet mountains shut the
    sky.

THE CROCUS

Out of the frozen earth below,
Out of the melting of the snow,
  No flower, but a film, I push to light ;
No stem, no bud, — yet I have burst
The bars of winter, I am the first,
  O Sun, to greet thee out of the night !

Bare are the branches, cold is the air,
Yet it is fire at the heart I bear,
  I come, a flame that is fed by none :
The summer hath blossoms for her delight,
Thick and dewy and waxen-white,
  Thou seest me golden, O golden Sun !

Deep in the warm sleep underground
Life is still, and the peace profound :
  Yet a beam that pierced, and a thrill
    that smote
Call'd me and drew me from far away ; —
I rose, I came, to the open day
  I have won, unshelter'd, alone, remote.

No bee strays out to greet me at morn,
I shall die ere the butterfly is born,
  I shall hear no note of the nightingale ;
The swallow will come at the break of
    green,
He will never know that I have been
  Before him here when the world was
    pale.

They will follow, the rose with the thorny
    stem,
The hyacinth stalk, — soft airs for them ;
  They shall have strength, I have but
    love :
They shall not be tender as I, —
Yet I fought here first, to bloom, to die,
  To shine in his face who shines above.

O Glory of heaven, O Ruler of morn,
O Dream that shap'd me, and I was born
  In thy likeness, starry, and flower of
    flame ;
I lie on the earth, and to thee look up,
Into thy image will grow my cup,
  Till a sunbeam dissolve it into the same.

POETS OF THE RENAISSANCE

Ford Madox Brown

FOR THE PICTURE, "THE LAST OF ENGLAND"

"THE last of England ! O'er the sea, my
    dear,
Our homes to seek amid Australian fields,
Us, not our million-acred island yields
The space to dwell in. Thrust out ! Forced
    to bear
Low ribaldry from sots, and share rough
    cheer
With rudely-nurtur'd men. The hope
    youth builds
Of fair renown, barter'd for that which
    shields
Only the back, and half-form'd lands that
    rear
The dust-storm blistering up the grasses
    wild.
There learning skills not, nor the poet's
    dream,
Nor aught so lov'd as children shall we see."
She grips his listless hand and clasps her
    child,
Through rainbow tears she sees a sunnier
    gleam,
She cannot see a void, where he will be.

O. M. B.

(DIED NOVEMBER, 1874)

As one who strives from some fast steamer's
    side
To note amid the backward-spinning foam
And keep in view some separate wreath
    therefrom,
That cheats him even the while he views it
    glide
(Merging in other foam-tracks stretching
    wide),
So strive we to keep clear that day our
    home
First saw you riven — a memory thence to
    roam,
A shatter'd blossom on the eternal tide !
O broken promises that show'd so fair !
O morning sun of wit set in despair !
O brows made smooth as with the Muse's
    chrism !
O Oliver ! ourselves Death's cataclysm
Must soon o'ertake — but not in vain —
    not where
Some vestige of your thought outspans the
    abysm !

Sir Joseph Noel Paton

REQUIEM

WITHER'D pansies faint and sweet,
  O'er his breast in silence shed,
Faded lilies o'er his feet,
  Waning roses round his head,
Where in dreamless sleep he lies —
Folded palms and sealed eyes —
  Young Love, within my bosom — dead.

Young Love that was so fond, so fair,
  With his mouth of rosy red,
Argent wing and golden hair,
  And those blue eyen, glory-fed

From some fount of splendor, far
Beyond or moon or sun or star —
  And can it be that he is dead ?

Ay ! his breast is cold as snow :
  Pulse and breath forever fled ;
If I kiss'd him ever so,
  To my kiss he were as lead ;
If I clipp'd him as of yore
He would answer me no more
  With lip or hand — for he is dead.

But breathe no futile sigh ; no tear
  Smirch his pure and lonely bed.

Let no foolish cippus rear
  Its weight above him.   Only spread
Rose, lily, pale forget-me-not,
  And pansies round the silent spot
    Where in his youth he lieth — dead.

THE LAST OF THE EURYDICE

The training-ship Eurydice —
  As tight a craft, I ween,
As ever bore brave men who lov'd
  Their country and their queen —
Built when a ship, sir, was a ship,
  And not a steam-machine.

Six months or more she had been out
  Cruising the Indian sea ;
And now, with all her canvas bent —
  A fresh breeze blowing free —
Up Channel in her pride she came,
  The brave Eurydice.

On Saturday it was we saw
  The English cliffs appear,
And fore and aft, from man and boy,
  Uprang one mighty cheer ;
While many a rough-and-ready hand
  Dash'd off the gathering tear.

We saw the heads of Dorset rise
  Fair in the Sabbath sun ;
We mark'd each hamlet gleaming white,
  The church spires, one by one ;
We thought we heard the church bells ring
  To hail our voyage done.

" Only an hour from Spithead, lads :
  Only an hour from home ! "
So sang the captain's cheery voice
  As we spurn'd the ebbing foam ;
And each young sea-dog's heart sang back
  " Only an hour from home ! "

No warning ripple crisp'd the wave
  To tell of danger nigh ;
Nor looming rack, nor driving scud —
  From out a smiling sky,
With sound as of the trump of doom,
  The squall broke suddenly.

A hurricane of wind and snow
  From off the Shanklin shore ;
It caught us in its blinding whirl
  One instant, and no more ;
For, ere we dream'd of trouble near,
  All earthly hope was o'er.

No time to shorten sail, — no time
  To change the vessel's course ;
The storm had caught her crowded masts
  With swift, resistless force.
Only one shrill, despairing cry
  Rose o'er the tumult hoarse.

And broadside the great ship went down,
  Amid the swirling foam ;
And with her nigh four hundred men
  Went down, in sight of home,
(Fletcher and I alone were sav'd)
  Only an hour from home !

Thomas Woolner

MY BEAUTIFUL LADY

I love my Lady ; she is very fair ;
Her brow is wan, and bound by simple hair ;
  Her spirit sits aloof, and high,
  But glances from her tender eye
    In sweetness droopingly.

As a young forest while the wind drives through,
My life is stirr'd when she breaks on my view ;
  Her beauty grants my will no choice
  But silent awe, till she rejoice
    My longing with her voice.

Her warbling voice, though ever low and mild,
Oft makes me feel as strong wine would a child ;
  And though her hand be airy light
  Of touch, it moves me with its might,
    As would a sudden fright.

A hawk high pois'd in air, whose nerv'd wing-tips
Tremble with might suppress'd, before he dips,
  In vigilance, scarce more intense
  Than I, when her voice holds my sense
    Contented in suspense.

Her mention of a thing, august or poor,
Makes it far nobler than it was before :
  As where the sun strikes life will gush,
  And what is pale receive a flush,
    Rich hues, a richer blush.

My Lady's name, when I hear strangers
  use,
Not meaning her, to me sounds lax mis-
  use ;
  I love none but my Lady's name ;
  Maud, Grace, Rose, Marian, all the
    same,
    Are harsh, or blank and tame.

My Lady walks as I have watch'd a swan
Swim where a glory on the water shone :
  There ends of willow branches ride,
  Quivering in the flowing tide,
    By the deep river's side.

Fresh beauties, howsoe'er she moves, are
  stirr'd :
As the sunn'd bosom of a humming bird
  At each pant lifts some fiery hue,
  Fierce gold, bewildering green or blue ;
    The same, yet ever new.

GIVEN OVER

THE men of learning say she must
Soon pass, and be as if she had not been.
To gratify the barren lust
Of Death, the roses in her cheeks are
  seen
To blush so brightly, blooming deeper
  damascene.

All hope and doubt, all fears, are vain :
The dreams I nurs'd of honoring her are
  past,
  And will not comfort me again.
I see a lurid sunlight throw its last
Wild gleam athwart the land whose shad-
  ows lengthen fast.

It does not seem so dreadful now,
The horror stands out naked, stark, and
  still ;
  I am quite calm, and wonder how
My terror play'd such mad pranks with my
  will.
The north winds fiercely blow, I do not feel
  them chill.

All things must die : somewhere I read
What wise and solemn men pronounce of
  joy ;
  No sooner born, they say, than dead ;
The strife of being, but a whirling toy
Humming a weary moan spun by capricious
  boy.

Has my soul reach'd a starry height
Majestically calm ? No monster, drear
And shapeless, glares me faint at night ;
I am not in the sunshine check'd for fear
That monstrous, shapeless thing is some-
  where crouching near ?

No ; woe is me ! far otherwise :
The naked horror numbs me to the bone ;
  In stupor calm its cold, blank eyes
Set hard at mine. I do not fall or groan,
Our island Gorgon's face has changed me
  into stone.

Dante Gabriel Rossetti

THE BLESSED DAMOZEL[1]

THE blessed damozel lean'd out
  From the gold bar of Heaven ;
Her eyes were deeper than the depth
  Of waters still'd at even ;
She had three lilies in her hand,
  And the stars in her hair were seven.

Her robe, ungirt from clasp to hem,
  No wrought flowers did adorn,

But a white rose of Mary's gift,
  For service meetly worn ;
Her hair that lay along her back
  Was yellow like ripe corn.

Herseem'd she scarce had been a day
  One of God's choristers ;
The wonder was not yet quite gone
  From that still look of hers ;
Albeit, to them she left, her day
  Had counted as ten years.

[1] Written in his 19th year, 1846–47.

(To one, it is ten years of years.
   . . . Yet now, and in this place,
Surely she lean'd o'er me — her hair
   Fell all about my face.   . . .
Nothing : the autumn-fall of leaves.
   The whole year sets apace.)

It was the rampart of God's house
   That she was standing on :
By God built over the sheer depth
   The which is Space begun ;
So high, that looking downward thence
   She scarce could see the sun.

It lies in Heaven, across the flood
   Of ether, as a bridge.
Beneath, the tides of day and night
   With flame and darkness ridge
The void, as low as where this earth
   Spins like a fretful midge.

Around her, lovers, newly met
   'Mid deathless love's acclaims,
Spoke evermore among themselves
   Their heart-remember'd names ;
And the souls mounting up to God
   Went by her like thin flames.

And still she bow'd herself and stoop'd
   Out of the circling charm ;
Until her bosom must have made
   The bar she lean'd on warm,
And the lilies lay as if asleep
   Along her bended arm.

From the fix'd place of Heaven she saw
   Time like a pulse shake fierce
Through all the worlds. Her gaze still strove
   Within the gulf to pierce
Its path ; and now she spoke as when
   The stars sang in their spheres.

The sun was gone now ; the curl'd moon
   Was like a little feather
Fluttering far down the gulf ; and now
   She spoke through the still weather.
Her voice was like the voice the stars
   Had when they sang together.

(Ah sweet ! Even now, in that bird's song,
   Strove not her accents there,
Fain to be hearken'd ?   When those bells
   Possess'd the mid-day air,
Strove not her steps to reach my side
   Down all the echoing stair ?)

" I wish that he were come to me,
   For he will come," she said.
" Have I not pray'd in Heaven ? — on earth,
   Lord, Lord, has he not pray'd ?
Are not two prayers a perfect strength ?
   And shall I feel afraid ?

" When round his head the aureole clings,
   And he is cloth'd in white,
I 'll take his hand and go with him
   To the deep wells of light ;
As unto a stream we will step down,
   And bathe there in God's sight.

" We two will stand beside that shrine,
   Occult, withheld, untrod,
Whose lamps are stirr'd continually
   With prayer sent up to God ;
And see our old prayers, granted, melt
   Each like a little cloud.

" We two will lie i' the shadow of
   That living mystic tree
Within whose secret growth the Dove
   Is sometimes felt to be,
While every leaf that His plumes touch
   Saith His Name audibly.

" And I myself will teach to him,
   I myself, lying so,
The songs I sing here ; which his voice
   Shall pause in, hush'd and slow,
And find some knowledge at each pause,
   Or some new thing to know."

(Alas ! we two, we two, thou say'st !
   Yea, one wast thou with me
That once of old.   But shall God lift
   To endless unity
The soul whose likeness with thy soul
   Was but its love for thee ?)

" We two," she said, " will seek the groves
   Where the lady Mary is,
With her five handmaidens, whose names
   Are five sweet symphonies,
Cecily, Gertrude, Magdalen,
   Margaret and Rosalys.

" Circlewise sit they, with bound locks
   And foreheads garlanded ;
Into the fine cloth white like flame
   Weaving the golden thread,
To fashion the birth-robes for them
   Who are just born, being dead.

" He shall fear, haply, and be dumb :
    Then will I lay my cheek
To his, and tell about our love,
    Not once abash'd or weak :
And the dear Mother will approve
    My pride, and let me speak.

" Herself shall bring us, hand in hand,
    To Him round whom all souls
Kneel, the clear-ranged unnumber'd heads
    Bow'd with their aureoles :
And angels meeting us shall sing
    To their citherns and citoles.

" There will I ask of Christ the Lord
    Thus much for him and me : —
Only to live as once on earth
    With Love, — only to be,
As then awhile, forever now
    Together, I and he."

She gazed and listen'd and then said,
    Less sad of speech than mild, —
" All this is when he comes."   She ceas'd.
    The light thrill'd towards her, fill'd
With angels in strong level flight.
    Her eyes pray'd, and she smil'd.

(I saw her smile.)   But soon their path
    Was vague in distant spheres :
And then she cast her arms along
    The golden barriers,
And laid her face between her hands,
    And wept.   (I heard her tears.).

THE PORTRAIT

THIS is her picture as she was :
    It seems a thing to wonder on,
As though mine image in the glass
    Should tarry when myself am gone.
I gaze until she seems to stir, —
Until mine eyes almost aver
    That now, even now, the sweet lips part
    To breathe the words of the sweet heart :
And yet the earth is over her.

Alas ! even such the thin-drawn ray
    That makes the prison - depths more rude, —
The drip of water night and day
    Giving a tongue to solitude.

Yet only this, of love's whole prize
Remains ; save what, in mournful guise,
    Takes counsel with my soul alone, —
    Save what is secret and unknown,
Below the earth, above the skies.

In painting her I shrin'd her face
    'Mid mystic trees, where light falls in
Hardly at all ; a covert place
    Where you might think to find a din
Of doubtful talk, and a live flame
Wandering, and many a shape whose name
    Not itself knoweth, and old dew,
    And your own footsteps meeting you,
And all things going as they came.

A deep, dim wood ; and there she stands
    As in that wood that day : for so
Was the still movement of her hands,
    And such the pure line's gracious flow.
And passing fair the type must seem,
Unknown the presence and the dream.
    'T is she : though of herself, alas !
    Less than her shadow on the grass,
Or than her image in the stream.

That day we met there, I and she,
    One with the other all alone ;
And we were blithe ; yet memory
    Saddens those hours, as when the moon
Looks upon daylight.   And with her
I stoop'd to drink the spring-water,
    Athirst where other waters sprang :
    And where the echo is, she sang, —
My soul another echo there.

But when that hour my soul won strength
    For words whose silence wastes and kills,
Dull raindrops smote us, and at length
    Thunder'd the heat within the hills.
That eve I spoke those words again
Beside the pelted window-pane ;
    And there she hearken'd what I said,
    With under-glances that survey'd
The empty pastures blind with rain.

Next day the memories of these things,
    Like leaves through which a bird has flown,
Still vibrated with Love's warm wings ;
    Till I must make them all my own
And paint this picture. So, 'twixt ease
Of talk and sweet, long silences,
    She stood among the plants in bloom
    At windows of a summer room,
To feign the shadow of the trees.

And as I wrought, while all above
And all around was fragrant air,
In the sick burthen of my love
It seemed each sun - thrill'd blossom
    there
Beat like a heart among the leaves.
O heart, that never beats nor heaves,
In that one darkness lying still,
What now to thee my love's great will,
Or the fine web the sunshine weaves ?

For now doth daylight disavow
Those days — nought left to see or
    hear.
Only in solemn whispers now
At night-time these things reach mine
    ear ;
When the leaf-shadows at a breath
Shrink in the road, and all the heath,
Forest and water, far and wide,
In limpid starlight glorified,
Lie like the mystery of death.

Last night at last I could have slept,
And yet delay'd my sleep till dawn,
Still wandering. Then it was I wept :
For unawares I came upon
Those glades where once she walk'd with
    me :
And as I stood there suddenly,
All wan with traversing the night,
Upon the desolate verge of light
Yearn'd loud the iron-bosom'd sea.

Even so, where Heaven holds breath and
    hears
The beating heart of Love's own breast, —
Where round the secret of all spheres
All angels lay their wings to rest, —
How shall my soul stand rapt and aw'd,
When, by the new birth borne abroad
Throughout the music of the suns,
It enters in her soul at once
And knows the silence there for God !

Here with her face doth memory sit
Meanwhile, and wait the day's decline,
Till other eyes shall look from it,
Eyes of the spirit's Palestine,
Even than the old gaze tenderer :
While hopes and aims long lost with her
Stand round her image side by side,
Like tombs of pilgrims that have died
About the Holy Sepulchre.

FROM "THE HOUSE OF LIFE: A SONNET-SEQUENCE"

INTRODUCTORY

A SONNET is a moment's monument, —
Memorial from the Soul's eternity
To one dead, deathless hour. Look that it
    be,
Whether for lustral rite or dire portent,
Of its own arduous fulness reverent :
Carve it in ivory or in ebony,
As Day or Night may rule ; and let Time
    see
Its flowering crest impearl'd and orient.
A Sonnet is a coin : its face reveals
The soul, — its converse, to what power 't is
    due : —
Whether for tribute to the august ap-
    peals
Of Life, or dower in Love's high retinue,
It serve ; or, 'mid the dark wharf's caver-
    nous breath,
In Charon's palm it pay the toll to Death.

LOVESIGHT

WHEN do I see thee most, beloved one ?
When in the light the spirits of mine eyes
Before thy face, their altar, solemnize
The worship of that Love through thee
    made known ?
Or when, in the dusk hours (we two alone),
Close-kiss'd, and eloquent of still replies
Thy twilight-hidden glimmering visage lies,
And my soul only sees thy soul its own ?
O love, my love ! if I no more should see
Thyself, nor on the earth the shadow of
    thee,
Nor image of thine eyes in any spring, —
How then should sound upon Life's darken-
    ing slope
The ground-whirl of the perish'd leaves of
    Hope,
The wind of Death's imperishable wing ?

HER GIFTS

HIGH grace, the dower of queens ; and
    therewithal
Some wood-born wonder's sweet simpli-
    city ;
A glance like water brimming with the sky
Or hyacinth-light where forest-shadows
    fall ;

Such thrilling pallor of cheek as doth in-
    thrall
The heart ; a mouth whose passionate
    forms imply
All music and all silence held thereby ;
Deep golden locks, her sovereign coronal ;
A round rear'd neck, meet column of
    Love's shrine
To cling to when the heart takes sanctuary;
Hands which forever at Love's bidding be,
And soft-stirr'd feet still answering to his
    sign : —
These are her gifts, as tongue may tell
    them o'er.
Breathe low her name, my soul ; for that
    means more.

THE DARK GLASS

Not I myself know all my love for thee :
How should I reach so far, who cannot
    weigh
To-morrow's dower by gage of yesterday ?
Shall birth and death, and all dark names
    that be
As doors and windows bar'd to some loud
    sea,
Lash deaf mine ears and blind my face with
    spray ;
And shall my sense pierce love, — the last
    relay
And ultimate outpost of eternity ?
Lo ! what am I to Love, the lord of all ?
One murmuring shell he gathers from the
    sand, —
One little heart-flame shelter'd in his hand.
Yet through thine eyes he grants me clear-
    est call
And veriest touch of powers primordial
That any hour-girt life may understand.

WITHOUT HER

What of her glass without her ? The
    blank gray
There where the pool is blind of the moon's
    face.
Her dress without her ? The toss'd empty
    space
Of cloud-rack whence the moon has pass'd
    away.
Her paths without her ? Day's appointed
    sway
Usurp'd by desolate night. Her pillow'd
    place

Without her ? Tears, ah me ! for love's
    good grace,
And cold forgetfulness of night or day.
What of the heart without her ? Nay,
    poor heart,
Of thee what word remains ere speech be
    still ?
A wayfarer by barren ways and chill,
Steep ways and weary, without her thou
    art,
Where the long cloud, the long wood's
    counterpart,
Sheds doubled darkness up the laboring
    hill.

BROKEN MUSIC

The mother will not turn, who thinks she
    hears
Her nursling's speech first grow articu-
    late ;
But breathless, with averted eyes elate
She sits, with open lips and open ears,
That it may call her twice.   'Mid doubts
    and fears
Thus oft my soul has hearken'd ; till the
    song,
A central moan for days, at length found
    tongue,
And the sweet music well'd and the sweet
    tears.
But now, whatever while the soul is fain
To list that wonted murmur, as it were
The speech-bound sea-shell's low, impor-
    tunate strain, —
No breath of song, thy voice alone is
    there,
O bitterly belov'd ! and all her gain
Is but the pang of unpermitted prayer.

INCLUSIVENESS

The changing guests, each in a different
    mood,
Sit at the roadside table, and arise :
And every life among them in like wise
Is a soul's board set daily with new food.
What man has bent o'er his son's sleep, to
    brood
How that face shall watch his when cold it
    lies ? —
Or thought, as his own mother kiss'd his
    eyes,
Of what her kiss was when his father
    woo'd ?

May not this ancient room thou sitt'st in
    dwell
In separate living souls for joy or pain ?
Nay, all its corners may be painted plain
Where Heaven shows pictures of some life
    spent well ;
And may be stamp'd, a memory all in vain,
Upon the sight of lidless eyes in Hell.

A SUPERSCRIPTION

Look in my face ; my name is Might-have-
    been ;
I am also call'd No-more, Too-late, Fare-
    well ;
Unto thine ear I hold the dead-sea shell
Cast up thy Life's foam-fretted feet be-
    tween ;
Unto thine eyes the glass where that is seen
Which had Life's form and Love's, but by
    my spell
Is now a shaken shadow intolerable,
Of ultimate things unutter'd the frail
    screen.
Mark me, how still I am ! But should there
    dart
One moment through thy soul the soft sur-
    prise
Of that wing'd Peace which lulls the breath
    of sighs, —
Then shalt thou see me smile, and turn apart
Thy visage to mine ambush at thy heart
Sleepless with cold commemorative eyes.

SONNETS ON PICTURES

A VENETIAN PASTORAL

BY GIORGIONE

(In the Louvre)

Water, for anguish of the solstice : — nay,
But dip the vessel slowly, — nay, but lean
And hark how at its verge the wave sighs
    in
Reluctant. Hush ! beyond all depth away
The heat lies silent at the brink of day :
Now the hand trails upon the viol-string
That sobs, and the brown faces cease to
    sing,
Sad with the whole of pleasure. Whither
    stray

Her eyes now, from whose mouth the slim
    pipes creep
And leave it pouting, while the shadow'd
    grass
Is cool against her naked side ? Let be : —
Say nothing now unto her lest she weep,
Nor name this ever. Be it as it was, —
Life touching lips with Immortality.

MARY MAGDALENE

AT THE DOOR OF SIMON THE PHARISEE

(For a Drawing by D. G. R.[1])

" Why wilt thou cast the roses from thine
    hair ?
Nay, be thou all a rose, — wreath, lips, and
    cheek.
Nay, not this house, — that banquet-house
    we seek ;
See how they kiss and enter ; come thou
    there.
This delicate day of love we two will
    share
Till at our ear love's whispering night
    shall speak.
What, sweet one, — hold'st thou still the
    foolish freak ?
Nay, when I kiss thy feet they 'll leave the
    stair."
" Oh loose me ! Seest thou not my Bride-
    groom's face
That draws me to Him ? For His feet my
    kiss,
My hair, my tears He craves to-day : —
    and oh !
What words can tell what other day and
    place
Shall see me clasp those blood-stain'd feet
    of His ?
He needs me, calls me, loves me : let me
    go ! "

SUDDEN LIGHT

I have been here before,
    But when or how I cannot tell :
I know the grass beyond the door,
    The sweet keen smell,
The sighing sound, the lights around the
    shore.

[1] In the drawing Mary has left a procession of revellers, and is ascending by a sudden impulse the steps of the house where she sees Christ. Her lover has followed her, and is trying to turn her back.

You have been mine before, —
How long ago I may not know :
But just when at that swallow's soar
Your neck turn'd so,
Some veil did fall, — I knew it all of yore.

Has this been thus before ?
And shall not thus time's eddying flight
Still with our lives our love restore
In death's despite,
And day and night yield one delight once
more ?

THE WOODSPURGE

THE wind flapp'd loose, the wind was still,
Shaken out dead from tree and hill :
I had walk'd on at the wind's will, —
I sat now, for the wind was still.

Between my knees my forehead was, —
My lips, drawn in, said not Alas !
My hair was over in the grass,
My naked ears heard the day pass.

My eyes, wide open, had the run
Of some ten weeds to fix upon ;
Among those few, out of the sun,
The woodspurge flower'd, three cups in
one.

From perfect grief there need not be
Wisdom or even memory :
One thing then learnt remains to me, —
The woodspurge has a cup of three.

THE SEA-LIMITS

CONSIDER the sea's listless chime :
Time's self it is, made audible, —
The murmur of the earth's own shell.
Secret continuance sublime
Is the sea's end : our sight may pass
No furlong further. Since time was,
This sound hath told the lapse of time.

No quiet, which is death's, — it hath
The mournfulness of ancient life,
Enduring always at dull strife.
As the world's heart of rest and wrath,
Its painful pulse is in the sands.
Last utterly, the whole sky stands,
Gray and not known, along its path.

Listen alone beside the sea,
Listen alone among the woods ;
Those voices of twin solitudes
Shall have one sound alike to thee :
Hark where the murmurs of throng'd men
Surge and sink back and surge again, —
Still the one voice of wave and tree.

Gather a shell from the strown beach
And listen at its lips : they sigh
The same desire and mystery,
The echo of the whole sea's speech.
And all mankind is thus at heart
Not anything but what thou art :
And Earth, Sea, Man, are all in each.

A LITTLE WHILE

A LITTLE while a little love
The hour yet bears for thee and me
Who have not drawn the veil to see
If still our heaven be lit above.
Thou merely, at the day's last sigh,
Hast felt thy soul prolong the tone ;
And I have heard the night-wind cry
And deem'd its speech mine own.

A little while a little love
The scattering autumn hoards for us
Whose bower is not yet ruinous
Nor quite unleav'd our songless grove.
Only across the shaken boughs
We hear the flood-tides seek the sea,
And deep in both our hearts they rouse
One wail for thee and me.

A little while a little love
May yet be ours who have not said
The word it makes our eyes afraid
To know that each is thinking of.
Not yet the end : be our lips dumb
In smiles a little season yet :
I 'll tell thee, when the end is come,
How we may best forget.

THE BALLAD OF DEAD LADIES

TRANSLATION FROM FRANÇOIS VILLON, 1450

TELL me now in what hidden way is
Lady Flora the lovely Roman ?
Where 's Hipparchia, and where is Thais,
Neither of them the fairer woman ?

Where is Echo, beheld of no man,
Only heard on river and mere, —
  She whose beauty was more than hu-
    man ? . . .
But where are the snows of yester-year ?

Where 's Héloise, the learned nun,
  For whose sake Abeillard, I ween,
Lost manhood and put priesthood on ?
  (From Love he won such dule and
    teen !)
  And where, I pray you, is the Queen
Who will'd that Buridan should steer
  Sew'd in a sack's mouth down the
    Seine ? . . .
But where are the snows of yester-year ?

White Queen Blanche, like a queen of
    lilies,
  With a voice like any mermaiden, —
Bertha Broadfoot, Beatrice, Alice,
  And Ermengarde the lady of Maine, —
  And that good Joan whom English-
    men
At Rouen doom'd and burn'd her there, —
  Mother of God, where are they
    then ? . . .
But where are the snows of yester-year ?

Nay, never ask this week, fair lord,
  Where they are gone, nor yet this year,
Save with thus much for an overword, —
  But where are the snows of yester-year ?

Richard Watson Dixon

ODE ON CONFLICTING CLAIMS

HAST thou no right to joy,
O youth grown old ! who palest with the
    thought
Of the measureless annoy,
The pain and havoc wrought
By Fate on man : and of the many men,
The unfed, the untaught,
Who groan beneath that adamantine chain
Whose tightness kills, whose slackness
    whips the flow
Of waves of futile woe :
Hast thou no right to joy ?

Thou thinkest in thy mind
In thee it were unkind
To revel in the liquid Hyblian store,
While more and more the horror and the
    shame,
The pity and the woe grow more and more,
Persistent still to claim
The filling of thy mind.

Thou thinkest that, if none in all the rout
Who compass thee about
Turn full their soul to that which thou de-
    sirest,
For seek to gain thy goal,
Beauty, the heart of beauty,
The sweetness, yea, the thoughtful sweet-
    ness,
The one right way in each, the best,

Which satisfies the soul,
The firmness lost in softness, touch of typi-
    cal meetness,
Which lets the soul have rest ;
Those things to which thyself aspirest : —
That they, though born to quaff the bowl
    divine,
As thou art, yield to the strict law of duty;
And thou from them must thine example
    take,
Leave the amaranthine vine,
And the prized joy forsake.

O thou, foregone in this,
Long struggling with a world that is amiss,
Reach some old volume down,
Some poet's book, which in thy bygone years
Thou hast consum'd with joys as keen as
    fears,
When o'er it thou wouldst hang with rap-
    turous frown,
Admiring with sweet envy all
The exquisite of words, the lance-like fall
Of mighty verses, each on each,
The sweetness which did never cloy,
(So wrought with thought ere touch'd with
    speech),
And ask again, Hast thou no right to joy ?
Take the most precious tones that thunder-
    struck thine ears
In gentler days gone by :
And if they yield no more the old ecstasy,
Then give thyself to tears.

HUMANITY

THERE is a soul above the soul of each,
A mightier soul, which yet to each be-
    longs :
There is a sound made of all human
    speech,
And numerous as the concourse of all
    songs :
And in that soul lives each, in each that
    soul,
Though all the ages are its lifetime vast ;
Each soul that dies, in its most sacred
    whole
Receiveth life that shall forever last.
And thus forever with a wider span
Humanity o'erarches time and death ;
Man can elect the universal man,
And live in life that ends not with his
    breath :
And gather glory that increases still
Till Time his glass with Death's last dust
    shall fill.

FROM "MANO: A POETICAL HISTORY"

THE SKYLARK

THOU only bird that singest as thou flyest,
    Heaven-mounting lark, that measurest
        with thy wing
The airy zones, till thou art lost in highest !
Upon the branch the laughing thrushes
    cling,
About her home the humble linnet wheels,
Around the tower the gather'd starlings
    swing ;
These mix their songs and weave their
    figur'd reels :
Thou risest in thy lonely joy away,
From the first rapturous note that from
    thee steals,
    Quick, quick, and quicker, till the exalted
        lay
Is steadied in the golden breadths of light,
'Mid mildest clouds that bid thy pinions
    stay.
    The heavens that give would yet sus-
        tain thy flight,
And o'er the earth for ever cast thy voice,
If but to gain were still to keep the height.
    But soon thou sinkest on the fluttering
        poise

Of the same wings that soar'd : soon
    ceasest thou
The song that grew invisible with joys.
    Love bids thy fall begin ; and thou art now
Dropp'd back to earth, and of the earth
    again,
Because that love hath made thy heart to
    bow.
    Thou hast thy mate, thy nest on lowly
        plain,
Thy timid heart by law ineffable
Is drawn from the high heavens where thou
    shouldst reign ;
    Earth summons thee by her most tender
        spell ;
For thee there is a silence and a song :
Thy silence in the shadowy earth must
    dwell,
    Thy song in the bright heavens cannot be
        long.
— And best to thee those fates may I com-
    pare
Where weakness strives to answer bidding
    strong.

OF A VISION OF HELL, WHICH A MONK HAD

OUT of this town there riseth a high hill,
    About whose sides live many anchorites
In cells cut in the rock with curious skill,
    And laid in terraces along the heights ;
This holy hill with that where stands the
    town
The ancient Roman aqueduct unites ;
    And passing o'er the vale her chain of
        stone
Cuts it in two with line indelible ;
A work right marvellous to gaze upon.
    To one of those grave hermits there
        befell
A curious thing, whereof the fame was new
In our sojourn ; the which I here will tell.
    He found himself when night had shed
        her dew,
In a long valley, narrow, deep, and straight
Like that which lay all day beneath his
    view.
    On each hand mountains rose precipitate
Whose tops for darkness he could nowise
    see,
Though wistful that high gloom to pene-
    trate ;
    And through this hollow, one, who
        seem'd to be

Of calm and quiet mien, was leading him
In friendly converse and society :
  But whom he wist not : neither could he
    trim
Memory's spent torch to know what things
    were said,
Nor about what, in that long way and
    dim.
  But as the valley still before him spread,
He saw a line, that did the same divide
Across in halves : which made him feel
    great dread.
  For he beheld fire burning on one side
Unto the mountains from the midmost
    vale ;
On the other, ice the empire did discide,
  Fed from the opposing hill with snow
    and hail.
So dreary was that haunt of fire and
    cold,
That nought on earth to equal might
    avail.
  Fire ended where began the frozen
    mould ;
Both in extreme at their conjunction :
So close were they, no severance might be
    told :
  No thinnest line of separation,
Like that which is by painter drawn to
    part
One color in his piece from other one,
  So fine as that which held these realms
    apart.
And through the vale the souls of men in
    pain
From one to the other side did leap and
    dart,
  From heat to cold, from cold to heat
    again :
And not an instant through their anguish
    great
In either element might they remain.
  So great the multitude thus toss'd by
    fate,
That as a mist they seem'd in the dark
    air.
To shrimper, who at half-tide takes his
    freight,
  When high his pole-net seaward he doth
    bear,
Ever beheld so thick a swarm to leap
Out of the brine on evening still and
    fair,
  Waking a mist mile-long 'twixt shore
    and deep.

Now while his mind was fill'd with ruth
    and fear,
And with great horror stood his eyeballs
    steep,
  Deeming that hell before him did ap-
    pear,
And souls in torment toss'd from brink to
    brink :
Upon him look'd the one who set him
    there,
  And said : " This is not hell, as thou dost
    think,
Neither those torments of the cold and
    heat
Are those wherewith the damned wail and
    shrink."
  And therewith from that place he turn'd
    his feet ;
And sometime on they walk'd, the while
    this man
In anguish shuddering did the effect re-
    peat :
  Such spasms of horror through his body
    ran,
Walking with stumbling, and with glazed
    eyes
Whither he knew not led, ghastly and wan.
  Then said the other : " In those agonies
No more than hell's beginning know : be-
    hold,
The doom of hell itself is otherwise."
  Therewith he drew aside his vesture's
    fold,
And show'd his heart : than fire more hot
    it burn'd
One half : the rest was ice than ice more
    cold.
  A moment show'd he this : and then he
    turn'd,
And in his going all the vision went :
And he, who in his mind these things dis-
    cern'd,
  Came to himself with long astonishment.

OF TEMPERANCE IN FORTUNE

HAPPY the man who so hath Fortune tried
  That likewise he her poor relation
    knows :
To whom both much is given and denied :
  To riches and to poverty he owes
An equal debt : of both he makes acquist,
  And moderate in all his mind he shows.
But ill befalls the man who hath not
    miss'd

Aught of his heart's desires, in plenty
  nurs'd :
For evil things he knows not to resist :
  And, aiding their assault, himself is
  worst
Against himself, with self-destructive
  rage.
But states are with another evil curs'd,
  For, falling into luxury with age,

They burst in tumults, swollen with bloody
  shame,
Which old exploits aggrieve and not as-
  suage.
Past temperance doth the present feast
  inflame ;
Past grandeur like too heavy armor
  weighs :
Great without virtue is an evil name.

William Morris

THE GILLYFLOWER OF GOLD

A GOLDEN gillyflower to-day
I wore upon my helm alway,
And won the prize of this tourney.
  Hah ! hah ! la belle jaune giroflée.

However well Sir Giles might sit,
His sun was weak to wither it,
Lord Miles's blood was dew on it :
  Hah ! hah ! la belle jaune giroflée.

Although my spear in splinters flew
From John's steel-coat, my eye was true ;
I wheel'd about, and cried for you,
  Hah ! hah ! la belle jaune giroflée.

Yea, do not doubt my heart was good,
Though my sword flew like rotten wood,
To shout, although I scarcely stood,
  Hah ! hah ! la belle jaune giroflée.

My hand was steady, too, to take
My axe from round my neck, and break
John's steel-coat up for my love's sake.
  Hah! hah ! la belle jaune giroflée.

When I stood in my tent again,
Arming afresh, I felt a pain
Take hold of me, I was so fain —
  Hah! hah ! la belle jaune giroflée —

To hear : *" Honneur aux fils des preux ! "*
Right in my ears again, and shew
The gillyflower blossom'd new.
  Hah! hah ! la belle jaune giroflée.

The Sieur Guillaume against me came,
His tabard bore three points of flame

From a red heart : with little blame —
  Hah ! hah ! la belle jaune giroflée —

Our tough spears crackled up like straw ;
He was the first to turn and draw
His sword, that had nor speck nor flaw, —
  Hah ! hah ! la belle jaune giroflée.

But I felt weaker than a maid,
And my brain, dizzied and afraid,
Within my helm a fierce tune play'd, —
  Hah ! hah ! la belle jaune giroflée.

Until I thought of your dear head,
Bow'd to the giliyflower bed,
The yellow flowers stain'd with red ; —
  Hah ! hah ! la belle jaune giroflée.

Crash ! how the swords met, *" giroflée ! "*
The fierce tune in my helm would play,
" La belle ! la belle jaune giroflée ! "
  Hah ! hah ! la belle jaune giroflée.

Once more the great swords met again,
" La belle ! la belle ! " but who fell then
Le Sieur Guillaume, who struck down
  ten ; —
  Hah ! hah ! la belle jaune giroflée.

And as, with maz'd and unarm'd face,
Toward my own crown and the Queen's
  place
They led me at a gentle pace, —
  Hak ! hah ! la belle jaune giroflée, —

I almost saw your quiet head
Bow'd o'er the gillyflower bed,
The yellow flowers stain'd with red, —
  Hah ! hah ! la belle jaune giroflée.

SHAMEFUL DEATH

THERE were four of us about that bed ;
  The mass-priest knelt at the side,
I and his mother stood at the head,
  Over his feet lay the bride ;
We were quite sure that he was dead,
  Though his eyes were open wide.

He did not die in the night,
  He did not die in the day,
But in the morning twilight
  His spirit pass'd away,
When neither sun nor moon was bright,
  And the trees were merely gray.

He was not slain with the sword,
  Knight's axe, or the knightly spear,
Yet spoke he never a word
  After he came in here ;
I cut away the cord
  From the neck of my brother dear.

He did not strike one blow,
  For the recreants came behind,
In a place where the hornbeams grow,
  A path right hard to find,
For the hornbeam boughs swing so
  That the twilight makes it blind.

They lighted a great torch then ;
  When his arms were pinion'd fast,
Sir John the knight of the Fen,
  Sir Guy of the Dolorous Blast,
With knights threescore and ten,
  Hung brave Lord Hugh at last.

I am threescore and ten,
  And my hair is all turn'd gray,
But I met Sir John of the Fen
  Long ago on a summer day,
And am glad to think of the moment when
  I took his life away.

I am threescore and ten,
  And my strength is mostly past,
But long ago I and my men,
  When the sky was overcast,
And the smoke roll'd over the reeds of the
    fen,
  Slew Guy of the Dolorous Blast.

And now, knights all of you,
  I pray you pray for Sir Hugh,
A good knight and a true,
  And for Alice, his wife, pray too.

THE BLUE CLOSET

The Damozels

LADY ALICE, Lady Louise,
Between the wash of the tumbling seas
We are ready to sing, if so ye please :
So lay your long hands on the keys ;
    Sing " *Laudate pueri.*"

*And ever the great bell overhead
Boom'd in the wind a knell for the dead,
Though no one toll'd it, a knell for the dead.*

Lady Louise

Sister, let the measure swell
Not too loud ; for you sing not well
If you drown the faint boom of the bell ;
    He is weary, so am I.

*And ever the chevron overhead
Flapp'd on the banner of the dead ;
(Was he asleep, or was he dead ?)*

Lady Alice

Alice the Queen, and Louise the Queen,
Two damozels wearing purple and green,
Four lone ladies dwelling here
From day to day and year to year :
And there is none to let us go ;
To break the locks of the doors below,
Or shovel away the heap'd-up snow ;
And when we die no man will know
That we are dead; but they give us leave,
Once every year on Christmas-eve,
To sing in the Closet Blue one song :
And we should be so long, so long,
If we dar'd, in singing ; for, dream on dream,
They float on in a happy stream ;
Float from the gold strings, float from the
    keys,
Float from the open'd lips of Louise :
But, alas ! the sea-salt oozes through
The chinks of the tiles of the Closet Blue ;

*And ever the great bell overhead
Booms in the wind a knell for the dead,
The wind plays on it a knell for the dead.*

(*They sing all together :*)

How long ago was it, how long ago,
He came to this tower with hands full of
    snow ?

"Kneel down, O love Louise, kneel down,"
he said,
And sprinkled the dusty snow over my head.

He watch'd the snow melting, it ran through
my hair,
Ran over my shoulders, white shoulders and
bare.

"I cannot weep for thee, poor love Louise,
For my tears are all hidden deep under the
seas;

"In a gold and blue casket she keeps all my
tears,
But my eyes are no longer blue, as in old
years;

"Yea, they grow gray with time, grow small
and dry,
I am so feeble now, would I might die."

*And in truth the great bell overhead
Left off his pealing for the dead,
Perchance because the wind was dead.*

Will he come back again, or is he dead?
O! is he sleeping, my scarf round his head?

Or did they strangle him as he lay there,
With the long scarlet scarf I used to wear?

Only I pray thee, Lord, let him come here!
Both his soul and his body to me are most
dear.

Dear Lord, that loves me, I wait to re-
ceive
Either body or spirit this wild Christmas-
eve.

*Through the floor shot up a lily red,
With a patch of earth from the land of the
dead,
For he was strong in the land of the dead.*

What matter that his cheeks were pale,
His kind kiss'd lips all gray?
"O, love Louise, have you waited long?"
"O, my lord Arthur, yea."

What if his hair that brush'd her cheek
Was stiff with frozen rime?
His eyes were grown quite blue again,
As in the happy time.

"O, love Louise, this is the key
Of the happy golden land!
O, sisters, cross the bridge with me,
My eyes are full of sand.
What matter that I cannot see,
If ye take me by the hand?"

*And ever the great bell overhead
And the tumbling seas mourn'd for the dead;
For their song ceased, and they were dead.*

FROM "THE EARTHLY PARA-
DISE"

THE SINGER'S PRELUDE

OF Heaven or Hell I have no power to
sing,
I cannot ease the burden of your fears,
Or make quick-coming death a little thing,
Or bring again the pleasure of past years,
Nor for my words shall ye forget your
tears,
Or hope again for aught that I can say,
The idle singer of an empty day.

But rather, when aweary of your mirth
From full hearts still unsatisfied ye sigh,
And, feeling kindly unto all the earth,
Grudge every minute as it passes by,
Made the more mindful that the sweet days
die. —
Remember me a little then, I pray,
The idle singer of an empty day.

The heavy trouble, the bewildering care
That weighs us down who live and earn our
bread,
These idle verses have no power to bear;
So let me sing of names remembered,
Because they, living not, can ne'er be dead,
Or long time take their memory quite
away
From us poor singers of an empty day.

Dreamer of dreams, born out of my due
time,
Why should I strive to set the crooked
straight?
Let it suffice me that my murmuring
rhyme
Beats with light wing against the ivory
gate,
Telling a tale not too importunate

To those who in the sleepy region stay,
Lull'd by the singer of an empty day.

Folk say, a wizard to a northern king
At Christmas-tide such wondrous things
    did show,
That through one window men beheld the
    spring,
And through another saw the summer
    glow,
And through a third the fruited vines
    a-row,
While still, unheard, but in its wonted
    way,
Pip'd the drear wind of that December
    day.

So with this Earthly Paradise it is,
if ye will read aright, and pardon me,
Who strive to build a shadowy isle of bliss
Midmost the beating of the steely sea,
Where toss'd about all hearts of men must
    be ;
Whose ravening monsters mighty men
    shall slay,
Not the poor singer of an empty day.

ATALANTA'S VICTORY

Through thick Arcadian woods a hunter
    went,
Following the beasts up, on a fresh spring
    day ;
But since his horn-tipp'd bow but seldom
    bent,
Now at the noontide nought had happ'd to
    slay,
Within a vale he call'd his hounds away,
Hearkening the echoes of his lone voice
    cling
About the cliffs, and through the beech-trees
    ring.

But when they ended, still awhile he
    stood,
And but the sweet familiar thrush could
    hear,
And all the day-long noises of the wood,
And o'er the dry leaves of the vanish'd
    year
His hounds' feet pattering as they drew
    anear,
And heavy breathing from their heads low
    hung,
To see the mighty cornel bow unstrung.

Then, smiling, did he turn to leave the
    place,
But with his first step some new fleeting
    thought
A shadow cast across his sun-burn'd face ;
I think the golden net that April brought
From some warm world his wavering soul
    had caught ;
For, sunk in vague, sweet longing, did he
    go
Betwixt the trees with doubtful steps and
    slow.

Yet, howsoever slow he went, at last
The trees grew sparser, and the wood was
    done ;
Whereon one farewell, backward look he
    cast,
Then, turning round to see what place was
    won,
With shaded eyes look'd underneath the
    sun,
And o'er green meads and new-turn'd fur-
    rows brown
Beheld the gleaming of King Schœneus'
    town.

So thitherward he turn'd, and on each
    side
The folk were busy on the teeming land,
And man and maid from the brown fur-
    rows cried,
Or 'midst the newly blossom'd vines did
    stand,
And, as the rustic weapon press'd the
    hand,
Thought of the nodding of the well-fill'd
    ear,
Or how the knife the heavy bunch should
    shear.

Merry it was : about him sung the
    birds,
The spring flowers bloom'd along the firm,
    dry road,
The sleek-skinn'd mothers of the sharp-
    horn'd herds
Now for the barefoot milking - maidens
    low'd ;
While from the freshness of his blue
    abode,
Glad his death-bearing arrows to for-
    get,
The broad sun blaz'd, nor scatter'd plagues
    as yet.

Through such fair things unto the gates
he came,
And found them open, as though peace
were there ;
Wherethrough, unquestion'd of his race or
name,
He enter'd, and along the streets 'gan fare,
Which at the first of folk were well-nigh
bare ;
But pressing on, and going more hastily,
Men hurrying, too, he 'gan at last to see.

Following the last of these, he still press'd
on,
Until an open space he came unto,
Where wreaths of fame had oft been lost
and won,
For feats of strength folk there were wont
to do.
And now our hunter look'd for something
new,
Because the whole wide space was bare,
and still'd
The high seats were, with eager people
fill'd.

There with the others to a seat he gat,
Whence he beheld a broider'd canopy,
'Neath which in fair array King Schœneus
sat
Upon his throne with councillors thereby ;
And underneath this well-wrought seat and
high
He saw a golden image of the sun,
A silver image of the Fleet-foot One.

A brazen altar stood beneath their feet
Whereon a thin flame flicker'd in the wind ;
Nigh this a herald clad in raiment meet
Made ready even now his horn to wind,
By whom a huge man held a sword, en-
twin'd
With yellow flowers ; these stood a little
space
From off the altar, nigh the starting place.

And there two runners did the sign
abide,
Foot set to foot, — a young man slim and
fair,
Crisp-hair'd, well knit, with firm limbs
often tried
In places where no man his strength may
spare :
Dainty his thin coat was, and on his hair

A golden circlet of renown he wore,
And in his hand an olive garland bore.

But on this day with whom shall he con-
tend ?
A maid stood by him like Diana clad
When in the woods she lists her bow to
bend,
Too fair for one to look on and be glad,
Who scarcely yet has thirty summers had,
If he must still behold her from afar ;
Too fair to let the world live free from war.

She seem'd all earthly matters to forget ;
Of all tormenting lines her face was clear :
Her wide gray eyes upon the goal were
set
Calm and unmov'd as though no soul were
near.
But her foe trembled as a man in fear,
Nor from her loveliness one moment turn'd
His anxious face with fierce desire that
burn'd.

Now through the hush there broke the
trumpet's clang
Just as the setting sun made eventide.
Then from light feet a spurt of dust there
sprang,
And swiftly were they running side by side ;
But silent did the thronging folk abide
Until the turning-post was reach'd at last,
And round about it still abreast they past.

But when the people saw how close they
ran,
When half-way to the starting-point they
were,
A cry of joy broke forth, whereat the man
Headed the white-foot runner, and drew
near
Unto the very end of all his fear;
And scarce his straining feet the ground
could feel,
And bliss unhop'd for o'er his heart 'gan
steal.

But 'midst the loud victorious shouts he
heard
Her footsteps drawing nearer, and the
sound
Of fluttering raiment, and thereat afeard
His flush'd and eager face he turn'd
around,
And even then he felt her past him bound

Fleet as the wind, but scarcely saw her
    there
Till on the goal she laid her fingers fair.

There stood she breathing like a little
    child
Amid some warlike clamor laid asleep,
For no victorious joy her red lips smil'd,
Her cheek its wonted freshness did but
    keep ;
No glance lit up her clear gray eyes and
    deep,
Though some divine thought soften'd all
    her face
As once more rang the trumpet through the
    place.

But her late foe stopp'd short amidst his
    course,
One moment gaz'd upon her piteously,
Then with a groan his lingering feet did
    force
To leave the spot whence he her eyes could
    see ;
And, changed like one who knows his time
    must be
But short and bitter, without any word
He knelt before the bearer of the sword ;

Then high rose up the gleaming deadly
    blade,
Bar'd of its flowers, and through the
    crowded place
Was silence now, and midst of it the
    maid
Went by the poor wretch at a gentle
    pace,
And he to hers upturn'd his sad white
    face ;
Nor did his eyes behold another sight
Ere on his soul there fell eternal night.

ATALANTA'S DEFEAT

Now has the lingering month at last gone
    by,
Again are all folk round the running
    place,
Nor other seems the dismal pageantry
Than heretofore, but that another face
Looks o'er the smooth course ready for the
    race,
For now, beheld of all, Milanion
Stands on the spot he twice has look'd
    upon.

But yet — what change is this that holds
    the maid ?
Does she indeed see in his glittering eye
More than disdain of the sharp shearing
    blade,
Some happy hope of help and victory ?
The others seem'd to say, " We come to
    die ;
Look down upon us for a little while,
That, dead, we may bethink us of thy
    smile."

But he — what look of mastery was this
He cast on her ? why were his lips so red ?
Why was his face so flush'd with happiness?
So looks not one who deems himself but
    dead,
E'en if to death he bows a willing head ;
So rather looks a god well pleas'd to find
Some earthly damsel fashion'd to his mind.

Why must she drop her lids before his
    gaze,
And even as she casts adown her eyes
Redden to note his eager glance of praise,
And wish that she were clad in other
    guise ?
Why must the memory to her heart arise
Of things unnoticed when they first were
    heard,
Some lover's song, some answering maiden's
    word ?

What makes these longings, vague, with-
    out a name,
And this vain pity never felt before,
This sudden languor, this contempt of
    fame,
This tender sorrow for the time past o'er,
These doubts that grow each minute more
    and more ?
Why does she tremble as the time grows
    near,
And weak defeat and woeful victory fear ?

But while she seem'd to hear her beat-
    ing heart,
Above their heads the trumpet blast rang
    out
And forth they sprang, and she must play
    her part ;
Then flew her white feet, knowing not a
    doubt,
Though, slackening once, she turn'd her
    head about,

But then she cried aloud and faster fled
Than e'er before, and all men deem'd him
    dead.

But with no sound he rais'd aloft his
    hand,
And thence what seem'd a ray of light
    there flew
And past the maid roll'd on along the sand ;
Then trembling she her feet together drew,
And in her heart a strong desire there
    grew
To have the toy ; some god she thought
    had given
That gift to her, to make of earth a
    heaven.

Then from the course with eager steps
    she ran,
And in her odorous bosom laid the gold.
But when she turn'd again, the great-
    limb'd man,
Now well ahead, she fail'd not to behold,
And, mindful of her glory waxing cold,
Sprang up and follow'd him in hot pur-
    suit,
Though with one hand she touch'd the
    golden fruit.

Note, too, the bow that she was wont to
    bear
She laid aside to grasp the glittering prize,
And o'er her shoulder from the quiver fair
Three arrows fell and lay before her eyes
Unnoticed, as amidst the people's cries
She sprang to head the strong Milanion,
Who now the turning-post had well-nigh
    won.

But as he set his mighty hand on it
White fingers underneath his own were
    laid,
And white limbs from his dazzled eyes did
    flit ;
Then he the second fruit cast by the maid,
But she ran on awhile, then as afraid
Waver'd and stopp'd, and turn'd and made
    no stay
Until the globe with its bright fellow lay.

Then, as a troubled glance she cast
    around,
Now far ahead the Argive could she see,
And in her garment's hem one hand she
    wound

To keep the double prize, and strenuously
Sped o'er the course, and little doubt had
    she
To win the day, though now but scanty
    space
Was left betwixt him and the winning
    place.

Short was the way unto such winged
    feet ;
Quickly she gain'd upon him, till at last
He turn'd about her eager eyes to meet,
And from his hand the third fair apple
    cast.
She waver'd not, but turn'd and ran so
    fast
After the prize that should her bliss fulfil,
That in her hand it lay ere it was still.

Nor did she rest, but turn'd about to
    win
Once more an unbless'd woeful victory —
And yet — and yet — why does her breath
    begin
To fail her, and her feet drag heavily ?
Why fails she now to see if far or nigh
The goal is ? why do her gray eyes grow
    dim ?
Why do these tremors run through every
    limb ?

She spreads her arms abroad some stay
    to find,
Else must she fall, indeed, and findeth
    this,
A strong man's arms about her body en-
    twin'd.
Nor may she shudder now to feel his kiss,
So wrapt she is in new unbroken bliss :
Made happy that the foe the prize hath
    won.
She weeps glad tears for all her glory
    done.

THE KING'S VISIT

So long he rode he drew anigh
A mill upon the river's brim,
That seem'd a goodly place to him,
For o'er the oily smooth millhead
There hung the apples growing red,
And many an ancient apple-tree
Within the orchard could he see,
While the smooth millwalls white and black
Shook to the great wheel's measur'd clack,

And grumble of the gear within ;
While o'er the roof that dull'd that din
The doves sat crooning half the day,
And round the half-cut stack of hay
The sparrows flutter'd twittering.
  There smiling stay'd the joyous king,
And since the autumn noon was hot
Thought good anigh that pleasant spot
To dine that day, and therewith sent
To tell the miller his intent :
Who held the stirrup of the king,
Bareheaded, joyful at the thing,
While from his horse he lit adown,
Then led him o'er an elm-beam brown,
New cut in February tide,
That cross'd the stream from side to side ;
So underneath the apple trees
The king sat careless, well at ease,
And ate and drank right merrily.
  To whom the miller drew anigh
Among the courtiers, bringing there
Such as he could of country fare,
Green yellowing plums from off his wall,
Wasp-bitten pears, the first to fall
From off the wavering spire-like tree,
Junkets, and cream and fresh honey.

SONG : TO PSYCHE

O PENSIVE, tender maid, downcast and shy,
  Who turnest pale e'en at the name of
    love,
And with flush'd face must pass the elm-
    tree by
Asham'd to hear the passionate gray dove
Moan to his mate, thee too the god shall
    move,
Thee too the maidens shall ungird one
    day,
And with thy girdle put thy shame away.

  What then, and shall white winter ne'er
    be done
Because the glittering frosty morn is fair ?
Because against the early-setting sun
Bright show the gilded boughs though
    waste and bare ?
Because the robin singeth free from care ?
Ah ! these are memories of a better day
When on earth's face the lips of summer
    lay.

  Come then, beloved one, for such as thee
Love loveth, and their hearts he knoweth
    well,

Who hoard their moments of felicity,
As misers hoard the medals that they
    tell,
Lest on the earth but paupers they should
    dwell :
" We hide our love to bless another day ;
The world is hard, youth passes quick,"
    they say.

  Ah, little ones, but if ye could forget
Amidst your outpour'd love that you must
    die,
Then ye, my servants, were death's con
    querors yet,
And love to you should be eternity
How quick soever might the days go by :
Yes, ye are made immortal on the day
Ye cease the dusty grains of time to
    weigh.

  Thou hearkenest, love ? O, make no
    semblance then
Thou art beloved, but as thy wont is
Turn thy gray eyes away from eyes of
    men,
With hands down-dropp'd, that tremble
    with thy bliss,
With hidden eyes, take thy first lover's
    kiss ;
Call this eternity which is to-day,
Nor dream that this our love can pass
    away.

A LAND ACROSS THE SEA

ACROSS the sea a land there is,
  Where, if fate will, men may have bliss,
For it is fair as any land :
There hath the reaper a full hand,
While in the orchard hangs aloft
The purple fig, a-growing soft ;
And fair the trellis'd vine-bunches
Are swung across the high elm-trees ;
And in the rivers great fish play,
While over them pass day by day
The laden barges to their place.
There maids are straight, and fair of face,
And men are stout for husbandry,
And all is well as it can be
Upon this earth where all has end.
  For on them God is pleas'd to send
The gift of Death down from above,
That envy, hatred, and hot love,
Knowledge with hunger by his side,
And avarice and deadly pride,

There may have end like everything
Both to the shepherd and the king :
Lest this green earth become but hell
If folk thereon should ever dwell.
  Full little most men think of this,
But half in woe and half in bliss
They pass their lives, and die at last
Unwilling, though their lot be cast
In wretched places of the earth,
Where men have little joy from birth
Until they die ; in no such case
Were those who till'd this pleasant place.
  There soothly men were loth to die,
Though sometimes in his misery
A man would say "Would I were dead ! "
Alas ! full little likelyhead
That he should live forever there.
  So folk within that country fair
Liv'd on unable to forget
The long'd-for things they could not get,
And without need tormenting still
Each other with some bitter ill ;
Yea, and themselves too, growing gray
With dread of some long-lingering day,
That never came ere they were dead
With green sods growing on the head ;
Nowise content with what they had,
But falling still from good to bad
While hard they sought the hopeless best ;
And seldom happy or at rest
Until at last with lessening blood
One foot within the grave they stood.

ANTIPHONY

Hæc

IN the white-flower'd hawthorn brake,
Love, be merry for my sake ;
Twine the blossoms in my hair,
Kiss me where I am most fair —
Kiss me, love ! for who knoweth
What thing cometh after death ?

Ille

Nay, the garlanded gold hair
Hides thee where thou art most fair ;
Hides the rose-tinged hills of snow —
Ah, sweet love, I have thee now !
Kiss me, love ! for who knoweth
What thing cometh after death ?

Hæc

Shall we weep for a dead day,
Or set Sorrow in our way ?

Hidden by my golden hair,
Wilt thou weep that sweet days wear ?
Kiss me, love ! for who knoweth
What thing cometh after death ?

Ille

Weep, O Love, the days that flit,
  Now, while I can feel thy breath ;
Then may I remember it
  Sad and old, and near my death.
Kiss me, love ! for who knoweth
What thing cometh after death ?

FROM "SIGURD THE
VOLSUNG"

OF THE PASSING AWAY OF BRYNHILD

THEY look'd on each other and spake not ;
    but Gunnar gat him gone,
And came to his brother Hogni, the wise-
    heart Giuki's son,
And spake : " Thou art wise, O Hogni ; go
    in to Brynhild the queen,
And stay her swift departing ; or the last
    of her days hath she seen."

"It is nought, thy word," said Hogni ;
    " wilt thou bring dead men aback,
Or the souls of kings departed midst the
    battle and the wrack ?
Yet this shall be easier to thee than the
    turning Brynhild's heart ;
She came to dwell among us, but in us she
    had no part ;
Let her go her ways from the Nib-
    lungs with her hand in Sigurd's
    hand.
Will the grass grow up henceforward where
    her feet have trodden the land ? "

" O evil day," said Gunnar, " when my
    queen must perish and die ! "

" Such oft betide," said Hogni, " as the lives
    of men flit by ;
But the evil day is a day, and on each day
    groweth a deed,
And a thing that never dieth ; and the
    fateful tale shall speed.
Lo now, let us harden our hearts and set
    our brows as the brass,
Lest men say it, ' They loath'd the evil and
    they brought the evil to pass. ' "

So they spake, and their hearts were heavy,
    and they long'd for the morrow
    morn,
And the morrow of to-morrow, and the new
    day yet to be born.

But Brynhild cried to her maidens : " Now
    open ark and chest,
And draw forth queenly raiment of the
    loveliest and the best,
Red things that the Dwarf-lords fashion'd,
    fair cloths that queens have sew'd
To array the bride for the mighty, and the
    traveller for the road."

They wept as they wrought her bidding
    and did on her goodliest gear ;
But she laugh'd mid the dainty linen, and
    the gold-rings fashion'd fair :
She arose from the bed of the Niblungs,
    and her face no more was wan ;
As a star in the dawn-tide heavens, mid the
    dusky house she shone ;
And they that stood about her, their hearts
    were rais'd aloft
Amid their fear and wonder : then she
    spake them kind and soft :

" Now give me the sword, O maidens,
    wherewith I shear'd the wind
When the Kings of Earth were gather'd to
    know the Chooser's mind."

All sheath'd the maidens brought it, and
    fear'd the hidden blade,
But the naked blue-white edges across her
    knees she laid,
And spake : " The heap'd-up riches, the
    gear my fathers left,
All dear-bought woven wonders, all rings
    from battle reft,
All goods of men desired, now strew
    them on the floor,
And so share among you, maidens, the
    gifts of Brynhild's store."

They brought them mid their weeping, but
    none put forth a hand
To take that wealth desired, the spoils of
    many a land :

There they stand and weep before her, and
    some are mov'd to speech,
And they cast their arms about her and
    strive with her, and beseech

That she look on her lov'd-ones' sorrow
    and the glory of the day.
It was nought ; she scarce might see
    them, and she put their hands
    away,
And she said : " Peace, ye that love
    me ! and take the gifts and the
    gold
In remembrance of my fathers and the
    faithful deeds of old."

Then she spake : " Where now is Gunnar,
    that I may speak with him ?
For new things are mine eyes behold-
    ing, and the Niblung house grows
    dim,
And new sounds gather about me, that
    may hinder me to speak
When the breath is near to flitting, and
    the voice is waxen weak."

Then upright by the bed of the Niblungs
    for a moment doth she stand,
And the blade flasheth bright in the cham-
    ber, but no more they hinder her
    hand
Than if a God were smiting to rend the
    world in two :
Then dull'd are the glittering edges, and
    the bitter point cleaves through
The breast of the all-wise Brynhild, and
    her feet from the pavement fail,
And the sigh of her heart is hearken'd mid
    the hush of the maidens' wail.
Chill, deep is the fear upon them, but they
    bring her aback to the bed,
And her hand is yet on the hilt, and side-
    long droopeth her head.

Then there cometh a cry from without-
    ward, and Gunnar's hurrying feet
Are swift on the kingly threshold, and
    Brynhild's blood they meet.
Low down o'er the bed he hangeth and
    hearkeneth for her word,
And her heavy lids are open'd to look on
    the Niblung lord,
And she saith : " I pray thee a prayer, the
    last word in the world I speak,
That ye bear me forth to Sigurd, and the
    hand my hand would seek ;
The bale for the dead is builded, it is
    wrought full wide on the plain,
It is rais'd for Earth's best Helper, and
    thereon is room for twain :

Ye have hung the shields about it, and the
    Southland hangings spread,
There lay me adown by Sigurd and my head
    beside his head :
But ere you leave us sleeping, draw his
    Wrath from out the sheath,
And lay that Light of the Branstock, and
    the blade that frighted death
Betwixt my side and Sigurd's, as it lay that
    while agone,
When once in one bed together we twain
    were laid alone :
How then when the flames flare upward
    may I be left behind ?
How then may the road he wendeth be hard
    for my feet to find ?
How then in the gates of Valhall may the
    door of the gleaming ring
Clash to on the heel of Sigurd, as I follow
    on my king ? "

Then she rais'd herself on her elbow, but
    again her eyelids sank,
And the wound by the sword-edge whisper'd,
    as her heart from the iron shrank,
And she moan'd : " O lives of man-folk, for
    unrest all overlong
By the Father were ye fashion'd ; and what
    hope amendeth wrong ?
Now at last, O my beloved, all is gone ; none
    else is near,
Through the ages of all ages, never sun-
    der'd, shall we wear. "

Scarce more than a sigh was the word, as
    back on the bed she fell,
Nor was there need in the chamber of the
    passing of Brynhild to tell ;
And no more their lamentation might the
    maidens hold aback,
But the sound of their bitter mourning was
    as if red-handed wrack
Ran wild in the Burg of the Niblungs, and
    the fire were master of all.

Then the voice of Gunnar the war-king
    cried out o'er the weeping hall :
" Wail on, O women forsaken, for the
    mightiest woman born !
Now the hearth is cold and joyless, and the
    waste bed lieth forlorn,
Wail on, but amid your weeping lay hand
    to the glorious dead,
That not alone for an hour may lie Queen
    Brynhild's head :

For here have been heavy tidings, and the
    Mightiest under shield
Is laid on the bale high-builded in the Nib-
    lungs' hallow'd field.
Fare forth ! for he abideth, and we do All-
    father wrong,
If the shining Valhall's pavement await
    their feet o'erlong."

Then they took the body of Brynhild in the
    raiment that she wore,
And out through the gate of the Niblungs
    the holy corpse they bore,
And thence forth to the mead of the people,
    and the high-built shielded bale ;
Then afresh in the open meadows breaks
    forth the women's wail
When they see the bed of Sigurd, and the
    glittering of his gear ;
And fresh is the wail of the people as Bryn-
    hild draweth anear,
And the tidings go before her that for twain
    the bale is built,
That for twain is the oak-wood shielded
    and the pleasant odors spilt.

There is peace on the bale of Sigurd, and
    the Gods look down from on high,
And they see the lids of the Volsung close
    shut against the sky,
As he lies with his shield beside him in the
    Hauberk all of gold,
That has not its like in the heavens, nor has
    earth of its fellow told ;
And forth from the Helm of Aweing are
    the sunbeams flashing wide,
And the sheathed Wrath of Sigurd lies still
    by his mighty side.
Then cometh an elder of days, a man of the
    ancient times,
Who is long past sorrow and joy, and the
    steep of the bale he climbs ;
And he kneeleth down by Sigurd, and
    bareth the Wrath to the sun
That the beams are gather'd about it, and
    from hilt to blood-point run,
And wide o'er the plain of the Niblungs
    doth the Light of the Branstock
    glare,
Till the wondering mountain-shepherds on
    that star of noontide stare,
And fear for many an evil ; but the ancient
    man stands still
With the war-flame on his shoulder, nor
    thinks of good or of ill,

Till the feet of Brynhild's bearers on the
    topmost bale are laid,
And her bed is dight by Sigurd's ; then he
    sinks the pale white blade
And lays it 'twixt the sleepers, and leaves
    them there alone —
He, the last that shall ever behold them, —
    and his days are well nigh done.

Then is silence over the plain ; in the moon
    shine the torches pale
As the best of the Niblung Earl-folk bear
    fire to the builded bale :
Then a wind in the west ariseth, and the
    white flames leap on high,
And with one voice crieth the people a
    great and mighty cry,
And men cast up hands to the Heavens, and
    pray without a word,
As they that have seen God's visage, and
    the face of the Father have heard.

They are gone — the lovely, the mighty, the
    hope of the ancient Earth :
It shall labor and bear the burden as before
    that day of their birth ;
It shall groan in its blind abiding for the
    day that Sigurd hath sped,
And the hour that Brynhild hath hasten'd,
    and the dawn that waketh the
    dead :
It shall yearn, and be oft-times holpen, and
    forget their deeds no more,
Till the new sun beams on Baldur, and the
    happy sealess shore.

THE BURGHERS' BATTLE

THICK rise the spear-shafts o'er the land
That erst the harvest bore ;
The sword is heavy in the hand,
And we return no more.
The light wind waves the Ruddy Fox,
Our banner of the war,
And ripples in the Running Ox,
And we return no more.
Across our stubble acres now
The teams go four and four ;
But outworn elders guide the plough,
And we return no more.
And now the women, heavy-eyed,
Turn through the open door
From gazing down the highway wide,
Where we return no more.

The shadows of the fruited close
Dapple the feast-hall floor ;
There lie our dogs and dream and doze,
And we return no more.
Down from the minster tower to-day
Fall the soft chimes of yore
Amidst the chattering jackdaws' play :
And we return no more.
But underneath the streets are still ;
Noon, and the market's o'er !
Back go the goodwives o'er the hill ;
For we return no more.
What merchant to our gates shall come ?
What wise man bring us lore ?
What abbot ride away to Rome,
Now we return no more ?
What mayor shall rule the hall we built ?
Whose scarlet sweep the floor ?
What judge shall doom the robber's guilt,
Now we return no more ?
New houses in the streets shall rise
Where builded we before,
Of other stone wrought otherwise ;
For we return no more.
And crops shall cover field and hill,
Unlike what once they bore,
And all be done without our will,
Now we return no more.
Look up ! the arrows streak the sky,
The horns of battle roar ;
The long spears lower and draw nigh,
And we return no more.
Remember how, beside the wain,
We spoke the word of war,
And sow'd this harvest of the plain,
And we return no more.
Lay spears about the Ruddy Fox !
The days of old are o'er ;
Heave sword about the Running Ox !
For we return no more.

A DEATH SONG

WHAT cometh here from west to east
    a-wending ?
And who are these, the marchers stern and
    slow ?
We bear the message that the rich are
    sending
Aback to those who bade them wake and
    know.
Not one, not one, nor thousands must they
    slay,
But one and all if they would dusk the day.

We ask'd them for a life of toilsome earning,
They bade us bide their leisure for our bread ;
We crav'd to speak to tell our woeful learning :
We come back speechless, bearing back our dead.

They will not learn ; they have no ears to hearken ;
They turn their faces from the eyes of fate;

Their gay-lit halls shut out the skies that darken.
But, lo ! this dead man knocking at the gate.

Here lies the sign that we shall break our prison ;
Amidst the storm he won a prisoner's rest ;
But in the cloudy dawn the sun arisen
Brings us our day of work to win the best.
Not one, not one, nor thousands must they slay,
But one and all if they would dusk the day.

Lord De Tabley

(JOHN LEICESTER WARREN)

A WOODLAND GRAVE

BRING no jarring lute this way
To demean her sepulchre,
Toys of love and idle day
Vanish as we think of her.
We, who read her epitaph,
Find the world not worth a laugh.

Light, our light, what dusty night
Numbs the golden drowsy head ?
Lo ! empath'd in pearls of light,
Morn resurgent from the dead ;
From whose amber shoulders flow
Shroud and sheet of cloudy woe.

Woods are dreaming, and she dreams :
Through the foliaged roof above
Down immeasurably streams
Splendor like an angel's love,
Till the tomb and gleaming urn
In a mist of glory burn.

Cedars there in outspread palls
Lean their rigid canopies ;
Yet a lark note through them falls,
As he scales his orient skies.
That aërial song of his,
Sweet, might come from thee in bliss.

There the roses pine and weep
Strong, delicious human tears ;
There the posies o'er her sleep
Through the years — ah ! through the years :

Spring on spring renew the show
Of their frail memorial woe.

Wreaths of intertwisted yew
Lay for cypress where she lies,
Mingle perfume from the blue
Of the forest violet's eyes.
Let the squirrel sleek its fur,
And the primrose peep at her.

We have seen three winters sow
Hoarfrost on thy winding-sheet :
Snows return again, and thou
Hearest not the crisping sleet.
Winds arise and winds depart,
Yet no tempest rocks thy heart.

We have seen with fiery tongue
Thrice the infant crocus born :
Thrice its trembling curtain hung
In a chink of frozen morn.
This can rear its silken crest :
Nothing thaws her ice-bound breast.

We have eaten, we have earn'd
Wine of grief and bread of care,
We, who saw her first inurn'd
In the dust and silence there.
We have wept — ah God ! not so :
Trivial tears dried long ago.

But we yearn and make our moan
For the step we us'd to know :
Gentle hand and tender tone,
Laughter in a silver flow :

All that sweetness in thy chain,
Tyrant Grave, restore again.

Bring again the maid who died :
We have wither'd since she went.
O unseal the shadowy side
Of her marble monument ;
Earth, disclose her as she lies
Doz'd with woodland lullabies.

A SIMPLE MAID

THOU hast lost thy love, poor fool,
Creep into thy bed and weep.
Loss must be a maiden's school,
Loss and love and one long sleep.
Half her time perplex'd with tears
Till the dust end all her years, —
All her fears.

Was thy love so gracious, lass ?
Never such a love before
In this old world came to pass,
Nor shall be for evermore.
Sweet and true, a king of men,
None like him shall come again, —
Come again.

Was thy bud so precious, lass,
Opening to a perfect rose ?
Till between the leaves, alas !
Winter fell in flaky snows.
Then, ah ! then, its crimson side
Brake upon the briers and died, —
Brake and died.

FORTUNE'S WHEEL

I HAD a true-love, none so dear,
And a friend both leal and tried :
I had a cask of good old beer,
And a gallant horse to ride.

A little while did Fortune smile
On him and her and me :
We sang along the road of life
Like birds upon a tree.

My lady fell to shame and hell,
And with her took my friend ;
My cask ran sour, my horse went lame,
So alone in the cold I end.

CIRCE

THIS the house of Circe, queen of charms, —
A kind of beacon-cauldron pois'd on high,
Hoop'd round with ember-clasping iron
bars,
Sways in her palace porch, and smoulder-
ingly
Drips out in blots of fire and ruddy stars :
But out behind that trembling furnace air
The lands are ripe and fair,
Hush are the hills and quiet to the eye.
The river's reach goes by
With lamb and holy tower and squares of
corn,
And shelving interspace
Of holly bush and thorn
And hamlets happy in an Alpine morn,
And deep-bower'd lanes with grace
Of woodbine newly born.

But inward o'er the hearth a torch-head
stands
Inverted, slow green flames of fulvous hue,
Echoed in wave-like shadows over her.
A censer's swing-chain set in her fair
hands
Dances up wreaths of intertwisted blue
In clouds of fragrant frankincense and
myrrh.
A giant tulip head and two pale leaves
Grew in the midmost of her chamber there.
A flaunting bloom, naked and undivine,
Rigid and bare,
Gaunt as a tawny bond-girl born to shame,
With freckled cheeks and splotch'd side
serpentine,
A gipsy among flowers,
Unmeet for bed or bowers,
Virginal where pure-handed damsels sleep :
Let it not breathe a common air with them,
Lest when the night is deep,
And all things have their quiet in the
moon,
Some birth of poison from its leaning stem
Waft in between their slumber-parted lips,
And they cry out or swoon,
Deeming some vampire sips
Where riper Love may come for nectar
boon !

And near this tulip, rear'd across a loom,
Hung a fair web of tapestry half done,
Crowding with folds and fancies half the
room :

Men eyed as gods, and damsels still as
    stone,
Pressing their brows alone,
In amethystine robes,
Or reaching at the polish'd orchard globes,
Or rubbing parted love-lips on their rind,
While the wind
Sows with sere apple-leaves their breast
    and hair.
And all the margin there
Was arabesqued and border'd intricate
With hairy spider things,
That catch and clamber,
And salamander in his dripping cave
Satanic ebon-amber ;
Blind worm, and asp, and eft of cumbrous
    gait,
And toads who love rank grasses near a
    grave,
And the great goblin moth, who bears
Between his wings the ruin'd eyes of
    death ;
And the enamell'd sails
Of butterflies, who watch the morning's
    breath,
And many an emerald lizard with quick
    ears
Asleep in rocky dales ;
And for outer fringe, embroider'd small,
A ring of many locusts, horny-coated,
A round of chirping tree-frogs merry-
    throated,
And sly, fat fishes sailing, watching all.

A SONG OF FAITH FORSWORN

Take back your suit.
It came when I was weary and distraught
With hunger. Could I guess the fruit you
    brought ?
I ate in mere desire of any food,
Nibbled its edge, and nowhere found it
    good.
Take back your suit.

Take back your love.
It is a bird poach'd from my neighbor's
    wood :
Its wings are wet with tears, its beak with
    blood.
'Tis a strange fowl with feathers like a
    crow :
Death's raven, it may be, for all we know.
Take back your love.

Take back your gifts.
False is the hand that gave them ; and the
    mind
That plann'd them, as a hawk spread in
    the wind
To poise and snatch the trembling mouse
    below,
To ruin where it dares — and then to go.
Take back your gifts.

Take back your vows.
Elsewhere you trimm'd and taught these
    lamps to burn ;
You bring them stale and dim to serve my
    turn.
You lit those candles in another shrine,
Gutter'd and cold you offer them on
    mine.
Take back your vows.

Take back your words.
What is your love ? Leaves on a woodland
    plain,
Where some are running and where some
    remain.
What is your faith ? Straws on a moun-
    tain height,
Dancing like demons on Walpurgis night.
Take back your words.

Take back your lies.
Have them again : they wore a rainbow
    face,
Hollow with sin and leprous with dis-
    grace :
Their tongue was like a mellow turret
    bell
To toll hearts burning into wide-lipp'd hell.
Take back your lies.

Take back your kiss.
Shall I be meek, and lend my lips again
To let this adder daub them with his
    stain ?
Shall I turn cheek to answer, when I hate ?
You kiss like Judas in the garden gate !
Take back your kiss.

Take back delight,
A paper boat launch'd on a heaving pool
To please a child, and folded by a fool ;
The wild elms roar'd : it sail'd — a yard
    or more.
Out went our ship, but never came to shore.
Take back delight.

Take back your wreath.
Has it done service on a fairer brow ?
Fresh, was it folded round her bosom snow ?
Her cast-off weed my breast will never
      wear :
Your word is 'love me ;' my reply, ' de-
      spair ! '
Take back your wreath.

THE TWO OLD KINGS

In ruling well what guerdon ?   Life runs
      low,
As yonder lamp upon the hour-glass lies,
Waning and wasted.   We are great and
      wise,
But Love is gone, and Silence seems to grow

Along the misty road where we must
      go.
From summits near the morning star's up-
      rise
Death comes, a shadow from the northern
      skies,
As, when all leaves are down, thence
      comes the snow.
Brother and king, we hold our last carouse.
One loving-cup we drain, and then fare-
      well.
The night is spent.   The crystal morning
      ray
Calls us, as soldiers laurell'd on our brows,
To march undaunted, while the clarions
      swell,
Heroic hearts, upon our lonely way.

Algernon Charles Swinburne

A MATCH

If love were what the rose is,
   And I were like the leaf,
Our lives would grow together
In sad or singing weather,
Blown fields or flowerful closes,
   Green pleasure or gray grief ;
If love were what the rose is,
   And I were like the leaf.

If I were what the words are,
   And love were like the tune,
With double sound and single
Delight our lips would mingle,
With kisses glad as birds are
   That get sweet rain at noon ;
If I were what the words are,
   And love were like the tune.

If you were life, my darling,
   And I your love were death,
We 'd shine and snow together
Ere March made sweet the weather
With daffodil and starling
   And hours of fruitful breath ;
If you were life, my darling,
   And I your love were death.

If you were thrall to sorrow,
   And I were page to joy,

We 'd play for lives and seasons
With loving looks and treasons
And tears of night and morrow
   And laughs of maid and boy ;
If you were thrall to sorrow,
   And I were page to joy.

If you were April's lady,
   And I were lord in May,
We 'd throw with leaves for hours
And draw for days with flowers,
Till day like night were shady
   And night were bright like day ;
If you were April's lady,
   And I were lord in May.

If you were queen of pleasure,
   And I were king of pain,
We 'd hunt down love together,
Pluck out his flying-feather,
And teach his feet a measure,
   And find his mouth a rein ;
If you were queen of pleasure,
   And I were king of pain.

HESPERIA

Out of the golden remote wild west where
      the sea without shore is,
Full of the sunset, and sad, if at all, with
      the fulness of joy,

As a wind sets in with the autumn that
  blows from the region of stories,
Blows with a perfume of songs and of
  memories belov'd from a boy,
Blows from the capes of the past oversea
  to the bays of the present,
Fill'd as with shadow of sound with the
  pulse of invisible feet,
Far out to the shallows and straits of the
  future, by rough ways or pleasant,
Is it thither the wind's wings beat ? is it
  hither to me, O my sweet ?
For thee, in the stream of the deep tide-
  wind blowing in with the water,
Thee I behold as a bird borne in with
  the wind from the west,
Straight from the sunset, across white
  waves whence rose as a daughter
Venus thy mother, in years when the
  world was a water at rest.
Out of the distance of dreams, as a dream
  that abides after slumber,
Stray'd from the fugitive flock of the
  night, when the moon overhead
Wanes in the wan waste heights of the
  heaven, and stars without number
Die without sound, and are spent like
  lamps that are burnt by the dead,
Comes back to me, stays by me, lulls me
  with touch of forgotten caresses,
One warm dream clad about with a fire
  as of life that endures ;
The delight of thy face, and the sound
  of thy feet, and the wind of thy
  tresses,
And all of a man that regrets, and all of
  a maid that allures.
But thy bosom is warm for my face and
  profound as a manifold flower,
Thy silence as music, thy voice as an
  odor that fades in a flame ;
Not a dream, not a dream is the kiss of thy
  mouth, and the bountiful hour
That makes me forget what was sin,
  and would make me forget were it
  shame.
Thine eyes that are quiet, thy hands that
  are tender, thy lips that are loving,
Comfort and cool me as dew in the dawn
  of a moon like a dream ;
And my heart yearns baffled and blind,
  mov'd vainly toward thee, and mov-
  ing
As the refluent seaweed moves in the
  languid exuberant stream,

Fair as a rose is on earth, as a rose under
  water in prison,
That stretches and swings to the slow
  passionate pulse of the sea,
Clos'd up from the air and the sun, but
  alive, as a ghost re-arisen,
Pale as the love that revives as a ghost
  re-arisen in me.
From the bountiful infinite west, from the
  happy memorial places
Full of the stately repose and the lordly
  delight of the dead,
Where the fortunate islands are lit with
  the light of ineffable faces,
And the sound of a sea without wind is
  about them, and sunset is red,
Come back to redeem and release me from
  love that recalls and represses,
That cleaves to my flesh as a flame, till
  the serpent has eaten his fill ;
From the bitter delights of the dark, and
  the feverish, the furtive caresses
That murder the youth in a man or ever
  his heart have its will.
Thy lips cannot laugh and thine eyes can-
  not weep ; thou art pale as a rose
  is,
Paler and sweeter than leaves that cover
  the blush of the bud ;
And the heart of the flower is compassion,
  and pity the core it incloses,
Pity, not love, that is born of the breath
  and decays with the blood.
As the cross that a wild nun clasps till the
  edge of it bruises her bosom,
So love wounds as we grasp it, and black-
  ens and burns as a flame ;
I have lov'd overmuch in my life : when
  the live bud bursts with the blos-
  som,
Bitter as ashes or tears is the fruit, and
  the wine thereof shame.
As a heart that its anguish divides is the
  green bud cloven asunder ;
As the blood of a man self-slain is the
  flush of the leaves that allure ;
And the perfume as poison and wine to the
  brain, a delight and a wonder ;
And the thorns are too sharp for a
  boy, too slight for a man, to en-
  dure.
Too soon did I love it, and lost love's rose ;
  and I car'd not for glory's :
Only the blossoms of sleep and of plea-
  sure were mix'd in my hair.

Was it myrtle or poppy thy garland was
    woven with, O my Dolores ?
Was it pallor or slumber, or blush as of
    blood, that I found in thee fair ?
For desire is a respite from love, and the
    flesh, not the heart, is her fuel ;
She was sweet to me once, who am fled
    and escap'd from the rage of her
    reign ;
Who behold as of old time at hand as I turn,
    with her mouth growing cruel,
And flush'd as with wine with the blood
    of her lovers, Our Lady of Pain.
Low down where the thicket is thicker with
    thorns than with leaves in the sum-
    mer,
In the brake is a gleaming of eyes
    and a hissing of tongues that I
    knew ;
And the lithe long throats of her snakes
    reach round her, their mouths over-
    come her,
And her lips grow cool with their foam,
    made moist as a desert with dew.
With the thirst and the hunger of lust
    though her beautiful lips be so
    bitter,
With the cold foul foam of the snakes
    they soften and redden and smile ;
And her fierce mouth sweetens, her eyes
    wax wide and her eyelashes glit-
    ter,
And she laughs with a savor of blood in
    her face, and a savor of guile.
She laughs, and her hands reach hither, her
    hair blows hither and hisses
As a low-lit flame in a wind, back-blown
    till it shudder and leap ;
Let her lips not again lay hold on my soul,
    nor her poisonous kisses,
To consume it alive and divide from thy
    bosom, Our Lady of Sleep.
Ah, daughter of sunset and slumber, if now
    it return into prison,
Who shall redeem it anew ? but we, if
    thou wilt, let us fly ;
Let us take to us, now that the white skies
    thrill with a moon unarisen,
Swift horses of fear or of love, take flight
    and depart and not die.
They are swifter than dreams, they are
    stronger than death ; there is none
    that hath ridden,
None that shall ride in the dim strange
    ways of his life as we ride :

By the meadows of memory, the highlands
    of hope, and the shore that is hidden,
Where life breaks loud and unseen, a
    sonorous invisible tide ;
By the sands where sorrow has trodden,
    the salt pools bitter and sterile,
By the thundering reef and the low sea
    wall and the channel of years,
Our wild steeds press on the night, strain
    hard through pleasure and peril,
Labor and listen and pant not or pause
    for the peril that nears ;
And the sound of them trampling the way
    cleaves night as an arrow asunder,
And slow by the sand-hill and swift by
    the down with its glimpses of grass,
Sudden and steady the music, as eight hoofs
    trample and thunder,
Rings in the ear of the low blind wind of
    the night as we pass ;
Shrill shrieks in our faces the blind bland
    air that was mute as a maiden,
Stung into storm by the speed of our
    passage, and deaf where we past ;
And our spirits too burn as we bound, thine
    holy but mine heavy-laden,
As we burn with the fire of our flight ;
    ah, love, shall we win at the last ?

IN MEMORY OF WALTER SAV-
AGE LANDOR

BACK to the flower-town, side by side,
    The bright months bring,
New-born, the bridegroom and the bride,
    Freedom and spring.

The sweet land laughs from sea to sea,
    Fill'd full of sun ;
All things come back to her, being free ;
    All things but one.

In many a tender wheaten plot
    Flowers that were dead
Live, and old suns revive ; but not
    That holier head.

By this white wandering waste of sea,
    Far north, I hear
One face shall never turn to me
    As once this year :

Shall never smile and turn and rest
    On mine as there,

Nor one most sacred hand be prest
    Upon my hair.

I came as one whose thoughts half linger,
    Half run before ;
The youngest to the oldest singer
    That England bore.

I found him whom I shall not find
    Till all grief end,
In holiest age our mightiest mind,
    Father and friend.

But thou, if anything endure,
    If hope there be,
O spirit that man's life left pure,
    Man's death set free,

Not with disdain of days that were
    Look earthward now ;
Let dreams revive the reverend hair,
    The imperial brow ;

Come back in sleep, for in the life
    Where thou art not
We find none like thee.   Time and strife
    And the world's lot

Move thee no more ; but love at least
    And reverent heart
May move thee, royal and release,
    Soul, as thou art.

And thou, his Florence, to thy trust
    Receive and keep,
Keep safe his dedicated dust,
    His sacred sleep.

So shall thy lovers, come from far,
    Mix with thy name
As morning-star with evening-star
    His faultless fame.

LOVE AT SEA

IMITATED FROM THÉOPHILE GAUTIER

WE are in love's land to-day ;
    Where shall we go ?
Love, shall we start or stay,
    Or sail or row ?
There 's many a wind and way,
And never a May but May ;
We are in love's hand to-day ;
    Where shall we go ?

Our landwind is the breath
Of sorrows kiss'd to death
    And joys that were ;
Our ballast is a rose ;
Our way lies where God knows
    And love knows where.
      We are in love's hand to-day —

Our seamen are fledged Loves,
Our masts are bills of doves,
    Our decks fine gold ;
Our ropes are dead maids' hair,
Our stores are love-shafts fair
    And manifold.
      We are in love's land to-day —

Where shall we land you, sweet ?
On fields of strange men's feet,
    Or fields near home ?
Or where the fire-flowers blow,
Or where the flowers of snow
    Or flowers of foam ?
      We are in love's hand to-day —

Land me, she says, where love
Shows but one shaft, one dove,
    One heart, one hand, —
A shore like that, my dear,
Lies where no man will steer,
    No maiden land.

FROM " ROSAMOND "

ROSAMOND AT WOODSTOCK

Rosamond.   Are you tir'd ?
But I seem shameful to you, shameworthy,
Contemnable of good women, being so bad,
So bad as I am. Yea, would God, would
    God,
I had kept my face from this contempt of
    yours.
Insolent custom would not anger me
So as you do ; more clean are you than I,
Sweeter for gathering of the grace of God
To perfume some accomplish'd work in
    heaven ?
I do not use to scorn, stay pure of hate,
Seeing how myself am scorn'd unworthily;
But anger here so takes me in the throat
I would speak now for fear it strangle me.
Here, let me feel your hair and hands and
    face ;
I see not flesh is holier than flesh,

Or blood than blood more choicely quali-
fied
That scorn should live between them.
Better am I
Than many women ; you are not over
fair,
Nor delicate with some exceeding good
In the sweet flesh ; you have no much
tenderer soul
Than love is moulded out of for God's
use
Who wrought our double need ; you are
not so choice
That in the golden kingdom of your eyes
All coins should melt for service. But I
that am
Part of the perfect witness for the world
How good it is ; I chosen in God's eyes
To fill the lean account of under men,
The lank and hunger-bitten ugliness
Of half his people ; I who make fair heads
Bow, saying, "Though we be in no wise
fair
We have touch'd all beauty with our eyes,
we have
Some relish in the hand, and in the lips
Some breath of it," because they saw me
once ;
I whose curl'd hair was as a strong stak'd
net
To take the hunters and the hunt, and bind
Faces and feet and hands ; a golden gin
Wherein the tawny-lidded lions fell,
Broken at ankle ; I that am yet, ah yet,
And shall be till the worm hath share in
me,
Fairer than love or the clean truth of
God,
More sweet than sober customs of kind
use
That shackle pain and stablish temper-
ance ;
I that have roses in my name, and make
All flowers glad to set their color by ;
I that have held a land between twin lips
And turn'd large England to a little kiss ;
God thinks not of me as contemptible ;
And that you think me even a smaller
thing
Than your own goodness and slight name
of good,
Your special, thin, particular repute, —
I would some mean could be but clear to
me
Not to contemn you.

FROM "ATALANTA IN CALYDON"

CHORUS : — "WHEN THE HOUNDS OF SPRING"

WHEN the hounds of spring are on winter's
traces,
The mother of months in meadow or
plain
Fills the shadows and windy places
With lisp of leaves and ripple of rain ;
And the brown bright nightingale amorous
Is half assuaged for Itylus,
For the Thracian ships and the foreign
faces,
The tongueless vigil, and all the pain.

Come with bows bent and with emptying of
quivers,
Maiden most perfect, lady of light,
With a noise of winds and many rivers,
With a clamor of waters, and with
might ;
Bind on thy sandals, O thou most fleet,
Over the splendor and speed of thy feet ;
For the faint east quickens, the wan west
shivers,
Round the feet of the day and the feet
of the night.

Where shall we find her, how shall we sing
to her,
Fold our hands round her knees, and
cling ?
O that man's heart were as fire and could
spring to her,
Fire, or the strength of the streams
that spring !
For the stars and the winds are unto her
As raiment, as songs of the harp-player ;
For the risen stars and the fallen cling to
her,
And the southwest-wind and the west-
wind sing.

For winter's rains and ruins are over,
And all the season of snows and sins ;
The days dividing lover and lover,
The light that loses, the night that
wins ;
And time remember'd is grief forgotten,
And frosts are slain and flowers begotten,
And in green underwood and cover
Blossom by blossom the spring begins.

The full streams feed on flower of rushes,
   Ripe grasses trammel a travelling foot,
The faint fresh flame of the young year
   flushes
   From leaf to flower and flower to fruit ;
And fruit and leaf are as gold and fire,
And the oat is heard above the lyre,
And the hoofed heel of a satyr crushes
   The chestnut-husk at the chestnut-
   root.

And Pan by noon and Bacchus by night,
   Fleeter of foot than the fleet-foot kid,
Follows with dancing and fills with delight
   The Mænad and the Bassarid ;
And soft as lips that laugh and hide
The laughing leaves of the trees divide,
And screen from seeing and leave in sight
   The god pursuing, the maiden hid.

The ivy falls with the Bacchanal's hair
   Over her eyebrows, hiding her eyes ;
The wild vine slipping down leaves bare
   Her bright breast shortening into
   sighs ;
The wild vine slips with the weight of its
   leaves,
But the berried ivy catches and cleaves
To the limbs that glitter, the feet that scare
   The wolf that follows, the fawn that
   flies.

FROM THE CHORUS, " WE HAVE SEEN
      THEE, O LOVE ! "

WE have seen thee, O Love, thou art fair ;
   thou art goodly, O Love ;
Thy wings make light in the air as the
   wings of a dove.
Thy feet are as winds that divide the
   stream of the sea ;
Earth is thy covering to hide thee, the gar-
   ment of thee.
Thou art swift and subtle and blind as a
   flame of fire ;
Before thee the laughter, behind thee the
   tears of desire ;
And twain go forth beside thee, a man with
   a maid ;
Her eyes are the eyes of a bride whom
   delight makes afraid ;
As the breath in the buds that stir is her
   bridal breath :
But Fate is the name of her ; and his name
   is Death.

FROM "CHASTELARD"

CHASTELARD AND MARY STUART

Scene. — *In Prison, before* Chastelard's
      Execution.

Queen. Would God my heart were
   greater ; but God wot
I have no heart to bear with fear and die.
Yea, and I cannot help you : or I know
I should be nobler, bear a better heart :
But as this stands — I pray you for good
   love,
As you hold honor a costlier thing than
   life —
Chastelard. Well ?
Queen.   Nay, I would not
   be denied for shame ;
In brief, I pray you give me that again.
Chast. What, my reprieve ?
Queen.   Even so ; deny me not.
For your sake mainly : yea, by God you
   know
How fain I were to die in your death's
   stead,
For your name's sake. This were no need
   to swear,
Lest we be mock'd to death with a re-
   prieve,
And so both die, being sham'd. What,
   shall I swear ?
What, if I kiss you ? must I pluck it out ?
You do not love me : no, nor honor.
   Come,
I know you have it about you : give it me.
Chast. I cannot yield you such a thing
   again ;
Not as I had it.
Queen.   A coward ? what shift now ?
Do such men make such cravens ?
Chast.   Chide me not :
Pity me that I cannot help my heart.
Queen. Heaven mend mine eyes that took
   you for a man !
What, is it sewn into your flesh ? take
   heed —
Nay, but for shame — what have you done
   with it ?
Chast. Why, there it lies, torn up.
Queen.   God help me, sir !
Have you done this ?
Chast.   Yea, sweet ; what should I do ?
Did I not know you to the bone, my sweet ?
God speed you well ? you have a goodly
   lord.

Queen. My love, sweet love, you are
more fair than he,
Yea, fairer many times : I love you much,
Sir, know you that ?
Chast. I think I know that well.
Sit here a little till I feel you through
¯n all my breath and blood for some sweet
while.
O gracious body that mine arms have had,
And hair my face has felt on it ! grave eyes
And low thick lids that keep since years
agone
In the blue sweet of each particular vein
Some special print of me ! I am right glad
That I must never feel a bitterer thing
Than your soft curl'd-up shoulder and
amorous arms
From this time forth ; nothing can hap to
me
Less good than this for all my whole life
through.
I would not have some new pain after this
Come spoil the savor. O, your round bird's
throat,
More soft than sleep or singing ; your calm
cheeks,
Turn'd bright, turn'd wan with kisses hard
and hot ;
The beautiful color of your deep curv'd
hands,
Made of a red rose that had changed to
white ;
That mouth mine own holds half the sweet-
ness of,
Yea, my heart holds the sweetness of it,
whence
My life began in me ; mine that ends here
Because you have no mercy, — nay, you
know
You never could have mercy. My fair
love,
Kiss me again, God loves you not the
less ;
Why should one woman have all goodly
things ?
You have all beauty ; let mean women's
lips
Be pitiful and speak truth : they will not
be
Such perfect things as yours. Be not
asham'd
That hands not made like these that snare
men's souls
Should do men good, give alms, relieve
men's pain ;

You have the better, being more fair than
they,
They are half foul, being rather good than
fair ;
You are quite fair : to be quite fair is
best.
Why, two nights hence I dream'd that I
could see
In through your bosom under the left
flower,
And there was a round hollow, and at
heart
A little red snake sitting, without spot,
That bit — like this, and suck'd up sweet
— like this,
And curl'd its lithe light body right and left,
And quiver'd like a woman in act to love.
Then there was some low flutter'd talk i'
the lips,
Faint sound of soft fierce words caressing
them —
Like a fair woman's when her love gets
way.
Ah, your old kiss — I know the ways of it :
Let the lips cling a little. Take them off,
And speak some word, or I go mad with
love.
Queen. Will you not have my chaplain
come to you ?
Chast. Some better thing of yours —
some handkerchief,
Some fringe of scarf to make confession
to —
You had some book about you that fell
out —
Queen. A little written book of Ron-
sard's rhymes,
His gift, I wear in there for love of him —
See, here between our feet.
Chast. Ay, my old lord's —
The sweet chief poet, my dear friend long
since ?
Give me the book. Lo you, this verse of
his :
With coming lilies in late April came
Her body, fashion'd whiter for their shame ;
And roses, touch'd with blood since Adon
bled,
From her fair color fill'd their lips with red :
A goodly praise : I could not praise you so.
I read that while your marriage-feast went
on.
Leave me this book, I pray you : I would
read
The hymn of death here over ere I die ;

I shall know soon how much he knew of
death
When that was written. One thing I
know now,
I shall not die with half a heart at least,
Nor shift my face, nor weep my fault alive,
Nor swear if I might live and do new
deeds
I would do better. Let me keep the book.
    Queen. Yea, keep it : as would God you
had kept your life
Out of mine eyes and hands. I am wrung
to the heart :
This hour feels dry and bitter in my mouth
As if its sorrow were my body's food
More than my soul's. There are bad
thoughts in me —
Most bitter fancies biting me like birds
That tear each other. Suppose you need
not die ?
    Chast. You know I cannot live for two
hours more.
Our fate was made thus ere our days were
made :
Will you fight fortune for so small a
grief ?
But for one thing I were full fain of death.
    Queen. What thing is that ?
    Chast. None need to name the thing.
Why, what can death do with me fit to
fear ?
For if I sleep I shall not weep awake ;
Or if their saying be true of things to
come,
Though hell be sharp, in the worst ache
of it
I shall be eas'd so God will give me back
Sometimes one golden gracious sight of
you —
The aureole woven flowerlike through your
hair,
And in your lips the little laugh as red
As when it came upon a kiss and ceas'd,
Touching my mouth.
    Queen. As I do now, this way,
With my heart after : would I could shed
tears,
Tears should not fail when the heart shud-
ders so.
But your bad thought ?
    Chast. Well, such a thought as this :
It may be, long time after I am dead,
For all you are, you may see bitter days ;
God may forget you or be wroth with you :
Then shall you lack a little help of me,

And I shall feel your sorrow touching you,
A happy sorrow, though I may not touch :
I that would fain be turn'd to flesh again,
Fain get back life to give up life for you,
To shed my blood for help, that long ago
You shed and were not holpen : and your
heart
Will ache for help and comfort, yea, for
love,
And find less love than mine — for I do
think
You never will be lov'd thus in your life.
    Queen. It may be man will never love
me more ;
For I am sure I shall not love man twice.
    Chast. I know not : men must love you
in life's spite,
For you will always kill them ; man by man
Your lips will bite them dead ; yea, though
you would,
You shall not spare one ; all will die of
you ;
I cannot tell what love shall do with these,
But I for all my love shall have no might
To help you more, mine arms and hands
no power
To fasten on you more. This cleaves my
heart,
That they shall never touch your body
more.
But for your grief — you will not have to
grieve ;
For being in such poor eyes so beautiful
It must needs be as God is more than I
So much more love he hath of you than
mine ;
Yea, God shall not be bitter with my love,
Seeing she is so sweet. ·
    Queen. Ah, my sweet fool,
Think you when God will ruin me for sin
My face of color shall prevail so much
With him, so soften the tooth'd iron's edge
To save my throat a scar ? Nay, I am sure
I shall die somehow sadly.
    Chast. This is pure grief ;
The shadow of your pity for my death,
Mere foolishness of pity : all sweet moods
Throw out such little shadows of them-
selves,
Leave such light fears behind. You, die
like me ?
Stretch your throat out that I may kiss all
round
Where mine shall be cut through : suppose
my mouth

The axe-edge to bite so sweet a throat in
   twain
With bitter iron, should not it turn soft
As lip is soft to lip ?
  Queen.   I am quite sure
I shall die sadly some day, Chastelard ;
I am quite certain.
  Chast.   Do not think such things ;
Lest all my next world's memories of you
   be
As heavy as this thought.
  Queen.   I will not grieve you ;
Forgive me that my thoughts were sick
   with grief.
What can I do to give you ease at heart ?
Shall I kiss now ?   I pray you have no
   fear
But that I love you.
  Chast.   Turn your face to me ;
I do not grudge your face this death of
   mine ;
It is too fair — by God, you are too fair.
What noise is that ?
  Queen. Can the hour be through so soon ?
I bade them give me but a little hour.
Ah ! I do love you ! such brief space for
   love !
I am yours all through, do all your will
   with me ;
What if we lay and let them take us fast,
Lips grasping lips.   I dare do anything.
  Chast. Show better cheer : let no man
   see you maz'd ;
Make haste and kiss me ; cover up your
   throat,
Lest one see tumbled lace and prate of it.
              Enter the guard.

FROM "BOTHWELL"

JOHN KNOX'S INDICTMENT OF THE QUEEN

God ye hear not, how shall ye hear me ?
Or if your eyes be seal'd to know not her,
If she be fit to live or no, can I
With words unseal them ? None so young
   of you
But hath long life enough to understand
And reason to record what he hath seen
Of hers and of God's dealings mutually
Since she came in.   Then was her spirit
   made soft,
Her words as oil, and with her amorous
   face

She caught men's eyes to turn them where
   she would,
And with the strong sound of her name of
   queen
Made their necks bend ; that even of God's
   own men
There were that bade refuse her not her
   will,
Deny not her, fair woman and great queen,
Her natural freedom born, to give God
   praise
What way she would, and pray what
   prayers ; though these
Be as they were, to God abominable
And venomous to men's souls.   So came
   there back
The cursed thing cast forth of us, and so
Out of her fair face and imperious eyes
Lighten'd the light whereby men walk in
   hell.
And I that sole stood out and bade not let
The lightning of this curse come down on
   us
And fly with feet as fire on all winds blown
To burn men's eyes out that beheld God's
   face,
That being long blind but now gat sight,
   and saw
And prais'd him seeing — I that then spake
   and said,
Ten thousand men here landed of our foes
Were not so fearful to me on her side
As one mass said in Scotland — that with-
   stood
The man to his face I lov'd, her father's
   son,
Then master'd by the pity of her, and
   made
Through that good mind not good — who
   then but I
Was tax'd of wrongful will, and for hard
   heart
Miscall'd of men ? And now, sirs, if her
   prayer
Were just and reasonable, and unjust I
That bade shut ears against it — if the mass
Hath brought forth innocent fruit, and in
   this land
Wherein she came to stablish it again
Hath stablish'd peace with honor — if in
   her
It hath been found no seed of shame, and
   she
That lov'd and serv'd it seem now in men's
   sight

No hateful thing nor fearful — if she
   stand
Such a queen proven as should prove hon-
   orable
The rule of women, and in her that thing
Be shown forth good that was call'd evil
   of me,
Blest and not curst — then have I sinn'd,
   and they
That would have cross'd me would have
   cross'd not God :
Whereof now judge ye. Hath she brought
   with her
Peace, or a sword ? and since her incoming
Hath the land sat in quiet, and the men
Seen rest but for one year ? or came not in
Behind her feet, right at her back, and
   shone
Above her crown'd head as a fierier crown,
Death, and about her as a raiment wrapt
Ruin ? and where her foot was ever turn'd
Or her right hand was pointed, hath there
   fallen
No fire, no cry burst forth of war, no sound
As of a blast blown of an host of men
For summons of destruction ? Hath God
   shown
For sign she had found grace in his sight,
   and we
For her sake favor, while she hath reign'd
   on us,
One hour of good, one week of rest, one
   day ?
Or hath he sent not for an opposite sign
Dissensions, wars, rumors of wars, and
   change,
Flight and return of men, terror with
   power,
Triumph with trembling ?
  .   .   .   .
God is not mock'd ; and ye shall surely
   know
What men were these, and what man he
   that spake
The things I speak now prophesying, and
   said
That if ye spare to shed her blood for
   shame,
For fear or pity of her great name or face,
God shall require of you the innocent blood
Shed for her fair face' sake, and from your
   hands
Wring the price forth of her bloodguilti-
   ness.
Nay, for ye know it, nor have I need again

To bring it in your mind if God ere now
Have borne me witness ; in that dreary
   day
When men's hearts fail'd them for pure
   grief and fear
To see the tyranny that was, and rule
Of this queen's mother, where was no light
   left
But of the fires wherein his servants died,
I bade those lords that clave in heart to
   God
And were perplex'd with trembling and
   with tears
Lift up their hearts, and fear not ; and
   they heard
What some now hear no more, the word I
   spake
Who have been with them, as their own
   souls know,
In their most extreme danger ; Cowper
   Moor,
Saint Johnston, and the Crags of Edin-
   burgh,
Are recent in my heart ; yea, let these
   know,
That dark and dolorous night wherein all
   they
With shame and fear were driven forth of
   this town
Is yet within my mind ; and God forbid
That ever I forget it. What, I say,
Was then my exhortation, and what word
Of all God ever promis'd by my mouth
Is fallen in vain, they live to testify
Of whom not one that then was doom'd to
   death
Is perish'd in that danger ; and their foes,
How many of these hath God before their
   eyes
Plague-stricken with destruction ! lo the
   thanks
They render him, now to betray his cause
Put in their hands to stablish ; even that
   God's
That kept them all the darkness through
   to see
Light, and the way that some now see no
   more,
But are gone after light of the fen's fire
And walk askant in slippery ways ; but ye
Know if God's hand have ever when I
   spake
Writ liar upon me, or with adverse proof
Turn'd my free speech to shame ; for in
   my lips

He put a word, and knowledge in my
    heart,
When I was fast bound of his enemies'
    hands
An oarsman on their galleys, and beheld
From off the sea whereon I sat in chains
The walls wherein I knew that I there
    bound
Should one day witness of him ; and this
    pledge
Hath God redeem'd not ?   Nay then, in
    God's name,
If that false word fell unfulfill'd of mine,
Heed ye not now nor hear me when I
    say
That for this woman's sake shall God cut
    off
The hand that spares her as the hand that
    shields,
And make their memory who take part
    with her
As theirs who stood for Baal against the
    Lord
With Ahab's daughter ; for her reign and
    end
Shall be like Athaliah's, as her birth
Was from the womb of Jezebel, that slew
The prophets, and made foul with blood
    and fire
The same land's face that now her seed
    makes foul
With whoredoms and with witchcrafts ; yet
    they say
Peace, where is no peace, while the adul-
    terous blood
Feeds yet with life and sin the murderous
    heart
That hath brought forth a wonder to the
    world
And to all time a terror ; and this blood
The hands are clean that shed, and they
    that spare
In God's just sight spotted as foul as
    Cain's.
If then this guilt shall cleave to you or no,
And to your children's children, for her
    sake,
Choose ye ; for God needs no man that is
    loth
To serve him, and no word but his own
    work
To bind and loose their hearts who hear
    and see
Such things as speak what I lack words to
    say.

SAPPHO

FROM "ON THE CLIFFS"

LOVE'S priestess, mad with pain and joy of
    song,
Song's priestess, mad with joy and pain of
    love,
Name above all names that are lights
    above,
We have lov'd, prais'd, pitied, crown'd,
    and done thee wrong,
O thou past praise and pity ; thou the sole
Utterly deathless, perfect only and whole
Immortal, body and soul.
For over all whom time hath overpast
The shadow of sleep inexorable is cast,
The implacable sweet shadow of perfect
    sleep
That gives not back what life gives death
    to keep ;
Yea, all that liv'd and lov'd and sang and
    sinn'd
Are all borne down death's cold, sweet,
    soundless wind
That blows all night and knows not whom
    its breath,
Darkling, may touch to death :
But one that wind hath touch'd and changed
    not, — one
Whose body and soul are parcel of the
    sun ;
One that earth's fire could burn not, nor
    the sea
Quench ; nor might human doom take hold
    on thee ;
All praise, all pity, all dreams have done
    thee wrong,
All love, with eyes love-blinded from
    above ;
Song's priestess, mad with joy and pain of
    love,
Love's priestess, mad with pain and joy of
    song.

Hast thou none other answer then for me
Than the air may have of thee,
Or the earth's warm woodlands girdling
    with green girth
Thy secret, sleepless, burning life on earth,
Or even the sea that once, being woman
    crown'd
And girt with fire and glory of anguish
    round,
Thou wert so fain to seek to, fain to crave

If she would hear thee and save
And give thee comfort of thy great green
    grave ?
Because I have known thee always who
    thou art,
Thou knowest, have known thee to thy
    heart's own heart,
Nor ever have given light ear to storied
    song
That did thy sweet name sweet unwitting
    wrong,
Nor ever have call'd thee nor would call
    for shame,
Thou knowest, but inly by thine only name,
Sappho — because I have known thee and
    lov'd, hast thou
None other answer now ?
As brother and sister were we, child and
    bird,
Since thy first Lesbian word
Flam'd on me, and I knew not whence I
    knew,
This was the song that struck my whole
    soul through,
Pierced my keen spirit of sense with edge
    more keen,
Even when I knew not, — even ere sooth
    was seen, —
When thou wast but the tawny sweet wing'd
    thing
Whose cry was but of spring.

HOPE AND FEAR

BENEATH the shadow of dawn's aerial
    cope,
With eyes enkindled as the sun's own sphere,
Hope from the front of youth in godlike
    cheer
Looks Godward, past the shades where
    blind men grope
Round the dark door that prayers nor
    dreams can ope,
And makes for joy the very darkness dear
That gives her wide wings play; nor dreams
    that fear
At noon may rise and pierce the heart of
    hope.
Then, when the soul leaves off to dream
    and yearn,
May truth first purge her eyesight to dis-
    cern
What once being known leaves time no
    power to appal ;

Till youth at last, ere yet youth be not,
    learn
The kind wise word that falls from years
    that fall —
" Hope thou not much, and fear thou not
    at all."

ON THE DEATHS OF THOMAS CARLYLE AND GEORGE ELIOT

Two souls diverse out of our human sight
Pass, follow'd one with love and each with
    wonder :
The stormy sophist with his mouth of thun-
    der,
Cloth'd with loud words and mantled in
    the might
Of darkness and magnificence of night ;
And one whose eye could smite the night
    in sunder,
Searching if light or no light were there-
    under,
And found in love of loving-kindness
    light.
Duty divine and Thought with eyes of fire
Still following Righteousness with deep
    desire
Shone sole and stern before her and
    above,
Sure stars and sole to steer by ; but more
    sweet
Shone lower the loveliest lamp for earthly
    feet,
The light of little children, and their love.

HERTHA

I AM that which began ;
    Out of me the years roll ;
    Out of me God and man ;
    I am equal and Whole ;
God changes, and man, and the form of
    them bodily ; I am the soul.

    Before ever land was,
    Before ever the sea,
    Or soft hair of the grass,
    Or fair limbs of the tree,
Or the flesh-color'd fruit of my branches,
    I was, and thy soul was in me.

    First life on my sources
    First drifted and swam ;

Out of me are the forces
   That save it or damn ;
Out of me man and woman, and wild-beast
   and bird ; before God was, I am.

Beside or above me
   Nought is there to go ;
Love or unlove me,
   Unknow me or know,
I am that which unloves me and loves ; I
   am stricken, and I am the blow.

I the mark that is miss'd
   And the arrows that miss,
I the mouth that is kiss'd
   And the breath in the kiss,
The search, and the sought, and the seeker,
   the soul and the body that is.

I am that thing which blesses
   My spirit elate ;
That which caresses
   With hands uncreate
My limbs unbegotten that measure the
   length of the measure of fate.

But what thing dost thou now,
   Looking Godward, to cry
"I am I, thou art thou,
   I am low, thou art high ? "
I am thou, whom thou seekest to find him;
   find thou but thyself, thou art I.

I the grain and the furrow,
   The plough-cloven clod
And the ploughshare drawn tho-
     rough,
   The germ and the sod,
The deed and the doer, the seed and the
   sower, the dust which is God.

Hast thou known how I fashion'd
   thee,
   Child, underground ?
Fire that impassion'd thee,
   Iron that bound,
Dim changes of water, what thing of all
   these hast thou known of or found ?

Canst thou say in thine heart
   Thou hast seen with thine eyes
With what cunning of art
   Thou wast wrought in what wise,
by what force of what stuff thou wast
   shapen, and shown on my breast to the
   skies ?

Who hath given, who hath sold it
   thee,
   Knowledge of me ?
Hath the wilderness told it thee ?
   Hast thou learnt of the sea ?
Hast thou commun'd in spirit with night ?
   have the winds taken counsel with thee ?

Have I set such a star
   To show light on thy brow
That thou sawest from afar
   What I show to thee now ?
Have ye spoken as brethren together, the
   sun and the mountains and thou ?

What is here, dost thou know it ?
   What was, hast thou known ?
Prophet nor poet
   Nor tripod nor throne
Nor spirit nor flesh can make answer, but
   only thy mother alone.

Mother, not maker,
   Born, and not made ;
Though her children forsake her,
   Allur'd or afraid,
Praying prayers to the God of their fashion,
   she stirs not for all that have pray'd.

A creed is a rod,
   And a crown is of night ;
But this thing is God,
   To be man with thy might,
To grow straight in the strength of thy
   spirit, and live out thy life as the light.

I am in thee to save thee,
   As my soul in thee saith,
Give thou as I gave thee,
   Thy life-blood and breath,
Green leaves of thy labor, white flowers of
   thy thought, and red fruit of thy death.

Be the ways of thy giving
   As mine were to thee ;
The free life of thy living,
   Be the gift of it free ;
Not as servant to lord, nor as master to
   slave, shalt thou give thee to me.

O children of banishment,
   Souls overcast,
Were the lights ye see vanish meant
   Alway to last,
Ye would know not the sun overshining the
   shadows and stars overpast.

I that saw where ye trod
  The dim paths of the night
  Set the shadow call'd God
    In your skies to give light ;
But the morning of manhood is risen, and
  the shadowless soul is in sight.

  The tree many-rooted
    That swells to the sky
  With frondage red-fruited,
    The life-tree am I ;
In the buds of your lives is the sap of my
  leaves : ye shall live and not die.

  But the Gods of your fashion
    That take and that give,
  In their pity and passion
    That scourge and forgive,
They are worms that are bred in the bark
  that falls off : they shall die and not live.

  My own blood is what stanches
    The wounds in my bark :
  Stars caught in my branches
    Make day of the dark,
And are worshipp'd as suns till the sunrise
  shall tread out their fires as a spark.

  Where dead ages hide under
    The live roots of the tree,
  In my darkness the thunder
    Makes utterance of me ;
In the clash of my boughs with each other
  ye hear the waves sound of the sea.

  That noise is of Time,
    As his feathers are spread
  And his feet set to climb
    Through the boughs overhead,
And my foliage rings round him and rustles,
  and branches are bent with his tread.

  The storm-winds of ages
    Blow through me and cease,
  The war-wind that rages,
    The spring-wind of peace,
Ere the breath of them roughen my tresses,
  ere one of my blossoms increase.

  All sounds of all changes,
    All shadows and lights
  On the world's mountain-ranges
    And stream-riven heights,
Whose tongue is the wind's tongue and lan-
  guage of storm-clouds on earth-shaking
  nights ;

  All forms of all faces,
    All works of all hands
  In unsearchable places
    Of time-stricken lands,
All death and all life, and all reigns and all
  ruins, drop through me as sands.

  Though sore be my burden
    And more than ye know,
  And my growth have no guerdon
    But only to grow,
Yet I fail not of growing for lightnings
  above me or deathworms below.

  These too have their part in me,
    As I too in these ;
  Such fire is at heart in me,
    Such sap is this tree's,
Which hath in it all sounds and all secrets
  of infinite lands and of seas.

  In the spring-color'd hours
    When my mind was as May's,
  There brake forth of me flowers
    By centuries of days,
Strong blossoms with perfume of man-
  hood, shot out from my spirit as
  rays.

  And the sound of them springing
    And smell of their shoots
  Were as warmth and sweet singing
    And strength to my roots ;
And the lives of my children made perfect
  with freedom of soul were my fruits.

  I bid you but be ;
    I have need not of prayer ;
  I have need of you free
    As your mouths of mine air ;
That my heart may be greater within me,
  beholding the fruits of me fair.

  More fair than strange fruit is
    Of faith ye espouse ;
  In me only the root is
    That blooms in your boughs;
Behold now your God that ye made you
  to feed him with faith of your vows.

  In the darkening and whitening
    Abysses ador'd,
  With dayspring and lightning
    For lamp and for sword,
God thunders in heaven, and his angels ar
  red with the wrath of the Lord.

O my sons, O too dutiful
  Toward Gods not of me,
Was not I enough beautiful ?
  Was it hard to be free ?
For behold, I am with you, am in you and
  of you ; look forth now and see.

Lo, wing'd with world's wonders,
  With miracles shod,
With the fires of his thunders
  For raiment and rod,
God trembles in heaven, and his angels are
  white with the terror of God.

For his twilight is come on him,
  His anguish is here ;
And his spirits gaze dumb on him,
  Grown gray from his fear ;
And his hour taketh hold on him stricken,
  the last of his infinite year.

Thought made him and breaks him,
  Truth slays and forgives ;
But to you, as time takes him,
  This new thing it gives,
Even love, the beloved Republic, that feeds
  upon freedom and lives.

For truth only is living,
  Truth only is whole,
And the love of his giving
  Man's polestar and pole ;
Man, pulse of my centre, and fruit of my
  body, and seed of my soul.

One birth of my bosom ;
  One beam of mine eye ;
One topmost blossom
  That scales the sky ;
Man, equal and one with me, man that is
  made of me, man that is I.

ÉTUDE RÉALISTE

I

A baby's feet, like sea-shells pink,
  Might tempt, should Heaven see meet,
An angel's lips to kiss, we think,
  A baby's feet.

Like rose-hued sea-flowers toward the heat
  They stretch and spread and wink
Their ten soft buds that part and meet.

No flower-bells that expand and shrink
  Gleam half so heavenly sweet
As shine on life's untrodden brink
  A baby's feet.

II

A baby's hands, like rosebuds furl'd,
  Whence yet no leaf expands,
Ope if you touch, though close upcurl'd,
  A baby's hands.

Then, even as warriors grip their brands
  When battle's bolt is hurl'd,
They close, clench'd hard like tightening
  bands.

No rosebuds yet by dawn impearl'd
  Match, even in loveliest lands,
The sweetest flowers in all the world —
  A baby's hands.

III

A baby's eyes, ere speech begin,
  Ere lips learn words or sighs,
Bless all things bright enough to win
  A baby's eyes.

Love, while the sweet thing laughs and lies,
  And sleep flows out and in,
Lies perfect in them Paradise.

Their glance might cast out pain and sin,
  Their speech make dumb the wise,
By mute glad godhead felt within
  A baby's eyes.

THE ROUNDEL

A ROUNDEL is wrought as a ring or a star-
  bright sphere,
With craft of delight and with cunning of
  sound unsought,
That the heart of the hearer may smile if
  to pleasure his ear
A roundel is wrought.

Its jewel of music is carven of all or of
  aught —
Love, laughter or mourning, remembrance
  of rapture or fear —
That fancy may fashion to hang in the ear
  of thought.

As a bird's quick song runs round, and the
    hearts in us hear
Pause answer to pause, and again the same
    strain caught,
So moves the device whence, round as a
    pearl or tear,
    A roundel is wrought.

A FORSAKEN GARDEN

In a coign of the cliff between lowland and
    highland,
    At the sea-down's edge between wind-
        ward and lee,
Wall'd round with rocks as an inland
    island,
    The ghost of a garden fronts the sea.
A girdle of brushwood and thorn encloses
    The steep, square slope of the blossom-
    less bed
Where the weeds that grew green from
    the graves of its roses
        Now lie dead.

The fields fall southward, abrupt and
    broken,
    To the low last edge of the long lone
    land.
If a step should sound or a word be
    spoken,
    Would a ghost not rise at the strange
    guest's hand?
So long have the gray, bare walks lain
    guestless,
    Through branches and briers if a man
    make way,
He shall find no life but the sea-wind's,
    restless
        Night and day.

The dense, hard passage is blind and stifled
    That crawls by a track none turn to
    climb
To the strait waste place that the years
    have rifled
    Of all but the thorns that are touch'd
    not of Time.
The thorns he spares when the rose is
    taken;
    The rocks are left when he wastes the
    plain.
The wind that wanders, the weeds wind-
    shaken,
        These remain.

Not a flower to be press'd of the foot that
    falls not;
    As the heart of a dead man the seed-
    plots are dry;
From the thicket of thorns whence the
    nightingale calls not,
    Could she call, there were never a rose to
    reply.
Over the meadows that blossom and wither
    Rings but the note of a sea-bird's song;
Only the sun and the rain come hither
        All year long.

The sun burns sere and the rain dishevels
    One gaunt bleak blossom of scentless
    breath.
Only the wind here hovers and revels
    In a round where life seems barren as
    death.
Here there was laughing of old, there was
    weeping,
Haply, of lovers none ever will know,
    Whose eyes went seaward a hundred
    sleeping
        Years ago.

Heart handfast in heart as they stood,
    "Look thither,"
    Did he whisper? "Look forth from the
    flowers to the sea;
For the foam-flowers endure when the rose-
    blossoms wither,
    And men that love lightly may die —
    but we?"
And the same wind sang and the same
    waves whiten'd,
    And or ever the garden's last petals
    were shed,
In the lips that had whisper'd, the eyes
    that had lighten'd,
        Love was dead.

Or they lov'd their life through, and then
    went whither?
    And were one to the end — but what end
    who knows?
Love deep as the sea as a rose must wither
    As the rose-red seaweed that mocks the
    rose.
Shall the dead take thought for the dead
    to love them?
    What love was ever as deep as a grave
They are loveless now as the grass above
    them
        Or the wave.

All are at one now, roses and lovers,
Not known of the cliffs and the fields
and the sea.
Not a breath of the time that has been
hovers
In the air now soft with a summer to
be.
Not a breath shall there sweeten the seasons
hereafter
Of the flowers or the lovers that laugh
now or weep,
When, as they that are free now of weeping
and laughter,
We shall sleep.

Here death may deal not again forever ;
Here change may come not till all change
end.
From the graves they have made they shall
rise up never,
Who have left nought living to ravage
and rend.
Earth, stones, and thorns of the wild
ground growing,
While the sun and the rain live, these
shall be ;
Till a last wind's breath upon all these
blowing
Roll the sea.

Till the slow sea rise and the sheer cliff
crumble,
Till terrace and meadow the deep gulfs
drink,
Till the strength of the waves of the high
tides humble
The fields that lessen, the rocks that
shrink,
Here now in his triumph where all things
falter,
Stretch'd out on the spoils that his own
hand spread,
As a god self-slain on his own strange
altar,
Death lies dead.

ON THE MONUMENT ERECTED TO MAZZINI AT GENOA

ITALIA, mother of the souls of men,
Mother divine,
Of all that serv'd thee best with sword or
pen,
All sons of thine,

Thou knowest that here the likeness of the
best
Before thee stands :
The head most high, the heart found faith-
fulest,
The purest hands.

Above the fume and foam of time that
flits,
The soul, we know,
Now sits on high where Alighieri sits
With Angelo.

Nor his own heavenly tongue hath hea-
venly speech
Enough to say
What this man was, whose praise no
thought may reach,
No words can weigh.

Since man's first mother brought to mortal
birth
Her first-born son,
Such grace befell not ever man on earth
As crowns this One.

Of God nor man was ever this thing said :
That he could give
Life back to her who gave him, that his
dead
Mother might live.

But this man found his mother dead and
slain,
With fast-seal'd eyes,
And bade the dead rise up and live again,
And she did rise :

And all the world was bright with her
through him :
But dark with strife,
Like heaven's own sun that storming clouds
bedim,
Was all his life.

Life and the clouds are vanish'd ; hate and
fear
Have had their span
Of time to hurt and are not : He is here
The sunlike man.

City superb, that hadst Columbus first
For sovereign son,
Be prouder that thy breast hath later nurst
This mightier One.

Glory be his forever, while this land
    Lives and is free,
As with controlling breath and sovereign
    hand
    He bade her be.

Earth shows to heaven the names by thou-
    sands told
    That crown her fame :
But highest of all that heaven and earth
    behold
    Mazzini's name.

John Payne

CADENCES

I

(MINOR)

THE ancient memories buried lie,
    And the olden fancies pass ;
The old sweet flower-thoughts wither and
    fly,
And die as the April cowslips die,
    That scatter the bloomy grass.

All dead, my dear ! And the flowers are
    dead,
    And the happy blossoming spring ;
The winter comes with its iron tread,
The fields with the dying sun are red,
    And the birds have ceas'd to sing.

I trace the steps on the wasted strand
    Of the vanish'd springtime's feet :
Wither'd and dead is our Fairyland,
For Love and Death go hand in hand
    Go hand in hand, my sweet !

II

(MAJOR)

OH, what shall be the burden of our
    rhyme,
And what shall be our ditty when the blos-
    som's on the lime ?
Our lips have fed on winter and on weari-
    ness too long :
We will hail the royal summer with a
    golden-footed song !

O lady of my summer and my spring,
We shall hear the blackbird whistle and
    the brown sweet throstle sing,
And the low clear noise of waters running
    softly by our feet,
When the sights and sounds of summer in
    the green clear fields are sweet.

We shall see the roses blowing in the
    green,
The pink-lipp'd roses kissing in the golden
    summer sheen ;
We shall see the fields flower thick with
    stars and bells of summer gold,
And the poppies burn out red and sweet
    across the corn-crown'd wold.

The time shall be for pleasure, not for
    pain ;
There shall come no ghost of grieving for
    the past betwixt us twain ;
But in the time of roses our lives shall grow
    together,
And our love be as the love of gods in the
    blue Olympic weather.

SIBYL

THIS is the glamour of the world antique :
The thyme-scents of Hymettus fill the air,
And in the grass narcissus-cups are fair.
The full brook wanders through the ferns
    to seek
The amber haunts of bees ; and on the
    peak
Of the soft hill, against the gold-marged
    sky,
She stands, a dream from out the days gone
    by.
Entreat her not. Indeed, she will not
    speak!
Her eyes are full of dreams ; and in her
    ears
There is the rustle of immortal wings ;
And ever and anon the slow breeze bears
The mystic murmur of the songs she
    sings.
Entreat her not : she sees thee not, nor
    hears
Aught but the sights and sounds of bygone
    springs.

THORGERDA

Lo, what a golden day it is !
 The glad sun rives the sapphire deeps
Down to the dim pearl-floor'd abyss
 Where, cold in death, my lover sleeps ;

Crowns with soft fire his sea-drench'd hair,
 Kisses with gold his lips death-pale,
Lets down from heaven a golden stair,
 Whose steps methinks his soul doth scale.

This is my treasure. White and sweet,
 He lies beneath my ardent eyne,
With heart that nevermore shall beat,
 Nor lips press softly against mine.

How like a dream it seems to me,
 The time when hand in hand we went
By hill and valley, I and he,
 Lost in a trance of ravishment !

I and my lover here that lies
 And sleeps the everlasting sleep,
We walk'd whilere in Paradise ;
 (Can it be true ?) Our souls drank deep

Together of Love's wonder-wine :
 We saw the golden days go by,
Unheeding, for we were divine ;
 Love had advanced us to the sky.

And of that time no traces bin,
 Save the still shape that once did hold
My lover's soul, that shone therein,
 As wine laughs in a vase of gold.

Cold, cold he lies, and answers not
 Unto my speech ; his mouth is cold
Whose kiss to mine was sweet and hot
 As sunshine to a marigold.

And yet his pallid lips I press ;
 I fold his neck in my embrace ;
I rain down kisses none the less
 Upon his unresponsive face :

I call on him with all the fair
 Flower-names that blossom out of love ;
I knit sea-jewels in his hair ;
 I weave fair coronals above

The cold, sweet silver of his brow :
 For this is all of him I have ;
Nor any Future more than now
 Shall give me back what Love once gave.

For from Death's gate our lives divide ;
 His was the Galilean's faith :
With those that serve the Crucified,
 He shar'd the chance of Life and Death.

And so my eyes shall never light
 Upon his star-soft eyes again ;
Nor ever in the day or night,
 By hill or valley, wood or plain,

Our hands shall meet afresh. His voice
 Shall never with its silver tone
The sadness of my soul rejoice,
 Nor his breast throb against my own.

His sight shall never unto me
 Return whilst heaven and earth remain :
Though Time blend with Eternity,
 Our lives shall never meet again, —

Never by gray or purple sea,
 Never again in heavens of blue,
Never in this old earth — ah me !
 Never, ah never ! in the new.

For me, he treads the windless ways
 Among the thick star-diamonds,
Where in the middle æther blaze
 The Golden City's pearl gate-fronds ;

Sitteth, palm-crown'd and silver-shod,
 Where in strange dwellings of the skies
The Christians to their Woman-God
 Cease nevermore from psalmodies.

And I, I wait, with haggard eyes
 And face grown awful for desire,
The coming of that fierce day's rise
 When from the cities of the fire

The Wolf shall come with blazing crest,
 And many a giant arm'd for war ;
When from the sanguine-streaming West,
 Hell-flaming, speedeth Naglfar.

LOVE'S AUTUMN

Yes, love, the Spring shall come again,
 But not as once it came :
Once more in meadow and in lane
 The daffodils shall flame,
The cowslips blow, but all in vain ;
 Alike, yet not the same.

The roses that we pluck'd of old
 Were dew'd with heart's delight ;

Our gladness steep'd the primrose-gold
　In half its lovely light :
The hopes are long since dead and cold
　That flush'd the wind-flowers' white.

Oh, who shall give us back our Spring ?
　What spell can fill the air
With all the birds of painted wing
　That sang for us whilere ?
What charm reclothe with blossoming
　Our lives, grown blank and bare ?

What sun can draw the ruddy bloom
　Back to hope's faded rose ?
What stir of summer re-illume
　Our hearts' wreck'd garden-close ?
What flowers can fill the empty room
　Where now the nightshade grows ?

'T is but the Autumn's chilly sun
　That mocks the glow of May ;
'T is but the pallid bindweeds run
　Across our garden way,
Pale orchids, scentless every one,
　Ghosts of the summer day.

Yet, if it must be so, 't is well :
　What part have we in June ?
Our hearts have all forgot the spell
　That held the summer noon ;
We echo back the cuckoo's knell,
　And not the linnet's tune.

What shall we do with roses now,
　Whose cheeks no more are red ?
What violets should deck our brow,
　Whose hopes long since are fled ?
Recalling many a wasted vow
　And many a faith struck dead.

Bring heath and pimpernel and rue,
　The Autumn's sober flowers :
At least their scent will not renew
　The thought of happy hours,
Nor drag sad memory back unto
　That lost sweet time of ours.

Faith is no sun of summertide,
　Only the pale, calm light
That, when the Autumn clouds divide,
　Hangs in the watchet height, —
A lamp, wherewith we may abide
　The coming of the night.

And yet, beneath its languid ray,
　The moorlands bare and dry
Bethink them of the summer day
　And flower, far and nigh,
With fragile memories of the May,
　Blue as the August sky.

These are our flowers : they have no
　　scent
To mock our waste desire,
No hint of bygone ravishment
　To stir the faded fire :
The very soul of sad content
　Dwells in each azure spire.

I have no violets : you laid
　Your blight upon them all :
It was your hand, alas ! that made
　My roses fade and fall,
Your breath my lilies that forbade
　To come at Summer's call.

Yet take these scentless flowers and pale,
　The last of all my year :
Be tender to them ; they are frail :
　But if thou hold them dear,
I 'll not their brighter kin bewail,
　That now lie cold and sere.

SONGS' END

The chime of a bell of gold
　That flutters across the air,
The sound of a singing of old,
The end of a tale that is told,
　Of a melody strange and fair,
　Of a joy that has grown despair :

For the things that have been for me
　I shall never have them again ;
The skies and the purple sea,
And day like a melody,
　And night like a silver rain
　Of stars on forest and plain.

They are shut, the gates of the day ;
　The night has fallen on me :
My life is a lightless way ;
I sing yet, while as I may !
　Some day I shall cease, maybe :
　I shall live on yet, you will see.

Robert Bridges

POOR WITHERED ROSE

POOR wither'd rose and dry,
Skeleton of a rose,
Risen to testify
To love's sad close :

Treasur'd for love's sweet sake,
That of joy past
Thou mightst again awake
Memory at last.

Yet is thy perfume sweet ;
Thy petals red
Yet tell of summer heat,
And the gay bed :

Yet, yet recall the glow
Of the gazing sun,
When at thy bush we two
Join'd hands in one.

But, rose, thou hast not seen,
Thou hast not wept,
The change that pass'd between
Whilst thou hast slept.

To me thou seemest yet
The dead dream's thrall ;
While I live and forget
Dream, truth, and all.

Thou art more fresh than I,
Rose, sweet and red :
Salt on my pale cheeks lie
The tears I shed.

I WILL NOT LET THEE GO

I WILL not let thee go.
Ends all our month-long love in this ?
Can it be summ'd up so,
Quit in a single kiss ?
I will not let thee go.

I will not let thee go.
If thy words' breath could scare thy deeds,
As the soft south can blow
And toss the feather'd seeds,
Then might I let thee go.

I will not let thee go.
Had not the great sun seen, I might ;
Or were he reckon'd slow
To bring the false to light,
Then might I let thee go.

I will not let thee go.
The stars that crowd the summer skies
Have watch'd us so below
With all their million eyes,
I dare not let thee go.

I will not let thee go.
Have we not chid the changeful moon,
Now rising late, and now
Because she set too soon,
And shall I let thee go ?

I will not let thee go.
Have not the young flowers been content,
Pluck'd ere their buds could blow,
To seal our sacrament ?
I cannot let thee go.

I will not let thee go.
I hold thee by too many bands :
Thou sayest farewell, and, lo !
I have thee by the hands,
And will not let thee go.

UPON THE SHORE

WHO has not walk'd upon the shore,
And who does not the morning know,
The day the angry gale is o'er,
The hour the wind has ceas'd to blow ?

The horses of the strong southwest
Are pastur'd round his tropic tent,
Careless how long the ocean's breast
Sob on and sigh for passion spent.

The frighten'd birds, that fled inland
To house in rock and tower and tree,
Are gathering on the peaceful strand,
To tempt again the sunny sea ;

Whereon the timid ships steal out
And laugh to find their foe asleep,
That lately scatter'd them about,
And drave them to the fold like sheep.

The snow-white clouds he northward chas'd
Break into phalanx, line, and band :
All one way to the south they haste,
The south, their pleasant fatherland.

From distant hills their shadows creep,
Arrive in turn and mount the lea,
And flit across the downs, and leap
Sheer off the cliff upon the sea ;

And sail and sail far out of sight.
And still I watch their fleecy trains,
That, piling all the south with light,
Dapple in France the fertile plains.

A PASSER-BY

WHITHER, O splendid ship, thy white sails
    crowding,
  Leaning across the bosom of the urgent
    West,
That fearest nor sea rising, nor sky cloud-
    ing,
  Whither away, fair rover, and what thy
    quest ?
Ah ! soon, when Winter has all our vales
    opprest,
  When skies are cold and misty, and hail is
    hurling,
  Wilt thou glide on the blue Pacific, or rest
In a summer haven asleep, thy white sails
    furling.

I there before thee, in the country so well
    thou knowest,
  Already arriv'd, am inhaling the odorous
    air ;
I watch thee enter unerringly where thou
    goest,
  And anchor queen of the strange shipping
    there,
  Thy sails for awnings spread, thy masts
    bare ;
Nor is aught, from the foaming reef to the
    snow-capp'd, grandest
  Peak that is over the feathery palms,
    more fair
Than thou, so upright, so stately, and still
    thou standest.

And yet, O splendid ship, unhail'd and
    nameless,
  I know not if, aiming a fancy, I rightly
    divine

That thou hast a purpose joyful, a courage
    blameless,
  Thy port assur'd in a happier land than
    mine.
But for all I have given thee, beauty
    enough is thine,
As thou, aslant with trim tackle and shroud-
    ing,
  From the proud nostril curve of a prow's
    line
In the offing scatterest foam, thy white sails
    crowding.

ELEGY

I HAVE lov'd flowers that fade,
Within whose magic tents
Rich hues have marriage made
With sweet unmemoried scents :
A honeymoon delight, —
A joy of love at sight,
That ages in an hour : —
My song be like a flower !

I have lov'd airs that die
Before their charm is writ
Along a liquid sky
Trembling to welcome it.
Notes, that with pulse of fire
Proclaim the spirit's desire,
Then die, and are nowhere : —
My song be like an air !

Die, song, die like a breath,
And wither as a bloom :
Fear not a flowery death,
Dread not an airy tomb !
Fly with delight, fly hence !
'T was thine love's tender sense
To feast ; now on thy bier
Beauty shall shed a tear.

THOU DIDST DELIGHT MY EYES

THOU didst delight my eyes :
Yet who am I ? nor first
Nor last nor best, that durst
Once dream of thee for prize ;
Nor this the only time
Thou shalt set love to rhyme.

Thou didst delight my ear :
Ah ! little praise ; thy voice
Makes other hearts rejoice

Makes all ears glad that hear ;
And short my joy : but yet,
O song, do not forget.

For what wert thou to me ?
How shall I say ? The moon,
That pour'd her midnight noon
Upon his wrecking sea ; —
A sail, that for a day
Has cheer'd the castaway.

AWAKE, MY HEART !

AWAKE, my heart, to be lov'd, awake,
    awake !
The darkness silvers away, the morn doth
    break,
It leaps in the sky : unrisen lustres slake
The o'ertaken moon. Awake, O heart,
    awake !

She, too, that loveth awaketh and hopes for
    thee ;
Her eyes already have sped the shades that
    flee,
Already they watch the path thy feet shall
    take :
Awake, O heart to be lov'd, awake, awake !

And if thou tarry from her, — if this could
    be, —
She cometh herself, O heart, to be lov'd, to
    thee ;
For thee would unasham'd herself for-
    sake :
Awake to be lov'd, my heart, awake,
    awake !

Awake! The land is scatter'd with light,
    and see,
Uncanopied sleep is flying from field and
    tree ;
And blossoming boughs of April in laughter
    shake :
Awake, O heart, to be lov'd, awake, awake!

Lo, all things wake and tarry and look for
    thee :
She looketh and saith, "O sun, now bring
    him to me.
Come, more ador'd, O ador'd, for his com-
    ing's sake,
And awake, my heart, to be lov'd, awake,
    awake ! "

O YOUTH WHOSE HOPE IS HIGH

O YOUTH whose hope is high,
Who doth to truth aspire,
Whether thou live or die,
O look not back nor tire.

Thou that art bold to fly
Through tempest, flood and fire,
Nor dost not shrink to try
Thy heart in torments dire, —

If thou canst Death defy,
If thy Faith is entire,
Press onward, for thine eye
Shall see thy heart's desire.

Beauty and love are nigh,
And with their deathless quire
Soon shall thine eager cry
Be number'd and expire.

SO SWEET LOVE SEEMED

So sweet love seem'd that April morn,
When first we kiss'd beside the thorn,
So strangely sweet, it was not strange
We thought that love could never change.

But I can tell — let truth be told —
That love will change in growing old ;
Though day by day is nought to see,
So delicate his motions be.

And in the end 't will come to pass
Quite to forget what once he was,
Nor even in fancy to recall
The pleasure that was all in all.

His little spring, that sweet we found,
So deep in summer floods is drown'd,
I wonder, bath'd in joy complete,
How love so young could be so sweet.

ASIAN BIRDS

IN this May-month, by grace
    of heaven, things shoot apace.
The waiting multitude
    of fair boughs in the wood, —
How few days have array'd
    their beauty in green shade !

What have I seen or heard?
  it was the yellow bird
Sang in the tree : he flew
  a flame against the blue ;
Upward he flash'd. Again,
  hark ! 't is his heavenly strain,

Another ! Hush ! Behold,
  many, like boats of gold,
From waving branch to branch
  their airy bodies launch.
What music is like this,
  where each note is a kiss ?

The golden willows lift
  their boughs the sun to sift :
Their silken streamers screen
  the sky with veils of green,

To make a cage of song,
  where feather'd lovers throng.

How the delicious notes
  come bubbling from their throats !
Full and sweet, how they are shed
  like round pearls from a thread !
The motions of their flight
  are wishes of delight.

Hearing their song, I trace
  the secret of their grace.
Ah, could I this fair time
  so fashion into rhyme,
The poem that I sing
  would be the voice of spring.

Arthur O'Shaughnessy

THE FAIR MAID AND THE SUN

O sons of men, that toil, and love with
    tears !

Know ye, O sons of men, the maid who
    dwells
Between the two seas at the Dardanelles ?
  Her face hath charm'd away the change
    of years,
And all the world is filled with her spells.

No task is hers forever, but the play
Of setting forth her beauty day by day :
  There in your midst, O sons of men that
    toil,
She laughs the long eternity away.

The chains about her neck are many-
    pearl'd,
Rare gems are those round which her hair
    is curl'd ;
  She hath all flesh for captive, and for
    spoil,
The fruit of all the labor of the world.

She getteth up and maketh herself bare,
And letteth down the wonder of her
    hair
  Before the sun ; the heavy golden locks
Fall in the hollow of her shoulders fair.

She taketh from the lands, as she may
    please,
All jewels, and all corals from the seas ;
  She layeth them in rows upon the rocks ;
Laugheth, and bringeth fairer ones than
    these.

Five are the goodly necklaces that deck
The place between her bosom and her
    neck ;
  She passeth many a bracelet o'er her
    hands ;
And, seeing she is white without a fleck,

And seeing she is fairer than the tide,
And of a beauty no man can abide,
  Proudly she standeth as a goddess stands,
And mocketh at the sun and sea for pride :

And to the sea she saith : " O silver sea,
Fair art thou, but thou art not fair like me ;
  Open thy white-tooth'd, dimpled mouths
    and try ;
They laugh not the soft way I laugh at
    thee."

And to the sun she saith : " O golden sun,
Fierce is thy burning till the day is done !
  But thou shalt burn mere grass and
    leaves, while I
Shall burn the hearts of men up every one.'

O fair and dreadful is the maid who
  dwells
Between the two seas at the Dardanelles, —
  As fair and dread as in the ancient
    years ;
And still the world is filled with her spells.

O sons of men, that toil, and love with tears !

HAS SUMMER COME WITHOUT THE ROSE ?

Has summer come without the rose,
  Or left the bird behind ?
Is the blue changed above thee,
  O world ! or am I blind ?
Will you change every flower that grows,
  Or only change this spot,
Where she who said, I love thee,
  Now says, I love thee not ?

The skies seem'd true above thee,
  The rose true on the tree ;
The bird seem'd true the summer through,
  But all prov'd false to me.
World, is there one good thing in you,
  Life, love, or death — or what ?
Since lips that sang, I love thee,
  Have said, I love thee not ?

I think the sun's kiss will scarce fall
  Into one flower's gold cup ;
I think the bird will miss me,
  And give the summer up.
O sweet place, desolate in tall
  Wild grass, have you forgot
How her lips lov'd to kiss me,
  Now that they kiss me not ?

Be false or fair above me ;
  Come back with any face,
Summer ! — do I care what you do ?
  You cannot change one place, —
The grass, the leaves, the earth, the dew,
  The grave I make the spot, —
Here, where she used to love me,
  Here, where she loves me not.

AT HER GRAVE

I have stay'd too long from your grave, it
    seems ;
  Now I come back again.

Love, have you stirr'd down there in your
    dreams
  Through the sunny days or the rain ?
Ah, no ! the same peace : you are happy
    so ;
  And your flowers, how do they grow ?

Your rose has a bud : is it meant for
    me ?
  Ah, little red gift put up
So silently, like a child's present, you see
  Lying beside your cup !
And geranium leaves, — I will take, if I
    may,
  Two or three to carry away.

I went not far. In yon world of ours
  Grow ugly weeds. With my heart,
Thinking of you and your garden of
    flowers,
  I went to do my part,
Plucking up, where they poison the human
    wheat,
  The weeds of cant and deceit.

'T is a hideous thing I have seen, and the
    toil
  Begets few thanks, much hate ;
And the new crop only will find the soil
  Less foul, — for the old 't is too late.
I come back to the only spot I know
  Where a weed will never grow.

SILENCES

'T is a world of silences. I gave a cry
  In the first sorrow my heart could not
    withstand ;
I saw men pause, and listen, and look sad,
  As though no answer in their hearts they
    had ;
Some turn'd away, some came and took
    my hand,
  For all reply.

I stood beside a grave. Years had pass'd
    by ;
  Sick with unanswer'd life I turn'd to
    death,
And whisper'd all my question to the
    grave,
And watch'd the flowers desolately wave,
  And grass stir on it with a fitful breath,
  For all reply.

I rais'd my eyes to heaven ; my prayer
   went high
Into the luminous mystery of the blue ;
My thought of God was purer than a
   flame,
And God it seem'd a little nearer came,
   Then pass'd ; and greater still the silence
     grew,
For all reply.

But you ! If I can speak before I die,
   I spoke to you with all my soul, and
     when
I look at you 't is still my soul you see.
Oh, in your heart was there no word for
   me ?
   All would have answer'd had you an-
     swer'd then
With even a sigh.

IF SHE BUT KNEW

IF she but knew that I am weeping
   Still for her sake,
That love and sorrow grow with keeping
   Till they must break,
My heart that breaking will adore her,
   Be hers and die ;
If she might hear me once implore her,
   Would she not sigh ?

If she but knew that it would save me
   Her voice to hear,
Saying she pitied me, forgave me,
   Must she forbear ?
If she were told that I was dying,
   Would she be dumb ?
Could she content herself with sighing ?
   Would she not come ?

Philip Bourke Marston

A GREETING

RISE up, my song ! stretch forth thy wings
   and fly
With no delaying, over shore and deep !
Be with my lady when she wakes from
   sleep ;
Touch her with kisses softly on each
   eye ;
And say, before she puts her dreaming
   by :
" Within the palaces of slumber keep
One little niche wherein sometimes to weep
For one who vainly toils till he shall die ! "
Yet say again, a sweeter thing than this :
" His life is wasted by his love for thee."
Then, looking o'er the fields of memory,
She 'll find perchance, o'ergrown with grief
   and bliss,
Some flower of recollection, pale and fair,
That she, through pity, for a day may wear.

A VAIN WISH

I WOULD not, could I, make thy life as
   mine ;
Only I would, if such a thing might be,
Thou shouldst not, love, forget me utterly ;
Yea, when the sultry stars of summer shine

On dreaming woods, where nightingales
   repine,
I would that at such times should come to
   thee
Some thought not quite unmix'd with pain,
   of me, —
Some little sorrow for a soul's decline.
Yea, too, I would that through thy brightest
   times,
Like the sweet burden of remember'd
   rhymes,
That gentle sadness should be with thee,
   dear ;
And when the gates of sleep are on thee
   shut,
I would not, even then, it should be
   mute,
But murmur, shell-like, at thy spirit's ear.

LOVE'S MUSIC

LOVE held a harp between his hands, and,
   lo !
The master hand, upon the harp-strings
   laid
By way of prelude, such a sweet tune
   play'd
As made the heart with happy tears o'er-
   flow ;

Then sad and wild did that strange music
grow,
And, — like the wail of woods by storm
gusts sway'd,
While yet the awful thunder's wrath is
stay'd,
And earth lies faint beneath the coming
blow, —
Still wilder wax'd the tune ; until at length
The strong strings, strain'd by sudden stress
and sharp
Of that musician's hand intolerable,
And jarr'd by sweep of unrelenting strength,
Sunder'd, and all the broken music fell.
Such was Love's music, — lo, the shatter'd
harp !

THE ROSE AND THE WIND

DAWN

The Rose

WHEN, think you, comes the Wind,
The Wind that kisses me and is so
kind ?
Lo, how the Lily sleeps ! her sleep is
light ;
Would I were like the Lily, pale and
white !
Will the Wind come ?

The Beech
Perchance for you too soon.

The Rose
If not, how could I live until the noon ?
What, think you, Beech-tree, makes the
Wind delay ?
Why comes he not at breaking of the day ?

The Beech
Hush, child, and, like the Lily, go to sleep.

The Rose
You know I cannot.

The Beech
Nay, then, do not weep.

(*After a pause*)

Your lover comes, be happy now, O Rose !
He softly through my bending branches
goes.
Soon he shall come, and you shall feel his
kiss.

The Rose
Already my flush'd heart grows faint with
bliss ;
Love, I have long'd for you through all the
night.

The Wind
And I to kiss your petals warm and bright.

The Rose
Laugh round me, Love, and kiss me ; it is
well.
Nay, have no fear, the Lily will not tell.

MORNING

The Rose
'T was dawn when first you came ; and
now the sun
Shines brightly and the dews of dawn are
done.
'T is well you take me so in your embrace ;
But lay me back again into my place,
For I am worn, perhaps with bliss extreme.

The Wind
Nay, you must wake, Love, from this child-
ish dream.

The Rose
'T is you, Love, who seem changed ; your
laugh is loud,
And 'neath your stormy kiss my head is
bow'd.
O Love, O Wind, a space will you not spare ?

The Wind
Not while your petals are so soft and fair.

The Rose
My buds are blind with leaves, they cannot
see, —
O Love, O Wind, will you not pity me ?

EVENING

The Beech
O Wind, a word with you before you pass ;
What did you to the Rose that on the grass
Broken she lies and pale, who lov'd you so ?

The Wind
Roses must live and love, and winds must
blow.

HOW MY SONG OF HER BEGAN

God made my lady lovely to behold, —
Above the painter's dream he set her face,
And wrought her body in divinest grace ;
He touch'd the brown hair with a sense of
    gold ;
And in the perfect form He did enfold
What was alone as perfect, the sweet heart ;
Knowledge most rare to her He did impart ;
And fill'd with love and worship all her
    days.
And then God thought Him how it would
    be well
To give her music ; and to Love He said,
" Bring thou some minstrel now that he
    may tell
How fair and sweet a thing My hands have
    made."
Then at Love's call I came, bow'd down
    my head,
And at His will my lyre grew audible.

THE OLD CHURCHYARD OF BONCHURCH

The churchyard leans to the sea with its
    dead, —
It leans to the sea with its dead so long.
Do they hear, I wonder, the first bird's
    song,
When the winter's anger is all but fled ;
The high, sweet voice of the west wind,
The fall of the warm, soft rain,
When the second month of the year
Puts heart in the earth again ?

Do they hear, through the glad April
    weather,
The green grasses waving above them ?
Do they think there are none left to love
    them,
They have lain for so long there together ?
Do they hear the note of the cuckoo,
The cry of gulls on the wing,
The laughter of winds and waters,
The feet of the dancing Spring ?

Do they feel the old land slipping sea-
    ward, —
The old land, with its hills and its graves, —
As they gradually slide to the waves,
With the wind blowing on them from lea-
    ward ?

Do they know of the change that awaits
    them, —
The sepulchre vast and strange ?
Do they long for the days to go over,
And bring that miraculous change ?

Or love they their night with no moonlight,
With no starlight, no dawn to its gloom ?
Do they sigh : " 'Neath the snow, or the
    bloom
Of the wild things that wave from our
    night,
We are warm, through winter and summer ;
We hear the winds rave, and we say :
' The storm-wind blows over our heads,
But we here are out of its way ' " ?

Do they mumble low, one to another,
With a sense that the waters that thunder
Shall ingather them all, draw them under :
" Ah, how long to our moving, my brother ?
How long shall we quietly rest here,
In graves of darkness and ease ?
The waves, even now, may be on us,
To draw us down under the seas ! "

Do they think 't will be cold when the waters
That they love not, that neither can love
    them,
Shall eternally thunder above them ?
Have they dread of the sea's shining daugh-
    ters,
That people the bright sea-regions
And play with the young sea-kings ?
Have they dread of their cold embraces,
And dread of all strange sea-things ?

But their dread or their joy, — it is bootless :
They shall pass from the breast of their
    mother ;
They shall lie low, dead brother by brother,
In a place that is radiant and fruitless ;
And the folk that sail over their heads
In violent weather
Shall come down to them, haply, and all
They shall lie there together.

GARDEN FAIRIES

Keen was the air, the sky was very light,
Soft with shed snow my garden was, and
    white,
And, walking there, I heard upon the night
    Sudden sound of little voices,
    Just the prettiest of noises.

It was the strangest, subtlest, sweetest
   sound :
It seem'd above me, seem'd upon the
   ground,
Then swiftly seem'd to eddy round and
   round,
Till I said : " To-night the air is
   Surely full of garden fairies."

And all at once it seem'd I grew aware
That little, shining presences were there, —
White shapes and red shapes danced upon
   the air ;
   Then a peal of silver laughter,
   And such singing followed after

As none of you, I think, have ever heard.
More soft it was than call of any bird,
Note after note, exquisitely deferr'd,
   Soft as dew-drops when they settle
   In a fair flower's open petal.

" What are these fairies ? " to myself I
   said ;
For answer, then, as from a garden's bed,
On the cold air a sudden scent was shed, —
   Scent of lilies, scent of roses,
   Scent of Summer's sweetest posies.

And said a small, sweet voice within my ear :
" We flowers, that sleep through winter,
   once a year
Are by our flower queen sent to visit here,
   That this fact may duly flout us, —
   Gardens can look fair without us.

" A very little time we have to play,
Then must we go, oh, very far away,
And sleep again for many a long, long day,
   Till the glad birds sing above us,
   And the warm sun comes to love us.

" Hark what the roses sing now, as we go ; "
Then very sweet and soft, and very low, —
A dream of sound across the garden snow, —
   Came the chime of roses singing
   To the lily-bell's faint ringing.

ROSES' SONG

" Softly sinking through the snow,
To our winter rest we go,
Underneath the snow to house
Till the birds be in the boughs,
And the boughs with leaves be fair,
And the sun shine everywhere.

" Softly through the snow we settle,
Little snow-drops press each petal.
Oh, the snow is kind and white, —
Soft it is, and very light ;
Soon we shall be where no light is,
But where sleep is, and where night is, —
Sleep of every wind unshaken,
Till our Summer bids us waken."

Then toward some far-off goal that singing
   drew ;
Then altogether ceas'd ; more steely blue
The blue stars shone ; but in my spirit grew
   Hope of Summer, love of Roses,
   Certainty that Sorrow closes.

LOVE AND MUSIC

I LISTEN'D to the music broad and deep :
I heard the tenor in an ecstasy
Touch the sweet, distant goal ; I heard the
   cry
Of prayer and passion ; and I heard the
   sweep
Of mighty wings, that in their waving keep
The music that the spheres make end-
   lessly ; —
Then my cheek shiver'd, tears made blind
   mine eye ;
As flame to flame I felt the quick blood leap,
And, through the tides and moonlit winds
   of sound,
To me love's passionate voice grew audible.
Again I felt thy heart to my heart bound,
Then silence on the viols and voices fell ;
But, like the still, small voice within a shell,
I heard Love thrilling through the void
   profound.

NO DEATH

I SAW in dreams a mighty multitude, —
Gather'd, they seem'd, from North, South,
   East, and West,
And in their looks such horror was exprest
As must forever words of mine elude.
As if transfix'd by grief, some silent stood,
While others wildly smote upon the breast,
And cried out fearfully, " No rest, no
   rest ! "
Some fled, as if by shapes unseen pursued.
Some laugh'd insanely. Others, shrieking,
   said :
" To think but yesterday we might have
   died ;

For then God had not thundered, 'Death
   is dead !' "
They gash'd themselves till they with blood
   were red.
"Answer, O God ; take back this curse!"
   they cried,
But "Death is dead," was all the voice
   replied.

AT THE LAST

BECAUSE the shadows deepen'd verily, —
Because the end of all seem'd near, for-
   sooth, —
Her gracious spirit, ever quick to ruth,
Had pity on her bond-slave, even on me.
She came in with the twilight noiselessly,
Fair as a rose, immaculate as Truth ;
She lean'd above my wreck'd and wasted
   youth ;
I felt her presence, which I could not see.
"God keep you, my poor friend," I heard
   her say ;
And then she kiss'd my dry, hot lips and
   eyes.
Kiss *thou* the next kiss, quiet Death, I pray ;
Be instant on this hour, and so surprise
My spirit while the vision seems to stay ;
Take thou the heart with the heart's Para-
   dise.

HER PITY

THIS is the room to which she came that
   day, —
Came when the dusk was falling cold and
   gray, —
Came with soft step, in delicate array,

And sat beside me in the firelight there ;
And, like a rose of perfume rich and rare,
Thrill'd with her sweetness the environing
   air.

We heard the grind of traffic in the street,
The clamorous calls, the beat of passing
   feet,
The wail of bells that in the twilight meet.

Then I knelt down, and dar'd to touch her
   hand, —
Those slender fingers, and the shining band
Of happy gold wherewith her wrist was
   spann'd.

Her radiant beauty made my heart re-
   joice ;
And then she spoke, and her low, pitying
   voice
Was like the soft, pathetic, tender noise

Of winds that come before a summer
   rain :
Once leap'd the blood in every clamorous
   vein ;
Once leap'd my heart, then, dumb, stood
   still again.

AFTER SUMMER

WE 'll not weep for summer over, —
    No, not we :
Strew above his head the clover, —
    Let him be !

Other eyes may weep his dying,
    Shed their tears
There upon him, where he 's lying
    With his peers.

Unto some of them he proffer'd
    Gifts most sweet ;
For our hearts a grave he offer'd, —
    Was this meet ?

All our fond hopes, praying, perish'd
    In his wrath, —
All the lovely dreams we cherish'd
    Strew'd his path.

Shall we in our tombs, I wonder,
    Far apart,
Sunder'd wide as seas can sunder
    Heart from heart,

Dream at all of all the sorrows
    That were ours, —
Bitter nights, more bitter morrows ;
    Poison-flowers

Summer gather'd, as in madness,
    Saying, "See,
These are yours, in place of gladness, —
    Gifts from me" ?

Nay, the rest that will be ours
    Is supreme,
And below the poppy flowers
    Steals no dream.

TO THE SPIRIT OF POETRY

ALL things are changed save thee, — thou
　art the same,
Only perchance more dear, as one friend
　grows
When other friends have turn'd away. Who
　knows
With what strange joy thou didst my life
　inflame
Before I took upon my lips the name
Which vows me to thy service ?　Come
　thou close ;
For to thy feet to-day my being flows,
As when, a boy, for comforting I came.
Thou, whose transfiguring touch makes
　speech divine, —
Whose eyes are deeper than deep seas or
　skies, —
Warm with thy fire this heart, these lips of
　mine,
Lighten the darkness with thy luminous
　eyes,
Till all the quivering air about me shine,
And I have gain'd my spirit's Paradise.

IF YOU WERE HERE

A SONG IN WINTER

O LOVE, if you were here
　This dreary, weary day, —
If your lips, warm and dear,
　Found some sweet word to say, —
Then hardly would seem drear
　These skies of wintry gray.

But you are far away, —
　How far from me, my dear !
What cheer can warm the day ?
　My heart is chill with fear,
Pierced through with swift dismay ;
　A thought has turn'd Life sere :

If you from far away
　Should come not back, my dear ;
If I no more might lay
　My hand on yours, nor hear
That voice, now sad, now gay,
　Caress my listening ear ;

If you from far away
　Should come no more, my dear, —
Then with what dire dismay
　Year joined to hostile year

Would frown, if I should stay
　Where memories mock and jeer !

But I would come away
　To dwell with you, my dear ;
Through unknown worlds to stray, —
　Or sleep ; nor hope, nor fear,
Nor dream beneath the clay
　Of all our days that were.

AT LAST

REST here, at last,
The long way overpast ;
Rest here, at home, —
　Thy race is run,
　Thy dreary journey done,
Thy last peak clomb.

'Twixt birth and death,
What days of bitter breath
Were thine, alas !
　Thy soul had sight
　To see by day, by night,
Strange phantoms pass.

Thy restless heart
In few glad things had part,
But dwelt alone,
　And night and day,
　In the old way,
Made the old moan.

But here is rest
For aching brain and breast,
Deep rest, complete,
　And nevermore,
　Heart-weary and foot-sore,
Shall stray thy feet, —

Thy feet that went,
With such long discontent,
Their wonted beat
　About thy room,
　With its deep-seated gloom,
Or through the street.

Death gives them ease ;
Death gives thy spirit peace ;
Death lulls thee, quite.
　One thing alone
　Death leaves thee of thine own, —
Thy starless night.

DRAMATISTS AND PLAYWRIGHTS

(See also : ROBERT BROWNING, BUCHANAN, LADY CURRIE, LORD DE TABLEY, SWINBURNE, LORD TENNYSON)

Tom Taylor

FROM "THE FOOL'S REVENGE"

THE JESTER AND HIS DAUGHTER

SCENE. — A room in the house of BERTUCCIO.

[BERTUCCIO *stands for a moment fondly contemplating* FIORDELISA. *He steps forward.*
Ber. My own !
Fio. [*Turning suddenly, and flinging herself into his arms with a cry of joy.*] My father !
Ber. [*Embracing her tenderly.*] Closer, closer yet !
Let me feel those soft arms about my neck,
This dear cheek on my heart ! No — do not stir —
It does me so much good ! I am so happy —
These minutes are worth years !
Fio. My own dear father !
Ber. Let me look at thee, darling — why, thou growest
More and more beautiful ! Thou 'rt happy here ?
Hast all that thou desirest — thy lute — thy flowers ?
She loves her poor old father ? — Blessings on thee —
I know thou dost — but tell me so.
Fio. I love you —
I love you very much ! I am so happy
When you are with me. Why do you come so late,
And go so soon ? Why not stay always here ?
Ber. Why not ! Why not ! Oh, if I could ! To live
Where there 's no mocking, and no being mock'd :
No laughter, but what 's innocent ; no mirth
That leaves an after bitterness like gall.
Fio. Now, you are sad ! There 's that black ugly cloud

Upon your brow — you promis'd, the last time,
It never should come when we were together.
You know, when you 're sad, I 'm sad too.
Ber. My bird !
I 'm selfish even with thee — let dark thoughts come,
That thy sweet voice may chase them, as they say
The blessed church-bells drive the demons off.
Fio. If I but knew the reason of your sadness,
Then I might comfort you ; but I know nothing —
Not even your name.
Ber. I 'd have no name for thee
But "father."
Fio. In the convent at Cesena,
Where I was rear'd, they us'd to call me orphan.
I thought I had no father, till you came.
And then they needed not to say I had one;
My own heart told me that.
Ber. I often think
I had done well to have left thee there, in the peace
Of that still cloister. But it was too hard !
My empty heart so hunger'd for my child,
For those dear eyes that look no scorn for me,
That voice that speaks respect and tenderness,
Even for me ! — My dove — my lily-flower —
My only stay in life ! — O God ! I thank thee
That thou hast left me this at least !
[*He weeps.*
Fio. Dear father !
You 're crying now — you must not cry — you must not —
I cannot bear to see you cry.

Ber. Let be !
'T were better than to see me laugh.
  Fio. But wherefore ?
You say you are so happy here, and yet
You never come but to weep bitter tears.
And I can but weep, too, — not knowing
  why.
Why are you sad ? Oh, tell me — tell me
  all !
  Ber. I cannot. In this house I am thy
  father ;
Out of it, what I am boots not to say ;
Hated, perhaps, or envied — fear'd, I hope,
By many — scorn'd by more — and lov'd
  by none.
In this one innocent corner of the world
I would but be to thee a father — some-
  thing
August and sacred !
  Fio. ⁕ And you are so, father.
  Ber. I love thee with a love strong as
  the hate
I bear for all but thee. Come, sit beside
  me,
With thy pure hand in mine — and tell me
  still,
" I love you," and " I love you," — only
  that.
Smile on me — so ! — thy smile is passing
  sweet !
Thy mother used to smile so once — O God !
I cannot bear it. Do not smile — it wakes
Memories that tear my heart-strings. Do
  not look
So like thy mother, or I shall go mad !
  Fio. Oh, tell me of my mother !
  Ber. [*Shuddering.*] No, no, no !
  Fio. She 's dead ?
  Ber. Yes.
  Fio. You were with her when she died?
  Ber No ! — leave the dead alone — talk
  of thyself —
Thy life here. Thou heed'st well my cau-
  tion, girl,
Not to go out by day, nor show thyself
There at the casement.
  Fio. Yes ; some day, I hope,
You will take me with you, but to see the
  town ;
'T is so hard to be shut up here alone —
  Ber. Thou hast *not* stirr'd abroad ?
  Fio. Only to vespers —
You said I might do that with good Bri-
  gitta ;
I never go forth or come in alone.

Ber. That 's well. I grieve that thou
  shouldst live so close.
But if thou knewest what poison 's in the
  air,
What evil walks the streets ; how innocence
Is a temptation, beauty but a bait
For desperate desires ! — no man, I hope,
Has spoken to thee ?
  Fio. Only one. ·
  Ber. Ha ! who ?
  Fio. I know not — 't was against my will.
  Ber. You gave
No answer ?
  Fio. No — I fled.
  Ber. He follow'd you ?
  Fio. A gracious lady gave me kind pro-
  tection,
And bade her train guard me safe home.
  Oh, father,
If you had seen how good she was, how
  gently
She sooth'd my fears, — for I was sore
  afraid, —
I 'm sure you 'd love her.
  Ber. Did you learn her name ?
  Fio. I ask'd it, first, to set it in my
  prayers,
And then that *you* might pray for her.
  Ber. Her name ? [*Aside.*] *I* pray !
  Fio. The Countess Malatesta.
  Ber. [*Aside.*] Count Malatesta's wife
  protect my child !
You have not seen her since ?
  Fio. No, though she urged me
So hard to come to her ; and ask'd my
  name ;
And who my parents were ; and where I
  liv'd.
  Ber. You did not tell her ?
  Fio. Who my parents were ?
How could I, when I must not know my-
  self ?
  Ber. Patience, my darling ; trust thy
  father's love,
That there is reason for this mystery !
The time may come when we may live in
  peace,
And walk together free, under free heaven ;
But that cannot be here — nor now !
  Fio. Oh, when —
When shall that time arrive ?
  Ber. When what I live for
Has been achiev'd !
  Fio. What *you* live for ?
  Ber. Revenge !

Fio. Oh, do not look so, father !
Ber.   Listen, girl.
You ask'd me of your mother ; it is time
You should know why all questioning of
    her
Racks me to madness.   Look upon me,
    child ;
Misshapen as I am, there once was one,
Who seeing me despis'd — mock'd, lonely,
    poor —
Lov'd me, I think, most for my misery ;
Thy mother, like thee — just so pure — so
    sweet.
I was a public notary in Cesena ;
Our life was humble, but so happy : thou
Wert in thy cradle then, and many a
    night
Thy mother and I sate hand in hand to-
    gether,
Watching thine innocent smiles, and build-
    ing up
Long plans of joy to come !
Fio.   Alas ! she died !
Ber.   Died !   There are deaths 't is com-
    fort to look back on :
Hers was not such a death.   A devil came
Across our quiet life, and mark'd her
    beauty,
And lusted for her ; and when she scorn'd
    his offers,
Because he was a noble, great and strong,
He bore her from my side — by force —
    and after
I never saw her more : they brought me
    news
That she was dead !
Fio.   Ah me !
Ber.   And I was mad
For years and years, and when my wits
    came back, —
If e'er they came, — they brought one
    haunting purpose,
That since has shap'd my life, — to have
    revenge !
Revenge upon her wronger and his order ;
Revenge in kind ; to quit him — wife for
    wife !
Fio.   Father, 't is not for me to question
    with you ;
But think ! — revenge belongeth not to
    man,
It is God's attribute — usurp it not !
Ber.   Preach abstinence to him that dies
    of hunger ;
Tell the poor wretch who perishes of thirst

There 's danger in the cup his fingers
    clutch :
But bid me not forswear revenge.   No
    word !
Thou know'st now why I mew thee up so
    close ;
Keep thee out of the streets ; shut thee
    from eyes
And tongues of lawless men — for in these
    days
All men are lawless.   'T is because I fear
To lose thee, as I lost thy mother.
Fio.   Father,
I 'll pray for her.
Ber.   Do — and for me ; good night !
Fio.   Oh, not so soon — with all these
    sad, dark thoughts,
These bitter memories.   You need my
    love :
I 'll touch my lute for you, and sing to
    it.
Music, you know, chases all evil angels.
Ber.   I must go : 't is grave business
    calls me hence —
[*Aside*] 'T is time that I was at my post.
    — My own,
Sleep in thine innocence.   Good !   Good
    night !
Fio.   But let me see you to the outer
    door.
Ber.   Not a step further, then.   God
    guard this place,
That here my flower may grow, safe from
    the blight
Of look or word impure, — a holy thing
Consecrate to my service and my love !

ABRAHAM LINCOLN

(FROM " PUNCH ")

You lay a wreath on murder'd Lincoln's
    bier,
    You, who with mocking pencil wont to
        trace,
Broad for the self - complaisant British
    sneer,
    His length of shambling limb, his fur-
        row'd face,

His gaunt, gnarl'd hands, his unkempt,
    bristling hair,
    His garb uncouth, his bearing ill at ease,
His lack of all we prize as debonair,
    Of power or will to shine, of art to please;

You, whose smart pen back'd up the pencil's laugh,
  Judging each step as though the way were plain ;
Reckless, so it could point its paragraph,
  Of chief's perplexity, or people's pain, —

Beside this corpse, that bears for winding-sheet
  The Stars and Stripes he liv'd to rear anew,
Between the mourners at his head and feet,
  Say, scurrile jester, is there room for *you?*

Yes : he had liv'd to shame me from my sneer,
  To lame my pencil and confute my pen ;
To make me own this hind of princes peer,
  This rail-splitter a true-born king of men.

My shallow judgment I had learn'd to rue,
  Noting how to occasion's height he rose;
How his quaint wit made home-truth seem more true ;
  How, iron-like, his temper grew by blows ;

How humble, yet how hopeful he could be ;
  How in good fortune and in ill the same ;
Nor bitter in success, nor boastful he,
  Thirsty for gold, nor feverish for fame.

He went about his work, — such work as few
  Ever had laid on head and heart and hand, —
As one who knows, where there's a task to do,
  Man's honest will must Heaven's good grace command ;

Who trusts the strength will with the burden grow,
  That God makes instruments to work his will,
If but that will we can arrive to know,
  Nor tamper with the weights of good and ill.

So he went forth to battle, on the side
  That he felt clear was Liberty's and Right's,

As in his peasant boyhood he had plied
  His warfare with rude Nature's thwarting mights, —

The unclear'd forest, the unbroken soil,
  The iron bark that turns the lumberer's axe,
The rapid that o'erbears the boatman's toil,
  The prairie hiding the maz'd wanderer's tracks,

The ambush'd Indian, and the prowling bear, —
  Such were the deeds that help'd his youth to train :
Rough culture, but such trees large fruit may bear,
  If but their stocks be of right girth and grain.

So he grew up, a destin'd work to do,
  And liv'd to do it ; four long-suffering years'
Ill fate, ill feeling, ill report liv'd through,
  And then he heard the hisses change to cheers,

The taunts to tribute, the abuse to praise,
  And took both with the same unwavering mood, —
Till, as he came on light from darkling days,
  And seem'd to touch the goal from where he stood,

A felon hand, between the goal and him,
  Reach'd from behind his back, a trigger prest,
And those perplex'd and patient eyes were dim,
  Those gaunt, long-laboring limbs were laid to rest.

The words of mercy were upon his lips,
  Forgiveness in his heart and on his pen,
When this vile murderer brought swift eclipse
  To thoughts of peace on earth, good will to men.

The Old World and the New, from sea to sea,
  Utter one voice of sympathy and shame.

Sore heart, so stopp'd when it at last beat
high !
Sad life, cut short just as its triumph
came !

A deed accurs'd ! Strokes have been
struck before
By the assassin's hand, whereof men
doubt

If more of horror or disgrace they bore ;
But thy foul crime, like Cain's, stands
darkly out,

Vile hand, that brandest murder on a strife,
Whate'er its grounds, stoutly and nobly
striven,
And with the martyr's crown crownest a life
With much to praise, little to be for-
given.

John Westland Marston

FROM "MARIE DE MERANIE"

THE PARTING OF KING PHILIP AND MARIE

SCENE. — A Room in the Palace. MARIE
alone.

Marie. Another night, and yet no tid-
ings come.
Day follows day to mock me in its round.
O Time ! that to all senseless things dost
bear
Succor and comfort, — the reviving heat
And freshening dew to tree and flower and
weed, —
Why dost thou pass the famish'd heart
and smile ?

Enter ANNE.

Anne. Dear lady !
Marie. [*Eagerly.*] Anne ! Well ? No ;
your face is void !
You have no tidings for me.
Anne. Alas ! none.
Marie. We must be patient, Anne. I
cannot think
The Council will bereave me of my lord.
Anne. Heaven touch their hearts with
gentleness !
Marie. Amen !
Anne. And keep the king — [*Faltering.*
Marie. Why falter ? Prayers should
breathe
Trust, and not fear.
Anne. Heaven keep King Philip faith-
ful
And worthy of your love.
Marie. I will not say
Amen to that. To pray he may be faithful

Were to misdoubt he is so.
Anne. All men, being tempted,
Are prone to fall ; most prone, ambitious
kings.
Marie. What dost thou mean ?
Anne. By thoughts on ill that may be
To shield your heart from worse.
Marie. Worse ? What were worse
Than treachery in my lord ? Rash girl,
that word
Stretches to woe so infinite, it fathoms
An ocean of despair ! Uncrown me, slay
me,
Honors and life must end. Not love ! The
grave
Is as a port where it unlades its wealth
For immortality. But rob or taint
The merchandise of love — then let the
bark
Drift helmless o'er the seas, or strike the
shoals !
They can but wreck a ruin.
Anne. Pardon, madam.
I would not thus have mov'd you ; but —
Marie. Be silent !
Thy look doth herald thoughts my soul re-
pels.
He did desert me once. You see I read
you.
No, Anne ! His love was changeless, but
he quell'd it
For duty and his country. O shame,
shame !
Listening thy treason, I adopt it. Go ! —
Nay, not unkindly. This suspense disturbs
me.
Leave me awhile. There, there !
[*Taking her hand,* ANNE *goes out.*
Another night !

It cannot last forever. Even now
The unregarding messenger despatch'd
To bear my doom his onward course may
    speed.
They could not part us, Philip, had they
    seen
Our happy solitude, our inner world
Of secret, holy, all-sufficing bliss.
They guess it not, nor feel it. At their
    knees,
Lock'd in my arms, I should have told
    them this,
And forced my heart an avenue to theirs
Through all their wiles, for hearts must
    answer hearts ;
But mine was dumb, and how could theirs
    reply ?
Woe 's me ! Who comes ?

Enter PHILIP.

    Philip — my lord ! — Say, say,
May I embrace thee ? — may I call thee
    mine ? —
Am I thy wife ?
Phil. Yes ; in the sight of Heaven.
Marie. And not of earth ? A doom
told in a breath ;
Brief, but so cold that it hath froze the
    fount
Whence sorrow gushes !
Phil.   I am dear to thee ?
Marie. What ! is there hope ? If not,
    encourage none.
Phil. Why should we be the slaves of
    Rome ?
Marie. Thou wilt
Resist his mandate ? Yet thy kingdom,
    love ?
Phil. Dearest, most faithful ! We may
    still remain
Bound to each other, and the Papal curse
Pass from the realm.
Marie. How ? Haste thee to disclose.
Phil. The Council has pronounced no
    sentence.
Marie. Yet
Thou art return'd !
Phil. Like to a criminal
I stood before the conclave. Every day
Brought some new contumely. The weight
    I bore
Of strain'd suspense and nice indignity
Was pleasant pastime for them ; and they
    linger'd,
Protracting their enjoyment, and inviting

The universe to look on haughty Philip
Crouch'd at their stools, and learn from
    thence how Rome
Would deal with rebel kings !
Marie. And yet you bore it ?
Phil. It was the Church's aim to judge
    my cause,
To plant its insolent foot upon my neck,
Humbling all crowns in mine. I look'd for
    this ;
I bore it long. At last scorn heap'd on
    scorn
Turn'd patience to revolt.
Marie. [*After a short pause.*] And then ?
    How then ?
Phil. [*Avoiding her look.*] Marie ! I said
    within my soul, my pomp,
My title, all my gilded shows of power,
Were not the links that bound thy love to
    mine.
Was I right there ?
Marie. Can Philip ask that question ?
Phil. Her trust doth sting me more
    than could reproach.
Too late, too late ! all must be told ! [*Aside.*
Marie. What follow'd ?
Phil. I will not hear your judgment,
    lords, I cried :
Not mov'd by you, but of my sovereign
    will,
I have resolv'd that Marie shall resign
The throne and empty state she never
    priz'd,
And Ingerburge to her lost dignities
Be straight restor'd. 'T is all that Den-
    mark seeks ;
Therefore dissolve the interdict !
Marie. *Thou* saidst this ? —
Heard I aright ?
Phil. [*Confused.*] Marie, thou didst.
Marie. And Philip
Could of his proper will cast Marie out !
I thought — I thought you said we should
    not part.
Phil. Part ? — never, never ! Part !
Marie. But have you not own'd Inger-
    burge your wife ?
I am no longer queen.
Phil. But for all this
We must not part.
Marie. Husband — I pray your par-
    don ;
I can't forget you were so — torture not
My mind with this perplexity ! How is 't
I can be thine, and Ingerburge thy wife ?

Phil. [*After a pause.*] She is but so in
   name ; thou wilt retain
The empire of my heart.
Marie.   Ha ! how the light —
The cruel light I could not see before —
Bursts on my sight ! No ; 't is some hide-
   ous dream.
Although I see, I shall not touch thy hand.
   [*Takes his hand as if to assure herself.*
It is reality ! And yet — forgive me !
A subtle tempter through my o'erwrought
   brain
Would stab my trust in thee. He shall
   not, love !
Even now I 'm calmer. Pray, repeat the
   words, —
The words you spake but now.
   Phil.   I said, my own,
Though Ingerburge might bear the name
   of queen,
Thou only shouldst rule Philip —
Marie.   Pause awhile.
Though Ingerburge might bear the name
   of queen,
I only should rule Philip —
          [*Signs to him to proceed.*
Phil.   Thou shouldst share
His hours of love — thou only; thou
   shouldst be —
          [*Hesitating, and averting his head.*
Marie. His paramour ! O God ! although
   his voice
Was sham'd from speech, this is the thing
   he means.   [*She turns from him.*
Phil. Thou wouldst not go ?
Marie.   I am already gone !
We measure distance by the heart.
Phil.   Yet hear me !
Marie. The Duke de Méran's daughter
   listens, sir.   [*She sits.*
Phil. [*About to kneel.*] If this humility
   may aught —
Marie.   No knee !
Respect so far my woe's reality,
As to put by these pageant semblances.
Phil. Oh ! has this grief no remedy ?
Marie.   None, none.
The faith of love no hand can wound but
   that
Was pledged to guard it. Then what hand
   can staunch ?
We strive no more with doom ; the sad
   mistake
May be endur'd, but not retriev'd. No,
   no !

Phil. By heaven, you do me wrong !
   'T is not in man
To conquer destiny. I made you queen.
Marie. You made me queen ! I made
   you more than king.
When my eyes rais'd their worship to thy
   face,
I saw no crown. I ask'd not if thy hand
Clos'd on a sceptre ; but mine press'd it
   close,
Because it rent the shackles of the slave.
'T was not thy grandeur won me. Had
   the earthquake
Engulfed thine empire, — had frowning
   Fate
Lower'd on thine arms and scourged thee
   from the field,
A fugitive ; if on thy forehead Rome
Had grav'd her curse, and all thy kind re-
   coil'd
In horror from thy side, — I yet had cried,
There is no brand upon thy heart ; let
   that,
In the vast loneliness, still beat to mine !
   Phil. [*Falling at her feet.*] You had ;
   you had ! the dust is on my head !
Sweet saint ! thou 'rt of a higher brood
   than we,
Hast right to spurn me from thee.
Marie.   Rise ! The feet,
By thorns on life's rough path so often
   pierced,
Are little like to spurn a stumbling brother.
Phil. [*Rising.*] Forgive, forgive me,
   Marie !
Marie.   You repent ?
'T was but delusion. You will be again
The Philip I ador'd ! That hope shall
   bless me
When we are far apart. And now for-
   ever
In this dark world farewell ! Another land
I seek, but ne'er shall find another home.
Shield him, all holy powers ! Philip —
          [*Extending her hand.*
Phil.   Go, go ;
I was not worthy thee !
Marie.   Not thus, not thus !
Phil. But one embrace. It is the last,
   the last !   [*They embrace.*
Go, Marie !
[MARIE *goes to the door. She reverts her
   head. They regard each other in silence
   for a few moments, after which* MARIE
   slowly disappears.

Phil. [*After a pause, sinking into a chair.*]
    I'm alone on earth ! She's gone,
And what is left me ?
    [*The roll of drums is heard without.*
[*He suddenly rises.*] Ha ! that clamor speaks
In stern reply ; a summons to the field !

Fate, that denies me love, has left me ven-
    geance.
Friends fail me, foemen swarm my coasts.
    'T is well !
Now, fiend of war, I am devote to thee !
    [*He rushes out*

William Gorman Wills

CROMWELL AND HENRIETTA MARIA

FROM THE STAGE TEXT OF "CHARLES THE FIRST"

SCENE. — Whitehall Palace. CROMWELL dis-
    covered seated.

Cromwell. On me and on my children !
So said the voice last night ! A lying
    dream !
This blood — this blood on me and on my
    children.
It is my wont to feel more heartiness
When face to face with action. But this
    deed
Doth wrap itself in doubt and fearfulness.
Do I best to confront him at this hour,
Even when yon scaffold waiteth for its vic-
    tim,
And his pale face doth look like martyrdom?
I will not. Out upon my sinking heart !
The standard-bearer fainteth, and my fol-
    lowers
Grow slack. I 'll hie me to them —
And yet, if by the granting him his life
He abdicate — no shifts — he abdicate !
Then — then this offer of the Prince of
    Wales —
This young Charles Stuart — he in our ab-
    solute power,
As he doth promise if we spare his father.
Why, if he come — I had not thought of
    that —
Both son and father given to our hands :
Then have we scotch'd the snake !

Enter an Attendant, *who hands* CROMWELL
    a letter.

Attend. My Lord-General — from the
    King !   [*Exit* Attendant.
Crom. [*Reads the letter.*] " Declines to see
me !"

Well — well —
    " *His last hour disturb'd !* "
            It shall be thy last hour.
    " *As touching the Prince of Wales' noble
offering of himself for me. Look back on my
past life, and thou art answer'd !* "
Past life ! Full of deceit and subtle car-
    riage.
    " *I pardon thee and all mine enemies, and
may Heaven pardon them !* "
What now doth stay to rend away this patch
On our new garment ?
England ! one hour — gray tyranny is dead!
And in this hand thy future destiny.

Enter QUEEN.

Madam, my daughter hardly did prevail
That I should grant you this last inter-
    view.
It must be brief and private, or I warn
    you
I cannot answer for your safe return.
Queen. [*Aside.*] Sainte Vierge, aidez-
    moi ! This is the man who holds
My husband's life within his hands. Ah !
    could I — *Sainte Marie, inspirez-moi,
    mettez votre force dans mes prières !*
I see him as the drowning swimmer sees
The distant headland he can never reach.
Sir, do not go. I wish to speak to you.
Crom. Madam, I wait.
Queen. Oh, sir ! the angels wait and
    watch your purpose :
Unwritten history pauses for your deed,
To set your name within a shining annal,
Or else to brand it on her foulest page !
Crom. Madam, 't is not for me to answer
    you.
And for unwritten history — thou nor I
Can brief it in our cause ; 't will speak the
    truth.
England condemns the King, and he shall
    die !

Queen. Oh, pity! pity! Hast a human heart?
How canst thou look at me so cruelly?
I look for pity on thy stubborn cheek
As I might place a mirror to dead lips
To find one stain of breath.
The brightest jewel ever set in crown
Were worthless to the glisten of one tear
Upon thy lid — one faint hope-star of mercy.
Be merciful! a queen doth kneel to thee.
Crom. Not to me! Nor am I now
A whit more mov'd because thou art a queen!
Queen. I am no queen; but a poor stricken woman,
On whom this dreadful hour is closing in.
        [*Chimes. The half-hour.*
Dost hear the clock? Each second quivering on
Is full of horror for both thee and me:
Endless remorse thy doom, and sorrow mine.
Crom. Madam, no more. I shall have no remorse
For an unhappy duty well perform'd.
Queen. Thou call'st it duty; but all heaven and earth
Shall raise one outraged cry and call it murder;
It shall be written right across the clouds
In characters of blood till Heaven hath judged it.
Crom. Nay, you forget! the righteous cause doth prosper.
If this be crime, the hand of Heaven not in it,
Then had thy husband flourish'd; on our side
God's heavy judgment fallen, shame and slaughter.
Queen. God speaketh not in thunder when he judges,
But in the dying moans of those we treasure,
And in the silence of our broken hearts!
Thou hast a daughter, and her cheek is pale;
Her days do balance between life and death,
Whether they wither or abide with thee.
Let him be cruel who hath none to love;
But let that father tremble who shall dare
Widow another's home! She loves the King.
Take now his sacred life, and hie thee home.
Smile on her, call her to thee, she will linger.
Ask for thy welcome, she will give it thee!

A shudder as she meets thee at the door:
A cry as thou wouldst think to touch her lips;
A sickening at thy guilty hands' caress!
The haunting of a mute reproach shall dwell
Forever in her eyes till they be dead!
Crom. [*Moved.*] Silence! You speak you know not what. No more!
Thou voice within, why dost thou seem so far?
Shine out, thou fiery pillar! Bring me up
From the dead wilderness —
Queen. Oh! yield not to that voice, hearken to mercy,
And I will join my prayers to thine henceforth
That thy Elizabeth may live for thee.
Crom. Madam, I came here with intent of mercy,
And with a hope of life.
Queen.   Of life — of life!
Crom. I offer'd him his life — he scorn'd my offer.
Queen. No — no — he shall not. I am somewhat faint;
The hope thou showest striketh me like lightning.
Life! didst thou say his life? Ask anything.
Crom. If he would abdicate and quit the kingdom.
Queen. And he shall do it. I will answer for it.
Give me but breathing-time to move him, sir.
Crom. Stay, madam. If we spare your husband's life
Your son has offer'd to submit his person
Into our hands, and set his sign and seal
To any proposition we demand.
Queen. "Thou strikest a fountain for me in the rock,
And ere my lips can touch it, it is dry!"
My husband first must abdicate, and then my son —
What was the answer of the King to thee?
Crom. He doth refuse our mercy, and elects
To carry to his death the name of King.
Queen. When all was lost at Newark, and thy King
Was bought and sold by his own countrymen,
'T was thou who with a fawning cozenage

Lur'd thy good master to undo himself,
To doubt where all his hope was to confide,
And blindly trust where every step was
  fatal !
'T was thou, when the repenting Parlia-
  ment
Were fain for reconcilement, brought thy
  soldiers —
Thou (jealous stickler for the Commons'
  rights)
Arrested every true man in the house,
And pack'd the benches with thy regicides !

Crom. What, madam, is the purpose of
  this railing ?
Queen. Thou think'st to make the mother
  a decoy,
And, holding the lost father in thy grip,
Secure the son who yet may punish thee !
  [*Chimes. Three quarters.*
Crom. Madam, the clock ! say, what
  dost thou intend ?

Queen. To choke my sighs, to hide each
  bitter tear,
To keep a calm and steadfast countenance,
To mask my anguish from his Majesty.
Crom. So ! it were well ; and then —
Queen. Then we will both be faithful to
  ourselves,
Even unto death !
Crom. Will you not, madam, use your
  influence ?
Queen. Never ! My husband, sir, shall
  die a King !
Crom. Thou shadow of a King, then art
  thou doom'd !
I wash mine hands of it. [*Aside.*
What melancholy doth raven on my heart ?
Thou child of many prayers, Elizabeth ! —
I 'll to the Generals. Fairfax relents.
That not will I. My hand is on the
  plough ;
I will not look behind. [*Exit* CROMWELL.

William Schwenck Gilbert

FROM "PYGMALION AND GALATEA"

SCENE. — PYGMALION's Studio, containing a
Statue of GALATEA, before which curtains
are drawn.

Pygmalion. "The thing is but a statue
  after all ! "
Cynisca little thought that in those words
She touch'd the key-note of my discontent.
True, I have powers denied to other men ;
Give me a block of senseless marble —
  well,
I 'm a magician, and it rests with me
To say what kernel lies within its shell ;
It shall contain a man, a woman — child —
A dozen men and women if I will.
So far the gods and I run neck and neck ;
Nay, so far I can beat them at their trade !
I am no bungler — all the men *I* make
Are straight-limb'd fellows, each magnifi-
  cent
In the perfection of his manly grace :
I make no crook-backs — all my men are
  gods,
My women goddesses — in outward form.
But there 's my tether ! I can go so far,
And go no farther ! At that point I stop,

To curse the bonds that hold me sternly
  back ;
To curse the arrogance of those proud
  gods,
Who say, " Thou shalt be greatest among
  man,
And yet infinitesimally small ! "
Galatea. Pygmalion !
Pyg.   Who called ?
Gal.   Pygmalion !

[PYGMALION *tears away curtain and discov-
  ers* GALATEA *alive.*

Pyg. Ye gods ! It lives !
Gal.   Pygmalion !
Pyg.   It speaks !
I have my prayer ! my Galatea breathes !
Gal. Where am I ? Let me speak,
  Pygmalion ;
Give me thy hand — both hands — how
  soft and warm !
Whence came I ?   [*Descends.*
Pyg.   Why, from yonder pedestal !
Gal. That pedestal ? Ah, yes ! I recol-
  lect
There was a time when it was part of me.
Pyg. That time has passed forever :
  thou art now

A living, breathing woman, excellent
In every attribute of womankind.
Gal.   Where am I, then ?
Pyg.   Why, born into the world
By miracle !
Gal.   Is this the world ?
Pyg.   It is.
Gal.   This room ?
Pyg.   This room is portion of a house ;
The house stands in a grove ; the grove
      itself
Is one of many, many hundred groves
In Athens.
Gal.   And is Athens, then, the world ?
Pyg.   To an Athenian — yes.
Gal.   And I am one ?
Pyg.   By birth and parentage, not by
      descent.
Gal.   But how came I to be ?
Pyg.   Well — let me see.
Oh — you were quarried in Pentelicus ;
I modell'd you in clay — my artisans
Then rough'd you out in marble — I, in
      turn,
Brought my artistic skill to bear on you,
And made you what you are — in all but
      life ;
The gods completed what I had begun,
And gave the only gift I could not give !
Gal.   Then this is life ?
Pyg.   It is.
Gal.   And not long since
I was a cold, dull stone ?   I recollect
That by some means I knew that I was
      stone :
That was the first dull gleam of conscious-
      ness ;
I became conscious of a chilly self,
A cold, immovable identity.
I knew that I was stone, and knew no more !
Then, by an imperceptible advance,
Came the dim evidence of outer things,
Seen — darkly and imperfectly, yet seen —
The walls surrounding me, and I alone.
That pedestal — that curtain — then a voice
That call'd on Galatea !   At that word,
Which seem'd to shake my marble to the
      core,
That which was dim before came evident ;
Sounds that had humm'd around me, indis-
      tinct,
Vague, meaningless, seem'd to resolve
      themselves
Into a language I could understand ;
I felt my frame pervaded by a glow

That seem'd to thaw my marble into flesh.
Its cold, hard substance throbb'd with
.   active life ;
My limbs grew supple, and I mov'd — I
      liv'd !
Liv'd in the ecstacy of new-born life !
Liv'd in the love of him that fashion'd me !
Liv'd in a thousand tangled thoughts of
      hope,
Love, gratitude, — thoughts that resolv'd
      themselves
Into one word, that word Pygmalion !
                      [*Kneels to him.*
Pyg.   I have no words to tell thee of my
      joy,
O woman — perfect in thy loveliness !
Gal.   What is that word ?   Am I a wo-
      man ?
Pyg.   Yes.
Gal.   Art thou a woman ?
Pyg.   No, I am a man.
Gal.   What *is* a man ?
Pyg.   A being strongly fram'd
To wait on woman, and protect her from
All ills that strength and courage can
      avert ;
To work and toil for her, that she may
      rest ;
To weep and mourn for her, that she may
      laugh ;
To fight and die for her, that she may
      live !
Gal.   [*After a pause.*]   I 'm glad I am
      a woman.
Pyg.   So am I.   [*They sit.*
Gal.   That I escape the pains thou hast
      to bear ?
Pyg.   That I may undergo those pains
      for thee.
Gal.   With whom, then, wouldst thou
      fight ?
Pyg.   With any man
Whose deed or word gave Galatea pain.
Gal.   Then there are other men in this
      strange world ?
Pyg.   There are, indeed !
Gal.   And other women ?
Pyg.   [*Taken aback.*]   Yes.
Though for a moment I 'd forgotten it !
Yes, other women.
Gal.   And for all of these
Men work, and toil, and mourn, and weep,
      and fight ?
Pyg.   It is man's duty, if he 's call'd
      upon,

To fight for all : he works for those he
loves.
Gal. Then by thy work I know thou
lovest me.
Pyg. Indeed, I love thee !
[*Embraces her.*
Gal. With what kind of love ?
Pyg I love thee [*recollecting himself and
releasing her*] as a sculptor loves his
work !
Aside.] There 's a diplomacy in that reply.
Gal. My love is different in kind to
thine :
I am no sculptor, and I 've done no work,
Yet I do love thee : say, what love is
mine ?
Pyg. Tell me its symptoms, then I 'll
answer thee.
Gal. Its symptoms ? Let me call them
as they come.
A sense that I am made *by* thee *for* thee ;
That I 've no will that is not wholly thine ;
That I 've no thought, no hope, no enter-
prise
That does not own *thee* as its sovereign ;
That I have life, that I may live for thee,
That I am thine — that thou and I are one !
What kind of love is that ?
Pyg. A kind of love
That I shall run some risk in dealing with !
Gal. And why, Pygmalion ?
Pyg. Such love as thine
A man may not receive, except indeed
From one who is, or is to be, his wife !
Gal. Then *I* will be thy wife !
Pyg. That may not be ;
I have a wife — the gods allow but one.
Gal. Why did the gods, then, send me
here to thee ?
Pyg. I cannot say — unless to punish
me
For unreflecting and presumptuous prayer.
I pray'd that thou shouldst live — I have
my prayer,
And now I see the fearful consequence
That must attend it !
Gal. Yet thou lovest me ?
Pyg. Who could look on that face and
stifle love ?
Gal. Then I am beautiful ?
Pyg. Indeed thou art.
Gal. I wish that I could look upon my-
self,
But that 's impossible.
Pyg. Not so indeed.

This mirror will reflect thy face. Behold !
[*Hands her a mirror.*
Gal. How beautiful ! I 'm very glad
to know
That both our tastes agree so perfectly ;
Why, my Pygmalion, I did not think
That aught could be more beautiful than
thou,
Till I beheld myself. Believe me, love,
I could look in this mirror all day long.
So I 'm a woman ?
Pyg. There 's no doubt of that !
Gal. Oh happy maid, to be so passing
fair !
And happier still Pygmalion, who can gaze,
At will, upon so beautiful a face !
Pyg. Hush, Galatea ! in thine inno-
cence
Thou sayest things that others would re-
prove.
Gal. Indeed, Pygmalion ? Then it is
wrong
To think that one is exquisitely fair ?
Pyg. Well, Galatea, it 's a sentiment
That every other woman shares with thee ;
They *think* it, but they keep it to them-
selves.
Gal. And is thy wife as beautiful as I ?
Pyg. No, Galatea, for in forming thee
I took her features — lovely in them-
selves —
And in the marble made them lovelier
still.
Gal. [*Disappointed.*] Oh ! then I 'm not
original ?
Pyg. Well — no —
That is — thou hast indeed a prototype ;
But though in stone thou didst resemble
her,
In life the difference is manifest.
Gal. I 'm very glad I am lovelier than
she.
And am I better ?
Pyg. That I do not know.
Gal. Then she has faults ?
Pyg. But very few indeed ;
Mere trivial blemishes, that serve to show
That she and I are of one common kin.
I love her all the better for such faults !
Gal. [*After a pause.*] Tell me some
faults and I 'll commit them now.
Pyg. There is no hurry ; they will come
in time :
Though, for that matter, it 's a grievous sin
To sit as lovingly as we sit now.

Gal. Is sin so pleasant ? If to sit and talk,
As we are sitting, be indeed a sin,
Why, I could sin all day ! But tell me, love,
Is this great fault, that I 'm committing now,
The kind of fault that only serves to show
That thou and I are of one common kin ?
Pyg. Indeed, I 'm very much afraid it is.
Gal. And dost thou love me better for such fault ?
Pyg. Where is the mortal that could answer " No " ?
Gal. Why, then I 'm satisfied, Pygmalion ;
Thy wife and I can start on equal terms.
She loves thee ?
Pyg. Very much.
Gal. I am glad of that.
I like thy wife.
Pyg. And why ?
Gal. Our tastes agree.
We love Pygmalion well, and, what is more,
Pygmalion loves us both. I like thy wife ;
I 'm sure we shall agree.
Pyg. [*Aside.*] I doubt it much !
Gal. Is she within ?
Pyg. No, she is not within.
Gal. But she 'll come back ?
Pyg. Oh, yes, she will come back.
Gal. How pleas'd she 'll be to know, when she returns,
That there was some one here to fill her place !
Pyg. [*Dryly.*] Yes, I should say she 'd be extremely pleas'd.
Gal. Why, there is something in thy voice which says
That thou art jesting ! Is it possible
To say one thing and mean another ?
Pyg. Yes,
It 's sometimes done.
Gal. How very wonderful !
So clever !
Pyg. And so very useful.
Gal. Yes.
Teach me the art.
Pyg. The art will come in time.
My wife will *not* be pleas'd ; there — that 's the truth.
Gal. I do not think that I *shall* like thy wife.
Tell me more of her.

Pyg. Well —
Gal. What did she say
When last she left thee ?
Pyg. Humph ! Well, let me see :
Oh ! true, she gave thee to me as my wife, —
Her solitary representative ;
She fear'd I should be lonely till she came
And counsell'd me, if thoughts of love should come,
To speak those thoughts to thee, as I am wont
To speak to her.
Gal. That 's right.
Pyg. But when she spoke
Thou wast a stone, now thou art flesh and blood,
Which makes a difference !
Gal. It 's a strange world !
A woman loves her husband very much,
And cannot brook that I should love him, too !
She fears he will be lonely till she comes,
And will not let me cheer his loneliness !
She bids him breathe his love to senseless stone,
And, when that stone is brought to life, be dumb !
It 's a strange world — I cannot fathom it !
Pyg. [*Aside.*] Let me be brave, and put an end to this.
[*Aloud.*] Come, Galatea — till my wife returns,
My sister shall provide thee with a home ;
Her house is close at hand.
Gal. [*Astonished and alarmed.*] Send me not hence,
Pygmalion — let me stay.
Pyg. It may not be.
Come, Galatea, we shall meet again.
Gal. [*Resignedly.*] Do with me as thou wilt, Pygmalion !
But we *shall* meet again ? — and very soon ?
Pyg. Yes, very soon.
Gal. And when thy wife returns,
She 'll let me stay with thee ?
Pyg. I do not know.
[*Aside.*] Why should I hide the truth from her ? [*Aloud.*] Alas !
I may not see thee then.
Gal. Pygmalion !
What fearful words are these ?
Pyg. The bitter truth.
I may not love thee — I must send thee hence.

Gal. Recall those words, Pygmalion,
    my love !
Was it for this that Heaven gave me life ?
Pygmalion, have mercy on me ; see,
I am thy work, thou hast created me ;
The gods have sent me to thee. I am thine,
Thine ! only and unalterably thine !
This is the thought with which my soul is
    charged.
Thou tellest me of one who claims thy
    love,
That thou hast love for her alone. Alas !
I do not know these things — I only know

That Heaven has sent me here to be with
    thee !
Thou tellest me of duty to thy wife,
Of vows that thou wilt love but her. Alas !
I do not know these things — I only know
That Heaven, who sent me here, has given
    me
One all-absorbing duty to discharge —
To love thee, and to make thee love again !

[*During this speech* PYGMALION *has shown
    symptoms of irresolution ; at its conclusion
    he takes her in his arms, and embraces her.*

Herman Charles Merivale

ÆTATE XIX

NINETEEN ! of years a pleasant number ;
    And it were well
If on his post old Time would slumber
    For Isabel :

If he would leave her, fair and girlish,
    Untouch'd of him
Forgetting once his fashions churlish,
    Just for a whim !

But no, not he ; ashore, aboard ship,
    Sleep we, or wake,
He lays aside his right of lordship
    For no man's sake ;

But all untiring girds his loins up
    For great and small ;
And, as a miser sums his coins up,
    Still counts us all.

As jealous as a nine-days' lover,
    He will not spare,
Spite of the wealth his presses cover,
    One silver hair ;

But writes his wrinkles far and near in
    Life's every page,
With ink invisible, made clear in
    The fire of age.

Child ! while the treacherous flame yet
    shines not
    On thy smooth brow,
There even Envy's eye divines not
    That writing now,

In this brief homily I read you
    There should be found
Some wholesome moral, that might lead
    you
    To look around,

And think how swift, as sunlight passes
    Into the shade,
The pretty picture in your glass is
    Foredoom'd to fade.

But, 'faith, the birthday genius quarrels
    With moral rhyme,
And I was never good at morals
    At any time ;

While with ill-omens to alarm you
    'T were vain to try, —
To show how little mine should harm you,
    Your mother's by !

And what can Time hurt me, I pray, with,
    If he insures
Such friends to laugh regrets away with
    As you — and yours ?

READY, AY, READY

OLD England's sons are English yet,
    Old England's hearts are strong ;
And still she wears her coronet
    Aflame with sword and song.
As in their pride our fathers died,
    If need be, so die we ;
So wield we still, gainsay who will,
    The sceptre of the sea.

England, stand fast ; let hand and heart be
steady ;
Be thy first word thy last, — Ready, ay,
ready !

We 've Raleighs still for Raleigh's part,
We 've Nelsons yet unknown ;
The pulses of the Lion Heart
Beat on through Wellington.
Hold, Britain, hold thy creed of old,
Strong foe and steadfast friend,
And, still unto thy motto true,
Defy not, but defend.
England, stand fast ; let heart and hand be
steady ;
Be thy first word thy last, — Ready, ay,
ready!

Men whisper'd that our arm was weak,
Men said our blood was cold,
And that our hearts no longer speak
The clarion-note of old ;
But let the spear and sword draw near
The sleeping lion's den,
His island shore shall start once more
To life with armed men.
England, stand fast ; let heart and hand be
steady ;
Be thy first word thy last, — Ready, ay,
ready !

THAISA'S DIRGE

THAISA fair, under the cold sea lying,
Sleeps the long sleep denied to her by
Earth ;
We, adding sighs unto the wild winds' sigh-
ing,
With all our mourning under-mourn her
worth :
The white waves toss their crested plumes
above her,
Round sorrowing faces with the salt spray
wet ;
All are her lovers that once learn'd to love
her,
And never may remember to forget ;
Shells for her pillow Amphitrite bring-
eth,
And sad nymphs of the dank weed weave
her shroud ;
Old Triton's horn her dirge to Ocean sing-
eth,
Whose misty caverns swell the echo
loud ;
And, while the tides rock to and fro her
bier,
What was Thaisa lies entombed here.

Augusta Webster

SONGS FROM DRAMAS

NEWS TO THE KING

"NEWS to the king, good news for all,"
The corn is trodden, the river runs red.
"News of the battle," the heralds call,
"We have won the field ; we have taken
the town ;
We have beaten the rebels and crush'd
them down."
And the dying lie with the dead.

"Who was my bravest ? " quoth the king,
The corn is trodden, the river runs red.
" Whom shall I honor for this great thing ? "
"Threescore were best, where none were
worst ;
But Walter Wendulph was aye the first."
And the dying lie with the dead.

"What of my husband ? " quoth the
bride,
*The corn is trodden, the river runs
red.*
" Comes he to-morrow ? how long will he
bide ? "
" Put off thy bridegear, busk thee in
black ;
Walter Wendulph will never come back.'
And the dying lie with the dead.

'TWEEN EARTH AND SKY

SEEDS with wings, between earth and sky
Fluttering, flying ;
Seeds of a lily with blood-red core
Breathing of myrrh and of giroflore :
Where winds drop them, there must they
lie,
Living or dying.

Some to the garden, some to the wall,
  Fluttering, falling ;
Some to the river, some to earth :
Those that reach the right soil get birth ;
None of the rest have liv'd at all.
  Whose voice is calling —

" Here is soil for wing'd seeds that near,
    Fluttering, fearing,
  Where they shall root and burgeon and
    spread.
  Lacking the heart-room the song lies
    dead:
Half is the song that reaches the ear,
  Half is the hearing " ?

DAY IS DEAD

DAY is dead, and let us sleep,
  Sleep a while or sleep for aye ;
'T were the best if we unknew
While to-morrow dawn'd and grew ;
It may bring us time to weep :
  We were glad to-day.
Joy for a little while is won,
Joy is ending while begun ;
Then the setting of the sun ;
  Afterwards is long to rue.

TELL ME NOT OF MORROWS, SWEET

TELL me not of morrows, sweet ;
All to-day is fair, and ours,
    Thine and mine ;
Mar not Now with needing more.
  Neither speak of yesterdays ;
  Lose not Now with backward gaze,
Lingering on what went before.
Watch for all to-day's new flowers,
    Mine and thine,
Else to-day were incomplete.

Nay, but speak of morrows, sweet ;
Lest to-day seem loss of ours,
    Thine and mine,
Leaving nought to come again.
  Nay, but speak of yesterdays,
  Lest, forgetting trodden ways,
We have trodden them in vain.
Take one love-time of all hours,
    Mine and thine,
Else to-day were incomplete.

THE DEATHS OF MYRON AND KLYDONE

FROM " IN A DAY "

SCENE. — A lighted Hall. Soft music playing
  without. A Bed placed in an alcove among
  flowers.

Enter MYRON, OLYMNIOS, RUFUS, LYSIS,
    and others.
Myr. Move me that jasmine further
  from the bed :
The perfume's sweetest coming faint
  through air.
That's well. And shut the nearest case-
  ment close :
The breeze is almost chill. Throw that
  one wide :
Let waking stars peep at their mimics here.
Now, Rufus, art thou ready ?
Ruf.   'T is, Art thou ?
Myr. Give me the cup, good Lysis.
  Pure wine first.
I drink to the Good Genius [*drinks*], whom,
    perchance,
I shall know presently by some nearer name.
Now, Lysis, that blent wine whose name is
    Sleep.   [*Drinks.*
  [*To Rufus.*] So, thou hast seen me drink,
    and know'st what draught,
Who saw'st it mix'd ; no need methinks to
    watch.
Go, prithee, try again my vintage wine :
I doubt thou wilt not ask to taste *this* brew.
Ruf. No, 'faith ! my thirst can wait a
    wholesomer tap.
I am sorry for thee, too.
Myr.   Well, go, my man ;
Thou canst come by-and-by and see 't was
    sure.
[*Exeunt all but* MYRON, OLYMNIOS, *and*
    LYSIS.
Now quick, boy ! fetch Klydone.
          [*Exit* LYSIS.
          'T is most strange
How death that is of all we know most sure,
Of all we know seems most impossible.
I shall not live an hour ; my mind grants
    that,
But grants it as a stage of argument,
Gives it but such belief as when, being told
" So many fathomless miles to reach that
    star,"
We learn the count unquestioning it for true,
But cannot shape conception of its reach.

I cannot, quick life still within my veins,
I cannot feel a faith that presently
My cold oblivious body shall lie there,
Void of the soul, an ended nothingness.

Olymn. Thou art too young, and death
unnatural.

Myr. Klydone thinks all death unnatu-
ral.

Olymn. If nature stood for perfectness,
it were.
And therein is the better after-hope :
For perfectness must be, since we conceive
it,
And, not being here, 't is in some second
life.

Myr. I 'll think my soul shall, like the
sunward swallows,
Having known but summer here, renew it
there.
Klydone comes not.

Olymn. That 's for want of wings.

Myr. I would she had them, to flee
hence and rest.
'T is a wild, long journey. Ah, poor child,
poor child !
May the gods send her happy.

Olymn. If they will ;
Pray rather they may send her as is best.

Myr. Let her not brood upon my death
too much,
And most of all persuade her from re-
morse ;
Tell her 't was destin'd, had she never
spoken ;
Hush her from her own blame till, by-and-
by,
It takes the strangeness of unworded
thoughts
That fade like bodiless ghosts beyond our
ken.

Olymn. No, Myron. Self-blame 's a
shrewd counsellor ;
I will not help Klydone from that good.

Myr. She is such a woman as some
griefs could kill.

Olymn. Better to die by an ennobling
grief
Than to live cheerful in too low content.

Myr. But spare her, if it be but for
my sake.

Olymn. Whom dost thou ask ? I spare
not nor chastise ;
That 's God's to do, who makes our self his
means :
Her sorrowing or her comfort lie in her.

Enter LYSIS.

Lys. Klydone, sir, Klydone — [*Stops.*

Myr. Comes she not ?
Tell her to make more speed, for I grow
heavy.

Lys. She comes ; she bade them carry
her ; she 's half dead.

Myr. I am awake, I think. Say it again.
Half dead ?

Lys. She took the poison at due time ;
She said 't was at due time by thine own
count;
She said thou shouldst have call'd her in
an hour,
And she was ready then : but 't was too
long,
More than an hour, and so she must go first
That did but mean to follow thee after-
wards.

Olymn. Well, 't is her right.

Myr. Is it a message, boy ?

Lys. She said it by gasps ; then bade
me, if she died,
Tell it thee for her, and thou 'dst know and
pardon.
She is coming.

Myr. She go first ! Klydone die !
Olymnios, hast thou heard ?

Olymn. I blame her not ;
Nor weep her going with thee. 'T is the
best.

Myr. I would have had her live : she
hated death.
But we go hand in hand, husband and wife.
Lysis, go bid them hasten, lest she sleep,
Or I, past waking, ere she come to me.

Enter Servants *carrying* KLYDONE *on a
couch.*

A Servant. 'T is over. She still breath'd
a minute since ;
But now 't is over.

Second Serv. 'T was but just " To-
soon ! "
As if she sigh'd in sleep ; then only breath'd
And now 't is over.

Myr. Oh, how fair she lies
She should have kept that smile to look o'
me.
Sweet, canst thou see me still ? How fai
she is !
Smile on, Klydone, death has wedded us.
Wife, wilt thou love me there, whither w
go ? [*Exit* OLYMNIO

Lys. Master, she stirr'd.
Myr. 'T was but my breath, my boy,
That mov'd that straying gossamer of her
    hair.
[*To the* Servants.] Come, lift her gently,
    lay her on the bed.
So.
  Olymn. [*Without.*] Both ! oh, both !
  A Servant.   Hark ! 'T was a fall.
  Go see.   [*Exeunt some* Servants.
  Myr. Where is Olymnios ?

    Reënter a Servant.

        What 's the noise we heard ?
Serv. Olymnios, master.
Myr.   Yes ?
Serv.   He died and fell.
Myr. When sorrow swells these iron-
    pent hearts they break.
Go, all of you. Keep stillness, wake me not.
I have room beside thee, love. [*Lies down
    on the bed.*] Go now, my friends.
Lysis, not thou. Sit where I do not see thee.
Send hence that music, and thou, sing me
    asleep.
Is it moonlight yet ?

Lys.   Yes.
Myr.   Throw the curtains back.
Put out those lights. Now sing until I
    sleep.   [*Exeunt* Servants.
No dirges, boy ; that song Klydone lov'd,
Philomel and the aloe flower, sing that.
  Lys. [*Sings.*]
Joy that 's half too keen and true
  Makes us tears.
Oh the sweetness of the tears !
If such joy at hand appears,
Snatch it, give thine all for it :
Joy that is so exquisite,
  Lost, comes not new.
(One blossom for a hundred years.)

Grief that 's fond, and dies not soon,
  Makes delight.
Oh the pain of the delight !
If thy grief be Love's aright,
Tend it close and let it grow :
Grief so tender not to know
  Loses Love's boon.
(Sweet Philomel sings all the night.)
Myr. [*Drowsily.*] Fair dreams, Klydone.
Waken me at dawn.   [*Sleeps.*

ELEGANTIÆ

ꜰꞃeꝺeꞃick 𝕷ockeꞃ-𝕷ampꟲon

(FREDERICK LOCKER)

TO MY GRANDMOTHER

SUGGESTED BY A PICTURE BY MR. ROMNEY

  THIS relative of mine,
  Was she seventy-and-nine
    When she died ?
  By the canvas may be seen
  How she look'd at seventeen,
    As a bride.

  Beneath a summer tree,
  Her maiden reverie
    Has a charm ;
  Her ringlets are in taste ;
  What an arm ! . . . what a waist
    For an arm !

  With her bridal-wreath, bouquet,
  Lace farthingale, and gay
    Falbala,
  Were Romney's limning true,
  What a lucky dog were you,
    Grandpapa !

  Her lips are sweet as love ;
  They are parting ! Do they move ?
    Are they dumb ?
  Her eyes are blue, and beam
  Beseechingly, and seem
    To say, " Come ! "

  What funny fancy slips
  From atween these cherry lips !
    Whisper me,

Sweet sorceress in paint,
What canon says I may n't
　　Marry thee ?

That good-for-nothing Time
Has a confidence sublime !
　　When I first
Saw this lady, in my youth,
Her winters had, forsooth,
　　Done their worst.

Her locks, as white as snow,
Once sham'd the swarthy crow :
　　By-and-by
That fowl's avenging sprite
Set his cruel foot for spite
　　Near her eye.

Her rounded form was lean,
And her silk was bombazine :
　　Well I wot
With her needles would she sit,
And for hours would she knit, —
　　Would she not ?

Ah, perishable clay !
Her charms had dropp'd away
　　One by one ;
But if she heav'd a sigh
With a burden, it was, " Thy
　　Will be done."

In travail, as in tears,
With the fardel of her years
　　Overpast,
In mercy she was borne
Where the weary and the worn
　　Are at rest.

Oh, if you now are there,
And sweet as once you were,
　　Grandmamma,
This nether world agrees
'T will all the better please
　　Grandpapa.

THE WIDOW'S MITE

A Widow, — she had only one !
A puny and decrepit son ;
　　But, day and night,
Though fretful oft, and weak and small,
A loving child, he was her all, —
　　The Widow's Mite.

The Widow's Mite — ay, so sustain'd,
She battled onward, nor complain'd
　　Though friends were fewer :
And while she toil'd for daily fare,
A little crutch upon the stair
　　Was music to her.

I saw her then, and now I see
That, though resign'd and cheerful, she
　　Has sorrow'd much :
She has, — He gave it tenderly, —
Much faith, and, carefully laid by,
　　A little crutch.

ON AN OLD MUFF

Time has a magic wand !
What is this meets my hand,
Moth-eaten, mouldy, and
　　Cover'd with fluff ?
Faded, and stiff, and scant ;
Can it be ? no, it can't,—
Yes, I declare, it 's Aunt
　　Prudence's muff !

Years ago, twenty-three,
Old Uncle Doubledee
Gave it to Aunty P.
　　Laughing and teasing :
" Prue of the breezy curls,
Whisper those solemn churls,
What holds a pretty girl's
　　Hand without squeezing ? "

Uncle was then a lad
Gay, but, I grieve to add,
Sinful, if smoking bad
　　Baccy 's a vice :
Glossy was then this mink
Muff, lined with pretty pink
Satin, which maidens think
　　" Awfully nice ! "

I seem to see again
Aunt in her hood and train
Glide, with a sweet disdain,
　　Gravely to Meeting :
Psalm-book, and kerchief new,
Peep'd from the Muff of Prue ;
Young men, and pious too,
　　Giving her greeting.

Sweetly her Sabbath sped
Then ; from this Muff, it 's said,
Tracts she distributed :
　　Converts (till Monday !),

Lur'd by the grace they lack'd,
Follow'd her. One, in fact,
Ask'd for — and got — his tract
   Twice of a Sunday !

Love has a potent spell ;
Soon this bold ne'er-do-well,
Aunt's too susceptible
   Heart undermining,
Slipp'd, so the scandal runs,
Notes in the pretty nun's
Muff, — triple-corner'd ones,
   Pink as its lining.

Worse follow'd : soon the jade
Fled (to oblige her blade !)
Whilst her friends thought that they'd
   Lock'd her up tightly :
After such shocking games
Aunt is of wedded dames
Gayest, and now her name's
   Mrs. Golightly.

In female conduct, flaw
Sadder I never saw.
Faith still I 've in the law
   Of compensation.
Once Uncle went astray,
Smok'd, jok'd, and swore away ;
Sworn by he 's now, by a
   Large congregation.

Changed is the Child of Sin ;
Now he 's (he once was thin)
Grave, with a double chin, —
   Blest be his fat form !
Changed is the garb he wore,
Preacher was never more
Priz'd than is Uncle for
   Pulpit or platform.

If all 's as best befits
Mortals of slender wits,
Then beg this Muff and its
   Fair Owner pardon :
All 's for the best, indeed
Such is my simple creed :
Still I must go and weed
   Hard in my garden.

TO MY MISTRESS

Countess, I see the flying year,
And feel how Time is wasting here :
Ay, more, he soon his worst will do,
And garner all your roses too.

It pleases Time to fold his wings
Around our best and fairest things ;
He 'll mar your blooming cheek, as now
He stamps his mark upon my brow.

The same mute planets rise and shine
To rule your days and nights as mine :
Once I was young and gay, and, see. . .
What I am now you soon will be.

And yet I boast a certain charm
That shields me from your worst alarm ;
And bids me gaze, with front sublime,
On all these ravages of Time.

You boast a gift to charm the eyes,
I boast a gift that Time defies :
For mine will still be mine, and last
When all your pride of beauty 's past.

My gift may long embalm the lures
Of eyes — ah, sweet to me as yours !
For ages hence the great and good
Will judge you as I choose they should.

In days to come, the peer or clown,
With whom I still shall win renown,
Will only know that you were fair
Because I chanced to say you were.

Proud Lady ! Scornful beauty mocks
At aged heads and silver locks ;
But think awhile before you fly,
Or spurn a poet such as I.

THE SKELETON IN THE CUP-BOARD

The characters of great and small
   Come ready-made, we can't bespeak one ;
Their sides are many, too, and all
   (Except ourselves) have got a weak one.
Some sanguine people love for life,
   Some love their hobby till it flings them.
How many love a pretty wife
   For love of the *éclat* she brings them !

A little to relieve my mind
   I 've thrown off this disjointed chatter,
But more because I 'm disinclin'd
   To enter on a painful matter :
Once I was bashful ; I 'll allow
   I 've blush'd for words untimely spoken ;
I still am rather shy, and now . . .
   And now the ice is fairly broken.

We all have secrets : you have one
　Which may n't be quite your charming
　　spouse's ;
We all lock up a skeleton
　In some grim chamber of our houses ;
Familiars, who exhaust their days
　And nights in probing where our smart
　　is,
And who, excepting spiteful ways,
　Are " silent, unassuming *parties*."

We hug this phantom we detest,
　Rarely we let it cross our portals ;
It is a most exacting guest :
　Now, are we not afflicted mortals ?
Your neighbor Gay, that jovial wight,
　As Dives rich, and brave as Hector, —
Poor Gay steals twenty times a night,
　On shaking knees, to see his spectre.

Old Dives fears a pauper fate,
　So hoarding is his ruling passion :
Some gloomy souls anticipate
　A waistcoat straiter than the fashion !

She childless pines, that lonely wife,
　And secret tears are bitter shedding ;
Hector may tremble all his life,
　And die, — but not of that he 's dreading

Ah me, the World ! — how fast it spins !
　The beldams dance, the caldron bubbles ;
They shriek, they stir it for our sins,
　And we must drain it for our troubles.
We toil, we groan ; the cry for love
　Mounts up from this poor seething city,
And yet I know we have above
　A FATHER infinite in pity.

When Beauty smiles, when Sorrow weeps,
　Where sunbeams play, where shadows
　　darken,
One inmate of our dwelling keeps
　Its ghastly carnival ; but hearken !
How dry the rattle of the bones !
　That sound was not to make you start
　　meant :
Stand by ! Your humble servant owns
　The Tenant of this Dark Apartment.

Robert Barnabas Brough

MY LORD TOMNODDY

MY Lord Tomnoddy 's the son of an Earl ;
His hair is straight, but his whiskers curl :
His Lordship's forehead is far from wide,
But there 's plenty of room for the brains
　inside.
He writes his name with indifferent ease,
He 's rather uncertain about the " d's ; "
But what does it matter, if three or one,
To the Earl of Fitzdotterel's eldest son ?

My Lord Tomnoddy to college went ;
Much time he lost, much money he spent;
Rules, and windows, and heads, he broke —
Authorities wink'd — young men will joke !
He never peep'd inside of a book :
In two years' time a degree he took,
And the newspapers vaunted the honors
　won
By the Earl of Fitzdotterel's eldest son.

My Lord Tomnoddy came out in the world ;
Waists were tighten'd and ringlets curl'd.
Virgins languish'd, and matrons smil'd —
T is true, his Lordship is rather wild ;

In very queer places he spends his life ;
There 's talk of some children by nobody's
　wife —
But we must n't look close into what is
　done
By the Earl of Fitzdotterel's eldest son.

My Lord Tomnoddy must settle down —
There 's a vacant seat in the family town !
('T is time he should sow his eccentric
　oats) —
He has n't the wit to apply for votes :
He cannot e'en learn his election speech,
Three phrases he speaks, a mistake in each
And then breaks down — but the borough
　is won
For the Earl of Fitzdotterel's eldest son.

My Lord Tomnoddy prefers the Guards,
(The House is a bore) so, it 's on the cards
My Lord 's a Lieutenant at twenty-three,
A Captain at twenty-six is he :
He never drew sword, except on drill ;
The tricks of parade he has learnt but ill
A full-blown Colonel at thirty-one
Is the Earl of Fitzdotterel's eldest son !

My Lord Tomnoddy is thirty-four ;
The Earl can last but a few years more.
My Lord in the Peers will take his place :
Her Majesty's councils his words will grace.

Office he 'll hold, and patronage sway ;
Fortunes and lives he will vote away ;
And what are his qualifications ? — ONE !
He 's the Earl of Fitzdotterel's eldest son.

Charles Stuart Calverley

COMPANIONS

A TALE OF A GRANDFATHER

I KNOW not of what we ponder'd
Or made pretty pretence to talk,
As, her hand within mine, we wander'd
Tow'rd the pool by the lime-tree walk,
While the dew fell in showers from the
    passion flowers
And the blush-rose bent on her stalk.

I cannot recall her figure :
Was it regal as Juno's own ?
Or only a trifle bigger
Than the elves who surround the throne
Of the Faëry Queen, and are seen, I ween,
By mortals in dreams alone ?

What her eyes were like I know not :
Perhaps they were blurr'd with tears ;
And perhaps in yon skies there glow not
(On the contrary) clearer spheres.
No ! as to her eyes I am just as wise
As you or the cat, my dears.

Her teeth, I presume, were " pearly : "
But which was she, brunette or blonde ?
Her hair, was it quaintly curly,
Or as straight as a beadle's wand ?
That I fail'd to remark : it was rather dark
And shadowy round the pond.

Then the hand that repos'd so snugly
In mine, — was it plump or spare ?
Was the countenance fair or ugly ?
Nay, children, you have me there !
My eyes were p'haps blurr'd ; and besides
    I'd heard
That it 's horribly rude to stare.

And I, — was I brusque and surly ?
Or oppressively bland and fond ?
Was I partial to rising early ?
Or why did we twain abscond,

When nobody knew, from the public view
To prowl by a misty pond ?

What pass'd, what was felt or spoken, —
Whether anything pass'd at all, —
And whether the heart was broken
That beat under that shelt'ring shawl, —
(If shawl she had on, which I doubt), —
    has gone,
Yes, gone from me past recall.

Was I haply the lady's suitor ?
Or her uncle ? I can't make out ;
Ask your governess, dears, or tutor.
For myself, I 'm in hopeless doubt
As to why we were there, who on earth
    we were,
And what this is all about.

BALLAD

PART I

THE auld wife sat at her ivied door,
    (*Butter and eggs and a pound of cheese*)
A thing she had frequently done before ;
    And her spectacles lay on her apron'd
        knees.

The piper he pip'd on the hill-top high,
    (*Butter and eggs and a pound of cheese*)
Till the cow said, " I die, " and the goose
        asked " Why ? "
    And the dog said nothing, but search'd
        for fleas.

The farmer he strode through the square
        farmyard ;
    (*Butter and eggs and a pound of cheese*)
His last brew of ale was a trifle hard,
    The connection of which with the plot
        one sees.

The farmer's daughter hath frank blue eyes;
    (*Butter and eggs and a pound of cheese*)

She hears the rooks caw in the windy skies,
  As she sits at her lattice and shells her
      peas.

The farmer's daughter hath ripe red lips ;
  (*Butter and eggs and a pound of cheese*)
If you try to approach her away she skips
  Over tables and chairs with apparent
      ease.

The farmer's daughter hath soft brown
      hair ;
  (*Butter and eggs and a pound of cheese*)
And I met with a ballad, I can't say where,
  Which wholly consisted of lines like
      these.

PART II

She sat with her hands 'neath her dimpled
      cheeks,
  (*Butter and eggs and a pound of cheese*)
And spake not a word. While a lady speaks
  There is hope, but she did n't even sneeze.

She sat with her hands 'neath her crimson
      cheeks ;   •
  (*Butter and eggs and a pound of cheese*)
She gave up mending her father's breeks,
  And let the cat roll in her best chemise.

She sat with her hands 'neath her burning
      cheeks,
  (*Butter and eggs and a pound of cheese*)
And gaz'd at the piper for thirteen weeks ;
  Then she follow'd him out o'er the misty
      leas.

Her sheep follow'd her, as their tails did
      them,
  (*Butter and eggs and a pound of cheese*)
And this song is consider'd a perfect gem ;
  And as to the meaning, it 's what you
      please.

ON THE BRINK

I WATCH'D her as she stoop'd to pluck
  A wild flower in her hair to twine ;
And wish'd that it had been my luck
    To call her mine ;

Anon I heard her rate with mad,
  Mad words her babe within its cot,
And felt particularly glad
    That it had not.

I knew (such subtle brains have men !)
  That she was uttering what she should n't ;
And thought that I would chide, and
      then
    I thought I would n't.

Few could have gaz'd upon that face,
  Those pouting coral lips, and chided :
A Rhadamanthus, in my place,
    Had done as I did.

For wrath with which our bosoms glow
  Is chain'd there oft by Beauty's spell ;
And, more than that, I did not know
    The widow well.

So the harsh phrase pass'd unreprov'd :
  Still mute — (O brothers, was it sin ?) —
I drank, unutterably mov'd,
    Her beauty in.

And to myself I murmur'd low,
  As on her upturn'd face and dress
The moonlight fell, " Would she say
      No, —
    By chance, or Yes ? "

She stood so calm, so like a ghost,
  Betwixt me and that magic moon,
That I already was almost
    A finish'd coon.

But when she caught adroitly up
  And sooth'd with smiles her little daugh-
      ter ;
And gave it, if I 'm right, a sup
    Of barley-water ;

And, crooning still the strange, sweet
      lore
  Which only mothers' tongues can utter,
Snow'd with deft hand the sugar o'er
    Its bread-and-butter ;

And kiss'd it clingingly (ah, why
  Don't women do these things in pri-
      vate ?) —
I felt that if I lost her, I
    Should not survive it.

And from my mouth the words nigh
      flew, —
  The past, the future, I forgat 'em, —
" Oh, if you 'd kiss me as you do
    That thankless atom ! "

But this thought came ere yet I spake,
  And froze the sentence on my lips :
" They err who marry wives that make
    Those little slips."

It came like some familiar rhyme,
  Some copy to my boyhood set ;
And that 's perhaps the reason I 'm
    Unmarried yet.

Would she have own'd how pleas'd she was,
  And told her love with widow's pride ?
I never found out that, because
    I never tried.

Be kind to babes and beasts and birds,
  Hearts may be hard though lips are coral ;
And angry words are angry words :
    And that 's the moral.

Joseph Ashby-Sterry

A MARLOW MADRIGAL

OH, Bisham Banks are fresh and fair,
  And Quarry Woods are green,
And pure and sparkling is the air,
  Enchanting is the scene !
I love the music of the weir,
  As swift the stream runs down,
For oh, the water 's deep and clear
  That flows by Marlow town !

When London 's getting hot and dry,
  And half the season 's done,
To Marlow you should quickly fly,
  And bask there in the sun.
There pleasant quarters you may find, —
  The " Angler " or the " Crown"
Will suit you well, if you're inclin'd
  To stay in Marlow town.

I paddle up to Harleyford,
  And sometimes I incline
To cushions take with lunch aboard,
  And play with rod and line ;
For in a punt I love to laze,
  And let my face get brown ;
And dream away the sunny days
  By dear old Marlow town.

I go to luncheon at the Lawn,
  I muse, I sketch, I rhyme ;
I headers take at early dawn,
  I list to All Saints' chime.
And in the river, flashing bright,
  Dull care I strive to drown, —
And get a famous appetite
  At pleasant Marlow town.

So when no longer London life
  You feel you can endure,

Just quit its noise, its whirl, its strife,
  And try the " Marlow cure. "
You 'll smooth the wrinkles on your brow,
  And scare away each frown, —
Feel young again once more, I vow,
  At quaint old Marlow town.

Here Shelley dream'd and thought and
    wrote,
  And wander'd o'er the leas ;
And sung and drifted in his boat
  Beneath the Bisham trees.
So let *me* sing, although I 'm no
  Great poet of renown,
Of hours that much too quickly go
  At good old Marlow town !

A PORTRAIT

IN sunny girlhood's vernal life
  She caused no small sensation,
But now the modest English wife
  To others leaves flirtation.
She 's young still, lovely, debonair,
  Although sometimes her features
Are clouded by a thought of care
  For those two tiny creatures.

Each tiny, toddling, mottled mite
  Asserts with voice emphatic,
In lisping accents, " Mite is right, " —
  Their rule is autocratic :
The song becomes, that charm'd mankind,
  Their musical narcotic,
And baby lips than Love, she 'll find,
  Are even more despotic.

Soft lullaby when singing there,
  And castles ever building,

Their destiny she 'll carve in air,
    Bright with maternal gilding :
Young Guy, a clever advocate,
    So eloquent and able !
A powder'd wig upon his pate,
    A coronet for Mabel !

THE LITTLE REBEL

PRINCESS of pretty pets,
Tomboy in trouserettes,
Eyes are like violets,
    Gleefully glancing !
Skin like an otter sleek,
Nose like a baby Greek,
Sweet little dimple-cheek,
    Merrily dancing !

Lark-like, her song it trills
Over the dale and hills.
Hark, how her laughter thrills !
    Joyously joking :
Yet, should she feel inclin'd,
I fancy you will find,
She, like all womankind,
    Oft is provoking.

Often she stands on chairs,
Sometimes she unawares
Slyly creeps up the stairs,
    Secretly hiding :

Then will this merry maid —
She is of nought afraid —
Come down the balustrade,
    Saucily sliding !

Books she abominates,
But see her go on skates,
And over five-barr'd gates
    Fearlessly scramble !
Climbing up apple-trees,
Barking her supple knees,
Flouting mamma's decrees,
    Out for a ramble.

Now she is good as gold,
Then she is pert and bold,
Minds not what she is told,
    Carelessly tripping.
She is an April miss,
Bounding to grief from bliss ;
Often she has a kiss, —
    Sometimes a whipping !

Naughty but best of girls,
Through life she gayly twirls,
Shaking her sunny curls,
    Careless and joyful.
Ev'ry one on her dotes,
Carolling merry notes,
Pet in short petticoats,
    Truly tomboyful !

William John Courthope

FROM "THE PARADISE OF BIRDS"

BIRDCATCHER'S SONG

WHEN at close of winter's night
    All the insect world 's a-wing ;
When anemones are white ;
    When the first Lent lilies spring ;
When the birds their troths do plight,
    And all feather'd lovers sing ;
Eggs of golden plovers reach
In London town a shilling each.

Sweet it is to see the gold
    Brightening on the cowslip tall ;
Sweet to hear on lonely wold
    Birds by dawn their lovers call ;

Sweet to smell the freshening mould ;
    But far sweeter than them all,
Flowers, sweet breath, or songs of lovers
Are shilling eggs of golden plovers.

Bid them pay, and men will buy
    For their palate magic taste ;
Shift the prices, woman's eye
    Leaves the diamond, likes the paste ;
If the market run not high,
    Heavenly nectar may go waste;
But each shilling paid discovers
Fresh flavor in the eggs of plovers.

ODE — TO THE ROC

O UNHATCH'D Bird, so high preferr'd,
    As porter of the Pole,

Of beakless things, who have no wings,
  Exact no heavy toll.
If this my song its theme should wrong,
  The theme itself is sweet ;
Let others rhyme the unborn time,
  I sing the Obsolete.

And first, I praise the nobler traits
  Of birds preceding Noah,
The giant clan, whose meat was Man,
  Dinornis, Apteryx, Moa.
These, by the hints we get from prints
  Of feathers and of feet,
Excell'd in wits the later tits,
  And so are obsolete.

I sing each race whom we displace
  In their primeval woods,
While Gospel Aid inspires Free-Trade
  To traffic with their goods.
With Norman Dukes the still Sioux
  In breeding might compete ;
But where men talk the tomahawk
  Will soon grow obsolete.

I celebrate each perish'd State ;
  Great cities plough'd to loam ;
Chaldæan kings ; the Bulls with wings ;
  Dead Greece, and dying Rome.
The Druids' shrine may shelter swine,
  Or stack the farmer's peat ;
'T is thus mean moths treat finest cloths,
  Mean men the obsolete.

Shall nought be said of theories dead ?
  The Ptolemaic system ?
Figure and phrase, that bent all ways
  Duns Scotus lik'd to twist 'em ?
Averrhoes' thought ? and what was taught
  In Salamanca's seat ?
Sihons and Ogs ? and showers of frogs ?
  Sea-serpents obsolete ?

Pillion and pack have left their track ;
  Dead is " the Tally-ho ; "
Steam rails cut down each festive crown
  Of the old world and slow ;
Jack-in-the-Green no more is seen,
  Nor Maypole in the street ;
No mummers play on Christmas-day ;
  St. George is obsolete.

O fancy, why hast thou let die
  So many a frolic fashion ?

Doublet and hose, and powder'd beaux ?
  Where are thy songs, whose passion
Turn'd thought to fire in knight and
    squire,
  While hearts of ladies beat ?
Where thy sweet style, ours, ours ere-
    while ?
  All this is obsolete.

In Auvergne low potatoes grow
  Upon volcanoes old ;
The moon, they say, had her young day,
  Though now her heart is cold ;
Even so our earth, sorrow and mirth,
  Seasons of snow and heat,
Check'd by her tides in silence glides
  To become obsolete.

The astrolabe of every babe
  Reads, in its fatal sky,
" Man's largest room is the low tomb —
  Ye all are born to die."
Therefore this theme, O Birds, I deem
  The noblest we may treat ;
The final cause of Nature's laws
  Is to grow obsolete.

IN PRAISE OF GILBERT WHITE

If Transmigration e'er compel
  A bird to live with human heart,
I pray that bird have choice to dwell
  From human ills apart.

When swallows through the world went
    forth,
  And watch'd affairs in every nation,
They found for ever, south and north,
  Vanity and Vexation.

So let him dwell not in the Town —
  There Trade and Penury roar and weep:
But 'neath the silence of a down
  Disturb'd by grazing sheep.

There, like his brook, his life shall glide,
  Far from State-party, plot, and treason,
Nor feel the flow of Fortune's tide,
  Beyond the change of season.

There he shall Learning woo, and Art,
  Without a rival to unthrone ;
Nor seek to pain another's heart,
  Since he may please his own.

Books he shall read in hill and tree ;
  The flowers his weather shall portend,
The birds his moralists shall be,
  And everything his friend.

Such man in England I have seen ;
  He mov'd my heart with fresh delight ;
And had I not the swallow been,
  I had been Gilbert White.

Sir Frederick Pollock

THE SIX CARPENTERS' CASE

(1 Smith, L. C. 133, 7th Ed.)

THIS case befell at four of the clock
  (now listeneth what I shall say),
and the year was the seventh of James the
    First,
  on a fine September day.
    The birds on the bough sing loud and
      sing low,
    what trespass shall be *ab initio*.

It was Thomas Newman and five his feres
  (three more would have made them nine),
and they entered into John Vaux's house,
  that had the Queen's Head to sign.
    The birds on the bough sing loud and
      sing low,
    what trespass shall be *ab initio*.

They called anon for a quart of wine
  (they were carpenters all by trade),
and they drank about till they drank it
    out,
  and when they had drunk they paid.
    The birds on the bough sing loud and
      sing low,
    what trespass shall be *ab initio*.

One spake this word in John Ridding's
    ear
  (white manchets are sweet and fine) :

"Fair sir, we are fain of a penn'orth of
    bread
  and another quart of wine."
    The birds on the bough sing loud and
      sing low,
    what trespass shall be *ab initio*.

Full lightly thereof they did eat and drink
  (to drink is iwis no blame).
"Now tell me eight pennies," quoth Mas-
    ter Vaux ;
  but they would not pay the same.
    The birds on the bough sing loud and
      sing low,
    what trespass shall be *ab initio*.

"Ye have trespassed with force and arms.
    ye knaves
  (the six be too strong for me),
but your tortious entry shall cost you
    dear,
  and that the King's Court shall see.
    The birds on the bough sing loud and
      nought low,
    your trespass was wrought *ab initio*."

Sed per totam curiam 't was well resolved
  (note, reader, this difference)
that in mere not doing no trespass is,
  and John Vaux went empty thence.
    The birds on the bough sing loud and
      sing low,
    no trespass was here *ab initio*.

"THE LAND OF WONDER-WANDER"

Edward Lear

THE JUMBLIES

THEY went to sea in a sieve, they did ;
In a sieve they went to sea ;
In spite of all their friends could say,
On a winter's morn, on a stormy day,
In a sieve they went to sea.
And when the sieve turn'd round and
round,
And every one cried, " You 'll be drown'd ! "
They call'd aloud, " Our sieve ain't big :
But we don't care a button ; we don't care
a fig :
In a sieve we 'll go to sea ! "
    Far and few, far and few,
      Are the lands where the Jumblies
      live :
    Their heads are green, and their hands
    are blue ;
    And they went to sea in a sieve.

They sail'd away in a sieve, they did,
In a sieve they sail'd so fast,
With only a beautiful pea-green veil
Tied with a ribbon, by way of a sail,
To a small tobacco-pipe mast.
And every one said who saw them go,
" Oh ! won't they be soon upset, you know :
For the sky is dark, and the voyage is
long ;
And, happen what may, it 's extremely
wrong
In a sieve to sail so fast."

The water it soon came in, it did ;
The water it soon came in :
So, to keep them dry, they wrapp'd their
feet
In a pinky paper all folded neat :
And they fasten'd it down with a pin.
And they pass'd the night in a crockery-
jar ;
And each of them said, " How wise we
are !
Though the sky be dark, and the voyage be
long,

Yet we never can think we were rash or
wrong,
While round in our sieve we spin."

And all night long they sail'd away ;
And, when the sun went down,
They whistled and warbled a moony song
To the echoing sound of a coppery gong,
In the shade of the mountains brown,
" O Timballoo ! how happy we are
When we live in a sieve and a crockery-
jar !
And all night long, in the moonlight pale,
We sail away with a pea-green sail
In the shade of the mountains brown."

They sail'd to the Western Sea, they did, —
To a land all cover'd with trees :
And they bought an owl, and a useful cart,
And a pound of rice, and a cranberry-tart,
And a hive of silvery bees ;
And they bought a pig, and some green
jackdaws,
And a lovely monkey with lollipop paws,
And forty bottles of ring-bo-ree,
And no end of Stilton cheese :

And in twenty years they all came back, —
In twenty years or more ;
And every one said, " How tall they 've
grown !
For they 've been to the Lakes, and the Tor-
rible Zone,
And the hills of the Chankly Bore."
And they drank their health, and gave
them a feast
Of dumplings made of beautiful yeast ;
And every one said, " If we only live,
We, too, will go to sea in a sieve,
To the hills of the Chankly Bore."
    Far and few, far and few,
      Are the lands where the Jumblies
      live :
    Their heads are green, and their hands
    are blue ;
    And they went to sea in a sieve.

William Brighty Rands

TOPSY-TURVY WORLD

IF the butterfly courted the bee,
And the owl the porcupine ;
If churches were built in the sea,
And three times one was nine ;
If the pony rode his master,
If the buttercups ate the cows,
If the cats had the dire disaster
To be worried, sir, by the mouse ;
If mamma, sir, sold the baby
To a gypsy for half a crown ;
If a gentleman, sir, was a lady, —
The world would be Upside-down !
If any or all of these wonders
Should ever come about,
I should not consider them blunders,
For I should be Inside-out !

Chorus

Ba-ba, black wool,
Have you any sheep ?
Yes, sir, a packfull,
Creep, mouse, creep !
Four-and-twenty little maids
Hanging out the pie,
Out jump'd the honey-pot,
Guy Fawkes, Guy !
Cross latch, cross latch,
Sit and spin the fire ;
When the pie was open'd,
The bird was on the brier !

POLLY

BROWN eyes,
Straight nose ;
Dirt pies,
Rumpled clothes ;

Torn books,
Spoilt toys ;
Arch looks,
Unlike a boy's ;

Little rages,
Obvious arts ;
(Three her age is,)
Cakes, tarts ;

Falling down
Off chairs ;
Breaking crown
Down stairs ;

Catching flies
On the pane ;
Deep sighs, —
Cause not plain ;

Bribing you
With kisses
For a few
Farthing blisses ;

Wide awake,
As you hear,
" Mercy 's sake,
Quiet, dear ! "

New shoes,
New frock,
Vague views
Of what 's o'clock,

When it 's time
To go to bed,
And scorn sublime
For what it said ;

Folded hands,
Saying prayers,
Understands
Not, nor cares ;

Thinks it odd,
Smiles away ;
Yet may God
Hear her pray !

Bedgown white,
Kiss Dolly ;
Goodnight ! —
That 's Polly.

Fast asleep,
As you see ;
Heaven keep
My girl for me !

DRESSING THE DOLL

THIS is the way we dress the Doll : —
You may make her a shepherdess, the Doll,
If you give her a crook with a pastoral hook,
But this is the way we dress the Doll.

Chorus
Bless the Doll, you may press the Doll,
But do not crumple and mess the Doll !
This is the way we dress the Doll.

First, you observe, her little chemise,
As white as milk, with ruches of silk ;
And the little drawers that cover her knees,
As she sits or stands, with golden bands,
And lace in beautiful filagrees.

Chorus

Now these are the bodies : she has two,
One of pink, with rouches of blue,
And sweet white lace ; be careful, do !
And one of green, with buttons of sheen,
Buttons and bands of gold, I mean,
With lace on the border in lovely order,
The most expensive we can afford her !

Chorus

Then, with black at the border, jacket
And this — and this — she will not lack it ;
Skirts ? Why, there are skirts, of course,
And shoes and stockings we shall enforce,
With a proper bodice, in the proper place,
(Stays that lace have had their days
And made their martyrs) ; likewise garters,
All entire. But our desire
Is to show you her night attire,
At least a part of it. Pray admire
This sweet white thing that she goes to
    bed in !
It 's not the one that 's made for her wed-
    ding :
That is special, a new design,
Made with a charm and a countersign,
Three times three and nine times nine :
These are only her usual clothes.
Look, there 's a wardrobe ! gracious knows
It 's pretty enough, as far as it goes !

So you see the way we dress the Doll :
You might make her a shepherdess, the
    Doll,
If you gave her a crook with pastoral hook,
With sheep, and a shed, and a shallow brook,
And all that, out of the poetry-book.

Chorus
Bless the Doll, you may press the Doll,
But do not crumple and mess the Doll !
This is the way we dress the Doll ;
If you had not seen, could you guess the
    Doll ?

I SAW A NEW WORLD

I SAW a new world in my dream,
Where all the folks alike did seem :
There was no Child, there was no Mother,
There was no Change, there was no Other.

For everything was Same, the Same ;
There was no praise, there was no blame ;
There was neither Need nor Help for it ;
There was nothing fitting or unfit.

Nobody laugh'd, nobody wept ;
None grew weary, so none slept ;
There was nobody born, and nobody wed ;
This world was a world of the living-dead.

I long'd to hear the Time-Clock strike
In the world where people were all alike ;
I hated Same, I hated Forever ;
I long'd to say Neither, or even Never.

I long'd to mend, I long'd to make ;
I long'd to give, I long'd to take ;
I long'd for a change, whatever came after,
I long'd for crying, I long'd for laughter.

At last I heard the Time-Clock boom,
And woke from my dream in my little room ;
With a smile on her lips my Mother was
    nigh,
And I heard the Baby crow and cry.

And I thought to myself, How nice it is
For me to live in a world like this,
Where things can happen, and clocks can
    strike,
And none of the people are made alike ;

Where Love wants this, and Pain wants
    that,
Where all our hearts want Tit for Tat
In the jumbles we make with our heads and
    our hands,
In a world that nobody understands,
But with work, and hope, and the right to
    call
Upon Him who sees it and knows us all !

Charles Lutwidge Dodgson

("LEWIS CARROLL")

JABBERWOCKY

'T was brillig, and the slithy toves
  Did gyre and gimble in the wabe ;
All mimsy were the borogoves,
  And the mome raths outgrabe.

" Beware the Jabberwock, my son !
  The jaws that bite, the claws that catch !
Beware the Jubjub bird, and shun
  The frumious Bandersnatch ! "

He took his vorpal sword in hand :
  Long time the manxome foe he sought —
So rested he by the Tumtum tree,
  And stood awhile in thought.

And as in uffish thought he stood,
  The Jabberwock, with eyes of flame,
Came whiffling through the tulgey wood,
  And burbled as it came !

One, two ! One, two ! And through and
    through
The vorpal blade went snicker-snack !
He left it dead, and with its head
  He went galumphing back.

" And hast thou slain the Jabberwock ?
  Come to my arms, my beamish boy !
O frabjous day ! Callooh ! Callay ! "
  He chortled in his joy.

'T was brillig, and the slithy toves
  Did gyre and gimble in the wabe ;
All mimsy were the borogoves,
  And the mome raths outgrabe.

FROM "THE HUNTING OF THE SNARK"

THE BAKER'S TALE

THEY rous'd him with muffins — they
  rous'd him with ice —
They rous'd him with mustard and
  cress —
They rous'd him with jam and judicious
  advice —
They set him conundrums to guess.

When at length he sat up and was able to
  speak,
  His sad story he offer'd to tell ;
And the Bellman cried "Silence ! Not
  even a shriek ! "
  And excitedly tingled his bell.

There was silence supreme ! Not a shriek,
  not a scream,
  Scarcely even a howl or a groan,
As the man they call'd "Ho ! " told his
  story of woe
  In an antediluvian tone.

" My father and mother were honest,
  though poor — "
" Skip all that ! " cried the Bellman in
  haste.
" If it once becomes dark, there 's no chance
  of a Snark —
  We have hardly a minute to waste ! "

" I skip forty years," said the Baker, in tears,
  " And proceed without further remark
To the day when you took me aboard of
  your ship
  To help you in hunting the Snark.

" A dear uncle of mine (after whom I was
  nam'd)
  Remark'd, when I bade him farewell — "
" Oh, skip your dear uncle ! " the Bellman
  exclaim'd,
  As he angrily tingled his bell.

" He remark'd to me then," said that mild·
  est of men,
  " 'If your Snark be a Snark, that is
    right :
Fetch it home by all means — you may
  serve it with greens,
And it 's handy for striking a light.

" 'You may seek it with thimbles — and
  seek it with care ;
You may hunt it with forks and hope ;
You may threaten its life with a railway-
  share ;
  You may charm it with smiles and
  soap — ' "

("That's exactly the method," the Bell-
man bold
In a hasty parenthesis cried,
"That's exactly the way I have always
been told
That the capture of Snarks should be
tried !")

"' But oh, beamish nephew, beware of the
day,
If your Snark be a Boojum ! For then
You will softly and suddenly vanish away,
And never be met with again !'

"It is this, it is this that oppresses my
soul,
When I think of my uncle's last words :
And my heart is like nothing so much as a
bowl
Brimming over with quivering curds !

" It is this, it is this — " " We have had
that before !"
The Bellman indignantly said.
And the Baker replied, " Let me say it
once more.
It is this, it is this that I dread !

" I engage with the Snark — every night
after dark —
In a dreamy, delirious fight :
I serve it with greens in those shadowy
scenes,
And I use it for striking a light :

" But if ever I meet with a Boojum, that day,
In a moment (of this I am sure),
I shall softly and suddenly vanish away —
And the notion I cannot endure ! "

OF ALICE IN WONDERLAND

A BOAT, beneath a sunny sky,
Lingering onward dreamily
In an evening of July ;

Children three that nestle near,
Eager eye and willing ear,
Pleased a simple tale to hear ; —

Long has paled that sunny sky :
Echoes fade and memories die,
Autumn frosts have slain July.

Still she haunts me, phantom-wise,
Alice moving under skies
Never seen by waking eyes.

Children yet, the tale to hear,
Eager eye and willing ear,
Lovingly shall nestle near.

In a Wonderland they lie,
Dreaming as the days go by,
Dreaming as the summers die :

Ever drifting down the stream,
Lingering in the golden gleam, —
Life, what is it but a dream ?

III

CLOSE OF THE ERA

(INTERMEDIARY PERIOD)

1875–1895

DEATH OF ALFRED, LORD TENNYSON: OCTOBER 6, 1892

ALFRED AUSTIN APPOINTED LAUREATE: JANUARY 1, 1896

IMPRESSION

In these restrained and careful times
Our knowledge petrifies our rhymes ;
Ah ! for that reckless fire men had
When it was witty to be mad,

When wild conceits were piled in scores,
And lit by flaring metaphors,
When all was crazed and out of tune, —
Yet throbbed with music of the moon.

If we could dare to write as ill
As some whose voices haunt us still,
Even we, perchance, might call our own
Their deep enchanting undertone.

We are too diffident and nice,
Too learnèd and too over-wise,
Too much afraid of faults to be
The flutes of bold sincerity.

For, as this sweet life passes by,
We blink and nod with critic eye ;
We 've no words rude enough to give
Its charm so frank and fugitive.

The green and scarlet of the Park,
The undulating streets at dark,
The brown smoke blown across the blue,
This colored city we walk through ; —

The pallid faces full of pain,
The field-smell of the passing wain,
The laughter, longing, perfume, strife,
The daily spectacle of life ; —

Ah ! how shall this be given to rhyme,
By rhymesters of a knowing time ?
Ah ! for the age when verse was glad,
Being godlike, to be bad and mad.

EDMUND GOSSE.

1894.

CLOSE OF THE ERA

(INTERMEDIARY PERIOD)

RECENT POETS OF GREAT BRITAIN

Austin Dobson

A DEAD LETTER

I

I DREW it from its china tomb ; —
It came out feebly scented
With some thin ghost of past perfume
That dust and days had lent it.

An old, old letter, — folded still !
To read with due composure,
I sought the sun-lit window-sill,
Above the gray enclosure,

That glimmering in the sultry haze,
Faint flowered, dimly shaded,
Slumbered like Goldsmith's Madam Blaize,
Bedizened and brocaded.

A queer old place ! You 'd surely say
Some tea-board garden-maker
Had planned it in Dutch William's day
To please some florist Quaker,

So trim it was. The yew-trees still,
With pious care perverted,
Grew in the same grim shapes ; and still
The lipless dolphin spurted ;

Still in his wonted state abode
The broken-nosed Apollo ;
And still the cypress-arbor showed
The same umbrageous hollow.

Only, — as fresh young Beauty gleams
From coffee-colored laces, —
So peeped from its old-fashioned dreams
The fresher modern traces ;

For idle mallet, hoop, and ball
Upon the lawn were lying ;
A magazine, a tumbled shawl,
Round which the swifts were flying ;

And, tossed beside the Guelder rose,
A heap of rainbow knitting,
Where, blinking in her pleased repose,
A Persian cat was sitting.

" A place to love in, — live, — for aye,
If we too, like Tithonus,
Could find some God to stretch the gray
Scant life the Fates have thrown us ;

" But now by steam we run our race,
With buttoned heart and pocket ;
Our Love 's a gilded, surplus grace, —
Just like an empty locket !

" ' The time is out of joint.' Who will,
May strive to make it better ;
For me, this warm old window-sill,
And this old dusty letter."

II

" Dear *John* (the letter ran), it can't, can't
be,
For Father 's gone to *Chorley Fair* with
Sam,
And Mother 's storing Apples, — *Prue* and
Me
Up to our Elbows making Damson Jam :
But we shall meet before a Week is
gone, —
' 'T is a long Lane that has no turning,' *John !*

"Only till Sunday next, and then you'll
    wait
Behind the White-Thorn, by the broken
    Stile —
We can go round and catch them at the
    Gate,
All to Ourselves, for nearly one long
    Mile ;
Dear *Prue* won't look, and Father he'll go
    on,
And *Sam's* two Eyes are all for *Cissy,*
    John!

"*John,* she's so smart, — with every ribbon
    new,
Flame-colored Sack, and Crimson Pade-
    soy ;
As proud as proud ; and has the Vapours
    too,
Just like My Lady ; — calls poor *Sam* a
    Boy,
And vows no Sweet-heart's worth the
    Thinking-on
Till he's past Thirty . . . I know better,
    John!

"My Dear, I don't think that I thought of
    much
Before we knew each other, I and
    you ;
And now, why, *John,* your least, least Fin-
    ger-touch,
Gives me enough to think a Summer
    through.
See, for I send you Something ! There,
    't is gone !
Look in this corner, — mind you find it,
    John!"

III

This was the matter of the note, —
    A long-forgot deposit,
Dropped in an Indian dragon's throat,
    Deep in a fragrant closet,

Piled with a dapper Dresden world, —
    Beaux, beauties, prayers, and poses, —
Bonzes with squat legs undercurled,
    And great jars filled with roses.

Ah, heart that wrote ! Ah, lips that kissed !
    You had no thought or presage
Into what keeping you dismissed
    Your simple old-world message !

A reverent one. Though we to-day
    Distrust beliefs and powers,
The artless, ageless things you say
    Are fresh as May's own flowers,

Starring some pure primeval spring,
    Ere Gold had grown despotic, —
Ere Life was yet a selfish thing,
    Or Love a mere exotic !

I need not search too much to find
    Whose lot it was to send it,
That feel upon me yet the kind,
    Soft hand of her who penned it ;

And see, through twoscore years of smoke,
    In by-gone, quaint apparel,
Shine from yon time-black Norway oak
    The face of Patience Caryl, —

The pale, smooth forehead, silver-tressed ;
    The gray gown, primly flowered ;
The spotless, stately coif whose crest
    Like Hector's horse-plume towered ;

And still the sweet half-solemn look
    Where some past thought was clinging,
As when one shuts a serious book
    To hear the thrushes singing.

I kneel to you ! Of those you were,
    Whose kind old hearts grow mellow, —
Whose fair old faces grow more fair
    As Point and Flanders yellow ;

Whom some old store of garnered grief,
    Their placid temples shading,
Crowns like a wreath of autumn leaf
    With tender tints of fading.

Peace to your soul ! You died unwed —
    Despite this loving letter.
And what of John ? The less that's said
    Of John, I think, the better.

A RONDEAU TO ETHEL

*(Who wishes she had lived —
"In teacup-times of hood and hoop,
Or while the patch was worn.")*

"IN teacup-times" ! The style of dress
Would suit your beauty, I confess ;
    BELINDA-like, the patch you'd wear ;
    I picture you with powdered hair, —
You'd make a charming Shepherdess !

And I — no doubt — could well express
Sir Plume's complete conceitedness, —
 Could poise a clouded cane with care
   " In teacup-times " !

The parts would fit precisely — yes :
We should achieve a huge success !
 You should disdain, and I despair,
 With quite the true Augustan air ;
But . . . could I love you more, or less, —
   " In teacup-times " ?

" WITH PIPE AND FLUTE "

With pipe and flute the rustic Pan
Of old made music sweet for man ;
 And wonder hushed the warbling bird,
 And closer drew the calm-eyed herd, —
The rolling river slowlier ran.

Ah ! would, — ah ! would, a little span,
Some air of Arcady could fan
 This age of ours, too seldom stirred
   With pipe and flute !

But now for gold we plot and plan ;
And, from Beersheba unto Dan,
 Apollo's self might pass unheard,
 Or find the night-jar's note preferred ; —
Not so it fared, when time began,
   With pipe and flute !

A GAGE D'AMOUR

Martiis cœlebs quid agam Kalendis,
—— miraris ? — Horace, iii, 8.

Charles, — for it seems you wish to
   know, —
You wonder what could scare me so,
And why, in this long-locked bureau,
 With trembling fingers, —
With tragic air, I now replace
This ancient web of yellow lace,
Among whose faded folds the trace
 Of perfume lingers.

Friend of my youth, severe as true,
I guess the train your thoughts pursue ;
But this my state is nowise due
 To indigestion ;
I had forgotten it was there,
A scarf that Some-one used to wear.
Hinc illæ lacrimæ, — so spare
 Your cynic question.

Some-one who is not girlish now,
And wed long since. We meet and bow ;
I don't suppose our broken vow
 Affects us keenly ;
Yet, trifling though my act appears,
Your Sternes would make it ground for
   tears ; —
One can't disturb the dust of years,
 And smile serenely.

" My golden locks " are gray and chill,
For hers, — let them be sacred still ;
But yet, I own, a boyish thrill
  Went dancing through me,
Charles, when I held you yellow lace ;
For, from its dusty hiding-place,
Peeped out an arch, ingenuous face
 That beckoned to me.

We shut our heart up nowadays,
Like some old music-box that plays
Unfashionable airs that raise
 Derisive pity ;
Alas, — a nothing starts the spring ;
And lo, the sentimental thing
At once commences quavering
 Its lover's ditty.

Laugh, if you like. The boy in me, —
The boy that was, — revived to see
The fresh young smile that shone when
   she,
 Of old, was tender.
Once more we trod the Golden Way, —
That mother you saw yesterday,
And I, whom none can well portray
 As young, or slender.

She twirled the flimsy scarf about
Her pretty head, and stepping out,
Slipped arm in mine, with half a pout
 Of childish pleasure.
Where we were bound no mortal knows,
For then you plunged in Ireland's woes,
And brought me blankly back to prose
 And Gladstone's measure.

Well, well, the wisest bend to Fate.
My brown old books around me wait,
My pipe still holds, unconfiscate,
 Its wonted station.
Pass me the wine. To Those that keep
The bachelor's secluded sleep
Peaceful, inviolate, and deep,
 I pour libation.

THE CRADLE

How steadfastly she worked at it !
How lovingly had drest
With all her would-be-mother's wit
That little rosy nest !

How longingly she 'd hung on it ! —
It sometimes seemed, she said,
There lay beneath its coverlet
A little sleeping head.

He came at last, the tiny guest,
Ere bleak December fled ;
That rosy nest he never prest . . .
Her coffin was his bed.

THE FORGOTTEN GRAVE

A SKETCH IN A CEMETERY

OUT from the City's dust and roar,
You wandered through the open door ;
Paused at a plaything pail and spade
Across a tiny hillock laid ;
Then noted on your dexter side
Some moneyed mourner's "love or pride ;"
And so, — beyond a hawthorn-tree,
Showering its rain of rosy bloom
Alike on low and lofty tomb, —
You came upon it — suddenly.

How strange ! The very grasses' growth
Around it seemed forlorn and loath ;
The very ivy seemed to turn
Askance that wreathed the neighbor
    urn.
The slab had sunk ; the head declined,
And left the rails a wreck behind.
No name ; you traced a "6," — a "7," —
Part of "affliction" and of "Heaven ;"
And then, in letters sharp and clear,
You read — O Irony austere !
" Tho' lost to Sight, to Mem'ry dear."

THE CURE'S PROGRESS

MONSIEUR the Curé down the street
Comes with his kind old face, —
With his coat worn bare, and his strag-
    gling hair,
And his green umbrella-case.

You may see him pass by the little
    " Grande Place,"
And the tiny " Hôtel-de-Ville ; "
He smiles as he goes to the fleuriste Rose,
And the pompier Théophile.

He turns, as a rule, through the " Marché "
    cool,
Where the noisy fish-wives call ;
And his compliment pays to the " belle
    Thérèse,"
As she knits in her dusky stall.

There 's a letter to drop at the locksmith's
    shop,
And Toto, the locksmith's niece,
Has jubilant hopes, for the Curé gropes
In his tails for a pain d'épice.

There 's a little dispute with a merchant of
    fruit,
Who is said to be heterodox,
That will ended be with a " Ma foi, oui ! "
And a pinch from the Curé's box.

There is also a word that no one heard
    To the furrier's daughter Lou ;
And a pale cheek fed with a flickering
    red,
And a " Bon Dieu garde M'sieu' ! "

But a grander way for the Sous-Préfet,
    And a bow for Ma'am'selle Anne ;
And a mock " off-hat " to the Notary's
    cat,
And a nod to the Sacristan : —

For ever through life the Curé goes
With a smile on his kind old face —
With his coat worn bare, and his strag-
    gling hair,
And his green umbrella-case.

"GOOD-NIGHT, BABETTE !"

Si viellesse pouvait !

SCENE. — A small neat Room. In a high Vol-
taire Chair sits a white-haired old Gentleman.
MONSIEUR VIEUXBOIS.   BABETTE.

M. VIEUXBOIS [turning querulously].

Day of my life ! Where can she get ?
Babette ! I say ! Babette ! — Babette !

BABETTE [*entering hurriedly*].

Coming, M'sieu'! If M'sieu' speaks
So loud, he won't be well for weeks!

M. VIEUXBOIS.

Where have you been?

BABETTE.

Why, M'sieu' knows: —
April! . . . Ville-d'Avray! . . . Ma'am'-
selle Rose!

M. VIEUXBOIS.

Ah! I am old, — and I forget.
Was the place growing green, Babette?

BABETTE.

But of a greenness! — yes, M'sieu'!
And then the sky so blue! — so blue! —
And when I dropped my *immortelle*,
How the birds sang!

[*Lifting her apron to her eyes.*
This poor Ma'am'selle!

M. VIEUXBOIS.

You're a good girl, Babette, but she, —
She was an Angel, verily.
Sometimes I think I see her yet
Stand smiling by the cabinet;
And once, I know, she peeped and laughed
Betwixt the curtains . . .
Where's the draught?

[*She gives him a cup.*
Now I shall sleep, I think, Babette; —
Sing me your Norman *chansonnette*.

BABETTE [*sings*].

Once at the Angelus
(Ere I was dead),
Angels all glorious
Came to my Bed; —
Angels in blue and white
Crowned on the Head.

M. VIEUXBOIS [*drowsily*].

She was an Angel . . . Once she
laughed . . .
What, was I dreaming?
Where's the draught?

BABETTE [*showing the empty cup*].

The draught, M'sieu'?

M. VIEUXBOIS.

How I forget!
I am so old! But sing, Babette!

BABETTE [*sings*].

One was the Friend I left
Stark in the Snow;
One was the Wife that died
Long, — long ago;
One was the Love I lost . . .
How could she know?

M. VIEUXBOIS [*murmuring*].

Ah, Paul! . . . old Paul! . . . Eulalie too!
And Rose . . . And O! . . . the sky so blue!

BABETTE [*sings*].

One had my Mother's eyes,
Wistful and mild;
One had my Father's face;
One was a Child:
All of them bent to me, —
Bent down and smiled!

He is asleep!

M. VIEUXBOIS [*almost inaudibly*].

How I forget!
I am so old . . . Good night, Babette!

ON A FAN

THAT BELONGED TO THE MARQUISE DE
POMPADOUR

CHICKEN-SKIN, delicate, white,
Painted by Carlo Vanloo,
Loves in a riot of light,
Roses and vaporous blue;
Hark to the dainty *frou-frou!*
Picture above, if you can,
Eyes that could melt as the dew, —
This was the Pompadour's fan!

See how they rise at the sight,
Thronging the Œil de Bœuf through,
Courtiers as butterflies bright,
Beauties that Fragonard drew,
Talon-rouge, falbala, queue,
Cardinal, Duke, — to a man,
Eager to sigh or to sue, —
This was the Pompadour's fan!

Ah, but things more than polite
Hung on this toy, *voyez-vous!*

Matters of state and of might,
Things that great ministers do ;
Things that, may be, overthrew
Those in whose brains they began ;
Here was the sign and the cue, —
This was the Pompadour's fan !

ENVOY

Where are the secrets it knew ?
Weavings of plot and of plan ?
— But where is the Pompadour, too ?
This was the Pompadour's Fan !

"O NAVIS"

SHIP, to the roadstead rolled,
What dost thou ? — O, once more
Regain the port. Behold !
Thy sides are bare of oar,
Thy tall mast wounded sore
Of Africus, and see,
What shall thy spars restore ! —
Tempt not thy tyrant sea !

What cable now will hold
When all drag out from shore !
What god canst thou, too bold,
In time of need implore !
Look ! for thy sails flap o'er,
Thy stiff shrouds part and flee,
Fast — fast thy seams outpour, —
Tempt not the tyrant sea !

What though thy ribs of old
The pines of Pontus bore !
Not now to stern of gold
Men trust, or painted prore !
Thou, or thou count'st it store
A toy of winds to be,
Shun thou the Cyclads' roar,—
Tempt not the tyrant sea !

ENVOY

Ship of the State, before
A care, and now to me
A hope in my heart's core, —
Tempt not the tyrant sea !

"O FONS BANDUSIÆ"

O BABBLING Spring, than glass more clear,
Worthy of wreath and cup sincere,
To-morrow shall a kid be thine

With swelled and sprouting brows for
    sign, —
Sure sign ! — of loves and battles near.

Child of the race that butt and rear !
Not less, alas ! his life-blood dear
Must tinge thy cold wave crystalline,
            O babbling Spring !

Thee Sirius knows not. Thou dost cheer
With pleasant cool the plough-worn
    steer, —
The wandering flock. This verse of
    mine
Will rank thee one with founts divine ;
Men shall thy rock and tree revere,
            O babbling Spring !

FOR A COPY OF THEOCRITUS

O SINGER of the field and fold,
Theocritus ! Pan's pipe was thine, —
Thine was the happier Age of Gold.

For thee the scent of new-turned mould,
The bee-hives, and the murmuring pine,
O Singer of the field and fold !

Thou sang'st the simple feasts of old, —
The beechen bowl made glad with wine . . .
Thine was the happier Age of Gold.

Thou bad'st the rustic loves be told, —
Thou bad'st the tuneful reeds combine,
O Singer of the field and fold !

And round thee, ever-laughing, rolled
The blithe and blue Sicilian brine . . .
Thine was the happier Age of Gold.

Alas for us ! Our songs are cold ;
Our Northern suns too sadly shine : —
O Singer of the field and fold,
Thine was the happier Age of Gold !

TO A GREEK GIRL

WITH breath of thyme and bees that hum,
Across the years you seem to come, —
    Across the years with nymph-like head,
    And wind-blown brows unfilleted ;
A girlish shape that slips the bud
    In lines of unspoiled symmetry ;
A girlish shape that stirs the blood
    With pulse of Spring, Autonoë !

Where'er you pass, — where'er you go,
I hear the pebbly rillet flow ;
　Where'er you go, — where'er you pass,
　There comes a gladness on the grass ;
You bring blithe airs where'er you tread, —
　Blithe airs that blow from down and
　　sea ;
You wake in me a Pan not dead, —
　Not wholly dead ! — Autonoë !

How sweet with you on some green sod
To wreathe the rustic garden-god ;
　How sweet beneath the chestnut's shade
　With you to weave a basket-braid ;
To watch across the stricken chords
　Your rosy-twinkling fingers flee ;
To woo you in soft woodland words,
　With woodland pipe, Autonoë !

In vain, — in vain ! The years divide :
Where Thamis rolls a murky tide,
　I sit and fill my painful reams,
　And see you only in my dreams ; —
A vision, like Alcestis, brought
　From under-lands of Memory, —
A dream of Form in days of Thought, —
　A dream, — a dream, Autonoë !

ARS VICTRIX

IMITATED FROM THÉOPHILE GAUTIER

Yes ; when the ways oppose —
　When the hard means rebel,
Fairer the work out-grows, —
　More potent far the spell.

O Poet, then, forbear
　The loosely-sandalled verse,
Choose rather thou to wear
　The buskin — strait and terse ;

Leave to the tiro's hand
　The limp and shapeless style ;
See that thy form demand
　The labor of the file.

Sculptor, do thou discard
　The yielding clay, — consign
To Paros marble hard
　The beauty of thy line ; —

Model thy Satyr's face,
　For bronze of Syracuse ;
In the veined agate trace
　The profile of thy Muse.

Painter, that still must mix
　But transient tints anew,
Thou in the furnace fix
　The firm enamel's hue ;

Let the smooth tile receive
　Thy dove-drawn Erycine ;
Thy Sirens blue at eve
　Coiled in a wash of wine.

All passes.　Art alone
　Enduring stays to us ;
The Bust outlasts the throne, —
　The Coin, Tiberius ;

Even the gods must go ;
　Only the lofty Rhyme
Not countless years o'erthrow, —
　Not long array of time.

Paint, chisel, then, or write ;
　But, that the work surpass,
With the hard fashion fight, —
　With the resisting mass.

THE LADIES OF ST. JAMES'S

A PROPER NEW BALLAD OF THE COUNTRY
AND THE TOWN

The ladies of St. James's
　Go swinging to the play ;
Their footmen run before them,
　With a "Stand by !　Clear the way !"
But Phyllida, my Phyllida !
　She takes her buckled shoon,
When we go out a-courting
　Beneath the harvest moon.

The ladies of St. James's
　Wear satin on their backs ;
They sit all night at *Ombre*,
　With candles all of wax :
But Phyllida, my Phyllida !
　She dons her russet gown,
And runs to gather May dew
　Before the world is down.

The ladies of St. James's !
　They are so fine and fair,
You 'd think a box of essences
　Was broken in the air :
But Phyllida, my Phyllida !
　The breath of heath and furze
When breezes blow at morning,
　Is not so fresh as hers.

The ladies of St. James's !
  They 're painted to the eyes ;
Their white it stays for ever,
  Their red it never dies :
But Phyllida, my Phyllida !
  Her color comes and goes ;
It trembles to a lily, —
  It wavers to a rose.

The ladies of St. James's !
  You scarce can understand
The half of all their speeches,
  Their phrases are so grand :
But Phyllida, my Phyllida !
  Her shy and simple words
Are clear as after rain-drops
  The music of the birds.

The ladies of St. James's !
  They have their fits and freaks ;
They smile on you — for seconds,
  They frown on you — for weeks :
But Phyllida, my Phyllida !
  Come either storm or shine,
From Shrove-tide unto Shrove-tide,
  Is always true — and mine.

My Phyllida ! my Phyllida !
  I care not though they heap
The hearts of all St. James's,
  And give me all to keep ;
I care not whose the beauties
  Of all the world may be,
For Phyllida — for Phyllida
  Is all the world to me !

A FAMILIAR EPISTLE

TO . . . ESQ. OF . . . WITH A LIFE OF THE
LATE INGENIOUS MR. WM. HOGARTH

DEAR Cosmopolitan, — I know
I should address you a *Rondeau,*
Or else announce what I 've to say
At least *en Ballade fratriseé ;*
But No : for once I leave Gymnasticks,
And take to simple *Hudibrasticks,*
Why should I choose another Way,
When this was good enough for GAY ?

You love, my FRIEND, with me I think,
That Age of Lustre and of Link ;
Of *Chelsea* China and long "s"es,
Of Bag-wigs and of flowered Dresses ;

That Age of Folly and of Cards,
Of Hackney Chairs and Hackney Bards ;
— No H-LTS, no K-G-N P-LS were then
Dispensing Competence to Men ;
The gentle Trade was left to Churls,
Your frowsy TONSONS and your CURLLS ;
Mere Wolves in Ambush to attack
The AUTHOR in a Sheep-skin Back ;
Then SAVAGE and his Brother-Sinners
In *Porridge Island* div'd for Dinners ;
Or doz'd on *Covent Garden* Bulks,
And liken'd Letters to the Hulks ; —
You know that by-gone Time, I say,
That aimless easy-moral'd Day,
When rosy Morn found MADAM still
Wrangling at *Ombre* or *Quadrille,*
When good SIR JOHN reel'd Home to
    Bed,
From *Pontack's* or the *Shakespear's Head ;*
When TRIP *convey'd* his Master's Cloaths,
And took his Titles and his Oaths ;
While BETTY, in a cast *Brocade,*
Ogled MY LORD at Masquerade ;
When GARRICK play'd the guilty *Richard,*
Or mouth'd *Macbeth* with Mrs. PRITCHARD;
When FOOTE grimaced his snarling Wit ;
When CHURCHILL bullied in the Pit ;
When the CUZZONI sang —
        But there !
The further Catalogue I spare,
Having no Purpose to eclipse
That tedious Tale of HOMER's Ships ; —
This is the MAN that drew it all
From *Pannier Alley* to the *Mall,*
Then turn'd and drew it once again
From *Bird - Cage - Walk* to *Lewknor's*
    Lane ; —
Its Rakes and Fools, its Rogues and
    Sots ;
Its brawling Quacks, its starveling Scots ;
Its Ups and Downs, its Rags and Garters,
Its HENLEYS, LOVATS, MALCOLMS, CHAR-
    TRES,
Its Splendor, Squalor, Shame, Disease ;
Its *quicquid agunt Homines ;* —
Nor yet omitted to pourtray
Furens quid possit Foemina ; —
In short, held up to ev'ry Class
NATURE's unflatt'ring looking-Glass ;
And, from his Canvas, spoke to All
The Message of a JUVENAL.

Take Him. His Merits most aver :
His weak Point is — his Chronicler !

"IN AFTER DAYS"

In after days when grasses high
O'er-top the stone where I shall lie,
Though ill or well the world adjust
My slender claim to honored dust,
I shall not question nor reply.

I shall not see the morning sky ;
I shall not hear the night-wind sigh ;
I shall be mute, as all men must
In after days !

But yet, now living, fain were I
That some one then should testify,
Saying — " He held his pen in trust
To Art, not serving shame or lust."
Will none ? — Then let my memory die
In after days !

Wilfrid Scawen Blunt

TO MANON

COMPARING HER TO A FALCON

Brave as a falcon and as merciless,
With bright eyes watching still the world,
thy prey,
I saw thee pass in thy lone majesty,
Untamed, unmated, high above the press.
The dull crowd gazed at thee. It could
not guess
The secret of thy proud aërial way,
Or read in thy mute face the soul which
lay
A prisoner there in chains of tenderness.
— Lo, thou art captured. In my hand to-
day
I hold thee, and awhile thou deignest to
be
Pleased with my jesses. I would fain be-
guile
My foolish heart to think thou lovest me.
See,
I dare not love thee quite. A little while
And thou shalt sail back heavenwards.
Woe is me !

TO THE SAME

ON HER LIGHTHEARTEDNESS

I would I had thy courage, dear, to
face
This bankruptcy of love, and greet despair
With smiling eyes and unconcerned em-
brace,
And these few words of banter at " dull
care."

I would that I could sing and comb my
hair
Like thee the morning through, and choose
my dress,
And gravely argue what I best should wear,
A shade of ribbon or a fold of lace.
I would I had thy courage and thy peace,
Peace passing understanding ; that mine
eyes
Could find forgetfulness like thine in sleep ;
That all the past for me like thee could
cease
And leave me cheerfully, sublimely wise,
Like David with washed face who ceased to
weep.

LAUGHTER AND DEATH

There is no laughter in the natural world
Of beast or fish or bird, though no sad
doubt
Of their futurity to them unfurled
Has dared to check the mirth-compelling
shout.
The lion roars his solemn thunder out
To the sleeping woods. The eagle screams
her cry.
Even the lark must strain a serious throat
To hurl his blest defiance at the sky.
Fear, anger, jealousy, have found a voice.
Love's pain or rapture the brute bosoms
swell.
Nature has symbols for her nobler joys,
Her nobler sorrows. Who had dared fore-
tell
That only man, by some sad mockery,
Should learn to laugh who learns that he
must die ?

GIBRALTAR

SEVEN weeks of sea, and twice seven days
of storm
Upon the huge Atlantic, and once more
We ride into still water and the calm
Of a sweet evening screened by either shore
Of Spain and Barbary. Our toils are o'er,
Our exile is accomplished. Once again
We look on Europe, mistress as of yore
Of the fair earth and of the hearts of men.
Ay, this is the famed rock, which Hercules
And Goth and Moor bequeathed us. At
this door
England stands sentry. God! to hear the
shrill
Sweet treble of her fifes upon the breeze,
And at the summons of the rock gun's roar
To see her red coats marching from the hill.

THE OLD SQUIRE

I LIKE the hunting of the hare
Better than that of the fox ;
I like the joyous morning air,
And the crowing of the cocks.

I like the calm of the early fields,
The ducks asleep by the lake,
The quiet hour which Nature yields
Before mankind is awake.

I like the pheasants and feeding things
Of the unsuspicious morn ;
I like the flap of the wood-pigeon's wings
As she rises from the corn.

I like the blackbird's shriek, and his rush
From the turnips as I pass by,
And the partridge hiding her head in a
bush,
For her young ones cannot fly.

I like these things, and I like to ride,
When all the world is in bed,
To the top of the hill where the sky grows
wide,
And where the sun grows red.

The beagles at my horse heels trot
In silence after me ;
There's Ruby, Roger, Diamond, Dot,
Old Slut and Margery,—

A score of names well used, and dear,
The names my childhood knew ;
The horn, with which I rouse their cheer,
Is the horn my father blew.

I like the hunting of the hare
Better than that of the fox ;
The new world still is all less fair
Than the old world it mocks.

I covet not a wider range
Than these dear manors give ;
I take my pleasures without change,
And as I lived I live.

I leave my neighbors to their thought ;
My choice it is, and pride,
On my own lands to find my sport,
In my own fields to ride.

The hare herself no better loves
The field where she was bred,
Than I the habit of these groves,
My own inherited.

I know my quarries every one,
The meuse where she sits low ;
The road she chose to-day was run
A hundred years ago.

The lags, the gills, the forest ways,
The hedgerows one and all,
These are the kingdoms of my chase,
And bounded by my wall ;

Nor has the world a better thing,
Though one should search it round,
Than thus to live one's own sole king,
Upon one's own sole ground.

I like the hunting of the hare ;
It brings me, day by day,
The memory of old days as fair,
With dead men passed away.

To these, as homeward still I ply
And pass the churchyard gate,
Where all are laid as I must lie,
I stop and raise my hat.

I like the hunting of the hare ;
New sports I hold in scorn.
I like to be as my fathers were,
In the days e'er I was born.

Frank T. Marzials

DEATH AS THE TEACHER OF LOVE–LORE

'T WAS in mid autumn, and the woods
    were still.
A brooding mist from out the marshlands
    lay
Like age's clammy hand upon the day,
Soddening it ; — and the night rose dank
    and chill.
I watched the sere leaves falling, falling,
    till
Old thoughts, old hopes, seemed fluttering
    too away,
And then I sighed to think how life's
    decay,
And change, and time's mischances, Love
    might kill.
Sudden a shadowy horseman, at full speed
Spurring a pale horse, passed me swiftly
    by,
And mocking shrieked, " Thy love is dead
    indeed,
Haste to the burial ! " — With a bitter cry
I swooned, and wake to wonder at my
    creed,
Learning from Death that Love can never
    die.

DEATH AS THE FOOL

IN the high turret chamber sat the sage,
Striving to wring its secret from the scroll
Of time ; — and hard the task, for roll on
    roll
Was blurred with blood and tears, or black
    with age.
So that at last a hunger seized him, a rage
Of richer lore than our poor life can dole,
And loud he called on Death to dower his
    soul
With the great past's unrifled heritage.
And lo, a creaking step upon the stair,
A croak of song, a jingle, — and Death
    came in
Humming in motley with a merry din
And jangle of bells, and droning this re-
    frain,
God help the fools who count on death
    for gain."
So had the sage death-bell and passing-
    prayer.

TWO SONNET–SONGS

I

The Sirens sing.

HIST, hist, ye winds, ye whispering wave-
    lets hist,
Their toil is done, their teen and trouble
    are o'er,
Wash them, ye waves, in silence to the shore,
Waft them, ye winds, with voices hushed
    and whist.
Hist, waves and winds, here shall their
    eyes be kist
By love, and sweet love-slumber, till the roar
Of forepast storms, now stilled, for ever-
    more,
Die on their dream-horizons like dim mist.
What of renown, ye winds, when storms
    are done ?
A faded foam-flower on a wearying wave.
All toil is but the digging of a grave.
Here let them rest awhile ere set the sun,
And sip the honey'd moments one by one —
So fleet, so sweet, so few to squander or
    save.

II

Orpheus and the Mariners make answer.

FLEET, fleet and few, ay, fleet the moments
    fly —
(*Lash to light live foam, ye oars, the dreaming
    seas*),
And shall we lie in swine-sloth here at
    ease —
(*Dip, dip, ye oars, and dash the dark seas by*),
In swine-sloth here while death is stealing
    nigh —
(*Sweep, oars, sweep, here ripples and sparkles
    the breeze*),
And work is ours to drain to the last lees ?
(*Drive oars and winds, we will dare and do
    ere we die*).
And if no sound of voice nor any call
Break the death-silence bidding us all hail,
And, even among the living, Fame should
    fail
To shrill our deeds, yet whatsoe'er befall,
As men who fought for good not guerdon
    at all,
Peal the glad Pæan ! (*Steady oars and
    sail.*)

George Cotterell

AN AUTUMN FLITTING

My roof is hardly picturesque —
It lacks the pleasant reddish brown
Of the tiled house-tops out of town,
And cannot even hope to match
The modest beauty of the thatch :
Nor is it Gothic or grotesque —
No gable breaks, with quaint design,
Its hard monotony of line,
And not a gargoyle on the spout
Brings any latent beauty out :
Its only charm — I hold it high —
Is just its nearness to the sky.

But yet it looks o'er field and tree,
And in the air
One breathes up there
A faint, fresh whiff suggests the sea.
And that is why, this afternoon,
The topmost slates above the leads
Were thick with little bobbing heads,
And frisking tails, and wings that soon
Shall spread, ah me !
For lands where summer lingers fair,
Far otherwhere.
I heard a muttering,
Saw a fluttering,
Pointed wings went skimming past,
White breasts shimmered by as fast,
Wheel and bound and spurt and spring —
All the air seemed all on wing.
Then, like dropping clouds of leaves,
Down they settled on the eaves —
All the swallows of the region,
In a number almost legion —
Frisked about, but did not stop
Till they reached the ridge atop.

Then what chirping, what commotion !
What they said I have no notion,
But one cannot err in stating
There was very much debating.
First a small loquacious swallow
Seemed to move a resolution ;
And another seemed to follow,
Seconding the subject-matter
With a trick of elocution.
After that the chirp and chatter
Boded some more serious end, meant

For a quarrelsome amendment ;
Bobbing heads and flapping wings,
Eloquent of many things,
Gathered into lively rows,
" Pros " and " cons " and " ayes " and
     " noes."
As the clatter reached my ears,
Now it sounded like " hear, hears " ;
But again a note of faction,
With a clash of beaks in action,
Gave an aspect to the scene
Not exactly quite serene.
Fretful clusters flew away,
All too much incensed to stay ;
Wheeled about, then took a tack,
Halted and came darting back.
Others, eager to be heard,
Perched upon the chimney-top,
Chirped, as they would never stop,
Loud and fluent every bird.

But the turmoil passed away :
How it happened I can't say, —
All I know is, there was peace.
Whether some more thoughtful bird
Said the quarrelling was absurd,
And implored that it should cease ;
Whether what appeared contention
Was a difference not worth mention,
Just some mere exchange of words
Not uncommon among birds,
I have only my own notion,
You may make a nearer guess ;
All at once the noise was over,
Not a bird was now a rover,
Some one seemed to put the motion,
And the little heads bobbed " Yes."

Oh, that sudden resolution,
So unanimously carried !
Would they 'd longer talked and tarried,
With their fiery elocution !
What it bodes I cannot doubt ;
They were planning when to go,
And they have settled it, I know ;
Some chill morning, when the sun
Does not venture to shine out,
I shall miss them — overnight
They will all have taken flight,
And the summer will be gone.

IN THE TWILIGHT

FAR off ?   Not far away
  Lies that fair land ;
Shut from the curious gaze by day,
  Hidden, but close at hand :
Let us seek it who may.

Lie by me and hold me, sweet,
  Clasp arms and sink ;
There needs no weariness of the feet,
  Neither to toil nor think ;
Almost the pulse may cease to beat.

Eyes made dim, and breathing low,
  Hand locked in hand,
Goodly the visions that come and go,
  Glimpses of that land
Fairer than the eyes can know.

Is it not a land like ours ?
  Nay, much more fair ;
Sweeter flowers than earthly flowers
  Shed their fragance there,
Fade not with the passing hours.

Soft are all the airs that blow,
  Breathing of love ;
Dreamily soft the vales below,
  The skies above,
And all the murmuring streams that
  flow.

There are daughters of beauty, the host
  Of nymphs of old time ;

All the loves of the poets who boast
  Of their loves in their rhyme, —
Loves won, and the sadder loves lost :

Fair, passionless creatures of thought,
  Most fair, most calm ;
The joy of whose beauty has brought
  To the soul its own balm ;
Not desire that cometh to naught.

The dreams that were dreamed long ago
  Lie treasured there still ;
For the things that the dreamers fore-
    know
  The years shall fulfil,
The fleet years and slow.

Dreams, memories, hopes that were
    bright,
  And hearts that were young ;
All the stars and the glories of night,
  All the glories of song, —
They are there, in that land of delight.

Wilt thou seek that land then, sweet ?
  Yea, love, with thee ;
Fleet, as thy soul's wings are fleet,
  Shall our passage be :
Soft, on wings of noiseless beat.

Bid my wings with thine expand ;
  So may we glide
Into the stillness of that land,
  Lovingly side by side,
Hopefully hand in hand.

Andrew Lang

BALLADES

TO THEOCRITUS, IN WINTER

ἐσορῶν τὰν Σικελὰν ἐς ἅλα. — ID. viii. 56.

AH ! leave the smoke, the wealth, the
    roar
Of London, leave the bustling street,
For still, by the Sicilian shore,
The murmur of the Muse is sweet.
Still, still, the suns of summer greet
The mountain-grave of Helikê,
And shepherds still their songs repeat
Where breaks the blue Sicilian sea.

What though they worship Pan no
    more
That guarded once the shepherd's seat,
They chatter of their rustic lore,
They watch the wind among the wheat :
Cicalas chirp, the young lambs bleat,
Where whispers pine to cypress tree ;
They count the waves that idly beat,
Where breaks the blue Sicilian sea.

Theocritus ! thou canst restore
The pleasant years, and over-fleet ;
With thee we live as men of yore,
We rest where running waters meet :

And then we turn unwilling feet
And seek the world — so must it be —
We may not linger in the heat
Where breaks the blue Sicilian sea !

Master, — when rain, and snow, and
    sleet
And northern winds are wild, to thee
We come, we rest in thy retreat,
Where breaks the blue Sicilian sea !

OF THE BOOK-HUNTER

In torrid heats of late July,
In March, beneath the bitter *bise*,
He book-hunts while the loungers fly,
He book-hunts, though December freeze ;
In breeches baggy at the knees,
And heedless of the public jeers,
For these, for these, he hoards his
    fees, —
Aldines, Bodonis, Elzevirs.

No dismal stall escapes his eye,
He turns o'er tomes of low degrees,
There soiled romanticists may lie,
Or Restoration comedies ;
Each tract that flutters in the breeze
For him is charged with hopes and fears,
In mouldy novels fancy sees
Aldines, Bodonis, Elzevirs.

With restless eyes that peer and spy,
Sad eyes that heed not skies nor trees,
In dismal nooks he loves to pry,
Whose motto evermore is *Spes !*
But ah ! the fabled treasure flees ;
Grown rarer with the fleeting years,
In rich men's shelves they take their
    ease, —
Aldines, Bodonis, Elzevirs !

ENVOY

Prince, all the things that tease and
    please, —
Fame, hope, wealth, kisses, cheers, and
    tears,
What are they but such toys as these, —
Aldines, Bodonis, Elzevirs ?

OF BLUE CHINA

There 's a joy without canker or cark,
There 's a pleasure eternally new,

'T is to gloat on the glaze and the mark
Of china that 's ancient and blue ;
Unchipp'd, all the centuries through
It has pass'd, since the chime of it rang,
And they fashion'd it, figure and hue,
In the reign of the Emperor Hwang.

These dragons (their tails, you remark,
Into bunches of gillyflowers grew), —
When Noah came out of the ark,
Did these lie in wait for his crew ?
They snorted, they snapp'd, and they slew,
They were mighty of fin and of fang,
And their portraits Celestials drew
In the reign of the Emperor Hwang.

Here 's a pot with a cot in a park,
In a park where the peach-blossoms blew,
Where the lovers eloped in the dark,
Lived, died, and were changed into two
Bright birds that eternally flew
Through the boughs of the may, as they
    sang ;
'T is a tale was undoubtedly true
In the reign of the Emperor Hwang.

ENVOY

Come, snarl at my ecstasies, do,
Kind critic ; your "tongue has a tang,"
But — a sage never heeded a shrew
In the reign of the Emperor Hwang.

OF LIFE

" ' Dead and gone,' — a sorry burden of the Ballad of
Life." — Death's Jest Book.

Say, fair maids, maying
    In gardens green,
In deep dells straying,
    What end hath been
    Two Mays between
Of the flowers that shone
    And your own sweet queen ? —
" They are dead and gone ! "

Say, grave priests, praying
    In dule and teen,
From cells decaying
    What have ye seen
    Of the proud and mean,
Of Judas and John,
    Of the foul and clean ? —
" They are dead and gone ! "

Say, kings, arraying
Loud wars to win,
Of your manslaying
What gain ye glean ?
" They are fierce and keen,
But they fall anon,
On the sword that lean, —
They are dead and gone ! "

ENVOY

Through the mad world's scene
We are drifting on,
To this tune, I ween,
" They are dead and gone ! "

OF HIS CHOICE OF A SEPULCHRE

HERE I 'd come when weariest !
Here the breast
Of the Windberg 's tufted over
Deep with bracken ; here his crest
Takes the west,
Where the wide-winged hawk doth hover.

Silent here are lark and plover ;
In the cover
Deep below, the cushat best
Loves his mate, and croons above her
O'er their nest,
Where the wide-winged hawk doth hover.

Bring me here, Life's tired-out guest,
To the blest
Bed that waits the weary rover, —
Here should failure be confest ;
Ends my quest,
Where the wide-winged hawk doth hover !

ENVOY

Friend, or stranger kind, or lover,
Ah, fulfil a last behest,
Let me rest
Where the wide-winged hawk doth hover !

ROMANCE

MY Love dwelt in a Northern land.
A gray tower in a forest green
Was hers, and far on either hand
The long wash of the waves was seen,
And leagues on leagues of yellow sand,
The woven forest boughs between !

And through the silver Northern night
The sunset slowly died away,
And herds of strange deer, lily-white,
Stole forth among the branches gray ;
About the coming of the light,
They fled like ghosts before the day !

I know not if the forest green
Still girdles round that castle gray ;
I know not if the boughs between
The white deer vanish ere the day ;
Above my Love the grass is green,
My heart is colder than the clay !

THE ODYSSEY

As one that for a weary space has lain
Lulled by the song of Circe and her wine
In gardens near the pale of Proserpine,
Where that Ææan isle forgets the main,
And only the low lutes of love complain,
And only shadows of wan lovers pine,
As such an one were glad to know the brine
Salt on his lips, and the large air again, —
So gladly, from the songs of modern speech
Men turn, and see the stars, and feel the
free
Shrill wind beyond the close of heavy
flowers,
And, through the music of the languid
hours,
They hear like ocean on a western beach
The surge and thunder of the Odyssey.

SAN TERENZO

MID April seemed like some November
day,
When through the glassy waters, dull as
lead,
Our boat, like shadowy barques that bear
the dead,
Slipped down the long shores of the Spezian
bay,
Rounded a point, — and San Terenzo lay
Before us, that gay village, yellow and red,
The roof that covered Shelley's homeless
head, —
His house, a place deserted, bleak and gray.
The waves broke on the doorstep ; fisher-
men
Cast their long nets, and drew, and cast
again.

Deep in the ilex woods we wandered free,
When suddenly the forest glades were
    stirred
With waving pinions, and a great sea bird
Flew forth, like Shelley's spirit, to the sea !

SCYTHE SONG

Mowers, weary and brown, and blithe,
    What is the word methinks ye know,
Endless over-word that the Scythe
    Sings to the blades of the grass below ?
Scythes that swing in the grass and clover,
    Something, still, they say as they pass ;
What is the word that, over and over,
    Sings the Scythe to the flowers and
        grass ?

Hush, ah hush, the Scythes are saying,
    Hush, and heed not, and fall asleep ;
Hush, they say to the grasses swaying ;
    Hush, they sing to the clover deep !
Hush — 't is the lullaby Time is singing —
    Hush, and heed not, for all things pass ;
Hush, ah hush ! and the Scythes are swinging
    Over the clover, over the grass !

MELVILLE AND COGHILL

(THE PLACE OF THE LITTLE HAND)

Dead, with their eyes to the foe,
    Dead, with the foe at their feet ;
Under the sky laid low
    Truly their slumber is sweet,
Though the wind from the Camp of the
        Slain Men blow,
    And the rain on the wilderness beat.

Dead, for they chose to die
    When that wild race was run ;
Dead, for they would not fly,
    Deeming their work undone,
Nor cared to look on the face of the sky,
    Nor loved the light of the sun.

Honor we give them and tears,
    And the flag they died to save,
Rent from the raid of the spears,
    Wet from the war and the wave,
Shall waft men's thoughts through the dust
        of the years,
    Back to their lonely grave !

PARAPHRASES

ERINNA

ANTIPATER OF SIDON

Brief is Erinna's song, her lowly lay,
    Yet there the Muses sing ;
Therefore her memory doth not pass away,
    Hid by Night's shadowy wing !
But we, — new countless poets, — heaped
        and hurled
All in oblivion lie ;
Better the swan's chant than a windy world
    Of rooks in the April sky !

TELLING THE BEES

ANONYMOUS

Naiads, and ye pastures cold,
    When the bees return with spring,
Tell them that Leucippus old
    Perished in his hare-hunting,
Perished on a winter night.
Now no more shall he delight
    In the hives he used to tend,
But the valley and the height
    Mourn a neighbor and a friend.

HELIODORE DEAD

MELEAGER

Tears for my lady dead,
    Heliodore !
Salt tears and ill to shed
    Over and o'er.
Tears for my lady dead,
    Sighs do we send,
Long love rememberèd,
    Mistress and friend.
Sad are the songs we sing,
    Tears that we shed,
Empty the gifts we bring,
    Gifts to the dead.
Go tears, and go lament !
    Fare from her tomb,
Wend where my lady went,
    Down through the gloom.
Ah, for my flower, my love,
    Hades hath taken !
Ah for the dust above,
    Scattered and shaken !
Mother of all things born,
    Earth, in thy breast
Lull her that all men mourn,
    Gently to rest !

A SCOT TO JEANNE D'ARC

DARK Lily without blame,
Not upon us the shame,
Whose sires were to the Auld Alliance
  true ;
They, by the Maiden's side,
Victorious fought and died ;
One stood by thee that fiery torment
  through,
Till the White Dove from thy pure lips
  had passed,
And thou wert with thine own St. Catherine
  at the last.

Once only didst thou see,
In artist's imagery,
Thine own face painted, and that precious
  thing
Was in an Archer's hand
From the leal Northern land.

THREE PORTRAITS OF PRINCE CHARLES

1731

BEAUTIFUL face of a child,
  Lighted with laughter and glee,
Mirthful, and tender, and wild,
  My heart is heavy for thee !

1744

Beautiful face of a youth,
  As an eagle poised to fly forth
To the old land loyal of truth,
  To the hills and the sounds of the
    North :
Fair face, daring and proud,
  Lo ! the shadow of doom, even now,
The fate of thy line, like a cloud,
  Rests on the grace of thy brow !

1773

Cruel and angry face,
  Hateful and heavy with wine,
Where are the gladness, the grace,
  The beauty, the mirth that were thine ?

Ah, my Prince, it were well, —
  Hadst thou to the gods been dear, —
To have fallen where Keppoch fell,
  With the war-pipe loud in thine ear !
To have died with never a stain
  On the fair White Rose of Renown,

To have fallen, fighting in vain,
  For thy father, thy faith, and thy
    crown !
More than thy marble pile,
  With its women weeping for thee,
Were to dream in thine ancient isle,
  To the endless dirge of the sea !
But the Fates deemed otherwise ;
  Far thou sleepest from home,
From the tears of the Northern skies,
  In the secular dust of Rome.
A city of death and the dead,
  But thither a pilgrim came,
Wearing on weary head
  The crowns of years and fame :
Little the Lucrine lake
  Or Tivoli said to him,
Scarce did the memories wake
  Of the far-off years and dim,
For he stood by Avernus' shore.
  But he dreamed of a Northern glen,
And he murmured, over and o'er,
  " *For Charlie and his men :* "
And his feet, to death that went,
  Crept forth to St. Peter's shrine,
And the latest Minstrel bent
  O'er the last of the Stuart line.

ÆSOP

HE sat among the woods ; he heard
  The sylvan merriment; he saw
The pranks of butterfly and bird,
  The humors of the ape, the daw.

And in the lion or the frog, —
  In all the life of 'moor and fen, —
In ass and peacock, stork and dog,
  He read similitudes of men.

" Of these, from those," he cried, " we
    come,
  Our hearts, our brains descend from
    these."
And, lo ! the Beasts no more were dumb,
  But answered out of brakes and trees :

" Not ours," they cried ; " Degenerate,
  If ours at all," they cried again,
" Ye fools, who war with God and Fate,
  Who strive and toil ; strange race of
    men.

" For *we* are neither bond nor free,
  For *we* have neither slaves nor kings ;

But near to Nature's heart are we,
  And conscious of her secret things.

"Content are we to fall asleep,
  And well content to wake no more ;
We do not laugh, we do not weep,
  Nor look behind us and before :

" But were there cause for moan or mirth,
  'T is *we*, not you, should sigh or scorn,
Oh, latest children of the Earth,
  Most childish children Earth has born."

   .   .   .   .

They spoke, but that misshapen slave
  Told never of the thing he heard,
And unto men their portraits gave,
  In likenesses of beast and bird !

ON CALAIS SANDS

On Calais Sands the gray began,
  Then rosy red above the gray ;
The morn with many a scarlet van
  Leaped, and the world was glad with
    May !

The little waves along the bay
  Broke white upon the shelving strands ;
The sea-mews flitted white as they
    On Calais Sands !

On Calais Sands must man with man
  Wash honor clean in blood to-day ;
On spaces wet from waters wan
  How white the flashing rapiers play, —
Parry, riposte ! and lunge ! The fray
  Shifts for a while, then mournful stands
The Victor : life ebbs fast away
    On Calais Sands !

On Calais Sands a little space
  Of silence, then the plash and spray,
The sound of eager waves that ran
  To kiss the perfumed locks astray,
To touch these lips that ne'er said " Nay,"
  To dally with the helpless hands,
Till the deep sea in silence lay
    On Calais Sands !

Between the lilac and the may
  She waits her love from alien lands ;
Her love is colder than the clay
    On Calais Sands !

William Canton

KARMA

In the heart of the white summer mist lay
  a green little piece of the world ;
And the tops of the beeches were lost in
  the mist, and the mist ringed us
  round ;
All the low leaves were silvered with dew,
  and the herbage with dew was im-
  pearled ;
And the turmoil of life was but vaguely
  divined through the mist as a sound.

In the heart of the mist there was warmth,
  for the soil full of sun was aglow,
Like a fruit when it colors, — and fragrance
  from flowers, and a scent from the
  soil ;
And a lamb in the grass, in the flowers,
  in the dew, nibbled, whiter than
  snow ;

And the white summer mist was a fold fo
  us both against sorrow and toil.

From the fields in the mist came a bleating
  a sound as of longing and need :
But the lamb from the grass in its lit
  tle green heaven never lifted it
  head :
It was innocent, whiter than snow ;
  was glad in the flowers, took n
  heed ;
But the sound from the fields in the mi
  made me grieve as for one that
  dead.

And behold ! 't was a dream I had dreame
  and a voice made me wake with
  start,
Saying : "Hark ! once again in the fle
  shall ye twain live your life for
  span ;

But since whiteness of snow is as nought
   in mine eyes without pity of heart,
Lo ! the lamb shall be born as a wolf, with
   a wolf's heart, but thou as a man ! "

LAUS INFANTIUM

In praise of little children I will say
God first made man, then found a better
   way
For woman, but his third way was the best.
Of all created things, the loveliest
And most divine are children. Nothing
   here
Can be to us more gracious or more dear.
And though, when God saw all his works
   were good,
There was no rosy flower of babyhood,
'T was said of children in a later day
That none could enter Heaven save such as
   they.

The earth, which feels the flowering of a
   thorn,
Was glad, O little child, when you were
   born ;
The earth, which thrills when skylarks
   scale the blue,
Soared up itself to God's own Heaven in
   you ;

And Heaven, which loves to lean down
   and to glass
Its beauty in each dewdrop on the grass, —
Heaven laughed to find your face so pure
   and fair,
And left, O little child, its reflex there.

A NEW POET

I WRITE. He sits beside my chair,
   And scribbles, too, in hushed delight ,
He dips his pen in charmèd air :
   What is it he pretends to write ?

He toils and toils ; the paper gives
   No clue to aught he thinks. What then ?
His little heart is glad ; he lives
   The poems that he cannot pen.

Strange fancies throng that baby brain.
   What grave, sweet looks ! What earnest
   eyes !
He stops — reflects — and now again
   His unrecording pen he plies.

It seems a satire on myself, —
   These dreamy nothings scrawled in air,
This thought, this work ! Oh tricksy elf,
   Wouldst drive thy father to despair ?

Despair ! Ah, no ; the heart, the mind
   Persists in hoping, — schemes and
   strives
That there may linger with our kind
   Some memory of our little lives.

Beneath his rock i' the early world
   Smiling the naked hunter lay,
And sketched on horn the spear he hurled,
   The urus which he made his prey.

Like him I strive in hope my rhymes
   May keep my name a little while, —
O child, who knows how many times
   We two have made the angels smile !

John Hartley

TO A DAISY

AH ! I 'm feared thou 's come too sooin,
   Little daisy !
Pray whativer wor ta doin' ?
   Are ta crazy ?
Winter winds are blowin' yet.
Tha 'll be starved, mi little pet !

Did a gleam o' sunshine warm thee;
   An' deceive thee ?

Niver let appearance charm thee ;
   Yes, believe me,
Smiles tha 'lt find are oft but snares
Laid to catch thee unawares.

An' yet, I think it looks a shame
   To talk sich stuff ;
I 've lost heart, an' thou 'lt do t' same,
   Ay, sooin enough !
An', if thou 'rt happy as tha art,
Trustin' must be t' wisest part.

Come ! I 'll pile some bits o' stoan
  Round thi dwellin' ;
They may cheer thee when I 've goan, —
  Theer 's no tellin' ;
An' when Spring's mild day draws near
I 'll release thee, niver fear !

An' if then thi pretty face
  Greets me smilin',
I may come an' sit by th' place,
  Time beguilin',
Glad to think I 'd paar to be
Of some use if but to thee !

Alexander Anderson

CUDDLE DOON

THE bairnies cuddle doon at nicht
  Wi' muckle faught an' din ;
" Oh try and sleep, ye waukrife rogues,
  Your faither 's comin' in."
They never heed a word I speak ;
  I try to gie a froon,
But aye I hap them up an' cry,
  " Oh, bairnies, cuddle doon."

Wee Jamie wi' the curly heid —
  He aye sleeps next the wa' —
Bangs up an' cries, " I want a piece ; "
  The rascal starts them a'.
I rin an' fetch them pieces, drinks,
  They stop awee the soun',
Then draw the blankets up an' cry,
  " Noo, weanies, cuddle doon."

But, ere five minutes gang, wee Rab
  Cries out, frae 'neath the claes,
" Mither, mak' Tam gie ower at ance,
  He 's kittlin' wi' his taes."
The mischief 's in that Tam for tricks,
  He 'd bother half the toon ;
But aye I hap them up and cry,
  " Oh, bairnies, cuddle doon."

At length they hear their faither's fit,
  An', as he steeks the door,
They turn their faces to the wa',
  While Tam pretends to snore.
" Hae a' the weans been gude ? " he
    asks,
  As he pits aff his shoon ;
" The bairnies, John, are in their beds,
  An' lang since cuddled doon."

An' just afore we bed oorsels,
  We look at our wee lambs ;
Tam has his airm roun' wee Rab's
    neck,
  And Rab his airm round Tam's.
I lift wee Jamie up the bed,
  An' as I straik each croon,
I whisper, till my heart fills up,
  " Oh, bairnies, cuddle doon."

The bairnies cuddle doon at nicht
  Wi' mirth that 's dear to me ;
But soon the big warl's cark an' care
  Will quaten doon their glee.
Yet, come what will to ilka ane,
  May He who rules aboon
Aye whisper, though their pows be bald,
  " Oh, bairnies, cuddle doon."

Emily Henrietta Hickey

A SEA STORY

SILENCE. A while ago
  Shrieks went up piercingly ;
But now is the ship gone down ;
  Good ship, well manned, was she.
There 's a raft that 's a chance of life for one,
  This day upon the sea.

A chance for one of two ;
  Young, strong, are he and he,

Just in the manhood prime,
  The comelier, verily,
For the wrestle with wind and weather and
    wave,
  In the life upon the sea.

One of them has a wife
  And little children three ;
Two that can toddle and lisp,
  And a suckling on the knee :

Naked they 'll go, and hunger sore,
　If he be lost at sea.

One has a dream of home,
　A dream that well may be :
He never has breathed it yet ;
　She never has known it, she.
But some one will be sick at heart
　If he be lost at sea.

"Wife and kids at home ! —
　Wife, kids, nor home has he ! —
Give us a chance, Bill ! "　Then,
　"All right, Jem ! "　Quietly
A man gives up his life for a man,
　This day upon the sea.

BELOVED, IT IS MORN

BELOVED, it is morn !
　A redder berry on the thorn,

A deeper yellow on the corn,
For this good day new-born.
　Pray, Sweet, for me
　That I may be
　Faithful to God and thee.

Beloved, it is day !
　And lovers work, as children play,
　With heart and brain untired alway :
Dear love, look up and pray.
　Pray, Sweet, for me
　That I may be
　Faithful to God and thee.

Beloved, it is night !
　Thy heart and mine are full of light,
　Thy spirit shineth clear and white,
God keep thee in His sight !
　Pray, Sweet, for me
　That I may be
　Faithful to God and thee.

Walter Crane

A SEAT FOR THREE

WRITTEN ON A SETTLE

"A SEAT for three, where host and
　　guest
May side-by-side pass toast or jest ;
　And be their number two or three,
　With elbow-room and liberty,
What need to wander east or west ?

" A book for thought, a nook for rest,
And meet for fasting or for fest,
　In fair and equal parts to be
　　A seat for three.

"Then give you pleasant company,
For youth or elder shady tree ;
　A roof for council or sequest,
　A corner in a homely nest ;
Free, equal, and fraternally,
　　A seat for three."

ACROSS THE FIELDS

ACROSS the fields like swallows fly
Sweet thoughts and sad of days gone by ;
　From Life's broad highway turned away,
　Like children, Thought and Memory play
Nor heed Time's scythe though grass be
　　high.

Beneath the blue and shoreless sky
Time is but told when seedlings dry
　By Love's light breath are blown, like
　　spray,
　　Across the fields.

Now comes the scent of fallen hay,
And flowers bestrew the foot-worn clay,
　And summer breathes a passing sigh
　As westward rolls the day's gold eye,
And Time with Labor ends his day
　　Across the fields.

Eugene Lee-Hamilton

SIR WALTER RALEIGH TO A CAGED LINNET

THOU tiny solace of these prison days,
Too long already have I kept thee here ;
With every week thou hast become more
    dear —
So dear that I will free thee : fly thy
    ways.

Man, the alternate slave and tyrant, lays
Too soon on others what he hath to bear.
Thy cage is in my cage ; but, never fear,
The sun once more shall bathe thee with
    its rays.

Fly forth, and tell the sunny woods how
    oft
I think of them, and stretch my limbs in
    thought
Upon their fragrant mosses green and soft ;

And whistle all the whistlings God hath
    taught
Thy throat, to other songsters high aloft —
Not to a captive who can answer nought.

IZAAK WALTON TO RIVER AND BROOK

WHICH is more sweet, — the slow mysteri-
    ous stream,
Where sleeps the pike throughout the long
    noon hours,
Which moats with emerald old cathedral
    towers,
And winds through tufted timber like the
    dream
That glides through summer sleep ; where
    white swans teem,
And dragonflies and broad-leaved floating
    flowers,
Where through the hanging boughs you see
    the mowers
Among the grasses whet their scythes that
    gleam ;

Or that blue brook where leaps the speckled
    trout,
That laughs and sings and dances on its way
Among a thousand bafflings in and out ;
Bubbling and gurgling through the livelong
    day
Between the stones, in riot, reel, and rout,
While rays of sun make rainbows in the
    spray ?

CHARLES II. OF SPAIN TO APPROACHING DEATH

MAKE way, my lords ! for Death now once
    again
Waits on the palace stairs. He comes to lay
His finger on my brow.   Make way ! make
    way,
Ye whispering groups that scent an ending
    reign !

Death, if I make thee a grandee of Spain,
And give thee half my subjects, wilt thou
    stay
Behind the door a little, while I play
With life a moment longer ?   I would fain.

Oh, who shall turn the fatal shadow back
On Ahaz' sundial now ?   Who 'll cure the
    king
When Death awaits him, motionless and
    black ?

Upon the wall the inexorable thing
Creeps on and on, with horror in its track.
The king is dying.   Bid the great bells ring.

TO MY TORTOISE CHRONOS

THOU vague dumb crawler with the groping
    head
As listless to the sun as to the showers,
Thou very image of the wingless Hours
Now creeping past me with their feet of
    lead :
For thee and me the same small garden
    bed
Is the whole world : the same half life is
    ours ;
And year by year, as Fate restricts my
    powers,
I grow more like thee, and the soul grows
    dead.

No, Tortoise : from thy like in days of
    old
Was made the living lyre ; and mighty
    strings
Spanned thy green shell with pure vibrat-
    ing gold.

The notes soared up, on strong but trem-
    bling wings,
Through ether's lower zones ; then, growing
    bold,
Spurned earth for ever and its wingless
    things.

SUNKEN GOLD

In dim green depths rot ingot-laden ships ;
And gold doubloons, that from the drowned
  hand fell,
Lie nestled in the ocean-flower's bell
With love's old gifts, once kissed by long-
  drowned lips ;
And round some wrought gold cup the sea-
  grass whips,
And hides lost pearls, near pearls still in
  their shell,
Where sea-weed forests fill each ocean
  dell
And seek dim sunlight with their restless
  tips.
So lie the wasted gifts, the long-lost hopes
Beneath the now hushed surface of myself,
In lonelier depths than where the diver
  gropes ;
They lie deep, deep ; but I at times behold
In doubtful glimpses, on some reefy shelf,
The gleam of irrecoverable gold.

SEA-SHELL MURMURS

The hollow sea-shell, which for years hath
  stood
On dusty shelves, when held against the
  ear
Proclaims its stormy parents ; and we hear
The faint far murmur of the breaking flood.
We hear the sea. The sea ? It is the
  blood
In our own veins, impetuous and near,
And pulses keeping pace with hope and
  fear
And with our feelings' every shifting mood.
Lo, in my heart I hear, as in a shell,
The murmur of a world beyond the grave,
Distinct, distinct, though faint and far it be.
Thou fool ; this echo is a cheat as well, —
The hum of earthly instincts ; and we
  crave
A world unreal as the shell-heard sea.

A FLIGHT FROM GLORY

Once, from the parapet of gems and glow,
An Angel said, "O God, the heart grows
  cold
On these eternal battlements of gold,
Where all is pure, but cold as virgin snow.

Here sobs are never heard ; no salt tears
  flow ;
Here there are none to help — nor sick nor
  old ;
No wrong to fight, no justice to uphold :
Grant me Thy leave to live man's life be-
  low."
"And then annihilation ? " God replied.
" Yes," said the Angel, "even that dread
  price ;
For earthly tears are worth eternal night."
" Then go," said God. — The Angel opened
  wide
His dazzling wings, gazed back on Heaven
  thrice,
And plunged for ever from the walls of
  Light.

WHAT THE SONNET IS

Fourteen small broidered berries on the
  hem
Of Circe's mantle, each of magic gold ;
Fourteen of lone Calypso's tears that
  rolled
Into the sea, for pearls to come of them ;
Fourteen clear signs of omen in the gem
With which Medea human fate foretold ;
Fourteen small drops, which Faustus,
  growing old,
Craved of the Fiend, to water Life's dry
  stem.
It is the pure white diamond Dante
  brought
To Beatrice ; the sapphire Laura wore
When Petrarch cut it sparkling out of
  thought ;
The ruby Shakespeare hewed from his
  heart's core ;
The dark, deep emerald that Rossetti
  wrought
For his own soul, to wear for evermore.

ON HIS "SONNETS OF THE WINGLESS HOURS "

I wrought them like a targe of hammered
  gold
On which all Troy is battling round and
  round ;
Or Circe's cup, embossed with snakes that
  wound
Through buds and myrtles, fold on scaly
  fold ;

Or like gold coins, which Lydian tombs
   may hold,
Stamped with winged racers, in the old
   red ground ;
Or twined gold armlets from the funeral
   mound
Of some great viking, terrible of old.

I know not in what metal I have wrought ;
Nor whether what I fashioned will be thrust
Beneath the clouds that hide forgotten
   thought ;
But if it is of gold it will not rust ;
And when the time is ripe it will be brought
Into the sun, and glitter through its dust.

Alfred Perceval Graves

THE WHITE BLOSSOM'S OFF
THE BOG

THE white blossom 's off the bog and the
   leaves are off the trees,
And the singing birds have scattered
   across the stormy seas :
   And oh ! 't is winter,
   Wild, wild winter !
With the lonesome wind sighing for ever
   through the trees.

How green the leaves were springing ! how
   glad the birds were singing !
When I rested in the meadow with my
   head on Patrick's knees !

   And oh ! 't was spring-time,
   Sweet, sweet spring-time !
With the daisies all dancing before in the
   breeze.

With the spring the fresh leaves they 'll
   laugh upon the trees,
And the birds they 'll flutter back with
   their songs across the seas,
But I 'll never rest again with my head on
   Patrick's knees ;
   And for me 't will be winter,
   All the year winter,
With the lonesome wind sighing for ever
   through the trees.

Frederika Richardson Macdonald

NEW YEAR'S EVE — MIDNIGHT

DEAD. The dead year is lying at my
   feet ;
In this strange hour the past and future
   meet ;
There is no present ; no land in the vast
   sea ;
Appalled, I stand here in Eternity.

Darkness upon me. On my soul it weighs ;
The gloom, that has crushed out the life of
   days
That once knew light, has crept into my
   heart ;
I have not strength to bid it thence depart.

Oh, what is Time ? and what is Life, the fire
That thrills my pulses with its large de-
   sire ?

Since at each step I rend a fragment of my
   soul,
And growth means dying, whither is the
   goal ?

The old, old question ! yet I do not
   shrink
From bitter truths ; I do not fear to
   drink
Even to the dregs the cup that tears may
   fill ;
I 'd know God's truth, though it were human
   ill.

I have cast down the idols in my mind
Which sought to comfort me for being
   blind ;
I need no pleasant lie to cheat the night,
I need God's Truth, that I may walk
   aright.

That, and that only ! with unflinching eyes
I would tear through the secret of the
    skies ;
Smile on, ye stars ; in me there is a might
Which dares to scale your large empyreal
    height.

Yet — yet — how shall it be ? Time sweeps
    me on,
And what one day I hold, the next is gone ;
The very Heavens are changed ! the face
    they wore,
A moment back, is lost to come no more.

My soul along the restless current drifts,
And to its sight the source of radiance
    shifts ;
Wildly I strive some gleam of truth to
    save,
And cry, " God help me ! " battling with
    the wave.

God help me ?   Well I know the prayer is
    vain,
Although it rush up to my lips again ;
I know His help was given with the Breath
That leads me thus to struggle against
    death.

No further help.   No help beyond the soul,
The fragment of Himself I hold in my
    control ;
From heaven, no stronger aid to lead me
    through the fight :
In heaven, no higher aim to bind me to
    the Right.

Thus stand I on the brink of this new year,
Darkness upon me — not the work of fear.
Powerless I know to check the river's
    sweep,
Powerful alone my own soul's truth to
    keep.

George Barlow

THE DEAD CHILD

But yesterday she played with childish
    things,
    With toys and painted fruit.
To-day she may be speeding on bright
    wings
    Beyond the stars !   We ask.   The stars
    are mute.

But yesterday her doll was all in all ;
    She laughed and was content.
To-day she will not answer, if we call :
    She dropped no toys to show the road
    she went.

But yesterday she smiled and ranged with
    art
    Her playthings on the bed.
To-day and yesterday are leagues apart !
    She will not smile to-day, for she is
    dead.

IF ONLY THOU ART TRUE

If only a single rose is left,
    Why should the summer pine ?

A blade of grass in a rocky cleft ;
    A single star to shine.
— Why should I sorrow if all be lost,
    If only thou art mine ?

If only a single bluebell gleams
    Bright on the barren heath,
Still of that flower the Summer dreams,
    Not of his August wreath.
— Why should I sorrow if thou art mine,
    Love, beyond change and death ?

If only once on a wintry day
    The sun shines forth in the blue,
He gladdens the groves till they laugh as
    in May
    And dream of the touch of the dew.
— Why should I sorrow if all be false,
    If only thou art true ?

THE OLD MAID

She gave her life to love.   She never knew
    What other women give their all to gain.
Others were fickle.   She was passing true.
    She gave pure love, and faith without a
    stain.

She never married. Suitors came and
went :
The dark eyes flashed their love on one
alone.
Her life was passed in quiet and content.
The old love reigned. No rival shared
the throne.

Think you her life was wasted ? Vale and
hill
Blossomed in summer, and white winter
came ;

The blue ice stiffened on the silenced rill ;
All times and seasons found her still the
same.

Her heart was full of sweetness till the
end.
What once she gave, she never took
away.
Through all her youth she loved one faith-
ful friend :
She loves him now her hair is growing
gray.

Frederic Edward Weatherly

LONDON BRIDGE

PROUD and lowly, beggar and lord,
Over the bridge they go ;
Rags and velvet, fetter and sword,
Poverty, pomp, and woe.
Laughing, weeping, hurrying ever,
Hour by hour they crowd along,
While, below, the mighty river
Sings them all a mocking song.
Hurry along, sorrow and song,
All is vanity 'neath the sun ;
Velvet and rags, so the world wags,
Until the river no more shall run.

Dainty, painted, powdered and gay,
Rolleth my lady by ;
Rags-and-tatters, over the way,
Carries a heart as high.
Flowers and dreams from country mea-
dows,
Dust and din through city skies,
Old men creeping with their shadows,
Children with their sunny eyes,—
Hurry along, sorrow and song,
All is vanity 'neath the sun ;
Velvet and rags, so the world wags,
Until the river no more shall run.

Storm and sunshine, peace and strife,
Over the bridge they go ;
Floating on in the tide of life,
Whither no man shall know.
Who will miss them there to-morrow,
Waifs that drift to the shade or sun ?
Gone away with their songs and sorrow ;
Only the river still flows on.

Hurry along, sorrow and song,
All is vanity 'neath the sun ;
Velvet and rags, so the world wags,
Until the river no more shall run.

NANCY LEE

OF all the wives as e'er you know,
Yeo-ho ! lads ho ! Yeo-ho ! Yeo-ho !
There 's none like Nancy Lee, I trow,
Yeo-ho ! lads ho ! Yeo-ho !
See there she stands an' waves her hands
upon the quay,
And ev'ry day when I 'm away, she 'll
watch for me,
An' whisper low, when tempests blow for
Jack at Sea,
Yeo-ho ! lads ho ! Yeo-ho !
The sailor's wife the sailor's star shall
be,
Yeo-ho ! we go across the sea ;
The sailor's wife the sailor's star shall
be,
The sailor's wife his star shall be.

The harbor 's past, the breezes blow :
Yeo-ho ! lads ho ! Yeo-ho ! Yeo-ho !
'T is long ere we come back, I know ;
Yeo-ho ! lads ho ! Yeo-ho !
But true an' bright from morn till night
my home will be,
An' all so neat, an' snug, an' sweet, for
Jack at sea,
An' Nancy's face to bless the place, an'
welcome me ;
Yeo-ho ! lads ho ! Yeo-ho !

The boa's'n pipes the watch below,
Yeo-ho ! lads ho ! Yeo-ho ! Yeo-ho !
Then here 's a health afore we go,
Yeo-ho ! lads ho ! Yeo-ho !
A long long life to my sweet wife and
mates at sea ;
An' keep our bones from Davy Jones
where'er we be,
An' may you meet a mate as sweet as
Nancy Lee ;
Yeo-ho ! lads ho ! Yeo-ho !
The sailor's wife the sailor's star shall
be,
Yeo-ho ! we go across the sea ;
The sailor's wife the sailor's star shall
be,
The sailor's wife his star shall be.

A BIRD IN THE HAND

THERE were three young maids of Lee,
They were fair as fair can be,
And they had lovers three times three,
For they were fair as fair can be,
These three young maids of Lee.
But these young maids they cannot find
A lover each to suit her mind;
The plain-spoke lad is far too rough,
The rich young lord is not rich enough,
And one is too poor and one too tall,
And one just an inch too short for them all.
" Others pick and choose and why not we ? "
" We can very well wait," said the maids
of Lee.
There were three young maids of
Lee,
They were fair as fair can be,
And they had lovers three times three,
For they were fair as fair can be,
These three young maids of Lee.

There are three old maids of Lee,
And they are old as old can be,
And one is deaf, and one cannot see,
And they all are cross as a gallows tree,
These three old maids of Lee.
Now if any one chanced — 't is a chance
remote —
One single charm in these maids to note,
He need not a poet nor handsome be,
For one is deaf and one cannot see ;
He need not woo on his bended knee,
For they all are willing as willing can
be.

He may take the one, or the two, or the
three,
If he 'll only take them away from Lee.
There are three old maids at Lee,
They are cross as cross can be,
And there they are, and there they 'll be
To the end of the chapter one, two,
three,
These three old maids of Lee.

DOUGLAS GORDON

" Row me o'er the strait, Douglas Gordon,
Row me o'er the strait, my love," said she,
" Where we greeted in the summer, Doug-
las Gordon,
Beyond the little Kirk by the old, old
trysting tree."
Never a word spoke Douglas Gordon,
But he looked into her eyes so tenderly,
And he set her at his side,
And away across the tide
They floated to the little Kirk,
And the old, old trysting tree.

" Give me a word of love, Douglas Gordon,
Just a word of pity, O my love," said she,
" For the bells will ring to-morrow, Douglas
Gordon,
My wedding bells, my love, but not for
you and me.
They told me you were false, Douglas
Gordon,
And you never came to comfort me ! "
And she saw the great tears rise,
In her lover's silent eyes,
As they drifted to the little Kirk,
And the old, old, trysting tree.

" And it 's never, never, never, Douglas
Gordon,
Never in this world that you may come
to me,
But tell me that you love me, Douglas
Gordon,
And kiss me for the love of all that used
to be ! "
Then he flung away his sail, his oars and
rudder,
And he took her in his arms so tenderly,
And they drifted on amain,
And the bells may call in vain,
For she and Douglas Gordon
Are drowned in the sea.

DARBY AND JOAN

DARBY dear, we are old and gray,
Fifty years since our wedding day,
Shadow and sun for every one
As the years roll on ;
Darby dear, when the world went wry,
Hard and sorrowful then was I —
Ah ! lad, how you cheered me then,
Things will be better, sweet wife, again !
Always the same, Darby my own,
Always the same to your old wife Joan.

Darby, dear, but my heart was wild
When we buried our baby child,
Until you whispered " Heav'n knows best ! "
And my heart found rest ;

Darby, dear, 't was your loving hand
Showed the way to the better land —
Ah ! lad, as you kiss'd each tear,
Life grew better, and Heaven more near ⸰
Always the same, Darby my own,
Always the same to your old wife Joan.

Hand in hand when our life was May,
Hand in hand when our hair is gray,
Shadow and sun for every one,
As the years roll on ;
Hand in hand when the long night-tide
Gently covers us side by side —
Ah ! lad, though we know not when,
Love will be with us forever then :
Always the same, Darby, my own,
Always the same to your old wife Joan.

Catherine C. Liddell

(C. C. FRASER–TYTLER)

JESUS THE CARPENTER

" IS N'T this Joseph's son ? " — ay, it is He ;
Joseph the carpenter — same trade as me —
I thought as I'd find it — I knew it was
       here —
    But my sight's getting queer.

I don't know right where as His shed must
       ha' stood —
But often, as I've been a-planing my wood,
I've took off my hat, just with thinking of
       He
    At the same work as me.

He war n't that set up that He could n't
       stoop down
And work in the country for folks in the
       town ;
And I'll warrant He felt a bit pride, like
       I've done
    At a good job begun.

The parson he knows that I'll not make
       too free,
But on Sunday I feels as pleased as can be,
When I wears my clean smock, and sits in
       a pew,
    And has thoughts a few.

I think of as how not the parson hissen,
As is teacher and father and shepherd o'
       men,
Not he knows as much of the Lord in that
       shed,
    Where He earned His own bread.

And when I goes home to my missus, says
       she,
" Are ye wanting your key ? "
For she knows my queer ways, and my love
       for the shed,
    (We've been forty years wed.)

So I comes right away by mysen, with the
       book,
And I turns the old pages and has a good
       look
For the text as I've found, as tells me as
       He
    Were the same trade as me.

Why don't I mark it ? Ah, many says
       so,
But I think I'd as lief, with your leaves, let
       it go :
It do seem that nice when I fall on it
       sudden —
    Unexpected, you know !

THE POET IN THE CITY

THE Poet stood in the sombre town,
And spake to his heart, and said,
" O weary prison, devised by man !
O seasonless place, and dead ! "
His heart was sad, for afar he heard
The sound of the Spring's light tread.

He thought he saw in the pearly east
The pale March sun arise,
The happy housewife beneath the thatch,
With hand above her eyes,
Look out to the cawing rooks, that built
So near to the quiet skies.

Out of the smoke, and noise, and sin
The heart of the Poet cried :
" O God ! but to be Thy laborer there,
On the gentle hill's green side,
To leave. the struggle of want and
wealth,
And the battle of lust and pride ! "

He bent his ear, and he heard afar
The growing of tender things,

And his heart broke forth with the travail-
ing earth,
And shook with the tremulous wings
Of sweet brown birds, that had never known
The dirge of the city's sins.

And later, — when all the earth was green
As the Garden of the Lord,
Primroses opening their innocent face,
Cowslips scattered abroad,
Bluebells mimicking summer skies,
And the song of the thrush outpoured —

The changeless days were so sad to him,
That the Poet's heart beat strong,
And he struggled as some poor caged lark,
And he cried : " How long, how long ?
I have missed a spring I can never see,
And the singing of birds is gone ! "

But when the time of the roses came,
And the nightingale hushed her lay,
The Poet, still in the dusty town,
Went quietly on his way —
A poorer poet by just one Spring,
And a richer man by one suffering.

Edmund Gosse

LYING IN THE GRASS

BETWEEN two golden tufts of summer
grass,
I see the world through hot air as through
glass,
And by my face sweet lights and colors
pass.

Before me, dark against the fading sky,
I watch three mowers mowing, as I lie :
With brawny arms they sweep in harmony.

Brown English faces by the sun burnt red,
Rich glowing color on bare throat and
head,
My heart would leap to watch them, were
I dead !

And in my strong young living as I lie,
I seem to move with them in harmony, —
A fourth is mowing, and that fourth am I.

The music of the scythes that glide and
leap,
The young men whistling as their great
arms sweep,
And all the perfume and sweet sense of
sleep,

The weary butterflies that droop their
wings,
The dreamy nightingale that hardly sings,
And all the lassitude of happy things,

Are mingling with the warm and pulsing
blood
That gushes through my veins a languid
flood,
And feeds my spirit as the sap a bud.

Behind the mowers, on the amber air,
A dark-green beech wood rises, still and
fair,
A white path winding up it like a stair.

And see that girl, with pitcher on her head,
And clean white apron on her gown of
    red, —
Her even-song of love is but half-said :

She waits the youngest mower. Now he
    goes ;
Her cheeks are redder than a wild blush-
    rose :
They climb up where the deepest shadows
    close.

But though they pass, and vanish, I am
    there.
I watch his rough hands meet beneath her
    hair,
Their broken speech sounds sweet to me
    like prayer.

Ah ! now the rosy children come to play,
And romp and struggle with the new-mown
    hay;
Their clear high voices sound from far
    away.

They know so little why the world is sad,
They dig themselves warm graves and yet
    are glad ;
Their muffled screams and laughter make
    me mad !

I long to go and play among them there ;
Unseen, like wind, to take them by the hair,
And gently make their rosy cheeks more
    fair.

The happy children ! full of frank surprise,
And sudden whims and innocent ecstasies ;
What godhead sparkles from their liquid
    eyes !

No wonder round those urns of mingled
    clays
That Tuscan potters fashioned in old days,
And colored like the torrid earth ablaze,

We find the little gods and loves portrayed,
Through ancient forests wandering undis-
    mayed,
And fluting hymns of pleasure unafraid.

They knew, as I do now, what keen delight
A strong man feels to watch the tender
    flight
Of little children playing in his sight ;

What pure sweet pleasure, and what sacred
    love,
Come drifting down upon us from above,
In watching how their limbs and features
    move.

I do not hunger for a well-stored mind ;
I only wish to live my life, and find
My heart in unison with all mankind.

My life is like the single dewy star
That trembles on the horizon's primrose-
    bar, —
A microcosm where all things living are.

And if, among the noiseless grasses, Death
Should come behind and take away my
    breath,
I should not rise as one who sorroweth ;

For I should pass, but all the world would
    be
Full of desire and young delight and glee,
And why should men be sad through loss
    of me ?

The light is flying ; in the silver-blue
The young moon shines from her bright
    window through :
The mowers are all gone, and I go too.

ON A LUTE FOUND IN A SARCOPHAGUS

WHAT curled and scented sun-girls, al-
    mond-eyed,
With lotos-blossoms in their hands and hair,
Have made their swarthy lovers call them
    fair,
With these spent strings, when brutes were
    deified,
And Memnon in the sunrise sprang and
    cried,
And love-winds smote Bubastis, and the
    bare
Black breasts of carven Pasht received the
    prayer
Of suppliants bearing gifts from far and
    wide !
This lute has out-sung Egypt ; all the lives
Of violent passion, and the vast calm art
That lasts in granite only, all lie dead ;
This little bird of song alone survives,
As fresh as when its fluting smote the heart
Last time the brown slave wore it garlanded.

THE PIPE-PLAYER

COOL, and palm-shaded from the torrid
heat,
The young brown tenor puts his singing by,
And sets the twin pipe to his lips to try
Some air of bulrush-glooms where lovers
meet ;
O swart musician, time and fame are fleet,
Brief all delight, and youth's feet fain to
fly !
Pipe on in peace ! To-morrow must we
die ?
What matter, if our life to-day be sweet !
Soon, soon, the silver paper-reeds that sigh
Along the Sacred River will repeat
The echo of the dark-stoled bearers' feet,
Who carry you, with wailing, where must
lie
Your swarthed and withered body, by and
by
In perfumed darkness with the grains of
wheat.

HANS CHRISTIAN ANDERSEN

1805–1875

A BEING cleaves the moonlit air,
With eyes of dew and plumes of fire,
New-born, immortal, strong and fair ;
Glance ere he goes !
His feet are shrouded like the dead,
But in his face a wild desire
Breaks like the dawn that flushes red,
And like a rose.

The stars shine out above his path,
And music wakes through all the skies ;
What mortal such a triumph hath,
By death set free ?
What earthly hands and heart are pure
As this man's, whose unshrinking eyes
Gaze onward through the deep obscure,
Nor quail to see ?

Ah ! this was he who drank the fount
Of wisdom set in speechless things,
Who, patient, watched the day-star mount,
While others slept.
Ah ! this was he whose loving soul
Found   heart-beats   under   trembling
wings,
And heard divinest music roll
Where wild springs leapt.

For poor dumb lips had songs for him
And children's dreamings ran in tune,
And strange old heroes, weird and dim,
Walked by his side.
The very shadows loved him well
And danced and flickered in the moon,
And left him wondrous tales to tell
Men far and wide.

And now no more he smiling walks
Through greenwood alleys full of sun,
And, as he wanders, turns and talks,
Though none be there ;
The children watch in vain the place
Where they were wont, when day was
done,
To see their poet's sweet worn face,
And faded hair.

Yet dream not such a spirit dies,
Though all its earthly shrine decay !
Transfigured under clearer skies,
He sings anew;
The frail soul-covering, racked with pain,
And scored with vigil, fades away,
The soul set free and young again
Glides upward through.

Weep not ; but watch the moonlit air !
Perchance a glory like a star
May leave what hangs about him there,
And flash on us ! . . .
Behold ! the void is full of light,
The beams pierce heaven from bar to bar,
And all the hollows of the night
Grow luminous !

DE ROSIS HIBERNIS

AMBITIOUS Nile, thy banks deplore
Their Flavian patron's deep decay ;
Thy Memphian pilot laughs no more
To see the flower-boat float away ;
Thy winter-roses once were twined
Across the gala-streets of Rome,
And thou, like Omphale, couldst bind
The vanquished victor in his home.

But if the barge that brought thy store
Had foundered in the Lybian deep,
It had not slain thy glory more,
Nor plunged thy rose in salter sleep ;
Nor gods nor Cæsars wait thee now,
No jealous Pæstum dreads thy spring,

Thy flower enfolds no augur's brow,
　Nor gives thy poet strength to sing.

Yet, surely, when the winds are low,
　And heaven is all alive with stars,
Thy conscious roses still must glow
　Above thy dreaming nenuphars ;
They recollect their high estate,
　The Roman honors they have known,
And while they ponder Cæsar's fate
　They cease to marvel at their own.

THEOCRITUS

THE poplars and the ancient elms
　Make murmurous noises high in air ;
The noon-day sunlight overwhelms
　The brown cicalas basking there ;
But here the shade is deep, and sweet
　With new-mown grass and lentisk-shoots,
And far away the shepherds meet
　With noisy fifes and flutes.

Their clamor dies upon the ear ;
　So now bring forth the rolls of song,
Mouth the rich cadences, nor fear
　Your voice may do the poet wrong ;
Lift up the chalice to our lips, —
　Yet see, before we venture thus,
A stream of red libation drips
　To great Theocritus.

We are in Sicily to-day ;
　And, as the honeyed metre flows,
Battos and Corydon, at play,
　Will lose the syrinx, gain the rose ;
Soft Amaryllis, too, will bind
　Dark violets round her shining hair,
And in the fountain laugh to find
　Her sun-browned face so fair.

We are in Sicily to-day ;
　Ah ! foolish world, too sadly wise,
Why didst thou e'er let fade away
　Those ancient, innocent ecstasies ?
Along the glens, in checkered flight,
　Hither to-day the nymphs shall flee,
And Pan forsake for our delight
　The tomb of Helice.

WITH A COPY OF HERRICK

FRESH with all airs of woodland brooks
　And scents of showers,

Take to your haunt of holy books
　This saint of flowers.

When meadows burn with budding May,
　And heaven is blue,
Before his shrine our prayers we say, —
　Saint Robin true.

Love crowned with thorns is on his staff, —
　Thorns of sweet briar ;
His benediction is a laugh,
　Birds are his choir.

His sacred robe of white and red
　Unction distils ;
He hath a nimbus round his head
　Of daffodils.

THE VOICE OF D. G. R.

FROM this carved chair wherein I sit to-
　night,
The dead man read in accents deep and
　strong,
Through lips that were like Chaucer's, his
　great song
About the Beryl and its virgin light ;
And still that music lives in death's despite,
And though my pilgrimage on earth be
　long,
Time cannot do my memory so much wrong
As e'er to make that gracious voice take
　flight.
I sit here with closed eyes ; the sound
　comes back,
With youth, and hope, and glory on its
　track,
A solemn organ-music of the mind ;
So, when the oracular moon brings back
　the tide,
After long drought, the sandy channel wide
Murmurs with waves, and sings beneath
　the wind.

SONG FOR MUSIC

COUNT the flashes in the surf,
　Count the crystals in the snow,
Or the blades above the turf,
　Or the dead that sleep below !
These ye count — yet shall not know, —
While I wake or while I slumber, —
　Where my thoughts and wishes go,
What her name, and what their number.

Ask the cold and midnight sea,
Ask the silent-falling frost,
Ask the grasses on the lea,
Or the mad maid, passion-crost!

They may tell of posies tost
To the waves where blossoms blow not,
Tell of hearts that staked and lost, —
But of me and mine they know not.

Théophile Marzials

A PASTORAL

FLOWER of the medlar,
Crimson of the quince,
I saw her at the blossom-time,
And loved her ever since!
She swept the draughty pleasance,
The blooms had left the trees,
The whilst the birds sang canticles,
In cherry symphonies.

Whiteness of the white rose,
Redness of the red,
She went to cut the blush-rose buds
To tie at the altar-head ;
And some she laid in her bosom,
And some around her brows,
And, as she passed, the lily-heads
All becked and made their bows.

Scarlet of the poppy,
Yellow of the corn,
The men were at the garnering,
A-shouting in the morn ;
I chased her to a pippin-tree, —
The waking birds all whist, —
And oh! it was the sweetest kiss
That I have ever kiss'd.

Marjorie, mint, and violets
A-drying round us set,
'T was all done in the faïence-room
A-spicing marmalet ;
On one tile was a satyr,
On one a nymph at bay,
Methinks the birds will scarce be home
To wake our wedding-day!

TWICKENHAM FERRY

" AHOY ! and O-ho ! and it 's who 's for
the ferry ? "
(The briar 's in bud and the sun going
down)

" And I 'll row ye so quick and I 'll row ye
so steady,
And 't is but a penny to Twickenham
Town."
The ferryman 's slim and the ferryman 's
young,
With just a soft tang in the turn of his
tongue ;
And he 's fresh as a pippin and brown as a
berry,
And 't is but a penny to Twickenham
Town.

" Ahoy ! and O-ho ! and it 's I 'm for the
ferry,"
(The briar 's in bud and the sun going
down)
" And it 's late as it is and I have n't a
penny —
Oh! how can I get me to Twickenham
Town ? "
She 'd a rose in her bonnet, and oh! she
look'd sweet
As the little pink flower that grows in
the wheat,
With her cheeks like a rose and her lips
like a cherry —
" It 's sure but you 're welcome to
Twickenham Town."

" Ahoy ! and O-ho ! " — You 're too late
for the ferry,
(The briar 's in bud and the sun has
gone down)
And he 's not rowing quick and he 's not
rowing steady ;
It seems quite a journey to Twicken-
ham Town.
" Ahoy ! and O-ho ! " you may call as
you will ;
The young moon is rising o'er Petersham
Hill ;
And, with Love like a rose in the stern of
the wherry,
There 's danger in crossing to Twick-
enham Town.

MAY MARGARET

IF you be that May Margaret
   That lived on Kendal Green,
Then where 's that sunny hair of yours
   That crowned you like a queen?
That sunny hair is dim, lad,
   They said was like a crown —
The red gold turned to gray, lad,
   The night a ship went down.

If you be yet May Margaret,
   May Margaret now as then,
Then where 's that bonny smile of yours
   That broke the hearts of men?
The bonny smile is wan, lad,
   That once was glad as day —
And oh! 't is weary smiling
   To keep the tears away.

If you be yet May Margaret,
   As yet you swear to me,
Then where 's that proud, cold heart of
     yours
   That sent your love to sea?
Ah! me, that heart is broken,
   The proud cold heart has bled
For one light word outspoken,
   For all the love unsaid.

Then Margaret, my Margaret,
   If all you say be true,
Your hair is yet the sunniest gold,
   Your eyes the sweetest blue.
And dearer yet and fairer yet
   For all the coming years —
The fairer for the waiting,
   The dearer for the tears!

LAST NIGHT

(FROM THE SWEDISH)

LAST night the nightingale waked me,
   Last night when all was still;
It sang in the golden moonlight
   From out the woodland hill.
I opened the window gently,
   And all was dreamy dew —
And oh! the bird, my darling,
   Was singing, singing of you!

I think of you in the day-time;
   I dream of you by night —
I wake — would you were near me
   And hot tears blind my sight.
I hear a sigh in the lime-tree,
   The wind is floating through,
And oh! the night, my darling,
   Is longing, longing for you.

Nor think I can forget you!
   I could not though I would!
I see you in all around me, —
   The stream, the night, the wood;
The flowers that sleep so gently,
   The stars above the blue,
Oh! heaven itself, my darling,
   Is praying, praying for you.

CARPE DIEM

TO-DAY, what is there in the air
That makes December seem sweet May?
   There are no swallows anywhere,
   Nor crocuses to crown your hair,
And hail you down my garden way.

Last night the full moon's frozen stare
   Struck me, perhaps; or did you say
Really,—you 'd come, sweet friend and fair!
       To-day?

To-day is here: — come! crown to-day
   With Spring's delight or Spring's despair,
Love cannot bide old Time's delay: —
Down my glad gardens light winds play,
   And my whole life shall bloom and bear
       To-day.

Walter Herries Pollock

BELOW THE HEIGHTS

I SAT at Berne, and watched the chain
   Of icy peaks and passes,
That towered like gods above the plain,
   In stern majestic masses.

I waited till the evening light
   Upon their heads descended;
They caught it on their glittering height,
   And held it there suspended.

I saw the red spread o'er the white,
   How like a maiden's blushing,

Till all were hid in rosy light
That seemed from heaven rushing ;

The dead white snow was flushed with life,
As if a new Pygmalion
Had sought to find himself a wife
In stones that saw Deucalion.

Too soon the light began to wane ;
It lingered soft and tender,
And the snow-giants sank again
Into their cold dead splendor.

And, as I watched the last faint glow,
I turned as pale as they did,
And sighed to think that on the snow
The rose so quickly faded.

A CONQUEST

I found him openly wearing her token ;
I knew that her troth could never be broken ;
I laid my hand on the hilt of my sword, —
He did the same, and he spoke no word ;
I faced him with his villainy ;
He laughed, and said, " She gave it me."
We searched for seconds, they soon were found ;
They measured our swords ; they measured the ground ;
They held to the deadly work too fast ;
They thought to gain our place at last.
We fought in the sheen of a wintry wood ;
The fair white snow was red with his blood ;
But his was the victory, for, as he died,
He swore by the rood that he had not lied.

FATHER FRANCIS

"I come your sin-rid souls to shrive ;
Is this the way wherein ye live ? "

We lightly think of virtue,
Enjoyment cannot hurt you.

" Ye love. Hear then of chivalry,
Of gallant truth and constancy."
We find new loves the meetest,
And stolen kisses sweetest.

" Voices ye have. Then should ye sing
In praise of heaven's mighty king."
We deem it is our duty
To chant our darlings' beauty.

" Strait are the gates of worldly pleasure ;
The joy beyond no soul can measure."
Alas ! we are but mortal,
And much prefer the portal.

" Nay, sons : then must I leave ye so ;
But lost will be your souls, I trow."
Nay, Father, make you merry ;
Come, drawer, bring some sherry.

" Me drink ? Old birds are not unwary —
Still less — Ha — well — 't is fine canary."
Mark how his old blood prances —
A stoup for Father Francis !

" Your wine, my sons, is wondrous good,
And hath been long time in the wood."
Mark how his old eye dances —
More wine for Father Francis !

" A man, my sons — a man, I say,
Might well drink here till judgment-day."
Now for soft words and glances —
But where is Father Francis ?

" Heed me, my sons, I pray, no more ;
I always sleep upon the floor."
Alas ! for old wine's chances ;
A shutter for Father Francis !

𝔐ichael 𝔉ield

FROM CANUTE THE GREAT "

Scene. — A room on the northern bank of the Thames.
Enter Canute.

Canute. She dared not wait my coming, and shall look

No more upon my face. — A vacancy,
A blank ! that scarf left trailing on the floor,
A shred too of her robe, — I must have trampled,
Have hurt her, as I thrust her off. A shred,

A tag, and is it thus that women suffer ?
We can inflict so little on such natures ;
We cannot make reprisals. Slavish tears
For Edric, and, — O Hel ! — a bloody
    gleam
Across her eyes, when I proclaimed the
    rights
Of Edmund's children. I am cut adrift,
Far, far from the great, civilizing God, —
Dull, speechless, unappraised.
[*A voice singing.*] Is that a child
At babble with his vespers ?—Silver sweet !
It minds me of the holy brotherhood,
Chanting adown the banks. As yesterday
I see all clear, how as they moved they
    chanted,
And made a mute procession in the stream.
            [*Gazing abstractedly on the water.*]

Merrily sang the monks of Ely,
As Canute the king passed by.
Row to the shore, knights, said the king,
And let us hear the Churchmen sing.

Still are they singing ? It was Candlemas,
My queen sat splendid at the prow and lis-
    tened
With heaving breast. 'T was then the
    passion seized me
To emulate, to let her know my ear
Had common pleasure with her, and I
    thrilled
The story out. The look she turned on
    me !
The choir shall sing this music. I resolved
In the glory of the verse to civilize
My blood, to sweeten it, to give it law,
To curb my wild thoughts with the rein of
    metre.
Row to the shore! So pleasantly it ran,
A ripple on the wave. I grew ambitious
To be a scholar like King Alfred, gather
Wise men about me, in myself possess
A treasure, an enchantment. For an
    instant
I looked round royally, and felt a king.
The abbey-chant, the stream, the meadow-
    land,
The willows glimmering in the sun ; — a
    poet
Wins things to come so close. A plash, a
    gurgle !
There 's a black memory for the river
    now ;
And hark ! strange, solemn, Latin words
    that toll,

And move on slowly to me . . . Up the
    stair.
Without the door. A wail, a litany !
        Enter Child *singing.*
  Child.   Miserere mei, Deus, secundam
    magnam misericordiam tuam ;
Et   secundum   multitudinem   miserationum
    tuarum, dele iniquitatem meam.
  Can. How perfectly he sings the
    music ! Child,
Who art thou with that voice, those dying
    cheeks ?
Art thou an angel sent to wring my heart,
Or is it mortal woe ? Thine arms are
    full.
  Child. Green, country herbs, they say,
    will staunch a wound,
And I have run about the fields and
    gathered
Those I could catch up quickly : — for the
    blood
Was leaping all the while. But here is
    clary,
The blessèd thistle, yarrow, sicklewort,
And all-heal red as gore. I knew a wood
So dark and cool, I crept for lily-leaves ;
Then it grew lonely, and I lost the way.
But, oh, you must not beat me ; it is done.
Father, I stabbed him, throw away the
    whip !
Now God will scourge me. So I plucked
    the flowers,
And sang for mercy in the holy words
Priest Sampson taught me, *Miserere !*
  Can.   This
Is Edric's child, the little murderer,
Who did my deed of treason. Edmund,
    turn
Those trustful eyes from off me.
  Child.   Take me back.
He will be dead . . . He fell, O father,
    fell,
And when I put my cheek against his side,
Gave a great pant. Let 's pray for him
    together.
Can you sing *Miserere ?* For I did it,
And then he looked . . . Once in the ivy-
    tod
I caught an owl, and hurt its wing. 'T was
    so
He looked. Oh, quickly tell me where he
    lies —
Next room ? or down the passage? Do
    you know
He was my uncle, and was kissing me,

One, two, three, on my head.
 Can.   Cease! From these lips,
White, childish penitents, how awful
 sounds
The wild avowal of their treachery.
Child, it was I who struck your uncle's
 side,
Who falsely kissed him; it was I who set
Your father on this wickedness; 't was I
Who drove your frantic innocence to work
The sin of my conception. Can you learn
That I alone am guilty, and God's wrath
Will visit me with judgment?
 Child.   Come along,
And take me where he is. How can I go?
I do not know the path or time of day.
The leaves are fading. Can the blood
 flow long
Before it kills? I saw it spirt and jump;
I could not see it now. I ran and ran . . .
Perchance I stayed too long about the fields.
'T is dark; no trees and hedges. He is gone,
And I am damned forever; the fresh herbs
Could once have saved me.
 Can. He is chill and fainting;
Give me these hands.
 Child. I am not much afraid.
Before I struck at him my skin was hot;
Now dew is falling on me; it is cool.
Let me lie in your arms where I can look
Up at the sky. There's some one . . . and
 he grows
So kindly. Oh, he smiles down all the way,
Quite golden in my eyes.
 Can.   He sees the moon.
How pale and cold he's growing! All the
 flowers
Are slipping down. I cannot bear his
 weight.
'T is condemnation. There is just a spot
Here on his garment, one bright drop of
 blood,
Sprinkling his spirit; he is saved; on him
It is the very mark of Christ; on me
The blot that makes illegible my name
I' the book of life.
 Child. If I should fall asleep,
It will not matter, for I could not see
The healing plants by night; besides, my
 eyes
Will open wide at morning. I must hold
The blessèd thistle in my hand, and pray;
And God may so forgive me. *Miserere!*
 Can. The child is dying on my breast.
He closes

His frightened eyes; the notes are on his
 lips,
His arm still round my shoulder.
 . . . . .
        Sharply flows
The Thames now he is dead; the rush, the
 hum,
Are like a conscience haunting me without.
I cannot bear it. I will fling him forth
To the engulfing river, and forget him.
Rank, pagan impulse! I would learn the
 prayer,
Recall the gracious song, — and stormy
 sagas
Come hurtling through my brain. I am a
 stranger
To our sweet Saviour Christ; I cannot pray;
I love the slaughter of my enemies,
And to exact full vengeance. Little one,
Thou shalt have fair, white cere-cloth, and
 a circlet
Of purest gold. Now that I look on thee,
It grows soft in my heart as when they
 chanted
Across the stream, — *Canute the king passed
 by,* —
And listened. They shall sing about thy
 grave.
[*He bows himself over the child and weeps.*]

THE BURIAL OF ROBERT BROWNING

Upon St. Michael's Isle
 They laid him for awhile
That he might feel the Ocean's full em-
 brace,
  And wedded be
  To that wide sea —
The subject and the passion of his race.
 As Thetis, from some lovely under-
 ground
 Springing, she girds him round
  With lapping sound
  And silent space:
Then, on more honor bent,
 She sues the firmament,
And bids the hovering, western clouds com-
 bine
To spread their sabled amber on her lus-
 trous brine.

  It might not be
  He should lie free

Forever in the soft light of the sea,
For lo ! one came,
Of step more slow than fame,
Stooped over him — we heard her breathe
    his name —
And, as the light drew back,
Bore him across the track
Of the subservient waves that dare not
    foil
That veiled, maternal figure of its
    spoil.

Ah ! where will she put by
Her journeying majesty ?
She hath left the lands of the air and sun ;
She will take no rest till her course be run.
Follow her far, follow her fast,
    Until at last,
Within a narrow transept led,
Lo ! she unwraps her face to pall her
    dead.

'T is England who has travelled far,
England who brings
Fresh splendor to her galaxy of
    Kings.
We kiss her feet, her hands,
Where eloquent she stands ;
Nor dare to lead
A wailful choir about the poet dumb
Who is become
Part of the glory that her sons would bleed
To save from scar ;
Yea, hers in very deed
    As Runnymede,
    Or Trafalgar.

WIND OF SUMMER

O WIND, thou hast thy kingdom in the trees,
    And all thy royalties
Sweep through the land to-day.
    It is mid June,
And thou, with all thine instruments in tune,
    Thine orchestra
Of heaving fields, and heavy, swinging fir,
    Strikest a lay
    That doth rehearse
Her ancient freedom to the universe.
    All other sound in awe
    Repeals its law ;
The bird is mute, the sea
Sucks up its waves, from rain
The burthened clouds refrain,

To listen to thee in thy leafery,
    Thou unconfined,
Lavish, large, soothing, refluent summer-
    wind.

THE DANCERS

I DANCE and dance ! Another faun,
A black one, dances on the lawn.
He moves with me, and when I lift
My heels his feet directly shift :
I can't outdance him though I try ;
He dances nimbler than I.
I toss my head, and so does he ;
What tricks he dares to play on me !
I touch the ivy in my hair ;
Ivy he has and finger there.
The spiteful thing to mock me so !
I will outdance him ! Ho, ho, ho !

LETTICE

LITTLE Lettice is dead, they say,
The brown, sweet child who rolled in the
    hay ;
    Ah, where shall we find her ?
    For the neighbors pass
    To the pretty lass,
In a linen cere-cloth to wind her.

If her sister were set to search
The nettle-green nook beside the church,
    And the way were shown her
    Through the coffin-gate
    To her dead playmate,
She would fly too frightened to own her.

Should she come at a noonday call,
Ah, stealthy, stealthy, with no footfall,
    And no laughing chatter,
    To her mother 't were worse
    Than a barren curse
That her own little wench should pat her.

Little Lettice is dead and gone !
The stream by her garden wanders on
    Through the rushes wider ;
    She fretted to know
    How its bright drops grow
On the hills, but no hand would guide her.

Little Lettice is dead and lost !
Her willow-tree boughs by storm are tost —

Oh, the swimming sallows ! —
Where she crouched to find
The nest of the wind
Like a water-fowl's in the shallows.

Little Lettice is out of sight !
The river-bed and the breeze are bright :
  Ay me, were it sinning
  To dream that she knows
  Where the soft wind rose
That her willow-branches is thinning ?

Little Lettice has lost her name,
Slipt away from our praise and our blame ;
  Let not love pursue her,
  But conceive her free
  Where the bright drops be
On the hills, and no longer rue her !

EARTH TO EARTH

I STOOD to hear that bold
Sentence of grit and mould,
  Earth to earth ; they thrust
  On his coffin dust ;
Stones struck against his grave :
Oh, the old days, the brave !

Just with a pebble's fall,
Grave-digger, you turn all
  Bliss to bereaving ;
  To catch the cleaving
Of Atropa's fine shears
Would less hurt human ears.

Live senses that death dooms !
For friendship in dear rooms,
  Slow-lighting faces,
  Hand-clasps, embraces,
Ashes on ashes grind :
Oh, poor lips left behind !

AN ÆOLIAN HARP

DOST thou not hear ? Amid dun, lonely
    hills
Far off a melancholy music shrills,
As for a joy that no fruition fills.

Who live in that far country of the wind ?
The unclaimed hopes, the powers but half-
    divined,
The shy, heroic passions of mankind.

And all are young in those reverberant
    bands ;
None marshals them, no mellow voice com-
    mands ;
They whirl and eddy as the shifting sands.

There, there is ruin, and no ivy clings ;
There pass the mourners for untimely
    things,
There breaks the stricken cry of crownless
    kings.

But ever and anon there spreads a boom
Of wonder through the air, arraigning
    doom
With ineffectual plaint as from a tomb.

IRIS

THE Iris was yellow, the moon was pale,
  In the air it was stiller than snow,
There was even light through the vale,
    But a vaporous sheet
    Clung about my feet,
  And I dared no further go.
I had passed the pond, I could see the
    stile,
The path was plain for more than a mile,
  Yet I dared no further go.

The iris-beds shone in my face, when,
    whist !
A noiseless music began to blow,
A music that moved through the mist,
    That had not begun,
    Would never be done, —
  With that music I must go :
And I found myself in the heart of the
    tune,
Wheeling around to the whirr of the moon,
  With the sheets of the mist below.

In my hands how warm were the little
    hands,
  Strange, little hands that I did not
    know :
I did not think of the elvan bands,
    Nor of anything
    In that whirling ring —
  Here a cock began to crow !
The little hands dropped that had clung so
    tight,
And I saw again by the pale dawnlight
  The iris-heads in a row.

Mathilde Blind

FROM "A LOVE-TRILOGY"

I CHARGE you, O winds of the West, O
  winds with the wings of the dove,
That ye blow o'er the brows of my Love,
  breathing low that I sicken for love.

I charge you, O dews of the Dawn, O tears
  of the star of the morn,
That ye fall at the feet of my love with the
  sound of one weeping forlorn.

I charge you, O birds of the Air, O birds
  flying home to your nest,
That ye sing in his ears of the joy that
  forever has fled from my breast.

I charge you, O flowers of the Earth, O
  frailest of things, and most fair,
That ye droop in his path as the life in me
  shrivels consumed by despair.

O Moon, when he lifts up his face, when
  he seeth the waning of thee,
A memory of her who lies wan on the
  limits of life let it be.

Many tears cannot quench, nor my sighs
  extinguish, the flames of love's fire,
Which lifteth my heart like a wave, and
  smites it, and breaks its desire.

I rise like one in a dream when I see the
  red sun flaring low,
That drags me back shuddering from sleep
  each morning to life with its woe.

I go like one in a dream ; unbidden my feet
  know the way
To that garden where love stood in blossom
  with the red and white hawthorn of
  May.

The song of the throstle is hushed, and the
  fountain is dry to its core,
The moon cometh up as of old ; she seeks,
  but she finds him no more.

The pale-faced, pitiful moon shines down
  on the grass where I weep,
My face to the earth, and my breast in an
  anguish ne'er soothed into sleep.

The moon returns, and the spring, birds
  warble, trees burst into leaf,
But love once gone, goes forever, and all
  that endures is the grief.

THE DEAD

THE dead abide with us ! Though stark
  and cold
Earth seems to grip them, they are with us
  still :
They have forged our chains of being for
  good or ill ;
And their invisible hands these hands yet
  hold.
Our perishable bodies are the mould
In which their strong imperishable will —
Mortality's deep yearning to fulfil —
Hath grown incorporate through dim time
  untold.
Vibrations infinite of life in death,
As a star's travelling light survives its star !
So may we hold our lives, that when we are
The fate of those who then will draw this
  breath,
They shall not drag us to their judgment-
  bar,
And curse the heritage which we bequeath.

FROM "LOVE IN EXILE"

I

WHY will you haunt me unawares,
  And walk into my sleep,
Pacing its shadowy thoroughfares,
  Where long-dried perfume scents the airs,
    While ghosts of sorrow creep,
Where on Hope's ruined altar-stairs,
  With ineffectual beams,
The Moon of Memory coldly glares
  Upon the land of dreams ?

My yearning eyes were fain to look
  Upon your hidden face ;
Their love, alas ! you could not brook,
But in your own you mutely took
  My hand, and for a space
You wrung it till I throbbed and shook,
  And woke with wildest moan
And wet face channelled like a brook
  With your tears or my own.

2

We met as strangers on life's lonely way,
And yet it seemed we knew each other
well ;
There was no end to what thou hadst to
say,
Or to the thousand things I found to
tell.
My heart, long silent, at thy voice that day
Chimed in my breast like to a silver
bell.

How much we spoke, and yet still left
untold
Some secret half revealed within our
eyes :

Didst thou not love me once in ages old ?
Had I not called thee with importunate
cries,
And, like a child left sobbing in the cold,
Listened to catch from far thy fond re-
plies ?

We met as strangers, and as such we part ;
Yet all my life seems leaving me with
thine ;
Ah, to be clasped once only heart to heart,
If only once to feel that thou wert mine !
These lips are locked, and yet I know thou
art
That all in all for which my soul did
pine.

Robert Louis Stevenson

PIRATE STORY

THREE of us afloat in the meadow by the
swing,
Three of us aboard in the basket on the
lea.
Winds are in the air, they are blowing in
the spring,
And waves are on the meadow like the
waves there are at sea.

Where shall we adventure, to-day that
we 're afloat,
Wary of the weather and steering by a
star ?
Shall it be to Africa, a-steering of the boat,
To Providence, or Babylon, or off to
Malabar ?

Hi ! but here 's a squadron a-rowing on
the sea —
Cattle on the meadow a-charging with a
roar !
Quick, and we 'll escape them, they 're as
mad as they can be,
The wicket is the harbor and the garden
is the shore.

FOREIGN LANDS

UP into the cherry tree
Who should climb but little me ?
I held the trunk with both my hands
And looked abroad on foreign lands.

I saw the next-door garden lie,
Adorned with flowers, before my eye,
And many pleasant faces more
That I had never seen before.

I saw the dimpling river pass
And be the sky's blue looking-glass ;
The dusty roads go up and down
With people tramping in to town.

If I could find a higher tree
Farther and farther I should see,
To where the grown-up river slips
Into the sea among the ships,

To where the roads on either hand
Lead onward into fairy land,
Where all the children dine at five,
And all the playthings come alive.

THE LAND OF COUNTERPANE

WHEN I was sick and lay a-bed,
I had two pillows at my head,
And all my toys beside me lay
To keep me happy all the day.

And sometimes for an hour or so
I watched my leaden soldiers go,
With different uniforms and drills,
Among the bed-clothes, through the hills ;

And sometimes sent my ships in fleets
All up and down among the sheets ;

Or brought my trees and houses out,
And planted cities all about.

I was the giant great and still
That sits upon the pillow-hill,
And sees before him, dale and plain,
The pleasant land of counterpane.

THE LAND OF NOD

FROM breakfast on through all the day
At home among my friends I stay,
But every night I go abroad
Afar into the land of Nod.

All by myself I have to go,
With none to tell me what to do —
All alone beside the streams
And up the mountain-sides of dreams.

The strangest things are there for me,
Both things to eat and things to see,
And many frightening sights abroad
Till morning in the land of Nod.

Try as I like to find the way,
I never can get back by day,
Nor can remember plain and clear
The curious music that I hear.

IN THE SEASON

IT is the season now to go
About the country high and low,
Among the lilacs hand in hand,
And two by two in fairy land.

The brooding boy, the sighing maid,
Wholly fain and half afraid,
Now meet along the hazelled brook
To pass and linger, pause and look.

A year ago, and blithely paired,
Their rough-and-tumble play they shared;
They kissed and quarrelled, laughed and
    cried,
A year ago at Eastertide.

With bursting heart, with fiery face,
She strove against him in the race ;
He unabashed her garter saw,
That now would touch her skirts with awe.

Now by the stile ablaze she stops,
And his demurer eyes he drops ;

Now they exchange averted sighs
Or stand and marry silent eyes.

And he to her a hero is
And sweeter she than primroses ;
Their common silence dearer far
Than nightingale and mavis are.

Now when they sever wedded hands,
Joy trembles in their bosom-strands,
And lovely laughter leaps and falls
Upon their lips in madrigals.

TO N. V. DE G. S.

THE unfathomable sea, and time, and tears,
The deeds of heroes and the crimes of
    kings
Dispart us ; and the river of events
Has, for an age of years, to east and west
More widely borne our cradles. Thou to
    me
Art foreign, as when seamen at the dawn
Descry a land far off and know not which.
So I approach uncertain ; so I cruise
Round thy mysterious islet, and behold
Surf and great mountains and loud river-
    bars,
And from the shore hear inland voices call.
Strange is the seaman's heart ; he hopes,
    he fears ;
Draws closer and sweeps wider from that
    coast ;
Last, his rent sail refits, and to the deep
His shattered prow uncomforted puts back.
Yet as he goes he ponders at the helm
Of that bright island ; where he feared to
    touch,
His spirit readventures ; and for years,
Where by his wife he slumbers safe at
    home,
Thoughts of that land revisit him ; he sees
The eternal mountains beckon, and awakes
Yearning for that far home that might
    have been.

IN THE STATES

WITH half a heart I wander here
    As from an age gone by,
A brother — yet though young in years,
    An elder brother, I.

You speak another tongue than mine,
    Though both were English born.

I towards the night of time decline,
  You mount into the morn.

Youth shall grow great and strong and
    free,
  But age must still decay :
To-morrow for the States — for me,
  England and Yesterday.

THE SPAEWIFE

OH, I wad like to ken — to the beggar-wife
    says I —
Why chops are guid to brander and nane
    sae guid to fry.
An' siller, that's sae braw to keep, is
    brawer still to gi'e.
It's gey an' easy spierin', says the beggar-
    wife to me.

Oh, I wad like to ken — to the beggar-wife
    says I —
Hoo a' things come to be whaur we find
    them when we try,
The lasses in their claes an' the fishes in
    the sea.
It's gey an' easy spierin', says the beggar-
    wife to me.

Oh, I wad like to ken — to the beggar-wife
    says I —
Why lads are a' to sell an' lasses a' to buy ;
An' naebody for dacency but barely twa or
    three.
It's gey an' easy spierin', says the beggar-
    wife to me.

Oh, I wad like to ken — to the beggar-wife
    says I —
Gin death's as shüre to men as killin' is to
    kye,
Why God has filled the yearth sae fu' o'
    tasty things to pree.
It's gey an' easy spierin', says the beggar-
    wife to me.

Oh, I wad like to ken — to the beggar-wife
    says I —
The reason o' the cause an' the wherefore
    o' the why,
Wi' mony anither riddle brings the tear
    into my e'e.
It's gey an' easy spierin', says the beggar-
    wife to me.

HEATHER ALE : A GALLOWAY
LEGEND

FROM the bonny bells of heather
  They brewed a drink long-syne,
Was sweeter far than honey,
  Was stronger far than wine.
They brewed it and they drank it,
  And lay in a blessed swound
For days and days together
  In their dwellings underground.

There rose a king in Scotland,
  A fell man to his foes,
He smote the Picts in battle,
  He hunted them like roes.
Over miles of the red mountain
  He hunted as they fled,
And strewed the dwarfish bodies
  Of the dying and the dead.

Summer came in the country,
  Red was the heather bell ;
But the manner of the brewing
  Was none alive to tell.
In graves that were like children's
  On many a mountain head,
The Brewsters of the Heather
  Lay numbered with the dead.

The king in the red moorland
  Rode on a summer's day ;
And the bees hummed, and the curlews
  Cried beside the way.
The king rode, and was angry ;
  Black was his brow and pale,
To rule in a land of heather
  And lack the Heather Ale.

It fortuned that his vassals,
  Riding free on the heath,
Came on a stone that was fallen
  And vermin hid beneath.
Rudely plucked from their hiding,
  Never a word they spoke :
A son and his aged father —
  Last of the dwarfish folk.

The king sat high on his charger,
  He looked on the little men ;
And the dwarfish and swarthy couple
  Looked at the king again.
Down by the shore he had them ;
  And there on the giddy brink —

"I will give you life, ye vermin,
For the secret of the drink."

There stood the son and father
And they looked high and low;
The heather was red around them,
The sea rumbled below.
And up and spoke the father,
Shrill was his voice to hear :
"I have a word in private,
A word for the royal ear.

"Life is dear to the aged,
And honor a little thing;
I would gladly sell the secret,"
Quoth the Pict to the King.
His voice was small as a sparrow's,
And shrill and wonderful clear :
"I would gladly sell my secret,
Only my son I fear.

"For life is a little matter,
And death is nought to the young;
And I dare not sell my honor
Under the eye of my son.
Take *him*, O king, and bind him,
And cast him far in the deep;
And it's I will tell the secret
That I have sworn to keep."

They took the son and bound him,
Neck and heels in a thong,
And a lad took him and swung him,
And flung him far and strong,
And the sea swallowed his body,
Like that of a child of ten ; —
And there on the cliff stood the father,
Last of the dwarfish men.

"True was the word I told you :
Only my son I feared ;
For I doubt the sapling courage
That goes without the beard.

But now in vain is the torture,
Fire shall never avail :
Here dies in my bosom
The secret of Heather Ale."

THE WHAUPS

TO S. R. C.

"Blows the wind to-day, and the sun and
the rain are flying —
Blows the wind on the moors to-day and
now,
Where about the graves of the martyrs the
whaups are crying,
My heart remembers how !

"Gray, recumbent tombs of the dead in
desert places,
Standing stones on the vacant, red-wine
moor,
Hills of sheep, and the homes of the silent
vanished races
And winds austere and pure !

"Be it granted me to behold you again in
dying,
Hills of home ! and I hear again the call —
Hear about the graves of the martyrs the
pee-wees crying,
And hear no more at all."

REQUIEM

Under the wide and starry sky,
Dig the grave and let me lie.
Glad did I live and gladly die,
And I laid me down with a will.

This be the verse you grave for me :
Here he lies where he longed to be ;
Home is the sailor, home from sea,
And the hunter home from the hill.

Gleeson White

A BALLADE OF PLAYING CARDS

To soothe a mad King's fevered brain
(So runs the legend), cards were
made,
When Gringonneur for Charles insane
"Diversely colored" heart and spade,

Diamond and club, the painted jade,
The light-heeled Jack, and beckoning
Called, to their royal cousin's aid,
Puppets of knave, and queen, and king.

Grim fancy ! that the playful train,
The quaint, grimacing cavalcade,

Should wreck such ills where they obtain
The victims to their sorry trade,
The player cozened by the played ;
Pasteboards supreme ; to this they bring
Both gallant buck and roystering blade,
Puppets of knave, and queen, and king.

From reckless play, what noble gain ?
One friend hard hit, the rest afraid
To show their pleasure at his pain,
Such sympathy might well persuade
The cards in garish heaps displayed
To join, with impish revelling,
And jeer as all his fortunes fade —
Puppets of knave, and queen, and king.

L'ENVOI

Prince ! after all, they are the shade,
The type of every earthly thing,
And we, through all life's masquerade,
Puppets of knave, and queen, and king.

SUFFICIENCY

A LITTLE love, of Heaven a little share,
And then we go — what matters it ? since
    where,
    Or when, or how, none may aforetime
    know,

Nor if Death cometh soon, or lingering
    slow,
Send on ahead his herald of Despair.

On this gray life, Love lights with golden
    glow ;
Refracted from The Source, his bright
    wings throw
Its glory round us, should Fate grant
    our prayer
    — A little' love !

A little ; 't is as much as we may bear,
For Love is compassed with such magic air
Who breathes it fully dies ; and, knowing
    so,
The Gods all wisely but a taste bestow
For little lives, — a little while they spare
    A little love.

A PRIMROSE DAME

SHE has a primrose at her breast,
I almost wish I were a Tory.
I like the Radicals the best ;
She has a primrose at her breast ;
Now is it chance she so is drest,
Or must I tell a story ?
She has a primrose at her breast,
I almost wish I *were* a Tory.

John Arthur Goodchild

SCHÖNE ROTHRAUT

TAKE as gold this old tradition
Of the royal-rendered wage,
Guerdon of love's mad ambition
In the true heart of a page.

He, his passion vainly hiding,
Worn and pale with hopeless pain,
Through the summer woods was riding
Close beside his mistress' rein.

"Why so sad, my page ? " and turning,
Gazed she straight into his eyes.
"T is thy thought my bosom burning
With a flame that never dies."

Flushed she then, but answered, "Carest
Thou to feed the flame I bring ?

Look me full, and if thou darest,
Kiss the daughter of the king."

Stark he stood, all wonders mingling,
Then from heart to finger-tips
Rushed the heated life-blood tingling
As he seized upon her lips.

Crushing newborn awe with laughter,
Said she, "Thus must end thy pain ;
See thou never more hereafter
Lookest for like grace again."

Spake he glad : "Each leaf that glit-
    ters
In the sun thy gift hath seen ;
Every bird that sings and twitters
Knoweth where my lips have been.

"And the winds from dawn to vesper,
Blow they north or blow they south,
Softly in my ear shall whisper,
'Thou hast kissed Schöne Rothraut's
    mouth.'

"Every floweret of the meadow,
Every bird upon the tree,
In life's sunshine or its shadow,
Shall bring back my joy to me."

A PARABLE OF THE SPIRIT

I CAME in light that I might behold
The shadow which shut me apart of old.
Lo, it was lying robed in white,
With the still palms crossed o'er a lily,
    bright
With salt rain of tears ; and everywhere
Around lay blossoms that filled the air
With perfume, snow of flowers that hid
The snow of the silken coverlid
With myrtle and orange bloom and store
Of jasmine stars, and a wreath it wore
Of stephanotis.   Still it lay,
For its time of travail had passed away.
"Of old it was never so fair as this,"
I said, as I bent me down to kiss
The cast swathing robe. "It is well that so
I see it before I turn to go —
Turn to depart that I may bless
The love that has shown such tenderness."

So I passed to my mother's side,
Where she lay sleepless and weary-eyed ;
Glided within, that I might see
The chamber her love had reserved for
    me.
It was wide and warm, and furnished forth
With the best she had, with gifts of worth,
Anxious watchings and tears and prayers
And ministrations of many years.
I bent me down o'er her wrinkled brow
And kissed it smooth, as I whispered low
Comfort and hope for her daughter dear,
Till my whisper drew forth the healing
    tear.
Last, I kissed her to slumber deep,
Kissed her to quiet rest and sleep.

I passed to my sister's heart, and there
I heard sweet notes of her soaring prayer ;
And, joining therewith, found the fair
    white shrine
That her love had set apart as mine.

On its alabaster altar stood
A vessel with sacrificial blood.
Incense of sweet unselfishness
Rose ever, a pillar of light to bless
That fair pure place with its flower-sweet
    fume.
Dimmed was that shrine by no cloud of
    gloom,
But bright shone that pillar which rose
    above
On her earthly jewels with its lambent
    love.
So I knew that any gift of mine
Was naught by her treasure of love divine,
Flowing freely down ; but a flower I lent
That would bloom in her bosom with sweet
    content,
'T was forget-me-not. "Though poor," I
    said,
"Mid her blossoms of living love, the dead
Would yet be loved, and I will that she
Keep this, and render it back to me."
I knew how my blossom would live and
    grow,
As I kissed it once ere I turned to go ;

Turned to go to my cousin Kate —
She who was rival to me of late,
Jealous, unhappy, but in the end
Nursed me and tended me like a friend.
I searched her heart, and soon I found
A plot of mine in her garden ground ;
Flowers were there which had ripened seed,
But among them many a yellow weed.
Still, I saw with a gladdened eye
The weeds were pining and like to die,
Whilst heartsease throve, and sprigs of
    rue
Watered well with remorseful dew.
So I bent down and rooted out
Nettles of envy, and round about
Cleared the ground that the flowers might
    live,
Live and blossom and grow and thrive.
Lastly, I drew with cords of love
A thistle of pride naught else might move,
Pressed her forehead and swiftly passed —
For I kept my best gifts to the last —
Treasures of comfort and hope to cheer
The heart which my own had held mos'
    dear.

I dreamed of the bliss that I should fee!
When that opened heart should to m·
    reveal

Its fulness, before but dimly seen,
As I lifted its veils and entered in —
Entered, and saw with mute amaze
How squalid and narrow was the place.
Still, I fancied, perchance for me
The best of that which is here may be.
Searching in dusk, I forced my way
To the secret place where my chamber
    lay,
Choked with the sordid piles o'erthrown
Of a miser's dust which had been my own,
Till but little space for me remained,
All being filthy and weather-stained ;
Whilst evil fungi, spawn of lust,
Pushed through the rotten floor, and
    thrust
Unsightly growths in that evil space,
And vanity pressed in the crowded space
Till room was scanty for me to tread.
I gazed shadowed a moment before I fled,

For no gift of mine of love or care
Might live in that pestilential air ;
Still, for the love of dreams bygone,
I could not leave him quite alone,
So I planted cypress to warn of death.
It might live, and its keen balsamic breath
Would wither these fungi one by one,
Giving entrance, perchance, to some ray of
    sun.

Then I departed, earth's lesson o'er.
Never henceforth shall I enter more ;
And the thought was mine of former
    dread
And former longings, and so I said,
" Blind I was when my dearest wish
Was ever to dwell in a home like this."
Knew, as I went forth to my rest,
My prayer was a child's, and God knew
    best.

Eric Mackay

THE WAKING OF THE LARK

O BONNIE bird, that in the brake, exultant,
    dost prepare thee,
As poets do whose thoughts are true, for
    wings that will upbear thee —
Oh ! tell me, tell me, bonnie bird,
    Canst thou not pipe of hope deferred ?
Or canst thou sing of naught but Spring
    among the golden meadows ?

Methinks a bard (and thou art one) should
    suit his song to sorrow,
And tell of pain, as well as gain, that waits
    us on the morrow ;
But thou art not a prophet, thou,
    If naught but joy can touch thee now ;
If, in thy heart, thou hast no vow that
    speaks of Nature's anguish.

Oh ! I have held my sorrows dear, and
    felt, though poor and slighted,
The songs we love are those we hear when
    love is unrequited ;
But thou art still the slave of dawn,
And canst not sing till night be gone,
Till o'er the pathway of the fawn the sun-
    beams shine and quiver.

Thou art the minion of the sun that rises
    in his splendor,
And canst not spare for Dian fair the songs
    that should attend her.
The moon, so sad and silver-pale,
Is mistress of the nightingale ;
And thou wilt sing on hill and dale no
    ditties in the darkness.

For Queen and King thou wilt not spare
    one note of thine outpouring ;
And thou 'rt as free as breezes be on Na-
    ture's velvet flooring.
The daisy, with its hood undone,
The grass, the sunlight, and the sun —
These are the joys, thou holy one, that pay
    thee for thy singing.

Oh, hush ! Oh, hush ! how wild a gush of
    rapture in the distance —
A roll of rhymes, a toll of chimes, a cry for
    love's assistance ;
A sound that wells from happy throats,
A flood of song where beauty floats,
And where our thoughts, like golden boats,
    do seem to cross a river.

This is the advent of the lark — the priest
    in gray apparel —
Who doth prepare to trill in air his sinless
    summer carol ;
This is the prelude to the lay
The birds did sing in Cæsar's day,
And will again, for aye and aye, in praise
    of God's creation.

O dainty thing, on wonder's wing, by life
    and love elated,
Oh ! sing aloud from cloud to cloud, till
    day be consecrated ;
Till from the gateways of the morn,
The sun, with all his light unshorn,
His robes of darkness round him torn, doth
    scale the lofty heavens !

MARY ARDEN

O THOU to whom, athwart the perished days
And parted nights, long sped, we lift our
    gaze,
Behold ! I greet thee with a modern
    rhyme,
Love-lit and reverent as befits the time,
To solemnize the feast-day of thy son.

And who was he who flourished in the
    smiles
Of thy fair face ? 'T was Shakespeare of
    the Isles,
Shakespeare of England, whom the world
    has known
As thine, and ours, and Glory's, in the zone
    Of all the seas and all the lands of
    earth.

He was unfamous when he came to thee,
But sound, and sweet, and good for eyes to
    see,
And born at Stratford, on St. George's
    Day,
A week before the wondrous month of
    May ;
And God therein was gracious to us all.

He loved thee, lady ! and he loved the
    world ;
And, like a flag, his fealty was unfurled ;
And kings who flourished ere thy son was
    born
Shall live through him, from morn to fur-
    thest morn,
In all the far-off cycles yet to come.

He gave us Falstaff, and a hundred quips,
A hundred mottoes from immortal lips ;
And, year by year, we smile to keep away
The generous tears that mind us of the
    sway
    Of his great singing, and the pomp
    thereof.

His was the nectar of the gods of Greece,
The lute of Orpheus, and the Golden
    Fleece
Of grand endeavor ; and the thunder-roll
Of words majestic, which, from pole to pole,
    Have borne the tidings of our English
    tongue.

He gave us Hamlet ; and he taught us
    more
Than schools have taught us ; and his fairy-
    lore
Was fraught with science ; and he called
    from death
Verona's lovers, with the burning breath
    Of their great passion that has filled the
    spheres.

He made us know Cordelia, and the man
Who murdered sleep, and baleful Caliban ;
And, one by one, athwart the gloom ap-
    peared
Maidens and men and myths who were
    revered
    In olden days, before the earth was sad.

Ay ! this is true. It was ordainéd so ;
He was thine own, three hundred years ago ;
But ours to-day ; and ours till earth be
    red
With doom-day splendor for the quick and
    dead,
    And days and nights be scattered like the
    leaves.

It was for this he lived, for this he died :
To raise to Heaven the face that never
    lied,
To lean to earth the lips that should be-
    come
Fraught with conviction when the mouth
    was dumb,
    And all the firm, fine body turned to
    clay.

He lived to seal, and sanctify, the lives
Of perished maids, and uncreated wives,

And gave them each a space wherein to
dwell ;
And for his mother's sake he loved them
well
And made them types undying of all
truth.

O fair and fond young mother of the boy
Who wrought all this — O Mary ! — in this
thy joy
Didst thou perceive, when, fitful from his
rest,
He turned to thee, that his would be the best
Of all men's chanting since the world
began ?

Didst thou, O Mary ! with the eye of trust
Perceive, prophetic through the dark and
dust
Of things terrene, the glory of thy son,
And all the pride therein that should be won
By toilsome men, content to be his
slaves ?

Didst thou, good mother ! in the tender
ways
That women find to fill the fleeting days,
Behold afar the Giant who should rise
With foot on earth, and forehead in the
skies,
To write his name and thine among the
stars ?

I love to think it ; and in dreams at night
I see thee stand, erect, and all in white,
With hands out-yearning to that mighty
form,
As if to draw him back from out the storm —
A child again, and thine to nurse withal.

I see thee, pale and pure, with flowing hair,
And big, bright eyes — far-searching in the
air
For thy sweet babe — and, in a trice of
time,
I see the boy advance to thee, and climb,
And call thee "Mother !" in ecstatic
tones.

Yet if my thought be vain — if, by a touch
Of this weak hand, I vex thee overmuch —
Forbear the blame, sweet Spirit ! and endow
My heart with fervor while to thee I bow
Athwart the threshold of my fading
dream.

For — though so seeming-bold in this my
song —
I turn to thee with reverence, in the throng
Of words and thoughts, as shepherds
scanned afar
The famed effulgence of that eastern star
Which ushered in the Crowned One of
the heavens.

In dreams of rapture I have seen thee
pass
Along the banks of Avon, by the grass,
As fair as that fair Juliet whom thy son
Endowed with life, but with the look of
one
Who knows the nearest way to some new
grave.

And often, too, I 've seen thee in the flush
Of thy full beauty, while the mother's
" Hush ! "
Hung on thy lip, and all thy tangled hair
Re-clothed a bosom that in part was bare
Because a tiny hand had toyed therewith !

Oh ! by the June-tide splendor of thy face
When, eight weeks old, the child in thine
embrace
Did leap and laugh — O Mary ! by the
same,
I bow to thee, subservient to thy fame,
And call thee England's Pride forever-
more !

ECSTASY

I CANNOT sing to thee as I would sing
If I were quickened like the holy lark,
With fire from Heaven and sunlight on his
wing,
Who wakes the world with witcheries of
the dark
Renewed in rapture in the reddening air.
A thing of splendor do I deem him then,
A feathered frenzy with an angel's throat,
A something sweet that somewhere seems
to float
'Twixt earth and sky, to be a sign to men.
He fills me with such wonder and despair !
I long to kiss thy locks, so golden bright,
As he doth kiss the tresses of the sun.
Oh ! bid me sing to thee, my chosen one,
And do thou teach me, Love, to sing
aright !

IN TUSCANY

DOST thou remember, friend of vanished
    days,
How, in the golden land of love and song,
We met in April in the crowded ways
Of that fair city where the soul is strong,
Ay! strong as fate, for good or evil
    praise?
And how the lord whom all the world
    obeys,

The lord of light to whom the stars belong,
Illumed the track that led thee through
    the throng?
Dost thou remember, in the wooded dale,
Beyond the town of Dante the Divine,
How all the air was flooded as with wine?
And how the lark, to drown the nightingale,
Pealed out sweet notes? I live to tell the
    tale.
But thou? Oblivion signs thee with a
    sign!

F. Wyville Home

AN ENGLISH GIRL

SPEAK, quiet lips, and utter forth my fate;
    Before thy beauty I bow down, I kneel,
Girl, and to thee my life I dedicate,
    And seal the past up with a dateless seal.

What delicate hours and seasons without
        storm
    Have nursed thee, and what happy Eng-
        lish dale?
For tenderer is thy light and gracile form
    Than any snowy wind-flower of the vale.

O wild-flower, though the bee that drinks
        thy wine
    Must soar past crags that front the leap-
        ing sea,
I climb to thee; thy beauty shall be mine;
    Or let the cold green wave go over me.

DOVER CLIFF

LAST April, when the winds had lost their
        chill,
I lay down dreamily upon the verge
Of Shakespeare's Cliff, where sea and sea-
        wind scourge
The eternal barrier that withstands them
        still.

I heard the billows break beneath and fill
The wide air with the thunder of the surge;
And near my cheek, half fearful to emerge,
A violet grew upon the grassy hill.
There while I lay, Poet, I dreamed of thee.
Thy very voice, whose matchless music yet
O'ermasters all the world's, surrounded me,
Singing, and in the sound of it there met
With all the might and passion of the sea
The utter sweetness of the violet.

IN A SEPTEMBER NIGHT

THERE the moon leans out and blesses
    All the dreamy hills below:
Here the willows wash their tresses
    Where the water-lilies blow
    In the stream that glideth slow.

High in heaven, in serried ranges,
    Cloud-wreaths float through pallid light,
Like a flock of swans that changes
    In the middle Autumn night
    North for South in ordered flight.

What know ye, who hover yonder,
    More than I, of that veiled good
Whither all things tend, I wonder,
    That ye follow the wind's mood
    In such patient quietude?

Francis William Bourdillon

EURYDICE

He came to call me back from death
  To the bright world above.
I hear him yet with trembling breath
  Low calling, "O sweet love!
Come back! The earth is just as fair;
The flowers, the open skies are there;
  Come back to life and love!"

Oh! all my heart went out to him,
  And the sweet air above.
With happy tears my eyes were dim;
  I called him, "O sweet love!
I come, for thou art all to me.
Go forth, and I will follow thee,
  Right back to life and love!"

I followed through the cavern black;
  I saw the blue above.
Some terror turned me to look back:
  I heard him wail, "O love!
What hast thou done! What hast thou
  done!"
And then I saw no more the sun,
  And lost were life and love.

A VIOLINIST

The lark above our heads doth know
A heaven we see not here below;
She sees it, and for joy she sings;
Then falls with ineffectual wings.

Ah, soaring soul! faint not nor tire!
Each heaven attained reveals a higher.
Thy thought is of thy failure; we
List raptured, and thank God for thee.

OLD AND YOUNG

Long ago, on a bright spring day,
I passed a little child at play;
And as I passed, in childish glee
She called to me, "Come and play with
  me!"

But my eyes were fixed on a far-off height
I was fain to climb before the night;
So, half-impatient, I answered, "Nay!
I am too old, too old to play."

Long, long after, in Autumn time —
My limbs were grown too old to climb —
I passed a child on a pleasant lea,
And I called to her, "Come and play with
  me!"

But her eyes were fixed on a fairy-book;
And scarce she lifted a wondering look,
As with childish scorn she answered,
  "Nay!
I am too old, too old to play!"

THE NIGHT HAS A THOUSAND EYES

The night has a thousand eyes,
  And the day but one;
Yet the light of the bright world dies
  With the dying sun.

The mind has a thousand eyes,
  And the heart but one;
Yet the light of a whole life dies
  When love is done.

Herbert Edwin Clarke

IN THE WOOD

Through laughing leaves the sunlight
  comes,
  Turning the green to gold;
The bee about the heather hums,
  And the morning air is cold

Here on the breezy woodland side,
  Where we two ride.

Through laughing leaves on golden hair
  The sunlight glances down,
And makes a halo round her there,
  And crowns her with a crown

Queen of the sunrise and the sun,
    As we ride on.

The wanton wind has kissed her face, —
    His lips have left a rose, —
He found her cheek so sweet a place
    For kisses, I suppose,
He thought he 'd leave a sign, that so
    Others might know.

The path grows narrower as we ride,
    The green boughs close above,
And overhead, and either side,
    The wild birds sing of Love :
But ah, she is not listening
    To what they sing !

Till I take up the wild-birds' song,
    And word by word unfold
Its meaning as we ride along, —
    And when my tale is told,
I turn my eyes to hers again, —
    And then, — and then, —

(The bridle path more narrow grows,
    The leaves shut out the sun ;)
Where the wind's lips left their one rose
    My own leave more than one :
While the leaves murmur up above,
    And laugh for love.

This was the place ; — you see the sky
    Now 'twixt the branches bare ;
About the path the dead leaves lie,
    And songless is the air ; —
All 's changed since then, for that, you
        know,
    Was long ago.

Let us ride on ! The wind is cold, —
    Let us ride on — ride fast ! —
'T is winter, and we knew of old
    That love could never last
Without the summer and the sun ! —
    Let us ride on !

A CRY

Lo, I am weary of all,
    Of men and their love and their hate ;
I have been long enough Life's thrall
    And the toy of a tyrant Fate.

I would have nothing but rest,
    I would not struggle again ;

Take me now to thy breast,
    Earth, sweet mother of men.

Hide me and let me sleep ;
    Give me a lonely tomb
So close and so dark and so deep
    I shall hear no trumpet of doom.

There let me lie forgot
    When the dead at its blast are gone ;
Give me to hear it not,
    But only to slumber on.

This is the fate I crave,
    For I look to the end and see
If there be not rest in the grave
    There will never be rest for me.

THE AGE

I

A PALE and soul-sick woman with wan
        eyes
Fixed on their own reflection in the glass,
Uncertain lips half-oped to say " Alas,
Naked I stand between two mysteries,
Finding my wisdom naught who am most
        wise."
Behind, the shapes and fiery shadows pass
Of fervent life ; no joy in them she has,
But gazing on herself she moans and sighs.
And yet of knowledge she doth hold the
        key,
And Power and Pleasure are her hand-
        maidens,
And all past years have given of their best
To make her rich and great and strong
        and free,
Who stands in slack and listless impotence,
Marvelling sadly at her own unrest.

II

Her children cluster round about her
        knees ;
The hoarded wealth and wisdom of the
        Dead
Of all past time they have inherited,
And still within their hands it doth
        increase ;
Yet in their eyes is mirrored her dis-peace,
Her weariness within their hearts is shed ;
Her dreary sorrow weighs each drooping
        head,
And each soul sickens with her fell disease.

Beneath their feet lie many broken toys,
They are too old to laugh, too wise to
          pray,
Or look to God for wage or chastise-
    ment :

They have known all sorrows, wearied of
    all joys,
Fed all desires, and none hath said them nay;
Two things alone they lack, Peace and
    Content.

Lady Charlotte Elliot

THE WIFE OF LOKI

CURSED by the gods and crowned with
    shame,
  Fell father of a direful brood,
Whose crimes have filled the heaven with
      flame
  And drenched the earth with blood ;

Loki, the guileful Loki, stands
  Within a rocky mountain-gorge ;
Chains gird his body, feet, and hands,
  Wrought in no mortal forge.

Coiled on the rock, a mighty snake
  Above him, day and night, is hung,
With dull malignant eyes awake,
  And poison-dropping tongue.

Drop follows drop in ceaseless flow,
  Each falling where the other fell,

To lay upon his blistered brow
  The liquid fire of hell.

But lo, beside the howling wretch
  A woman stands, devoid of dread,
And one pale arm is seen to stretch
  Above his tortured head !

All through the day is lifted up,
  And all the weary night-time through,
One patient hand that holds a cup
  To catch the poison-dew.

Sometimes the venom overfills
  The cup, and she must pour it forth ;
With Loki's curses then the hills
  Are rent from south to north.

But she in answer only sighs,
  And lays her lips upon his face,
And, with love's anguish in her eyes,
  Resumes her constant place.

William James Dawson

A CHILD'S PORTRAIT

HER face is hushed in perfect calm,
  Her lips half-open hint the psalm
The angels sing, who wear God's palm :
  And in her eyes a liquid light,
With somewhat of a starry sheen,
  Comes welling upward from the white
And vestal soul that throbs within.

A golden tangle is her hair
  That holds the sunlight in its snare ;
And one pure lily she doth wear
  In her white robe : and she doth seem
A flower-like creature, who will fade

If suns strike down too rude a beam,
  Or winds blow roughly on her shade.

The golden ladders of the Dawn
  Meet at her feet, where on the lawn
She stands, in tender thought withdrawn :
  And little wonder would it be,
If on those slanting stairs she trod,
  And, with one farewell smile toward me,
Were caught into the smile of God.

BIRD'S SONG AT MORNING

O THOU that cleavest heaven
  With such unmastered flight,

To whom the fates have given
For sport the sky's blue height;
Where cloud with cloud is meeting,
I see thy bright wings beating,
And flashing and retreating
Against the morning light !

No toilsome task thou knowest,
No day with tears begun,
Lighthearted forth thou goest
At morn to meet the sun ;
All day thy song thou triest
From lowest note to highest,
And all unweary fliest
Until the day be done.

Thou knowest no toil for raiment,
No pain of mocked desire ;
The skies are thy song's payment,
The sun thy throne of fire.
Thou askest and receivest,
And if perchance thou grievest,
At will the world thou leavest
On wings that never tire.

Yet we of grosser stature
Have in thy flight a part,
We share thy tameless nature,
We have a nobler art.
When thou art tired returning,
There mount in love and yearning,
Toward suns of keener burning,
The winged thoughts of our heart.

Within our souls are folden
The wings thou canst not share,
We see a dawn more golden,
We breathe diviner air :
In sleep when toil is ended,
In prayer with hope attended,
We traverse ways more splendid,
And see a world more fair.

Yet oft, when day is gleaming
On sleepless eyes, we vow
We would exchange our dreaming
To be one hour as thou !
Such discontent we borrow,
That we forget in sorrow
We have the long to-morrow,
Thou only hast the NOW.

IDEAL MEMORY

IF in the years that come such thing should
   be
That we should part, with tears or deadly
   strife,
That we should cease to share a common life,
Or walk estranged in voiceless misery,
Then by this night of love remember me.

For tired hearts at last an end shall be,
For tired feet the pitfall grave doth wait :
Can we escape this common trick of fate ?
More fortunate than all beside are we ?
Wherefore by this night's love remember
   me.

Not by my worst, when dull or bitterly
The mind moved, and the evil in my blood
Worked words of anger thy meek will
   withstood,
Not by the hours I sinned 'gainst love and
   thee,
Oh, not by these, dear love, remember me.

First in our mind live things that perfect be,
All shapes of joy or beauty, — day's low
   light
Dying along the seaward edge of night,
The first sweet violet, music's ecstasy,
Making the heart leap, — so remember me.

For I would have thy mind and memory
A chamber of sweet sounds and fragrances.
Let the ill pass : its power to hurt was less
Than joy's to bless us. I remember thee
By thy first kiss ; Oh, thus remember me !

There was an hour wherein a god's degree
And stature seemed to clothe me, and I
   stood
Supremely strong, and high, and great, and
   good :
Oh, by that hour, when all I aimed to be
I did appear, by that remember me !

TO A DESOLATE FRIEND

O FRIEND, like some cold wind to-day
Your message came, and chilled the light ;
Your house so dark, and mine so bright, —
I could not weep, I could not pray !

My wife and I had kissed at morn,
My children's lips were full of song ;
O friend, it seemed such cruel wrong,
My life so full, and yours forlorn !

We slept last night clasped hand in hand,
Secure and calm — and never knew
How fared the lonely hours with you,
What time those dying lips you fanned.

We dreamed of love, and did not see
The shadow pass across our dream ;
We heard the murmur of a stream,
Not death's, for it ran bright and free.

And in the dark her gentle soul
Passed out, but oh ! we knew it not !
My babe slept fast within her cot,
While yours woke to the slow bell's toll.

She paused a moment, — who can tell ? —
Before our windows, but we lay
So deep in sleep she went away,
And only smiled a sad farewell !

It would be like her ; well we know
How oft she waked while others slept —
She never woke us when she wept,
It would be like her thus to go !

Ah, friend ! you let her stray too far
Within the shadow-haunted wood,
Where deep thoughts never understood
Breathe on us and like anguish are.

One day within that gloom there shone
A heavenly dawn, and with wide eyes
She saw God's city crown the skies,
Since when she hasted to be gone.

Too much you yielded to her grace ;
Renouncing self, she thus became
An angel with a human name,
And angels coveted her face.

Earth's door you set so wide, alack
She saw God's gardens, and she went
A moment forth to look ; she meant
No wrong, but oh ! she came not back !

Dear friend, what can I say or sing,
But this, that she is happy there ?
We will not grudge those gardens fair
Where her light feet are wandering.

The child at play is ignorant
Of tedious hours ; the years for you
To her are moments : and you too
Will join her ere she feels your want.

The path she wends we cannot track :
And yet some instinct makes us know
Hers is the joy, and ours the woe, —
We dare not wish her to come back !

THE ANGEL AT THE FORD

I sought to hold her, but within her
    eyes
I read a new strange meaning ; faint they
    prayed,
" Oh, let me pass and taste the great sur-
    prise ;
Behold me not reluctant nor afraid ! "

" Nay, I will strive with God for this ! " I
    cried,
" As man with man, like Jacob at the brook,
Only be thou, dear heart, upon my side ! "
" Be still," she answered, " very still, and
    look ! "

And straightway I discerned with inward
    dread
The multitudinous passing of white souls,
Who paused, each one with sad averted
    head,
And flashing of indignant aureoles.

Frances Isabel Parnell

AFTER DEATH

Shall mine eyes behold thy glory, O my
    country ? Shall mine eyes behold
    thy glory ?
Or shall the darkness close around them,
    ere the sun-blaze break at last upon
    thy story ?

When the nations ope for thee their
    queenly circle, as a sweet new sister
    hail thee,
Shall these lips be sealed in callous death
    and silence, that have known but to
    bewail thee ?

Shall the ear be deaf that only loved thy
    praises, when all men their tribute
    bring thee ?
Shall the mouth be clay that sang thee in
    thy squalor, when all poets' mouths
    shall sing thee ?

Ah, the harpings and the salvos and the
    shoutings of thy exiled sons return-
    ing !
I should hear, though dead and mouldered,
    and the grave-damps should not
    chill my bosom's burning.

Ah, the tramp of feet victorious ! I should
    hear them 'mid the shamrocks and
    the mosses,

And my heart should toss within the shroud
    and quiver as a captive dreamer
    tosses.

I should turn and rend the cere-clothes
    round me, giant sinews I should bor-
    row —
Crying, "O my brothers, I have also
    loved her in her loneliness and sor-
    row.

" Let me join with you the jubilant pro-
    cession ; let me chant with you her
    story ;
Then contented I shall go back to the
    shamrocks, now mine eyes have seen
    her glory ! "

Alice Meynell

THE MODERN POET

A SONG OF DERIVATIONS

I COME from nothing ; but from where
Come the undying thoughts I bear ?
    Down, through long links of death and
      birth,
    From the past poets of the earth.
My immortality is there.

I am like the blossom of an hour.
But long, long vanished sun and shower
    Awoke my breath i' the young world's air.
    I track the past back everywhere
Through seed and flower and seed and
    flower.

Or I am like a stream that flows
Full of the cold springs that arose
    In morning lands, in distant hills ;
    And down the plain my channel fills
With melting of forgotten snows.

Voices I have not heard possessed
My own fresh songs ; my thoughts are
    blessed
    With relics of the far unknown ;
    And mixed with memories not my own
The sweet streams throng into my breast.

Before this life began to be,
The happy songs that wake in me

Woke long ago, and far apart
Heavily on this little heart
Presses this immortality.

SONG

My Fair, no beauty of thine will last,
Save in my love 's eternity.
Thy smiles, that light thee fitfully,
Are lost forever — their moment past —
Except the few thou givest to me.

Thy sweet words vanish day by day,
As all breath of mortality ;
Thy laughter, done, must cease to be,
And all thy dear tones pass away,
Except the few that sing to me.

Hide then within my heart, oh, hide
All thou art loath should go from thee.
Be kinder to thyself and me.
My cupful from this river's tide
Shall never reach the long sad sea.

CHANGELESS

A POET of one mood in all my lays,
Ranging all life to sing one only love,
Like a west wind across the world I
    move,
Sweeping my harp of floods mine own wild
    ways.

The countries change, but not the west-wind days
Which are my songs. My soft skies shine above,
And on all seas the colors of a dove,
And on all fields a flash of silver grays.
I make the whole world answer to my art
And sweet monotonous meanings. In your ears
I change not ever, bearing, for my part,
One thought that is the treasure of my years,
A small cloud full of rain upon my heart
And in mine arms, clasped, like a child in tears.

RENOUNCEMENT

I MUST not think of thee ; and, tired yet strong,
I shun the thought that lurks in all delight —
The thought of thee — and in the blue Heaven's height,
And in the sweetest passage of a song.
Oh, just beyond the fairest thoughts that throng
This breast, the thought of thee waits, hidden yet bright ;

But it must never, never come in sight ;
I must stop short of thee the whole day long.
But when sleep comes to close each difficult day,
When night gives pause to the long watch I keep,
And all my bonds I needs must loose apart,
Must doff my will as raiment laid away, —
With the first dream that comes with the first sleep
I run, I run, I am gathered to thy heart.

SONG OF THE NIGHT AT DAYBREAK

ALL my stars forsake me,
And the dawn-winds shake me :
Where shall I betake me ?

Whither shall I run
Till the set of the sun,
Till the day be done ?

To the mountain-mine,
To the boughs o' the pine,
To the blind man's eyne,

To a brow that is
Bowed upon the knees,
Sick with memories.

Pakenham Beatty

CHARLES LAMB

THOUGH our great love a little wrong his fame,
And seeing him with such familiar eyes
We say " how kind " more often than " how wise,"
Such is the simple reverence he would claim ;
He would not have us call him by a name
Higher than that of friend, — yet by this grave
We feel the saint not pure, nor hero brave,
And all the martyr's patience put to shame.
Brother, we leave thee by thy sister's side ;
Whom such a love bound let not death divide ;

She is at peace, now, brother, thou canst rest;
Thy long sad guardianship of love is o'er,
And gentle Shakespeare on the dead men's shore
Salutes thy gentle ghost that praised him best.

THE DEATH OF HAMPDEN

SCENE. — A tent in the Parliamentary camp. HAMPDEN lies wounded, and CROMWELL is bending over him.

Hampden. Spare all who yield ; alas, that we must pierce
One English heart for England !
Cromwell. How he raves ! The fever is at height.
Hamp. I thank you, sir. My wound is nothing ; a little loss of blood :

I fear much more must flow from worthier
    veins
Ere England's hurt be healed.
Crom. How powerful are base things to
    destroy !
The brute's part in them kills the god's in
    us,
And robs the world of many glorious
    deeds ;
In all the histories of famous men
We never find the greatest overthrown
Of such as were their equals, but the head,
Screened of its laurels from the lightning's
    flash,
Falls by some chance blow of an obscure
    hand,
And glory cannot guard the hero's heart
Against the least knave's dagger.
    Hamp.   You cannot help me.
Save yourself, sir ; my best prayers keep
    you safe —
I fain would win as far as yonder house ;
It was my dear dead wife's ; such shapes
    are there
As I would see about my dying bed,
To make me sure of heaven — Forgive
    me, love,
That I am loath to come yet to thy heart ;
I have only lived without thee, O my best,
That I might live for England ! Is Crom-
    well come ?
    Crom. How is it with you, cousin ?
    Hamp.   Very well ;
With hope to be soon better ; gentle cou-
    sin,
I have scant time to speak and much to
    say,
That thou must hear — Men's eyes more
    clearly see,
Ere the long darkness ; and thus plagues,
    and wars,
Earthquake, and overthrow of prosperous
    states,
Have been foretold by lips of dying men,
Who saw their country's end before their
    own ;
But I die happy ; with a joy too keen
For this weak wounded body, and delight
Of eager youth that dreams of noble deeds ;
Knowing the greatness in thee, which occa-
    sion
Has not yet shown the world, and thine
    own self
Hast only dimly guessed at — These
    hands I hold

Shall bear the weight of England's great-
    ness up ;
Thy name, mine own dear kinsman's, shall
    have sound
More royal than all crownèd kings' ; the
    slave
Shall murmur it in dreams of liberty,
The patriot in his dungeon, and endure,
The tyrant, and grow merciful for fear ;
And when thou hast done high and song
    worthy deeds,
At length shall come thy poet, whose purer
    eyes
God shall seclude from sight of our gross
    Earth,
And for the dull light of our darker day
Give all heaven to his vision, star with
    star
Shining, and splendid and sonorous spheres
To make him music ; and those sacred lips,
More eloquent than the Mantuan's, prais-
    ing thee,
Shall make thy fame a memory for all
    time,
And set a loftier laurel on thy head
Than any gathered from red fields of war ;
So great shall England's great need make
    thee, Cromwell ;
Whom thou forget not still to love and
    serve,
Holding thy greatness given to make her
    great,
Thy strength to keep her strong ; then
    (since oblivion
Is what men chiefly fear in death), dear
    cousin,
I would not be forgotten of thy love.
And now I am loath the last words I shall
    speak
Must be of strife — yet I must utter them ;
Be not of those that vex the angry times
With meek-mouthed proffers of rejected
    peace ;
When men have set the justice of their
    cause
To sharp arbitrament of answering arms,
Tongues should keep mute, and steel hold
    speech with steel,
Till victory can plead the conquered's
    cause,
And make soft mercy no more dangerous.
We must o'ercome our foes to make them
    friends. . . .
Thy hand, dear cousin . . . Sweet, I hear
    thy voice

That calls me, and leave England for thy
    sake ;
Kiss me, dear love, and take my soul to
    God ! . . .
Receive my soul, Lord Jesus ! O God,
    save
My country — God be merciful to —
Crom. O Lord of Hosts, if thou wilt only
    give me
An England with but three such English-
    men,

My life shall be as noble as this man's. . . .
Farewell, dear cousin, perfect heart that
    beats
No more for England — Think of me in
    Heaven,
And help to make me all thou saidst I
    should be, —
[*Kneels down by the bed. Rising, and look-
    ing steadfastly at the dead body of* HAMP-
    DEN.]
                            Yea, and I shall be.

Oliver Madox Brown

BEFORE AND AFTER

AH ! long ago since I or thou
Glanced past these moorlands brow to
    brow,
    Our mixed hair streaming down the
    wind —
        So fleet ! so sweet !
I loved thy footsteps more than thou
Loved my whole soul or body through —
    So sweet ! so fleet ! ere Fate outgrew the
    days wherein Life sinned !

And ah ! the deep steep days of shame,
Whose dread hopes shrivelled ere they
    came,
    Or vanished down Love's nameless
    void —
        So dread ! so dead !
Dread hope stripped dead from each soul's
    shame,

Soulless alike for praise or blame —
    Too dead to dread the eternities whose
    heaven its shame destroyed.

LAURA'S SONG

ALAS ! who knows or cares, my love,
    If our love live or die, —
If thou thy frailty, sweet, should prove,
    Or my soul thine deny ?
Yet merging sorrow in delight,
Love's dream disputes our devious night.

None know, sweet love, nor care a thought
    For our heart's vague desire,
Nor if our longing come to naught,
    Or burn in aimless fire ;
Let them alone, we 'll waste no sighs :
Cling closer, love, and close thine eyes !

Edward Cracroft Lefroy

A SHEPHERD MAIDEN

ON shores of Sicily a shape of Greece !
Dear maid, what means this lonely com-
    muning
With winds and waves ? What fancy,
    what caprice,
Has drawn thee from thy fellows ? Do
    they fling

Rude jests at thee ? Or seekest thou sur-
    cease
Of drowsy toil in noonday shepherding ?
Enough : our questions cannot break thy
    peace ;
Thou art a shade, — a long-entombéd
    thing.
But still we see thy sun-lit face, O sweet,
Shining eternal where it shone of yore ;

Still comes a vision of blue-veinéd feet
That stand forever on a pebbly shore ;
While round, the tidal waters flow and fleet
And ripple, ripple, ripple, evermore.

A SICILIAN NIGHT

COME, stand we here within this cactus-
brake,
And let the leafy tangle cloak us round :
It is the spot whereof the Seer spake —
To nymph and faun a nightly trysting-
ground.
How still the scene ! No zephyr stirs to
shake
The listening air. The trees are slumber-
bound
In soft repose. There 's not a bird awake
To witch the silence with a silver sound.
Now haply shall the vision trance our eyes,
By heedless mortals all too rarely scanned,
Of mystic maidens in immortal guise,
Who mingle shadowy hand with shadowy
hand,
And, moving o'er the lilies circle-wise,
Beat out with naked feet a saraband.

A FOOTBALL–PLAYER

IF I could paint you, friend, as you stand
there,
Guard of the goal, defensive, open-eyed,
Watching the tortured bladder slide and
glide
Under the twinkling feet ; arms bare
head bare,
The breeze a-tremble through crow-tufts
of hair ;
Red-brown in face, and ruddier having
spied
A wily foeman breaking from the side,
Aware of him, — of all else unaware :
If I could limn you, as you leap and fling
Your weight against his passage, like a
wall ;
Clutch him, and collar him, and rudely
cling
For one brief moment till he falls — you
fall :
My sketch would have what Art can never
give —
Sinew and breath and body ; it would
live.

May Probyn

THE BEES OF MYDDELTON MANOR

17TH CENTURY

BUZZING, buzzing, buzzing, my golden-
belted bees :
My little son was seven years old — the
mint-flower touched his knees ;
Yellow were his curly locks ;
Yellow were his stocking-clocks ;
His plaything of a sword had a diamond in
its hilt ;
Where the garden beds lay sunny,
And the bees were making honey,
"For God and the king — to arms ! to
arms !" the day long would he lilt.

Smock'd in lace and flowered brocade, my
pretty son of seven
Wept sore because the kitten died, and
left the charge uneven.
" I head one battalion, mother —
Kitty," sobbed he, " led the other !

And when we reach'd the bee-hive bench
We used to halt and storm the trench :
If we could plant our standard here,
With all the bees a-buzzing near,
And fly the colors safe from sting,
The town was taken for the king !"
Flitting, flitting over the thyme, my bees
with yellow band —
My little son of seven came close, and
clipp'd me by the hand ;
A wreath of mourning cloth was wound
His small left arm and sword-hilt round,
And on the thatch of every hive a wisp of
black was bound.
" Sweet mother, we must tell the bees, or
they will swarm away :
Ye little bees !" he called, " draw nigh,
and hark to what I say,
And make us golden honey still for our
white wheaten bread,
Though never more
We rush on war
With Kitty at our head :

Who 'll give the toast
When swords are cross'd,
Now Kitty lieth dead ? "

Buzzing, buzzing, buzzing, my bees of yel-
low girth :
My son of seven changed his mood, and
clasp'd me in his mirth.
" Sweet mother, when I grow a man and
fall on battle-field,"
He cried, and down in the daisied grass
upon one knee he kneel'd,
" I charge thee, come and tell the bees
how I for the king lie dead ;
And thou shalt never lack fine honey for
thy wheaten bread ! "

. . . .

Flitting, flitting, flitting, my busy bees,
alas !
No footstep of my soldier son came clink-
ing through the grass.
Thrice he kiss'd me for farewell,
And far on the stone his shadow fell ;
He buckled spurs and sword-belt on, as the
sun began to stoop,
Set foot in stirrup, and sprang to horse,
and rode to join his troop.
To the west he rode, where the winds
were at play,
And Monmouth's army mustering lay ;
Where Bridgewater flew her banner
high,
And gave up her keys, when the Duke
came by ;
And the maids of Taunton paid him court
With colors their own white hands had
wrought ;
And red as a field, where blood doth run,
Sedgemoor blazed in the setting sun.

Broider'd sash and clasp of gold, my
soldier son, alas !
The mint was all in flower, and the clover
in the grass :
" With every bed
In bloom," I said,
" What further lack the bees,
That they buzz so loud,
Like a restless cloud,
Among the orchard trees ? "
No voice in the air, from Sedgemoor
field,
Moan'd out how Grey and the horse had
reel'd ;

Met me no ghost, with haunting eyes,
That westward pointed 'mid its sighs,
And pull'd apart a bloody vest,
And show'd the sword-gash in its breast.

Empty hives, and flitting bees, and sunny
morning hours :
I snipp'd the blossom'd lavender, and the
pinks, and the gillyflowers ;
No petal trembled in my hold —
I saw not the dead stretched stark and
cold
On the trampled turf at the shepherd's
door,
In the cloak and the doublet Monmouth
wore,
With Monmouth's scarf and headgear
on,
And the eyes, not clos'd, of my soldier
son ;
I knew not how, ere the cocks did crow,
the fight was fought in the dark,
With naught for guide but the enemy's
guns, when the flint flash'd out a
spark,
Till, routed at first sound of fire, the cav-
alry broke and fled,
And the hoofs struck dumb, where they
spurn'd the slain, and the meadow
stream ran red ;
I saw not the handful of horsemen spur
through the dusk, and out of sight,
My soldier son at the Duke's left hand,
and Grey that rode on his right.

Buzzing, buzzing, buzzing, my honey-mak-
ing bees,
They left the musk, and the marigolds
and the scented faint sweet-peas ;
They gather'd in a darkening cloud, and
sway'd, and rose to fly ;
A blackness on the summer blue, they
swept across the sky.
Gaunt and ghastly with gaping wounds —
(my soldier son, alas !)
Footsore and faint, the messenger came
halting through the grass.
The wind went by and shook the leaves —
the mint-stalk shed its flower —
And I miss'd the murmuring round the
hives, and my boding heart beat
slower.
His soul we cheer'd with meat and
wine ;
With women's craft and balsam fine

We bath'd his hurts, and bound them
soft,
While west the wind played through the
croft,
And the low sun dyed the pinks blood red,
And, straying near the mint-flower shed,
A wild bee wanton'd o'er the bed.

He told how my son, at the shepherd's
door, kept guard in Monmouth's
clothes,
While Monmouth donned the shepherd's
frock, in hope to cheat his foes.
A couple of troopers spied him stand,
And bade him yield to the King's com-
mand :
"Surrender, thou rebel as good as
dead,
A price is set on thy traitor head !"
My soldier son, with secret smile,
Held both at bay for a little while,
Dealt them such death-blow as he fell,
Neither was left the tale to tell ;
With dying eyes, that asked no grace,
They stared on him for a minute's
space,
And felt that it was not Monmouth's
face.
Crimson'd through was Monmouth's cloak,
when the soldier dropped at their
side —
"Those knaves will carry no word," he
said, and he smil'd in his pain, and
died.
"Two days," told the messenger, "did we
lie
Hid in the field of peas and rye,
Hid in the ditch of brake and sedge,
With the enemy's scouts down every
hedge,
Till Grey was seized, and Monmouth seized,
that under the fern did crouch,
Starved, and haggard, and all unshaved,
with a few raw peas in his pouch."

. . . .

No music soundeth in my ears, but a pass-
ing bell that tolls
For gallant lords with head on block —
sweet Heaven receive their souls !

And a mound, unnamed, in Sedgemoor
grass,
That laps my soldier son, alas !
The bloom is shed —
The bees are fled —
Myddelton luck it 's done and dead.

"IS IT NOTHING TO YOU ? '

WE were playing on the green together,
My sweetheart and I —
Oh ! so heedless in the gay June weather,
When the word went forth that we must
die.
Oh ! so merrily the balls of amber
And of ivory tossed we to the sky,
While the word went forth in the King's
chamber,
That we both must die.

Oh ! so idly, straying through the pleas-
aunce,
Plucked we here and there
Fruit and bud, while in the royal presence
The King's son was casting from his hair
Glory of the wreathen gold that crowned it,
And, ungirdling all his garments fair,
Flinging by the jewelled clasp that bound it,
With his feet made bare,

Down the myrtled stairway of the palace —
Ashes on his head,
Came he, through the rose and citron
alleys,
In rough sark of sackcloth habited,
And in a hempen halter — oh ! we jested,
Lightly, and we laughed as he was led
To the torture, while the bloom we breasted
Where the grapes grew red.

Oh ! so sweet the birds, when he was dying
Piped to her and me —
Is no room this glad June day for sighing —
He is dead, and she and I go free !
When the sun shall set on all our pleasure
We will mourn him — What, so you
decree
We are heartless — Nay, but in what
measure
Do you more than we ?

Mackenzie Bell

SPRING'S IMMORTALITY

THE buds awake at touch of Spring
From Winter's joyless dream ;
From many a stone the ouzels sing
By yonder mossy stream.

The cuckoo's voice, from copse and vale,
Lingers, as if to meet
The music of the nightingale
Across the rising wheat —

The bird whom ancient Solitude
Hath kept forever young,
Unaltered since in studious mood
Calm Milton mused and sung.

Ah, strange it is, dear heart, to know
Spring's gladsome mystery
Was sweet to lovers long ago —
Most sweet to such as we —

That fresh new leaves and meadow flowers
Bloomed when the south wind came ;
While hands of Spring caressed the bowers,
The throstle sang the same.

. . . .

Unchanged, unchanged the throstle's song,
Unchanged Spring's answering breath,
Unchanged, though cruel Time was strong,
And stilled our love in death.

AT THE GRAVE OF DANTE GABRIEL ROSSETTI

HERE of a truth the world's extremes are
met :
Amid the gray, the moss-grown tombs of
those

Who led long lives obscure till came the
close
When, their calm days being done, their
suns were set —
Here stands a grave, all monumentless
yet,
Wrapped like the others in a deep repose ;
But while yon wakeful ocean ebbs and
flows
It is a grave the world shall not forget,
This grave on which meek violets grow
and thyme,
Summer's fair heralds ; and a stranger
now
Pauses to see a poet's resting-place,
But one of those who will in many a clime
On each return of this sad day avow
Fond love's regret that ne'er they saw his
face.

AT STRATFORD-ON-AVON

SHAKESPEARE, thy legacy of peerless song
Reveals mankind in every age and place,
In every joy, in every grief and wrong :
'T is England's legacy to all our race.
Little we know of all thine inner life,
Little of all thy swift, thy wondrous years —
Years filled with toil, rich years whose days
were rife
With strains that bring us mirth, that bring
us tears.
Little we know, and yet this much we
know,
Sense was thy guiding star — sense guided
thee
To live in this thy Stratford long ago,
To live content in calm simplicity ;
Greatest of those who wrought with soul
aflame
At honest daily work — then found it fame.

Toru Dutt

OUR CASUARINA TREE

LIKE a huge Python, winding round and
round
The rugged trunk, indented deep with
scars,

Up to its very summit near the stars,
A creeper climbs, in whose embraces
bound
No other tree could live. But gallantly
The giant wears the scarf, and flowers are
hung

In crimson clusters all the boughs among,
  Whereon all day are gathered bird and
    bee ;
And oft at nights the garden overflows
With one sweet song that seems to have no
    close,
Sung darkling from our tree, while men
    repose.

When first my casement is wide open
    thrown
At dawn, my eyes delighted on it rest ;
Sometimes, and most in winter, — on its
    crest
A gray baboon sits statue-like alone
  Watching the sunrise ; while on lower
    boughs
His puny offspring leap about and play ;
And far and near kokilas hail the day ;
  And to their pastures wend our sleepy
    cows ;
And in the shadow, on the broad tank cast
By that hoar tree, so beautiful and vast,
The water-lilies spring, like snow enmassed.

But not because of its magnificence
  Dear is the Casuarina to my soul :
  Beneath it we have played ; though
    years may roll,
O sweet companions, loved with love in-
    tense,
For your sakes, shall the tree be ever
    dear.
Blent with your images, it shall arise
In memory, till the hot tears blind mine
    eyes !
What is that dirge-like murmur that I
    hear

Like the sea breaking on a shingle-beach ?
It is the tree's lament, an eerie speech,
That haply to the unknown land may reach.

Unknown, yet well-known to the eye of
    faith !
  Ah, I have heard that wail far, far away
  In distant lands, by many a sheltered bay,
When slumbered in his cave the water-
    wraith
And the waves gently kissed the classic
    shore
Of France or Italy, beneath the moon,
When earth lay trancèd in a dreamless
    swoon :
  And every time the music rose, — before
Mine inner vision rose a form sublime,
Thy form, O Tree, as in my happy prime
I saw thee, in my own loved native clime.

Therefore I fain would consecrate a lay
  Unto thy honor, Tree, beloved of those
  Who now in blessed sleep for aye re-
    pose, —
Dearer than life to me, alas, were they !
  Mayst thou be numbered when my days
    are done
With deathless trees — like those in Bor-
    rowdale,
Under whose awful branches lingered pale
  "Fear, trembling Hope, and Death, the
    skeleton,
And Time the shadow ;" and though weak
    the verse
That would thy beauty fain, oh, fain re-
    hearse,
May Love defend thee from Oblivion's
    curse.

William Sharp

THE LAST ABORIGINAL

I SEE him sit, wild-eyed, alone,
  Amidst gaunt, spectral, moonlit gums ;
He waits for death : not once a moan
  From out his rigid fixed lips comes ;
His lank hair falls adown a face
  Haggard as any wave-worn stone,
And in his eyes I dimly trace
The memory of a vanished race.

The lofty ancient gum-trees stand,
  Each gray and ghostly in the moon,

The giants of an old strange land
  That was exultant in its noon
When all our Europe was o'erturned
  With deluge and with shifting sand,
With earthquakes that the hills inurned
And central fires that fused and burned.

The moon moves slowly through the vast
  And solemn skies ; the night is still,
Save when a warrigal springs past
  With dismal howl, or when the shrill
Scream of a parrot rings which feels
  A twining serpent's fangs fixed fast,

Or when a gray opossum squeals, —
Or long iguana, as it steals

From bole to bole, disturbs the leaves :
But hushed and still he sits — who knows
That all is o'er for him who weaves
With inner speech, malign, morose,
A curse upon the whites who came
And gathered up his race like sheaves
Of thin wheat, fit but for the flame —
Who shot or spurned them without shame.

He knows he shall not see again
The creeks whereby the lyre-birds sing ;
He shall no more upon the plain,
Sun-scorched, and void of water-spring,
Watch the dark cassowaries sweep
In startled flight, or, with spear lain
In ready poise, glide, twist, and creep
Where the brown kangaroo doth leap.

No more in silent dawns he 'll wait
By still lagoons, and mark the flight
Of black swans near : no more elate
Whirl high the boomerang aright
Upon some foe. He knows that now
He too must share his race's night —
He scarce can know the white man's plough
Will one day pass above his brow.

Last remnant of the Austral race
He sits and stares, with failing breath :
The shadow deepens on his face,
For 'midst the spectral gums waits death :
A dingo's sudden howl swells near —
He stares once with a startled gaze,
As half in wonder, half in fear,
Then sinks back on his unknown bier.

THE COVES OF CRAIL

THE moon-white waters wash and leap,
The dark tide floods the Coves of Crail ;
Sound, sound he lies in dreamless sleep,
Nor hears the sea-wind wail.

The pale gold of his oozy locks
Doth hither drift and thither wave ;
His thin hands plash against the rocks,
His white lips nothing crave.

Afar away she laughs and sings —
A song he loved, a wild sea-strain —
Of how the mermen weave their rings
Upon the reef-set main.

Sound, sound he lies in dreamless sleep,
Nor hears the sea-wind wail,
Though with the tide his white hands creep
Amid the Coves of Crail.

THE ISLE OF LOST DREAMS

THERE is an Isle beyond our ken,
Haunted by Dreams of weary men.
Gray Hopes enshadow it with wings
Weary with burdens of old things :
There the insatiate water-springs
Rise with the tears of all who weep :
And deep within it, — deep, oh, deep ! —
The furtive voice of Sorrow sings.
    There evermore,
        Till Time be o'er,
Sad, oh, so sad ! the Dreams of men
Drift through the Isle beyond our ken.

THE DEATH-CHILD

SHE sits beneath the elder-tree
And sings her song so sweet,
And dreams o'er the burn that darksomely
Runs by her moonwhite feet.

Her hair is dark as starless night,
Her flower-crowned face is pale,
But oh, her eyes are lit with light
Of dread ancestral bale.

She sings an eerie song, so wild
With immemorial dule —
Though young and fair, Death's mortal
    child
That sits by that dark pool.

And oft she cries an eldritch scream,
When red with human blood
The burn becomes a crimson stream,
A wild, red, surging flood :

Or shrinks, when some swift tide of tears —
The weeping of the world —
Dark eddying 'neath man's phantom-fears
Is o'er the red stream hurled.

For hours beneath the elder-tree
She broods beside the stream ;
Her dark eyes filled with mystery,
Her dark soul rapt in dream.

The lapsing flow she heedeth not
Through deepest depths she scans :

Life is the shade that clouds her thought,
As Death's the eclipse of man's.

Time seems but as a bitter thing
Remembered from of yore :
Yet ah (she thinks) her song she 'll sing
When Time's long reign is o'er.

Erstwhiles she bends alow to hear
What the swift water sings,
The torrent running darkly clear
With secrets of all things.

And then she smiles a strange sad smile
And lets her harp lie long ;
The death-waves oft may rise the while,
She greets them with no song.

Few ever cross that dreary moor,
Few see that flower-crowned head ;
But whoso knows that wild song's lure
Knoweth that he is dead.

FROM "SOSPIRI DI ROMA"

SUSURRO

BREATH o' the grass,
Ripple of wandering wind,
Murmur of tremulous leaves :
A moonbeam moving white
Like a ghost across the plain :
A shadow on the road :
And high up, high,
From the cypress-bough,
A long sweet melancholy note.
Silence.
And the topmost spray
Of the cypress-bough is still
As a wavelet in a pool :
The road lies duskily bare :
The plain is a misty gloom :
Still are the tremulous leaves ;
Scarce a last ripple of wind,
Scarce a breath i' the grass.
Hush : the tired wind sleeps :
Is it the wind's breath, or
Breath o' the grass ?

RED POPPIES

IN THE SABINE VALLEYS NEAR ROME

THROUGH the seeding grass,
And the tall corn,
The wind goes :
With nimble feet,

And blithe voice,
Calling, calling,
The wind goes
Through the seeding grass,
And the tall corn.

What calleth the wind,
Passing by —
The shepherd-wind ?
Far and near
He laugheth low,
And the red poppies
Lift their heads
And toss i' the sun.
A thousand thousand blooms
Tossed i' the air,
Banners of joy,
For 't is the shepherd-wind
Passing by,
Singing and laughing low
Through the seeding grass
And the tall corn.

THE WHITE PEACOCK

HERE where the sunlight
Floodeth the garden,
Where the pomegranate
Reareth its glory
Of gorgeous blossom ;
Where the oleanders
Dream through the noontides ;
And, like surf o' the sea
Round cliffs of basalt,
The thick magnolias
In billowy masses
Front the sombre green of the ilexes:
Here where the heat lies
Pale blue in the hollows,
Where blue are the shadows
On the fronds of the cactus,
Where pale blue the gleaming
Of fir and cypress,
With the cones upon them
Amber or glowing
With virgin gold :
Here where the honey-flower
Makes the heat fragrant,
As though from the gardens
Of Gulistân,
Where the bulbul singeth
Though a mist of roses,
A breath were borne :
Here where the dream-flowers,
The cream-white poppies

Silently waver,
And where the Scirocco,
Faint in the hollows,
Foldeth his soft white wings in the sun-
    light,
And lieth sleeping
Deep in the heart of
A sea of white violets :
Here, as the breath, as the soul of this
    beauty
Moveth in silence, and dreamlike, and
    slowly,
White as a snow-drift in mountain valleys
When softly upon it the gold light lingers :
White as the foam o' the sea that is driven
O'er billows of azure agleam with sun-
    yellow :
Cream-white and soft as the breasts of a
    girl,
Moves the White Peacock, as though
    through the noon-tide
A dream of the moonlight were real for a
    moment.
Dim on the beautiful fan that he spreadeth,
Foldeth and spreadeth abroad in the sun-
    light,
Dim on the cream-white are blue adum-
    brations,
Shadows so pale in their delicate blueness
That visions they seem as of vanishing vio-
    lets,
The fragrant white violets veinèd with
    azure,
Pale, pale as the breath of blue smoke in
    far woodlands.

Here, as the breath, as the soul of this
    beauty,
White as a cloud through the heats of the
    noontide
Moves the White Peacock.

SONG

LOVE in my heart : oh, heart of me, heart
    of me !
Love is my tyrant, Love is supreme.
What if he passeth, oh, heart of me, heart
    of me !
Love is a phantom, and Life is a dream !

What if he changeth, oh, heart of me, heart
    of me !
Oh, can the waters be void of the wind ?
What if he wendeth afar and apart from
    me,
What if he leave me to perish behind ?

What if he passeth, oh, heart of me, heart
    of me !
A flame i' the dusk, a breath of Desire ?
Nay, my sweet Love is the heart and the
    soul of me,
And I am the innermost heart of his fire !

Love in my heart : oh, heart of me, heart
    of me !
Love is my tyrant, Love is supreme.
What if he passeth, oh, heart of me, heart
    of me !
Love is a phantom, and Life is a dream !

Oscar Wilde

AVE IMPERATRIX

SET in this stormy Northern sea,
    Queen of these restless fields of tide,
England ! what shall men say of thee,
    Before whose feet the worlds divide ?

The earth, a brittle globe of glass,
    Lies in the hollow of thy hand,
And through its heart of crystal pass,
    Like shadows through a twilight land,

The spears of crimson-suited war,
    The long white-crested waves of fight,

And all the deadly fires which are
    The torches of the lords of Night.

The yellow leopards, strained and lean,
    The treacherous Russian knows so
        well,
With gaping blackened jaws are seen
    To leap through hail of screaming
        shell.

The strong sea-lion of England's wars
    Hath left his sapphire cave of sea,
To battle with the storm that mars
    The star of England's chivalry.

The brazen-throated clarion blows
  Across the Pathan's reedy fen,
And the high steeps of Indian snows
  Shake to the tread of armèd men.

And many an Afghan chief, who lies
  Beneath his cool pomegranate-trees,
Clutches his sword in fierce surmise
  When on the mountain-side he sees

The fleet-foot Marri scout, who comes
  To tell how he hath heard afar
The measured roll of English drums
  Beat at the gates of Kandahar.

For southern wind and east wind meet
  Where, girt and crowned by sword and
    fire,
England with bare and bloody feet
  Climbs the steep road of wide empire.

O lonely Himalayan height,
  Gray pillar of the Indian sky,
Where saw'st thou last in clanging fight
  Our wingèd dogs of Victory ?

The almond groves of Samarcand,
  Bokhara, where red lilies blow,
And Oxus, by whose yellow sand
  The grave white-turbaned merchants go ;

And on from thence to Ispahan,
  The gilded garden of the sun,
Whence the long dusty caravan
  Brings cedar and vermilion ;

And that dread city of Cabool
  Set at the mountain's scarpèd feet,
Whose marble tanks are ever full
  With water for the noonday heat,

Where through the narrow straight Bazaar
  A little maid Circassian
Is led, a present from the Czar
  Unto some old and bearded khan, —

Here have our wild war-eagles flown,
  And flapped wide wings in fiery fight ;
But the sad dove, that sits alone
  In England — she hath no delight.

In vain the laughing girl will lean
  To greet her love with love-lit eyes :
Down in some treacherous black ravine,
  Clutching his flag, the dead boy lies.

And many a moon and sun will see
  The lingering wistful children wait
To climb upon their father's knee ;
  And in each house made desolate

Pale women who have lost their lord
  Will kiss the relics of the slain —
Some tarnished epaulette — some sword —
  Poor toys to soothe such anguished pain.

For not in quiet English fields
  Are these, our brothers, lain to rest,
Where we might deck their broken shields
  With all the flowers the dead love best.

For some are by the Delhi walls,
  And many in the Afghan land,
And many where the Ganges falls
  Through seven mouths of shifting sand.

And some in Russian waters lie,
  And others in the seas which are
The portals to the East, or by
  The wind-swept heights of Trafalgar.

O wandering graves ! O restless sleep !
  O silence of the sunless day !
O still ravine ! O stormy deep !
  Give up your prey ! Give up your prey !

And those whose wounds are never healed,
  Whose weary race is never won,
O Cromwell's England ! must thou yield
  For every inch of ground a son ?

Go ! crown with thorns thy gold-crowned
    head,
  Change thy glad song to song of pain ;
Wind and wild wave have got thy dead,
  And will not yield them back again.

Wave and wild wind and foreign shore
  Possess the flower of English land —
Lips that thy lips shall kiss no more,
  Hands that shall never clasp thy hand.

What profit now that we have bound
  The whole round world with nets of gold,
If hidden in our heart is found
  The care that groweth never old ?

What profit that our galleys ride,
  Pine-forest like, on every main ?
Ruin and wreck are at our side,
  Grim warders of the House of pain.

Where are the brave, the strong, the
    fleet ?
Where is our English chivalry ?
Wild grasses are their burial-sheet,
    And sobbing waves their threnody.

O loved ones lying far away,
    What word of love can dead lips send ?
O wasted dust ! O senseless clay !
    Is this the end ? is this the end ?

Peace, peace ! we wrong the noble dead
    To vex their solemn slumber so ;
Though childless, and with thorn-crowned
    head,
    Up the steep road must England go,

Yet when this fiery web is spun,
    Her watchmen shall descry from far
The young Republic like a sun
    Rise from these crimson seas of war.

Douglas B. W. Sladen

A CHRISTMAS LETTER FROM AUSTRALIA

'T is Christmas, and the North wind blows ;
    't was two years yesterday
Since from the Lusitania's bows I looked
    o'er Table Bay,
A tripper round the narrow world, a pil-
    grim of the main,
Expecting when her sails unfurled to start
    for home again.

'T is Christmas, and the North wind blows ;
    to-day our hearts are one,
Though you are 'mid the English snows
    and I in Austral sun ;
You, when you hear the Northern blast,
    pile high a mightier fire,
Our ladies cower until it 's past in lawn and
    lace attire.

I fancy I can picture you upon this Christ-
    mas night,
Just sitting as you used to do, the laughter
    at its height :
And then a sudden, silent pause intruding
    on your glee,
And kind eyes glistening because you
    chanced to think of me.

This morning when I woke and knew 't was
    Christmas come again,
I almost fancied I could view white rime
    upon the pane,
And hear the ringing of the wheels upon
    the frosty ground,
And see the drip that downward steals in
    icy casket bound.

I daresay you 'll be on the lake, or sliding
    on the snow,
And breathing on your hands to make the
    circulation flow,
Nestling your nose among the furs of which
    your boa 's made, —
The Fahrenheit here registers a hundred in
    the shade.

It is not quite a Christmas here with this
    unclouded sky,
This pure transparent atmosphere, this sun
    midheaven-high ;
To see the rose upon the bush, young leaves
    upon the trees,
And hear the forest's summer hush or the
    low hum of bees.

But cold winds bring not Christmastide,
    nor budding roses June,
And when it 's night upon your side we 're
    basking in the noon.
Kind hearts make Christmas — June can
    bring blue sky or clouds above ;
The only universal spring is that which
    comes of love.

And so it 's Christmas in the South as or
    the North-Sea coasts,
Though we are starved with summer-drouth
    and you with winter frosts.
And we shall have our roast beef here, and
    think of you the while,
Though all the watery hemisphere cuts off
    the mother isle.

Feel sure that we shall think of you, we
    who have wandered forth,

And many a million thoughts will go to-day
  from south to north ;
Old heads will muse on churches old, where
  bells will ring to-day —
The very bells, perchance, which tolled
  their fathers to the clay.

And now, good-night ! and I shall dream
  that I am with you all,
Watching the ruddy embers gleam athwart
  the panelled hall ;
Nor care I if I dream or not, though sev-
  ered by the foam,
My heart is always in the spot which was
  my childhood's home.

SUNSET ON THE CUNIMBLA VALLEY, BLUE MOUNTAINS

I SAT upon a windy mountain height,
On a huge rock outstanding from the
  rest ;
The sun had sunk behind a neighboring
  crest,
Leaving chill shade ; but looking down, my
  sight
Beheld the vale still bathed in his warm
  light
And of the perfect peace of eve pos-
  sessed,
No wave upon the forest on its breast
And all its park-like glades with sunshine
  bright.
It put me into mind of the old age
Of one who leaves ambition's rocks and
  peaks
To those inhabited by nobler rage,
And still existence in life's valleys seeks ;
His is the peaceful eve ; but then one
  hour
Of mountain life is worthy his twenty-
  four.

THE TROPICS

LOVE we the warmth and light of tropic
  lands,
The strange bright fruit, the feathery fan-
  spread leaves,
The glowing mornings and the mellow
  eves,
The strange shells scattered on the golden
  sands,

The curious handiwork of Eastern hands,
The little carts ambled by humpbacked
  beeves,
The narrow outrigged native boat which
  cleaves,
Unscathed, the surf outside the coral
  strands.
Love we the blaze of color, the rich red
Of broad tiled-roof and turban, the bright
  green
Of plantain-frond . and paddy-field, nor
  dread
The fierceness of the noon. The sky serene,
The chill-less air, quaint sights, and tropic
  trees,
Seem like a dream fulfilled of lotus-ease.

FROM THE DRAMA OF "CHARLES II"

REFRAIN

COME and kiss me, mistress Beauty,
I will give you all that 's due t' ye.

I will taste your rosebud lips
Daintily as the bee sips ;
At your bonny eyes I 'll look
Like a scholar at his book :

On my bosom you shall rest,
Like a robin on her nest :
Round my body you shall twine,
I 'll be elm, and you be vine :

In a bumper of your breath
I would drain a draught of death :
In the tangles of your hair
I 'd be hanged and never care.

Then come kiss me, mistress Beauty,
I will give you all that 's due t' ye.

SALOPIA INHOSPITALIS

TOUCH not that maid :
She is a flower, and changeth but to fade.
Fragrant is she, and fair
As any shape that haunts this lower air ;
In form as graceful and as free
As honeysuckles and the lilies be ;
Insensible, and shrinking from caress
As flowers, which you peril when you
  press.

Gaze not on her ;
She is a being of another sphere.
Brilliant is she, and bright
As any star illuminate at night ;
Of stuff as sober and as fine
As hers whose glory through the moon doth
    shine ;
Unliker to come down to this thy love
Than any orb that 's fixed for aye above.

Heed her no more :
She is a gem whose heart thou canst not
    bore ;
Glistering is she, and grand
As any stone that decks a monarch's hand ;
In face as free from flaw or stain
As diamond from mine, or pearl from main :
But she thy fire and fever never felt,
For adamant can neither waste nor melt.

Henry Charles Beeching

A SUMMER DAY

GREEN leaves panting for joy with the
    great wind rushing through ;
A burst of the sun from cloud and a
    sparkle on valley and hill,
Gold on the corn, and red on the poppy,
    and on the rill
Silver, and over all white clouds afloat in
    the blue.

Swallows that dart, a lark unseen, innume-
    rous song
Chirruped and twittered, a lowing of
    cows in the meadow grass,
Murmuring gnats, and bees that suck
    their honey and pass :
God is alive, and at work in the world : —
    we did it wrong.

Human eyes, and human hands, and a
    human face
Darkly beheld before in a vision, not
    understood,
Do I at last begin to feel as I stand and gaze
Why God waited for this, then called
    the world very good ?

TO MY TOTEM

" Sub tegmine fagi."

THY name of old was great :
    What though sour critics teach
" The beech by the Scæan gate
    Was not indeed a beech,"
That sweet Theocritus
    The ilex loved, not thee ? —
These are made glorious
    Through thy name, glorious tree.

And sure 't was 'neath thy shade
    Tityrus oft did use
(The while his oxen strayed)
    To meditate the Muse.
To thee 't was Corydon
    (Sad shepherd) did lament
Vain hopes, and violets wan
    To fair Alexis sent.

Our singers loved thee, too :
    In Chaucer's liquid verse
Are set thy praises due
    The ages but rehearse ;
Though later poets bring
    Their homage still, and I
The least of those who sing
    Thy name would magnify.

For long ago my sires,
    Ere Hengist crossed the sea
To map our English shires,
    Gave up their heart to thee,
And vowed if thou wouldst keep
    Their lives from fire and foe,
Thou too shouldst never weep
    The axe's deadly blow.

Thou hast my heart to-day :
    Whether in June I sit
And watch the leaves at play,
    The flickering shadows flit ;
Or whether, when leaves fall
    And red the autumn mould,
I pace the woodland hall
    Thy stately trunks uphold.

Thou hast my heart, and here
    In scattered fruit I see
An emblem true and clear
    Of what my heart must be : —

Hard sheath and scanty fare,
Yet forced on every side
To break apart and share
Small gifts it fain would hide.

KNOWLEDGE AFTER DEATH

Siccine separat amara mors ?
Is death so bitter ?   Can it shut us fast
Off from ourselves, that future from this
      past,
When Time compels us through those nar-
      now doors ?
Must we, supplanted by ourselves in the
      course,
Changelings, become as they who know at
      last
A river's secret, never having cast
One guess, or known one doubt, about its
      source ?
Is it so bitter ?   Does not knowledge here
Forget her gradual growth, and how each
      day
Seals up the sum of each world-conscious
      soul ?
So, though our ghosts forget us, waste no
      tear ;
We being ourselves would gladly be as
      they,
And we being they are still ourselves made
      whole.

PRAYERS

I

God who created me
      Nimble and light of limb,
In three elements free,
      To run, to ride, to swim :
Not when the sense is dim,
      But now from the heart of joy,
I would remember Him :
      Take the thanks of a boy.

II

Jesu, King and Lord,
      Whose are my foes to fight,
Gird me with thy sword
      Swift, and sharp, and bright.
Thee would I serve if I might,
      And conquer if I can,
From day-dawn till night :
      Take the strength of a man.

III

Spirit of Love and Truth,
      Breathing in grosser clay,
The light and flame of youth,
      Delight of men in the fray,
Wisdom in strength's decay ;
      From pain, strife, wrong, to be free
This best gift I pray :
      Take my spirit to Thee.

John William Mackail

AN ETRUSCAN RING

I

Where, girt with orchard and with olive-
      yard,
The white hill-fortress glimmers on the
      hill,
Day after day an ancient goldsmith's
      skill
Guided the copper graver, tempered hard
By some lost secret, while he shaped the
      sard
Slowly to beauty, and his tiny drill,
Edged with corundum, ground its way
      until
The gem lay perfect for the ring to
      guard.

Then seeing the stone complete to his de-
      sire,
With mystic imagery carven thus,
And dark Egyptian symbols fabulous,
He drew through it the delicate golden
      wire,
And bent the fastening ; and the Etrurian
      sun
Sank behind Ilva, and the work was done.

II

What dark-haired daughter of a Lucumo
Bore on her slim white finger to the
      grave
This the first gift her Tyrrhene lover
      gave,
Those five-and-twenty centuries ago ?

What shadowy dreams might haunt it,
   lying low
So long, while kings and armies, wave on
   wave,
Above the rock-tomb's buried architrave
Went million - footed trampling to and
   fro ?

Who knows ? but well it is so frail a thing,
Unharm'd by conquering Time's supremacy,
Still should be fair, though scarce less old
   than Rome.
Now once again at rest from wandering
Across the high Alps and the dreadful sea,
In utmost England let it find a home.

J. B. B. Nichols

LINES BY A PERSON OF QUALITY

THE loves that doubted, the loves that dis-
   sembled,
That still mistrusted themselves and trem-
   bled,
That held back their hands and would
   not touch ;
Who strained sad eyes to look more nearly,
And saw too curiously and clearly
What others blindly clutch ;

To whom their passion seemed only seeming,
Who dozed and dreamed they were only
   dreaming,
And fell in a dusk of dreams on sleep ;
When dreams and darkness are rent asun-
   der,
And morn makes mock of their doubts and
   wonder,
What should they do but weep ?

A PASTORAL

MY love and I among the mountains strayed
   When heaven and earth in summer heat
   were still,
Aware anon that at our feet were laid
   Within a sunny hollow of the hill
A long-haired shepherd-lover and a maid.

They saw nor heard us, who a space above,
   With hands clasped close as hers were
   clasped in his,

Marked how the gentle golden sunlight
   strove
To play about their leaf-crowned curls,
   and kiss
Their burnished slender limbs, half-bared
   to his love.

But grave or pensive seemed the boy to
   grow,
For while upon the grass unfingered lay
The slim twin-pipes, he ever watched with
   slow
   Dream-laden looks the ridge that far away
Surmounts the sleeping midsummer with
   snow.

These things we saw ; moreover we could
   hear
The girl's soft voice of laughter, grown
   more bold
With the utter noonday silence, sweet and
   clear :
   " Why dost thou think ? By thinking
   one grows old ;
Wouldst thou for all the world be old, my
   dear ? "

Here my love turned to me, but her eyes told
   Her thought with smiles before she spake
   a word ;
And being quick their meaning to behold
   I could not choose but echo what we
   heard :
" Sweet heart, wouldst thou for all the
   world be old ? "

Mrs. Darmesteter

(A. MARY F. ROBINSON)

DAWN-ANGELS

ALL night I watched awake for morning,
  At last the East grew all aflame,
The birds for welcome sang, or warning,
  And with their singing morning came.

Along the gold-green heavens drifted
  Pale wandering souls that shun the light,
Whose cloudy pinions, torn and rifted,
  Had beat the bars of Heaven all night.

These clustered round the moon, but higher
  A troop of shining spirits went,
Who were not made of wind or fire,
  But some divine dream-element.

Some held the Light, while those remaining
  Shook out their harvest-colored wings,
A faint unusual music raining,
  (Whose sound was Light) on earthly
      things.

They sang, and as a mighty river
  Their voices washed the night away,
From East to West ran one white shiver,
  And waxen strong their song was Day.

COCKAYNE COUNTRY

NEAR where yonder evening star
  Makes a glory in the air,
Lies a land dream-found and far
  Where it is light alway.
There those lovely ghosts repair
  Who in Sleep's enchantment are,
In Cockayne dwell all things fair.
  (But it is far away.)

Through the gates — a goodly sight —
  Troops of men and maidens come,
There shut out from Heaven at night
  Belated angels stray ;
Down those wide-arched groves they roam
  Through a land of great delight,
Dreaming they are safe at home.
  (But it is far away.)

There the leaves of all the trees
  Written are with a running rhyme,
There all poets live at peace,
  And lovers are true, they say.

Earth in that unwintered clime
  Like a star incarnate sees
The glory of her future time.
  (But it is far away.)

Hard to find as it is far !
  Dark nights shroud its brilliance rare,
Crouching round the cloudy bar
  Under the wings of day.
But if thither ye will fare,
  Love and Death the pilots are, —
Might either one convey me there !
  (But it is far away.)

CELIA'S HOME-COMING

MAIDENS, kilt your skirts and go
  Down the stormy garden-ways,
Pluck the last sweet pinks that blow,
  Gather roses, gather bays,
Since our Celia comes to-day
That has been too long away.

Crowd her chamber with your sweets -
  Not a flower but grows for her !
Make her bed with linen sheets
  That have lain in lavender ;
Light a fire before she come
Lest she find us chill at home.

Ah, what joy when Celia stands
  By the leaping blaze at last,
Stooping down to warm her hands
  All benumbèd with the blast,
While we hide her cloak away
To assure us she shall stay.

Cyder bring and cowslip wine,
  Fruits and flavors from the East,
Pears and pippins too, and fine
  Saffron loaves to make a feast:
China dishes, silver cups,
For the board where Celia sups !

Then, when all the feasting 's done,
  She shall draw us round the blaze,
Laugh, and tell us every one
  Of her far triumphant days —
Celia, out of doors a star,
By the hearth a holier Lar !

FROM "TUSCAN CYPRESS"

(RISPETTI)

I

When I am dead and I am quite forgot,
  What care I if my spirit lives or dies ?
To walk with angels in a grassy plot,
  And pluck the lilies grown in Paradise ?

Ah, no — the heaven of all my heart has
    been
To hear your voice and catch the sighs be-
    tween.
Ah, no — the better heaven I fain would
    give,
But in a cranny of your soul to live.

II

Ah me, you well might wait a little while,
  And not forget me, Sweet, until I die !
I had a home, a little distant isle,
  With shadowy trees and tender misty sky.

I had a home ! It was less dear than thou,
And I forgot, as you forget me now.
I had a home, more dear than I could tell,
And I forgot, but now remember well.

III

Love me to-day and think not on to-morrow,
  Come, take my hands, and lead me out
    of doors,
There in the fields let us forget our sorrow,
  Talking of Venice and Ionian shores ; —

Talking of all the seas innumerable
Where we will sail and sing when I am well ;
Talking of Indian roses gold and red,
Which we will plait in wreaths — when I
    am dead.

ROSA ROSARUM

Give me, O friend, the secret of thy heart
  Safe in my breast to hide,
So that the leagues which keep our lives
    apart
  May not our souls divide.

Give me the secret of thy life to lay
  Asleep within my own,
Nor dream that it shall mock thee any day
  By any sign or tone.

Nay, as in walking through some convent-
    close,
  Passing beside a well,
Oft have we thrown a red and scented
    rose
  To watch it as it fell ;

Knowing that never more the rose shall
    rise
  To shame us, being dead ;
Watching it spin and dwindle till it lies
  At rest, a speck of red —

Thus, I beseech thee, down the silent
    deep
  And darkness of my heart,
Cast thou a rose ; give me a rose to keep,
  My friend, before we part.

For, as thou passest down thy garden-
    ways,
  Many a blossom there
Groweth for thee : lilies and laden bays,
  And rose and lavender.

But down the darkling well one only rose
  In all the year is shed ;
And o'er that chill and secret wave it
    throws
  A sudden dawn of red.

DARWINISM

When first the unflowering Fern-forest
  Shadowed the dim lagoons of old,
A vague unconscious long unrest
  Swayed the great fronds of green and
    gold.

Until the flexible stems grew rude,
  The fronds began to branch and bower,
And lo ! upon the unblossoming wood
  There breaks a dawn of apple-flower

Then on the fruitful Forest-boughs
  For ages long the unquiet ape
Swung happy in his airy house
  And plucked the apple and sucked the
    grape.

Until in him at length there stirred
  The old, unchanged, remote distress,
That pierced his world of wind and bird
  With some divine unhappiness.

Not Love, nor the wild fruits he sought ;
  Nor the fierce battles of his clan
Could still the unborn and aching thought
  Until the brute became the man.

Long since. . . . And now the same unrest
  Goads to the same invisible goal,
Till some new gift, undreamed, unguessed,
  End the new travail of the soul.

A BALLAD OF ORLEANS

1429

THE fray began at the middle-gate,
  Between the night and the day ;
Before the matin bell was rung
  The foe was far away.
There was no knight in the land of France
  Could gar that foe to flee,
Till up there rose a young maiden,
  And drove them to the sea.

Sixty forts around Orleans town,
  And sixty forts of stone !
Sixty forts at our gates last night —
  To-day there is not one !

Talbot, Suffolk, and Pole are fled
  Beyond the Loire, in fear —

Many a captain who would not drink,
  Hath drunken deeply there —
Many a captain is fallen and drowned,
  And many a knight is dead,
And many die in the misty dawn
  While forts are burning red.

The blood ran off our spears all night
  As the rain runs off the roofs —
God rest their souls that fell i' the fight
  Among our horses' hoofs !
They came to rob us of our own
  With sword and spear and lance,
They fell and clutched the stubborn
  earth,
  And bit the dust of France !

We fought across the moonless dark
  Against their unseen hands —
A knight came out of Paradise
  And fought among our bands.
Fight on, O maiden knight of God,
  Fight on and do not tire —
For lo ! the misty break o' the day
  Sees all their forts on fire !

Sixty forts around Orleans town,
  And sixty forts of stone !
Sixty forts at our gates last night —
  To-day there is not one !

John Davidson

HARVEST–HOME SONG

THE frost will bite us soon ;
  His tooth is on the leaves :
Beneath the golden moon
  We bear the golden sheaves :
We care not for the winter's spite,
We keep our Harvest-home to-night.
    Hurrah for the English yeoman !
      Fill full, fill the cup !
    Hurrah ! he yields to no man !
      Drink deep ; drink it up !

The pleasure of a king
  Is tasteless to the mirth
Of peasants when they bring
  The harvest of the earth.
With pipe and tabor hither roam
All ye who love our Harvest-home.

The thresher with his flail,
  The shepherd with his crook,
The milkmaid with her pail,
  The reaper with his hook —
To-night the dullest blooded clods
Are kings and queens, are demigods.
    Hurrah for the English yeoman !
      Fill full ; fill the cup !
    Hurrah ! he yields to no man !
      Drink deep ; drink it up !

A BALLAD OF HEAVEN

HE wrought at one great work for years ;
  The world passed by with lofty look :
Sometimes his eyes were dashed with
    tears ;
Sometimes his lips with laughter shook

His wife and child went clothed in rags,
  And in a windy garret starved :
He trod his measures on the flags,
  And high on heaven his music carved.

Wistful he grew, but never feared ;
  For always on the midnight skies
His rich orchestral score appeared
  In stars and zones and galaxies.

He sought to copy down his score :
  The moonlight was his lamp : he said,
" Listen, my love ; " but on the floor
  His wife and child were lying dead.

Her hollow eyes were open wide ;
  He deemed she heard with special zest :
Her death's-head infant coldly eyed
  The desert of her shrunken breast.

" Listen, my love : my work is done ;
  I tremble as I touch the page
To sign the sentence of the sun
  And crown the great eternal age.

" The slow adagio begins ;
  The winding-sheets are ravelled out
That swathe the minds of men, the sins
  That wrap their rotting souls about.

" The dead are heralded along ;
  With silver trumps and golden drums,
And flutes and oboes, keen and strong,
  My brave andante singing comes.

" Then like a python's sumptuous dress
  The frame of things is cast away,
And out of time's obscure distress
  The thundering scherzo crashes Day.

" For three great orchestras I hope
  My mighty music shall be scored :
On three high hills they shall have scope,
  With heaven's vault for a sounding-board.

Sleep well, love ; let your eyelids fall ;
  Cover the child ; good-night, and if . . .
What ? Speak . . . the traitorous end of
    all !
Both . . . cold and hungry . . . cold and
    stiff !

But no, God means us well, I trust :
  Dear ones, be happy, hope is nigh :

We are too young to fall to dust,
  And too unsatisfied to die."

He lifted up against his breast
  The woman's body stark and wan ,
And to her withered bosom prest
  The little skin-clad skeleton.

" You see you are alive," he cried.
  He rocked them gently to and fro.
" No, no, my love, you have not died ;
  Nor you, my little fellow ; no."

Long in his arms he strained his dead
  And crooned an antique lullaby ;
Then laid them on the lowly bed,
  And broke down with a doleful cry.

" The love, the hope, the blood, the
    brain,
  Of her and me, the budding life,
And my great music, — all in vain !
  My unscored work, my child, my wife !

" We drop into oblivion,
  And nourish some suburban sod :
My work, this woman, this my son,
  Are now no more : there is no God.

" The world's a dustbin ; we are due,
  And death's cart waits : be life accurst ! "
He stumbled down beside the two,
  And, clasping them, his great heart
    burst.

Straightway he stood at heaven's gate,
  Abashed and trembling for his sin :
I trow he had not long to wait,
  For God came out and let him in.

And then there ran a radiant pair,
  Ruddy with haste and eager-eyed,
To meet him first upon the stair,
  His wife and child beatified.

They clad him in a robe of light,
  And gave him heavenly food to eat ;
Great seraphs praised him to the height,
  Archangels sat about his feet.

God, smiling, took him by the hand,
  And led him to the brink of heaven :
He saw where systems whirling stand,
  Where galaxies like snow are driven.

Dead silence reigned ; a shudder ran
  Through space ; Time furled his wearied
    wings ;
A slow adagio then began
  Sweetly resolving troubled things.

The dead were heralded along :
  As if with drums and trumps of flame,
And flutes and oboes keen and strong,
  A brave andante singing came.

Then like a python's sumptuous dress
  The frame of things was cast away,
And out of Time's obscure distress
  The conquering scherzo thundered
    Day.

He doubted ; but God said, " Even so ;
  Nothing is lost that's wrought with
    tears :
The music that you made below
  Is now the music of the spheres."

LONDON

ATHWART the sky a lowly sigh
  From west to east the sweet wind carried;
The sun stood still on Primrose Hill ;
  His light in all the city tarried ;
The clouds on viewless columns bloomed
Like smouldering lilies unconsumed.

" Oh sweetheart, see ! How shadowy,
  Of some occult magician's rearing,
Or swung in space of heaven's grace
  Dissolving, dimly reappearing,
Afloat upon ethereal tides
St. Paul's above the city rides ! "

A rumor broke through the thin smoke,
  Enwreathing abbey, tower, and palace,
The parks, the squares, the thoroughfares,
  The million-peopled lanes and alleys,
An ever-muttering prisoned storm,
The heart of London beating warm.

Rosa Mulholland

LOVE AND DEATH

IN the wild autumn weather, when the rain
  was on the sea,
And the boughs sobbed together, Death
  came and spake to me :
" Those red drops of thy heart I have come
  to take from thee ;
As the storm sheds the rose, so thy love
  shall broken be,"
    Said Death to me.

Then I stood straight and fearless while
  the rain was in the wave,
And I spake low and tearless : " When
  thou hast made my grave,
Those red drops from my heart then thou
  shalt surely have ;
But the rose keeps its bloom, as I my love
  will save
    All for my grave."

In the wild autumn weather a dread sword
  slipped from its sheath ;
While the boughs sobbed together, I fought
  a fight with Death,

And I vanquished him with prayer, and I
  vanquished him by faith :
Now the summer air is sweet with the
  rose's fragrant breath
    That conquered Death.

SISTER MARY OF THE LOVE OF GOD

THIS is the convent where they tend the
  sick,
Comfort the dying, make the ailing
  strong ;
Covered, you see, with ivy, very thick ;
  Haunt of the birds, alive with bloom and
  song.

The happy sick are smiling in their beds,
  The happy sisters flitting to and fro ;
Ah, blessings on the wise and gentle heads
  That planned this place a hundred year
  ago !

To build the walls a woman crossed the
  sea,
  Travelled with tender feet a weary road

I 'll tell you now the little history
Of Sister Mary of the Love of God.

A lovely maiden of a high estate,
She danced away her days in careless
glee ;
A bird beside her window came and sate,
And piped and sang, " *The Lord has need
of thee !* "

Deep in the night, when everything was
still,
The restless dance, the music's merry
clang,
That bird would perch upon the window sill:
" *The Lord hath need of thee,*" it piped
and sang.

She rose and fled her chamber in affright,
And roused with eager call the minstrel
gray ;
" The birds are singing strange things in
the night ;
Tune me, O minstrel, something blythe
and gay ! "

The minstrel struck his harp with ready
power ;
The laughing echoes wakened merrily ;
The lady turned as white as lily-flower, —
The music trilled, " *The Lord has need
of thee !* "

Her guests came round her and her ball-
room blazed,
While lively footsteps on the floor did
beat ;
The lady led the dance with looks
amazed, —
" *The Lord doth need thee !* " said the
dancers' feet.

The feast was spread, and flowed the
rarest wine
In golden goblets clinking round the
board ;
The flashing cups from hand to hand did
shine,
And rang and chimed " *Go, give thee to
the Lord !* "

Within her chamber long the lady sate,
Then raised her downcast face, all pale
and sweet :
" There is a beggar lying at the gate —
Go, bring him in, that I may wash his
feet."

They looked upon her robes of satin sheen,
They looked upon her eyes so strange
and glad ;
They whispered, " She is not as she hath
been ; "
Her damsels wept, " Our lady hath gone
mad ! "

But in the night she stole away alone.
Then sang the minstrels many a mourn-
ful rhyme,
Till some forgot her as one never known,
And others said, " She hath some heavy
crime."

Ah me, it is a hundred years ago ! —
This ivy on the walls is thick, you see ;
The world would laugh if I should tell it so
Of Sister Mary's little history.

Another dances in her shoes to-day ;
One wears that gem of hers, another this ;
But she is happy and the poor are gay,
The sick are smiling and the dead in
bliss !

Edith Nesbit Bland

BALLAD OF A BRIDAL

Oh, fill me flagons full and fair,
Of red wine and of white,
nd, maidens mine, my bower prepare,
It is my wedding night !

Braid up my hair with gem and flower,
And make me fair and fine,

The day has dawned that brings the
hour
When my desire is mine ! "

They decked her bower with roses blown,
With rushes strewed the floor,
And sewed more jewels on her gown
Than ever she wore before.

She wore two roses in her face,
  Two jewels in her e'en ;
Her hair was crowned with sunset rays,
  Her brows shone white between.

"Tapers at the bed's foot," she saith,
  "Two tapers at the head ! "
(It seemed more like the bed of death
  Than like a bridal bed.)

He came. He took her hands in his :
  He kissed her on the face :
" There is more heaven in thy kiss
  Than in Our Lady's grace ! "

He kissed her once, he kissed her twice,
  He kissed her three times o'er,
He kissed her brow, he kissed her eyes,
  He kissed her mouth's red flower.

" Oh, love ! What is it ails thy knight ?
  I sicken and I pine —
Is it the red wine or the white,
  Or that sweet kiss of thine ? "

" No kiss, no wine or white or red
  Can make such sickness be : —
Lie down and die on thy bride-bed,
  For I have poisoned thee !

" And though the curse of saints and men
  Be for the deed on me,
I would it were to do again,
  Since thou wert false to me !

" Thou shouldst have loved or one or none,
  Nor *she* nor I loved twain ;
But we are twain thou hast undone,
  And therefore art thou slain.

" And when before my God I stand,
  With no base flesh between,
I shall hold up my guilty hand,
  And He shall judge it clean ! "

He fell across the bridal bed,
  Between the tapers pale.
" I, first, shall see our God " — he said,
  " And *I* will tell thy tale ;

" And, if God judge thee as I do
  Then art thou justified :
I loved thee, and I was not true,
  And that was why I died.

" If I might judge thee — thou shouldst be
  First of the saints on high,
But, ah, I fear God loveth thee
  Not half so dear as I ! "

Constance C. W. Naden

THE PANTHEIST'S SONG OF IMMORTALITY

BRING snow-white lilies, pallid heart-
  flushed roses,
  Enwreathe her brow with heavy scented
    flowers ;
In soft undreaming sleep her head reposes,
  While, unregretted, pass the sunlit
    hours.

Few sorrows did she know — and all are
  over ;
  A thousand joys — but they are all for-
    got ;
Her life was one fair dream of friend and
  lover,
  And were they false — ah, well, she
    knows it not.

Look in her face and lose thy dread of
  dying ;
  Weep not that rest will come, that toil
    will cease ;
Is it not well to lie as she is lying,
  In utter silence, and in perfect peace ?

Canst thou repine that sentient days are
  numbered ?
  Death is unconscious Life, that waits
    for birth ;
So didst thou live, while yet thine embryo
  slumbered,
  Senseless, unbreathing, even as heaven
    and earth.

Then shrink no more from Death, though
  Life be gladness,
  Nor seek him, restless in thy lonely pain

The law of joy ordains each hour of sadness,
And firm or frail, thou canst not live in
vain.

What though thy name by no sad lips be
spoken,
And no fond heart shall keep thy mem-
ory green ?
Thou yet shalt leave thine own enduring
token,
For earth is not as though thou ne'er
hadst been.

See yon broad current, hasting to the ocean,
Its ripples glorious in the western red :
Each wavelet passes, trackless ; yet its
motion
Has changed for evermore the river bed.

Ah, wherefore weep, although the form and
fashion

Of what thou seemest fades like sunset
flame ?
The uncreated Source of toil and passion
Through everlasting change abides the
same.

Yes, thou shalt die : but these almighty
forces,
That meet to form thee, live for ever-
more ;
They hold the suns in their eternal courses,
And shape the tiny sand-grains on the
shore.

Be calmly glad, thine own true kindred
seeing
In fire and storm, in flowers with dew
impearled ;
Rejoice in thine imperishable being,
One with the essence of the boundless
world.

Rennell Rodd

A ROMAN MIRROR

THEY found it in her hollow marble bed,
There where the numberless dead cities
sleep,
They found it lying where the spade
struck deep,
A broken mirror by a maiden dead.

These things — the beads she wore about
her throat
Alternate blue and amber all untied,
A lamp to light her way, and on one
side
The toll men pay to that strange ferry-
boat.

No trace to-day of what in her was fair !
Only the record of long years grown
green
Upon the mirror's lustreless dead sheen,
Grown dim at last, when all else withered
there.

Dead, broken, lustreless ! It keeps for
me
One picture of that immemorial land,

For oft as I have held thee in my hand
The dull bronze brightens, and I dream to
see

A fair face gazing in thee wondering
wise,
And o'er one marble shoulder all the
while
Strange lips that whisper till her own
lips smile,
And all the mirror laughs about her eyes.

It was well thought to set thee there, so
she
Might smooth the windy ripples of her
hair
And knot their tangled waywardness, or
ere
She stood before the queen Persephone.

And still it may be where the dead folk
rest
She holds a shadowy mirror to her
eyes,
And looks upon the changelessness, and
sighs
And sets the dead land lilies in her breast.

ACTEA

WHEN the last bitterness was past, she bore
Her singing Cæsar to the Garden Hill,
Her fallen pitiful dead emperor.
She lifted up the beggar's cloak he wore
— The one thing living that he would not
    kill —
And on those lips of his that sang no more,
That world-loathed head which she found
    lovely still,
Her cold lips closed, in death she had her
    will.
Oh wreck of the lost human soul left free
To gorge the beast thy mask of manhood
    screened !
Because one living thing, albeit a slave,
Shed those hot tears on thy dishonored
    grave,
Although thy curse be as the shoreless sea,
Because she loved, thou art not wholly
    fiend.

IMPERATOR AUGUSTUS

Is this the man by whose decree abide
The lives of countless nations, with the
    trace
Of fresh tears wet upon the hard cold
    face ?
— He wept, because a little child had
    died.
They set a marble image by his side,
A sculptured Eros, ready for the chase ;
It wore the dead boy's features, and the
    grace
Of pretty ways that were the old man's
    pride.
And so he smiled, grown softer now, and
    tired
Of too much empire, and it seemed a joy
Fondly to stroke and pet the curly head,
The smooth round limbs so strangely like
    the dead,
To kiss the white lips of his marble boy
And call by name his little heart's-desired.

THE DAISY

WITH little white leaves in the grasses,
    Spread wide for the smile of the sun,

It waits till the daylight passes
    And closes them one by one.

I have asked why it closed at even,
    And I know what it wished to say :
There are stars all night in the heaven,
    And I am the star of day.

"WHEN I AM DEAD"

WHEN I am dead, my spirit
    Shall wander far and free,
Through realms the dead inherit
    Of earth and sky and sea ;
Through morning dawn and gloaming,
    By midnight moons at will,
By shores where the waves are foaming,
    By seas where the waves are still.
I, following late behind you,
    In wingless sleepless flight,
Will wander till I find you,
    In sunshine or twilight ;
With silent kiss for greeting
    On lips and eyes and head,
In that strange after-meeting
    Shall love be perfected.
We shall lie in summer breezes
    And pass where whirlwinds go,
And the northern blast that freezes
    Shall bear us with the snow.
We shall stand above the thunder,
    And watch the lightnings hurled
At the misty mountains under,
    Of the dim forsaken world.
We shall find our footsteps' traces,
    And passing hand in hand
By old familiar places,
    We shall laugh, and understand.

THEN AND NOW

THERE never were such radiant noons,
    Such roses, such fair weather,
Such nightingales, such mellow moons,
    As while we were together !

But now the suns are poor and pale,
    The cloudy twilight closes,
The mists have choked the nightingale,
    The blight has killed the roses.

William Watson

EPIGRAMS

TO A SEABIRD

FAIN would I have thee barter fates with
    me, —
Lone loiterer where the shells like jewels
    be,
Hung on the fringe and frayed hem of the
    sea.
But no, — 't were cruel, wild-wing'd Bliss!
    to thee.

THE PLAY OF "KING LEAR"

HERE Love the slain with Love the slayer
    lies ;
Deep drowned are both in the same sun-
    less pool.
Up from its depths that mirror thundering
    skies
Bubbles the wan mirth of the mirthless
    Fool.

BYRON THE VOLUPTUARY

Too avid of earth's bliss, he was of those
    Whom Delight flies because they give
        her chase.
Only the odor of her wild hair blows
    Back in their faces hungering for her
        face.

ON DÜRER'S *MELENCOLIA*

WHAT holds her fixed far eyes nor lets
    them range ?
Not the strange sea, strange earth, or
    heav'n more strange ;
But her own phantom dwarfing these great
    three,
More strange than all, more old than
    heav'n, earth, sea.

EXIT

IN mid whirl of the dance of Time ye start,
    Start at the cold touch of Eternity,
And cast your cloaks about you, and de-
    part :
    The minstrels pause not in their min-
        strelsy.

LACHRYMÆ˙ MUSARUM

(6TH OCTOBER, 1892)

Low, like another's, lies the laurelled
    head :
The life that seemed a perfect song is o'er :
Carry the last great bard to his last bed.
Land that he loved, thy noblest voice is
    mute.
Land that he loved, that loved him ! never-
    more
Meadow of thine, smooth lawn or wild sea-
    shore,
Gardens of odorous bloom and tremulous
    fruit,
Or woodlands old, like Druid couches
    spread,
The master's feet shall tread.
Death's little rift hath rent the faultless
    lute :
The singer of undying songs is dead.

Lo, in this season pensive-hued and grave,
While fades and falls the doomed, reluc-
    tant leaf
From withered Earth's fantastic coronal,
With wandering sighs of forest and of
    wave
Mingles the murmur of a people's grief
For him whose leaf shall fade not, neither
    fall.
He hath fared forth, beyond these suns and
    showers.
For us, the autumn glow, the autumn flame,
And soon the winter silence shall be ours :
Him the eternal spring of fadeless fame
Crowns with no mortal flowers.

Rapt though he be from us,
Virgil salutes him, and Theocritus ;
Catullus, mightiest-brained Lucretius, each
Greets him, their brother, on the Stygian
    beach ;
Proudly a gaunt right hand doth Dante
    reach ;
Milton and Wordsworth bid him welcome
    home ;
Bright Keats to touch his raiment doth
    beseech ;
Coleridge, his locks aspersed with fairy
    foam,

Calm Spenser, Chaucer suave,
His equal friendship crave :
And godlike spirits hail him guest, in
    speech
Of Athens, Florence, Weimar, Stratford,
    Rome.

What needs his laurel our ephemeral
    tears,
To save from visitation of decay ?
Not in this temporal sunlight, now, that
    bay
Blooms, nor to perishable mundane ears
Sings he with lips of transitory clay ;
For he hath joined the chorus of his peers
In habitations of the perfect day :
His earthly notes a heavenly audience
    hears,
And more melodious are henceforth the
    spheres,
Enriched with music stolen from earth
    away.

He hath returned to regions whence he
    came.
Him doth the spirit divine
Of universal lovelinesss reclaim.
All nature is his shrine.
Seek him henceforward in the wind and
    sea,
In earth's and air's emotion or repose,
In every star's august serenity,
And in the rapture of the flaming rose.
There seek him if ye would not seek in
    vain,
There, in the rhythm and music of the
    Whole ;
Yea, and forever in the human soul
Made stronger and more beauteous by his
    strain.

For lo ! creation's self is one great
    choir,
And what is nature's order but the rhyme
Whereto the worlds keep time,
And all things move with all things from
    their prime ?
Who shall expound the mystery of the
    lyre ?
In far retreats of elemental mind
Obscurely comes and goes
The imperative breath of song, that as the
    wind
Is trackless, and oblivious whence it
    blows.

Demand of lilies wherefore they are white,
Extort her crimson secret from the rose,
But ask not of the Muse that she disclose
The meaning of the riddle of her might :
Somewhat of all things sealed and recon-
    dite,
Save the enigma of herself, she knows.
The master could not tell, with all his
    lore,
Wherefore he sang, or whence the mandate
    sped :
Even as the linnet sings, so I, he said ; —
Ah, rather as the imperial nightingale,
That held in trance the ancient Attic shore,
And charms the ages with the notes that
    o'er
All woodland chants immortally prevail !
And now, from our vain plaudits greatly
    fled,
He with diviner silence dwells instead,
And on no earthly sea with transient roar,
Unto no earthly airs, he trims his sail,
But far beyond our vision and our hail
Is heard forever and is seen no more.

No more, O never now,
Lord of the lofty and the tranquil brow
Whereon nor snows of time
Have fallen, nor wintry rime,
Shall men behold thee, sage and mage
    sublime.
Once, in his youth obscure,
The maker of this verse, which shall en-
    dure
By splendor of its theme that cannot die,
Beheld thee eye to eye,
And touched through thee the hand
Of every hero of thy race divine,
Even to the sire of all the laurelled line,
The sightless wanderer on the Ionian strand,
With soul as healthful as the poignant
    brine,
Wide as his skies and radiant as his seas,
Starry from haunts of his Familiars nine,
Glorious Mæonides.
Yea, I beheld thee, and behold thee yet :
Thou hast forgotten, but can I forget ?
The accents of thy pure and sovereign
    tongue,
Are they not ever goldenly imprest
On memory's palimpsest ?
I see the wizard locks like night that
    hung,
I tread the floor thy hallowing feet have
    trod ;

I see the hands a nation's lyre that strung,
The eyes that looked through life and
  gazed on God.

The seasons change, the winds they shift
  and veer ;
The grass of yesteryear
Is dead ; the birds depart, the groves de-
  cay :
Empires dissolve and peoples disappear :
Song passes not away.
Captains and conquerors leave a little dust,
And kings a dubious legend of their reign ;
The swords of Cæsars, they are less than
  rust :
The poet doth remain.
Dead is Augustus, Maro is alive ;
And thou, the Mantuan of our age and
  clime,
Like Virgil shalt thy race and tongue sur-
  vive,
Bequeathing no less honeyed words to
  time,
Embalmed in amber of eternal rhyme,
And rich with sweets from every Muse's
  hive ;
While to the measure of the cosmic rune
For purer ears thou shalt thy lyre attune,
And heed no more the hum of idle praise
In that great calm our tumults cannot
  reach,
Master who crown'st our immelodious days
With flower of perfect speech.

THE FIRST SKYLARK OF SPRING

Two worlds hast thou to dwell in, Sweet, —
  The virginal, untroubled sky,
And this vexed region at my feet. —
    Alas, but one have I !

To all my songs there clings the shade,
  The dulling shade, of mundane care ;
They amid mortal mists are made, —
    Thine, in immortal air.

My heart is dashed with griefs and fears ;
  My song comes fluttering, and is gone.
O high above the home of tears,
    Eternal Joy, sing on !

Not loftiest bard, of mightiest mind,
  Shall ever chant a note so pure,

Till he can cast this earth behind
    And breathe in heaven secure.

We sing of Life, with stormy breath
  That shakes the lute's distempered string:
We sing of Love, and loveless Death
    Takes up the song we sing.

And born in toils of Fate's control,
  Insurgent from the womb, we strive
With proud, unmanumitted soul
    To burst the golden gyve.

Thy spirit knows nor bounds nor bars ;
  On thee no shreds of thraldom hang :
Not more enlarged, the morning stars
    Their great Te Deum sang.

But I am fettered to the sod,
  And but forget my bonds an hour ;
In amplitude of dreams a god,
    A slave in dearth of power.

And fruitless knowledge clouds my soul,
  And fretful ignorance irks it more.
Thou sing'st as if thou knew'st the whole,
    And lightly held'st thy lore !

Sing, for with rapturous throes of birth,
  And arrowy labyrinthine sting,
There riots in the veins of Earth
    The ichor of the Spring !

Sing, for the beldam Night is fled,
  And Morn the bride is wreathed and gay;
Sing, while her revelling lord o'erhead
    Leads the wild dance of day !

The serpent Winter sleeps upcurled :
  Sing, till I know not if there be
Aught else in the dissolving world
    But melody and thee !

Sing, as thou drink'st of heaven thy fill,
  All hope, all wonder, all desire —
Creation's ancient canticle
    To which the worlds conspire !

Somewhat as thou, Man once could sing,
  In porches of the lucent morn,
Ere he had felt his lack of wing,
    Or cursed his iron bourn.

The springtime bubbled in his throat,
  The sweet sky seemed not far above,

And young and lovesome came the note ; —
  Ah, thine is Youth and Love !

Thou sing'st of what he knew of old,
  And dreamlike from afar recalls ;
In flashes of forgotten gold
    An orient glory falls.

And as he listens, one by one
Life's utmost splendors blaze more nigh ;
  Less inaccessible the sun,
    Less alien grows the sky.

For thou art native to the spheres,
  And of the courts of heaven art free,
And carriest to his temporal ears
    News from eternity ;

And lead'st him to the dizzy verge,
  And lur'st him o'er the dazzling line,
Where mortal and immortal merge,
    And human dies divine.

SONG IN IMITATION OF THE ELIZABETHANS

SWEETEST sweets that time hath rifled
  Live anew on lyric tongue —
Tresses with which Paris trifled,
  Lips to Antony's that clung.
These surrender not their rose,
Nor their golden puissance those.

Vain the envious loam that covers
  Her of Egypt, her of Troy :
Helen's, Cleopatra's lovers
  Still desire them, still enjoy.
Fate but stole what Song restored :
Vain the aspic, vain the cord.

Idly clanged the sullen portal,
  Idly the sepulchral door :
Fame the mighty, Love the immortal,
  These than foolish dust are more :
Nor may captive Death refuse
Homage to the conquering Muse.

Arthur Reed Ropes

IN PACE

WHEN you are dead some day, my dear,
  Quite dead and under ground,
Where you will never see or hear
  A summer sight or sound,
What shall remain of you in death,
When all our songs to you
Are silent as the bird whose breath
  Has sung the summer through ?

I wonder, will you ever wake,
  And with tired eyes again
Live for your old life's little sake
  An age of joy or pain ?
Shall some stern destiny control
  That perfect form, wherein
I hardly see enough of soul
  To make your life a sin ?

For, we have heard, for all men born
  One harvest-day prepares
Its golden garners for the corn,
  And fire to burn the tares ;
But who shall gather into sheaves,
  Or turn aside to blame
The poppies' puckered helpless leaves,
  Blown bells of scarlet flame ?

No hate so hard, no love so bold
  To seek your bliss or woe ;
You are too sweet for hell to hold,
  And heaven would tire you so.
A little while your joy shall be,
  And when you crave for rest
The earth shall take you utterly
  Again into her breast.

And we will find a quiet place
  For your still sepulchre,
And lay the flowers upon your face
  Sweet as your kisses were,
And with hushed voices void of mirth
  Spread the light turf above,
Soft as the silk you loved on earth
  As much as you could love.

Few tears, but once, our eyes shall shed,
  Nor will we sigh at all,
But come and look upon your bed
  When the warm sunlights fall.
Upon that grave no tree of fruit
  Shall grow, nor any grain,
Only one flower of shallow root
  That will not spring again.

ON THE BRIDGE

ALL the storm has rolled away,
  Only now a cloud or two
Drifts in ragged disarray
  Over the deep darkened blue ;
And the risen golden moon
  Shakes the shadows of the trees
  Round the river's stillnesses
And the birdsong of the June.

Under me the current glides,
  Brown and deep and dimly lit,
Soundless save against the sides
  Of the arch that narrows it ;
And the only sound that grieves
  Is a noise that never stops,
Footsteps of the falling drops
  Down the ladders of the leaves.

John Arthur Blaikie

ABSENCE

IF not now soft airs may blow
  From thy haven unto me,
If not now last Autumn's glow
  Thrill delight 'twixt me and thee,
Call up Memory, oh, entreat her,
In the present there's none sweeter.

One true thought and constant only
  To that pleasurable time
Me sufficeth to make lonely
  All the void and mocking prime
Of this summertide, whose story
Pales in that exceeding glory.

SONG

IN thy white bosom Love is laid ;
  His rosy cheek within that nest
Another dawning there hath made,
  Causing in me a new unrest.
Like as the sun the hills with fire
He wakes anew my old desire.

But ah, thou dost defy the boy,
  Too strong for him and me dost prove,

The freezing snows proclaim thee coy,
  Purloin the blushing hope of Love
Who flies, alas for thy disdain !
The throne where he alone should reign.

LOVE'S SECRET NAME

SIGH his name into the night
  With the stars for company,
From thy lips 't will take fair flight,
  Doing thee no injury,
If by the sea or trysting-tree
Thou breathe it in no company.

Whisper it from thy full heart,
  Let none hear thy passion moan,
Safe from cruel pang or smart,
  To the cold world unbeknown,
By darkling tree or silent sea
With Love alone for company.

In thy heart of hearts let sleep
  All thy rapture ; and his name
True in purity shall keep
  All its vital force and flame ;
Fickle speech and falsest jar
Come from lips that loudest are.

Francis Thompson

TO A POET BREAKING SILENCE

Too wearily had we and song
Been left to look and left to long,
Yea, song and we to long and look,
Since thine acquainted feet forsook

The mountain where the Muses hymn
For Sinai and the Seraphim.
Now in both the mountains' shine
Dress thy countenance, twice divine !
From Moses and the Muses draw
The Tables of thy double Law !

His rod-born fount and Castaly
Let the one rock bring forth for thee,
Renewing so from either spring
The songs which both thy countries sing :
Or we shall fear lest, heavened thus long,
Thou shouldst forget thy native song,
And mar thy mortal melodies
With broken stammer of the skies.

Ah ! let the sweet birds of the Lord
With earth's waters make accord ;
Teach how the crucifix may be
Carven from the laurel-tree,
Fruit of the Hesperides
Burnish take on Eden-trees,
The Muses' sacred grove be wet
With the red dew of Olivet,
And Sappho lay her burning brows
In white Cecilia's lap of snows !

Thy childhood must have felt the stings
Of too divine o'ershadowings ;
Its odorous heart have been a blossom
That in darkness did unbosom,
Those fire-flies of God to invite,
Burning spirits, which by night
Bear upon their laden wing
To such hearts impregnating.
For flowers that night-wings fertilize
Mock down the stars' unsteady eyes,
And with a happy, sleepless glance
Gaze the moon out of countenance.
I think thy girlhood's watchers must
Have took thy folded songs on trust,
And felt them, as one feels the stir
Of still lightnings in the hair,
When conscious hush expects the cloud
To speak the golden secret loud
Which tacit air is privy to ;
Flasked in the grape the wine they knew,
Ere thy poet-mouth was able
For its first young starry babble.
Keep'st thou not yet that subtle grace ?
Yea, in this silent interspace,
God sets His poems in thy face !

The loom which mortal verse affords,
Out of weak and mortal words,
Wovest thou thy singing-weed in,
To a rune of thy far Eden.
Vain are all disguises ! ah,
Heavenly *incognita !*
Thy mien bewrayeth through that wrong
The great Uranian House of Song !

As the vintages of earth
Taste of the sun that riped their birth,
We know what never cadent Sun
Thy lampèd clusters throbbed upon,
What plumèd feet the winepress trod ;
Thy wine is flavorous of God.
Whatever singing-robe thou wear
Has the Paradisal air ;
And some gold feather it has kept
Shows what Floor it lately swept !

DREAM-TRYST

THE breaths of kissing night and day
    Were mingled in the eastern Heaven :
Throbbing with unheard melody
    Shook Lyra all its star-chord seven :
        When dusk shrunk cold, and light trod
            shy,
        And dawn's gray eyes were troubled
            gray ;
        And souls went palely up the sky,
            And mine to Lucidé.

There was no change in her sweet eyes
    Since last I saw those sweet eyes shine ;
There was no change in her deep heart
    Since last that deep heart knocked at
        mine.
        Her eyes were clear, her eyes were
            Hope's,
        Wherein did ever come and go
        The sparkle of the fountain-drops
            From her sweet soul below.

The chambers in the house of dreams
    Are fed with so divine an air
That Time's hoar wings grow young
        therein,
    And they who walk there are most fair.
        I joyed for me, I joyed for her,
        Who with the Past meet girt about :
        Where our last kiss still warms the air,
            Nor can her eyes go out.

DAISY

WHERE the thistle lifts a purple crown
    Six foot out of the turf,
And the harebell shakes on the windy
    hill —
    O the breath of the distant surf ! —

The hills look over on the South,
And southward dreams the sea ;
And, with the sea-breeze hand in hand,
Came innocence and she.

Where 'mid the gorse the raspberry
Red for the gatherer springs,
Two children did we stray and talk
Wise, idle, childish things.

She listened with big-lipped surprise,
Breast-deep mid flower and spine :
Her skin was like a grape, whose veins
Run snow instead of wine.

She knew not those sweet words she spake,
Nor knew her own sweet way ;
But there 's never a bird, so sweet a song
Thronged in whose throat that day !

Oh, there were flowers in Storrington
On the turf and on the spray ;
But the sweetest flower on Sussex hills
Was the Daisy-flower that day !

Her beauty smoothed earth's furrowed face!
She gave me tokens three : —
A look, a word of her winsome mouth,
And a wild raspberry.

A berry red, a guileless look,
A still word, — strings of sand !
And yet they made my wild, wild heart
Fly down to her little hand.

For standing artless as the air,
And candid as the skies,
She took the berries with her hand,
And the love with her sweet eyes.

The fairest things have fleetest end :
Their scent survives their close,
But the rose's scent is bitterness
To him that loved the rose !

She looked a little wistfully,
Then went her sunshine way : —
The sea's eye had a mist on it,
And the leaves fell from the day.

She went her unremembering way,
She went and left in me
The pang of all the partings gone,
And partings yet to be.

She left me marvelling why my soul
Was sad that she was glad ;
At all the sadness in the sweet,
The sweetness in the sad.

Still, still I seemed to see her, still
Look up with soft replies,
And take the berries with her hand,
And the love with her lovely eyes.

Nothing begins, and nothing ends,
That is not paid with moan ;
For we are born in others' pain,
And perish in our own.

James Kenneth Stephen

LAPSUS CALAMI

TO R. K.

WILL there never come a season
Which shall rid us from the curse
Of a prose which knows no reason
And an unmelodious verse :
When the world shall.cease to wonder
At the genius of an ass,
And a boy's eccentric blunder
Shall not bring success to pass :

When mankind shall be delivered
From the clash of magazines,
And the inkstand shall be shivered
Into countless smithereens :

When there stands a muzzled stripling,
Mute, beside a muzzled bore :
When the Rudyards cease from kipling
And the Haggards ride no more.

A THOUGHT

IF all the harm that women have done
Were put in a bundle and rolled into one,
Earth would not hold it,
The sky could not enfold it,
It could not be lighted nor warmed by the
sun ;
Such masses of evil
Would puzzle the devil
And keep him in fuel while Time's wheels
run.

But if all the harm that's been done by men
Were doubled and doubled and doubled again,
And melted and fused into vapor and then
Were squared and raised to the power of ten,
There would n't be nearly enough, not near,
To keep a small girl for the tenth of a year.

A SONNET

Two voices are there: one is of the deep;
It learns the storm-cloud's thunderous melody,
Now roars, now murmurs with the changing sea,
Now bird-like pipes, now closes soft in sleep :
And one is of an old half-witted sheep
Which bleats articulate monotony,
And indicates that two and one are three,
That grass is green, lakes damp, and mountains steep :
And, Wordsworth, both are thine · at certain times,
Forth from the heart of thy melodious rhymes
The form and pressure of high thoughts will burst :
At other times — good Lord ! I 'd rather be
Quite unacquainted with the A. B. C.
Than write such hopeless rubbish as thy worst.

Rosamund Marriott Watson

("GRAHAM R. TOMSON")

LE MAUVAIS LARRON

(SUGGESTED BY WILLETTE'S PICTURE)

THE moorland waste lay hushed in the dusk of the second day,
Till a shuddering wind and shrill moaned up through the twilight gray ;
Like a wakening wraith it rose from the grave of the buried sun,
And it whirled the sand by the tree —
(there was never a tree but one —)
But the tall bare bole stood fast, unswayed with the mad wind's stress,
And a strong man hung thereon in his pain and his nakedness.
His feet were nailed to the wood, and his arm strained over his head ;
'T was the dusk of the second day, and yet was the man not dead.
The cold blast lifted his hair, but his limbs were set and stark,
And under their heavy brows his eyes stared into the dark :
He looked out over the waste, and his eyes were as coals of fire,
Lit up with anguish and hate, and the flame of a strong desire.

The dark blood sprang from his wounds, the cold sweat stood on his face,
For over the darkening plain came a rider riding apace.
Her rags flapped loose in the wind ; the last of the sunset glare
Flung dusky gold on her brow and her ·bosom broad and bare.
She was haggard with want and woe, on a jaded steed astride,
And still, as it staggered and strove, she smote on its heaving side,
Till she came to the limbless tree where the tortured man hung high —
A motionless crooked mass on a yellow streak in the sky.

" 'T is I — I am here, Antoine — I have found thee at last," she said ;
" O the hours have been long, but long ! and the minutes as drops of lead.
Have they trapped thee, the full-fed flock, thou wert wont to harry and spoil ?
Do they laugh in their town secure o'er their measures of wine and oil ?
Ah God ! that these hands might reach where they loll in their rich array ;

Ah God, that they were but mine, all mine,
   to mangle and slay !
How they shuddered and shrank, ere-
   while, at the sound of thy very
   name,
When we lived as the gray wolves live,
   whom torture nor want may tame :
And thou but a man ! and still a scourge
   and a terror to men,
Yet only my lover to me, my dear, in the
   rare days then.
O years of revel and love ! ye are gone as
   the wind goes by,
He is snared and shorn of his strength, and
   the anguish of hell have I —
I am here, O love, at thy feet; I have
   ridden far and fast
To gaze in thine eyes again, and to kiss
   thy lips at the last."
She rose to her feet and stood upright on
   the gaunt mare's back,
And she pressed her full red lips to his
   that were strained and black.
" Good-night, for the last time now — good-
   night, beloved, and good-bye — "
And his soul fled into the waste between a
   kiss and a sigh.

DEID FOLKS' FERRY

'T is They, of a veritie —
   They are calling thin an' shrill ;
We maun rise an' put to sea,
   We maun gi'e the deid their will,
We maun ferry them owre the faem,
   For they draw us as they list;
We maun bear the deid folk hame
   Through the mirk an' the saft sea-
   mist.

" But how can I gang the nicht,
   When I 'm new come hame frae sea ?
When my heart is sair for the sicht
   O' my lass that langs for me ? "
" O your lassie lies asleep,
   An' sae do your bairnies twa ;
The cliff-path 's stey an' steep,
   An' the deid folk cry an' ca'."

O sae hooly steppit we,
   For the nicht was mirk an' lown,

Wi' never a sign to see,
   But the voices all aroun'.
We laid to the saut sea-shore,
   An' the boat dipped low i' th' tide,
As she micht hae dipped wi' a score,
   An' our ain three sel's beside.

O the boat she settled low,
   Till her gunwale kissed the faem,
An' she didna loup nor row
   As she bare the deid folk hame ;
But she aye gaed swift an' licht,
   An' we naething saw nor wist
Wha sailed i' th' boat that nicht
   Through the mirk an' the saft sea-mist.

There was never a sign to see,
   But a misty shore an' low ;
Never a word spak' we,
   But the boat she lichtened slow,
An' a cauld sigh stirred my hair,
   An' a cauld hand touched my wrist,
An' my heart sank cauld and sair
   I' the mirk an' the saft sea-mist.

Then the wind raise up wi' a maen,
   ('T was a waefu' wind, an' weet),
Like a deid saul wud wi' pain,
   Like a bairnie wild wi' freit ;
But the boat rade swift an' licht,
   Sae we wan the land fu' sune,
An' the shore showed wan an' white
   By a glint o' the waning mune.

We steppit oot owre the sand
   Where an unco' tide had been,
An' Black Donald caught my hand
   An' coverit up his een :
For there, in the wind an' weet,
   Or ever I saw nor wist,
My Jean an' her weans lay cauld at my
   feet,
   In the mirk an' the saft sea-mist.

An' it 's O for my bonny Jean !
   An' it 's O for my bairnies twa,
It 's O an' O for the watchet een
   An' the steps that are gane awa' —
Awa' to the Silent Place,
   Or ever I saw nor wist,
Though I wot we twa went face to face
   Through the mirk an' the saft sea-mist.

HEREAFTER

SHALL we not weary in the windless days
Hereafter, for the murmur of the sea,
The cool salt air across some grassy lea ?
Shall we not go bewildered through a maze
Of stately streets with glittering gems
    ablaze,
Forlorn amid the pearl and ivory,
Straining our eyes beyond the bourne to see
Phantoms from out Life's dear, forsaken
    ways ?
Give us again the crazy clay-built nest,
Summer, and soft unseasonable spring,
Our flowers to pluck, our broken songs to
    sing,
Our fairy gold of evening in the West ;
Still to the land we love our longings
    cling,
The sweet, vain world of turmoil and un-
    rest.

THE FARM ON THE LINKS

GRAY o'er the pallid links, haggard and
    forsaken,
  Still the old roof-tree hangs rotting over-
    head,
Still the black windows stare sullenly to
    seaward,
  Still the blank doorway gapes, open to
    the dead ;

What is it cries with the crying of the
    curlews ?
  What comes apace on those fearful,
    stealthy feet,
Back from the chill sea-deeps, gliding o'er
    the sand-dunes,
  Home to the old home, once again to
    meet ?

What is to say as they gather round the
    hearth-stone,
  Flameless and dull as the feuds and
    fears of old ?
Laughing and fleering still, menacing and
    mocking,
  Sadder than death itself, harsher than
    the cold.

Woe for the ruined hearth, black with dule
    and evil,
  Woe for the wrong and the hate too
    deep to die !

Woe for the deeds of the dreary days past
    over,
  Woe for the grief of the gloomy days
    gone by !

Where do they come from ? furtive and
    despairing,
  Where are they bound for ? those that
    gather there,
Slow, with the sea-wind sobbing through
    the chambers, —
  Soft, with the salt mist stealing up the
    stair ?

Names that are nameless now, names of
    dread and loathing,
  Banned and forbidden yet, dark with
    spot and stain :
Only the old house watches and remem-
    bers,
  Only the old home welcomes them again.

TO MY CAT

HALF loving-kindliness and half disdain,
Thou comest to my call serenely suave,
With humming speech and gracious ges-
    tures grave,
In salutation courtly and urbane ;
Yet must I humble me thy grace to gain,
For wiles may win thee though no arts
    enslave,
And nowhere gladly thou abidest save
Where naught disturbs the concord of thy
    reign.
Sphinx of my quiet hearth ! who deign'st
    to dwell
Friend of my toil, companion of mine
    ease,
Thine is the lore of Ra and Rameses ;
That men forget dost thou remember
    well,
Beholden still in blinking reveries
With sombre, sea-green gaze inscrutable.

AVE ATQUE VALE

FAREWELL, my Youth ! for now we needs
    must part,
For here the paths divide ;
Here hand from hand must sever, heart
    from heart, —
Divergence deep and wide.

You'll wear no withered roses for my sake,
Though I go mourning for you all day long,
Finding no magic more in bower or brake,
  No melody in song.

Gray Eld must travel in my company
To seal this severance more fast and sure.
A joyless fellowship, i' faith, 't will be,
Yet must we fare together, I and he,
Till I shall tread the footpath way no more.

But when a blackbird pipes among the
  boughs,

On some dim, iridescent day in spring,
Then I may dream you are remembering
  Our ancient vows.

Or when some joy foregone, some fate
  forsworn,
Looks through the dark eyes of the violet,
I may re-cross the set, forbidden bourne,
  I may forget
Our long, long parting for a little while,
Dream of the golden splendors of your
  smile,
Dream you remember yet.

Lizzie M. Little

LIFE

O LIFE! that mystery that no man
  knows,
And all men ask: the Arab from his
  sands,
The Cæsar's self, lifting imperial hands,
And the lone dweller where the lotus
  blows;
O'er trackless tropics, and o'er silent snows,
She dumbly broods, that Sphinx of all the
  lands;

And if she answers, no man understands,
And no cry breaks the blank of her repose.
But a new form rose once upon my pain,
With grave, sad lips, but in the eyes a
  smile
Of deepest meaning dawning sweet and
  slow,
Lighting to service, and no more in vain
I ask of Life, "What art thou?" — as ere-
  while —
For since Love holds my hand I seem to
  know!

Katharine Tynan Hinkson

SHEEP AND LAMBS

ALL in the April evening,
  April airs were abroad,
The sheep with their little lambs
  Passed me by on the road.

The sheep with their little lambs
  Passed me by on the road;
All in the April evening
  I thought on the Lamb of God.

The lambs were weary, and crying
  With a weak, human cry.
I thought on the Lamb of God
  Going meekly to die.

Up in the blue, blue mountains
  Dewy pastures are sweet,
Rest for the little bodies,
  Rest for the little feet,

But for the Lamb of God,
  Up on the hill-top green,
Only a Cross of shame
  Two stark crosses between.

All in the April evening,
  April airs were abroad,
I saw the sheep with their lambs,
  And thought on the Lamb of God.

DE PROFUNDIS

You must be troubled, Asthore,
  Because last night you came
And stood on the moonlit floor,
  And called again my name.
In dreams I felt your tears,
  In dreams mine eyes were wet ;
O, dead for seven long years !
  And can you not forget ?
Are you not happy yet ?
  The mass-bell shall be rung,
  The mass be said and sung,
  And God will surely hear ;
  Go back and sleep, my dear !

You went away when you heard
  The red cock's clarion crow.
You have given my heart a sword,
  You have given my life a woe,
I, who your burden bore,
  On whom your sorrows fell ;
You had to travel, Asthore,
  Your bitter need to tell,
And I — was faring well !
  The mass-bell shall be rung,
  The mass be said and sung,
  And God will surely hear ;
  Go back and sleep, my dear !

SINGING STARS

" What sawest thou, Orion, thou hunter of
    the star-lands,
On that night star-sown and azure when
    thou cam'st in splendor sweeping,
And amid thy starry brethren from the
    near lands and the far lands
All the night above a stable on the earth
    thy watch wert keeping ? "

" Oh, I saw the stable surely, and the
    young Child and the Mother,
And the placid beasts still gazing with
    their mild eyes full of loving.
And I saw the trembling radiance of the
    Star, my lordliest brother,
Light the earth and all the heavens as he
    kept his guard unmoving.

" There were kings that came from East-
    ward with their ivory, spice, and
    sendal,
With gold fillets in their dark hair, and
    gold broidered robes and stately,

And the shepherds, gazing star-ward, over
    yonder hill did wend all,
And the silly sheep went meekly, and the
    wise dog marvelled greatly.

" Oh we knew, we stars, the stable held
    our King, His glory shaded,
That His baby hands were poising all the
    spheres and constellations ;
Berenice shook her hair down, like a shower
    of stardust braided,
And Arcturus, pale as silver, bent his
    brows in adorations.

" The stars sang all together, sang their
    love-songs with the angels,
With the Cherubim and Seraphim their
    shrilly trumpets blended.
They have never sung together since that
    night of great evangels,
And the young Child in the manger, and
    the time of bondage ended."

THE SAD MOTHER

O when the half-light weaves
  Wild shadows on the floor,
How ghostly come the withered leaves
  Stealing about my door !

I sit and hold my breath,
  Lone in the lonely house ;
Naught breaks the silence still as death,
  Only a creeping mouse.

The patter of leaves, it may be,
  But liker patter of feet,
The small feet of my own baby
  That never felt the heat.

The small feet of my son,
  Cold as the graveyard sod ;
My little, dumb, unchristened one
  That may not win to God.

" Come in, dear babe," I cry,
  Opening the door so wide.
The leaves go stealing softly by ;
  How dark it is outside !

And though I kneel and pray
  Long on the threshold-stone,
The little feet press on their way,
  And I am ever alone.

THE DEAD COACH

At night when sick folk wakeful lie,
I heard the dead coach passing by,
And heard it passing wild and fleet,
And knew my time was come not yet.

Click-clack, click-clack, the hoofs went past,
Who takes the dead coach travels fast,
On and away through the wild night,
The dead must rest ere morning light.

If one might follow on its track
The coach and horses, midnight black,
Within should sit a shape of doom
That beckons one and all to come.

God pity them to-night who wait
To hear the dead coach at their gate,
And him who hears, though sense be
dim,
The mournful dead coach stop for him.

He shall go down with a still face,
And mount the steps and take his place,
The door be shut, the order said !
How fast the pace is with the. dead !

Click-clack, click-clack, the hour is chill,
The dead coach climbs the distant hill.
Now, God, the Father of us all,
Wipe Thou the widow's tears that fall !

May Kendall

A PURE HYPOTHESIS

(*A Lover, in Four-dimensioned space, describes
a Dream.*)

Ah, love, the teacher we decried,
  That erudite professor grim,
In mathematics drenched and dyed,
  Too hastily we scouted him.
He said : " The bounds of Time and Space,
  The categories we revere,
May be in quite another case
  In quite another sphere."

He told us : " Science can conceive
  A race whose feeble comprehension
Can't be persuaded to believe
  That there exists our Fourth Dimen-
    sion,
Whom Time and Space for ever balk ;
  But of these beings incomplete,
Whether upon their heads they walk
  Or stand upon their feet —

" We cannot tell, we do not know,
  Imagination stops confounded ;
We can but say ' It *may* be so,'
  To every theory propounded."
Too glad were we in this our scheme
  Of things, his notions to embrace, —
But — I have dreamed an awful dream
  Of *Three-dimensioned* Space !

I dreamed — the horror seemed to stun
  My logical perception strong —
That everything beneath the sun
  Was *so unutterably wrong.*
I thought — what words can I com-
    mand ? —
  That nothing ever did come right.
No wonder *you* can't understand :
  I could not, till last night !

I would not, if I could, recall
  The horror of those novel heavens,
Where Present, Past, and Future all
  Appeared at sixes and at sevens,
Where Capital and Labor fought,
  And, in the nightmare of the mind,
No contradictories were thought
  As truthfully combined !

Nay, in that dream-distorted clime,
  These fatal wilds I wandered through,
The boundaries of Space and Time
  Had got most frightfully askew.
" What *is* ' askew ' ? " my love, you cry ;
  I cannot answer, can't portray ;
The sense of Everything awry
  No language can convey.

I can't tell what my words denote,
  I know not what my phrases mean ;
Inexplicable terrors float
  Before this spirit once serene.

Ah, what if on some lurid star
  There should exist a hapless race,
Who live and love, who think and are,
  In Three-dimensioned Space !

A BOARD SCHOOL PASTORAL

ALONE I stay ; for I am lame,
I cannot join them at the game,
  The lads and lasses ;
But many a summer holiday
I sit apart and watch them play,
And well I know : my heart can say,
  When Ella passes.

Of all the maidens in the place,
'T is Ella has the sunniest face,
  Her eyes are clearest.
Of all the girls, or here or there,
'T is Ella's voice is soft and rare,
And Ella has the darkest hair,
  And Ella 's dearest.

Oh, strong the lads for bat or ball,
But I in wit am first of all
  The master praises.
The master's mien is grave and wise ;
But, while I look into his eyes,
My heart, that o'er the schoolroom flies,
  At Ella gazes.

And Hal 's below me every day ;
For Hal is wild, and he is gay,
  He loves not learning.
But when the swiftest runners meet,
Oh, who but Hal is proud and fleet,
And there 's a smile I know will greet
  His glad returning.

They call me moody, dull, and blind,
They say with books I maze my mind,
  The lads and lasses ;
But little do they know — ah me !
How with my book upon my knee
I dream and dream, but ever see
  Where Ella passes.

A LEGEND

AY, an old story, yet it might
  Have truth in it — who knows ?
Of the heroine's breaking down one night
  Just ere the curtain rose.

And suddenly, when fear and doubt
  Had shaken every heart,
There stepped an unknown actress out
  To take the heroine's part.

But oh the magic of her face,
  And oh the songs she sung,
And oh the rapture in the place,
  And oh the flowers they flung !

But she never stooped : they lay all night
  As when she turned away
And left them — and the saddest light
  Shone in her eyes of gray.

She gave a smile in glancing round,
  And sighed, one fancied, then —
But never they knew where she was bound,
  Or saw her face again.

But the old prompter, gray and frail,
  They heard him murmur low :
" It only could be Meg Coverdale,
  Died thirty years ago,

" In that old part who took the town ;
  And she was fair, as fair
As when they shut the coffin down
  On the gleam of her golden hair ;

" And it was n't hard to understand
  How a lass so fair as she
Could never rest in the Promised Land
  Where none but angels be."

THE PAGE OF LANCELOT

So I arm thee for the final night,
  And for thy one defeat ;
For God upon his side shall fight
  When thou and he shall meet.
I know, for good or evil, thine
  Will be a well-fought field —
For good or evil, master mine,
  If I may bear thy shield !

Now art thou the unfaithfullest
  Of all that bore the vow —
Yet some there are that love thee best,
  Most honor, even now.
I see the face I held divine
  Ah, yet divine revealed !
For good or evil, master mine,
  If I may bear thy shield !

Amy Levy

A LONDON PLANE-TREE

GREEN is the plane-tree in the square,
  The other trees are brown ;
They droop and pine for country air ;
  The plane-tree loves the town.

Here from my garret-pane, I mark
  The plane-tree bud and blow,
Shed her recuperative bark,
  And spread her shade below.

Among her branches, in and out,
  The city breezes play ;
The dun fog wraps her round about ;
  Above, the smoke curls gray.

Others the country take for choice,
  And hold the town in scorn ;
But she has listened to the voice
  On city breezes borne.

BETWEEN THE SHOWERS

BETWEEN the showers I went my way,
  The glistening street was bright with
    flowers ;
It seemed that March had turned to May
    Between the showers.

Above the shining roofs and towers
  The blue broke forth athwart the gray ;
Birds carolled in their leafless bowers.

Hither and thither, swift and gay,
  The people chased the changeful hours ;
And you, you passed and smiled that day,
    Between the showers.

IN THE MILE END ROAD

How like her ! But 't is she herself,
  Comes up the crowded street,
How little did I think, the morn,
  My only love to meet !

Whose else that motion and that mien ?
  Whose else that airy tread ?
For one strange moment I forgot
  My only love was dead.

TO VERNON LEE

ON Bellosguardo, when the year was
    young,
We wandered, seeking for the daffodil
And dark anemone, whose purples fill
The peasant's plot, between the corn-shoots
    sprung.
Over the gray, low wall the olive flung
Her deeper grayness ; far off, hill on
    hill
Sloped to the sky, which, pearly-pale and
    still,
Above the large and luminous landscape
    hung.
A snowy blackthorn flowered beyond my
    reach ;
You broke a branch and gave it to me
    there ;
I found for you a scarlet blossom rare.
Thereby ran on of Art and Life our
    speech ;
And of the gifts the gods had given to
    each —
Hope unto you, and unto me Despair.

Elizabeth Craigmyle

SOLWAY SANDS

TWA race doon by the Gatehope-Slack,
  When nicht is wearin' near to the noon,
He on the gray and she on the black ;
Her faither and brithers are hard on the
    track,
  And Solway sands are white in the moon.

Strong is their love, but their loves may be
    twined
  Or ever the lady grant love's boon ;
Elliots and Armstrongs hold chase behind,
Their shouts and curses ring down the
    wind,
  And Solway sands stretch white in the
    moon.

Annan rins fu' frae brae to bank,
  But Katharine's lover is nae coward
    loon ;
Into the good gray's foam-flecked flank
In the rowels o' the gray steel sank,
  And Solway sands wait white in the
    moon.

The water's up to his bandelier,
  It's up to the waist o' her satin goon ;
" We 'll win to the shore and never fear,
There 's never a Elliot will follow here,"
  And Solway sands glint white in the
    moon.

The steeds and the riders are safely
    o'er,
  Through the swirl o' waters that waste
    and droon ;
" We try the swimming this night no
    more,
The boat is waiting on Solway shore,
  And Solway sands shine white in the
    moon."

Through the gray tide-water their horses
    splash,
  Through the salt pools left on the sea-
    sand broon ;
Then on to the waiting boat they dash, —

Their midnight riding is wild and rash,
  And Solway sands gleam white in the
    moon.

" To-night the boat's rough deck I trow,
  Next night the bridal in Carlisle toon."
But nights shall come and nights shall
    go,
O'er their bride-bed deep in the quick-
    sand's flow,
  And Solway sands stand white in the
    moon.

The boat rocks light on the Solway wave,
  The turn of the tide is coming soon,
But slowly they sink in their ghastly grave,
Wrapped round in the dark with none to
    save,
  And Solway sands laugh white in the
    moon.

The cloud wrack breaks, and the stars
    shine fair,
  The sea's voice sounds like a mystic
    rune,
The skipper looks out, but none are there,
The glimmering coast-line is wide and
    bare,
  And Solway Sands are white in the
    moon.

Ernest Rhys

LONDON FEAST

O WHERE do you go, and what 's your will,
My sunburnt herdsmen of the hill,
  That leave your herds no pastoral priest,
And take the road where, sad and dun,
The smoke-cloud drapes the April sun ? —
    " We go to taste
    Of London feast."

O country-lads, this April tide,
Why do you leave the country-side ?
  The new-come Spring stirs bird and
    beast ;
The winter storm is over now,
And melted the December snow : —
    " We go to taste
    Of London feast ! "

O village maidens, April girls,
With dancing eyes and country curls,
  Is April naught, the maypole ceased,
That you must leave the daisied places
That painted all your pretty faces ? —
    " We go to taste
    Of London feast."

And ancient dalesmen of the north,
That leave your dales, and the sweet brown
    earth,
  Are country acres so decreased,
And Cumbrian fells no longer ringing
With bleating lambs, and blackbirds sing-
    ing ? —
    " We go to taste
    Of London feast."

O sailor lads, that love the sea,
Are you, too, of this company ? —
   The shifting wind 's no longer east ;
Yet you have put the helm about,
To come ashore, and join the rout ? —
     " *We go to taste*
     Of London feast."

Too late, my golden mariners !
I have seen there these many years,
   How Most grew more, and less grew
     Least ;
And now you go too late ; the board
Cannot one crumb to you afford :
     You cannot taste
     Of London feast.

Too late, dear children of the sun ;
For London Feast is past and gone !
   I sat it out, and now released
Make westward from its weary gate.
Fools and unwise, you are too late :
     You cannot taste
     Of London feast.

They did not heed, they would not stay ;
I saw the dust on London way
   By denser thousands still increased :
My cry was vain. As they went by
Their murmur ran, for all reply : —
     " *We go to taste*
     Of London feast."

AN AUTOBIOGRAPHY

WALES England wed ; so I was bred.
   'T was merry London gave me
   breath.
I dreamt of love, and fame : I strove.
   But Ireland taught me love was
   best :
And Irish eyes, and London cries, and
   streams of Wales, may tell the
   rest.
What more than these I asked of life, I
   am content to have from Death.

DIANA

THIS new Diana makes weak men her
   prey,
   And, making captive, still would fain
   pursue,

And still would keep, and still would drive
   away, —
   So day by day,
Hate, hunt, do murder, and yet love
   them too ;
     Ah, dear Diana !

'T were well, poor fools, to shun her cruel
   spear,
   More fatal far than that which slew of
   old ;
Her spear is wit, that she so brings to
   bear ;
   Then laughs to hear
When it has struck, and one more heart
   runs cold ;
     Ah, dear Diana !

Be wise, O fools, and shun her cruel
   eyes,
   Which, when you see, you straight must
   love, to death.
This new Diana has such sorceries,
   Who loves her, dies ;
   And dying, cries still, with his latest
   breath, —
     Ah, dear Diana !

BRECHVA'S HARP SONG

LITTLE harp, at thy cry,
   He shall come in good time ;
And thy sword-song on high,
   High shall chime.

Little harp, in his brain
   Is the fire ; in his hand
Are the sword and the rein
   Of command.

Little harp, like the wind
   Is his strength ; like thy song
Are his words, to unbind
   Wales ere long !

Little harp, if his name
   Be unknown, ye shall hear
How the stars tell his fame
   Far and near.

Little harp, if unknown
   He come, ye shall sing
When Eryri shall throne
   Him All King !

WHITE ROSES

No sleep like hers, no rest,
  In all the earth to-night :
Upon her whiter breast
  Our roses lie so light.

She had no sins to lose,
  As some might say ;
But calmly keeps her pale repose
  Till God's good day.

SONG OF THE WULFSHAW LARCHES

HEART of Earth, let us be gone,
From this rock where we have stayed
While the sun has risen and shone
Ten thousand times, and thrown our shade
Always in the self-same place.

Now the night draws on apace :
The day is dying on the height,

The wind brings cold sea - fragrance
    here,
And cries, and restless murmurings,
Now night is near, —
Of wings and feet that take to flight,
Of furry feet and feathery wings
That take their joyous flight at will
Away and over the hiding hill,
And into the land where the sun has
    fled.
O let us go, as they have sped, —
The soft swift shapes that left us
    here,
The gentle things that came and went
And left us in imprisonment !
Let us be gone, as they have gone,
Away, and into the hidden lands ; —
From rock and turf our roots uptear,
Break from the clinging keeping bands,
Out of this long imprisoning break ;
At last, our sunward journey take,
And far, to-night, and farther on, —
Heart of Earth, let us be gone !

Arthur Christopher Benson

KNAPWEED

BY copse and hedgerow, waste and wall,
  He thrusts his cushions red ;
O'er burdock rank, o'er thistles tall,
  He rears his hardy head :
Within, without, the strong leaves press,
  He screens the mossy stone,
Lord of a narrow wilderness,
  Self-centred and alone.

He numbers no observant friends,
  He soothes no childish woes,
Yet nature nurtures him, and tends
  As duly as the rose ;
He drinks the blessed dew of heaven,
  The wind is in his ears,
To guard his growth the planets seven
  Swing in their airy spheres.

The spirits of the fields and woods
  Throb in his sturdy veins :
He drinks the secret, stealing floods,
  And swills the volleying rains :
And when the birds' note showers and
    breaks
  The wood's green heart within,

He stirs his plumy brow and wakes
  To draw the sunlight in.

Mute sheep that pull the grasses soft
  Crop close and pass him by,
Until he stands alone, aloft,
  In surly majesty.
No fly so keen, no bee so bold,
  To pierce that knotted zone,
He frowns as though he guarded gold,
  And yet he garners none.

And so when autumn winds blow late,
  And whirl the chilly wave,
He bows before the common fate,
  And drops beside his grave.
None ever owed him thanks or said
  " A gift of gracious heaven."
Down in the mire he droops his head ;
  Forgotten, not forgiven.

Smile on, brave weed ! let none inquire
  What made or bade thee rise :
Toss thy tough fingers high and higher
  To flout the drenching skies.
Let others toil for others' good,
  And miss or mar their own ;

Thou hast brave health, and fortitude
To live and die alone !

REALISM

AND truth, you say, is all divine ;
'T is truth we live by ; let her drench
The shuddering heart like potent wine ;
No matter how she wreck or wrench

The gracious instincts from their throne,
Or steep the virgin soul in tears ; —
No matter ; let her learn her own
Enormities, her vilest fears,

And sound the sickliest depths of crime,
And creep through roaring drains of woe,
To soar at last, unstained, sublime,
Knowing the worst that man can know ;

And having won the firmer ground,
When loathing quickens pity's eyes,
Still lean and beckon underground,
And tempt a struggling foot to rise.

Well, well, it is the stronger way !
Heroic stuff is hardly made ;
But one, who dallies with dismay,
Admires your boldness, half-afraid.

He deems that knowledge, bitter-sweet,
Can rust and rot the bars of right,
Till weakness sets her trembling feet
Across the threshold of the night.

She peers, she ventures ; growing bold,
She breathes the enervating air,
And shuns the aspiring summits, cold
And silent, where the dawn is fair.

She wonders, aching to be free,
Too soft to burst the uncertain band,
Till chains of drear fatality
Arrest the feeble willing hand.

Nay, let the stainless eye of youth
Be blind to that bewildering light !
When faith and virtue falter, truth
Is handmaid to the hags of night.

AN ENGLISH SHELL

I WAS an English shell,
Cunningly made and well,
With a heart of fire in an iron frame,
Ready to break in fury and flame,
Slice through the ranks my raging way,
Dying myself, to slay.

Out from the heart of the battle-ship,
Yelling a song of death, I rose,
Brake from the cannon's smoky lip
Into a land of foes : —
How was I baffled ? I soared and sank
Over the bastion, across the hill,
Into the lap of a grassy bank,
Impotent there to kill.
Slowly the thunder died away ; —
My merry comrades, how you roared,
Loud and jubilant, while I lay
Sunk in the slothful sward !
Peace came back with her corn and wine,
Smiling faint with a bleeding breast,
While in the offing, over the brine
My battle-ship steered to the West.

Then were the long slopes crowned again
With clustering vines and waving grain,
Winter by winter the stealing rain
Fretted me rotting there.
Suddenly once as I sadly slept,
Tinkling, the slow team over me stept, —
Jarring the ploughshare, — I was swept
Into the breezy air.
Why did he tempt me ? I had lain
Year by year in the peaceful rain,
Till my lionlike heart had grown
Dull and motionless, heavy as stone ; —
Mocking, he smote me : —
                            Then I leapt
Out in my anger, and screamed and swept
Him as he laughed in a storm of blood,
Shattered sinew and flying brain,
Brake the cottage and scarred the wood,
Roaring across the plain.
How should you blame me ? Ay, 't was
        peace !
War was the word I had learned to know ; —
Think you, I was an English shell,
Trained one lesson alone to spell —
I had vowed as I lay below,
Vowed to perish and find release
Slaying an English foe.

AFTER CONSTRUING

LORD CÆSAR, when you sternly wrote
The story of your grim campaigns,
And watched the ragged smoke-wreath float
Above the burning plains,

Amid the impenetrable wood,
  Amid the camp's incessant hum,
At eve, beside the tumbling flood
  In high Avaricum,

You little recked, imperious head,
  When shrilled your shattering trumpet's
    noise,
Your frigid sections would be read
  By bright-eyed English boys.

Ah me ! who penetrates to-day
  The secret of your deep designs ?
Your sovereign visions, as you lay
  Amid the sleeping lines ?

The Mantuan singer pleading stands ;
  From century to century
He leans and reaches wistful hands,
  And cannot bear to die.

But you are silent, secret, proud,
  No smile upon your haggard face,
As when you eyed the murderous
    crowd
Beside the statue's base.

I marvel : that Titanic heart
  Beats strongly through the arid page,
And we, self-conscious sons of art,
  In this bewildering age,

Like dizzy revellers stumbling out
  Upon the pure and peaceful night,
Are sobered into troubled doubt,
  As swims across our sight

The ray of that sequestered sun,
  Far in the illimitable blue, —
The dream of all you left undone,
  Of all you dared to do.

Norman Gale

SONG

THIS peach is pink with such a pink
  As suits the peach divinely ;
The cunning color rarely spread
  Fades to the yellow finely ;
But where to spy the truest pink
Is in my Love's soft cheek, I think.

The snowdrop, child of windy March,
  Doth glory in her whiteness ;
Her golden neighbors, crocuses,
  Unenvious praise her brightness !
But I do know where, out of sight,
My sweetheart keeps a warmer white.

SONG

WAIT but a little while —
  The bird will bring
A heart in tune for melodies
  Unto the spring,
Till he who 's in the cedar there
Is moved to trill a song so rare,
And pipe her fair.

Wait but a little while —
  The bud will break ;

The inner rose will open and glow
  For summer's sake ;
Fond bees will lodge within her breast
Till she herself is plucked and prest
  Where I would rest.

Wait but a little while —
  The maid will grow
Gracious with lips and hands to thee,
  With breast of snow.
To-day Love 's mute, but time hath sown
A soul in her to match thine own,
Though yet ungrown.

A PRIEST

NATURE and he went ever hand in hand
Across the hills and down the lonely lane ;
They captured starry shells upon the
    strand
And lay enchanted by the musing main.
So She, who loved him for his love of her,
Made him herself the heir to traceries and signs
On tiny children nigh too small to stir
In great green plains of hazel leaf or
    vines.
She taught the trouble of the nightingale ;
Revealed the velvet secret of the rose ;

She breathed divinity into his heart,
That rare divinity of watching those
Slow growths that make a nettle learn to
 dart
The puny poison of its little throes.

Her miracles of motion, butterflies,
Rubies and sapphires skimming lily-crests,
Carved on a yellow petal with their eyes
Tranced by the beauty of their powdered
 breasts,
Seen in the mirror of a drop of dew,
He loved as friends and as a friend he knew.
The dust of gold and scarlet underwings
More precious was to him than nuggets torn
From all invaded treasure-crypts of time,
And every floating, painted, silver beam
Drew him to roses where it stayed to
 dream,
Or down sweet avenues of scented lime.

And Nature trained him tenderly to know
The rain of melodies in coverts heard.
Let him but catch the cadences that flow
From hollybush or lilac, elm or sloe,
And he would mate the music with the bird.
The faintest song a redstart ever sang
Was redstart's piping, and the whitethroat
 knew
No cunning trill, no mazy shake that rang
Doubtful on ears unaided by the view.

But in his glory, as a young pure priest
In that great temple, only roofed by stars,
An angel hastened from the sacred East
To reap the wisest and to leave the least.
And as he moaned upon the couch of death,
Breathing away his little share of breath,
All suddenly he sprang upright in bed !
Life, like a ray, poured fresh into his face,
Flooding the hollow cheeks with passing
 grace.
He listened long, then pointed up above ;
Laughed a low laugh of boundless joy and
 love —
That was a plover called, he softly said,
And on his wife's breast fell, serenely
 dead !

THE COUNTRY FAITH

HERE in the country's heart
Where the grass is green,
Life is the same sweet life
As it e'er hath been.

Trust in a God still lives,
And the bell at morn
Floats with a thought of God
O'er the rising corn.

God comes down in the rain,
And the crop grows tall —
This is the country faith,
And the best of all !

A DEAD FRIEND

IT hardly seems that he is dead,
 So strange it is that we are here
Beneath this great blue shell of sky
 With apple-bloom and pear :
It scarce seems true that we can note
The bursting rosebud's edge of flame,
Or watch the blackbird's swelling throat
 While he is but a name.

No more the chaffinch at his step
 Pipes suddenly her shrill surprise,
For in an ecstasy of sleep
 Unconsciously he lies,
Not knowing that the sweet brown lark
From off her bosom's feathery lace
Shakes down the dewdrop in her flight
 To fall upon his face.

CONTENT

THOUGH singing but the shy and sweet
Untrod by multitudes of feet,
Songs bounded by the brook and wheat,
 I have not failed in this,
The only lure my woodland note,
To win all England's whitest throat !
O bards in gold and fire who wrote,
 Be yours all other bliss !

THE FIRST KISS

ON Helen's heart the day were night !
 But I may not adventure there :
Her breast is guarded by a right,
 And she is true as fair.

And though in happy days her eyes
 The glow within mine own could please,
She 's purer than the babe who cries
 For empire on her knees.

Her love is for her lord and child,
And unto them belongs her snow ;
But none can rob me of her wild
Young kiss of long ago !

TO MY BROTHERS

O BROTHERS, who must ache and stoop
O'er wordy tasks in London town,
How scantly Laura trips for you —
A poem in a gown !
How rare if Grub-street grew a lawn !
How sweet if Nature's lap could spare
A dandelion for the Strand,
A cowslip for Mayfair !

But here, from immaterial lyres,
There rings in easy confidence
The blackbird's bright philosophy
On apple-spray or fence :
For ploughmen wending home from toil
Some patriot thrush outpours his lay,
And voices, wildly eloquent,
The diary of his day.

These living lyrics you may hear
Remembering the lane's romance,
All hung in wicker heels to chirp
Thin ghosts of utterance :
But where the gusts of liberty
Make Ragged Robin wisely bend,
They quicken hedgerows with their song,
Melodiously unpenned.

If souls of mighty singers leave
The vacant body to its hush,
Does Shelley linger in the lark,
Or Keats possess the thrush ?
The end is undecaying doubt,
And in some blackbird's bosom still

Great Tennyson may sweeten eve
And whistle on the hill.

Come, brothers, to this clean delight,
And watch the velvet-headed tit.
Here 's honest sorrel in the grass
And sturdy cuckoo-spit :
What shepherds hear you shall not miss,
And at deliverance of dawn
Shall see a miracle of bloom
Across the sparkling lawn.

The forest musically begs
To fan you with its leafy love ;
Oh, fall asleep upon this moss
Entreated by the dove !
Here shall that sweet Conservative,
Dear Mother Nature, lend to you
Her lovely rural elements
Beneath the primal blue.

O brothers, who must ache and stoop
O'er wordy tasks in London town,
How scantly Laura trips for you —
A poem in a gown !
How good if Fleet-street grew a lawn !
How sweet if garden-plots could spare
A bed of cloves to scent the Strand,
A pansy for Mayfair !

DAWN AND DARK

GOD with His million cares
Went to the left or right,
Leaving our world ; and the day
Grew night.

Back from a sphere He came
Over a starry lawn,
Looked at our world ; and the dark
Grew dawn.

𝔄. 𝔗. 𝔔uiller-𝔠ouch

THE SPLENDID SPUR

NOT on the neck of prince or hound
Nor on a woman's finger twin'd,
May gold from the deriding ground
Keep sacred that we sacred bind :
Only the heel
Of splendid steel

Shall stand secure on sliding fate,
When golden navies weep their freight.

The scarlet hat, the laurell'd stave
Are measures, not the springs, of
worth ;
In a wife's lap, as in a grave,
Man's airy notions mix with earth.

Seek other spur
Bravely to stir
The dust in this loud world, and tread
Alp-high among the whisp'ring dead.

Trust in thyself, — then spur amain :
So shall Charybdis wear a grace,
Grim Ætna laugh, the Libyan plain
Take roses to her shrivell'd face.
This orb — this round
Of sight and sound —
Count it the lists that God hath built
For haughty hearts to ride a-tilt.

THE WHITE MOTH

If a leaf rustled, she would start :
And yet she died, a year ago.
How had so frail a thing the heart
To journey where she trembled so ?
And do they turn and turn in fright,
Those little feet, in so much night ?

The light above the poet's head
Streamed on the page and on the cloth,
And twice and thrice there buffeted
On the black pane a white-winged moth :
'T was Annie's soul that beat outside
And " Open, open, open ! " cried :

" I could not find the way to God ;
There were too many flaming suns
For signposts, and the fearful road
Led over wastes where millions
Of tangled comets hissed and burned —
I was bewildered and I turned.

" O, it was easy then ! I knew
Your window and no star beside.
Look up, and take me back to you ! "
— He rose and thrust the window wide.
'T was but because his brain was hot
With rhyming ; for he heard her not.

But poets polishing a phrase
Show anger over trivial things ;
And as she blundered in the blaze
Towards him, on ecstatic wings,
He raised a hand and smote her dead ;
Then wrote " *That I had died instead !* "

Jane Barlow

A CURLEW'S CALL

Ἔκλυον ἄν ἐγὼ οὐδ' ἄν ἤλπισ' αὐδάν.

WHETHEN is it yourself, Mister Hagan ?
an' lookin' right hearty you are ;
'T is a thrate to behold you agin. You 'll
be waitin' to take the long car
For Kilmoyna, the same as meself, sir ?
They 're late at the cross-roads to-
night,
For I mind when the days 'ud be long,
they 'd be here ere the droop of the
light,
Yet out yonder far over the bog there 's
the sunset beginnin' to burn
Like the red of a camp-fire raked low, and
no sign of thim roundin' the turn. —

So the dark 'll git ahead of us home on this
jaunt ; we 've good ten mile to go,
And thin afther the rain-pours this mornin',
we 're apt to be draggin' an' slow —
Ay, you 're right, sir : alongside the road
I 've been thravellin' you 'd scarce
count that far ;

You 'll cross dark an' light times and agin
between Creggan and Kandahar.

And is Norah along wid you ? Well, Norah
jewel, how 's yourself all this year ?
Sure she 's thin grown and white, sir, to
what I remember her last time we
were here.
Took could in the spring ? Ah, begorrah,
the March win 's as bad as a blight ;
But the weather we git in Afghanistan,
troth, 't would destroy her outright.
For in summer Ould Horny seems houldin'
the earth in the heat of his hand,
And in winther the snow 's the great ghost
of a world settled down on the land,
Wid a blast keenin' over it fit to be freezin'
the sun where he shone ;
If they 'd lease you that counthry rint-free,
you 'd do righter to let it alone.

Glad enough to be ought of it ? Well, in
a way, but I 've this on me mind,
That I 'm come like the winther's worst day,
after lavin' me betthers behind ;

An' the nearer I git to the ould place at
　　home, it's the stranger I seem,
Missin' thim I 'll behold there no more till
　　me furlough I take in a dream.
But the divil a dream's in it now, and I 'd
　　liefer dream ugly than think
What Jack Connolly's folk 'll remember
　　whinever they notice the blink
Of me coat past their hedge, and I goin'
　　their road. Jack's poor mother be-
　　like
'Ill be feedin' her hins in the door, or else
　　gath'rin' her clothes at the dyke,
And it's down to the gate she 'll be runnin'
　　and callin', an' biddin' me step in ;
And she 'll say to me : " Well, Dan, you 're
　　home, and I 'm glad, sure, to see
　　you agin."
Quare an' glad, I 'll be bound, wid the
　　thought in her heart of how long
　　she might wait,
Ere she 'd see her own slip of a redcoat
　　come route-marchin' in at her gate ;
He that 's campin' apart from us, joined
　　wid the throop who shift quarters
　　no more ;
Crep' in under the tent that's wide worlds
　　beyond call, tho' 't was pitched at
　　your door.
Ah, the crathur: 't is poor bits of hope
　　folk take up wid whin luck's turnin'
　　bad !
She that not so long since 'ud be thinkin'
　　she 'd soon git a sight of the lad,
There she 'll stand wid her eyes on me
　　face, till I see all as plain 's if I
　　heard
How she 's wond'rin', an dhreadin' to ask,
　　have I brought her so much as a
　　word.
That 's the notion's come home wid me ;
　　faix, I get thinkin' it every odd
　　while,
Maybe oft as a lamed horse shrinks his fut
　　in the len'th of a stony mile.

You 'll remember Jack Connolly, sir ? Ay,
　　for sure, 't is good neighbors you 've
　　been
Since he was n't the height of your stick,
　　and meself but a bit of spalpeen.
Great the pair of us both were ; out most
　　whiles off over the bog and away,
But the end of it happint us yonder at sun-
　　set last Pathrick's Day.

The way of it ? Our picket was ridin' in
　　be the wall of the little white town,
That 's stuck like a blaiched wasps' nest in
　　the gap where the ridge of the hills
　　breaks down,
And the big flat plain spreads out and
　　about, you might say 't was a bog
　　gone dhry,
Lookin' nathural enough till you notice
　　pricked up 'gin the light in the sky,
Their two thin towers, like an ould snail's
　　horns be the shell of their haythin
　　dome,
Peerin' out of a purpose to put you in
　　mind where you 've thravelled from
　　home.
We were ridin' too close ; I remember
　　along on the white of the wall
The front men's helmets went bob, bob,
　　bob, in blue shadow, sthretched
　　won'erful tall,
For the sunbames were raichin' their fur-
　　thest aslant from the edge of the
　　day,
Where the light ran, dhrained over the
　　earth, like a wave turnin' back to
　　the say,
All hot gold. Howane'er, when we past
　　where their straight - archin' door
　　opened black,
Wid the dust - thracks they thramp into
　　roads glamin' in at it, off went a
　　crack,
And ere ever an echo got rappin' the hills,
　　or the smoke riz to float,
'T was a plunge, and a thud, and Jack Con-
　　nolly down wid him, shot in the
　　throat.

So be raison of we two bein' neighbors,
　　they bid me mind Jack while they
　　went
To make out what the mischief at all the
　　rapscallion that potted him meant ;
Some ould objic' wisped up in his rags head
　　and fut, the crow's notice to quit,
Wid a quare carabine 'ud scarce fright
　　e'er a bird who 'd a scrumption of
　　wit.
But it was able enough for that job, and
　　be hanged to it ; Jack's business was
　　done,
As you could n't misdoubt. All the west
　　swam clear fire round the smooth,
　　redhot sun,

Dropped down steady as a shell thro' still
    wather ; but 't would n't be sunk out
    of sight
Ere the lad had got finished wid dyin', and
    gone beyond darkness and light.
And between whiles 't was divil as much
    could I do to be helpin' him ; just
Keep beside him, and dhrive the black fly-
    buzz, and lift up his head from the
    dust,
And hear tell had he aught in his mind.
But, och man, if his heart was to
    break,
Every whisper of voice he had in him was
    kilt, not a word could he spake.
Sure now that was conthrary. An instant
    before 't was no odds what he said,
And he 'd laughed, and he 'd gabbed on
    galore, any blathers come into his
    head ;
But wid on'y a minit to hold all his speech
    in for ever and a day,
Just one breath of a word like a hand
    raichin' worlds' worlds an' years'
    years away,
'T is sthruck dumb he was, same as his
    crathur of a baste that stood watch-
    in' us there,
Wid big eyes shinin' fright, and snuffin'
    the throuble up out of the air.

'T was a throuble swep' nearer, an' blacker,
    an' surer ; the whole world stood
    still ;
You 'd as aisy turn back a cloud's shadow,
    that 's tuk to slide over a hill.
There was Jack wid the life failin' out
    of him fast as the light from the
    sky,
That came fingerin' the grass wid long
    rays, blade be blade, an' thin twin-
    klin' up high
On the gold spark atop their green dome.
    And I thought to meself how the
    same
Blamed ould sunset 'ud thrapese away to
    the west till the shine of it came,
Flarin' red in the bog-houles, an' bright
    past the turf-stacks, and in at the
    door
Of the little ould place down the lonin',
    that Jack 'ud set fut in no more,
And 't would dance on their bits of gilt
    jugs, till they glittered like stars in
    a row,

And the people widin at their suppers
    ne'er thinkin' no great while ago
It was dazzlin' Jack's eyes as he looked for
    me face wid the last of his sight.
And sez I to him, " What is it, lad ? " but
    I knew I might listen all night
And no answer ; the sorra a chance to
    be bringin' thim a word we 'd ha'
    found,
On'y Jack had more sinse in him yet
    than meself that was hearty and
    sound ;
For he looked towards the rim of the west
    wid the sun hangin' ready to fall,
And he whistled two notes quick and low —
    well I knew it : the curlew's call.

I 'd not aisy mistake it ; sure out on these
    bogs scarce a minit goes by,
But anear or afar on the win' comes a
    flicker of the crathur's cry —
Faith I heard wan just thin — and on many
    a day, ere the sun 'ud be up,
And around and around stood the gray of
    the air like a big empty cup
Fit to hold every sound ever stirred, and to
    catch all the light ever shone,
I 'd be out wid me on to our bogland, all
    desolit lyin', and lone
As they say whin you 've watched the low
    shore till it dips where the ridges
    rowl green,
And I 'd spy was there e'er a wan out, and
    belike not a sowl to be seen
Save Jack whistlin' away to me down be
    the lough ; you 'd ha' swore 't was
    the bird,
Barrin' just the laste differ ; Jack done it
    the likest that ever I heard.
And there 's plenty that thry at it. Seldom
    a sunsit throops out of the west
But some lad 'll be whistlin' his sweet-
    heart, that 's sittin' and listenin' her
    best,
While the corners grow dark, and she 's
    reckonin' the shadows for 'fraid he
    might fail.
So his call lit the world like a star. Ne'er
    a sweetheart had Jack, I 'll go bail,
For the truth is his mind was tuk up
    wid his own folk ; it could n't be
    tould
The opinion he had and consait of the
    whole of thim, young wans and
    ould,

And it 's there where I 'm bothered en-
    tirely to think how he got the idee
To go soldierin' off to the ends of the
    earth wid no comrade but me.
Howanever, he went off suddint, afore we
    knew right what was on ;
And I thought to meself the ould place
    'ud be quare wid Jack Connolly
    gone,
So I up and I down to the barracks below,
    an' the shillin' I tuk —
That 's the way it fell out, and belike
    't was himself had the best of the
    luck.

And continted and aisy he went, wanst he
    saw he 'd made shift to conthrive
That the message he had in his mind 'ud
    go safe. For sez I : " Man alive,
I 'll be tellin' your people at home the first
    chance I can git, good or bad,
How thimselves, and the ould place you
    quit, was the last thought that ever
    you had ;
And I 'll bid thim be thinkin' of you,
    whin they hear the bird cry on our
    bog.
Your poor mother, an' father, an' the
    childher, an' their little ould rogue
    of a dog,
Ne'er a wan you 're forgettin'," sez I ; and
    bedad any fool might ha' known,
For the manin' he meant wid his call was
    as clear as a bugle blown.
And our rifles wint crack be the gateway,
    and now and again wid a plop
Come a bullet dhruv deep in the sand —
    't was the divil dhrill-sowin' his
    crop —
And a priest legged it up to the top of the
    tower, and stood risin' a yell
For the rest to be sayin' their prayers, like
    as if 't was our angely bell.
But it 's little Jack heeded ; for sure his
    own folk, and th' ould counthry, and
    all

Were come nearer than near, and gone fur-
    ther than far, along wid that cur-
    lew's call.

Ah, but Norah, you 're perished an'
    thrimblin' wid could sittin' here in
    the win' ;
Did you bring ne'er a wrap to rowl round
    you, machree, now the night 's closin'
    in ?
For there 's mists curlin' white on the pools,
    and the air gets an edge whin they
    lift.
Ay, the moon 's up, just on'y a breath 'gin
    the blue, where the cloud comes
    adrift,
Sthreelin' by like a haystack on fire, wid
    the flame blowin' off be the way
In bright bundles and wisps, as if some
    wan 'ud harvest the light of the day.
'T is n't that fashion dark falls, out there
    in the aist. Wanst the sun goes on
    lave,
Ne'er a thrace of a glame bides to show
    where he passed, like the foam of
    a wave ;
He 'll be blazin' wan minit, and thin 't is the
    same as if somebody shut ·
A black door on the blink of a hearth, or
    kicked over a lamp wid his fut.
So the rest of us rode thro' a night blindin'
    dark, till we 'd half the plain
    crossed,
And the moon riz ice-clear, wid a shine
    lyin' thick on the grass as hoar-
    frost
You could gather up. And, troth, if our
    tongues had froze stiff, 't is as much
    we 'd ha' said,
Wid Jack Connolly's baste saddle-empty,
    and jerkin' the reins as I led.
Sure poor Jack had a dale of good-nature ;
    he 'd fooled the ould mare all he
    could,
And the crathur went slow-fut and heavy ;
    you might think that she understood.

Selwyn Image

THE PROTESTATION

Dear Eyes, set deep within the shade
    Of Love's pale alabaster brow ;

Of what strange substance are ye
    made,
    That such enchantments on me now,
Resistless, by your grace are laid ?

Ye are the stars, that do control
  The tides of my obedient mind :
Ye are the founts whereat my soul
  In thirst may cool assuagement find :
The soothing balm to make me whole.

Ye are the deeps, in whose retreat
  Refuge I find from bounding sin :
Ye are the paths, by which my feet
  Move onward to God's peace within :
The abode where all pure memories meet.

Dear Eyes, dear Eyes, my health ye bring
  'Mid every circumstance of fate !
In what true numbers shall I sing
  The glory and virtues of your state,
Whence for my soul all grace doth spring ?

A PRAYER

DEAR, let me dream of love,
  Ah ! though a dream it be !
I 'll ask no boon, above
  A word, a smile, from thee :
At most, in some still hour, one kindly
  thought of me.

Sweet, let me gaze awhile
  Into those radiant eyes !
I 'll scheme not to beguile
  The heart, that deeper lies

Beneath them, than yon star in night's
  pellucid skies.

Love, let my spirit bow
  In worship at thy shrine !
I 'll swear thou shalt not know
  One word from lips of mine,
An instant's pain to send through that shy
  soul of thine.

HER CONFIRMATION

WHEN my Clorinda walks in white
Unto her Confirmation Rite,
  What sinless dove can show to heaven
A purer sight ?

Beneath a lawn, translucent crown
Her lovely curls conceal their brown ;
  Her wanton eyes are fastened, even,
Demurely dòwn.

And that delicious mouth of rose
No words, no smile, may discompose :
  All of her feels the approaching awe,
And silent grows.

Come, then, Thou noiseless Spirit, and rest
Here, where she waits Thee for her Guest :
  Pass not, but sweetly onward draw,
Till heaven 's possessed !

Herbert P. Horne

AMICO SUO

WHEN on my country walks I go,
  I never am alone :
Though whom 't were pleasure then to know
Are gone, and you are gone ;
From every side discourses flow.

There are rich counsels in the trees,
  And converse in the air ;
All magic thoughts in those and these
  And what is sweet and rare ;
And everything that living is.

But most I love the meaner sort,
  For they have voices too ;
Yet speak with tongues, that never hurt,
  As ours are apt to do :
The weeds, the grass, the common wort.

FORMOSAE PUELLAE

Tot tibi tamque dabit formosas Roma puellas ;
Haec habet, ut dicas, quidquid in orbe fuit.

OH ! had you eyes, but eyes that move
Within the light and realm of love,
  Then would you, on the sudden, meet
A Helen walking down the street.

Here in this London 'mid the stir,
The traffic, and the burdened air,
  Oh ! could your eyes divine their home,
Then this were Greece, or that were Rome.

The state of Dian is not gone,
The dawn she fled is yet the dawn ;
  Her crystal flesh the years renew
Despite her bodice, skirt, and shoe.

Nor is she only to be seen
With Juno's height, and Pallas' sheen ;
The knit, all-wondrously wrought, form
Of Cytherea, soft and warm,

Yet, like her jewelled Hesperus,
Puts forth its light, and shines on us ;
Whene'er she sees, and would control,
Love, at the windows of the soul.

NANCY DAWSON

NANCY DAWSON, Nancy Dawson,
  Not so very long ago
    Some one wronged you from sheer love,
  . dear ;
    Little thinking it would crush, dear,
  All I cherished in you so.
But now, what 's the odds, my Nancy ?
Where 's the guinea, there 's the fancy.
Are you Nancy, that old Nancy ?
    Nancy Dawson.

Nancy Dawson, Nancy Dawson,
  I forget you, what you were ;

Till I feel the sad hours creep, dear,
  O'er my heart ; as o'er my cheek,
    dear,
Once of old, that old, old hair :
And then, unawares, my Nancy,
I remember, and I fancy
You are Nancy, that old Nancy ;
    Nancy Dawson.

"IF SHE BE MADE OF WHITE AND RED"

IF she be made of white and red,
As all transcendent beauty shows ;
If heaven be blue above her head,
And earth be golden, as she goes :
Nay, then thy deftest words restrain ;
Tell not that beauty, it is vain.

If she be filled with love and scorn,
As all divinest natures are ;
If 'twixt her lips such words are born,
As can but Heaven or Hell confer :
Bid Love be still, nor ever speak,
Lest he his own rejection seek.

Margaret L. Woods

REST

To spend the long warm days
Silent beside the silent-stealing streams,
To see, not gaze, —
To hear, not listen, thoughts exchanged for
    dreams :

See clouds that slowly pass
Trailing their shadows o'er the far faint
    down,
  And ripening grass,
While yet the meadows wear their starry
    crown :

To hear the breezes sigh
Cool in the silver leaves like falling rain,
  Pause and go by,
Tired wanderers o'er the solitary plain :

See far from all affright
Shy river creatures play hour after hour,

  And night by night
Low in the West the white moon's folding
    flower.

  Thus lost to human things,
To blend at last with Nature and to hear
  What songs she sings
Low to herself when there is no one near.

TO THE FORGOTTEN DEAD

To the forgotten dead,
Come, let us drink in silence ere we part.
To every fervent yet resolved heart
That brought its tameless passion and its
    tears,
Renunciation and laborious years,
To lay the deep foundations of our race,
To rear its stately fabric overhead
And light its pinnacles with golden grace.
To the unhonored dead.

To the forgotten dead,
Whose dauntless hands were stretched to
grasp the rein
Of Fate and hurl into the void again
Her thunder-hoofèd horses, rushing blind
Earthward along the courses of the wind.
Among the stars, along the wind in vain
Their souls were scattered and their blood
was shed,
And nothing, nothing of them doth remain.
To the thrice-perished dead.

YOUNG WINDEBANK

THEY shot young Windebank just here,
By Merton, where the sun
Strikes on the wall. 'T was in a year
Of blood the deed was done.

At morning from the meadows dim
He watched them dig his grave.
Was this in truth the end for him,
The well-beloved and brave ?

He marched with soldier scarf and sword,
Set free to die that day,

And free to speak once more the word
That marshalled men obey.

But silent on the silent band,
That faced him stern as death,
He looked, and on the summer land,
And on the grave beneath.

Then with a sudden smile and proud
He waved his plume, and cried,
" The king ! the king ! " and laughed aloud,
" The king ! the king ! " and died.

Let none affirm he vainly fell,
And paid the barren cost
Of having loved and served too well
A poor cause and a lost.

He in the soul's eternal cause
Went forth as martyrs must —
The kings who make the spirit laws
And rule us from the dust ;

Whose wills unshaken by the breath
Of adverse Fate endure,
To give us honor strong as death
And loyal love as sure.

Richard Le Gallienne

ORBITS

TWO stars once on their lonely way
Met in the heavenly height,
And they dreamed a dream they might
shine alway
With undivided light ;
Melt into one with a breathless throe,
And beam as one in the night.

And each forgot in the dream so strange
How desolately far
Swept on each path, for who shall change
The orbit of a star ?
Yea, all was a dream, and they still must go
As lonely as they are.

LOVE'S POOR

YEA, love, I know, and I would have it
thus ;
I know that not for us

Is springtide Passion with his fire and
flowers,
I know this love of ours
Lives not, nor yet may live,
By the dear food that lips and hands can
give.
Not, love, that we in some high dream
despise
The common lover's common Paradise ;
Ah, God, if Thou and I
But one short hour their blessedness might
try,
How could we poor ones teach
Those happy ones who half forget them
rich :
For if we thus endure,
'T is only, love, because we are so poor.

REGRET

ONE asked of Regret,
And I made reply :

To have held the bird,
    And let it fly ;
To have seen the star
    For a moment nigh,
And lost it
    Through a slothful eye ;
To have plucked the flower
    And cast it by ;
To have one only hope —
    To die.

THE WONDER-CHILD

" OUR little babe," each said, " shall be
Like unto thee " — " Like unto *thee !* "
    " Her mother's " — " Nay, his father's "
    — " eyes,"
" Dear curls like thine " — but each re-
    plies,
" As thine, all thine, and naught of me."

What sweet solemnity to see
The little life upon thy knee,
    And whisper as so soft it lies, —
      " Our little babe ! "

For, whether it be he or she,
A David or a Dorothy,
    " As mother fair," or " father wise,"
    Both when it 's " good," and when it
      cries,
One thing is certain, — it will be
    Our little babe.

AN OLD MAN'S SONG

YE are young, ye are young,
    I am old, I am old ;
And the song has been sung
    And the story been told.

Your locks are as brown
    As the mavis in May,
Your hearts are as warm
    As the sunshine to-day,
But mine white and cold
    As the snow on the brae.

And Love, like a flower,
    Is growing for you,
Hands clasping, lips meeting,
    Hearts beating so true ;
While Fame like a star
In the midnight afar
Is flashing for you.

For you the To-come,
    But for me the Gone-by,
You are panting to live,
    I am waiting to die ;
The meadow is empty,
    No flower groweth high,
And naught but a socket
    The face of the sky.

Yea, howso we dream,
    Or how bravely we do ;
The end is the same,
    Be we traitor or true :
And after the bloom
    And the passion is past,
Death cometh at last.

THE PASSIONATE READER TO HIS POET

DOTH it not thrill thee, Poet,
    Dead and dust though thou art,
To feel how I press thy singing
    Close to my heart ?

Take it at night to my pillow,
    Kiss it before I sleep,
And again when the delicate morning
    Beginneth to peep ?

See how I bathe thy pages
    Here in the light of the sun,
Through thy leaves, as a wind among roses,
    The breezes shall run.

Feel how I take thy poem
    And bury within it my face
As I pressed it last night in the heart of a
    flower,
    Or deep in a dearer place.

Think, as I love thee, Poet,
    A thousand love beside,
Dear women love to press thee too
    Against a sweeter side.

Art thou not happy, Poet ?
    I sometimes dream that I
For such a fragrant fame as thine
    Would gladly sing and die.

Say, wilt thou change thy glory
    For this same youth of mine ?
And I will give my days i' the sun
    For that great song of thine.

Rudyard Kipling

DANNY DEEVER

" WHAT are the bugles blowin' for ? "
    said Files-on-Parade.
" To turn you out, to turn you out," the
    Color-Sergeant said.
" What makes you look so white, so
    white ? " said Files-on-Parade.
" I 'm dreadin' what I 've got to watch,"
    the Color-Sergeant said.
For they 're hangin' Danny Deever,
    you can hear the Dead March play,
The regiment 's in 'ollow square —
    they 're hangin' him to-day ;
They 've taken of his buttons off an'
    cut his stripes away,
An' they 're hangin' Danny Deever in
    the mornin'.

" What makes the rear-rank breathe so
    'ard ? " said Files-on-Parade.
" It 's bitter cold, it 's bitter cold," the
    Color-Sergeant said.
" What makes that front-rank man fall
    down ? " says Files-on-Parade.
" A touch o' sun, a touch o' sun," the Color-
    Sergeant said.
They are hangin' Danny Deever, they
    are marchin' of 'im round,
They 'ave 'alted Danny Deever by 'is
    coffin on the ground ;
An' 'e 'll swing in 'arf a minute for
    a sneakin' shootin' hound —
O they 're hangin' Danny Deever in
    the mornin' !

" 'Is cot was right-'and cot to mine," said
    Files-on-Parade.
" 'E 's sleepin' out an' far to-night," the
    Color-Sergeant said.
" I 've drunk 'is beer a score o' times," said
    Files-on-Parade.
" 'E 's drinkin' bitter beer alone," the Color-
    Sergeant said.
They are hangin' Danny Deever, you
    must mark 'im to 'is place,
For 'e shot a comrade sleepin' — you
    must look 'im in the face ;
Nine 'undred of 'is county an' the reg-
    iment's disgrace,
While they 're hangin' Danny Deever
    in the mornin'.

" What 's that so black agin the sun ? "
    said Files-on-Parade.
" It 's Danny fightin' 'ard for life," the
    Color-Sergeant said.
" What 's that that whimpers over'ead ? "
    said Files-on-Parade.
" It 's Danny's soul that 's passin' now," the
    Color-Sergeant said.
For they 're done with Danny Deever,
    you can 'ear the quickstep play,
The regiment 's in column, an' they 're
    marchin' us away ;
Ho ! the young recruits are shakin',
    an' they 'll want their beer to-day,
After hangin' Danny Deever in the
    mornin'.

" FUZZY-WUZZY "

(SOUDAN EXPEDITIONARY FORCE)

WE 'VE fought with many men acrost the
    seas,
An' some of 'em was brave an' some was
    not,
The Paythan an' the Zulu an' Burmese ;
    But the Fuzzy was the finest o' the lot.
We never got a ha'porth's change of
    'im :
'E squatted in the scrub an' 'ocked our
    'orses,
'E cut our sentries up at Suakim,
An' 'e played the cat an' banjo with our
    forces.
So 'ere's to you, Fuzzy-Wuzzy, at your
    'ome in the Soudan ;
You 're a pore benighted 'eathen but
    a first-class fightin' man ;
We gives you your certificate, an' if
    you want it signed
We 'll come an' 'ave a romp with you
    whenever you 're inclined.

We took our chanst among the Kyber
    'ills,
The Boers knocked us silly at a mile,
The Burman give us Irriwaddy chills,
An' a Zulu *impi* dished us up in style :
But all we ever got from such as they
    Was pop to what the Fuzzy made us
    swaller ;

We 'eld our bloomin' own, the papers
　　say,
But man for man the Fuzzy knocked us
　　'oller.
Then 'ere 's *to* you, Fuzzy-Wuzzy, an'
　　the missis and the kid ;
Our orders was to break you, an' of
　　course we went an' did.
We sloshed you with Martinis, an' it
　　was n't 'ardly fair ;
But for all the odds agin' you, Fuzzy-
　　Wuz, you broke the square.

'E 'as n't got no papers of 'is own,
　'E 'as n't got no medals nor rewards,
So we must certify the skill 'e 's shown
In usin' of 'is long two-'anded swords :
When 'e 's 'oppin' in an' out among the
　　bush
With 'is coffin-'eaded shield an' shovel-
　　spear,
An 'appy day with Fuzzy on the rush
　Will last an 'ealthy Tommy for a
　　year.
　　So 'ere 's *to* you, Fuzzy-Wuzzy, an'
　　　your friends which are no more,
　　If we 'ad n't lost some messmates we
　　　would 'elp you to deplore ;
　　But give an' take 's the gospel, an'
　　　we 'll call the bargain fair,
　　For if you 'ave lost more than us, you
　　　crumpled up the square !

'E rushes at the smoke when we let
　　drive,
　An', before we know, 'e 's 'ackin' at our
　　'ead ;
'E 's all 'ot sand an' ginger when alive,
　An' 'e 's generally shammin' when 'e 's
　　dead.
'E 's a daisy, 'e 's a ducky, 'e 's a lamb !
　'E 's a injia-rubber idiot on the spree,
'E 's the on'y thing that does n't give a
　　damn
　For a Regiment o' British Infantree !
　　So 'ere 's *to* you, Fuzzy-Wuzzy, at your
　　　'ome in the Soudan ;
　　You 're a pore benighted 'eathen but a
　　　first-class fightin' man ;
　　An' 'ere 's *to* you, Fuzzy-Wuzzy, with
　　　your 'ayrick 'ead of 'air —
　　You big black boundin' beggar — for
　　　you broke a British square !

THE BALLAD OF EAST AND WEST

OH, *East is East, and West is West, and*
　　never the twain shall meet,
Till Earth and Sky stand presently at God's
　　great Judgment Seat ;
But there is neither East nor West, Border,
　　nor Breed, nor Birth,
When two strong men stand face to face, tho'
　　they come from the ends of the earth !

Kamal is out with twenty men to raise the
　　Border side,
And he has lifted the Colonel's mare that
　　is the Colonel's pride :
He has lifted her out of the stable-door
　　between the dawn and the day,
And turned the calkins upon her feet, and
　　ridden her far away.
Then up and spoke the Colonel's son that
　　led a troop of the Guides :
" Is there never a man of all my men can
　　say where Kamal hides ? "
Then up and spoke Mahommed Khan, the
　　son of the Ressaldar,
" If ye know the track of the morning-mist,
　　ye know where his pickets are.
At dusk he harries the Abazai — at dawn
　　he is into Bonair,
But he must go by Fort Bukloh to his own
　　place to fare,
So if ye gallop to Fort Bukloh as fast as
　　a bird can fly,
By the favor of God ye may cut him off
　　ere he win to the Tongue of Jagai,
But if he be passed the Tongue of Jagai,
　　right swiftly turn ye then,
For the length and the breadth of that
　　grisly plain is sown with Kamal's
　　men.
There is rock to the left, and rock to the
　　right, and low lean thorn between,
And ye may hear a breech-bolt snick where
　　never a man is seen."
The Colonel's son has taken a horse, and a
　　raw rough dun was he,
With the mouth of a bell and the heart of
　　Hell, and the head of the gallows-
　　tree.
The Colonel's son to the Fort has won, they
　　bid him stay to eat —
Who rides at the tail of a Border thief, he
　　sits not long at his meat.

He's up and away from Fort Bukloh as
    fast as he can fly,
Till he was aware of his father's mare in
    the gut of the Tongue of Jagai,
Till he was aware of his father's mare with
    Kamal upon her back,
And when he could spy the white of her
    eye, he made the pistol crack.
He has fired once, he has fired twice, but
    the whistling ball went wide.
"Ye shoot like a soldier," Kamal said.
    "Show now if ye can ride."
It's up and over the Tongue of Jagai, as
    blown dust-devils go,
The dun he fled like a stag of ten, but the
    mare like a barren doe.
The dun he leaned against the bit and
    slugged his head above,
But the red mare played with the snaffle-
    bars, as a maiden plays with a glove.
There was rock to the left and rock to the
    right, and low lean thorn between,
And thrice he heard a breech-bolt snick
    tho' never a man was seen.
They have ridden the low moon out of
    the sky, their hoofs drum up the
    dawn,
The dun he went like a wounded bull, but
    the mare like a new-roused fawn.
The dun he fell at a water-course — in a
    woful heap fell he,
And Kamal has turned the red mare back,
    and pulled the rider free.
He has knocked the pistol out of his hand
    — small room was there to strive,
"'T was only by favor of mine," quoth he,
    "ye rode so long alive:
There was not a rock for twenty mile,
    there was not a clump of tree,
But covered a man of my own men with
    his rifle cocked on his knee.
If I had raised my bridle-hand, as I have
    held it low,
The little jackals that flee so fast, were
    feasting all in a row:
If I had bowed my head on my breast, as
    I have held it high,
The kite that whistles above us now were
    gorged till she could not fly."
Lightly answered the Colonel's son : — "Do
    good to bird and beast,
But count who come for the broken meats
    before thou makest a feast.
If there should follow a thousand swords
    to carry my bones away,

Belike the price of a jackal's meal were
    more than a thief could pay.
They will feed their horse on the stand-
    ing crop, their men on the garnered
    grain,
The thatch of the byres will serve their
    fires when all the cattle are slain.
But if thou thinkest the price be fair, —
    thy brethren wait to sup,
The hound is kin to the jackal-spawn, —
    howl, dog, and call them up!
And if thou thinkest the price be high, in
    steer and gear and stack,
Give me my father's mare again, and I'll
    fight my own way back!"
Kamal has gripped him by the hand and
    set him upon his feet.
"No talk shall be of dogs," said he, "when
    wolf and gray wolf meet.
May I eat dirt if thou hast hurt of me in
    deed or breath;
What dam of lances brought thee forth to
    jest at the dawn with Death?"
Lightly answered the Colonel's son : "I
    hold by the blood of my clan:
Take up the mare for my father's gift —
    by God, she has carried a man!"
The red mare ran to the Colonel's son, and
    nuzzled against his breast,
"We be two strong men," said Kamal
    then, "but she loveth the younger
    best.
So she shall go with a lifter's dower, my
    turquoise-studded rein,
My broidered saddle and saddle-cloth, and
    silver stirrups twain."
The Colonel's son a pistol drew and held it
    muzzle-end,
"Ye have taken the one from a foe," said
    he ; "will ye take the mate from a
    friend?"
"A gift for a gift," said Kamal straight;
    "a limb for the risk of a limb.
Thy father has sent his son to me, I'll
    send my son to him!"
With that he whistled his only son, that
    dropped from a mountain-crest —
He trod the ling like a buck in spring, and
    he looked like a lance in rest.
"Now here is thy master," Kamal said,
    "who leads a troop of the Guides,
And thou must ride at his left side as
    shield on shoulder rides.
Till Death or I cut loose the tie, at camp
    and board and bed,

Thy life is his — thy fate it is to guard him
    with thy head.
So thou must eat the White Queen's meat,
    and all her foes are thine,
And thou must harry thy father's hold for
    the peace of the border-line.
And thou must make a trooper tough and
    hack thy way to power —
Belike they will raise thee to Ressaldar
    when I am hanged in Peshawur."

They have looked each other between the
    eyes, and there they found no fault,
They have taken the Oath of the Brother-
    in-Blood on leavened bread and salt :
They have taken the Oath of the Brother-
    in-Blood on fire and fresh-cut sod,
On the hilt and the haft of the Khyber knife,
    and the Wondrous Names of God.
The Colonel's son he rides the mare and
    Kamal's boy the dun,
And two have come back to Fort Bukloh
    where there went forth but one.
And when they drew to the Quarter-Guard,
    full twenty swords flew clear —
There was not a man but carried his feud
    with the blood of the mountaineer.
" Ha' done ! ha' done ! " said the Colonel's
    son. " Put up the steel at your
    sides !
Last night ye had struck at a Border
    thief — to-night 't is a man of the
    Guides ! "

Oh, East is East, and West is West, and
    never the two shall meet,
Till Earth and Sky stand presently at God's
    great Judgment Seat ;
But there is neither East nor West, Border,
    nor Breed, nor Birth,
When two strong men stand face to face, tho'
    they come from the ends of the earth.

THE CONUNDRUM OF THE WORKSHOPS

WHEN the flush of a new-born sun fell first
    on Eden's green and gold,
Our father Adam sat under the Tree and
    scratched with a stick in the mould ;
And the first rude sketch that the world
    had seen was joy to his mighty heart,
Till the Devil whispered behind the leaves,
    " It 's pretty, but is it Art ? "

Wherefore he called to his wife, and fled
    to fashion his work anew —
The first of his race who cared a fig for the
    first, most dread review ;
And he left his lore to the use of his sons
    — and that was a glorious gain
When the Devil chuckled " Is it Art ? " in
    the ear of the branded Cain.

They builded a tower to shiver the sky and
    wrench the stars apart,
Till the Devil grunted behind the bricks :
    " It 's striking, but is it Art ? "
The stone was dropped at the quarry-side
    and the idle derrick swung,
While each man talked of the aims of Art,
    and each in an alien tongue.

They fought and they talked in the North
    and the South, they talked and they
    fought in the West,
Till the waters rose on the pitiful land, and
    the poor Red Clay had rest —
Had rest till the dank, blank-canvas dawn
    when the dove was preened to start,
And the Devil bubbled below the keel :
    " It 's human, but is it Art ? "

The tale is as old as the Eden Tree — and
    new as the new-cut tooth —
For each man knows ere his lip-thatch
    grows he is master of Art and Truth ;
And each man hears as the twilight nears,
    to the beat of his dying heart,
The Devil drum on the darkened pane :
    " You did it, but was it Art ? "

We have learned to whittle the Eden Tree
    to the shape of a surplice-peg,
We have learned to bottle our parents
    twain in the yelk of an addled egg,
We know that the tail must wag the dog,
    for the horse is drawn by the cart ;
But the Devil whoops, as he whooped of
    old : " It 's clever, but is it Art ? "

When the flicker of London sun falls faint
    on the Club-room's green and gold,
The sons of Adam sit them down and scratch
    with their pens in the mould —
They scratch with their pens in the mould
    of their graves, and the ink and the
    anguish start,
For the Devil mutters behind the leaves :
    " It 's pretty, but is it Art ? "

Now, if we could win to the Eden Tree
   where the Four Great Rivers flow,
And the Wreath of Eve is red on the turf
   as she left it long ago,
And if we could come when the sentry
   slept and softly scurry through,
By the favor of God we might know
   as much — as our father Adam
   knew.

THE LAW OF THE JUNGLE

Now this is the Law of the Jungle — as old
   and as true as the sky ;
And the Wolf that shall keep it may prosper,
   but the Wolf that shall break it must
   die.
As the creeper that girdles the tree-trunk the
   Law runneth forward and back —
For the strength of the Pack is the Wolf,
   and the strength of the Wolf is the
   Pack.

Wash daily from nose-tip to tail-tip ; drink
   deeply, but never too deep ;
And remember the night is for hunting, and
   forget not the day is for sleep.

The Jackal may follow the Tiger, but, Cub,
   when thy whiskers are grown,
Remember the Wolf is a hunter — go forth
   and get food of thine own.

Keep peace with the Lords of the Jun-
   gle — the Tiger, the Panther, and
   Bear ;
And trouble not Hathi the Silent, and mock
   not the Boar in his lair.

When Pack meets Pack in the Jungle, and
   neither will go from the trail,
Lie down till the leaders have spoken — it
   may be fair words shall prevail.

When ye fight with a Wolf of the Pack, ye
   must fight him alone and afar,
Lest others take part in the quarrel, and the
   Pack be diminished by war.

The Lair of the Wolf is his refuge, and
   where he has made him his home,
Not even the Head Wolf may enter, not
   even the Council may come.

The Lair of the Wolf is his refuge, but
   where he has digged it too plain,
The Council shall send him a message, and
   so he shall change it again.

If ye kill before midnight, be silent, and
   wake not the woods with your bay,
Lest ye frighten the deer from the crops.
   and thy brothers go empty away.

Ye may kill for yourselves, and your mates,
   and your cubs as they need, and ye
   can ;
But kill not for pleasure of killing, and
   seven times never kill Man.

If ye plunder his Kill from a weaker, de-
   vour not all in thy pride ;
Pack-Right is the right of the meanest; so
   leave him the head and the hide.

The Kill of the Pack is the meat of the
   Pack.   Ye must eat where it lies ;
And no one may carry away of that meat
   to his lair, or he dies.

The Kill of the Wolf is the meat of the
   Wolf.   He may do what he will,
But, till he has given permission, the Pack
   may not eat of that Kill.

Cub-Right is the right of the Yearling.
   From all of his Pack he may claim
Full-gorge when the killer has eaten ; and
   none may refuse him the same.

Lair-Right is the right of the Mother.
   From all of her year she may claim
One haunch of each kill for her litter, and
   none may deny her the same.

Cave-Right is the right of the Father — to
   hunt by himself for his own ;
He is freed of all calls to the Pack ; he is
   judged by the Council alone.

Because of his age and his cunning, be-
   cause of his gripe and his paw,
In all that the Law leaveth open, the word
   of the Head Wolf is Law.

Now these are the Laws of the Jungle, and
   many and mighty are they ;
But the head and the hoof of the Law and
   the haunch and the hump is — Obey !

THE LAST CHANTEY

" And there was no more sea."

THUS said the Lord in the Vault above the
   Cherubim,
  Calling to the Angels and the Souls in
    their degree : —
   " Lo ! Earth has passed away
   On the smoke of Judgment Day,
That Our Word may be established shall
    we gather up the Sea ? "

Loud sang the souls of the jolly, jolly Mari-
    ners : —
  " Plague upon the hurricanes that made
    us furl and flee !
   But the war is done between us,
   In the deep the Lord hath seen us —
Our bones we 'll leave the barracout' ;
    and God may sink the Sea ! "

Then said the soul of Judas that betrayed
   Him : —
  " Lord, hast Thou forgotten Thy covenant
    with me ?
   How once a year I go
   To cool me on the floe,
  And Ye take my Day of Mercy if Ye
    take away the Sea ! "

Then said the Soul of the Angel of the Off-
   Shore Wind : —
  (He that bits the Thunder when the bull-
    mouthed breakers flee)
   " I have watch and ward to keep
   O'er thy wonders on the deep,
  And Ye take mine Honor from me if Ye
    take away the Sea ! "

Loud sang the souls of the jolly, jolly Mari-
    ners : —
  " Nay, but we were angry and a hasty
    folk are we !
   If we worked the ship together
   Till she foundered in foul weather,
Are we babes that we should clamor for
    a vengeance on the Sea ? "

Then said the souls of the slaves that men
   threw overboard : —
  " Kennelled in the picaroon a weary band
    were we :
   But Thy arm was strong to save,
   And it touched us on the wave,

And we drowsed the long tides idle till
   Thy trumpets tore the Sea."

Then cried the soul of the stout Apostle
   Paul to God :
  " Once we frapped a ship, and she labored
    woundily.
   There were fourteen score of these,
   And they blessed Thee on their knees
When they learned Thy Grace and Glory
   under Malta by the sea."

Loud sang the souls of the jolly, jolly Mari-
    ners,
  Plucking at their harps, and they plucked
    unhandily —
   " Our thumbs are rough and tarred
   And the tune is something hard —
  May we lift the Dipsea Chantey such as
    seamen use at sea ? "

Then said the souls of the Gentlemen-
   Adventurers —
  Fettered wrist-to-bar all for red iniquity :
   " Ho, we revel in our chains
   O'er the sorrow that was Spain's ;
  Heave or sink it, leave or drink it, we
    were Masters of the Sea ! "

Up spake the soul of a grey Gothavn
   'speckshioner : —
  (He that led the flinching in the fleets of
    fair Dundee)
   " Ho, the ringer and right whale,
   And the fish we struck for sale,
  Will ye whelm them all for wantonness
    that wallow in the sea ? "

Loud sang the souls of the jolly, jolly Mari-
    ners,
  Crying : — " Under Heaven here is nei-
    ther lead nor lee !
   Must we sing for evermore
   On the windless glassy floor ?
  Take back your golden fiddles, and we 'll
    beat for open sea ! "

Then stooped the Lord, and He called the
   good Sea up to Him,
  And 'stablished his borders unto all Eter-
    nity,
   That such as have no pleasure
   For to praise the Lord by measure
They may enter into galleons and serve
   Him on the Sea.

Sun, wind, and cloud shall fail not from the
*   face of it,*
Stinging, ringing spindrift nor the fulmar
*   flying free,*

And the ships shall go abroad
To the glory of the Lord
Who heard the silly sailor-men and gave
*   them back their Sea!*

Arthur Symons

AT FONTAINEBLEAU

IT was a day of sun and rain,
Uncertain as a child's swift moods ;
And I shall never spend again
So blithe a day among the woods.

Was it because the Gods were pleased
That they were awful in our eyes,
Whom we in very deed appeased
With barley-cakes of sacrifice ?

The forest knew her and was glad,
And laughed for very joy to know
Her child was with her ; then, grown
    sad,
She wept, because her child must go.

And Alice, like a little Faun,
Went leaping over rocks and ferns,
Coursing the shadow-race from dawn
Until the twilight-flock returns.

And she would spy and she would cap-
    ture
The shyest flower that lit the grass ;
The joy I had to watch her rapture
Was keen as even her rapture was.

The forest knew her and was glad,
And laughed and wept for joy and
    woe.
This was the welcome that she had
Among the woods of Fontainebleau.

JAVANESE DANCERS

TWITCHED strings, the clang of metal,
    beaten drums,
Dull, shrill, continuous, disquieting ;
And now the stealthy dancer comes
Undulantly with cat-like steps that cling ;

Smiling between her painted lids a smile
Motionless, unintelligible, she twines

Her fingers into mazy lines,
Twining her scarves across them all the
    while.

One, two, three, four step forth, and, to
    and fro,
Delicately and imperceptibly,
Now swaying gently in a row,
Now interthreading slow and rhythmi-
    cally,

Still with fixed eyes, monotonously still,
Mysteriously, with smiles inanimate,
With lingering feet that undulate,
With sinuous fingers, spectral hands that
    thrill,

The little amber-colored dancers move,
Like little painted figures on a screen,
Or phantom-dancers haply seen
Among the shadows of a magic grove.

DURING MUSIC

THE music had the heat of blood,
    A passion that no words can reach ;
We sat together, and understood
    Our own heart's speech.

We had no need of word or sign,
    The music spoke for us, and said
All that her eyes could read in mine
    Or mine in hers had read.

TO A PORTRAIT

A PENSIVE photograph
    Watches me from the shelf —
Ghost of old love, and half
    Ghost of myself !

How the dear waiting eyes
    Watch me and love me yet —
Sad home of memories,
    Her waiting eyes !

Ghost of old love, wronged ghost,
　　Return : though all the pain
Of all once loved, long lost,
　　Come back again.

Forget not, but forgive !
　　Alas, too late I cry.
We are two ghosts that had their chance to
　　live,
And lost it, she and I.

Dollie Radford

IF ALL THE WORLD

IF all the world were right,
　　How fair our love would grow,
At what a golden height
　　Its spotless flower could blow.

Through what untroubled air
　　Its fragrant boughs would spread,
On fruit how sweet and rare
　　Should we be freely fed.

But ah, what could we tend,
　　With sorrow and delight,
Our hearts how should we spend,
　　If all the world were right ?

AH, BRING IT NOT

AH, bring it not so grudgingly,
　　The gift thou bringest me,
Thy kind hands shining from afar
　　Let me in welcome see,
And know the treasure that they hold,
　　For purest gold.

And with glad feet that linger not,
　　Come through the summer land,
Through the sweet fragrance of the
　　　flowers,
　　Swiftly to where I stand,
And in the sunshine let me wear
　　Thy token rare.

Fairer for me will be the day,
　　Fair all the days will be,
And thy rich gift upon my breast
　　Will make me fair to see ;
And beautiful, through all the years,
　　In joys and tears.

Ah come, and coming do not ask
　　The answering gift of mine ;

Thou hast the pride of offering,
　　Taste now the joy divine,
And come, content to pass to-day
　　Empty away.

MY LITTLE DEAR

MY little dear, so fast asleep,
　　Whose arms about me cling,
What kisses shall she have to keep,
　　While she is slumbering ?

Upon her golden baby-hair,
　　The golden dreams I 'll kiss
Which Life spread through my morn-
　　　ing fair,
　　And I have saved, for this.

Upon her baby eyes I 'll press
　　The kiss Love gave to me,
When his great joy and loveliness
　　Made all things fair to see.

And on her lips, with smiles astir,
　　Ah me, what prayer of old
May now be kissed to comfort her,
　　Should Love or Life grow cold.

A MODEL

YEAR after year I sit for them,
　　The boys and girls who come and go,
Although my beauty's diadem
　　Has lain for many seasons low.

When first I came n. hair was bright, —
　　How hard, they said, to paint its gold,
How difficult to catch the light
　　Which fell upon it, fold on fold, —

How hard to give my happy youth
　　In all its pride of white and red ;

None would believe, in very truth,
A maiden was so fair, they said.

How could they know they gave to me
The daily hope which made me fair,
Sweet promises of things to be,
The happy things I was to share.

The flowers painted round my face,
The magic seas and skies above,
And many a fair enchanted place
Full of the summer time and love.

They set me in a fairy-land,
So much more real than they knew,
And I was slow to understand
The pictures could not all come true.

But one by one, they died somehow,
The waking dreams which kept me
glad,
And as I sat, they told me now,
None would believe a maid so sad.

They paint me still, but now I sit
Just for my neck and shoulder lines,
And for the little lingering bit
Of color in my hair that shines.

And as a figure worn and strange
Into their groups I sometimes stray,
To break the light, to mark their range
Of sun and shade, of grave and gay.

And evermore they come and go,
With life and hope so sweet and high, —
In all the world how should they know
There is no one so tired as I.

OCTOBER

FROM falling leaf to falling leaf,
How strange it was, through all the year,
In all its joy and all its grief,
You did not know I loved you dear ;
Through all the winter-time and spring,
You smiled and watched me come and go,
Through all the summer blossoming,
How strange it was you did not know.

Your face shone from my earth and sky,
Your voice was in my heart always,
Days were as dreams when you were by,
And nights of dreaming linked the days ;
In my great joy I craved so much,
My life lay trembling at your hand,
I prayed you for one magic touch,
How strange you did not understand !

From leaf to leaf, the trees are bare,
The autumn wind is cold and stern,
And outlined in the clear sharp air
Lies a new world for me to learn ;
Stranger than all, dear friend, to-day,
You take my hand and do not know
A thousand years have passed away,
Since last year — when I loved you so.

William Butler Yeats

AN INDIAN SONG

O WANDERER in the southern weather,
Our isle awaits us ; on each lea
The pea-hens dance ; in crimson feather
A parrot swaying on a tree
Rages at his own image in the enamelled
sea.

There dreamy Time lets fall his sickle
And Life the sandals of her fleetness,
And sleek young Joy is no more fickle,
And Love is kindly and deceitless,
And all is over save the murmur and the
sweetness.

There we will moor our lonely ship
And wander ever with woven hands,

Murmuring softly, lip to lip,
Along the grass, along the sands —
Murmuring how far away are all earth's
feverish lands :

How we alone of mortals are
Hid in the earth's most hidden part,
While grows our love an Indian star,
A meteor of the burning heart,
One with the waves that softly round us
laugh and dart ;

One with the leaves ; one with the dove
That moans and sighs a hundred days ;
How when we die our shades will rove,
Dropping at eve in coral bays
A vapory footfall on the ocean's sleepy
blaze.

AN OLD SONG RESUNG

Down by the salley gardens my love and I
    did meet ;
She passed the salley gardens with little
    snow-white feet.
She bid me take love easy as the leaves
    grow on the tree ;
But I, being young and foolish, with her
    would not agree.

In a field by the river my love and I did
    stand,
And on my leaning shoulder she laid her
    snow-white hand.
She bid me take life easy as the grass
    grows on the weirs ;
But I was young and foolish, and now am
    full of tears.

THE ROSE OF THE WORLD

Who dreamed that beauty passes like a
    dream ?
For these red lips with all their mourn-
    ful pride,
Mournful that no new wonder may betide,
Troy passed away in one high funeral
    gleam,
And Usna's children died.

We and the laboring world are passing
    by : —
Amid men's souls that day by day gives
    place,
More fleeting than the sea's foam-fickle
    face,
Under the passing stars, foam of the sky,
Lives on this lonely face.

Bow down, archangels, in your dim abode :
Before ye were or any hearts to beat,
Weary and kind one stood beside His
    seat ;
He made the world, to be a grassy road
Before her wandering feet.

THE WHITE BIRDS

I would that we were, my beloved, white
    birds on the foam of the sea :
We tire of the flame of the meteor, before
    it can pass by and flee ;

And the flame of the blue star of twilight,
    hung low on the rim of the sky,
Has awaked in our hearts, my beloved, a
    sadness that never may die.

A weariness comes from those dreamers,
    dew-dabbled, the lily and rose,
Ah, dream not of them, my beloved, the
    flame of the meteor that goes,
Or the flame of the blue star that lingers
    hung low in the fall of the dew :
For I would we were changed to white birds
    on the wandering foam—I and you.

I am haunted by numberless islands, and
    many a Danaan shore,
Where Time would surely forget us, and
    Sorrow come near us no more :
Soon far from the rose and the lily, the
    fret of the flames, would we be,
Were we only white birds, my beloved,
    buoyed out on the foam of the sea.

THE FOLK OF THE AIR

O'Driscoll drove with a song
    The wild duck and the drake
From the tall and the tufted weeds
    Of the drear Heart Lake.

And he saw how the weeds grew dark
    At the coming of night tide,
And he dreamed of the long dim hair
    Of Bridget his bride.

He heard while he sang and dreamed
    A piper piping away,
And never was piping so sad,
    And never was piping so gay.

And he saw young men and young girls
    Who danced on a level place,
And Bridget his bride among them,
    With a sad and a gay face.

The dancers crowded about him,
    And many a sweet thing said,
And a young man brought him red wine,
    And a young girl white bread.

But Bridget drew him by the sleeve,
    Away from the merry bands,
To old men playing at cards
    With a twinkling of ancient hands.

The bread and the wine had a doom,
For these were the folk of the air ;
He sat and played in a dream
Of her long dim hair.

He played with the merry old men,
And thought not of evil chance,
Until one bore Bridget his bride
Away from the merry dance.

He bore her away in his arms,
The handsomest young man there,
And his neck and his breast and his
    arms
Were drowned in her long dim hair.

O'Driscoll got up from the grass
And scattered the cards with a cry ;
But the old men and dancers were gone
As a cloud faded into the sky.

He knew now the folk of the air,
And his heart was blackened by dread,
And he ran to the door of his house ;
Old women were keening the dead ;

But he heard high up in the air
A piper piping away ;
And never was piping so sad
And never was piping so gay.

THE SONG OF THE OLD MOTHER

I RISE in the dawn, and I kneel and blow
Till the seed of the fire flicker and glow.
And then I must scrub, and bake, and
    sweep,
Till stars are beginning to blink and
    peep ;
But the young lie long and dream in their
    bed
Of the matching of ribbons, the blue and
    the red,
And their day goes over in idleness,
And they sigh if the wind but lift up a
    tress ;·
While I must work, because I am old
And the seed of the fire gets feeble and
    cold.

George William Russell

("A. E.")

SELF-DISCIPLINE

WHEN the soul sought refuge in the place
    of rest,
Overborne by strife and pain beyond con-
    trol,
From some secret hollow, whisper soft-
    confessed,
Came the legend of the soul.

Some bright one of old time laid his scep-
    tre down,
So his heart might learn of sweet and bit-
    ter truth ;
Going forth bereft of beauty, throne, and
    crown,
And the sweetness of his youth.

So the old appeal and fierce revolt we
    make
Through the world's hour dies within our
    primal will ;

And we justify the pain and hearts that
    break,
And our lofty doom fulfilled.

KRISHNA

"I am Beauty itself among beautiful things."—
                            BHAGAVAD-GITA.

THE East was crowned with snow-cold
    bloom
And hung with veils of pearly fleece :
They died away into the gloom,
Vistas of peace — and deeper peace.

And earth and air and wave and fire
In awe and breathless silence stood ;
For One who passed into their choir
Linked them in mystic brotherhood.

Twilight of amethyst, amid
Thy few strange stars that lit the heights,

Where was the secret spirit hid ?
Where was Thy place, O Light of Lights ?

The flame of Beauty far in space —
Where rose the fire : in Thee ? in Me ?
Which bowed the elemental race
To adoration silently ?

THE GREAT BREATH

Its edges foamed with amethyst and rose,
Withers once more the old blue flower of
    day :
There where the ether like a diamond glows
    Its petals fade away.

A shadowy tumult stirs the dusky air ;
Sparkle the delicate dews, the distant
    snows ;
The great deep thrills, for through it every-
    where
    The breath of Beauty blows.

I saw how all the trembling ages past,
Moulded to her by deep and deeper breath,
Neared to the hour when Beauty breathes
    her last
    And knows herself in death.

THE MAN TO THE ANGEL

I HAVE wept a million tears.
Pure and proud one, where are thine ?
What the gain, though all thy years
In unbroken beauty shine ?

All your beauty cannot win
Truth we learn in pain and sighs :
You can never enter in
To the Circle of the Wise.

They are but the slaves of light
Who have never known the gloom,
And between the dark and bright
Willed in freedom their own doom.

Think not in your pureness there
That our pain but follows sin :
There are fires for those who dare
Seek the throne of might to win.

Pure one, from your pride refrain :
Dark and lost amid the strife,

I am myriad years of pain
Nearer to the fount of life.

When defiance fierce is thrown
At the god to whom you bow,
Rest the lips of the Unknown
Tenderest upon my brow.

OM

A MEMORY

FAINT grew the yellow buds of light
Far flickering beyond the snows,
As leaning o'er the shadowy white
Morn glimmered like a pale primrose.

Within an Indian vale below
A child said " OM " with tender heart,
Watching with loving eyes the glow
In dayshine fade and night depart.

The word which Brahma at his dawn
Outbreathes and endeth at his night,
Whose tide of sound so rolling on
Gives birth to orbs of pearly light ;

And beauty, wisdom, love, and youth,
By its enchantment gathered grow
In agelong wandering to the Truth,
Through many a cycle's ebb and flow.

And here the voice of earth was stilled,
The child was lifted to the Wise :
A strange delight his spirit filled,
And Brahm looked from his shining eyes.

IMMORTALITY

WE must pass like smoke or live within
    the spirit's fire,
For we can no more than smoke unto the
    flame return,
If our thought has changed to dream or
    will unto desire.
As smoke we vanish though the fire may
    burn.

Lights of infinite pity star the gray dusk
    of our days :
Surely here is soul ; with it we have eter-
    nal breath :
In the fire of love we live or pass by many
    ways,
By unnumbered ways of dream to death.

Theodore Wratislaw

THE MUSIC-HALL

THE curtain on the grouping dancers falls,
The heaven of color has vanished from our
    eyes ;
Stirred in our seats we wait with vague
    surmise
What haply comes that pleases or that
    palls.
Touched on the stand the thrice-struck
    baton calls,
Once more I watch the unfolding curtain
    rise,
I hear the exultant violins premise
The well-known tune that thrills me and
    enthralls.
Then trembling in my joy I see you flash
Before the footlights to the cymbals' clash,
With laughing lips, swift feet, and brilliant
    glance,
You, fair as heaven and as a rainbow
    bright,
You, queen of song and empress of the
    dance,
Flower of mine eyes, my love, my heart's
    delight !

EXPECTATION

COME while the afternoon of May
Is sweet with many a lilac-spray,
Come while the sparrows chirping fare
From branch to branch across the square.

Come like the dawn and bring to me
The fresh winds of an open sea,
Come like the stars of night and bear
All consolation in thine hair.

Bring me release from ancient pain,
Bring me the hopes of joy found vain,
Bring me thy sweetness of the dove,
Come, sweet, and bring thyself and love !

A VAIN DESIRE

DEAR, did you know how sweet to me
    Was every glance of yours, how sweet
The laugh that lights your face with glee,
    The passing murmur of your feet,

And seeing perchance with grief how
    vain
    The love that makes you sadly dear
Did grant for my unuttered pain
    A whispered word, a smile, a tear

Dropped like a star from Paradise,
    Then might I bless my weary state,
Though you behold me from the skies
    And I on earth am desolate.

Mary C. G. Byron

(M. C. GILLINGTON)

THE TRYST OF THE NIGHT

OUT of the uttermost ridge of dusk,
    where the dark and the day are
    mingled,
The voice of the Night rose cold and
    calm—it called through the shadow-
    swept air ;
Through all the valleys and lone hillsides,
    it pierced, it thrilled, it tingled —
It summoned me forth to the wild sea-
    shore, to meet with its mystery
    there.

Out of the deep ineffable blue, with palpi-
    tant swift repeating
Of gleam and glitter and opaline glow,
    that broke in ripples of light —
In burning glory it came and went, — I
    heard, I saw it beating,
Pulse by pulse, from star to star, — the
    passionate heart of the Night !

Out of the thud of the rustling sea — the
    panting, yearning, throbbing
Waves that stole on the startled shore,
    with coo and mutter of spray —

The wail of the Night came fitful-faint, —
  I heard her stifled sobbing :
The cold salt drops fell slowly, slowly,
  gray into gulfs of gray.

There through the darkness the great
  world reeled, and the great tides
  roared, assembling —
Murmuring hidden things that are past,
  and secret things that shall be ;
There at the limits of life we met, and
  touched with a rapturous trem-
  bling —
One with each other, I and the Night,
  and the skies, and the stars, and
  sea.

THE FAIRY THRALL

On gossamer nights when the moon is low,
  And stars in the mist are hiding,
Over the hill where the foxgloves grow
  You may see the fairies riding.
    Kling ! Klang ! Kling !
  Their stirrups and their bridles ring,

And their horns are loud and their
  bugles blow,
When the moon is low.

They sweep through the night like a whis-
  tling wind,
  They pass and have left no traces ;
But one of them lingers far behind
  The flight of the fairy faces.
    She makes no moan,
    She sorrows in the dark alone,
  She wails for the love of human kind,
    Like a whistling wind.

" Ah ! why did I roam where the elfins
  ride,
  Their glimmering steps to follow ?
They bore me far from my loved one's
  side,
To wander o'er hill and hollow.
    Kling ! Klang ! Kling !
  Their stirrups and their bridles ring,
But my heart is cold in the cold night-
  tide,
Where the elfins ride."

Alice E. Gillington

THE SEVEN WHISTLERS

Whistling strangely, whistling sadly,
  whistling sweet and clear,
The Seven Whistlers have passed thy
  house, Pentruan of Porthmeor ;
It was not in the morning, nor the noon-
  day's golden grace,
It was in the dead waste midnight, when
  the tide yelped loud in the Race ;
The tide swings round in the Race, and
  they're plaining whisht and low,
And they come from the gray sea-marshes,
  where the gray sea-lavenders grow ;
And the cotton grass sways to and fro ;
  And the gore-sprent sundews thrive
  With oozy hands alive.
Canst hear the curlews' whistle through
  thy dreamings dark and drear,
How they're crying, crying, crying, Pen-
  truan of Porthmeor ?

Shall thy hatchment, mouldering grimly in
  yon church amid the sands,

Stay trouble from thy household ? Or the
  carven cherub-hands
Which hold thy shield to the font ? Or
  the gauntlets on the wall
Keep evil from its onward course, as the
  great tides rise and fall ?
The great tides rise and fall, and the cave
  sucks in the breath
Of the wave when it runs with tossing spray,
  and the ground-sea rattles of Death ;
" I rise in the shallows," 'a saith,
  " Where the mermaid's kettle sings,
  And the black shag flaps his wings ! "
Ay, the green sea-mountain leaping may
  lead horror in its rear,
When thy drenched sail leans to its yawn-
  ing trough Pentruan of Porthmeor !

Yet the stoup waits at thy doorway for its
  load of glittering ore,
And thy ships lie in the tideway, and thy
  flocks along the moor ;
And thine arishes gleam softly when the
  October moonbeams wane,

When in the bay all shining the fishers set
  the seine ;
The fishers cast the seine, and 't is " Heva ! "
  in the town,
And from the watch-rock on the hill the
  huers are shouting down ;
And ye hoist the mainsail brown,
  As over the deep-sea roll
  The lurker follows the shoal ;
To follow and to follow, in the moonshine
  silver-clear,
When the halyards creak to thy dipping
  sail, Pentruan of Porthmeor !

And wailing, and complaining, and whis-
  tling whisht and clear,
The Seven Whistlers have passed thy house,
  Pentruan of Porthmeor !
It was not in the morning, nor the noon-
  day's golden grace, —
It was in the fearsome midnight, when the
  tide-dogs yelped in the Race :
— The tide swings round in the Race, and
  they 're whistling whisht and low,
And they come from the lonely heather,
  where the fur-edged foxgloves blow ;
And the moor-grass sways to and fro ;
  Where the yellow moor-birds sigh,
  And the sea-cooled wind sweeps by.
Canst hear the curlews' whistle through
  the darkness wild and drear, —
How they 're calling, calling, calling, Pen-
  truan of Porthmeor ?

THE ROSY MUSK–MALLOW

(ROMANY LOVE-SONG)

THE rosy musk-mallow blooms where the
  south wind blows,
  O my gypsy rose !
In the deep dark lanes where thou and I
  must meet ;
  So sweet !
Before the harvest moon's gold glints over
  the down,
Or the brown-sailed trawler returns to the
  gray sea-town,
The rosy musk-mallow sways, and the south
  wind's laughter
Follows our footsteps after !

The rosy musk-mallow blooms by the
  moor-brook's flow,
  So daintily O !

Where thou and I in the silence of night
  must pass,
  My lass !
Over the stream with its ripple of song,
  to-night,
We will fly, we will run together, my
  heart's delight !
The rosy musk-mallow sways, and the moor-
  brook's laughter
Follows our footsteps after !

The rosy musk-mallow blooms within sound
  of the sea ;
  It curtseys to thee,
O my gypsy-queen, it curtseys adown to
  thy feet ;
  So sweet !
When dead leaves drift through the dusk
  of the autumn day,
And the red elf-lanthorns hang from the
  spindle-spray,
The rosy musk-mallow sways, and the
  sea's wild laughter
Follows our footsteps after !

The rosy musk-mallow blooms where the
  dim wood sleeps,
  And the bind-weed creeps ;
Through tangled wood-paths unknown we
  must take our flight,
  To-night !
As the pale hedge-lilies around the dark
  elder wind,
Clasp thy white arms about me, nor look
  behind.
The rosy musk-mallow is closed, and the
  soft leaves' laughter
Follows our footsteps after !

THE DOOM–BAR

O D' YOU hear the seas complainin', and
  complainin', whilst it 's rainin' ?
Did you hear it mourn in the dimorts,[1]
  when the surf woke up and sighed ?
  The choughs screamed on the sand,
  And the foam flew over land,
And the seas rolled dark on the Doom-
  Bar at rising of the tide.

I gave my lad a token, when he left me
  nigh heart-broken,
To mind him of old Padstow town, where
  loving souls abide ;

[1] Twilight.

'T was a ring with the words set
All round, " Can Love Forget ? "
And I watched his vessel toss on the Bar
with the outward-turning tide.

D' you hear the seas complainin', and com-
plainin', while it 's rainin' ?
And his vessel has never crossed the Bar
from the purple seas outside ;
And down the shell-pink sands,
Where we once went, holding hands,
Alone I watch the Doom-Bar and the ris-
ing of the tide.

One day — 't was four years after — the
harbor-girls, with laughter
So soft and wild as sea-gulls when they 're
playing seek-and-hide,
Coaxed me out — for the tides were
lower
Than had ever been known before ;
And we ran across the Doom-Bar, all
white and shining wide.

I saw a something shinin', where the long,
wet weeds were twinin'

Around a rosy scallop ; and gold a ring lay
inside ;
And around its rim were set
The words " Can Love Forget ? " —
And there upon the Doom-Bar I knelt and
sobbed and cried.

I took my ring and smoothed it where the
sand and shells had grooved it ;
But O ! St. Petrock bells will never ring
me home a bride ! —
For the night my lad was leavin'
Me, all tearful-eyed and grievin',
He had tossed my keepsake out on the
Bar to the rise and fall of the
tide !

Do you hear the seas complainin', and com-
plainin', while it 's rainin' ?
Did you hear them call in the dimorts,
when the surf woke up and sighed ?
Maybe it is a token
I shall go no more heart-broken —
And I shall cross the Doom-Bar at the
turning of the tide.

Dora Sigerson

ALL SOULS' NIGHT

O MOTHER, mother, I swept the hearth, I
set his chair and the white board
spread,
I prayed for his coming to our kind Lady
when Death's sad doors would let
out the dead ;
A strange wind rattled the window-pane,
and down the lane a dog howled on.
I called his name and the candle flame
burnt dim, pressed a hand the door-
latch upon.
Deelish ! Deelish ! my woe forever that
I could not sever coward flesh from
fear.
I called his name and the pale Ghost came ;
but I was afraid to meet my dear.
O mother, mother, in tears I checked the
sad hours past of the year that 's
o'er,

Till by God's grace I might see his face
and hear the sound of his voice once
more ;
The chair I set from the cold and wet, he
took when he came from unknown
skies
Of the land of the dead ; on my bent brown
head I felt the reproach of his sad-
dened eyes ;
I closed my lids on my heart's desire,
crouched by the fire, my voice was
dumb ;
At my clean-swept hearth he had no
mirth, and at my table he broke no
crumb.
Deelish ! Deelish ! my woe forever that I
could not sever coward flesh from
fear :
His chair put aside when the young cock
cried, and I was afraid to meet my
dear.

Percy Addleshaw

("PERCY HEMINGWAY")

THE HAPPY WANDERER

HE is the happy wanderer, who goes
Singing upon his way, with eyes awake
To every scene, with ears alert to take
The sweetness of all sounds ; who loves and
        knows
The secrets of the highway, and the rose
Holds fairer for the wounds the briars make;
Who welcomes rain, that he his thirst may
        slake, —
The sun, because it dries his dripping
        clothes ;
Treasures experience beyond all store,
Careless if pain or pleasure he shall win,
So that his knowledge widens more and
        more
Ready each hour to worship or to sin ;
Until tired, wise, content, he halts before
The sign o' the Grave, a cool and quiet inn.

TRAVELLERS

WE shall lodge at the sign of the Grave,
        you say ;
Well, the road is a long one we trudge, my
        friend,

So why should we grieve at the break of
        the day ?
Let us sing, let us drink, let us love, let us
        play, —
We can keep our sighs for the journey's
        end.

We shall lodge at the sign o' the Grave,
        you say ;
Well, since we are nearing our journey's
        end,
Our hearts should be happy while yet they
        may :
Let us sing, let us drink, let us love, let
        us play,
For perhaps it's a comfortless inn, my
        friend.

IT MAY BE

IT may be we shall know in the here-
        after
Why we, begetting hopes, give birth to
        fears,
And why the world's too beautiful for
        laughter,
Too gross for tears.

Olive Custance

THE WAKING OF SPRING

SPIRIT of Spring, thy coverlet of snow
Hath fallen from thee, with its fringe of
        frost,
And where the river late did overflow

Sway fragile white anemones, wind-tost,
And in the woods stand snowdrops, half
        asleep,
With drooping heads — sweet dreamers so
        long lost.

Spirit, arise ! for crimson flushes creep
Into the cold gray east, where clouds as-
        semble
To meet the sun : and earth hath ceased to
        weep.

Her tears tip every blade of grass, and
        tremble,
Caught in the cup of every flower. O
        Spring !
I see thee spread thy pinions,— they re-
        semble

Large delicate leaves, all silver-veined,
        that fling
Frail floating shadows on the forest sward ;
And all the birds about thee build and
        sing !

Blithe stranger from the gardens of our
        God,
We welcome thee, for one is at thy side
Whose voice is thrilling music, Love, thy
        Lord,

Whose tender glances stir thy soul, whose
wide
Wings wave above thee, thou awakened
bride !

TWILIGHT

SPIRIT of Twilight, through your folded
wings
I catch a glimpse of your averted face,
And rapturous on a sudden, my soul
sings
"Is not this common earth a holy
place ? "

Spirit of Twilight, you are like a song
That sleeps, and waits a singer, — like a
hymn
That God finds lovely and keeps near Him
long,
Till it is choired by aureoled cherubim.

Spirit of Twilight, in the golden gloom
Of dreamland dim I sought you, and I
found
A woman sitting in a silent room
Full of white flowers that moved and
made no sound.

These white flowers were the thoughts you
bring to all,
And the room's name is Mystery where
you sit,
Woman whom we call Twilight, when
night's pall
You lift across our Earth to cover it.

THE PARTING HOUR

NOT yet, dear love, not yet : the sun is high ;
You said last night "At sunset I will go."
Come to the garden, where when blossoms
die
No word is spoken ; it is better so :
Ah ! bitter word " Farewell."

Hark ! how the birds sing sunny songs of
spring !
Soon they will build, and work will si-
lence them ;
So we grow less light-hearted as years
bring
Life's grave responsibilities — and then
The bitter word " Farewell."

The violets fret to fragrance 'neath your
feet,
Heaven's gold sunlight dreams aslant
your hair :
No flower for me ! your mouth is far more
sweet.
O, let my lips forget, while lingering
there,
Love's bitter word " Farewell."

.   .   .   .

Sunset already ! have we sat so long ?
The parting hour, and so much left un-
said !
The garden has grown silent — void of
song,
Our sorrow shakes us with a sudden
dread !
Ah ! *bitter* word " Farewell."

IV

COLONIAL POETS

(INDIA — AUSTRALASIA — DOMINION OF CANADA)

1837-1894

ENGLAND AND HER COLONIES

SHE stands, a thousand-wintered tree,
  By countless morns impearled;
Her broad roots coil beneath the sea,
  Her branches sweep the world;
Her seeds, by careless winds conveyed,
  Clothe the remotest strand
With forests from her scatterings made,
New nations fostered in her shade,
  And linking land with land.

O ye by wandering tempest sown
  'Neath every alien star,
Forget not whence the breath was blown
  That wafted you afar!
For ye are still her ancient seed
  On younger soil let fall —
Children of Britain's island-breed,
To whom the Mother in her need
  Perchance may one day call.

WILLIAM WATSON.

POEMS: 1893.

COLONIAL POETS

(INDIA — AUSTRALASIA — DOMINION OF CANADA)

INDIA

See TORU DUTT, RUDYARD KIPLING, *in the preceding division of this Anthology.*
See also, in the second division, SIR EDWIN ARNOLD, SIR ALFRED LYALL, *poets of English birth, and sometime resident in India*

AUSTRALASIA

(*See also:* A. DOMETT, R. H. HORNE, W. SHARP, D. B. W. SLADEN)

Percy Russell

THE BIRTH OF AUSTRALIA

NOT 'mid the thunder of the battle guns,
Not on the red field of an Empire's wrath,
Rose to a nation Australasia's sons,
Who tread to greatness Industry's pure path.
Behold a people, through whose annals runs
No damning stain of falsehood, force, or fraud ;
Whose sceptre is the ploughshare — not the sword —
Whose glory lives in harvest-ripening suns !
Where 'mid the records of old Rome or Greece
Glows such a tale? Thou canst not answer, Time.
With shield unsullied by a single crime,
With wealth of gold, and still more golden fleece,
Forth stands Australia, in her birth sublime,
The only nation from the womb of Peace !

Charles Harpur

A MIDSUMMER'S NOON IN THE AUSTRALIAN FOREST

NOT a sound disturbs the air,
There is quiet everywhere ;
Over plains and over woods
What a mighty stillness broods !
All the birds and insects keep
Where the coolest shadows sleep ;
Even the busy ants are found
Resting in their pebbled mound ;
Even the locust clingeth now
Silent to the barky bough :
Over hills and over plains
Quiet, vast and slumbrous, reigns.

Only there's a drowsy humming
From yon warm lagoon slow-coming :
'T is the dragon-hornet — see !
All bedaubed resplendently
Yellow on a tawny ground —
Each rich spot not square nor round,
Rudely heart-shaped, as it were
The blurred and hasty impress there
Of a vermeil-crusted seal
Dusted o'er with golden meal.
Only there's a droning where
Yon bright beetle shines in air,
Tracks it in its gleaming flight
With a slanting beam of light
Rising in the sunshine higher,
Till its shards flame out like fire.

Every other thing is still,
Save the ever-wakeful rill,
Whose cool murmur only throws
Cooler comfort round repose ;
Or some ripple in the sea,
Of leafy boughs, where, lazily,
Tired summer, in her bower
Turning with the noontide hour,
Heaves a slumbrous breath ere she
Once more slumbers peacefully.

Oh, 't is easeful here to lie
Hidden from noon's scorching eye,
In this grassy cool recess
Musing thus of quietness.

AN ABORIGINAL MOTHER'S LAMENT

STILL farther would I fly, my child,
  To make thee safer yet
From the unsparing white man,
  With his dread hand murder-wet !

I 'll bear thee on as I have borne
  With stealthy steps wind-fleet,
But the dark night shrouds the forest,
  And thorns are in my feet.

    O moan not ! I would give this braid —
      Thy father's gift to me —
    But for a single palmful
      Of water now for thee.

Ah, spring not to his name — no more
  To glad us may he come —
He is smouldering into ashes
  Beneath the blasted gum ;
All charred and blasted by the fire
  The white man kindled there,
And fed with our slaughtered kindred
  Till heaven-high went its glare !

And but for thee, I would their fire
  Had eaten me as fast !
Hark ! Hark ! I hear his death-cry
  Yet lengthening up the blast !
But no — when his bound hands had signed
  The way that we shound fly,
On the roaring pyre flung bleeding —
  I saw thy father die !

No more shall his loud tomahawk
  Be plied to win our cheer,
Or the shining fish pools darken
  Beneath his shadowing spear ;
The fading tracks of his fleet foot
  Shall guide not as before,
And the mountain-spirits mimic
  His hunting call no more !

    O moan not ! I would give this braid —
      Thy father's gift to me —
    For but a single palmful
      Of water now for thee.

Robert Lowe, Viscount Sherbrooke

SONG OF THE SQUATTER

THE commissioner bet me a pony — I won,
So he cut off exactly two-thirds of my run ;
For he said I was making a fortune too fast,
And profit gained slower the longer would last.

He remarked, as devouring my mutton he sat,
That I suffered my sheep to grow sadly too fat ;
That they wasted waste land, did prerogative brown,
And rebelliously nibbled the droits of the Crown ;

That the creek that divided my station in
two
Showed that Nature designed that two
fees should be due.
Mr. Riddle assured me 't was paid but for
show,
But he kept it and spent it, that's all that
I know.

The commissioner fined me because I for-
got
To return an old ewe that was ill of the
rot,
And a poor wry-necked lamb that we kept
for a pet ;
And he said it was treason such things to
forget.

The commissioner pounded my cattle be-
cause
They had mumbled the scrub with their
famishing jaws
On the part of the run he had taken away,
And he sold them by auction the costs to
defray.

The border police they were out all the
day
To look for some thieves who had ran-
sacked my dray ;
But the thieves they continued in quiet
and peace,
For they'd robbed it themselves, had the
border police !

When the white thieves had left me the
black thieves appeared,
My shepherds they waddied, my cattle
they speared ;
But from fear of my license I said not a
word,

For I knew it was gone if the Government
heard.

The commissioner's bosom with anger was
filled
Against me because my poor shepherd was
killed ;
So he straight took away the last third of
my run,
And got it transferred to the name of his
son.

The son had from Cambridge been lately
expelled,
And his license for preaching most justly
withheld !
But this is no cause, the commissioner says,
Why he should not be fit for my license to
graze.

The cattle, that had not been sold at the
pound,
He took with the run at five shillings all
round,
And the sheep the blacks left me at six-
pence a head, —
A very good price, the commissioner said.

The Governor told me I justly was served,
That commissioners never from duty had
swerved ;
But that if I'd a fancy for any more land
For one pound an acre he'd plenty on hand.

I'm not very proud ! I can dig in a bog,
Feed pigs, or for firewood can split up a
log,
Clean shoes, riddle cinders, or help to boil
down —
Anything that you please, but graze lands
of the Crown !

Adam Lindsay Gordon

HOW WE BEAT THE FAVORITE

A LAY OF THE LOAMSHIRE HUNT CUP

"AYE, squire," said Stevens, "they back
him at evens ;
The race is all over, bar shouting, they
say ;

The Clown ought to beat her ; Dick Neville
is sweeter
Than ever — he swears he can win all
the way.

"A gentleman rider — well, I'm an out-
sider,
But if he's a gent who the mischief's a
jock ?

You swells mostly blunder, Dick rides for
the plunder,
He rides, too, like thunder — he sits like
a rock.

" He calls 'hunted fairly' a horse that has
barely
Been stripped for a trot within sight of
the hounds,
A horse that at Warwick beat Birdlime
and Yorick,
And gave Abdelkader at Aintree nine
pounds.

" They say we have no test to warrant a
protest ;
Dick rides for a lord and stands in with
a steward ;
The light of their faces they show him —
his case is
Prejudged and his verdict already se-
cured.

" But none can outlast her, and few travel
faster,
She strides in her work clean away from
The Drag ;
You hold her and sit her, she could n't be
fitter,
Whenever you hit her she 'll spring like
a stag.

" And p'raps the green jacket, at odds
though they back it,
May fall, or there 's no knowing what
may turn up.
The mare is quite ready, sit still and ride
steady,
Keep cool ; and I think you may just
win the Cup."

Dark-brown with tan muzzle, just stripped
for the tussle,
Stood Iseult, arching her neck to the curb,
A lean head and fiery, strong quarters and
wiry,
A loin rather light, but a shoulder superb.

Some parting injunction, bestowed with
great unction,
I tried to recall, but forgot like a dunce,
When Reginald Murray, full tilt on White
Surrey,
Came down in a hurry to start us at
once.

" Keep back in the yellow ! Come up on
Othello !
Hold hard on the chestnut ! Turn
round on The Drag !
Keep back there on Spartan ! Back you,
sir, in tartan !
So, steady there, easy," and down went
the flag.

We started, and Kerr made strong running
on Mermaid.
Through furrows that led to the first
stake-and-bound,
The crack, half extended, looked bloodlike
and splendid,
Held wide on the right where the head-
land was sound.

I pulled hard to baffle her rush with the
snaffle,
Before her two-thirds of the field got
away,
All through the wet pasture where floods
of the last year
Still loitered, they clotted my crimson
with clay.

The fourth fence, a wattle, floored Monk
and Blue-bottle ;
The Drag came to grief at the black-
thorn and ditch,
The rails toppled over Redoubt and Red
Rover,
The lane stopped Lycurgus and Leices-
tershire Witch.

She passed like an arrow Kildare and Cock
Sparrow,
And Mantrap and Mermaid refused the
stone wall ;
And Giles on The Greyling came down at
the paling,
And I was left sailing in front of them all.

I took them a burster, nor eased her nor
nursed her
Until the Black Bullfinch led into the
plough,
And through the strong bramble we bored
with a scramble —
My cap was knocked off by the hazel-
tree bough.

Where furrows looked lighter I drew the
rein tighter ;

Her dark chest all dappled with flakes
of white foam,
Her flanks mud-bespattered, a weak rail
she shattered :
We landed on turf with our heads turned
for home.

Then crashed a low binder, and then close
behind her
The sward to the strokes of the favorite
shook ;
His rush roused her mettle, yet ever so little
She shortened her stride as we raced at
the brook.

She rose when I hit her. I saw the stream
glitter,
A wide scarlet nostril flashed close to
my knee,
Between sky and water The Clown came
and caught her, —
The space that he cleared was a caution
to see.

And forcing the running, discarding all
cunning,
A length to the front went the rider in
green ;
A long strip of stubble, and then the big
double,
Two stiff flights of rails with a quickset
between.

She raced at the rasper, I felt my knees
grasp her,
I found my hands give to her strain on
the bit,
She rose when The Clown did — our silks
as we bounded
Brushed lightly, our stirrups clashed loud
as we lit.

A rise steeply sloping, a fence with stone
coping —
The last — we diverged round the base
of the hill ;
His path was the nearer, his leap was the
clearer,
I flogged up the straight, and he led sit-
ting still.

She came to his quarter, and on still I
brought her,
And up to his girth, to his breast-plate
she drew ;

A short prayer from Neville just reached
me, — " The Devil,"
He muttered, — locked level the hurdles
we flew.

A hum of hoarse cheering, a dense crowd
careering,
All sights seen obscurely, all shouts
vaguely heard ;
" The green wins ! " " The crimson ! "
The multitude swims on,
And figures are blended and features are
blurred.

" The horse is her master ! " " The green
forges past her ! "
" The Clown will outlast her ! " " The
Clown wins ! " " The Clown ! "
The white railing races with all the white
faces,
The chestnut outpaces, outstretches the
brown.

On still past the gateway she strains in the
straightway,
Still struggles, " The Clown by a short
neck at most,"
He swerves, the green scourges, the stand
rocks and surges,
And flashes, and verges, and flits the
white post.

Ay ! so ends the tussle, — I knew the tan
muzzle
Was first, though the ring-men were
yelling " Dead heat ! "
A nose I could swear by, but Clarke said
" The mare by
A short head." And that 's how the
favorite was beat.

THE SICK STOCK-RIDER

HOLD hard, Ned ! Lift me down once more,
and lay me in the shade.
Old man, you 've had your work cut out
to guide
Both horses, and to hold me in the saddle
when I swayed,
All through the hot, slow, sleepy, silent
ride.
The dawn at " Moorabinda " was a mist
rack dull and dense,
The sun-rise was a sullen, sluggish lamp ;

I was dozing in the gateway at Arbuthnot's
    bound'ry fence,
I was dreaming on the Limestone cattle
    camp.
We crossed the creek at Carricksford, and
    sharply through the haze,
And suddenly the sun shot flaming forth ;
To southward lay " Katâwa," with the sand
    peaks all ablaze,
And the flushed fields of Glen Lomond
    lay to north.
Now westward winds the bridle-path that
    leads to Landisfarm,
And yonder looms the double-headed
    Bluff ;
From the far side of the first hill when the
    skies are clear and calm,
You can see Sylvester's woolshed fair
    enough.

Five miles we used to call it from our
    homestead to the place
Where the big tree spans the roadway
    like an arch ;
'T was here we ran the dingo down that
    gave us such a chase
Eight years ago — or was it nine ? —
    last March.
'T was merry in the glowing morn among
    the gleaming grass,
To wander as we 've wandered many a
    mile,
And blow the cool tobacco cloud, and watch
    the white wreaths pass,
Sitting loosely in the saddle all the while.
'T was merry 'mid the blackwoods, when
    we spied the station roofs,
To wheel the wild scrub cattle at the yard,
With a running fire of stock whips and a
    fiery run of hoofs ;
Oh ! the hardest day was never then too
    hard !

Aye ! we had a glorious gallop after " Star-
    light " and his gang,
When they bolted from Sylvester's on
    the flat ;
How the sun-dried reed-beds crackled, how
    the flint-strewn ranges rang,
To the strokes of " Mountaineer " and
    " Acrobat," —
Hard behind them in the timber, harder
    still across the heath,
Close beside them through the tea-tree
    scrub we dashed ;

And the goldentinted fern leaves, how
    they rustled underneath :
And the honeysuckle osiers, how they
    crashed !
We led the hunt throughout, Ned, on the
    chestnut and the gray,
And the troopers were three hundred
    yards behind,
While we emptied our six-shooters on the
    bush-rangers at bay,
In the creek with stunted box-trees for
    a blind !
There you grappled with the leader, man
    to man, and horse to horse,
And you rolled together when the chest-
    nut rear'd.
He blazed away and missed you in that
    shallow water-course —
A narrow shave — his powder singed
    your beard !

In these hours when life is ebbing, how
    those days when life was young
Come back to us ; how clearly I recall
Even the yarns Jack Hall invented, and
    the songs Jem Roper sung ;
And where are now Jem Roper and
    Jack Hall ?

Aye ! nearly all our comrades of the old
    colonial school,
Our ancient boon companions, Ned, are
    gone ;
Hard livers for the most part, somewhat
    reckless as a rule,
It seems that you and I are left alone.

There was Hughes, who got in trouble
    through that business with the cards,
It matters little what became of him ;
But a steer ripped up Macpherson in the
    Cooramenta yards,
And Sullivan was drowned at Sink-or-
    swim ;
And Mostyn — poor Frank Mostyn — died
    at last, a fearful wreck,
In the "horrors" at the Upper Wandinong,
And Carisbrooke, the rider, at the Horse-
    fall broke his neck —
Faith ! the wonder was he saved his
    neck so long !
Ah ! those days and nights we squandered
    at the Logans' in the glen —
The Logans, man and wife, have long
    been dead.

Elsie's tallest girl seems taller than your
little Elsie then ;
And Ethel is a woman grown and wed.

I 've had my share of pastime, and I 've
done my share of toil,
And life is short — the longest life a
span ;
I care not now to tarry for the corn or for
the oil,
Or for wine that maketh glad the heart
of man.
For good undone, and gifts misspent, and
resolutions vain,
'T is somewhat late to trouble. This I
know —
I should live the same life over, if I had to
live again ;
And the chances are I go where most
men go.

The deep blue skies wax dusky, and the
tall green trees grow dim,
The sward beneath me seems to heave
and fall ;
And sickly, smoky shadows through the
sleepy sunlight swim,
And on the very sun's face weave their
pall.
Let me slumber in the hollow where the
wattle blossoms wave,
With never stone or rail to fence my
bed ;
Should the sturdy station children pull the
bush-flowers on my grave,
I may chance to hear them romping
overhead.

VALEDICTORY

LAY me low, my work is done,
I am weary. Lay me low,

Where the wild flowers woo the sun,
Where the balmy breezes blow,
Where the butterfly takes wing,
Where the aspens, drooping, grow,
Where the young birds chirp and
sing —
I am weary, let me go.

I have striven hard and long
In the world's unequal fight,
Always to resist the wrong,
Always to maintain the right.
Always with a stubborn heart,
Taking, giving blow for blow ;
Brother, I have played my part,
And am weary, let me go.

Stern the world and bitter cold,
Irksome, painful to endure ;
Everywhere a love of gold,
Nowhere pity for the poor.
Everywhere mistrust, disguise,
Pride, hypocrisy, and show ;
Draw the curtain, close mine eyes,
I am weary, let me go.

Other chance when I am gone
May restore the battle-call,
Bravely lead the good cause on
Fighting in the which I fall.
God may quicken some true soul
Here to take my place below
In the heroes' muster roll —
I am weary, let me go.

Shield and buckler, hang them up,
Drape the standards on the wall,
I have drained the mortal cup
To the finish, dregs and all ;
When our work is done, 't is best,
Brother, best that we should go —
I am weary, let me rest,
I am weary, lay me low.

James Brunton Stephens

THE DOMINION OF AUSTRALIA

(A FORECAST)

SHE is not yet, but he whose ear
Thrills to that finer atmosphere

Where footfalls of appointed things,
Reverberant of days to be,
Are heard in forecast echoings,
Like wave-beats from a viewless sea —
Hears in the voiceful tremors of the sky
Auroral heralds whispering " She is nigh."

She is not yet ; but he whose sight
Foreknows the advent of the light,
Whose soul to morning radiance turns
　　Ere night her curtain hath withdrawn,
And in its quivering folds discerns
　　The mute monitions of the dawn,
With urgent sense strained onward to de-
　　scry
Her distant tokens, starts to find her nigh.

Not yet her day.　How long "not yet ? "
There comes the flush of violet !
And heavenward faces, all aflame
　　With sanguine imminence of morn,
Wait but the sun-kiss to proclaim
　　The Day of the Dominion born.
Prelusive baptism ! — ere the natal hour
Named with the name and prophecy of
　　power.

Already here to hearts intense
A spirit force, transcending sense,
In heights unscaled, in deeps unstirred,
　　Beneath the calm, above the storm,
She waits the incorporating word
　　To bid her tremble into form :
Already, like divining-rods, men's souls
Bend down to where the unseen river rolls ;

For even as, from sight concealed,
By never flush of dawn revealed,
Nor e'er illumed by golden noon,
　　Nor sunset-streaked with crimson bar,
Nor silver-spanned by wake of moon,
　　Nor visited of any star,
Beneath these lands a river waits to bless
(So men divine) our utmost wilderness, —

Rolls dark, but yet shall know our skies,
Soon as the wisdom of the wise
Conspires with nature to disclose
　　The blessing prisoned and unseen,
Till round our lessening wastes there glows
　　A perfect zone of broadening green, —
Till all our land Australia Felix called,
Become one Continent-Isle of Emerald ; —

So flows beneath our good and ill
A viewless stream of common will,
A gathering force, a present might,
　　That from its silent depths of gloom
At Wisdom's voice shall leap to light,
　　And hide our barren fields in bloom,
Till, all our sundering lines with love o'er-
　　grown,
Our　bounds　shall　be　the　girdling　seas
　　alone.

George Gordon M'Crae

FORBY SUTHERLAND

A STORY OF BOTANY BAY

A. D. 1770

A LANE of elms in June ; — the air
　　Of eve is cool and calm and sweet.
See ! straying here a youthful pair,
　　With sad and slowly moving feet,

On hand in hand to yon gray gate,
　　O'er which the rosy apples swing ;
And there they vow a mingled fate,
　　One　day　when　George　the　Third　is
　　　king.

The ring scarce clasped her finger fair,
　　When, tossing in their ivied tower,
The distant bells made all the air
　　Melodious with that golden hour.

Then sank the sun out o'er the sea,
　　Sweet day of courtship fond, . . . the
　　　last !
The holy hours of twilight flee
　　And speed to join the sacred Past.

The house-dove on the moss-grown thatch
　　Is murmuring love-songs to his mate,
As lovely Nell now lifts the latch
　　Beneath the apples at the gate.

A plighted maid she nears her home,
　　Those gentle eyes with weeping red ;
Too soon her swain must breast the foam,
　　Alas ! with that last hour he fled.

And, ah ! that dust-cloud on the road,
　　Yon　heartless　coach - guard's　blaring
　　　horn ;
But naught beside, that spoke or showed
　　Her sailor to poor Nell forlorn.

She dreams ; and lo ! a ship that ploughs
  A foamy furrow through the seas,
As, plunging gaily, from her bows
  She scatters diamonds on the breeze.

Swift, homeward bound, with flags displayed
  In pennoned pomp, with drum and fife,
And all the proud old-world parade
  That marks the man-o'-war man's life.

She dreams and dreams ; her heart's at sea ;
  Dreams while she wears the golden ring ;
Her spirit follows lovingly
  One humble servant of the king.

And thus for years, since Hope survives
  To cheer the maid and nerve the youth.
" Forget-me-not ! " — how fair it thrives
  Where planted in the soil of Truth !

The skies are changed ; and o'er the sea,
  Within a calm, sequestered nook,
Rests at her anchor thankfully
  The tall-sterned ship of gallant Cook.

The emerald shores ablaze with flowers,
  The sea reflects the smiling sky,
Soft breathes the air of perfumed bowers —
  How sad to leave it all, and die !

To die, when all around is fair
  And steeped in beauty ; — ah ! 't is hard
When ease and joy succeed to care,
  And rest, to " watch " and " mounted
    guard."

But harder still, when one dear plan,
  The end of all his life and cares,
Hangs by a thread ; the dying man
  Most needs our sympathy and prayers !

'T was thus with Forby as he lay
  Wan in his narrow canvas cot ;
Sole tenant of the lone " sick bay,"
  Though " mates " came round, he heard
    them not.

'or days his spirit strove and fought,
  But, ah ! the frame was all too weak.
ome phantom strange it seemed he sought,
  And vainly tried to rise and speak.

At last he smiled and brightened up,
  The noonday bugle went ; and he
Drained ('t was his last) the cooling cup
  A messmate offered helpfully.

His tongue was loosed — " I hear the horn !
  Ah, Nell ! *my number's flying.* See ! —
The horses too ; — they 've had their
    corn.
  Alas, dear love ! . . . I part from thee ! "

He waved his wasted hand, and cried,
  " Sweet Nell ! Dear maid ! My own
    true Nell !
The coach won't wait for me ! " . . . and
    died —
  And this was Forby's strange farewell.

Next morn the barge, with muffled oars,
  Pulls slowly forth, and leaves the slip
With flags half-mast, and gains the shores,
  While silence seals each comrade's lip.

They bury him beneath a tree,
  His treasure in his bosom hid.
What was that treasure ? Go and see !
  Long since it burst his coffin-lid !

Nell gave to Forby, once in play,
  Some hips of roses, with the seeds
Of hedgerow plants, and flowerets gay
  (In England such might count for weeds).

" Take these," cries smiling Nell, " to
    sow
  In foreign lands ; and when folk see
The English roses bloom and grow,
  Some one may bless an unknown me."

The turf lies green on Forby's bed,
  A hundred years have passed, and
    more,
But twining over Forby's head
  Are Nell's sweet roses on that shore.

The violet and the eglantine,
  With sweet-breathed cowslips, deck the
    spot,
And nestling 'mid them in the shine,
  The meek, blue-eyed " Forget - me-
    not ! "

Henry Clarence Kendall

TO A MOUNTAIN

To thee, O father of the stately peaks,
Above me in the loftier light — to thee,
Imperial brother of those awful hills,
Whose feet are set in splendid spheres of
    flame,
Whose heads are where the gods are, and
    whose sides
Of strength are belted round with all the
    zones
Of all the world, I dedicate these songs.
And if, within the compass of this book,
There lives and glows one verse in which
    there beats
The pulse of wind and torrent — if one
    line
Is here that like a running water sounds,
And seems an echo from the lands of leaf,
Be sure that line is thine. Here, in this
    home,
Away from men and books and all the
    schools,
I take thee for my Teacher. In thy voice
Of deathless majesty, I, kneeling, hear
God's grand authentic gospel ! Year by
    year,
The great sublime cantata of thy storm
Strikes through my spirit — fills it with a
    life
Of startling beauty ! Thou my Bible art
With holy leaves of rock, and flower, and
    tree,
And moss, and shining runnel. From each
    page
That helps to make thy awful volume, I
Have learned a noble lesson. In the psalm
Of thy grave winds, and in the liturgy
Of singing waters, lo ! my soul has heard
The higher worship ; and from thee, in-
    deed,
The broad foundations of a finer hope
Were gathered in ; and thou hast lifted
    up
The blind horizon for a larger faith.
Moreover, walking in exalted woods
Of naked glory, in the green and gold
Of forest sunshine, I have paused like one
With all the life transfigured : and a flood
Of life ineffable has made me feel
As felt the grand old prophets caught
    away

By flames of inspiration ; but the words
Sufficient for the story of my dream
Are far too splendid for poor human lips !
But thou, to whom I turn with reverent
    eyes —
O stately Father, whose majestic face
Shines far above the zone of wind and
    cloud,
Where high dominion of the morning is —
Thou hast the Songs complete of which my
    songs
Are pallid adumbrations ! Certain sounds
Of strong authentic sorrow in this book
May have the sob of upland torrents —
    these,
And only these, may touch the great
    World's heart ;
For lo ! they are the issues of that grief
Which makes a man more human, and his
    life
More like that frank exalted life of thine.
But in these pages there are other tones
In which thy large, superior voice is
    not —
Through which no beauty that resembles
    thine
Has ever shown. These are the broken
    words
Of blind occasions, when the World has
    come
Between me and my dream. No song is
    here
Of mighty compass ; for my singing robes
I 've worn in stolen moments. All my
    days
Have been the days of a laborious life,
And ever on my struggling soul has burned
The fierce heat of this hurried sphere.
    But thou,
To whose fair majesty I dedicate
My book of rhymes — thou hast the per-
    fect rest
Which makes the heaven of the highest
    gods !
To thee the noises of this violent time
Are far, faint whispers, and, from age to
    age,
Within the world and yet apart from it,
Thou standest ! Round thy lordly capes the
    sea
Rolls on with a superb indifference
Forever ; in thy deep, green, gracious glen

The silver fountains sing forever. Far
Above dim ghosts of waters in the caves,
The royal robe of morning on thy head
Abides forever ! Evermore the wind
Is thy august companion ; and thy peers
Are cloud, and thunder, and the face sublime
Of blue mid-heaven ! On thy awful brow
Is Deity ; and in that voice of thine
There is the great imperial utterance
Of God forever ; and thy feet are set
Where evermore, through all the days and
    years,
There rolls the grand hymn of the deathless
    wave.

COOGEE

SING the song of wave-worn Coogee, Coo-
    gee in the distance white,
With its jags and points disrupted, gaps
    and fractures fringed with light ;
Haunt of gledes, and restless plovers of the
    melancholy wail,
Ever lending deeper pathos to the mel-
    ancholy gale.
There, my brothers, down the fissures,
    chasms deep and wan and wild,
Grows the sea-bloom, one that blushes like
    a shrinking, fair, blind child ;
And amongst the oozing forelands many a
    glad green rock-vine runs,
Getting ease on earthy ledges, sheltered
    from December suns.

Often, when a gusty morning, rising cold
    and gray and strange,
Lifts its face from watery spaces, vistas
    full with cloudy change,
Bearing up a gloomy burden which anon
    begins to wane,
Fading in the sudden shadow of a dark de-
    termined rain,
Do I seek an eastern window, so to watch
    the breakers beat
Round the steadfast crags of Coogee, dim
    with drifts of driving sleet :
Hearing hollow mournful noises sweeping
    down a solemn shore,
While the grim sea-caves are tideless, and
    the storm strives at their core.

Often when the floating vapors fill the silent
    autumn leas,
Dreaming memories fall like moonlight
    over silent sleeping seas,

Youth and I and Love together ! other
    times and other themes
Come to me unsung, unwept for, through
    the faded evening gleams.
Come to me and touch me mutely — I that
    looked and longed so well,
Shall I look and yet forget them ? — who
    may know or who foretell ?
Though the southern wind roams, shadowed
    with its immemorial grief,
Where the frosty wings of Winter leave
    their whiteness on the leaf.

Friend of mine beyond the waters, here
    and there these perished days
Haunt me with their sweet dead faces and
    their old divided ways.
You that helped and you that loved me,
    take this song, and when you read
Let the lost things come about you, set
    your thoughts, and hear and heed.
Time has laid his burden on us — we who
    wear our manhood now,
We would be the boys we have been, free
    of heart and bright of brow,
Be the boys for just an hour, with the
    splendor and the speech
Of thy lights and thunders, Coogee, flying
    up thy gleaming beach.

Heart's desire and heart's division ! who
    would come and say to me,
With the eyes of far-off friendship, " You
    are as you used to be ? "
Something glad and good has left me here
    with sickening discontent,
Tired of looking, neither knowing what it
    was or where it went.
So it is this sight of Coogee, shining in the
    morning dew,
Sets me stumbling through dim summers
    once on fire with youth and you—
Summers pale as southern evenings when
    the year has lost its power
And the wasted face of April weeps above
    the withered flower.

Not that seasons bring no solace, not that
    time lacks light and rest,
But the old things were the dearest, and
    the old loves seem the best.
We that start at songs familiar, we that
    tremble at a tone
Floating down the ways of music, like a
    sigh of sweetness flown,

We can never feel the freshness, never
   find again the mood
Left among fair-featured places, bright-
   ened of our brotherhood.
This and this we have to think of when the
   night is over all,
When the woods begin to perish, and the
   rains begin to fall.

SEPTEMBER IN AUSTRALIA

GRAY Winter hath gone, like a wearisome
   guest,
And, behold, for repayment,
September comes in with the wind of the
   West
And the Spring in her raiment !
The ways of the frost have been filled of
   the flowers,
While the forest discovers
Wild wings, with the halo of hyaline hours,
And a music of lovers.

September, the maid with the swift silver
   feet !
She glides, and she graces
The valleys of coolness, the slopes of the
   heat,
With her blossomy traces ;
Sweet month, with a mouth that is made
   of a rose,
She lightens and lingers
In spots where the harp of the evening
   glows,
Attuned by her fingers.

The stream from its home in the hollow
   hill slips
In a darling old fashion ;
And the day goeth down with a song on its
   lips
Whose key-note is passion ;
Far out in the fierce, bitter front of the sea
I stand, and remember
Dead things that were brothers and sisters
   of thee,
Resplendent September.

The West, when it blows at the fall of the
   noon
And beats on the beaches,
So filled with a tender and tremulous tune
That touches and teaches ;

The stories of Youth, of the burden of
   Time,
And the death of Devotion,
Come back with the wind, and are themes
   of the rhyme
In the waves of the ocean.

We, having a secret to others unknown,
In the cool mountain-mosses,
May whisper together, September, alone
Of our loves and our losses.
One word for her beauty, and one for the
   place
She gave to the hours ;
And then we may kiss her, and suffer her
   face
To sleep with the flowers.

High places that knew of the gold and the
   white
On the forehead of Morning
Now darken and quake, and the steps of
   the Night
Are heavy with warning !
Her voice in the distance is lofty and loud
Through its echoing gorges ;
She hath hidden her eyes in a mantle of
   cloud,
And her feet in the surges !

On the tops of the hills, on the turreted
   cones —
Chief temples of thunder—
The gale, like a ghost, in the middle watch
   moans,
Gliding over and under.
The sea, flying white through the rack and
   the rain,
Leapeth wild at the forelands ;
And the plover, whose cry is like passion
   with pain,
Complains in the moorlands.

Oh, season of changes — of shadow and
   shine —
September the splendid !
My song hath no music to mingle with
   thine,
And its burden is ended ;
But thou, being born of the winds and the
   sun,
By mountain, by river,
May lighten and listen, and loiter and run
With thy voices forever.

THE LAST OF HIS TRIBE

HE crouches, and buries his face on his
    knees,
And hides in the dark of his hair ;
For he cannot look up to the storm-smitten
    trees,
    Or think of the loneliness there —
    Of the loss and the loneliness there.

The wallaroos grope through the tufts of
    the grass,
And turn to their covers for fear ;
But he sits in the ashes and lets them
    pass
    Where the boomerangs sleep with the
      spear —
    With the nullah, the sling, and the
      spear.

Uloola, behold him ! The thunder that
    breaks
On the top of the rocks with the rain,
And the wind which drives up with the salt
    of the lakes,
    Have made him a hunter again —
    A hunter and fisher again.

For his eyes have been full with a smoul-
    dering thought ;
    But he dreams of the hunts of yore,
And of foes that he sought, and of fights
    that he fought
    With those who will battle no more —
    Who will go to the battle no more.

It is well that the water which tumbles and
    fills,
Goes moaning and moaning along ;
For an echo rolls out from the sides of the
    hills,
    And he starts at a wonderful song —
    At the sounds of a wonderful song.

And he sees through the rents of the scat-
    tering fogs,
The corroboree warlike and grim,
And the lubra who sat by the fire on the
    logs,
    To watch, like a mourner, for him —
    Like a mother and mourner for him.

Will he go in his sleep from these desolate
    lands,
    Like a chief, to the rest of his race,

With the honey-voiced woman who beck-
    ons and stands,
    And gleams like a dream in his face —
    Like a marvellous dream in his face ?

THE VOICE IN THE WILD OAK

TWELVE years ago, when I could face
    High heaven's dome with different eyes,
In days full-flowered with hours of grace,
    And nights not sad with sighs,
I wrote a song in which I strove
To shadow forth thy strain of woe,
Dark widowed sister of the grove —
    Twelve wasted years ago.

But youth was then too young to find
    Those high authentic syllables
Whose voice is like the wintering wind
    By sunless mountain fells ;
Nor had I sinned and suffered then
    To that superlative degree
That I would rather seek, than men,
    Wild fellowship with thee.

But he who hears this autumn day
    Thy more than deep autumnal rhyme,
Is one whose hair was shot with gray
    By grief instead of time.
He has no need, like many a bard,
    To sing imaginary pain,
Because he bears, and finds it hard,
    The punishment of Cain.

No more he sees the affluence
    Which makes the heart of Nature glad ;
For he has lost the fine first sense
    Of beauty that he had.
The old delight God's happy breeze
    Was wont to give, to grief has grown ;
And therefore, Niobe of trees,
    His song is like thine own.

But I, who am that perished soul,
    Have wasted so these powers of mine,
That I can never write that whole,
    Pure, perfect speech of thine.
Some lord of words august, supreme,
    The grave, grand melody demands ;
The dark translation of thy theme
    I leave to other hands.

Yet here, where plovers nightly call
    Across dim melancholy leas —

Where comes by whistling fen and fall
  The moan of far-off seas —
A gray old Fancy often sits
  Beneath thy shade with tired wings,
And fills thy strong, strange rhyme by fits
  With awful utterings.

Then times there are when all the words
  Are like the sentences of one
Shut in by fate from wind and birds
  And light of stars and sun !
No dazzling dryad, but a dark
  Dream-haunted spirit, doomed to be
Imprisoned, cramped in bands of bark,
  For all eternity.

Yea, like the speech of one aghast
  At Immortality in chains,
What time the lordly storm rides past
  With flames and arrowy rains :
Some wan Tithonus of the wood,
  White with immeasurable years —
An awful ghost, in solitude
  With moaning moors and meres !

And when high thunder smites the hill
  And hunts the wild dog to his den,
Thy cries, like maledictions, shrill
  And shriek from glen to glen,
As if a frightful memory whipped

Thy soul for some infernal crime
That left it blasted, blind, and stripped —
  A dread to Death and Time !

But when the fair-haired August dies,
  And flowers wax strong and beautiful,
Thy songs are stately harmonies
  By wood-lights green and cool,
Most like the voice of one who shows
  Through sufferings fierce, in fine relief,
A noble patience and repose —
  A dignity in grief.

But, ah ! conceptions fade away,
  And still the life that lives in thee,
The soul of thy majestic lay,
  Remains a mystery !
And he must speak the speech divine,
  The language of the high-throned lords,
Who 'd give that grand old theme of thine
  Its sense in faultless words.

By hollow lands and sea-tracts harsh,
  With ruin of the fourfold gale,
Where sighs the sedge and sobs the marsh,
  Still wail thy lonely wail ;
And, year by year, one step will break
  The sleep of far hill-folded streams,
And seek, if only for thy sake,
  Thy home of many dreams.

Percy F. Sinnett

THE SONG OF THE WILD STORM-WAVES

(AFTER THE LOSS OF THE " TARARUA ")

Oh, ye wild waves, shoreward dashing,
  What is your tale to-day ?
O'er the rocks your white foam splashing,
  While the moaning wind your spray
  Whirls heavenwards away
    In the mist ?
Have ye heard the timbers crashing
  Of the good ship out at sea ?
Seen the masts the dank ropes lashing,
  While the sailors bend the knee,
  And vainly call on Heaven
    To assist ?

Oh, ay ! we 've seen and heard —
  Oh, ay ! we 've heard and seen

More than ever you could gather —
  More than ever you could glean
    From our tale.
We have seen, and heard, and laughed,
As we tossed the shattered craft,
  While those on board, aghast,
  Every moment thought their last,
    In the gale.

We tossed them like a plaything,
  And rent their riven sail ;
And we laughed our loud Ha ! ha !
  With the demons of the gale
    In their ears.
We have laughed, and heard, and seen,
In the lightning's lurid sheen,
  And the growling thunder's blast ;
  And we drowned them all at last
    For their fears.

There were mothers there on board
  With their little ones in arms ;
There were maidens there on board
  More lovely in their charms
    Than the day ;
And again we heard, and laughed
As we dashed across the craft ;
  While our master shrieked and roared,
  As we swept them overboard,
    And away.

And they battled all in vain,
  With their puny human strength.
In our grasp they were as nothing ;
  Down, down, they sank at length
    In the sea ;
And still again we screamed,
As the lurid flashes gleamed,
  And o'er their heads we swept,
  And for joy we danced and leapt
    In our glee.

This, this, now is the tale
  We have to tell to-day,
And now to you we 've sung it
  In our merry, mocking way.
    Do you hear ?
How our havoc we have wrought,
And to destruction brought
  The treasures of the Earth,
  Held by man in price, and worth,
    Very dear ?

Oh ! ye cruel waves up-dashing,
  Why rejoice you so to-day ?
As shoreward ye come crashing
  From your cruel, cruel play ;
  Why fling ye up your spray
    On the shore ?
The sand your salt spume splashing,
  As ye frolic in your glee ;
As the iron rocks ye 're lashing,
  Ye scourges of the sea, —
Will ye never then be glutted
    Any more ?

𝔄. ℭ. 𝔖mith

THE WAIF

HE went into the bush, and passed
  Out of the sight of living men,
None knows the nook that held him last,
  None ever saw his face again.

It may be, in the wildering wood
  He wandered, weary, spent of breath,
Till the all-mastering solitude
  Sank to the deeper hush of death.

Perchance he crawled where the low bush,
  More verdant, whispered streams were
    nigh,
Hopeful, but desperate, made a rush,
  And found, O God ! the bed was dry !

He was a waif, and friends had none ;
  Who knows but in some distant land
A mother mourns her errant son,
  A sister longs to clasp his hand ?

He was a waif, but with him died
  A world of yearnings deep within —
Yearning to loftiest things allied,
  But wrecked by cruel fate, or sin.

None heard the lone one's dying prayer
  Save Infinite Pity bending o'er,
Who, haply, bore him quietly where
  They hunger and they thirst no
    more.

O ye vast woods ! what fond life-dreams
  Ye close ! what broken lives ye hide !
Darkly absorbed, like hopeful streams,
  That in dry desert lands subside.

Stranger the tales ye could unfold
  Than wild romancer ever penned,
Remaining buried in the mould
  Till time shall cease, and mystery
    end !

Frances Tyrrell Gill

BENEATH THE WATTLE BOUGHS

THE wattles were sweet with September's
    rain,
We drank in their breath and the breath
    of the spring :
" Our pulses are strong with the tide of
    life,"
I said, " and one year is so swift a thing ! "

The land all around was yellow with
    bloom,
The birds in the branches sang joyous and
    shrill,
The blue range rose 'gainst the blue of the
    sky,
Yet she sighed, " But death may be stronger
    still ! "

Then I reached and gathered a blossomy
    bough,
And divided its clustering sprays in twain,
" As a token for each " (I closed one in her
    hand)
" Till we come to the end of the year
    again ! "

Then the years sped on, strung high with
    life ;
And laughter and gold were the gifts they
    gave,
Till I chanced one day on some pale dead
    flowers,
And spake, shaking and white, " One more
    gift I crave."
" Nay," a shadow voice in the air replied,
" 'Neath the blossoming wattles you 'll find
    a grave ! "

Sarah Welch

THE DIGGER'S GRAVE

HE sought Australia's far-famed isle,
Hoping that Fortune on his lot would smile,
In search for gold. When one short year
    had flown,
He wrote the welcome tidings to his own
Betrothèd ; told how months of toiling
    vain
Made ten-fold sweeter to him sudden
    gain;
With sanguine words, traced with love's
    eager hand,
He bade her join him in this bright south
    land.
Oft as he sat, his long day's labor o'er,
In his bush hut, he dreamed of home once
    more ;
His thoughts to the old country home in
    Kent
Returned. 'T was Christmas-day, and they
    two went
O'er frost and snow ; the Christmas anthem
    rang
Through the old church, which echoed as
    they sang.

That day had Philip courage gained to tell
His tale of love to pretty Christabel ;
And she, on her part, with ingenuous grace,
Endorsed the tell-tale of her blushing face.
Dream on, true lover ! never, never thou
Shalt press the kiss of welcome on her brow.
E'en now a comrade, eager for thy gold,
Above thy fond true heart the knife doth
    hold —
One stroke, the weapon 's plunged into his
    breast ;
So sure the aim that, like a child at rest,
The murdered digger lies, — a happy smile
Parts the full manly bearded lips the while.

Next day they found him. In his death-
    cold hand,
He held his last home letter, lately scanned
With love-lit eyes ; and next his heart they
    found
A woman's kerchief which, when they un-
    wound,
Disclosed a lock of silken auburn hair
And portrait of a girl's face, fresh and fair
Dyed with the life-blood of his faithful
    heart.

To more than one eye, tears unbidden start ;
With reverent hands, and rough, uncon-
scious grace,
They laid him in his lonely resting-place.

The bright-hued birds true nature's re-
quiem gave,
And wattle-bloom bestrews the digger's
grave.

Arthur Patchett Martin

LOVE AND WAR

THE Chancellor mused as he nibbled his
pen
(Sure no Minister ever looked wiser),
And said, "I can summon a million of
men
To fight for their country and Kaiser ;

"While that shallow charlatan ruling o'er
France,
Who deems himself deeper than Merlin,
Thinks he and his soldiers have only to
dance
To the tune of the *Can-can* to Berlin.

"But as soon as he gets to the bank of the
Rhine,
He 'll be met by the great German
army."
Then the Chancellor laughed, and he said,
"I will dine,
For I see nothing much to alarm me."

Yet still as he went out he paused by the
door
(For his mind was in truth heavy laden),
And he saw a stout fellow, equipped for
the war,
Embracing a fair-haired young maiden.

"Ho ! ho !" said the Chancellor, "this
will not do,
For Mars to be toying with Venus,
When these Frenchmen are coming — a
rascally crew ! —
And the Rhine only flowing between us."

So the wary old fox, just in order to hear,
Strode one or two huge paces nearer ;
And he heard the youth say, "More than
life art thou dear ;
But, O loved one, the Fatherland's
dearer."

Then the maid dried her tears and looked
up in his eyes,
And she said, "Thou of loving art
worthy :
When all are in danger no brave man e'er
flies,
And thy love should spur on — not deter
thee."

The Chancellor took a cigar, which he
lit,
And he muttered, "Here's naught to
alarm me ;
By Heaven ! I swear they are both of them
fit
To march with the great German army."

THE CYNIC OF THE WOODS [1]

I COME from busy haunts of men,
With nature to commune,
Which you, it seems, observe, and then
Laugh out, like some buffoon.

You cease, and through the forest drear
I pace, with sense of awe ;
When once again upon my ear
Breaks in your harsh guffaw.

I look aloft to yonder place,
Where placidly you sit,
And tell you to your very face,
I do not like your wit.

I 'm in no mood for blatant jest,
I hate your mocking song,
My weary soul demands the rest
Denied to it so long.

Besides, there passes through my brain
The poet's love of fame —
Why should not an Australian strain
Immortalize my name ?

[1] The giant kingfisher, or "laughing jackass."

And so I pace the forest drear,
　Filled with a sense of awe,
When louder still upon my ear
　Breaks in your harsh guffaw.

Yet truly, Jackass, it may be,
　My words are all unjust :
You laugh at what you hear and see,
　And laugh because you must.

You 've seen Man civilized and rude,
　Of varying race and creed,
The black-skinned savage almost nude,
　The Englishman in tweed.

And here the lubra oft has strayed,
　To rest beneath the boughs,
Where now, perchance, some fair-haired
　　maid
　May hear her lover's vows ;

While you from yonder lofty height
　Have studied human ways,

And, with a satirist's delight,
　Dissected hidden traits.

Laugh on, laugh on ! Your rapturous
　　shout
　Again on me intrudes ;
But I have found your secret out,
　O cynic of the woods !

Well ! I confess, grim mocking elf,
　Howe'er I rhapsodize,
That I am more in love with self
　Than with the earth or skies.

So I will lay the epic by,
　That I had just begun :
Why do I babble ? Let me lie
　And bask here in the sun.

And let me own, were I endowed
　With your fine humorous sense,
I, too, should laugh — ay, quite as loud,
　At all Man's vain pretence.

Ethel Castilla

AN AUSTRALIAN GIRL

She has a beauty of her own,
A beauty of a paler tone
　Than English belles.
The Southern sun and Southern air
Have kissed her cheeks until they wear
The dainty tints that oft appear
　On rosy shells.

Her frank, clear eyes bespeak a mind
Old-world traditions fail to bind.
　She is not shy

or void, but simply self-possessed ;
Her independence adds a zest
Unto her speech, her piquant jest,
　Her quaint reply.

O'er classic volumes she will pore
With joy ; and some scholastic lore
　Will often gain.
In sports she bears away the bell,
Nor under music's siren spell
To dance divinely, flirt as well,
　Does she disdain.

Eleanor Montgomery

A NEW ZEALAND REGRET

Come ! in this cool retreat,
Under the chestnut's shade,
Far from all noise and heat —
Distant and faint the beat

Of the great city — we two have strayed
Come, linnet, sing to me,
Sing my soul across the sea.

Sing ! let each rippling note
Carry my soul away ;

Sweeter than wild bird's throat,
Backward my memory float,
On music's wing my heart convey,
Where southern stars in beauty glow,
And Egmont lifts her brow of snow.

Again I 'll see our long lost home
Upon Wairoa's grassy plain ;
Among the fern the cattle roam ;
With idle rein upon his arm o'erthrown
The shepherd guards his flocks again,
And his shrill whistle with his dog's bark
    blends,
As down the hill the woolly stream descends.

Or now, the early "muster" over,
With Jim and Tom I 'm slowly riding
Through the home-paddock white with
    clover,
And followed close by Nip and Rover,
Their warm allegiance now dividing,
For Tom's fair sisters here we meet,
And welcoming smiles their weary swains
    do greet.

Here in the world's great heart abiding,
We two have left the happy isle ;
Australian grass Tom's face is hiding,
Jim in the spirit-land is riding.
From weary thoughts my heart beguile !
Sing, linnet, sing to me,
Sing my soul across the sea.

Yes ! now my wings I feel,
Once more the isle I see ;
Let sleep my eyelids seal
While to those scenes I steal,
Borne thus on melody ;
So sweetly you have sung to me,
Sung my soul across the sea.

ADIEU

O SHEPHERDS ! take my crook from me,
For I no longer here can stay.
There comes a whisper from the sea,
Calling my soul from you away ;
Friends of my heart ! long tried and true,
O let me leave my crook with you.
    An idle shepherd have I lain,
    Dreaming while sheep-dogs barked in
        vain,
    Or chasing rhymes to wreathe the strain
        Which from sweet musing grew.

Above the stars I drift in thought,
Melodious murmurings in my ears ;
As though the upborne spirit caught
Soft echoes from the higher spheres.
But see ! far up the azure height,
Bright Sirius hails me with his light !
My soul, impatient of delay,
Rides on the wings of thought away,
My heart alone with you can stay :
My Shepherds dear — Good night !

DOMINION OF CANADA

Susanna Strickland Moodie

CANADIAN HUNTER'S SONG

THE Northern Lights are flashing
    On the rapids' restless flow,
But o 'er the wild waves dashing
    Swift darts the light canoe :
    The merry hunters come, —
    "What cheer ? What cheer ? "
    "We 've slain the deer ! "
"Hurrah ! you 're welcome home ! "

The blithesome horn is sounding,
    And the woodman's loud halloo ;
And joyous steps are bounding
    To meet the birch canoe.
    "Hurrah ! the hunters come ! "
        And the woods ring out
        To their noisy shout,
As they drag the dun deer home !

The hearth is brightly burning,
    The rustic board is spread ;

To greet their sire returning
The children leave their bed.
With laugh and shout they come,

That merry band,
To grasp his hand
And bid him welcome home !

Charles Dawson Shanly

THE WALKER OF THE SNOW

SPEED on, speed on, good master !
The camp lies far away ;
We must cross the haunted valley
Before the close of day.

How the snow-blight came upon me
I will tell you as we go, —
The blight of the Shadow-hunter,
Who walks the midnight snow.

To the cold December heaven
Came the pale moon and the stars,
As the yellow sun was sinking
Behind the purple bars.

The snow was deeply drifted
Upon the ridges drear,
That lay for miles around me
And the camp for which we steer.

'T was silent on the hillside,
And by the solemn wood
No sound of life or motion
To break the solitude,

Save the wailing of the moose-bird
With a plaintive note and low,
And the skating of the red leaf
Upon the frozen snow.

And said I, — " Though dark is falling,
And far the camp must be,
Yet my heart it would be lightsome,
If I had but company."

And then I sang and shouted,
Keeping measure, as I sped,
To the harp-twang of the snow-shoe
As it sprang beneath my tread ;

Nor far into the valley
Had I dipped upon my way,
When a dusky figure joined me,
In a capuchon of gray,

Bending upon the snow-shoes,
With a long and limber stride ;
And I hailed the dusky stranger,
As we travelled side by side.

But no token of communion
Gave he by word or look,
And the fear-chill fell upon me
At the crossing of the brook.

For I saw by the sickly moonlight,
As I followed, bending low,
That the walking of the stranger
Left no footmarks on the snow.

Then the fear-chill gathered o'er me,
Like a shroud around me cast,
As I sank upon the snow-drift
Where the Shadow-hunter passed.

And the otter-trappers found me,
Before the break of day,
With my dark hair blanched and
whitened
As the snow in which I lay.

But they spoke not as they raised
me ;
For they knew that in the night
I had seen the Shadow-hunter,
And had withered in his blight.

Sancta Maria speed us !
The sun is falling low, —
Before us lies the valley
Of the Walker of the Snow !

Charles Heavysege

SCENES FROM "SAUL"

DAVID EXORCISING MALZAH, THE EVIL
SPIRIT FROM THE LORD

SCENE. — A chamber of the palace. DAVID
playing on his harp. SAUL enters and listens,
and at length DAVID ceases.

Saul. Still more, still more : I feel the
demon move
Amidst the gloomy branches of my breast,
As moves a bird that buries itself deeper
Within its nest at stirring of the storm.
[DAVID *plays again.*
Were ever sounds so sweet ! — where am
I ? O,
I have been down in hell, but this is
heaven !
It grows yet sweeter, — 't is a wondrous air.
Methinks I lately died a hideous death,
And that they buried me accursed and
cursing.
But this is not the grave ; for, surely,
music
Comes not to reanimate man 'neath the
clods.
Let me not think on 't ! yet a fiend fierce
tore me.
Ah, I remember now, too much remember ;
But I am better : still methinks I fainted ;
Or was the whole a fearful, nightmare
dream ?
Nay, am I yet not dreaming ? No ; I wake :
And, as from dream or as from being born,
Without the outcry of a mother's travail ;
Or, as if waking from a revery,
I to myself am ushered by strange music,
That, in its solemn gentleness, falls on me
Like a superior's blessing. Give me more
Of this sweet benefit.
[*After having listened again.*
Who is this stranger ? Yes, I know him
now.
'T is not a heavenly spirit, though so like one,
With curving arms encompassing the harp,
As clasps the landscape the aërial bow :
It is the minstrel youth from Bethlehem ;
In form, indeed, surpassing beautiful.
Methinks he doth address himself to sing :
I 'll listen, for I love him as he sits
Rapt, like a statue conjured from the air.
Hist !

David. [*Sings, accompanying himself on
his harp.*]
O Lord, have mercy on the king ;
The evil spirit from him take ;
His soul from its sore suffering
Deliver, for thy goodness' sake.

Saul. [*Aside.*] He for me prays.

O, heal thine own Anointed's hurt ;
Let evil from his thoughts be driven ;
And breathe upon his troubled heart
The balmy sense of fault forgiven.

Saul. [*Aside.*] I would not hide my
faults ; amen.

Great God, thou art within this place ;
The universe is filled with thee :
To all thou givest strength and grace ;
O, give the king thy grace to see.

Saul. [*Aside.*] What have I done de-
served the loss of grace ?
I cannot say "amen" ; — and if I did,
My feeble amen would be blown away
Before it had reached heaven. I cannot
say it :
There disbelief takes prisoner my tongue !

As after winter cometh spring,
Make joy unto his soul return ; —
And me, in thy good pleasure, bring
To tend my flock where I was born.

Saul. [*Aside.*] So able, yet so humble !
[*Aloud.*] David, no ;
Thou shalt remain and be mine armor-
bearer.
What, wouldst thou seek again the idle
downs,
'Midst senseless sheep, to spend the listless
day,
Watching the doings of thy ewes and rams !
Thou shalt go with me to the martial field
And see great deeds thereon.
Myself will teach thee military lessons ;
To tell the enemy's numbers ; to discover
His vulnerable points ; by stratagem
To draw him from his posts of vantage ;
how
Swift to advance ; how to surprise the foe ;

And how to leaven others with thy courage ;
How win from Ammon and the strong
    Philistine,
And how at last to drink triumphantly,
From goblet of victorious return,
The blood-red wine of war.
Meantime, thy lyric pleasures need not end ;
For the fair maidens of the court affect
Music and song. Go now and tell the
    Queen
All the advantage thou hast been to me.
                  [*Exit David.*
How potent is the voice of music ! stronger
Even than is a king's command. How oft
In vain have I adjured this demon hence !
O Music, thou art a magician ! Strange,
Most strange, we did not sooner think of
    thee,
And charm us with thy gentle sorcery.

THE FLIGHT OF MALZAH

Malzah. Music, music hath its sway ;
Music's order I obey :
I have unwound myself at sound
From off Saul's heart, where coiled I lay.
'T is true, awhile I 've lost the game ;
Let fate and me divide the blame.
And now away, away ; but whither,
Whither, meantime, shall I go ?
Erelong I must returned be hither.
There's Jordan, Danube, and the Po,
And Western rivers huge, I know :
There's Ganges, and the Euphrates,
Nilus and the stretching seas :
There 's many a lake and many a glen
To rest me, as in heaven, again ;
With Alps, and the Himalayan range : —
And there 's the Desert for a change.
Whither shall I go ?
                I 'll sit i' the sky,
And laugh at mortals and at care ;
(Not soaring, as before, too high,
And bring upon myself a snare ;)
But out my motley fancies spin
Like cobwebs on the yellow air;
Laugh bright with joy, or dusky grin
In changeful mood of seance there.
The yellow air ! the yellow air !
He 's great who 's happy anywhere.

To be the vassals and the slaves of music
Is weakness that afflicts all heaven-born
    spirits.
But touch whom with the murmur of a lute,

Or swell and fill whom from the harmo-
    nious lyre,
And man may lead them wheresoe'er he
    wills,
And stare to see the nude demoniac
Sit clothed and void of frenzy. I 'll be-
    gone,
And take a posy with me from Saul's garden
[*Exit ; and soon re-enters, bearing a huge*
    nosegay, and thereat snuffing.
Shall I fling it in the earth's face, whence
    I took it !
Albeit I 've seen, perhaps, flowers as mean
    in heaven.
Well, I will think that these are heaven's.
    Alack,
This is a poor excuse for asphodel ;
And yet it has the true divine aroma.
Here 's ladslove, and the flower which even
    death
Cannot unscent, the all-transcending rose.
Here 's gilly-flower, and violets dark as eyes
Of Hebrew maidens. There 's convolvulus,
That sickens ere noon and dies ere evening.
Here 's monkey's-cap. — Egad ! 't would
    cap a monkey
To say what I have gathered ; for I spread
    my arms
And closed them like two scythes. I have
    crushed many ;
I 've sadly mangled my lilies. However,
    here
Is the august camellia, and here 's marigold,
And, as I think, i' the bottom two vast sun-
    flowers.
There are some bluebells, and a pair of fox-
    gloves
(But not of the kind that Samson's foxes
    wore).
That 's mint ; and here is something like a
    thistle
Wherewith to prick my nose should I grow
    sleepy.
O, I 've not half enumerated them !
Here 's that and that, and many trifling
    things,
Which, had I time, and were i' the vein for
    scandal,
I could compare to other trifling things,
But shall not. Ah, here 's head-hanging-
    down narcissus,
A true and perfect emblem of myself.
I 'll count it my own likeness ; and so leave
    it
For delectation of my radiant mistress,

Who,lieu of keeping watch and ward o'er me,
May keep it over my pale effigy.
          [Drops the narcissus.
I 'll hang this matchless rose upon my lips,
And whilst I 'm flying will inhale its breath.
          [Exit.

MALZAH AND THE ANGEL ZELEHTHA

SCENE. — The Alps. Time, night, with stars.
    Enter MALZAH, walking slowly.

Malzah. So, so ; I feel the signal.
It seems to reach me through the air,
To Saul it prompts me to repair.
I wish 't would cease ; it doth not please
Me now to terminate my leisure.
I was alone ; and here to groan
At present is my greatest pleasure.
I 'll come anon ; I say begone ;
What is the wayward King to me ?
I say begone ; I 'll come anon.
O, thou art strong ; I 'll follow thee.
  [Exit, and enter the angel Zelehtha.
Zelehtha. He flees, he flees, across the
    seas
That eastward lead to Canaan's land ;
And Heaven commands me not to cease
To urge, yet guide, his hand.
          [Looking upwards.
How every star reminds me of my lover !
When we did part, he on me cast his eyes,
Bright as those orbs. Yet over them
    suffusion
Came like the mists o'er evening, as he
    charged me
Still to him to return (if so I might
Return afresh to him, my home and goal),
What time the earth returned day's light
    to heaven.
So would I now swift soar unto his bosom,
But I must not abandon this foul fiend,
Until his work is done. Hence do I follow
Him through the spaces of the universe,
Still tracking him in silence, as I track
Him now across these heaven-piercing
    heights,
O'er which the quiet, congregated stars
Dance, twinkling-footed, and, in gladness,
    make
Mute immemorial measure, without song.
Yet hearken ; the immeasurable yawn
Methinks awakens, and, by me evoked,
This grave of silence gives a ghost of sound.
What song is that which wanders hither-
    ward,

Falling as faintly and as dewlike down
Into the urn of my night-opened ear,
As might, like incense, to the nostril come
The floating fragrance of a far-off flower ?
It is the voice of some desiring seraph,
That lonely sings unto her absent love ;
And, in the breathing of her languishment,
Gives more than words unto the dumb
    abyss.
I 'll also sing, since some ascending angel
May hear it, and repeat it to my cherub.
          [Sings.
I said, farewell,
And smiled, — for tears yet never fell in
    heaven ;
But thou didst sigh,
" Farewell," didst sigh ; " return to me
    at even."

But why at even
Didst thou to thee solicit my return ?
Since distance cannot
Divide us who in old embraces burn.

Then let 's unsay
" Farewell," — which we ought never to
    have said,
But, each to each,
Words of rejoicing and delight instead.

Lorn thoughts from thee
Put far, then, since, though now from
    thee apart,
I soon shall be
Again thy love-mate, whereso'er thou art.

Lo, where yon demon, with increasing
    speed,
Makes his dim way across the nighthung
    flood,
Due to the Hebrew King, with onward heed,
Like to a hound that snuffs the scent of
    blood.
I 'll follow him.   *[Exit.*

TWILIGHT

THE day was lingering in the pale north-
    west,
    And light was hanging o'er my head,
    Night where a myriad stars were spread ;
While down in the east, where the light
    was least,
    Seemed the home of the quiet dead.

And, as I gazed on the field sublime
To watch the bright pulsating stars,
Adown the deep, where the angels
    sleep,
Came drawn the golden chime

Of those great spheres that sound the years
For the horologe of time ; —
Millenniums numberless they told,
Millenniums a millionfold
From the ancient hour of prime !

John Hunter-Duvar

FROM THE DRAMA OF "DE
ROBERVAL"

OHNÁWA

SCENE. — Within the fort of Quebec. Soldiers
    carousing.

One sings :

Fill, comrades, fill the bowl right well,
  Trowl round the can with mirth and
    glee,
Zip-zip, huzza, Noël ! Noël !
  A health to me, a health to thee
        And Normandie.

Chorus :

Pass, comrades, pass the reaming can,
And swig the draught out every man !

Another round as deep as last,
  Down to the bottom peg, pardie !
Eyes to the front, — half pikes, — stand
    fast !
  A health to me, a health to thee
        And Picardie.

Chorus :

Pass, comrades, pass the reaming can,
And swig the draught out every man !

Though this be naught but soldiers' tap,
  None better wine none ne'er did see,
It riped on our own crofts mayhap,
  So here's a health to thee, to me
        And fair Lorraine,
          Again —
            Lorraine !

Chorus :

May he be shot that shirks the can !
Quick, drain the draught out every man !

Enter OHNÁWA : Soldiers *crowd around her.*

1st Soldier. Whom have we here ? This
  is a shapely wench.

2d Sold. Clean-limbed.
3d Sold. Round-armed.
4th Sold. Svelte.
5th Sold. And lithe and lissome.
6th Sold. Like a Provençale in her mum-
  ming garb
On Pope Unreason's day. But where 's her
  dog ?
7th Sold. I saw one like that one in
  Italy ;
A statue like her as two peas. They called
  her
Bronze something, — I forget. They dug
  her up,
And polished her, and set her up on end.
1st Sold. Hi ! graven image, hast thou
  ne'er a tongue ?
2d Sold. How should she speak but as
  a magpie chatters,
Chat, chat ! pretty Mag !
3d Sold. Leave her alone, now.
4th Sold. Lay hold on her and see if she
  feels warm.
        [OHNÁWA *draws a knife.*
All. Aha ! well done ! encore the scene !
  well played !
[ROBERVAL *approaches ; she advances to-*
        wards him.
Soldiers. [Retiring.] Meat for our master.
Rob. Ohnāwa !
Ohn. Great Chief !
Rob. What then, my wild fawn, has 't
  indeed come in,
A live pawn for thy people ? Then I hope
'T will be long time ere they make mat-
  ters up,
So that we still may keep thee hostage
  here.
But say, do practised warriors, shrewd and
  cunning,
Send such bright eyes as thine to armèd
  camp,
To glancing catch full note of our weak
  points

Or of our strength ? We hang up spies,
  Ohnāwa.
Ohn. I am no spy. No warrior sent
  me here.
Rob. Why didst thou come ?
Ohn. Didst thou thyself not ask me ?
Rob. I did, i' faith ; and now, thou being
  here
Shalt see such wonders as are to be seen.
They will impress thy untutored savage
  mind.
Not'st thou those arms upon that slender
  mast,
Whose fingers, sudden moving, form new
  shapes ?
By that we speak, without the aid of words,
Long leagues away.
Ohn. This is not new to me.
Our braves, on journeys, speak in silent
  signs
By leaves, grass, mosses, feathers, twigs
  and stones,
So that our people can o'ertake the trail,
And tell a message after many moons.
Rob. I have heard of the woodland sema-
  phore.
'T is a thing to be learned, — and acted
  on.
Ohn. Why dost thou raise thy head-gear
  to that blanket ?
Rob. Blanket ! young savage, — 't is the
  flag of France,
The far most glorious flag of earth and sea,
That, floating over all this continent,
Shall yet surmount the red brick towers of
  Spain.
But, pshaw ! why do I speak.
  Gunner, fire off a fauconet.
  [*Gun.*
What, not a wink ? Art thou, then, really
  bronze,
Insensible to wonder ?
Ohn. All is new.
Rob. Then why not show astonishment ?
  Young maids,
When marvels are presented to their view,
Clasp their fore-fingers, or put hand to
  ears,
Simper, cry " O, how nice ! " look down
  and giggle,
And show the perturbation of weak minds.
Ohn. I see new marvels that I ne'er
  have seen,
But when I once have seen them they are
  old.

Rob. These are the stables where the
  chargers are.
  [*Horse led out ;* Groom *gallops.*
No wonder in thine eyes even at this sight ?
Canst thou look on this steed, and yet not
  feel
No sight so beautiful in all the world ?
Ohn. I have seen herds of these brave
  gallant beasts.
Rob. [*Quickly.*] When ? where was
  this ?
Ohn. When that I was a child
A tribe came scouting from the sinking sun,
The hatchet buried, on a pilgrimage
To take salt water back from out the sea,
As is their custom in their solemn rites.
They all were mounted, every one, on steeds.
Rob. Indeed !
Ohn. Our brethren, who live six moons
  nearer night,
And many more in number than the stars,
With steeds in number many more than
  they,
Dwell on the boundless, grassy, hunting-
  plains,
Beyond which mountains higher than the
  clouds,
And on the other side of them the sea.
Rob. Important this, but of it more
  anon.
  [*They enter the caserne.*
These are called books. These are the
  strangest things
Thou yet hast seen. I take one of them
  down,
And lo ! a learned dead man comes from
  his grave,
Sits in my chair and holds discourse with me.
And these are pictures.
Ohn. They are good totem.
Rob. These, maps.
Ohn. I, with a stick, upon the sand
Can trace the like.
Rob. By 'r Lady of St. Roque
That shalt thou do ! The Pilot missed it
  there ;
These savages must know their country
  well.
This girl shall be my chief topographer,
By her I 'll learn the gold and silver coast
That Cartier could not find.
Come hither to this window. Music, ho !
  [*Band plays.*
Art thou not pleased with these melodious
  sounds ?

Ohn. The small sounds sparkle like a
  forest fire,
The big horn brays like lowing of the
  moose,
The undertone is as Niagara.
Rob. Have ye no music, enfans, in the
  woods ?
No brave high ballad that your warriors sing
To cheer them on a march ?
Ohn. We have music,
But our braves sing not. We have tribal
  bards
Who see in dreams things to make music of.
They tell our squaws, and the good mothers
  croon
Them over to their little ones asleep.
Rob. Sing me a forest song, one of thine
  own.
[OHNÁWA *goes to a drum and beats softly
  with her hand, humming the while.*
This verily is music without words.
Explain, now, what its purport most may
  mean.
Ohn. The cataracts in the forests have
  many voices,
They talk all day and converse beneath the
  stars,
The mists hide their faces from the moon.
The spirits of braves come down from the
  hunting-grounds ;
They swim in the night rainbows, and stalk
  among the trees,
Hearing the voice of the waters.
Rob. Poetic, by my soul. Why, Ohnáwa,
I 've found a treasure in thee. Go now,
  child ;
Halt e'er thou goest !
Here are our wares for trading with the
  tribes ;
Take something with thee for remembrance,
Bright scarlet cloth, beads, buttons, rosaries,
Ribbons and huswifes, scissors, looking-
  glasses —
To civilized and savage women dear.
Take one, take anything, nay, lade thyself.·
Nothing ? Shrewd damsel, but that shall
  not be ;
No visitor declines a souvenir.
What hast thou ta'en ? A dagger double-
  edged :
Good, 't is a choice appropriate ; guard it
  well,
And hide it in thy corset, — I forget,
Thou wear'st none. Go now, girl, — and
  come again.

ADIEU TO FRANCE

ADIEU to France ! my latest glance
  Falls on thy port and bay, Rochelle ;
The sun-rays on the surf-curls dance,
  And springtime, like a pleasing spell,
Harmonious holds the land and sea.
  How long, alas, I cannot tell,
Ere this scene will come back to me !

The hours fleet fast, and on the mast
  Soon shall I hoist the parting sail ;
Soon will the outer bay be passed,
  And on the sky-line eyes will fail
To see a streak that means the land.
  On, then ! before the tides and gale,
Hope at the helm, and in God's hand.

What doom I meet, my heart will beat
  For France, the débonnaire and gay ;
She ever will in memory's seat
  Be present to my mind alway.
Hope whispers my return to you,
  Dear land, but should Fate say me
  nay,
And this should be my latest view,
  Fair France, loved France, *my* France,
  adieu !
Salut à la France, salut !

TWILIGHT SONG

THE mountain peaks put on their hoods,
  Good-night !
And the long shadows of the woods
Would fain the landscape cover quite ;
The timid pigeons homeward fly,
Scared by the whoop owl 's eerie cry,
  Whoo-oop ! whoo-oop !
As like a fiend he flitteth by ;
The ox to stall, the fowl to coop,
The old man to his nightcap warm,
Young men and maids to slumbers light,
Sweet Mary, keep our souls from harm !
  Good-night ! good-night !

THE GALLANT FLEET

A GALLANT fleet sailed out to sea
With the pennons streaming merrily.

On the hulls the tempest lit,
And the great ships split
  In the gale,
And the foaming fierce sea-horses

Hurled the fragments in their forces
  To the ocean deeps,
  Where the kraken sleeps,
    And the whale.

The men are in the ledges' clefts,
  Dead, — but with motion of living guise
    Their bodies are rocking there ;
Monstrous sea-fish and efts
  Stare at them with glassy eyes
  As their limbs are stirred and their
    hair.

    Moan, O sea !
O death at once and the grave,
And sorrow in passing, O cruel wave !
  Let the resonant sea-caves ring,
  And the sorrowful surges sing,
For the dead men rest but restlessly.

We do keep account of them
And sing an ocean requiem
    For the brave.

BRAWN OF ENGLAND'S LAY

THE villeins clustered round the bowl
At merrie Yule to make good cheer,
And drank with froth on beard and jowl :
  " Was-hael to the Thane !
May never Breton taste our beer,
    Nor Dane."

Till the red cock on the chimney crew,
And each man cried with a mighty yawn
As the tapster one more flagon drew :
  " To the Saxon land was-hael !
May we never want for mast-fed brawn
    Nor ale ! "

The thane took up the stirrup-cup
And blew off the reaming head,
And at one draught he swigged it up
And smacked his lips and said :
  " Was-hael to coulter and sword !
  Was-hael to hearth and hall !
  To Saxon land and Saxon lord
    And thrall."

Charles Mair

FROM "TECUMSEH: A DRAMA"

LEFROY IN THE FOREST

THIS region is as lavish of its flowers
As Heaven of its primrose blooms by night.
This is the Arum, which within its root
Folds life and death ; and this the Prince's
  Pine,
Fadeless as love and truth — the fairest
  form
That ever sun-shower washed with sudden
  rain.
This golden cradle is the Moccasin Flower,
Wherein the Indian hunter sees his hound ;
And this dark chalice is the Pitcher-Plant,
Stored with the water of forgetfulness.
Whoever drinks of it, whose heart is pure,
Will sleep for aye 'neath foodfull asphodel,
And dream of endless love.

   .   .   .   .

There was a time on this fair continent
When all things throve in spacious peace-
  fulness.

The prosperous forests unmolested stood,
For where the stalwart oak grew there it
  lived
Long ages, and then died among its kind.
The hoary pines — those ancients of the
  earth —
Brimful of legends of the early world,
Stood thick on their own mountains unsub-
  dued ;
And all things else illumined by the sun,
Inland or by the lifted wave, had rest.
The passionate or calm pageants of the skies
No artist drew ; but in the auburn west
Innumerable faces of fair cloud
Vanished in silent darkness with the day.
The prairie realm — vast ocean's para-
  phrase —
Rich in wild grasses numberless, and flowers
Unnamed save in mute Nature's inventory,
No civilized barbarian trenched for gain.
And all that flowed was sweet and uncor-
  rupt :
The rivers and their tributary streams,
Undammed, wound on forever, and gave up
Their lonely torrents to weird gulfs of sea,

And ocean wastes unshadowed by a sail.
And all the wild life of this western world
Knew not the fear of man ; yet in those
　woods,
And by those plenteous streams and mighty
　lakes,
And on stupendous steppes of peerless plain,
And in the rocky gloom of canyons deep,
Screened by the stony ribs of mountains hoar
Which steeped their snowy peaks in purg-
　ing cloud,
And down the continent where tropic suns
Warmed to her very heart the mother
　earth,
And in the congealed north where silence
　self
Ached with intensity of stubborn frost,
There lived a soul more wild than barba-
　rous ;
A tameless soul — the sunburnt savage
　free —
Free and untainted by the greed of gain,
Great Nature's man, content with Nature's
　food.

IENA'S SONG

FLY far from me,
　Even as the daylight flies,
And leave me in the darkness of my pain !
Some earlier love will come to thee again,
　And sweet new moons will rise,
And smile on it and thee.

Fly far from me,
　Even whilst the daylight wastes —
Ere thy lips burn me in a last caress ;
Ere fancy quickens, and my longings press,
　And my weak spirit hastes
For shelter unto thee !

Fly far from me,
　Even whilst the daylight pales —
So shall we never, never meet again !
Fly ! for my senses swim — Oh, Love ! Oh,
　Pain ! —
Help ! for my spirit fails —
I cannot fly from thee !

THE BUFFALO HERDS

Lefroy.　　　　　　　　　We left
The silent forest, and, day after day,
Great prairies swept beyond our aching
　sight

Into the measureless West : uncharted
　realms,
Voiceless and calm, save when tempestuous
　wind
Rolled the rank herbage into billows vast,
And rushing tides, which never found a
　shore.
And tender clouds, and veils of morning
　mist
Cast flying shadows, chased by flying light,
Into interminable wildernesses,
Flushed with fresh blooms, deep perfumed
　by the rose,
And murmurous with flower-fed bird and
　bee.
The deep-grooved bison-paths like furrows
　lay,
Turned by the cloven hoofs of thundering
　herds
Primeval, and still travelled as of yore.
And gloomy valleys opened at our feet —
Shagged with dusk cypresses and hoary
　pine ;
And sunless gorges, rummaged by the
　wolf,
Which through long reaches of the prairie
　wound,
Then melted slowly into upland vales,
Lingering, far - stretched amongst the
　spreading hills.
　Brock. What charming solitudes ! And
　　life was there !
　Lefroy. Yes, life was there ! inexpli-
　　cable life,
Still wasted by inexorable death.
There had the stately stag his battle-field —
Dying for mastery among his hinds.
There vainly sprung the affrighted ante-
　lope,
Beset by glittering eyes and hurrying feet.
The dancing grouse, at their insensate
　sport,
Heard not the stealthy footstep of the
　fox ;
The gopher on his little earthwork stood,
With folded arms, unconscious of the fate
That wheeled in narrowing circles over-
　head,
And the poor mouse, on heedless nibbling
　bent,
Marked not the silent coiling of the snake.
At length we heard a deep and solemn
　sound —
Erupted moanings of the troubled earth
Trembling beneath innumerable feet.

A growing uproar blending in our ears,
With noise tumultuous as ocean's surge,
Of bellowings, fierce breath and battle
  shock,
And ardor of unconquerable herds.
A multitude whose trampling shook the
  plains,
With discord of harsh sound and rumblings
  deep,
As if the swift revolving earth had struck,
And from some adamantine peak recoiled —

Jarring. At length we topped a high-
  browed hill —
The last and loftiest of a file of such —
And, lo ! before us lay the tameless stock,
Slow - wending to the northward like a
  cloud !
A multitude in motion, dark and dense —
Far as the eye could reach, and farther
  still,
In countless myriads stretched for many a
  league.

John E. Logan

("BARRY DANE")

THE NOR'-WEST COURIER

Up, my dogs, merrily,
  The morn sun is shining,
  Our path is uncertain,
  And night's sombre curtain
May drop on us, verily,
  Ere time for reclining ;
So, up, without whining,
You rascals, instanter,
  Come into your places
There, stretch out your traces,
And off, at a canter.

Up, my dogs, cheerily,
  The noon sun is glowing ;
  Fast and still faster,
  Come, follow your master ;
Or to-night we may wearily,
Tired and drearily,
  Travel, not knowing
  What moment disaster
May sweep in the storm-blast,
And over each form cast
  A shroud in its blowing.

On, my dogs, steadily,
  Though keen winds are shifting
  The snowflakes, and drifting
  Them straight in your faces ;
Come, answer me readily,
Not wildly nor headily,
  Plunging and lifting
  Your feet, keep your paces ;
For yet we shall weather
The blizzard together,
  Though evil our case is.

Sleep, my dogs, cosily,
  Coiled near the fire,
  That higher and higher
Sheds its light rosily
Out o'er the snow and sky ;
  Sleep in the ruddy glow,
  Letting Keewaydin blow
Fierce in his ire.
Sleep, my dogs, soundly ;
  For to-morrow we roundly
  Must buffet the foe.

A BLOOD-RED RING HUNG ROUND THE MOON

A BLOOD-RED ring hung round the moon,
  Hung round the moon. Ah me ! Ah
  me !
I heard the piping of the Loon,
  A wounded Loon. Ah me !
And yet the eagle feathers rare,
I, trembling, wove in my brave's hair.

He left me in the early morn,
  The early morn. Ah me ! Ah me !
The feathers swayed like stately corn,
  So like the corn. Ah me !
A fierce wind swept across the plain,
The stately corn was snapped in twain.

They crushed in blood the hated race,
  The hated race. Ah me ! Ah me !
I only clasped a cold, blind face,
  His cold, dead face. Ah me !
A blood-red ring hangs in my sight,
I hear the Loon cry every night.

A DEAD SINGER

FAIR little spirit of the woodland mazes,
Thou liest sadly low,
No more the purple vetch and star-eyed
daisies
Thy mating hymn shall know.

No more the harebell by the silent river
Shall bend her dainty ear,
When nigh thou fliest, and her petals
quiver
With maiden joy to hear.

No more to flit among the yellow mustard,
Imperial thistle tops,
And intertwining woodbine, thickly clus-
tered
With tendrils of wild hops.

No more the dragon's darting course to
follow
O'er golden, sunlit sheaves ;
No more to catch, within the shady hollow,
The dew from spangled leaves.

No more above the scented rose to hover,
Sipping its fragrant fee ;
No more to chase, across the billowy clover,
The velvet-coated bee.

What fatal stroke has torn the downy cinc-
ture,
Round thy once tuneful throat
And pulseless bosom, where a deathly tinc-
ture
Dyes thy soft feathery coat ?

No gentle mate and thou shalt wing to-
gether,
With tender chicks, your way,
To sunnier southern fields, when autumn
weather
Chills the short northern day.

Dead is the soul of love and song and
laughter,
That thrilled thy fragile breast, —
There is no more for thee, but dead here-
after
Of unbegotten rest.

George Murray

TO A HUMMING BIRD IN A GARDEN

BLITHE playmate of the Summer time,
Admiringly I greet thee ;
Born in old England's misty clime,
I scarcely hoped to meet thee.

Com'st thou from forests of Peru,
Or from Brazil's savannahs,
Where flowers of every dazzling hue
Flaunt, gorgeous as Sultanas ?

Thou scannest me with doubtful gaze,
Suspicious little stranger !
Fear not, thy burnished wings may
blaze
Secure from harm or danger.

Now here, now there, thy flash is
seen,
Like some stray sunbeam darting,

With scarce a second's space between
Its coming and departing.

Mate of the bird that lives sublime
In Pat's immortal blunder,
Spied in two places at a time,
Thou challengest our wonder.

Suspended by thy slender bill,
Sweet blooms thou lov'st to rifle ;
The subtle perfumes they distil
Might well thy being stifle.

Surely the honey-dew of flowers
Is slightly alcoholic,
Or why, through burning August hours,
Dost thou pursue thy frolic ?

What though thy throatlet never rings
With music, soft or stirring ;
Still, like a spinning-wheel, thy wings
Incessantly are whirring.

How dearly I would love to see
Thy tiny *cara sposa*,
As full of sensibility
As any coy mimosa !

They say, when hunters track her nest
Where two warm pearls are lying,
She boldly fights, though sore distrest,
And sends the brigands flying.

What dainty epithets thy tribes
Have won from men of science !
Pedantic and poetic scribes
For once are in alliance.

Crested Coquette, and Azure Crown,
Sun Jewel, Ruby-Throated,
With Flaming Topaz, Crimson Down,
Are names that may be quoted.

Such titles aim to paint the hues
That on the darlings glitter,
And were we for a week to muse,
We scarce could light on fitter.

Farewell, bright bird ! I envy thee,
Gay rainbow-tinted rover ;
Would that my life, like thine, were free
From care till all is over !

A LESSON OF MERCY

BENEATH a palm-tree by a clear cool spring
God's Prophet, Mahomet, lay slumbering,
Till, roused by chance, he saw before him
    stand
A foeman, Durther, scimitar in hand.
The chieftain bade the startled sleeper rise ;
And with a flame of triumph in his eyes,
" Who now can save thee, Mahomet ? " he
    cried.
" God," said the Prophet, " God, my friend
    and guide."
Awe-struck the Arab dropped his naked
    sword,
Which, grasped by Mahomet, defied its lord :
And, " Who can save thee now thy blade
    is won ? "
Exclaimed the Prophet. Durther answered,
    " None ! "
Then spake the victor : " Though thy hands
    are red
With guiltless blood unmercifully shed,
I spare thy life, I give thee back thy steel :
Henceforth, compassion for the helpless
    feel."
And thus the twain, unyielding foes of yore,
Clasped hands in token that their feud was
    o'er.

George Frederick Cameron

THE GOLDEN TEXT

YOU ask for fame or power ?
Then up, and take for text : —
This is my hour,
And not the next, nor next !

Oh, wander not in ways
Of ease or indolence !
Swift come the days,
And swift the days go hence.

Strike ! while the hand is strong :
Strike ! while you can and may :
Strength goes ere long, —
Even yours will pass away.

Sweet seem the fields, and green,
In which you fain would lie ;
Sweet seems the scene
That glads the idle eye ;

Soft seems the path you tread,
And balmy soft the air, —
Heaven overhead
And all the earth seems fair ;

But, would your heart aspire
To noble things, — to claim
Bard's, statesman's fire —
Some measure of their fame ;

Or, would you seek and find
The secret of success
With mortal kind ?
Then, up from idleness !

Up — up ! all fame, all power
Lies in this golden text :
This is my hour —
And not the next nor next !

STANDING ON TIPTOE

STANDING on tiptoe ever since my youth,
  Striving to grasp the future just above,
I hold at length the only future — Truth,
  And Truth is Love.

I feel as one who being awhile confined
  Sees drop to dust about him all his bars : —
The clay grows less, and, leaving it, the mind
  Dwells with the stars.

WHAT MATTERS IT

WHAT reck we of the creeds of men ?
  We see them — we shall see again.
What reck we of the tempest's shock ?
What reck we where our anchor lock,
  On golden marl or mould,
In salt-sea flower or riven rock,
  What matter, so it hold ?

What matters it the spot we fill
  On Earth's green sod when all is said ?
When feet and hands and heart are still
  And all our pulses quieted ?
When hate or love can kill nor thrill,
  When we are done with life and dead ?

So we be haunted night nor day
  By any sin that we have sinned,
What matter where we dream away
  The ages ? In the isles of Ind,
In Tybee, Cuba, or Cathay,
  Or in some world of winter wind ?

It may be I would wish to sleep
  Beneath the wan, white stars of June,
And hear the southern breezes creep
  Between me and the mellow moon ;
But so I do not wake to weep
  At any night or any moon,

And so the generous gods allow
  Repose and peace from evil dreams,
It matters little where or how
  My couch be spread : by moving streams,
Or on some eminent mountain's brow
  Kissed by the morn's or sunset's beams.

For we shall rest ; the brain that planned,
  That thought or wrought or well or ill,
At gaze like Joshua's moon shall stand,
  Not working any work or will,
While eye and lip and heart and hand
  Shall all be still — shall all be still !

Isabella Valancey Crawford

THE CANOE

MY masters twain made me a bed
Of pine-boughs resinous, and cedar ;
Of moss, a soft and gentle breeder
Of dreams of rest ; and me they spread
With furry skins, and, laughing, said, —
" Now she shall lay her polished sides
As queens do rest, or dainty brides,
Our slender lady of the tides ! "

My masters twain their camp-soul lit,
Streamed incense from the hissing cones ;
Large crimson flashes grew and whirled,
Thin golden nerves of sly light curled,
Round the dun camp, and rose faint zones
Half-way about each grim bole knit,
Like a shy child that would bedeck
With its soft clasp a Brave's red neck,

Yet sees the rough shield on his breast,
The awful plumes shake on his crest,
And fearful drops his timid face,
Nor dares complete the sweet embrace.

Into the hollow hearts of brakes
Yet warm from sides of does and stags,
Passed to the crisp dark river flags,
Sinuous, red as copper, snakes, —
Sharp-headed serpents, made of light,
Glided and hid themselves in night.

My masters twain the slaughtered deer
Hung on forked boughs, with thongs of leather.
Bound were his stiff, slim feet together,
His eyes like dead stars cold and drear;
The wandering firelight drew near
And laid its wide palm, red and anxious,

On the sharp splendor of his branches ;
On the white foam grown hard and sere
  On flank and shoulder.
Death, hard as breast of granite boulder,
  And under his lashes,
Peered through his eyes at his life's gray
    ashes.

My masters twain sang songs that wove
(As they burnished hunting blade and rifle)
A golden thread with a cobweb trifle,
Loud of the chase, and low of love.

" O Love ! art thou a silver fish,
Shy of the line and shy of gaffing,
Which we do follow, fierce, yet laughing,
Casting at thee the light-winged wish ?
And at the last shall we bring thee up
From the crystal darkness under the cup
  Of lily folden,
  On broad leaves golden ?

" O Love ! art thou a silver deer ?
Swift thy starred feet as wing of swallow,
While we with rushing arrows follow :
And at the last shall we draw near,
And over thy velvet neck cast thongs,
Woven of roses, of stars, of songs,
  New chains all moulden
  Of rare gems olden ? "

They hung the slaughtered fish like swords
On saplings slender ; like scimitars
Bright, and ruddied from new-dead wars,
Blazed in the light the scaly hordes.

They piled up boughs beneath the trees,
Of cedar-web and green fir tassel ;
Low did the pointed pine tops rustle,
The camp fire blushed to the tender breeze.

The hounds laid dew-laps on the ground,
With needles of pine sweet, soft and
    rusty,
Dreamed of the dead stag stout and lusty ;
A bat by the red flames wove its round.

The darkness built its wigwam walls
Close round the camp, and at its curtain
Pressed shapes, thin woven and uncertain,
As white locks of tall waterfalls.

THE AXE

HIGH grew the snow beneath the low-hung
    sky,
And all was silent in the wilderness ;
In trance of stillness Nature heard her God
Rebuilding her spent fires, and veiled her
    face
While the Great Worker brooded o'er His
    work.

" Bite deep and wide, O Axe, the tree !
What doth thy bold voice promise me ? "

" I promise thee all joyous things
That furnish forth the lives of kings !

" For every silver ringing blow,
Cities and palaces shall grow ! "

" Bite deep and wide, O Axe, the tree !
Tell wider prophecies to me."

" When rust hath gnawed me deep and
    red,
A nation strong shall lift his head.

" His crown the very Heavens shall
    smite,
Æons shall build him in his might ! "

" Bite deep and wide, O Axe, the tree ;
Bright Seer, help on thy prophecy ! "

Max smote the snow-weighed tree, and
    lightly laughed.
" See, friend," he cried to one that looked
    and smiled,
" My axe and I — we do immortal tasks —
We build up nations — this my axe and I ! "

William Douw Schuyler-Lighthall

THE CONFUSED DAWN

WHAT are the Vision and the Cry
  That haunt the new Canadian soul ?
Dim grandeur spreads we know not why
  O'er mountain, forest, tree and knoll,
And murmurs indistinctly fly.
Some magic moment sure is nigh.
  O Seer, the curtain roll !

The Vision, mortal, it is this :
  Dead mountain, forest, knoll and tree,
Awaken all endued with bliss,
  A native land — O think ! to be
Thy native land ! and, ne'er amiss,
Its smile shall like a lover's kiss
  From henceforth seem to thee.

The Cry thou couldst not understand,
  Which runs through that new realm of
      light,
From Breton's to Vancouver's strand
  O'er many a lovely landscape bright,
It is their waking utterance grand,
The great refrain " A Native Land ! "
  Thine be the ear, the sight.

PRÆTERITA EX INSTANTIBUS

How strange it is that, in the after age, —
When Time's clepsydra will be nearer dry,
That all the accustomed things we now
    pass by
Unmarked, because familiar, shall engage
The antique reverence of men to be ;
And that quaint interest which prompts the
    sage
The silent fathoms of the past to gauge
Shall keep alive our own past memory,
Making all great of ours, the garb we
    wear,
Our voiceless cities, reft of roof and spire,
The very skull whence now the eye of
    fire
Glances bright sign of what the soul can
    dare.
So shall our annals make an envied lore,
And men will say, "Thus did the men of
    yore."

THE BATTLE OF LA PRAIRIE

1691

THAT was a brave old epoch,
  Our age of chivalry,
When the Briton met the French-
    man
  At the fight of La Prairie ;
And the manhood of New England,
  And the Netherlanders true
And Mohawks sworn, gave battle
  To the Bourbon's lilied blue.

That was a brave old governor
  Who gathered his array,
And stood to meet, he knew not what,
  On that alarming day.
Eight hundred, amid rumors vast
  That filled the wild wood's gloom,
With all New England's flower of
    youth,
  Fierce for New France's doom.

And the brave old half five hundred !
  Theirs should in truth be fame ;
Borne down the savage Richelieu,
  On what emprise they came !
Your hearts are great enough, O few :
  Only your numbers fail, —
New France asks more for conquerors
  All glorious though your tale.

It was a brave old battle
  That surged around the fort,
When D'Hosta fell in charging,
  And 't was deadly strife and short ;
When in the very quarters
  They contested face and hand,
And many a goodly fellow
  Crimsoned yon La Prairie sand.

And those were brave old orders
  The colonel gave to meet
That forest force with trees entrenched
  Opposing the retreat :
" De Callière's strength 's behind us,
  And in front your Richelieu ;
We must go straightforth at them ;
  There is nothing else to do."

And then the brave old story comes,
Of Schuyler and Valrennes,
When "Fight" the British colonel called,
Encouraging his men,
" For the Protestant Religion
And the honor of our King ! " —
" Sir, I am here to answer you ! "
Valrennes cried, forthstepping.

Were those not brave old races ?
Well, here they still abide ;
And yours is one or other,
And the second 's at your side ;
So when you hear your brother say,
" Some loyal deed I 'll do,"
Like old Valrennes, be ready with
" I 'm here to answer you ! "

MONTREAL

REIGN on, majestic Ville Marie !
Spread wide thine ample robes of state ;
The heralds cry that thou art great,
And proud are thy young sons of thee.
Mistress of half a continent,
Thou risest from thy girlhood's rest ;
We see thee conscious heave thy breast
And feel thy rank and thy descent.

Sprung of the saint and chevalier !
And with the Scarlet Tunic wed !
Mount Royal's crown upon thy head,
And, past thy footstool, broad and clear
St. Lawrence sweeping to the sea ;
Reign on, majestic Ville Marie !

Charles G. D. Roberts

CANADA

O CHILD of Nations, giant-limbed,
Who stand'st among the nations now,
Unheeded, unadored, unhymned,
With unanointed brow :

How long the ignoble sloth, how long
The trust in greatness not thine own ?
Surely the lion's brood is strong
To front the world alone !

How long the indolence, ere thou dare
Achieve thy destiny, seize thy fame;
Ere our proud eyes behold thee bear
A nation's franchise, nation's name ?

The Saxon force, the Celtic fire,
These are thy manhood's heritage !
Why rest with babes and slaves ? Seek
higher
The place of race and age.

I see to every wind unfurled
The flag that bears the Maple-Wreath ;
Thy swift keels furrow round the world
Its blood-red folds beneath ;

Thy swift keels cleave the furthest seas ;
Thy white sails swell with alien gales ;
To stream on each remotest breeze
The black smoke of thy pipes exhales.

O Falterer, let thy past convince
Thy future : all the growth, the
gain,
The fame since Cartier knew thee, since
Thy shores beheld Champlain !

Montcalm and Wolfe ! Wolfe and Mont-
calm !
Quebec, thy storied citadel
Attest in burning song and psalm
How here thy heroes fell !

O Thou that bor'st the battle's brunt
At Queenston, and at Lundy's Lane :
On whose scant ranks but iron front
The battle broke in vain !

Whose was the danger, whose the day,
From whose triumphant throats the
cheers,
At Chrysler's Farm, at Chateauguay,
Storming like clarion-bursts our ears ?

On soft Pacific slopes, — beside
Strange floods that northward rave and
fall, —
Where chafes Acadia's chainless tide, —
Thy sons await thy call.

They wait ; but some in exile, some
With strangers housed, in stranger
lands ;

And some Canadian lips are dumb
  Beneath Egyptian sands.

O mystic Nile ! Thy secret yields
  Before us ; thy most ancient dreams
Are mixed with far Canadian fields
  And murmur of Canadian streams.

But thou, my Country, dream not thou !
  Wake, and behold how night is done, —
How on thy breast, and o'er thy brow,
  Bursts the uprising sun !

THE ISLES

FAITHFUL reports of them have reached
    me oft !
  Many their embassage to mortal court,
  By golden pomp, and breathless-heard
    consort
    Of music soft, —
By fragrances accredited, and dreams.
  Many their speeding heralds, whose light
    feet
Make pause at wayside brooks, and fords
    of streams,
  Leaving transfigured by an effluence
    fleet
  Those wayfarers they meet.

No wind from out the solemn wells of night
  But hath its burden of strange messages,
  Tormenting for interpreter ; nor less
    The wizard light
That steals from noon-stilled waters, woven
    in shade,
  Beckons somewhither, with cool fingers
    slim.
No dawn but hath some subtle word con-
    veyed
  In rose ineffable at sunrise rim,
  Or charactery dim.

One moment throbs the hearing, yearns the
    sight.
  But though not far, yet strangely hid,
    the way,
  And our sense slow ; nor long for us
    delay
    The guides their flight !
The breath goes by ; the word, the light,
    elude ;
  And we stay wondering. But there comes
    an hour

Of fitness perfect and unfettered mood,
  When splits her husk the finer sense with
    power,
  And — yon their palm-trees tower !

Here Homer came, and Milton came, though
    blind.
  Omar's deep doubts still found them nigh
    and nigher,
  And learned them fashioned to the heart's
    desire.
    The supreme mind
Of Shakespeare took their sovereignty, and
    smiled.
  Those passionate Israelitish lips that
    poured
  The Song of Songs attained them ; and the
    wild
Child-heart of Shelley, here from strife
    restored,
  Remembers not life's sword.

BURNT LANDS

ON other fields and other scenes the morn
Laughs from her blue, — but not such
    scenes are these,
Where comes no cheer of Summer leaves
    and bees,
And no shade mitigates the day's white
    scorn.
These serious acres vast no groves adorn ;
But giant trunks, bleak shapes that once
    were trees,
Tower naked, unassuaged of rain or breeze,
Their stern gray isolation grimly borne.
The months roll over them, and mark no
    change ;
But when spring stirs, or autumn stills, the
    year,
Perchance some phantom leafage rustles
    faint
Through their parched dreams, — some old-
    time notes ring strange,
When in his slender treble, far and clear,
Reiterates the rain-bird his complaint.

THE FLIGHT OF THE GEESE

I HEAR the low wind wash the softening
    snow,
The low tide loiter down the shore. The
    night,

Full filled with April forecast, hath no
    light.
The salt wave on the sedge-flat pulses slow.
Through the hid furrows lisp in murmurous
    flow
The thaw's shy ministers ; and hark ! The
    height
Of heaven grows weird and loud with un-
    seen flight
Of strong hosts prophesying as they go !
High through the drenched and hollow
    night their wings
Beat northward hard on winter's trail.
    The sound
Of their confused and solemn voices, borne
Athwart the dark to their long arctic morn,
Comes with a sanction and an awe pro-
    found,
A boding of unknown, foreshadowed things.

THE NIGHT SKY

O DEEP of Heaven, 't is thou alone art
    boundless,
'T is thou alone our balance shall not weigh,
'T is thou alone our fathom-line finds sound-
    less, —
Whose infinite our finite must obey !
Through thy blue realms and down thy
    starry reaches
Thought voyages forth beyond thy furthest
    fire,
And homing from no sighted shoreline,
    teaches
Thee measureless as is the soul's desire.
O deep of Heaven ! No beam of Pleiad
    ranging
Eternity may bridge thy gulf of spheres !
The ceaseless hum that fills thy sleep un-
    changing
Is rain of the innumerable years.
Our worlds, our suns, our ages, — these
    but stream
Through thine abiding like a dateless
    dream.

THE DESERTED CITY

THERE lies a little city leagues away.
Its wharves the green sea washes all day
    long.
Its busy, sun-bright wharves with sailors'
    song
And clamor of trade ring loud the live-long
    day.

Into the happy harbor hastening, gay
With press of snowy canvas, tall ships
    throng.
The peopled streets to blithe-eyed Peace
    belong,
Glad housed beneath these crowding roofs
    of gray.
'T was long ago this city prospered so,
For yesterday a woman died therein.
Since when the wharves are idle fallen, I
    know,
And in the streets is hushed the pleasant
    din ;
The thronging ships have been, the songs
    have been ; —
Since yesterday it is so long ago.

AUTOCHTHON

I AM the spirit astir
    To swell the grain,
When fruitful suns confer
    With laboring rain ;
I am the life that thrills
    In branch and bloom ;
I am the patience of abiding hills,
    The promise masked in doom.

When the sombre lands are wrung,
    And storms are out,
And giant woods give tongue,
    I am the shout ;
And when the earth would sleep,
    Wrapped in her snows,
I am the infinite gleam of eyes that keep
    The post of her repose.

I am the hush of calm,
    I am the speed,
The flood-tide's triumphing psalm,
    The marsh-pool's heed ;
I work in the rocking roar
    Where cataracts fall ;
I flash in the prismy fire that dances o'er
    The dew's ephemeral ball.

I am the voice of wind
    And wave and tree,
Of stern desires and blind,
    Of strength to be ;
I am the cry by night
    At point of dawn,
The summoning bugle from the unseen
    height,
    In cloud and doubt withdrawn.

I am the strife that shapes
   The stature of man,
The pang no hero escapes,
   The blessing, the ban ;
I am the hàmmer that moulds
   The iron of our race,
The omen of God in our blood that a people
      beholds,
   The foreknowledge veiled in our face.

MARSYAS

A LITTLE gray hill-glade, close-turfed, with-
      drawn
Beyond resort or heed of trafficking feet,
Ringed round with slim trunks of the moun-
   tain ash.
Through the slim trunks and scarlet
      bunches flash —
Beneath the clear chill glitterings of the
   dawn —
Far off, the crests, where down the rosy
      shore
The Pontic surges beat.
The plains lie dim below. The thin airs
      wash
The circuit of the autumn-colored hills,
And this high glade, whereon
The satyr pipes, who soon shall pipe no
   more.
He sits against the beech-tree's mighty
      bole, —
He leans, and with persuasive breathing fills
The happy shadows of the slant-set lawn.
The goat-feet fold beneath a gnarlèd root ;
And sweet, and sweet the note that steals
      and thrills
From slender stops of that shy flute.
Then to the goat-feet comes the wide-eyed
      fawn
Hearkening ; the rabbits fringe the glade,
      and lay
Their long ears to the sound ;
In the pale boughs the partridge gather
      round,
And quaint hern from the sea-green river
   reeds ;
The wild ram halts upon a rocky horn
O'erhanging ; and, unmindful of his prey,
The leopard steals with narrowed lids to
      lay
His spotted length along the ground.
The thin airs wash, the thin clouds wander
      by,

And those hushed listeners move not. All
      the morn
He pipes, soft-swaying, and with half-shut
      eye,
In rapt content of utterance, —
                           nor heeds
The young God standing in his branchy
      place,
The languor on his lips, and in his face,
Divinely inaccessible, the scorn.

EPITAPH FOR A SAILOR BURIED ASHORE

HE who but yesterday would roam
   Careless as clouds and currents range,
In homeless wandering most at home,
   Inhabiter of change ;

Who wooed the west to win the east,
   And named the stars of north and south,
And felt the zest of Freedom's feast
   Familiar in his mouth ;

Who found a faith in stranger speech,
   And fellowship in foreign hands,
And had within his eager reach
   The relish of all lands —

How circumscribed a plot of earth
   Keeps now his restless footsteps still,
Whose wish was wide as ocean's girth,
   Whose will the water's will !

THE KEEPERS OF THE PASS

(WHEN ADAM DULAC AND HIS COMRADES,
SWORN NOT TO RETURN ALIVE, SAVED MONT-
REAL FROM THE IROQUOIS)

Now heap the branchy barriers up.
   No more for us shall burn
The pine-logs on the happy hearth,
   For we shall not return.

We 've come to our last camping-ground.
   Set axe to fir and tamarack.
The foe is here, the end is near,
   And we shall not turn back.

In vain for us the town shall wait,
   The home-dear faces yearn,
The watchers on the steeple watch, —
   For we shall not return.

For them we're come to these hard straits,
To save from flame and wrack
The little city built far off ;
And we shall not turn back.

Now beat the yelling butchers down.
Let musket blaze, and axe-edge burn.
Set hand to hand, lay brand to brand,
But we shall not return.

For every man of us that falls
Their hordes a score shall lack.
Close in about the Lily Flag !
No man of us goes back.

For us no morrow's dawn shall break.
Our sons and wives shall learn
Some day from lips of flying scout
Why we might not return.

A dream of children's laughter comes
Across the battle's slack,
A vision of familiar streets, —
But we shall not go back.

Up roars the painted storm once more.
Long rest we soon shall earn.
Henceforth the city safe may sleep,
But we shall not return.

And when our last has fallen in blood
Between these waters black,
Their tribe shall no more lust for war, —
For we shall not turn back.

In vain for us the town shall wait,
The home-dear faces yearn,
The watchers in the steeple watch,
For we shall not return.

THE BIRD'S SONG, THE SUN, AND THE WIND

The bird's song, the sun, and the wind —
The wind that rushes, the sun that is still,
The song of the bird that sings alone,
And wide light washing the lonely hill !

The Spring's coming, the buds and the brooks —
The brooks that clamor, the buds in the rain,

The coming of Spring that comes unprayed for,
And eyes that welcome it not for pain !

AFOOT

Comes the lure of green things growing,
Comes the call of waters flowing —
And the wayfarer desire
Moves and wakes and would be going.

Hark the migrant hosts of June
Marching nearer noon by noon !
Hark the gossip of the grasses
Bivouacked beneath the moon !

Long the quest and far the ending
When my wayfarer is wending —
When desire is once afoot,
Doom behind and dream attending !

In his ears the phantom chime
Of incommunicable rhyme,
He shall chase the fleeting camp-fires
Of the Bedouins of Time.

Farer by uncharted ways,
Dumb as death to plaint or praise,
Unreturning he shall journey,
Fellow to the nights and days ;

Till upon the outer bar
Stilled the moaning currents are,
Till the flame achieves the zenith,
Till the moth attains the star,

Till through laughter and through tears
Fair the final peace appears,
And about the watered pastures
Sink to sleep the nomad years !

DOMINE, CUI SUNT PLEIADES CURAE

Father, who keepest
The stars in Thy care,
Me, too, Thy little one,
Childish in prayer,
Keep, as Thou keepest
The soft night through
Thy long, white lilies
Asleep in Thy dew.

William Wilfred Campbell

TO THE LAKES

WITH purple glow at even,
　With crimson waves at dawn,
Cool bending blue of heaven,
　O blue lakes pulsing on ;
Lone haunts of wilding creatures dead to
　　　wrong ;
　Your trance of mystic beauty
　Is wove into my song.

I know no gladder dreaming
　In all the haunts of men,
I know no silent seeming
　Like to your shore and fen ;
No world of restful beauty like your world
　Of curvèd shores and waters,
　In sunlight vapors furled.

I pass and repass under
　Your depths of peaceful blue ;
You dream your wild, hushed wonder
　Mine aching heart into ;
And all the care and unrest pass away
　Like night's gray, haunted shadows
　At the red birth of day.

You lie in moon-white splendor
　Beneath the northern sky,
Your voices soft and tender
　In dream-worlds fade and die,
In whispering beaches, haunted bays and
　　　capes,
　Where mists of dawn and midnight
　Drift past in spectral shapes.

Beside your far north beaches
　Comes late the quickening spring ;
With soft, voluptuous speeches
　The summer, lingering,
Fans with hot winds your breast so still
　　　and wide,
　Where June, with trancèd silence,
　Drifts over shore and tide.

Beneath great crags the larches,
　By some lone, northern bay,
Bend, as the strong wind marches
　Out of the dull, north day,
Horning along the borders of the night,
　With icèd, chopping waters
　Out in the shivering light.

Here the white winter's fingers
　Tip with dull fires the dawn,
Where the pale morning lingers
　By stretches bleak and wan ;
Kindling the icèd capes with heatless glow,
　That renders cold and colder
　Lone waters, rocks and snow.

Here in the glad September,
　When all the woods are red
And gold, and hearts remember
　The long days that are dead ;
And all the world is mantled in a haze ;
　And the wind, a mad musician,
　Melodious makes the days ;

And the nights are still, and slumber
　Holds all the frosty ground,
And the white stars whose number
　In God's great books are found,
Gird with pale flames the spangled, frosty
　　　sky ;
　By white, moon-curvèd beaches
　The haunted hours go by.

A CANADIAN FOLK-SONG

THE doors are shut, the windows fast,
Outside the gust is driving past,
Outside the shivering ivy clings,
While on the hob the kettle sings.
　Margery, Margery, make the tea,
　Singeth the kettle merrily.

The streams are hushed up where they
　　　flowed,
The ponds are frozen along the road,
The cattle are housed in shed and byre,
While singeth the kettle on the fire.
　Margery, Margery, make the tea,
　Singeth the kettle merrily.

The fisherman on the bay in his boat
Shivers and buttons up his coat ;
The traveller stops at the tavern door,
And the kettle answers the chimney's roar
　Margery, Margery, make the tea,
　Singeth the kettle merrily.

The firelight dances upon the wall,
Footsteps are heard in the outer hall,

And a kiss and a welcome that fill the
   room,
And the kettle sings in the glimmer and
   gloom.
Margery, Margery, make the tea,
Singeth the kettle merrily.

A LAKE MEMORY

THE lake comes throbbing in with voice of
   pain
Across these flats, athwart the sunset's
   glow,
I see her face, I know her voice again,
   Her lips, her breath, O God, as long ago.

To live the sweet past over I would fain,
   As lives the day in the red sunset's fire,
That all these wild, wan marshlands now
   would stain,
   With the dawn's memories, loves and
   flushed desire.

I call her back across the vanished years,
   Nor vain — a white-armed phantom fills
   her place ;
Its eyes the wind-blown sunset fires, its tears
   This rain of spray that blows about my
   face.

THE WERE-WOLVES

THEY hasten, still they hasten,
   From the even to the dawn ;
And their tired eyes gleam and glisten
   Under north skies white and wan.
Each panter in the darkness
   Is a demon-haunted soul,
The shadowy, phantom were-wolves,
   Who circle round the Pole.

Their tongues are crimson flaming,
   Their haunted blue eyes gleam,
And they strain them to the utmost
   O'er frozen lake and stream ;
Their cry one note of agony,
   That is neither yelp nor bark,
These panters of the northern waste,
   Who hound them to the dark.

You may hear their hurried breathing,
   You may see their fleeting forms,
At the pallid polar midnight
   When the north is gathering storms ;
When the arctic frosts are flaming,
   And the ice-field thunders roll ;

These demon-haunted were-wolves,
   Who circle round the Pole.

They hasten, still they hasten,
   Across the northern night,
Filled with a frighted madness,
   A horror of the light ;
Forever and forever,
   Like leaves before the wind,
They leave the wan, white gleaming
   Of the dawning far behind.

Their only peace is darkness,
   Their rest to hasten on
Into the heart of midnight,
   Forever from the dawn.
Across far phantom ice-floes
   The eye of night may mark
These horror-haunted were-wolves
   Who hound them to the dark.

All through this hideous journey,
   They are the souls of men
Who in the far dark-ages
   Made Europe one black fen.
They fled from courts and convents,
   And bound their mortal dust
With demon wolfish girdles
   Of human hate and lust.

These who could have been god-like,
   Chose, each a loathsome beast,
Amid the heart's foul graveyards,
   On putrid thoughts to feast ;
But the great God who made them
   Gave each a human soul,
And so 'mid night forever
   They circle round the Pole ;

A praying for the blackness,
   A longing for the night,
For each is doomed forever
   By a horror of the light ;
And far in the heart of midnight,
   Where their shadowy flight is hurled,
They feel with pain the dawning
   That creeps in round the world.

Under the northern midnight,
   The white, glint ice upon,
They hasten, still they hasten,
   With their horror of the dawn ;
Forever and forever,
   Into the night away
They hasten, still they hasten
   Unto the judgment day.

Frederick George Scott

KNOWLEDGE

THEY were islanders, our fathers were,
　And they watched the encircling seas,
And their hearts drank in the ceaseless stir,
　And the freedom of the breeze ;
Till they chafed at their narrow bounds
And longed for the sweep of the main,
And they fretted and fumed like hounds
Held in within sight of the plain,
　　And the play
　　And the prey.

So they built them ships of wood, and sailed
　To many an unknown coast ;
They braved the storm and battles hailed,
　And danger they loved most ;
Till the tiny ships of wood
Grew powerful on the globe,
And the new-found lands for good
They wrapped in a wondrous robe
　　Of bold design,
　　Our brave ensign.

And islanders yet in a way are we,
　Our knowledge is still confined,
And we hear the roar of encircling sea,
　To be crossed in the ship of the mind ;
And we dream of lands afar,
　Unknown, unconquered yet,
And we chafe at the bounds there are,
　And our spirits fume and fret
　　For the prize
　　Of the wise.

But we 'll never do aught, I know, unless
　We are brave as our sires of old,
And face like them the bitterness
　Of the battle and storm and cold ;
Unless we boldly stand,
　When men would hold us back,
With the helm-board in our hand,
　And our eyes to the shining track
　　Of what may be
　　Beyond the sea.

There are rocks out there in that wide, wide
　　sea,
　'Neath many a darkling stream,
And souls that once sailed out bold and
　　free
Have been carried away in a dream ;

For they never came back again —
　On the deep the ships were lost ;
But in spite of the danger and pain,
　The ocean has still to be crossed,
　And only they do
　Who are brave and true.

TIME

I SAW Time in his workshop carving faces ;
Scattered around his tools lay, blunting
　　griefs,
Sharp cares that cut out deeply in reliefs
Of light and shade ; sorrows that smooth
　　the traces
Of what were smiles. Nor yet without fresh
　　graces
His handiwork, for ofttimes rough were
　　ground
And polished, oft the pinched made smooth
　　and round ;
The calm look, too, the impetuous fire re-
　　places.
Long time I stood and watched ; with hid-
　　eous grin
He took each heedless face between his
　　knees,
And graved and scarred and bleached with
　　boiling tears.
I wondering turned to go, when, lo ! my
　　skin
Feels crumpled, and in glass my own face
　　sees
Itself all changed, scarred, careworn, white
　　with years.

SAMSON

PLUNGED in night, I sit alone
Eyeless on this dungeon stone,
Naked, shaggy and unkempt,
Dreaming dreams no soul hath dreamt.

Rats and vermin round my feet
Play unharmed, companions sweet,
Spiders weave me overhead
Silken curtains for my bed.

Day by day the mould I smell
Of this fungus-blistered cell ;

Nightly in my haunted sleep
O'er my face the lizards creep.

Gyves of iron scrape and burn
Wrists and ankles when I turn,
And my collared neck is raw
With the teeth of brass that gnaw.

God of Israel, canst Thou see
All my fierce captivity?
Do thy sinews feel my pains?
Hearest Thou the clanking chains?

Thou who madest me so fair,
Strong and buoyant as the air,
Tall and noble as a tree,
With the passions of the sea,

Swift as horse upon my feet,
Fierce as lion in my heat,
Rending, like a wisp of hay,
All that dared withstand my way,

Canst Thou see me through the gloom
Of this subterranean tomb, —
Blinded tiger in his den,
Once the lord and prince of men?

Clay was I; the potter Thou
With Thy thumb-nail smooth'dst my brow,
Roll'dst the spital-moistened sands
Into limbs between Thy hands.

Thou didst pour into my blood
Fury of the fire and flood,
And upon the boundless skies
Thou didst first unclose my eyes.

And my breath of life was flame;
God-like from the source it came,
Whirling round like furious wind
Thoughts upgathered in the mind.

Strong Thou mad'st me, till at length
All my weakness was my strength;
Tortured am I, blind and wrecked,
For a faulty architect.

From the woman at my side,
Was I woman-like to hide
What she asked me, as if fear
Could my iron heart come near?

Nay, I scorned and scorn again
Cowards who their tongues restrain;

Cared I no more for Thy laws
Than a wind of scattered straws.

When the earth quaked at my name
And my blood was all aflame,
Who was I to lie, and cheat
Her who clung about my feet?

From Thy open nostrils blow
Wind and tempest, rain and snow;
Dost Thou curse them on their course,
For the fury of their force?

Tortured am I, wracked and bowed,
But the soul within is proud;
Dungeon fetters cannot still
Forces of the tameless will.

Israel's God, come down and see
All my fierce captivity;
Let Thy sinews feel my pains,
With Thy fingers lift my chains.

Then, with thunder loud and wild,
Comfort Thou Thy rebel child,
And with lightning split in twain
Loveless heart and sightless brain.

Give me splendor in my death —
Not this sickening dungeon breath,
Creeping down my blood like slime,
Till it wastes me in my prime.

Give me back, for one blind hour,
Half my former rage and power,
And some giant crisis send
Meet to prove a hero's end.

Then, O God, Thy mercy show —
Crush him in the overthrow
At whose life they scorn and point,
By its greatness out of joint.

VAN ELSEN

God spake three times and saved Van
    Elsen's soul;
He spake by sickness first and made him
    whole;
    Van Elsen heard him not,
    Or soon forgot.

God spake to him by wealth, the world out-
    poured

Its treasures at his feet, and called him
  Lord ;
Van Elsen's heart grew fat
And proud thereat.

God spake the third time when the great
  world smiled,
And in the sunshine slew his little child ;
Van Elsen like a tree
Fell hopelessly.

Then in the darkness came a voice which
  said,
"As thy heart bleedeth, so my heart hath
  bled,
As I have need of thee,
Thou needest me."

That night Van Elsen kissed the baby
  feet,
And, kneeling by the narrow winding sheet,
  Praised Him with fervent breath
  Who conquered death.

AD MAJOREM DEI GLORIAM

THY glory alone, O God, be the end of all
  that I say ;
Let it shine in every deed, let it kindle the
  prayers that I pray ;
Let it burn in my innermost soul, till the
  shadow of self pass away,
And the light of Thy glory, O God, be un-
  veiled in the dawning of day.

Elizabeth Gostwycke Roberts

IN THE GOLDEN BIRCH

How the leaves sing to the wind !
  And the wind with its turbulent voices
    sweet
  Gives back the praise of the leaves, as is
    meet,
To the soft blue sky, where the cumulous
  clouds are thinned,
  And driven away, like a flock of fright-
    ened sheep,
  By the wind that waketh and putteth to
    sleep.

Here, in the golden birch,
  Folded in rapture of golden light,
  I taste the joy of the birds in their flight ;
And I watch the flickering shadows, that
  sway and lurch
  And flutter, like dancing brownies, over
    the green,
  And the birch is singing wherein I lean.

From over the purple hills
  Comes the wind with its strange sweet
    song to the land ;
  And the earth looks bright, as it might
    when planned
By the Maker, and left unblemished of
  human ills ;
  And the river runs, like a child to its
    mother's knee,
  To the heart of the great unresting
    sea.

How perfect the day, and sweet !
  Over me, limitless heavens of blue ;
  Close to me, leaves that the wind sifts
    through ;
And the one sweet song, that the wind and
  the leaves repeat,
  Till the mild, hushed meadows listen,
    crowned with light,
  And the hill-tops own its might !

Archibald Lampman

HEAT

From plains that reel to southward, dim,
  The road runs by me white and bare ;
Up the steep hill it seems to swim
  Beyond, and melt into the glare.
Upward half way, or it may be
  Nearer the summit, slowly steals
A hay-cart, moving dustily
  With idly clacking wheels.

By his cart's side the wagoner
  Is slouching slowly at his ease,
Half-hidden in the windless blur
  Of white dust puffing to his knees.
This wagon on the height above,
  From sky to sky on either hand,
Is the sole thing that seems to move
  In all the heat-held land.

Beyond me in the fields the sun
  Soaks in the grass and hath his will ;
I count the marguerites one by one ;
  Even the buttercups are still.
On the brook yonder not a breath
  Disturbs the spider or the midge.
The water-bugs draw close beneath
  The cool gloom of the bridge.

Where the far elm-tree shadows flood
  Dark patches in the burning grass,
The cows, each with her peaceful cud,
  Lie waiting for the heat to pass.
From somewhere on the slope near by
  Into the pale depth of the noon
A wandering thrush slides leisurely
  His thin revolving tune.

In intervals of dreams I hear
  The cricket from the droughty ground ;
The grasshoppers spin into mine ear
  A small innumerable sound.
I lift mine eyes sometimes to gaze :
  The burning sky-line blinds my sight ;
The woods far off are blue with haze ;
  The hills are drenched in light.

And yet to me not this or that
  Is always sharp or always sweet ;
In the sloped shadow of my hat
  I lean at rest, and drain the heat ;

Nay more, I think some blessed power
  Hath brought me wandering idly here :
In the full furnace of this hour
  My thoughts grow keen and clear.

BETWEEN THE RAPIDS

The point is turned ; the twilight shadow
    fills
  The wheeling stream, the soft receding
    shore,
And on our ears from deep among the hills
  Breaks now the rapids' sudden quicken-
    ing roar.
Ah, yet the same ! or have they changed
    their face,
  The fair green fields, and can it still be
    seen,
The white log cottage near the mountain's
    base,
  So bright and quiet, so home-like and
    serene ?
Ah, well I question, for as five years go,
How many blessings fall, and how much
    woe.

Aye there they are, nor have they changed
    their cheer,
  The fields, the hut, the leafy mountain
    brows ;
Across the lonely dusk again I hear
  The loitering bells, the lowing of the
    cows,
The bleat of many sheep, the stilly rush
  Of the low whispering river, and, through
    all,
Soft human tongues that break the deep-
    ening hush
  With faint-heard song or desultory call :
O comrades, hold ! the longest reach is
    past ;
The stream runs swift, and we are flying
    fast.

The shore, the fields, the cottage, just the
    same,
  But how with them whose memory makes
    them sweet ?
Oh, if I called them, hailing name by name,
  Would the same lips the same old shouts
    repeat ?

Have the rough years, so big with death
    and ill,
Gone lightly by and left them smiling
    yet?
Wild black-eyed Jeanne whose tongue was
    never still,
    Old wrinkled Picaud, Pierre and pale
    Lisette,
The homely hearts that never cared to
    range,
While life's wide fields were filled with
    rush and change.

And where is Jacques, and where is Ver-
    ginie?
I cannot tell ; the fields are all a blur.
The lowing cows whose shapes I scarcely
    see,
    Oh, do they wait and do they call for her?
And is she changed, or is her heart still
    clear
As wind or morning, light as river foam?
Or have life's changes borne her far from
    here,
    And far from rest, and far from help
    and home?
Ah comrades, soft, and let us rest awhile,
For arms grow tired with paddling many a
    mile.

The woods grow wild, and from the rising
    shore
    The cool wind creeps, the faint wood
    odors steal ;
Like ghosts adown the river's blackening
    floor
The misty fumes begin to creep and reel.
Once more I leave you, wandering toward
    the night,
    Sweet home, sweet heart, that would
    have held me in ;
Whither I go I know not, and the light
Is faint before, and rest is hard to win.
Ah, sweet ye were and near to heaven's
    gate ;
But youth is blind and wisdom comes too
    late.

Blacker and loftier grow the woods, and
    hark !
    The freshening roar ! The chute is near
    us now,
And dim the canyon grows, and inky dark
    The water whispering from the birchen
    prow.

One long last look, and many a sad adieu,
    While eyes can see and heart can feel
    you yet,
I leave sweet home and sweeter hearts to
    you,
    A prayer for Picaud, one for pale Lisette,
A kiss for Pierre, my little Jacques, and
    thee,
A sigh for Jeanne, a sob for Verginie.

Oh, does she still remember ? Is the dream
    Now dead, or has she found another
    mate ?
So near, so dear ; and ah, so swift the
    stream ;
    Even now perhaps it were not yet too
    late.
But, oh, what matter ; for, before the night
    Has reached its middle, we have far to
    go :
Bend to your paddles, comrades ; see, the
    light
Ebbs off apace ; we must not linger so.
Aye thus it is ! Heaven gleams and then
    is gone.
Once, twice, it smiles, and still we wander
    on.

A FORECAST

WHAT days await this woman, whose
    strange feet
Breathe sweet spells, whose presence makes men
    dream like wine,
Tall, free and slender as the forest pine,
Whose form is moulded music, through
    whose sweet
Frank eyes I feel the very heart's least
    beat,
Keen, passionate, and full of dreams and
    fire :
How in the end, and to what man's desire
Shall all this yield, whose lips shall these
    lips meet?
One thing I know : if he be great and
    pure,
This love, this fire, this beauty shall endure
Triumph and hope shall lead him by the
    palm :
But if not this, some differing thing he be,
That dream shall break in terror ; he shall
    see
The whirlwind ripen, where he sowed the
    calm.

THE LOONS

ONCE ye were happy, once by many a
    shore,
Wherever Glooscap's gentle feet might
    stray,
Lulled by his presence like a dream, ye
    lay
Floating at rest ; but that was long of yore.
He was too good for earthly men ; he bore
Their bitter deeds for many a patient day,
And then at last he took his unseen way.
He was your friend, and ye might rest no
    more :
And now, though many hundred altering
    years
Have passed, among the desolate northern
    meres
Still must ye search and wander queru-
    lously,
Crying for Glooscap, still bemoan the light
With weird entreaties, and in agony
With awful laughter pierce the lonely night.

THE CITY OF THE END OF THINGS

BESIDE the pounding cataracts
Of midnight streams unknown to us,
'T is builded in the dismal tracts
And valleys huge of Tartarus.
Lurid and lofty and vast it seems ;
It hath no rounded name that rings,
But I have heard it called in dreams
The City of the End of Things.

Its roofs and iron towers have grown
None knoweth how high within the night,
But in its murky streets far down
A flaming terrible and bright
Shakes all the stalking shadows there,
Across the walls, across the floors,
And shifts upon the upper air
From out a thousand furnace doors ;
And all the while an awful sound
Keeps roaring on continually,
And crashes in the ceaseless round
Of a gigantic harmony.
Through its grim depths reëchoing,
And all its weary height of walls,
With measured roar and iron ring,
The inhuman music lifts and falls.
Where no thing rests and no man is,
And only fire and night hold sway,

The beat, the thunder, and the hiss
Cease not, and change not, night nor day.

And moving at unheard commands,
The abysses and vast fires between,
Flit figures that, with clanking hands,
Obey a hideous routine.
They are not flesh, they are not bone,
They see not with the human eye,
And from their iron lips is blown
A dreadful and monotonous cry.
And whoso of our mortal race
Should find that city unaware,
Lean Death would smite him face to face,
And blanch him with its venomed air ;
Or, caught by the terrific spell,
Each thread of memory snapped and cut,
His soul would shrivel, and its shell
Go rattling like an empty nut.

It was not always so, but once,
In days that no man thinks upon,
Fair voices echoed from its stones,
The light above it leaped and shone.
Once there were multitudes of men
That built that city in their pride,
Until its might was made, and then
They withered, age by age, and died ;
And now of that prodigious race
Three only in an iron tower,
Set like carved idols face to face,
Remain the masters of its power ;
And at the city gate a fourth,
Gigantic and with dreadful eyes,
Sits looking toward the lightless north,
Beyond the reach of memories :
Fast-rooted to the lurid floor,
A bulk that never moves a jot,
In his pale body dwells no more
Or mind or soul, — an idiot !

But some time in the end those three
Shall perish and their hands be still,
And with the masters' touch shall flee
Their incommunicable skill.
A stillness, absolute as death,
Along the slacking wheels shall lie,
And, flagging at a single breath,
The fires shall smoulder out and die.
The roar shall vanish at its height,
And over that tremendous town
The silence of eternal night
Shall gather close and settle down.
All its grim grandeur, tower and hall,
Shall be abandoned utterly,

And into rust and dust shall fall
From century to century.
Nor ever living thing shall grow,
Or trunk of tree or blade of grass ;
No drop shall fall, no wind shall blow,

Nor sound of any foot shall pass.
Alone of its accursèd state
One thing the hand of Time shall spare,
For the grim Idiot at the gate
Is deathless and eternal there !

Bliss Carman

MARIAN DRURY

MARIAN DRURY, Marian Drury,
How are the marshes full of the sea !
Acadie dreams of your coming home
All year through, and her heart gets
free, —

Free on the trail of the wind to travel,
Search and course with the roving tide,
All year long where his hands unravel
Blossom and berry the marshes hide.

Marian Drury, Marian Drury,
How are the marshes full of the surge !
April over the Norland now
Walks in the quiet from verge to
verge.

Burying, brimming, the building billows
Fret the long dikes with uneasy foam.
Drenched with gold weather, the idling
willows
Kiss you a hand from the Norland
home.

Marian Drury, Marian Drury,
How are the marshes full of the sun !
Blomidon waits for your coming home,
All day long where the white wings
run.

All spring through they falter and follow,
Wander, and beckon the roving tide,
Wheel and float with the veering swallow,
Lift you a voice from the blue hill-
side.

Marian Drury, Marian Drury,
How are the marshes full of the rain !
April over the Norland now
Bugles for rapture, and rouses pain, —

Halts before the forsaken dwelling,
Where in the twilight, too spent to
roam,

Love, whom the fingers of death are quell-
ing,
Cries you a cheer from the Norland
home.

Marian Drury, Marian Drury,
How are the marshes filled with you !
Grand Pré dreams of your coming home, —
Dreams while the rainbirds all night
through,

Far in the uplands calling to win you,
Tease the brown dusk on the marshes
wide ;
And never the burning heart within you
Stirs in your sleep by the roving tide.

A SEA CHILD

THE lover of child Marjory
Had one white hour of life brim full ;
Now the old nurse, the rocking sea,
Hath him to lull.

The daughter of child Marjory
Hath in her veins, to beat and run,
The glad indomitable sea,
The strong white sun.

GOLDEN ROWAN

SHE lived where the mountains go down to
the sea,
And river and tide confer.
Golden Rowan, in Menalowan,
Was the name they gave to her.

She had the soul no circumstance
Can hurry or defer.
Golden Rowan, of Menalowan,
How time stood still for her !

Her playmates for their lovers grew,
But that shy wanderer,
Golden Rowan, of Menalowan,
Knew love was not for her.

Hers was the love of wilding things ;
  To hear a squirrel chir
    In the golden rowan of Menalowan
  Was joy enough for her.

She sleeps on the hill with the lonely sun,
  Where in the days that were,
    The golden rowan of Menalowan
  So often shadowed her.

The scarlet fruit will come to fill,
  The scarlet spring to stir
    The golden rowan of Menalowan,
  And wake no dream for her.

Only the wind is over her grave,
  For mourner and comforter ;
    And " Golden Rowan, of Menalowan,"
  Is all we know of her.

SPRING SONG

MAKE me over, mother April,
  When the sap begins to stir !
When thy flowery hand delivers
All the mountain-prisoned rivers,
And thy great heart beats and quivers
  To revive the days that were,
Make me over, mother April,
  When the sap begins to stir !

Take my dust and all my dreaming,
Count my heart-beats one by one,
Send them where the winters perish ;
Then some golden noon recherish
And restore them in the sun,
Flower and scent and dust and dreaming,
  With their heart-beats every one !

Set me in the urge and tide-drift
Of the streaming hosts a-wing !
Breast of scarlet, throat of yellow,
Raucous challenge, wooings mellow —
Every migrant is my fellow,
  Making northward with the spring.
Loose me in the urge and tide-drift
Of the streaming hosts a-wing !

Shrilling pipe or fluting whistle,
  In the valleys come again ;
Fife of frog and call of tree-toad,
All my brothers, five or three-toed,
With their revel no more vetoed,
  Making music in the rain ;
Shrilling pipe or fluting whistle,
  In the valleys come again.

Make me of thy seed to-morrow,
  When the sap begins to stir !
Tawny light-foot, sleepy bruin,
Bright-eyes in the orchard ruin,
Gnarl the good life goes askew in,
  Whiskey-jack, or tanager, —
Make me anything to-morrow,
  When the sap begins to stir !

Make me even (How do I know ?)
  Like my friend the gargoyle there ;
It may be the heart within him
Swells that doltish hands should pin him
Fixed forever in mid-air.
Make me even sport for swallows,
  Like the soaring gargoyle there !

Give me the old clue to follow,
  Through the labyrinth of night !
Clod of clay with heart of fire,
Things that burrow and aspire,
With the vanishing desire,
  For the perishing delight, —
Only the old clue to follow,
  Through the labyrinth of night !

Make me over, mother April,
  When the sap begins to stir !
Fashion me from swamp or meadow,
Garden plot or ferny shadow,
Hyacinth or humble burr !
Make me over, mother April,
  When the sap begins to stir !

Let me hear the far, low summons,
  When the silver winds return ;
Rills that run and streams that stammer,
Goldenwing with his loud hammer,
Icy brooks that brawl and clamor
  Where the Indian willows burn ;
Let me hearken to the calling,
  When the silver winds return,

Till recurring and recurring,
Long since wandered and come back,
Like a whim of Grieg's or Gounod's,
This same self, bird, bud, or Bluenose,
Some day I may capture (Who knows ?)
  Just the one last joy I lack,
Waking to the far new summons,
  When the old spring winds come back.

For I have no choice of being,
  When the sap begins to climb, —
Strong insistence, sweet intrusion,
Vasts and verges of illusion, —

So I win, to time's confusion,
The one perfect pearl of time,
Joy and joy and joy forever,
Till the sap forgets to climb !

Make me over in the morning
From the rag-bag of the world !
Scraps of dream and duds of daring,
Home-brought stuff from far sea-faring,
Faded colors once so flaring,
Shreds of banners long since furled !
Hues of ash and glints of glory,
In the rag-bag of the world !

Let me taste the old immortal
Indolence of life once more ;
Not recalling nor foreseeing,
Let the great slow joys of being
Well my heart through as of yore !
Let me taste the old immortal
Indolence of life once more !

Give me the old drink for rapture,
The delirium to drain,
All my fellows drank in plenty
At the Three Score Inns and Twenty
From the mountains to the main !
Give me the old drink for rapture,
The delirium to drain !

Only make me over, April,
When the sap begins to stir !
Make me man or make me woman,
Make me oaf or ape or human,
Cup of flower or cone of fir ;
Make me anything but neuter
When the sap begins to stir !

A MORE ANCIENT MARINER

THE swarthy bee is a buccaneer,
A burly velveted rover,
Who loves the booming wind in his ear
As he sails the seas of clover.

A waif of the goblin pirate crew,
With not a soul to deplore him,
He steers for the open verge of blue
With the filmy world before him.

His flimsy sails abroad on the wind
Are shivered with fairy thunder ;
On a line that sings to the light of his wings
He makes for the lands of wonder.

He harries the ports of the Hollyhocks,
And levies on poor Sweetbrier ;
He drinks the whitest wine of Phlox,
And the Rose is his desire.

He hangs in the Willows a night and a
day ;
He rifles the Buckwheat patches ;
Then battens his store of pelf galore
Under the tautest hatches.

He woos the Poppy and weds the Peach,
Inveigles Daffodilly,
And then like a tramp abandons each
For the gorgeous Canada Lily.

There 's not a soul in the garden world
But wishes the day were shorter,
When Mariner B. puts out to sea
With the wind in the proper quarter.

Or, so they say ! But I have my doubts ;
For the flowers are only human,
And the valor and gold of a vagrant bold
Were always dear to woman.

He dares to boast, along the coast,
The beauty of Highland Heather, —
How he and she, with night on the sea,
Lay out on the hills together.

He pilfers from every port of the wind,
From April to golden autumn ;
But the thieving ways of his mortal days
Are those his mother taught him.

His morals are mixed, but his will is fixed ;
He prospers after his kind,
And follows an instinct, compass-sure,
The philosophers call blind.

And that is why, when he comes to die,
He 'll have an easier sentence
Than some one I know who thinks jus'
so,
And then leaves room for repentance.

He never could box the compass round ;
He does n't know port from starboard ;
But he knows the gates of the Sundown
Straits,
Where the choicest goods are harbored.

He never could see the Rule of Three,
But he knows a rule of thumb

Better than Euclid's, better than yours,
Or the teachers' yet to come.

He knows the smell of the hydromel
As if two and two were five ;
And hides it away for a year and a day
In his own hexagonal hive.

Out in the day, hap-hazard, alône,
Booms the old vagrant hummer,
With only his whim to pilot him
Through the splendid vast of summer.

He steers and steers on the slant of the
    gale,
Like the fiend or Vanderdecken ;
And there's never an unknown course to
    sail
But his crazy log can reckon.

He drones along with his rough sea-song
And the throat of a salty tar,
This devil-may-care, till he makes his
    lair
By the light of a yellow star.

He looks like a gentleman, lives like a
    lord,
And works like a Trojan hero ;
Then loafs all winter upon his hoard,
With the mercury at zero.

A WINDFLOWER

BETWEEN the roadside and the wood,
    Between the dawning and the dew,
A tiny flower before the wind,
    Ephemeral in time, I grew.

The chance of straying feet came by, —
    Nor death nor love nor any name
Known among men in all their lands, —
    Yet failure put desire to shame.

To-night can bring no healing now,
    The calm of yesternight is gone ;
Surely the wind is but the wind,
    And I a broken waif thereon.

How fair my thousand brothers wave
    Upon the floor of God's abode :
Whence came that careless wanderer
    Between the woodside and the road !

THE MENDICANTS

WE are as mendicants who wait
Along the roadside in the sun.
Tatters of yesterday and shreds
Of morrow clothe us every one.

And some are dotards, who believe
And glory in the days of old ;
While some are dreamers, harping still
Upon an unknown age of gold.

Hopeless or witless ! Not one heeds,
As lavish Time comes down the way
And tosses in the suppliant hat
One great new-minted gold To-day.

Ungrateful heart and grudging thanks,
His beggar's wisdom only sees
Housing and bread and beer enough ;
He knows no other things than these.

O foolish ones, put by your care !
Where wants are many, joys are few ;
And at the wilding springs of peace,
God keeps an open house for you.

But that some Fortunatus' gift
Is lying there within his hand,
More costly than a pot of pearls,
His dulness does not understand.

And so his creature heart is filled ;
His shrunken self goes starved away.
Let him wear brand-new garments still,
Who has a threadbare soul, I say.

But there be others, happier few,
The vagabondish sons of God,
Who know the by-ways and the flowers,
And care not how the world may plod.

They idle down the traffic lands,
And loiter through the woods with spring ;
To them the glory of the earth
Is but to hear a bluebird sing.

They too receive each one his Day ;
But their wise heart knows many things
Beyond the sating of desire,
Above the dignity of kings.

One I remember kept his coin,
And laughing flipped it in the air ;

But when two strolling pipe-players
Came by, he tossed it to the pair.

Spendthrift of joy, his childish heart
Danced to their wild outlandish bars ;
Then supperless he laid him down
That night, and slept beneath the stars.

SONG

Love, by that loosened hair
Well now I know
Where the lost Lilith went
So long ago.

Love, by those starry eyes
I understand
How the sea maidens lure
Mortals from land.

Love, by that welling laugh
Joy claims his own
Sea-born and wind-wayward
Child of the sun.

HACK AND HEW

Hack and Hew were the sons of God
In the earlier earth than now :
One at his right hand, one at his left,
To obey as he taught them how.

And Hack was blind, and Hew was dumb,
But both had the wild, wild heart ;
And God's calm will was their burning will,
And the gist of their toil was art.

They made the moon and the belted stars,
They set the sun to ride ;
They loosed the girdle and veil of the sea,
The wind and the purple tide.

Both flower and beast beneath their hands
To beauty and speed outgrew, —
The furious, fumbling hand of Hack,
And the glorying hand of Hew.

Then, fire and clay, they fashioned a
man,
And painted him rosy brown ;
And God himself blew hard in his eyes :
"Let them burn till they smoulder
down ! "

And " There ! " said Hack, and " There ! "
thought Hew,
" We 'll rest, for our toil is done."
But " Nay," the Master Workman said,
" For your toil is just begun.

" And ye who served me of old as God
Shall serve me anew as man,
Till I compass the dream that is in my
heart,
And perfect the vaster plan."

And still the craftsman over his craft,
In the vague white light of dawn,
With God's calm will for his burning will,
While the mounting day comes on,

Yearning, wind-swift, indolent, wild,
Toils with those shadowy two, —
The faltering, restless hand of Hack,
And the tireless hand of Hew.

ENVOY

I

Have little care that Life is brief,
And less that Art is long.
Success is in the silences
Though Fame is in the song.

II

With the Orient in her eyes,
Life my mistress lured me on.
" Knowledge," said that look of hers,
" Shall be yours when all is done."

Like a pomegranate in halves,
" Drink me," said that mouth of hers,
And I drank who now am here
Where my dust with dust confers.

S. Frances Harrison

("SERANUS")

CHATEAU PAPINEAU

(AFLOAT)

I

THE red tiled towers of the old Château,
  Perched on the cliff above our bark,
Burn in the western evening glow.

The fiery spirit of Papineau
  Consumes them still with its fever spark,
The red tiled towers of the old Château !

Drift by and mark how bright they show,
  And how the mullioned windows —
    mark !
Burn in the western evening glow !

Drift down, or up, where'er you go,
  They flame from out the distant park,
The red tiled towers of the old Château.

So was it once with friend, with foe ;
  Far off they saw the patriot's ark
Burn in the western evening glow.

Think of him now ! One thought bestow,
  As, blazing against the pine trees dark,
The red tiled towers of the old Château
Burn in the western evening glow !

(ASHORE)

II

Within this charmèd cool retreat
  Where bounty dwelt and beauty waits,
The Old World and the New World meet.

Quitting the straggling village street,
  Enter, — passing the great gray gates,
Within this charmèd cool retreat.

Where thrives a garden, ancient, neat,
  Where vulgar noise ne'er penetrates,
The Old World and the New World meet.

For mouldering vault and carven seat
  Tell us that France predominates
Within this charmèd cool retreat,

Though Canada be felt in beat
  Of summer pulse that enervates:
The Old World and the New World meet

In dial, arbor, tropic heat.
  Enter ! And note, how clear all states
That, in this charmèd cool retreat,
The Old World and the New World meet.

III

The garden's past. 'T is forest now
  Encircling us with leafy tide,
Close clustering in green branch and bough.

So beautiful a wood, we vow,
  Was never seen, so fresh, so wide.
The garden's past, 't is forest now,

'T is more, 't is Canada, and how
  Should feudal leaven lurk and hide
Close clustering in green branch and
    bough ?

Quaintly the dial on the brow
  Of yonder open glade is spied ;
The garden's past, 't is forest now,

Yet doth the dial straight endow
  The green with glamor undenied,
Close clustering in green branch and bough.

Such relics who would disallow ?
  We pause and ponder ; turn aside ;
The garden's past, 't is forest now,
Close clustering in green branch and bough.

IV

The glint of steel, the gleam of brocade,
  "Monseigneur" up in his tarnished frame,
A long low terrace, half sun, half shade ;

Tapestry, dusty, dim and frayed,
  Fauteuil and sofa, a flickering flame,
A glint of steel, a gleam of brocade ;

"Mdme" on the wall as a roguish maid,
  Later — some years — as a portly dame,
The long low terrace, half sun, half shade,

Where " Mdme's " ghost and " Monsieur's "
    parade,
And   play   at   *ombre*,   their   favorite
    game !
The glint of steel, the gleam of brocade,

Hang over hall and balustrade.
Paceth a spectral peacock tame
The long low terrace, half sun, half
    shade.

Waketh a nightly serenade
    Where daylight now we see proclaim
The glint of steel, the gleam of brocade,
The long low terrace, half sun, half
    shade !

v

The spell of Age is over all,
The lichened vault, the massive keep,
The shaded walks, the shadowy hall,

And mediæval mists enthrall
The senses bathed in beauty sleep, —
The spell of age is over all !

No marvel if a silken shawl
Be sometimes heard to trail and sweep
The shaded walks, the shadowy hall.

No marvel if a light footfall
Adown the stair be heard to creep, —
The spell of age is over all.

A foot — we muse — both arched and small,
Doth often tread this terrace steep,
Those shaded walks, this shadowy hall

A foot as white as trilliums tall —
Musing, the wall we lightly leap.
The spell of Age is over all !
The shaded walks — the shadowy hall.

SEPTEMBER

I

BIRDS that were gray in the green are black
    in the yellow.
Here where the green remains rocks one
    little fellow.

Quaker in gray, do you know that the
    green is going ?
More than that — do you know that the
    yellow is showing ?

II

Singer of songs, do you know that your
    youth is flying ?
That Age will soon at the lock of your life
    be prying ?

Lover of life, do you know that the brown
    is going ?
More than that — do you know that the
    gray is showing ?

Duncan Campbell Scott

ABOVE ST. IRÉNÉE

I RESTED on the breezy height,
    In cooler shade and clearer air,
        Beneath a maple tree ;
        Below, the mighty river took
Its sparkling shade and sheeny light
Down to the sombre sea,
        And clustered by the leaping brook
The roofs of white St. Irénée.

The sapphire hills on either hand
    Broke down upon the silver tide,
        The river ran in streams,
        In streams of mingled azure-gray

With here a broken purple band,
    And whorls of drab, and beams
        Of shattered silver light astray,
        Where far away the south shore
            gleams.

I walked a mile along the height
    Between the flowers upon the road,
        Asters and golden-rod ;
        And in the gardens pinks and
            stocks,
And gaudy poppies shaking light,
    And daisies blooming near the sod,
        And lowly pansies set in flocks
With purple monkshood overawed.

And there I saw a little child
Between the tossing golden-rod,
Coming along to me ;
  She was a tender little thing,
So fragile-sweet, so Mary-mild,
  I thought her name Marie ;
  No other name methought could
    cling
To any one so fair as she.

And when we came at last to meet,
  I spoke a simple word to her,
"Where are you going, Marie ? "
  She answered and she did not smile,
But oh, her voice, — her voice so sweet,
  "Down to St. Irénée,"
And so passed on to walk her mile,
And left the lonely road to me.

A LITTLE SONG

THE sunset in the rosy west
  Burned soft and high ;
A shore-lark fell like a stone to his nest
  In the waving rye.

A wind came over the garden beds
  From the dreamy lawn,
The pansies nodded their purple heads,
  The poppies began to yawn.

One pansy said : It is only sleep,
  Only his gentle breath :
But a rose lay strewn in a snowy heap,
  For the rose it was only death.

Heigho, we've only one life to live,
  And only one death to die :
Good-morrow, new world, have you nothing
    to give ? —
  Good-bye, old world, good-bye.

AT LES ÉBOULEMENTS

THE bay is set with ashy sails,
With purple shades that fade and flee,
And curling by in silver wales
The tide is straining from the sea.

The grassy points are slowly drowned,
The water laps and overrolls
The wicker pêche ; with shallow sound
A light wave labors on the shoals.

The crows are feeding in the foam,
  They rise in crowds tumultuously,
"Come home," they cry, "come home, —
    come home,
And leave the marshes to the sea."

OTTAWA

CITY about whose brow the north winds
    blow,
Girdled with woods and shod with river
    foam,
Called by a name as old as Troy or Rome,
Be great as they but pure as thine own
    snow ;
Rather flash up amid the auroral glow,
The Lamia city of the northern star,
Than be so hard with craft or wild with
    war,
Peopled with deeds remembered for their
    woe.
Thou art too bright for guile, too young for
    tears,
And thou wilt live to be too strong for
    Time ;
For he may mock thee with his furrowed
    frowns,
But thou wilt grow in calm throughout the
    years,
Cinctured with peace and crowned with
    power sublime,
The maiden queen of all the towered towns.

AT THE CEDARS

YOU had two girls — Baptiste —
One is Virginie —
Hold hard — Baptiste !
Listen to me.

The whole drive was jammed,
In that bend at the Cedars ;
The rapids were dammed
With the logs tight rammed
And crammed ; you might know
The Devil had clinched them below.

We worked three days — not a budge !
"She's as tight as a wedge
On the ledge,"
Says our foreman :
"Mon Dieu ! boys, look here,
We must get this thing clear."

He cursed at the men,
And we went for it then ;
With our cant-dogs arow,
We just gave he-yo-ho,
When she gave a big shove
From above.

The gang yelled, and tore
For the shore ;
The logs gave a grind,
Like a wolf's jaws behind,
And as quick as a flash,
With a shove and a crash,
They were down in a mash,
But I and ten more,
All but Isaàc Dufour,
Were ashore.

He leaped on a log in the front of the rush,
And shot out from the bind
While the jam roared behind;
As he floated along
He balanced his pole
And tossed us a song.
But, just as we cheered,
Up darted a log from the bottom,
Leaped thirty feet fair and square,
And came down on his own.

He went up like a block
With the shock ;
And when he was there,
In the air,
Kissed his hand
To the land.
When he dropped
My heart stopped,
For the first logs had caught him
And crushed him ;
When he rose in his place
There was blood on his face.

There were some girls, Baptiste,
Picking berries on the hillside,
Where the river curls, Baptiste,
You know, — on the still side
One was down by the water,
She saw Isaàc
Fall back.

She did not scream, Baptiste,
She launched her canoe ;
It did seem, Baptiste,
That she wanted to die too,
For before you could think
The birch cracked like a shell

In that rush of hell,
And I saw them both sink —

Baptiste !
He had two girls,
One is Virginie ;
What God calls the other
Is not known to me.

IN NOVEMBER

THE ruddy sunset lies
  Banked along the west ;
In flocks with sweep and rise
  The birds are going to rest.

The air clings and cools,
  And the reeds look cold,
Standing above the pools,
  Like rods of beaten gold.

The flaunting golden-rod
  Has lost her worldly mood,
She 's given herself to God,
  And taken a nun's hood.

The wild and wanton horde,
  That kept the summer revel,
Have taken the serge and cord,
  And given the slip to the Devil.

The winter 's loose somewhere,
  Gathering snow for a fight ;
From the feel of the air
  I think it will freeze to-night.

THE REED-PLAYER

BY a dim shore where water darkening
  Took the last light of spring,
I went beyond the tumult, hearkening
  For some diviner thing.

Where the bats flew from the black elms
    like leaves,
  Over the ebon pool,
Brooded the bittern's cry, as one that
    grieves
  Lands ancient, bountiful.

I saw the fire-flies shine below the wood,
  Above the shallows dank,
As Uriel, from some great altitude,
  The planets rank on rank.

And now unseen along the shrouded mead
One went under the hill ;
He blew a cadence on his mellow reed,
That trembled and was still.

It seemed as if a line of amber fire
Had shot the gathered dusk,
As if had blown a wind from ancient
Tyre
Laden with myrrh and musk.

He gave his luring note amid the fern ;
Its enigmatic fall
Haunted the hollow dusk with golden
turn
And argent interval.

I could not know the message that he
bore,
The springs of life from me
Hidden ; his incommunicable lore
As much a mystery.

And as I followed far the magic player
He passed the maple wood,
And when I passed the stars had risen
there,
And there was solitude.

LIFE AND DEATH

I THOUGHT of death beside the lonely
sea
That went beyond the limit of my sight,
Seeming the image of his mastery,
The semblance of his huge and gloomy
might.

But firm beneath the sea went the great
earth,
With sober bulk and adamantine hold,

The water but a mantle for her girth,
That played about her splendor fold on fold.

And life seemed like this dear familiar
shore
That stretched from the wet sand's last
wavy crease,
Beneath the sea's remote and sombre roar,
To inland stillness and the wilds of peace.

Death seems triumphant only here and
there ;
Life is the sovereign presence everywhere.

THE END OF THE DAY

I HEAR the bells at eventide
Peal slowly one by one,
Near and far off they break and glide,
Across the stream float faintly beauti-
ful
The antiphonal bells of Hull ;
The day is done, done, done,
The day is done.

The dew has gathered in the flowers
Like tears from some unconscious deep,
The swallows whirl around the towers,
The light runs out beyond the long
cloud bars,
And leaves the single stars ;
'T is time for sleep, sleep, sleep,
'T is time for sleep.

The hermit thrush begins again,
Timorous eremite,
That song of risen tears and pain,
As if the one he loved was far away :
" Alas ! another day —"
" And now Good-Night, Good-Night, "
" Good-Night."

Gilbert Parker

SONNETS FROM "A LOVER'S DIARY"

LOVE'S OUTSET

As one would stand who saw a sudden light
Flood down the world, and so encompass
him,

And in that world illumined Seraphim
Brooded above and gladdened to his sight ;
So stand I in the flame of one great thought,
That broadens to my soul from where she
waits,
Who, yesterday, drew wide the inner gates
Of all my being to the hopes I sought.

Her words came to me like a summer-
song,
Blown from the throat of some sweet night-
ingale ;
I stand within her light the whole day
long,
And think upon her till the white stars
fail :
I lift my head towards all that makes life
wise,
And see no farther than my lady's eyes.

A WOMAN'S HAND

I

NONE ever climbed to mountain height of
song,
But felt the touch of some good woman's
palm ;
None ever reached God's altitude of calm,
But heard one voice cry, "Follow !" from
the throng.
I would not place her as an image high
Above my reach, cold, in some dim recess,
Where never she should feel a warm
caress
Of this my hand that serves her till I
die.
I would not set her higher than my heart, —
Though she is nobler than I e'er can be, —
Because she placed me from the crowd
apart,
And with her tenderness she honored me.
Because of this, I hold me worthier
To be her kinsman, while I worship her.

II

A WOMAN'S hand. Lo, I am thankful now
That with its touch I have walked all my
days ;
Rising from fateful and forbidden ways,
To find a woman's hand upon my brow,
Soft as a pad of rose-leaves, and as pure
As upraised palms of angels, seen in
dreams :
And soothed by it, to stand as it beseems
A man who strives to conquer and endure.
A woman's hand ! — There is no better
thing
Of all things human ; it is half divine ;
It hath been more to this lame life of
mine,
When faith was weakness, and despair was
king.

Man more than all men, Thou wast glad to
bless
A woman's sacrifice and tenderness.

ART

I

ART'S use ; what is it but to touch the
springs
Of nature ? But to hold a torch up for
Humanity in Life's large corridor,
To guide the feet of peasants and of
kings !
What is it but to carry union through
Thoughts alien to thoughts kindred, and to
merge
The lines of color that should not diverge,
And give the sun a window to shine through !
What is it but to make the world have
heed
For what its dull eyes else would hardly
scan !
To draw in a stark light a shameless
deed,
And show the fashion of a kingly man !
To cherish honor, and to smite all shame,
To lend hearts voices, and give thoughts a
name !

II

BUT wherein shall art work ? Shall beauty
lead
It captive, and set kisses on its mouth ?
Shall it be strained unto the breast of
youth,
And in a garden live where grows no
weed ?
Shall it, in dalliance with the flaunting
world,
Play but soft airs, sing but sweet-tempered
songs ?
Veer lightly from the stress of all great
wrongs,
And lisp of peace 'mid battle-flags un-
furled ?
Shall it but pluck the sleeve of wanton-
ness,
And gently chide the folly of our time ?
But wave its golden wand at sin's duress,
And say, "Ah me ! ah me !" to fallow
crime ?
Nay; Art serves Truth, and Truth, with
Titan blows,
Strikes fearless at all evil that it knows.

INVINCIBLE

WHY, let them rail ! God's full anointed
ones
Have heard the world exclaim, " We know
you not ! "
They who by their soul's travailing have
brought
Us nearer to the wonder of the suns.
Yet, who can stay the passage of the stars ?
Who can prevail against the thunder-
sound ?
The wire that flashes lightning to the ground
Diverts, but not its potency debars.
So, men may strike quick stabs at Cæsar's
worth, —
They only make his life an endless force,
'Scaped from its penthouse, flashing through
the earth,
And whelming those who railed about his
corse.
Men's moods disturb not those born truly
great :
They know their end ; they can afford to
wait.

ENVOY

WHEN you and I have played the little
hour,
Have seen the tall subaltern Life to
Death
Yield up his sword ; and, smiling, draw
the breath,
The first long breath of freedom ; when
the flower
Of Recompense hath fluttered to our
feet,
As to an actor's ; and the curtain down,
We turn to face each other all alone —
Alone, we two, who never yet did meet,
Alone, and absolute, and free : oh, then,
Oh, then, most dear, how shall be told the
tale ?
Clasped hands, pressed lips, and so clasped
hands again ;
No words. But as the proud wind fills the
sail,
My love to yours shall reach, then one
deep moan
Of joy ; and then our infinite Alone.

E. Pauline Johnson

THE SONG MY PADDLE SINGS

WEST wind, blow from your prairie nest,
Blow from the mountains, blow from the
west.
The sail is idle, the sailor too ;
O wind of the west, we wait for you !
Blow, blow !
I have wooed you so,
But never a favor you bestow.
You rock your cradle the hills between,
But scorn to notice my white lateen.

I stow the sail and unship the mast :
I wooed you long, but my wooing 's past ;
My paddle will lull you into rest :
O drowsy wind of the drowsy west,
Sleep, sleep !
By your mountains steep,
Or down where the prairie grasses sweep,
Now fold in slumber your laggard wings,
For soft is the song my paddle sings.

August is laughing across the sky,
Laughing while paddle, canoe and I
Drift, drift,
Where the hills uplift
On either side of the current swift.

The river rolls in its rocky bed,
My paddle is plying its way ahead,
Dip, dip,
When the waters flip
In foam as over their breast we slip.

And oh, the river runs swifter now ;
The eddies circle about my bow :
Swirl, swirl !
How the ripples curl
In many a dangerous pool awhirl !
And far to forward the rapids roar,
Fretting their margin for evermore ;
Dash, dash,
With a mighty crash,
They seethe and boil and bound and splash.

Be strong, O paddle ! be brave, canoe !
The reckless waves you must plunge into.
Reel, reel,
On your trembling keel,
But never a fear my craft will feel.

We 've raced the rapids ; we 're far ahead :
The river slips through its silent bed.
Sway, sway,
As the bubbles spray
And fall in tinkling tunes away.

And up on the hills against the sky,
A fir tree rocking its lullaby
Swings, swings,
Its emerald wings,
Swelling the song that my paddle sings.

AT HUSKING TIME

At husking time the tassel fades
To brown above the yellow blades
  Whose rustling sheath enswathes the corn
  That bursts its chrysalis in scorn
Longer to lie in prison shades.

Among the merry lads and maids
The creaking ox-cart slowly wades
'Twixt stalks and stubble, sacked, and torn
  At husking time.

The prying pilot crow persuades
The flock to join in thieving raids ;
  The sly raccoon with craft inborn
  His portion steals, — from plenty's horn
His pouch the saucy chipmunk lades
  At husking time.

THE VAGABONDS

What saw you in your flight to-day,
Crows a-winging your homeward way ?

Went you far in carrion quest,
Crows that worry the sunless west ?

Thieves and villains, you shameless
  things !
Black your record as black your wings.

Tell me, birds of the inky hue,
Plunderous rogues — to-day have you

Seen with mischievous, prying eyes
Lands where earlier suns arise ?

Saw you a lazy beck between
Trees that shadow its breast in green,

Teased by obstinate stones that lie
Crossing the current tauntingly ?

Fields abloom on the farther side
With purpling clover lying wide,

Saw you there as you circled by,
Vale-environed a cottage lie —

Girt about with emerald bands,
Nestling down in its meadow lands ?

Saw you this on your thieving raids ?
Speak — you rascally renegades.

Thieved you also away from me
Olden scenes that I long to see ?

If O crows ! you have flown since morn
Over the place where I was born,

Forget, will I, how black you were
Since dawn, in feather and character ;

Absolve, will I, your vagrant band,
Ere you enter your slumber-land.

Arthur Weir

SNOWSHOEING SONG

Hilloo, hilloo, hilloo, hilloo !
Gather, gather, ye men in white ;
The winds blow keenly, the moon is bright,
The sparkling snow lies firm and white ;
Tie on the shoes, no time to lose,
We must be over the hill to-night.

Hilloo, hilloo, hilloo, hilloo !
Swiftly in single file we go,
The city is soon left far below,
Its countless lights like diamonds glow ;
And as we climb we hear the chime
Of church bells stealing o'er the
snow.

Hilloo, hilloo, hilloo, hilloo !
Like winding-sheet about the dead,
O'er hill and dale the snow is spread,
And silences our hurried tread ;
The pines bend low, and to and fro
The magpies toss their boughs o'erhead.

Hilloo, hilloo, hilloo, hilloo !
We laugh to scorn the angry blast,
The mountain top is gained and past.
Descent begins, 't is ever fast —
One short quick run, and toil is done,
We reach the welcome inn at last.

Shake off, shake off the clinging snow ;
Unloose the shoe, the sash untie,
Fling tuque and mittens lightly by ;

The chimney fire is blazing high,
And, richly stored, the festive board
Awaits the merry company.

Remove the fragments of the feast !
The steaming coffee, waiter, bring
Now tell the tale, the chorus sing,
And let the laughter loudly ring ;
Here 's to our host, drink down the toast,
Then up ! for time is on the wing.

Hilloo, hilloo, hilloo, hilloo !
The moon is sinking out of sight,
Across the sky dark clouds take fligh.,
And dimly looms the mountain height ;
Tie on the shoes, no time to lose,
We must be home again to-night.

Ethelwyn Wetherald

THE WIND OF DEATH

The wind of death that softly blows
The last warm petal from the rose,
The last dry leaf from off the tree,
To-night has come to breathe on me.

There was a time I learned to hate,
As weaker mortals learn to love ;
The passion held me fixed as fate,
Burned in my veins early and late,
But now a wind falls from above —

The wind of death that silently
Enshroudeth friend and enemy.

There was a time my soul was thrilled
By keen ambition's whip and spur ;
My master forced me where he willed,
And with his power my life was filled,
But now the old time pulses stir

How faintly in the wind of death,
That bloweth lightly as a breath !

And once, but once at Love's dear feet,
I yielded strength, and life, and heart ;
His look turned bitter into sweet,
His smile made all the world complete ;
The wind blows loves like leaves apart —

The wind of death that tenderly
Is blowing 'twixt my love and me.

O wind of death, that darkly blows
Each separate ship of human woes
Far out on a mysterious sea,
I turn, I turn my face to thee.

THE HOUSE OF THE TREES

Ope your doors and take me in,
Spirit of the wood,
Wash me clean of dust and din,
Clothe me in your mood.

Take me from the noisy light
To the sunless peace,
Where at mid day standeth Night
Signing Toil's release.

All your dusky twilight stores
To my senses give ;
Take me in and lock the doors,
Show me how to live.

Lift your leafy roof for me,
Part your yielding walls :
Let me wander lingeringly
Through your scented halls.

Ope your doors and take me in,
Spirit of the wood ;
Take me — make me next of kin
To your leafy brood.

THE SNOW STORM

THE great soft downy snow storm like a
cloak
Descends to wrap the lean world head to
feet ;
It gives the dead another winding sheet,
It buries all the roofs until the smoke
Seems like a soul that from its clay has
broke.
It broods moon-like upon the Autumn
wheat,
And visits all the trees in their retreat
To hood and mantle that poor shivering
folk.

With wintry bloom it fills the harshest
grooves
In jagged pine stump fences.   Every
sound
It hushes to the footstep of a nun.
Sweet Charity ! that brightens where it
moves
Inducing darkest bits of churlish ground
To give a radiant answer to the sun.

TO FEBRUARY

BUILD high your white and dazzling pal-
aces,
Strengthen your bridges, fortify your
towers,
Storm with a loud and a portentous lip.
And April with a fragmentary breeze,
And half a score of gentle golden hours,
Will leave no trace of your stern
workmanship.

BIOGRAPHICAL NOTES

BIOGRAPHICAL NOTES

These Notes are restricted, for the most part, to the simplest biographical data concerning the poets quoted in this volume, with mention of their leading works. In "Victorian Poets" — the book, by the present editor, to which "A Victorian Anthology" is adapted — a critical review is essayed of those among the following authors who became known earlier than the fiftieth year of Her Majesty's reign.

Where records of birth, death, etc., differ from those previously accepted, there is good authority for the statements made.[1]

ADAMS, Sarah Fuller (Flower), b. Harlow, 1805; d. 1848. Daughter of Benjamin Flower, journalist and politician. In 1834 she married William Bridges Adams. Was connected with the religious society at Finsbury, under the care of William Johnson Fox. "Vivia Perpetua," her dramatic poem, was published in 1841.

ADDLESHAW, Percy, barrister, b. Bowden, Cheshire, 186-. Was graduated at Christchurch, Oxford. Was called to the bar, 1893. Has written articles, poems, and reviews for various publications, and under the pseudonym of "Percy Hemingway" published "Out of Egypt," a volume of short stories, 1894, and "The Happy Wanderer and other Poems," 1895.

AÏDÉ, C. Hamilton, dramatist and songwriter, b. Paris, 1829. Educated at the University of Bonn. Has written a number of novels, and is well known as the author of many favorite songs, set to music by Blumenthal and others. His "Eleonore, and other Poems" appeared in 1856; "The Romance of the Scarlet Leaf, and other Poems," 1865; "Songs without Music," 1882.

AIRD, Thomas, journalist, b. Bowden, 1802; d., Castle Bank, Dumfries, 1876. Educated at Edinburgh University. Editor of the "Dumfries Herald" and later of the "Edinburgh Weekly Journal." In 1852 brought out the works of D. M. Moir, with a memoir, and in 1856 a collective edition of his own poems. Contributor to "Blackwood's."

ALEXANDER, Cecil Frances (Humphries), b. Strabane, Ireland, 182-. Daughter of Major Humphries. Married Rev. William Alexander, afterwards Bishop of Derry, in 1850. Her publications, consisting of stories and poems for children, were issued anonymously. Edited the "Sunday Book of Poetry," of the "Golden Treasury" Series. D. Londonderry, 1895.

ALFORD, Henry, divine, b. London, 1810; d. Canterbury, 1871. Educated at Trinity College, where he took a fellowship in 1834. From 1853 to 1857 preached in the Quebec Street Chapel. In 1857 succeeded to the deanery of Canterbury. First editor of the "Contemporary Review," and author of a standard critical edition of the Greek Testament. The fourth edition of his poems appeared in 1865.

ALLINGHAM, William, editor and balladist, b. Ballyshannon, 1824; d. Whitby, 1889. Contributed to the "Athenæum" and other periodicals, and edited "Fraser." In 1850 his first volume, "Poems," appeared, and in 1855 an enlarged edition of "Day and Night Songs," illustrated by Rossetti, Millais, and A. Hughes. Author of "Songs, Poems and Ballads," 1877; "Evil May-Day," 1883; "Ashby Manor," a drama, 1883; and "Blackberries," 1884.

ANDERSON, Alexander, railway laborer, b. Kirkconnel, Dumfriesshire, Scotland, 1845. Adopted the pseudonym of "Surfaceman," and has published "Songs of Labor," 1873; "The Two Angels and other Poems: with Introductory Sketch by George Gilfillan," 1875; "Songs of the Rail," 1877, 1881; "Ballads and Sonnets," 1879.

ARMSTRONG, G. F. — See *G. F. Savage-Armstrong*.

ARNOLD, Sir Edwin, editor and Sanscrit scholar, b. Sussex, 1832. Educated at King's College, London, and University College, Oxford. Was made Principal of the Government Sanscrit College at Poona and Fellow of the University of Bombay. In 1861 he returned to England and went on the staff of the London "Daily Telegraph," during his connection with which he brought about the expedition of George Smith to Assyria in 1873, and that of Henry M. Stanley to Africa in 1874. When the Queen was proclaimed Empress of India, he was named a Companion of the Star of

[1] Where an author has died since the preparation of these biographies the date of decease is appended.

India; the King of Siam conferred upon him the decoration of the Order of the White Elephant; and in 1876 he received the Second Class of the Imperial Order of the Medjidie from the Sultan of Turkey. Visited America, 1892, and gave readings from his poems. As will be seen from the following list of his principal poetical works, he has devoted his muse to the idealization of the Oriental legendary, and especially the Buddhist faith, making this a field of his own, as compared with any English poet since Sir William Jones. Was knighted by the Queen in 1888. Author of "Poems Narrative and Lyrical," 1853; "Griselda and other Poems," 1856; "The Poets of Greece," 1869; "The Light of Asia," 1879; "Indian Poetry," 1881; "Pearls of the Faith," 1883; "India Revisited," 1886; "Lotus and Jewel," 1887; "The Light of the World," 1891; "Japonica," 1891; "Potiphar's Wife and other Poems," 1892. (D. London, 1904.)

ARNOLD, Matthew, critic of life, letters, and belief, b. Laleham, 24 December, 1822; d. Liverpool, 15 April, 1888. Eldest son of Dr. Thomas Arnold, the renowned master of Rugby. Educated at Winchester, Rugby, and Balliol College, Oxford. Scholar of Balliol, 1840; winner of the Newdigate prize by his poem of "Cromwell," 1843; Fellow of Oriel College, 1845. Professor of Poetry, Oxford, 1857-67. Eminently a university man and equally an independent thinker, he made and retained his hold on Oxford thought as no other man of his generation, arousing younger minds to a fine enthusiasm. Was a comrade of Clough, — the subject of his poem, "The Scholar Gypsy," and of the pastoral elegy, "Thyrsis," — and with him experienced the unsettling effect of the Tractarian movement. A noble melancholy thenceforth tinged his writings. He arrived at something like agnosticism, and warred against dogma of every kind; but emancipated thought, and was the rebuker of vulgarity and the apostle of true culture. Was the greatest of Victorian critics, as may be seen from his lectures "On Translating Homer," 1861; "Celtic Literature," 1868, etc.; and from his typical books of social and theological criticism: "Culture and Anarchy," 1869; "St. Paul and Protestantism," 1870; "Literature and Dogma," 1873; "Literature and Science," 1882. His earliest poems were "The Strayed Reveller," etc., 1848; "Empedocles on Etna," 1855. These were followed by "Merope," 1861; "New Poems," 1868. The prefaces to some of his own editions, and to editions of Wordsworth and Byron, are of the highest order. For years he held official positions as Inspector of Schools and Commissioner on Education. Received the following degrees : LL. D., Edinburgh, 1869; Oxford, 1870; Cambridge, 1883. Cp. "Victorian Poets," chaps. iii, xii. [E. C. S.]

ASHBY-STERRY, Joseph, essayist, poet, and novelist, b. London, 1838. Resident in London, where he is an authority on matters con-

nected with pleasure-boating on the Thames, of which he has always been an ardent devotee. Much of his writing is related to his out-door life. Besides his contributions to magazines, he has written regularly for the press, and is a member of the editorial staff of the London "Graphic." Among his best known works are "Shuttlecock Papers," 1873; "Tiny Travels," 1874; "Boudoir Ballads," 1876; "Cucumber Chronicles," 1887; "The Lazy Minstrel," 1887; "Nutshell Novels," 1890; "A Naughty Girl," 1893.

ASHE, Thomas, instructor, b. Stockport, Cheshire, 1836; d. 1889. Was graduated at St. John's, Cambridge; was ordained and became a teacher. Afterwards was curate of Silverstorn, Northamptonshire, but in a short time resigned and resumed teaching. Author of several volumes of verse, the first appearing in 1859. Published a drama, "The Sorrows of Hypsipyle." "Songs Now and Then" appeared in 1875, and in 1886 a complete edition of his poems was issued.

AUSTIN, Alfred, journalist and critic, b. Headingley, near Leeds, 1835. Educated at Stonyhurst, and at St. Mary's College, Oscott. Took a degree at the University of London, 1853; was called to the bar in 1857, but devoted himself almost entirely to literature. Has been a writer for the "Standard" and the "Quarterly Review," and editor of the "National Review." Author of notable criticism on "The Poetry of the Period," of various essays, three novels, and of many volumes of poems and poetic dramas. Among the latter are : "The Human Tragedy," 1872, 1876; "Savonarola," 1881; "At the Gate of the Convent," 1885; "English Lyrics," 1890; "Prince Lucifer," 1891; "Narrative Poems," 1891; "Fortunatus the Pessimist," 1892. See p. 710.

AYTOUN, William Edmonstoune, professor, b. Edinburgh, 1813; d. Blackhills, near Elgin, 1865. Author of "Lays of the Scottish Cavaliers," 1848, and many other poems, and also of stories published in "Blackwood's." He was at one time a member of the staff of "Blackwood's" and then professor of rhetoric and belles-lettres in the University of Edinburgh. In addition to his other literary labors, he collected and annotated the ballads of Scotland. "Firmilian," 1854, was a brilliant take-off, satirizing the "Spasmodic School" of poetry. The racy "Bon Gaultier's Book of Ballads," 1856, was the joint work of Aytoun and Sir Theo. Martin.

BAILEY, Philip James, barrister, b. Nottingham, 1816. Studied at the University of Glasgow. Admitted to the bar in 1840. "Festus," his extended poem, was first published in 1839, and after numerous editions the enlarged "Jubilee Edition" was brought out in 1889, and included most of his other poems, viz. : "The Angel World," 1850; "The Mystic," "The Spiritual Legend," and "The Universal Hymn," 1868. (D. Nottingham, 1902.)

BALLANTINE, James, artist, b. Edinburgh, 1808; d. 1877. Published "The Gaberlunzie's Wallet," 1843; "The Miller of Dearbaugh," and a collective edition of his poems, in 1856. Known also as a painter on glass. Some of his art work may be found in Westminster Palace.

BANIM, John, dramatist and novelist, b. Kilkenny, 1798; d. 1842. With his brother Michael, wrote a series of novels dealing with Irish life. "Tales of the O'Hara Family" vividly portray the condition of the Irish peasantry. His few poems are published chiefly in a volume entitled "The Chant of the Cholera: Songs for the Irish People."

BARHAM, Richard Harris, clerical wit, b. Canterbury, 1788; d. 1845. Known as "Thomas Ingoldsby," and contributed a series of quaint and comical stories in rhyme, "The Ingoldsby Legends," to "Bentley's Miscellany." These were afterwards collected in book form, and are still famous in their kind. Also wrote a novel, "My Cousin Nicholas." Appointed minor canon of St. Paul's and became vicar of the City churches of St. Augustine and St. Faith.

BARING-GOULD, Sabine, clergyman, b. Exeter, 1834. Took the degree of M. A. at Clare College, Cambridge, 1856. Appointed incumbent of Dalton, Thirsh, 1869, and rector of East Mersea, Colchester, 1871. In 1881 became rector of Lew-Trenchard. Has written extensively on religious subjects, and of late years has become well known as a novelist. Brought out a volume of poems in 1868.

BARLOW, George, b. London, 1847. Educated at Harrow School and at Exeter College, Oxford. His first book, "Poems and Sonnets," 1871, appeared while he was an undergraduate. Since then, a fluent lyrical writer, he has written many volumes of poetry, of which "The Pageant of Life," 1888, has gained the most attention.

BARLOW, Jane, b. Clontarf, County Dublin, 1860, in which locality she has always resided. Daughter of the Rev. James Barlow, of Dublin University. Her verses picturing Irish life and sentiment have been issued in both England and the United States. "Bogland Studies," her first book, was published in 1892. This was followed by "Irish Idyls," 1893; "Kerrigan's Quality," 1894. Encouraged by the favor awarded to these sketches and poems, Miss Barlow is engaged upon other work. "The End of Elfintown," a fairy tale in verse, and an English rendering of the "Batrachomyomachia," are announced for publication.

BARNES, William, clergyman, b. Dorset, 1801; d. 1886. Was an engraver in his youth, but meanwhile took up the study of Oriental languages. In 1847 became curate of Whitcombe, and in 1862 rector of Winterbourne Came. His poems in Dorset dialect were published in 1844, and again in 1856. "Poems of Rural Life," 1868, is a translation into ordinary English of some of his unpublished poems. Was author, also, of important works bearing on philology and early English history.

BAYLY, Thomas Haynes, song-writer, b. Bath, 1797; d. Boulogne-sur-Mer, 1839. Studied theology and law. Began writing poetry when young. At one time his ballads were quite popular among the English upper classes; some of the best known are, "The Rose that all are Praising," "O, no! We never mention Her," and "Gaily the Troubadour."

BEACONSFIELD, Benjamin Disraeli, Earl of, novelist, statesman, and Premier of the Realm, b. London, 1804; d. London, 1881. Educated under tutors. Entered Parliament, 1837. Chancellor of the Exchequer in 1852 and again in 1858, and prime minister in 1868 and 1874-80. In 1877 was raised to the peerage and created Earl of Beaconsfield. His novels, "Coningsby," 1844, and "Sybil," 1845, revolutionized certain political methods of the time and gave him a brilliant reputation as a novelist of politics and high-life which he maintained to his closing years, "Lothair," 1870, having been read still more widely than his earlier works. "The Wondrous Tale of Alroy" appeared in 1833; "Rise of Iskander" and the "Revolutionary Epic," 1834; "Tragedy of Count Alarcos," 1839. "Endymion," his last novel, was issued in 1880.

BEATTY, Pakenham Thomas, b. 1855. Author of "To my Lady," 1878; "Three Women of the People," 1881; and "Marcia, a Tragedy," 1884.

BEDDOES, Thomas Lovell, physiologist, b. Clifton, 1803; d. Basle, Switzerland, 1849. Son of Thomas Beddoes, M. D., an eminent savant. Took his degree at Pembroke College, Oxford; adopted his father's profession, but having means, studied in Germany and mastered and advanced the science of physiology. A precocious genius, he wrote plays and lyrics while yet a youth, publishing "The Bride's Tragedy" in 1822. This gained the critical favor of George Darley, like whom he was indeed "a belated Elizabethan." The maturer and more powerful drama, "Death's Jest Book," appeared after his death, in the Pickering collection of his plays and poems, 1851.

BEECHING, Henry Charles, clergyman, b. 185-. Rector of Yattendon, Berks. Edited some of Shakespeare's plays, and in conjunction with J. W. Mackail and J. B. B. Nichols wrote "Love in Idleness," published in 1883, and "Love's Looking Glass," 1891, both volumes of verse. Author of "In a Garden," a volume of lyrics, 1895.

BELL, H. T. Mackenzie, critic, b. Liverpool, 1856. He has had an active literary career, contributing to the "Academy" and other periodicals, and writing many critical and biographical notices of Victorian authors. Has published in verse "The Keeping of the Vow," 1879; "Verses of Varied Life," 1882; "Old

Year Leaves," 1883. In 1884 brought out a biographical and critical monograph on Charles Whitehead, of which an enlarged edition has since appeared. "Spring's Immortality and other Poems" was issued in 1893. Is now about to publish a monograph on Christina Rossetti.

BENNETT, William Cox, journalist, b. Greenwich, 1820. Has always taken an active interest in educational matters and in the establishment of local institutions for the benefit of the people. Has written several volumes of verse, the first of which appeared in 1843. Was a member of the staff of the "Weekly Dispatch," the London "Figaro," and other periodicals. Received the degree of LL. D. from the University of Tusculum in 1869. D. 1895.

BENSON, Arthur Christopher, educator, b. Wellington College (of which his father was then head-master), Wokingham, 1862. Eldest surviving son of Edward White Benson, Archbishop of Canterbury. Educated at Eton and King's College, Cambridge. Took a first class in the Classical Tripos, 1884. Assistant master at Eton College, 1885, a position which he still holds. Has published "Memoirs of Arthur Hamilton," 1886, under the pseudonym of "Christopher Carr;" "Life of Archbishop Laud," 1887; "Poems," 1893; "Lyrics," 1885.

BESANT, Sir Walter. See *Addenda,* p. 710.

BLACKIE, John Stuart, professor, b. Glasgow, 1809; d. 1895. Educated at Aberdeen and Edinburgh Universities; also studied in Germany and Italy. In 1841 became Professor of Humanity at Marischal College, Aberdeen, and in 1852 Professor of Greek in the University of Edinburgh. Author of "Homer and the Iliad," 1868, and "Lays and Legends of Ancient Greece," 1869. In 1860 his "Lyrical Poems" appeared, and in 1869 "Musa Burschicosa," a book of rollicking student songs. Much sturdy and characteristic verse came from the pen of this fine old Greek and German scholar. His nature was of a Scotch-Homeric cast, his person and manner not to be forgotten, and he left his impress upon all who came within his range.

BLAIKIE, John Arthur, b. London, 1850. Was on the staff of the "Saturday Review." Published his first book, "Poems by Two Friends," with Mr. Edmund Gosse.

BLANCHARD, Laman, journalist and humorist, b. Great Yarmouth, 1804; d. 1845. Became secretary to the Zoölogical Society in 1827. Issued his first book of poems, 1828. Wrote for many magazines and papers; editor of the "Courier" and sub-editor of the "Examiner." In 1876 an edition of his poems was published, with a memoir by Blanchard Jerrold.

BLAND, Edith (Nesbit), b. 1858. Wrote verses before her twelfth year. Her first published poems appeared in the "Sunday Magazine" and "Good Words." In 1879 married Mr. Bland. Published "Lays and Legends," 1886, and "Leaves of Life," 1888. Has also

been a successful writer of children's stories and verse.

BLEW, William John, clergyman, b. about 1806; d. 1894. Was graduated at Wadham College, Oxford, 1830; ordained, 1832. Has published several religious works.

BLIND, Mathilde, b. 1850. A noteworthy article on Shelley which appeared in the "Westminster Review" was her first published work. "The Prophecy of Oran," a narrative poem, was issued in 1881; "Heather on Fire," 1886; "The Ascent of Man," a poem on evolution, 1889; "Songs and Sonnets," 1893. Translated the journal of Marie Bashkirtseff. D. 1896.

BLUNT, Wilfrid Scawen, b. Crabbet Park, Crawley, Sussex, 1840. Educated at Stonyhurst, and at St. Mary's College, Oscott. Member of the diplomatic service from 1858 to 1869. In the latter year married Lady Anne Isabella Noel, granddaughter of Lord Byron. Has spent much time in the East. He favored the cause of Arabi Pasha, and is an ardent advocate of justice to Ireland. Author of "The Love Sonnets of Proteus," 1881; "In Vinculis," and "The New Pilgrimage," both issued in 1889.

BONAR, Horatius, divine, b. Edinburgh, 1808. Educated at the University of Edinburgh. In 1837 was ordained; became the pastor of the Presbyterian church at Kelso, and while there began the publication of the "Kelso Tracts." Joined the Free Church movement in 1843, and since 1866 has been the pastor of the Chalmers Memorial Free Church in Edinburgh. At one time editor of "The Journal of Prophecy," and "The Christian Treasury." Published several volumes of hymns.

BOURDILLON, Francis William, educator, b. Woolbedding, 1852. Son of Rev. Francis Bourdillon, author of many religious works. Educated at Worcester College, Oxford. For some years private resident tutor to the sons of Prince and Princess Christian. Some of his published works as "Among the Flowers and other Poems," 1874; "Ailes d'Alouette," republished in the United States, 1891; "A Lost God," 1892; and "Sursum Corda," 1893.

BOWRING, Sir John, scholar and diplomatist, b. Exeter, 1792; d. 1872. An editor of the "Westminster Review." Took an active part in political and social questions. Elected to Parliament in 1835, and afterwards filled diplomatic positions in China and India. Was knighted in 1854. He was widely famous as a linguist, and published translations of the poetry of many lands.

BRIDGES, Robert Seymour, physician, b. 1844. Educated at Eton, and Corpus Christi College, Oxford. After travelling in foreign countries, studied medicine in London and practised until 1882. A number of his poems, under the title of "The Growth of Love," were beautifully printed at the private press of a friend. "Shorter Poems," published in 1890, and enlarged in 1894, contains the greater portion of his lyrical work. He has written several classical plays.

BRONTË, Emily and Anne. Emily, b. Yorkshire, 1818; d. 1848. Anne, b. Yorkshire, 1820; d. 1849. Daughters of Rev. Patrick Brontë. Educated at home and at a school for clergymen's daughters. Emily adopted the pseudonym of "Ellis Bell," and Anne that of "Acton Bell." In conjunction with their sister, Charlotte Brontë, they published a book of verse, "Poems," 1846. Emily also wrote one novel, "Wuthering Heights," 1846; and Anne produced two, "Agnes Grey," 1846, and "The Tenant of Wildfell Hall," 1848.

BROOKE, Stopford Augustus, clergyman, b. Letterkenny, Donegal, 1832. Educated at Trinity College, Dublin. Curate of St. Matthew, Marylebone, and afterwards of Kensington; minister of St. James' Chapel, 1866-75; appointed Chaplain in Ordinary to the Queen, 1872; and in 1876 became minister of Bedford Chapel. In 1880 seceded from the Church of England. He has published several theological works, besides "Riquet of the Tuft," 1880; "Poems," 1888; "Tennyson: His Art in Relation to Modern Life," 1894; and "Life and Letters of the late Frederick W. Robertson," which appeared in 1865.

BROUGH, Robert Barnabas, dramatist and journalist, b. 1828; d. 1860. His early literary work consisted of amusing dramas produced at the Olympic and other theatres, and of journalism in a light vein. Later endeavored to do more serious work. Published "Songs of the Governing Classes," 1855; and a collection of "tales in prose and verse."

BROWN, Ford Madox, artist, b. Calais, 1821; d. 1893. A veteran leader in the Pre-Raphaelite school, and wrote and lectured on art. Was engaged for eleven years on a fresco series in the Manchester Town Hall.

BROWN, Oliver Madox, son of Ford Madox Brown, b. Finchley, 1855; d. 1874. He possessed unwonted literary and artistic gifts. Exhibited pictures at the Royal Academy, and showed marked precocity as a writer of verse and prose. "The Black Swan," his prose romance, was revised and published as "Gabriel Denver," but the original and better text appears in his collected works, edited in two volumes after his premature death, by Mr. W. M. Rossetti and Dr. Hueffer.

BROWNING, Elizabeth Barrett (Moulton-Barrett), the most inspired of womanpoets, b. Coxoe Hall, Durham, 6 March, 1806; d. Florence, Italy, 29 June, 1861. The record of her birth is now substantiated, it having been given, until recently, as "at Hope End, Ledbury, 1809." She was, therefore, six years older than her husband, and in her forty-third year when Robert Barrett Browning, their only child, was born. Her youth was passed in Ledbury, at the home of her father, a rich Jamaican, Mr. Moulton, who had added the name

of Barrett to his own. In childhood, her precocity and love of study were marvellous. She wrote verse, delighted in the classics, and, as she grew older, learned Hebrew and Italian. She read Greek poetry and philosophy in the original texts, and even the Greek Christian Fathers, — often in company with Hugh Stuart Boyd, as exquisitely related in "Wine of Cyprus." Published anonymously her first book of verse, "An Essay on Mind," 1827. Her translation of the "Prometheus Bound" appeared, with poems of her own, 1833. In 1837 she ruptured a blood-vessel, and thenceforth was always fragile, — confined for years at a time to her room, where she pursued her work and studies, and, until after her marriage, saw only her near and devoted friends. Meantime her reputation increased with "The Seraphim," 1838; "The Romaunt of the Page," 1839; and "A Drama of Exile," 1844; and in the last-named year she brought out the first collective edition of her poems. John Kenyon made her acquainted, 1845, with Robert Browning, who was gratified by an allusion to himself in "Lady Geraldine's Courtship." The poets fell in love, but Mr. Barrett absolutely forbade his daughter to contract marriage. Disregarding his mandate, she wedded Browning, 12 Sept., 1846, and went with him to Italy, never again seeing her father, and being relentlessly unforgiven by him to the end. After her marriage her poetry increased in beauty and power; she wrote her most sustained works and noblest lyrics, and her fame, despite her technical shortcomings, became world-wide. America loved her, and was loved by her in turn. A poet of humanity, freedom, and enthusiasm, she sang spontaneously, and from a glowing heart. Her masterpiece of art and feeling is the "Sonnets from the Portuguese," 1850, — inspired by her love and marriage, and unequalled by any English sonnet-series except Shakespeare's own. "Casa Guidi Windows," 1851, is her chief tribute to the Italian cause; "Aurora Leigh," her longest work, a highly subjective romantic tale, embodying her humane and liberal views, appeared in 1856; and "Poems before Congress" in 1860. Her "Last Poems" were edited by her husband the year after her death. Her only prose relics are her letters, and the Essays on the Greek - Christian and English Poets, contributed to the "Athenæum," 1842. Her remains lie in the English burying-ground at Florence. — Cp. R. H. Horne, J. Kenyon, and "Victorian Poets," chap. iv. [E. C. S.]

BROWNING, Robert, the poet of dramatic psychology, and in years, genius, and fame the Laureate's only peer, b. Camberwell, near London, 7 May, 1812; d. Venice, Dec. 12, 1889. On his father's side he was of somewhat humble English stock, and inherited West Indian creole blood from his paternal grandmother. On his mother's side he was Scottish and German. His father's means were limited, but young Browning attended lectures at the University of London, and was afterward enabled to travel on the Continent. From the first he showed originality, and was little affected by current modes of art and thought. His earliest book was the fragmentary "Pauline," 1833, afterward suppressed, but latterly included in the "complete editions." This was followed by "Paracelsus," 1835, which secured for the poet a small set of firm adherents. "Strafford," his first acting drama, was played by Macready at Covent Garden, 1837. The enigmatical "Sordello," 1840, made it plain that he was no candidate for immediate popularity, but took his appeal to the intellectual few. From 1841 to 1846, however, many of his most beautiful and dramatic lyrics and idyls came out in the eight parts of "Bells and Pomegranates;" which embraced, also, the great series of earlier dramas : "Pippa Passes," 1840 ; "King Victor and King Charles," 1842 ; "The Return of the Druses," 1843 ; "A Blot in the 'Scutcheon," 1843 ; "Colombe's Birthday," 1844 ; "Luria," 1846 ; and "A Soul's Tragedy," 1846. These intensely wrought and penetrating studies of human life, thought, and circumstance, fervid with color, and saturated with learning, came from the brain of one who could be as melodious or as rugged as he chose, and at will impassioned or analytic. They impressed careful readers with his greatness ; but he failed to reach the common people, or gain the fame then won by Tennyson, until the afternoon of his vigorous life. Meantime he wrote ceaselessly ; his marriage with Miss Barrett, of itself, with their life in Rome, invested him with interest, and finally such works as "Men and Women," 1855, "Dramatis Personæ," 1864, "The Ring and the Book," 1868-69, were as eagerly welcomed by the English-reading world as by those who so long had recognized his gifts. After his marriage (related in the preceding notice), the thoroughly ideal life of "the wedded poets" was something that has become historic, no other union of two poets so individually great having ever occurred. When Mrs. Browning died, Browning left Florence, and resided chiefly in London for many years. Among his volumes hitherto unmentioned are "Balaustion's Adventure," 1871 ; "Fifine at the Fair," 1872 ; "Red Cotton Night-Cap Country," 1873 ; "Aristophanes' Apology," 1875 ; "The Inn Album," 1875 ; "La Saisiaz," 1878 ; "Dramatic Idyls," 1879, 1880 ; "Jocoseria," 1883 ; "Ferishtah's Fancies," 1884 ; "Parleyings," etc., 1887 ; and the small collection of his last lyrics, "Asolando," 1889. Browning, after all this prodigal work, and a hale and optimistic old age, died serenely, and was buried in Westminster Abbey. For years before his death his name had been as splendid as it was formerly obscure. The original Browning Club was founded in 1881, for the study and exposition of his works. His extreme votaries rank him with Shakespeare, praise him for his more involved and prosaic labors, and look askance at other modern poets, — Tennyson not excepted. But these are they who care less for absolute poetry than for metaphysics. Of late a finer discrimination is exercised, and the poet's

highest qualities are more clearly comprehended, even by the Browning societies. His truest lover is one who takes him at his best, as an affluent artist, and the most profound modern revealer of the human soul, without over-valuing his excess of analysis and didacticism. Cp. "Victorian Poets," chaps. ix, xii.
[E. C. S.]

BUCHANAN, Robert, dramatist and novelist, b. Glasgow, 1841. Educated at the University of Glasgow, where he met the poet David Gray, with whom he afterwards occupied lodgings in London. He is a versatile and polemic man of letters, has won distinction in various departments of literature, and is an active writer of plays for the stage. Has been a regular contributor to the "Contemporary Review" for a number of years. Author of "Undertones," 1860 ; "Idyls and Legends of Inverburn," 1865; "London Poems," 1866; "The Book of Orm," 1870 ; "Ballads of Life, Love, and Humor," 1882. He has also written several novels. Among his plays are "A Nine Days' Queen," "Lady Clare," "Storm-Beaten," and "Sophia." A beautiful edition of his poems, in three volumes, came out in 1874. Cp. "Victorian Poets," ch. x. (D. London, 1901.)

BULWER, Sir Edward Lytton. See *Edward, Lord Lytton.*

BURBIDGE, Thomas, b. 1816. Author of "Poems, Longer and Shorter," 1838 ; "Hours and Days," 1851. Published, in connection with A. H. Clough, "Ambarvalia, and other Poems," 1849.

BYRON, Mary C. G. (Mary C. Gillington), b. Cheshire, 1861. Became associate of the Royal Academy of Music, 1887. Married George F. Byron in 1892. Joint author, with her sister, of "Poems," 1892, and is a contributor of both verse and prose to English and American journals.

CALL, Wathen Marks Wilks, reformer, b. 1817 ; d. 1890. Was graduated at Cambridge ; took Holy Orders, but withdrew from the church in 1856. Contributed to the "Leader," and the "Westminster," "Theological," and "Fortnightly" Reviews. Interested in social and political reform. Published, in verse, "Reverberations," 1842, and "Golden Histories," in addition to an early volume which contained some fine translations.

CALVERLEY, Charles Stuart, educator and lecturer, b. Martley, Worcestershire, 1831 ; d. 1884. Educated at Balliol College, Oxford, and Christ's College, Cambridge. Translated successfully from the Latin, and wrote clever parodies and humorous verse. Published "Verses and Translations," 1862 ; a "Verse Translation of Theocritus," 1869 ; "Fly Leaves," 1872. Resided in Cambridge, teaching and lecturing at college. Studied law, and became a member of the Inner Temple, 1865.

CAMERON, George Frederick, journalist, b. New Glasgow, Nova Scotia, 1854 ; d. 1887.

Educated at Queen's University, Kingston. Resided in the United States for several years, and wrote for the American and Canadian periodicals. Author of "Lyrics on Freedom, Love, and Death." A writer of promise, whose loss was deeply regretted.

CAMPBELL, William Wilfred, government service, b. Western Ontario, 1861. Educated at University College, Toronto, and Cambridge, Mass. His verse appears in American magazines. Has held an appointment in the Department of the Secretary of State at Ottawa since 1893. Author of "Lake Lyrics," 1889; "The Dread Voyage," 1893; "Mordred, a Tragedy," and "Hildebrand," dramas in blank verse, 1895.

CANTON, William, journalist, b. Island of Chusan, off the coast of China, 1845. Passed his childhood in Jamaica and was educated in France. Removed to Scotland and joined the staff of the Glasgow "Herald." "A Lost Epic and other Poems" was published in 1887.

CARLYLE, Jane Welsh, b. Haddington, 1801; d. London, 1866. Married Thomas Carlyle, 1826. A collection of her letters was made and edited by J. A. Froude, 1883. Her verse, of which at one time she wrote a great deal, was spirited and original.

CARLYLE, Thomas, essayist and historian, b. Ecclefechan, Scotland, 1795; d. Chelsea, London, 1881. Educated at Edinburgh University. Studied for the ministry, but gave that up for law, which he also shortly abandoned. He taught school and was tutor in a private family. Owing to his individual style, he did not take his proper place in literature until the publication of the "French Revolution," 1837. Most of his verse was contributed to magazines between 1823 and 1833. Was made Lord Rector of Edinburgh University in 1866. Among his works are "Sartor Resartus," 1833–34; "Chartism," 1839; "Heroes and Hero-Worship," 1841; "Oliver Cromwell's Letters and Speeches," 1845; "History of Frederick the Great," 1858–65.

CARMAN, Bliss, man of letters, b. Fredericton, N. B., 1861. Was graduated at the University of New Brunswick, 1881, receiving the degree of M. A., 1884. During the past few years has resided chiefly in the United States, where he has been actively engaged as an editor and writer. Member of the editorial staff of several periodicals, including the New York "Independent" and the Chicago "Chap-Book." A frequent contributor of poetry and critical articles to the mazagines. His published books are, "Low Tide on Grand Pré," 1893; and "Songs from Vagabondia," with Richard Hovey as joint author, 1894.

"CARROLL, Lewis." — See Charles Lutwidge Dodgson.

CASTILLA, Ethel, resident of Victoria, Australia. "An Australian Girl" was contributed to a Melbourne newspaper.

CLARKE, Herbert Edwin, b. Chatteris, Isle of Ely, 1852. Educated in schools conducted by the Society of Friends, of which denomination his parents were members. Published "Songs in Exile," 1879; "Storm-Drift," 1882.

CLEPHANE, Elizabeth Cecilia, b. Edinburgh, 1830; d. Melrose, 1869. Her poem, "The Ninety and Nine," made famous by the singing evangelist, Ira D. Sankey, first appeared in the "Family Treasury," and afterwards in the "Christian Age."

CLOUGH, Arthur Hugh, educator, b. Liverpool, 1819; d. Florence, Italy, 1861. Spent most of his childhood in the United States, but later was sent to Rugby, and was a favorite pupil of Dr. Arnold. He took the Balliol Scholarship in 1836 and went to Oxford. Subsequently he was appointed Fellow and tutor at Oriel. Visited Rome and Paris, and wrote a notable series of letters from both places. In 1852 he came to the United States and established himself at Cambridge, Mass., where he lectured, taught, and contributed to various periodicals. During his American sojourn he won the friendship and alliance of the selectest leaders of the Harvard literary group. At Oxford he is remembered with Matthew Arnold and the struggle for freedom of opinion. His life and death inspired Arnold's "The Scholar Gypsy," and elegy of "Thyrsis." In 1853 he returned to England, accepting office in the Education Department of the Privy Council, which he held until his death. "The Bothie of Tober-na-Vuolich" was published in 1848, and a volume of poems, "Ambarvalia," which he wrote with Thomas Burbidge, appeared in 1849. Completed his revision of Dryden's "Plutarch," 1859. After his death, his collected poems were brought out, 1862, with a memoir by his friend, Prof. C. E. Norton.

COLERIDGE, Hartley, son of Samuel Taylor Coleridge, b. Clevedon, 1796; d. 1849. Attended Merton College, Oxford, and obtained a Fellowship at Oriel College. Attempted a literary career in London, and afterward started a boys' school at Ambleside, but was unsuccessful in both. Met Wordsworth when a boy and formed a friendship with him that lasted until his death. Contributed to "Blackwood's." Published a volume of poems in 1833. His works were edited and republished by his brother in 1851.

COLERIDGE, Sara, daughter of Samuel Taylor Coleridge, b. Keswick, 1802; d. 1852. For a number of years made her home with her uncle, Robert Southey. In 1829, married her cousin, Henry Nelson Coleridge. Did some valuable editorial work, and translating. "Phantasmion," a fairy tale, appeared in 1837.

COLLINS, Mortimer, novelist and journalist, b. Plymouth, 1827; d. Richmond, 1876. Published his first book of verse, "Idyls and Rhymes," in 1855, while master of mathematics at Queen Elizabeth's College, Guernsey. In

1856 gave up this position and devoted himself entirely to writing. "Summer Songs" appeared in 1860. Was the author of a number of novels, of which "Sweet Anne Page," 1868, is one of the best known. Contributed to newspapers and magazines.

COOK, Eliza, b. Southwark, 1812; d. 1889. In her youth her writings were published in periodicals and attracted a great deal of notice. Established "Eliza Cook's Journal," a weekly periodical, 1849, but owing to failing health discontinued it in 1854. "Lays of a Wild Harp" appeared in 1835, and her collected "Poems," 1840; "New Echoes," 1864; and "Diamond Dust," 1865. Her poems attained wide popularity and have passed through various editions.

COOPER, Thomas, "The Chartist," b. Leicester, 1805; d. 1892. Self-educated, and pursued his studies under great disadvantages. Took an active part in political reform and devoted his time to lecturing in England and Scotland. Collected his poetical works in 1878.

CORY, William, educator, b. 1823; d. 1892. Known as William Johnson during the greater part of his life, and while bearing this name published "Ionica," a book of chaste and exquisite verse, 1858, and several text-books on the classics. Was educated at Eton, and held a Fellowship at King's College, Cambridge. Assistant master at Eton, 1847-71. Soon after leaving Eton, adopted the name of Cory, and brought out a "Guide to Modern English History." A new edition of "Ionica" appeared in 1891.

COTTERELL, George, journalist, b. Walsall, in the English Midlands, 1839. Studied law and practised for some years, but afterwards entered literature as a profession. For eight years he has been the editor of the "Yorkshire Daily Herald." Published "Poems: Old and New," 1894; also two privately printed volumes of verse, 1870, 1887. The "Banquet," a satire, appeared in 1884.

COURTHOPE, William John, b. Sussex, 1842. Educated at Harrow and New College, Oxford. Contributed to the "Quarterly Review," and was one of the founders of the "National Review." Appointed Civil Service Commissioner, 1887. At present Fellow of New College, Cambridge, and the most prominent candidate for the Chair of Poetry at Oxford, soon to be vacated by Prof. Palgrave. Author of "Ludibria Lunæ," 1869; "The Paradise of Birds," 1870; "Addison" in the "English Men of Letters," 1884. The first volume of his masterwork, "A History of English Poetry," has now (1895) appeared.

CRAIGMYLE, Elizabeth. Published "Poems and Translations," 1886; "A Handful of Pansies," 1888.

CRAIK, Dinah Maria (Mulock), novelist, b. Stoke-upon-Trent, 1826; d. 1887. Married George Lillie Craik, Jr., 1865. Received a pension of £60 in consideration of her literary labors.

Published her first novel, "The Ogilvies," in her twenty-third year. "John Halifax, Gentleman," her best known work, appeared in 1856-57; "A Life for a Life," 1860. Collected her poems in a volume entitled "Thirty Years, being Poems New and Old," 1881.

CRANE, Walter, painter, b. Liverpool, 1845. Also a decorative designer and illustrator of books. President of the Arts and Crafts Exhibition Society, founded 1888. "The Sirens Three," a poem written and illustrated by himself, appeared in 1886. He is also the author of illustrated books for children.

CRAWFORD, Isabella Valancey, b. about 1857; d. Toronto, 1887. Published "Old Spooks's Pass; Malcolm's Katie, and other Poems," in 1884.

CRAWFORD, Louise (Macartney). One of the active contributors to Chapman and Hall's "Metropolitan Magazine." Beginning about 1835, she published therein a series of "Autobiographical Sketches," and also collaborated with Prof. F. Nicholls Crouch, the well-known composer, in the issue of several books of songs, she writing the words for his music. "Kathleen Mavourneen," as given in this Anthology, appeared in "Echoes from the Lakes," the first of the series. It was subsequently elongated for dramatic representation, by three supplementary songs, in the same measure, of which "Dermot Astore" begins as follows:—

" Oh, Dermot Astore! between waking and sleeping
I heard thy dear voice, and wept to its lay;
Every pulse of my heart the sweet measure was keeping,
Till Killarney's wild echoes had borne it away."

CROSS, Mary Ann Evans (Lewes), "George Eliot," novelist, b. Kirk Hallam, Derbyshire, 1819; d. London, 1880. Educated at the village school and at a boarding school at Nuneaton. Became associate editor of the "Westminster Review," and meeting George Henry Lewes, she formed an alliance with him, although for legal reasons they could not marry. Mr. Lewes died in 1878, and she was married to J. W. Cross, 1880. Her first book of fiction was "Scenes from Clerical Life," written in 1856, and published under the pseudonym of "George Eliot." Author also of "Adam Bede," 1859; "The Mill on the Floss," 1860; "Silas Marner," 1861; "Romola," 1863; "Felix Holt," 1866; "Middlemarch," 1871-72; "Daniel Deronda," 1876. Of her poetry, "The Spanish Gypsy" was published, 1868; "Agatha," 1869; "The Legend of Jubal and other Poems," 1864. "How Lisa loved the King" appeared after her death.

CURRIE, Mary Montgomerie (Lamb) Lady, b. 184-, known as "Violet Fane," eldest daughter of Savile Montgomery Lamb, of Beauport, Sussex, and great-granddaughter of Archibald, Earl of Eglinton. Was married to Henry Sydenham Singleton, 1864; after his death in 1893, she became the wife of Si. Philip Currie, British ambassador to Turkey, and resides at present in Constantinople. Her first book of verse appeared in 1872. Since then she has published five volumes of poetry and a number of prose works. An eclectic edition of her Poems, in two volumes, appeared in 1892.

CUSTANCE, Olive, b. Weston Park, Norwich, 1874. Daughter of Colonel Custance. Her work appears in the leading English periodicals.

DARLEY, George, critic and mathematician, b. Dublin, 1795 ; d. 1846. Took his B. A. at Trinity College, Dublin, 1820. Going to London, he wrote critical and other papers for the magazines, and finally, after a period of travel, went on the staff of the "Athenæum." At intervals, from the first, he produced highly lyrical dramas, children of the Elizabethan fantasy, born out of time. Of these the most noted and poetic is "Sylvia, or the May Queen," 1827. Darley is well called by Mr. Ingram "a laureate of fairyland." To his songs and melodies given in this Anthology the following lyric may be added as a foil : —

THE FALLEN STAR

A star is gone ! a star is gone !
There is a blank in Heaven,
One of the cherub choir has done
His airy course this even.

He sat upon the orb of fire
That hung for ages there,
And lent his music to the choir
That haunts the nightly air.

But when his thousand years are passed,
With a cherubic sigh
He vanished with his car at last,
For even cherubs die !

Hear how his angel-brothers mourn —
The minstrels of the spheres —
Each chiming sadly in his turn
And dropping splendid tears.

The planetary sisters all
Join in the fatal song,
And weep this hapless brother's fall
Who sang with them so long.

But deepest of the choral band
The Lunar Spirit sings,
And with a bass according hand
Sweeps all her sullen strings.

From the deep chambers of the dome
Where sleepless Uriel lies,
His rude harmonic thunders come
Mingled with mighty sighs.

The thousand car-borne cherubim,
The wandering eleven,
All join to chant the dirge of him
Who fell just now from Heaven.

DARMESTETER, Agnes Mary Frances Robinson), b. Leamington, 1857. Studied at he University College, paying special attention) Greek literature. Was married to M. James)armesteter, the eminent Orientalist, in 1888, ud has since resided in Paris. Author of veral volumes of verse, among which are " A

Handful of Honeysuckle," 1878 ; " An Italian Garden," 1886 ; " Lyrics," 1891 ; and " Retrospect," 1893. Has written, also, a novel and several prose essays, and translated the " Crowned Hippolytus " of Euripides.

DAVIDSON, John, b. Barrhead, Renfrewshire, 1857. Educated at the Highlanders Academy, Greenock, and Edinburgh University. His " In a Music Hall and other Poems," appeared in 1891 ; " Fleet Street Eclogues," 1893 ; " Ballads and Poems," 1895. In addition to these he has written several dramas in verse.

DAVIS, Thomas Osborn, b. Mallow, County Cork, 1814 ; d. Dublin, 1845. Was graduated from Trinity College, Dublin, 1836. Intensely patriotic, he was one of the most effective contributors to the " Nation," — the revolutionary Irish journal established by Chas. Gavan Duffy in 1842. His poems and essays were collected after his death and published in Duffy's " Library of Ireland."

DAWSON, William James, clergyman, b. Towcester, Northamptonshire, 1854. Entered the Wesleyan ministry, 1875. In 1892 resigned from the Wesleyan ministry and entered the Congregational. Has been a successful historical lecturer. His " Arvalon, a first Poem," appeared in 1878 ; " A Vision of Souls," 1884 ; and " Poems and Lyrics," 1893.

DE TABLEY, Lord (John Byrne Leicester Warren), b. 1835. Took his degree at Christ Church College, Oxford, 1856. Called to the Bar, 1860. His early work appeared under the assumed name of " William P. Lancaster." Author of " Eclogues and Monodramas," 1864 ; " Orestes," a drama in verse, 1867 ; " Rehearsals," 1870 ; " Searching the Net," 1873 ; " The Soldier of Fortune," 1876. After years of retirement as a poet, Lord De Tabley brought out his later " Poems," 1893, and a second series, 1894. Both these collections are distinguished for rare lyrical qualities, and have been warmly received by select lovers of poetry. D. 1895.

DE VERE, Aubrey Thomas, b. Curragh Chase, Limerick, 1814. Third son of Sir Aubrey de Vere Hunt. Educated at Trinity College, Dublin. Author of " The Waldenses ; or the Fall of Rora," 1842 ; " The Search after Proserpine, Recollections of Greece and other Poems," 1843 ; and of several volumes of verse and two volumes of essays. A selection of his poems, edited by Prof. G.E. Woodberry, appeared in New York, 1894. (D. birthplace, 1902.)

DICKENS, Charles. — See page 710.

DISRAELI, Benjamin. — See *Earl of Beaconsfield.*

DIXON, Richard Watson, clergyman, b. London, 1833. Educated at King Edward's School, Birmingham, and Pembroke College, Oxford. With Edward Burne-Jones, William Morris, and others, started the " Oxford and Cambridge Magazine " as an advocate of Pre-Raphaelite ideas. Curate at Lambeth, 1868, and later vicar of Warksworth and honorary canon of Carlisle. Author of " Christ's Com pany and other Poems," 1861; "Mano," 1883; "Odes and Eclogues," 1884; "Lyrical Poems," 1886; and "The Story of Eudocia and her Brothers," 1888.

DOBELL, Sydney Thompson, b. Cranbrook, Kent, 1824; d. 1874. Succeeded his father in the wine trade, but found time to produce several volumes of poetry, and a political pamphlet on reform in parliamentary elections. His first work, "The Roman," a dramatic poem, appeared 1850; followed by "Balder," 1854; "Sonnets of the War," in which he collaborated with Alexander Smith, 1855; "England in Time of War," 1856. In early days he used the pen-name of "Sydney Yendys."

DOBSON, Henry Austin, Civil Service, b. Plymouth, 1840. Educated in Wales and on the Continent. In 1856 received a clerkship in the Board of Trade, and has since remained in official life. In the early seventies he attracted attention by novel and charming lyrics in light but thoroughly poetic vein; and upon the issue of his first collection, in Rhyme, "Vignettes in Rhyme, and Vers de Société," 1873, it was evident that a new and artistic master of "Society Verse" had arisen. From that time, advancing in both art and feeling, he has stood at the head of his own school. Is the foremost writer upon the mode of Queen Anne's time, and quite imbued with its atmosphere. Since 1873 has issued, in verse, "Proverbs in Porcelain," 1877; "Old World Idyls," 1883; "At the Sign of the Lyre," 1885; "Ballade of Beau Brocade," 1892. All of these have been brought out in select and elegant editions, both in England and America. As a prose writer he has given us Lives of Hogarth, Fielding, Steele, and Goldsmith, and various critical works. Cp. "Victorian Poets," pp. 273, 473.

DODGSON, Charles Lutwidge, clergyman and scholar, b. about 1833; d. 1898. Popularly known by his pseudonym "Lewis Carroll." Educated at Christ Church, Oxford. Entered the Church, but became a lecturer on mathematics. His first story for children, "Alice's Adventures in Wonderland," was published in 1865. Author also of "Phantasmagoria," a collection of poems and parodies, 1869; "Through the Looking-Glass," 1872; "The Hunting of the Snark," 1876; "Doublets," 1879; and "Rhyme and Reason," 1883.

DOMETT, Alfred, colonial statesman, b. Camberwell Grove, Surrey, 1811; d. London, 1887. Studied at St. John's College, Cambridge. Was called to the bar, 1841. Went to New Zealand in 1842, and remained there for thirty years, during which time he held important political offices. Published his first book of poems in 1833. Some of his verses, which appeared in "Blackwood's Magazine" in 1837, attracted a great deal of attention. "Ranolf and Amohia" was issued in 1872: and "Flotsam and Jetsam; Rhymes Old and New," 1877. He was thought to be the "Waring" of Browning's poem by that name.

DOWDEN, Edward, critic, b. Cork, 1843. Was graduated with honors at Trinity College, Dublin. A divinity student for two years, and, later, President of the Philosophical Society. At the age of twenty-four was appointed Professor of English Literature at Trinity. An accomplished student and editor of Shakespeare. His "Poems" appeared in 1877. "Studies in Literature," 1878, has been supplemented by a collection of more recent essays, "New Studies in Literature," 1895. One of the most important of his later works is the "Life of Percy Bysshe Shelley," in two volumes.

DOWLING, Bartholomew, b. Limerick, Ireland, 182-. Was clerk to the treasurer of the Corporation of Limerick. Resided for a time in the United States. Is known by his lyric, "The Brigade at Fontenoy," and by "The Revel." The latter poem has been erroneously attributed to Alfred Domett.

DOWNING, Ellen Mary Patrick, b. Cork, 1828; d. 1869. In her youth contributed to the "Nation," and was known as "Mary of the Nation."

DOYLE, Sir Francis Hastings, barrister, b. Nunappleton, Yorkshire, 1810; d. 1888. Educated at Eton and Christ Church, Oxford. Called to the bar, 1831. Held an appointment in the Customs, and was made Professor of Poetry at Oxford, 1867, occupying the chair for ten years. Published his first volume, 1840, selections from which were reprinted in "The Return of the Guards, and other Poems," 1866. His "Reminiscences" appeared in 1886.

DUFFERIN, Helen Selina (Sheridan), Lady, afterwards Lady Gifford, granddaughter of Richard Brinsley Sheridan, and sister of the Hon. Mrs. Norton, b. 1807; d. 1867. Married Mr. Price Blackwood, who became Lord Dufferin in 1839, and died in 1841. She wrote many beautiful songs and lyrics. A posthumous collection of her poems, edited by her son, Lord Dufferin, has recently (1895) appeared.

DUFFY, Sir Charles Gavan, journalist, b. Cork, 1816. Editor and one of the founders of the "Nation." Joined the Irish Confederacy, a branch of the Young Ireland Party, in 1847. Went to Australia in 1856, where he held several important offices. Was knighted in 1877. (D. Nice, 1903.)

DUTT, Toru, b. Calcutta, 1856; d. Calcutta, 1877. In 1869, her father, a high-caste Hindu, took her with her sister Aru to Europe to study English and French. After visiting Italy and England she returned to her Indian home, in 1873. Her first book, "Sheaf Gleaned in French Fields," was published at Bhowanipore, 1876. The little volume of her poems, "Ancient Ballads and Legends of Hindustan," with a memoir by Edmund Gosse, came out in 1882.

DUVAR, J. H. — See *John Hunter-Duvar.*

EDMESTON, James, architect, b. Wapping, London, 1791; d. Homerton, 1867. A well-known writer of hymns. Published hi first volume of poems in 1817, and another in 1847, the latter being a select collection.

"ELIOT, GEORGE." — See *M. A. E.* (*Lewes*) *Cross.*

ELLIOT, Lady Charlotte, b. 183-. Daughter of Sir James Carnegie, and sister of the sixth earl of Southesk. Was married to F. F. Scrymsoure-Fothringham in 1860. Her second husband was Frederick Boileau Elliot. Her " Medusa and other Poems " appeared in 1878.

ELLIOTT, Charlotte, b. Brighton, 1789; d. 1871. Became a confirmed invalid, but for many years edited " The Christian Remembrancer Pocket-Book," and contributed largely to and revised the " Invalid's Hymn Book."

ELLIOTT, Ebenezer, known as the " Corn Law Rhymer," b. Wasborough, Yorkshire, 1781 ; d. Argilt Hill, 1849. Son of a poorly-paid clerk in an iron foundry, his opportunities for acquiring an education were limited. The beginning of his business career was a failure : but in 1821 he started as an ironworker in Sheffield, and in 1841 was able to retire to a small estate near Barnsley Hill, where he passed the remainder of his days. " Corn Law Rhymes," with " The Ranter," appeared in 1827 ; " The Village Patriarch," 1829. Was also a contributor to Bulwer's " New Monthly Magazine."

EVANS, Sebastian, barrister and journalist, b. Market Bosworth, Leicestershire, 1830. Was graduated at Emmanuel College, Cambridge, 1853. Received degree of LL.D., 1868. Editor of the " Birmingham Daily Gazette " for three years. Called to the bar, 1873, and some years later became editor of the " People," a conservative journal. " Brother Fabian's Manuscript and other Poems " was issued in 1865, and " In the Studio " in 1875.

FABER, Frederick William, churchman, b. Yorkshire, 1814 ; d. 1863. Educated at Harrow and Oxford. Entered the Church of England, but in 1845 became a Roman Catholic. Was received into the Oratory of St. Philip Neri, and in 1849 was appointed Superior of the Oratory at London. Published several prose works, but is known chiefly by his hymns, a complete edition of which appeared in 1862.

"FATHER PROUT." — See *Francis Mahoney.*

FERGUSON, Sir Samuel, scholar, b. Belfast, 1810 ; d. 1886. Educated at Trinity College, Dublin. Admitted to the Bar, 1838. Was made Deputy Keeper of the Records of Ireland, 1867, knighted in 1878, and elected President of the Royal Irish Academy, 1882. Author of " Lays of the Western Gael," 1865 ; " Congal," an epic poem, 1867, and of several articles on Irish antiquities.

FIELD, Michael, the Parnassian name of two unmarried ladies, aunt and niece, whose reserve is properly held in respect by the editorial guild. Authors of " Calirrhoë " and " Fair Rosamond," 1884 ; " The Father's Tragedy," etc., 1885 ; " Canute the Great," 1887 ; " The

Tragic Mary," 1890, and other vigorous poetic dramas, as well as the lyrical volumes entitled " Long Ago," 1889 ; " Sight and Song," 1892, and " Under the Bough," 1893.

FITZGERALD, Edward, b. Suffolk, 1809 ; d. Norfolk, 1883. Took a degree at Trinity College, Cambridge. His translations from the Spanish, the Greek, and the Persian, most of which were issued anonymously, reproduce the quality of the originals with such taste and poetic feeling as to be almost original works in themselves. His best known translations are " Euphranor, a Dialogue on Youth," 1851 ; " Polonius, a Collection of Wise Saws and Modern Instances," 1852 ; " Six Dramas of Calderon," 1853 ; and the " Rubáiyát of Omar Khayyám," his greatest work, 1859. A superb American edition of the Rubáiyát, illustrated by Elihu Vedder's imaginative series of designs, was brought out in 1884.

FOX, William Johnson, preacher and man of letters, b. Suffolk, 1786 ; d. 1864. Studied for the Orthodox ministry, and finally became a radical Unitarian pastor at Chichester, and at the celebrated Finsbury Chapel, London. Wrote for various periodicals and was an eloquent speaker. Greatly interested in questions of reform. A memorial edition of his works was published in twelve volumes, 1868.

FRASER-TYTLER, C. C. — See *Catherine C. Liddell.*

GALE, Norman, b. Kew, Surrey, 1862. Educated at Oxford and then took up teaching, but since 1892 has devoted his time almost entirely to literature. " A Country Muse " appeared in 1892, followed by " Orchard Songs " and " A Country Muse : Second Series," in 1893, and " A June Romance " (prose) and " Cricket Songs," 1894.

GARNETT, Richard, librarian, b. Lichfield, 1835. Became an assistant in the Library of the British Museum at the age of sixteen, and has risen to his present dignity of Keeper, and is widely known and esteemed. In 1883 the University of Edinburgh conferred upon him the degree of LL. D. His " Primula and other Poems " appeared in 1858 ; " Io in Egypt," 1859 ; " Iphigenia in Delphi," 1890 ; and " Poems," a collective edition, 1893. (D. London, 1906.)

GILBERT, William Schwenck, dramatist, b. London, 1836. Educated at Great Ealing and at King's College. Obtained a clerkship and afterwards became a barrister, but finally gave all his time to literature. Has collaborated with Sir Arthur Sullivan in the production of many popular light operas. Author of " Bab Ballads " and a number of dramas.

GILFILLAN, Robert, b. Dunfermline, 1798 ; d. Leith, 1850. The son of a master weaver, he was apprenticed to a cooper, but after acting as merchants' clerk for several years, finally became collector of police rates at Leith. Contributed to various Scotch periodicals and to the anthology, " Whistle Binkie." A collection of his works, with a prefatory biography, was published after his death in 1851.

GILL, Frances Tyrrell, Victoria, Australia. No collection of her poems has been made, although she contributed much to Australian periodicals.

GILLINGTON, Alice E., b. Cheshire. Is the daughter of a clergyman, and has passed much of her life in the south of England. Conjointly with her sister she published "Poems" in 1892. Is a frequent contributor to periodicals in England and the United States.

GILLINGTON, M. C.—See *Mary C. Byron.*

GOODCHILD, John Arthur, physician, b. 1851. Educated at the Philberds, Maidenhead, and St. George's Hospital. Practiced medicine at Ealing, and for the past fifteen years at Bordighera, Italy. Has published three series of "Somnia Medici," the first appearing in 1884. "Lyrics and Tales in Verse" was issued in 1893.

GORDON, Adam Lindsay, b. Fayal in the Azores, 1833 ; d. 1870. Son of a distinguished English officer. After receiving a college education and developing a somewhat wild and adventurous spirit, he left England in 1853 for South Australia. There he was a trooper in the mounted police, and afterwards followed various occupations, but without continued success. About 1867 he settled in Melbourne, and was considered "the best amateur steeple-chase rider in the colonies." Here he published his first book, "Sea Spray and Smoke Drift," 1868. His racy ballads of the bush and turf made him the most striking figure among the Australian poets. Disappointment and exposure undermined his health, and in a fit of despair he died by his own hand. Collective editions of his poems, with a memoir, are published in London and Melbourne.

GOSSE, Edmund (William), critic and literary historian, b. London, 1849. Son of Philip Henry Gosse, the naturalist. Was assistant librarian at the British Museum, 1867, and after 1875 translator to the Board of Trade. Elected Clark Lecturer in English Literature at Trinity College, Cambridge, and during the season of 1884–85 delivered the Lowell Lectures in the United States. Mr. Gosse is a Norse scholar, and an authoritative writer upon Scandinavian literature. Is actively engaged in critical journalism. Has published "Madrigals, Songs and Sonnets," 1870 ; "On Viol and Flute," 1873 ; "King Erik," a drama, and "New Poems," 1879 ; "Firdausi in Exile, and other Poems," 1886 ; "In Russet and Silver," 1894.

GRAVES, Alfred Perceval, Civil Service, b. Dublin, 1846. Son of the Bishop of Limerick. Educated in England and at Trinity College, Dublin. Has held various positions in the Civil Service, London. His "Songs of Killarney" was published in 1873 ; "Irish Songs and Ballads," 1882 ; "Songs of Irish Wit and Humor," 1894 ; "The Irish Song Book," 1894.

GRAY, David, b. Kirkintulloch, 1838 ; d.

1861. His home was on the banks of the Luggie, the little stream celebrated in his poem. In 1860 he went to London, but met with disappointments, and, his health failing, he went home to die. "The Luggie and other Poems," including a series of sonnets, "In the Shadows," was published after his death, with an introduction by Lord Houghton.

GREENWELL, Dora (Dorothy), b. on the family estate, Greenwell Ford, Lanchester, Durham, 1821 ; d. Clifton, 1882. Remained at Greenwell Ford until 1848. Afterwards resided at Northumberland, Durham, and London. Contributed to the "Contemporary Review." Author of several books of poetry, among which are "Carmina Crucis," 1871, and "Songs of Salvation," 1873.

GRIFFIN, Gerald, novelist, b. Limerick, 1803 ; d. Cork, 1840. Went to London at the age of nineteen. In 1827 published his first volume of Irish stories, "Holland Tide." This was followed by another series of tales and by his novel, "The Collegians." Joined the order of the Christian Brothers in 1838. After his death his works were brought together in a uniform edition.

HAKE, Thomas Gordon, anatomist, b. Leeds, 1809 ; d. 1894. Educated at Christ's Church School, London, and studied medicine at Edinburgh, the University of Glasgow, and in France. Became a specialist in comparative osteology, and wrote a number of treatises on that and kindred subjects. Published "Madeline and Other Poems," 1871 ; "Parables and Tales," 1872 ; "New Symbols," 1876 ; "Legends of the Morrow," 1879 ; "Maiden Ecstasy," 1880 ; "The Serpent Play," 1883 ; "The New Day," a book of sonnets, 1890.

HALL, Christopher Newman, clergyman, b. Maidstone, Kent, 1816. Graduate of London University, Pastor of Albion Chapel, Hull, and of Surrey Chapel, London. Often visited America. His church tower was named "Lincoln," after the Emancipator. (D. London, 1902.)

HALLAM, Arthur Henry, b. London, 1811 ; d. Vienna, 1833. Son of Henry Hallam, historian, and comrade of Tennyson, who commemorated him in "In Memoriam." Took his degree at Trinity College, Cambridge, 1832. Author of some noteworthy essays and of poems which were to have been published with those of the friend who afterward became his elegist.

HAMERTON, Philip Gilbert, artist and art-critic, b. Laneside, Lancashire, 1834 ; d. Boulogne-sur-Seine, 1894. Educated at Burnley and Doncaster Grammar Schools, and prepared for Oxford but did not matriculate. Studied art in Paris, and in 1861 took up a permanent residence in France. In 1869 founded "The Portfolio," which he edited until his death. His "Etching and Etchers," 1868, has never been supplanted as an authority on the art of etching. Author, also, of "The Intellectual Life," 1873 ; "The Graphic Arts," 1882 ; "Human Intercourse," 1884 ; "Land scape," 1885; "Man in Art," 1893. His early volume of poetry, "The Isles of Loch Awe," appeared in 1859.

HANMER, John, 1st Lord, politician, b. 1809; d. Knotley Hall, near Tunbridge Wells, 1881. Educated at Eton and Christ Church, Oxford. An advocate of political reform. Published "Fra Cipolla and Other Poems," 1839; "Sonnets," 1840.

HARPUR, Charles, government service, b. New South Wales, 1817; d. 1868. Educated at the Government School. Originally a squatter and farmer, he was appointed to the gold commissionership at Araluen in 1858. Published a volume of sonnets in 1840, and an edition of his poems appeared in 1883.

HARRISON, S. Frances ("Seranus") b. Toronto, Canada, of Irish parentage. In 1879 was married to Mr. J. W. F. Harrison, an English professor of music. She has contributed to Canadian periodicals for a number of years, using the pseudonym "Seranus." In addition to her poems, "Pine, Rose, and Fleur de Lys," 1890, she has compiled an anthology of the Canadian poets, and has produced a volume of short stories.

HARTLEY, John, a Yorkshire miner, whose volume of poems was published in 1872. His poem, "To a Daisy," was given to the present editor from memory by Mr. David Christie Murray.

HAVERGAL, Frances Ridley, daughter of the Rev. W. H. Havergal, b. Astley, 1836; d. Swanna, South Wales, 1879. A fine musician and linguist. Contributed to religious periodicals, and has published several little volumes of hymns and verse.

HAWKER, Robert Stephen, clergyman, b. Plymouth, 1804; d. Plymouth, 1875. Educated at Pembroke College, Oxford. A stalwart and heroic character. In 1834 became Vicar of Morwenstow, a lonely parish on the Cornish coast. His "Echoes from Old Cornwall" appeared in 1845; "Cornish Ballads," in 1869. Joined the Roman Catholic Church shortly before his death. His poetical works, memoir, etc., were published in 1879.

HEAVYSEGE, Charles, journalist, b. Yorkshire, 1816; d. Montreal, 1869. A woodcarver by trade, and mainly self-educated. Emigrated to Montreal, 1853, where he became a writer for the press. "Saul: a Drama in three Parts," appeared in 1857, and impressed Nathaniel Hawthorne, then consul at Liverpool, to such an extent that he brought it to the notice of the "North British Review," in which it was reviewed at length in 1858. Heavysege's "Ode on Shakespeare" and "Jephtha's Daughter" were published in 1855.

HERVEY, Thomas Kibble, editor, b. Paisley, 1799; d. Kentish Town, London, 1859. Studied law, but soon adopted a literary career. Went to London about 1820. Contributed to the "Art Journal," and edited the "Athe-

næum" for several years. His poems were collected and published, with a memoir, by his widow, in 1866.

HICKEY, Emily Henrietta, b. Wexford County, Ireland, 1845. Contributed to the "Cornhill Magazine," "Academy," and other periodicals. "A Sculptor and Other Poems" appeared in 1881, and in the same year she assisted in founding the Browning Society. "Verse Tales, Lyrics and Translations" was published in 1889, and "Michael Villiers, Idealist, and Other Poems," in 1891.

HINKSON, Katharine (Tynan), b. Dublin, 1861. Educated at the Dominican Convent of St. Catherine of Siena, Drogheda. Published her first book, "Louise de la Vallière and other Poems," 1885. "Shamrocks" appeared in 1887; "Ballads and Lyrics," in 1892; and "Cuckoo Songs," in 1894. Contributes to leading journals in England and the United States.

HOME, F. Wyville, b. Edinburgh, 1851. Author of "Songs of a Wayfarer," 1878; "Lay Canticles and Other Poems," 1883; "The Wrath of the Fay," 1887.

HOOD, Thomas, journalist, b. London, 1799; d. London, 1845. Studied engraving, but, that profession disagreeing with his health, he turned his attention to literature. Was employed as sub-editor on the "London Magazine," and his early work comprised examples of nearly all the styles of composition in which he afterward excelled. The two series of "Whims and Oddities" appeared 1826-27, and were followed by the now entirely forgotten "National Tales." Then came the "Plea of the Midsummer Fairies," the dramatic romance "Lamia," "Tylney Hall," and many exquisite songs and ballads. "Miss Kilmansegg," a lyrical extravaganza, is the best example of his serio-comic style. "The Song of the Shirt" and "The Bridge of Sighs" are everywhere familiar. Was editor successively of the "Gem" and the "New Monthly Magazine." Afterwards established "Hood's Magazine," and published the "Comic Annual." He had the faculty of blending mirth and pathos in his poetry as in his life, his own experience being a struggle against poverty and ill health, which he maintained with cheerful fortitude. In 1854 a monument was erected above his grave in Kensal Green, adorned with bas-reliefs suggested by "The Dream of Eugene Aram" and "The Bridge of Sighs," and inscribed with the legend, "He sang the Song of the Shirt." Cp. "Victorian Poets," chap. iii.

HORNE, Herbert P., architect, b. London, 1864. About 1882, began the study of art with Selwyn Image, and with him, in 1886, started the "Hobby Horse," but afterwards assumed the sole editorship of that magazine. An expert with relation to printing and the decoration of books. "Diversi Colores," a small volume of verse, appeared in 1891.

HORNE, Richard Hengist (originally Henrv), dramatist and poet, b. London, 1803 ; d. Margate, 1884. An adventurous wanderer of the purely English type of Trelawny, Domett, and Oliphant. Spent years in Australia and other lands, and served in the Mexican army during the war with the United States. In his old age settled down in London, poor in means, but a picturesque and impressive figure. He began his literary career in 1828, with a poem in the "Athenæum," and developed virile, almost Elizabethan, dramatic genius as a poet. He was throughout life a prolific, uneven writer of prose and verse, but among his superior dramas are "Cosmo de' Medici," 1837 ; "The Death of Marlowe," 1837 ; "Gregory VII," 1840 ; "Judas Iscariot," 1848 ; "Prometheus the Fire-Bringer," 1864. His still famous allegorical epic of "Orion" was first issued at the price of a farthing. In 1844, conjointly with Mrs. Browning and Robert Bell, he published "A New Spirit of the Age," a series of critical essays. It was after his visit to Australia that he styled himself "Hengist." Mrs. Browning's letters to him were published in two volumes, 1877.   [E. C. S.]

HOUGHTON, Richard Monckton Milnes, Lord, parliamentarian, b. London, 1809 ; d. Vichy, 1885. Educated at Trinity College, Cambridge, where he formed friendships with Tennyson, Hallam, Trench, and others. Entered Parliament in 1837, and during his political career took an active part in leading movements of the time. Was raised to the peerage by Lord Palmerston in 1863. He was always ready to befriend young writers and artists, and gathered about him a circle of the most brilliant men of the day. Published several volumes of travel on the Continent, and "Poems of Many Years," 1838 ; "Memorials of Many Seasons," 1840 ; "Poetry for the People," 1840 ; "Poems, Legendary and Historical," 1844 ; "Palm Leaves," 1844 ; "Life and Letters of Keats," 1848.

HOWITT, William and Mary, miscellaneous writers. William b. Derbyshire, 1792 ; d. Rome, 1879. Mary (Botham) b. Coleford, in the Forest of Dean, about 1799 ; d. Rome, 1888. Married in 1820, and worked together in a kind of literary partnership. Published their first volume of poems, "The Forest Minstrel," in 1823, followed by "The Desolation of Eyam," 1827. William Howitt was the author of "The Book of the Seasons," 1831, and "The Homes and Haunts of the British Poets," 1847. Mrs. Howitt translated the works of Frederika Bremer into English, and wrote a number of children's stories.

HUNTER-DUVAR, John, b. England, 1830. Has lived most of his life in Canada. For a time held an appointment in the Canadian Civil Service. His prose and verse have appeared in English and American periodicals, and he has made a number of translations. Published "De Roberval," a drama of early Canadian romance, 1888 ; "The Triumph of Constancy," 18— ; "Annals of the Court of Oberon," 1895.

HUXLEY, Thomas Henry, scientist, b. Ealing, Middlesex, 1825 ; d. Eastbourne, Sussex, 1895. In 1846 took the diploma of the Royal College of Surgeons, and entered the royal navy as assistant surgeon. Rose to eminence as a biologist, and has held many important professorships. Was a strong supporter of the Darwinian theory, and the comrade of Tyndall and Spencer. Author of scientific works of the highest grade. President of the Royal Society, 1873–85. The following lines, written by Mrs. Huxley, have been carved upon his tombstone, in compliance with his own request:

And if there be no meeting past the grave,
If all is darkness, silence, yet 't is rest.
Be not afraid, ye waiting hearts that weep,
For God still giveth His beloved sleep.
And if an endless sleep He wills — so best !

IMAGE, Selwyn, artist, b. about 1850. Educated at Brighton College and Marlborough, and took a degree at New College, Oxford, 1872. Was ordained in the same year, and continued in orders until 1880, when he gave up clerical work altogether and began the study of art. With Mr. Herbert Horne, he started the "Hobby Horse," 1886.

INGELOW, Jean, b. Boston, Lincolnshire, about 1830. In addition to her poetical works, has written several popular novels, and some stories for children. Published "A Rhyming Chronicle of Incident and Feeling," 1850 ; a first series of "Poems" in 1863, which instantly won the public affection in both England and America, and was followed by others in 1865, 1867, 1879, 1881, and 1886. Died, London, 1897.

"INGOLDSBY, Thomas." — See Richard Harris Barham.

INGRAM, John Kells, political economist, b. Newry, near Belfast, 1823. Fellow and professor of Trinity College, Dublin. His poem, "Ninety-Eight," first appeared in the Dublin "Nation."

JAMESON, Anna Brownell, b. Dublin, 1794 ; d. Ealing, Middlesex, 1860. Eldest daughter of D. Brownell Murphy, a miniature-painter. Became a governess at the age of sixteen, and in 1825 married Robert Jameson. In 1846 she visited Italy to collect material for her "Sacred and Legendary Art."

JAPP, Alexander Hay, journalist and critic, b. Forfarshire, Scotland, 1840. Educated at the University of Edinburgh. Became a contributor to Scottish journals, but removed to London, where he formed connections with "Good Words" and the "Sunday Magazine." Has been an industrious and successful writer, signing the pseudonym, "H. A. Page," to many of his most important works. Among his prose books are "Three Great Teachers of our Time," "Thomas De Quincey : his Life and Writings," and "Hours in my Garden." His latest volumes in verse are "Circle of the Year, a Sonnet Sequence," privately printed in 1893 and "Dramatic Pictures, English Rispetti Sonnets, and other Verse," 1894. (D. 1905.)

JOHNSON, E. Pauline, b. on the Grand

River Indian Reserve, Ontario, 1862. Daughter of the head chief of the Mohawks, her mother being an Englishwoman. Has written verse for English and American journals, a collection of which is announced for publication in England.

JONES, Ebenezer, agitator, b. Islington, 1820; d. Brentwood, 1860. Was reared in a Calvinistic atmosphere, but being of a passionate nature, found restraint most irksome. Took a clerkship in 1837, and at the same time began his literary work, which he pursued under difficulties. Issued his book of poems, "Studies in Sensation and Event," in 1843, but subsequently devoted himself to prose writing on political subjects.

JONES, Ernest Charles, barrister, b. Berlin, Germany, 1819; d. Manchester, 1868. Educated at St. Michael's College, Lüneburg. Called to the Bar in London, 1844. Sacrificed the best years of his life to writing and speaking in behalf of social reform, and, in 1848, was imprisoned for two years on a charge of sedition. Author of "The Battle Day," 1855; "The Emperor's Vigil and other Waves of War," 1856; "Corydon and Other Poems," 1860.

JOYCE, Robert Dwyer, physician and journalist, b. Glenosheen, County Limerick, 1830; d. Dublin, 1883. Went to the United States in 1866, and took up his residence in Boston, where he practised medicine and wrote continually. A sturdy balladist and legendary poet. His "Ballads of Irish Chivalry" were first collected into a volume in Boston, 1872. These were followed in the eighties by "Deirdrè," an Irish epic, and "Blanid," the former of which brought its author into general repute.

KEBLE, John, divine, b. Fairford, 1792; d. Bournemouth, 1866. Educated at Oxford. Became a college tutor, and afterward accepted a curacy. Was professor of Poetry at Oxford, 1831-41. Vicar of Hursley from 1835 until his death. Author of several prose works in addition to "The Christian Year," 1827; "Lyra Innocentium," 1845; and "Poems," issued after his death. Was a leader in the High Church movement, afterwards called Tractarianism. Keble College, Oxford, founded after his design, now bears his name.

KELLY, Mary Eva (Mrs. Kevin O'Doherty), b. Galway, and now living in Australia. Was one of the regular contributors to the "Nation."

KEMBLE, Frances Anne, actress, b. London, 1809; d. 1893. Daughter of Charles Kemble, the actor, and niece of Mrs. Siddons. Began to write for the stage at an early age. Appeared first as Juliet, at the Covent Garden Theatre, 1809. Made a professional tour of America in 1832. Married Mr. Pierce Butler, of South Carolina, and was divorced in 1839. Lived in the United States for twenty years, and then took up her residence in England. Was a frequent prose writer, and published two volumes of verse.

KENDALL, Henry Clarence, government service, b. New South Wales, 1841; d. near Sydney, 1882. Held an appointment at one time in the Civil Service, wrote for the press, and occupied several mercantile positions. In 1881 was made Inspector of Forests. Published "Leaves from an Australian Forest," 1869, and "Songs from the Mountains," 1880. His collected poems, with a memoir by Alexander Sutherland, were issued in London.

KENDALL, May, b. Bridlington, Yorkshire, 1861. Author of "From a Garret," "White Poppies," "Such is Life," "Dreams to Sell," 1887; "Songs from Dreamland," 1894.

KENT, William Charles Mark (known as Charles Kent), journalist, b. London, 1823. Educated at Prior Park and Oscott Colleges. Editor of "The Sun" and the "Weekly Register." Was called to the Bar, Inner Temple, 1859. His collected "Poems" appeared in 1870.

KENYON, John, b. Jamaica, 1784; d. Cowes, 1856. Educated at Peterhouse, Cambridge. Took up his residence at Woodlands, Somerset, where he made the acquaintance of Coleridge, Wordsworth, Southey, Lamb, and other noted authors. He was a distant relative of Elizabeth Barrett, and first made her acquainted with the poetry of Browning and with the poet himself, and afterward remained the beloved friend of both, bequeathing six thousand guineas to Mrs. Browning, and four thousand to her husband. His "Poems for the most part Occasional" appeared in 1838; "A Day at Tivoli, with Other Verse," 1849.
[E. C. S.]

KING, Harriet Eleanor (Hamilton), b. Edinburgh, 1840. Daughter of Admiral W. A. B. Hamilton. In 1863 married Mr. Henry S. King. Author of "Aspromonte," 1869; "The Disciple," 1873; "Book of Dreams," 1883.

KINGSLEY, Charles, clergyman and novelist, b. Holne Vicarage, Devonshire, 1819; d. Eversley, 1875. Educated at Clifton and at Magdalene College, Cambridge. Ordained in 1842, and became rector of Eversley in 1844. An active worker in the cause of social reform, he became one of the most conspicuous leaders of the Chartist movement, and, in 1849, published his novel, "Alton Locke," an exposition of the aims and views of Chartism. Was made canon of Chester in 1869, and canon of Westminster in 1873. Of his poetical works, "The Saint's Tragedy" was published in 1848, and "Andromeda and Other Poems," in 1858. Author of literary essays and of many noted prose works, of which "Yeast," 1851, "Hypatia," 1853, "Glaucus, or the Wonders of the Shore," 1855, "Westward Ho!" 1855, "The Water-Babies, a Book for Children," 1863, and "Prose Idylls," 1873, are, perhaps, the best known.

KIPLING, Rudyard, romancer and balladist, b. Bombay, 1865. Educated in England, but returned to India and went on the staff of the "Lahore Civil and Military Gazette," and contributed to the Indian daily press until 1889, when he went to England, and quickly achieved a reputation throughout the English-speaking world by his dramatic and original tales and poems of Anglo-Indian life. Married Miss Balestier, sister of Wolcott Balestier, and took up a residence in the United States, where he now lives. His first volume of verse," Departmental Ditties," appeared in 1886, and " Plain Tales from the Hills" in 1888. " Soldiers Three" and " Barrack Room Ballads" were published in America in 1891. Has written two novels, in one of which, " The Naulahka," he collaborated with Wolcott Balestier. " The Jungle Book," 1894, is a unique and imaginative production, and immediately became a favorite with young and old.

KNOX, Isa (Craig), b. Edinburgh, 1831. Took an active interest in social science. Her Ode on Burns won the place in the competition on the occasion of the Burns Centenary. Was married to her cousin, Mr. John Knox, of London. Published her first book of poems in 1856. " Songs of Consolation" appeared in 1874.

LAING, Alexander, b. Brechin, Scotland, 1787; d. Brechin, 1857. Engaged in the business of flax-dressing, and afterwards became a pedler. Contributed to local newspapers and to " Smith's Scottish Minstrels," " Harp of Renfrewshire," and " Whistle Binkie." Published a collection of his poems, called " Wayside Flowers," in 1846.

LAMPMAN, Archibald, Civil Service, b. Western Ontario, 1861. The son of an Anglican clergyman. Educated and took a degree at the University of Trinity College, Toronto. In 1883 received an appointment in the Civil Service at Ottawa, where he has since remained. His "Among the Millet and Other Poems" was published in 1888. His lyrics appear in the leading American magazines. (D. Ottawa, 1899.)

LANDOR, Walter Savage, b. Warwick, 30 Jan., 1775; d. Florence, Italy, 17 Sept., 1864. Was a classical enthusiast of a very genuine type, and held a unique position in literature. Never popular in the sense of being widely read by the common people, he is known better as a prose-writer than as a poet. Spent the latter years of his life in Italy. As an epigrammatist in verse, a writer of elegant bits of satire, elegy, gallantry, and social rhyme, he had no master in the English tongue. He was a man of impetuous temper, which involved him in unfortunate quarrels and complications, but all through his life he showed nobility of sentiment and great powers of tenderness and sympathy. He was an ardent Republican, devoted to liberty, and scornful of tyranny in all forms. Author of " Imaginary Conversations," 1824; " Pericles and Aspasia," 1836; " The Citation of William Shakespeare," 1834; and the " Pentameron," 1837. His plays include " Andrea of Hungary," " Giovanna of Naples," and " Fra Rupert." His Latin poetry, " Poemata et Inscriptiones," was published in 1847. In the same year, the exquisite " Hellenics" also appeared, and his last book, " Heroic Idyls," was issued in 1863. His Life, written at great length

by John Forster, 1867-69, is the detailed record of a restless, versatile, in some respects heroic, and wonderfully prolonged, literary career. Cp. " Victorian Poets," chap. ii.

LANG, Andrew, critic and essayist, b. 1844. Educated at St. Andrew's University, and Balliol College, Oxford. Was made a Fellow of Merton, 1868. He has made notable translations of Homer, Theocritus, and the Greek Anthology, and, in prose, has written numerous biographical and critical essays. Author of " Ballads and Lyrics of Old France," 1872; " XXII Ballades in Blue China," 1880; " Helen of Troy," 1882; " Rhymes à la Mode," 1884; " Grass of Parnassus," 1888; also of several books of fairy tales; " Letters to Dead Authors," 1886; " Myth, Ritual, and Religion," 1887; and is in the front rank of the most active and authoritative English men of letters.

LANGHORNE, Charles Hartley, b. Berwick-on-Tweed, 1818; d. 1845. Educated at Glasgow University and Oxford. Was studying law at the time of his premature death.

LAYCOCK, Samuel, b. Marsden, Yorkshire, 1825; d. Blackpool, 1893. Was employed in a mill, but began writing verse in his youth. Published " Lancashire Rhymes; or Homely Pictures of the People," 1864; " Lancashire Songs," 1866; " Lancashire Poems, Tales and Recitations," 1875. Shortly before his death, brought out a collective edition of his works.

LEAR, Edward, artist, b. Holloway, London, 1812; d. San Remo, 1888. Resided in Italy for a number of years. Painter of animals and landscape. Published several volumes of catching " Nonsense Verse."

LEE-HAMILTON, Eugene, b. London, 1845. Educated in France and Germany, and went to Oxford in 1864. Entered the diplomatic service, but while Secretary of Legation at Lisbon, 1873, a cerebro-spinal disorder developed, and from that time until recently, when his condition is somewhat improved, he has been unable to leave his couch. He is a half-brother of Miss Violet Paget (" Vernon Lee "). In addition to several other volumes of verse, he has published " The Fountain of Youth," 1891, and " Sonnets of the Wingless Hours," 1894.

LEFROY, Edward Cracroft, clergyman, b. Westminster, 1855. Related to Jane Austen and Sir John Franklin. His two sisters were married to Charles and Alfred Tennyson. Educated at Blackheath School and Keble College. Entered the church, and held curacies at Lambeth, Truro, and other places, until 1882. Author of " Echoes of Theocritus and other Sonnets," 1885. D. 1891.

LE GALLIENNE, Richard, b. Birkenhead, 1865. Educated at the Liverpool College. Entered upon a business career, but soon gave it up for the profession of letters. Has done successful work in prose as well as verse. His first volume of poetry was privately printed in 1887. Later works are " Volumes in Folio,"

1889; "George Meredith: some Characteristics," 1890; "The Book-Bills of Narcissus," 1891; "English Poems," 1892; "Prose Fancies," 1894. He has also edited an edition of William Hazlitt's "Liber Amoris," 1893.

LEIGHTON, Robert, merchant, b. Dundee, 1822; d. Liverpool, 1869. Resided chiefly at Ayr.

LEVY, Amy, novelist, b. Clapham, 1861; d. London, 1889. Her parents were of the Jewish faith. Educated at Brighton and Newnham College. Was of a melancholy temperament, and died by her own hand. Her "Xantippe and Other Poems" was published in 1881, a great part of the volume reappearing in "A Minor Poet and Other Verse," 1884. "Reuben Sachs," a novel, and the volume of verse, "A London Plane Tree," came out in 1889.

LIDDELL, Catherine C. (Fraser-Tytler), b. 1848. Married Mr. Edward Liddell. Is author of "Songs in Minor Keys," published in 1881.

LIGHTHALL, W. D.—See *W. D. Schuyler-Lighthall.*

LINDSAY, Blanche Elizabeth (FitzRoy), Lady, b. 1844. Daughter of the Rt. Hon. Henry FitzRoy, second son of the 3d Lord Southampton, and of Hannah Meyer, daughter of the late Baron Nathan-Meyer Rothschild. In 1864 married Sir Coutts Lindsay, Bart., of Balcarres, the founder of the Grosvenor Gallery, and a painter. She is a successful prose writer, and an accomplished musician and painter in watercolors. Published, in verse, "Lyrics," 1890; "A Child's Dream," and "A String of Beads," 1893.

LINTON, William James, b. London, 1812. Noted as a wood-engraver, a political agitator, and a man of letters. He did much to advance wood-engraving in America, where he lived for some years, and he contributed largely to literature both in prose and verse. In 1854 he founded "The English Republic," a periodical devoted to social science. "Claribel and Other Poems" was published in 1865; "A History of Wood Engraving in America," 1882; "Poems and Translations," 1889. He edited "Golden Apples of Hesperus," 1882; and a superb work, "The Masters of Wood Engraving," 1889. Linton had a notable career, having participated in the Corn Law, Irish, and Italian struggles, and was always in the van as a Radical. From his private press, the "Appledore," at New Haven, Conn., he issued frequent metrical brochures, and published his "Reminiscences," 1894. Died in that city, 1898.

LITTLE, Lizzie M. Author of "Persephone, and Other Poems," 1884.

LOCKER-LAMPSON, Frederick, b. near London, 1821; d. at his place, "Rowfant," Sussex, 1895. Clerk and précis writer in the Admiralty for a number of years. Added the surname Lampson to his own after the death of Sir Curtis Lampson, Bart., of Rowfant, father of his second wife. He made a rare collection of books, manuscripts, and autographs. His daughter, now Mrs. Augustine Birrell, was first married to Lionel Tennyson, son of the Laureate. Published "London Lyrics" in 1862, and "Patchwork" (prose and verse), 1879, and edited the "Lyra Elegantiarum," 1867.

LOGAN, John E., insurance adjuster, b. Hamilton, Canada, 1852; about twenty years later removed to Montreal, where, with the exception of a few years, spent in the Canadian Northwest, he has since lived. Under the pseudonym of "Barry Dane" he has contributed a number of poems to the newspapers and periodicals, but they have never been published in book form.

LOVER, Samuel, novelist and painter, b. Dublin, 1797; d. Jersey, 1868. Was successful as a miniature painter, and became a member of the Irish Academy of Arts. Wrote several very popular ballads of Irish peasant life, which he set to music of his own composition. Went to London, where he was very popular. Illustrated his prose works with his own etchings. "Songs and Ballads" appeared in 1839, and "Handy Andy," an Irish novel, in 1842.

LOWE, Robert, Viscount Sherbrooke, statesman, b. Nottinghamshire, England, 1811; d. London, 1892. Educated at Winchester and University College, Oxford. Went to Australia in 1843, where he held legislative positions; returned to London in 1851. Prominent figure in English politics; was Chancellor of the Exchequer, 1868-1873, and Home Secretary, 1873-1874. "Poems of Life" appeared in London, 1855.

LYALL, Sir Alfred Comyns, K. C. B., b. Coulston, Surrey, 1835. Educated at Eton; and entered the Indian civil service, in which he has held offices of high distinction. Has published a book of religious and social studies relating to Asia; a Biography of Warren Hastings, and a volume of poems, "Verses Written in India," 1889.

LYTE, Henry Francis, clergyman, b. Ednam, near Kelso, Scotland, 1793; d. Nice, 1847. Educated at Trinity College, Dublin. Entered the ministry of the Church of England in 1815. Changed parishes several times, but finally became "perpetual curate" of Lower Brixham, Devonshire. Published "Poems, chiefly Religious," 1833, and "Spirit of the Psalms," 1834. An eclectic volume of his poems was brought out in 1868.

LYTTON, Edward, Lord (Edward George Earle Lytton Bulwer-Lytton), novelist, dramatist, and parliamentarian, b. London, 1803, d. 1873. During his earlier literary career he was popularly known as "Bulwer." The most fertile and brilliant, after Sir Walter Scott, of the romantic school of novelists. Of his many, and often overwrought, romances, "The Last Days of Pompeii," 1834, and "Rienzi," 1835, will always have a place in English literature. In later years, his novels took on a more intellectual tinge, as is seen in " The Caxtons," 1850, and " My Novel," 1853. Like Disraeli, he wrote to his dying day, and found a world of readers, " Kenelm Chillingly " and " The Parisians," both 1873, rivalling Beaconsfield's " Lothair " and " Endymion." He was graduated at Cambridge, 1826 ; was in Parliament 1831–41, 1852–66, and an ambitious orator ; was Lord Rector of Glasgow University, 1856, and Colonial Secretary, under Lord Derby, 1858. Raised to the peerage, 1866. His eagerness for fame, and his versatile gifts and industry, were always in evidence. As a dramatist and playwright he succeeded well, — " The Lady of Lyons," 1838, and " Richelieu," 1838, still holding the stage. Since industry and ambition cannot make a poet, Bulwer's intense longing to obtain a lyric crown was of no avail. His " New Timon," a satire, 1846, brought him cause for regret. His epic, " King Arthur," 1848, and " The Lost Tales of Miletus," 1866, showed few traces of the divine fire. His dramatic verse, after all, was his best metrical work ; but in addition to the extract from " Richelieu," and the song given in this Anthology, it is but just to reprint the following stanzas which have passion and lyrical quality.

[E. C. S.]

ABSENT YET PRESENT

As the flight of a river
That flows to the sea,
My soul rushes ever
In tumult to thee.

A twofold existence
I am where thou art ;
My heart in the distance
Beats close to thy heart.

Look up, I am near thee,
I gaze on thy face ;
I see thee, I hear thee,
I feel thine embrace.

As a magnet's control on
The steel it draws to it,
Is the charm of thy soul on
The thoughts that pursue it.

And absence but brightens
The eyes that I miss,
And custom but heightens
The spell of thy kiss.

It is not from duty,
Though that may be owed, -
It is not from beauty,
Though that be bestowed ;

But all that I care for,
And all that I know,
Is that, without wherefore,
I worship thee so.

Through granite it breaketh
A tree to the ray,
As a dreamer forsaketh
The grief of the day,

My soul in its fever
Escapes unto thee ;

O dream to the griever,
O light to the tree !

A twofold existence
I am where thou art ;
Hark, hear in the distance
The beat of my heart !

LYTTON, Earl of (Edward Robert Bulwer-Lytton), diplomatist, b. London, 1831, d. Paris, 1891. Son of Edward, Lord Lytton. Educated at Harrow and Bonn. Began his diplomatic career as attaché at Washington, D. C., and was subsequently connected with the British legations in most of the important European capitals. Appointed Viceroy to India in 1876, and advanced in the peerage as Earl of Lytton and Viscount Knebworth, 1880. Scholar, diplomatist, magistrate, courtier, and man of letters, he touched life at many points. " Clytemnestra, the Earl's Return, and Other Poems " appeared in 1859 under the pseudonym of " Owen Meredith," followed by " The Wanderer, A Collection of Poems in Many Lands," 1858 ; " Lucile, a Poem," 1860 ; " Fables in Song," 1874 ; " Speeches of Edward, Lord Lytton, with a Memoir," 1874 ; and " Glenaveril, or the Metamorphoses," 1885. Among his later poetical works, " Orval, or the Fool of Time," 1869, reflects the Polish mystical school. " King Poppy," 1892, is a brilliant satire.

McCRAE, George Gordon, government service, b. Scotland. Holds an appointment in the civil service in Victoria. Contributes to the Australian periodicals but has never published his collected poems. Has embodied many of the legends of the aborigines in verse, of which " Mamba, the Bright-eyed " and " The Story of Balladeadro," both published in 1867, are the best known.

McGEE, Thomas D'Arcy, journalist, b. Carlingford, Ireland, 1825 ; killed at Ottawa, Canada, 1868. Emigrated to America, 1842, and became editor of the Boston " Pilot." Returned to Ireland in 1845 to edit the " Freeman's Journal," but soon became connected with " The Nation." During the riots in 1848, he was obliged to flee to America, and here for nine years published " The New York Nation." In 1857 moved to Montreal, and soon entered the Canadian Parliament. While going home from a night session, he was assassinated for his opposition to the Fenians.

MACAULAY, Thomas Babington, Lord, historian, b. in Rothley Temple, Leicestershire, 1800 ; d. Kensington, 1859. Displayed remarkable precocity, reading incessantly from the age of three, and possessed unique powers of memory throughout life. He was generous and devoted to his sisters, and died unmarried. Was noted in Parliament, and spent three years and a half in India as a member of the supreme council. " The History of England " was his greatest literary achievement, although he was the author of many brilliant essays, published mostly in the " Edinburgh Review," and then collected into volumes. His poetry consists of the " Lays of Ancient Rome " and other ballads. He became a peer in 1857. He was buried in Westminster Abbey, 9 Jan., 1860. His grave is in the Poets' Corner, at the foot of Addison's statue.

MacCARTHY, Denis Florence, b. Dublin, 1817; d. 1882. Educated at Trinity College; called to the Bar, but devoted himself mainly to literature. Contributed to "The Nation." Professor of Poetry in the Irish Catholic University. Translated several of Calderon's dramas into English verse. A collective edition of his own poems appeared in 1884.

MACDONALD, Frederika Richardson. Author of "Nathaniel Vaughan, Priest and Man," 1874; "Puck and Pearl"; Wanderings of two English Children in India," 1886.

MACDONALD, George, novelist, b. Huntley, Aberdeenshire, 1824. Took his degree from King's College, Aberdeen. Studied for the ministry, and was first pastor of an Independent church at Arundel, for a short time. Joined the Church of England and settled in London, devoting himself to literature. "Within and Without," a dramatic poem, was published in 1856; "A Hidden Life," 1857; and "The Disciples and Other Poems," 1867. Author of many novels. (D. London, 1905.)

MACKAIL, John William, author of "Thermopylæ: Newdigate Verse," 1881; and "Virgil's Æneid in English Prose," 1885. As a poet, associated with Rev. H. C. Beeching and Mr. J. B. B. Nichols in the production of "Love in Idleness," 1883, and "Love's Looking-glass," 1891.

MACKAY, Charles, journalist and song writer, b. Perth, 1814; d. 1889. Issued his first volume of poems in 1834. While sub-editor of the "Morning Chronicle" published "The Hope of the World." Afterwards editor of the "Glasgow Argus," and "The Illustrated London News," and founder of the "London Review." Lectured in the United States, 1857-58, and during the Civil War was New York correspondent of the "Times."

MACKAY, Eric, b. London, 1851. Son of the late Dr. Charles Mackay. Educated in Scotland, and afterwards passed a number of years in Italy. Has published "Love Letters of a Violinist," 1885; followed by "Gladys the Singer," and "A Lover's Litanies." His "Nero and Actaea," a dramatic work, appeared in 1891. Died in London, 1898.

MACLEOD, Fiona. -- See *William Sharp.*

MAGINN, William, b. Cork, 1793; d. Walton-on-Thames, 1842. Attended Trinity College, Dublin, when but ten years of age, and received the degree of LL. D. at the age of twenty-three. Was connected with "Blackwood's" and "Fraser's." His irregular habits stood in the way of a success proportionate to his genius. Author of a series of Homeric Ballads.

MAHONY, Francis Sylvester ("Father Prout"), priest and humorist, b. Cork, 1805; d. Paris, 1866. Was ordained as a priest, but in 1837 adopted the profession of literature. Contributed to "Fraser's" and other periodicals, and collected his magazine articles in a volume entitled "The Reliques of Father Prout." A brilliant author, witty and sarcastic.

MAIR, Charles, b. 1840, Province of Ontario. Educated at Queen's University, Kingston. His letters to Canadian journals from the Northwest Territory gave the first impetus to immigration to that region. He took an active part in putting down the insurrections led by Louis Riel. Engaged in the fur-trade for a time, but is now occupied solely with literary work. "Dreamland and other Poems" was issued in 1868, and "Tecumseh," a drama, in 1886.

MANGAN, James Clarence, b. Dublin, 1803; d. 1849. Received a common school education, and at the age of fifteen entered a solicitor's office. Here he remained for several years, the sole support of the family, working early and late. In 1830, began contributing remarkable translations to Dublin periodicals and obtained a position in Trinity College Library. Continued his translations and wrote some odes for "The Nation." Dissipation enfeebled his constitution, and he succumbed to an attack of cholera.

MARSTON, John Westland, dramatist, b. Boston, Lincolnshire, 1819; d. 1890. Studied law, but relinquished it for literature. His first play, "The Patrician's Daughter," was written when he was twenty-two years of age. "Strathmore" appeared in 1849, and was followed by several other dramas. In 1888, published "Recollections of our Recent Actors." For many years led the life of a London editor, contributor, and man of letters.

MARSTON, Philip Bourke, b. London, 1850; d. London, 1887. Only son of Dr. Westland Marston, and godson of Dinah Maria Mulock (Mrs. Craik). It was to him she addressed her poem "Philip, My King." Notwithstanding his blindness, caused by an injury to his eyes when he was a young child, he began to dictate verses from his early youth. The loss through death of his betrothed (Miss Nesbit), his two sisters, his brother-in-law, Arthur O'Shaughnessy, and his friend, Oliver Madox Brown, all occurred within the space of a few years. Rossetti encouraged his genius, and said of some of his verse that it was "worthy of Shakespeare in his subtlest lyrical moods." "Song-Tide and Other Poems" was issued in 1871, and was followed by "All in All" in 1875, and "Wind Voices," 1883. A collection of all his poems was edited with a memoir by his devoted friend, Mrs. Louise Chandler Moulton, in 1892.

MARTIN, Arthur Patchett, journalist, b. Woolwich, England, 1851, and taken to Australia in 1852. Educated at Melbourne University. Held an appointment in the civil service for a time. Was one of the founders of the

"Melbourne Review," and its editor for six years. Author of "A Sweet Girl Graduate" and "An Easter Omelette," 1878; "Fernshawe," a volume of prose and verse, published in Australia in 1881, and republished in London, 1885; and "The Withered Jester, and other Verses," 1895.

MARTINEAU, Harriet, b. Norwich, 1802; d. 1876. An advocate of free thought and social reform, and a voluminous writer on political economy, history, and biography. Contributed to the "Monthly Repository" and the "Daily News."

MARZIALS, Frank T., b. Lille, France, 1840. At an early age entered the English war office, where he still remains. Has written various biographies. Edited the Academy series of "Great Writers," and has contributed articles on art and French literature to leading periodicals. His poetical writings are included in "Death's Disguises," 1889.

MARZIALS, Théophile Julius Henry, musician and composer, b. 1850. Of French descent. "The Passionate Dowsabella," a pastoral poem, was first printed privately in 1872. It was included in "A Gallery of Pigeons and Other Poems," published in 1873. Has composed many artistic and captivating songs.

MASSEY, Gerald, b. Tring, Hertfordshire, 1828. Began to work in a silk factory when a mere lad. Edited "The Spirit of Freedom" at the age of twenty-one, and in the following year became one of the secretaries of the "Christian Socialists." Brought out his first volume of poems in 1850. Has lectured upon psychological subjects, and of late years has been engaged in forming societies to promote spiritualism and socialism. "My Lyrical Life," published in 1890, contains selections from his four previously published works.

MEREDITH, George, novelist, b. Hampshire, about 1828. Studied in Germany and was prepared for the law, but took up literature instead. He published "Poems" in 1851; "The Shaving of Shagpat," 1856; "The Ordeal of Richard Feverel," 1859; "Evan Harrington," 1861; "Modern Love," a volume of poems, 1862; "Emilia in England," 1864; "Rhoda Fleming," 1865; "Vittoria," 1867; "The Adventures of Harry Richmond," 1871; "Beauchamp's Career," 1876; "The Egoist," 1879; "The Tragic Comedians," 1881; "Poems and Lyrics of the Joy of Earth," 1883; "Diana of the Crossways," 1885; "Ballads and Poems of a Tragic Life," 1887; "A Reading of Earth," 1888; "Lord Ormont and his Aminta," 1894.

"MEREDITH, Owen." — See *Robert, Earl of Lytton.*

MERIVALE, Herman Charles, dramatist and novelist, b. London, 1839. Educated at Harrow and Oxford. Called to the Bar in 1864, at the Inner Temple. Edited "Annual Register" for ten years. Author of several successful plays. "The White Pilgrim and Other Poems" was published in 1883; "Florien and Other Poems," 1884.

MEYNELL, Alice (Thompson), b. London. Educated at home, and spent much of her childhood in Italy. In 1875 brought out a volume of poems, "Preludes," which was illustrated by her sister, Lady Butler. Married Mr. Wilfred Meynell, editor of "Merry England," in 1877. Since then has written chiefly prose, and published a book of essays, "The Rhythm of Life," in 1893; "The Color of Life," 1896; "The Children," 1896; "The Flower of the Mind, an Anthology," 1898.

MILLER, Thomas, novelist, b. Gainsborough, 1807; d. London, 1874. While employed as a basket-maker, published his first book of verse, "Songs of the Sea Nymphs," 1832. "A Day in the Woods" (verse) appeared in 1836. Contributed to the annuals and the "London Journal," and wrote a number of books for children.

MILLER, William, b. Bridgegate, Glasgow, Scotland, 1810; d. 1872. Followed the trade of wood-turner at Glasgow. Contributed to "Whistle Binkie," and published "Scottish Nursery Songs and Other Poems," 1863. The charm of his poems of children made them so popular that he has been called by Robert Buchanan the "Laureate of the Nursery."

MILMAN, Henry Hart, divine, b. London, 1791; d. Sunninghill, 1868. Educated at Oxford; ordained in 1816, and became a curate at Reading. Professor of Poetry at Oxford for ten years; rector of St. Margaret's, Westminster, 1835, and dean of St. Paul's, 1849. Author of several poetical and historical works, the most important of the latter being "The History of Latin Christianity," 1854-55.

MILNES, Richard Monckton. As the bearer of this name the author of "The Brook-Side," before his elevation to the peerage. achieved his reputation as a writer of verse and prose, and performed most of his literary work. See *Lord Houghton.*

MITFORD, John, clergyman and editor, b. 1781; d. 1859. In 1814 edited Gray's works, and in 1851, those of Milton. Also edited Parnell's works for the "Aldine Poets." A collection of his own verse, entitled "Miscellaneous Poems," appeared in 1858.

MOIR, David Macbeth, physician, b. Musselburgh, 1798; d. Dumfries, 1851. Granted a surgeon's diploma from University of Edinburgh, 1816. Contributed to "Blackwood's:" published "Legends of Genevieve, with Other Tales and Poems," 1824. Author of several prose works. After his death a collection of his poems was published, edited by Thomas Aird.

MONKHOUSE, Cosmo, art critic, b. London, 1840. Educated at St. Paul's School. At the age of seventeen he secured a position in the Board of Trade, where he still remains, and is now assistant secretary for finance. In 1865 published "A Dream of Idleness and other Poems," and twenty-five years later, "Corn and Poppies," the volume containing his best lyrical work. Has written the life of Turner in the "Great Artists" series, and the life of Leigh Hunt in the "Great Writers" series. Is well known as an authoritative writer on art and letters. (D. 1901.)

MONSELL, John Samuel Bewley, clergyman, b. St. Columb's, Londonderry, Ireland, 1811; d. Guildford, Surrey, 1875. Was graduated from Trinity College, Dublin, 1832. Rector of Ramoan, chancellor of Connor, and rector of St. Nicholas', Guildford, Surrey. His poems are nearly all of a religious nature. Many of them appeared in "Hymns of Love and Praise for the Church's Year," 1863.

MONTGOMERY, Eleanor Elizabeth, b. New Zealand, and lives there on a cattle ranch. Employs the pseudonym of "The Singing Shepherd." Author of "Songs of the Singing Shepherd," issued in Wauganui, New Zealand, 1885.

MONTGOMERY, James, journalist, b. Ayrshire, Scotland, 1771; d. 1854. Spent most of his life in Sheffield, where he edited a liberal newspaper. In addition to devotional poems he wrote "The Wanderer in Switzerland;" "The West Indies," a poem against the slave trade; "The World before the Flood;" "Greenland;" and "The Pelican Island."

MOODIE, Susanna Strickland, b. Reydon Hall, Suffolk, England, 1803; d. Toronto, Canada, 1885. Sister of Agnes Strickland. Married John Wedderburn Dunbar Moodie, ex-naval officer, and traveller and author of several books on Holland, South Africa, and settlers' life in Canada. She came to Canada with Mr. Moodie, and resided for many years in Toronto. Author of "Enthusiasm and Other Poems," 1829; "Roughing it in the Bush, or Life in Canada," 1852; "Life in the Clearings versus the Bush," 1853. Also wrote several novels.

MORRIS, Sir Lewis, b. in Caermarthen, 1833. Educated at Sherborne School and Jesus College, Oxford, where he was awarded the Chancellor's prize in 1855, and the English Essay prize in 1858. Called to the Bar in 1861, and practised for many years. In 1881 he stood in the Liberal interest for the Caermarthen Boroughs, but retired before election. Contested the Pembroke Boroughs in 1886, but was defeated. Is an Honorary Fellow of Jesus College, a Knight of the Order of the Saviour (Greece), and a Justice of the Peace for his native county. In 1890 his collected poetical "Works" appeared in one volume. This included the three series of "Songs of Two Worlds," "Epic of Hades," "Gwen," "Ode of Life," "Songs Unsung," "Gycia," and

"Songs of Britain." "A Vision of Saints" also appeared in 1890. He was knighted by the Queen in 1895.

MORRIS, William, decorative artist, b. Walthamstow, 1834. Educated at Marlborough and Exeter College, Oxford, and studied architecture under George Edmund Street. Established "The Oxford and Cambridge Magazine." Made a special study of artistic design and founded the firm of Morris, Marshall, Faulkner & Co., which is now conducted under his name alone, and which produces materials used in fine art decoration. More recently has established the Kelmscott Press, from which costly reprints, in the highest style of Caxton's art, are issued. Among his many publications are "The Defence of Guenevere and Other Poems," 1858; "The Life and Death of Jason," 1867; "The Earthly Paradise," 1868-70; "Love is enough," 1873; "A Tale of the House of the Wolfings," 1889. In collaboration with Eiríkr Magnússon he has begun a translation of the Icelandic Sagas, the first volume of which was published in 1891. Of late years he has been an ardent advocate of social reform, often lecturing to the working classes. In poetry Chaucer was his master, but he is unrivalled in the strength, learning, and felicity with which he has reproduced the Germanic and Norse legendaries in his affluent English verse. In art, beginning with Pre-Raphaelite affiliations, he has practically applied the secrets of beauty throughout the range of decorative construction. Cp. "Victorian Poets," ch. x. D. London, 1896. [E. C. S.]

MULHOLLAND, Rosa, novelist, b. Belfast. Has contributed to the "Cornhill" and "All the Year Round," and has written a number of novels and tales. Published a volume of poems in 1886. Now Lady Gilbert.

MULOCK, Dinah Maria.—See *D. M. Craik.*

MUNBY, Arthur Joseph, barrister, b. in the Wapentake of Bulmer, Yorkshire, 1828. His London quarters are in the Temple, and he resorts for a country life to his farm in Surrey. A truly pastoral lyrist and idyllist, delighting in the simple lives of the English peasantry and farm and house servants, which he realistically depicts. His "Dorothy," written in elegiac verse, became a favorite in England and America, 1880. He had previously published "Verses New and Old," 1865. Author, also, of "Vestigia Retrorsum," 1891; "Vulgar Verses," mostly dialect poems (under the pseudonym of "Jones Brown"), 1891; "Susan," 1893. [E. C. S.]

MURRAY, George, educator, b. London, England. Was graduated with honors at Oxford. Went to Montreal and was made classical master of the High School. He has made a number of metrical translations from the French. Author of "Verses and Versions," 1891.

MYERS, Ernest, classicist, b. Keswick, 1844. Educated at Cheltenham College and at Balliol College, Oxford. Was a Fellow of

Wadham College and classical lecturer there and at Balliol. Younger brother of Frederic W. H. Myers. Author of "The Puritans," 1869; "Poems," 1870; "The Defence of Rome and Other Poems," 1880; "The Judgment of Prometheus and Other Poems," 1886. He collaborated with Andrew Lang and W. Leaf in the "Translation of the Iliad," published in 1883.

MYERS, Frederic William Henry, investigator, b. Keswick, 1843. Son of Rev. Frederic Myers, author of "Catholic Thoughts." Educated at Cheltenham College and at Trinity College, Cambridge. Inspector of Schools for a number of years, and assisted in establishing the "Psychical Research Society." "St. Paul" appeared in 1865; "Poems," 1870; "The Renewal of Youth," 1882. Is also a prose-writer, and was part author of "Phantasms of the Living," 1886. (D. Rome, 1901.)

NADEN, Constance Caroline Woodhill, b. Edgbaston, 1858; d. London, 1889. Author of "Songs and Sonnets of Springtime," 1881, and "The Modern Apostle and Other Poems," 1887.

NEWMAN, John Henry, Cardinal, theologian, b. London, 1801; d. Birmingham, 1890. Was graduated with honor from Trinity College, 1820. Fellow of Oriel College, and afterwards tutor at the same. Vice-principal of St. Alban's under Dr. Whately; incumbent of St. Mary's, Oxford. One of the leaders of the Tractarian movement. Left the Church of England and joined the Church of Rome in 1845. Was created a Cardinal Deacon by the Pope in 1879. Published two volumes of verse, and contributed to the "Lyra Apostolica." An eminent master of English prose, and the author of several theological and historical works.

NICHOL, John, scholar, b. Montrose, 1833; d. 1894. Son of John Pringle Nichol, the astronomer. Took his degree, with honor, from Balliol College, Oxford, 1859. Became Professor of English Literature in Glasgow University; received the degree of LL. D. from the University of St. Andrews, 1873. Besides critical and other works, he published "Hannibal: an Historical Drama," 1873; and "The Death of Themistocles, and Other Poems," 1881.

NICHOLS, J. B. B. Associated with Rev. H. C. Beeching and J. W. Mackail in the authorship of "Love in Idleness," 1883, and "Love's Looking-glass," 1891.

NICOLL, Robert, b. Auchtergaven in Perthshire, 1814; d. 1837. While engaged in humble employments he trained himself for a literary career. Became editor of the "Leeds Times," a Liberal weekly. Published "Poems and Lyrics" in 1835.

NOEL, Hon. Roden Berkeley Wriothesley, b. 1834; d. Maintz, 1894. Son of the Earl of Gainsborough (second creation). His childhood was passed at Exton Park, Rutlandshire. Much of his descriptive poetry was the result of his visit to his grandfather Lord Roden's beautiful place in Ireland. Took his degree from Cambridge, and travelled extensively in the East. Author of "Beatrice and Other Poems," 1868; "The Red Flag," 1872; "A Little Child's Monument," 1881; and "A Modern Faust," 1888. In prose is known as a critic, biographer, and philosopher.

NORTON, Caroline Elizabeth Sarah (Sheridan), afterwards Lady Stirling-Maxwell, b. 1808; d. 1877. Daughter of Thomas Sheridan, and granddaughter of Richard Brinsley Sheridan. In 1827 she married Mr. George Norton, but the union was an unhappy one. She wrote several successful novels. Of her poetry, "The Sorrows of Rosalie" appeared in 1829; "The Undying One," in 1831; "The Child of the Island," in 1845, and "The Lady of la Garaye," in 1863. She married Sir William Sterling-Maxwell three months before her death.

O'LEARY, Ellen, b. Tipperary, 1831; d. Dublin, 1889. Contributed to various Irish publications, and with her brother John O'Leary was active in the Fenian movement of 1864. After 1885 she made her home in Dublin. A collected edition of her poems was published, with a memoir, in 1890.

O'SHAUGHNESSY, Arthur William Edgar, b. London, 1844 (as given in his own MS.); d. London, 1881. Connected with the British Museum, first holding a subordinate position in the Library, and afterwards being transferred to the Department of Natural History. Married Eleanor, the daughter of Dr. Westland Marston and sister of the blind poet, Philip Bourke Marston. "An Epic of Women" appeared in 1870; "Lays of France" in 1872; and "Music and Moonlight" in 1874. His posthumous poems, "Songs of a Worker," were published in 1831. A selection from his poems, edited by his friend, Mrs. Moulton, appeared in 1894.

PALGRAVE, Francis Turner, critic, b. 1824. Son of Sir Francis Palgrave, historian. Took his degree from Balliol College in 1847, and was elected Fellow of Exeter College. From 1850 to 1855 was vice-principal (under Dr. Temple, subsequently bishop of London) of the Training College at Kneller Hall. Became one of the secretaries of the Committee of Council on Education; and afterwards professor of Poetry at Oxford. In 1878, was created an honorary LL. D. of Edinburgh. Editor of admirable collections of poetry, and author of "Lyrical Dreams," 1871, and "The Vision of England," 1881. Died in London, 1897.

PARKER, Gilbert, b. Canada, 1862. Educated at the University of Trinity College, Toronto, and was afterwards a lecturer there in English literature. Studied for the Church, but owing to a severe illness went to the South Seas, where he joined the staff of the "Sydney Morning Herald," and was special commissioner for that paper in the South Seas. Has published "Pierre and His People," 1892; "Mrs. Falchion," 1893; "The Translation of a Savage," 1894; "A Lover's Diary," 1894; "The Trail of the Sword," 1895. Well known in the United States by his novels, and a prominent contributor to American magazines.

PARNELL, Frances Isabel (Fanny), b. 1854; d. 1882. Sister of Charles Stewart Parnell and granddaughter of Charles Stewart, the historic commander of the U. S. frigate "Constitution." Her poems have never been collected.

PATMORE, Coventry Kearsey Deighton, b. Woodford, 1823. In 1844 brought out his first volume of poems; in 1847, became assistant librarian in the British Museum. Published "The Angel in the House," "The Betrothal," 1854, and "The Espousals," 1856. After his wife's death he retired from the Museum and has since lived at Hastings. "The Unknown Eros" appeared in 1877; "Amelia," and a collected edition of his poems, in 1878. Edited "The Children's Garland" in the Golden Treasury Series. D. Lymington, 1896.

PATON, Sir Joseph Noel, painter, b. Dunfermline, 1821. Studied at the Royal Academy, London. Twice succeeded in securing the prize at the Westminster Hall competitions; appointed Queen's Limner for Scotland, 1865; knighted in 1867, and made LL. D. of Edinburgh University in 1876. "Poems by a Painter" appeared in 1861, and "Spindrift" in 1867.

PAYNE, John, solicitor, b. 1842. Published "A Masque of Shadows," 1870; "Intaglios," 1871; "Songs of Life and Death," 1872; "Lautrec," 1878; and "New Poems, 1880." Translated, for the Villon Society, Villon's Poems, the "Thousand Nights and One Night," and "The Decameron." Is a most learned scholar, and a master of English prose, to which a skilful archaic quality lends artistic effect.

PEACOCK, Thomas Love, novelist, b. Weymouth, 1785; d. Lower Halliford, 1866. One of the best classical scholars of his time, though self-educated. Became the intimate friend of Shelley, and was his executor. Was connected with the India House as chief examiner from 1819 to 1856. Wrote several novels, of which "Headlong Hall," published in 1815, was the first. "Rhododaphne," a long poem, appeared in 1818; "Nightmare Abbey," in 1818; "Maid Marian," in 1822; "Gryll Grange," in 1860.

PFEIFFER, Emily (Davis), b. Wales, 1841; d. 1890. Daughter of Mr. R. Davis of Oxfordshire, an officer in the army. Lack of means prevented her receiving a systematic education. After a tour abroad she married Mr. Pfeiffer, a rich German merchant who settled in London. Though suffering for years from ill-health, she wrote, chivalrously encouraged by her husband, many volumes of poetry,

and contributed articles on "Woman's Work" to the "Contemporary Review."

POLLOCK, Sir Frederick, 3d Bart., barrister, b. 1845. Eldest son of Sir William Frederick Pollock, Bart. Fellow of Trinity College, Cambridge, 1868. Made Corpus Prof. Jur., Oxford, 1883, and Prof. of Common Law, Inns of Court, 1884. Also editor of the "Law Quarterly Review" and author of various legal works. Has written a book on Spinoza, and in verse, the witty "Leading Cases Done into English," 1876, from which "The Six Carpenters' Case," given in this Anthology, is taken.

POLLOCK, Walter Herries, editor, b. London, 1850. Brother of the preceding. Graduated from Trinity College, Cambridge, 1871. Called to the bar at the Inner Temple, 1874. Has lectured at the Royal Institution, London, and other places. Long the editor of the "Saturday Review." In addition to a volume of lectures and a novel, he has published "Verses of Two Tongues," "The Poet and the Muse," translated from A. de Musset, and "Songs and Rhymes," 1882.

PRAED, Winthrop Mackworth, parliamentarian, b. London, 1802; d. 1839. Entered Eton in 1814, and Trinity College, Cambridge, 1821. While at Eton, he published the "Etonian," and at both institutions was noted for his brilliant scholarship. The elegant and gifted pioneer of modern society-verse. Contributed to the "Quarterly Magazine." Entered Parliament in 1830. An edition of his poems was brought out by Rev. Derwent Coleridge, 1864.

PROBYN, May. Author of "Poems," 1881; "A Ballad of the Road and Other Poems," 1883; and works of fiction. Her verse was well received by the public. It is understood that, having entered an order of the Roman Catholic Church, for a time she ceased to write, but a new volume of her poetry has been announced.

PROCTER, Adelaide Anne, b. London, 1825; d. 1864. Daughter of Bryan Waller Procter, "Barry Cornwall." Her verses were first published over the signature of "Mary Berwick," and were sent to her father's friend, Charles Dickens, then editor of "Household Words." The success of her efforts led her to disclose her identity. She became a Roman Catholic and was indefatigable in charitable work. An enlarged edition of "Legends and Verses" was issued in 1861. "A Chaplet of Verses" appeared in 1862, and a complete edition of her poems, with an introduction by Charles Dickens, was issued not long after her death.

PROCTER, Bryan Waller, barrister, b. London, 1787; d. London, 1874. Educated at Harrow. He was called to the bar in 1831. Held the post of Commissioner of Lunacy from 1831 to 1861. His first work was published under the pen-name of "Barry Cornwall." Author of "Dramatic Scenes and Other Poems," 1819; "Mirandola," a play that had a successful run at Covent Garden, 1821; "A Sicilian

Story," 1821; "Flood of Thessaly," 1823; "English Songs," 1832; and memoirs of Shakespeare, Lamb, and others. A natural and exquisite song-writer, associated in literary annals with our traditions of Lamb, Hunt, Landor, Keats, Shelley, and the post-Georgian school. Cp. "Victorian Poets," chap. iii.

QUILLER-COUCH, Arthur Thomas, romancer, b. Bodwin in Cornwall, 1863. Educated at Clifton College and Trinity College, Oxford. Has published "The Splendid Spur," 1889; "The Delectable Duchy," 1893; "Green Bays" and "The White Moth" (verse), 1893.

RADFORD, Dollie, b. 1858. Author of "A Light Load," 1891; "Songs and other Verses," 1895. Was Miss Dollie Maitland before her marriage to the well-known writer Ernest Radford.

RANDS, William Brighty, b. 1823; d. 1880. Wrote under the pseudonyms of "Henry Holbeach," "Matthew Browne," and "Timon Fielding." Was reporter in the Committee Rooms of the House of Commons. Wrote "The Literary Lounger" in the "Illustrated Times"; contributed to other periodicals. "Lilliput Levee" appeared in 1864; "Chaucer's England," in 1869; "Lilliput Lectures," in 1871.

RHYS, Ernest, editor, b. London, 1859. Educated at schools in Bishop Stootford and Newcastle-on-Tyne. Became a mining engineer, and followed his profession in County Durham, but after awhile devoted himself to letters. Having resided as a boy in South Wales, he has paid special attention to the translation of Welsh literature. Editor of the "Camelot Series," sixty-five volumes, 1885-90, of popular reprints and translations. Author of "The Great Cockney Tragedy," 1891; "A London Rose and Other Rhymes," 1894; "Life of Sir Frederick Leighton, P. R. A.," 1895. Member of the Rhymers' Club, and a contributor to its "First" and "Second Books," 1893-94.

ROBERTS, Charles George Douglas, professor, b. New Brunswick, 1860. The son of a clergyman, he was educated at home under his father's instruction, and at the University of New Brunswick. Was made head master of Chatham Grammar School in 1879. Two years later edited the Toronto "Week" for a short time. In 1885 became professor of Modern Literature in King's College, Windsor, N. S. Author of "Orion and Other Poems," 1880; "In Divers Tones," 1887; "Songs of the Common Day," 1893. Has now resigned his professorship to devote himself more freely to literature. He has been an influential leader of the new and promising Canadian group of writers.

ROBERTS, Jane Elizabeth Gostwycke, b. Westcock, New Brunswick. Sister of C. G. D. Roberts.

ROBINSON, A. Mary F.—See *A. M. F. Darmesteter.*

RODD, Rennell, diplomatist, b. 1858. His poem on Sir Walter Raleigh won for him the Newdigate prize at Oxford, in 1880. Appointed to the Berlin Embassy in 1884, and afterwards connected with the Legation at Athens. In addition to "Feda and Other Poems," 1886, has published some volumes of verse and two prose works.

ROPES, Arthur Reed, b. near London, 1859. Son of an American merchant who settled in England, and nephew of John C. Ropes, the writer on military history. Fellow of King's College, Cambridge, 1884-90. Published "Poems" in 1884, and has since written lyrics for the stage under the name of "Adrian Roos." Edited, also, selections from the letters of Lady Mary Wortley Montagu.

ROSCOE, William Caldwell, b. Liverpool, 1823; d. 1859. Took his degree at University College, London, 1843. Called to the Bar, 1850, but owing to ill-health he was obliged to give up practice. His "Poems and Essays," in two volumes, were edited with a memoir, by his brother-in-law, Richard Holt Hutton, after his death.

ROSSETTI, Christina Georgina, b. London, 1830; d. London, 1894. Daughter of Gabriel Rossetti, an Italian political exile and distinguished student of Dante, and sister of Dante Gabriel Rossetti. In the front rank of modern women poets. Her later work is devotional in sentiment, and consists chiefly of poetical commentaries on religious subjects. Collective editions of her poems have been published in England and America. Author of "Goblin Market and Other Poems," 1862; "The Prince's Progress and Other Poems," 1866; "Sing-Song, a Nursery Rhyme-book," 1872; "Annus Domini, a Collect for Each Day of the Year," 1874; "A Pageant and Other Poems," 1881; "Letter and Spirit, Notes on the Commandments," 1883; "Time Flies, a Reading Diary," 1885.

ROSSETTI, Dante Gabriel (Gabriel Charles Dante), painter, b. London, 1828; d. Westgate-on-Sea, 1882. Son of Gabriel Rossetti and brother of Christina Rossetti. Educated at King's College School; studied art at the Royal Academy Antique School and in Ford Madox Brown's studio. He was confessedly the leader and exemplar of the Pre-Raphaelite School, both in painting and poetry. In 1850, with the assistance of a few associates of the Pre-Raphaelite Brotherhood, he founded "The Germ," which was the organ of the order, and in which "The Blessed Damozel" appeared in 1850. His pictures are distinguished by the same subtle quality that marks his verse, and exercised as great an influence in art as the latter did in literature. His "Early Italian Poets," a translation, appeared in 1861; "Poems," in 1870; "Dante and His Circle," also a translation, in 1874; and "Ballads and Sonnets," in 1881. "Cp. "Victorian Poets," chap. x and p. 439.

ROSSLYN, 4th Earl of, Francis Robert St. Clair Erskine, b. 1833; d. 1890. Published his "Sonnets" in 1883.

RUSKIN, John, critic and virtuoso, and Slade Professor of Fine Arts at Oxford, b. London, 8 Feb., 1819 ; d. Brentwood, near Coniston, 20 Jan., 1900. Educated at Oxford, where he took the Newdigate prize in 1829. Devoted himself to art, and in 1843 published the first volume of "Modern Painters," which work finally consisted of five volumes, illustrated by himself. Besides many noble books on the fine arts, composed in his fervent and cumulative style, he published two architectural treatises. His writings often involved a criticism of life, from an idealist's point of view, and bore upon social problems. Under the title "Praeterita," 1885–1889, he issued what is practically his autobiography.

RUSSELL, George William ("A. E."), b. Durgan, a town in the North of Ireland, 1867. Moved to Dublin with his family at the age of ten. Formed the acquaintance of a group of literary people, of which W. B. Yeats and Katharine Tynan were conspicuous members. He studied art for a short time. His poems have been published under the initials "A. E." "Homeward Songs by the Way" was reissued in the United States, 1895.

RUSSELL, Percy, Australian journalist and poet, now living in London. Author of "King Alfred and Other Poems," 1880 ; "My Strange Wife," 1886.

SAVAGE-ARMSTRONG, George Francis, b. County Dublin, 1845. Educated at Trinity College, Dublin. Professor of History and English Literature in Queen's College, Cork, and a professor of the Queen's University, Ireland. Edited the works of his deceased brother, Edmund J. Armstrong, with a biography. Made Litt. D., Queen's University, 1882, and is a Fellow of the Royal University of Ireland. Author of many poetical works, among which are "Poems, Lyrical and Dramatic," 1879 ; "Ugone, a Tragedy," 1870 ; "The Tragedy of Israel" (a trilogy), 1872–76 ; "Stories of Wicklow," 1886 ; "One in the Infinite," 1891. An edition of all his poetry, in 10 volumes, was issued in 1892.

SCHUYLER - LIGHTHALL, William Douw, advocate, b. Hamilton, Ontario, 1857. Published several volumes on Canadian national life. "Thoughts, Moods, and Ideals," a small book of verse, was printed for private circulation in 1887. He also edited "Songs of the Great Dominion," 1889.

SCOTT, Clement William, dramatist and dramatic critic, b. Hoxton, London, 1841. Son of Rev. William Scott. Educated at Marlborough College, Wiltshire. Appointed to a clerkship in the War Office, 1860, and in 1879 retired on a pension. Has contributed to many of the leading English periodicals. Became dramatic critic to the London "Daily Telegraph" in 1879. "Lays of a Londoner" appeared in 1882 ; "Lays and Legends," in 1888. Is the author of several successful plays, among which are "The Cape Mail," "Odette," and

"Sister Mary," in which he collaborated with Wilson Barrett. (D. London, 1904.)

SCOTT, Duncan Campbell, b. Ottawa, 1862. Lived in Ottawa, and subsequently in Quebec, until 1879, when he entered the Indian Department of the Civil Service, and is now chief clerk of that department. He published "The Magic House" in 1893.

SCOTT, Frederick George, clergyman, b. 1861. In charge of a church at Drummondville, Quebec. Author of "The Soul's Quest," 1888, and "My Lattice and Other Poems," 1894.

SCOTT, William Bell, painter and etcher, b. near Edinburgh, 1811 ; d. Ayrshire, 1890. Educated at the Edinburgh High School and studied art at the Government Academy and the British Museum. Established a Government art school at Newcastle, 1844. His early poems appeared in the Edinburgh magazines. "Poems of a Painter" was published in 1854, and "A Poet's Harvest Home" in 1882. His personal reminiscences, largely concerned with the Pre-Raphaelite group of poets and painters, were published after his death.

SHAIRP, John Campbell, critic, b. Linlithgowshire, 1819 ; d. 1885. Educated at Glasgow and Oxford. Assistant professor at Rugby and afterward professor of Humanity at the University of St. Andrews. In 1864 published a volume of poems, "Kilmahoe, a Highland Pastoral ; " and in 1868, "Studies in Poetry and Philosophy." Principal of the united college of St. Salvator and St. Leonard in the University of St. Andrews. Elected Professor of Poetry at Oxford in 1877.

SHANLY, Charles Dawson, journalist, b. Dublin, Ireland, 1811 ; d. Florida, U. S., 1875. Educated at Trinity College, Dublin. Went to Canada and finally to New York, where he wrote regularly for the newspapers and magazines, but is claimed as a Canadian poet.

SHARP, William,[1] author and critic, b. Garthland Place, Scotland, 1856. Educated at the University of Glasgow. In youth was intimate with Dante Rossetti, whose biography he wrote, 1882, as also that of Browning in after years. His travels have been extensive, including a sojourn in Australia, and visits to Continental Europe, Northern Africa, and the United States. His earliest book of poetry was " The Human Inheritance, Transcripts from Nature, and Other Poems," 1882. Since this have appeared: "Earth's Voices," 1884 ; "Romantic Ballads," 1888 ; "Sospiri di Roma," 1891; "Flower of the Vine," 1892, an American reprint of the last two works; and "Vistas," 1894, weirdly symbolic dramas, but of an individual cast. Has written several novels, etc., and is editor of the "Canterbury Poets" series. (D. Sicily, 1905.)

SIGERSON, Dora, b. Dublin, 187-. Daughter of Dr. George Sigerson, the writer and balladist. Author of "Verses," 1893. Now Mrs. Clement Shorter.

[1] See Addenda, p. 710.

SIMMONS, Bartholomew, b. Kilworth, Ireland, 18—; d. 1850. Obtained a situation in the Excise Office, after removing to London. Contributed to various magazines. Published "Legends, Lyrics, and Other Poems," 1843.

SINNETT, Percy F., b. Norwood, South Australia, 18—; d. North Adelaide, at the age of twenty-two. He wrote a number of political poems. "The Song of the Wild Storm-Waves" was written, when he was eighteen, on the loss of the "Tararua."

SKIPSEY, Joseph, b. near North Shields, 1832. Much of his life, since his seventh year, has been spent in the coal-pits, at hard physical labor. "A Book of Miscellaneous Lyrics," published in 1878, attracted the attention of the Pre-Raphaelite poets. In 1886, "Carols from the Coalfields" was issued, and in 1892, "Songs and Lyrics."

SLADEN, Douglas Brooke Wheelton, man of letters, b. London, 1856. Studied at Cheltenham and Oxford, went to Australia, 1879, and for a time was professor of History in the University of Sydney. From 1882 to 1890 he published many volumes of poems, among them: "Frithjof and Ingebjorg," 1882; "Australian Lyrics," 1883, 1888; "A Poetry of Exiles," 1884; "A Summer Christmas," 1885; "In Cornwall and Across the Sea," 1885; "Edward the Black Prince" (drama), 1886; "The Spanish Armada," 1888. Editor of Australian and Canadian Anthologies, which have been of service to the present work. An extensive traveller and industrious writer, he latterly has paid more attention to prose, his books "The Japs at Home," and "On the Cars and Off" (Canadian travel), 1894, having been well received, — to which he has added a novel, "A Japanese Marriage," 1895. Is honorary secretary of the Authors' Club, London.

SMEDLEY, Menella Bute, b. 1820; d. 1877. Her delicate health made it necessary for her to reside for many years at Tenby, a sea-coast town. She published three volumes of verse, many of the poems in "Child-World" and "Poems Written for a Child," and several successful prose tales.

SMITH, A. C., clergyman. Was in charge of a Presbyterian church in Victoria, Australia, but afterward moved to Queensland.

SMITH, Alexander, b. Kilmarnock, 31 December, 1829; d. 1867. While he was a pattern designer at Glasgow, some of his verse was published in the "Glasgow Citizen" and afterwards in the "British Critic." In 1852 "The Life Drama" came out and made a sensation. (See *W. E. Aytoun*.) He became secretary to the University of Edinburgh in 1854. Edited an edition of Burns, and with Mr. Sidney Dobell wrote "Sonnets on the Crimean War." "City Poems" appeared in 1857; "Edwin of Deira," in 1861.

SMITH, Walter C., clergyman, b. 1824. Since 1876 has been pastor of the Free High Church, Edinburgh. Author of the following books of poetry, some of which have passed through several editions: "Olrig Grange," "Borland Hill," "Hilda," "Raban," "Bishop Walk and Other Poems;" also of "North Country Folk," 1883; "Kildrostan, a Dramatic Poem," 1884; "A Heretic," 1891.

SOUTHESK, Earl of, (Sir James Carnegie, 6th Earl of Southesk, Scotland, and Baron Balinhard, U. K.), b. 1827. Author of "Herminius: a Romance," 1862; "Jonas Fisher: a Poem in Brown and White," 1876; "Meda Maiden," 1877; "The Burial of Isis, with Other Poems," 1884.

STANLEY, Arthur Penrhyn, divine, b. Alderly, Cheshire, 1815; d. London, 1881. Educated at Rugby and Oxford, where he was distinguished for scholarship. For twelve years tutor in the University. Canon of Canterbury and of Christ Church, and Professor of Ecclesiastical History at Oxford. In 1863 was appointed to the Deanery at Westminster, and in the same year married Lady Augusta Bruce, daughter of the 7th Earl of Elgin. Published several prose works but no collected edition of his poems.

STEPHEN, James Kenneth, "J. K. S.," b. 1859; d. London, 1892. Son of Sir James Fitzjames Stephen. Educated at Eton and at King's College, Cambridge. A Fellow of King's, and for a time tutor of Prince Albert Victor. Called to the Bar at the Inner Temple, 1884. Author of "International Law and International Relations," 1885; "Lapsus Calami," 1891, which reached its fourth edition in the same year; and "Quo, musa, tendis?" 1891.

STEPHENS, James Brunton, instructor, b. Linlithgowshire, Scotland, 1835. Emigrated to Queensland, 1866. At one time head master in one of the State schools. Author of "Miscellaneous Poems," 1880; "Convict Once and Other Poems," 1885.

STERLING, John, b. Kames Castle in Bute, 1806; d. 1844. Educated at Glasgow University and Trinity College, Cambridge. For a time editor of the "Athenæum." Ordained curate in 1834, but owing to ill-health soon gave up his orders. Published "Poems" in 1839, and "Strafford," a drama, in 1843. After his death his essays and tales were collected and edited by Archdeacon Hare. The memoir prefixed to these caused Thomas Carlyle, who was his intimate friend, to write the "Life of John Sterling."

STEVENSON, Robert Louis Balfour, novelist, b. Edinburgh, 1850; d. in Samoa, 1894. Grandson of Robert Stevenson, an eminent engineer. His people having been engineers to the Board of Northern Lighthouses for three generations, he was at first trained for the same profession. Called to the bar in 1875, but after a short practice abandoned it. Owing to ill-health, much of his time was spent in travelling, until he finally built for himself a picturesque tropical home near Apia, in the

Samoan Islands. The best of his prose romances and his eminence among recent writers of fiction are familiar to all readers of English literature. In verse he published "A Child's Garden of Verses," 1885; "Underwoods," 1887; "Ballads," 1890. The noble Edinburgh edition of his Complete Works, in 20 volumes, was just beginning to appear at the time of his lamented death.

SWAIN, Charles, song-writer, b. Manchester, 1803; d. 1874. Was an engraver in his native place. Contributed to the "Literary Gazette," and published "Metrical Essays," 1827; "The Mind and Other Poems," 1831; "Dramatic Chapters and Other Poems," 1847; "English Melodies," 1849; "The Letters of Laura d'Auverne and Other Poems," 1853; besides several later volumes of verse.

SWINBURNE, Algernon Charles, b. Pimlico, 5 April, 1837. Son of Admiral Swinburne, and, on his mother's side, grandson of the 3d Earl of Ashburnham. Educated at Balliol College, Oxford, where he contributed to "Undergraduate Papers," edited by John Nichol. Left Oxford, 1860, without taking his degree, but is distinguished for his command of the Greek and Latin tongues, and the languages and literatures derived from them. Like Shelley, was from the first devoted to liberty and republicanism. The friend and eulogist of Landor, Mazzini, and Hugo, he has been the lyrist of revolutionary struggles in Italy and other lands, though impulsively patriotic where British supremacy is at stake. His early plays, "The Queen Mother" and "Rosamond," appeared in 1860. "Atalanta in Calydon," a classical drama, 1865, displayed his unrivalled rhythmical genius, and of itself placed him at the head of the new poets. "Poems and Ballads," 1866, a collection of his lyrics to that date, excited the criticism of moralists, and the poet defended himself in the pamphlet, "Notes on Poems and Reviews." Titles of various later poetical works are as follows: "Ode on the Proclamation of the French Republic," 1870; "Songs before Sunrise" (a majestic series of lyrics), 1871; "Songs of Two Nations," 1875; "Erectheus" (another *nova antica*), 1876; "Poems and Ballads," Second and Third Series, 1878, 1889; "Songs of the Spring-Tides," 1880; "Tristram of Lyonesse," 1882; "A Century of Rondels," 1883; "A Midsummer Holiday," etc., 1884; "Marino Faliero" (drama), 1885; "Astrophel and Other Poems," 1894. His trilogy of Mary Stuart consists of three dramas: "Chastelard," 1865; "Bothwell," 1874; "Mary Stuart," 1881. Author, also, of many learned, critical, often controversial, literary essays and studies, written in a swift and eloquent style. Though Mr. Swinburne is of a somewhat delicate physique, no modern writer has surpassed him in the extent and vigor of his printed works. Since the deaths of Tennyson and Browning, he has been, in the common judgment of his guild, the poet best qualified by genius and achievements to inherit the laureateship. Cp. "Victorian Poets," ch. xi, and pp. 434–439. [E. C. S.]

SYMONDS, John Addington, critic and essayist, b. Bristol, 1840; d. Rome, 1893. Educated at Harrow and at Balliol College, Oxford, and was made Fellow of Magdalen, 1862. Although a life-long sufferer from nervous maladies which forced him to travel continually in search of a fostering climate, his activity in literary work was unflagging, and he produced sketches of travel, biographies, critical studies in art and literature, and several volumes of verse. A biography of him has been compiled from his journal and letters by his friend Horatio F. Brown. Among his poetical works are "The Sonnets of Michael Angelo and Campanella," 1878; "Animi Figura," 1882; "Wine, Women, and Song," a collection and translation of the songs of the mediæval Latin students, 1884. His great prose work is the "Renaissance Work in Italy," 1875-86.

SYMONS, Arthur, critic, b. Wales, 1865 A contributor to the "Academy" and other periodicals. Published "Days and Nights," 1889; "Silhouettes," 1892.

TAYLOR, Sir Henry, b. 1800; d. 1886. He went to sea as a midshipman in 1814, but left the service at the end of the voyage. In 1823 he entered the civil service at the Colonial Office, London. In consideration of his official work and as a reward for his achievements in literature, he was made a Knight Commander of the Order of St. Michael and St. George in 1869. He published "Isaac Comnenus" in 1827; "Philip Van Artevelde," 1834; "Edwin the Fair," 1842; "Poems," 1845; "The Eve of the Conquest and other Poems," 1847; "Notes from Books," 1849; "A Sicilian Summer," 1850; "St. Clement's Eve," 1862; and his notable Autobiography in 1886.

TAYLOR, Tom, dramatist, b. Sunderland, 1817; d. 1880. Educated at the Universities of Glasgow and Cambridge. Author of "The Ticket-of-Leave Man," and a series of historical plays. Editor of "Punch," 1874-80, and art critic to the "Times" and "Graphic."

TENNYSON, Alfred, 1st Lord ("Baron Tennyson, of Aldworth, Surrey, and Farringford, Freshwater, Isle of Wight."[1] — *Burke's Peerage*, 1892), — poet-laureate of England, and chief of the Victorian composite or "idyllic" school, — b. Somersby, Lincolnshire, 6 August, 1809; d. Aldworth House, Haslemere, Surrey, 6 October, 1892. Through his father, Rev. G. C. Tennyson, Rector of Somersby, he was of ancient Norman lineage. To a secluded and observant life in youth, passed with his poet-brothers in Lincolnshire and near the sea, we owe much of the landscape, atmosphere, and truth to nature, of his poetry, and its exquisitely idyllic, rather than dramatic, characteristics. With Charles Tennyson, he brought out the "Poems by Two Brothers," now so rare, in 1827. Entering Trinity College, Cambridge, 1828, he there became attached to Arthur Henry

[1] See Addenda, page 710.

Hallam, against whom as a competitor he won the Newdigate Prize by his poem, "Timbuctoo," 1829. During his college years he wrote much verse (some of which first saw the light half a century later), and published " Poems, Chiefly Lyrical," 1830, in which volume his distinctive quality was indicated. It was, however, the " Poems," 1832-33, that more clearly bore the signs of coming greatness, and included some of his still most cherished pieces. On the whole, this volume was Pre-Raphaelite, and, though it preceded the rise of the group known by that name, equalled in the archaic beauty of certain ballads the extreme reach afterward attained by poets who could not follow Tennyson's advance to the higher and broader domains of song. The poet left Cambridge without his degree, about March, 1831, and certainly not yet appreciated by critics and the public, — to whom he made no further appeal until 1842, when the two-volume edition of his " Poems," containing so many of his finest lyrics and idylls, brought him universal recognition. In 1845 he was awarded a yearly pension of £200 by the Queen. His next works were "The Princess," 1847, and " In Memoriam," 1850. The masterpiece last named, an elegiac poem in memory of Hallam, is at the highest mark of its author's mature wisdom and genius; it reflects the utmost advance of speculative religious thought and scientific research at the date of its production, and is both the sweetest and the noblest intellectual poem of the typical " Victorian Epoch." Wordsworth having passed away, the laureateship was awarded to Tennyson in 1850, and by these two masters that office was reinvested with a dignity which had been unworn by it since the Elizabethan age. The laureate's " Ode on the Death of the Duke of Wellington," and other national lyrics, were included with " Maud and Other Poems," 1855. Of his epical romances, " Idylls of the King," begun with the early " Morte d'Arthur," four parts appeared in 1859, and brought him to the height of renown. The series was finally completed in 1885. In 1855 Oxford gave him the degree of D. C. L., and he was elected, 1859, to an honorary fellowship of his own college, Trinity, Cambridge. Was made F. R. S. in 1865. The most noted of his later volumes, other than dramatic, are: " Enoch Arden," 1864; " Ballads and Other Poems," 1880; " Tiresias and Other Poems," 1885; " Locksley Hall, Sixty Years After," 1886; " Demeter and Other Poems," 1889; " The Death of Œnone," etc., 1892. Several of these books exhibit much of the lyrical freshness and beauty of his earlier song, reinforced by imagination, wisdom, and mental power. But throughout his work the expression of the " master-passion " is at most one of reserve, and there is a lack of the gift to combine and put in action types of human personality. It was not strange, then, that his repeated efforts to compose enduring dramas were unsuccessful, judged by the standard of his other productions. His successive plays, of course, were skilfully arranged and

intellectually wrought, and some of them, brought out by Irving, had every advantage of the English stage; but they were the tours-de-force of a perfect artist, and essentially undramatic, from first to last of the following series: " Queen Mary," 1875; " Harold," 1876; " The Falcon " and " The Lover's Tale," 1879; " The Cup," 1881; " The Promise of May," 1882; " Becket," 1884; " The Foresters," 1892. In 1884, Tennyson was raised to the peerage. No conferred title could increase his name and fame, but his new station, in view of his liberal conservatism and intensely English allegiance, and as the logical recognition of genius, — whether military, political, or creative,— in a monarchical country, was one plainly within his liberties to accept for himself and his inheritors. After many years' residence at Farringford, Isle of Wight, — near which a beacon is to be erected by English and American subscribers, — he died at Aldworth, full of honors such as no English poet had received before him. He was buried, 12 October, 1892, near the grave of Chaucer, in Westminster Abbey, the fit resting-place of a bard and laureate " certainly to be regarded, in time to come, as, all in all, the fullest representative of the refined, speculative, complex Victorian age." Cp. *F. Tennyson, C. Tennyson Turner, A. H. Hallam.* See, also, " Victorian Poets," chh. v and vi, and pp. 417-424.   [E. C. S.]

TENNYSON, Charles. — See *Charles Tennyson Turner.*

TENNYSON, Frederick, b. Louth, 1807. An elder brother of Alfred Tennyson. Educated at Eton and Trinity College, Cambridge. Married an Italian girl and lived in Florence, but returned to England in 1859 and took up a residence in Jersey. Author of " Days and Hours," 1854; " The Isles of Greece," 1890; " Daphne and Other Poems," 1891; " Poems of the Day and Year," 1895. Died in London, 1898.

THACKERAY, William Makepeace, one of the two greatest Victorian novelists, b. Calcutta, 1811; d. London, 1863. After his early childhood in India, was sent to England, and to the Charterhouse School; then passed a year at Trinity, Cambridge, but left without a degree, wishing to become an artist. His knack as a draughtsman, however, and his student-life in Paris, combined merely to aid him in the literary career upon which circumstances, and the bent of his true genius, were soon to start him. As Dickens made his novels profit by a youthful acquaintance with low life, and by his service as a law-clerk and newspaper-reporter, so Thackeray's novels of society would have been impossible but for his good birth and breeding, his touch of university and studio life, and his travel on the Continent. As an author he began by contributing to " Fraser's," 1837-42, a series of writings, among which the " Yellowplush Papers," and the really powerful " Luck of Barry Lyndon," of themselves would place him among the foremost of modern satirists. He also wrote for " Punch," wherein the

"Ballads of Policeman X." appeared, 1842. In fact, beside his ability to illustrate his story effectively, if faultily, with drawings of his own, he had equally a turn for verse, was a born balladist, and his poems — avowedly "minor" pieces — are delightful with the mirth and tenderness of his rich nature. In 1855, he gathered them, from his own books and from various periodicals, into a little volume published simultaneously in England and America. Was the first editor of the "Cornhill," 1859–62. Of his greater work in fiction, the masterpieces are: "Vanity Fair," 1848; "Pendennis," 1850; "Henry Esmond," 1852; "The Newcomes," 1854. [E. C. S.]

THOM, William, the "Inverary poet," b. Aberdeen, 1798; d. Dundee, 1848. For many years a weaver in humble circumstances. The publication of a poem in the "Aberdeen Herald," 1841, called attention to his talent. Through the influence of friends he visited London, where he was warmly received. Published "Rhymes and Recollections of a Handloom Weaver" in 1844.

THOMPSON, Francis, b. about 1859. Was educated at a Catholic college and was urged by his family to become a medical student. Believing that literature offered the only suitable career for him, he left home and underwent great privations in the pursuit of his chosen calling. His poetry was collected and published in 1894 under the title of "Poems," and is followed by another volume, "Songs Wing-to-Wing: an Offering to Two Sisters," 1895.

THOMSON, James, b. Port Glasgow, 1834; d. London, 1882. He was assistant schoolmaster at an army station, and later a clerk in a solicitor's office. Subsequently he visited the United States in the interests of a mining company, and, returning in a short time from that mission, he went to Spain as the representative of the "New York World" during the Carlist insurrections. A singular, but undoubted genius, whose life and death were infelicitous, but who has left his mark on English verse. Author of "The Doom of a City," 1857; "Sunday at Hampstead," 1863; "Sunday up the River," 1868; "The City of Dreadful Night," 1874; "Vane's Story," 1880; "Insomnia," 1882. Cp. "Victorian Poets," pp. 435–437.

THORNBURY, George Walter, man of letters, b. 1828; d. 1876. Son of a London solicitor. When seventeen, contributed a series of prose articles to the "Bristol Journal." Published his first volume of verse, "Lays and Legends, or Ballads of the New World," in 1851. This was followed by one or two prose works, after which he spent some time in travelling in the East. In 1857, issued his best volume of poetry, "Songs of the Cavaliers and Roundheads," and in 1875, "Legendary and Historic Ballads." His prose writings were continuous.

TODHUNTER, John, physician, b. Dublin, 1839. Educated at Trinity College, Dublin,

and at Paris and Vienna. Took his medical degree in 1866, but is chiefly devoted to letters. Professor of English Literature at Alexandra College, Dublin, from 1870 to 1874. Among his published works are "Laurella and Other Poems," 1876; "Forest Songs," 1881; "Helena in Troas," a drama, 1886; "The Banshee and Other Poems," 1888.

TOMSON, Graham R. — See *Rosamund Marriott Watson.*

TOWNSHEND, Chauncey Hare, b. 1800; d. 1868. Educated at Trinity Hall, Cambridge, and took the degree of M. A. in 1824. Author of "Jerusalem," 1828; "Sermons in Sonnets, with Other Poems," 1851; "The Shell Gates," 1859.

TRENCH, Richard Chenevix, divine, b. Dublin, 1807; d. 1886. Was educated at Harrow and Cambridge. Dean of Westminster and Archbishop of Dublin, 1864–1884. Author of "The Study of Words," 1851; "English, Past and Present," 1855; and other prose works. His poems were collected and published in 1865.

TURNER, Charles Tennyson, clergyman, b. 1808; d. Cheltenham, 1879. Elder brother of Alfred, Lord Tennyson. In 1827, "Poems by Two Brothers," written by himself and Alfred, was published. He was graduated at Trinity College, Cambridge, 1832; and ordained in 1835. Became vicar of Grasby. Married Louisa Sellwood, sister of Lady Tennyson, in 1836. In 1835, by the death of his great-uncle, Samuel Turner, he succeeded to the estate of Caistor and took the name of Turner. An authoritative collection of his sonnets was published in 1880, after his death.

TYNAN, Katharine. — See *Katharine Tynan Hinkson.*

TYRWHITT, Reginald (or Richard?) St. John, clergyman, b. about 1826. Was graduated at Oxford, 1849. Vicar of St. Mary Magdalen, Oxford, 1858–72. Author of several works upon symbolic art, etc., and of "Free Field Lyrics, chiefly Descriptive," 1888. — Owing to the lateness with which the foregoing notes were obtained, the spirited hunting-ballad by this poet is somewhat out of chronological order, among the selections from Victorian "Balladists and Lyrists." D. Oxford, 1895.

VEITCH, John, philosopher and critic, b. Peebles, near Edinburgh, 1829; d. there, 1894. Educated at the Grammar School and the University of Edinburgh. Professor of Logic, Metaphysics, and Rhetoric, in the University of St. Andrews, and afterwards of Logic in Glasgow University. Prose writer and author of "The Tweed and Other Poems," 1875; "Merlin and Other Poems," 1889.

VELEY, Margaret, b. 1843; d. 1887. Daughter of Augustus Charles Veley, a solicitor in Braintree, Essex. Began writing verse at an early age. Contributed both prose and poetry to the leading periodicals of London and America. Her poems were collected and published in 1889, with a biographical preface by Leslie Stephen.

"VIOLET FANE." — See *Lady Currie.*

WADDINGTON, Samuel, b. Boston Spa, Yorkshire, 1844. Took his degree from Brasenose College, Oxford, 1865. Obtained an appointment at the Board of Trade. In 1881, published "English Sonnets by Living Writers." His first book of original verse appeared in 1884, entitled "Sonnets and Other Verse."

WADE, Thomas, dramatist, b. 1805; d. Jersey, 1875. Issued his first volume of verse in 1825. Was a friend of W. J. Linton, and one of the band of radicals and poet-reformers who flourished in 1836-50. Wrote several dramas, some of which were played with success at Covent Garden. Edited "The British Press" and contributed to "The National" and other periodicals. Issued "Mundi et Cordis Carmina," a collection of poems, in 1835; "The Contention of Death and Love," "Helena," "The Shadow-Seeker," 1837; "Prothanasia," 1839.

WALKER, William Sidney, scholar and critic, b. Pembroke, South Wales, 1795; d. 1846. Educated at Eton and at Trinity College. When but seventeen wrote an epic poem, "Gustavus Vasa." Later, he edited a "Corpus Poetarum Latinorum." His Shakespearean notes appeared in 1854 and 1860, and his "Poetical Remains" in 1852.

WALLER, John Francis, barrister, b. Limerick, 1810; d. 1894. Author of a number of poems, but is more widely known as a critic and essayist.

WARREN, John Leicester. — See *Lord De Tabley.*

WATSON, Rosamund Marriott ("Graham R. Tomson"), b. London, 1860. Under the latter designation she gained her repute as the author of "The Bird-Bride, a Volume of Ballads and Sonnets," published in 1889; "A Summer Night and Other Poems," 1891; "After Sunset," 1895. Has edited several anthologies. This poet announces that hereafter her writings will appear with the signature, "Rosamund Marriott Watson." Has contributed to English and American periodicals under the name of "R. Armytage."

WATSON, William, b. Burley-in-Wharfedale, 1858. The latter part of his childhood and early manhood were spent near Liverpool. In 1875 some of his poems appeared in "The Argus," a Liverpool periodical. "The Prince's Quest and Other Poems" was published in 1880. "Epigrams" was issued in 1884. In 1885, he contributed to the "National Review" a sonnet-sequence, "Ver Tenebrosum." Came into high repute through his stately and imaginative poems on Wordsworth, Shelley, and Tennyson, the last of which is reprinted in this Anthology. His collected "Poems" appeared

iu 1893, followed by "Odes and Other Poems," 1894.

WATTS, Theodore, critic, b. St. Ives, 1836. Originally trained as a naturalist, but afterwards studied law, and passed his examination in 1863. Has resided chiefly in London. Intimately associated with D. G. Rossetti and others of the Pre-Raphaelites, and now a devoted friend and companion of Mr. Swinburne. Contributed articles to the "Encyclopædia Britannica," expounding the principles of the "Romantic movement," the Nature of Poetry, etc. Contributed to the "Nineteenth Century" and the "Examiner," and is leading critic of the "Athenæum" in poetry and the arts. A collection of his poems and sonnets has long been promised.

WAUGH, Edwin, "the Laureate of Lancashire," b. Rochdale, 1818; d. 1890. A printer and bookseller, who finally devoted himself to literature, and won regard by the truth to nature of his poems in the Lancashire dialect, and by his local tales and sketches. Author of "Lancashire Sketches," "Poems and Lancashire Songs," etc., and much other prose and verse. His complete works, in 10 volumes, were published 1881-83.

WEATHERLY, Frederic Edward, barrister, b. Portishead, 1848. Published his first volume of verse, "Muriel and Other Poems," 1870. Took his degree from Brasenose College, Oxford, 1871. Called to the Bar, 1887. Many of his lyrics have been set to music by leading composers and are very popular. He has also written librettos, and several books for children.

WEBSTER, Augusta (Davies), b. Poole, Dorsetshire, 1840; d. 1894. Daughter of Vice-Admiral George Davies. In 1860 published "Blanche Lisle and Other Poems," using the pseudonym "Cecil Home." In 1863 married Mr. Thomas Webster, Fellow and Law Lecturer of Trinity College, Cambridge, but now a solicitor in London. "A Woman Sold and Other Poems" appeared in 1867. Author of several metrical dramas, and of some fine translations of Greek tragedies. "In a Day," a drama, appeared in 1882.

WEIR, Arthur, banker, b. Montreal, 1864. Educated at Montreal High School and McGill University. Held editorial positions on Canadian newspapers for several years, and then became an analytical chemist, but gave up science to enter his father's bank. "Fleurs de Lys" appeared in 1887, and "The Romance of Sir Richard, Sonnets, and Other Poems" in 1890.

WELCH, Sarah. Lives in Adelaide, South Australia, and is a nurse in hospitals. Author of "The Dying Chorister, and the Chorister's Funeral," 1879.

WELDON, Charles, 18— -1856. In Linton and Stoddard's "English Verse," Weldon is set down as an Englishman, whose poems appeared over the signature "O. O." in the New York "Tribune," 1850-56.

WELLS, Charles Jeremiah, b. 1800; d. Marseilles, 1879. In his youth became acquainted with the Keats brothers, and with R. H. Horne. In 1822 he published, anonymously, "Stories after Nature," and in 1824, "Joseph and His Brethren, a Scriptural Drama: in Two Acts," using the pseudonym "H. L. Howard." This was revived in 1876, with an introduction by Mr. Swinburne. Practised law early in life, and at one time held a professorship at Quimper. His closing years were passed at Marseilles.

WESTWOOD, Thomas, b. 1814; d. 1888. In youth became an intimate friend of Charles Lamb. Was enthusiastic on the subject of angling, and published in 1864 "The Chronicle of the Complete Angler." His first volume of verse, "Poems," appeared in 1840. In 1844 he removed to Belgium as a railway official. "Gathered in the Gloaming," issued in 1885, is a collection of poems previously printed.

WETHERALD, Ethelwyn, b. in Ontario, Can., of English Quaker parentage. Educated at a Friends' boarding-school in New York State, and at Pickering College, Ontario. She is a journalist, and has contributed poems and verse to periodicals in the United States and Canada. No collected volume of her works has yet been published.

WHITE, Gleeson, art editor, b. 1851. Now follows his profession in London, where he has been editor of "The Studio" and other select journals; but for a time resided in the United States, and conducted the N. Y. "Art Amateur." Writer of historical and critical papers on art, and a designer of book-plates, title-pages, etc. Is also a contributor to the Century Guild's "Hobby Horse," and has edited "Ballades and Rondeaus," a selection of poems by Dobson, Lang and others, with a chapter on the various ballad "forms," 1887.

WHITEHEAD, Charles, novelist, b. London, 1804; d. Melbourne, 1862. For a time was engaged in commercial pursuits, but finally resorted to literature, and gained the friendship of Charles Dickens. Published "The Solitary," a poem, 1831, and in 1834, "The Autobiography of Jack Ketch," a work of fiction, which includes "The Confession of James Wilson." His most important novel was "Richard Savage," 1842. A collective edition of his poems appeared in 1849. An admirable critical biography of Whitehead, by H. T. Mackenzie Bell, appeared in 1884, and since then has been revised for a new edition.

WHITWORTH, William Henry. In Sharp's "Sonnets of the Century" it is stated that Mr. Whitworth was head master in a large public school. Author of various sonnets which have been preserved.

WILBERFORCE, Samuel, divine, b. Clapham Common, 1805; d. 1873. Son of William Wilberforce; educated at Oxford. Ordained in 1828, and after several appointments became Bishop of Oxford and Winchester.

WILDE, Jane Francesca Speranza (Elgee), Lady, widow of Sir William Wilde, who died in 1869, an archæologist of Dublin, and surgeon-oculist to the Queen. Contributed to "The Nation," as "Speranza." In addition to various prose works and translations from the French and German, has published "Ugo Bassi," 1857; and "Poems," 1864. D. 1896.

WILDE, Oscar Fingall O'Flahertie Wills, dramatist, b. Dublin, 1856. Son of Sir William and Lady Wilde ("Speranza"). Educated at Trinity College, Dublin, and Magdalen College, Oxford, taking his Oxford degree in 1878. In both colleges excelled in prose and poetical composition, and was winner of the Newdigate prize at Oxford. Published his early "Poems" in 1881. Became "an apostle of artistic house decoration and dress reform," and the author of successful plays. "Salome," a drama in French, based on the story of Herod and Herodias, appeared in 1893. (D. Paris, 1900.)

WILLIAMS, Sarah ("Sadie"), b. London, 1841; d. 1868, while engaged in preparing her poems for publication. "Twilight Hours: A Legacy of Verse," was issued shortly after her death, and contained a prefatory memoir by the late Dean Plumptre.

WILLS, William Gorman, painter and dramatist, b. Kilkenny Co., Ireland, 1828; d. London, 1891. Educated at Trinity College, Dublin. Studied art at the Royal Irish Academy and acquired some reputation as a portrait-painter. Wrote a large number of dramas, the first of which, "The Man o' Airlie," was produced in 1867. "Charles I.," with Henry Irving in the title character, ran for two hundred nights at the "Lyceum" in 1872. Collaborated with Sydney Grundy and with Westland Marston.

WOODS, James Chapman, author of "A Child of the People and Other Poems," 1879; "Guide to Swansea and the Mumbles, Gower and Other Places," 1883; a lecture on "Old and Rare Books," 1885, and "In Foreign Byways," 1887.

WOODS, Margaret L., daughter of Dean Bradley and wife of President Woods of Trinity College, Oxford. Author of "A Village Tragedy," 1887; "Lyrics and Ballads," 1889," "Esther Vanhomrigh," 1891; and "Vagabonds," 1894.

WOOLNER, Thomas, sculptor, b. Hadleigh, in Suffolk, 1825; d. London, 1892. Educated at Ipswich, and began to study sculpture in the studio of William Behnes, when but thirteen years of age. Exhibited his first model at the Royal Academy in 1843. His next, a group, "The Death of Boadicea," established his reputation. Contributed verse to "The Germ," the magazine published by the "Pre-Raphaelite Brotherhood." "My Beautiful

Lady" appeared in 1868; "Pygmalion" in 1881; "Silenus" and "Tiresias" in 1886.

WORDSWORTH, Christopher, divine, b. Braintree, Essex, 1807; d. 1885. Nephew of William Wordsworth, the laureate. Educated at Winchester School and at Trinity College, Cambridge. Canon of Westminster Abbey, and in 1869 appointed Bishop of Lincoln. Published a volume of poems, "The Holy Year."

WRATISLAW, Theodore, b. Rugby, 1871, of an old Bohemian family settled in England for a century. In 1892 he published two small books of verse, and in 1893, "Caprices."

YEATS, William Butler, critic, b. Sandymount, Dublin, 1866. Spent the greater part of his childhood at Sligo. Has contributed to the "National Observer," and other periodicals. Among his publications are "Fairy and Folk Tales of the Irish Peasantry," 1888; "Irish Tales," a volume of selections from the Irish novelists, issued in 1891; "John Sherman and Dhoya" (Pseudonym Library), 1891; "The Countess Kathleen," Cameo Series, 1892; and edited in conjunction with Mr. E. J. Ellis, "The Works of William Blake," 3 vols., 1893.

ADDENDA

BESANT, Sir Walter, author, b. Portsmouth, 14 Aug., 1836. Educated at King's College, London, and later at Christ's College, Cambridge, where he graduated with honors. He soon became Senior Professor in the Royal College of Mauritius. A few years later ill health forced him to return to England, where he has since resided. He served as Secretary of the Palestine Exploration Fund until 1885, and then was made Hon. Secretary. His first work appeared in 1868: "Studies in Early French Poetry." In collaboration with the late Professor Palmer he wrote a "History of Jerusalem," 1871. In this same year he began his literary partnership with the late James Rice. The associates produced many novels, and two plays, one of which was enacted at the Court Theatre. Among Walter Besant's publications under his own name are: "The French Humorists," 1873; "Coligny," 1879; "The Revolt of Man;" "Dorothy Forster," 1884; "Armorel of Lyonnesse," 1890; "Beyond the Dreams of Avarice," 1895; "The City of Refuge," 1896; "The Rise of the British Empire," 1897. His world-famous novel "All Sorts and Conditions of Men," 1882, led to the founding and erection of the People's Palace in the East End of London. He is the editor of the series of biographies entitled "The New Plutarch," and of an extensive work, "The Survey of Western Palestine." In 1896 he was knighted. As Chairman and the leading spirit of the "Incorporated Society of Authors," Sir Walter's services to his own craft have been from first to last courageous and far-reaching. He is held in honor and affection by all professional writers of the English tongue. The charming lyric "To Daphne" is from his novel "Dorothy Forster," where it is attributed to the gallant Lord Derwentwater, who suffered in the cause of the Pretender, A.D. 1716. (D. Hampstead, Eng., 10 June, 1901.)

DICKENS, Charles, the great Victorian novelist of the common people, b. Landport, Portsmouth, 1812; d. Gadshill Place, near Rochester, 1870. "The Ivy Green" is given in this volume, as it originally appeared in the "Pickwick Papers." The more even but less spontaneous version, as set to music by Henry Russell, can be found in various song-books and collections.

In the notice of Lord Tennyson, p. 705, the designation of his title is taken from "Burke's Peerage," but its correctness may be open to question. Mr. Eugene Parsons, of Chicago, having instituted a search at Heralds' College, finds "that the Patent, creating Alfred Tennyson, Esquire, a Baron of the United Kingdom by the name, style, and title of *Baron Tennyson of Aldworth in Sussex, and of Freshwater in the Isle of Wight,* is dated January 24, 1884.

Since the death of William Sharp, it has been announced that he and "Fiona Macleod" were the same person. The poems and other writings purporting to be the work of a Scottish woman thus named were in the front rank of those of the pioneers in the modern "Celtic revival," and contain possibly the most lasting memorials which Mr. Sharp produced. Among the publications bearing his pseudonym are: "Pharais: a Romance of the Isles," 1894; "The Mountain Lovers," 1895; "From the Hills of Dream," 1896; "The Washer of the Ford," 1896; "Other Studies in Spiritual History," 1900.

On January 1, 1896, **Alfred Austin** was appointed to the Laureateship, which office until then had remained vacant after the death of Lord Tennyson in 1892.

INDEXES

INDEX OF FIRST LINES

INDEX OF TITLES

INDEX OF POETS